Current Biography Yearbook 2012

H. W. Wilson
A Division of EBSCO Publishing
Ipswich, Massachusetts

SEVENTY-THIRD ANNUAL CUMULATION—2012

International Standard Serial No. 0084-9499

International Standard Book No. 978-0-8242-1144-8

Library of Congress Catalog Card No. 40-27432

Printed in the United States of America

CONTENTS

LIST OF BIOGRAPHICAL SKETCHES

List of Biographical Sketches

LIST OF OBITUARIES

List of Obituaries

List of Obituaries

Current Biography Yearbook 2012

Current Biography Yearbook 2012

Marguerite Abouet

Born: 1971
Occupation: Graphic novelist

Born in the West African nation of Ivory Coast, Marguerite Abouet has been living in France since the age of twelve and currently lives near Paris with her husband and son. In her early thirties, she began work on a graphic novel about the everyday issues and concerns of a group of friends, young adults living in an Ivory Coast city in the late 1970s. The graphic novel, simply titled *Aya*, was published in France in 2005 and has sold more than 200,000 copies. In 2007, it was published in English in North America. Subsequent English translations of sequels followed: *Aya of Yop City* (2008), *Aya: The Secrets Come Out* (2009), *Aya: Life in Yop City* (2012), and *Aya: Love in Yop City* (2012).

In a review of *Aya of Yop City* for the *Wall Street Journal* (5 Sep. 2008), Davide Berretta observed that the book "aims to show a new side of Africa." That observation is equally valid for all five parts of the *Aya* series. Abouet was well aware that the news coverage of Africa—particularly in Europe and the United States—often focused on AIDS, famine, and civil wars; although she has not denied that those are serious problems, Abouet wanted to make the case that there is much more to Africa—something universal, such as adults and adolescents dealing with love, romance, friendship, and financial concerns. *Aya* has been translated into more than a dozen languages. Abouet, who wrote and outlined *Aya*, collaborated with her husband, Clément Oubrerie, an artist who illustrated the graphic novel. An animated film version of *Aya*, written and co-directed by Abouet, is scheduled to be released in 2013.

EARLY LIFE IN ABIDJAN

Abouet was born in 1971 in Abidjan, Ivory Coast. Her childhood in Ivory Coast and her subsequent visits to her home country in later years provided the foundation for the descriptions and characters that populate *Aya*. By the time Abouet was born, Ivory Coast had achieved its independence from France; it had been a French colony until 1960. In an interview with Angela Ajayi for the online magazine

AFP/Getty Images

Wild River Review (July 2012), Abouet offered a summary of the cultural and economic movements that followed the Ivory Coast's independence from France. She describes the new middle class of young, educated people who moved to Abidjan." Helped along by the economy of the time, all these new graduates found jobs. For relaxation, they formed clubs where they met after work or on weekends. That is also where they socialized and married. Their parents no longer had great influence on their life choices; they had been surpassed by the changes in the country and by this new freedom brought about by the 'Ivorian miracle.'" Abouet goes on to say that middle class women in Abidjan at this time enjoyed a newfound liberation. "They no longer yielded to their parents' authority in choosing a husband. Their level of education made them aware of their rights: the right to divorce, access to the pill, opportunities for professional careers." In fact, Abouet's parents were both products of this middle class.

AN AVID READER MOVES TO FRANCE

From a young age, Abouet loved stories, and she became an avid reader. However, one of her earliest influences, she told an interviewer for *The Brown Bookshelf* blog (31 Jan. 2010), was her grandfather. "I have always treasured the stories that my maternal grandfather told me around the fire during the holidays in the village," she said. "All of those stories in our oral tradition were rich, imaginative accounts of mythology, wonderful tales. He taught me to pay attention to what occurred around me, to listen to the stories, and then become a storyteller. These stories of the Ivory Coast provided fertile ground for my imagination."

When Abouet was twelve years old, she and her older brother were sent by their parents to Paris, France, where they lived with their great-uncle and pursued educations. Even though Abouet was in a new culture and a new country; she was familiar with the language because even after independence, French remained the official language of the Ivory Coast (although there are many dialects spoken in the country). In France she loved going to the library, reading the works of a variety of authors, such as William Shakespeare, science-fiction writer Jules Verne, and mystery writers such as Agatha Christie and Sir Arthur Conan Doyle.

TELLING HER STORIES, HER WAY

Despite living in France, far away from her place of birth, Abouet did not forget her home country and her upbringing. In fact, the idea to write about both had long been brewing inside her. Her idea was not only about the characters and stories, she told Ajayi, but also about fixing what she believed was a one-sided view of Africa in the mainstream Western media: "I had always felt the need to recollect my youth down there, the silliness I got into, the unbelievable stories about the quartier [the quarter], the families, the neighbors. I did not want to forget that part of my life, to hold on to those memories, and the desire to recount them got stronger with age. I felt a little guilty for being content in another country, far away from my family; in addition, I got so annoyed at the way in which the media systematically showed the bad side of the African continent, habitual litanies of wars, famine, of the 'sida,' and other disasters, that I wished to show the other side, to tell about daily modern life that also exists in Africa."

Prior to gaining success with the *Aya* series, Abouet worked as a legal assistant in Paris. She also wrote and tried to publish novels for young adults. However, as she has revealed in various interviews, she had a hard time getting those novels published—and ultimately gave up trying—because the publishers wanted to edit her books in a way that stripped them of all frank discussions of topics like sex and other mature themes.

GETTING STARTED AS A GRAPHIC NOVELIST

Abouet did not set out to become a graphic novelist. In fact, her introduction to that world came through comics, about which she had mixed feelings. "I feel like girls were not really involved in comics, and comics were not really for girls," Abouet told John Zuarino for *Bookslut* (May 2007). "I hated when I was young to read [stories of] superheroes. Except for Spider-Man. He was a normal guy—he was having affairs with girls. He had complicated stories with girls and his aunt and everything, so I felt he was closer to me. And he was beautiful also. I was in love with Spider-Man. But otherwise I didn't feel close to the superheroes. I wasn't concerned with them."

Marjane Satrapi, the author of the autobiographical graphic novel *Persepolis: The Story of a Childhood* (2002), which is about growing up in Iran, became a big influence on Abouet, inspiring her to write her graphic novel about a girl living in Abidjan, Ivory Coast, in the late 1970s. Abouet wanted to tell a real story about the adolescents and adults living in a city that at one point was her home. She based many of the characters on people she used to know, but the situations and events, albeit realistic, were fictionalized. In addition to relying on her memories of her upbringing in Ivory Coast, Abouet used the memories and experiences of her recent trips to Abidjan to provide her with inspiration.

Abouet has admitted many times that she cannot draw. On the other hand, her husband, Oubrerie, is an artist, so she asked him to illustrate her graphic novel. Abouet wrote the story and made storyboards, then she and her husband worked on the story together. Once the plot and storyboards were complete, Oubrerie began to work on the color illustrations. Not only was Oubrerie familiar with the story of Abouet's upbringing, but he had also traveled to the Ivory Coast many times.

AYA

The graphic novel the couple produced, *Aya*, was a big success in France, where it was first published in 2005 before being published in English in North America by Drawn & Quarterly, in 2007. The book would ultimately be translated into more than a dozen languages and win the 2006 Angouleme International Comics Festival prize for "first album."

Aya is about the title character, a nineteen-year-old girl, and her friends Adjoua and Bintou, as well as their families and friends. It is a lively, lighthearted, real, humorous tale of life in the Yopougon neighborhood during Ivory Coast's so-called Ivorian miracle, which was a relatively prosperous time for the West African nation. In a review for *Library Journal* (9 Jan. 2007), Melissa Aho called the book a "fun and charming story of a bygone era." Aho then concluded: "Mature themes and issues will appeal to adult audiences, but the unique Ivory Coast setting and the female central characters make this book ideal for harder-to-please older teenage girls." The stories and problems into which Abouet delves in the graphic novel are universal. Many young people can relate to stories of drinking and dancing, the desire to find companionship with a special someone, and the confusion and heartache that can come with romance—especially when it goes wrong. There are other problems, too. For example, Aya wants to study to become a doctor, whereas her father is more concerned with her finding a good husband and marrying well. Although Aya is certainly part of the story, much of the time she is simply the witness and observer. Toward the end of the book, Aya's friend Adjoua gives birth to a baby boy (the pregnancy was not planned). Adjoua says the father is a young man named Moussa, who is the son of a wealthy local man named Bonaventure Sissoko. The claim is suspicious, which becomes apparent in the sequel.

THE AYA SERIES

The sequel, *Aya of Yop City*, picks up where *Aya* leaves off. In the first few pages of the book, Bonaventure Sissoko is standing over the baby and asks Adjoua, her father, and others gathered around, "Tell me the truth, when you see this baby, does he look like my son Moussa?" While Adjoua's father tries pitifully to explain, Bonaventure does not buy the explanations. The answer is obviously no. In fact, it later becomes apparent that the baby looks like Mamadou, a local playboy. Mamadou may be good-looking and charming, but Adjoua cannot depend on him for support. Mamadou is not the only undependable man in the story. Aya's friend Bintou falls for Gregoire, who claims to be successful.

The overlapping stories of Yop City would have little impact in a graphic novel without the proper illustration style, one that captures the mood, language, and culture of the time. In a review for the website *ComicMix* (27 Oct. 2008), Andrew Wheeler focuses on the drawings: "As in the first book, Oubrerie's loose, vibrant art captures the feel of Ivory Coast—his sunlight has an almost physical quality and his line delights in the possibilities of the many bold patterns worn by the women of Yop City. His character's expressions can sometimes feel a bit flat—he draws them without eyelids, so eyes are always wide open, with only size and shape to define emotion—but their body language makes up for that." At the time of Wheeler's review, four graphic novels in the *Aya* series had been published in France, where they had sold more than 200,000 copies. Furthermore, because of Abouet's efforts, her French publisher, Édition Gallimard, sold inexpensive, softcover copies of the *Aya* series in the Ivory Coast.

In *Aya: The Secrets Come Out*, published in English in 2009, Abouet continues telling the stories of the everyday lives of the young people of Yop City. In a review for *Library Journal* (7 Jan. 2010), Martha Cornog wrote: "With much of the story focusing on a Miss Yop City beauty pageant, the level-headed Aya helps family and friends with their problems while allowing them to find their own way. *Aya's* setting and detail conjure the appeal of a different place and time, whereas the characters resonate in the universality of their hopes." Abouet continued to tell the delightfully funny and touching story of Aya and her friends, family, and neighbors in *Aya: Life in Yop City* and *Aya: Love in Yop City*. The latter contains the last three chapters of the *Aya* series, in which are mature themes: For example, Aya must deal with a shady professor who has taken advantage of her. However, the volume, unlike all previous *Aya* editions, contains additional material, such as an afterword from Abouet, as well as recipes, sketches, and a guide to the slang of the Ivory Coast.

SUGGESTED READING

Abouet, Marguerite. "Drawing on the Universal in Africa: An Interview with Marguerite Abouet." Interview by Angela Ajayi. *Wild River Review*. Wild River Review, July 2012. Web. 21 Aug. 2012.

Aho, Melissa. "*Aya*." Review of *Aya*, by Marguerite Abouet and Clement Oubrerie. *Library Journal*. Library Journal, 15 Jan. 2007. Web. 21 Aug. 2012.

Berretta, Davide. "The Cartoon Heart of Africa." *Wall Street Journal*. Dow Jones, 5 Sep. 2008. Web. 23 Aug. 2012.

Cornog, Martha. "From *Aya* to *Zapt!*: Twenty-Four Graphic Novels for African American History Month." Review of *Aya*, by Marguerite Abouet and Clement Oubrerie. *Library Journal*. Library Journal, 7 Jan. 2010. Web. 21 Aug. 2012.

Wheeler, Andrew. "Review: *Aya of Yop City* by Marguerite Abouet and Clement Oubrerie." *ComicMix*. ComicMix, 27 Oct. 2008. Web. 21 Aug. 2012.

—*Dmitry Kiper*

Jad Abumrad

Born: April 18, 1973
Occupation: Radio host and producer

Jad Abumrad is the cohost and producer of the popular radio show *Radiolab*. Making use of his background in music and creative writing, Abumrad created the program in 2002 for WNYC, the New York City affiliate of National Public Radio (NPR). *Radiolab* delves into difficult philosophical and scientific questions with an earnest curiosity and enthusiasm. Since its inception, the show has tackled such topics as number theory, the science of laughter, and humankind's capacity for cruelty. Veteran financial and science reporter Robert Krulwich is Abumrad's *Radiolab* cohost.

EARLY LIFE AND EDUCATION

An only child, Jad Abumrad was born on April 18, 1973 in Syracuse, New York. Abumrad's mother, a scientist, and his father, a doctor, came to Syracuse from Lebanon. His father conducted his residency in surgery at the State University of New York (SUNY) Upstate Medical University. When Abumrad was twelve years old, the family moved to Nashville, Tennessee, after both of his parents took positions at Vanderbilt University. During his youth, Abumrad fell in love with music and learned to play the guitar and piano. Unlike many young people who love playing instruments, Abumrad did not dream of becoming a rock star. Instead, he was interested in writing music scores for films.

Abumrad attended Oberlin College, a private liberal arts school in Oberlin, Ohio, where he majored in creative writing and minored in music composition. He received his bachelor's degree in 1995. After graduating, Abumrad worked in web design and wrote music for short films. He soon decided to try his hand at radio. In an interview with Orli Van Mourik for the *Villager* (1 Aug. 2007), Abumrad recalled what his thinking process was at the time: "I was like: Well, I like writing and I like music and I'm not terribly good at either in isolation. Radio felt like an intersection of those two things."

GETTING STARTED IN RADIO

Abumrad got his start in radio by volunteering at the listener-supported New York City radio station WBAI, 99.5 FM. Soon after that, he began freelancing for National Public Radio (NPR) and WNYC, the New York City affiliate of NPR. As a freelancer, Abumrad went on to report and produce radio pieces for various NPR programs such as *On the Media, All Things Considered, Morning Edition,* and *Studio 360.*

In 2000, Abumrad reported a story for *Weekend Edition* (11 June 2000) about the local activist Luis Garden Acosta and his El Puente

Courtesy the John D. & Catherine T. MacArthur Foundation

community center. The center is located in the Williamsburg neighborhood of the New York City borough of Brooklyn. By the year 2000, Williamsburg had become popular with young people, but this was not the case when Acosta founded the center seventeen years prior. Williamsburg was very dangerous then—so dangerous, Abumrad reported, that CBS called it "the killing fields." In his report, Abumrad also covered a relatively recent addition to the center, an accredited public high school, which offered writing classes in Spanish and English, as well as subjects like global studies. Five months after the September 11, 2001 terrorist attacks on New York City, Abumrad filed a report for the NPR program *Morning Edition* (25 Feb. 2002) about the use of video surveillance in New York City. He profiled Bill Brown, an ardent privacy-rights supporter who was giving walking tours of "heavily surveilled neighborhoods in Manhattan" while pointing out various hidden cameras. The majority of cameras in the city, Abumrad stated in his report, are private—belonging to banks, residential buildings, and the like. In his report, Abumrad addressed the issue of finding a balance between security and privacy. He also discussed the potential of Visionics, a brand of face-recognition software.

STARTING *RADIOLAB*

In 2002, WNYC offered Abumrad a three-hour slot on late Sunday nights for his own radio show. Abumrad experimented with sound, music, and narrative. The show, which Abumrad called

Radiolab, was trimmed from three hours to two hours and then, in 2004, to one hour—which became the show's standard length. Because of the time and effort the show took to produce, WNYC featured only five *Radiolab* episodes per year.

In November 2003, NPR science correspondent Robert Krulwich began appearing as a guest on *Radiolab*, and he soon joined the show as cohost. By the time Abumrad met Krulwich, the latter was a well-respected, experienced journalist who specialized in matters of science and finance. Krulwich was a fan of early *Radiolab* shows. In an interview with Robert K. Elder of the *Chicago Tribune* (22 Oct. 2008), Krulwich recalled thinking that Abumrad "wasn't a beginner or even an intermediate. He was doing a kind of radio jazz that I had never heard before. And I wanted to do it too." Despite their differences in age and experience, Abumrad and Krulwich had a strong intellectual connection, and partook in philosophical discussions about science and culture.

Those discussions served as the basis for the engaging and novel approach of *Radiolab*. "On first listen, the bantering tone struck by Abumrad and Krulwich, and their palpable chemistry, stands out," wrote Rob Walker for the *New York Times* (10 Apr. 2011). "They joke, challenge, openly admit to not fully understanding their expert guests, and give the general impression that they're having a ball." Walker also pointed out how the addition of Krulwich as cohost both changed and did not change the show: "While working with Krulwich loosened up Abumrad's on-air presence, and he learned the ropes of professional journalism, Abumrad never really stopped thinking like a composer. That is, he thinks like someone interested in how sound makes a listener feel. When he talks about influences, the most prominent name is Walter Murch, a legendary film editor and sound designer. Listen more closely to a *Radiolab* episode, and once you get past the cutting up and the jumpiness, you'll notice just how intricate the underlying soundscapes are."

SEASONS 1–3

The first season of *Radiolab* featured five episodes, with each one tackling a particular topic. The episode "Who Am I?" explored the meaning of identity and consciousness by asking the question, "How does the brain make me?" Abumrad talked to such experts as neurologist Paul Broks and neuroscientist V.S. Ramachandran. Another episode, titled "Time," delved deep into the concept of time (and how humans perceive it) by talking to physicist Brian Greene, neurologist Oliver Sacks, and many others. Part of the conversation had to do with time and music, for which Abumrad played pieces of Beethoven's "Ninth Symphony" that had been stretched from

its original one-hour running time to twenty-four hours. "Time" aired on WNYC in the spring of 2004, and by the fall of 2006, it was airing on numerous NPR affiliates nationwide. *Radiolab* shows were often rebroadcast, which fit with the ideas Abumrad had about the show's durability. Abumrad's melding of interviews, music, sound effects, and his conversations with Krulwich, make *Radiolab* shows seem like pieces of music. Each has its own rhythms, textures, and can be replayed many times. The show's large podcast audience is also a testament to the lasting impact of each episode.

In fact, in the second season, in an episode titled "Musical Language," *Radiolab* explored the line between language and music, asking such fundamental questions as "What is music?" Abumrad delved into how the brain processes music and talked with various guests, including the popular science writer Jonah Lehrer. The show's second season also explored such topics as morality, and the human brain's sense of location. Season 3 of *Radiolab* discussed mortality, memory, the placebo, and sleep. The "Sleep" episode began with the fact that every animal sleeps, and examined the various ways rats, iguanas, and human beings enact sleep behavior. The following season covered laughter, deception, pop music, and even featured the show's first live episode, "War of the Worlds," which discussed the 1938 Orson Welles spoof radio broadcast that chronicled a Martian invasion of the United States. That episode explored how and why so many people were fooled by the broadcast, and how it spawned imitators, including one in Ecuador in 1949 that resulted in twenty casualties.

SEASONS 4 AND 5

By Season 4, *Radiolab* was airing on 150 stations across the nation, with nearly a million listeners on radio and about 350,000 listeners online. Season 5, which debuted in November 2008, covered such topics as choice, reproduction, and race. The "Race" episode served as a good example of Abumrad's willingness to explore a complicated, sensitive topic, examining the relationship between race and DNA, between race and medicine, and how well (or not so well) people can tell someone's race based on their appearance. During the show's fifth season, the London-based *Guardian* (11 Aug. 2008) listed *Radiolab* as one of the best radio programs on the Internet, demonstrating the show's popularity outside of the United States.

Jaya Saxena, writing for *Gothamist* (7 Apr. 2011), asked Abumrad where he and Krulwich get their ideas. "We read a lot," Abumrad replied. "We make lots of phone calls. We send each other a million articles with the subject line 'interesting?'. . .So we spend a long time looking . . . but at this point all of us share a gut. When something has that poetic spookiness, we all know it." One of the things that has made the show popular among media critics is the fact that Krulwich and Abumrad discuss, debate, and sometimes disagree with one another—and they often disagree with scientists, too. "If anything, *Radiolab* is a wrestling match between science and mystery," Abumrad told Saxena. "And speaking personally—Robert and I disagree on this point—I have no allegiance to physicists or biologists or neuroscientists. I root for mystery. What pulls me through the intensely long hours of producing this show is the chance to stand in awe of the world around me. But the key—and this is where the science comes in—that awe can't be a cheap awe. I want the awe that's hard fought, that you only get after interviewing impenetrable researchers and fighting with them a little." Yet while guests and scientists provide many insights and answers—and even pose new questions—the foundation of the show is the dialogue between the cohosts, which is a blend of improvised and scripted conversation. "This is where it feels to me like music, like we're a pair of instruments, riffing," Krulwich told Saxena. "Almost from the beginning, we could do this. It's not like ordinary conversation, or even ordinary radio conversation; it's always been a duet."

SEASON 6 AND BEYOND
Season 6 of *Radiolab* debuted with an episode titled "Stochasticity," which is another word for randomness. Abumrad and Krulwich examined patterns and chance in things as varied as sporting events and the workings of cells in the human body. Other episodes looked at number theory, parasites, and the moment between life and death. Season 7 tackled the minds of animals, the lives of apes, tumors, and the limits of the human mind, and whether it is possible to really know someone. *Radiolab* continues to interweave themes found in both science and philosophy. Season 9 kicked off with an episode that asked: What does evolution tell us about altruism? The episode explored why acts like sharing not only make for a better society but also have roots in natural selection. That season also featured another live-recorded *Radiolab* episode, with musical accompaniment and guests such as astrophysicist Neil deGrasse Tyson. Other stories from that season explored our sense of direction and gaining control of our urges. *Radiolab*'s tenth season featured ten episodes instead of five. It explored such themes as human-like robots, the dark side of human nature (the capacity for murder and cruelty), escaping prison, the digestive system, and the human ability to see color.

Radiolab received a Peabody Award in 2010. The following year, Abumrad received a MacArthur Foundation grant of approximately $500,000. The show's audience numbers approximately one million listeners and its *Radiolab.org* podcast audience is an estimated 1.8 million listeners. In March 2011, Abumrad and Krulwich took *Radiolab* on its first national tour, performing in venues in New York, Los Angeles, and Seattle. They performed the episode on symmetry with accompaniment from cellist Zoe Keating.

Jad Abumrad and his wife, television producer Karla Murthy, have one child.

SUGGESTED READING
Battaglia, Andy. "Jad Abumrad and Robert Krulwich." *Onion* 24 Apr. 2008: AV Club.
Elder, Robert K. "Putting 'Radio Lab' under the Microscope." *Chicago Tribune* 22 Oct. 2008: C5.
Van Mourik, Orli. "Tuning into Radio Lab's Strange Frequency." *New York Villager* 1–7 Aug. 2007.
Walker, Rob. "The Sweet Sound of Science." *New York Times* 10 Apr. 2011: MM42.

—*Dmitry Kiper*

Jay Adelson
Born: September 7, 1970
Occupation: Internet entrepreneur

Tech entrepreneur Jay Adelson has been involved in numerous ventures related to the Internet. He created a commercial browser that allowed average users to access the World Wide Web, helped develop a network that enabled e-commerce companies to serve larger customer bases, and spoke to the US House Select Committee on Homeland Security regarding cybersecurity. Yet Adelson is arguably best known for his tenure as the chief executive officer (CEO) of Digg, a news-aggregation website on which users determine which stories are the most interesting and popular. At the height of Digg's popularity, Adelson was named in the "2008 *Time* 100," *Time* magazine's annual list of the one hundred most influential people in the world.

EARLY LIFE AND EDUCATION
Adelson was born on September 7, 1970, in Detroit, Michigan. He and his older brother, Scott, were raised in the suburb of Southfield. Their great-grandfather had founded an electrical supply company located on Detroit's iconic Eight Mile Road, a highway that divides the city from its suburbs.

Adelson's father was a schoolteacher by training, but he later assumed control of the company from his father. The business was heavily dependent upon the fortunes of the automobile industry and thus experienced periodic fluctuations

Michigan. He excelled at the school and was particularly active with its campus radio station. Upon graduating from Cranbrook in 1988, Adelson entered Boston University.

A longtime film buff, Adelson majored in film and broadcasting and he minored in computer science. He earned his bachelor's degree in 1992 and moved to California to accept an unpaid internship at Skywalker Sound, a comprehensive post-production facility affiliated with filmmaker George Lucas.

EARLY CAREER

Needing to earn a living, Adelson began looking for a job involving his college minor, computer science. "A friend was helping start the very first commercial IP (Internet provider) in the US," Adelson told an interviewer for the Cranbrook Schools' online feature "Alumni Stories" (9 Mar. 2012). "It was the first time you could dial into the Internet. He said he'd pay me a salary and benefits and I was like, 'What are benefits?'" In 1993, Adelson joined Netcom, which had been founded in 1988 by Bob Rieger, a former Lockheed information systems engineer, who wanted to start a service that would allow Bay Area students to access university networks even when they were not on campus.

At Netcom, Adelson started as an installation coordinator and was soon promoted to director of network operations. He was instrumental in the creation of a Windows 3.1–based program called NetCruiser, a commercial browser that allowed ordinary users to access the expanding World Wide Web. "I was learning at the pace the Internet was evolving," Adelson told Cranbrook Schools. "It was the frontier days of the Internet when there were literally thousands of Internet service companies."

PAIX

As the Web expanded, it became evident that the existing infrastructure was becoming woefully inadequate. "There was a horrible problem with the 'inter' part of 'Internet,'" he explained to Cranbrook Schools. "There were many thousands of networks like spider webs controlled by single companies like AOL and Verizon. Someone using AOL needed to be able to send an e-mail to Verizon." In 1996, Adelson left Netcom to work for Albert M. Avery IV at the Digital Equipment Corporation's Palo Alto–based Network System Laboratory, with the aim of building a physical plant at which the networks could connect. Known as the Palo Alto Internet Exchange, or PAIX, the facility proved to be a boon to California-area businesses. While he served as the operations manager of PAIX until 2003, Adelson concurrently sought to leverage his new expertise on a more global level.

in its own revenues. Adelson and his brother have recalled being roused from bed at five in the morning during the summers and loaded into the family station wagon for the trip to Eight Mile Road. There, as their father worked, they found cubbyholes or boxes in which to sleep until nine o'clock, when they woke up to begin helping customers. Adelson has credited his father's work ethic—as well as the prevailing blue-collar ethos of the neighborhood—with shaping his own work habits.

Adelson, who wore what he remembers as thick, unfashionable eyeglasses at an early age, was always a quiet child who preferred indoor pursuits. His brother, Scott, often tried to coax him out of his room to play hockey or basketball, invitations that Adelson politely deflected.

Toward the end of the 1970s, the family purchased an early home computer model, and Adelson became fascinated by its pulsating green display screen and the distinctive sound the modem made as it connected. Although he has joked with journalists about presenting a stereotypical picture of a young computer geek with Coke-bottle glasses, holed up antisocially in his room, Adelson has also said that he was not a lonely or solitary teen. Using rudimentary online bulletin boards, he connected with other computer enthusiasts. He was, in effect, as socially connected online as it was possible to be during the early days of the Internet.

Adelson attended the Cranbrook Kingswood School, an academically rigorous institution located in the wealthy Bloomfield Hills area of

EQUINIX

In 1998, Adelson and Avery co-founded Equinix. He explained the idea behind the new venture to Heather Havenstein for *ComputerWorld* (28 May 2007, online): "When the Internet became a commercial medium in 1994, [it] had been funded and operated by the government and universities. When it switched over to one operated by telecommunication companies, a very strong hierarchy developed. Tier 1 ISPs, the top five players in the world, would collect a dime on every packet that flowed throughout the Internet." He continued, "Part of the reason was all the Internet networks had to interconnect with each other using these antiquated network access points operated by carriers. Equinix replaced these single, network-owned facilities with Internet business exchanges where anyone could exchange packets with anyone in a neutral playing field."

Thanks to Equinix and its Internet Business Exchange (IBX) centers, e-commerce companies and content providers were able to serve larger customer bases, deliver content faster and more reliably over multiple networks, and reduce costs. "[We] allowed the dot-coms like Yahoo and Google and others to really exert their might," Adelson told Havenstein.

In his capacity as chief technology officer of Equinix, in 2003 Adelson testified in front of the US House Select Committee on Homeland Security's Subcommittee on Cybersecurity, Science, and Research and Development, chaired by Representative Mac Thornberry, a Republican from Texas. The purpose of the hearing was to hear industry perspectives on issues related to cybersecurity. Attempting to explain Equinix to the subcommittee members, Adelson said, "A good analogy for an exchange point is that we function as an international airport for Internet networks and services, though our airlines are networks, and our travelers are data bits and bytes." He continued, "While my distinguished [fellow] panel members are part of well-known large vendors and network service providers, the chances are while you may not have been exposed to Equinix in the past, you've sent or received e-mails that have traversed our exchange points and surfed websites housed in our facilities."

Equinix held its initial public offering (IPO) in 2000, raising more than $270 million of capital. Despite the company's success, Adelson found his life exceptionally stressful. Although he remained affiliated with Equinix until 2005, he moved with his family to upstate New York for a long sabbatical.

KEVIN ROSE AND DIGG

In 2003, Adelson was interviewed by Internet entrepreneur Kevin Rose, who was producing and cohosting an episode of a show called the *Screen Savers* for TechTV, a San Francisco–based cable and satellite channel that broadcast information about technology and the Internet. The following year, Rose approached Adelson with an idea for a website that would aggregate stories from all over the Web, with users voting for their favorites. The idea reminded Adelson of what he had been trying to do with Equinix. Referencing how IBX centers had leveled the playing field for e-businesses, he told Havenstein, "Digg does a very similar thing to the media. I have had an incredible passion about communication and how to break down the barriers for establishing a voice of the people."

News sites and blogs of all types began displaying "Digg" icons so that readers could easily click to vote a piece of writing onto the site. The pieces with the most votes won the most prominent placement. Because items were always being added, rankings changed constantly, making the site a dynamic place to visit on a regular basis. Adelson told Brian Deagon for *Investor's Business Daily* (3 Apr. 2007): "Digg represents a reflection of the crowd's interest in what's on the Web at any given time in various categories. All the content on Digg comes from links that are submitted by our regular users and then by other users who come to the Digg website. If that content becomes popular enough, it gets promoted to Digg's home page. At that point a very interesting secondary effect happens. You suddenly get this flood of interest in that particular article or content." He concluded, "We believe that Digg is democratizing media and doing it in a very effective and very level way."

Some early commentators expressed fears that rather than "democratizing" the Web, Digg's system might lead to an online mob mentality, with users ganging up to either promote or bury divisive stories. Adelson acknowledged that Digg attracted passionate users, but he explained that the system had checks and balances built in. "There is no such thing as a single mob in the Digg world," he told Havenstein. Others wondered what would happen if a false or spurious story gained traction on the website; Adelson was forced to admit that there was always a danger of that happening.

In 2007 Digg administrators, fearful that intellectual-property laws would be violated, tried to prevent users from linking to a story about an encryption code used to illegally copy DVDs. An uproar ensued, and Adelson subsequently backed down, allowing the content to be posted. Observers hailed this as a victory for openness and freedom on the user-generated Web 2.0. Another controversy broke out the following year, when the Associated Press mounted a campaign to prevent blogs and other websites from using too much of its material. While observers predicted that such a move could severely impede Digg, Adelson claimed to be unconcerned. "While I definitely love the idea of syndication and democratization of information, I tend to sympathize with the A.P.," he told Saul Hansell for the *New York Times* (18 June 2008, online). "It is their decision how their content gets used." He continued, "The way we designed Digg was to protect copyright owners, not abuse them. Digg's job is to direct you to the source." In 2008, Adelson was named in *Time* magazine's annual list of the world's one hundred most influential people.

Meanwhile, Adelson and Rose teamed up on another venture in 2005, an Internet video site called Revision3. Although the advertising for the venture claimed that it would "kill your television," Revision3's content could not be viewed on a television set unless the shows—which included *Diggnation*, hosted by Rose; *Geekdrome*; *Mysteries of Science Explained*; and the cooking program *Ctrl + Alt + Chicken* —were downloaded as video podcasts to a TiVo box. Adelson believed that "Internet television" had several advantages over traditional or cable networks, which tended to pander to a mass audience and were exceedingly expensive. "A very good television show has a million dollar budget for an episode," he told Thomas Claburn for InformationWeek (25 Sep. 2006, online). "Our budgets are certainly less than $50,000 and can be as low as $500. The podcasting generation, what it did was it created distributing and editing technologies, where the costs are just significantly less than traditional media." He pointed out that younger viewers were "more focused on the quality of the talent and the content than whether or not you have a $2 million set behind them." By mid-2006, *Diggnation*, which featured two people drinking beer and conversing while sitting on a sofa, was being downloaded some 250,000 times a week, making it among the most popular offerings in Apple's iTunes podcast listings.

Almost since its founding, rumors circulated that Digg was up for sale, but Adelson and Rose always denied such stories and affirmed their loyalty to the company. Industry observers were thus somewhat surprised in April 2010, when Adelson announced that he would be stepping down as CEO and that Rose, widely considered to be the more sociable and gregarious figure, would be taking over the leadership role. Many theorized that the move had been forced by the company's investors, who were presumably unhappy that Digg was not performing as well as originally hoped. Don Takahashi wrote for *VentureBeat* (25 Oct. 2010, online): "Digg has become a Silicon Valley fable because it didn't sell out when it was hot and allowed itself to be surpassed by other hot social networks such as Facebook. The conventional wisdom is that Adelson and founder Kevin Rose should have taken big offers from the likes of Google . . . when [Digg] had the chance."

Adelson, who denied that big offers had rolled in, wrote on the company blog that he had simply been subject to a new "entrepreneurial calling" and intended to "incubate some new business ideas over the next twelve months."

RECENT VENTURES

In late 2010, Adelson became the CEO of SimpleGeo, a platform that helps developers build location-based services and apps. A year later, he oversaw the company's acquisition by Urban Airship, a tech company focused on mobile apps, and remained onboard as a strategic adviser. Adelson also appears on the Revision3 program *Ask Jay*, on which he provides advice to aspiring entrepreneurs.

Adelson and his wife, Brenda Shea, were married in 1996. They have three children.

SUGGESTED READING

Bilton, Nick. "Digg Founder Kevin Rose to Replace Jay Adelson as CEO" *Bits*. The New York Times Company, 5 Apr. 2010. Web. 9 Apr. 2012.

Deagon, Brian. "When Viewers Dig a Story on This Site, They Digg It." *Investor's Business Daily*. 3 Apr. 2007: A6. Print.

Hansell, Saul. "Jay Adelson Diggs the A.P." *Bits*. The New York Times Company, 18 June 2008. Web. 9 Apr. 2012.

Havenstein, Heather. "The Grill: Digg.com's Jay Adelson on the Hot Seat." *Networking*. Computerworld Inc., 28 May 2007. Web. 9 Apr. 2012.

Takahashi, Dean. "Digg's Former CEO Jay Adelson Has 'No Regrets' About Not Taking Offers." *VentureBeat/Social*. VentureBeat, 25 Oct. 2010. Web. 9 Apr. 2012.

—*Mari Rich*

Sylviane Agacinski

Born: May 4, 1945
Occupation: Feminist philosopher, educator, writer

The French philosopher Sylviane Agacinski, who teaches at the École des hautes études en sciences sociales (EHESS, the School for Advanced Studies in the Social Sciences), in Paris, is one of France's leading feminist thinkers and has published several books. Internationally she is better known as the wife of the French politician Lionel Jospin, who served as his country's prime minister from 1997 to 2002.

Her diary-like account of his failed bid for the presidency, *Journal interrompu: 24 janvier–25 mai 2002*, was a sensation in France, prompting Pat Donnelly to write for the *Montreal Gazette* (April 12, 2003), "It's unfortunate that Agacinski's best-selling trifle, a journal written last year during the ill-fated political campaign of her husband, . . . has upstaged her more serious work."

Among the serious volumes to which Donnelly referred are Agacinski's treatise *Aparté: Conceptions et morts de Soren* Kierkegaard (1977, published in English in 1988 as *Aparté: Conceptions and Deaths of Soren Kierkegaard*) and *Politique des sexes* (1998, published as *Parity of the Sexes* in 2001). In the latter book Agacinski "begins with the notion that sexual difference should be affirmed rather than denied," according to the Web site of Columbia University Press, which published the translated edition. "Sex, Agacinski points out, is not a social, cultural, or ethnic characteristic—it is a universal human trait. In her argument for the necessary recognition of sexual difference, she enters into today's most controversial social territory." Thanks in some part to Agacinski's influence over Jospin, in 2000 a law went into effect in France requiring each of the country's political parties to name women to fill at least 50 percent of all candidacies for public office in certain elections.

EARLY LIFE AND EDUCATION

Sylviane Agacinski was born on May 4, 1945, in Nades, a village in the Auvergne region in central France. Her father, Henri, an immigrant from Poland, worked as a mining engineer. Her mother is mentioned in English-language sources simply as being "employed in trade." Agacinski's older sister, Sophie, was an actress who was known for her work in French TV movies and mini-series during the 1960s, '70s, and '80s.

Agacinski studied at a high school in Lyon, France, named for Juliette Recamier (1777–1849), a French socialite who ran a salon for a small but influential circle of writers and politicians. She next entered the University of Lyon, where she took several classes with Gilles Deleuze (1925–1995), a philosopher known for his writings on identity, literary theory, and cinema. Agacinski, who worked in the late 1960s as a journalist for *Paris Match*, later passed the *agrégation* (a competitive exam certifying her as a professor) in philosophy and embarked on a career in academia, teaching at the Lycée Carnot, in Paris, among other schools. In Paris she met the postmodernist philosopher Jacques Derrida (1930–2004), who introduced the term *deconstruction*, or *deconstructionism*, into the lexicon of critical theory. Deconstructionism, according to a posting on PBS.org, "is a challenge to the attempt to establish any ultimate or secure meaning in a text. Basing itself in language analysis,

Courtesy of Patrick Kovarik/AFP/Getty Images

it seeks to 'deconstruct' the ideological biases (gender, racial, economic, political, cultural) and traditional assumptions that infect all histories, as well as philosophical and religious 'truths.'" Derrida was one of the most celebrated and controversial philosophers of his generation, and "he cut a dashing, handsome figure at the lectern, with his thick thatch of prematurely white hair, tanned complexion, and well-tailored suits," Jonathan Kandall wrote for the *New York Times* (October 10, 2004, online). In 1983 Agacinski helped Derrida found the Collège international de philosophie (CIPh, the International College of Philosophy), an institute of higher learning that sought to open the study of philosophy to a wider segment of the population, free from the constraints of traditional institutional authority. Derrida, who had been married since 1957 to Marguerite Aucouturier, a psychoanalyst, became romantically involved with Agacinski; she gave birth to their son, Daniel, in 1984.

CAREER

Although neither as celebrated nor as polarizing as Derrida, Agacinski became well known in academia in her own right. Among her well-received early works was her aforementioned study of the 19th-century Danish philosopher and theologian Søren Kierkegaard. According to an article by Jon Stewart for *Kierkegaard Research: Sources, Reception and Research* (Volume 8, 2009), in *Aparté: Conceptions et morts de Søren Kierkegaard*, Agacinski "argues that Kierkegaard's mother, about whom he says nothing in his journals or published writing, represents an other, something apart. She is the secret to the authorship that Kierkegaard wishes never to be revealed." Agacinski later wrote another book that focused on Kierkegaard: *Critique de l'egocentrisme: L'evenement de l'autre* (1996, "A critique of egocentrism: The event as the other").

In 1991 Agacinski became affiliated with the EHESS, one of France's *grands établissements*, prestigious public institutions under ministerial charter, where she continues to teach. The following year she published a volume on architecture, *Philosophies et politiques de l'architecture*. A translated description of the book for the *Journal de l'Architecte* (April 8, 2010, online) lauds Agacinski's examination of the "original and rigorous challenges to which the phenomena of 'space' continue to send us."

Earlier, in 1983, at her sister's wedding to the actor Jean-Marc Thibault, Agacinski had met Lionel Jospin. Jospin was active in France's Parti Socialiste (PS), a center-left, socialist-democratic political party. A longtime member of the National Assembly, he had become the head of the party in 1981, after François Mitterrand, the former head, was elected president of France, and he subsequently served in Mitterrand's government as an education minister. Jospin and Agacinski met again in 1989, when she approached the Ministry of Education to discuss issues facing professors of philosophy. A romance was kindled, and they married in 1994. The following year Jospin was chosen to run against Jacques Chirac, the longtime mayor of Paris, in France's 1995 presidential election. Although Chirac won by a narrow margin, Jospin's relatively strong showing earned him the leadership of the PS once again. He set about building a new coalition with several other left-wing parties, and in 1997, when Chirac called an early election for the National Assembly, the coalition garnered a parliamentary majority, and Jospin became prime minister.

Despite her spouse's new national role, Agacinski stayed largely out of the political spotlight, as had long been traditional among politicians' wives in France; she continued to teach and write. She told journalists that she rarely even visited her husband at his office in the Hôtel Matignon (the official residence of French prime ministers), asserting to Victoria Main for the Wellington, New Zealand, *Dominion* (March 16, 1999), "Matignon? I never go there, except to lunch from time to time." She accompanied Jospin on overseas trips only when the destination interested her.

POLITICS

In 1998 Agacinski published *Politique des sexes*, in which she wrote, as quoted by Judith Warner in the *Washington Post* (June 3, 2001), "We want to keep the freedom to be seduced—and

to seduce. . . . There will never be a war of the sexes in France." In that book, which was translated into English in 2001, Agacinski discussed how the concept of *parité* (parity, the state of being equivalent) could be applied in a political context. The Columbia University Press Web site explained, "Agacinski's model of parity does not strive for the nebulous ideal of 'equality' between the sexes; instead, it demands a concrete formula for political contests: an equal number of female and male candidates in every election. It is a theory that has sparked impassioned debate across France: Are female politicians necessarily different from male politicians? Is parity democratic? Is it truly feminist?" In an article for the *New Republic* (March 26, 2001), Judith Warner quoted Agacinski as saying, "The people and their representatives are sexed individuals, masculine and feminine." "In her formulation," Warner wrote, parity is "the political interpretation of sexual difference." Warner added, "In other words, France needs equal representation not so women can express their fundamental equality with men but so they can express their fundamental difference, thereby bringing greater femininity to public life."

Agacinski's views drew loosely upon those of a group of prominent feminists, including Françoise Gaspard, who had published a book of essays in 1992 titled *Au pouvoir, citoyennes!: Liberté, égalité, parité*, playing on France's national motto, "Liberté, égalité, fraternité" (*pouvoir* means "power" or "governing"). Although Agacinski had told the *Dominion* reporter, "Frankly, nobody asks for my opinion," most observers easily discerned her hand in the passage of a new law on May 3, 2000, requiring that in certain elections the country's political parties fill at least half of all candidacies with women or risk being fined or losing state campaign funding. In an article for the *New Yorker* (May 29, 2000), Jane Kramer wrote, "[People] say that, if Françoise Gaspard 'baked the cake,' Sylviane Agacinski 'put on the icing' that made men try it."

Both Agacinski and the new law were subject to their share of vitriol. Some critics worried that quotas for women might reinforce or lead to discrimination against other groups. The philosopher and feminist Elisabeth Badinter told Kramer, "The French should be thinking less about the number of women in the National Assembly than about the fact that there isn't a single North African." Others found the idea of enforced parity demeaning to women. The jurist Evelyne Pisier asserted to Kramer, "*Parité* leads to an idea I cannot accept—that women have a different way of thinking."

"But, most of all," Kramer wrote, "Agacinski's enthusiasm for *parité* on what she called 'anthropological principle' did not endear her to the intellectuals in Paris's gay community . . . who thought that Agacinski's (in the words of one gay critic) 'two-headed hydra called humanity' flew in the face of contemporary understandings of sexuality. . . . They thought that her argument about sexual duality being 'the only universal difference' idealized the rights of a certain kind of people and, by implication, discredited the demands of anyone who wasn't that kind of people."

Over the ensuing years the uproar quieted. Kramer wrote for the *New Yorker* (July 25, 2011), "A decade later, the National Assembly looks much as it did in 2000; most political parties have simply chosen to pay the fines that exempt them from compliance, and women still account for less than a fifth of the country's deputies. On the other hand, the idea of parity in French life and politics has become respectable. Ségolène Royal was the Socialists' candidate for President in 2007. Today, Martine Aubry is their party leader. Even the National Front—the far-right party founded in the early seventies by the virulently macho Jean-Marie Le Pen—is currently in the hands of his daughter Marine."

In 2002 Jospin ran in France's presidential election against the incumbent, Chirac, and—unusually for a political campaign in France—Agacinski found herself in the public eye. "The French voters are yawning in apathy," Susan Bell wrote for the *Scotsman* (April 12, 2002), "at what they perceive as a boring two-horse race for the presidential elections between Gaullist incumbent Jacques Chirac and Socialist Prime Minister Lionel Jospin. So the two rivals, in a desperate effort to inject some passion into their lacklustre campaigns, have each reached for a secret weapon—their wives. And suddenly things begin to look more interesting. Because while the electorate is complaining that it can't tell the difference between the manifestos of 'Chirpin and Jospac,' as the wits have dubbed them, the front-runners' wives couldn't be more different." Bell continued, "In the blue corner, sporting her trademark tweeds, twinset and sensible shoes, is the coifed blonde Mme Bernadette Chirac—née Chodron de Courcel—a 68-year-old aristocrat from one of France's oldest families. . . . In the red corner, wearing a slinky number by avant-garde Paris designer Sonia Rykiel, is the sleek brunette Mme Jospin, although only the very brave would dare to address her as such." (During the campaign Agacinski used the hyphenated name Agacinski-Jospin; she later returned to using only her own name.)

For Agacinski, being a potential first lady was a trying experience. She told Bell, "It's like a chiaroscuro painting. The light shines on the wife who at the same time must remain in the shadow of the husband. It isn't easy." Scrutiny by journalists extended even to the manner in which the husbands and wives addressed each other, with much attention paid to the fact that the Chiracs still used the formal *vous* after more than four decades of marriage, while Agacinski and Jospin used the informal (and presumably more affectionate) *tu*.

International observers were stunned when Jospin was knocked out of the race in the first round by the far-right National Front candidate, Le Pen, who went on to lose to Chirac in the second round. Physically exhausted and gravely disappointed, Jospin withdrew from public life and settled into a period of self-imposed exile at his vacation home on the Isle of Rhe. Agacinski, seemingly used to the political spotlight by then, was vocal in her defense of her husband and publicly excoriated those whom she felt had contributed to his loss. A few months after the election, she published *Journal interrompu*, in which she characterized Chirac as "cynical" and "sinister" and railed against what she termed "the infantile Left," whose members did not support Jospin adequately. (Chirac's wife, too, published a book about her husband.)

Agacinski's recent books are *Engagements* (2007), a further examination of the differences between the sexes, and *La plus belle histoire des femmes* (2011, "The most beautiful history of women"), which she co-wrote with Françoise Héritier, Michelle Perrot, and Nicole Bacharan.

Agacinski is the stepmother of Jospin's son and daughter, Hugo and Eva, from his first marriage, which ended in divorce. Her son, Daniel, is pursuing a doctorate at the University of Toulouse, in France.

SUGGESTED READING

"Autour de 'Volume. Philosophies et politiques de l'architecture." *Journal de l'Architecte*. Journal de l'Architecte, 8 Apr. 2010. Web. 16 Dec. 2011.

Bell, Susan. "The First Wives Club Each Other." *Scotsman* 12 Apr. 2002: 2. Print.

"Deconstructionism." *PBS.org*. Public Broadcasting Service, n.d. Web. 16 Dec. 2011.

Donnelly, Pat. "Singing the Blue-Met's-Over Blues: Five-Day Festival Featured 117 Events. Exposure to a New Array of Authors Makes One's Reading List Grow Exponentially." *Gazette* [Montreal, Quebec] 12 Apr. 2003: H2. Print.

Kandell, Jonathan. "Jacques Derrida, Abstruse Theorist, Dies at 74." *New York Times*. New York Times, 10 Oct. 2004. Web. 16 Dec. 2011.

Kramer, Jane. "Against Nature: Elisabeth Badinter's Contrarian Feminism." *New Yorker* 25 July 2011: 44–55. Print.

---. "Liberty, Equality, Sorority: French Women Demand Their Share." *New Yorker* 29 May 2000: 112–117. Print.

Main, Victoria. "Woman Trouble for Unworldly Jospin." *Dominion* [Wellington, New Zealand] 16 Mar. 1999: Features 6. Print.

"Parity of the Sexes." *Columbia University Press.* Columbia University Press, n.d. Web. 16 Dec. 2011.

Warner, Judith. "Same Difference." *New Republic* 26 Mar. 2001: 16. Print.

---. "Who Knew? The French Got Femininity Right." *Washington Post* 3 June 2001: B1. Print.

SELECTED WORKS

Aparte: Conceptions and Deaths of Søren Kierkegaard, 1998; *Parity of the Sexes,* 2001; *Time Passing: Modernity and Nostalgia,* 2003

—*Mari Rich*

Angela Ahrendts

Born: June 7, 1960
Occupation: CEO of Burberry

Bloomberg via Getty Images

Angela Ahrendts, the chief executive officer (CEO) of the multibillion-dollar luxury fashion company Burberry since 2006, "wasn't raised with handmade elegance and can't claim a pedigree from École Polytechnique or reminisce about the family château," Nancy Hass wrote for the *Wall Street Journal Magazine* (9 Sep. 2010, online). Hass continued, "She doesn't even have the rapid-fire, cosmopolitan panache of her predecessor, Rose Marie Bravo. . . . But her homespun roots in Middle America . . . may be fundamental to her success." Ahrendts's down-to-earth manner, a rarity in her industry, has helped her to win the loyalty of her workers and has been a key ingredient in her considerable success. She began her career in the early 1980s at Damon, a line of men's clothing, and then went on, successively, to high-level positions at the fashion houses Warnaco, Carmelo Pomodoro, Donna Karan, Henri Bendel, and Liz Claiborne. Ahrendts "truly doesn't care about image, about ego, about seeming cool or exclusive," Paul Charron, the CEO of Liz Claiborne during Ahrendts's tenure there, told Hass. "That's why she's been able to do all this. People want to work for her because she's completely unadorned and she has a life. She's all talent and no pretension." Among other honors, Ahrendts was number eight (up from thirteen the previous year) on the *Financial Times* (15 Nov. 2011, online) list of the fifty "Women at the Top," and in 2004 she was included on the ten-woman "power list" of fashion executives compiled by the magazine *Time Style & Design*.

At the UK-based Burberry, Ahrendts has continued the mission begun by Bravo in the late 1990s: making the once-stodgy company relevant to young customers without sacrificing longtime buyers of its products. Ahrendts's efforts in that direction have centered largely on the Internet: For example, she started a Burberry social-networking site, and the company's annual runway shows can be streamed online in real time. As a result, Burberry's online sales have skyrocketed. "In her relatively short tenure," Julia Werdigier wrote for the *New York Times* (10 Nov. 2009), "Ms. Ahrendts has done well by doing the surprising." She has also done the prudent: Thanks to the substantial but careful cost-cutting Ahrendts undertook during the economic crisis that began in 2008, Burberry weathered the storm more successfully than any other firm in the United Kingdom. "Balance . . . to an almost mechanical degree, is what seems to motivate Ahrendts," Hass observed. "While other brands have made themselves slaves to the pursuit of a new 'it' bag or leverage everything on the discovery of a new silhouette each season, she is dogged about hedging risk." Ahrendts said to Werdigier, "The biggest thing that keeps me up at night is how can we continue to evolve this organization in order to stay ahead of the curve. My job is always to look two to three years ahead and look round the corner and see what's coming."

EARLY LIFE AND EDUCATION

The third of six children (five of them girls) to come along within seven years, Angela Ahrendts was born on June 7, 1960 and raised in New Palestine, Indiana, a town of just over 2,000. Her father, Richard Ahrendts, was an entrepreneur in the town; her mother, Jean, was a former model. The family was Methodist. "We were really, really close," Ahrendts told the *Financial Times* (15 Nov. 2011). The eight family members slept in four bedrooms, which did not make for a great deal of privacy; Ahrendts's solution was to claim a space below a stairwell, where she "installed black lights and put in shelves" and "lit candles she'd hand-dipped," as her sister Carrie recalled to Nancy Hass. "It was famous in the neighborhood. Everyone came to see Angela's place."

While growing up, Ahrendts struck others as friendly and not particularly assertive. Dana Knight reported for the *Indianapolis Star* (19 Dec. 2005) that she was "the kind of girl whose order at a restaurant could arrive completely wrong and she would just smile sheepishly and eat it up." Her mother told Knight, "As a child, she just floated along, and I prayed no one would take advantage of her." The exception to her general behavior involved clothes. One morning, for example, she was running late for school and realized that the shade of blue of her socks did not match that of her skirt; angry that she had dressed herself in mismatched clothes, she vented her feelings at her family members, who were shocked. As a teen, Ahrendts collected clothing and could often be found at her sewing machine, making her own clothes. While she did not give the appearance of being ego-driven, Ahrendts impressed her teachers, one of whom, Marvin Shepler, told Peter Gumbel for CNNmoney.com (15 Oct. 2007), "She stood out. You knew she was going to be successful whatever she ended up doing."

Ahrendts enrolled at Ball State University, in Muncie, Indiana, where she studied fashion design and merchandising. She was also a standout tennis player at the school. During that period she also listened to Christian music, which "brought her closer to her faith," as Nancy Hass wrote. While she was a student at Ball State, Ahrendts took a trip to New York City and visited the studios of fashion designers, which fueled her desire to enter the field.

CAREER

One course short of earning her undergraduate degree, Ahrendts moved to New York to work as an account manager for Damon, a line of men's clothing. Before long she moved to Warnaco, a designer and seller of intimate apparel and sportswear, working under Linda Wachner, a CEO renowned for her toughness. At Warnaco she began as sales manager for Geoffrey Beene sportswear; she later moved up to vice president in charge of Geoffrey Beene as well as the Valentino and Ungaro lines of intimate apparel. Wachner told Nancy Hass about Ahrendts, "She was one of the few people who knew not to take things personally. She never flinched, never

whined, never shirked. She was a class act, and I can't say that about too many people." Ahrendts said to the *Financial Times*, "Linda is very left-brain analytical: a wizard with the numbers, so smart. [At] Warnaco I sharpened my left brain. To win in that corporation, you had to."

In 1989, Ahrendts became vice president for marketing and sales at the sportswear-design company Carmelo Pomodoro. There, she tripled sales and was later named the firm's president. In April 1992 she joined the fashion company Donna Karan, and within a short time she was president of Donna Karan International, overseeing the design, production, and sales operations for the Donna Karan Collection and Donna Karan Signature. Dana Knight wrote that "Ahrendts was a creative genius, according to Karan, and had a knack for balancing that creative vision with the business side of things." Ahrendts told the *Financial Times* that while Linda Wachner at Warnaco had been left-brain oriented, Donna Karan was "a very right-brain driven company. Donna is the epitome of creative." She came to understand, she added, that in the fashion business "marrying that extreme left with the extreme right is critical." Peter Gumbel quoted her as saying that the chief lesson she learned at Karan is that "great design alone isn't going to yield the results investors are expecting."

In 1996 Leslie Wexner, the CEO of Limited Brands, hired Ahrendts as executive vice president of Henri Bendel, a high-end seller of women's fashion accessories. Ahrendts was charged with expanding Henri Bendel, which was centered in New York, to fifty new outlets around the country. She said to Gumbel, "Part of me is very entrepreneurial. I loved the challenge of doing that with the support of a big corporation behind me." Eighteen months later, however, the board of Henri Bendel withdrew that support, ending plans for the expansion, in what Ahrendts called "the most devastating blow in my career." Nonetheless, she had won the esteem of her staff. Philip Monaghan, the head of marketing during Ahrendts's tenure at the company, told Hass that Ahrendts's workers "would walk through fire for her." Hass wrote in 2010, "Unlike corporate chiefs who favor an inaccessible, imperial style, Ahrendts seems comfortable with dissent; her executives joke easily with her, and aren't afraid to press their points."

The fashion house Liz Claiborne took Ahrendts on in 1998 as vice president for merchandising. The company's CEO, Paul Charron, had set out to acquire fashion brands and companies, and Ahrendts advised him during that process. He did not always take the advice readily. When she approached him about buying Juicy Couture, a line of casual wear, "I thought it was a little crazy," Charron recalled to Gumbel. "I said, 'Angela, it's a damn track suit.'" Ahrendts and Juicy Couture's two founders persuaded him, however, and the line went on to become one of Liz Claiborne's most successful. Eleven months after starting at the company, Ahrendts became group president; she was later promoted to executive vice president and oversaw more than twenty brands, among them Lucky jeans, Kenneth Cole New York, Dana Buchman, and Sigrid Olsen—making for 40 percent of company revenues in total. In her years at Liz Claiborne, sales shot from $2.5 billion to $4.6 billion. Ahrendts told the *Financial Times* that during her tenure there, Charron taught her leadership.

Ahrendts has said that she made one of the most difficult decisions of her career when offered the chance to become CEO of the UK-based Burberry. She nearly declined the offer because she was "in love with" her post at Liz Claiborne, as she told Dana Knight. She added, however, "One night a little voice in my head said, 'If you don't do this, will it ever come along again?' There are not a lot of CEO opportunities for women in the world." Ahrendts joined Burberry in late 2005. After a period of training under the company's outgoing CEO, Rose Marie Bravo, Ahrendts officially assumed that position in July 2006.

Burberry was founded in 1856 by Thomas Burberry, who started a shop in Hampshire, England, with the aim of providing durable clothing for sportsmen. Burberry invented gabardine, which he patented in 1888, and during the 1890s his company brought out the first trench coat. During World War I, British officers were clad in Burberry products. Over the course of the twentieth century, the company was seen strictly as a maker of raincoats and umbrellas and known for its red, black, beige, and white check (plaid) pattern. After becoming Burberry's CEO, in 1997, Bravo remade the firm into a provider of luxury items, greatly increasing sales by pursuing a younger clientele without alienating established customers.

Among Ahrendts's challenges when she succeeded Bravo were to continue to woo the youth market and to address the overexposure of the Burberry check pattern, which had been copied by less-exclusive labels and worn extensively by second- and third-tier celebrities. Ahrendts's strategy was to remove the check from about 90 percent of Burberry's products while greatly increasing the use of Thomas Burberry's signature and the company's century-old logo, featuring an equestrian knight carrying a flag that reads "Prorsum," Latin for "forward." In order to pursue younger customers while keeping the business of more traditional buyers, Ahrendts separated Burberry's clothing into three distinct lines: Prorsum, made up of luxurious evening wear seen on such A-list celebrities as actor Gwyneth Paltrow; Burberry London, the everyday-clothing and office-wear line; and Burberry Brit, for more casual items.

Ahrendts counted among her early successes at Burberry the introduction of $2,000 handbags to mark the company's 150th anniversary, in 2006. The bags saw phenomenal sales. A pitfall that year followed Ahrendts's decision to close Burberry's shirt factory in Wales and shift production to China; workers organized protests, and the move drew criticism from British celebrities such as actor Emma Thompson and even Prince Charles, who expressed skepticism that Burberry could maintain its British air if it stopped making its products at home. Ahrendts apparently smoothed over relations with Prince Charles, as she has since been invited on several occasions to Buckingham Palace.

Ahrendts's plan for winning and maintaining the loyalty of younger purchasers involved creative use of the Internet; she was inspired partly by the example of her daughters, who buy much of their clothing online. She has also given a great deal of freedom to Burberry's creative director, Christopher Bailey, who has had significant input in terms of marketing and is not advised or hampered by any outside design firms. Ahrendts said to Andrea Catherwood for *Analyst Wire* (24 Feb. 2010), "We said a couple of years ago that there was a digital tsunami coming our way. And we could either ride the greatest wave of our life or be crushed. And Christopher said let's so surfing." The company has pursued purchasers through Twitter and YouTube and, as of early 2012, had nearly eleven million fans on Facebook. At its 2010 runway show, the company introduced Burberry Retail Theatre, passing out iPads complete with customized apps to allow attendees to prepurchase the items on display. Ahrendts also pioneered a social-networking site for Burberry, Artofthetrench.com, on which Internet viewers can submit photos of themselves in Burberry trench coats. As a result of those moves, in 2010 Burberry saw its Internet sales increase 60 percent from the previous year. Ahrendts told Hass, "If I look to any company as a model, it's Apple. They're a brilliant design company working to create a lifestyle, and that's the way I see us."

Like many companies, Burberry was hit hard by the worldwide financial crisis that began in 2008; that year its revenues fell by 14 percent in one quarter. Facing an emergency, Ahrendts aimed to lower the firm's expenses by $78 million. To that end, she reduced the company's workforce by 10 percent, postponed plans to revamp six major outlets, froze salary increases, and put off giving bonuses. "Our recession strategy was do not stop investing in anything the consumer sees," Ahrendts told Catherwood. "And anything the consumer doesn't see, maybe we need to tighten and pull that in a little bit." That plan appeared to pay off: According to at least one research company, Burberry performed better than any other British company in 2009, and between late 2009 and late 2010, the value of its stock doubled. In 2009 the firm's beefed-up line of children's clothing, in particular, sold so well that Burberry had trouble meeting demand.

In terms of business in other countries, Burberry has been active in the Asian market, maintaining dozens of stores in China and also establishing a solid presence in Japan. At the same time, Ahrendts has been careful to control use of the Burberry label outside the United Kingdom. For example, under Bravo, the company's Spanish partner, Burberry Spain, created products unrelated to those of the British firm and sold them under the Burberry label, making for 20 percent of Burberry's revenue. Despite that enormous source of revenue, Ahrendts—in order to protect the integrity of the company's products—discontinued that practice, developing a line of Burberry-made items to sell in Spain. "If you can't control everything, you can't control anything, not really," Ahrendts said to Hass.

PERSONAL LIFE
Werdigier called Ahrendts "tall [and] charismatic," and Hass referred to her "sharp blue eyes." Ahrendts met her husband, Gregg, the founder and former head of a contracting business in New York City, when both were in elementary school in Indiana. The couple have two daughters, Sommer and Angelina, and a son, Jennings. When Ahrendts interviewed for her position at Burberry, "I said, 'I have three full-time jobs that you need to know about upfront,'" Ahrendts recalled to Dana Knight. "I've been with my husband 27 years, and that's full time. I do have three children, and that's full time. And I have a full-time job. And all three of them are critically important to me." Knight noted in 2005 that Ahrendts "is the kind of mom who gets down on the floor to play" with her children. She also reads the Bible daily. As for her career, Ahrendts told Catherine Curan for *Crain's New York Business* (1999, online), "I've never considered it work. It's a natural extension of my life."

SUGGESTED READING
Gumbel, Peter. "Burberry's New Boss Doesn't Wear Plaid." *CNNMoney*. Cable News Network, 1 Oct. 2007. Web. 17 Feb. 2012.

Hass, Nancy. "Earning Her Stripes." *Wall Street Journal Magazine* 9 Sep. 2010. Web. 17 Feb. 2012.

Knight, Dana. "Mad for Plaid: Hoosier Angela Ahrendts Taking Helm of Venerable Fashion Firm Burberry." *Indianapolis Star* 19 Dec. 2005: C1. Print.

Prosser, David. "Angela Ahrendts: Exactly the Right Material." *Independent*. Independent. co.uk, 28 May 2011. Web. 17 Feb. 2012.

Werdigier, Julia. "Still Chic, As Time Goes By." *New York Times* 10 Nov. 2009, nat. ed.: B1. Print.

—*Clifford Thompson*

Samir Amin

Born: September 3, 1931
Occupation: Economist and educator

Samir Amin is the director of the Third World Forum, a group of intellectuals working in Africa, Latin America, and Asia that is dedicated to encouraging social and economic growth in poor or oppressed regions. He has been called, in some quarters, one of the world's foremost political economists and one of the most enlightened thinkers of his generation. Amin is the author of dozens of books and regularly publishes articles in small left-leaning journals. Not surprisingly, he has received little attention in other media outlets, as most of his views are far outside of the mainstream. He has repeatedly asserted, for example, that the United States, western Europe, and Japan constitute an "imperialist triad." On the subject of the terrorist attacks of September 11, 2001, he told Fatemah Farag for *Al-Ahram Weekly* (30 Oct. 2002), "I sometimes wonder if the whole thing was not fabricated. . . . considering the degree of the stupidity of the likes of [Osama] Bin Laden he was successfully exploited within the plan of the US military control scenario."

EARLY LIFE AND EDUCATION
Amin was born on September 3, 1931, in Cairo, Egypt. Born prematurely, he remained sickly and jaundiced for much of his first year. His mother, Odette, was of French descent. His father, Farid, was a native of Egypt. Farid could trace his lineage to what was known as the Coptic aristocracy, a wealthy and educated group whose members often intermarried in an attempt at insularity. His paternal grandfather was a railroad engineer who mounted a sly protest during Great Britain's occupation of Egypt by pretending not to speak English when approached by the British. Both of Amin's parents were medical doctors; Farid served as a public-health official in Port Said, and Odette worked in a private clinic, charging her wealthy patients enough to subsidize her after-hours care of the indigent. It was unusual for a woman of her generation and social standing to work in Egypt, but Farid, who believed in democratic and secular reform, fully supported her decision. (Farid belonged to the Wafd Party, a nationalist movement that emerged after World War I.) Amin and his older sister, Leila, were raised with the help of a kind

AFP/Getty Images

housekeeper, whom he remembers with great fondness.

Thanks in large part to his parents' example, Amin exhibited a strong sense of social justice at an early age. "I would not necessarily say [they were] socialist, but in the end it came to more or less the same thing," he wrote in *A Life Looking Forward: Memoirs of an Independent Marxist* (2006). "In the privileged class to which I belonged, people were insensitive to the wretched lot of the working classes and considered it quite 'natural.' Father and Mother, however, never stopped telling me that it was neither natural nor acceptable, and that all it meant was that society was badly constructed." Once, when he was about six years old, Amin accompanied his mother to a poor neighborhood in Port Said and witnessed a child eating from a garbage can. When Odette explained that society sometimes forced people to live like that, he vowed solemnly that when he grew up he would change society. "When she told this story forty years later to [a friend] who had asked her at what age I became a communist, she said: 'As you see, since he was six.'" The family sympathized deeply with the USSR, and for a time Farid and Odette allowed the Soviets to use a portion of the large family home as a consulate.

Amin, who had been educated as a child in Egypt's French-run schools, traveled to Paris to study in 1947. (Part of his journey took place on an oil tanker, whose captain was willing to accept paying passengers.) Amin had never before been outside of Egypt and had rarely left the small region around Cairo, Port Said, and Suez. He became a boarder at the Lycée Henri IV (a public secondary school), where his studies focused on math. He has recalled that a homeless person with a math background regularly stationed himself outside of the school gates and offered to do homework in exchange for a cheap bottle of wine; Amin has admitted that he availed himself of this service from time to time.

While at the Lycée, Amin joined the Communist Party, and much of his social life revolved around party functions, as he considered his politically uninvolved fellow students to be bourgeois and elitist. He enjoyed math but began to have doubts about making it the basis of a career. Much to the displeasure of his instructors, he decided in 1949 to focus instead on political science and economics. In 1952, Amin earned a diploma from the Institute of Political Science, and the following year he earned a law degree (a prerequisite for the serious study of economics). Concurrently, he remained active in France's Communist Party, which maintained a cell at the Institute of Political Science. In 1950, Amin also met his future wife, Isabelle, at the Institute.

In addition to the Communist Party, Amin was a member of the French students' union, whose protests often turned violent, and he helped to edit the leftist student paper *Étudiants anticolonialistes*. In 1954, he received an advanced degree in political economics, and two years later he earned a mathematical statistician's diploma from France's Institute of Statistics.

Amin remained in France until 1957 and considers that decade, which coincided almost exactly with the country's Fourth Republic, to have been an exceptionally formative time for him. Amin wrote in his memoir that "our image of the Fourth Republic was certainly colorless during my student days in Paris. When I say 'our,' I mean the revolutionary young communists and numerous former members of the Resistance." While he and his compatriots did not give up all hope of a glorious Soviet-style "people's republic," their movement gradually lost steam. "Once history has taken its course, it always seems to have been inevitable," he wrote. "Those who fitted into it appear as realistic—history 'proved them right'—while the others appear as utopian. I belonged, and still belong, to the latter group."

RETURN TO EGYPT

Soon after Gamal Abdel Nasser Hussein assumed the presidency of Egypt in 1956, he announced the nationalization of the largely French-owned Suez Canal Company, which built the canal in the mid-nineteenth century and had operated it since. A crisis ensued, precipitated in part by the nationalization, and Amin was deeply worried for his parents, who lived so close to the center of hostilities that some of their furniture was riddled with bullet holes.

Once the Suez Canal Crisis calmed, Nasser nationalized many of Egypt's other foreign entities, including the construction, steel, tobacco, pharmaceutical, and chemical industries. (He did, however, allow enough property to remain in the private sector to encourage growth.) A new institution for economic management was formed, and Ismail Abdullah, the Marxist economist who had originally conceived of the organization, was made head of its economic research unit. (Nasser would not grant him oversight of the entire institution because of Abdullah's Communist affiliation.) Abdullah ensured that Amin, who had returned to his native country after defending his doctoral thesis and marrying Isabelle, was appointed to a research position. In this capacity, Amin prepared weekly reports to guide the managers of the newly nationalized enterprises and offered in-depth studies of the economic problems in relevant sectors.

SEEF AND MOVING TO AFRICA
In January 1960, Amin traveled to Paris to work at the Service des Études Économiques et Financières (SEEF). There, he teamed with a mathematician to study relative prices (an economic term describing the price of one commodity in relation to others) and determine a way in which France's pricing system could be "delinked" from those of other countries, allowing for more efficient social policies. "Of course, World Bank officials could never have conceived of such a model," he sniped in A Life Looking Forward, "trapped as they are by their idiotic preconception of the market as self-regulating by nature. Still today the Bank sees relative prices simply as crude data."

Amin left SEEF in September, although officials there were eager for him to stay. He realized, however, that he was putting his talents and energies to use in the service of capitalism, a prospect he found distressing. "Why not try to place them at the service of liberation and progress somewhere in the Third World," he wrote.

As a student, Amin had met many activists of African descent, including those who had founded the Fédération des Étudiants d'Afrique Noire en France. One of his colleagues at SEEF had been advising the new government of Mali (formerly the Sudanese Republic) and he recommended opportunities in the area to Amin. Intrigued, Amin and Isabelle traveled to the Malian capital of Bamako, where he began working as an advisor to the economics and planning ministry. In that role, he was responsible for drafting various programs relating to education, mass vaccination, agricultural production, and public finance reform, among other areas. "The idea was not to dream up some spectacular advance on the highway of progress," he wrote, "but to predict the dangers on the winding road ahead."

That highway, as Amin predicted, contained several roadblocks. He had to contend with ill-informed technocrats; a misguided love of large prestige projects, such as sports stadiums, rather than more needed structures; a tendency to prioritize political gain over economic reality; and incompetence at every occupational and social level. With widespread computer use several years in the future, Amin relied heavily on an engineering slide rule, but he never found that much of an impediment; he was convinced, as he has explained, that any calculation needed in Africa boiled down to compound interest and the so-called rule of three (a type of cross-multiplication).

The government housed the couple in a villa in Koulouba, overlooking the city, and although Isabelle, who had found a job teaching, was once attacked by a monkey, their life was otherwise ordered and pleasant, with regular dinner parties and trips to the open-air cinema.

Amin was proud of the economic model that he helped to formulate for Mali and believed that its results were largely positive. Still, he has admitted, "the plan left scope for discussion of various options important both socially and politically and in terms of economic efficiency." He remarked, "The rot set in later": Mali is now among the poorest nations in the world.

IDEP AND OTHER ACTIVITIES
Amin always had preferred to work not in "stuffy libraries," as he often characterized academia, but in a "close and living relationship" with practical action. Still, he was interested to hear of a job at the African Institute for Economic Development and Planning (IDEP), a Pan-African institution formed in 1962 by the United Nations General Assembly. In 1963, he left Bamako for Dakar, where IDEP maintained its headquarters. The organization, which has more than fifty member states, was charged with training policy makers and development officials, advising African governments, encouraging original research on Africa's policy issues, and ensuring the economic independence of individual countries.

Amin agreed to join IDEP's small teaching staff. He was given responsibility for courses in national accounting and African planning techniques; however, he quickly suspected that he may have made a career misstep. He enjoyed little autonomy as an instructor and found his students to be extremely unprepared for the level of work required. Adding to the difficulty was the fact that some spoke only French, while others spoke just English. Amin tried to mitigate the situation by lecturing in each language on alternate days.

A colleague suggested that attempting France's grueling civil-service exam would expand Amin's career choices and give him a chance at a professorship in political economics. Although most candidates spend several years in preparation for the competitive test, Amin decided to try on the spur of the moment. He was delighted to pass. Although he remained affiliated with IDEP, he found several other teaching posts. As a foreign-born graduate of the exam, he was assigned, in 1966, to a provincial school, the University of Poitiers.

In the wake of the mass student protests and general strike of 1968, French officials founded a new, less traditional school called the Centre Universitaire Expérimental de Vincennes, which later changed its name to the University of Paris VIII Vincennes à Saint-Denis. With its policies of openness and experimentation, it was a good match for Amin, who became a well-liked professor there. Additionally, he taught for a time at Dakar University.

Despite his early misgivings about IDEP, when the UN reassessed the organization and determined that its main focus should be planning and development strategies—which its education programs then had to be reformulated to reflect—Amin agreed to step in as director. He held that leadership spot from 1970 to 1980, but his tenure did not always go smoothly. "I conducted IDEP's affairs as one wages a war," he recalled in his memoir. His combativeness stemmed largely from his view that the United States was forcing the UN to bow to its demands, and to those of its allies, including Israel. During his time as head of IDEP, Amin was also instrumental in the founding of the Council for Development of Social Science Research in Africa and served as the organization's first executive secretary, from 1973 to 1975.

THIRD WORLD FORUM AND BEYOND
In 1980, Amin became the director of the Third World Forum, also known as the Forum du Tiers Monde, which is based in Dakar. "The aim was to create an independent international association of intellectuals of the Third World," he explained to Naima Bouteldja for Z *Magazine* (Aug. 2003). "We wanted to organize an exchange of ideas and have a discussion centered . . . on the challenges that global capitalism poses to the people of the Third World. Those challenges are not only economic; they are cultural, political, and geo-strategic." In 1997, realizing the need for a similar group on a global level, he helped create the Cairo-based World Forum for Alternatives (WFA). (The Third World Forum is now one of the constituent groups of the WFA.)

The World Economic Forum (WEF) brings together many of the top political and business leaders from around the globe in the group's annual meeting in Davos, Switzerland.

Starting in 1999, the WFA, in conjunction with the Third World Forum and other organizations, began staging "another Davos" event as an alternative to the WEF's meeting. Called the World Social Forum, it seeks to strengthen the ties among groups that "work against both neo-liberal globalization and US hegemony," as Amin told Bouteldja. Among the speakers have been such well-known figures as American linguist and philosopher Noam Chomsky and Indian novelist Arundhati Roy. The involvement of such luminaries has lead to charges that the WFA is relying hypocritically on celebrities; however, others have argued that the presence of such figures ensures media attention.

Amin has written several books, some of which have been translated into English. Among them are *Unequal Development* (1976), *The Arab Nation* (1978), *Eurocentrism* (1989), *Maldevelopment in Africa and in the Third World* (1990), *Capitalism in the Age of Globalization* (1997), *Obsolescent Capitalism: Contemporary Politics and Global Disorder* (2004), *Europe and the Arab World: Patterns and Prospects for the New Relationship* (2005), and *Beyond U.S. Hegemony?: Assessing the Prospects for a Multipolar World* (2006). Many of these are published by the London-based Zed Books, an independent company focused on nonfiction works in such areas as economics, gender studies, and development studies. The company has no shareholders and is operated as a cooperative. Some of Amin's other works are published by the book-publishing arm of the *Monthly Review*, an independent Socialist magazine to which Amin frequently contributes articles.

PERSONAL PHILOSOPHY
Although he has sometimes held highly prominent positions, Amin has always remained true to the values expressed in his works. "I like equality," he wrote in *A Life Looking Forward*. "I like to hear other people's points of view and to discuss them. All those who have worked with me . . . can testify that I have never resorted to even mildly repressive methods. The whole idea disgusts me." Although his memoir makes plain that he enjoys the small comforts and pleasures of life, he added, "A pathological attachment to the external manifestations of power—prestigious office, large car, and so on—has never tempted me in any way."

SUGGESTED READING
Amin, Samir. *A Life Looking Forward: Memoirs of an Independent Marxist.* London: Zed Books, 2006.

Bouteldja, Naima. "Third World Forum: Naima Bouteldja Interviews Samir Amin." Z *Magazine.* Z Communications, Aug. 2003. Web. 20 Mar. 2012.

Farag, Fatemah. "Empire of Chaos Challenged: An Interview with Samir Amin." *Al-Ahram Weekly*. Al-haram Weekly, 24–30 Oct. 2002. Web. 20 Mar. 2012.

Foster, John Bellamy. "Samir Amin at 80." *Monthly Review*. Monthly Review, Oct. 2011. Web. 20 Mar. 2012.

Motta, Sara. "In Conversation: Samir Amin." *Ceasefire Magazine*. Ceasefire Magazine, 5 Dec. 2011. Web. 20 Mar. 2012.

—*Mari Rich*

Getty Images for TechCrunch

Michael Arrington

Born: March 13, 1970
Occupation: Founder of *TechCrunch*

Michael Arrington, founder of the technology blog *TechCrunch*, is an influential blogger and Internet start-up investor. In 2005, he founded the company *TechCrunch* to aid his research into user-driven Internet start-ups, collectively known as Web 2.0 companies. Almost immediately, he attracted a large readership that included entrepreneurs, innovators, and investors. Within two years of its founding, *TechCrunch* was the fourth most-linked-to blog on the Internet, and Arrington's articles could make or break a start-up. His success allowed him to acquire a team of writers and begin hosting a series of major industry conferences.

As Arrington's company and reputation grew, he became known both for his intelligent tech analysis and sharp writing, as well as his assertive personality, which contributed to a number of high-profile arguments with other influential figures in the tech industry. In September 2010, Arrington sold *TechCrunch* to AOL for about $25 million, with the understanding that the Internet services and media company would not interfere with Arrington's editorial freedom. However, a year later, Arrington was forced to leave *TechCrunch* amid controversy surrounding his cofounding of CrunchFund, a venture capital fund focusing on tech start-ups.

After his departure from AOL, Arrington started a new blog, *Uncrunched*, where he continues to be one of the strongest and most distinctive voices in the industry. Throughout his career, Arrington has garnered controversy for investing in many of the same companies he writes about, leading to routine accusations of conflicts of interest. His success and influence has sparked conversations about the role of bloggers in traditional journalism.

EARLY LIFE

J. Michael Arrington was born on March 13, 1970, in Huntington Beach, California. He attended Claremont McKenna College, a small liberal arts school located on the eastern border of Los Angeles, California, where he received a BA degree in economics in 1992. Three years later, he earned a JD degree from Stanford Law School in Stanford, California.

After law school, Arrington worked for a few years as a corporate and securities lawyer at a series of firms, including Wilson Sonsini Goodrich & Rosati (WSGR), one of Silicon Valley's top technology law firms. While specializing in helping companies prepare for initial public offerings, Arrington worked with numerous venture funds and investment banks, as well as such companies as Idealab, Netscape, Pixar, and Apple. Although he was, in his own words, "an exceptionally average attorney," as quoted by Fred Vogelstein for *Wired* (22 June 2007, online), Arrington found that he enjoyed working with entrepreneurs, whose spirit he greatly admired. "Entrepreneurs are crazy," he told Vogelstein. "It makes no sense to quit a job as a lawyer or an investment banker making $200,000 a year to take a one-in-ten chance of getting rich."

INTERNET START-UPS

In 1999, Arrington left WSGR to work for a series of Internet start-up companies. His entrance into the tech world coincided with the peak of the dot-com boom, the period of time from 1996 to 2000 when Internet companies saw their stock values grow rapidly. Arrington first served as the vice president of business development and general counsel for RealNames, a company founded in 1997 by the British tech entrepreneur Keith Teare. RealNames aimed to create a system to replace domain names with intuitive keywords typed directly into the address bar of the Internet browser Microsoft Explorer. Around the same time, Arrington cofounded an online-payment company called Achex. By 2001, however, Achex could no longer compete with the e-commerce start-up PayPal, and Arrington and his partners were forced to sell Achex to the e-commerce payment company First Data Corp for $32 million.

In the three years after selling Achex, Arrington worked for companies in England, Denmark, Canada, and Los Angeles, buying and selling domain names. By mid-2004, after having saved several hundred thousand dollars, he left business for a beach condominium in Los Angeles for nine months. In 2005, Arrington teamed back up with Teare to start an online classified advertisement website called Edgeio, which they hoped would be able to compete with Craigslist, the dominant classified ad website on the Internet. Having been out of touch with Internet developments for almost a year, Arrington spent time researching the business models of various new web companies, such as Flickr and Facebook. Those and other websites have allowed users to collaborate, share information, and establish online communities. Arrington discovered that accurate information about such companies was difficult to find. To aid in his research, he started the tech blog *TechCrunch*, which featured original reviews and analyses of technology companies, websites, and products. Arrington did not initially have high aspirations for the blog. "I figured, at the very least, I'd use it as a networking tool," Arrington told Vogelstein.

TECHCRUNCH

As Arrington added more entries and began to attract a large following of readers, it became clear that *TechCrunch* was providing a needed service to the tech community. Arrington quit Edgeio after just six months to focus on *TechCrunch*. He also began hosting parties for his readers at his home in Atherton, California. The parties progressively increased in size, and by his fourth gathering, Arrington was forced to rent a large tent for the five hundred people who attended. "I stopped having parties at my house because it was getting trashed," he wrote for *Inc.* magazine (1 Oct. 2010, online). The parties were not just social events; they were opportunities for entrepreneurs to pitch ideas about start-ups to Arrington. A mention on his blog meant more website traffic and, sometimes, investment offers from venture capitalists.

The event that marked Arrington's emergence as a power broker in the tech world may have been his October 9, 2006, blog post, in which he broke the news that Google had purchased the video-sharing website YouTube for $1.65 billion in stock. Since its launch in February 2005, YouTube had exploded in popularity as a pioneer of grassroots video-sharing technology. When it sold, it was providing one hundred million new videos a day. In his entry announcing the sale, Arrington posted notes he took during a conference call held by Google CEO Eric Schmidt, Google senior vice president David Drummond, YouTube CEO and cofounder Chad Hurley, and YouTube cofounder Stephen Yen. When the mainstream media reported on Google's acquisition of YouTube the following day, journalists were forced to credit Arrington with providing the first analysis on the story. Alan Kohler wrote for the *Sydney Morning Herald* (11 Oct. 2006, online): "Just when you think blogs are either meaningless noise or journalist chat . . . you start finding a lot of serious journalism on blogs being supported by advertisers. In other words, flourishing small journalism businesses."

By 2007, Arrington had written about some five hundred start-ups, and *TechCrunch* was the fourth most-linked-to blog on the Internet. Though *TechCrunch* did not garner the most traffic of any blog, it exerted significant market influence. The website itself had also expanded. Arrington hired several writers and researchers who produced up to ten posts a day. He also hired Heather Harde, a former Fox Interactive Media executive, as CEO. *TechCrunch* had expanded to include *CrunchNotes*, an opinion blog; *CrunchGear*, a gadget blog; *Crunch Jobs*, a website featuring classified ads; and *Mobile Crunch*, a portable computing blog. Through sales advertisements and job postings, the website was bringing about $200,000 a month in revenue. Also in 2007, Arrington began hosting a series of technology conferences with his friend and fellow web entrepreneur Jason Calacanis. The conferences, called TechCrunch40 and TechCrunch50, gave hundreds of Internet start-up companies the opportunity to make pitches to venture capitalists, corporations, entrepreneurs, and media. The conferences lasted until 2009, when Arrington and Calacanis parted ways. The next year, Arrington launched a similar series of conferences called TechCrunch Disrupt.

In July 2008, Arrington began what would ultimately become a failed attempt to enter the hardware market when he issued a challenge to readers of *TechCrunch* to design a "dead simple and dirt cheap touch screen Web tablet" (21 July 2008). Arrington aimed to create an affordable tablet that allowed users to browse the Internet, check email, and watch videos—and nothing more. He partnered with Singapore-based Chandrasekar Rathakrishnan, of the start-up development studio Fusion Garage, to begin creating the device, called the CrunchPad. For over a year, Arrington devoted much of his time to the

CrunchPad, and in October 2009, the tablet, not yet for sale, was honored with an award from *Popular Mechanics* magazine. A month later, however, Fusion Garage announced that due to pressure from shareholders, it planned to continue developing the product under the name JooJoo—without Arrington and *TechCrunch*. In response, Arrington filed a federal lawsuit, seeking damages and to keep the company from profiting from the JooJoo. After many delays, the tablet was released in 2010.

Meanwhile, as *TechCrunch* rose to success, Arrington was named one of *Time* magazine's "100 Most Influential People" of 2008. Arrington became something of an icon in the tech world, known for his brashness and a level of confidence that many thought approached arrogance. Arrington also routinely criticized mainstream media for being inept and was always quick to use his blog to fire back at his critics. "I'm human," he told Vogelstein. "I've put my entire life into this blog, and when I'm attacked, it's emotional. I'm going to react sometimes—that's just me."

Arrington had begun angel investing in 2007, providing funding for various start-up companies. Some of the companies he wrote checks to included a social network for dogs called Doggster, a video-aggregation website called Seesmic, and a social-networking website for dancing fans called DanceJam, among other companies. Though Arrington regularly disclosed the times when he wrote about companies to which he had provided financial backing, he was routinely accused of behaving unethically. By the summer of 2008, Arrington began receiving death threats, which he took to the police. In March 2009, he announced that he had stopped investing in start-ups.

PARTNERING WITH AOL

On September 28, 2010, AOL CEO Tim Armstrong announced that AOL had acquired *Tech-Crunch* for $25 million. The deal was made public and the contract signed onstage at a TechCrunch conference in San Francisco. At that time, AOL was in the midst of redefining its business after spinning off from its partnership with TimeWarner. AOL had also purchased the *Huffington Post*, another popular blog, and had begun building a core business around curating original content. That same date, Arrington posted on *TechCrunch* his reasoning behind selling to AOL. He stated that he had been persuaded to join with AOL because of its promise to allow Arrington to retain full editorial freedom, and that the arrangement would allow him to devote more time to writing. "I fully intend to stay with AOL for a very, very long time," Arrington wrote. "And the entire team has big incentives to stay on board for at least three years." At the time of the transaction, the *New York Times* reported that *TechCrunch* was generating $10 million in annual revenue and $3.5 million in profits, and that it attracted 3.8 million visitors per month.

TechCrunch's partnership with AOL did not temper Arrington's outspoken nature. For example, in January 2011, he posted a series of *Tech-Crunch* entries in which he sharply criticized Engadget, AOL's other tech blog, for a variety of reasons, at one point referring to it as "a plasticized caricature of a real blog" (11 Jan. 2011). In June 2011, Arrington launched a much-publicized attack on entrepreneur Catarina Fake for refusing to allow *TechCrunch* to break the news about her new start-up, Hunch.

In the spring of 2011, Arrington announced that he had resumed investing in tech start-ups, sparking a new round of accusations of conflicts of interest. On September 1, 2011, Arrington and Armstrong made another announcement—the establishment of a new venture capital fund, called CrunchFund, to invest in tech start-ups. This resulted in more aggressive criticisms of Arrington, given that the fund's backers included some of the biggest names in the tech world, such as AOL, which had given about $8 million to CrunchFund's $20 million total. Nicholas Carlson for *Business Insider* said of the fund, "It's hard to think of a company that *TechCrunch* covers that is not in some way backed by these people. We can't help but wonder if that will influence coverage" (1 Sep. 2011, online).

In the wake of the negative response to CrunchFund, AOL executives disagreed on what Arrington's role at the company would be going forward. Armstrong defended Arrington and stated during the September 1 announcement that *TechCrunch* writers were not bound by the same rules as other AOL journalists. As quoted by David Carr for the *New York Times* (4 Sep. 2011), Armstrong said that "*TechCrunch* is a different property and they have different standards." Several days later, however, Arianna Huffington, the head of AOL's editorial operations, claimed that Arrington had already left AOL to become a venture capitalist. As reported by Carr (4 Sep. 2011), Huffington said that Arrington "could continue to write . . . but as an unpaid blogger." Arrington responded to the controversy in a September 6, 2011, *TechCrunch* blog post, commenting that AOL should either stick to its promise of allowing *TechCrunch* total editorial independence or sell it back to its original shareholders. "Editorial independence was never supposed to be an easy thing for AOL to give us. But it was never meaningful if it shatters the first time it is put to the test."

Despite the many pleas by *TechCrunch* writers and others in the tech industry to allow Arrington to continue to serve both as venture capitalist and tech journalist, AOL announced on September 12, 2011, that Arrington had decided to "move on." The announcement was widely understood to mean that Arrington had been pushed out of AOL, and many news outlets reported that he had been fired. "The episode has riveted the tech and media worlds," Claire Cain Miller wrote for the *New York Times* (12 Sep. 2011, online), "raising one of the most pressing questions that media organizations grapple with today: Do the old rules of journalism apply to Internet bloggers?"

AFTER TECHCRUNCH

Erick Schonfeld, the former coeditor of *Tech-Crunch*, replaced Arrington. Just days after the shake up, Arrington made an unexpected appearance at the TechCrunch Disrupt conference in San Francisco, where he wore a t-shirt that read "unpaid blogger," a reference to Huffington's description of his role at AOL. On September 23, 2011, Arrington began a new blog, called *Uncrunched*. Two days later, he posted an entry entitled, "What Exactly Am I Doing Here at *Uncrunched*?" In answer to that question, he wrote: "I'm going to do the same thing I've been doing since 2005. I'm going to write about start-ups, and the people who build them, and the people who fund them, and the people who use them. I'm going to break stories and I'm going to write my opinion, and I'm going to do whatever the hell else I feel like in between."

In the months since Arrington's departure, *TechCrunch* has remained influential, even while its web traffic has steadily declined. In February 2012, the digital journalism website PaidContent.org reported that *TechCrunch*'s traffic had declined by at least 35 percent since the same time a year before (29 Feb. 2012). Several senior *TechCrunch* employees also left, including Harde and writers MG Siegler and Paul Carr. On February 29, 2012, Arrington responded to the news that Schonefeld had left *TechCrunch* two days before. His *Uncrunched* blog post criticized AOL executives for their poor management of *TechCrunch*—especially Huffington. Arrington returned to *TechCrunch* temporarily in April 2012 as a guest blogger.

In addition to writing for *Uncrunched*, Arrington has continued to invest in start-ups through CrunchFund, which he runs with co-founders Siegler and Patrick Gallagher.

PERSONAL LIFE

Arrington lives in Seattle, Washington, with his two Labrador retrievers, Laguna and Buddy. He volunteers at local animal shelters and regularly writes posts encouraging people to adopt dogs and cats from shelters. In recent years, Arrington has been romantically linked to Meghan Asha, founder of the website Nonsociety.com.

SUGGESTED READING

Arrington, Michael. "An Update to My Investment Policy." *TechCrunch*. AOL Inc., 27 Apr. 2011.

——. "The Way I Work." *Inc.com* Inc. Magazine, 1 Oct. 2010. Web. 14 May 2012.

——. "Why We Sold *TechCrunch* to AOL and Where We Go From Here." *TechCrunch*. AOL Inc., 28 Sep. 2010. Web. 14 May 2012.

Carr, David. "A Tech Blogger Who Leaps Over the Line." *New York Times* New York Times, 4 Sep. 2011. Web. 14 May 2012.

Miller, Claire Cain. "Tech Blogger Parts with AOL." *New York Times* New York Times, 12 Sep. 2011. Web. 14 May 2012.

Vogelstein, Fred. "*TechCrunch* Blogger Michael Arrington Can Generate Buzz . . . and Cash." *Wired*. Condé Nast Publications, 22 June 2007. Web. 14 May 2012.

—*Margaret Roush Mead*

Charles Askegard

Born: 1969
Occupation: Ballet dancer

Charles Askegard is a former principal dancer with the New York City Ballet (NYCB) and the founding artistic director, with former American Ballet Theatre (ABT) principal dancer Michele Wiles, of the New York dance company Ballet Next. The forty-two-year-old dancer retired from NYCB after a long career that also included ten years as a corps member and soloist with ABT. NYCB ballerinas who knew Askegard for his partnering skills were especially sad to see Askegard move on. Writing for the Associated Press (Oct. 10, 2011), Jocelyn Noveck said, "It's a crucial role in a company. Male dancers who excel at partnering are not always the flashiest, don't always jump the highest, but they save their partners from disaster, allow them to shine, and give them the security to take risks, elevating the performance for everyone." Askegard began honing his partnering technique as a teenage dancer in Minnesota. "I always thought that partnering a woman was such a huge part of ballet, and I loved it," he told Gia Kourlas for *Time Out New York* (Sep. 23, 2011, online). As one of a handful of boys in his ballet classes, Askegard partnered with ballerinas of all shapes and sizes. His own size made learning technique difficult; by his own account, he did not stop growing until he was twenty-one. He now stands six feet, four inches tall. "Few men of Chuck's height can do what he can do," principal dancer and frequent partner Wendy Whelan told Roslyn Sulcas for the *International Herald Tribune* (Oct. 6, 2011).

Askegard admits that he would like to choreograph one day, perhaps through his most recent endeavor, Ballet Next. "When you're in a company you are allowed some freedom in performance," Askegard told Janet Babin for the

Robert Pitts/Landov

WQXR blog (Nov. 21, 2011, online). "But you don't have freedom to choose what you want to dance, when you perform, how often you perform a ballet. None of those choices are yours." As one of the founders of Ballet Next, Askegard can now make such choices. The troupe, composed of dancer friends of Askegard and Wiles, premiered on November 21, 2011, in the intimate Joyce Theater, accompanied by a chamber orchestra. Not all of the reviews of the evening were positive, but the cross-company collaborators—including ABT soloist Misty Copeland and NYCB principal Jennie Somogyi—generated some excitement. Askegard's own contributions to the premiere were praised. "I will continue dancing for a little bit—not on the same schedule as NYCB, which is so physically demanding," he told Joseph Carman for *Dance* magazine (Oct. 1, 2011). "You know when it's time."

EARLY LIFE AND EDUCATION

Charles Askegard was born in 1969 in Minneapolis, Minnesota, to Douglas Askegard and Darla Boggs. He has an older sister, Dorothy, and a younger sister, Johanna. Encouraged by their mother, who had studied dance as a teenager, the siblings were all dancers as children, though Charles Askegard was the only one to pursue a professional career. Askegard began taking classes with Loyce Houlton, the director of the Minnesota Dance Theatre, at the age of five. At six, he made his stage debut as a mouse in Houlton's

Nutcracker Fantasy. But as Askegard told Kourlas, he fell in love with ballet during his first Saturday morning classes with a Minnesota Dance Theatre company member. "We were doing all kinds of fun stuff in that class, jumping over each other and exploring movement in a very fun way," he said, "and it captured our imaginations." During his teen years he endured frequent teasing from his peers but found solace in the studio every day after school. Askegard first learned to partner from Eugene Collins, a former dancer with the Ballet Russe de Monte Carlo.

Even as a teenager Askegard was tall for a dancer, but Collins paired him with dancers of every size for practice. Askegard spent his summers training with companies in various cities, studying with the San Francisco Ballet; the School of American Ballet (SAB) at NYCB, where he worked with instructors Stanley Williams, Richard Rapp, and Andrei Kramarevsky; and the ABT. Askegard graduated from Washburn High School in Minneapolis at sixteen and moved to New York to train with legendary ballet instructor Maggie Black, becoming her sole scholarship student. Black's class, he told Kourlas, "was the most intense class around. . . . I felt like it was where I could really learn to dance. It was a very odd choice to make because it was connected to nothing, no company." Askegard was still growing at the time, and finding his balance and core strength proved difficult. Black emphasized technique and strength. Speaking of Black's guidance, he told Kourlas, "It was helpful in strengthening my weaknesses. She made a huge difference, and having that strong technique is great. It really set me up for a good, long career." When Black retired from teaching in the early 1990s, Askegard began training with ballet instructor David Howard.

CAREER

In 1987 Askegard joined ABT, then under the artistic direction of famed dancer Mikhail Baryshnikov, at the age of eighteen. He was selected by choreographer Glen Tetley to perform Igor Stravinsky's *The Rite of Spring* and then by British dancer Michael Somes for Frederick Ashton's *Symphonic Variations*. He was promoted to soloist in the company in 1992. The repertoire at ABT was largely classical, and Askegard danced some of ballet's most famous roles, including leads in *Giselle*, *Romeo and Juliet*, *La bayadère*, *The Nutcracker*, *Le corsaire*, and *Apollo*. He also appeared in such modern ballets as Kenneth MacMillan's *Manon*, Glen Tetley's *Voluntaries*, and Agnes de Mille's *Rodeo* and *Fall River Legend*.

In a review (June 11, 1993) of the ABT performance of Harald Lander's Études, *New York Times* dance critic Jennifer Dunning wrote, "Charles Askegard's long legs and feet did astonishing things to his beats, in a role debut as the Danish cavalier. Mr. Askegard also stood out for the elegant lyricism of his arms, an ebullient attack and partnering that was as exquisitely attuned as ever to his ballerina." A critic for the *Washington Post* (Mar. 7, 1995) wrote of his performance in *La bayadère*, "Askegard . . . is so likeable a presence onstage that even his thoughtful facial expressions are enjoyable." However, not all of Askegard's early reviews were unreservedly positive. Jack Anderson for the *New York Times* (June 10, 1995) criticized Askegard's portrayal of Romeo in the ballet adaptation of Shakespeare's *Romeo and Juliet*, calling him "boyish" and adding, "Unfortunately, as Mr. Askegard characterized him, the rush of tragic events did not mature Romeo but merely seem to bewilder him. This was an interesting sketch for an interpretation that deserves to be developed further."

Despite his success performing leading roles with ABT, Askegard was frustrated that he remained a soloist. "I was a soloist but doing mostly principal work," he told Kourlas, "and it felt like I'd plateaued." He decided to leave the company in 1997. He had no specific plan but was working with Valentina Kozlova, a veteran of both the Bolshoi Ballet and NYCB, and the choreographer and dancer Margo Sappington. For a short time Askegard considered moving to Europe and joining the Royal Danish Ballet, but after performing with Whelan he began to think seriously about NYCB. At ABT, Askegard had been considered better suited for classical pieces than for those by George Balanchine, the famed choreographer who dominated the NYCB repertoire. Nevertheless, Askegard auditioned for ballet master and choreographer Peter Martins, who hired him on the spot. This was an unusual decision on Martins's part; nearly all NYCB dancers begin at the School of American Ballet (SAB), the company's academy, and rise through the ranks, but Askegard joined the company as a soloist. Rick Nelson, writing for the Minneapolis *Star Tribune* (Mar. 3, 1999) described Askegard's ascent as "meteoric."

NEW YORK CITY BALLET

Askegard estimated that it took him nearly two years to become a "Balanchine dancer." He told Kourlas, "It was all so new, and there were a lot of things that had to be changed and learned, and it wasn't just the dancing technique: it was the partnering technique as well." Martins paired Askegard with Kyra Nichols, Darci Kistler, and Maria Kowroski, the last of whom, nearly six feet tall when en pointe, became one of Askegard's most frequent partners. The way the ballerinas danced at NYCB, Askegard said, was "not how ballerinas danced at ABT—or pretty much anywhere else. . . . They were big risk-takers. It was just so exciting." He recalled a particular moment early in his NYCB career when he was

called upon at the last minute to perform *The Nutcracker* that evening with Nichols; he had never performed the ballet with NYCB nor had he ever danced with Nichols, but after a fifteen-minute rehearsal he did both. "I remember it going really well," he told Kourlas. The ballerinas also demanded a different, and in some respects lesser, kind of support from their partners. "The tendency is to want to hold the girl and make sure that everything is okay," Askegard explained to Kourlas of his pre-NYCB technique, "but to back off from all of that and give her a little bit of what she needs—that took a long time."

Askegard worked with legendary choreographer Jerome Robbins a few months before Robbins's death in 1998, performing in a revival of his 1985 ballet *In Memory of.. . .* Askegard reprised the role throughout his NYCB career. He performed more than a dozen roles his first year with NYCB and saw the stage nearly every day. "I'm dancing six times a week, four different roles a week," he told Minneapolis *Star Tribune* critic Rick Nelson. "I wouldn't get this variety at ABT." Askegard admitted that the schedule was grueling—he estimated that he was often dancing thirty-five to forty hours each week—but that the pain paid off in performance. Askegard told Sean Evans for the New York *Daily News* (Nov. 30, 2008) that he thrived on the energy of an audience. He said, "They're so quiet you can hear a pin drop. But that means their full attention is focused on you when you're on stage, and that's a fantastic feeling." At the end of 1998 Askegard was promoted to principal dancer.

The NYCB repertoire draws heavily from the choreography of Balanchine, Robbins, and Martins, and Askegard became well versed in the work of all three. He danced featured roles in many Balanchine pieces, including *The Four Temperaments*, *Firebird*, *Liebeslieder Walzer*, *Cortège hongrois*, and the masterpiece *Serenade*. He appeared in Robbins's *The Four Seasons*, *In the Night*, and *Ives, Songs*, and he originated featured roles in Martins's *Harmonielehre*, *Swan Lake*, and *Viva Verdi*. He also danced Helgi Tomasson's *Prism*, Robert La Fosse's "Rockin' in Rhythm" from *Duke!*, and Christopher Wheeldon's *Carnival of the Animals*. After announcing his retirement in 2011, Askegard worked with Martins to devise a farewell program incorporating some of his favorite pieces. On October 9, 2011, Askegard appeared in familiar roles including the pas de deux from the "Diamonds" segment of Balanchine's *Jewels*, partnered with Kowroski. Alistair Macaulay for the *New York Times* (Oct. 11, 2011) recalled of that particular piece, "During my time watching his career, there have been many . . . "Diamonds" performances when a ballerina has been way off balance, but Mr. Askegard, supporting her with seeming nonchalance, has made the angle of her body look not only right, but also exciting."

Askegard also appeared in Balanchine's *Episodes* and *Western Symphony* and performed in his career favorite, Robbins's *In Memory of . . .*, with Jared Angle and Whelan.

BALLET NEXT

Askegard's Ballet Next premiered at the Joyce Theater in New York City on November 21, 2011. The first half of the program featured works by Balanchine and Marius Petipa, while the program's second half was more contemporary, with recent works including a world-premiere duet choreographed by Mauro Bigonzetti and set to a composition by Antonio Vivaldi. The venue was uncharacteristically small for a ballet, and the music was performed by six musicians without a conductor. "There's usually a distance between musicians and dancers, and we're taking away that separation," Askegard told WQXR blogger Janet Babin. Claudia La Rocco for the *New York Times* (Nov. 23, 2011) praised the intimate nature of the evening as well as several individual performances—she called Askegard and Jennie Somogyi's interpretation of Sappington's *Entwined* the "night's only real bright spot"—but criticized the lack of cohesion. She wrote that the "half-classical, half-contemporary" program was forgettable and seemed "stuck together with no real sense of a governing vision or even personality."

Askegard has been a guest artist with many companies, including the National Ballet of Canada, Phillipine Ballet Theatre, and Pacific Northwest Ballet. In addition to his many performances on stage, Askegard has appeared in several films and television broadcasts. While a member of ABT he appeared in the 1995 documentary *Ballet*, directed by Fred Wiseman. In 2001 Martins choreographed the animated children's film *Barbie in the Nutcracker*. Askegard, who danced as the Nutcracker and Prince Eric, and other NYCB dancers wore bodysuits covered with sensors, allowing the animators to track their movements and body positions with computers for use in the film. Askegard told Ellen Dunkel for the Bergen County *Record* (Nov. 30, 2001) that he hoped the film would inspire young audiences to take an interest in dance. "*Nutcracker* is basically how a lot of us, in America anyway, get into dance," he said, adding that "[The video is] not just a cartoon drawing of it, it's actual people actually doing it. So it's a really nice thing for little kids to see and open up their eyes to it and hopefully get some more people involved in it." Askegard went on to dance for *Barbie of Swan Lake* (2003) and *Barbie in the 12 Dancing Princesses* (2006). In 2002 he appeared in "New York City Ballet's Diamond Project: Ten Years of New Choreography," a broadcast of *Live from Lincoln Center* in which he danced *Them Twos*, with music by Wynton Marsalis. Askegard danced *Vienna Waltzes* in the 2004 *Live from Lincoln Center* broadcast "Lincoln Center Celebrates Balanchine 100."

PERSONAL LIFE

Askegard married ABT ballerina Ashley Tuttle in 1993 at the age of twenty-four. The couple later divorced. In 2002 he met *Sex and the City* writer Candace Bushnell at an NYCB company gala; they were wed several months later. The couple filed for divorce in 2011.

SUGGESTED READING

Babin, Janet. "Two Dance Luminaries Take Big Leap with Ballet Next." *WQXR Blog*. WQXR, 21 Nov. 2011. Web. 9 Jan. 2012.

Carman, Joseph. "Charles Askegard Will Retire from New York City Ballet." *Dance* 1 Oct. 2011: 73. Print.

Dunkel, Ellen. "Playing Ballet Barbie, Animatedly: Dancers Deliver 3-D Performance." *Record* [Bergen County, NJ] 30 Nov. 2001: 17. Print.

Dunning, Jennifer. "A Display of Pyrotechnics by New Leads in 'Etudes.'" *New York Times* 11 June 1993: C32. Print.

Evans, Sean. "Leap of Faith." *Daily News* [New York] 30 Nov. 2008, Sunday Now sec.: 8. Print.

"Grand Finale: New York City Ballet." *Metroland* [Albany, NY] 1 Aug. 2002: 34. Print.

Kourlas, Gia. "Charles Askegard." *Time Out New York*. Time Out New York, 23 Sep. 2011. Web. 9 Jan. 2012.

La Rocco, Claudia. "A New Troupe Begins with Blend of Then and Now." *New York Times* 24 Nov. 2011: C14. Print.

Macaulay, Alistair. "A Goodbye, Understated but Riveting in Its Duets." *New York Times* 11 Oct. 2011: C1. Print.

Nelson, Rick. "Askegard Takes Leap to the Top in Ballet." *Star Tribune* [Minneapolis] 3 Mar. 1999: E1. Print.

Sulcas, Roslyn. "Star Leaps into the Unknown: At 42, Charles Askegard is leaving New York City Ballet to Form a Company." *International Herald Tribune* 6 Oct. 2011, Leisure sec.: 13. Print.

"Tharp and Petipa, Deftly Delivered." *Washington Post* 7 Mar. 1995: E2. Print.

—Molly Hagan

Harold Augenbraum

Born: March 31, 1953
Occupation: Executive director of the National Book Foundation

In 2004, Harold Augenbraum began serving as the executive director of the National Book Foundation (NBF), which determines the winners of the annual National Book Awards (NBA). He is fluent in Spanish and French with an expertise in Latino literature and is a writer, translator, editor, and a self-described "obsessive reader." Augenbraum is described by the Boston University (BU) website as "a scholar to whom community is as important as intellectualism."

Following his 1976 college graduation from BU, Augenbraum taught English in Spain for several years, and in the 1980s, he held a series of jobs that made use of his skills in publicity, fundraising, community outreach, and program development. His arrival at the venerable Mercantile Library in 1990 led to that institution's rebirth and its return to sound financial footing. After fourteen years there, he felt prepared for his NBF job "in the sense that I came from a world of literature, and so I [was] familiar with the writer's side of things," he told Barbara Hoffert for *Library Journal* (15 May 2005). "I was able to walk in and say, literary education works with adults."

In an essay for the Concordia College online publication *Ascent* (Mar. 2011), Augenbraum wrote, "As the director of the National Book Foundation, I am, in essence, a book marketer. My job, each year, is to take twenty golden books called National Book Award Finalists and transform them into cultural currency, no matter what technology you might use to imbibe them." He told Barbara Hoffert, "I don't have an outlook that says, you should always read hoity-toity literary books. . . . In fact, I think that drawing a line between literary and commercial fiction is killing fiction. I read Proust and I read Sara Paretsky; one of my favorite writers of all time is Eric Ambler. In the long run, I hope I can use this broad experience to expand what the National Book Foundation is."

EARLY YEARS, EDUCATION, AND EARLY CAREER

Harold Augenbraum was born on March 31, 1953, in New York City to Samuel Augenbraum, an insurance broker, and Ada Baker Augenbraum, a homemaker. His mother died in 1966, shortly before his thirteenth birthday, and his father died in 1972, a few days after Augenbraum turned nineteen. After Augenbraum completed high school, he enrolled in Boston University (BU) where he majored in English. During his senior year he had a job washing floors in the Student Union every weeknight. In an interview

AP Photo

for the English Department's "Featured Alumni" section of the BU website, Augenbraum explained that his coworkers spoke only Spanish, "so if I wanted to talk to anyone I had to burnish my Spanish pretty quickly," he recalled. Also that year he and a fellow student started an informal literary discussion group that met in the English Department office every Wednesday afternoon. "The only requirement was that you bring a bottle of wine," Augenbraum told the BU interviewer. By the end of that year, "fifteen of us were crammed into that tiny office every week." Augenbraum graduated *cum laude* in 1976 with a bachelor's degree.

After graduation, Augenbraum moved to Barcelona, Spain, where he taught English as a foreign language. (His planned stay of six months stretched into three and a half years.) While living and working in Barcelona—an experience he has described as "life-changing"—he abandoned the idea of pursuing an advanced degree in comparative literature. In 1980, after his return to New York, he got a job as an account executive with the United Way of New York City. The next year he was hired as a staff consultant for the Bruce Porter Company, which handled fundraising from private sources for schools, hospitals, research groups, and other nonprofit organizations. One of its clients was the Burden Center for the Aging, which offers social services and programs to help elderly New Yorkers remain in their own homes. In 1984, Augenbraum joined the Brookdale Center for Healthy Aging and Longevity, an arm of Hunter College of the

City University of New York. For three years he served as the director of external affairs for the center, which, according to its website, "serves as a critical bridge between gerontological education, research, policy, practice, and advocacy" and collaborates with community and government agencies.

In his next job, which he held from 1987 to 1989, Augenbraum was the associate director for external affairs at the Museum of the City of New York. The museum, which opened in 1923, is a private, nonprofit institution that offers, in addition to exhibitions, programs for educators, school groups, families, and the general public and includes lectures, symposiums, and hands-on demonstrations that focus on such topics as famous or little-known New Yorkers and places, events, and conditions in the city, past and present.

THE MERCANTILE LIBRARY

In 1990, Augenbraum was named the director of the Mercantile Library, a nonprofit institution that is open to fee-paying members and draws additional financial support from donations, grants, and an endowment. The library has been operating in New York City since 1821, and by 1870, its membership totaled almost 11,000 with a collection of over 140,000 books. In the ensuing decades, the library occupied a series of buildings each of which contained a reading room, offices, spaces rented to publishing companies and others, and accommodations for writers; one of the first to write there was Edgar Allan Poe. Virtually from the beginning, the most popular among the library's books were works of fiction.

With the opening of the New York Public Library's main building at Fifth Avenue and Forty-Second Street in 1912 and the expansion of the tax-supported, free New York public library system of neighborhood branches, membership in the Mercantile Library dwindled. By 1920, the number of subscribers had shrunk to about 3,000, and by 1940, to about 1,400; the number "kept falling through the 1950s and 60s," Christopher Gray wrote for the *New York Times* (6 May 2001). Desperate for funds, the library's board of trustees sold several of its collections in the 1970s. Membership had dropped to 375 when, in August 1989, the board closed the library. The trustees continued to meet, however, with hopes of resurrecting the facility. By the end of the year, they had hired Augenbraum to head the library and guide its revival. According to Gray, the new director "got the trustees to agree to finance the library for a year and a half while searching for a new mission." The board and Augenbraum "decided to refine the focus to fiction and to special programs."

The Mercantile Library (now called The Center for Fiction) reopened in early 1990. In his interview with Barbara Hoffert, Augenbraum said that when he worked there, he "felt like this tiny little mouse in this great monstrosity of a metropolis, with people going by and not even knowing we were there. It was a sort of semi-monkish existence," but as the library's director, Augenbraum was far from isolated socially. As he told Hoffert, "I did a lot of public speaking . . . at the library because I ran one hundred-odd literary programs a year. I was always getting up making introductions, socializing, and talking to people." The programs, supported by grants and occasionally organized in collaboration with the New York Historical Society, the PEN American Center, or other groups, included lecture series and panel discussions on, for example, French or Latino literature, renowned authors, and topics ranging from food and adultery in literature to the grand tours of Europe undertaken by writers and artists in the eighteenth century.

THE PROUST SOCIETY

In 1997, Augenbraum founded the Proust Society of America. For several years the society marked Proust's birthday with a dinner that included madeleines, the small cakes that inspired Proust to write the seven-volume novel known in English as *In Search of Lost Time* (or *Remembrance of Things Past*). Groups for beginning and advanced Proust readers would meet once a month at the library to discuss one of the novels. In 1999, Augenbraum helped to organize the first annual New York Festival of Mystery, which was called Murder in the City that year. "We wanted a fan conference and an academic conference," he told a *New York Times* (17 May 1999) reporter. "This will cross the two." The two-day festival's symposiums and walking tours to places mentioned in New York crime fiction attracted more than 200 scholars and mystery aficionados. Another widely attended program that Augenbraum organized celebrated the one hundredth anniversary of John Steinbeck's birth, in 2002. With Susan Shillinglaw, he wrote the guide *How to Organize a Steinbeck Book or Film Discussion Group* (2002).

THE NATIONAL BOOK FOUNDATION

In 2004, Augenbraum left the Mercantile Library to become the executive director of the National Book Foundation, which among other things presents the National Book Awards, the US literary awards introduced in 1950 that are "given to writers by writers." The NBF was established in 1989 "to broaden [the] scope" of the awards and "to develop programs to promote reading and literacy," the then chairman Al Silverman told Edwin McDowell for the *New York Times* (5 July 1989). According to the NBF website, the awards are given to writers of fiction, nonfiction, and poetry "who have helped shape the foundation of American literature." First Lady Eleanor Roosevelt served as the keynote speaker at the first awards ceremony, and writer and television personality Clifton Fadiman was the master of ceremonies.

When Barbara Hoffert asked Augenbraum if the awards "really matter," he responded that because of the recognition it represented, he never knew an author who didn't want an award. Furthermore, Augenbraum added, "awards help sales, [and] winning the NBA shows that they have backed the right author." (Only a book's publisher can nominate it for an award.) When Hoffert asked in what way the NBA matters to the public, Augenbraum explained that because there are fewer book reviews available to the public, the awards are "recommendations by people who supposedly know what they are doing." Not everyone agrees with the foundation's choices for annual winners, which Augenbraum believes to be a good thing: "Every once in a while someone will say, 'I read that book that won the NBA, and it was terrible,' but I love that they read the book."

The NBA honors books written by Americans and published by American companies in the categories of fiction, nonfiction, poetry, and young-people's literature. Books in each category are nominated from among hundreds read by a panel of five judges, one of whom acts as the panel's chair. Each panel selects five finalists and chooses the winner from among those five. "Judges are published writers who are known to be doing great work in their genre or field, and, in some cases, are past NBA finalists or winners," the NBF website explains. The chair "acts as the voice of the panel and the liaison to the NBF. The foundation staff takes no part in the deliberations, except to verify a submission's eligibility." Like the public, Augenbraum and his board and staff learn the names of the winners at the awards ceremony. In an interview with Liz Funk for inReads.com (8 Aug. 2011), he acknowledged, "There are going to be high quality books that will only be published as e-books and we will need to figure out how to handle that with our judges."

PUBLICATIONS AND REVIEWS

By his own account, a program about Latino literature that Augenbraum arranged at the Mercantile Library led to the publication of two books: Augenbraum's *Latinos in English: A Selected Bibliography of Latino Fiction Writers of the United States* (1992) and *Growing Up Latino: Memoirs and Stories* (1993), the latter of which he edited with Ilan Stavans. "I am not Latino," he wrote for *Contemporary Authors* in the early 1990s. "I am, however, excited about the ability of the Latino community of writers to infuse literature in the United States with new energy, themes, and settings. . . . I have made (or helped

to make) my two books in order to share with a broad audience the pleasures I have had as a reader." Augenbraum also wrote that he intended to "continue to seek out 'hidden' literatures, especially those written in English, which have not had much consideration because of political, social, geographic, or other reasons."

With Margarite *Fernández* Olmos, Augenbraum edited *The Latino Reader: An American Literary Tradition from 1542 to the Present*, 1997, and *U.S. Latino Literature: A Critical Guide for Students and Teachers*, 2000. His revised and annotated version of Fanny Bandelier's 1905 translation of Alvar Núñez Cabez de Vaca's *Chronicle of the Narváez Expedition* was published in 2002.

Augenbraum has coedited several books with Ilan Stavans, including the four-volume *Encyclopedia Latina: History, Culture, and Society in the United States*, 2005; *Lengua Fresca: Latinos Writing on the Edge*, 2006; *The Norton Anthology of Latino Literature*, 2011; and a translation of Juan Rulfo's 1953 collection of short stories, *El llano en llamas*, which has been retitled *The Plain in Flames*. Augenbraum has also translated two books by José Rizal (1861–1896), a Filipino polymath and national hero: *Noli Me Tangere (Touch Me Not*, 2006) and *El filibusterismo*, 2011.

Reviewers have greeted Augenbraum's books enthusiastically. In one representative assessment, Sylvia V. Meisner, writing for *School Library Journal* (Feb. 2001), described *U.S. Latino Literature* as "an essential reference tool for high schools and public libraries." Diana Kirby, writing for *Booklist*, noted that *Encyclopedia Latina* had benefited from "the expertise of an editorial board and staff and contributions from approximately 200 Latino researchers, professors, journalists, scholars, and others," and she declared, "its broad historical sweep and multidisciplinary coverage make it an indispensable reference resource" (1 Oct. 2005). In an enthusiastic critique of *Lengua Fresca* for *Library Journal* (15 Nov. 2008), Nedra Crowe-Evers wrote that each "entry is unique, e.g., a tongue-in-cheek menu from a Puerto Rican restaurant, hip-hop lyrics, a treatise on Mexican food. . . . The more traditional selections include stories from hope-to-hear-more-of authors Oscar Casares, Nelly Rosario, and Miguel Jaime-Becerra." Crowe-Evers concluded, "Recommended for all public libraries."

PERSONAL LIFE AND ADDITIONAL INTERESTS

In 1989, Augenbraum married Carla Scheele, who has served as the director of endowment and special gifts at the Bank Street College of Education. They live in the Riverdale section of New York City and maintain a home in the Catskill Mountains region of New York State. They have a grown daughter, Audrey.

Augenbraum has taught courses in Latino literature at Amherst College, and he is a member of the advisory board of the literary and photography magazine *Common*, which is published at that school. He served for ten years as treasurer of the board of the Asian American Writers Workshop and six years as a member of the Brooklyn Literary Council. As of 2011, Augenbraum had won eight grants from the National Endowment for the Humanities and had received grants from the New York Council for the Humanities in 1991 and 1993; he was a member of the council's board from 1993 to 1998 and its vice chairman in 1996. His honors include the 2000 Raven Award from the Mystery Writers of America and the 2010 Concordia College President's Medallion. According to Augenbraum's personal website, he writes the "sometime" blog *Reading Ahead: The Future of Reading*.

SUGGESTED READING

Augenbraum, Harold. "In Praise of the Obsessive Reader: An Exercise in Taxonomy." *Ascent*. Concordia College. 30 Mar. 2011. Web. 14 Feb. 2012.

Funk, Liz. "Inside the National Book Awards—A Q&A with Harold Augenbraum." *InReads*. WETA, 8 Aug. 2011. Web. 14 Feb. 2012.

Gray, Christopher. "Streetscapes/17 East 47th Street: The Mercantile Library Finds a New Literary Life." *nytimes.com*. New York Times, 6 May 2001. Web. 23 Jan. 2012.

"Harold Augenbraum: Life Among Languages." *bu.edu*. Boston University, n.d. Web. 23 Jan. 2012.

Hoffert, Barbara. "Harold Augenbraum: Into the Limelight." *Library Journal* 15 May 2005: 30–31. Print.

Tomassi, Noreen. "A History of the Mercantile Library of New York." *centerforfiction.org*. The Center for Fiction, n.d. Web. 23 Jan. 2012.

—*Miriam Helbok*

Francisco Ayala

Born: March 12, 1934
Occupation: Evolutionary biologist

Francisco J. Ayala is regarded as one the world's foremost authorities in the field of evolutionary biology. He pioneered the use of molecular biology techniques to study the process of evolution. "Before Ayala," Andrei Tatarenkov, a former researcher in Ayala's lab, told Gordy Slack for *UC Irvine Today* (29 Aug. 2002), "theories about the origin of the species were mostly based on mathematical models. The early work of Ayala and [mentor] Dobzhansky was really the first experimental work."

© Paul Rodriguez/ZUMA Press/Corbis

Ayala's research with *Drosophila* (a fruit fly genus that he used as a model organism) has provided insight into not only the lineage of species but also into the prevalence of genetic variation, the hierarchical population structure, and evolutionary rates. In recent years Ayala has dedicated himself to the research of protozoan parasites, namely those responsible for Chagas disease and malaria, in an effort to find a cure for various tropical diseases. Ayala, a former priest, has also garnered attention in scientific circles for being opposed to the encroachment of religion into science—a stance that is reflected in his books *Darwin and Intelligent Design* (2006), *Darwin's Gift to Science and Religion* (2007), and *Am I a Monkey? Six Questions about Evolution* (2010).

EARLY LIFE AND INTERESTS

Francisco José Ayala Pereda was born in Madrid, Spain, on March 12, 1934. He is the fourth of Soledad (Pereda) and Francisco Ayala's six children. His mother was a homemaker, and his father worked as a businessman. The younger Ayala grew up in the shadow of the Spanish Civil War, a failed military uprising against the country's republican government that escalated into a violent, protracted conflict. After a three-year struggle (1936–39), the government was eventually overthrown by the rebels, whose leader, Francisco Franco, ruled Spain with an iron fist for four decades.

Ayala developed an early interest in science while he was attending a private Catholic school in Madrid. In 1951, upon completing his secondary education at Colegio de San Fernando, Ayala enrolled at the University of Madrid, where he majored in physics. After receiving his BS degree in 1955, he spent the next five years at the Pontifical Faculty of San Esteban, in Salamanca, studying theology and preparing for the priesthood. While there, Ayala became fascinated with genetics. "I had studied science as an undergraduate at the University of Madrid, and I continued to be interested in it," he recalled to Rachel Saslow for the *Washington Post* (27 Apr. 2010). "When I was studying theology, I started to read much more about human evolution and genetics."

COLUMBIA UNIVERSITY

After his ordination as a Dominican priest in 1960, Ayala decided to leave the priesthood. In 1961 he traveled to New York City, and with the help of renowned evolutionary biologist Theodosius Dobzhansky, who would become his mentor, Ayala entered the graduate program in evolutionary biology and genetics at Columbia University.

Ayala first became aware of the ongoing debate between science and religion while studying at Columbia. "It was an unexpected turn of events for me, coming from conservative Spain, to discover that there was in the United States a strong creationist current that saw [Charles] Darwin and the theory of evolution as contrary to religious beliefs," Ayala wrote in his 2007 book, *Darwin's Gift to Science and Religion*. "In Salamanca, in my theological studies, evolution had been perceived as a friend, not an enemy, of the Christian faith."

Under Dobzhansky's guidance, Ayala performed genetic experiments on fruit flies (*Drosophila*) and observed the process by which new biological species are formed (also known as speciation). In 1964, a year after earning his MA degree in genetics, Ayala was awarded a PhD in genetics. It was while conducting research for his thesis, however, that he discovered new ways of calculating population fitness (the capacity of an organism to survive and reproduce successfully). Additionally, Ayala was able to show that the evolutionary rate (how quickly a new species evolves) of a species is dependent on its degree of genetic variation, which is critical to its ability to adapt to changes in the environment.

TEACHING POSITIONS

Following his time at Columbia University, Ayala underwent a year of postdoctoral training at Rockefeller University, also in New York City. In 1965 he joined the faculty at Rhode Island's Providence College as an assistant professor of biology. He returned to New York—and Rockefeller University—in 1967, after accepting a similar position.

During his four years or so at Rockefeller, Ayala observed several closely related *Drosophila* species in an effort to find a link between the amount of genetic polymorphism (DNA sequence variations among populations) and the rate at which a new species evolves. One area of investigation focused on rainforest *Drosophila* species (*D. birchii* and *D. serrata*) and the effects of radiation-induced genetic mutations on the ability of those populations to quickly adapt to a changing environment. Ayala discovered that the adaptation rate of the populations exposed to radiation was significantly greater than those of the nonirradiated populations. He concluded that natural selection plays a larger role in populations that have a greater variety of genotypes available for selection.

In 1971, the same year he became a naturalized citizen, Ayala was appointed assistant professor of genetics at the University of California (UC) at Davis, where Dobzhansky joined him. Three years later Ayala was promoted to full professor, a post he held until 1987. From 1977 to 1981 he served as the school's associate dean for environmental studies, the director of the Institute of Ecology, and the chair of the division of environmental studies.

POPULATION GENETICS RESEARCH

While teaching at UC Davis, Ayala employed revolutionary molecular genetic techniques, including electrophoresis (an innovative method that sorts and measures DNA strands to analyze genetic variation) and gene cloning (manipulating DNA to create multiple copies of a single gene), to observe the amount and pattern of genetic differences between several groups of species across a broad geographic distribution.

The adaptive importance of genetic variation was another focus of Ayala's research. He examined the effect of environmental factors—such as population density (the average number of individuals living in a unit of area), food supply, and temperature—on the selection of genetic variants, or alleles (different version of the same genes). His findings supported the view that natural selection is the driving force affecting genetic polymorphism.

Ayala also teamed up with noted paleontologist James W. Valentine to examine the fossil record (fossilized plant and animal remains) in an attempt to gain awareness regarding which components contribute to the increasing diversification as well as to understand the sudden decline of many species. Ayala collaborated with other colleagues on a series of experiments comparing the genetic differences between living species found in habitats that are stable and replete with natural resources, like coral reefs, and those found in similarly homogeneous environments with fewer resources. The diverse organisms collected from both the resource-rich and the resource-poor areas displayed high levels of genetic diversity, confirming that stable environments maintain genetic variation. This is attributed to the fact that these species become better adapted to the various environmental factors and resources; as a result there may be little natural selection among the well-adapted organisms. In 1980, Ayala was invited to join the National Academy of Sciences (NAS) for his pioneering work on population genetics.

In 1981, Ayala testified as an expert witness for the defense in *McLean v. Arkansas Board of Education*, a federal court case that contested Arkansas' Act 590, which dictated that both evolution and creationism be taught in public school science classrooms. "Frank Press, the newly elected president of the National Academy of Sciences, asked me whether I thought the academy should get involved," Ayala told Slack. "I said it should. What was at stake was not a particular branch of science, but the survival of rationality in this country. If we allowed the Book of Genesis to be taught as science, that would be as bad for science as it would be for religion." The judge agreed; he overturned Act 590 on the basis that it was unconstitutional.

PARASITIC PROTOZOA RESEARCH

In addition to his studies with *Drosophila* fruit flies, Ayala conducted joint research with French doctor Michel Tibayrenc on *Trypanosoma cruzi*, the protozoan parasite that is responsible for Chagas disease, an incurable, potentially deadly disease that is native to Latin America and affects nearly twenty million people worldwide. Tibayrenc thought that *T. cruzi* might actually be more than one species.

In January 1985, after receiving a government fellowship, Tibayrenc traveled with his family from France to California, where he collaborated with Ayala. Over the next twenty months, they employed molecular genetic methods to study the genetic diversity of natural populations of *T. cruzi* and made several important findings. Although Tibayrenc's initial theory about *T. cruzi* was incorrect, the team found that the parasite reproduces primarily by cloning itself. They also discovered that other disease-causing protozoa, including those that cause sleeping sickness and malaria, also reproduce by cloning.

In 1987 Ayala accepted the position of distinguished professor of biological sciences at the University of California, Irvine. In 1989 he served as the Donald Bren Professor of Biological Sciences and founding director of the Bren Fellows Program while also teaching philosophy. In 1990 Ayala and Tibayrenc's findings were published in the scientific journal *Proceedings of the National Academy of Sciences of the United States of America* (*PNAS*), in an article entitled "A Clonal Theory of Parasitic Protozoa."

FOCUS ON MALARIA

During his time as a member of the National Advisory Council for the Human Genome Project between 1990 and 1993, Ayala recommended that a portion of the budget (between three and five percent) should be allocated toward figuring out the ethical, legal, and social ramifications of the project's outcome. In 1994 President Bill Clinton named Ayala to the US President's Committee of Advisors on Science and Technology, a post he held until 2001.

In the early 1990s Ayala also turned his attention to *Plasmodium falciparum*, a protozoan parasite commonly found in Africa that is responsible for the most virulent, or infective, form of human malaria. At the time, the disease affected between three hundred and five hundred million people around the world each year and resulted in more than a million deaths annually, chiefly among African children. With the help of colleagues, Ayala observed the genetic diversity among several *Plasmodium* species and determined that *P. falciparum* was more closely related to *P. reichenowi*, a parasite commonly found in chimpanzees, than to other *Plasmodium* species that infect humans (*P. vivax, P. malariae*) or birds (*P. gallinaceum, P. lophurae*).

In 1998 Ayala teamed up with Stephen Rich, a former UC Irvine graduate student, to examine the amount of genetic variation that existed among DNA from diverse strains of *P. falciparum*. They analyzed the DNA arrangement of ten genes in thirty strains of *P. falciparum*, relying mainly on published data. After discovering only slight variation, Ayala and Rich reasoned that all thirty strains had descended from the same ancestral strain (a "malarial Eve") within the last 57,500 years.

The finding contradicted earlier investigations by others who had observed noticeable differences among the genes for antigenic proteins (those foreign proteins that are targeted by the human immune system). To explain this inconsistency, Ayala and his colleagues determined that these mutations had occurred in response to the human immune system. Ayala and Rich also concluded that the spread of *P. falciparum* from its origins in Africa to tropical and subtropical regions around the world had occurred within the last 5,000 years and coincided with the evolution of farming in Africa.

ADDITIONAL DISCOVERIES

Since 2000 Ayala has been a professor of logic and the philosophy of science at UC Irvine. In 2003 he was named a University Professor in the UC system—a distinguished title he still holds. From 2004 to 2006 Ayala served as president of the nonprofit scientific society Sigma Xi.

In 2009 Ayala and his colleagues garnered attention with a paper that was published in the September issue of *PNAS*. The article traced the

origin of *Plasmodium falciparum* to a closely related species, *P. reichenowi*, which infects chimpanzees. This time the team was able to study
not just one isolate of the chimpanzee parasite,
but eight other isolates from chimps born in the
wild. The team concluded that *P. falciparum*
came from a single branch of *P. reichenowi*,
probably via a single chimp-mosquito-human
transmission.

Ayala also made headlines the following
January, for another paper that appeared in
PNAS. In this article, he wrote that strains of
the human parasite *P. falciparum* had recently
been found in apes, suggesting that even if malaria were stamped out, the human population
could still be at risk via contagion from gorillas
or chimpanzees.

HONORS AND PUBLICATIONS

In addition to the Templeton Prize (2010), Ayala's many accolades include the Medal of the
College of France (1979); the W. E. Key Award
from the American Genetics Association (1985);
the Scientific Freedom and Responsibility Award
of the American Association for the Advancement of Science (1987); the Gold Medal of the
Italian National Academy of Sciences (1998);
the William Procter Prize for Scientific Achievement (2000) from Sigma Xi; the National Medal
of Science (2001); and the American Institute of
Biological Sciences (AIBS) Distinguished Scientist Award (2007).

Ayala spent three years (1993–96) as president and board chairman of the American Academy of Arts and Sciences (AAAS); he also had a
two-year stint (2004–06) as president of Sigma
Xi. In addition to his memberships in the AAAS
and the National Academy of Sciences, Ayala
has been elected a foreign member of the Royal
Academy of Sciences of Spain; the Russian
Academy of Sciences; the Russian Academy of
Natural Sciences; and the Serbian Academy of
Sciences and Arts.

Ayala has more than seven hundred publications to his name. In addition to the books and
scientific articles mentioned previously, he has
also published *Studies in the Philosophy of Biology* (1977); *Population and Evolutionary Genetics: A Primer* (1982); *Modern Genetics* (second
edition, 1984); *Genetics and The Origin of Species* (1997); and *Human Evolution: Trails from
the Past* (2007).

PERSONAL LIFE

In April 2010, UC Irvine announced that it
would rename its science library the Francisco
J. Ayala Science Library. In October 2011, Ayala
made a $10 million endowment—one million
each year for the next decade—to UC Irvine's
School of Biological Sciences; it is the largest
endowment to date by a faculty member. The
donation was amassed from the proceeds of his

two-thousand-acre vineyard, located in northern
San Joaquin and Sacramento counties. Ayala
grows grapes for his own private label and for
other wineries.

Since 1985, Ayala has been married to his
second wife, Dr. Hana (Lostakova) Ayala, an
ecologist. The couple live in Irvine. Ayala has
two sons, Francisco José and Carlos Alberto,
from his first marriage to Mary Henderson.

SUGGESTED READING

Davies, Caroline. "Pro-Religion Scientist Wins
£1m Templeton Prize." *The Guardian*. Guardian Media Group, 5 May 2010. Web. 14 Aug.
2012.

Dean, Cornelia. "Francisco J. Ayala: Roving De-
fender of Evolution, and of Room for God."
New York Times. New York Times, 29 Apr.
2008. Web. 31 July 2012.

Gale, Elaine. "God Welcome in Biologist's Lab:
Ex-Priest's Unique Perspective Bridges Gap
Between Science, Religion." *Los Angeles
Times*. Tribune Co., 4 Sep. 1999. Web. 14
Aug. 2012.

Saslow, Rachel. "Genetics Researcher Francisco
Ayala Discusses His Life, His Work and Cre-
ationism." *Washington Post*. Washington Post
Co., 26 Apr. 2010. Web. 31 July 2012.

Slack, Gordy. "A Good Life." *UC Irvine Today*.
UCI Communications, 29 Aug. 2002. Web.
12 Aug. 2012.

—*Bertha Muteba*

Alison Balsom

Born: October 7, 1978
Occupation: Trumpeter

Known as the "trumpet crumpet"—a name she
gave herself when she was just ten—the British trumpet-soloist Alison Balsom is considered
among the most talented classical musicians of
her generation. The fact that she is a woman—
and a glamorous one at that—has added to her
distinction, given the traditional view that the
trumpet is a macho instrument predominantly
played by men. Balsom has insisted the stereotypes about her chosen instrument and its typical players are unfounded, and she has embraced
the mission of demonstrating the instrument's
versatility. "People do think of the trumpet as a
brutish, loud, masculine instrument—which it
doesn't have to be," Balsom told Arminta Wallace for the Dublin, Ireland, *Irish Times* (Sep. 9,
2009, online). "You can play musical lines any
way you want. You can play in a lyrical way. You
can play in a singing way. And if the music is
good, and it's romantic music, then why can you
not do it on the trumpet?"

Getty Images

Since her debut album, *Music for Trumpet and Organ* (2002), when she was twenty-two, Balsom has released five acclaimed solo albums, performed before packed audiences the world over, and won numerous honors including three Classical BRIT Awards. Although her oft-noted striking beauty has undoubtedly broadened her audience, critics praise her for her talent as a musician. "The days are long gone when blowing a brass instrument was a male preserve," Geoff Brown noted for the London *Times* (June 20, 2006). "Even so, the young trumpeter Alison Balsom remains a singular figure. It's not that she's long and blonde; it's the roar of her talent that makes her stand out, along with her knack for breaking down barriers and making the trumpet so much more than a toot machine."

EARLY LIFE AND EDUCATION

Balsom was born in England on October 7, 1978, in the county of Hertfordshire and grew up in the town of Royston. Her father, Bill, was a builder, while her mother, Zena, worked at an agency placing children in foster homes. Balsom's parents were educated and sophisticated, but neither played an instrument.

Balsom began playing the trumpet in primary school after first trying out several other instruments. She was particularly attracted to the trumpet's versatility. Balsom explained to Hugh Canning for the London *Sunday Times* (Nov. 15, 2009), "The trumpet has so many colours. It can do so much. It's not just loud, loud, loud—or it doesn't have to be."

As a child, Balsom and her mother would go to the library and take out cassette tapes of trumpeters including the twentieth-century jazz trumpeter Dizzy Gillespie, whose work would influence Balsom throughout her career. She was inspired to become a soloist at age nine or ten when she attended a concert by the Swedish trumpet virtuoso Håkan Hardenberger at the Barbican, a large arts center in London. "I remember that concert as if it was a week ago," she told Antonia Hoyle for the London *Daily Mail* (May 17, 2009). "I just thought, that's what I want to do—stand up there and play trumpet solos. And even as I grew up and it became apparent that this wasn't what most trumpet players did—they mostly sit at the back of orchestras—my ambition was still to be a soloist." She later went on to study with Hardenberger from 2001–04.

Balsom took early lessons from music instructor Adrian Jacobs at Greneway School. She also joined the local brass band in her hometown of Royston, along with her brother, Richard, who played the tuba. (Richard later retired from music and became a firefighter.) At thirteen, Balsom enrolled in the junior department of London's Guildhall School of Music and Drama before attending the senior school, where her teachers included Stephen Keavy and Paul Benniston. Balsom was so focused on her future that she made few friends. She recalled to Louette Harding for the *Daily Mail* (Dec. 10, 2011), "I was a bit of an outsider." After she finished at Guildhall, she spent a year at the Paris Conservatory of Music, where she trained to become a virtuoso. There her playing improved dramatically. "The French trumpet-playing way is much more solo-oriented, much less orchestra-focused, than in Britain," she explained to Antonia Hoyle. Balsom also played in the prestigious National Youth Orchestra in the United Kingdom. She won her big break in 1998 when she won the brass category of the BBC Young Musician of the Year competition.

Balsom was not aware that the trumpet was traditionally thought to be a man's instrument when she first began studying the instrument. "I come from a family with no gender bias," she told Harding. "I wanted to play the trumpet brilliantly and they encouraged me. It never occurred to me that other people found a female doing this surprising." Although Balsom's gender presented no obstacle, finding good material proved to be a challenge. The trumpet is an ancient instrument, but the modern trumpet—composed of valves that allow musicians to reach a wide range of notes—was developed in the early to mid-nineteenth century, long after many masters had written their great works for other instruments such as violin or piano. Balsom worked hard to find pieces written for classical trumpet, and when she could not find what she wanted, she adapted pieces composed for other instruments.

AWARD-WINNING RECORDINGS

Balsom was represented for about three years by Radio 3 New Generation Artists, a project organized by the BBC radio station to foster young musical talent. During that time, she performed with the London Chamber Orchestra. She released her first solo album, *Music for Trumpet and Organ* (2002), which included the works of George Thalben-Ball, Henri Tomasi, Henry Purcell, Jan Pieterszoon Sweelinck, and J. S. Bach—all hand selected by Balsom. The debut received enthusiastic reviews. Balsom played trumpet on the Hyperion record *The Fam'd Italian Masters* (2003), alongside trumpet soloist Crispian Steele-Perkins and the Parley of Instruments.

In 2004, she signed a three-record deal with the company EMI Classics. For *Bach: Works for Trumpet and Organ* (2005), her first album for the main label and second solo album, Balsom adapted Bach concertos originally written for other instruments—such as the cello, the keyboard, or the choir. Some of the adjustments Balsom made were including breaks for breathing, since a trumpeter cannot play continuously the way a violinist or organist can. Balsom's trumpet playing on the record was accompanied by organ, violin, and continuo. Like her debut, the record won rave reviews. "Britain's new trumpet star Alison Balsom goes for baroque in this disc composed, despite the title, of works Bach didn't write for trumpet at all," Geoff Brown noted for the London *Times* (Jan. 20, 2006). Describing her tone as "gleaming but flexible," the writer found Balsom's performance of Bach's concertos the most rewarding of the pieces.

Balsom also adapted most of the music for trumpet on her next record, *Caprice* (2006), released just a year later. That album received mixed assessments. In a review for the Melbourne, Australia, *Sunday Herald Sun* (Aug. 8, 2007), Bob Crimeen noted some weaknesses in the record but concluded, "*Caprice* sees Balsom venturing beyond tradition to embrace tango, opera, piano, violin and song. . . . Balsom rarely fails to project the music's mood." James Manishen wrote for the *Winnipeg Free Press* (Dec. 23, 2006), "Young British trumpet star Alison Balsom's virtuosity comes born from the music, but is not externally applied; a sort of art concealing art with the fireworks sounding truly integral rather than in and of themselves." The album went on to win the 2006 Solo CD of the Year from *Brass Band World* magazine. That same year Balsom won her first Classical BRIT Award in the category of young British classical performer.

Balsom's fourth solo album, *Haydn, Hummel: Trumpet Concertos* (2008), contained four of the earliest and best-known concertos for the trumpet. Balsom considers Haydn's Trumpet Concerto in E Flat Major (1796) particularly important because it was the first piece written specifically for a trumpet that could play a full scale. Balsom explained to Rachel Devine for the London *Sunday Times* (Mar. 9, 2008), "Before that, in the baroque period, trumpets could only play the notes in the harmonic series, which means they had to play extremely high before they could even play scales. "[Haydn's concerto] was the first piece that took the trumpet to a new level where it could be accepted as a solo instrument for the first time—very subtle, very simple, but so well crafted." A reviewer for the *New York Times* (Nov. 27, 2008) noted, "Those who associate the trumpet with brash fanfares should listen to Alison Balsom's poetic renditions of concertos . . . all performed with a clear, soaring tone, virtuosic technique and elegant phrasing."

Nominated for her second Classical BRIT Award in 2009, Balsom attended the ceremony at the Royal Albert Hall wearing a sparkling minidress and borrowed diamond jewelry worth a reported £1 million. Asked during an interview to comment on her notoriously glamorous dress, Balsom said, "Classical music has a reputation for being incredibly harsh and staid. . . . I'm not trying to dumb down in any way and I wouldn't wear a short dress on stage, but why not wear a cool rock-chick dress instead of a ball gown?" as quoted by Antonia Hoyle in the London *Daily Mail* (May 17, 2009). She has said on other occasions that the style of her dress helps her feel confident when walking out on stage. Balsom ultimately took home the award for female artist of the year.

Balsom's fifth solo album, *Italian Concertos* (2010), was EMI Classic's best-selling album that year. It included the trumpeter's own transcriptions of Italian baroque concertos originally written for violin and oboe, with accompaniment by the Scottish Ensemble led by music director Jonathan Morton. Jon Terauds described the music for the *Toronto Star* (Jan. 4, 2011, online) as "sparkling, nicely textured music dominated by Balsom's almost supernaturally smooth and assured playing. Not a dull note to be heard."

IN PERFORMANCE

As she recorded and released album after album, Balsom maintained a rigorous concert schedule. Her 2009 schedule included stops in the United Kingdom, Germany, Russia, Turkey, and the United States. On her tours she performed with such notable groups as the Los Angeles Philharmonic, Orchestre de Paris, San Francisco Symphony Orchestra, Orchestre National de France, Orchestra Sinfonica di Milano Giuseppe Verdi, Philharmonia Orchestra, and City of Birmingham Symphony Orchestra. She played a range of music, from the jazz of Dizzy Gillespie to the classical compositions of Claude Debussy to the popular music of George Gershwin. Many have noted that Balsom's early jazz influences are most evident in her rhythm and phrasing during live performances. In 2009 Balsom performed Haydn's Trumpet Concerto on BBC's annual concert Last Night of the Proms before an estimated worldwide television audience of 200 million. Balsom made her US television debut on December 8, 2010, when she performed with the Orchestra of St. Luke's on *The Late Show with David Letterman*—a rare and remarkable feat for a classical performer.

In February 2011 Balsom performed the world premiere of renowned Scottish composer James MacMillan's three-movement trumpet concerto *Seraph* at Wigmore Hall in London. The performance was part of a Scottish Ensemble program contrasting twentieth- and twenty-first-century British music with Italian baroque concerts by famed composers Tomaso Albinoni and Antonio Vivaldi. A writer for the London *Times* (Feb. 12, 2011) noted, "As the composer James MacMillan points out, a seraph is a 'celestial being usually associated with trumpets.' So he seems to have found the right person to premiere *Seraph* . . . as Alison Balsom is probably the most exciting thing to happen to brass instruments since the euphonium." In May 2011 Balsom was again named Female Artist of the Year at the annual Classical BRIT ceremony, beating out pianist Mitsuoko Uchida and violinist Nicola Benedetti. Later in the evening she performed a piece from her 2010 album, *Italian Concertos*.

CHALLENGES

In December 2011 Balsom was recording her next album, *Seraph: Trumpet Concertos* (2012), which reportedly includes some of her most challenging material yet. It features trumpet concertos written by such composers as Alexander Arutiunian, Bernd Alois Zimmermann, and James MacMillan, including the world premiere of MacMillan's latest trumpet concerto. "I love to show the versatility of the instrument," Balsom told Jessica Duchen for the London *Independent* (May 30, 2011, online). "We don't have as a big a repertoire as other instruments, but we do have as wide a scope."

Balsom has performed on the same live ticket as pop and hip-hop artists. One musician she has expressed her desire to collaborate with is the rapper Eminem. "I think he's a great artist," she told Arminta Wallace, "He's so unselfconscious in what he does: he doesn't do it to please his audiences, or his record label, or the masses, or anything. He just does something that is genuinely how he wants to perform and what he wants to say." She added, "I think that goes across all genres. It's about doing the best you can for yourself with conviction and without compromising."

Balsom has often discussed the unique stresses of being a soloist, a life she describes as very isolating. She explained to Louette Harding, "I exist with the terror of the deadline always, the steam train of doing my exercises, regardless of whatever else is going on in my life. I'm only as good as my last concert. Every time I'm on stage I have to prove so much—be amazing, move people, make it technically assured. And if it didn't go well, it might plant a seed of doubt in my head, which would affect the next performance." She continued, "There is a conductor, an orchestra and me. The orchestra is not my friend. . . . The closest it comes is a polite handclap when I'm introduced, but you can practically hear what they're thinking: 'Are you any good? If you're not, we'll let you know.'"

PERSONAL LIFE

As one of classical music's most glamorous practitioners, Balsom's love life has been the focus of the media and many curious fans. She had a brief romantic relationship with the Russian violinist Maxim Vengerov, who has continued to be a musical inspiration to her. In 2006 she met the conductor Edward Gardner while both of them were working with the Colorado Symphony Orchestra. Gardner became musical director for the prestigious English National Opera (ENO) in 2006. During his tenure, he was credited with turning the ENO into one of the finest opera companies in Europe. Balsom invited Gardner to serve as the conductor on her 2006 album, *Caprice*. The two performed together several times before embarking on a romantic relationship in 2009. Despite the attention they received from the press, Balsom and Gardner—who is four years her senior—strived to keep the romance low key, limiting performances and interviews. Still, the pair was hailed as one of the most exciting in the classical-music world. Balsom told Andy Whalen and Allan Hall for the London *Daily Mail* (Apr. 17, 2011, online), "To have someone so talented and passionate, who can understand the highs and lows of being a musician, all the irrational thoughts and emotions, that's amazing."

When Balsom unexpectedly became pregnant with Gardner's child in 2009, she decided that she was ready for the challenges of motherhood. "I'd done concerts when I had missed my train connection, the orchestra sounded terrible, someone made life difficult for me, and I'd gone on and somehow made it work," Balsom told Louette Harding. "I've survived those experiences and I think once you get to that point, then it's a good time to introduce a child into the mix." Balsom gave birth to a son named Charlie in March 2010. But by early 2011 she and Gardner had separated. Both moved out of their shared home in London, and the classical-music community mourned the loss of their golden couple.

Balsom regularly brings her son—as well as a nanny—with her to concerts. She told Louette Harding, "I'm really loving being a single mother. I'm not putting a brave face on it. I'm not looking for my life to be different to what it is now. I am happily single." In May 2011, when Balsom accepted her third Classical BRIT Award, she dedicated it to her son, whom she called her "happy, perfect touring companion."

Balsom's hobbies include skiing and yachting, which she has done competitively. She told Arminta Wallace, "I love going skiing, and I do loads of things that could be conceived as dangerous. But they can't stop you living your life—and I don't think they would want to, either. That's part of my personality, and they're things that I do quite frequently. Anyway, crossing the road is dangerous."

Another of Balsom's interests is philanthropic work, particularly her involvement with War Child, an international network of independent organizations that work to benefit children affected by war. "I think I might be the first classical ambassador they've had since Pavarotti," she told Wallace, "and I really am excited about it because they have this infrastructure where they put on concerts to raise money. So I can do something really helpful for them." Balsom also serves as a patron of London mayor Boris Johnson's initiative to provide music scholarships for local schoolchildren.

SUGGESTED READING

"Alison Balsom." *Times* [London] 12 Feb. 2011: 17. Print.

Brown, Geoff. "Alison Balsom." *Times* [London] 20 Jan. 2006: 16. Print.

---. "Alison Balsom/Manson Ensemble." *Times* [London] 20 Jun. 2006: 22. Print.

Canning, Hugh. "I Don't Think It Has Been Played by a Pregnant Trumpeter before." *Sunday Times* [London] 15 Nov. 2009: 32–33. Print.

Crimeen, Bob. "Instrumental." *Sunday Herald* [Melbourne] 5 Aug. 2007: E14. Print.

Cummings, Robert. "Alison Balsom." *Allmusic.com*. Rovi Corporation, 2012. Web. 19 Jan. 2012.

Devine, Rachel. "Girl with a Golden Horn." *Sunday Times* [London] 9 Mar. 2008: 14. Print.

Duchen, Jessica. "The Classical Star Landing a Blow for Brass." *Independent* [London]. Independent, 30 May 2011. Web. 18 Jan. 2012.

Harding, Louette. "Fanfare for the Modern Woman." *Daily Mail* [London] 10 Dec. 2011: 34–38. Print.

Hoyle, Antonia. "The Triumph of the Trumpet Majorette." *Daily Mail* [London] 17 May 2009: 40. Print.

Manishen, James. "Alison Balsom, Gothenburg Symphony Orchestra Caprice." *Winnipeg Free Press* 16 Dec. 2006: C4. Print.

Schweitzer, Vivien. "Classical Music." *New York Times*. New York Times, 27 Nov. 2008. Web. 18 Jan. 2012.

Terauds, John. "New Nutcracker and Classics Tweaked for Trumpet." *Toronto Star*. Toronto Star, 3 Jan. 2011. Web. 18 Jan. 2012.

Tyler, Jon. "Life Size Chunk of Fame for Trumpeter Alison Balsom." *Royston-crow.co.uk*. Archant Community Media, 12 May 2011. Web. 18 Jan. 2012.

Wallace, Arminta. "Classical, and All That Jazz." *Irish Times* [Dublin]. Irish Times, 9 Sep. 2009. Web. 18 Jan. 2012.

Whalen, Andy, and Allan Hall. "The Music Dies for 'Trumpet Crumpet' Alison Balsom and Her Proms Conductor." *Daily Mail* [London]. Associated Newspapers, 17 Apr. 2011. Web. 18 Jan. 2012.

Winn, Steven. "CD Reviews: Alison Balsom—Classical." *San Francisco Chronicle* 1 Oct. 2007: N42. Print.

SELECTED WORKS

Music for Trumpet and Organ, 2002; *Bach: Works for Trumpet and Organ*, 2005; *Caprice*, 2006; *Haydn, Hummel: Trumpet Concertos*, 2008; *Italian Concertos*, 2010; *Seraph: Trumpet Concertos*, 2012

—Maggie Mead

Maria Bamford

Born: September 3, 1970
Occupation: Comedian

Maria Bamford's stand-up comedy has been described as kooky, clever, and personal. She switches seamlessly among dozens of different voices—high-pitched, low-pitched, sweet, nervous, excited, condescending, unstable, creepy—impersonating a variety of characters, including her mother, father, sister, ex-boyfriend, agent, and therapist, the Baby Jesus, coworkers, sexually harassing bosses, and the singer Alicia Keys. In her performances, which are less like a typical stand-up-comedy set than like one-woman shows, Bamford covers common topics, such as romantic relationships, food obsessions, and the entertainment industry; she also openly discusses her mental-health problems, which she has had since childhood. Her humor is often dark, surreal, and absurd, but never meanspirited. On stage, as in life, Bamford is from all accounts a genuinely nice person. (Her website includes the unironically titled section "Nice Lady," where viewers can see her baby pictures and send e-mail messages to her mother.)

FilmMagic

Bamford may not be a household name, but there are those who think she should be. A writer for the *Los Angeles Times* (6 Dec. 2009) called her "underrated" and was "thankful she's finally getting more exposure without compromising her wonderfully weird perspective." Bamford has a strong following among both comedy fans and her fellow comedians. John Oliver of the *Daily Show*, Judd Apatow, and Patton Oswalt, for example, have all praised her. Bamford's career received a boost when she was featured, along with Oswalt, Brian Posehn, and Zach Galifianakis, in the documentary *The Comedians of Comedy* (2005). Her latest CD, *Unwanted Thoughts Syndrome* (2009), was named "one of the best comedy albums of the decade" by the *A.V. Club* (16 Nov. 2009). In an interview with *Current Biography* (the source of quotes for this article unless otherwise noted), asked whether she finds performing comedy to be therapeutic, Bamford replied, "Yes, yes, yes!" She added, "I was very quiet as a kid, and it's a really wonderful feeling to have—perceived—control, where everybody's listening to me and I am amplified and lit and I have 45 minutes for people to really take in what I have to say."

EARLY LIFE AND EDUCATION

Maria Elizabeth Sheldon Bamford was born at a US Navy hospital on September 3, 1970 in Port Hueneme, California, where her father, Joel, was serving in the navy at the time. A few years later the family moved to Duluth, Minnesota, where her father practiced dermatology;

her mother, Marilyn, was a homemaker, taking care of Maria and her older sister, Sarah. Her mother also regularly attended Bible study at an Episcopal church and was outspoken about her beliefs—which, Bamford said, were relatively liberal. (Episcopalianism, she said, "is sort of like Catholicism, but without the guilt.") Bamford was a quiet child. She began playing the violin at age three, made paper dolls, watched a lot of television, and enjoyed listening to comedy albums and programs with her father, including the records of Steve Martin and Eddie Murphy and Garrison Keillor's National Public Radio program *Prairie Home Companion*. Bamford herself showed comedic talent during those years, making her sister laugh with dead-on impressions of their parents.

By the age of eleven, Bamford was already suffering from several serious mental-health problems, including depression, anxiety, thoughts of suicide, and obsessive-compulsive disorder (OCD). Around that time she began seeing a therapist who incorporated Christian teachings in her sessions, a process Bamford did not find helpful; she found more relief a few years later, when she started seeing a psychologist.

Every year at Marshall High School in Duluth, Bamford ran for student council—not because she wanted to serve (she did not, particularly) but so that she could give funny speeches. More comfortable on stage than in everyday interaction with people, she appeared in plays during her school years. Although she enjoyed performing, she never considered becoming a comedian or an actor. "Specifically, I remember wanting to be a doctor in South America that played the violin," Bamford told Ben Kharakh for the *Gothamist* (21 Aug. 2006). "I liked the drama of my family never seeing [me] again and that they'd have to admire me [from afar for] my individuality."

GETTING HER START IN COMEDY

After high school Bamford studied for two years at Bates College, in Lewiston, Maine; during her junior year she attended the University of Edinburgh, in Scotland. She finished her college education at the University of Minnesota–Minneapolis, where she earned a bachelor's degree in English literature. She had considered studying acting but took classes in the subject and "didn't really enjoy it. I didn't really understand it. And I still don't really understand it. I love to see it—I wish desperately that I understood it—but I don't think it's my gift." She gave her first stand-up performance at a student union talent show; she talked about being from Minnesota. After graduating Bamford continued to do stand-up, finding Minneapolis to be a supportive environment for theater and comedy performers; she appeared at a handful of comedy clubs but more often in coffee shops and performance-art venues. Even then, Bamford's act, while not yet as sharp and polished as it would become, was offbeat and different from those of many comedians in being somewhat theatrical; her material was primarily about her personal life and her family. Bamford considered moving to Boston, Massachusetts, or New York City to further her stand-up career, but she decided against it because she was "super sensitive," in her words, and feared that she would not be able to handle hecklers. Raised in a culture that encouraged everyone "to be pleasant and never be loud . . . I was terrified of people telling me 'shut up' or 'you suck,'" she said. At the age of twenty-four, Bamford found a job playing a *Star Trek* character—though she was not a *Star Trek* fan—at the Mall of America, in Bloomington, Minnesota. When, a month later, the troupe was hired to perform at several malls in Los Angeles, California, Bamford moved with them.

After a year of that work, Bamford decided to spend more time on her own comedy. In that period, compared with her later work, "I wasn't as good at being conversational or social as a comedian," she told Kharakh. "I used to play the violin in my act. I'd say what I'd perceive to be a joke, play a violin solo, and then go into something else. When I think about it now, it was a bit passive aggressive. And I was bald too. I shaved my head and wore long floral dresses. It was a, 'Why are you looking at me?' kind of thing. 'Because you're bald playing a violin and telling jokes.' . . . Now I'd like to say that I'm more myself onstage. I still do characters and get the same type of reviews where it says, 'She's crazy. She's Sybil. She's schizophrenic.' My joke in response to that is, 'The actual diagnosis is clinical depression.'"

TELEVISION AND DOCUMENTARY APPEARANCES

Newly recognized for her quirky humor, in 1999 Bamford began to appear on nationally broadcast television programs, such as *Late Night with Conan O'Brien* and *The Tonight Show with Jay Leno*. *Variety* (17–23 July 2000) placed Bamford on its "10 Comics to Watch" list, along with such performers as Mitch Hedberg, Louis C. K., and Patton Oswalt. In 2001 Bamford appeared in her own half-hour stand-up TV special, *Comedy Central Presents*, and the following year she was seen on the Comedy Central stand-up variety show *Premium Blend*. Despite her growing success, on occasion Bamford still worked for temp agencies, which gave her plenty of material for her act. One joke, in which she adopted the voice of a temp agent, was, "Hello, Maria, this is T&R staffing! Here it is—the best offer! Thailand. You are sold into prostitution! $6.50 an hour and that's not all; there's free parking!" In addition to increased recognition in the United States, Bamford was starting to gain popularity in the United Kingdom and Australia. In 2004,

on a tour of Australia as a relatively unknown comic, Bamford came away with the Melbourne Comedy Festival's Barry Award for most outstanding show.

With the release of *The Comedians of Comedy* (2005), Bamford attained a new level of exposure. That documentary film follows four up-and-coming comedians on their US tour: Bamford, Patton Oswalt, Brian Posehn, and Zach Galifianakis; snippets of stand-up performances are mixed with an abundance of backstage and on-the-road footage. "I'm a bit more theatrical than [the other three comedians], so it was very nice for them to have me on the show," Bamford told Kyle Ryan for the *A.V. Club* (20 Apr. 2009). "Sometimes Patton would introduce me like, 'Hey guys? You guys, she's really great, a supernice person . . .' It was just awesome, and it was really nice to see everybody work on their jokes, try different jokes. I just love that part of comedy, where you see somebody's jokes develop. . . . It was a great learning experience." The documentary was also shown serially on Comedy Central, as six half-hour episodes, and an entire live performance, titled *The Comedians of Comedy: Live at the El Rey*, was released on DVD in 2007. The documentary itself received mixed reviews. In an assessment for the *New York Times* (11 Nov. 2005), Laura Kern did not find the performances to be very funny. "Offstage," she added, "the mostly unglamorous lifestyle of traveling comedians is accurately conveyed, but insight into their interactions, real-life personalities and creative processes is rare. . . . The camera's constant gaze doesn't seem to allow the troupe members to relax. In other words, they are always performing." Paul Brownfield, writing for the *Los Angeles Times* (11 Nov. 2005), disagreed: the comedians, he wrote, do not appear to be "on" when offstage. "*The Comedians of Comedy*," Brownfield added, "is a kind of hybrid of documentary and sitcom that gets the viewer closer to how comedians live and breathe, but only so close." The writer for the *Los Angeles Times* (6 Dec. 2009) felt that Bamford "nearly stole" the show.

"PLAN B"

In 2005 Bamford went on tour with her new stand-up act, titled "Plan B," in which she portrayed a dozen characters: her mother, father, sister, and high school nemesis, a comedy-club heckler, and others. The premise of the performance was that Bamford—or a very similar alter ego, also named Maria Bamford—suffers a breakdown while performing onstage and leaves Los Angeles to live with her parents in Duluth, Minnesota. The events Bamford depicted take place in her hometown of Duluth, mostly in her parents' house. Bamford switches among the characters, seamlessly altering her voice and facial expressions. Impersonating her mother talking to her,

Bamford says, "Honey, when you don't wear make-up, you look mentally ill." At another point Bamford, on an absurd shopping trip with her mother at Target, runs into Christie, her archenemy from high school, who tells Bamford in a smug, disgusted voice, "It's just like in high school. You're not funny. You're just weird." Bamford's friend and fellow comic Jackie Kashian told Gerard Wright for the Melbourne, Australia, *Sunday Age* (20 Mar. 2005) about Bamford's work, "It's very much comedy coming from tragedy. For me, it's some of the best. It's not shock comedy, it's dark. You have to be over everything you're talking about. When you're talking about your family, you have to be over the crazy things they've done to you." Bamford agreed, telling Wright, "It's an odd form of therapy, obviously, because you're saying something that may be shameful to say, but if you say it to a group of people and they laugh, then you know, 'Oh, I'm not by myself, everybody knows about this sort of stuff.' This isn't stand-up. It's totally in terms of a one-person show. They're probably too theatrical or long for people to listen to." In a mock-empathetic voice, she added, "Which I can totally understand."

The following year Bamford took her material to the United Kingdom. At the Edinburgh Fringe Festival—the world's largest arts festival—Bamford's show was a hit. In a review of "Plan B" for the London *Guardian* (14 Aug. 2006), Brian Logan wrote, "What's impressive is the economy with which Bamford animates this community of family and friends. Her transformations aren't self-consciously artful. She's just a terrific mimic, who can bring characters to keen comic life with the slightest phrase or mannerism. Or noise. Some of the show's funniest lines are actually whimpers, grunts or sotto voce muttering. Her ageing dad is a symphony of wheezes and throat-clearing. . . . Bamford's triumph, both personal and artistic, is to fashion such an entertaining and affectionate portrait from all this mutual resentment and disappointment." Bamford's live performance of the material at the Varsity Theater, in Minneapolis, was released on DVD as Plan B in 2010. After recording the stand-up show, Bamford did a one-woman sitcom version of "Plan B," filmed in her parents' home in Duluth; titled *The Maria Bamford Show*, the series' twenty five-minute episodes found her playing the characters in an even more exaggerated fashion, thanks to different outfits and quick cuts. The show initially aired on the now defunct comedy website *Super Deluxe*. (Episodes are now available on the video-sharing site YouTube.) Also, for one day in July 2011, *The Maria Bamford Show* was screened at the Museum of Art and Design, in New York. In 2007 she released an audio CD, *How to Win*, which included lengthier versions of the material in "Plan B" as well as new material.

UNWANTED THOUGHTS SYNDROME AND OTHER PROJECTS

Bamford's latest comedy album is *Unwanted Thoughts Syndrome* (2009). The name refers to an actual psychological condition, one of many variations of OCD, in which people have graphically sexual, violent, or simply bizarre thoughts that they cannot control. For the CD's liner notes, Bamford wrote, "I was unable to sleep at night for fear of being a rapist or a murderer or a genocider, and would have constant anxious thoughts of doing those things—to friends, family, babies, kitties, etc.—and it was especially powerful the more taboo or inappropriate the situation." Bamford had been having such thoughts since the age of ten and had seen various therapists about the problem over the years, without much success. Then, at the age of thirty-four, she consulted a psychologist who told her to record herself describing her unwanted thoughts and then listen repeatedly to what she had said. The idea was that by listening to herself, Bamford would realize how absurd and unthreatening her thoughts were. The strategy worked: within a few months the thoughts stopped. On *Unwanted Thoughts Syndrome* Bamford again demonstrated her vocal dexterity and comic timing. Among other subjects, she talks about taking painting classes taught by a man called the Wizard of Art—"who used to open for The Doors"—whom she impersonates in an overeager hippie-guru voice. Bamford also discusses getting older: "My body's changing. My skin's getting softer. But that makes my bones jut out—so I'm half soft, half *sharp*." In an *A.V. Club* (16 Nov. 2009) review that named *Unwanted Thoughts Syndrome* one of the "best albums of the decade," Scott Gordon wrote: "Bamford uses her barrage of exaggerated voices to chip her way toward some pretty elusive ideas and trick the brain into thinking about some pretty weird [expletive]. That's what *Unwanted Thoughts Syndrome* is all about: dwelling on the weird tension of planning lunch with your office mates, phone messages from Baby Jesus, performing as a *Star Trek* character in the mall. These aren't impressions, they're complete scenes, and they all sink in slowly and uncomfortably, in spite of Bamford's twitchy energy."

In addition to her stand-up comedy, Bamford has been involved in various side projects. She served as a writer on sixty-three episodes of *The Martin Short Show*, from 1999 to 2000, and she had a small role as Wendy the Waitress in the Nora Ephron–directed crime-comedy film *Lucky Numbers* (2000), which starred John Travolta and Lisa Kudrow. While the movie was universally panned, viewers got a chance to see Bamford improvise during a memorable press-conference scene. In the late 1990s, after she had lived in Los Angeles for several years, Bamford began auditioning frequently for sitcoms;

with the exception of a onetime appearance on *Dharma & Greg*, in 1999, she was unsuccessful. She went on to lend her voice to such animated TV cartoons as *Hey Arnold!*, *CatDog*, and *Home Movies*, in 1999; the animated film *Stuart Little 2* (2002); the TV shows *Hey Monie!* (2003), *Home Movies* (2004), *American Dad!* (2007), and *Adventure Time* (2010–11); and the Emmy Award–winning educational PBS superhero cartoon *WordGirl* (2007– 11). In 2009 and 2010 Bamford appeared in holiday ads for Target, in which she played a kooky, overenthusiastic shopper.

The petite Bamford lives in Los Angeles with her two pugs.

SUGGESTED READING

Kharakh, Ben. "Maria Bamford, Comedian." *Gothamist*. Gothamist, 21 Aug. 2006. Web. Jan. 2012.

Logan, Brian. "Maria Bamford: Assembly Rooms." (London) *Guardian*. Guardian News and Media, 14 Aug. 2006. Web. Jan. 2012.

"Maria Bamford." *IMDB*. IMDB.com, n.d. Web. Jan. 2012.

Maria Bamford. Maria Bamford, 2007–2012. Web. Jan. 2012.

Ryan, Kyle. "Interview: Maria Bamford." *A.V. Club*. Onion, 20 Apr. 2009. Web. Jan. 2012.

Zabel, Jason. "Interview: Maria Bamford." *A.V. Club*. Onion, 12 May 2011. Web. Jan. 2012.

—*Dmitry Kiper*

Pam Belluck

Occupation: *New York Times* science writer, journalist

The *New York Times* staff writer Pam Belluck has worked in journalism since her college years, when she served a summer internship with the *National Journal*. She later interned with the *Wall Street Journal* and then, as a Fulbright scholar, wrote for the *San Francisco Chronicle*, filing stories from Southeast Asia—work that earned her, at age twenty-three, an award for international reporting from the World Affairs Council of Northern California in 1987. After her return to the United States, she reported for the *Atlanta Journal-Constitution*, where she was part of a team of reporters who were finalists for a Pulitzer Prize in general reporting. At her next job, with the *Philadelphia Inquirer*, she was part of a team of reporters who were finalists for a Pulitzer in spot news reporting.

Belluck started at the *Times* as a general-assignment reporter. In her next positions, she headed the *Times*' bureau in Queens, briefly covered New York City schools, and was then

©David Beyda Studio, NYC

selected to be a national bureau chief, first in the Midwest and then in New England. In 2009, she joined the *Times*' stable of science and health writers. Belluck has won seven *Times* Publisher's Awards.

In thousands of published articles, Belluck has covered a wide variety of subjects and events, among them cattle rustling, embryo adoption, the bombing of the federal building in Oklahoma City in 1995, the crash of TWA Flight 800 in 1996, the introduction of same-sex marriage in Massachusetts, and the passage of a landmark health care overhaul in that state in 2006. She has written in-depth reports about the demolition of a public housing project in Chicago notorious for its omnipresent crime, end-of-life decisions, and the search for explanations for the Columbine High School massacre of 1999. She told *Current Biography* that she has "also written about quintessentially American quirkiness, including the fight between two Iowa farmers over whose property is the honest-to-goodness 'Field of Dreams,' [in reference to the 1989 movie by that name] and the mayor of a North Dakota town who won [an] election by a flip of a coin." She added: "My approach to journalism has always been driven by the desire to discover facts that are surprising or counterintuitive; to write stories that can reveal contradictions, problems, or injustices regarding issues that are important to the way people live; to probe beneath the surface of a subject and unearth its complexity and nuance; and to write with an arched eyebrow about the delightful idiosyncrasies of America."

In the foreword to Belluck's first book, *Island Practice: Cobblestone Rash, Underground Tom and Other Adventures of a Nantucket Doctor* (2012), Nathaniel Philbrick, a National Book Award winner, states: "Much in this book by Pam Belluck comes as a revelation. Some of it is fascinating; some of it is hilarious; and some of it is sad and very troubling. In *Island Practice*, Belluck has created a remarkable portrait of a physician and the island community to which he remains steadfastly devoted." The best-selling author Warren St. John wrote, "Pam Belluck has crafted an elegant and wildly entertaining depiction of the struggle to maintain humanity and empathy in the face of health care's ongoing industrialization."

EDUCATION AND EARLY CAREER

Pamela Joan Belluck was born in New York State to Raymond Belluck and Frances (Schell) Belluck. Her father, an engineering manager for the Sperry division of Unisys, and her mother, a medical social worker, are retired. She grew up on Long Island, New York, with her older brother, David Belluck, a partner in an investment firm, and her younger brother, Joseph Belluck, an attorney. After she graduated from Herricks High School in New Hyde Park, Belluck entered the Woodrow Wilson School of Public and International Affairs at Princeton University, in New Jersey. She majored in international relations, with a minor in Asian studies, and studied Mandarin throughout college, becoming skilled in that language as well as maintaining her knowledge of French. Her extracurricular activities included writing for the *Daily Princetonian*. During the summer of 1984, she worked in Washington, DC, as a reporting intern at the *National Journal*, a nonpartisan weekly focusing on politics and government. She earned a BA with honors in 1985.

For the next six months, Belluck worked in New York City as a *Wall Street Journal* reporting intern. She won a Fulbright scholarship, and for over a year and a half beginning in January 1986, she wrote freelance articles as the Southeast Asia correspondent of the *San Francisco Chronicle*. She covered events in the Philippines, where she was based, as well as in China, Hong Kong, South Korea, Thailand, and Burma (Myanmar). In 1987, the World Affairs Council of Northern California recognized the excellence of her work in Southeast Asia with its award for international reporting.

THE ATLANTA JOURNAL-CONSTITUTION

From August 1987 to March 1989, Belluck reported for the *Atlanta Journal-Constitution*, which serves the Atlanta, Georgia, metropolitan area. The subjects she wrote about included crimes by individuals, an investigation of a local charity for fraud, and efforts by the state and Atlanta bar associations to spur Georgia law firms to hire more members of minority groups. She also wrote about the prevalence of health and safety violations in Georgia nursing homes and the absence of effective state regulations of them, as well as the significant differences in care delivered to wealthy patients and poor patients in such places. Belluck was part of an *Atlanta Journal-Constitution* team that covered an eleven-day crisis at the Atlanta Federal Penitentiary, during which Cuban inmates held dozens of people hostage. For their "sustained coverage" of the crisis, the team became finalists for a 1988 Pulitzer Prize in general reporting. The team also won a Georgia Associated Press Award for spot news.

REPORTING FOR THE PHILADELPHIA INQUIRER

Belluck joined the *Philadelphia Inquirer* in March 1989. A daily morning paper, the *Inquirer* provides news of special interest to people in and around Philadelphia, along with some national and international news. Its online archive lists 319 articles with Belluck's byline, some as coauthor. In April 1991, she and other *Inquirer* journalists reported on the collision of a small airplane and a helicopter over an elementary school in Lower Merion Township, Pennsylvania, in which US senator H. John Heinz III of Pennsylvania, two first-graders, and four others were killed. The staff of the *Inquirer* were finalists for a Pulitzer Prize in the category of spot news reporting for their coverage of the tragedy, and the Pennsylvania Newspaper Association Foundation honored them with its 1992 Keystone Press Award in the same category. Earlier, in 1991, Belluck held a Case Media Fellowship from Indiana University, and that year she and her *Inquirer* team won the Society of Professional Journalists' Sigma Delta Chi Award for deadline reporting.

The *Inquirer* promoted Belluck to Atlantic City/Jersey Shore bureau chief in May 1992. The southern shore of New Jersey is known as a vacation and tourist destination. A major attraction is Atlantic City, which is famous for its gambling casinos and convention centers. Belluck's approach, which has been typical of her career, was to write about the little-known side of the city and the region. She spent time with her subjects, sometimes in difficult or risky situations. In March 1994, she spent days and nights with Mona Griffith, a sixteen-year-old homeless girl in Atlantic City, reporting what resulted in a front-page article: "A Few Days in a Life on the Edge." Belluck wrote: "To survive on the streets, kids hock what they have: their bodies, their brawn, their street savvy, their desperation. They take big chances for pitiful gains: They courier drugs for underwear. They pose for porno pictures for a chance to spend the night on a bare floor. They 'clock,' selling cocaine for dealers, sometimes in large quantities called 'eight balls.' And they carry drugs for dealers by slicing up their sneakers and stuffing the drugs into the gashes." That story won a first-place Keystone Press Award in 1995. Other reporting from Atlantic City and the Jersey Shore earned Belluck a New Jersey Society of Professional Journalists award for daily enterprise reporting.

In July 1994, Belluck was promoted again, this time to cover public health and urban issues for the *Inquirer*. Among other subjects, she reported on the deplorable conditions that prevailed in many so-called personal-care homes and boarding houses in Pennsylvania that received government funds as care providers for indigent clients. One article was headlined "The Bottom Rung of Board-and-Care. Linda Pennyfeather's Career Shows What Can Happen When Government Doesn't Regulate. Anyone Can Get Into the Boarding Home Business." That front-page article appeared on March 7, 1995, after Belluck's departure from the *Inquirer*.

COVERAGE FOR THE NEW YORK TIMES

Belluck had joined the staff of the *New York Times* earlier in 1995, working as a general-assignment reporter for its metropolitan desk. From March 1995 to October 1996, Belluck served as the *Times* bureau chief for the New York City borough of Queens. Her work earned her a Front Page Award from the Newswomen's Club of New York for deadline news.

One month after she took the bureau chief post, Belluck was assigned to cover what turned out to be the worst act of terrorism on US soil up to that date: the destruction of the Alfred P. Murrah Federal Building in Oklahoma City on April 20, 1995, by a seven-thousand-pound truck bomb. The bomb killed 149 adults and 19 children, injuring 800 others. On the next day, the *Times* began a series called "Terror in Oklahoma City." In Belluck's first article in the series, "Identifying Injured Loved Ones by Clues of Hair and Birthmarks," she observed parents on a desperate quest to find their children. "It was the birthmark on the child's tiny thigh that told Jim Denny he had finally found his son," Belluck wrote. "There was no other way to tell. There was nothing in the bloodied and bandaged face that resembled three-year-old Brandon." The *Times* kept Belluck stationed in Oklahoma for a month, longer than its other reporters. She wrote more than a dozen articles while there, including ones about Timothy J. McVeigh, who had been apprehended as a suspect in the bombing. One of her articles broke new ground in indicating that McVeigh had acknowledged responsibility for the crime. McVeigh was convicted on June 2, 1997, and sentenced to death. In her last article on the Oklahoma City bombing, dated June 11, 2001, Belluck described the scene outside

a federal penitentiary in Indiana when McVeigh was executed by lethal injection.

From July 1997 until September 2001, Belluck held the post of Midwest bureau chief for the *Times* and was based in Chicago. During that time, she wrote about the massacre that occurred on April 20, 1999, at Columbine High School in Littleton, Colorado. Two seniors—Eric Harris and Dylan Klebold—had planted a powerful bomb in the school cafeteria (which failed to detonate) and then shot to death twelve students and a teacher, wounding twenty-one others before killing themselves. Through their own investigations and with the help of information gathered by several other *Times* reporters, Belluck cowrote, with Jodi Wilgoren, a lengthy front-page article that considered possible causes or explanations for the massacre.

During her time in the Midwest, Belluck covered eleven states and dealt with a wide diversity of subjects. She chronicled the economic, political, and environmental changes unfolding in the region, including: the Missouri River, creationism in Kansas, the "brain drain" of young people from Nebraska, and the election of the wrestler Jesse "The Body" Ventura as governor of Minnesota. She wrote about race in stories dealing with poverty, crime, suicide, and disparities in school achievement in the middle class. On American Indian reservations in Nebraska and South Dakota, she wrote about welfare, cigarette manufacturing, casinos, and education. She co-authored a detailed investigation of food safety problems in the country. She also covered the birth of septuplets in Iowa and spent days in a convent in Minnesota, where scientists have been studying the brains of nuns for clues to Alzheimer's disease.

Continuing her penchant for rooting out unusual stories, Belluck wrote about Mrs. O'Leary's cow, which urban legend has blamed for starting the Chicago Fire of 1871. She also wrote about the remarkable find that a fisherman in Conneaut, Ohio, had kept preserved in his freezer since 1962—a fish that scientists believe might have been a species that was long considered extinct. In Rochelle, Illinois, Belluck wrote about evangelical truck drivers: "A red feather in his black derby, a black leather biker's jacket drawn against the cold, Brother Jay [Jay LeRette], as he likes to be called, strode up to each gargantuan rig and asked the drivers to come to an evangelical Christian prayer service. He made the same pitch on the public address system in the Iron Skillet diner to truckers digging into their chicken-fried steak breakfasts. Mr. LeRette has been cursed at on occasion, even spit upon. Many truckers simply say no. But this day, as often happens, he drummed up about fifteen people, almost as many as can comfortably sit in his chapel, since the chapel itself is an eighteen-wheeler—although one with a red neon cross on top, the Bible verse John 3:16 on the back, and the words 'Transport for Christ' on the side."

In one of the last articles that carried Belluck's byline while she was the Midwest bureau chief, she wrote about the Chicago city government's plan to weed out obsolete laws. The article, dated September 10, 2001, was published on September 11, when, as thousands of people were reading their copies of the *Times*, terrorists attacked the World Trade Center in New York. The September 12, 13, 14, 15, and 17 editions carried articles written or coauthored by Belluck about the effects of the attacks on the nation's transportation system.

By the end of that month, Belluck had been named the *Times'* New England bureau chief, based in Boston, Massachusetts. She covered the clergy sex abuse scandal in the Catholic church; the "shoe-bomber" who tried to blow up an airplane bound from Paris to Miami, using explosives encased in his black high-top sneakers; the devastating Rhode Island nightclub fire that killed one hundred people; the ultimately successful struggle to make Massachusetts the first state to allow same-sex marriage; and the state's landmark passage of a law requiring health insurance coverage for nearly everyone—a law that would become the model for key aspects of national health care law enacted under President Barack Obama. Belluck's reporting fleshed out new issues sweeping the nation: concierge medicine, parent coaching, methadone as a killer drug, children and hunting, embryonic stem cells, emergency contraception, schools paying students to improve their school attendance, and brain exercise programs.

Belluck also wrote stories about offbeat subjects that made it onto the front page. One in 2005 about islands that float was headlined "And Sometimes, the Island is Marooned on You." A 2004 story that readers have continued to ask about was datelined Lake Chargoggagogg-manchauggagoggchaubunagungamaugg, Massachusetts. Belluck wrote: "It is spelled just the way it sounds. Unless you spell it differently, like in the sign put up by the chamber of commerce at the southern end of town, which has an O for one of the U's and an H for one of the N's. Or the postcards at Waterfront Mary's, the lake's best-known restaurant, which have smuggled an extra 'gaug' into the name. Even for the locals, this sprawling central Massachusetts lake with the even more sprawling name, Lake Chargogga-goggmanchauggagoggchaubunagungamaugg— the longest place name in the country—is not for the tied of tongue." Belluck's front-page article "How to Catch Fish in Vermont: No Bait, No Tackle, Just Bullets" (11 May 2004), was included in the anthology *The Best American Sports Writing 2005*. In it she wrote, "Fish shooting is a sport in Vermont, and every spring, hunters break out their artillery—high-caliber pistols, shotguns, even AK-47's—and head to the marshes to exercise their right to bear arms against fish."

In "Living with Love, Chaos, and Haley" (22 Oct. 2006), a long front-page article, Belluck wrote about Haley Abaspour, a severely mentally disturbed ten-year-old. She covered the profound effects of Haley's illness on her parents and older sister, their struggles regarding how much to reveal to relatives and friends about Haley's problems, the ultimately ineffective drugs prescribed for her, and Haley's growing self-awareness. The article earned Belluck an award in 2006 from the American Academy of Child and Adolescent Psychiatry.

In 2007, Belluck was awarded a Knight Fellowship to study science journalism at the Massachusetts Institute of Technology and Harvard University. She took a leave of absence from the *Times* and spent an academic year attending classes, seminars, and workshops, many of them focusing on brain science, cognitive psychology, and issues in health and medicine. Since 2009, as a science and health writer based in New York for the *Times,* she has written on such topics as a new type of artificial arm that can be controlled by its wearer's thoughts and federal efforts to improve health care on American Indian reservations.

For a groundbreaking series on Alzheimer's disease, Belluck reported from Medellin, Colombia, and remote mountain areas caught up in a drug-fueled guerrilla conflict. She covered the plight of the world's largest family to be afflicted with Alzheimer's—an extended family of about five thousand members, many of whom develop dementia in their forties. In South Korea, Belluck reported on a remarkable campaign to deal with the nation's growing Alzheimer's population. The campaign has been "training thousands of people, including children, as 'dementia supporters,' to recognize symptoms and care for patients." Belluck explored the scientific underpinnings for effective caregiving approaches for Alzheimer's, spending time at a Phoenix, Arizona, nursing home that allows dementia patients "practically anything that brings comfort," including consuming as much chocolate as they want and choosing their own times for eating, sleeping, and bathing. In San Luis Obispo, California, Belluck spent several days in a men's prison, where first-degree murderers have been deputized as caregivers for an increasing number of aging inmates who have developed dementia but cannot leave prison because they are serving life sentences for murder.

Belluck's article "Test Subjects Who Call the Scientist Mom or Dad" (18 Jan. 2009) is reprinted in *The Best American Science Writing 2010*. "It makes sense that scientists' curious minds would be inspired by something they see every day: their children," Belluck wrote for the book.

"But I was struck to find scientists studying their children as research subjects, and how common academics said it was, given that universities and review boards were often unaware. . . . I was interested in ethical dimensions, effects on parent-child relationships, and how it was contributing to scientific discoveries."

Belluck married Bill Dedman, an accomplished investigative reporter, in 1993, and they have two children. Avocationally, Belluck plays jazz flute and composes music.

SUGGESTED READING

"Ask a Reporter: Pam Belluck." *New York Times.* New York Times, Apr. 2007. Web. 10 Apr. 2012.

"Times Topics: Pam Belluck." *New York Times.* New York Times, 12 Mar. 2012. Web. 10 Apr. 2012.

—*Miriam Helbok*

Miranda Pettengill

Franny Billingsley

Born: July 3, 1954
Occupation: Fantasy writer

The middle-grade and young-adult fantasy novelist Franny Billingsley is the author of three successful novels—*Well Wished* (1997), *The Folk Keeper* (1999), and *Chime* (2011)—as well as one children's picture book—*Big Bad Bunny* (2008). Billingsley was a finalist for the 2011 National Book Award in the young people's fiction category for *Chime*, while *The Folk Keeper* earned the 2000 Boston Globe–Horn Book Award and the Mythopoeic Fantasy Award in the Children's Literature category, among other honors.

EARLY LIFE: STORIES, SONGS, AND TRAVEL

The oldest of five children, Frances "Franny" Billingsley was born on July 3, 1954. Her father was a professor of mathematics and statistics at the University of Chicago, but he often accepted teaching assignments at other institutions. As a result, during Franny's childhood the family lived variously in Chicago, Illinois; Princeton, New Jersey; Washington, DC; Yokohama, Japan; England; and Copenhagen, Denmark. The time in Copenhagen, when Billingsley was in fifth grade, was particularly influential in shaping her later artistic sensibilities. As she recalls on her website, FrannyBillingsley.com (2011): "Denmark was a fairytale place, home of the great fairytale writer Hans Christian Andersen. I read his stories over and over, especially *The Snow Queen* and *The Little Mermaid*."

Family life in the Billingsley household also influenced her later writing. "[O]ur house was

always filled with shouts and yells and bangs and crashes," she states on her website. When it was time for bed, Billingsley would dream up stories. Her father also sang Irish and Scottish ballads, two for each of his children at bedtime. "Those ballads, with their melancholy stories and haunting melodies, seeped into my blood; they flavored the stories I wrote inside my head, a new installment every night, night after night."

Despite her nighttime story-creating, in her youth, Billingsley had no inclination to become an author. Even though she wrote most of a novel in fourth grade and experimented with poetry, especially limericks and haikus, in middle school and high school, a career as a writer was far from her mind. "In fact, I never thought I'd be much of anything," she says on FrannyBillingsley.com, "because I was such a lousy student. I daydreamed instead of listening to the teachers; I read instead of doing my homework. Reading was the only thing I was any good at. I was rather shy and solitary, but I don't think I was lonely. After all, I had a universe of friends inside my head."

Along with the works of Hans Christian Andersen, Billingsley enjoyed Noel Langley's *The Land of Green Ginger* (1936) and A. A. Milne's *Once on a Time* (1917) as she was growing up. Though she read widely, Billingsley took a special liking to fantasy works, especially Barbara Sleigh's *Carbonel* series (1955–78). As she got older, her tastes evolved, and she read works from a variety of genres and a wide array of authors. She told Michael Levy for *Publishers*

Weekly (24 Feb. 2011, online): "I was a big fan of romance and when I got a little bit older I would read a Harlequin romance or a Georgette Heyer novel and then [Charles Dickens's] *David Copperfield* [1849], and then another genre book and then Irving Stone's *The Agony and the Ecstasy* [1961]. I was that kind of reader. One book that I loved was *I Capture the Castle* [1948] by Dodie Smith. I loved voice and that book had it in spades. And then of course I grew into loving [Charlotte Brontë's] *Jane Eyre* [1847]."

TURNING AWAY FROM MAGIC

Billingsley's daydreaming and her nights spent crafting stories separated her from her peers, and as she grew older, she noticed how little she fit in. During her late teenage years she decided to reign in her imagination and try to conform. "In order to join the crowd, I thought, I had to set aside my nighttime imaginings," Billingsley states on FrannyBillingsley.com. "And so I did. I had been spinning stories for seventeen years; it took only a moment to stop. I remember that moment vividly, the moment I turned away from magic. I remember my bedroom, the brown carpet, the blue sleeping bag, the deep afternoon shadows. Yes, it was the decision of a moment, but it lasted for years. I spent years pretending to be just like everyone else—pretending even to myself—and after college, I went to law school, just like everyone else."

Billingsley graduated from the University of Chicago High School in 1971. For the next year, she studied music at the Cambridge College of Arts and Technology, in the United Kingdom, completing an A level degree (similar to Advanced Placement exams in the United States). Returning to the United States from overseas, she began her college education, matriculating at the University of New Mexico, where she spent her freshman year. She returned to Europe for her second year of college, studying at the Institute of European Studies in Paris, France. From there, she transferred to Tufts University in Medford, Massachusetts, graduating summa cum laude with a bachelor's of arts degree in 1976. Thereafter, she continued her studies at Boston University School of Law, completing her juris doctor (JD) in 1979.

For the next five years, Billingsley earned her living as an attorney in Boston and Chicago. The long hours and monotonous work sapped her of her creativity. As she wrote on her website, "Law school was miserable; practicing law was even worse."

A RETURN TO STORYTELLING

A trip to visit her sister in Barcelona, Spain, in 1983, broke Billingsley out of the rut that her law career had dug for her. While her sister lacked the financial security Billingsley enjoyed as an attorney, she made up for it in other ways. Leading a life free from the stresses of a demanding career, she had time to pursue her interests and cultivate a supportive circle of friends. Her example had a powerful influence on Billingsley. "That trip to Barcelona jolted me out of my misery and boredom," she comments on her website. "I saw clearly that I had chosen a false life for myself, and within two weeks, I had decided to quit my job and live in Spain."

Back in the United States, Billingsley started saving money. Once she had set enough aside, she resigned from her job and boarded an airplane back to Spain, loaded down with the books she had loved as a child. Billingsley was not entirely certain why she had crossed the ocean with so many books, though they were a departure from the dry legal documents she had been reading for the past five years. Later, she realized something else had been at work. "I'm convinced now there was something very smart operating below the level of my conscious mind," she states on FrannyBillingsley.com, "something that knew what it was I needed. Once I began reading, I thought, 'I love these books! How could I have gotten so far from what I truly love!' From there, it was just a small step to beginning to write them myself. And so it was that I came around full circle, back to my oldest, truest passion." She spent the next two years in Spain, where she re-embraced the storytelling of her youth and began penning her own works.

Though it would be more than a decade before any of her books were published, when she returned to Chicago in 1985, Billingsley dedicated herself to her vocation as a writer. Instead of taking another legal position, she went to work as a book buyer for 57th Street Books, a large independent bookstore, where she remained for approximately the next thirteen years. During her time at 57th Street Books, she performed a number of different functions in addition to book buying. She managed the children's department, worked the register, and organized story hours several times each week. In addition, she served as a creative writing instructor at Chicago's Columbia College and at the University of Chicago's Graham School. When not working or teaching, she focused on her own writing and on getting published. Her initial efforts were undistinguished. "My early books were simply awful," she told Sharron L. McElmeel for *Book Report* (Jan./Feb. 2001, online), "but I did not let rejections and criticism stop me from writing."

WELL WISHED

As the years progressed, Billingsley honed her skills and settled on fantasy writing as her genre of choice. Though she knew it was her calling, writing was difficult, and she often questioned her abilities. Other doubts crept in as well. When working at 57th Street Books, she told Levy, "Sometimes I would see all of the books coming in and I would think, 'What the hell am I doing? There are so many books out there; why should I write another book?'" She kept writing, however, and eventually her determination paid off. In 1997, Atheneum Books published her first book, *Well Wished*, a fantasy novel for middle grade students. The inspiration for *Well Wished* had first come to Billingsley when she went to donate blood in the summer of 1985. There, she met a women suffering from an autoimmune disease that made her severely weak, so weak that she could not even open jars. "As we were talking," Billingsley recalled in an interview with author Cynthia Leitich Smith (June 2012, online), "I got to thinking, what would it be like to be the kind of person I am, active and energetic, and be stuck in a body like that? And so the idea for my story came to me."

Billingsley had finished a first draft of the book in January 1993 and began sending it out to publishers soon thereafter. "I got a lot of rejections," she told Smith, "but was pretty lucky, really. I received a letter from the person who turned out to be my editor in December '94, saying she'd love to see a revision. So I submitted for almost two years, revised it for her for another fifteen months: it was finished in the spring of '96 and published in the spring of '97."

Well Wished is set in Bishop Mayne, a small village with a mysterious wishing well. The well grants each person one wish during the course of his or her life, but most people stay away because the wishes it grants tend to go wrong. One wish had even caused all of the children in town to vanish. The protagonist of the story is an eleven-year-old girl named Nuria, an orphan, who moves to Bishop Mayne to live with her grandfather, the Avy, after years with an abusive aunt. Though her grandfather cares for her, Nuria is lonely and misses children her own age. Recognizing this, her grandfather makes a wish at the wishing well, asking for the town's children to return so that his granddaughter might have friends and so Bishop Mayne will not die out. But the wish is only partially fulfilled. Just one child, Catty Winter, returns, and she is in a wheelchair, her legs withered. A friendship blossoms between Nuria and Catty, and soon Nuria promises Catty that she will make a wish so that her friend can walk again. Ignoring her grandfather's warnings, Nuria makes her wish, asking that Catty have a body like hers. The well gives Catty Nuria's body. In exchange, Nuria finds herself in Catty's wheelchair, in Catty's body, her legs crippled.

Billingsley's novel received positive reviews. "This is a promising debut for Billingsley, who has created a complete society in her story," Charlotte Decker wrote for *Library Talk* (Nov./Dec. 1997). Commenting on the novel for *Booklist*, Susan Dove Lempke wrote (1997): "First-time author Billingsley wraps an intriguing fantasy

around a convincing and endearing character, using the fantasy elements to explore the very earthly question, What makes me, me? as Nuria struggles with the frustrations of having her own mind and spirit inside someone else's body. . . . The rich storytelling, vibrant and insightful characterization, and elegant writing style make Billingsley an author to watch." *School Library Journal* named *Well Wished* a Best Book and *Booklist* named it a Top Ten First Novels for Youth. The novel earned the 2000–2001 Utah Children's Book Award and was listed as a 1997–98 honor book for the Anne Spencer Lindbergh Prize for the best fantasy writing.

Shortly before her second novel went to press, Billingsley decided to leave 57th Street Books. The impetus for the move was the April 20, 1999, massacre at Columbine High School near Littleton, Colorado. "My daughter was in fourth grade and I just thought, 'I have to be home with my kids,'" Billingsley told Levy. "So I quit and we sort of struggled along for a few years and then my husband got a job teaching at a college in the northern suburbs of Chicago and things improved."

THE FOLK KEEPER

In the fall of 1999, Billingsley followed up *Well Wished* with *The Folk Keeper*, a fantasy novel for young adults that she had been working on since 1993. Written in diary form, *The Folk Keeper* is the story of Corinna Stonewall, a silver-haired orphan who disguises herself as a boy and sits for hours in a damp cellar at a home for foundlings, using food and charms to fend off underground-dwelling creatures called the Folk. When unappeased, the Folk spoil milk, ruin crops, and create other sorts of mischief. Soon Corinna is called to leave her cellar to serve as the Folk Keeper for a wealthy family on their island estate. Out in the world, Corinna learns about herself and her heritage, confronts challenges from the Folk and other antagonists, and falls in love with the heir to the estate on which she is employed. "The author's ear for language, her use of classic motifs and her stalwart heroine make this novel an evocative, unforgettable read," a *Publishers Weekly* (18 Oct. 1999) reviewer wrote. "True folklore is often fierce, especially when it hasn't been prettied up or dumbed down for fear of frightening children." Betsy Hearne for the *New York Times Book Review* also praised the novel (16 Jan. 2000): "*The Folk Keeper* respects that power and combines the foreboding romance of ballads with the Gothic drama of ancient legends. . . . The story of Corinna's survival sustains a lyrical narrative. There's poetry not only in the style but also in the story elements themselves."

The Folk Keeper earned a number of honors. In addition to the 2000 Boston Globe–Horn Book Award for fiction, it won the 2000

Mythopoeic Fantasy Award in the Children's Literature category and was named a Booklist Editors' Choice, a Booklist Top Ten Fantasy Books for Youth selection, a School Library Journal Best Book, and an American Library Association (ALA) Notable Book for Children.

BIG BAD BUNNY

After the publication of *The Folk Keeper*, it was more than eight years before Billingsley produced another book. In *Big Bad Bunny*, published in 2008, Billingsley departed from her métier. Instead of a fantasy novel, she penned a children's picture book, with illustrations by G. Brian Karas. The big bad bunny of the title is not a bunny at all, but the alter ego of Baby Boo-Boo, a young mouse in a bunny suit. Baby Boo-Boo runs away from home and is tracked down by her mother, Mama Mouse. A writer for *Kirkus Reviews* (1 Mar. 2008) wrote that the book "works on every level: narrative arc, patterning, graphic-design elements (cue delighted dramatic reader), pacing, illustrations that express the comic mood and natural movement of the story." Ieva Bates for *School Library Journal* (Apr. 2008) said that the book "is a perfect choice for children who have felt big and bad one minute, and in need of their mothers the next." The recipient of multiple starred reviews, *Big Bad Bunny* was also named in Oprah Winfrey's Book Club in the Kids' Reading List category, for ages three to five years.

CHIME

Billingsley's next publication was *Chime* (2011), another fantasy novel for young adults. The main character is seventeen-year-old Briony Larkin, a troubled young woman burdened with dark secrets. Raised in the town of Swampsea, she blames herself for her stepmother's death and her twin sister's crippling fall. She also possesses magical powers and often retreats deep into the swamp where she communicates with the Old Ones, a supernatural race of swamp dwellers unhappy with the encroaching forces of civilization. If her otherworldly powers ever came to light, Briony could be put to death. Her world is transformed when she meets, Eldric, the young son of an engineer sent to drain the swamp. *Booklist* reviewer Angela Leeper wrote of the novel (2011): "Exploring the powers of guilt and redemption, Billingsley . . . has crafted a dark, chilling yet stunning world. Briony's many mysteries and occasional sardonic wit make her a force to be reckoned with. Exquisite to the final word." A critical success, *Chime* received starred reviews from *School Library Journal*, *Publishers Weekly*, and *Booklist*, among other publications, and was a finalist for the 2011 National Book Award in the Young People's Literature Category.

PERSONAL LIFE

Franny Billingsley has two children, Nathaniel and Miranda, and lives in San Miguel de Allende, Mexico. In addition to her writing, Billingsley is on the faculty of the Vermont College of Fine Arts, in Montpelier, Vermont, where she is part of the master of fine arts (MFA) program in writing for children and young adults. In her spare time, she enjoys stenciling and decorating her house. Asked what advice she would give to aspiring writers, Billingsley told Alice Pope for *Writers Digest* (11 Mar. 2008), "I think if you keep at it, you can catch on. Don't give up. Just don't give up. Just keep writing. It's really 99.9 percent determination."

SUGGESTED READING

Billingsley, Franny. "*Boston Globe*—Horn Book Award Acceptance." *Horn Book*. The Horn Book, Inc., Jan./Feb. 2001. Web. 18 May 2012.

___. *FrannyBillingsley*. Franny Billingsley, 2011. Web. 18 May 2012.

Levy, Michael. "Q & A with Franny Billingsley." *Publishers Weekly*. PWxyz, LLC, 24 Feb. 2011. Web. 18 May 2012.

McElmeel, Sharron L. "Franny Billingsley." *Book Report* 19.4 (2001): 26. *Ebscohost*. Web. 18 May 2012.

Pope, Alice. "Q&A with *Boston Globe*-Horn Book Award Winner Franny Billingsley." *Writers Digest*. F+W Media, Inc., 11 Mar. 2008. Web. 18 May 2012.

Smith, Cynthia Leitich. "Interview with Children's Book Author Franny Billingsley." *Cynthia Leitich Smith*. Cynthia Leitich Smith, June 2000. Web. 21 May 2012.

SELECTED WORKS

Well Wished, 1997; *The Folk Keeper*, 1999; *Big Bad Bunny*, 2008; *Chime*, 2011

—*Paul McCaffrey*

Paul Bloom

Born: December 24, 1963
Occupation: Psychologist and educator

Paul Bloom is a psychology professor at Yale University and the author of several science books for the general public. His books—*How Children Learn the Meanings of Words* (2000), *Descartes' Baby* (2004), and *How Pleasure Works* (2010)—all explore his research interests, primarily how children and adults understand their social and physical environments. In *How Pleasure Works*, Bloom examines the human appreciation of "higher pleasures," such as art and fiction. In

©Sigrid Estrada

TEACHING CAREER

In 1990 Bloom began his teaching career, starting with a stint as a lecturer in psychology at Brandeis University, in Waltham, Massachusetts. Later that year he joined the teaching faculty at the University of Arizona in Tucson, where from 1990 to 1996 he served as assistant professor at the Department of Psychology and eventually as an associate professor from 1996 to 1999. Also, from 1997 to 1998 he was a visiting professor at the Cognitive Development Unit at University College London, in the United Kingdom. In 1999 Bloom joined the faculty of the Department of Psychology at Yale University, in New Haven, Connecticut, where he held the title of professor until 2011. That year he was promoted to the post of Brooks and Suzanne Ragen Professor of Psychology and Cognitive Science.

At Yale University Bloom regularly teaches an undergraduate Introduction to Psychology course. He has also taught undergraduate and graduate courses including Language Development; Language and Perception; Language and Thought; Moral Psychology; Children, Psychology, and the Law; Cognitive Development; Evolution of Cognition; The Cognitive Sciences; The Cognitive Science of Fiction and the Imagination; The Cognitive Science of Pleasure; and The Cognitive Science of Good and Evil.

PUBLICATIONS

Bloom's first book was *How Children Learn the Meanings of Words*, intended for both general readers interested in language, psychology, and cognition, as well as for researchers and academics in these fields. The book describes the cognitive aspects of language acquisition related to topics including inference, syntactic structure, memory, and word learning. The way children learn the meaning of words is so complex, Bloom argues, that it is still largely unknown. In the concluding chapter of *How Children Learn the Meanings of Words*, Bloom explicitly states: "Any adequate theory needs to cover a range of phenomena that have been ignored in this book and in most of the literature as well." The book received notice in the academic community, but it was little discussed in mainstream media publications and programs. It won two awards: the 2000 Award for Excellence in Psychology from the Association for American Publishers and the 2002 Eleanor Maccoby Award from the American Psychological Association.

In his second book, *Descartes' Baby: How the Science of Child Development Explains What Makes Us Human*, Bloom makes the argument that human beings are naturally born dualists—that most believe that people are made up of both a material body and an immaterial soul. As he did in his first book, Bloom drew on his extensive expertise in child development, but he also deeply explored the beliefs of adults, concluding

addition to writing for scientific journals, such as *Science* and *Nature*, Bloom has written for mainstream outlets, including the *Atlantic Monthly*, the *New York Times*, and the *Guardian*. His book *Just Babies*, about the moral cognition and action of children, is due for release in 2013.

EARLY LIFE AND EDUCATION

Paul Bloom was born on December 24, 1963, in Montreal, Quebec. He attended Montreal's McGill University on a James McGill Scholarship from 1983 to 1985 and graduated with a bachelor's degree in psychology. Bloom then went on to attend the Massachusetts Institute of Technology (MIT) in Cambridge, Massachusetts. Renowned psychologist Steven Pinker, a fellow Montreal native, who had joined MIT as a professor in 1982, served as a mentor for Bloom.

In 1989, when Bloom was a year away from earning his doctorate degree, he and Pinker cowrote a paper in which they argued that language is not much different from other complex human abilities—like vision—in that it also gradually evolved by way of natural selection. Pinker and Bloom presented their paper at MIT, after which they published it in *Behavioral and Brain Sciences*, a prominent scientific journal. The paper was somewhat of a turning point, in that it made it more acceptable and respectable for researchers to pursue the study of language (and its origins) from an evolutionary perspective. In 1990 Bloom received his PhD in cognitive psychology from MIT.

that not much changes from early to late stages in life with regard to dualist assumptions.

To illustrate the point, writing on this theme for the *New York Times* (10 Sep. 2004), Bloom related the following story:

> "I once asked my six-year-old son, Max, about the brain, and he said that it is very important and involved in a lot of thinking—but it is not the source of dreaming or feeling sad, or loving his brother. Max said that's what he does, though he admitted that his brain might help him out. Studies from developmental psychology suggest that young children do not see their brain as the source of conscious experience and will. They see it instead as a tool we use for certain mental operations. It is a cognitive prosthesis, added to the soul to increase its computing power.
>
> This understanding might not be so different from that of many adults. People are often surprised to find out that certain parts of the brain are shown to be active—they 'light up'—in a brain scanner when subjects think about religion, sex or race. This surprise reveals the tacit assumption that the brain is involved in some aspects of mental life but not others."

Furthermore, Bloom wrote, the idea that souls are material—in the physical brain—is troubling to many people because it conflicts with their belief that the soul survives the death of the body. Bloom's arguments and observations are descriptive: he is pointing out a phenomenon. Yet he, as well as a great majority of psychologists and neuroscientists, makes the case that *all* mental phenomena (considered by most people to be part of the mind or the soul) take place in the brain. In other words: dualism is wrong, yet it still persists as a commonly held belief for most members of the general public. *Descartes' Baby* received more mainstream press coverage than its predecessor, and the reviews were mostly good. A review in *Time Out* (11 Aug. 2004) made the case that the book is for the most part a "fascinating read, penetrating but not off-puttingly so, and of far more intellectual weight than the average pop-psychology offering." Bloom also received the Eleanor Maccoby Award from the American Psychological Association in 2005.

In November 2008, while working on his upcoming book about the science of how pleasure works, Bloom wrote an essay for the *Atlantic Monthly* in which he explored the relationship between pleasure and the "multiple selves" contained within each human being. Titled "First Person Plural," the article made the argument—based on recent studies of psychology, economics, neuroscience, and neuroeconomics—that the question "What makes people happy?" is quite misguided. The question "How can I be happy?" should not only be concerned with defining happiness, Bloom wrote, but defining *I*. "Many researchers now believe, to varying degrees, that each of us is a community of competing selves, with the happiness of one often causing the misery of another," Bloom wrote. "This theory might explain certain puzzles of everyday life, such as why addictions and compulsions are so hard to shake off, and why we insist on spending so much of our lives in worlds—like TV shows and novels and virtual-reality experiences—that don't actually exist." Within each brain, Bloom wrote, "different selves are continually popping in and out of existence. They have different desires, and they fight for control—bargaining with, deceiving, and plotting against one another."

People have evolved to have a sense of continuity—of having a sense of a unitary self—but even from experience most people are aware of the many selves that reside within. The notion of knowing oneself occurs when an individual is aware of his personality and behavior and makes adjustments to his actions to achieve desired results; this can be as simple as anticipating distractions or removing temptations that he knows could be problematic. Memory and the particular situation one is in play a big role in bringing out a specific personality in individuals. For example, Bloom cites an experiment that shows that pleasant smells make people kinder to one another, while unpleasant smells make people more judgmental. A more extreme example is the series of experiments performed by Stanley Milgram in the 1960s, in which average people gave strangers electric shocks because someone they deemed an authority figure told them to. (They did not actually shock anyone but only thought they did. Experiments such as the Milgram study are no longer performed because they are viewed as unethical.) In the essay Bloom went on to make the case that our ability to "spawn multiple selves is central to pleasure." Reading a story or watching a movie requires a certain ability to "try on the identities of other people, adopting their perspectives so as to share their experiences."

How Pleasure Works: The New Science of Why We Like What We Like was released in 2010 to generally positive reviews. *How Pleasure Works* is not a self-help book about becoming happier. It is, in fact, a scientific and philosophical investigation. The *New York Times* review of *How Pleasure Works* noted, "[Bloom] analyzes how our minds have evolved certain cognitive tricks that help us negotiate the physical and social world—and how those tricks lead us to derive pleasure in some rather unexpected places"

(27 June 2010). Bloom covers quite a variety of unexpected topics in the book, such as sexual fetishes, cannibalism, and rubber vomit; the digressions all contribute to Bloom's broader points. Yet a mixed review in the *New Yorker* pointed out: "The examples have a way of piling up, however, and there are few unifying explanations, perhaps because pleasure basically works as one would expect, springing from a mixture of experience, context, physiology, and biology" (9 Aug. 2010).

The most important theme of *How Pleasure Works* is Bloom's idea that human beings are "natural-born essentialists," who see the world with a belief in the "underlying reality" or "true nature" of things. That idea, according to Bloom, helps explain quite a variety of phenomena, such as someone paying thousands of dollars for a tape measure once owned by John F. Kennedy; most people finding the idea of wearing a sweater that once belonged to a serial killer distasteful; people feeling more pleasure—as measured by an fMRI machine—when they drink wine if they think the wine is expensive as opposed to the same wine if they think it is cheap; and why knowing that a particular work of abstract art was painted by Jackson Pollock (for those who admire his work) will make the experience of looking at the painting more pleasurable. In fact, thinking about essentialism is how Bloom got started on the book. "I'm a developmental psychologist. I'm interested in how children make sense of the world," Bloom told the National Public Radio program "Talk of the Nation" (23 July 2010). "And one dominant idea in that field is that when children—and adults but even young children—name something or categorize something or make sense of something, they do so not just based on its physical properties, on its superficial features, but on its deeper nature, what they think is its essence. . . . And then the idea I began to explore is maybe essence affects not just how we think about things and talk about things, but how much we like things, and at a visceral level."

In addition to the books he wrote, Bloom has coedited the books *Language and Space* (1996) and *Language Logic and Concepts: Essays in Honor of John Macnamara* (1999, 2002). He has served as editor for the book *Language Acquisition: Core Readings* (1993). He is also a coeditor of several book series, including *Oxford Series in Cognitive Development* (from 2001) and *Foundations of Cognition* (from 2006). Starting in 2003, Bloom has served as the coeditor of the journal *Behavioral and Brain Sciences* as well.

In addition to the universities cited above, Bloom has also served as a visiting professor at the Benjamin N. Cardozo School of Law in New York City (spring 2004), Korea University in Seoul, South Korea (summer 2006), and the University of British Columbia in Canada (2008).

Bloom has received many honors and grants during his distinguished career. His accolades include the Alfred P. Sloan Research Fellowship from 1993 to 1996 and the 2003 Stanton Prize from the Society for Philosophy and Psychology. He became an American Psychological Society fellow in 2006, and some years later, he was made a visiting distinguished SAGE fellow at the SAGE Center for the Study of Mind, at the University of California, Santa Barbara, in 2010.

PERSONAL LIFE

Bloom has described himself as culturally Jewish—but he does not practice Judaism and considers himself to be an atheist. He and his wife, Karen Wynn, have two children, Max and Zachary, who were born in 1996 and 1998, respectively. Wynn received her PhD from MIT in cognitive science in 1990, and in 1999 she joined the Department of Psychology at Yale University, where she is a professor. Wynn is head of the Infant Cognition Center at Yale University, where she and Bloom have worked together on studies.

SUGGESTED READING

Bloom, Paul. "First Person Plural." *Atlantic Monthly* (Nov. 2008): 90–98. Print.

---. *How Pleasure Works: The New Science of Why We Like What We Like.* New York: Norton, 2010. Print.

---. "The Duel between Body and Soul." *New York Times* 10 Sep. 2004: A25. Print.

Brooks, Michael. "Natural Born Believers." *New Scientist* 7 Feb. 2009: 30–33. Print.

Marantz Henig, Robin. "The Psychology of Bliss." *New York Times Book Review* 27 June, 2010: 6. Print.

— *Dmitry Kiper*

Raymond S. Bradley

Born: June 13, 1948
Occupation: Climatologist, research director

In the past century, global temperatures have reached record heights due to increased levels of carbon dioxide and other greenhouse gases in the atmosphere, caused by rapid population growth and unrestrained fossil-fuel consumption. This unprecedented rise in temperature has come to be known as global warming, a phenomenon irrevocably linked in recent years to human activity. Raymond S. Bradley, an internationally recognized climatologist and the director of the Climate System Research Center at the University of Massachusetts at Amherst (UMass Amherst), is one of many scientists who have

Courtesy of Raymond S. Bradley

played significant roles in formulating an understanding of human-induced global warming.

In a nearly four-decade career, Bradley has coauthored numerous studies investigating changes in the earth's climate over time. He has specialized in paleoclimatology, the study of climate prior to the mid-nineteenth century, when temperatures were first recorded. Through the study and analysis of climate proxies such as tree rings, ice cores, coral layers, and sediment beds, as well as other statistical data, Bradley has been able to reconstruct temperature records across the Northern Hemisphere over centuries of time. He is best known for coauthoring the 1998 paper in the prestigious science journal *Nature* that first introduced the now-iconic "hockey stick" graph, which depicts temperatures in the late twentieth century as being exceptionally higher than at any other time over most of the last millennium.

The graph received widespread media attention and became a symbol of humanity's contribution to global warming after it was highlighted prominently in the 2001 Intergovernmental Panel on Climate Change (IPCC) Third Assessment Report. (The IPCC is a United Nations body of scientists that periodically assesses and reviews the latest information on climate change.) As their hockey-stick graph found itself at the center of the climate-change debate, Bradley and his colleagues unwillingly became embroiled in a political firestorm over the validity of their scientific findings. In 2005, an investigation led by

US congressmen Joe Barton (R-Texas) and Ed Whitfield (R-Kentucky) demanded complete detailed histories of their research into human-induced climate change.

Despite having their careers and reputations as climate scientists threatened, their findings were ultimately supported by the science community. Bradley and many of his peers went on to achieve a major victory in 2007 when the IPCC was awarded the Nobel Peace Prize (shared with former US vice president and environmentalist Al Gore) for its contribution to the understanding of human-induced climate change. As director of the Climate System Research Center, Bradley has regularly led studies on climate change in the Arctic and other mountainous environments.

EARLY LIFE AND EDUCATION

Raymond S. Bradley was born on June 13, 1948, in Birkenhead, a town in the Merseyside region of northwest England. He has recalled being raised by hardworking parents; his father worked in a steel factory, his mother in a bakery. He developed a passion for science at an early age and started building his own weather stations while he was still in grade school.

After graduating from Ellesmere Port Grammar School, Bradley attended the University of Southampton in southern England, where he received a bachelor of science degree in 1969. He then completed his graduate and postgraduate studies at the Institute of Arctic and Alpine Research (INSTAAR) of the University of Colorado–Boulder. Following his first year of graduate school, Bradley traveled for the first time to the Canadian Arctic, where he and other graduate students studied glaciers on Baffin Island in the remote northern Canadian territory of Nunavut. Despite freezing temperatures and unappetizing freeze-dried foods, he told Irene Sege for the *Boston Globe* (25 Aug. 2005), "the magic of the Arctic cast its spell." Bradley earned his MA (1971) and PhD (1974) degrees in climatology, and he received a DSc (doctor of science) from Southampton University in 2003.

CAREER

Bradley joined the faculty at UMass Amherst in 1975 as an assistant professor in the Department of Geosciences, where he continues to teach. He was promoted to associate professor in 1978 and professor in 1984, and he served as head of the department from 1993 to 2003. In the 1970s Bradley studied climate variations using some of the earliest temperature records from around the world, including records from remote ocean regions and early nineteenth-century military outposts in the western United States. Over the next two decades, he broadened his focus to include climate change on a wide range of time scales, and he started using climate proxies to study temperature variations before the mid-nineteenth century. Bradley also led numerous field studies in the Arctic and other mountainous regions, investigating glacial advances and collecting lake and loess (deposits of windblown silt) sediments in such places as Ellesmere Island and Cornwallis Island in the Canadian High Arctic, the Venezuelan Andes, Czechoslovakia, Austria, and China. Recalling one of his early expeditions to China, he told Sege, "We went to villages that had never seen a white person before."

Bradley's belief in the connection between human activity and global warming came about gradually as the field of climatology progressed in the 1970s and 1980s. During those decades, the world saw record-breaking temperatures that Bradley believes are attributable to increased levels of carbon dioxide and other greenhouse gases in the atmosphere. Rapid advances in computer technology and climate modeling allowed Bradley and other scientists to understand why temperatures were rising. In his book *Global Warming and Political Intimidation* (2011), Bradley explained, "Dramatic advances in climate modeling made it possible to simulate . . . how future climate will evolve if the concentration of carbon dioxide and other greenhouse gases in the atmosphere continues to rise. . . . I was never an evangelist about [global warming]. . . . But as I've learned more about the subject and scientific evidence has accumulated . . . I've become convinced that global warming is a critical issue that requires urgent attention."

By the mid-1990s, Bradley had already been studying human-induced climate change for years when he began working on a collaborative project with the geophysicist and climatologist Michael Mann, who then left Yale University to accept a postdoctoral fellowship at UMass Amherst. Interested in understanding why and how the global climate system has changed over time, the two teamed up with Malcolm Hughes, a professor of dendrochronology (tree-ring dating) at the University of Arizona, to reconstruct past global climate variations. The three men gathered data from a wide range of climate proxies, including tree rings, ice cores from polar ice sheets and glaciers, deep-sea corals, and lake sediments, as well as other historical records, then used groundbreaking statistical methods to determine temperature patterns. Their research resulted in the seminal paper "Global-Scale Temperature Patterns and Climate Forcing over the Past Six Centuries," which was published in the journal *Nature* in April 1998. The paper, for which Mann served as lead author, includes the then-yet-to-be-named hockey-stick graph, which shows relatively average temperatures across the Northern Hemisphere for centuries dating back to AD 1400 before a sharp rise in the twentieth century. It concludes that a dramatic

upsurge in greenhouse-gas emissions caused by human activities, not natural factors like volcanic eruptions and increases in solar activity, was ultimately responsible for such climate anomalies in the twentieth century.

In March 1999, Mann, Bradley, and Hughes published a follow-up paper, "Northern Hemisphere Temperatures during the Past Millennium: Inferences, Uncertainties, and Limitations," in the journal *Geophysical Research Letters*. For this new paper, they investigated temperatures stretching back even further, to AD 1000. While the paper points out in its title the complications inherent in accurately reconstructing temperature records for earlier periods, it ultimately concludes that the 1990s were likely the warmest decade, and 1998 the warmest year, of the last millennium. (The word *likely*, according to IPCC jargon, means that a statement has more than a 60 percent probability of being right.) These conclusions led to national media headlines, and a graph that was dubbed the "hockey-stick graph" for having a curve similar to the blade of a hockey stick emerged as an icon—or "sacrificial lamb," as Bradley put it in *Global Warming*—in what was becoming an increasingly contentious and highly politicized climate-change debate. (Jerry Mahlman, a former director of the Geophysical Fluid Dynamics Lab in Princeton, New Jersey, is credited with giving the graph its famous nickname after Michael Mann gave a talk at his lab about the study.)

The growing accumulation of scientific evidence supporting human-induced climate change prompted the US Senate Committee on Commerce, Science, and Transportation to hold a hearing on "the science behind global warming." In May 2000, Bradley was one of five scientists asked to testify before the committee, which was then chaired by US senator John McCain (R-Arizona). Though the hearing helped raise a greater awareness and understanding of global warming and its potentially calamitous effects, it also created more dissension in Congress, which had been firmly divided on the issue since the adoption of the highly controversial Kyoto Protocol, a December 1997 international treaty in which select United Nations member states agreed to put limits on their greenhouse-gas emissions. (As of 2012, the US is the only United Nations member state to have signed the protocol without ratifying it.)

Bradley and his colleagues reluctantly found themselves at the center of this congressional dissent in 2001 when the IPCC decided to highlight the hockey-stick graph in the condensed twenty-page summary of its Third Assessment Report, which comprised over 880 pages and more than two hundred figures. Despite the fact that it covered less than one page of the exhaustive report and was highlighted without its caveats concerning limitations and uncertainties, the graph was chosen by media outlets to represent all of the report's findings on human-induced global warming. Criticism began appearing not long after the release of the report, and skeptics used the graph as a vehicle for disputing global warming altogether.

Richard Monastersky for the *Chronicle of Higher Education* (8 Sep. 2006) described the hockey-stick graph as "one of the most scrutinized scientific graphs in recent memory," and one of the most noteworthy papers that scrutinized the graph appeared in the British journal *Energy & Environment* in June 2003. The paper, written by Canadian authors Stephen McIntyre and Ross McKitrick, points out a series of flaws such as "poor data handling" and "incorrect calculation of principal components" that allegedly disprove the graph. Bradley and his colleagues subsequently identified several minor errors in their original study, but they found that those errors had no effect on their previous results. Bradley noted in *Global Warming*, "Their analysis of our work was shoddy and inadequate; they did not follow the procedure we had used, and they eliminated certain sets of data. Not surprisingly, therefore, they came up with a different result." Nonetheless, McIntyre and Mc-Kitrick's findings gradually found their way onto the Internet and into newspapers, including the *Wall Street Journal*, which published an article about their efforts on February 14, 2005.

Four months after the *Wall Street Journal* article appeared, Bradley, along with Mann and Hughes, became the target of an investigation led by Republican congressmen Joe Barton, then the chairman of the House Energy Committee, and Ed Whitfield, then chairman of the House Subcommittee on Oversight and Investigations. Bradley received an e-mail from the congressmen demanding detailed information about the hockey-stick studies and all other studies he had conducted on climate change during the course of his career. The investigation sparked outrage among scientific organizations and even fellow politicians, who felt that the two congressmen were trying to discredit Bradley, his colleagues, and other climate scientists for the sake of protecting their own special interests in energy and other industries. Especially coming to the scientists' defense was Sherwood Boehlert, a Republican congressman from New York then chairing the House Committee on Science, who wrote a letter to Barton stating that the purpose of his investigation seemed "to be to intimidate scientists rather than to learn from them," as Sege noted.

Bradley and his colleagues, who never testified before the two committees, were eventually vindicated in 2006, when the National Academy of Sciences issued a report supporting their conclusions. In October of the following year, the Norwegian Nobel Committee announced its plans to award the IPCC and Al Gore that year's Nobel Peace Prize "for their efforts to build up and disseminate greater knowledge about man-made climate change, and to lay the foundations for the measures that are needed to counteract such change," as noted on the official Nobel Prize website. Bradley was one of many researchers and scientists who contributed to the IPCC's Nobel Prize–winning reports.

In addition to *Global Warming and Political Intimidation*, which chronicles Bradley's experiences dealing with the politics and science of global warming, he has written or edited eleven other books on climate change. Among these is *Paleoclimatology: Reconstructing Climates of the Quaternary* (1999), which has been described as "an indispensable work of reference for scientists and students alike," as posted on Amazon.com. Bradley has also published more than 180 peer-reviewed articles and chapters on the subject. He has received several awards and honors for his work, including the Chancellor's Medal from the University of Massachusetts (1995); the Outstanding Research Award from UMass Amherst's College of Natural Sciences, then the College of Natural Sciences and Mathematics (2005); an honorary doctoral degree from Lancaster University in England (2006); and the Hans Oeschger Medal from the European Geosciences Union (2007). He holds fellowships with the Arctic Institute of North America, the American Geophysical Union, and the American Association for the Advancement of Science and is a foreign member of the Finnish Academy of Science and Letters. In addition, he has served as an advisor for numerous government and international agencies. He is a cofounder of RealClimate.org, a website aimed at providing the public with accurate assessments and explanations of the latest climate science.

Bradley is a distinguished professor of geosciences at UMass Amherst. He has served as director of the university's Climate System Research Center since 1986. According to its website, the center's research focuses "on the climate system, climatic variability and global change issues, from contemporary climate variations, their causes and consequences, to paleoclimatic and paleoenvironmental changes." Since 2002, Bradley has led research expeditions to Ellesmere Island in the Canadian Arctic, the Lofoten Islands in Norway, Mount Kilimanjaro in East Africa, the Quelccaya Ice Cap in Peru, and Greenland. Despite being repeatedly targeted with other climate scientists in other global-warming disinformation campaigns, including the "Climategate" email hacking scandal of 2009, Bradley has remained optimistic about the future. In an article posted on the UMass Amherst website, he explained, "If the politicians would only take action to put a price on carbon, which is what we need to do to get control of greenhouse gas emissions, it would mean a tremendous boost to the economy. Numerous studies have shown that it would spur tremendous development, create jobs, and lead to economic growth rather than economic stagnation, which is what the fear mongers say. There's an awesome set of activities going on in technology development, so my optimism is more about replacing fossil fuel use rather than hoping for any real change in the political landscape."

PERSONAL LIFE

In her article for the *Boston Globe*, Irene Sege described Bradley as an "adventurous, white-haired, white-bearded, bespectacled professor who regularly leads expeditions to the northern Arctic." Bradley, who became a US citizen in 2005, lives in western Massachusetts with his wife, Jane, and their son, Stephen. According to Sege, he practices energy conservation on a daily basis by turning off lights and other appliances when not in use and driving a fuel-efficient car. In his spare time, he is an enthusiastic collector of rare books on the history of Arctic exploration. One of his graduate students told Sege, "There's some of that old-style British explorer in him."

SUGGESTED READING

Bradley, Gwendolyn. "Congressman Investigates Climate Scientists." *Academe* 91.6 (2005): 6.

Bradley, Raymond S. *Global Warming and Political Intimidation: How Politicians Cracked Down on Scientists as the Earth Heated Up.* Amherst: U of Massachusetts P, 2011.

Monastersky, Richard. "Climate Science on Trial." *Chronicle of Higher Education* 8 Sep. 2006: 10.

Pfarrer, Steve. "Baring the Battle Scars: UMass Climatologist Raymond Bradley Describes His War with Global-Warming Naysayers." *GazetteNET*. Daily Hampshire Gazette, 5 Aug. 2011. Web. 23 Apr. 2012.

Sege, Irene. "Inhospitable Climate: Political Storm over Global Warming Swirls around a UMass Professor." *Boston Globe* 25 Aug. 2005: E1.

—*Chris Cullen*

Daniel C. Burbank

Born: July 27, 1961
Occupation: Astronaut

Since joining NASA in 1996, Astronaut Daniel C. Burbank has been to outer space three times. His first time was in September 2000 as a crewmember of the space shuttle *Atlantis*, a mission that lasted twelve days. His second time was six years later, on another *Atlantis* mission, which also lasted twelve days. During his third space

Getty Images

journey, as the commander of Expedition 30, Burbank spent nearly six months in space aboard the International Space Station, where he and his crew conducted experiments and did maintenance on the station's hardware and software. Burbank has also served as a US Coast Guard helicopter pilot and as a professor of engineering at the US Coast Guard Academy.

EARLY LIFE AND EDUCATION

Daniel Christopher Burbank was born on July 27, 1961, in Manchester, Connecticut, to parents Dan and Joan Burbank. Burbank has a sister, Suzanne. When he was eleven years old, the family moved to Tolland, Connecticut. At school, Burbank excelled in mathematics and science, particularly physics, and became fascinated by the stars, looking out at them through his telescope. He also read science fiction and developed a fascination with space travel after seeing the *Apollo* space missions on television. Yet he was not just interested in space flight: he was also interested in sailing the oceans and seas, an obsession that began after watching the movie *The Boatniks* (1970). Burbank graduated from Tolland High School in 1979.

Burbank attended the US Coast Guard Academy, in New London, Connecticut, where he studied electrical engineering. He received his bachelor's degree in 1985. Five years later, while serving in the US Coast Guard, he received his master's degree in aeronautical science from Embry-Riddle Aeronautical University in Daytona Beach, Florida.

US COAST GUARD

In 1985, Burbank joined the US Coast Guard. He was assigned to the Coast Guard cutter *Gallatin* as deck watch officer and law enforcement and boarding officer. For a year, starting in January 1987, he attended naval flight training in Pensacola, Florida, where he learned to fly a helicopter. In 1988, he received two awards for the excellence he demonstrated during his naval flight training: the Orville Wright Achievement Award by the Order of Daedalians, and the Texas Society of the Daughters of the American Revolution Achievement Award.

After completing his training, Burbank was sent to work at the Coast Guard Air Station in Elizabeth City, North Carolina, where he flew an HH-3F Pelican as an aircraft commander. Following that, he flew an HH-60J Jayhawk, by which point he was not only an aircraft commander but also an instructor pilot. His career in the Coast Guard led to a great many experiences and also to new locations all over the United States. After finishing his aviation maintenance and administration training in Elizabeth City, Burbank went on to work, in 1992, at the Coast Guard Air Station in Cape Cod, Massachusetts, where he served as the rotary wing engineering officer; he also served as an aircraft commander and instructor pilot, flying an HH-60J helicopter.

Three years later, Burbank made another move, this time to Alaska. He served as the aeronautical engineering officer and aircraft commander, flying an HH-60J helicopter, at the Coast Guard Air Station in Sitka, Alaska, where he remained until 1996. According to his official NASA biography, Burbank has "logged over 4,000 flight hours, primarily in Coast Guard helicopters, and has flown more than 1,800 missions, including more than 300 search and rescue missions." In 1991, Burbank flew a rescue mission off the coast of the Atlantic Ocean—with wind gusts blowing over one hundred miles per hour—that would later be portrayed in the movie *The Perfect Storm* (2000), based on a book of the same name.

Inspired by fellow Coast Guard member Bruce E. Melnick's acceptance into NASA's space program and career as an astronaut, Burbank was inspired to apply to the space program himself in 1991. After being rejected, he reapplied two years later but was again rejected. Yet Burbank did not give up, and he was finally accepted in 1996. That year he left the Coast Guard to begin training at the Johnson Space Center in Houston, Texas.

NASA TRAINING

Starting in the summer of 1996, Burbank spent two years training at the Johnson Space Center. In 1998, he began work for the Astronaut Office Operations Planning Branch and the International Space Station (ISS) Branch. In addition to his experience with the US Coast Guard and two years of training at NASA, his electrical engineering degree came into use, as he was assigned to work out technical issues by testing and evaluating space shuttle software and hardware. Burbank spent some time outside of Houston as well, traveling to Russia to gain familiarity with the country's components for the International Space Station. Of particular interest to the United States was the making of good hardware that could last a long time in outer space. By the summer of 1998, Burbank was already practicing for going into outer space, where his electrical engineering skills and recently acquired expertise would be essential. For the many engineering, strategic, and scientific tasks awaiting him in space, Burbank had to prepare not only his mind but also his body. He was, for example, exposed to "weightlessness" in a deep-water pool, wore a virtual reality helmet that simulated the mission, and endured physically demanding tasks while wearing a space suit.

FIRST SPACE MISSION: STS-106 *ATLANTIS*

On September 8, 2000, Burbank and six fellow astronauts took off into outer space from the Kennedy Space Center at Cape Canaveral, Florida. On the way to orbit, the space shuttle *Atlantis* flew as fast as 17,500 miles per hour. During a news conference conducted while the astronauts were still in space—in Earth's orbit and about 235 miles above Earth—Burbank recalled an awe-inspiring moment: when *Atlantis* first entered orbit, he saw and photographed the fuel tank floating away after it had been ejected. "It was just so stunning," Burbank recalled, as quoted by C. Bryson Hull for the Associated Press (18 Sep. 2000). "I've seen plenty of IMAX films and videos and movies, just as everyone else has. I've seen a lot of still photography, but none of that, none of that at all comes close to seeing the Earth scroll by below you like that. It just took my breath away and was just the most amazing thing I could ever imagine."

One of the main goals of the twelve-day mission of STS-106 *Atlantis* was to prepare the International Space Station for long-term occupancy—which meant that the station's hardware and software needed to be in good shape and there also had to be a good supply of provisions. The ISS was a joint collaboration between sixteen countries, including Russia and the United States. It cost approximately $95 billion.

After a few days in space, Burbank guided the American astronaut Edward Lu and the Russian cosmonaut Yuri Malenchenko on a six-hour space walk up and around the outside of the ISS. Burbank, according to Hull (11 Sep. 2000), gave such commands as, "Watch your head" and "Bring your legs straight up." While giving these commands, Burbank watched the space walk from inside the cockpit of the *Atlantis*. The mission also included an upgrade to the station's battery system. In another Associated Press piece (13 Sep. 2000), Hull summarized the mission thus far, including a problem that the crew encountered: "Four small nutplates, riveted to Zarya's floor, obstructed a pair of bolts that Burbank and Morukov needed to loosen to replace a voltage converter that goes with the new battery. Mission Control quickly went to its bullpen of engineers in Houston and Russia for a solution. Their high-tech answer: Knock the nutplates free with a hammer and chisel. Mission Control sent Burbank to retrieve the space station's tool kit, with a motherly reminder to remember his safety goggles."

The astronauts moved more than 6,600 pounds of equipment—which Burbank was also in charge of—to the ISS from their shuttle, *Atlantis*, and the Russian supply ship that had docked with *Zvezda*, the Russian service module and latest ISS addition. The crew also installed the station's first toilet, as well as an oxygen generator, a treadmill, power converters, and five new batteries. Speaking of the ISS—from space, while still on the mission—Burbank told Marcia Dunn for the Associated Press (14 Sep. 2000), "It's a little bit like a home, a little bit like a space station and, for now anyway, a little bit like a construction site." *Atlantis* eventually undocked from the ISS and the astronauts headed back to Earth, returning on September 20, 2000.

SECOND SPACE MISSION: STS-115 *ATLANTIS*

The launch of the space shuttle *Atlantis* that carried Burbank on his first mission to space carried him on his second mission almost exactly six years later. On his second mission, STS-115 *Atlantis*, which lasted twelve days in orbit, Burbank was the flight engineer. He was joined by Commander Brent W. Jett Jr., pilot Christopher J. Ferguson, spacewalker Joseph R. Tanner, mission specialist Heidemarie M. Stefanyshyn-Piper, and Canadian astronaut Steve MacLean. The launch was originally scheduled for late August 2006, but was delayed for two weeks because of bad weather and technical issues. The technical issues carried a particular significance because this mission happened only a few years after the 2003 *Columbia* space shuttle disaster, in which all seven astronauts on board were killed when the shuttle broke apart during its reentry.

As was the case on his first mission, the main goal of Burbank's second mission was to work on the International Space Station. As part of the mission, Tanner and Stefanyshyn-Piper went on a space walk during which they attached a 35,000-pound power supply truss to the space station. They also connected various hydraulic, power, and data cables. According to John Schwartz, a writer for the *New York Times* (13 Sep. 2006), the walk involved some "extraordinarily complex choreography." During

a space walk of that duration, wrote Schwartz, astronauts usually receive about two hundred commands from ground control; this time they received 1,631 commands. As he did during the previous mission, Burbank helped direct the space walk.

The following day, Burbank and MacLean spent approximately seven hours on a space walk, mainly removing restraints and launch locks so that the station's solar panels could follow the sun, thereby receiving a maximum amount of energy. They removed a total of 243 bolts. Yet a serious situation started to unfold when a bolt got stuck and threatened to impede the movement of the solar panels. It took both astronauts about twenty minutes of hard work to remove that one bolt. According to Traci Watson for *USA Today* (14 Sep. 2006), when the bolt finally came out, Burbank yelled, "Woohoo!" The astronauts inside the shuttle and the NASA team on the ground all experienced a sigh of relief. According to a summary of the mission that appears on the official NASA biography of Burbank, "The crew also performed unprecedented robotics activity using the Shuttle and ISS robotic arms. Burbank made one EVA"—Extravehicular Activity, or space walk—"that completed truss installation, activated the solar alpha rotary joint, and enabled the solar arrays to be deployed."

During this mission, Burbank's children, Emily and Daniel, were teenagers. Playing their cellos, they recorded two Scottish sea chanteys, "Da Full Rigged Ship" and "Da New Rigged Ship," for their father. A few days after the launch of *Atlantis* into orbit, they played him those recordings while he was in space. Burbank and his fellow astronauts returned to Earth on *Atlantis* on September 21, 2006.

THIRD SPACE MISSION: ISS EXPEDITION 29 AND 30

Burbank's third time in space was by far his longest and most demanding. It was also different for other reasons. He did not fly on an American spacecraft, because NASA had put an end to its space shuttle program in July 2011. Burbank, as commander, along with two Russian flight engineers, Anton Shkaplerov and Anatoly Ivashin, flew on the *Soyuz TMA-22* spacecraft. They took off from the Baikonur Cosmodrome, in Kazakhstan, on November 14, 2011. The three of them spent 165 days in space—nearly half a year.

Upon arriving at the International Space Station, Burbank and the Russian flight engineers were greeted by station commander Michael Fossum, of Expedition 29, and flight engineers Sergei Volkov and Satoshi Furukawa. The latter three spent about four days getting the newly arrived crew familiar with the station, after which they flew back to Earth. (Burbank and his crew had also learned a great deal about the station prior to the space flight.) When the Fossum-led crew left, Burbank became the commander of Expedition 30.

In early December 2011, Burbank performed experiments in the ISS on the effects of vibration on particles suspended in fluid, among other experiments. Burbank and his crew also performed routine maintenance tasks, checking the quality of the station's air and water, as well as many other tasks. Later that December, a Russian Soyuz spacecraft docked with the ISS; the ship carried three astronauts on board: a Russian, an American, and a Dutchman. For the most part, Burbank and his crew, as well as the new crew, spent their months in space performing a variety of more than 180 experiments—from human adaptation to space flight, to the combustion of solids, to the workings of robots.

Burbank, along with Shkaplerov and Ivashin, returned to Earth in a Soyuz spacecraft on April 27, 2012. On June 14, 2012, Burbank gave a multimedia presentation of his experiences during Expedition 30, to both colleagues and the general public, at the Johnson Space Center in Houston.

AWARDS AND PERSONAL LIFE

According to his official NASA biography, Burbank has been the recipient of many honors, including the NASA Exceptional Service Medal, two NASA Space Flight Medals, two Defense Superior Service Medals, the Legion of Merit medal, the Air Medal, two Coast Guard Commendation Medals, and the Coast Guard Achievement Medal.

Burbank and his wife, Roslyn, a retired US Coast Guard captain, have two children: Emily and Daniel. Some of Burbank's hobbies include astronomy, playing guitar, sailing, skiing, and hiking.

SUGGESTED READING

"Embry-Riddle Grad to Be on Shuttle." *Orlando Sentinel* 12 Aug. 2000: D7.

Foster, Lee. "That's a Long Way to Fall." *Hartford Courant* 5 July 1998: H1.

Herszenhorn, David M. "Russian Soyuz Rocket Gives NASA a Lift to Space Station." *New York Times* 15 Nov. 2011 late ed.: A1.

Hull, C. Bryson. "Astronaut, Cosmonaut Take Flawless Spacewalk—Up the Space Station." *Associated Press State & Local Wire* 11 Sep. 2000.

Lyndon B. Johnson Space Center. "Biographical Data: Daniel C. Burbank (Captain, USCG, Ret), NASA Astronaut." *NASA.* National Aeronautics and Space Administration, May 2012. Web. 10 July 2012.

Watson, Traci. "Spacewalkers Tested as Tool Breaks, Bolt Balks." *USA Today* 14 Sep. 2006 final ed.: A4.

—*Dmitry Kiper*

Hannibal Buress

Born: February 4, 1983
Occupation: Stand-up comedian, television writer

The Chicago-born comedian Hannibal Buress, who is known for his observational humor and deadpan delivery, is one of the fastest-rising stars in comedy today. Frequently compared to the late comic Mitch Hedberg (1968–2005), who earned a cult following in the 1990s with his slipshod demeanor and his un-conventional style, Buress has won popularity for his offbeat, absurdist stand-up routine, which has featured what Chris Jones described for the *Chicago Tribune* (10 July 2011) as a persona that "is quite the compelling cocktail of listlessness underpinned by anger on slow burn." Moira McCormick wrote in another article for the same publication (2 May 2008) that Buress's "left-field, casually cerebral observations on such things as the Fire Department SUV, medieval barbarians, Microsoft Word font Courier New, and twenty-four-hour pawnshops are proffered with laid-back self-assurance and effortless cool."

Buress began his stand-up career in 2002 while a student at Southern Illinois University (SIU). After establishing his reputation on the Chicago club circuit and late-night talk shows, he moved to New York City in 2008, where he landed high-profile positions as a writer for the popular NBC shows *Saturday Night Live* and *30 Rock.* Those gigs helped increase Buress's profile within comedy circles, leading to greater stand-up exposure, other career opportunities, and the support of such prominent comedians as Louis C.K. and Chris Rock. Louis C.K. described Buress to Christopher Borrelli for the *Chicago Tribune* (16 June 2011) as an "original" with a "fresh voice," while Rock was quoted on Buress's official website as saying, "If Steven Wright, Mos Def, and Dave Chappelle had a baby, that would be disgusting, but it would sound like Hannibal Buress. The funniest young comic I've seen in years."

Since leaving his position as a staff writer on *30 Rock* in 2011, Buress has focused on his stand-up act and other endeavors, which include hosting a weekly comedy showcase at the Knitting Factory in Brooklyn, developing an upcoming Fox sitcom with comedic actor and writer Jonah Hill, and cohosting the Adult Swim late-night talk show *The Eric Andre Show.* He has released two comedy albums, *My Name Is Hannibal* (2010) and *Animal Furnace* (2012). The latter was issued in conjunction with Buress's first one-hour Comedy Central special, *Hannibal Buress: Animal Furnace,* which premiered in May 2012. "When people see my full set, it's a lot more than just observational," Buress

Getty Images

explained to Blake Hannon for the Lexington, Kentucky, *Herald Leader* (11 Sep. 2011). "You can watch stand-up on TV, but it's meant to be watched live. That's the feel."

EARLY LIFE AND EDUCATION

The youngest of four children, Hannibal Buress was born on February 4, 1983, in Chicago, Illinois. His father works for Union Pacific Railroad and his mother is a teacher at St. Paul Lutheran School, located in the Austin neighborhood on Chicago's West Side, where he grew up. Buress's father named him after the ancient Carthaginian general Hannibal Barca, who famously led an army of war elephants over the Alps into northern Italy to fight the Romans during the Second Punic War. Buress has frequently poked fun at his name during comedy routines, explaining how people have forever associated him with Dr. Hannibal Lecter, the fictional cannibalistic serial killer memorably portrayed by actor Anthony Hopkins in the 1991 Academy Award–winning film *Silence of the Lambs*. In fact, Buress's debut comedy album, *My Name Is Hannibal*, features an eponymous track dedicated to the frustrating encounters he has had with strangers as a result of his name; on it, he laments, "Why can't I be Hannibal from [the popular 1980s television series] *The A-Team* sometimes? He was cool. He hung out with Mr. T. They went on missions."

Because he was twelve years younger than his closest sibling, Buress had a mostly solitary childhood, and "he spent a lot of time playing video games alone," Steve Heisler noted for the

cultural magazine *Time Out Chicago* (4 Nov. 2008). While he was never a die-hard comedy fan, Buress remembers having plenty of experiences during his childhood and adolescence that helped shape his unique observational comedic style. Recalling times that he hung out with friends, Buress told Heisler, "My area wasn't that dangerous, but my mom didn't like when people were hanging out by her car, in the street, things like that. I'd be hanging out with those people, and she'd be calling the police on me. So I had the stigma of being the kid whose mom was known as the neighborhood snitch. I'd just try to be cool and . . . be like, 'I don't know what's wrong with her.'"

Buress attended Charles P. Steinmetz Academic Centre, formerly Steinmetz High School, a public high school located on Chicago's Northwest Side. As a senior he joined the school's debate team, which served as "a great training ground for learning how to frame an argument (constructing a joke) and holding up under cross-examination (taking down hecklers)," Heisler wrote. Buress, who had played football before getting kicked off the team for failing gym class, became a standout on the junior varsity debate squad and advanced to the semifinals in his division at the 1999–2000 Chicago Debate Championship.

"Debate was definitely an enjoyable time for me in high school," he recalled in an article posted on the official Chicago Debate League (CDL) website. "I was awarded for being a smart aleck. It taught me to be quick on my feet. It definitely shaped what I do in comedy and writing right now." Peter Bavis, Buress's high school debate coach, described him in the same article as having "a 'cool grit'—a combination of coolness under pressure and determination to succeed. I remember him in cross-examination using the same posture and delivery that he now deploys to take on hecklers during his stand-up shows. This has obviously paid dividends in the world of stand-up comedy where every audience member is a judge and the competition fierce." In 2010, Buress was named the CDL Alumnus of the Year.

After graduating from Steinmetz in 2000, Buress enrolled at Southern Illinois University (SIU) in Carbondale, Illinois, where he studied communications and befriended Todd Thomas, a fellow student who was performing comedy routines at open-mike nights on and around campus. Buress joined Thomas on the local open-mike circuit after realizing he could do better than the other fledgling comics, most of whom were "really bad," as he told Brian Raftery for *New York Entertainment* (27 Mar. 2011). He then honed his comedic skills by creating and hosting his own weekly dorm-room show, "The Hangover," which became popular among students. Buress described the show to Steve

Heisler as his "version of what a poorly produced Leno or Letterman would be." Meanwhile, as his passion for comedy picked up, he told Borrelli, "I started to lose focus in school, then just stopped going." Buress dropped out of SIU in 2003 to focus on his burgeoning comedy career.

EARLY STAND-UP CAREER

After leaving college, Buress started performing at comedy clubs around Chicago, "where he developed a sweetly comedic voice that is stylistically observational and sonically laconic—Seinfeld by way of [rapper] Humpty Hump," Raftery wrote. Buress first made a name for himself in 2003, when he was a finalist in the Laugh Across America comedy contest and was invited to perform at the associated Las Vegas Comedy Festival. He subsequently spent the next few years doing as many open-mike nights as he could find around Chicago, establishing his reputation on the city's highly competitive comedy scene with a stand-up act that included absurdist musings on such offbeat topics as computer fonts and pickle juice. "A lot of my sketches come from ideas, not attacking anybody," he told Kyra Kyles for *RedEye* (12 Nov. 2009).

In 2005, Buress was a finalist in NBC's annual Stand-Up for Diversity showcase, in which emerging comedians from select US cities compete to perform in front of entertainment industry professionals in Los Angeles. The following year he performed as part of the New Faces showcase at the prestigious Montreal Just for Laughs Comedy Festival, the largest international comedy festival in the world, and appeared on the popular Dutch television series *The Comedy Factory*. While tirelessly working Chicago's comedy-club circuit, Buress supported himself by taking on a number of odd jobs, including passing out flyers and other promotional products.

In the fall of 2007, Buress made his national television debut on CBS's *The Late Late Show with Craig Ferguson* and was named "Funniest Person in Chicago" by *Time Out Chicago*. Also that year, he competed in Comedy Central's inaugural *Open Mic Fight*, a multi-platform stand-up contest. Buress's participation in the latter event helped him land a coveted spot in Comedy Central's television showcase *Live at Gotham*, which featured up-and-coming stand-up comics performing live at New York's famed Gotham Comedy Club. His performance aired on the network in July 2008, and three months later he moved from Chicago to New York to further raise his stand-up profile.

Moving with just four hundred dollars, Buress recalled to Matthew Love for *Time Out New York* (11 Apr. 2012) that on the day he arrived in New York, he immediately went to an open-mike show in the Chelsea section of Manhattan and then did two more shows before dropping off his luggage at the place he was living at the time.

Buress would spend much of the next year working the New York comedy circuit, during which he received very little income, sometimes leading to bouts of homelessness that forced him to sleep on subways and in other public places.

Buress's big break came in the summer of 2009, when he was invited to perform on NBC's *Late Night with Jimmy Fallon* after a scheduled comedian called in sick. "I had submitted to get on the show maybe a month before," he recalled to Brad Gillman for the Ogden, Utah, *Standard-Examiner* (13 May 2011). "They needed a last minute fill-in and I was available." Buress's short set, which featured ruminations on the Amish, apple juice, mustaches, and rap videos, caught the attention of producers at *Saturday Night Live* (SNL), who sent a video of his set to the show's head writer, Seth Meyers. Impressed, Meyers contacted Buress's agent two weeks later to schedule a meeting and then immediately hired him as a staff writer based on his stand-up reputation. Buress accepted the job despite having no sketch-writing experience, with the exception of a few classes he had taken at New York's Peoples Improv Theater (or The PIT). "I was just doing stand-up on TV, hoping to book club dates from it," he told Mike Thomas for the *Chicago Sun-Times* (29 Mar. 2010), adding that getting hired by SNL was "extremely unexpected."

WRITING FOR TELEVISION

Buress joined SNL in September 2009 and spent the next year writing for the show, during which time he helped build and rewrite scripts and created jokes for cast members. He also wrote and pitched sketches every week, but only one of his sketches made it on the air: "Barkley Golf," which aired in early January 2010 and poked fun at Hall of Fame basketball player Charles Barkley's unusual golf swing. According to Buress, his cousin Percy Wilson came up with the idea for the sketch.

Buress has said that the transition from stand-up comedian to writer was difficult, and creating sketches week after week that failed to make it on air was hard to take at times. "At SNL, you would write a sketch that you thought was funny because you finished it at three in the morning and you were slightly delirious and sleepy," he explained to Chandler Levack for the *Toronto Star* (17 July 2011). "You go into the writer's room and it bombs and it hurts. And because it's out of your hands, you can feel like a helpless villain sometimes. That's easy for some people, but because I was very new, it was a struggle for me to be constantly thinking up new ideas."

Despite those struggles, Buress has credited SNL with fostering his development as a writer, noting that other esteemed comedy writers like Larry David, best known as the cocreator of the hit television series *Seinfeld*, also failed to get many sketches on air during their respective stints as writers for the show. Seth Meyers told Mike Thomas that Buress was "great at the re-write table," adding "a lot of value to the weekly process," and that he was "bar none, the funniest person" in pitch meetings, which he would often begin with short stand-up sets.

After leaving SNL in the summer of 2010, Buress was hired to write for NBC's Emmy Award–winning comedy series *30 Rock*, about a fictitious sketch-comedy show. He was recruited to the series by its star and creator, Tina Fey, whom he had met during one of her hosting stints on SNL. He wrote for *30 Rock's* fifth season, which aired from September 2010 to May 2011, and was credited as a cowriter of that season's finale, titled "Respawn." He also acted on the series, appearing in a recurring role as a homeless man. Buress has said that *30 Rock*, unlike SNL, featured a much more collaborative writing process, with every writer offering up story ideas and contributing to rewrites. He received a prime-time Emmy nomination for his writing contributions to SNL in 2010 and Writers Guild Award nominations as part of *30 Rock's* writing staff in 2011 and 2012.

During his stints on SNL and *30 Rock*, Buress continued to perform several times a week at comedy clubs and other venues around the city, including the Knitting Factory in Brooklyn, where he has hosted a weekly Sunday-night comedy showcase since November 2009. He also took his stand-up act to music festivals such as Chicago's Pitchfork Music Festival, Tennessee's Bonnaroo Music and Arts Festival, and the Gathering of the Juggalos, an annual hip-hop festival held in Illinois. In 2010, Buress starred in the Comedy Central special *The Awkward Comedy Show* and appeared on Louis C.K.'s FX sitcom *Louie*. In January 2011, he landed a high-profile slot on CBS's *Late Show with David Letterman*, which Jessica Iredale hailed for *Women's Wear Daily* (10 Feb. 2011) as a "triumph."

STAND-UP TOURS AND COMEDY ALBUMS

Buress left *30 Rock* in the spring of 2011 to devote more time to stand-up and touring. He has since taken his act to comedy clubs, college campuses, and other venues, including the legendary Zanies Comedy Night Club in downtown Chicago, where he gave an exclusive two-week run of performances in July 2011. He has also performed overseas, appearing at the 2011 Melbourne International Comedy Festival in Australia and the 2011 Edinburgh Fringe Festival in Scotland, and was nominated for the Best Newcomer Award at the Foster's Edinburgh Comedy Awards.

In addition to stand-up, Buress has embarked on other entertainment endeavors. In October 2011 he reached a deal with the Fox Network to cowrite and produce his own comedy series in collaboration with comedic actor and writer Jonah Hill, creator and star of the Fox animated comedy series *Allen Gregory*. The following May, Buress began cohosting a parody talk show on the Adult Swim cable channel called *The Eric Andre Show* with fellow stand-up comic Eric Andre. He is scheduled to appear on the upcoming Comedy Central series *The Nick Kroll Show* and on the third season of *John Oliver's New York Stand-Up Show*.

Buress's debut full-length comedy album, *My Name Is Hannibal*, was released in July 2010 and garnered mostly positive reviews. The hour-long album, recorded live at the now-defunct Lakeshore Theater in Chicago in January 2009, reached the number-one spot on the iTunes comedy-album chart shortly after its release. It captures Buress's offbeat style and features his observational musings on a wide array of topics, from kicking pigeons to the benefits of leftover pickle juice. In a review for the online commentary site Pitchfork (20 Aug. 2010), Zach Kelly wrote that listening to Buress's comedy set "feels something like indulging a friend in a strange late-night discussion where weed-induced analytical precision is applied to goofy but commonplace ideas. . . . His relaxed approach . . . draws attention to the fact that he's doing a bit and somehow managing to make it feel chatty and off-the-cuff."

Buress's second comedy album, *Animal Furnace*, was released on May 22, 2012, with an accompanying DVD of the same name, directed by Michael Dimich and Susan Locke. His first one-hour stand-up special, *Hannibal Buress: Animal Furnace*, premiered on Comedy Central and included skits based on some of Buress's bizarre touring experiences and encounters. In an undated review for About.com, Patrick Bromley wrote that the album transforms Buress "from the oddball observer of minutiae found on his first album . . . to a more caustic, more cynical critic of the world. It represents not just a refinement of his voice, but a big step forward for him as a comic." He added, "Where once he was laid back and quirky, he's now more aggressive. And quirky. And though he's able to get worked up about a lot of things this time around, his comedy is never mean-spirited. . . . *Animal Furnace* isn't political. It has no agenda besides doing what any really good comedy album should do: be funny and be true to the voice of the comic."

Buress launched a tour in support of *Animal Furnace* that included both US and international performances, including runs at the Soho Theatre in London and the Parkteatret Bar in Oslo, Norway, as well as a performance at the 2012 Edinburgh Fringe Festival. "Sometimes there's shows where it's hard to be a comedian," he explained to Chandler Levack. "And it feels like work, just to make it easy for people to enjoy themselves. I've made a serious commitment and I enjoy it when it's fun. But it's like . . . I gotta keep moving from city to city because people get tired of me after a few days. Then I gotta move on and find love again."

Buress lives in New York. He has been named a "Comic to Watch" by such publications as *Variety, Esquire, Entertainment Weekly, Rolling Stone,* and *New York Magazine.* In 2012, he was named "Best Club Comic" at the second annual Comedy Awards, held at Hammerstein Ballroom in New York.

SUGGESTED READING

Borrelli, Christopher. "Hannibal Heat: The Next King of Comedy Comes Back to His Hometown with a Reputation for Being Electric Onstage, Inscrutable Off." *Chicago Tribune* 16 June 2011: C1. Print.

Gillman, Brad. "Biology Blow-Up Triggers Comedy Career." *Getting Out! Standard-Examiner,* 13 May 2011. Web. 21 June 2012.

Hannon, Blake. "Comic Hannibal Buress Rides Observational Humor to Success." *Herald Leader* [Lexington] 11 Sep. 2011: F4. Print.

Heisler, Steve. "Slowly but Surely: Hannibal Buress Measures Success Inch by Inch." *Time Out Chicago.* Time Out Chicago, 4 Nov. 2008. Web. 21 June 2012.

Iredale, Jessica. "Can Hannibal Buress Conquer Comedy?" *Women's Wear Daily.* Condé Nast, 10 Feb. 2011. Web. 21 June 2012.

Jones, Chris. "Chicago Comic Takes No Prisoners." *Chicago Tribune* 11 July 2011: C1. Print.

Kyles, Kyra. "Comic Heroes: Chicago Comics Breaking into the Spotlight on Their Own Terms." *RedEye* [Chicago] 12 Nov. 2009: 30. Print.

Levack, Chandler. "When Hannibal Buress Stands Up, Chillarity Ensues: Horseshoe Welcomes Ex-*30 Rock* Comedy Dude Who Performs His Personality for a Living." *Toronto Star* 17 July 2011: E1. Print.

Raftery, Brian. "A Trip to Weird: Hannibal Buress's Hyperexaggerated Reality." *New York Entertainment.* New York Media, 27 Mar. 2011. Web. 21 June 2012.

Thomas, Mike. "Hannibal Kingdom: Still New Guy at 'SNL,' but On Stage, the Rising Comic Rules." *Chicago Sun-Times* 29 Mar. 2010, Features sec.: 30. Print.

Zinoman, Jason. "Off-Kilter, Laid-Back Stand-Up." *New York Times* 4 Nov. 2011: C1. Print.

—*Chris Cullen*

Erin Burnett

Born: July 2, 1976 (some sources list May 3, 1976)
Occupation: CNN news anchor and journalist

Few media figures have enjoyed as rapid an ascent in recent years as Erin Burnett, the host of the Cable News Network (CNN)'s *Erin Burnett OutFront.* Prior to *OutFront's* October 2011 debut, Burnett served as a financial journalist with stints as an on-air host for Bloomberg Television, where she anchored *Bloomberg on the Markets* and *In Focus* from 2003 to 2005. In 2005, she moved to CNBC, where she soon became the cohost of *Squawk on the Street* with Mark Haines and, not long after, assumed the anchor's chair of *Street Signs* as well. At CNBC, Burnett's impact was immediate. As Suzanna Andrews commented for *Vanity Fair* (Nov. 2008), "Within a year the ratings on both her shows soared among core viewers—92 percent at *Street Signs* and more than 100 percent at *Squawk on the Street.* With sultry blue eyes, sharp, almost perfect features, dimples, and a lazy, bedroomy smile, Burnett not only was knowledgeable about financial issues but had a knack for translating them into plain English." Thereafter, Burnett became a regular on a number of higher-profile programs owned by NBC, CNBC's parent company, developing into one of the network family's premiere commentators.

Since coming to CNN, Burnett has not been able to reverse the network's diminishing ratings. Nor has her performance been universally applauded. Based on what some saw as her dismissive attitude toward Occupy Wall Street (OWS) protests and overly sympathetic treatment of the financial industry, Glenn Greenwald, for *Salon* (5 Oct. 2011), declared, "Financial reporters like [Burnett] have the same relationship to Wall Street titans as most national security reporters have to military and intelligence officials: subservience, reverence, and a desperate desire to identify with them." Despite such criticism, based on her talent and appeal, Burnett is likely to be a mainstay of television news for some time to come.

EARLY LIFE AND EDUCATION

The youngest of three daughters, Erin Isabella Burnett was born on July 2, 1976 (some sources say May 3, 1976), in Mardela Springs, Maryland, to Kenneth King Burnett, a corporate lawyer, and the former Esther Margaret Stewart. Raised on a farm in rural Mardela Springs on Maryland's Eastern Shore, Burnett enjoyed a pastoral upbringing. For her early education, she went to primary school in neighboring Salisbury, at an institution her parents had helped establish.

For her secondary education, Burnett attended the St. Andrews School, a preparatory academy in Middletown, Delaware, where her

Getty Images

teachers and peers recognized her journalistic bent. As one of her history instructors, John Lyons, recalled to Howard Kurtz for the *Washington Post* (27 Aug. 2007), "she told me she had once written to [the news anchors] Dan Rather and Peter Jennings, and that's what she wanted to do one day. She had an impetuous sense of humor and always had a twinkle in her eye. This kid was enthralled by ideas and never showed any sign of sweat." Burnett graduated from St. Andrews in 1994; in their class yearbook, her fellow students had voted her "Most Likely to Host a Talk Show." Though many thought she was destined for television, Burnett was not so sure. "I wish I could say I was one of those people that grew up wanting to be [television journalist and former NBC host] Jane Pauley," she commented to Caroline Palmer for *Broadcasting & Cable* (3 June 2007). "But we only had three channels. There was no cable, no satellite; there wasn't even an NBC affiliate in my town. I remember having a big crush on Dan Rather, and I remember watching the *MacNeil-Lehrer News Hour*, but I didn't want to be a television journalist."

Following in the footsteps of her two older sisters, Burnett pursued her undergraduate studies at Williams College in Williamstown, Massachusetts. She played on the school's lacrosse and field hockey squads. Describing her to Kurtz, one of her former field hockey teammates, Melissa Winstanley, remarked, "She was a top scorer, and incredibly studious." Burnett graduated with her BA in political economy in

1998. Her senior thesis examined comparative labor standards and how to monitor them.

A CAREER TAKES OFF

After graduation, Burnett went to work in New York City as an analyst for Goldman Sachs, one of the world's leading investment banking and securities firms. There she focused on corporate finance and mergers and acquisitions. "Investment banking is just really, really long hours for junior people," Burnett recalled to Jonathan Soroff for the *Improper Bostonian*. "It's about not sleeping for a long period of your life." Dissatisfied with her career track after a year at Goldman, she wrote what she described to Brian Stelter for the *New York Times* (20 July 2008) as a "stalker letter" to Willow Bay, who had just been hired by CNN to cohost the financial news program *Moneyline*. Impressed with Burnett, Bay took her on as an assistant. Burnett excelled in her new role and soon earned a promotion, becoming a writer and booker for *Moneyline*.

Still, Burnett was not sure if television was a good fit for her. "For some people, it's love at first sight, but it wasn't for me," she explained to Stelter. Subsequently, she moved from CNN back to the banking sector, taking up a position as a vice president at Citigroup, where she led the development of the firm's web-based financial news service for investors. Despite her misgivings, when the new service needed someone on camera, Burnett gave it a try. Recollecting her on-air duties for Citigroup to Kurtz, Burnett described, "doing thousands of interviews that very few people watched." The experience was a valuable one, helping her sharpen her skills as an interviewer and as a journalist.

Now committed to an on-air career, in 2003, Burnett sent a query to Matthew Winkler, editor in chief of Bloomberg, the financial news giant. First hired as a producer, after a few months of voice training, she soon landed hosting duties for the program *Bloomberg on the Markets* on Bloomberg Television. As a result of her strong performance, Burnett eventually began anchoring Bloomberg's *In Focus* program as well.

CNBC

In November 2005, a serendipitous meeting with Bob Wright, the head of the NBC television network, set the stage for the next step in Burnett's career. Wright had stopped by at the Bloomberg studios for an interview with the acclaimed journalist Charlie Rose. Recognizing an opportunity, Burnett talked Wright into doing an interview on her show as well. "I was thinking: 'I'm going to stick it to CNBC,'" she stated as quoted by Stelter. "'They're going to see their boss on our air.'"

Not only did Wright give Burnett a scoop, referring to NBC as a "desperate network," he forwarded a recording of the interview to Mark

Hoffman, the president of CNBC, NBC's financial news cable network. At the time, Hoffman was looking for ways to increase CNBC's appeal to younger viewers and fend off a challenge from News Corporation, the company behind the Fox News Channel, which was starting its own financial news channel, the Fox Business Network. Burnett, with her photogenic appearance and sharp wit, seemed like just the sort of television personality the network needed.

Barely a month after meeting Wright, Burnett started work at CNBC's offices in Englewood Cliffs, New Jersey. Established by NBC in 1989 and known until 1991 as the Consumer News and Business Channel, CNBC is one of the world's leading financial and business information resources both on television and the Internet. Its cable news channel is available in nearly 100 million homes in the United States and Canada and 340 million homes worldwide. According to its website, "Viewers of CNBC business news programming are business executives and financial professionals that have significant purchasing power."

On December 19, 2005, about two and a half weeks after arriving, Burnett made her CNBC debut, appearing as cohost with Mark Haines on the inaugural installment of *Squawk on the Street*, a morning business news program airing at 9 a.m. and reporting on Wall Street and the financial markets from the floor of the New York Stock Exchange. Haines and Burnett were an unlikely pairing. A grizzled veteran of CNBC, Haines was known as much for his rumpled appearance and gruff demeanor as for his combative interviewing style. Burnett, meanwhile, with her youth, good looks, and personable charm offered a compelling contrast. Though at first, as Burnett told Kurtz, they "were like two dogs circling around," the anchors quickly developed a rapport both on and off the set. "We hit it off immediately," Haines observed to Kurtz. "She's very bright, funny. She's not a diva. She understands the markets. She works like a dog. It's just a ball to work with her."

Burnett's early tenure with *Squawk on the Street* went so well CNBC offered her another anchoring opportunity within a matter of months. In addition to cohosting *Squawk on the Street*, she now would helm *Street Signs*, an afternoon business news program. Burnett's presence proved a ratings boon. "Since Haines and Burnett launched 'Squawk on the Street,'" Kurtz remarked, "the show is up 44 percent in the ratings, to 326,000 viewers, and 144 percent in the key 25-to-54 age group."

With her success at CNBC, NBC executives quickly recognized they had a rising star on their hands and expanded Burnett's profile even further, as Burnett took on assignments outside the confines of CNBC, becoming a regular contributor on a number of other NBC-affiliated programs, among them, MSNBC's *Morning Joe* with Joe Scarborough and *Hardball* with Chris Matthews, and NBC's *Meet the Press* and *NBC Nightly News*. An occasional correspondent for the program, Burnett filled in as a host on NBC's *Today Show* from time to time, substituting for regular anchor Meredith Vieira. She also appeared on the morning show's weekend installment, *Weekend Today*, a seasoning ground for up-and-coming NBC talent. Burnett was a guest on *Late Night with Conan O'Brien* and in 2008 served as an adviser to the real estate developer and television personality Donald Trump on multiple episodes of *The Apprentice* reality program. She also hosted such documentaries as *On Assignment: Iraq*; *The Russian Gamble*; *Dollars & Danger: Africa, the Final Investment Frontier*; *India Rising: The New Empire*; and *City of Money and Mystery*. Her reporting assignments took her across the globe, from Iran and India to Nigeria and Egypt, and sometimes there were elements of danger. For example, while covering Arab Spring demonstrations in Cairo, Egypt, Burnett and her crew narrowly avoided gunfire and had warning shots fired at them by the Egyptian armed forces.

Regarding her performance at CNBC and elsewhere, commentators made a habit of noting her beauty as well as her strong work ethic, intellectual savvy, and humor. In a typical description, Kurtz characterized her as, "razor sharp, works crazy hours, is comfortable discussing liquidity or collateralized debt obligations—and everyone keeps talking about her looks. Under the lights, in a smoky blue dress that matches her eyes as well as her shoes, her flowing dark hair perfectly teased, she is not exactly hard on the eyes." Burnett acknowledges that her appearance played a role in her success. "There is an element of TV that is visual. You can't deny that," she admitted to Stelter. "But you're not going to be able to move to the next level without the passion, the contacts, the journalistic drive."

In July 2008, six months before her previous contract expired, Burnett signed another agreement with CNBC that would keep her there for the next three years. By that time, the running length of *Squawk on the Street* had been extended to two hours each morning, which, combined with the hour-long *Street Signs*, meant that Burnett was on the air three hours a day. "[A]t 32," Stelter observed, "Ms. Burnett is the youngest person on television to anchor three hours of business news every weekday."

During her time at CNBC and the larger NBC family of networks, Burnett did not always generate positive reviews. In a November 2007 appearance on *Morning Joe*, describing a public appearance featuring the president and other world leaders, she referred to George W. Bush as "the monkey in the middle," a comment for which she later apologized. On

Hardball with Chris Matthews, in response to a question about the frequent recalls of Chinese-made toys due to lead paint and other health threats, Burnett declared, as quoted by Kurtz, "If China were to revalue its currency, or China is to start making, say, toys that don't have lead in them or food that isn't poisonous, their costs of production are going to go up, and that means prices at Wal-Mart here in the United States are going to go up too." Burnett's unusual construction became fodder for late-night co-medians, with Jon Stewart, the host of Comedy Central's *Daily Show*, leading the way. For her part, Burnett told Kurtz, "Certainly I could have said it better."

As Burnett's three-year contract with CNBC wound down, she started to think about her next move career-wise. While she had made her name as a financial reporter, her other assignments for NBC led her to think about broadening her purview. As she explained to Stelter for the *New York Times* (29 Apr. 2011), "I had a lot of opportunities that made me realize, 'Hey, I like doing more than markets,'" NBC was interested in keeping her in the fold, offering what Burnett described to Stelter as "some really exciting opportunities." Burnett also held discussions with both the CBS and ABC television networks. Then CNN, the cable news channel that had launched Burnett's television career, sought to lure her back. CNN executives proposed she host an hour-long general-interest news program in a desirable time slot. Burnett accepted their offer, and the deal was announced in late April 2011.

On May 6, 2011, Burnett filmed her last segment with Chris Haines after more than five years together on *Squawk on the Street*. In an emotional moment, the normally acerbic Haines gave her a heartfelt tribute, declaring, as quoted by Carmine Gallo for *Forbes* (27 May 2011), "Coming to work for the last five-and-a-half years has been an absolute joy. You are the best. The absolute best. We wish you the best of luck. We're going to miss you a lot." Haines passed away just over two weeks after Burnett moved on to CNN.

ERIN BURNETT OUTFRONT

Burnett came to CNN during a period of transition for the network. Its chief competitors, Fox News and MSNBC, had each embraced partisan politics, filling their daily schedules with political commentators. Fox News, dominated by the likes of Sean Hannity and Bill O'Reilly, offered a largely conservative perspective, while MSNBC, with Rachel Maddow and Chris Matthews, among others, had a liberal slant. CNN had long sought a middle ground, striving for objectivity and straight, unbiased reporting. Unfortunately, the approach has not yielded the desired ratings, and CNN regularly finds itself falling behind both its competitors. By hiring

emerging media stars such as Burnett, the network hoped to turn the ratings' tide.

Erin Burnett OutFront premiered on CNN on October 3, 2011, in the 7 p.m. time slot, with an encore installment at 11 p.m., garnering almost immediate headlines, though not necessarily the kind the network wanted. On her second broadcast, in a segment dubbed, "Seriously?!" Burnett went down to New York City's Financial District to interview those involved in OWS. Adopting the slogan, "We Are the 99%," the protesters sought to draw attention to what they saw as the undue influence of the richest 1 percent on the levers of power in the United States and throughout the globe. Some perceived Burnett's treatment of the demonstrators and their concerns as flippant, misleading, and openly contemptuous. David Weigel, for *Slate*, characterized her performance as "hippie punching," according to Adam Clark Estes for the *Atlantic Wire* (6 Oct. 2011), who went on to comment, "Burnett grilled protesters on the specifics of their outrage, many say, from a point-of-view that's not befitting of a network that's often boasted of its objective journalism." To many liberals, Burnett's takedown of OWS and her earlier statements on Chinese toy recalls, among other subjects, fit into a recurring pattern. In their view, as a journalist Burnett is too much of an advocate for Wall Street and other financial interests. As a result, the progressive website *Salon* ranked Burnett fourth on its 2011 Hack List. Nevertheless, Burnett did not back down from her treatment of the protests and CNN stood by her comments.

Keeping up the frenetic travel schedule she established at CNBC, Burnett and her *OutFront* crew crisscross the globe in pursuit of the news, broadcasting from a wide variety of locations. In one of her most notable scoops to date, in April 2012, she flew to Israel to interview Prime Minister Benjamin Netanyahu. Ratings-wise, however, Burnett's early tenure at CNN has been disappointing and has failed to counteract the network's ongoing decline in viewership, which reached a twenty-year low in May 2012. In November 2011, its strongest month, *OutFront* generated an average viewership of 510,000 per night. In early May 2012, that had declined by more than 100,000 viewers.

PERSONAL LIFE

Burnett is engaged to David Rubulotta, an executive at Citigroup, whom she met while working on Citigroup's financial news service. She is a member of the Council on Foreign Relations (CFR) and was named to *Forbes* magazine's Top 40 Under 40 list in 2009. As for her future plans, Burnett does not have any long-term strategy plotted out, observing that in the current media environment there is no one established model for ascent in the industry. "There used to be a 'way' to TV success," she explained to Stelter. "You'd spend time being a war correspondent and then you'd be on the fast track for the evening news. I think the new paradigm is that there is no 'way.'"

SUGGESTED READING

Andrews, Suzanna. "Who Is Wall Street's Queen B.?" *Vanity Fair.* Condé Nast Digital, Nov. 2008. Web. June 22, 2012.

Irvine, Don. "Erin Burnett's 'Out Front' Is in Back." *Accuracy in Media.* Accuracy in Media (AIM), 10 May 2012. Web. 22 June 2012.

Kurtz, Howard. "Looking Good at CNBC (Pretty, Too)." *Washington Post.* Washington Post Co., 27 Aug. 2007. Web. 22 June 2012.

Stelter, Brian. "Needing a Star, CNBC Made One." *New York Times.* New York Times Co., 20 July 2008. Web. 22 June 2012.

---. "CNBC's Burnett Is Said Ready to Jump to CNN." *New York Times.* New York Times Co., 28 April 2011. Web. 22 June 2012.

—*Paul McCaffrey*

Getty Images

Chris Carpenter

Born: April 27, 1975
Occupation: Baseball player with the St. Louis Cardinals

"What sets him apart is focus," St. Louis Cardinals pitcher Adam Wainwright told Tom Verducci about teammate Chris Carpenter in an interview for *Sports Illustrated* (20 Oct. 2011). "From pitch to pitch, his focus puts him a cut above other pitchers with good stuff. . . . with Carp, it's not because he has the best stuff that makes him someone you want to copy. It's the work ethic." It is this same drive that helped the highly touted pitching prospect persevere through injuries during his first major-league stint with the Toronto Blue Jays and eventually become the ace of the Cardinals' pitching staff. Over the eight years spent in St. Louis, Carpenter helped lead his team to the National League (NL) Championship Series on four occasions and two World Series titles.

EARLY LIFE AND CAREER

Christopher John Carpenter was born on April 27, 1975, to Penny and Bob Carpenter in Exeter, New Hampshire, and grew up in the town of Raymond. Carpenter, who first developed an interest in baseball when he was five, played for his local Little League and Babe Ruth League teams. At the age of fifteen, he pitched for Manchester Post 79, an American Legion-sponsored amateur squad, often competing against eighteen- and nineteen-year-olds. "The big thing I saw from [Chris] was a competitiveness and focus. He always knew where to make the play," Carpenter's father, an assistant coach for the team, recalled to Kevin Gray for the *New Hampshire Union Leader* (18 Oct. 2011).

However, baseball was not the only sport in which Carpenter excelled. While attending Trinity High School, Carpenter not only played for the Pioneers baseball team, he was also a defenseman for his school's hockey squad. In 1992 he helped the Pioneers win the New Hampshire Interscholastic Athletic Association Class L championships (now called Division I). As a senior he was named the 1992–93 Gatorade New Hampshire Baseball Player of the Year and a Boston Globe All-Scholastic All-Star in 1993. During his last three years of high school, Carpenter also earned all-state honors in hockey, attracting the interest of scouts from two professional clubs in the National Hockey League—the Chicago Blackhawks and the Boston Bruins. However, Carpenter, who decided to forego college, pursued baseball instead and was selected as the fifteenth overall pick in the 1993 Major League Baseball Amateur Draft.

Carpenter was assigned to the Medicine Hat Blue Jays, the club's Rookie League affiliate located in Alberta, Canada. In 1994, his first professional season, he pitched just over eighty-two innings and struck out a team-leading eighty batters while only giving up twenty-six earned runs and thirty-nine walks. In addition to his win-loss record of six and three, Carpenter had an earned run average (ERA) of 2.76/below three. He started the 1995 season with the Dunedin Blue Jays, the team's Class A-Advanced affiliate in the Florida State League. Despite a three win and five loss record, he maintained his ERA below three and gave up only twenty-four earned runs in ninety-nine innings of work.

After fifteen starts with Dunedin, Carpenter was promoted to the Double-A level but initially struggled while pitching for the Knoxville Smokies in the Southern League. Along with the seventy-one hits and thirty-seven earned runs that he yielded in just over sixty-four innings, Carpenter compiled three wins and seven losses in twelve starts and finished with an ERA over five (5.18). His performance improved in 1996—his first full year with the Knoxville Smokies; he was the team leader in two categories—innings pitched and strikeouts. He also lowered his ERA under four (3.94) and doubled his win total, with seven victories. A year later Carpenter joined the pitching rotation of the Syracuse SkyChiefs, Toronto's Triple-A affiliate in the International League at the time.

MAJOR-LEAGUE DEBUT

On May 12, 1997, Carpenter made his major-league debut against the Minnesota Twins but lasted only three innings, allowing eight hits and five earned runs in a ten-run loss. He had two more starts (on May 18 and May 23)—losses to the Cleveland Indians and the Anaheim Angels, respectively—before being sent back down to the Triple-A level. After being recalled to the major leagues on July 29, Carpenter pitched alongside veterans Roger Clemens, Woody Williams, and Pat Hentgen in the Toronto Blue Jays' starting rotation. His first major-league victory came on August 19, against the Chicago White Sox. Carpenter finished his 1997 rookie season with three victories, seven losses, and an ERA over five for the Blue Jays, who compiled a record of seventy-six wins and eighty-six losses and finished last in the American League (AL) East Division.

In 1998, his first full season in the majors, Carpenter was named to the Blue Jays' starting rotation and quickly emerged as one of the team's best pitchers. He had the second-lowest ERA on the team, behind Roger Clemens; his twelve victories were instrumental in helping lead the team to third place in the AL East. Following an off-season trade that sent Clemens to the New York Yankees for fellow veteran pitcher David Wells, Carpenter struggled during the early part of the 1999 season with chronic pain to his right elbow that landed him on the fifteen-day disabled list in June.

Three months later Carpenter, whose chronic elbow inflammation was attributed to bone spurs, underwent arthroscopic elbow surgery. Despite the elbow pain Carpenter pitched 150 innings and only allowed 73 earned runs and 48

walks, although he did give up 177 hits. For the second straight year, Carpenter, who had nine victories and eight defeats, finished with an ERA below five (4.38), and his team placed third in the AL East division.

Carpenter's injury woes persisted in 2000. During a March preseason game against the Los Angeles Dodgers, he was hit on his surgically treated right elbow by a line drive but did not suffer any broken bones. Although he avoided a stint on the disabled list, Carpenter was sidelined in mid-September, after taking a line drive to the face during a game against the Chicago White Sox; he returned to the mound on September 28. Carpenter struggled throughout most of the season, surrendering 204 hits and 122 earned runs (the fourth highest in the majors) in 175 innings. Carpenter also posted an ERA over six but still managed ten wins for his team, who had a third consecutive third-place finish in the AL East.

In 2001 Carpenter rebounded from his injury-plagued season, pitching 215 innings and yielding only 75 walks and 98 earned runs, despite giving up nearly 230 hits—the sixth-most in the AL. He also led the pitching staff in victories, with eleven, and had the second-lowest ERA (4.09). The Blue Jays remained the AL East's perennial third-place finishers.

In anticipation of a strong season for Carpenter in 2002, the Blue Jays designated him the starting pitcher for the team's home opener on April 1. However, he lasted less than three innings and yielded six earned runs (including four home runs) to the Boston Red Sox, who suffered a one-run loss. On April 5 he was placed on the fifteen-day disabled list with a shoulder injury. Carpenter's struggles on the mound continued in his next start on April 21, against the New York Yankees. He gave up three runs and four hits in only three innings and was the losing pitcher in the Yankees' nine-to-two victory. Four days later Carpenter required another stint on the disabled list for tendinitis in his right shoulder, which kept him sidelined for nearly two months. He managed to make eleven more starts before his season was cut short due to a torn labrum in his right shoulder.

Carpenter finished the 2002 season with four wins and five losses and an ERA over five; once again, the Blue Jays finished third in the AL East division. On September 4, Carpenter underwent arthroscopic surgery to repair the torn labrum in his shoulder.

SECOND CHANCE IN ST. LOUIS

In early October the Blue Jays demoted Carpenter to the Triple-A level. Since he had more than four years of major-league service time, Carpenter refused the assignment and decided instead to become a free agent. On December 13, 2002, he signed a one-year contract with the St. Louis

Cardinals for $300,000, the league minimum; the deal also included an option for 2004, also worth $300,000. As a precaution Carpenter started the 2003 season on the sixty-day disabled list before embarking on a minor-league rehabilitation assignment in June and July. After pitching for the team's advanced-A affiliate, as well as its double and triple-A squads, he showed no improvement, and on July 29 he had season-ending surgery to remove scar tissue from his right shoulder.

In 2004 the Cardinals picked up Carpenter's option and named him to the Cardinals' starting rotation, which included Matt Morris, Jason Marquis, Jeff Suppan, and Woody Williams, his former Blue Jays teammate. Carpenter was off to an impressive start; only two months into the season, he had already amassed seven wins and one loss. He continued to pitch well and finished with a record of fifteen victories. During the regular season the St. Louis Cardinals won 105 games—the most in the major leagues—and claimed the NL Central Division title. Carpenter was left off the postseason roster, as a result of his nerve-related injury.

After defeating the Dodgers in the best-of-five NL Division Series, the Cardinals advanced to the National League Championship Series, where they narrowly beat out the Houston Astros in seven games to earn a World Series berth—their first since 1987. The Cardinals proved to be no match for the Boston Red Sox, who completed a four-game sweep to win their first World Series championship in eighty-six years.

BREAKTHROUGH 2005 SEASON
Impressed by Carpenter's strong 2004 performance, the St. Louis Cardinals signed him to a two-year contract extension, with a one-year option, in mid-April 2005. Carpenter had his best season to date, helping the Cardinals win their second consecutive Central Division title. He led the major leagues with seven complete games, and his twenty-one victories—a team-high and personal best—tied for the second-most in the majors. For the first time in his career, Carpenter posted an ERA under three (fifth-best in the NL); he also finished among the top five in several other categories, including innings pitched, strikeouts, and shutouts. Carpenter's performance earned him the NL Cy Young Award; he was also ninth in the voting for the NL Most Valuable Player Award. Other honors included the Sporting News NL Pitcher of the Year Award, as well as his first All-Star Game appearance.

Carpenter was named the starting pitcher in the opening game of the NL Division Series against the San Diego Padres. He set the tone, throwing six scoreless innings for the game 1 victory. The Cardinals won the next two games to complete the sweep and advance to the NL

Championship Series against the Houston Astros. Carpenter was called upon again to pitch the series opener. He gave up five hits and only two earned runs in eight innings of work to help the Cardinals claim game 1 of the NL Championship Series; the Astros went on to win the next three games. Carpenter struggled in the fifth game of the series, surrendering four runs and nine hits before leaving the game in the bottom of the seventh inning. The Cardinals, who were down by two runs at the time, came from behind to win, and Carpenter was awarded a no-decision. The Astros advanced to the World Series, after eliminating the Cardinals.

FIRST WORLD SERIES RING
Carpenter followed up his Cy Young Award–winning season with an equally solid effort in 2006. Carpenter, who appeared in his second All-Star Game, reached a career milestone on September 16, 2006, with his one hundredth career victory, against the San Francisco Giants. For the second consecutive year, he led the team in wins, with fifteen—seventh-best in the NL; he also had the NL's second-best ERA (3.09). In the race for the NL Cy Young Award, Carpenter came in third. Despite only winning eighty-three games, the Cardinals managed to capture the title in a weak NL Central Division.

Carpenter was instrumental in the NL Division Series, with victories, in game 1 and game 4, against the San Diego Padres, whom the Cardinals defeated to advance to the Championship Series against the New York Mets. However, he initially struggled in the series, giving up six hits, two home runs, and five earned runs in game 2 before being taken out after five innings. The Cardinals, who were down one run, came from behind to win the game by a score of nine to six. Carpenter pitched better in game 6, only giving up two earned runs in six innings. Despite this the Mets scored a total of four runs to defeat the Cardinals, who managed only two runs. Carpenter reached the World Series for the first time, following the Cardinals' victory in game 7.

Carpenter's World Series debut—and only appearance—came in game 3. He proved far too dominant for the Detroit Tigers, pitching eight scoreless innings and allowing only three hits to secure the shutout victory. With Carpenter's game 3 win, the Cardinals took a two-to-one lead in the best-of-seven series; the team won the next two games and became World Series champions. In early December, a month after earning his first World Series ring, Carpenter renegotiated his contract with the Cardinals, agreeing to a five-year deal worth $65 million that includes an option for 2012.

INJURY AND COMEBACK
On April 1, 2007, Carpenter took the mound for the Cardinals' season opener against the Mets.

He did not pitch well, giving up five earned runs and nine hits while only striking out three batters. Eight days later Carpenter, who complained of discomfort in his right elbow, was placed on the fifteen-day disabled list. In May he underwent arthroscopic surgery to clear bone chips from his right elbow. Two months later Carpenter experienced swelling and stiffness in his elbow and received the grim diagnosis that he would need season-ending ligament replacement surgery, also known as Tommy John surgery.

Following the surgery on July 24, Carpenter was sidelined for a year. He returned to the mound on July 30, 2008 and reverted to form against the Atlanta Braves, only surrendering an earned run, two walks, and five hits. The Cardinals eventually won the game by a score of seven to two, although he received a no-decision. However, Carpenter saw limited action during the rest of the season; he had two more starts in August and made one relief appearance in September. For the second straight year, the Cardinals missed the postseason, following their fourth place result in the NL Central Division.

Carpenter's first start of the 2009 season came on April 9, against the Pittsburgh Pirates. He pitched brilliantly, tossing seven scoreless innings and striking out seven batters while walking only two to secure the one-run victory for the Cardinals. Five days later Carpenter made his next start against the Arizona Diamondbacks but was forced to leave the game after three innings, due to an injury to his left rib cage. Carpenter, who was placed on the disabled list on April 15, was later diagnosed with a torn left oblique muscle, which sidelined him for a month.

He returned to action on May 20 and pitched well against the Chicago Cubs, allowing no runs, three hits, and two walks and striking out five to win the game. Despite the slow start Carpenter quickly re-established himself as one of baseball's premier pitchers. Carpenter had his best all-around game on October 1, in his final regular-season start against the Cincinnati Reds. Not only did he throw five scoreless innings of three-hit ball, striking out six and walking only one in the Cardinals' thirteen-run shutout, but he also hit his first home run—a grand slam.

Carpenter finished the regular season with seventeen wins (second-best in the NL) and also led the league in ERA (2.24). He earned NL Comeback Player of the Year honors for a second time and received the Tony Conigliaro Award. Carpenter was the runner-up for the NL Cy Young Award. The Cardinals won ninety-one regular-season games to reclaim the NL Central Division title, after two straight years of missing the postseason. Carpenter pitched respectably in the first game of the NL Division Series, but the Dodgers ultimately eliminated the Cardinals from postseason play.

Carpenter followed up his Cy Young–caliber season with another solid showing in 2010. He made a league-leading thirty-five starts and finished with sixteen wins while also appearing as a reserve player on the NL All-Star team. The Cardinals eventually finished second to the Cincinnati Reds in the NL Central division.

RETURN TO THE WORLD SERIES

Carpenter had a slow start to his 2011 season, losing his first five games. His first victory came on April 29; he did not win his second game until June 23. He went on to win nine more games, including the Cardinals' Wild Card–clinching victory on September 28. Carpenter finished the regular season with a record of eleven wins and nine losses. He made thirty-four starts, tying him for the major-league lead, and also had the fourth-highest number of innings pitched, with just over 237 innings.

The Cardinals entrusted Carpenter with the ball in game 2 of the NL Division Series. He lasted just three innings, allowing four earned runs and five hits against the Philadelphia Phillies. The Cardinals eventually overcame the four-run deficit to win by a score of five to four; Carpenter earned the no-decision. He was far more impressive in game 5, pitching a complete game—and a three-hit shutout at that—to eliminate the Phillies. Carpenter's next start came in game 3 of the NL Championship Series. He managed to get the win despite giving up three earned runs and six hits in five innings. The victory gave the Cardinals a two-to-one series lead; the team went on to capture games 5 and 6 to defeat the Brewers and advance to the World Series for the first time since 2006.

In the series opener Carpenter faced off against C. J. Wilson of the Texas Rangers. Carpenter followed up his game 1 win with a powerful effort in game 5. His seven-inning, two-run performance helped the Cardinals take a three-to-two lead in the series. Carpenter proved his mettle in the deciding seventh game, only allowing two earned runs and six hits in six innings. The Cardinals eventually won the game, by a score of six to two, and clinched the World Series.

During spring training Carpenter was diagnosed with a bulging disk in his neck. He was treated and ordered to avoid baseball-related activity for two weeks. A day after throwing a batting practice session, Carpenter complained of neck discomfort and weakness in his pitching shoulder, caused by an unrelated nerve irritation problem. Although Carpenter was slated to be the Opening Day starter for 2012, he has been sidelined indefinitely.

Carpenter lives in Bedford, New Hampshire during the off-season, with his wife, Alyson, and their two children, Sam and Ava.

SUGGESTED READING

Baseball-Reference. "Chris Carpenter Statistics and History." *Baseball-Reference.com.* Sports Reference, 2012. Web. 10 June 2012.

Gray, Kevin. "Kevin Gray's On Baseball: Carpenter Career In Focus." *Union Leader.com.* Union Leader Corp., 18 Oct. 2011. Web. 22 May 2012.

Korac, Louie. "Cardinal Ace Carpenter Tries His Luck on Skates." *NHL.com.* National Hockey League, 3 Nov. 2011. Web. 22 May 2012.

Verducci, Tom. "Carpenter Unseats Gibson in Cards History with Vintage Performance." *SI.com.* Turner Broadcasting System, 20 Oct. 2011. Web. 31 May 2011.

—*Bertha Muteba*

Wirelmage

Kris Carr

Born: August 31, 1971
Occupation: Actor, documentary filmmaker

Filmmaker and *New York Times* best-selling author Kris Carr never set out to be a self-proclaimed "wellness warrior" and health guru. In fact, Carr was happily settled in New York City working as an actor when she discovered, at the age of thirty-one, that she had a rare and incurable form of vascular cancer. The diagnosis, stage 4 epithelioid hemangioendothelioma (EHE), came in 2003. Carr decided to take control of her situation—and her life—by picking up a video camera and filming her road to physical, spiritual, and emotional recovery. The footage, culled from over four years of doctors' appointments, retreats, and candid moments, was edited into a full-length documentary called *Crazy Sexy Cancer,* after the subject heading of the mass e-mails she would send to her family and friends.

The film was a success at several independent film festivals and aired on The Learning Channel (TLC) in 2007. Carr became a popular cultural figure after appearing on the *Oprah Winfrey Show* the same year. Her books *Crazy Sexy Cancer Tips* (2007) and *Crazy Sexy Cancer Survivor: More Rebellion and Fire for Your Healing Journey* (2008) followed soon after. Most recently, Carr published *Crazy Sexy Diet: Eat Your Veggie, Ignite Your Spark, and Live Like Your Mean It!* (2011), which became her first *New York Times* best seller. She has expressed hopes that the success of the book will propel her past what she calls her "cancerlebrity" status and into the realm of wellness guru, a status enjoyed by the likes of another Oprah favorite, Dr. Oz.

"I knew when I was diagnosed with cancer that the only things I could control were what I ate, what I drank, and what I would think," Carr told Dr. Oz in a segment for the *Oprah Winfrey Show* on October 22, 2007. Carr touts what she learned on her journey as the "crazy sexy life," which is also the name of her website. She endorses yoga and meditation as well as a vegan raw diet, and when it comes time for an enema, she advises patients to transform their bathrooms into "ashrams" of beauty with flowers and decorations. Her personal motto is "make juice, not war." Carr embodies the healthiest iteration of a burgeoning concept: "Cancer's been my guru," she says in her film *Crazy Sexy Cancer.* "It's my teacher, and it teaches me every day." With more and more Americans living with cancer, Carr is helping change the face of the disease by encouraging a healthy lifestyle.

Some are critical, however. Carr has been accused of glossing over the less "sexy" aspects of the disease (chemotherapy, lost limbs) and of contributing to the cultural narrative of defeating terminal illness by sheer will. Carr's story is atypical for most cancer patients. During the filming of *Crazy Sexy Cancer,* Carr combated her particularly asymptomatic disease the best way she knew how—diet and exercise. The film concludes with Carr announcing that her tumors have stabilized, and as Mireille Silcoff wrote for the *New York Times Magazine* (14 Aug. 2011), "While it's all very well to attribute this to her diet and lifestyle changes, when she is presented as a spokeswoman for a disease that ravages the lives of millions, her message can be harder to swallow. . . . To a person currently undergoing hardcore combination chemotherapy, the idea that now's the time to be 'pHabulous' might make that person want to throw Carr's chipper empowerment out the window."

EARLY LIFE

Carr was born on August 31, 1971, in Pawling, New York. She was raised in a converted one-room schoolhouse by her mother, Aura. Her adoptive father, Ken, began dating Aura when Carr was a child; he officially adopted Carr when she was fourteen. Carr also has a younger sister named Leslie. Carr and her family later moved to New Milford, Connecticut. She attended the Wooster School in Danbury, graduating in 1990.

Carr attended Sarah Lawrence College before moving to New York City at age nineteen. She graduated from Marymount Manhattan College with an English degree and spent the next eleven years pursuing an acting and modeling career. She also worked as a professional photographer, specializing in actor headshots, and held faculty positions with the Playwright's Horizons Theater School and Stone Street Studios, both affiliated with New York University's Tisch School of the Arts. She appeared in several independent movies, including the critically acclaimed short *Kalin's Prayer* (1999) and the award-winning feature film *The Hidden* (2002).

In 1998, Carr appeared in the play *Mr. Peter's Connections*, written by the late Arthur Miller and staged at the Signature Theater Company. The production starred Peter Falk. Carr played the character Cathy Mae, whom *New York Times* reviewer Ben Brantley described as a "helpless woman child with a dazzling physique" (18 May 1998) because Carr appeared on stage in the nude. Her character drew comparisons to Marilyn Monroe, who was once married to Miller. In the opening of her first book, *Crazy Sexy Cancer Tips*, Carr cites the role as the reason she was able to see her doctor so quickly after first experiencing stomach pains. He remembered her from the show and offered to see her right away.

Carr also appeared in a touring production of the musical *Chicago*; on an episode of *Law and Order* called "Swept Away" in 2001, a rite of passage for any serious New York actor; and in several commercials, including two Bud Light advertisements that aired during the 2003 Super Bowl. She played a yoga instructor in one commercial, foreshadowing her eventual wellness lifestyle. The advertisements put her in high demand for the short period before her diagnosis, with her agent touting her as "the Julia Roberts of advertising." Yet despite her apparent successes, Carr was unhappy. Citing medication for depression and a diet of microwave dinners and Wild Turkey, Carr told Silcoff, "I was not satisfied with my life, and I was treating myself like garbage."

DIAGNOSIS

In February 2003, Carr had just returned from a week of drinking and celebration at the Sarasota Film Festival, where a film she had acted in had premiered. She told herself that she would spend the next month detoxing, with more exercise and no alcohol. She attended a Jivamukti-style yoga class, during which she overexerted herself. The next day, she started experiencing intense pain in her abdomen. At first she thought it was just a sign that her body was out of shape, but by evening the cramping had become so acute that she made a doctor's appointment for the following day. After a quick examination, her doctor told her that she was having gallbladder trouble. He prescribed her painkillers and sent her for an ultrasound to confirm his diagnosis. But the ultrasound showed something else.

The doctors found a number of lesions spotting Carr's liver and lungs. After a barrage of tests, she learned that she was suffering from a rare form of cancer called epithelioid hemangioendothelioma (EHE). According to HEARD (Hemangioendothelioma, Epithelioid Hemangioendothelioma, and Related Vascular Disorders), the support group for EHE patients and those suffering from related diseases, there are only about twenty new cases of EHE diagnosed each year in the United States. (Silcoff reports that the number is closer to between forty and eighty.) EHE is classified as incurable, and it is only since the mid-1990s that researchers have understood that the disease generally behaves in one of two ways, either very passively or very aggressively. Though it was not immediately clear to her doctors, Carr suffers from the former. Patients with slow-moving EHE, even ones with numerous growths, can live largely asymptomatic lives. Before any of this was clear to Carr, she wrote in her diary on the day she was diagnosed—February 14, 2003—"Happy Valentine's Day! You have cancer."

In her documentary, Carr famously interviewed potential doctors—after hers recommended a triple organ transplant—to find one whom she felt had her best interests in mind. (In the film, she advises others to treat their health like running a business, having appointed herself the CEO of "Save My Ass Technologies, Inc.") After a lengthy search, Carr "hired" Dr. George Demetri, the director of the Center for Sarcoma and Bone Oncology at the Dana-Farber Cancer Institute in Boston, Massachusetts. The treatment he advised was somewhat controversial; he advocated no treatment at all. In the film, he says that he would rather "let cancer make the first move." Following the documentary, Demetri and Carr continued to monitor her tumors, but because there is no known cure for EHE and because Carr remained in stable condition, no treatment remained their plan of action. Despite the positive nature of the prognosis, Carr found that it fundamentally changed her world-view. She embarked on a journey of healing to reconcile living a full life with having a terminal illness.

CRAZY SEXY CANCER

Carr made the decision to film her journey two weeks after her diagnosis. When asked what gave her the idea, she told Jennifer May for *Chronogram* magazine (21 Dec. 2007) that the process gave her a modicum of control: "When I was a director, I was not a patient. When I was an artist, I was not feeling like a victim." Carr put her acting career on hold indefinitely and sold her Manhattan apartment to support herself. She pursued, she often says jokingly, a "PhD from Google University," meaning that she dedicated all of her time to researching her medical options as well as ways to make her life healthier.

The video journal she had begun for herself soon included the stories of four other women that Carr met after her diagnosis. Melissa Gonzalez, a young mother, was diagnosed with Hodgkin's lymphoma at age twenty-eight; Jackie Farry, a former MTV host and rock-and-roll tour manager, was diagnosed with a rare blood cancer in 2003; playwright Oni Faida Lampley was a breast-cancer survivor; and Erin Zammett Ruddy, an editor for the magazine *Glamour*, had been diagnosed with leukemia. The women became Carr's "cancer posse," not only reinforcing Carr's desire to overcome the disease but also reminding her that cancer affects young women as well as older ones. The revelation inspired Carr to spread her "crazy sexy" message. In the film, she is adamant that young women suffering from the disease should not let it define them.

After four years, Carr's cancer stabilized. She embarked on a vegan raw diet and lifestyle and married Brian Fassett, her videographer and film editor. *Crazy Sexy Cancer* was completed by her and Fassett's production company, Red House Pictures; it premiered at the South by Southwest Film Festival in Austin, Texas, in 2007. The Learning Channel (TLC) bought the film in the fall of 2006 and aired it on the network on August 29, 2007.

By most accounts, the allure of the film, which follows Carr from visits to the oncology ward to experiments in holistic medicine, is its honesty. Though Carr jokes her way through most of the film, she included her most vulnerable moments in the final cut as well. The result is a jarring and complex portrait of illness that captured the attention of celebrities such as musician and cancer survivor Sheryl Crow and designer Donna Karan, who lost her husband to cancer. Karan threw a launch party for the film that was covered in the magazine *Vanity Fair*. Months later, Carr found herself on the *Oprah Winfrey Show*, sharing her experience with the world. According to Carr, the whirlwind process

was predestined. A year into her journey, she had written in her journal, "Oprah, I'm coming, save me a seat!"

CRAZY SEXY REVOLUTION

"I'm not saying that cancer is sexy," Carr stressed to Lisa Stein for *Scientific American* (16 July 2008). "What I'm saying is that we are still empowered. We are still alive and whole. I might have cancer, but I'm dealing with it and I'm still all that. The most important thing is to have a voice and use it." After the success of the film, Carr did not stop using her voice. She published a book called *Crazy Sexy Cancer Tips* in 2007, with a foreword written by Sheryl Crow. Part autobiography and part interactive scrapbook, the book pulls together Carr's advice after devoting years of her life to wellness. Her advice ranges from the practical ("Max out your insurance," she advises) to the lighthearted (a daily dance routine), all written in the expletive-laced, whimsical voice for which Carr is well known.

Carr's first book was so popular that it spawned a sequel, *Crazy Sexy Cancer Survivor: More Rebellion and Fire for Your Healing Journey*, published in 2008. With a foreword by spiritual activist Marianne Williamson, Carr's follow-up is focused more on well-being than on illness and cancer. It was the beginning of Carr's move into the mainstream, which she completed with the publication of a vegan raw cookbook in 2011, *Crazy Sexy Diet: Eat Your Veggie, Ignite Your Spark, and Live Like You Mean It!* This was the first of Carr's books to hit the *New York Times* best-seller list.

Crazy Sexy Diet boasts an array of contributors: Dr. Dean Ornish, founder of the Preventative Medicine Research Institute; Dr. Brian Clement, director of the Hippocrates Health Institute; Dr. Neal Bernard, author of *Food for Life* (1993); Rory Freedman, coauthor of the popular vegan guide *Skinny Bitch* (2005); and many others. Rather than focusing on those who are already suffering from illness, *Crazy Sexy Diet* aims for prevention, and the book has been praised for making an overwhelming life change seem palatable. Carr is not only anti-meat, dairy, and gluten but also anti-chemical, which means that she is against pharmaceuticals, caffeine, alcohol, and cosmetics that are not all natural. Though a number of doctors support Carr's claims, her approach may not be easy for the average person to follow. She recommends supplementing a plant-based, alkaline-balanced diet with colon cleanses, arduous dry brushing, and juice fasts.

On her own journey for health and wellness, Carr went back to school. She received a nutrition certification from the Hippocrates Health Institute in West Palm Beach, Florida, where she evolved her macrobiotic diet into the raw vegan principles she would later share with the world. In addition to doling out dieting advice,

Carr advocates for fresher foods in hospitals and schools as well as environmentally friendly consumption. She says that she wants everyone to wear the armor of a "wellness warrior" to start a "crazy sexy revolution."

ON THE ROAD

Much like the health gurus that guided Carr on her road to wellness, Carr is now in high demand as a lecturer and personal life coach. She maintains a popular website and syndicated blog at crazysexylife.com. She also films frequent vlogs, or video blog entries, in which she instructs her followers on such topics as how to meditate and how to make her favorite green juice. Carr spends a lot of time on the lecture circuit, visiting various schools and other organizations, such as Harvard University, and encouraging people to actively participate in their own health.

Carr, a natural blonde, is known for the streak of hot pink in her hair. She and her husband were married in the fall of 2006. They live on a farm in Woodstock, New York, with Lola, their rescue dog.

SUGGESTED READING

Brantley, Ben. "Theater Review: Peter Falk's Search for Meaning." *New York Times.* New York Times, 18 May 1998. Web. 17 Feb. 2012.

May, Jennifer. "Lust for Life." *Chronogram.* Luminary Pub., 21 Dec. 2007. Web. 19 Feb. 2012.

Silcoff, Mireille. "Every Cancer Has a Silver Lining." *New York Times Magazine* 14 Aug. 2011, late ed.: 18. Print.

Stein, Lisa. "Living with Cancer: Kris Carr's Story." *Scientific American.* Scientific American, 16 July 2008. Web. 19 Feb. 2012.

SELECTED BOOKS

Crazy Sexy Cancer Tips, 2007; *Crazy Sexy Cancer Survivor: More Rebellion and Fire for Your Healing Journey*, 2008; *Crazy Sexy Diet: Eat Your Veggie, Ignite Your Spark, and Live Like You Mean It!*, 2011

SELECTED FILMS

An Argentinian in New York, 1998; *Kalin's Prayer*, 1999: *Rendezvous with Jack*, 2000; *Queenie in Love*, 2001; *The Hidden*, 2002; *Luther*, 2009

—Molly Hagan

Michael Chabon

Born: May 24, 1963
Occupation: Writer

"[Michael] Chabon is more or less incapable of writing a boring sentence," Steve Almond wrote for the *Los Angeles Times* (4 Oct. 2009). That sentiment is frequently echoed by others; Chabon, who won a Pulitzer Prize for *The Amazing Adventures of Kavalier & Clay* (2000), about a pair of cousins who strike it big during the golden age of comic books, has been called one of the most gifted writers of his generation. Michael Hayward wrote for the quarterly Canadian magazine *Geist* that Chabon's "genre-defying success with *The Amazing Adventures of Kavalier & Clay* . . . and *The Yiddish Policemen's Union* demonstrate that 'popular success' and 'critical success' need not be mutually exclusive categories." Commenting on an additional dichotomy, a reviewer for the *St. Paul Pioneer Press* (17 May 2007) marveled, "He may be the only novelist in history to write for both the *New York Review of Books*, where he recently had a ravishing essay on Cormac McCarthy and apocalypse fiction, and *Details*, where his latest contribution concerned 'the man purse.'" Chabon explained his wide-ranging sensibilities to Charles Matthews for the *San Jose Mercury News* (11 Nov. 2007): "I hate to see great works of literature ghettoized, whereas others that conform to the rules, conventions, and procedures of the genre we call literary fiction get accorded greater esteem and privilege. To me, it's about pleasure, and the pleasure of reading, and I like to define pleasure broadly."

EARLY YEARS

Chabon (pronounced SHAY-bon) was born on May 24, 1963, in Washington, DC. His father, Robert Chabon, was a medical student who went on to become a noted pediatrician. His mother, Sharon (née Cohen), was a homemaker. Chabon's father also earned a law degree, and later in life was a litigator in cases related to medicine and health care. The family moved frequently during Chabon's early years, living in Pennsylvania, New York, and Arizona, among other places. When he was five years old, his younger brother, Stephen, was born. Chabon wrote in *Manhood for Amateurs* (2009), his book of personal essays, "I had learned to work a record player, tell lies, read the funny pages, and feel awkward at parties. But it was not until that morning, in early September 1968, that my story truly began. Until my brother was born, I had no one to tell it to."

The following year the family settled in Columbia, Maryland, a planned community established in 1967 and designed to be racially and economically integrated. Chabon has said that

Getty Images

watching the town grow had a profound effect on his future career. "It was this incredibly powerful demonstration of what an imagination could accomplish in the real world," he told Stephen Kiehl for the *Baltimore Sun* (May 13, 2007). "It was like an act of magic. It was like somebody saying abracadabra. And here, in this place where there was nothing, there is now a house and a shopping center and a pool." He continued, "It made this powerful, magical impression on me that you could say you were going to do something and, in a way, all you needed to do was name it. . . . By naming streets, by naming villages, by naming neighborhoods . . . by doing that, you could cause things to come into existence." Chabon occupied himself by wandering the town's vacant lots and playgrounds, playing in the neighbors' yards, and riding his bicycle. He was also an avid baseball fan.

In 1975, Chabon's parents divorced. Chabon's father moved to Pennsylvania to become the chief of pediatrics at a Pittsburgh hospital. Michael and his brother spent summers and holidays with their father and new stepmother, Shelley, a speech pathologist. The city of Pittsburgh, like the town of Columbia, became immensely important to Chabon, and is featured in much of writing.

Following her divorce, Chabon's mother enrolled at the University of Baltimore, earning a law degree when Michael and Stephen were ages fourteen and nine, respectively. When she took a new job at a federal agency that required a long commute, Chabon took over many of the household tasks, including cooking.

As a teenager, Chabon was socially awkward and semi-reclusive, holing up in his room to listen to music and read. He was particularly fond of science fiction novels and comic books, and still often describes himself to interviewers as a "geek." "My secret confederates were the works of Monty Python, H. P. Lovecraft, the cartoonist Vaughan Bodé, and the Ramones, among many others; they kept me watered and fed," he wrote in an op-ed piece for the *New York Times* (13 Apr. 2004). "It was not long before I began to write: stories, poems, snatches of autobiographical jazz. . . . But the main reason I wrote stories—and the reason that I keep on writing them today—was not to express myself. I started to write because once it had been nourished, stoked, and liberated by those secret confederates, I could not hold back the force of my imagination. I had been freed."

EDUCATION
After a brief stint at Carnegie-Mellon University, Chabon entered the University of Pittsburgh, where he edited the student literary magazine for a year and read such authors as William Faulkner and Jorge Luis Borges for the first time. In 1984, he earned a bachelor's degree in literature. He then entered the MFA program at the University of California, Irvine. As his master's thesis, he turned in a coming-of-age novel he titled *The Mysteries of Pittsburgh*. Chabon's professor, Donald Heiney (himself a novelist who wrote under the pen name MacDonald Harris), was so impressed by the manuscript that he sent it off to an agent without informing Chabon. A bidding war ensued among publishers, and Chabon ultimately earned a six-figure advance, a noteworthy accomplishment for a young, unknown author. "I'm kind of a poster boy for the more tangible benefits that a good writing program can bestow," he quipped in an essay included in *Manhood for Amateurs*.

THE LAUNCH OF A LITERARY CAREER
The Mysteries of Pittsburgh was published in 1988. The book takes place during the summer after its protagonist, Art Bechstein, has graduated from the University of Pittsburgh. The son of a mafia money launderer, Art wants only to enjoy a last summer of adventure before embarking on adult life and a career as a stockbroker. He soon becomes romantically involved with both Arthur Lecomte, a charismatic gay man, and Phlox Lombardi, a shy and somewhat odd young woman.

Because the novel was widely assumed to be semi-autobiographical, conjecture about Chabon's sexuality raged in literary circles. He was included by the editors of *Newsweek* in a feature on up-and-coming gay writers and felt compelled to issue a public denial. He asserted, however, that he was not upset about the mistake, because it had introduced his work to a whole new group of fans. Chabon later confirmed that he had once been engaged for a time in a same-sex relationship, and he employed gay characters and themes in several of his later works.

Amid the media interest in the amount of his advance and his sexual predilections, *The Mysteries of Pittsburgh* generated excitement in the book world. Alice McDermott's review for the *New York Times* (3 Apr. 1988), for example, was measured but still greatly enthusiastic. She wrote, "Here is a first novel by a talented young writer that is full of all the delights, and not a few of the disappointments, inherent in any early work of serious fiction. There is the pleasure of a fresh voice and a keen eye, of watching a writer clearly in love with language and literature, youth and wit, expound and embellish upon the world as he sees it, balanced by a scarcity of well-developed characters. . . . [Chabon] has learned well from the writers he appears to admire—F. Scott Fitzgerald especially—and his control over his story, the wonderful use he makes of each description, of Pittsburgh itself, are often astonishing." She concluded, "[T]here is much to admire here, and what the novel lacks in insight it compensates for in language, wit, and ambition, in the sheer exuberance of its voice: the voice of a young writer with tremendous skill as he discovers, joyously, just what his words can do."

In the wake of the publicity, Chabon—who declined both an offer to model jeans for a Gap ad campaign and a chance to be on *People* magazine's "Fifty Most Beautiful" list—remained characteristically modest. "I was one of the last first-novelists to get in that period when New York publishing was looking for the next hot thing," he told Sam Whiting for the *San Francisco Chronicle* (31 Mar. 1999). In 2008, *The Mysteries of Pittsburgh* was made into a film featuring Nick Nolte as the mobster father, and a young actor named Jon Foster as Art.

SOPHOMORE NOVEL

In 1990, Chabon published a short-story collection, *A Model World and Other Stories*, that was well received. He struggled for years with his next novel, which had as its main character an architect endeavoring to construct the ideal baseball park. After writing more than 1,000 words, he abandoned the effort in 1992. (An annotated fragment of the unfinished book, which had the working title *Fountain City*, was published in the literary magazine *McSweeney's* in December 2010.) Within a few months of turning his focus from *Fountain City*, Chabon completed *Wonder Boys*. Published in 1995, the novel follows the travails of Grady Tripp, a middle-aged writing instructor and novelist who had once been considered one of the most exceptional literary talents of his generation. Grady, who lives and works in Pittsburgh, now spends his days conducting an extramarital affair with his college's female chancellor (whose husband chairs the school's English Department) and drinking to excess. He is thus unable to complete a long-awaited magnum opus and must convince his flamboyantly gay editor that the manuscript is almost ready for publication. Over the course of the novel, Grady and one of his students, James, become embroiled in a series of comical criminal adventures. The character of Grady is based on Chuck Kinder, a University of Pittsburgh professor.

Most reviewers felt that Chabon, despite the lengthy period between novels, had avoided the sophomore slump. "Mr. Chabon is that rare thing, an intelligent lyrical writer," Robert Ward wrote for the *New York Times Book Review* (9 Apr. 1995, on-line). "Because his comedy always reins in his romantic impulses, his work seems to reflect a nature that is at once passionate and satirical. The result is a tone of graceful melancholy punctuated by a gentle and humane good humor." In 2000, *Wonder Boys* became a feature film starring Michael Douglas as Grady, and Tobey Maguire as James.

THE AMAZING ADVENTURES OF KAVALIER & CLAY

Chabon published another collection of short stories in 1999. The collection, *Werewolves in Their Youth*, was credited in part to August Van Zorn, a fictitious pulp writer who had appeared briefly in *Wonder Boys*. In 2000, Chabon published *The Amazing Adventures of Kavalier & Clay*. The Pulitzer Prize–winning novel traces the lives of two cousins: Josef Kavalier, who has come to New York City after escaping Nazi-occupied Prague, and Sammy Klayman, the son of a vaudeville strongman named the Mighty Molecule. It's the golden age of comic book publishing, and together the two develop such popular titles as *The Escapist*, *The Monitor*, and *Luna Moth*. *The Amazing Adventures of Kavalier & Clay* was based, in part, on Joe Shuster and Jerry Siegel, the creators of Superman, who had sold the rights to their character to DC Comics for a few hundred dollars in the late 1930s. The *Escapist* storylines described in the novel were later adapted as comic stories and released in three graphic novels.

In addition to winning the Pulitzer, *The Amazing Adventures of Kavalier & Clay* met with near-unanimous critical acclaim. In a representative review, Donna Seaman wrote for *Booklist* (Aug. 2000), "Virtuoso Chabon takes intense delight in the practice of his art, and never has his joy been more palpable than in this funny and profound tale of exile, love, and magic." In the flurry of interviews that followed his Pulitzer win, Chabon explained to journalists how important comics had been to him as a child, particularly after he discovered the iconic work of Jack

Kirby at Marvel. "These characters were more screwed up, had neuroses, problems," he told Lewis Buzzbee for the *New York Times* (24 Sep. 2000). "The idea that it would be lonely to be a superhero. It makes it easier to identify with—wow, Spider-Man is lonely, too." Additionally, comic books provided a connection to his father, who was also a fan, and the two often browsed comic shops together.

THE YIDDISH POLICEMAN'S UNION

In 2007, Chabon published *The Yiddish Policeman's Union*, a hard-boiled detective story set in Sitka, Alaska. A work of alternative history, the book takes as its premise that the Jews of Eastern Europe, displaced by World War II, have been allowed to settle in a remote corner of Alaska. (Chabon drew upon the little-known fact that Franklin Roosevelt's secretary of the interior had once proposed a similar plan.) In the fictional enclave, alcoholic police detective Meyer Landsman and his sidekick, Berko Shemets, must solve a mystery involving a murder, a mafia-like group called the Verbovers, and a Zionist geopolitical plot.

Writing a book featuring Jewish criminals and pidgin Yiddish left Chabon, who is Jewish, open to charges of being a self-hating anti-Semite. "Its satire has the effect, intended or not, of treating Israel as something simultaneously fanatical and ridiculous," Samuel Freedman wrote for the *Jewish Exponent* (26 Jul. 2007). "One of the running gags of the novel is the absurdity of shtetl life transplanted into Alaska. The unspoken inference is that it is just as unnatural for Jews to have plopped themselves down in a Middle Eastern desert. And when Chabon refers to the Sitka Jews having pushed out the indigenous Tlingit Indians, his metaphor needs no footnote to be understood." Despite such criticism, most reviewers were dazzled. Terrence Rafferty, writing for the *New York Times* (13 May 2007), called it a "funny, humane, wised-up novel," and in the *Washington Post* (13 May 2007), Elizabeth McCracken enthused, "Reading *The Yiddish Policemen's Union* is like watching a gifted athlete invent a sport using elements of every other sport there is—balls, bats, poles, wickets, javelins and saxophones." McCracken continued, "The pure reach and music and weight of Chabon's imagination are extraordinary, born of brilliant ambition you don't even notice because it is so deeply entertaining. He invents every corner of this strange world—the slang of the 'Sitkaniks,' their history, discount houses, divey bars, pie shops. Despite the complications of the plot, the details of the world are every bit as enthralling."

Chabon published *Telegraph Avenue* in 2012. The plot of the novel revolves around the intertwined lives of two families, one black and one white, who co-own a used-record store on the iconic street in Oakland,

California. The actual Telegraph Avenue that inspired the book extends almost five miles, from the downtown section of Oakland to the campus of the University of California, Berkeley. The street's nature changes every few blocks—with some sections lined with public housing and others filled with trendy clothing shops and unique bookstores. "I guess that for a guy who likes hanging around the borderlands—between genres, cultures, musics, legacies, styles—the appeal of Telegraph lies in the way it reflects a local determination to find your path irrespective of boundary lines, picking up what you can, shaking off what you can, along the way," Chabon wrote for the *Atlantic* (10 Jan. 2011).

OTHER WORKS

Chabon is also the author of *Summerland* (2002), a baseball-themed fantasy novel for young adults, and *The Astonishing Secret of Awesome Man* (2011), a picture book for children. His other books include the short Sherlock Holmes pastiche *The Final Solution: A Story of Detection* (2004); the novel *Gentlemen of the Road: A Tale of Adventure* (2007), which had been originally published in serial form in the *New York Times Magazine*; and the essay collection *Maps and Legends: Reading and Writing along the Borderlands* (2008). He has contributed to the occasional screenplay, including those for *Spider-Man 2* (2004) and *John Carter* (2012).

PERSONAL LIFE

In 1987, Chabon married the poet Iola "Lollie" Groth. He wrote in *Manhood for Amateurs* that the marriage had been, "in a way that I found almost intoxicating—the way slamming a trunk lid on your hand or missing a step as you climb a stairway in the dark can be intoxicating—a great mistake." The couple divorced in 1990. Two years later, Chabon met Ayelet Waldman, an Israeli-born attorney, on a blind date. They married in 1993. In addition to writing poetry, Waldman is also an essayist and mystery writer. She and Chabon have four children—Sophie, Zeke, Rosie, and Abe.

In 2010, Chabon, who lives with his family in Berkeley, was elected chairman of the MacDowell Colony, the oldest artists' colony in the United States. In 2012, he was inducted into the Academy of American Letters. Chabon was also featured on a 2006 episode of *The Simpsons* along with writers Tom Wolfe, Gore Vidal, and Jonathan Franzen.

SUGGESTED READING

Almond, Steve. "Manhood Bound." *Los Angeles Times* 4 Oct. 2009: E12. Print.
Chabon, Michael. *Manhood for Amateurs*. New York: HarperCollins, 2009. Print.

---. "That's Why I Came" *Atlantic*. Atlantic Monthly Group, 10 Jan. 2011. Web. 5 June 2012.

Cohen, Patricia. "The Frozen Chosen." *New York Times* 29 Apr. 2007: B1. Print.

Freedman, Samuel. "Chabon's Choice." *Jewish Exponent* 26 July 2007: 25. Print.

Kiehl, Stephen. "NovelBuilder." *Baltimore Sun*. 13 May 2007: E1. Print.

Kirschling, Gregory. "The New Adventures of Michael Chabon." *EW.com*. Entertainment Weekly, 9 May 2007. Web. 6 June 2012.

Whiting, Sam. "Writer's 'Wonder Year.'" *San Francisco Chronicle*. 31 Mar. 1999: E1. Print.

—*Mari Rich*

Dan Chaon

Born: June 11, 1964
Occupation: Writer, educator

Courtesy of Philip Chaon

"Riveting. Hypnotic. Unnerving. These are just a few of the adjectives used to describe author Dan Chaon's works," Krysta Brown wrote for the *Missourian*'s magazine section, *Vox* (February 1, 2011, online). Those works include the short-story collections *Fitting Ends* (1995; reissued in 2003) and *Among the Missing* (2001) and the novels *You Remind Me of Me* (2004) and *Await Your Reply* (2009). When Molly Antopol, writing for the *Rumpus* (September 15, 2009, online), asked the author to describe a "typical Dan Chaon story," Chaon—a native of Nebraska who now lives in Ohio—replied, "Sad people from the Midwest who are disturbed in some sort of existential way." He told Edward Champion for the literary podcast the *Bat Segundo Show* (July 16, 2010), "A lot of the energy that I get from the landscape of the Midwest is fed into my inspiration for writing. A lot of times I'll start out with landscape. And a lot of times, I'll start out with these isolated places that, for whatever reason, are emotional touchstones for me."

In an illustration of the scope of Chaon's appeal, *Await Your Reply* was listed as one of the best books of the year by sources as disparate as the American Library Association and *Entertainment Weekly*. His fiction has been greeted with rapturous reviews. In a representative assessment of Chaon's oeuvre, Henry D. Shapiro wrote for the Cleveland Arts Prize Web site, "Few novels can survive repeated readings and almost no short stories. . . . Chaon's delight again and again." Chaon's honors include Pushcart and O. Henry prizes and the 2002 Cleveland Arts Prize for Literature, and he was a finalist for the National Book Award for *Among the Missing*. In 2006 he won the Academy Award in Literature from the American Academy of Arts and Letters.

EARLY LIFE AND EDUCATION

Daniel Dean Chaon was born on June 11, 1964, in Omaha, Nebraska. He was adopted as an infant by Earl D. Chaon, an electrician and construction worker, and his wife, Teresa (Tallmage) Chaon. He was raised in Sidney, a town in western Nebraska that had fewer than seven thousand residents, most of them poor or, like his adoptive parents, working class. Chaon told Tom Barbash for the *Believer* (June 2004) that he grew up "with the sense that there's another life out there that I might have had, or multiple lives: Who were my biological parents? What if they'd kept me? What if I'd been adopted by a different family?" He added that part of his interest in alternate lives "has to do with coming from a small-town working-class background, being the first person in my family to go to college, and finding myself in this very different, upper-middle-class college-professor life."

As a boy Chaon loved to read; he told Krysta Brown, "One of the greatest things we had growing up was the Bookmobile. I didn't even know what I was looking for, but I'd come back with a stack of 15–20 books." As he grew older he became particularly drawn to works of horror and the supernatural by such writers as Stephen King, Shirley Jackson, and Peter Straub, all of whom he has cited as major influences. Chaon told Derek Handley for *Hot Metal Bridge* (Spring 2011, online), an online publication of the University of Pittsburgh's M.F.A. program, "I think all the formulas for fiction—whether you're talking about SF or Romance or Western or Horror or whatever—all these sometimes formulaic genres have also produced great works of fiction. It just depends on how the individual writers have responded and adapted and made use of those forms. There are people like the Brontë sisters, for example, who were responding to the gothic form in an interesting way. So I don't really think that the term 'genre fiction' is a useful workshop term. I think there are plenty of really good writers who are stuck in that ghetto with that 'genre' label."

Chaon was inspired to submit his own work to publishers when he was a teenager. "I was a ridiculously nerdy kid," he recalled to Barbash. "While the other kids in my high school were having sex and drinking beer, I was writing odd, creepy stories and sending them to the *New Yorker* and various literary journals under the nom de plume D. Dean Chaon. Don't ask me why I thought the initial was cool, but I did. Then, when I was a junior, I sent a story to *Tri-Quarterly*"—Northwestern University's literary magazine—"and the editor there, Reginald Gibbons, was very kind to send a note back, and then when he found out I was sixteen years old, he encouraged me to come to Northwestern."

Chaon took that advice, and after completing high school he entered Northwestern University, in Evanston, Illinois. "When I left Nebraska for college at Northwestern, I'd read an enormous amount but had spent so much time in my own head that I didn't have extensive social skills," he told Antopol. "Suddenly I was in this world where I was surrounded by these incredibly polished and wealthy kids who had gone to prep schools, and I felt daunted by them. I don't think people were aware of how full of anxiety I was. . . . For a long time I felt like I was living in a place where I shouldn't have been." Chaon graduated with a BA degree in 1986. He then held a series of odd jobs, including bartender and disk jockey, before entering Syracuse University, in New York, where he earned an MA degree in creative writing in 1990.

CAREER

In 1988, Chaon had married one of his undergraduate instructors, the writer Sheila Schwartz, who was 11 years his senior; they had two sons together. After he completed the master's program, the family moved to Cleveland, Ohio, where Schwartz had joined the English Department at Cleveland State University. "I got a job with a catering company until I was fired," Chaon told Handley. "Then I knew a guy who was a grad student at Cleveland State and he thought it would be really awesome if we didn't pursue academia at all, if we just became construction workers. So we started a roofing business and that went on for a little while until I fell off a roof. So my wife told me I couldn't do that anymore, because she was afraid I was going to die.

So then I got a job working with youth in a literacy program."

Meanwhile Chaon continued to write, thanks in large part to his wife's encouragement. He and Schwartz had regularly discussed writing and books before their marriage. "Looking back," he wrote for the *Rumpus* (January 8, 2009, online), "I can see that as the major turning point of my life, I see how knowing Sheila created a pathway that I wouldn't have been brave enough, or wise enough, to have chosen without her." In October 1995 (many sources state 1996), *Fitting Ends* was published by Northwestern University Press. (It had been edited by Chaon's mentor at Northwestern, Reginald Gibbons.) Although the collection received little attention until it was reissued in 2003, the notices it did garner were positive. A reviewer for *Publishers Weekly* (October 23, 1995, online), for example, praised the stories as "deftly written and brilliantly structured" and wrote, "Anyone who has ever toyed with the idea of staying in school an extra year in order to delay the sobering responsibilities of adulthood will identify with the people in Chaon's first collection. Familial burdens, sexual confusion, and unchallenging jobs are just a few of the impediments to the happiness of these 20-something characters, leaving them disillusioned and powerless to move on. It is especially poignant in 'Rapid Transit,' when the transition from fair-haired collegian to entry-level lackey stirs up some scary emotions. In 'Fraternity,' a party-boy rejects reality even as 'the music faded, the lights came up.' Many seek constancy from family members, only to find that they too are changing beyond their control. One man looks to his ailing grandmother for some order, while another hunts down his biological mother to provide 'whatever's missing' in his life." The title tale, in which the adult narrator looks back on his troubled relationship with his brother, Del, who was hit by a train and killed during his teens, was included in *The Best American Stories 1996*.

After the publication of *Fitting Ends*, Chaon found work teaching creative writing as an adjunct professor. In 2000 he was hired as a permanent faculty member at Oberlin College, in Ohio, where he is currently the Delaney Associate Professor of Creative Writing. An exceedingly popular figure on campus, Chaon told Michael Emerson Dirda for the Oberlin News and Media Web site (January 20, 2010), "I want creative writing students to find a voice that feels unique to them and that expresses some essential part of themselves. As a result, I've had students who are primarily writing science fiction. I've had students who are writing very personal biography. I've had students writing realism. I've had students writing fantasy. And I'm not particularly concerned about the content of their work as long as it's beautiful and it has that personal spark that makes the work unique to them."

His students were thrilled when Chaon was nominated for a National Book Award for his short-story collection *Among the Missing*, published in 2001. "I gave a reading at Oberlin shortly after the nominations were announced, and it was packed with people I've had in class, all of them cheering," he told Anita Lancaster for the Oberlin News and Media Web site. "That's the best thing that's happened to me since the nominations were announced, and the thing that made me happiest." Although the volume ultimately lost to *The Corrections*, by Jonathan Franzen, reviews were almost universally positive. "Despite their grim uncertainties, the stories in *Among the Missing* sneak resolutely up on you, like new weather that hits before you know it," Beverly Lowry wrote for the *New York Times Book Review* (August 5, 2001, online). In an assessment for *Publishers Weekly* (July 3, 2001, online), a critic wrote, "In the 12 quietly accomplished stories of his second collection, Chaon explores the complicated geography of human relationships, from the unintentional failures and minute betrayals of daily existence to the numbing grief caused by abandonment, disappearance, or death. Specific and disquieting absences—an uncle who killed himself, a mother who vanished, a friend who was kidnapped—haunt the protagonists, and a series of metaphoric and literal stand-ins take the place of what's missing. In 'Safety Man,' a dummy intended for crime deterrence—propped in the passenger seat, it looks like a male companion—becomes a kind of surrogate husband for a young widow, and for her daughters, an inflatable father; in 'I Demand to Know Where You're Taking Me,' a woman caring for her incarcerated brother-in-law's macaw comes to loathe the bird, its ugly talk transforming it into a symbol of everything wrong and incomprehensible about him. By and large, Chaon's characters are citizens of the emotional hinterlands, lonely even when surrounded. . . . And yet these stories are neither morbid nor even particularly melancholic. Singularly dedicated to an examination of all the profundity and strangeness of the quotidian, they are, in their best moments, unsettling, moving, even beautiful." One story from the collection, "Big Me," won a prestigious O. Henry Award, and another, "The Illustrated Encyclopedia of the Animal Kingdom," was included in a volume of Pushcart Prize winners.

Chaon next published a novel, *You Remind Me of Me* (2004), about the complex and often dysfunctional relationships among a group of midwestern characters. "Dan Chaon's extraordinary first novel is powerful evidence that an author whose reputation has been made in short fiction can successfully make the transition to novels," Logan Browning wrote for the *Houston Chronicle* (July 18, 2004, online). "As in Chaon's short-story collections, *Fitting Ends* and *Among the Missing*, the prose mesmerizes with its deliberative, mournful plenitude. But here he pieces together vignettes from multiple points of view across several decades into a rich narrative mosaic, and instead of one or two souls in search of self-knowledge, there are many." Browning continued, "The real wonder of Chaon's writing is its resolute refusal to treat any of its many misfits, loners or sufferers with condescension or sarcasm. Whenever Chaon inhabits one of his characters' consciousnesses, he abandons judgment entirely, working instead with the complete sympathy that only full understanding can produce. . . . The three main characters—Jonah, Troy and Nora—and not a few of the minor ones stumble through the roles of father, mother, child, grandparent, friend, spouse and lover, [and] regardless of their particular psychological or physical disfigurements, all are represented by Chaon with warm, gentle affection as they attempt to exorcise their unique collections of ghosts and guilt, struggling to expiate their shortcomings and sins."

The novel touched repeatedly on the topic of adoption. As an unwed teenager, Nora had been forced to give up her firstborn son, and her second child, Jonah, embarks on a quest to find his lost half-brother. Meanwhile, Troy, adopted as an infant by parents who soon divorce, is struggling to regain custody of his own son. "For me, the adoption stuff has continued to complicate my life in a whole variety of ways well into adulthood," Chaon told Jason Chambers and Jonathan Evison for the online literary magazine the *Nervous Breakdown* (November 19, 2009). "I met my biological father when I was in my late twenties, and I've had a very close relationship with him and his family ever since. . . . At the same time, I have a separate, and complicated relationship with my adoptive family (my adoptive parents both died in 1996) and there's also my biological mother, who I have only spoken to a couple times, and who has kept my existence a secret from her own family."

The three main protagonists in *Await Your Reply*, Chaon's second novel (2009), seem at first to be unrelated: Ryan Schuyler, whom we meet as he is being rushed to the hospital with his severed hand in a cooler, has dropped out of Northwestern University; the teenage Lucy Lattimore, hoping for love and adventure, has run off with her high-school history teacher; and Miles Cheshire, who works in a run-down magic store, has been searching for years for his brilliant, mentally ill twin brother. It becomes apparent as the story progresses that the three are deeply entwined—in sometimes shocking ways. The novel, which explores themes of identity and betrayal, earned Chaon some of the most enthusiastic reviews of his career. "Chaon is a dark, provocative writer, and *Await Your Reply* is a dark, provocative book," Lucinda Rosenfeld wrote for the *New York Times Book Review* (August 23, 2009, online). "In bringing its three strands together, Chaon has fashioned a braid out of barbed wire." "*Await Your Reply* is my favorite book of fall 2009. And that's saying a lot," Michele Filgate wrote for *BookSlut.com* (October 2009). "The number of major authors with new books out is overwhelming. I'll save you time right now by suggesting you move *Await Your Reply* to the very top of your to-be-read pile. His novel is beautifully written but also has a compelling plot. It's hard to find a combination of both in literary fiction, and Dan Chaon expertly provides an entertaining but literary read. . . . Chaon is one of the best writers of fiction in America, and this is, by far, his best work yet."

"When I started out, I didn't have any idea how the three threads were connected. I just knew that they were—somehow," Chaon told Edan Lepucki for the *Millions* (August 25, 2009, online). "The first hundred pages of the book took me about two years to write. I revised and revised, and fiddled around with the personalities of the characters, and added and deleted subplots and minor characters—basically trying to frame out the farmland that I was going to be working with, cutting brush and taking rocks out of the soil and so forth. The second hundred pages took about nine months. This was when I began to use cliff-hangers at the end of each chapter, leaving each thread with an unanswered question that I had to figure out, and that pushed things forward for me more quickly. . . . The last hundred pages was written in a little less than two months, but it really wasn't until the final few chapters that I truly had everything figured out. The last bit of plot clicked into place the way a difficult math problem sometimes does. Bing! Suddenly it seems so obvious!"

Chaon's wife, Sheila, died of ovarian cancer in November 2008, shortly after he completed his final revisions on *Await Your Reply*. Schwartz's short-story collection, *Imagine a Great White Light*, published by the Pushcart Press in 1993, won Pushcart's editor's award for "overlooked manuscripts of enduring literary value." Her novel, *Lies Will Take You Somewhere*, was published posthumously, in early 2009. "*Lies Will Take You Somewhere* is a family drama, both tragic and darkly funny, with odd gothic undertones that emerge and recede as the story progresses," Chaon wrote for the *Rumpus*. "It's the story of the Rosen family: Saul, a rabbi; his wife Jane; and their three daughters. This was not the life that Sheila led, though maybe it was one that she once imagined for herself, back when she was a middle-class Jewish girl growing up in Philadelphia, back before she decided to marry a much younger gentile boy from the redneck end of Nebraska."

Chaon's next book, the short-story collection *Stay Awake*, will be published in February 2012. Chaon writes occasional op-ed pieces and book reviews for such publications as the *New York Times* and the *Washington Post*.

Chaon lives in Cleveland Heights, Ohio, with his teenage sons, Philip and Paul.

SUGGESTED READING

Antopol, Molly. "The Rumpus Interview with Dan Chaon." *Rumpus*. Rumpus, 19 Dec. 2009. Web. 26 Sep. 2011.

Brown, Krysta. "Recap: Writer Dan Chaon on the Future of Literature." *Vox*. Columbia Missourian, 1 Feb. 2011. Web. 19 Dec. 2011.

Champion, Edward. "The Bat Segundo Show: Dan Chaon." *Reluctant Habits*. Edward Champion, 16 July 2010. Web. 19 Dec. 2011.

Dirda, Michael Emerson. "Celebrated Author and Oberlin Professor Dan Chaon Makes His Mark on Aspiring Writers." *Oberlin College*. Oberlin College, 20 Jan. 2010. Web. 19 Dec. 2011.

Shapiro, Henry D. "Dan Chaon, Writer: 2002 Cleveland Arts Prize for Literature." *Cleveland Arts Prize*. Cleveland Arts Prize. n.d. Web. 19 Dec. 2011.

SELECTED WORKS

Fitting Ends, 1995; *Among the Missing*, 2001; *You Remind Me of Me*, 2004; *Await Your Reply*, 2009; *Stay Awake*, 2012

—*Mari Rich*

Paul D. Clement

Born: June 24, 1966
Occupation: Lawyer and government official

Widely considered the most skilled advocate of his generation, Paul Clement is known for his nimble, straightforward style of delivering arguments before the US Supreme Court. After preparing for an average of one hundred hours for each appearance, he impressively presents his cases without notes, recalling from memory specific quotations and page numbers. His preparation allows him to gesture with his hands and make eye contact with the justices while directly answering their questions. "He just internalizes every single aspect of the case," Viet D. Dinh, Clement's law partner at Bancroft LLC, told Kevin Sack for the *New York Times* (26 Oct. 2011). "He makes the argument not from memory but from total immersion."

Since 2000, Clement has argued more cases before the Supreme Court than any

Bloomberg via Getty Images

raised in Cedarburg, Wisconsin, a small suburb located in the state's southeastern region. His father, Jerry Clement, served as a chief financial officer for a company, and his mother, Jean, stayed at home to raise her children and to volunteer in the community. Paul Clement attended Cedarburg's public school system and was a member of the debate team at Cedarburg High School. After graduating from high school in 1984, he attended Georgetown University's School of Foreign Service in Washington, DC. There he took part in the American Parliamentary Debate Association. After graduating summa cum laude from Georgetown in 1988, he received a master's degree in economics from Darwin College, one of the constituent schools of Cambridge University in England.

Clement began attending Harvard Law School in 1989 and graduated magna cum laude in 1992. During Clement's time at Harvard, the student body was sharply divided along ideological lines. Though an outspoken conservative, Clement maintained a good reputation among both liberals and conservatives. "Paul's a master of making a position, whatever the position is, seem reasonable. He has respect from both sides," Eric Sacks, one of Clement's classmates at Harvard, told Natalie Singer for the *Harvard News Bulletin* (Winter 2012). During law school, Clement developed a fascination with appellate and constitutional laws. He served as Supreme Court editor of the *Harvard Law Review* during his senior year, one year after Barack Obama had served as the publication's editor in chief. Also during his senior year, Clement was involved in a controversy surrounding the *Harvard Law Review* and its parody issue that mocked the work of a feminist law professor who had been murdered. The issue was published on the first anniversary of her death. Clement was one of eight editors who signed an apology letter for the incident and, in doing so, avoided punishment.

EARLY CAREER

Clement became a clerk for Judge Laurence H. Silberman, a member of the US Court of Appeals for the DC Circuit, who is considered among the most conservative federal judges in the country. From 1993 to 1994, Clement served as a clerk for associate Supreme Court Justice Antonin Scalia, also known for his consistently conservative votes as well as his colorful rhetoric. After completing those clerkships, Clement served briefly in the Washington, DC, office of the prestigious law firm Kirkland & Ellis, where notable Republican prosecutor Kenneth Starr was a partner. In 1995, Clement accepted a position as chief counsel of the US Senate Subcommittee on the Constitution, Federalism, and Property Rights. John Ashcroft, then a junior senator from Missouri, had appointed Clement to the post after becoming chair of the subcommittee

other attorney, and he has garnered a winning record, taking on many landmark cases representing some of the most politically sensitive issues of the day. Among his forty-nine Court appearances during his time as solicitor general and principal deputy solicitor in the George W. Bush administration (2001–08), Clement defended many of Bush's most controversial policies that were put in place after the terrorist attacks of September 11, 2001. After leaving the Bush administration in 2008, Clement continued to take on high-profile cases as a private attorney and has become something of a go-to representative for the Republican Party. He was hired by House majority leader John Boehner and the House Republicans to defend the 1996 Defense of Marriage Act (DOMA) against constitutional challenges, and in March 2012, he represented twenty-six states suing the federal government over the constitutionality of the 2010 Patient Affordability and Protection Act. Clement is noted for his ability to argue hot-button political issues on purely legal principles, a quality that has endeared him to members of the legal profession from both parties. Sack has quoted Walter Dellinger, a former solicitor general in the Clinton administration, as saying, "Paul is such a good advocate and such a cheerful friend that it's easy to forget how conservative he is."

EARLY LIFE AND EDUCATION

Paul Drew Clement is the youngest of four children; he has two sisters and one brother. He was following the 1994 elections that gave Republicans a majority in the Senate. Clement served on that subcommittee for three years, during which he worked on a variety of issues, including the Digital Millennium Copyright Act, which put into place two treaties passed by the World Intellectual Property Organization (WIPO) in 1996 to protect intellectual property rights. He also worked on the 1998 impeachment hearings of President Bill Clinton.

At the end of the Clinton impeachment hearings in 1998, Clement returned to private legal work, becoming the head of appellate practice for the international law firm King & Spalding. That same year Clement began working as an adjunct professor at the Georgetown University Law Center, teaching a seminar on the separation of powers. In February 2001, just three years after leaving public service, Clement returned to government service. John Ashcroft, who had recently been appointed US attorney general by President George W. Bush, selected Clement to become principal deputy to the new solicitor general, Theodore Olson. Unlike other deputies working under the solicitor general who are typically career attorneys and remain in their positions after the end of an administration, the principal deputy is, in part, a political position that is appointed at the start of each administration to support the solicitor general. The solicitor general's main responsibility is to represent the federal government in matters before the US Supreme Court and to file amicus briefs in cases involving issues that greatly affect the federal government.

Working alongside Theodore Olson gave Clement the chance to argue his first cases before the Supreme Court. His parents traveled from Wisconsin to watch him argue his first case. "Somebody said, 'Well, isn't it going to make you nervous that your parents are there?'" Clement recalled to Nina Totenberg for National Public Radio's *All Things Considered* (23 Mar. 2012), "and I said, 'How could I be any more nervous than I already am?'" Despite his initial discomfort before the justices, Clement proved to be a skilled arguer during his time as deputy solicitor general, arguing eighteen cases before the Supreme Court. He would eventually become known for his ease before the justices. Today Clement is widely praised for his clear, straightforward manner of speaking; his style is to banter with the justices rather than to deliver lengthy dramatic speeches.

NOTABLE CASES

In one of his most notable cases, *McConnell v. the Federal Election Commission* (2003), Clement defended the 2002 Bipartisan Campaign Reform Act, also known as the McCain-Feingold Act, which aimed to restrict the kinds of contributions individuals and corporations could make either to candidates for public office or to groups that ran ads in support of candidates. Clement managed to win a 5–4 decision that upheld the law by proving that it was in keeping with the past several generations of campaign finance reform. Observers praised the vigor with which Clement defended the statute, especially given the fact that he was representing a side that did not align with his personal politics. Another of Clement's notable Supreme Court wins was in the 2004 case *Tennessee v. Lane,* which expanded the rights of individuals with disabilities.

Some of Clement's most notable cases as deputy solicitor general involved enemy combatants detained during President George W. Bush's declared War on Terror. In the cases *Padilla v. Bush* and *Hamdi v. Rumsfeld,* which were considered by the Supreme Court together in April 2004, Clement defended the federal government's detention of American citizens alleged to have conspired against the United States. In both cases, the arrested parties were defined as "enemy combatants," transferred to military custody, and detained without access to legal counsel. Clement argued that it was legal to detain the men given the Court's long history of allowing the capture of enemies during times of war. Asked by Justice Ruth Bader Ginsburg whether the president had the power to order prisoners to be subjected to "mild torture" in order to obtain information, Clement boldly replied, "Well, our executive doesn't [allow that]. You have to recognize that in situations . . . where the government is on a war footing, that you have to trust the executive" (Totenberg). Just eight hours after Clement made that statement, televised images appeared on CBS News from Abu Ghraib prison in Iraq and showed what many perceived as acts of torture at the hands of US soldiers. The Supreme Court ultimately dismissed *Padilla v. Bush* on technical grounds. (Clement would represent the government again when the case reached federal court in 2005.) However, in the controlling opinion on *Hamdi v. Rumsfeld,* written by Sandra Day O'Connor, the Court ruled that Bush was authorized to hold the enemy combatants. If they were US citizens, however, they had the right to challenge their enemy combatant status before an impartial judge. The Court ruled that Hamdi had been deprived of his constitutional right to due process of law because he had been unable to appear before a judge or challenge the government's evidence against him. Many observers were impressed that Clement's reputation was not harmed after making such a public mistake in his arguments in these cases. Rather, as Zengerle points out for *New York* magazine (18 Mar. 2012), "conservatives and liberals rallied to his defense."

Clement became the acting solicitor general on July 11, 2004, upon Olson's resignation. In March 2005, he was formally nominated to the solicitor general post, and he was confirmed the following June. At age thirty-eight, he was the youngest solicitor general in 115 years. He argued before the Supreme Court in a number of influential cases, such as *Gonzales v. Raich* (2005), *Gonzales v. Oregon* (2005), *United States v. Georgia* (2005), and *Gonzales v. Carhart* (2006). The last was a 5–4 decision that upheld the 2003 Partial Birth Abortion Ban Act, which disallowed a specific type of late-term abortion. Clement also defended the Bush administration's controversial War on Terror policies in lower federal courts. According to members of the administration, Clement made efforts to convince the White House to relax its expansive claims about the government's right to detain and interrogate terrorism suspects. Clement served as acting attorney general for one day, September 17, 2007, after the resignation of embattled Attorney General Alberto Gonzales and before the president nominated former assistant attorney general Peter Keisler to the position. Benjamin Wittes, of the nonprofit public policy organization Brookings Institution, told Zengerle that Clement "was one of a very small number of senior lawyers in the Bush administration who worked on nearly all of the tough counterterrorism issues and came through with their reputations enhanced."

Upon resigning from the solicitor general post in June 2008, Clement was sought after by private law firms and was described by Dan Slater for the *Wall Street Journal* (27 Oct. 2008) as "the LeBron James of law firm recruiting." He ultimately joined the large Atlanta-based firm King & Spalding, heading its appellate practice in Washington, DC, where his reported salary was about $5 million. His high-profile clients included the National Rifle Association, whom he represented in the landmark 2010 Supreme Court decision *National Rifle Association v. City of Chicago, Illinois*, which struck down the city's 1982 handgun ban and ruled that the Second Amendment's guaranteed right to firearm ownership applies to each of the fifty states. Clement also represented the National Football League during the 2011 stalled negotiations over a new collective bargaining agreement, which led to a league lockout from March to July. Later that year, Clement represented the owners of the National Basketball Association in a labor dispute with the league's players union.

CONSERVATIVE CAUSES

Meanwhile, in April 2011, Clement was hired by House majority leader John Boehner and a bipartisan legal advisory group formed from House members to represent the 1996 Defense of Marriage Act (DOMA) in the face of constitutional challenges. Passed by large majorities in both houses and signed into law by Democratic President Bill Clinton, DOMA defined marriage for all federal purposes as a legal union between one man and one woman. It also prevented states from being required to respect same sex marriages that took place in other states. Since its passage, the law has been contentious; several states have issued bans on gay marriage while several others have legalized gay marriage. In February 2011, the Justice Department under President Barack Obama (who had promised during his 2008 presidential campaign to repeal DOMA) announced that it would no longer defend DOMA against legal challenges because the administration viewed it as unconstitutional. One week after Clement had agreed to represent DOMA, he was asked by King & Spalding to drop the case after the firm received numerous complaints from certain clients, partners, and gay rights groups. Clement, however, refused to abandon his client; instead, he resigned from the firm and joined the small Washington, DC, law firm Bancroft PLLC, founded by Viet D. Dinh, a law school classmate. In his resignation letter, Clement noted that his decision to leave the firm was not motivated by politics. He wrote, "Instead, I resign out of the firmly held belief that a representation should not be abandoned because the client's legal position is extremely unpopular in certain quarters. Defending unpopular positions is what lawyers do." Though he was criticized by gay rights groups, Clement was widely praised by lawyers and legal scholars from across the political spectrum for his decision to stand by his client. Supreme Court Justice Elena Kagan praised his "professionalism and honor" and noted that his critics "misunderstand the traditions and ethics of the legal profession." As of August of 2012, DOMA had not been reviewed by the Supreme Court.

Clement has continued to argue in favor of traditionally conservative causes. In January 2012, he appeared before the Court to argue on behalf of Texas governor Rick Perry after his redistricting plan was accused of being intentionally designed to prevent the formation of new minority districts. In April 2012 Clement defended the state of Arizona's controversial 2010 anti-immigration law, which, among other actions, made it a crime for illegal immigrants to be present in the state and allowed the government to arrest suspected illegal aliens without issuing warrants. On June 25, 2012, the Court ruled in a 5–3 decision that three of the four provisions were unconstitutional because they either interfered with federal enforcement efforts or they operated in areas that were solely controlled by federal policy. The Court allowed the provision that gives police the authority to arrest and hold anyone they believe had committed a crime and whom they believe was in the country illegally. Furthermore, suspects can be held until their immigration status is confirmed.

Certainly Clement's case with the farthest reaching consequences is the challenge to the Obama administration's controversial 2010 Patient Protection and Affordability Act, designed to provide health insurance to more than thirty million Americans, reform various aspects of the private health insurance industry, and require all Americans to purchase some form of health insurance or pay a fine, among other provisions. Clement was hired as lead counsel for the governors of twenty-six states in the latter case who sued the federal government shortly after the act became law in an effort to have it overturned. In August 2011, Clement and his co-counsel, Michael A. Carvin, had won the only appellate ruling to overturn the act's most controversial provision: the requirement all Americans obtain medical insurance beginning in 2014; the decision in the 11th Circuit Court directly contradicted an earlier ruling by the 6th Circuit, both of which were appealed to the Supreme Court.

In March 2012, the Supreme Court heard arguments from Clement and US Solicitor General Donald B. Verrilli over four aspects of the Patient Care and Affordability Act, including whether the individual mandate requiring the purchase of health insurance is constitutional and, if it's not, whether it can be severed from the rest of the law. Clement argued that while the Constitution's Commerce Clause in Article I allows Congress to regulate certain commercial activities, it does not allow Congress to compel commerce for the purpose of regulation, which Clement argued was the ultimate result of the health care law. Furthermore, Clement maintained, without the individual mandate to buy health insurance, other key features of the law—such as a requirement that insurers not reject clients due to preexisting conditions—cannot function as intended. Therefore, the entire law, or at least the key provisions that are affected, should be overturned. On June 28, 2012, the Court ruled in a 5–4 victory for President Obama that the individual mandate was constitutional because it was a tax and was not an application of Congressional power under the Commerce Clause. Writing for *USA Today* (29 June 2012), Wolf and Jackson reported on the decision and quoted Chief Justice John Roberts as explaining that "because the constitution permits such a tax, it is not our role to forbid it, or to pass upon its wisdom or fairness."

Clement has managed to retain a stellar reputation among legal scholars from both parties despite his penchant for taking on cases that echo tenets of the Republican Party platform. Clement himself has acknowledged that he holds conservative views but insists that his caseload is more balanced than people make it out to be. Though he is often mentioned as a possible Supreme Court nominee for a Republican president, there are many who believe his caseload has been too partisan for him to be confirmed by a bipartisan Congress. "I do hope, at least for the profession, that it doesn't become disqualifying just to take on kind of unpopular clients," Clement told Totenberg, "because I think they're the entities that most need good representation in our system."

PERSONAL LIFE

Clement's wife, Alexandra, is a graduate of Harvard Business School. They have three sons, Thomas, Theodore, and Paul, and live in Alexandria, Virginia. Clement differs from other powerful lawyers in Washington in his idiosyncratic style. For instance, rather than suits, he wears khakis and oxfords at his office and frequently commutes to work by bicycle, wearing a yellow bike helmet with a Green Bay Packers logo. An admirer of alternative rock music, he regularly attends concerts at Washington's 9:30 club, and he told Kate Murphy for the *New York Times* (7 Apr. 2012) that he counted Nirvana and the Kooks among his favorite artists. In the same interview he named Norman Lewis and P. G. Wodehouse as go-to writers when he wasn't reading old Supreme Court decisions, law briefs, or *The Federalist Papers*.

SUGGESTED READING

McDonough, Molly. "Clement Has No Regrets Over Abrupt Exit from King & Spalding." *ABA Journal.* American Bar Association, 5 July 2011. Web. 16 August 2012.

Murphy, Kate. "Paul Clement." *New York Times Sunday Review.* New York Times Co., 7 Apr. 2012. Web. 16 Aug. 2012.

Sack, Kevin. "Lawyer Opposing Health Law Is Familiar Face to Justice." *New York Times.* New York Times Co., 26. Oct. 2011. Web. 16 Aug. 2012.

Singer, Natalie. "Defending Unpopular Positions Is What Lawyers Do: In an Era of Ideological Fencing, Paul Clement '92 Won't Be Fenced In." *Harvard Law Bulletin.* President and Fellows of Harvard College, Winter 2012. Web. 16 Aug. 2012.

Slater, Dan. "Paul Clement: The LeBron James of Law Firm Recruiting." *Wall Street Journal.* Dow Jones & Co., Inc., 27 Oct. 2008. Web. 16 August 2012.

Totenberg, Nina. "The Legal Wunderkind Challenging the Health Law." *NPR.* NPR, 23 Mar. 2012. Web. 16 Aug. 2012.

Zengerle, Jason. "The Paul Clement Court." *New York.* New York Media LLC, 18 Mar. 2012. Web. 16 Aug. 2012.

—Margaret Roush Mead

Kathy Cloninger

Born: June 24, 1951
Occupation: CEO of Girl Scouts of America

Kathy Cloninger, chairman emeritus and former chief executive officer (CEO) of the Girl Scouts of the USA (GSUSA), the head division of the nation's top leadership development organization for girls, is widely regarded as a foremost voice on issues affecting women and girls. A Girl Scout in her youth, Cloninger began her career in the social services sector in the 1970s, working as an executive with the Young Women's Christian Association (YWCA). After earning an MS from East Texas State University (now Texas A&M University-Commerce) in the early 1980s, Cloninger started working for the Girl Scouts, where she held various leadership roles, including serving as CEO of Girl Scout councils in Colorado, Texas, and Tennessee, before being appointed the eighteenth CEO of the organization in 2003.

During her eight-year tenure as Girl Scouts CEO, Cloninger overhauled the one-hundred-year-old organization to make it more relevant to girls in the twenty-first century and to expand its public image beyond the famous cookies it produces, which rake in more than $700 million in annual sales. She led efforts to better prepare girls for future leadership roles and became known for her deep commitment to diversity, establishing outreach programs to expand the scope of the Girl Scout experience in traditionally underserved communities.

In 2011 Cloninger stepped down as GSUSA CEO to retire, moving into the honorary role of chairman emeritus. That year she released the book *Tough Cookies: Leadership Lessons from 100 Years of the Girl Scouts* (coauthored with the freelance writer Fiona Soltes), which provides an overview of the Girl Scouts and its guiding principles. "I love listening to girls," she said in an interview for *Pride* (Fall 2010), the alumni magazine of Texas A&M University-Commerce. "Every morning I wake up wondering 'what's on the mind of young women?' It's important to not only find out what's on their mind, but to discover what the world looks like through their lens." She concluded, "girls need to listen to their inner voice that says, 'I am important, I can be somebody and I can make a difference in the world.' If they believe that, they will achieve amazing things."

EARLY LIFE AND EDUCATION

One of three daughters, Kathy Cloninger was born on June 24, 1951, and grew up in Dallas, Texas. Her father worked as a mid-level manager at Sears Roebuck and Co.; her mother worked as a secretary for the Internal Revenue Service (IRS) and later for the Bureau of Alcohol,

Getty Images

Tobacco, and Firearms. Cloninger's affiliation with the Girl Scouts began in the second grade when she joined a local troop led by her mother. Cloninger has said that being a Girl Scout helped bring her closer to her mother and provide her with an early leadership model, and it was an outlet for fun outdoor experiences and activities normally not available to low-income, working-class families like her own. She recalled to Sarah Seltzer for the website *Women's eNews* (3 Jan. 2010) that her family "couldn't afford much in [the] way of after-school activities, so scouting is the place where I got that girl energy and learned to connect in a sisterhood. It really did change my life." Cloninger fondly remembers traveling to South Padre Island, Texas, on her first Girl Scout trip, which her troop funded entirely through cookie sales. "The whole experience was empowering," she told Patricia R. Olsen for the *New York Times* (10 July 2005). "We were able to just be girls, we didn't have to worry about what any boys would think of us." Cloninger remained involved in the Girl Scouts as a member of her mother's troop until the sixth grade.

Cloninger attended Bryan Adams High School, in Dallas, Texas, where she excelled academically. She achieved straight As and consistently ranked among the top of her class in grade-point average. Nonetheless, by the time she completed high school in 1969, Cloninger was directionless. "I come from a family with no track record of attending college," she explained in the interview for *Pride*. "I never thought I had the option of going to a university after high school, and honestly the idea of it was intimidating." Following the advice of a guidance counselor, Cloninger enrolled in a secretarial school shortly after her high-school graduation but dropped out after only a few weeks. She started working as a waitress at a folk music coffeehouse in Dallas called the Rubaiyat, where she stayed for five years. During that time she took courses at El Centro Community College, in downtown Dallas. "At that point," Cloninger recalled in *Tough Cookies* (2011), "I wasn't focused on getting a college degree, nor on any particular life plan. Life seemed to be pulling me along, and the pulls were intriguing enough to follow."

While waitressing and taking community college courses, Cloninger broadened her interests to include politics and worked on the Texas gubernatorial campaigns of Frances "Sissy" Farenthold in 1972 and 1974. She eventually continued her education at the University of Texas Health Science Center in Dallas, and paid her tuition there with money earned from waitressing and other jobs. One of those jobs included serving as program director at a halfway house for women with mild mental disabilities. After earning a bachelor's degree in rehabilitation counseling from the University of Texas, Cloninger spent two years working at the Job Corps, where she served as a counselor to disadvantaged male youths. She then worked a series of other social service jobs, including serving as a vocational advisor, before being hired to run two YWCA branches in the Dallas–Fort Worth Metroplex area in the early 1980s. As a YWCA director, Cloninger ran child care and economic development programs and worked with troubled women in juvenile detention centers. During her time with the YWCA, she earned an MS degree in counseling and business management from what is now Texas A&M University-Commerce by attending classes during weekends.

EARLY CAREER WITH THE GIRL SCOUTS

Cloninger's career with the Girl Scouts began in 1983 when she answered an advertisement in the paper for a leadership position at the Mountain Prairie Girl Scout Council in Greeley, Colorado. She recalled in *Tough Cookies*, "I knew nothing about Girl Scouts except that it had been fun to be one as a girl. The job leading a small Girl Scout council serving northeast Colorado quickly began to change my life." Cloninger served as CEO of the Greeley council for two years, during which she traveled around the country participating in Girl Scout–sanctioned think tanks and committees, learning invaluable business and leadership skills. It was also during this time that she met the pioneering nonprofit leader Frances Hesselbein, who was then serving as the CEO of Girl Scouts. Hesselbein headed the Girl Scouts from 1976 until 1990, and she is credited with

ushering the organization into the modern era, increasing the number of minority members, and launching the Daisy Scout program for kindergartners and first-graders. Hesselbein later became the founder, president, and CEO of the Leader to Leader Institute (formerly the Peter F. Drucker Foundation), which she currently runs. Cloninger explained in her interview for *Pride* that it was Hesselbein's "wise counsel and behind-the-scenes support" that gave her the confidence and courage to pursue greater leadership roles within the organization.

In 1986 Cloninger returned to Dallas to work as a national management consultant for the GSUSA, where she spent a year guiding and advising small Girl Scout councils in Arkansas, Kansas, and Oklahoma. She was then hired to run the San Antonio Area Council of Girl Scouts, which prospered under her leadership. In 1991 Cloninger left the Girl Scouts to accept a position with the W. K. Kellogg Foundation in Battle Creek, Michigan, as an executive grantmaker. She held that role for the next two years. Though the position paid well and offered her new career opportunities, Cloninger has said that the Kellogg job was not a good fit for her and that she ultimately missed being a part of an organization led by women. She returned to the Girl Scouts in 1993, when she became CEO of the Girl Scout Council of Cumberland Valley in Nashville, Tennessee. In *Tough Cookies*, Cloninger wrote, "Leaving Kellogg and going back to being a Girl Scout council CEO . . . [meant] a major pay cut and a return to local, not national work. But it absolutely felt like the right move."

As head of the Cumberland Valley council, a position she held for ten years until 2003, Cloninger oversaw girls from thirty-eight of the ninety-five counties in Tennessee. During her tenure she helped increase membership by 38 percent, from 18,000 to more than 25,000, and she implemented community outreach projects aimed at attracting minority and underprivileged girls. These projects included creating an "innovation team," which successfully led efforts to make the Girl Scouts more prominent in and accessible to African American and Hispanic communities as well as to girls living in public housing. "Our team knocked on doors, talked to girls and parents, used a grassroots approach," Cloninger recalled on the Girl Scouts website. "These families had never been approached before. So we made a commitment to these relationships." In 2000 Cloninger was named Nonprofit CEO of the Year by the Center for Nonprofit Management and she was honored with the National Conference of Community and Justice (NCCJ) Human Relations Award for her outreach efforts. While serving as Cumberland Valley CEO, she cofounded Tennessee's Association of Nonprofit Executives and served as a director of the Center for Nonprofit Management, Leadership

Nashville, and the United Way of Metropolitan Nashville.

CEO OF GSUSA

Cloninger had no intentions of becoming CEO of the Girl Scouts of the USA, when its head, Marsha Johnson Evans, resigned to become president and CEO of the Red Cross in 2002. However, after an unsuccessful months-long search for a replacement, she was contacted by the GSUSA's national search committee, which asked her to consider applying for the position. Despite the many challenges the job presented and despite having doubts about her own qualifications, Cloninger, at the urging of Frances Hesselbein, agreed to apply. She told Seltzer, "[w]hen I had the opportunity to come to a national leadership role, I thought, 'I've known the impact it has on girls on a community level, but I don't know if the world knows that.'" Cloninger was soon hired on the basis of her expansive leadership experience and appointed the eighteenth CEO of the GSUSA, officially stepping into the role in October 2003. In the process she became only the second council CEO (after Hesselbein) to be promoted directly to the top spot and one of just a handful of leaders to be hired from within the organization. Several months after her hiring, former Girl Scout president Cynthia B. Thompson spoke of Cloninger's "warm and inclusive management style, her skill at partnering and her deep commitment to diversity and Girl Scouting," as quoted on the official Girl Scouts website.

GIRL SCOUTS IN THE TWENTY-FIRST CENTURY

Founded in 1912 in Savannah, Georgia, by Juliette Gordon Low (1860–1927) as the women's counterpart to the Boy Scouts, the Girl Scouts started with a troop of eighteen girls but has since grown into the largest leadership development and educational organization for girls in the world, with more than ten million members in 145 countries worldwide. As head of the New York City–based GSUSA, the largest member organization of the World Association of Girl Guides and Girl Scouts (WAGGGS) and parent organization all national Girl Scout councils, Cloninger represented nearly one-third of those members and nearly one million more adult volunteers. Soon after becoming GSUSA CEO, she launched a massive overhaul of the organization to keep it relevant for girls in the twenty-first century in the wake of declining membership and changing demographics. She revamped the GSUSA's business model to focus on girl-centered leadership and led the first national restructuring of the organization since its founding, consolidating the number of Girl Scout councils to create a more streamlined and efficient corporate structure. She also "threw out the old handbooks, dramatically redesigned

them, and overhauled the badges," as she noted to Jenna Goudreau for *Forbes.com* (7 Nov. 2011), and she then unveiled new badges covering such fields as science, technology, engineering, and math. In an undated interview with the nonprofit organization Business Innovation Factory (BIF), Cloninger said, "The first question we asked is, what is it that we are best in the world at? We discovered that we were very fragmented. We are concerned about esteem, environmental issues, community service and character building. But our clear focus is that we are a leadership organization. We are very concerned about getting girls into leadership roles right now."

Among Cloninger's other initiatives as GSUSA CEO, she has focused on diversity and pluralism. Her tenure saw the development of numerous outreach programs that helped bring the Girl Scout experience to girls in minority and low-income neighborhoods, homeless shelters, and juvenile detention centers. Cloninger also launched a national brand campaign and a wide variety of programs geared toward preparing girls for future leadership roles. She has said that the Girls Scouts' annual cookie sale is one of the top early leadership experiences for girls in the United States and much more than simply selling tasteful varieties of cookies. "The cookie sale is the best financial literacy training program and best business entrepreneurship program for girls in the country," she told David Mielach for the online business resource BusinessNewsDaily (18 Oct. 2011). "The girls have to set a sales goal, have a plan to diversify their customer base, invest money over the long term and, most importantly, work with teams of people to get the job done and achieve success." Each year nearly two hundred million boxes of Girl Scout cookies are sold, generating over $700 million in annual sales.

RETIRED BUT STILL INVOLVED

In October 2011, Cloninger published the book *Tough Cookies: Leadership Lessons from 100 Years of the Girl Scouts*, which chronicles her nearly three decades of experience with the Girl Scouts. It also provides a background and history of the organization and offers a guide to becoming a successful female leader. The following month, Cloninger stepped down as CEO of the GSUSA to retire after serving at the helm for eight years. She was appointed to the honorary position of chairman emeritus, and she continues to work toward empowering girls. Cloninger's replacement, Anna Maria Chávez, former head of the Girl Scouts of Southwest Texas, is of Mexican American heritage and is the first woman of color to lead the organization.

On March 12, 2012, the GSUSA honored the one-hundredth anniversary of its founding by Juliette Low with celebratory events all over the country. The following month President

Barack Obama posthumously awarded Low the Presidential Medal of Freedom, the nation's highest civilian award, for her lasting contribution to girls around the world. Since the founding of GSUSA, more than fifty million alumnae have gone on to make a significant impact on the world: over 70 percent of female elected officials, 70 percent of female executives, and 100 percent of female astronauts were former Girl Scouts. However, with female CEOs currently representing just a little more than three percent of Fortune 500 companies, Cloninger hopes leadership organizations like the Girl Scouts will reverse such trends in the future. She explained to Goudreau, "[w]e define leadership in this country with a pretty narrow, masculine lens: strong, powerful, top-down, decisive, tough. In our research, girls and women are saying leadership is more collaborative and is striving to make a difference in the greater world while we're also serving the company. . . . In Girl Scouts we're focusing on helping girls start out from the beginning believing in themselves and developing strong confidence, life skills, integrity and values. We can do a lot to help girls, but at some point the rest of the world has to step up and help."

Cloninger is a member of the board of directors of American Humanics and the National Assembly of Human Services. She also serves on the advisory boards of the National Association of Corporate Boards, See Jane, and America's Promise. In 2007 she received the Award for Excellence in National Executive Leadership from the National Human Services Assembly and was listed in the *Nonprofit Times* as one of the fifty most powerful and influential people in nonprofits.

Cloninger is married to the folk singer-songwriter Mike Williams, whom she first met while working as a waitress at the Rubaiyat. They live in the West Meade neighborhood of Nashville. Both are avid country music fans and have hosted hundreds of music gatherings at their home.

SUGGESTED READING

Cloninger, Kathy, and Fiona Soltes. *Tough Cookies: Leadership Lessons from 100 Years of the Girl Scouts.* Hoboken: Wiley, 2011. Print.

"Dream Big." *Pride Alumni Magazine* (Fall 2010): 24–25. Print.

Goudreau, Jenna. "One Tough Cookie: Girl Scouts CEO Kathy Cloninger on Selling Women's Leadership." *Forbes.com.* Forbes.com LLC, 7 Nov. 2011. Web. 23 July 2012.

"Kathy Cloninger." *Businessinnovationfactory.com.* Business Innovation Factory, 2005–11. Web. 23 July 2012.

"Meet Kathy Cloninger: Chief Executive Officer." *Girlscouts.org.* Girl Scouts of the USA, 2012. Web. 23 July 2012.

Mielach, David. "Smart Cookies: 5 Handy Business Lessons from the Girl Scouts." *Busniessnewsdaily.com.* TechMediaNetwork.com, 18 Oct. 2011. Web. 23 July 2012.

Olsen, Patricia R. "Beyond the Cookie Sale." *Nytimes.com.* New York Times Co., 10 July 2005. Web. 23 July 2012.

Seltzer, Sarah. "2010—Seven Who Invent a Better Future." *Womensenews.org.* Women's eNews Inc., 3 Jan. 2010. Web. 23 July 2012.

—*Chris Cullen*

Lyor Cohen

Born: October 3, 1959
Occupation: North American Chairman and CEO of Recorded Music for Warner Music Group (WMG)

Rick Rubin, the cofounder of Def Jam Records, described the label's former CEO, Lyor Cohen, to Tim Arango for the *New York Post* (1 Feb. 2004): "I think Lyor knows how to connect with artists and sell records better than anyone in the business." Cohen first made his mark in the world of hip-hop as the tour manager for the pioneering group Run-D.M.C. His strategy of generating buzz through an innovative use of street marketing helped the band achieve mainstream status and helped to put Def Jam on the map. As a partner at Def Jam, Cohen became a guiding force behind the careers of many popular rappers, such as Jay-Z, Ja Rule, and DMX. Cohen showed himself to be equally adept at representing artists from other musical genres as head of the Island Def Jam Music Group. Since joining the Warner Music Group in 2004, Cohen has been at the forefront of the company's shift to digital music markets, while also serving as an advocate for new artists.

EARLY LIFE AND CAREER

Lyor Cohen was born on October 3, 1959, in New York City. He is one of two children of Elisha Cohen and Ziva Sirkis. Cohen's parents, both Israeli Jews, met during Israel's 1948 War of Independence. His father was hospitalized with an eye wound while serving in the Palmach, an elite fighting unit under the command of Yitzhak Rabin, and his mother was the nurse assigned to care for him. After moving to New York City in the 1950s, Elisha Cohen worked as a security guard at the Israeli consulate while studying mechanical engineering. By the time Cohen was three years old, his parents had divorced, and he went to live with his mother in Los Angeles, where she worked as a paralegal and cofounded the nonprofit firm Levitt and Quinn Family Law Center. At the time, Sirkis was remarried to

FilmMagic

Phillip Shulman, a psychiatrist, with whom she had two children, Daniel and Motti Shulman. At age thirteen, Cohen first developed a love for hip-hop music while visiting his older brother, Harel, a teacher at a South Central Los Angeles high school, where he would attend basketball games. During half time, he would listen to live musicians playing drum sets and bass in a kind of early form of hip-hop. "I knew something important had happened," he told David Lipsky for *W* magazine (Oct. 2011).

After graduating from John Marshall High School in 1977, Cohen studied global marketing and finance at the University of Miami's School of Business in Coral Gables, Florida. Upon receiving his bachelor's degree in business administration in 1981, the aspiring entrepreneur spent time in Ecuador and made an unsuccessful attempt at launching a shrimp farming enterprise. In the wake of his failure, Cohen returned to Los Angeles and accepted a position as a financial analyst at the Beverly Hills branch of Bank Leumi, one of Israel's leading banking institutions.

FROM RUN-D.M.C. TO DEF JAM

While working at Bank Leumi, Cohen came up with the idea of borrowing $700 from his mother to organize a concert featuring rap and punk rock groups. "I found out this one radio DJ was putting 20,000 kids into a municipal arena, just to listen to hip-hop. But the authorities didn't like 20,000 African-American kids together, so they shut it down at eleven sharp," he told Tom

Horan for the London *Telegraph* (21 Sep. 2002). "I figured, they're over by eleven, let me bring the artists to Hollywood afterwards." Among the local rock bands scheduled to perform were Social Distortion, the Circle Jerks, Fishbone, and the Red Hot Chili Peppers. The popular New York rap trio Run-D.M.C. was selected as the headline act. Cohen arranged for the concert to be held at the Stardust Ballroom on Sunset Boulevard, and the event was a hit, grossing $36,000—more than fifty times the original investment. Although Cohen had considerably less success promoting his second show, which featured the hip-hop group Whodini as the headliner, he resigned from his banking job to join Rush Productions, a New York City–based artist management company owned by Russell Simmons, the older brother of Run-D.M.C. member Joseph Simmons.

After moving to the Big Apple in the early 1980s, Cohen quickly made his mark. "So I arrive in New York to join the company," he recalled to Horan. "But when I get to the office, which is the size of this table, everyone's depressed. Run DMC are due to play London, the tour manager has gone AWOL and no one else has a passport. So I go back to the airport, meet the band, say 'Hi, I'm Lyor, I'm the new tour manager.'" In his new role, Cohen proved adept at managing crises. Shortly before Run-D.M.C.'s first show in London—a sold-out gig at the Electric Ballroom venue—he was approached by Jam Master Jay, the group's DJ, who informed Cohen that he had left his collection of vinyl records at the hotel. (Jam Master Jay would manipulate the records on a turntable to create the scratching sound that defined Run-D.M.C.'s signature sound.) "Suddenly it comes to me. I go out on stage: 'A lot of you been asking for autographs, but we have to prioritize here. So anyone with records to sign, pass them to the front,'" he told Horan. "The crowd [passed] a dozen 12-inch singles to the front and we use them to play the show. That's when I earned respect from Run DMC."

Spending the next three years as Run-D.M.C.'s tour manager, Cohen was also instrumental in promoting the group's music, which was not receiving radio airplay, through an innovative marketing strategy. "What did we do? We went into the parking lot and put fliers on everyone's windshields. We were the first street team," Cohen told Phyllis Furman for the *New York Daily News* (17 May 1999). Other promotional techniques included posting fliers on telephone poles and the sides of buildings.

Cohen negotiated the group's endorsement deal, the first such deal for a hip-hop act. In 1986, following the release of "My Adidas," the first single from their third album, *Raising Hell*, Cohen invited the Adidas's head of US marketing to one of the group's concerts at Madison Square Garden in New York City. During the performance of the song, the fans in the audience held their Adidas sneakers above their heads; as a result, the group signed a lucrative million-dollar contract to publicize the sneakers. At the time, Cohen was overseeing the Raising Hell tour, which showcased rap artists signed to Def Jam Recordings, a music label cofounded by Russell Simmons and Rick Rubin. These artists included the Beastie Boys, Public Enemy, and LL Cool J. Run-D.M.C. made history in December 1986, becoming the first rappers to appear on the cover of *Rolling Stone*. In 1987, Cohen was in charge of supervising a tour that headlined Run-D.M.C. and the Beastie Boys and was dubbed as the "Together Forever" tour.

One year later, after Rubin left Def Jam Recordings to launch his own record company, Simmons named Cohen as the president of the label. In his new role, Cohen signed several acts to the Def Jam roster, including the rapper Slick Rick, the interracial hip-hop trio 3rd Bass, and the rap duo EPMD.

FROM BANKRUPTCY TO PROFITABILITY

Also in 1988, the Def Jam label entered into a joint venture deal with Sony. Under the terms of the agreement, Sony provided Def Jam with cash—in the form of larger advances, higher royalties, and money to hire more staff—and in turn received a 50 percent stake in Simmons's label. "Our joint venture was, on paper, a fifty-fifty deal with Sony. But in reality the numbers were slanted their way. It was only fifty-fifty after they took 30 percent off the top," Simmons recalled in his 2001 autobiography *Life and Def: Sex, Drugs, Money, and God*.

In 1990, Cohen teamed up with Simmons to create Rush Associated Labels, a subsidiary of Def Jam Recordings comprised of several different labels formed by various artists and producers on the Def Jam Recordings roster. Record labels under the Rush umbrella included JMJ Records, an imprint founded by Jam Master Jay, and P.R.O. Division, founded by Chuck D. of the rap group Public Enemy. "We attempted to replicate the Sony structure with us being the mother label to several smaller ones, but all of them were unsuccessful," Simmons wrote. "But it was very difficult to put out those records and assist them with the limited resources we had. . . . Instead of being a new source of revenue, the labels were a drain. Eventually we folded them."

In 1994, after a falling-out with Sony, the Dutch entertainment company PolyGram paid over $30 million to acquire Sony's 50 percent interest in Def Jam Recordings, which was on the verge of financial bankruptcy. Over the next few years, the label's fortunes began to improve, largely due to several successful signings by Cohen. These included West Coast rapper Warren G, whose album *Warren G's Regulate . . . G Funk Era* (1994) sold three million copies

domestically, and New York rapper Foxy Brown, whose 1996 debut album *Ill Na Na* achieved platinum status in the United States.

With the help of Def Jam A&R executive Irving Lorenzo Jr. (known professionally as Irv Gotti), Cohen made two other major signings, both of which hail from the Big Apple: Jay-Z, whose 1997 album *In My Lifetime, Vol. 1* went platinum stateside, and DMX, who impressed Cohen during his audition despite his jaw being wired shut. DMX's 1998 debut *It's Dark and Hell Is Hot* sold four million copies in the United States. Cohen's unconventional strategy of releasing DMX's sophomore record in the same calendar year paid off: in the States, *Flesh of My Flesh, Blood of My Blood* went triple platinum. In the same year, Jay-Z's third studio album and his second on the Def Jam label, *Vol. 2 . . . Hard Knock Life*, reached the top of Billboard's 200 chart, sold more than five million copies domestically, and, in 1999, earned a Grammy Award. Cohen oversaw Jay-Z's Hard Knock Life tour, one of rap's most successful tours.

In December 1998, the Seagram Company's Universal Music Group, impressed by the label's annual revenues and profits ($180 million in sales and $40 million in profits), purchased PolyGram's interest in Def Jam. The following February, Seagram bought Cohen's and Simmons's stakes in Def Jam for a reported $100 million (other sources listing the amount at $130 million).

TAKING THE REINS AT ISLAND DEF JAM

Subsequent to the buyout, Cohen was named copresident of the Island Def Jam Music Group, which is comprised of Island Records, Def Jam Recordings, and Mercury Records. In his newly expanded role at Island Def Jam, Cohen inherited a roster that included Def Jam artists as well as performers from outside the hip-hop genre, including pop icon Elton John; singer-songwriters Melissa Etheridge, Elvis Costello, and Ryan Adams; country artists Shania Twain and Willie Nelson; the rock groups Bon Jovi and Nickelback; and the heavy metal band Slipknot. During the late 1990s, Cohen also partnered with Gotti to launch the Murder Inc. record label, a joint venture.

In an effort to boost the sales of new albums, Cohen came up with the idea of slashing prices during the first week of an album's release and raising them the following week—a strategy that has since become common practice in the music industry. To promote the label's diverse roster and raise its global profile, Cohen launched several sub-labels: Def Soul Recordings, an imprint devoted to rhythm and blues; Def Jam South, another imprint geared toward Southern rap artists, such as Ludacris; Def Jam Japan, whose roster included Teriyaki Boyz and Nitro Microphone Underground; and Def Jam Germany, whose roster included local rappers Spezializtz and Philly MC.

Cohen made headlines in May 2002 when he signed pop singer Mariah Carey to a three-album deal worth $20 million. EMI had bought out Carey's contract following her nervous breakdown and the disappointing sales of the *Glitter* soundtrack (2001). "I never once looked at Mariah as washed up," Cohen told Chuck Philips for the *Los Angeles Times* (9 May 2002). "I've always viewed her as this amazing artist—a great singer and a great songwriter. We were dying to sign her." Other notable additions during the early 2000s included the rock bands Sum 41 and Hoobastank, as well as Everlast, a white rapper turned singer-songwriter. Among Cohen's successes were releases from artists on the Murder Inc. label, most notably Ja Rule, whose platinum-selling debut *Venni Vetti Vecci* (1999) was eclipsed by the triple-platinum albums *Rule 3:36* (2000) and *Pain Is Love* (2001); and Ashanti, who followed up her 2002 eponymous debut with the double-platinum *Chapter II* (2003).

LEGAL TROUBLES

Cohen's tenure with the Island Def Jam Music Group was not without controversy. After signing the R and B group 112 in July 2002, he received a temporary restraining order from Sean "Puffy" Combs, the founder of the group's label Bad Boy Records. Combs contended that 112 was still signed to his label. The dispute was eventually settled, with both labels deciding to jointly promote and market the quartet and split the profits from their future recordings. Bad Boy Records would retain the rights to the song catalog from their first three albums, and Island Def Jam would be responsible for their distribution of the catalog.

In 2002, Cohen found himself at the center of a lawsuit filed by Steve Gottlieb, founder of the New York–based independent label TVT Records. The suit maintained that TVT Records had obtained verbal permission from Cohen to collaborate with Ja Rule, a former TVT artist, and Irv Gotti, a former scout at the label, on an album of new and unreleased material from Cash Money Click, Ja Rule's former group. Gottlieb further alleged that TVT had agreed to provide Island Def Jam with a cut of the album's profits. According to Gottlieb, Cohen blocked the deal months prior to the album's November 2002 release date, in anticipation of Ja Rule's upcoming Def Jam record, which was also scheduled to be released around that time. Gottlieb claimed that Cohen initially had consented in an attempt to appease Gotti in order to facilitate the renegotiation of Gotti's contract.

In March 2003, a federal jury ruled in favor of TVT Records, ordering Island Def Jam to pay $132 million in total—$24 million in compensation and $108 million in punitive damages; they also held Cohen personally liable for $56 million of that amount. In September 2003, following a first appeal by Cohen and the Island Def Jam Music Group, a US District Court judge reduced the total jury award to $53 million, of which Cohen was ordered to pay $3 million. Cohen had greater success with his second appeal. In June 2005, a US appellate court, citing insufficient evidence, overturned the $53 million judgment, instead granting TVT Records $126,720 for breach of contract.

Cohen came under scrutiny in early 2003, after the FBI raided the offices of Murder Inc. Records as part of an investigation regarding Gotti's relationship with his longtime friend Kenneth "Supreme" McGriff, a drug kingpin. Gotti was investigated on allegations that he used his record label for money laundering, drug trafficking, and gang activities. He was acquitted in December 2005 due to lack of evidence.

WARNER MUSIC GROUP

By 2004, Cohen had left Island Def Jam Music Group and accepted a position with the recently acquired Warner Music Group (WMG) as the chairman and chief executive officer in charge of the label's US recorded music division. Cohen spearheaded the company's shift from physical formats to digital music. "The CD made us sleepy . . . A lot of people got rich and nobody wanted it to stop," Cohen told Joel Brown for *Billboard.biz* (27 Apr. 2011). "The hustle of having one hit and locking it up on a $19 CD . . . was not consumer friendly." Additionally, Cohen has been a proponent of the 360 record deal. In the words of Jeff Leeds for the *New York Times* (11 Nov. 2007), the 360 record deal is "a rising new model for developing talent, one in which artists share not just revenue from their album sales but concert, merchandise and other earnings with their label in exchange for more comprehensive career support."

Within three years, WMG moved up the ranks from the fourth-largest to the third-largest recorded music and music publishing company in the world. Cohen's division also had the company's highest US album share in a decade for the fiscal years 2007 and 2008. In 2008, Cohen was named the chairman and CEO of WMG's recorded music division in North America, vice chairman of WMG, and chairman and CEO of the recorded music division in the Americas and the United Kingdom. WMG reached another milestone in November 2008 when their Atlantic Records label became the first to have its digital revenues in the United States eclipse its physical sales; it was also the first record company whose digital products (iTunes downloads and cell phone ringtones, for example) comprised more than half of its US music sales. In 2009, Atlantic Records was ranked first in the digital album market, with a share of nearly 8.5 percent.

Since July 20, 2011, Cohen has served as the director and the chairman and CEO of Recorded Music of Warner Music Group. In 2012, he ranked in the top fifty of *Billboard*'s annual Power 100 list.

Cohen lives in New York City and has two children, Az and Bea, from his marriage to Amy Cohen, whom he divorced in 2006. He is currently in a relationship with Tory Burch, a fashion designer.

SUGGESTED READING

Arango, Tim. "Lyor's Poker; Music Big Cohen Makes Risky Move to Warner." *New York Post*. NYP Holdings, 1 Feb. 2004. Web. 9 July 2012.

Fitzgerald, Michael. "Take Us to the River." *Fast Company*. Mansueto Ventures, 1 July 2010. Web. 8 June 2012.

Leeds, Jeff. "The New Deal: Band as Brand." *New York Times*. New York Times Co., 11 Nov. 2007. Web. 8 June 2012.

Lipsky, David. "Lyor's Got Game." *W* magazine. Conde Nast, Oct. 2011. Web. 2 June 2012.

Murray, Sonia. "Street Marketing Does the Trick." *Advertising Age*. Crain Communications, 20 Mar. 2000. Web. 10 June 2012.

Simmons, Russell, and Nelson George. *Life and Def: Sex, Drugs, Money, and God*. New York: Crown, 2001.

—*Bertha Muteba*

Suzanne Collins

Born: 1962
Occupation: Television writer and novelist

Children's fiction author Suzanne Collins is best known for her imaginative, fantastical book *The Hunger Games* (2008), as well as its sequels, *Catching Fire* (2009) and *Mockingjay* (2010). Set in a future dystopia, the books tell the story of Katniss Everdeen, a sixteen-year-old girl who takes part in a fight-to-the-death competition put on by the ruling class of Panem, the totalitarian state that now covers North America. All three books in the series became best sellers, received generally glowing reviews, and were placed on best-of lists by the *New York Times*, the *Los Angeles Times*, *Time* magazine, and other publications. In 2010 Collins was put on *Time* magazine's list of the 100 most influential people in the world. In 2012 the film version of *The Hunger Games* (Collins cowrote the screenplay) came out in theaters. The book trilogy has been translated into many languages and has also been a best seller as an e-book. Collins is also

Wirelmage

the author of the Underland Chronicles, a series of five books for middle school students. Prior to becoming an author, Collins wrote for children's television programs.

EARLY YEARS

The youngest of four children—she has two older sisters and an older brother—Suzanne Collins was born in 1962 into a military family that moved around often. Her father served in the US Air Force; he also held a doctorate in political science. When Collins was a young child, her father had a stint teaching military history at the United States Military Academy at West Point in upstate New York. When Collins was about six years old, the family moved yet again, this time to Indiana. That year, her father was deployed to fight in the Vietnam War. When he returned a year later, he was a changed man. In an interview with Susan Dominus for the *New York Times* (8 Apr. 2011), Collins recalled how after coming back from Vietnam her father had ongoing "nightmares, and that lasted his whole life." Sometimes she would wake up and hear him crying out in his sleep.

However, because of her father, Collins was exposed to military history. When Collins was about twelve years old, the family moved to Brussels, Belgium, where, Dominus writes, her father took the children to see battlefields and monuments and spoke often of both World Wars. "He was very interesting, fortunately," Collins recalled. "My God, it would have been hell if he wasn't." He would also tell stories of his childhood during the Great Depression, when he and his family would hunt so that they could eat. All these stories—the hunting, the military history, battle strategies, and the like—would decades later inform Collins's books, particularly the Hunger Games series.

Like many children, Collins also spent time hanging out with her friends; she also did gymnastics and read books. During her teen years, she read such classics as Betty Smith's *A Tree Grows in Brooklyn*, George Orwell's *1984*, William Golding's *Lord of the Flies*, and Ray Bradbury's *Dandelion Wine*. In 1980 she graduated from high school at the Alabama School of Fine Arts in Birmingham.

HIGHER EDUCATION AND WRITING

Following high school, Collins attended Indiana University's College of Arts and Sciences, where she pursued a double major in telecommunications and theater. There, she met her future husband, Cap Pryor. She received her bachelor's degree in 1985. She and Pryor moved to New York City, where she pursued a master of fine arts degree in dramatic writing at New York University.

In the early 1990s, Collins started writing for children's television programs. She started out by writing a few episodes for the Nickelodeon show *Clarissa Explains It All*, and later for *The Mystery Files of Shelby Woo* on the same network. She also wrote a few episodes of *Little Bear*, for preschool-age viewers, and the Christmas special *Santa, Baby!* (2001), as well as *Clifford's Puppy Days*, *Generation O!*, and *Wow! Wow! Wubbzy!*

THE UNDERLAND CHRONICLES

Collins was encouraged to write books for children by James Proimos, a children's author, with whom she was working on *Generation O!* from 2000 to 2001. Collins was living in New York City at the time, which got her thinking about a kind of gritty version of *Alice in Wonderland*— about fantastical worlds behind real city dangers such as manholes and rodents. This led her to imagine a world that would become the Underland Chronicles, the first volume of which was titled *Gregor the Overlander* (2003). The book, written for middle school students, features Gregor, a New York City kid, as its hero. After the boy's young sister, Boots, falls into an air duct in a laundry room, Gregor jumps in after her, and they end up in another world, called the Underland. As it turns out, that world had a prophecy that predicted the boy's coming. In that world he encounters rats, cockroaches, bats, and human beings with violet eyes. This story of fantasy and adventure was listed as a 2003 Editor's Choice by Kirkus Reviews and received the 2004 children's novel award from the New Atlantic Independent Bookseller's Association (NAIBA). It was also put on the New York Public Library's 100 Titles for Reading and Sharing list.

The second volume in the series, *Gregor and the Prophecy of Bane* (2004), continues the story of eleven-year-old Gregor. This time his young sister, Boots, is abducted by giant cockroaches, so he once again goes into the Underland to save her. A giant white rat named Bane is out to get her, and Gregor is expected not only to save his sister but also to defeat the rat. *Gregor and the Prophecy of Bane* was a children's literature finalist for the 2005 Connecticut Book Award. The end of the book left plenty of room for a sequel.

The third volume, *Gregor and the Curse of the Warmbloods* (2005), again finds Gregor and Boots in the Underworld, where there is a prophecy—the Curse of the Warmbloods—that threatens to wreak havoc on the Underland's mammals. As before, rats and bats occupy this strange world, and friendships and rivalries are a matter of life and death. The book received the 2006 Oppenheim Toy Portfolio Gold Award.

Volume four, *Gregor and the Marks of Secret* (2006), continues to develop Gregor's character, as he and Queen Luxa go looking for answers as to why the mice are disappearing. Gregor eventually discovers a secret, the resolution of which comes in the final installment of the Underground Chronicles, titled *Gregor and the Code of Claw* (2007). It turns out, according to the Prophecy of Time, that Gregor has been destined to die—a fate he must fight against. He is helped in his adventures by his rat friend, Ripred, and his bright sister Lizzie. Aside from Gregor's life, the fate of the mice is also on the line. In the book, as in the other books of the series, Collins does not shy away from themes of war, violence, and loss.

THE HUNGER GAMES
The following year saw the publication of *The Hunger Games* (2008), the first volume of a series that would make Collins a star of the young-adult fiction world. Unlike the adventures of Gregor, the Hunger Games series is intended for slightly older students—ages twelve and up. Yet, like the Harry Potter series, these books are also read by some adults. *The Hunger Games* is set sometime in the future in a world where most people live in poverty. The poor reside in one of twelve districts, where they primarily do manual labor, whereas the ruling class lives in the Capitol, a lavish city. Once a year a lottery is held: Two children between the ages of twelve and eighteen are selected from each district for the Hunger Games, a televised spectacle in which twenty-four children fight to the death in a large, landscaped arena. The book's main character is Katniss Everdeen, a sixteen-year-old girl who volunteers to fight in the Hunger Games so that her younger sister, who was selected in the lottery, does not have to go.

Once selected, the kids are pulled from their poverty and treated like reality-television stars;

they are also well fed and lavishly clothed. Katniss, growing up in District 12, had become a very good hunter as a matter of survival; and when it comes to the bloody Games, Katniss puts her skills to use. She does what she must to survive. This disturbing, imaginative book received many positive reviews. "Whereas Katniss kills with finesse, Collins writes with raw power," Lev Grossman wrote for *Time* magazine (7 Sep. 2009). "After a life spent in freezing poverty, Katniss experiences pleasure—warmth, food, pretty clothes—with almost unbearable intensity, and that's where Collins' writing comes alive. (Not sex, though. *The Hunger Games* isn't just chaste, like *Twilight*; it's oddly non-erotic.) Likewise, Collins brings a cold, furious clarity to her accounts of physical violence. You might not think it would be possible, or desirable, for a young-adult writer to describe, slowly and in full focus, a teenage girl getting stung to death by a swarm of mutant hornets. It wasn't, until Collins did it. But rather than being repellent, the violence is strangely hypnotic. It's fairytale violence, Brothers Grimm violence—not a cheap thrill but a symbol of something deeper." The book became a best seller and was listed as one the best children's fiction books of 2008 by many organizations and publications, including the *New York Times*, the *Los Angeles Times*, the Barnes & Noble bookstore, and the New York Public Library.

ALLEGORY OR WAR STORY?

As the book's popularity soared, there was more discussion as to its message. Collins made no secret of the fact that the idea for the book came to her when she was watching television, flipping between footage of the Iraq War and some reality television show. In her *New Yorker* (14 June 2010) essay on dystopian fiction for young adult readers, Laura Miller made the case that the book "is not an argument," meaning it is not an indictment of war or reality television. For one thing, Miller wrote, "as a tool of practical propaganda, the games don't make much sense. They lack that essential quality of the totalitarian spectacle: ideological coherence. You don't demoralize and dehumanize a subject people by turning them into celebrities and coaching them on how to craft an appealing persona for a mass audience."

Miller then went on to give her interpretation of what the book is all about: "If, on the other hand, you consider the games as a feverdream allegory of the adolescent social experience, they become perfectly intelligible. Adults dump teenagers into the viper pit of high school, spouting a lot of sentimental drivel about what a wonderful stage of life it's supposed to be. The rules are arbitrary, unfathomable, and subject to sudden change. A brutal social hierarchy prevails, with the rich, the good-looking, and the

athletic lording their advantages over everyone else. . . . Everyone's always watching you, scrutinizing your clothes or your friends and obsessing over whether you're having sex or taking drugs or getting good enough grades, but no one cares who you really are or how you really feel about anything." Simply put, Miller views the Games as a metaphor for high school.

However, in a rare profile of the media-shy author for the *New York Times* (8 Apr. 2011), Susan Dominus observed that although many *Hunger Games* readers see the book "through this prism," Collins herself does not. "I don't write about adolescence," Collins told Dominus. "I write about war. For adolescents."

CATCHING FIRE

The second book in the Hunger Games series, *Catching Fire* (2009), came out one year after the first one. This time it was met with a great deal of expectation. The first installment of the series ends with Katniss as the winner of the Games, so in *Catching Fire* she and Peeta, a boy from her district that she might have feelings for, travel on a sort of victory tour throughout all twelve districts in the land—which is how Katniss learns that the world is even more sinister than it appears. She learns that the very district she once called home is in danger. In a review for the *New York Times* (11 Oct. 2009), Gabrielle Zevin sang the book's praises, saying she loves it even more than the first. Zevin also pointed out that the book's hero is a "real girl," because she does not have any superpowers. "Katniss is more sophisticated in this book, and her observations are more acute," Zevin wrote. "We see this when she notices how much more difficult it is to kill people once you know them, or when she observes the decadent (and for the reader perhaps uncomfortably familiar) citizens of the Capitol gorging and then taking pills to make themselves vomit, or with her gradual realization that she may just stand for something greater than herself. All this is accomplished with the light touch of a writer who truly understands writing for young people: the pacing is brisk and the message tucked below the surface." The book became a best seller and was listed as one of the best children's fiction books of 2009 by various publications, including *People*, *Publisher's Weekly*, *Time*, the *Los Angeles Times*, and the *New York Times*.

MOCKINGJAY

The third installment in the series, *Mockingjay* (2010), was well received both by fans and critics alike. At the beginning of the book, Katniss walks the streets of District 12, looking at the rubble and burned human remains. Most of the people are dead. The few that remain alive have gone off to live in District 13, which is full of revolutionaries who are intent on overthrowing the government and its evil leader, President Snow. The rebels want Katniss, who is now seventeen years old, to help them in their revolution. Like Katniss, they are morally complex, with various motivations. Also in this book, Katniss finally decides between her romantic interests, Peeta and Gale. In a review of the book for the *Los Angeles Times* (23 Aug. 2010), Susan Carpenter wrote, "Unfolding in Collins' engaging, intelligent prose and assembled into chapters that end with didn't-see-that-coming cliffhangers, this finale is every bit the pressure cooker of its forebears. Where *The Hunger Games* set the stage for the unusual post-apocalyptic world in which Katniss first rose up from her inconsequential and impoverished life as an ace archer to win fame as a killer with a heart (and to become an unpredictable antihero for the masses), and *Catching Fire* uses that same stage to prime the pump for a brewing rebellion, *Mockingjay* takes readers into new territories and an even more brutal and confusing world: one where it's unclear what sides the characters are on, one where presumed loyalties are repeatedly stood on their head." *Mockingjay*, like the first two volumes of the series, became a best seller. It also was put on the best of 2010 children's fiction list by National Public Radio, the *Christian Science Monitor*, the *New York Times*, *Publisher's Weekly*, and others.

FILM ADAPTATIONS

The motion picture version of *The Hunger Games* (cowritten by Collins) came out in 2012. Starring Jennifer Lawrence as Katniss, it follows the plot of the book fairly closely. The movie also stars Josh Hutcherson, Woody Harrelson, Willow Shields, Lenny Kravitz, Elizabeth Banks, and Liam Hemsworth. There was much anticipation surrounding the release of the film, and many excited fans went to see it. Although a number of movie critics praised the film, there was no shortage of mixed reviews, some of which criticized Gary Ross's directing style as too slick for the story's troubling content. Movie versions of part two and three of the Hunger Games series have been announced and are slated for arrival in November of 2013, 2014, and 2015 (the adaptation of the final book will be split across two films).

In addition to the books mentioned above, Collins is also the author of books for young children: *When Charlie McButton Lost Power* (2005) and *When Charlie McButton Gained Power* (2009). They feature illustrations by Mike Lester.

Collins lives with her husband, Cap Pryor, an actor, in Connecticut. The couple moved there in 2003 from New York City, where they had been living for sixteen years. They have two children.

SUGGESTED READING

Carpenter, Susan. "Book Review: *Mockingjay*." *Los Angeles Times*. Los Angeles Times, 23 Aug. 2010. Web. 17 July 2012.

Dominus, Susan. "Suzanne Collins's War Stories for Kids." *New York Times*. New York Times, 8 Apr. 2011. Web. 17 July 2012.

Grossman, Lev. "*Catching Fire*: Suzanne Collins' Hit Young-Adult Novels." *Time*. Time, 7 Sep. 2009. Web. 17 July 2012.

Miller, Laura. "Fresh Hell." *New Yorker*. Condé Nast, 14 June 2010. Web. 17 July 2012.

Zevin, Gabrielle. "Constant Craving." *New York Times*. New York Times, 9 Oct. 2009. Web. 17 July 2012.

—*Dmitry Kiper*

Common

Born: March 13, 1972
Occupation: Rapper, actor

"In a field of one-trick ponies, Common is truly a rare breed: a hip-hop artist capable of expressing a full range of emotions," Scott McLennan wrote for the Worcester, Massachusetts, *Telegram & Gazette* (October 4, 2007) about the Grammy Award-winning hip-hop artist and actor. "Not content to cash in on whatever trend is pleasing the masses at a given moment, Common has a track record of stretching his skills across a broad assortment of songs, conjuring stuff that is thoughtful, funny, provocative or romantic all within a single album's span. If he needs any sort of label, let it simply be 'diverse.'" Formerly known by the stage name Common Sense, the recording artist has been credited with pioneering socially conscious rap—an introspective brand of hip-hop that focuses on social and cultural issues. He has been lauded for his rich, baritone voice and laid-back style and for crafting "eloquent, heartfelt lyrics about faith, family, and everyday life in the African American community at a time when macho bragging and gangsta posing were the norm," as Jim DeRogatis noted for the *Chicago Sun-Times* (May 22, 2005).

Common, who is part of a prominent group of Chicago-based rappers that includes Kanye West and Lupe Fiasco, made his recording debut in 1992 with the album *Can I Borrow a Dollar?*, followed by *Resurrection* (1994) and *One Day It'll All Make Sense* (1997), both of which earned him a strong cult following on the underground hip-hop scene. After signing a major-label deal with MCA Records, he achieved critical and commercial acclaim with his fourth studio effort, *Like Water for Chocolate* (2000), which included the singles "The 6th Sense" and

Courtesy of Angela Weiss/Getty Images for Virgin Unite

Pittsburgh Pipers during the 1969–70 season, before substance abuse and behavioral problems derailed his career and his marriage. "At six foot eight, he had NBA size and the skills to match. . . . But he talked back to coaches. He missed practice. He developed a [drug] habit. He was out of the league before his career really began," the rapper recounted in his 2011 memoir, *One Day It'll All Make Sense*. "Around the same time, his relationship with my mother was falling apart. He was getting high, keeping drugs right out in the open on the nightstand. One time my mother locked him out of our apartment, and he shot out all the windows. When he was sober, he was a loving man, but when he was high, he was somebody else." (Common's father would later appear as a guest performer on several of the rapper's albums.)

Common first developed an interest in hiphop during his early teens, while visiting relatives in Cincinnati, Ohio. "My cousin and I would hang out with his crew just talking and listening to music. Afrika Bambaataa and Soulsonic Force. Egyptian Lover. And the biggest group in Cincinnati, the Bond Hill Crew," he was quoted as saying in Yale University Press's *Anthology of Rap*. He has recalled that he wrote his first rap verse at the age of 12.

Common's passion for hip-hop music was rivaled only by his love of basketball. The rapper, who served as an NBA ball boy for the Chicago Bulls during Michael Jordan's rookie season (1984–85), was a standout point guard on Luther South High School's varsity basketball squad. His impressive basketball skills reportedly caught the attention of the NBA coaching legend and Hall of Famer Larry Brown. However, after being sidelined by an eye injury during his sophomore year, Common devoted his focus solely to music and began to make a name for himself around Chicago as a rapper. The summer after his junior year, he formed the rap group CDR with two of his friends, Corey and Dion. (According to some sources, the initials stood for the three group members' names—with the "R" representing Common's birth name, Rashid; however, in *One Day It'll All Make Sense*, Common noted that CDR also stood for Compact Disc Recorders and Controllers of Devastating Rhymes.)

The hip-hop trio recorded several demo taps that received airplay on the University of Chicago's radio station WHPK. They also served as an opening act for such hip-hop icons as N.W.A. and Big Daddy Kane before disbanding in the late 1980s. Common continues to collaborate with his former band mate Dion (now known as No I.D.), a renowned producer widely referred to as the "Godfather of Chicago hip-hop" and currently the executive vice president of A&R for Def Jam Recordings.

In the fall of 1989 Common won an academic scholarship to attend Florida Agricultural and

the Grammy-nominated "The Light." Following the release of the ambitiously eclectic but commercially disappointing *Electric Circus* (2002), Common returned to his hip-hop roots for his next two albums, *Be* (2005) and *Finding Forever* (2007), both of which helped catapult Common into mainstream consciousness. The two recordings received a combined seven Grammy nominations and sold more than 500,000 copies each. Common's latest studio album, *The Dreamer/ The Believer*, was released in late 2011 on the Warner Brothers label. In addition to his music, Common has branched out into acting, with roles in a number of films, including *Smokin' Aces*, *American Gangster*, *Street Kings*, *Wanted*, *Terminator Salvation*, *Date Night*, and *Just Wright*.

EARLY LIFE AND EDUCATION

The artist was born Lonnie Rashid Lynn Jr. on March 13, 1972, in Chicago, Illinois, to Lonnie Lynn Sr. and Dr. Mahalia Ann Hines, a teacher and principal in the Chicago public-school system. (She later became her son's manager.) The couple divorced when Common was a child. He was raised by Hines and his stepfather, Ralph, in Avalon Park, a middle-class neighborhood on Chicago's South Side. However, Common remained close to his biological father, a youth counselor and former basketball player who had spent just one season in the defunct American Basketball Association (ABA), appearing in 52 combined games with the Denver Rockets (now called the Denver Nuggets) and the

Mechanical University (FAMU) in Tallahassee. He majored in business administration while continuing to write rap lyrics and perform in his free time. After two years, however, he dropped out to pursue a music career full time, despite his mother's objections. As Mahalia Hines recalled to Marti Yarbrough for *Jet* (June 27, 2005), "When he decided to leave FAMU to pursue rap, we had a good talk about it. I was extremely upset. I didn't know what rap was. We agreed that if he did not do well in three years, he would go back to school."

RECORDING CAREER

Common's music career took off in 1991, when Relativity Records offered him a contract after one of his demo tapes (produced by No I.D.) was featured in *The Source* magazine's "Unsigned Hype" column, which had become known as a launching pad for other up-and-coming rappers, including the Notorious B.I.G. and Mobb Deep (and later DMX, Eminem, and 50 Cent). Common, who flew back to Chicago to sign the contract, told Cindy Pearlman for the *Chicago Sun-Times* (June 22, 2008), "I took three propeller planes to get there because I couldn't afford anything more than the cheapest airline tickets. But I had to do anything to sign a contract. I would have signed anything. I didn't care what the contract said. It was my beginning."

Using the stage name Common Sense, the rapper made his solo debut in 1992 with *Can I Borrow a Dollar?*, which No I.D. produced. The album, which featured the singles "Charms Alarm," "Take It EZ," "Breaker 1/9," and "Soul by the Pound," earned Common an underground following but had a polarizing effect on hip-hop critics and sold only a few thousand copies. "I faced the obstacle of people not paying attention because it was coming from a new area [of the country]," the rapper told Soren Baker for the *Los Angeles Times* (March 19, 2000). "The mentality seemed like, 'It's either East Coast or West Coast, or we aren't dealing with it.' Then there were barriers of dialect, because being from Chicago, we've got different slang." In a review for the All Music Guide (online), Stanton Swihart called the album "an antidote to the exaggeratedly hardcore rhymes of a lot of early-'90s hip-hop" and "one of the most underrated hip-hop debuts of the '90s."

Common's next album, *Resurrection* (1994), earned critical acclaim despite attracting little commercial attention. Produced by No I.D. and the deejay Ynot, the album included the standout track "I Used to Love H.E.R.," an allegorical diatribe against the commercialization of hip-hop. He rapped in the first verse: "I met this girl, when I was 10 years old/ And what I loved most, she had so much soul/ She was old school, when I was just a shorty/ Never knew throughout my life she would be there

for me/ On the regular, not a church girl, she was secular/ Not about the money, no studs was mic checkin' her/ But I respected her, she hit me in the heart." The song then continued, "I might've failed to mention that the chick was creative/ But once the man got to her, he altered the native/ Told her if she got an image and a gimmick/ That she could make money, and she did it like a dummy."

While "I Used to Love H.E.R." reached number 31 on *Billboard*'s rap-singles chart and was widely praised by music critics, it unintentionally started a feud with the rapper Ice Cube, who took particular offense to what he perceived as the song's direct criticism of West Coast gangsta rap. Ice Cube and the group Westside Connection, which included the rappers Mack 10 and WC, recorded a "diss track" called "Westside Slaughterhouse," in which they mentioned Common by name. Common subsequently countered with the song "The Bitch in Yoo," which mocked Ice Cube's posturing. (The exchange between Common and Ice Cube continued until 1997, when Nation of Islam leader Louis Farrakhan helped broker a truce between the two; Farrakhan was attempting to prevent further violence in the hip-hop community in the wake of the murders of Tupac Shakur and the Notorious B.I.G.)

Following the release of *Resurrection*, Common was forced to change his stage name when a California-based ska band with the same name sued him. In *One Day It'll All Make Sense*, the rapper recalled, "At first I didn't like Common without the Sense. Common? I'm not everyday. I'm extraordinary, not *extra* ordinary. But the more I lived with it, the more I heard the name coming out of the mouths of my fans, the better I felt about it. I started thinking about what the name represents. Common. The everyday person. The everyman. The common folk. The blue-collar worker. I strive to represent that in all that I do."

The artist's critically acclaimed third studio album, *One Day It'll All Make Sense*, was released in September 1997 and included collaborations with such artists as Lauryn Hill, Q-Tip, De La Soul, Erykah Badu, Cee-Lo, and Chantay Savage. The album's lead single, "Retrospect for Life," which featured Hill and sampled portions of Stevie Wonder's "Never Dreamed You'd Leave in Summer" and Donny Hathaway's "A Song For You," drew upon Common's real-life transition to fatherhood, with lyrics discussing the pros and cons of abortion. Ben Wener, writing for the *Orange County Register* (January 29, 1998), called the song "one of the most astonishingly honest rap cuts in ages." *One Day It'll All Make Sense* sold some 250,000 copies and reached number 12 on *Billboard*'s R&B/hip-hop-albums chart.

One Day It'll All Make Sense helped raise Common's profile in the hip-hop world, and in

1998, he landed his first major-label deal with MCA Records. Shortly thereafter, he moved from Chicago to the New York City borough of Brooklyn, where he began collaborating with the newly formed Soulquarians, a neo-soul and hip-hop collective comprised of such artists and rappers as the Roots, Talib Kweli, D'Angelo, Mos Def, Q-Tip, J Dilla, and Erykah Badu, among others. Common made guest appearances on Mos Def and Talib Kweli's album *Black Star* (1998), the Roots' *Things Fall Apart* (1999), and on the Rawkus Records compilation *Soundbombing II* (1999), before releasing his MCA debut, *Like Water for Chocolate*, in March 2000. Executive produced by Ahmir "Questlove" Thompson and named for Laura Esquivel's acclaimed 1989 novel of the same title, the album retained the same socially conscious nature of his previous work while achieving notable mainstream success. Among the album's 16 tracks was "The Light," a love song believed to have been written for Badu, whom he was then dating. The song reached number 44 on the *Billboard* Hot 100 singles chart and earned Common a Grammy nomination for best rap solo performance. *Like Water for Chocolate* received widespread praise from critics, reached number 16 on the *Billboard* 200 chart, and sold more than 750,000 copies. In an article for the *Chicago Sun-Times* (February 5, 2006), Jim DeRogatis made note of the album's "often mellow and always soulful and entrancing grooves" and called it the "crowning achievement" of Common's career. Common recalled to DeRogatis, "I sat down with a plan, a goal, and a wish list of things that I wanted to do musically. I wanted to make an album where you listen to the stories and look at the whole picture; I wanted you to see the portrait and not separate the colors in it. It's all one story, one movie."

Common adopted the same approach for his experimental follow-up, *Electric Circus*, which was released in December 2002. The album reflected Common's growing interest in other genres of music and featured an eclectic mix of hip-hop, pop, soul, and psychedelic rock. Its ambitious nature won over a number of critics but divided Common's fans. Consequently, *Electric Circus* was not a commercial success, selling fewer than 300,000 copies, and the album spawned only one single, the Mary J. Blige duet "Come Close," which peaked at number 65 on the *Billboard* Hot 100 chart. "Obviously, I wanted *Electric Circus* to receive a better response," Common told Gail Mitchell for *Billboard* (May 28, 2005). "But I don't apologize for the record. It was me being true to what I feel as an artist. Like Miles Davis, it's my *Bitches Brew*. It's a part of my musical evolution."

In 2003 Common won his first Grammy Award for best R&B song for "Love of My Life (An Ode to Hip-Hop)," a duet with Badu that

was featured on the soundtrack to the film *Brown Sugar* (2002). The following year fellow Chicago rapper Kanye West signed Common to his Geffen Records imprint, Getting Out Our Dreams (GOOD) Records. West, whose multiplatinum debut, *The College Dropout* (2004), had established him as one of hip-hop's most innovative figures, produced nine of the 11 tracks on Common's next studio album, *Be*, which was released in May 2005. Marking a return to his hip-hop roots with such hard-hitting singles as "The Corner" and "Testify," the disc debuted at number one on *Billboard*'s R&B/hip-hop chart. It became the second of Common's albums to earn gold status—selling more than 800,000 copies—and was declared an instant classic by many music insiders. In a review for the All Music Guide (online), Andy Kellman called *Be* "one of the most tightly constructed albums of any form within recent memory," and Jim Carroll described the album for the *Irish Times* (July 15, 2005) as "a sparkling, funky, feel-good behemoth." *Be* earned four Grammy nominations, including one for best rap album.

Common also worked with West on *Finding Forever*, which was released in July 2007 and debuted at number one on the *Billboard* 200 chart. *Finding Forever* achieved gold status and received three Grammy Award nods, including a win for best rap performance by a duo or group for the song "Southside" (featuring Kanye West); it lost out, however, to West's *Graduation* for best rap album. *Universal Mind Control*, his eighth studio album, was released in the fall of 2008. The album contained more up-tempo beats and a frenetic, electronic-based sound, and despite receiving mixed reviews from critics, it reached number 12 on the *Billboard* 200 chart and earned a Grammy nomination for best rap album. He followed up with the albums *Use Common Sense* (2009) and *Something in Common* (2010).

In the spring of 2011 Common was among a select group of entertainers and literary figures invited by First Lady Michelle Obama to appear at the White House for an evening celebrating poetry and the arts. The invitation caused a stir among some Republicans, including Karl Rove, a former senior advisor to President George W. Bush, who described Common as a "thug" and cited writings that allegedly advocated violence against Bush and the police. (One specific line in question was: "Burn a Bush cos for peace he push no button/ Killing over oil and grease/ No weapons of destruction.") Despite the controversy, Common performed at the event and later wrote a post on the social-networking site Facebook declaring his support for police officers and military troops.

In June 2011 Common signed a deal with Warner Brothers Records. His Warner debut, *The Dreamer/The Believer*, produced by No I.D., was released in December 2011; its first single, "Ghetto Dreams," featured the rapper Nas.

ACTING AND OTHER WORK

Common has also carved out a successful career as an actor. In 2006 he made his feature-film debut as a menacing bodyguard in Joe Carnahan's star-studded crime film *Smokin' Aces*, and the following year he appeared in Ridley Scott's critically acclaimed crime drama *American Gangster*, portraying the brother of real-life Harlem drug kingpin Frank Lucas (played by Denzel Washington). In 2008 Common had a supporting role in David Ayer's *Street Kings*, a crime film starring Keanu Reeves and Forest Whitaker; he also starred opposite Angelina Jolie and Morgan Freeman in the film adaptation of the comic book *Wanted*. In 2009 he appeared in the highly anticipated sci-fi reboot *Terminator Salvation*, followed by major roles in two romantic comedies: the Steve Carell/Tina Fey vehicle *Date Night* (2010), in which he played a corrupt cop, and *Just Wright* (2010), in which he starred as a professional basketball player who falls in love with his physical therapist (played by Queen Latifah). In 2011 Common lent his voice to the animated big-screen sequel *Happy Feet Two*. On the small screen he currently stars in *Hell on Wheels*, a Western that airs on the cable channel AMC.

Common, who has a daughter, Omoye Assata Lynn, currently has three children's novels to his credit, and in September 2011 he released a memoir, *One Day It'll All Make Sense*, which appeared on the *New York Times* best-seller list. He has recently become a fixture in the gossip pages for his relationship with tennis player Serena Williams.

In addition to being featured in ad campaigns for the Gap and Converse, Common has served as the face of the men's fragrance, Only the Brave. The socially conscious performer has supported such causes as HIV/AIDS awareness and vegetarianism, and he is the creator of the Common Ground Foundation, a Chicago-based organization that helps disadvantaged youth develop leadership and life skills. "I want to inspire kids to think critically," Common explained to Cindy Pearlman for the *Chicago Sun-Times*. "Through hip-hop, I have a voice. And I know kids are listening and they will respond. What better way to talk to the kids than educate and empower them about life?"

SUGGESTED READING

Baker, Soren. "Ready for the Majors." *Los Angeles Times*. 19 Mar. 2000, Calendar: 5. Print.
Carroll, Jim. "Do the Right Thing." *Irish Times* 15 July 2005, The Ticket: 3. Print.
Common and Adam Bradley. *One Day It'll All Make Sense*. New York: Atria, 2011. Print.
Kellman, Andy. "Rev. of *Be*, by Common." *AllMusic*. Rovi, n.d. Web. 19 Dec. 2011.
McLennan, Scott. "Common Has Unique Approach; Rapper's Songs Run the Gamut." Worcester, Massachusetts, *Telegram & Gazette* 4 Oct. 2007: E1. Print.
Pearlman, Cindy. "Common's Invincible Summer Gets Hotter." *Chicago Sun-Times*. 22 June 2008: D1. Print.

—*Christopher Cullen*

Tim Cook

Born: November 1, 1960
Occupation: CEO of Apple

When Timothy D. Cook took over as chief executive officer (CEO) of the Apple corporation in August 2011, he replaced outgoing CEO Steve Jobs, who was ailing and would later die of pancreatic cancer on October 5, 2011. As the face of Apple, Jobs was a cult-like figure among technology workers, businesspeople, and consumers. Both revered and feared, he was widely considered a technology pioneer and a genius. Cook faced intense scrutiny as the man appointed to fill Jobs's shoes, though he did so for several months in 2004, when Jobs was recovering from cancer surgery. Speculation regarding Cook's ability to lead the company—or more accurately, to fulfill Jobs's ongoing vision for the company—began as early as 2008, when Jobs appeared at a company event looking emaciated and pale. But Cook was already playing a significant role in the leadership of the company behind the scenes as its chief operating officer (COO). By the time he officially took over as CEO in 2011, he had also already spent (collectively) over a year in the position as the interim chief executive.

As COO, Cook had developed new ways to cut costs by eradicating leftover inventory while he also supervised an overhaul of Apple's manufacturing and distribution. Some might argue that Cook is to Apple's supply chain what Jobs was to the company's signature design. Both were revolutionary in their approach to overseeing the company. "My most significant discovery so far in my life was the result of one single decision, my decision to join Apple," Cook told students in a 2010 commencement address at his alma mater, Auburn University, as quoted by a reporter in the London *Guardian* (25 Aug. 2011). Cook added: "Working at Apple was never in any plan that I outlined for myself, but was without a doubt the best decision that I ever made."

EARLY LIFE AND CAREER

Cook was born on November 1, 1960, in Robertsdale, Alabama, to Donald and Geraldine

ChinaFotoPress via Getty Images

as a friendly and hardworking employee; he often worked holidays to complete orders for the company.

After twelve years with IBM, Cook was asked to join the staff of Intelligent Electronics, a small Colorado electronics distributor. Cook accepted a position as the firm's senior vice president in 1994. A year later, he was promoted to COO where he doubled the company's revenues. However, he then engineered the sale of the company to Ingram Micro, putting himself out of a job.

Cook was hired by the Houston-based computer company Compaq as the vice president of corporate materials in 1997. Eight months later, he received a call to interview for an executive position at a struggling electronics company in Palo Alto, California. Apple Computers, founded by Steve Jobs and Steve Wozniak in 1976, was nearing bankruptcy. Apple had become a popular producer of personal computers in the 1980s, but by the next decade that popularity was in rapid decline.

COOK AND JOBS

After being ousted as CEO in 1985, Jobs returned to Apple in 1996 and was looking for employees who could reverse the fate that many deemed inevitable. In 1996, a Forrester Research analyst said, as quoted by David Pogue for the *New York Times* (20 Sep. 2006): "Whether they stand alone or are acquired, Apple as we know it is cooked. It's so classic. It's so sad." Cook at first turned down the opportunity to interview for the position as Apple's senior vice president of worldwide operations. It took some convincing, but he finally relented, taking a Friday night red-eye flight to California to meet with Jobs for a Saturday morning interview in 1998.

Jobs was notoriously brusque in the interviews he conducted for Cook's position. Cook's meeting, however, went so well that he reportedly decided to take the position five minutes into his interview with Jobs. Outsiders were shocked by Cook's decision. Cook himself later admitted to the *Guardian*, "I listened to my intuition, not the left side of my brain." Cook and Jobs had a lot in common—they were both competitive, fiercely intelligent, and respected among their peers—but they differed in ways that gave an essential balance to the company. Jobs had an eye for design, but could be short-tempered, aggressive, and solitary. Cook is more analytical and a master of operations; he is also soft-spoken and described by colleagues as unflappable.

Cook began working for Apple in 1998, and his effect on the company was immediate. In the previous fiscal year, Apple had reported a $1 billion loss; the profits the company reported the next year exceeded Wall Street's projections by 38 percent. Jobs made a slew of changes to the company as CEO—including a severe edit

Cook. He has two brothers named Mike and Gerald; Cook is the middle child. Cook excelled at Robertsdale High School where he was elected president of the National Honor Society. He enjoyed mathematics, played trombone in the band, and was voted "Most Studious" by his classmates. He graduated in 1978 at the top of his class.

Cook attended Auburn University in Auburn, Alabama. In a commencement address he gave at the school in 2010, Cook said that the school "played a key role in my life and continues to mean a lot to me." He is a devoted Auburn football fan. As an undergraduate, he studied Industrial Engineering and also enjoyed business classes, thinking that an engineering degree would serve him well in the business world. This proved to be true; Cook caught the attention of an IBM executive with a speech he gave at the Institute of Industrial Engineers while still at Auburn. While completing his degree, Cook began working for Scott Paper Company in Mobile. He graduated in 1982 and began working as an industrial engineer for IBM.

Cook earned his MBA from the Fuqua School of Business at Duke University in 1988 while still working for IBM. He became the director of North American facilities in the company's personal computer division, where he oversaw the work of 6,000 employees. That number, he remarked to Ray Garner for *Technology Alabama* (1999), was "more people than are in Robertsdale today." Cook became known of Apple's products, from fifteen to four—and put Cook in charge of inventory. With the rate of change in the personal computer business, products left sitting on a shelf "lose value almost as fast as eggs" at the supermarket, David Kirkpatrick wrote in *Fortune* magazine (9 Nov. 1998). Cook reduced the amount of stock left lying around (which would have been recorded as a loss) from $400 million to $78 million in a little under a year.

When Jobs returned to Apple, he also introduced the iMac, a sleek desktop computer. To meet demand, Apple executives like Cook worked around the clock. In addition to inventory, Cook oversaw distribution and manufacturing. During that time, Cook called a meeting with his staff to discuss a problem at the Asia plant. "Someone should be in China driving this," Cook told *CNN Money* (10 Nov. 2008). Less than an hour later, Cook turned to an operations executive named Sabih Khan and asked, "Why are you still here?" Khan was on the next flight to China without a return ticket.

BEHIND THE SCENES

Cook's ability to manage inventory was invaluable to Apple; it allowed the company to keep production costs low while also charging premium prices for products. Apple is able to charge more than their competitors because their devices are often unrivaled in functionality, or at least in aesthetics. Apple's marketing and design appeal to consumers and make their devices desirable. For instance, in 2005, Apple introduced a new iPod called the Nano. The Nano was exciting because of its flash memory capabilities. Cook anticipated the incredible demand for the product and paid suppliers Samsung and Hynix nearly $1.25 billion in advance to effectively corner the market in the Nano's particular memory until 2010. His approach to Apple's supply chain was unusual as well. Most managers are focused on cutting costs—as is, to a large extent, Cook— but by securing the suppliers before even introducing the product to consumers, Cook took a gamble by paying to solve a problem before it even existed. Kevin O'Marah, a chief strategist for AMR Research told *CNN Money*, "That's the sort of thing [Apple] wouldn't have thought of in the days before Tim Cook." Cook has employed this method ever since; competitors are unable to manufacture the same goods as Apple because the company controls the components of their products.

In addition to supply chain management, Cook took over sales and customer support in 2000. At the time, Macs were sold at retailers like Best Buy. Cook began replacing those salespeople with Apple's own trained sales staff. Today, Apple stores offer the same support. Consumers can visit the store's "Genius Bar" to ask questions about their Macs or other Apple devices.

TRANSITIONS

Cook took over the Macintosh division in 2004, and stepped in as CEO while Jobs underwent surgery for pancreatic cancer. At the time, the computers were switching from PowerPC to Intel chips. The transition allowed Macs to run Microsoft Word, and encouraged millions of computer users to switch to a Mac. Cook became Apple's COO, in charge of the company's daily operations, in 2007. In 2008, Cook once again stepped in as CEO for the six months that Jobs was on medical leave. During this time, Cook was able to improve Apple's financial performance in the middle of the economic downturn. In August 2011, when Jobs stepped down from Apple's helm for the last time, Cook was named as the new CEO.

Cook has taken Jobs's parting advice to him as the new CEO of Apple to heart. Jobs told Cook, as quoted by Nick Wingfield for the *New York Times* (30 May 2012), "Never ask what [Steve] would do. Just do what's right." It was a lesson Jobs had learned from Walt Disney; after the great animator died, the company produced a slew of misguided movies thinking that they would have been what Disney would have chosen. Cook is already making different choices than his predecessor might have made, but still acting in the best interests of the company. So far his strategy has been working; as of 2012, Apple surpassed ExxonMobil as the world's most valuable company.

The day before Jobs's death, Cook unveiled the new iPhone model. It was his first public event as Apple's CEO. He has also overseen the debut of a new version of the MacBook Pro, the iPhone—most notably with the voice command, Siri—and the iPad. Cook maintains an aura of secrecy surrounding new products at the company. While, unlike Jobs, he is noticeably present at industry functions, Cook refuses to offer much in response to questions of Apple's direction, save a few tantalizing hints. Cook has said that he would like to work with social media powerhouse, Facebook. There has also been speculation that Apple will develop a television product.

IMPROVING THE SUPPLY CHAIN

Partnerships with external manufacturers have been a major factor in Apple's—and Cook's— success. In its early days, Apple touted itself as an American-made company. Outsourcing began under Cook's major plan to revolutionize the company's supply chain. During his tenure, Jobs was famously terse on the subject; reportedly telling President Obama in early 2011 that the manufacturing jobs Apple had taken overseas were never coming back.

Many of Apple's manufacturers are in Asia. In 2012, one of those manufacturers, a Taiwanese company called Foxconn, came under fire for poor labor practices at their plants. In an unprecedented step for Apple, Cook visited one of the Foxconn plants in China and subsequently issued an audit criticizing the company for long hours and dangerous working conditions. Foxconn subsequently agreed to reduce hours and increase wages at their plants. Cook seems determined to improve conditions in Apple's overseas factories perhaps in part because he had spent time working in factories himself. In February 2012 he told investors that he had spent time working in a paper mill in Alabama and an aluminum plant in Virginia. Daniel Diermeier, a professor who studies reputation management at Northwestern University, told the *New York Times* (2 Apr. 2012), "I think he probably has a deeper understanding, and this is more personal for him than it might be for other executives."

In 2012, Cook released the names of Apple's 156 suppliers and an audit of conditions within those plants—something Apple had never done before. Under Cook, Apple also became the first technology company to join the nonprofit global monitoring group, the Fair Labor Association (FLA). Cook invited the FLA to inspect its factories in China. The group found numerous violations of Chinese labor laws and Foxconn regulation that they reported to Apple.

Cook appears to be committed to improving conditions on the supply chain. In 2008, Apple inspectors discovered that a supplier had forced foreign workers to hand over their passports, making it difficult to leave their jobs. Apple demanded that the passports be returned. Still, as the FLA findings suggest, Apple has a lot of work to do. Cook notes that several of the suppliers are consistent violators, but conditions are improving. Because of its tough stance on labor, Apple stands to set the tone for the rest of the tech industry.

PERSONAL LIFE

Cook raised eyebrows in 2011 when Apple awarded him a $378 million salary and a ten-year stock grant, making him the highest paid CEO in the United States. Despite his income, he lives in a modest four-bedroom condo in Palo Alto. In 2012, *Gawker* reported that the neighboring condo is owned by Google executive Bill Maris.

Known for his dedication to fitness and his love of energy bars, Cook is an avowed Auburn football fan and cycling devotee. He also has great admiration for cyclist Lance Armstrong and late politician Robert Kennedy, referencing them frequently. He was voted as the most powerful gay or lesbian person of 2011 by *Out* magazine. Although Cook has never publicly come out and does not usually comment on his personal life,

he has acknowledged that he is gay within Apple and Silicon Valley circles.

SUGGESTED READING

Garner, Ray, and Chris McFadyen. "Alabama Native and Apple Interim CEO Tim Cook Shares His Career History." *Technology Alabama*. Technology Alabama, 2011. Web. 10 July 2012.

Kirkpatrick, David, and Tyler Maroney. "The Second Coming of Apple through a Magical Fusion of Man—Steve Jobs—and Company, Apple Is Becoming Itself Again: The Little Anticompany That Could." *CNN Money: Fortune*. Cable News Network, 9 Nov. 1998. Web. 11 July 2012.

Lashinsky, Adam. "The Genius behind Steve." *CNN Money*. Cable News Network, 10 Nov. 2008. Web. 11 July 2012.

Pogue, David. "When Apple Hit Bottom." *New York Times*. New York Times Co., 20 Sep. 2006. Web. 10 July 2012.

"Tim Cook: The Man Taking over from Steve Jobs at Apple." *Guardian*. Guardian News and Media Ltd., 25 Aug. 2011. Web. 10 July 2012.

Wingfield, Nick. "Fixing Apple's Supply Lines." *New York Times*. New York Times Co., 2 Apr. 2012. Web. 13 July 2012.

---. "Apple's Tim Cook on Steve Jobs, Leadership, and Manufacturing." *New York Times*. New York Times Co., 30 May 2012. Web. 13 July 2012.

—Molly Hagan

Natalie Coughlin

Born: August 23, 1982
Occupation: Swimmer

Gold medalist Natalie Coughlin is one of the most decorated female swimmers of all time. As a sixteen-year-old teen sensation, Coughlin qualified for an astounding fourteen events leading up to the 2000 Olympic Games, only to suffer a debilitating shoulder injury that prevented her from making the team at all. She dropped from public view to attend the University of California, Berkeley and retool her stroke. A few years later, she emerged more formidable than before, becoming the first woman to break the one-minute mark in the long-course 100-meter backstroke. (A long course, or Olympic-size swimming pool, is fifty meters long, while a typical collegiate pool is a short course, twenty-five meters long.) She is the only woman to win back-to-back Olympic gold medals in the event, a feat she achieved at the 2004 and 2008 Olympic Games. Coughlin

Getty Images for Sports Illustrated

EARLY LIFE

Coughlin was born on August 23, 1982, in the California city of Vallejo, northeast of San Francisco. Her father, Jim, is a retired police officer, and her mother, Zennie, is a paralegal. The family had a pool in their backyard, and the Coughlins decided to enroll Natalie and her younger sister, Megan, in swimming lessons at an early age.

Coughlin began swimming competitively with neighborhood clubs at the age of six. She was an enthusiastic swimmer, and although she won her races, her technique was not refined. Her early coach, Ray Mitchell, characterized her as a "determined thrasher." He added to Gorney, "The kid had one speed, and that was all out." In the backstroke, she sometimes powered so hard into the finish that she hit her head on the wall. "Natalie was always goal oriented," her father was quoted as saying in Coughlin's autobiography, *Golden Girl: How Natalie Coughlin Fought Back, Challenged Conventional Wisdom, and Became America's Olympic Champion* (2006), cowritten with Michael Silver. "No matter what she did, she had to know everything about it. And when it came to swimming, whatever level she was on, she'd pick out the fastest person around and make a point of saying, 'That's the one I'm going to beat.'"

Mitchell coached the Terrapins, a swim club based in Concord, California, about half an hour from the Coughlins' home. The Terrapins, a member club of the Pacific Swimming Association of USA Swimming, boast a rigorous training schedule and have groomed many national contenders. The Coughlins hoped that their daughter might be good enough to win a college scholarship, so they sent her to train with Mitchell at age thirteen.

Coughlin's first big meet was a Junior Nationals competition in Washington State, where she swam the grueling 1,000-yard freestyle event (twenty laps in a short-course pool). Mitchell recalled that Coughlin went out so fast that her first four laps were ahead of pace for the American adult record in the event. She pulled ahead of the pack by twenty-five yards but lost steam, finishing near the middle. The loss did not faze her; she went on to win three events as well as the meet trophy for single swimmer performance. It was clear that Coughlin was a talented swimmer, but Junior Nationals proved that she had the potential to become a world-class athlete.

TERRAPINS TRAINING

At fifteen, Coughlin's family moved from their home in Benicia to Concord, where she and her sister attended Carondolet High School. They were also closer to Coughlin's Terrapin practices, though Coughlin insists that swimming was not the only factor prompting them to move;

won eleven Olympic medals during that time, one for every event she entered and one shy of record holder Jenny Thompson, who earned twelve medals over the course of four Olympic Games.

For her speed, technique, and unusually large lung capacity, Coughlin has been touted as one of the most dynamic athletes the swimming world has ever seen. Though she is well versed in all four strokes—butterfly, backstroke, breaststroke, and freestyle—she has become most famous for her powerful underwater kick. At the start of the backstroke race and coming off of the wall at the turn, swimmers take advantage of their gained momentum by kicking underwater in a streamlined position for up to fifteen meters. Most prefer the alternating motion of the flutter kick, but Coughlin employs the more powerful (and more difficult) butterfly kick, holding her legs together and undulating her entire body to propel herself through the water, a motion similar to the cracking of a whip.

Coaches and fellow swimmers agree that there is an intangible quality to Coughlin's greatness. "Statistically, most people are swimming at relatively the same times they did thirty years ago, so people who are anomalies in this culture, like Natalie, really jump out at you," coach Bill Boomer told Cynthia Gorney for the *New Yorker* (5 July 2004). "There's something special going on here, and it isn't velocity. . . . She's swimming like she was in the womb, and we need to teach that."

Jim and the girls had been in a serious car accident while commuting to Concord. Still, the new home made Coughlin's twice-daily practice schedule more manageable.

Soon, Coughlin had her sights set on the 2000 Olympic Games in Sydney, Australia. The games were still a year and a half away, and Coughlin, who was sixteen at the time, was training harder than ever. She had set three national high school records and was poised to make the Olympic team in several strokes. At the age of fifteen, she had become the first US swimmer to qualify for all fourteen events at US Nationals, as well as the first high school sophomore to be named national swimmer of the year.

The pressure started to take its toll on both Coughlin and her coach. Mitchell pushed his swimmers and was known to dole out punishment—in the form of extra laps or a public dressing-down—when they did not live up to his standards. By several accounts, chronicled by Silver and Coughlin in *Golden Girl*, Mitchell was authoritarian in his coaching style. He monitored his swimmers both in and out of the water, taking meticulous note not only of their physical condition but also of their social activities and relationships. As Silver wrote, "diverse interests" to Mitchell meant that a swimmer swam for the Terrapins as well as their high school team. Before the 2000 Olympic trials, Mitchell advised Coughlin, who had just begun dating Terrapin breaststroker Ethan Hall, to put her relationship on hold. When she refused, he berated the couple, telling them that they were "uncoachable."

The tension came to a head in March of 1999 after Coughlin completed a particularly hard butterfly set at an afternoon practice. Late that night, Coughlin awoke with a stabbing pain in her left shoulder. Though its intensity brought her to tears, she was determined to swim through the pain—an oft-used phrase in elite swimming. However, the next morning Coughlin could barely move her arm. She had torn her labrum, the cartilage surrounding her shoulder, and required surgery.

Afraid that surgery might jeopardize her career, Coughlin instead opted to try physical therapy. She began working with Lisa Giannone of San Francisco's ActiveCare clinic, strengthening the surrounding muscles in her back to compensate for her shoulder. Mitchell accompanied Coughlin to all of her appointments, still hoping that she would be able to swim even though Giannone told her to rest. Often Coughlin would use a kickboard through practice and swim sets, using only her legs. Mitchell was disappointed with his star and told Coughlin so.

Coughlin graduated from high school in 2000. Despite her injury, she was heavily recruited by college teams, including Stanford and the University of California, Berkeley. Coughlin's parents pushed for her to attend Stanford, but as she began to recoil from the overbearing Mitchell, Coughlin became more and more attracted to UC Berkeley's easygoing coach, Teri McKeever. Coughlin's injury persisted. She told herself that she would retire from swimming; she no longer found joy in the pool and hoped only to make it through the season with a full-ride scholarship to college.

By the time the Olympic trials rolled around, Coughlin had all but given up. She entered the 200-meter individual medley, and though she recalled feeling surprisingly strong, she came in a disappointing fourth place. Mitchell took the loss especially hard, but Coughlin was resigned to the fact that her swimming career might have come to an end. Though she would keep the good memories of her early years with the Terrapins, Coughlin would never forget her traumatic last season. "Ray [Mitchell] has been quoted as saying that I have a tendency to fixate on that last year," Coughlin told Silver, "and that's absolutely true. That last year was such a betrayal to me—and to all the work, time, and emotional effort that I have put in over five years."

TERI MCKEEVER AND THE COMEBACK KID

Coughlin's college decision put added pressure on her Olympic trials year, and against her parents' urging she chose to attend UC Berkeley. She reasoned that she felt comfortable with coach McKeever, mostly because McKeever and Mitchell were polar opposites. While Mitchell had been controling, McKeever took a decidedly hands-off approach with her swimmers, encouraging them to develop facets of their personality outside of swimming. McKeever trusted that her team took the sport seriously enough not to ruin their training with college overindulgence. McKeever also encouraged what swimmers call "dry land" activities, which include conditioning exercises like Pilates and yoga that take place out of the water. Unlike Mitchell, who was mostly interested in endurance, McKeever stressed body awareness, technique, and balance. Swim practice was fresh and exciting; swimmers could show up expecting more than just mundane laps. Coughlin took to McKeever's philosophy immediately, but she still was not ready to reclaim her star potential.

"When I started coaching her," McKeever told Gorney, "I just thought, Here's someone who's had a tough relationship with the sport, in the sense that it gave her a lot of things, and then her body turned on her." After a few months, McKeever invited coach and renowned stroke consultant Milt Nelms to watch Coughlin swim. Nelms was surprised by what he saw; Coughlin's body was, he told Gorney, curiously asymmetrical. The muscles on her injured left side were exaggerated from therapy, yet when she moved through the water, she seemed to overcompensate on her right side, letting her injured shoulder glide along beside her. Nelms, who calls Coughlin a physical genius in the water, recalled her remarkable ability to absorb his coaching advice that day. She seemed to put his words into action almost instantaneously and spent the next few years completely reengineering her stroke.

Within a year, Coughlin was competing at the 2001 World Championships in Japan. She took home a gold medal in the 100-meter backstroke and a bronze in the 50-meter backstroke. In 2002, she won five national titles, the first person to do so in one meet since swimming legend Tracy Caulkins in 1978. The same year, Coughlin broke the American record in the 200-meter backstroke and the world record in the 100-meter backstroke, her time of 59.58 in the latter making her the first woman to ever break one minute. Coughlin was named the NCAA Swimmer of the Year in 2001, 2002, and 2003. "If Natalie had made that 2000 Olympic team and things had all gone back together smoothly, maybe she wouldn't be doing what she's doing now," McKeever told Bill Ward for the *Tampa (Florida) Tribune* (14 July 2003). "You just got to believe that in her case things happened for a reason. The best things that happen are sometimes the hardest journeys to reach them. But they teach you things that allow you to be even better."

GOLDEN GIRL

Despite having her Olympic hopes dashed in 2000, Coughlin emerged as a world record holder on the eve of the 2004 Games in Athens, Greece. Her story did not escape the press, who hailed her as a "golden girl" poised to overtake Mark Spitz's 1972 record of seven gold medals won at a single Games. Coughlin argued that due to the increase in preliminary races, merely entering seven events could be a challenge in itself. Still, she had a year to strategize.

In 2003, Coughlin attended the World Championships in Barcelona, Spain. Spanish newspapers trumpeted Coughlin as *la polivalencia*, "the versatile one," weeks before her arrival. Even the meet programs officially ceded two events, the 100- and 200-meter backstroke, to Coughlin. The race, it read, would be for second place. But again, as in the months leading up to the 2000 trials, Coughlin's body betrayed her. Due to a high fever, she turned in disappointing performances in all of her events (she fell in twenty-second place in the 100-meter backstroke), failing to place in any. The fluke reinforced the importance of the upcoming trials for Coughlin, as well as the fickle nature of the sport. All of her energy would go toward staying healthy and practicing for hours every day for the one race on the one day that would take her less than one minute to complete.

Coughlin completed the 2004 trials without illness or injury, though she was conservative in choosing her events. She chose to forgo both the 200-meter freestyle and the 100-meter butterfly so that she would not be swimming multiple events on one day in Athens. Instead, she focused on two individual events (the 100-meter backstroke and the 100-meter freestyle) and three relays (the 4 × 100- and 4 × 200-meter freestyle relays and the 4 × 100-meter medley) and made the team in all of them.

In Athens, Coughlin and her 4 × 100 freestyle relay team, which included Kara Lynn Joyce, Amanda Weir, and Jenny Thompson, won silver. Her 4 × 200 relay team—with Carly Piper, Dana Vollmer, and Kaitlin Sandeno—won gold and smashed the longest-standing world record in swimming by two seconds, clocking in at 7:53.42. The record had been set in 1987 by the East German team. Additionally, Coughlin, who led the relay, posted a time that would have won her a gold medal in the individual 200-meter freestyle event. She won bronze in the 100-meter freestyle, and her 4 × 100 medley relay with Amanda Beard, Jenny Thompson, and Kara Lynn Joyce won silver.

But it was her signature event, the 100-meter backstroke, that captured popular imagination. Coughlin was racing Zimbabwe's Kirsty Coventry, to whom she had lost the only race in her four-year college career just five months earlier in College Station, Texas, at the NCAA Championships. In *Golden Girl*, Coughlin recalls the dread she experienced during the Olympic finals when, with only twenty meters left to go, she felt her energy draining, her legs throbbing, and her whole body beginning to slow. She bit down hard on her lip to distract herself from the pain and powered into the wall. She did not break any records, but she out-touched Coventry to win gold. Her lip was still bleeding when she accepted her medal on the podium.

BACK ON TOP

Coughlin graduated from UC Berkeley with a degree in psychology in 2005. She was a five-time medalist at both the 2005 and 2007 World Championships. In 2005, she tied for silver in the 100-meter freestyle and won bronze in the 100-meter backstroke (where she was beaten by Coventry), bronze in the 4 × 100 freestyle relay, gold in the 4 × 200 freestyle relay, and silver in the 4 × 100 medley relay. In 2007, she took gold in the 100-meter backstroke and the 4 × 200 freestyle relay, silver in the 4 × 100 freestyle relay and the 4 × 100 medley relay, and bronze in the 100-meter butterfly.

In 2006, Coughlin teamed up with Silver to pen *Golden Girl*, touted as a "tell-all" for its frank discussion of her time with Mitchell. Coughlin, who was hesitant at first to air her grievances with her old coach so publicly, decided that she needed to be honest to address what she saw as larger problems within the swimming world.

Coughlin also addressed eating disorders among female swimmers in the book, another taboo in swimming circles. All in all, the book was evidence that Coughlin felt more comfortable in her own skin after the 2004 Olympics. Although she had already posted multiple world records, the added validation of being an Olympic gold medalist was undeniable. "Now, anytime you go to a meet, you're known as Olympic gold medalist Natalie Coughlin," she told Jennifer Starks for the *Contra Costa (California) Times* (2 June 2006). "I've always held on to a high standard. Without the gold medal, [former swimmer] Rowdy Gaines said you're not validated in this sport until you get that. It sounds harsh, but it's very true."

Leading up to the 2008 Olympic Games in Beijing, China, Coughlin was facing pressure to repeat her 2004 performance, not only in the 100-meter backstroke, but also in other events. She began swimming the 200-meter individual medley again, though she had vowed never to swim that race after her disappointment at the 2000 trials, and was surprised at the times she was posting. In turn, she surprised fans when she decided to swim the event at trials. But the real show came in the 100-meter backstroke. Coughlin's closest competitor, Haley McGregory, had snatched Coughlin's world record in the preliminaries, only to have Coughlin take it back less than five minutes later in the next heat. Going into finals, tensions were high. Coughlin was the reigning champion in the event, but McGregory was determined; it was her third Olympic trials and she had yet to make the cut. The race was frighteningly close until Coughlin pulled ahead out of the turn. She touched the wall in world-record time: 58.97 seconds.

In Beijing, Coughlin became the only female to retain gold in the 100-meter backstroke, besting Coventry again with a time of 58.96. She also won two silver medals, in the 4 × 100-meter medley relay and the 4 × 100-meter freestyle relay, and won bronze in the 100-meter freestyle, the 200-meter individual medley, and the 4 × 200-meter freestyle relay.

After the 2008 Olympics, Coughlin took an eighteen-month break from swimming. In 2009, she was a contestant on the reality television show *Dancing with the Stars*, where she was paired with dancer Alec Mazo. Though they were praised by the judges, Coughlin and Mazo were voted off the show midseason. Coughlin also shared recipes on the *Today Show* and served as an on-air commentator for MSNBC during the 2006 Olympic Winter Games in Torino, Italy.

Out of the pool, Coughlin is an avid cook and often posts recipes on her blog and website. She grows organic produce and raises chickens in her backyard. Coughlin remained with boyfriend Hall from her Terrapin years, and the two were married in 2009. They live in Lafayette, California, with their two dogs.

SUGGESTED READING

Gorney, Cynthia. "A Feel for the Water." *New Yorker* 5 July 2004: 72. Print.

Silver, Michael, and Natalie Coughlin. *Golden Girl: How Natalie Coughlin Fought Back, Challenged Conventional Wisdom, and Became America's Olympic Champion.* Emmaus, PA: Rodale, 2006. Print.

Starks, Jennifer. "Swimmer, Olympic Gold Medalist Savors Success, Tells All in New Book." *SwimStars.org News Archive.* Suzdawg Productions, 2 June 2006. Web. 13 Mar. 2012.

Ward, Bill. "Coughlin Carries Golden Hopes, Look of Success." *Tampa Tribune* 14 July 2003, final ed.: 1. Print.

—*Molly Hagan*

Fabien Cousteau

Born: October 1967
Occupation: Aquatic filmmaker and oceanographer

For over half of a century, the name Cousteau has been synonymous with the exploration of the undersea world, so it comes as no shock that Fabien Cousteau, as a third-generation oceanographic explorer and documentary filmmaker, has chosen the same career path of his esteemed father Jean-Michel Cousteau and legendary grandfather Jacques-Yves Cousteau. Cousteau, a graduate of Boston University (BU), has managed to carve out his own unique identity within the Cousteau family: he has made two nationally aired documentaries, *Attacks of the Mystery Shark* (2002), about the real-life Jersey Shore shark attacks of 1916, and *Shark: Mind of a Demon* (2006), in which he observed the behavior of sharks from inside a shark-shaped submarine. Cousteau has also been actively involved in numerous marine conservation organizations and programs in efforts to protect the world's oceans and endangered marine species. He partnered with his father and sister Celine for the multipart Public Broadcasting Service (PBS) series *Ocean Adventures*, which aired from 2006 to 2009. Cousteau has also launched other television and media projects through his production company Natural Entertainment. In 2010 he created a not-for-profit program called Plant-A-Fish, which leads initiatives to repair marine environments.

Though some observers would view the task of living up to a legacy like that of Jacques-Yves Cousteau's to be more of a burden than a blessing, Fabien Cousteau has maintained that he has never tried to fill his grandfather's shoes and was never pressured into going into the family business. Instead, he has chosen to carry on

WireImage

Jacques-Yves Cousteau's eldest two sons, Jean-Michel and Philippe, both followed in his footsteps. Jean-Michel, Fabien's father, served for over ten years as executive vice president of the Cousteau Society, his father's Hampton, Virginia–based nonprofit environmental education organization, before venturing out on his own as a documentary film producer and marine conservationist. He established the underwater production company Deep Ocean Odyssey and is the founder and president of the Ocean Futures Society, a nonprofit organization dedicated to educating people about the world's oceans. Philippe Cousteau, meanwhile, was an ocean explorer and environmentally-conscious documentary filmmaker who coproduced and starred in many of his father's films before dying tragically in a PBY Catalina flying boat crash in the Tagus river near Lisbon, Portugal, in 1979. He had two children, Alexandra (born in 1976) and Philippe Jr. (born in 1980, six months after his father's death), both of whom have worked to carry on his legacy as oceanographers and environmentalists through their organization EarthEcho International. In September 2006 Philippe Jr. was working with the famed Australian "Crocodile Hunter" Steve Irwin as an apprentice cohost on the iconic television personality's nature documentary *Ocean's Deadliest* when Irwin was fatally pierced in the chest by a stingray while snorkeling off the coast of Queensland, Australia. Philippe went on to finish hosting the documentary himself and later served as chief ocean correspondent for the nature-centric cable channels Animal Planet and Planet Green.

Along with his younger sister, Celine, Fabien Cousteau grew up immersed in the family business. He spent a good portion of his childhood observing his grandfather on expeditions aboard his famous research ship *Calypso*, where both his parents worked—his father as an explorer and researcher, and his mother as an expedition photographer. Meanwhile, he started diving "before many kids take off their training wheels," as Tim Stoddard wrote for *Bostonia* (Summer 2003, online), the quarterly magazine for alumni of Boston University (BU). When Cousteau was four years old, his grandfather built him custom scuba gear, and he began diving in his family's swimming pool in Sherman Oaks, California; soon afterward he was diving in the ocean. At seven, Cousteau went on his first *Calypso* expedition with his father and grandfather to Papua New Guinea. His first job was scrubbing barnacles off his grandfather's ship, but on later expeditions, he would be assigned to less menial, even glamorous roles as part of the crew. Cousteau recalled, as quoted in the Dublin, Ireland, *Sunday Independent* (9 Nov. 2008), "While other kids were at Disneyland, I was learning how to steer the *Calypso*."

the family legacy out of passion and as a matter of personal responsibility. He told journalist Ron Gluckman, in an article for the luxury travel magazine *Centurion* (Nov. 2012) posted on Gluckman's official website, "I think once you take a peek under the great blue, it's hard to turn your back. I'm addicted to ocean exploration. We're facing some very real challenges in this world, and we have to start fixing things."

CHILDHOOD AND THE FAMILY BUSINESS

The older of the two children of Jean-Michel and Anne-Marie Cousteau, Fabien Cousteau was born in October 1967 in Paris, France, the first grandchild of the pioneering ocean explorer, filmmaker, and researcher Jacques-Yves Cousteau. Considered the founding father of scuba diving, Jacques-Yves Cousteau coinvented the Aqua-Lung, an underwater breathing apparatus now known as the diving regulator, with the French engineer Emile Gagnan in 1943. He was also instrumental in the development of the first underwater cameras. He won Academy Awards for his groundbreaking undersea documentaries *The Silent World* (1956, codirected with the noted French filmmaker Louis Malle) and *World Without Sun* (1964), and rose to international fame as the host and star of the cult television series *The Undersea World of Jacques Cousteau*, which aired from 1968 to 1976 and inspired generations of ocean explorers. A prolific documentary filmmaker, he produced around 140 documentaries before dying, in 1997, at the age of eighty-seven.

While accompanying his grandfather and father on expeditions to some of the world's most remote places, Cousteau was instilled with an appreciation and respect for the ocean and its ecosystems. From an early age he developed a particular fascination with sharks, and he fondly remembers wanting to actually become a shark as a child after reading a book about the Belgian comic book character Tintin and his dog Snowy, titled *Red Rackham's Treasure* (1944), in which the two embark on a treasure hunt in a shark-shaped submarine; the book would later serve as the inspiration for Cousteau's 2006 documentary *Shark: Mind of a Demon*. His fascination was piqued even further after watching director Steven Spielberg's 1975 blockbuster thriller *Jaws* for the first time, when he snuck into a viewing of the film on a cruise ship where his father was giving a lecture. Based on author Peter Benchley's 1974 best-selling novel of the same name, the film helped perpetuate popular misperceptions about sharks and their behavior and was also largely responsible for scaring away generations of people from the water. Cousteau snuck into the film against his parents' orders, for which he was consequently grounded, he recalled to Stoddard, adding, "I walked out of there completely mystified because it went against everything I'd ever been taught." The film would ultimately inspire him to become a tireless advocate for sharks.

EDUCATION

Cousteau has noted that he moved twenty-four times growing up, due to his family's business. Consequently, he attended schools all over France and the United States. "Making new friends every time I started a new school may have been challenging," he wrote in an article for the London *Telegraph* (12 Aug. 2011, online), "but I got to experience the weird things out in the ocean world that most children never had a chance to." By the age of twelve, Cousteau had become a regular crew member on the *Calypso*, which resulted in him spending the rest of his teenage years in and out of school.

In 1987, after attending an all-male boarding school in Connecticut, Cousteau enrolled at Boston University's College of General Studies (CGS), in Boston, Massachusetts, which offers a two-year general education program. It was during this time that he first started exploring career endeavors outside of the family business, encouraged by his grandfather and parents. "My life experience up until then had been nothing but marine biology," he recalled to Stoddard. "So I wanted a flavor of something else. BU was a turning point in my life, because those were the years when I established myself outside of my family." After completing his core curriculum requirements at CGS in 1989, he entered BU's Metropolitan College (MET), where he majored in environmental economics. He earned a bachelor's degree in environmental economics from MET in 1991.

CAREER

After graduating from BU, Cousteau spent some time in fields outside the family business. He worked briefly in graphic design and sales management before joining the Burlington, Vermont–based environmental products development company Seventh Generation, where he worked in new product development. In that division he helped develop and market environmentally sustainable products. Cousteau has said that he purposely took on jobs after college that would force him to be more assertive and that would help him later on in his dealings as an independent filmmaker and businessman. He told Stoddard, "When you're sitting at the negotiating table with ABC executives, or raising funds for an expedition, it's essential to be able to speak their language, and to be able to translate your passion into words they understand."

Cousteau enjoyed success in the business world, but the work he was doing ultimately made him feel "kind of empty," as he told Ann Oldenburg for *USA Today* (27 June 2006). As a result he returned to the family business with a reinvigorated sense of passion and commitment. In the late 1990s he joined Deep Ocean Odyssey, the family's production company, and began working on documentaries with his father. He first came to international attention as an ocean explorer in 2000, when he accompanied his father on a documentary shoot in South Africa. Two years later he was pegged to host his first television special, *Attacks of the Mystery Shark*, as a correspondent for MSNBC's *National Geographic Explorer* documentary series. The hour-long special examined the deadly shark attacks that had occurred along the coast of New Jersey during a two week span in July 1916. The attacks had claimed four lives and wounded another, with three of those victims having been attacked upstream in Matawan Creek, located several miles from the ocean. The attacks were blamed on a great white shark and created a nationwide frenzy as people began perpetuating the theory that all sharks were human-eating predators. These attacks served as the inspiration for Benchley's novel *Jaws* (1974) and Steven Spielberg's 1975 film of the same name, as well as for numerous other media representations of sharks.

For *Attacks of the Mystery Shark*, Cousteau traveled to the site of the attacks in New Jersey, as well as to India's Ganges River Delta, the Bahamas, and Pacific Ocean, in efforts to give viewers a better understanding of sharks and their behavior. Contrary to the popular belief that a great white shark had been responsible for the attacks, Cousteau's film suggests that they were most likely committed by a rogue bull shark, a smaller but more aggressive and unpredictable shark species. The film also contends that shark attacks are almost always a case of mistaken identity, with sharks mistaking humans for fish. Viewers learn that of the eighty or so shark attacks against humans each year, only a handful are fatal, and that the public's grave misperceptions about sharks is contributing to their demise. *Attacks of the Mystery Shark* attracted mainstream media attention and Cousteau's good looks led *People* magazine to name him "Sexiest Man of the Sea" in 2002.

Cousteau spent several years working on his next project, a self-produced documentary centering on the behavior of great white sharks. For the project, he revisited the premise of his favorite Tintin story to create a first-of-its-kind shark-shaped submarine. In order to realize his vision, Cousteau enlisted the help of family friend Eddie Paul, a renowned Hollywood engineer, inventor, and prop maker who has coordinated stunts and special effects for numerous feature films, including *Grease* (1978), *E.T.: The Extra-Terrestrial* (1982), and *The Terminator* (1984). (Paul had previously built a robotic shark for Cousteau's father in the 1980s, but it was destroyed by a great white shark off the coast of Southern Australia when it started malfunctioning.) The end result was a fourteen-foot, 1200-pound wet sub, or a submarine designed to flood when underwater, that looked, moved, and sounded as much like a great white shark as possible. The sub featured hidden video cameras and a high-pressure pneumatic propulsion system, and it was covered in a rubber-like skin called Skinflex. The prototype, named "Troy" and costing over $100,000, allowed Cousteau to swim silently with great white sharks and observe them in their undisturbed natural habitat, as opposed to filming them from a conventional steel cage. Because Troy's steel-enforced cavity was built to fill with water after being submerged, Cousteau had to wear a wet suit and use scuba gear in order to breathe while piloting the mechanism.

The resulting one-hour special *Shark: Mind of a Demon* premiered on CBS in the summer of 2006 and helped debunk the popular myth that great white sharks are mindless killers and eating machines. It chronicled the trials and tribulations of Cousteau and his crew, including Paul, the shark expert Mark Marks, and Cousteau's sister Celine, following them over a two-year period as they tried to launch Troy in the great white shark–infested waters and feeding grounds near Guadalupe Island off the west coast of Mexico in the Pacific Ocean. Despite experiencing several mechanical issues with Troy during the course of filming, Cousteau was able to make some successful dives in the shark sub without being harmed.

The year 2006 also saw Cousteau collaborate with both his father and sister for a three-year PBS documentary series called *Ocean Adventures*, which followed the trio and their expedition team as they examined different types of marine life from all over the world. The series premiered in April of that year with the special *Voyage to Kure*, which explored the remote Kure Atoll of the northwestern Hawaiian Islands. Other specials in the *Ocean Adventures* series include *Sharks at Risk* (2006), which focused on gray sharks in French Polynesia and great white sharks in South Africa; *The Gray Whale Obstacle Course* (2006), which followed gray whale migration routes; *America's Underwater Treasures* (2006), a two-part episode that investigated all thirteen of the US National Marine Sanctuaries and the Northwestern Hawaiian Islands Marine National Monument; *Return to the Amazon* (2008), a ten-month expedition through the Amazon that explored the devastating effects of deforestation and development in the biodiverse region; *Sea Ghosts* (2009), an examination of the effects of climate change on Arctic-dwelling Beluga whales; and *Call of the Killer Whale* (2009), which shed light on the similarities between humans and orcas, or killer whales.

Cousteau has continued to lead and take part in expeditions all over the world. He has also cofounded a production company called Natural Entertainment, which develops television and other media projects related to ocean exploration and environmental awareness. In 2010, in honor of the one-hundredth anniversary of his grandfather's birth, he established Plant-A-Fish, a nonprofit organization that works to educate and empower individuals and communities through the replanting of ocean animals and plants. Cousteau explained to Gluckman that he wants the organization to "help influence the world to be a better place, specifically, to reconnect with the ocean and to feel the same passion most people felt when they first saw my grandfather's documentaries. It's a daunting task, but we can do it." Plant-A-Fish has launched programs to plant one billion oysters in the New York City area, one billion sea turtles in El Salvador, and one million corals in Florida and the Maldives.

Cousteau's other endeavors include writing and public speaking. He has written articles for the *Huffington Post* and other publications and is working on a children's book trilogy "about the future of our planet, a fictional account based on reality," as he told Gerri Miller for Mother Nature Network. He has also spoken on a wide range of environmental issues at conferences and educational institutions all over the world. While acknowledging his grandfather's lasting influence on his life, Cousteau told Stoddard, "I don't want people to think of me as Jacques Cousteau's grandson. I'd like to continue in the spirit of my grandfather, but no one can fill his shoes, and I wouldn't pretend to do that." He added, in his essay for the London *Telegraph*, "I remember clearly my grandfather saying to me when I was a child that the two fundamental things we need to live are air and water, and we are treating both as a garbage can. He created a consciousness about our oceans, and taking better care is more urgent now than ever before, so I try my best to carry on his message."

PERSONAL LIFE

Cousteau divides his time between New York City and the South of France. He serves on the board of the New York Harbor School, a public high school located on Governor's Island that offers special marine-based programs, and he is a member of the Water Innovations Alliance, which works to raise awareness of water issues by bringing them to the attention of corporate executives. Cousteau spends most of the year traveling but enjoys mountain biking and wind surfing in his spare time. He is also an avid rider and collector of vintage motorcycles, with at least eight vintage bikes in his collection. He told Ingrid Skjong for *Gotham* magazine (1 Aug. 2009, online) that he goes to bed "exhausted" every night and wakes up "every morning ready to do it again."

SUGGESTED READING

Cousteau, Fabien. "Biography." *Fabien Cousteau: The Adventure of Discovery*. Fabien Cousteau, n.d. Web. 5 Apr. 2012.
Cutter, Kimberly. "Who Is the Nouveau Cousteau?" *Men's Journal* (2008): n. pag. Print.
Finn, Robin. "PUBLIC LIVES; Heir to an Undersea World, Swimming With Sharks." *New York Times* 31 July 2002: 2. Print.
Miller, Gerri. "Cousteau, the Next Generation." *Arts & Culture*. MNN Holdings, LLC, 21 Apr. 2009. Web. 5 Apr. 2012.
Stoddard, Tim. "The Underseen World of Fabien Cousteau." *Bostonia*. Boston University, Summer 2003. Web. 5 Apr. 2012.

—*Chris Cullen*

Pavel Datsyuk

Born: July 20, 1978
Occupation: Hockey player

Since his National Hockey League (NHL) debut in 2001, Pavel Datsyuk has developed a reputation as a skilled offensive player, with his remarkable hand-eye coordination, his deceptive speed, and his stick-handling ability. He is consistent, scoring twenty or more goals in seven consecutive seasons (2003 to 2010). However, Datsyuk has not only garnered

NHLI via Getty Images

attention for his offensive abilities; he is also widely regarded for his defensive play. "If you're down a goal in the last minute, who do you want out there—[Alexander] Ovechkin, [Sidney] Crosby, [Evgeni] Malkin or Datsyuk? Any of them," said Detroit Red Wings coach Mike Babcock to Mitch Albom for the *Detroit Free Press* (19 Apr. 2009). "But if you're up a goal in the last minute and need to protect the lead, who would you want? You'd want Pav." Over three consecutive seasons (2008 to 2010) Datsyuk was the recipient of the Frank J. Selke Trophy, which recognizes the league's best defensive forward. In the 2007 and 2008 season he led the NHL in takeaways, with 144, a league record. During his eleven years in Detroit, Datsyuk has helped lead his team to two Stanley Cup titles.

EARLY LIFE

Pavel Valerievich Datsyuk was born on July 20, 1978, in Ekaterinburg (formerly known as Sverdlovsk), the fourth-largest city in Russia and one of the country's industrial and economic hubs. His father, Valery, worked as a van driver, and his mother, Galina, was a cook for a military post. Datsyuk lived with his parents and older sister in a cramped, three-room apartment. The building also overlooked a makeshift ice skating rink, where he first learned to play hockey.

Datsyuk honed his skills at the Yunost Sports Academy, in Ekaterinburg, and trained under the watchful eye of Valeri Goloukhov. Growing up,

Datsyuk also played for the local youth hockey team Yunost Ekaterinburg. However, he almost gave up the sport, following the untimely death of his mother, who passed away from cancer when he was sixteen years old—an event that affected him deeply. "I felt guilty," he told Albom. "I didn't know she was so sick. I thought she would get better. When I look back, I think she took that last vacation with me because she knew she was going to die." At first, a grieving Datsyuk struggled to cope with her death. "I lost myself," he admitted to Albom.

PROFESSIONAL HOCKEY IN RUSSIA

Despite his grief, Datsyuk eventually returned to the hockey rink. The eighteen-year-old center started the 1996 and 1997 season playing for SKA Yekaterinburg in the Pervaya Liga, a feeder league for the now-defunct Russian Superleague (RSL). In his position as center, Datsyuk's role is that of the playmaker, passing between the two wings to set up a goal.

Datsyuk scored two goals and had two assists in eighteen games for SKA Yekaterinburg before signing with Spartak Yekaterinburg, a team that competed in the RSL, which was not only the country's top professional ice hockey league but also ranked as the second-best league in the world, after the NHL. The Kontinental Hockey League (KHL), also regarded as the premier association in Europe, has since replaced the RSL.

In his 1996 and 1997 season with Spartak, Datsyuk appeared in thirty-six games, in which he had twelve goals and ten assists. He spent the 1997 and 1998 with Dynamo-Energiya Yekaterinburg, the farm club for HC Dynamo Moscow, a hockey team competing in the Western Conference of the KHL. After making twenty-four appearances and amassing three goals and five assists for the Dynamo squad, Datsyuk scored seven goals and had eight assists in twenty-two games for Dynamo-Energiya Yekaterinburg 2, the team's minor-league affiliate in the Pervaya Liga (also referred to as RUS-3).

NHL DRAFT PICK

During the 1997 and 1998 season, Datsyuk unexpectedly caught the attention of Hakan Andersson, the European director of scouting for the Detroit Red Wings of the NHL. "I travelled out to see [defensive prospect] Dmitri Kalinin play. His team was playing Datsyuk's team. Kalinin was an 18-year-old and Datsyuk in his last junior season," Andersson told Steve Simons for *Canoe.ca* (28 May 2008). "I went to see him one more time. I put him on the list. My main concern was he was small. I was afraid he would make the world junior team. That would have exposed him."

In June 1998 Datsyuk was the 171st player selected overall by the Detroit Red Wings, in the sixth round of the NHL Entry Draft. He had been previously passed over in the 1996 and 1997 NHL drafts, mainly over concerns about his size; at the time Datsyuk's height was five feet seven and he weighed about 150 pounds, which was considered undersized by league standards. After being drafted into the NHL, Datsyuk remained in Russia, where he continued to develop his skills. He began the 1998 and 1999 season with minor-league affiliate Dynamo-Energiya Yekaterinburg 2. After appearing in ten games and recording an equal number of goals and assists—fourteen—for the team, Datsyuk was subsequently assigned to Dynamo-Energiya Yekaterinburg, where he amassed twenty-one goals and twenty-three assists in thirty-five games to close out the season.

Datsyuk followed that up with a one-goal, three-assist performance for Dynamo-Energiya Yekaterinburg in 1999 and 2000. The next season he played for Ak Bars Kazan, a dominant club in the RSL. Despite suffering a leg injury, he still managed nine goals and seventeen assists in forty-two games. Datsyuk was also a member of the Russian team that competed at the 2001 International Ice Hockey Federation (IIHF) World Championship.

NHL DEBUT AND THE FIRST STANLEY CUP

In 2001 Datsyuk received an invitation to the Detroit Red Wings' training camp, where his impressive play quickly turned heads. "His first day of training camp he had the flu," former Red Wings teammate Steve Yzerman told Helene St. James in an interview that appeared in *USA Today* (20 Jan. 2009). "From the second day on, he wowed us." Datsyuk earned a spot on the club's 2001 and 2002 NHL roster, which also included veterans Brendan Shanahan, Niklas Lidstrom, and Chris Chelios; fellow Russians Igor Larionov and Sergei Fedorov; and newly signed free agents Brett Hull and Luc Robitaille.

During the eighty-two-game regular season, Datsyuk became a fixture in the Detroit Red Wings' starting lineup. He was part of an effective forward line with second-year player Boyd Devereaux and Hull, who dubbed the trio "Two Kids and an Old Goat." (The forward line, which consists of a left wing, a center, and a right wing, is responsible for most of the team's scoring.) Hull's veteran presence proved to be a benefit to the rookie Datsyuk, whose eleven goals and twenty-four assists in seventy games helped his team capture the Western Conference Central Division title as well as the NHL Presidents' Trophy.

After defeating the Vancouver Canucks and St. Louis Blues, the Red Wings advanced to the best-of-seven Western Conference championship, where they beat out the Colorado Avalanche and earned a berth to the Stanley Cup finals, another best-of-seven contest. The Carolina Hurricanes proved to be no match for the Red Wings, who won the series in five games. During his team's playoff run, Datsyuk appeared in twenty-one games, racking up three goals and three assists en route to his first Stanley Cup victory. That year he was part of the Western Conference squad that competed in the NHL YoungStars, an exhibition game among the league's top rookies that is held during the NHL All-Star weekend in January. He scored one of the team's thirteen goals en route to a six-run victory over their Eastern Conference counterparts.

PROMINENCE WITH THE RED WINGS
In his sophomore season (2002 and 2003), Datsyuk managed to notch twelve goals and thirty-nine assists despite being sidelined by a strained right knee injury that limited him to sixty-four regular-season games. He was again paired on the forward line with Hull; Henrik Zetterberg, a highly regarded rookie prospect from Sweden, replaced Devereaux. For the second straight season, the Detroit Red Wings won the Western Conference division and advanced to the Stanley Cup playoffs, where the upstart Mighty Ducks of Anaheim swept the defending champions in the first round. Datsyuk went scoreless in the four-game series.

In June 2003 Datsyuk signed a one-year $1.5 million contract, which included an option to remain with the Red Wings for the 2004 and 2005 season. In each of his first two seasons, he had earned less than a million dollars. Following the exodus of Sergei Fedorov, who had signed a five-year $40 million deal with the Ducks, Datsyuk was expected to play a larger role in the Red Wings' offense during the 2003 and 2004 season. For the last two seasons, Fedorov had been one of the team's scoring leaders, along with Hull and Shanahan.

In 2003 and 2004 Datsyuk received more ice time, averaging eighteen minutes and sixteen seconds per game, up from the fifteen minutes and twenty-eight seconds he averaged the previous season. With the increased playing time, he improved his offensive production, scoring a team-high thirty goals and thirty-eight assists in seventy-five games for the Red Wings, who won a league-best forty-eight games to clinch their third consecutive division title. After defeating the Nashville Predators four games to two in the first round of the Stanley Cup playoffs, Detroit was eliminated in the second round by the Calgary Flames. Datsyuk went scoreless with six assists in twelve playoff games. He also made his first NHL All-Star appearance as a reserve for the Western Conference team, who was defeated by the Eastern squad. Internationally, Datsyuk represented Russia at the 2003 IIHF World Championship and the 2004 World Cup of Hockey.

CORNERSTONE OF THE RED WINGS FRANCHISE
On September 15, 2004, the NHL collective bargaining agreement (CBA) expired, provoking a labor disagreement between league owners and the players association that resulted in the cancellation of the entire 2004 to 2005 season. In anticipation of the NHL lockout, Datsyuk agreed to terms with his former club HC Dynamo Moscow. During the 2004–2005 season, he scored fifteen goals and seventeen assists in forty-seven games, earning MVP honors while helping Dynamo Moscow claim the 2005 Russian Superleague Championship.

In July 2005 the owners and the players association reached a new CBA that set the league-wide salary cap at $39 million—more than half of what the Red Wings had previously spent. Despite the cap constraints, the Red Wings managed to sign Datsyuk, a restricted free agent, to a two-year, $7.8 million deal in late September. In 2005 and 2006 he recorded twenty-eight goals in seventy-five games. Datsyuk also ranked among the league's top ten in assists, with fifty-nine, for the Red Wings, who amassed a league-best fifty-eight victories to win the Presidents' Trophy. However, the team failed to advance past the first round of the 2006 Stanley Cup playoffs, losing to the Edmonton Oilers in six games; Datsyuk notched three assists in five of those games. Following the playoffs, Datsyuk, who had only logged twenty-two penalty minutes during the regular season, was presented with the Lady Byng Memorial Trophy for sportsmanlike conduct. He also competed with the national team, winning his second bronze at the 2005 IIHF World Championship and finishing fourth at the 2006 Winter Olympics in Turin, Italy.

In 2006 and 2007 Datsyuk was a model of consistency and durability, putting up numbers similar to the previous season. His twenty-seven goals and sixty assists in seventy-nine games helped lead the Red Wings to another Western Conference division title. Less than a week before the playoffs, Datsyuk agreed to a seven-year contract extension worth nearly $47 million. His team improved on last season's playoff performance, advancing past the Calgary Flames and San Jose Sharks in the first and second rounds, respectively. However, the Red Wings were defeated in the Western Conference finals by the Ducks, the eventual Stanley Cup champions. During the team's playoff run, Datsyuk was the scoring leader, with eight goals; he also had eight assists. Datsyuk was also the recipient of the Lady Byng award for the second consecutive time.

SECOND STANLEY CUP
Datsyuk's breakthrough season came in 2007 and 2008. He recorded a personal best of thirty-one goals, as well as a team-high sixty-six assists, while appearing in all eighty-two regular-season

games. Another individual accomplishment included his second All-Star selection. For the third straight season, the Red Wings captured the Central Division West; they were also winners of the Presidents' Trophy for the second time in three years.

Datsyuk and his teammates faced off against the Nashville Predators in the first-round playoff series, which the Red Wings won in six games. They proved dominant in the second round, sweeping the Colorado Avalanche in four to reach the Western Conference finals. Datsyuk had a memorable performance in game 3 of the series; he scored three goals against the Dallas Stars to record his first career hat trick. The Red Wings went on to eliminate the Stars in six games and advance to the 2008 Stanley Cup Finals, which they won four games to two against the Pittsburgh Penguins. In the championship series, Datsyuk notched a total of three assists in two of the team's victories: one in game 4 and two in the deciding game 6. His lone goal came during a triple overtime loss in game 5.

2008 TO 2010

Following the Stanley Cup playoffs, Datsyuk was honored with the Lady Byng Trophy for the third year in a row, becoming the first NHL player to achieve this feat in more than seventy years. He was also awarded the Frank J. Selke Trophy, which recognizes the best defensive forward in the league. Datsyuk garnered further recognition for being one of only two players to receive both the Lady Byng and Selke trophies during their careers.

Datsyuk's offensive numbers in 2008 and 2009 were nearly identical to those of the prior season. In eighty-one appearances, he amassed a career high of thirty-two goals as well as sixty-five assists, the second-most of his career. The Red Wings finished the season with fifty-one victories, the best record in the Central West and the second-best record in the Western Conference. After completing a four-game sweep of the Columbus Blue Jackets in the first round of the playoffs, the Red Wings advanced to the second round, where they defeated the Ducks in seven games. They dominated the Chicago Blackhawks in the Western Conference finals, winning four out of five games to earn their second straight berth in the finals of the Stanley Cup. In a rematch of last year's championship series, the Red Wings went head-to-head with the Penguins, who overcame a three games-to-two deficit to win the Stanley Cup. Datsyuk recorded one goal and eight assists in sixteen postseason games. His 2008 and 2009 honors included a fourth consecutive Lady Byng Trophy; a second straight Selke Trophy; and an ESPY nod for Best NHL Player Award.

Datsyuk continued to provide an offensive spark for the team during the 2009 and 2010 season, scoring twenty-seven goals and forty-three assists in eighty games. The Red Wings, winners of forty-four regular-season games, finished second in the Central division and fifth overall in the conference. Datsyuk not only led his team in goals scored, with twenty-seven, but he also had forty-three assists, which was the second-highest total, behind Zetterberg. After besting the Phoenix Coyotes in seven games during the first round of the playoffs, the Red Wings fell in five games to the San Jose Sharks in the second round. Datsyuk, the recipient of a third consecutive Selke Trophy, was voted to his third All-Star game but did not participate due to a hip injury. He also competed at the 2010 IIHF World Championship in Germany, where the Russian national team earned a second-place finish, behind the gold-medal winning Czech Republic squad. Datsyuk, who scored six goals and one assist over the course of the tournament, was named best forward.

2010 TO 2012

Despite an injury-plagued 2010 and 2011 season, Datsyuk still managed to record twenty goals and thirty-six assists in fifty-six games. His team regained the Central Division title, after playing forty-seven regular-season games. For the second straight season, the Red Wings met the Coyotes in the first round of the playoffs. However, this time they defeated the Coyotes in four straight games and went on to face the Sharks, in a rematch of the last season's second round. The Red Wings were unceremoniously eliminated from the Stanley Cup playoffs after losing to the Sharks in seven games.

In 2011 and 2012 Datsyuk remained one of his team's offensive leaders, recording nineteen goals and a team-leading forty-eight assists in seventy games for the Red Wings, who finished third in the Central and fifth in the conference. However, their postseason was short-lived; they failed to make it past the first round after being defeated in five games by the Nashville Predators. Datsyuk was nominated for the Selke Trophy, which was ultimately awarded to Patrice Bergeron of the Boston Bruins.

Datsyuk has established the PD13 Hockey School in his native city of Ekaterinburg—PD13 incorporates his initials and his jersey number. He lives in Detroit, Michigan, with his wife, Svetlana and their daughter, Elizabeth.

SUGGESTED READING

Cannella, Stephen. "The NHL." *Sports Illustrated*. Time Inc., 22 Dec. 2003. Web. 10 Aug. 2012. Cazeneuve, Brian. "Disgusting, but in A Good Way." *Sports Illustrated*. Time Inc., 2 May 2011. Web. 10 Aug. 2012.

Farber, Michael. "Staring down the End." *Sports Illustrated*. Time Inc., 15 Mar. 2010. Web. 10 Aug. 2012.

---. "The Third Russian." *Sports Illustrated*. Time Inc., 13 Apr. 2009. Web. 10 Aug. 2012.

Helka, Mike. "Datsyuk, Red Wings Destined for Each Other." *ESPN.com*. ESPN Internet Ventures, 26 Jan. 2004. Web. 11 Aug. 2012.

Simons, Steve. "Diamonds in The Rough." *Slam! Sports*. Canoe Inc., 28 May 2008. Web. 10 Aug. 2012.

St. James, Helene. "Red Wings' Datsyuk Puckish but Very Productive." *USA Today*. Gannett, 20 Jan. 2009. Web. 11 Aug. 2012.

—Bertha Muteba

Wirelmage

Zooey Deschanel

Born: January 17, 1980
Occupation: Actress and musician

Zooey Deschanel is the star of the television sitcom *New Girl*. She has also appeared in such mainstream films as *Almost Famous* (2000), *Elf* (2003), *Failure to Launch* (2006), and *Yes Man* (2008). Deschanel is also closely identified with such independent films as *All the Real Girls* (2003) and *(500) Days of Summer* (2009). "She's an actress. She's a singer. She's the girl that bespectacled guys dream about in physics class. Zooey Deschanel does blockbusters, and she does indie movies. She stars in sitcoms, and she makes jokey videos for Funny or Die. She's a comedian, a cute friend, a dramatic lead and a lifelong singer," Robert Isenberg wrote for *MSN* (11 Feb. 2012, online). "Deschanel has done pretty much everything you can do in Hollywood."

Nonetheless, Deschanel's varied success in music, movies, and television has caused some to criticize her. "[T]he perception of her as a sort of standard-bearer for all things sincere and nostalgic (or mannered and twee, depending on your point of view) has made her a figure of both adoration and exasperation," Jada Yuan wrote for *New York* magazine (11 Sep. 2011). Those who adore Deschanel, however, tend to do so wholeheartedly. Many of her female fans copy her trademark bangs, and her male admirers can be unabashedly effusive. "Maybe it's the way she stares at you with those huge blue eyes," Glenn Whipp wrote for the *Los Angeles Daily News* (14 Feb. 2003). "Maybe it's her ability to speak with equal authority on Fellini and chocolate milk."

EARLY LIFE AND EDUCATION

Deschanel (pronounced day-shuh-NEL) was born on January 17, 1980 in Los Angeles, California. She is named after Zooey Glass, a male character in the work of novelist J. D. Salinger. Her father, Caleb Deschanel, is an Oscar-nominated cinematographer whose credits include *The Right Stuff* (1983), *The Natural* (1984), and *The Passion of the Christ* (2004). Her mother, Mary Jo Deschanel, is an actress who has had roles in the television shows *Twin Peaks*, *JAG*, *Law & Order*, and *House M.D.*, as well as in the occasional film. Deschanel's older sister, Emily, is the star of the television crime drama *Bones*. As children, Deschanel and her sister accompanied their parents to movie sets on occasion, traveling to Africa, London, and Italy, among other places.

Deschanel developed an interest in acting at an early age. "My nursery school did a production of *The Three Little Pigs*," she told Glenn Whipp. "I played the third pig. When the wolf knocked on my door, I refused to get up and answer it because, to me, he was knocking the wrong way. I just laid there, snoring away on stage, fully immersed in my character. My Dad turned to my Mom and said, 'Dustin Hoffman.'" Her parents, understanding firsthand the hardships posed by the profession, allowed Deschanel to take acting lessons, but made her wait until she was old enough to have a driver's license before giving her permission to attend auditions.

CAREER BEGINNINGS

Deschanel attended a Los Angeles private school called Crossroads, where she had roles in several student productions, including *Our Town* and *The Mikado*. (Her classmates included actors Kate Hudson and Jake Gyllenhaal.) She appeared in her first professional production when she was sixteen, playing Red Riding Hood in an

Interact Theatre Company staging of the musical *Into the Woods*. John Rubinstein, a family friend, headed the theatre company. In the audience for one performance was an agent named Sarah Jackson, who told a reporter for *Back Stage* (8 July 2009, online), "Rarely in my career do you see somebody who has something special and you know will go all the way. But you could tell with her, even at that young age. She had no professional experience at all, but she held her own with this amazing cast, and you couldn't take your eyes off her."

With Jackson representing her, Deschanel won a guest spot on the sitcom *Veronica's Closet* in 1998, and the following year she appeared in her first film, playing a troubled teenager in the Lawrence Kasdan comedy-drama *Mumford*.

Deschanel attended Northwestern University, in Illinois, for less than a year before dropping out to accept a role in *Almost Famous* (2000), a semi-autobiographical movie written and directed by Cameron Crowe. "[School] was fun, but . . . acting is very much something . . . where you learn by doing it," she told Evan Henerson for the *Los Angeles Daily News* (20 Oct. 2004). "I figured I'm not going to turn down an opportunity to work with Cameron Crowe and Frances McDormand."

Almost Famous tells the story of William Miller, a fifteen-year-old who talks the editors of *Rolling Stone* magazine into letting him tour with and write about a rock band called Stillwater. (A teenaged Crowe had actually toured with and written about the Allman Brothers Band for *Rolling Stone*.) Deschanel was cast as William's older sister, Anita. Upon leaving home, Anita bequeaths her vinyl records to her brother, assuring him, in one of the film's most touching moments, "One day you'll be cool." Crowe told Whipp that he had been smitten with Deschanel immediately. "The moment Zooey walked into our office [to audition], we were no longer in L.A.," he recalled. "She wore an oversize, knee-length antique coat, an exotic flower behind her ear and a mischievous smile. Suddenly, a whiff of Paris was in the air. I pictured her with a cello, sneaking into the Ritz Hotel, a young girl abroad and looking for trouble."

Deschanel next appeared in the film *Manic* (2001), which starred Joseph Gordon-Levitt as a teen confined to a mental hospital. She appeared alongside Jennifer Aniston in the 2002 film *The Good Girl*. The two play coworkers at the discount store Retail Rodeo, where Deschanel's character, Cheryl, is known for making wisecracks over the store's public address system. Demoted to the makeup counter, she tells one customer that a new color palette is called "Cirque du Face" and asserts, "It's all the rage with the Frenchies." While *The Good Girl* was not a huge hit at the box office, it was praised by many critics and increased Deschanel's profile as an actor.

Deschanel also appeared in the 2002 thriller *Abandon* (2002), starring Katie Holmes. Although the part was small, she caught the eye of several critics, including Roger Ebert, who wrote for the *Chicago Sun-Times* (18 Oct. 2002), "Deschanel's drunk scene . . . is an example of material that is spot-on." Following a role in the ensemble comedy *Big Trouble* (2002), Deschanel took on a part in *The New Guy* (2002), about a geeky teen who transfers to a different high school in an attempt to change his image. While critics described the movie as sophomoric, Deschanel again won favorable attention, with Elvis Mitchell writing for the *New York Times* (10 May 2002), "The able cast also includes the protean young actress Zooey Deschanel, who has yet to give a bad performance in her brief career."

STARRING ROLES

In 2003, Deschanel starred in the independent feature *All the Real Girls*, alongside Paul Schneider and Patricia Clarkson. Set in a North Carolina town, the story revolves around Paul (played by Schneider), a working-class heartthrob who falls in love with Noel (played by Deschanel), his best friend's virginal younger sister. In a review for *Salon* (21 Feb. 2003, online), Stephanie Zacharek quoted one of Deschanel's lines, "I had a dream that you grew a garden on a trampoline and I was so happy that I invented peanut butter," and opined, "The good news is that Deschanel doesn't make the mistake of playing Noel as a google-eyed charmer; she's off in the ether just enough that she can sometimes be fascinating to watch. As Deschanel plays her, you can't write Noel off as a cutie-pie flake (her dreams about garden trampolines and peanut butter notwithstanding); we see that she's really a refuge of resolve and good sense in this godforsaken town." Kenneth Turan, the critic for the *Los Angeles Times* (14 Feb. 2003), was also impressed, writing, "Deschanel . . . is all she should be and more as Noel, perfectly capturing that pivotal moment of balance between childhood and the adult world, when vulnerability, confidence, confusion and yearning all collide in an emotional maelstrom. Previously known for small comic roles . . . Deschanel's best, most alive qualities have been liberated by [director David Gordon] Green's deliberate style, and she's unlikely to be known for small roles again."

Turan's prediction seemed to be fulfilled when Deschanel next starred opposite Will Ferrell in the holiday comedy *Elf* (2003). Ferrell's character, Buddy, a full-sized human who has been raised by elves at the North Pole, comes to New York City to seek out his birth father. While there he meets and falls in love with Deschanel's character, who finds his elfin idiosyncrasies charming. The movie proved to be an enormous hit at the box office and was also popular with critics, who praised its lack of irony and timeless appeal. "I wanted a spot in the . . . culture that will last," Deschanel told Matt Lauer on the *Today Show* (7 Nov. 2003). "I wanted to be in a movie like *Miracle on 34th Street*."

A VARIED CAREER

Although she won good reviews appearing alongside Matthew McConaughey and Sarah Jessica Parker in *Failure to Launch* (2006) and opposite Jim Carrey in *Yes Man* (2008), Deschanel did not choose to make such big-budget fare the focus of her career. She appeared instead in a variety of projects. These included *Eulogy* (2004), a black comedy in which a family gathers for the funeral of its patriarch, and *The Hitchhiker's Guide to the Galaxy* (2004), a big-screen adaptation of Douglas Adams science fiction novel. In 2005, Deschanel appeared alongside Ferrell again in *Winter Passing*, which also featured Deschanel's mother in a small role. Deschanel appeared in the road-trip picture *The Go-Getter* in 2006, and the film adaptation of the young-adult novel *The Bridge to Terabithia* in 2008. She appeared in director M. Night Shyamalan's thrilled *The Happening* and the romantic comedy *Gigantic* in 2008.

In 2009, Deschanel again starred opposite Joseph Gordon-Levitt, this time in the film *(500) Days of Summer*, a romantic comedy. Gordon-Levitt's character, Tom, falls in love with Deschanel's character, Summer, but as the narrator warns in the opening moments of the film, "Boy meets girl—but it is not a love story." Summer, whose winsome manner is irresistible to Tom, is uninterested in a meaningful, long-term relationship, preferring to live fancy-free and unencumbered. "Deschanel . . . simply embodies that girl, the one who hit the center of the target without trying," wrote Michael Ordona for the *Los Angeles Times* (17 July 2009). "Her elusiveness makes her moments of vulnerability all the more effective. She convinces the audience of not only Summer's charm, but also her uniqueness, making no mystery of why Tom falls so hard. It's a rare performance." The Backstage.com reporter echoed that enthusiasm: "[She's] the girl next door in the coolest neighborhood in town."

In 2011, Deschanel appeared in the comedy *Our Idiot Brother* and the knights-in-shining-armor spoof *Your Highness*. She also embarked on the most high-profile project of her career: starring in her own television sitcom, New Girl. The show features Deschanel as Jess Day, a loveable but awkward young woman who tends to break into song when she is nervous. Newly single because she has discovered her boyfriend cheating on her, she moves into a loft apartment with three male friends. "Jess is the keystone of the show and Deschanel, with her impossibly

blue eyes peeking out from behind her horn rims and up from under unkempt bangs, fills her with the charming and willful childishness usually reserved for characters played by male comedians— Will Ferrell in *Elf*, Adam Sandler in, well, just about anything," the television critic Mary McNamara wrote for the *Los Angeles Times* (20 Sep. 2011). "Deschanel's essential sexiness is impossible to eradicate, but she uses all its elements—the eyes, that voice, those curves—to fine comedic effect, playing dorky the way Judy Holliday, Carole Lombard or even Lucille Ball played dumb. Which is to say, with the occasional sensual growl and knowing twinkle in her eye, letting everyone know that Jess is in on the joke." The show was nominated for a 2011 Golden Globe Award as best television comedy of the year. Deschanel also received a best-actress nomination.

MUSIC CAREER

In addition to acting, Deschanel sings and plays multiple instruments, including the ukulele. She occasionally works as part of a cabaret act known as Pretty Babies, which performs standards from the 1920s and 1930s. (The other member of the duo is Samantha Shelton.)

She also performs in a band called She & Him, which she formed with folk rocker Matt Ward (known as M. Ward), whom she met on the set of The Go-Getter. They have released three albums to date: Volume One (2008), Volume Two (2010), and A Very She & Him Christmas (2011). Although several critics admitted the temptation to treat She & Him as merely a novelty act, the pair quickly earned widespread respect and acclaim. "After a few spins of [Volume One], one could make a compelling case that Deschanel could quit her day job," Tim Sendra wrote for the online music guide Allmusic, echoing sentiments expressed by many. "Deschanel's songs are simple and sad tales of heartbreak and missed connections, with hooky melodies and not a single artless moment to be found. For sure, there's not a single instance that sounds like she got the gig because of who she is instead of what she can do." He concluded, "If you run screaming at the thought of singing actresses, give She & Him a chance and they might calm your fears" (18 Mar. 2008).

She & Him can also be heard on the soundtrack to the 2011 Disney film *Winnie the Pooh*. They perform five tunes, including the classic theme song and an original end-credit song, which Deschanel wrote.

OTHER ROLES

Deschanel has also acted in several skits posted on the comedy website Funny or Die. She is also one of the founders of Hello Giggles, an entertainment website aimed at women. The site includes recipes, off-beat beauty tips, and how-to articles, as well as a live "Kitten Cam," which can be found in a section labeled "Cuteness."

PERSONAL LIFE

Deschanel was romantically linked to actor Jason Schwartzman from 2003 to 2005. In 2009, she married Ben Gibbard, the front man of the indie-rock band Death Cab for Cutie. They amicably separated in late 2011, and have since divorced.

Deschanel is fond of flea markets and vintage clothing, and she has told interviewers that she does research before she travels so that she knows where to find the best shops. She has admitted that she owns so many coats she must store them on rolling racks. Journalists often comment on her unique style. "In an era in which the red carpet can seem as if it's been styled by a single person (One-shoulder dresses are in! Everyone wear red!), Deschanel's independent sartorial spirit makes her a Hollywood anomaly," Sara Stewart wrote for the *New York Post* (4 July 2010). Deschanel told Shahesta Shaitly for the *London Observer* (22 May 2010), "I don't follow trends. . . . I don't go to a lot of fashion shows or pay attention to what other people are wearing. The red-carpet thing of premieres and parties is probably my least favorite part of my job."

Deschanel is also different from many other young actresses in that she is rarely featured in the tabloid press. "It's pretty easy to avoid being caught drunk at a club," she explained to Peta Hellard for the Melbourne, Australia *Herald-Sun* (1 Jan. 2009). "Just don't go to the club and don't get drunk."

Deschanel has become of the entertainment industry's best recognized talents, and is likely to remain a familiar in movies, television, and music for years to come.

SUGGESTED READING

Isenberg, Robert. "The Quirky, Fun Life of Zooey Deschanel." MSN.com. 11 Feb. 2012. Web. 28 Mar. 2012.

Shaitly, Shahesta. "Five Things I Know About Style." (London) *Observer*. 22 May 2010. Web. 28 Mar. 2012.

Stewart, Sara. "Zooey Zowie! Why Everyone's Infatuated with the Indie Ingenue." *New York Post*. 04 July 2010: 41.

Whipp, Glenn. "Zooey Story." *Los Angeles Daily News* 14 Feb. 2003: U7.

Yuan, Jada. "The Pinup of Williamsburg." New York. 11 Sep. 2011. Web. 28 Mar. 2012.

—*Mari Rich*

Susan Desmond-Hellmann

Born: 1957
Occupation: Oncologist and translational scientist

Dr. Susan Desmond-Hellman was named the first female chancellor of the University of California, San Francisco (UCSF) on August 3, 2009. The school is among the top health-care training facilities in the United States, and Desmond-Hellmann is an alumna of the residency program there. After presiding over product development at the drug developer Genentech, where she oversaw the production of several of the most effective cancer-fighting drugs on the market, Desmond-Hellmann returned to UCSF to train a new generation of oncologists (as well as other physicians, researchers, and pharmacists). As Julian Guthrie wrote for the *San Francisco Chronicle* (11 Apr. 2010), Desmond-Hellmann's successes at Genentech have "made her a millionaire hundreds of times over," but she is far more interested in UCSF's potential to foster important and life-saving research than she is a paycheck.

Advancements in technology have led to better drugs for cancer patients, but the cost of research—among a host of other factors—has driven up prices on the most effective drugs, which has adversely affected patient treatment. One oncologist at the Mayo Clinic said that she avoided discussing a particular drug with patients she knew could not afford it. "I don't want them to feel bad," Dr. Angela Dispenzieri told Alex Berenson for the *New York Times* (12 July 2005). With the recent economic downturn, investment in biotechnologies is also down, but Desmond-Hellmann, who hopes to raise $100 million for UCSF by 2016, remains undeterred. Given the lack of funding for UCSF within the University of California (UC) system, Desmond-Hellmann is taking steps to make the school more autonomous by securing funding from a variety of new sources. She even began the fundraising initiative by donating $1 million of her own money. "We need to make drug development faster, cheaper, and more predictable," Desmond-Hellmann told Guthrie. "We need to get to the point where when a patient hears the words, 'You have cancer,' the patient also hears, 'And here is what we have for you.'"

Desmond-Hellmann, who spent two years conducting AIDS research in Uganda with her husband, has been the recipient of a number of awards and honors. When she was with Genentech, *Fortune* magazine listed her among the "Top 50 Most Powerful Women in Business" in 2001 and from 2003 to 2008. In 2007, she was inducted into the Biotech Hall of Fame. In 2005 and again in 2006, the *Wall Street Journal*

Bloomberg via Getty Images

selected Desmond-Hellmann for its annual "50 Women to Watch" list, and in 2009 she was awarded the Edison Achievement Award for leadership in innovation (past awardees include the late Steve Jobs of Apple and Ted Turner of Time Warner).

EARLY LIFE AND EDUCATION

The second of seven children, Desmond-Hellmann was born in 1957 in Napa, California, and was raised in Reno, Nevada. Her father, Frank Desmond, is a retail pharmacist who ran a Keystone Owl Rexall Drugstore when Desmond-Hellmann was growing up. Her mother, Jennie Desmond, is a breast cancer survivor (as is Desmond-Hellman's older sister) and a former English teacher.

Desmond-Hellmann worked as a bookkeeper in her father's pharmacy. She enjoyed watching him interact with customers, but it was the family physician, Dr. Noah Smirnoff, who impressed her with his bedside manner during a visit to treat her father when he had the flu. Before high school, she knew that she wanted to be a doctor. It was a career path that fit Desmond-Hellmann's self-described "nerdy" nature, which she felt was embraced and encouraged by her family. "There was a lot of emphasis on being a good student, on studying, and discussion about science and about medicine," she told Joanna Breitstein for the website PharmExec (1 Apr. 2006). "When I was growing up, I was very much the nerdy student. I admired people who were smart."

After graduating as valedictorian from her high school, Desmond-Hellmann enrolled in the University of Nevada, Reno, so that she could live at home and save money. She finished her undergraduate premedical degree in three years and stayed in Reno to earn her medical degree beginning in 1978. She planned to pursue sports medicine, but a month-long rotation with an oncologist named Dr. Stephen Hall at the Veterans Administration Hospital in Reno changed her mind. Desmond-Hellmann shifted her focus to internal medicine and then oncology.

When it came time to apply for an internship and residency, UCSF was Desmond-Hellmann's first choice. Despite her stellar grades, winning a spot at UCSF was a long shot—most of the students in the applicant pool came from Ivy League schools. Lloyd "Holly" Smith, the former chair of the UCSF Department of Medicine, recalled Desmond-Hellmann's application to Guthrie: "Sue came from the University of Nevada, an institution we hadn't had any experience with. We took a chance on her because the university had written these letters filled with superlative descriptions. They said they had not seen a student like her."

Despite the support, Desmond-Hellmann felt like an underdog because of her background and gravitated toward another state-school student, Nick Hellmann from the University of Kentucky, who would later become her husband. Desmond-Hellmann distinguished herself by becoming board-certified in both internal medicine and oncology and serving as an assistant professor of hematology-oncology at UCSF. Like her husband—an infectious disease specialist—and a number of researchers in San Francisco during the 1980s, Desmond-Hellmann was concerned about the deadly AIDS epidemic. In particular, her concern focused on Kaposi's sarcoma, a viral cancer common in patients with AIDS. To educate herself about the epidemic and help fight it, she sought and earned a master's degree in public health in 1988 from the University of California, Berkeley.

UGANDA CANCER INSTITUTE AND PRIVATE PRACTICE

In 1989, Desmond-Hellmann and her husband received an offer from the Rockefeller Foundation, one of the oldest foundations devoted to public health, to study the heterosexual transmission of HIV/AIDS in Uganda. For two years, Desmond-Hellmann and her husband lived in Uganda where they conducted research at the Uganda Cancer Institute at Makerere University in Kampala, where they were also visiting faculty members. "It completely changed what I expected of myself," she told Carolyn Johnson of the experience in an interview for ABC 7 News, KGO-TV San Francisco (5 Apr. 2012). "I felt like I was so privileged and was incredibly fortunate compared to everyone I met in Uganda so I raised the personal bar of what I expected of myself in a powerful way."

The couple returned to the United States in 1991, and Desmond-Hellmann opened up a private oncology practice in her husband's home state of Kentucky. But Desmond-Hellmann was unsatisfied, particularly with the treatment options available to her patients. "We needed better weapons against cancer," she told a reporter for the journal *Nature Reviews: Drug Discovery* (July 2005), "and I wanted to be a part of that."

BRISTOL-MYERS SQUIBB

Upon returning to the United States, Hellmann's husband was offered a job with the biopharmaceutical company Bristol-Myers Squibb in Connecticut. In 1993, Desmond-Hellmann began to work for the company as well. As associate director of clinical cancer research, she helped to develop the breast cancer drug Taxol (the same drug her mother would later use after being diagnosed with breast cancer). Taxol, officially approved by the Food and Drug Administration (FDA) to treat early stage breast cancer in 1998, was a breakthrough in what is known as "targeted drug" therapy, which "aimed at destroying tumors without the side effects of traditional chemotherapy," Berenson reported for the *New York Times* in 2005.

However, government officials and patients were outraged by the cost of Taxol, which in 1992 was $4,000 a year. Drug prices, particularly prices for anticancer drugs, have risen significantly since Taxol.

Still, Desmond-Hellmann was exhilarated by the difficult work, and in 1995, she was recruited by the biotechnology corporation Genentech in San Francisco.

GENENTECH

Desmond-Hellmann began her career with Genentech as a clinical scientist, where she applied the work of doctors Frederic de Sauvage, now the vice president of molecular biology at Genentech, and Dan Eaton, now the director of protein chemistry, to clinical study. De Sauvage and Eaton identified the hormone thrombopoietin as a key regulator of blood platelets. The resulting drug was unsuccessful, but Desmond-Hellmann quickly distinguished herself among her colleagues. Within a year of her hiring, she was put in charge of all clinical trials. After that, Arthur D. Levinson, the former CEO of Genentech and current chair of the board at Apple, told Guthrie: "Every six to twelve months, I was promoting her. Her instincts were excellent."

In 1999, Desmond-Hellmann became the executive vice president of development and product operations; in March 2004, she became president of product development. During her time at Genentech, the company became the number-one producer of anticancer drug treatments in the United States, largely thanks to her work and willingness to approach cancer treatments in a new way. The journal *Nature Reviews: Drug Discovery* wrote of Desmond-Hellmann's "try anything" attitude. The company that many considered to be an upstart in the pharmaceutical industry became the steward of a new era in cancer treatment. Of the early research that she saw to fruition, Desmond-Hellmann told Guthrie, "The period from 1997 to 2001 was an amazing time in oncology. It was a special time because there was such an unmet need." Among the drugs that Desmond-Hellmann and Genentech developed were the breast cancer drug Herceptin, which many consider to be her crowning achievement, and Avastin, which was originally developed to treat colon cancer. Other drugs that received FDA approval during Desmond-Hellmann's time with Genentech include Lucentis, which treats the "wet" form of macular degeneration; Tarceva, for advanced nonsmall cell lung cancer; Rituxan, for certain types of non-Hodgkin's lymphoma; and Xolair to treat allergy-related asthma.

DEVELOPMENT OF HERCEPTIN AND AVASTIN

The development of Herceptin was revolutionary because it was the first drug to target a particular mutation, associated with a specific type of breast cancer, in which cells overproduce a protein called HER2. Before the drug, the same treatments were applied to all patients with breast cancer, though researchers and doctors now understand that there are several distinct forms of the disease that require different, personalized therapies. HER2-positive breast cancer was considered to be one of the most deadly forms, but with Herceptin, it has become one of the most treatable. According to a number of sources, Desmond-Hellmann's father shares a story in which he and his wife, who was receiving chemotherapy at the time, overheard a doctor talking to another patient whose tumor had recurred. The doctor comforted the woman with "good news"; he was prescribing her an "incredible new drug called Herceptin." Pointing to Jennie Desmond, the doctor added, "You can thank the daughter of this lady for bringing it to you." The drug, like other anticancer medications, is expensive, however. Herceptin cost patients $20,000 per year in 1998, and according to several sources it can cost almost twice that today.

Avastin was the first drug to work by effectively blocking the blood cells that feed cancerous tumors. This restricts the tumor's growth and reduces the cancer's ability to spread to other areas of the body. Avastin, approved by the FDA to treat colon and lung cancer in 2006, was also approved through an accelerated approval process to treat metastatic breast cancer in 2008. The FDA revoked the latter decision in a 2011 split vote, citing potentially life-threatening risks that might outweigh the drug's benefits. Avastin remains on the market, however, and doctors and patients can still choose to use the drug to treat certain cancers.

CHANCELLOR OF UCSF

Genentech merged with the Swiss pharmaceutical giant Roche in March 2009. Desmond-Hellmann resigned her position with the company in April, though Roche executives reportedly asked her to stay. Later that year, on August 3, 2009, Desmond-Hellmann became the ninth chancellor of UCSF. During her first three years in the position, Desmond-Hellmann looked for ways to combat the school's increasing financial troubles with budget cuts while maintaining the funding necessary to run a research-based institution. Unlike its sister schools under the UC umbrella, UCSF does not have an undergraduate program, and tuition accounts for only 1 percent of the school's annual budget. (Most schools raise tuition or increase enrollment in the face of financial woes.) UCSF derives only 5 percent of its revenues from the state, finding most of its revenues from its patient-care services like medical centers, a children's hospital, and a number of clinics owned and operated by the school. The school received $532.8 million from the US National Institutes of Health in 2011, making UCSF the recipient of the largest grant among public institutions, second overall to the private research university Johns Hopkins University in Baltimore.

But with a state budget in disarray, shake-ups within the UC system had a negative impact on UCSF. In 2012, Desmond-Hellmann's team projected that the university will be losing money by 2015—the same year the school is scheduled to open a brand new medical center at Mission Bay. In January 2012, Desmond-Hellmann presented these figures to the regents of the nine UC branches. "What we have here," she said in reference to UCSF's current relationship to UC, as quoted by Nanette Asimov for the *San Francisco Chronicle* (20 Jan. 2012), "is not sustainable."

According to Asimov, Desmond-Hellmann further pointed out that UCSF devotes the most money to the UC system, yet sees the least in return. She also proposed her solution: a system in which UCSF maintains a more flexible relationship with UC, without seceding or becoming a private institution. If her proposal is accepted, UCSF would maintain its own board of directors.

Desmond-Hellmann has expressed an interest in partnering research facilities with pharmaceutical companies, and encouraging students to begin their own start-ups. "Increasingly, big biotech and big pharma are coming straight to academia for innovation. We're testing this,"

she told Kerry Dolan for *Forbes* (30 Apr. 2012). Desmond-Hellmann added that the school had already partnered with Pfizer. In addition to working directly with UCSF scientists, Pfizer provides funds for research projects. The program has been an experiment, Desmond-Hellmann noted. "I don't know if this will work," she told Dolan, "but we're going to test it and we're going to measure outcomes and I'm very convinced that Pfizer and others will come back for more if it is successful."

BOARD APPOINTMENTS AND PERSONAL LIFE

In addition to her work at UCSF, Desmond-Hellmann was appointed to the California Academy of Sciences board of trustees in 2008, and in 2009, she joined the Federal Reserve Bank of San Francisco's Economic Advisory Council for a three-year term. She served a three-year term as a member of the American Association for Cancer Research board of directors from 2005 to 2008. At the Biotechnology Industry Organization, Desmond-Hellmann served on the executive committee of the board of directors from 2001 until 2009. From 2004 to 2009, she served on the corporate board of the Santa Clara–based biotech company Affymetrix.

Desmond-Hellmann and her husband, who is currently the executive vice president of medical and scientific affairs at the Elizabeth Glaser Pediatric AIDS Foundation, were married in 1987. Desmond-Hellmann is a sports enthusiast; she skies, mountain bikes, and wakes up before five in the morning on weekdays to run.

SUGGESTED READING

Asimov, Nanette. "UCSF seeks to ease ties with UC." *San Francisco Chronicle*. Hearst Communications, 20 Jan. 2012. Web. 15 Sep. 2012.

Berenson, Alex. "Cancer Drugs Offer Hope, but at a Huge Expense." *New York Times*. New York Times, 12 July 2005. Web. 10 Sep. 2012.

Breitstein, Joanna. "HBA [Healthcare Businesswomen's Association] Woman of the Year: Susan Desmond-Hellmann." *PharmExec.com*. Advanstar Communications, 1 Apr. 2006. Web. 13 Sep. 2012.

Dolan, Kerry. "UCSF Chancellor Susan Desmond-Hellmann On How Healthcare is Changing." *Forbes*. Forbes, 30 Apr. 2012. Web. 9 Sep. 2012.

"From Uganda to San Francisco, the President of Product Development at Genentech describes her 'chaotic' career." *Nature Reviews: Drug Discovery*. Nature Publishing Group, July 2005. Web. 12 Sep. 2012.

Guthrie, Julian. "Cancer warrior takes the helm of UCSF." *San Francisco Chronicle*. Hearst Communications, 11 Apr. 2010. Web. 9 Sep. 2012.

Johnson, Carolyn. "UCSF chancellor honored by Commonwealth Club." *KGO-TV San Francisco*. ABC 7, 5 Apr. 2012. Web. 9 Sep. 2012.

—*Molly Hagan*

Guy Deutscher

Born: June 20, 1969
Occupation: Linguist

Guy Deutscher, the Israeli-born ling-uist, first made a name for himself in the popular press with the publication of *The Unfolding of Language: An Evolutionary Tour of Mankind's Greatest Invention* (2005), his first book for the general public. In that book Deutscher discussed—with humor and insight—how languages all over the world have evolved over thousands of years. He then gained even more acclaim with his second book, *Through the Language Glass: Why the World Looks Different in Other Languages* (2010), in which he methodically lays out cases where one's native language does indeed color one's thinking and perception of the world and goes out of his way to dismiss old notions of how language affects those processes. In an interview with Mark de Silva of the *Paris Review* (November 9, 2010), Deutscher elaborated on one of the central claims of his book: "What the anthropologist and linguist Franz Boas explained in the beginning of the twentieth century was that the grammar of each language determines which aspects of experience must be expressed. In the 1950s Roman Jakobson turned Boas's insight into a pithy maxim: Languages differ essentially in what they *must* convey, not in what they *may* convey (for in theory, every thought can be expressed in every language). Languages differ in what types of information they force the speakers to mention when they describe the world. (For example, some languages require you to be more specific about gender than English does, while English requires you to be more specific about tense than some other languages. Some require you to be more specific about color differences, and so on.) And it turns out that if your language routinely obliges you to express certain information whenever you open your mouth; it forces you to pay attention to certain types of information and to certain aspects of experience that speakers of other languages may not need to be so attentive to. These habits of speech can then create habits of mind that go beyond mere speech, and affect things like memory, attention, association, even practical skills like orientation."

Through the Language Glass has received a good deal of praise from critics. The *Economist* put it on its "Best Books of 2010" list and

Courtesy of United Agents

the *New York Times* (September 12, 2010) selected it as an "Editor's Choice." In 2011 it was placed on the long list for the Samuel Johnson prize, the United Kingdom's top literary award for nonfiction.

EARLY LIFE AND EDUCATION

Guy Deutscher was born on June 20, 1969, in Tel Aviv, Israel. Deutscher and his brother, Elad, were raised by a mother who was a musician and a father who was a businessman. "They were good Jewish parents," Deutscher told *Current Biography* (the source of all quotes unless otherwise noted). "They always tried to provide us with intellectual stimulation." But his parents were not particularly interested in language—certainly not to the degree that their young son was. In addition to studying English and Arabic in school, Deutscher studied Latin and German, the latter at a German cultural center. (As a young boy, his father had come to Israel from Germany.) So even as a teenager, aside from Hebrew (his native tongue) Deutscher was learning four other languages.

But in college, at the University of Cambridge, in England, Deutscher studied mathematics. He didn't major in linguistics for two reasons: in high school he was very good at math, and in Israel, said Deutscher, there was almost an understanding that if you're good at math or science, that's what you go on to do. It never occurred to him that language is something that could be pursued as his main focus; he loved it, but he saw it as a hobby. "I think I needed a certain maturity," he recalls, "to realize that I could make language not just a hobby but my main subject." In Cambridge, studying language on his own, Deutscher was most fascinated by questions of origin: Where did language come from? How did it come about? How did it evolve? (Years later Deutscher would go on to answer those questions in his book *The Unfolding of Language*.)

After getting his bachelor's degree in math from Cambridge, Deutscher remained at the university to pursue a PhD in linguistics. During that time he took a year off to live in Norway and travel throughout Scandinavia, where he studied Norwegian, Swedish, and Danish—three related languages. During his time at Cambridge, Deutscher recalls, he was not fed any particular ideology about language. If you studied linguistics at a particular university, Deutscher said, you were likely to be exposed to a one-sided view of debates within the field. The main fault-line in linguistics is between nativists, who believe that some rules of grammar are hard-wired in the brain, and those who argue that the acquisition of language is more a function of nurture than nature. The most famous example of the former is at the Massachusetts Institute of Technology (MIT), where linguist Noam Chomsky made famous his concept of a "universal grammar," which states that human understanding of the most important aspects of grammar—in any language—is innate. Deutscher likes to point out that when linguists argue about what is or is not innate, they are speculating, because we cannot observe grammar rules in the neurons of a child's brain. However, Deutscher, like every respectable linguist, admits that babies and young children have an innate ability to learn any language—how could babies pick up language otherwise?—but that doesn't mean the capacity for grammar is both hard-wired and universal.

After getting his PhD, in 1999, Deutscher stayed at Cambridge for four years as a research fellow, which allowed him to pursue his own interests in linguistics. He did a lot of work on Semitic languages, such as Akkadian—one of the earliest languages—and was very proud of what he was doing, but at a certain point it dawned on him that he was writing for a very small, specialized audience of linguists. That work yielded a great many papers and the book *Syntactic Change in Akkadian: The Evolution of Sentential Complementation* (2000). Around 2002 Deutscher started work on *The Unfolding of Language*. "I wanted to make it as accessible as I could," Deutscher said, "but I didn't want to dumb it down." Aside from being accessible and engaging, the book is also quite entertaining. That, said Deutscher, came fairly naturally. Even in his scholarly articles he would occasionally be amusing or ironic—which "raised some eyebrows," he said.

THE UNFOLDING OF LANGUAGE

In the introduction to *The Unfolding of Language*, Deutscher writes: "Of all mankind's manifold creations, language must take pride of place. Other inventions—the wheel, agriculture, sliced bread—may have transformed our material existence, but the advent of language is what made us human. Compared to language, all other inventions pale in significance, since everything we have ever achieved depends on language and originates from it. Without language, we could never have embarked on our ascent to unparalleled power over all other animals, and even over nature itself. . . . Language is mankind's greatest invention—except, of course, that it was never invented." In fact, as the book's subtitle, "an evolutionary tour of mankind's greatest invention," indicates, language evolved over time. Early humans started out with utterances equivalent to "man throw spear," but language has come a long way since then. In the book, Deutscher focuses on the evolution of language over the last 5,000 years, when human beings started writing things down. Artifacts and fossils cannot establish with certainty when language started to develop, writes Deutscher. Researchers estimate that language emerged sometime between 40,000 and 1.5 million years ago—quite a range.

As the evolution of language in the last few thousand years has demonstrated, languages are not static. Languages change, Deutscher writes, by both "forces of destruction" and "forces of creation." With regard to the former, Deutscher argues that all languages "decay" in such a way that they evolve from being more regular and complex to more simple and crude. For example, classical Latin was more bound by rules and regularity than medieval Latin; and Anglo-Saxon was more complex than modern English. One of the factors involved is what Deutscher calls "the principle of least effort," in which words are shortened from two syllables to one, or multiple case markings of Old English are gotten rid of. But along with "forces of destruction" there are also "forces of creation," and the latter allows languages to stretch out and grow. For example, via what he calls "expressiveness," languages take on long phrases that are (strictly speaking) redundant or unnecessary: instead of saying "no," people often say "no way" or "not in a million years"; instead of saying "decision making," people say "decision-making process." So languages evolve via a complicated mix of destruction and creation.

The book was well received, although some critics pointed out that in his attempt to write for a general audience Deutscher unnecessarily—or unsuccessfully—tries to be funny and amusing. In a review for the London *Independent* (May 15, 2005), John Morrish made precisely that argument, but insisted that even though "Deutscher is no comedian. . . . What he can do, and has done, is give us a brilliant solution to a quandary that has puzzled people for many centuries. There was no need to whack readers round the head with a pig's bladder on a stick while explaining it. But that's enough about the book's failings. It is, on the whole, extremely thought-provoking. I wouldn't say it read like a thriller, and not only because I try to avoid clichés. It's a book of comparative philology, so you wouldn't expect that. You'd expect some brow-furrowing ideas and that's what you get. And Deutscher, when he's not attempting to tickle your ribs, is very good at explaining them." Although Jan Freeman of the *Boston Globe* (August 7, 2005) also took a shot at Deutscher's prose—"uncertainly pitched, ranging from dense to doggedly folksy"—she wrote that "any curious reader . . . will find something worth knowing in *The Unfolding of Language*." And Nathan Bierma, in a review for the *Chicago Tribune* (July 6, 2005), called the book "an engaging introduction for the general reader to language history and change."

THROUGH THE LANGUAGE GLASS

In his second book for a general audience, *Through the Language Glass: Why the World Looks Different in Other Languages* (2010), Deutscher brought forth solid scientific evidence that our mother tongue can indeed affect how we think and how we perceive the world. But before laying out his case in full, Deutscher spends a good deal of time explaining and disproving *old* notions of how our mother tongue can affect our thoughts and perception—namely "linguistic relativity," or the Sapir-Whorf hypothesis, a point of view advocated by American linguists Edward Sapir and Benjamin Lee Whorf in the 1930s. To Whorf and Sapir, one's native language was more or less a metaphorical prison. For example, Sapir argued that the appearance in the Nootka language (on Vancouver Island in Canada) of such expressions as "it stones down"—instead of "the stone falls"—means the Nootka speakers perceive the world differently, because of that strange fusion of verb and noun. Deutscher asserts the ridiculousness of this position by pointing out that in English the expression "it's raining"—instead of "rain is falling"—does not mean that English speakers cannot understand the distinction between water and the action of falling.

Deutscher then goes on to dismiss arguments that the tense system of a language determines its speakers' understanding of time, or that not having certain words in one's mother tongue prevents one from understanding the concepts they represent. "Eventually," wrote Deutscher in the *New York Times* (August 26, 2010) in a summary of his book, "Whorf's theory crash-landed on hard facts and solid common sense, when it transpired that there had never actually been any evidence to support his fantastic claims. The

reaction was so severe that for decades, any attempts to explore the influence of the mother tongue on our thoughts were relegated to the loony fringes of disrepute. But 70 years on, it is surely time to put the trauma of Whorf behind us. And in the last few years, new research has revealed that when we learn our mother tongue, we do after all acquire certain habits of thought that shape our experience in significant and often surprising ways."

To illustrate that point Deutscher first introduces his readers to a maxim by the Russian-American linguist Roman Jakobson: "Languages differ essentially in what they *must* convey and not in what they *may* convey." For example, if you say in English, "I went to the movies with my neighbor," you do not indicate the gender of said neighbor; whereas in many languages, such as French or Russian, you have to—you have no choice. In English, of course, you *may* say whether the neighbor was male or female, but you don't have to; in various other languages, however, you *must*. There's no way around it. "When your language routinely obliges you to specify certain types of information," Deutscher wrote in the *New York Times*, "it forces you to be attentive to certain details in the world and to certain aspects of experience that speakers of other languages may not be required to think about all the time. And since such habits of speech are cultivated from the earliest age, it is only natural that they can settle into habits of mind that go beyond language itself, affecting your experiences, perceptions, associations, feelings, memories, and orientation in the world." But is there any evidence?

In *Through the Language Glass*, Deutscher gives three empirically proven examples, which he discusses at length. The most powerful and striking of his examples is the aboriginal Australian language of Guugu Yimithirr, which does not use egocentric coordinates, such as "left," "right" "in front of" or "behind." Instead, Guugu Yimithirr speakers use cardinal directions, such as north, south, east, and west, which are absolute. In their language, they say things like "move over to the western chair" and "there's an ant on your northern foot." Even if they are watching television and someone on the screen is coming toward them, they will still give compass-like directions: if the TV is facing north and the hero is coming toward the screen, then they will say he was "coming northward." There are other languages, Deutscher points out—in various parts of Mexico, Bali, and other regions—that also rely primarily on geographic coordinates. Keeping in mind what Deutscher first argued, it is important to understand that speakers of such languages can learn concepts of left and right; but the question is whether *their* system of coordination affects how they think and perceive the world. After all, to speak such a language one would have to know which way north and south is at every moment—something native speakers start to develop by age two and more or less master by age seven. (That does not imply that English speakers cannot learn such masterful coordination; however, they do not *have* to know it as part of their language). In the book, Deutscher goes on to offer several experiments that underscore how differently Guugu Yimithirr-style speakers see the world. *Through the Language Glass* was well-received in the critics. For example, in a review for the *New Scientist* (June 5, 2010) Christine Kenneally wrote that the book is "so robustly researched and wonderfully told that it is hard to put down."

From 2004 to 2007 Deutscher held a research position at Leiden University in the Netherlands. In 2009 he joined the University of Manchester in England as a researcher, a post for which he is not required to teach. Deutscher and his wife, Jane, live in the London area. They have two daughters, Alma and Hellen.

SUGGESTED READING

Bierma, Nathan. "Linguistic History Bogged Down in Details." Rev. of *The Unfolding of Language*, by Guy Deutscher. *Chicago Tribune* 6 July, 2005, Tempo: C2. Print.

de Silva, Mark. "Guy Deutscher on *Through the Language Glass*." *Paris Review*. Paris Review, 9 Nov. 2010. Web. 21 Dec. 2011.

Deutscher, Guy. "Does Your Language Shape How You Think?" *New York Times*. New York Times, 26 Aug. 2010. Web. 21 Dec. 2011.

Freeman, Jan. "Not Dead Yet." Rev. of *The Unfolding of Language*, by Guy Deutscher. *Boston Globe* 7 Aug. 2005: E3. Print.

Kenneally, Christine. "Say Red to See It." Rev. of *Through the Language Glass*, by Guy Deutscher. *New Scientist*. Reed Business Information, 8 June 2010. Web. 21 Dec. 2011.

Morrish, John. "Why Metaphor Is a Lethal Weapon." Rev. of *The Unfolding of Language*, by Guy Deutscher. *(London) Independent* 15 May 2005, Features: 31. Print.

—*Dmitry Kiper*

Mahasweta Devi

Born: January 14, 1926
Occupation: Author, activist

The Indian writer and activist Mahasweta Devi, in a career spanning six decades, has published dozens upon dozens of short-story collections and novels—mostly in her native language of Bengali. Some of her best known works of fiction that have been translated into English include *The Queen of Jhansi* (1956), *Mother of 1084*

Courtesy of Ernesto Ruscio/Getty Images

(1974), and *Breast Stories* (1997). Her works often deal with the issues and causes closest to her heart, such as the poor living conditions and mistreatment of India's indigenous population. Upon being placed on the 2009 Man Booker International Prize long list, she spoke to a reporter for the New York-based publication *India Abroad* (March 27, 2009): "I have always believed that the real history is made by ordinary people," Devi said. "The reason and inspiration for my writing are those people who are exploited and used, and yet do not accept defeat. For me, the endless source of ingredients for writing is in these amazingly noble, suffering human beings. Why should I look for my raw material elsewhere, once I have started knowing them? Sometimes it seems to me that my writing is really their doing."

EARLY LIFE AND EDUCATION

Mahasweta Devi was born into an educated, middle-class family on January 14, 1926 in Dhaka, Bangladesh, a country in South Asia that was then part of British India. She grew up in West Bengal, a state in the eastern part of India. Her father, Manish Chandra Ghatak, wrote poetry and prose; her mother, Dharitri Devi, was a writer, translator, and social activist who promoted literacy among poor children. Devi and her siblings were raised on a love of many art forms—music, film, theater—and were encouraged to read broadly. "My family was very cultivated and talented," Devi told Francoise Chipaux for the *Manchester Guardian Weekly* (September 6,

2000). "Back as far as my grandmother's generation they were all educated, though they never went to school. They had large libraries and read a lot. My grandmother was very committed to the freedom movement against the British."

Devi, however, did attend various schools, most notably one in Santiniketan, in West Bengal, which was founded by the poet Rabindranath Tagore, who had won the Nobel Prize for Literature in 1913, the first Asian to do so. After getting her high school diploma from the Beltala Girls' School in Calcutta, Devi attended Vishvabharati University in Santiniketan, where she received a BA in English in 1946. Upon her graduation from Vishvabharati University, Devi married the playwright Bijon Bhattacharya, who was also a member of the Communist Party of India. After India gained its independence from Great Britain in 1947, great political turmoil and social instability followed. The following year Devi and her husband had a son, Nabarun, who would go on to be a writer. Because Devi's husband was a communist and a prominent party member, he had a hard time finding a job; and Devi, because she was married to a communist, had a hard time keeping one. Starting in 1948, for a period of two years, Devi held various positions, such as school teacher, private tutor, and post-office clerk. In the early 1950s she started writing short pieces of genre fiction under a pen name for *Sachitra Bharat*, a weekly newspaper.

CAREER

Devi's writing career really began with the publication of her debut novel, *Jhansir Rani* (1956), which was translated into English as *The Queen of Jhansi*. It is a work of historical fiction that takes place in the middle of the 19th century in India, when the country was ruled by the British. *The Queen of Jhansi* tells the story of Lakshmi Bai, a female ruler of a state in northern India who, in 1857, led the first popular revolt against the British. "I was drawn to her as a character because, according to historical documents, it was a genuine people's rebellion," Devi told Chipaux. Two years prior to writing the novel, Devi used both journalistic and scholarly techniques in researching her subject: she traveled to what is now the northern Indian state of Uttar Pradesh to collect documents, talk to people, and walk the land. Following the publication of *The Queen of Jhansi*, Mahasweta Devi gained notice as a writer. She then published several books, all about the everyday lives of Indian people, before the end of the decade: *Nati* (1957), *Madhurey Madhur* (1958), *Yamuna Key Teer* (1958), *Etotuka Asha* (1959), and *Premtara* (1959).

In the 1960s Devi went through a great deal of personal and professional change. In 1962 she divorced her husband, leaving him to care for their 14-year-old son. The following year she earned a master's degree in literature from the University of Calcutta. In 1964 she became a lecturer in English at Bijoygarh Jyotish Roy College in Calcutta, a post she would hold for 20 years. She also published *Bioscoper Baksho* (1964), about the constraints imposed on women in traditional, middle-class circles. In 1965, after a trip to the poverty-stricken district of Bihars, Devi became a social activist—a role she would soon intertwine with her work as a writer.

In Bihars she saw with her own eyes how tribal people—India's indigenous population—live in very poor conditions. In an interview three decades later with Archana Masih for the Indian Web site Rediff (December 24, 1997), when asked about the best way to help the tribal people, Devi said, "Security. Security that they are not evicted. Education, at least functional literacy. Drinking water, irrigation water, doctor and medicinal facility, crop training." But, Masih asked, is it possible to integrate the tribal people into mainstream Indian society? "Who tried to integrate them into Indian society?" Devi asked rhetorically. "It is said they are cut off from mainstream society. Who tried to integrate them? And what is there so beautiful in mainstream Indian society that they should get integrated and lose their tribal entity? I don't see it like that. I see that they get the minimum human benefit, food, electricity, water, education, work, training for women, for men also, childcare. . . . And since many will not get job opportunities, it is best to make them self-employed by giving various kinds of training."

In the early years of her activism, Devi published the novels *Jewel in Darkness* (1966) and *The Life and Death of Poet Bandyoghoti Gayin* (1966), both about class struggles in Bengal, with the latter set in the 15th century and the former set in the 18th. In 1973 she began writing the novel *Mother of 1084*, which, after its publication the following year, would become one of the author's best-known works. In *Mother of 1084*, a middle-class woman remembers her recently deceased son and tries to comprehend the nature of his participation in the militant-communist Naxalite movement, which was prevalent in parts of India from the late 1960s to the mid-1970s. That novel was followed by many more books: *Right to the Forest* (1977), a work of historical fiction about the 19th-century Munda rebellion against the British; *The Fire Within* (1978), a series of four long stories about the Naxalite movement; and *Chotti and His Arrow* (1979), which mostly takes place in the first half of the 20th century and tells the story of a tribe in eastern India. *Subhaga Basanta* (1980), a set of two novels, one about slavery in the 11th century and the other about the practice of *sati*—burning alive a widowed woman along with the body of her dead husband—takes place in the early 18th century; and *Sidhu Kanhur Daakey* (1981) is set in the mid-19th century during the Santhal rebellion, another tribal insurrection against the British.

In 1980 Devi co-founded the bonded-labor organization Palamau (Bahar) Zilla Bandhua Samiti, which set out to inform the public of the practice of bonded labor. Also known as debt bondage, it is essentially a form of slavery in which an individual's labor is pledged as a means of repaying a loan; the person is then trapped or deceived into working over a long term for very little or no pay, often every day of the week. Devi also figured out a way to give a voice to the voiceless poor workers in her region. According to Resil B. Mojares, writing for the Web site of the Ramon Magsaysay Award (a Philippine literary and public service prize awarded to Devi in 1997), "The year after her father died in 1979, Devi started editing the Bengali quarterly *Bortika*, an obscure literary periodical her father had edited. She turned it into a forum where tribals, small peasants, agricultural laborers, factory workers, and rickshaw pullers wrote about their life and problems. Impatient with abstract, theoretical, and academic research, Devi turned *Bortika* into a publication that gave precedence to the view-from-below and the documentation of social and economic conditions through surveys and reports done by the local people themselves."

Devi herself wrote about the plight of the poor starting in 1982, for the Bengali paper *Jugantar*. The following year she founded the Kheria-Sabar Welfare Society, meant to help the people of the Kheria and Sabar tribes; the organization has been involved in a variety of projects, including ones to promote literacy and farming skills. By 1984, having left her post at Calcutta University, Devi was devoting all of her time to her writing and her causes. That year she put out the long-story collection *Daulati* (1984), which covered the topic of bonded labor. The following year she published the novel *Srinkhalito* (1985), which tells the story of a writer who must decide between a simple and apathetic life, on the one hand, and an engaged, socially involved one, on the other. The following year she organized the Ancient Tribes Union, a group made up of representatives from dozens of West Bengali tribes.

AWARDS AND RECENT WORK

Her work did not go unnoticed by the Indian government. In 1986 she received the Padmasree award, which the Indian government grants to notable citizens. The following decade, more awards followed, both for her activism and her writing. In 1996 Devi received the Jnanpith Award, India's highest literary prize; South African president and civil-rights leader Nelson Mandela attended the ceremony in New Delhi, India. And the following year Devi received the Ramon Magsaysay Award for Journalism, Literature, and the Creative Communication Arts—given, according to Mojares, "in recognition of

her compassionate crusade through art and activism to claim for tribal peoples a just and honorable place in India's national life." As quoted by Mojares, in her acceptance speech Devi said: "I will have a sense of fulfillment if more and more young writers took to unbeaten tracks. My India still lives behind a curtain of darkness. A curtain that separates the mainstream society from the poor and the deprived. But then why my India alone? Cannot one say the same for so many countries and societies today? As the century comes to an end, it is important that we all make an attempt to tear the curtain of darkness, see the reality that lies beyond and see our own true faces in the process."

In the 1990s Devi gained some more attention in the West with the publication of *Breast Stories* (1997), a tragic account of a woman becoming a professional wet nurse and then contracting breast cancer. That year also saw the release of *Five Plays: Mother of 1084, Aajir, Bayen, Urvashi and Johnny, Water* (1997), stories that were adapted as plays. By this point 40 years had passed since Devi published her first novel. Bhaswati Chakravorty, writing for the Malaysia *New Straights Times* (October 1, 1997), offered a complimentary analysis of Devi's fiction writing: "One of her driving passions is an anger—an anger she began to feel when she imperceptibly began to move into her subjects' lives in the urge to record real-life truths with accuracy. The power of her fiction springs from a unique combination of relentless documentary details, the smell and feel of earth, leaves, blood, breath and skin and a passionate conviction which spins the raw material into gut-wrenching plots and scenes." Then, offering a more subtle analysis, he added: "It is perfectly justifiable to see her fiction as daring, radical and experimental. Yet critics of her work home in on melodrama in plots and artificialities in language, claiming that extra-literary concerns invariably damage the literary value of fiction. With work as powerful—and conscience stirring—as Mahasweta Devi's it is obviously difficult to segregate 'high art' and propaganda. Maybe it is the proportional relationship between inventiveness and moral fervour, which may vary from work to work. Or perhaps it is the limitation of range—gloom, tragedy, grief, horror, black sarcasm and little lightness of touch." Chakravorty then concludes his critical analysis with this: "The real problem about Mahasweta Devi is not that she is political, but whether criticism of her work should ignore the driving extra-literary passion behind her work. A moral conscience is surely unnecessary and distracting baggage in the world of literary criticism. But a writer like Mahasweta Devi, whose fiction is moulded by the moral conscience, makes categorical decisions on this score impossible."

In the new millennium the octogenarian Devi has continued to be politically active and receive recognition for her writing. In 2010 she joined in protest with farmers in the eastern Indian state of Jharkhand who were resisting the takeover of their land for construction of a government steel plant. The following year, Devi demanded the unconditional release of political prisoners in West Bengal. In 2009 she was placed on the long list of nominees for the Man Booker International Prize, which also included such notable writers as V. S. Naipaul, Peter Carey, and E. L. Doctorow. (The award ultimately went to Alice Munro.) Devi lives and works in Calcutta.

SUGGESTED READING

Chakravorty, Bhaswati. "The Art of Passion." Malaysia *New Straits Times* 1 Oct. 1997, Literary: 6. Print.

Chipaux, Françoise. "Power of a Pen." *Manchester Guardian Weekly* 6 Sep. 2000: 26. Print.

Devi, Mahasweta. Interview by Archana Masih. *Rediff on the Net*. Rediff, 24 Dec. 1997. Web. 21 Dec. 2011.

Mojares, Resil B. "Biography for Mahasweta Devi." *1997 Ramon Magsaysay Award for Journalism, Literature, and Creative Communication Arts*. Ramon Magsaysay Award Foundation, 1997. Web. 22 Dec. 2011.

"World Wakes Up to a Legend." *India Abroad* 27 Mar. 2009: A3. Print.

—*Dmitry Kiper*

AP Photo

Peter Diamond

Born: April 29, 1940
Occupation: Economist and educator

Peter Diamond, an economics professor at the Massachusetts Institute of Technology (MIT), first came to widespread public attention in early 2010, when President Barack Obama nominated him for a seat on the Federal Reserve's Board of Governors. Later that year, he was awarded the Nobel Prize in economics for his "analysis of markets with search frictions," as his citation states. Given the approbation of the Nobel committee and the international acclaim being accorded Diamond, his supporters assumed that his seat on the Federal Reserve would be virtually assured. Republican lawmakers questioned his qualifications to serve on that body, however, and began to obstruct the proceedings. Diamond ultimately withdrew himself from consideration and wrote an op-ed headlined "When a Nobel Prize Isn't Enough," which was published in the *New York Times* (5 June 2011). In the piece, he bemoaned the partisan bickering to which he had been subjected and wrote, "We should

all worry about how distorted the confirmation process has become, and how little understanding of monetary policy there is among some of those responsible for its Congressional oversight."

EARLY LIFE AND EDUCATION

Diamond, a third-generation American, was born on April 29, 1940, in New York City. In many respects, his family's story is a classic tale of immigration, hard work, and eventual success. His maternal grandparents came to the United States from Poland at the beginning of the twentieth century, while his paternal grandparents hailed from Romania and Russia. His parents were born soon after their families settled in New York.

After graduating from high school, Diamond's parents began working. His mother found a job as a bookkeeper, earning fifteen dollars a week, and his father sold shoes during the day while getting a college education at night. He ultimately earned a degree from Brooklyn Law School, and in his early years of practice earned about five dollars a week. The couple married right before the Great Depression, and Diamond's older brother, Richard, was born in 1934.

Diamond lived and attended public school in the Bronx until he was in second grade, when he moved to the town of Woodmere, in suburban Long Island, with his family. Although the move to the suburbs was a step up socially and economically, the family's new home was so close to the Long Island Rail Road tracks that they woke to a train thundering by each day.

Diamond attended Yale University. Although he initially considered studying engineering, he soon settled upon math, studying game theory and topology. Exceedingly generous about paying tribute to teachers and other mentors, he has cited Shizuo Kakutani, one of his first math professors at Yale, as an influence. He has also credited Charles Berry with introducing him to economics. His mentor, Edward Budd, taught an economics honors seminar that was so compelling, Diamond dropped his French classes to take more economics courses. Diamond also studied with Gerard Debreu, who won a Nobel Prize in 1983.

Diamond graduated summa cum laude from Yale in 1960. In the summer of that year, he worked as a research assistant for another future laureate, Tjalling C. Koopmans, who won the Nobel Prize in 1975 for his work on the theory of resource allocation. Koopmans was responsible for Diamond's first publishing credit, listing Diamond as a cowriter on a 1964 paper titled "Stationary Utility and Time Perspective."

Diamond studied for his graduate degree at MIT, where he took courses in micro- and macroeconomics, statistics, economic history, and public finance. His thesis was supervised by Robert Solow, whom he considers a major role model. (Solow won the Nobel Prize in 1987, for his work on the theory of economic growth; the neoclassical Solow–Swan growth model is named, in part, for him.) In 1963, Diamond earned his doctoral degree in economics from MIT, and he was recruited to teach at University of California, Berkeley.

ACADEMIC CAREER

Diamond served as an assistant professor at Berkeley from 1963 to 1965, when he was appointed an acting associate professor. It was an exciting time to be at the school, which was an epicenter of political activism and the free-speech movement. Diamond taught micro- and macroeconomics and public finance, and he found his schedule, which allowed for a combination of research and teaching, to be exhilarating. While at Berkeley, he authored a well-received 1965 paper on the national debt and also spent time as a visiting fellow at the Churchill College, University of Cambridge.

In 1966, while he was in the United Kingdom, Diamond received an airmail letter from Solow, asking if he had any interest in joining the faculty of MIT. He accepted immediately and served as an associate professor from 1966 to 1970 and a full professor from 1970 to 1988, serving as the head of MIT's economics department from 1985 to 1986. In 1989, Diamond was named the John and Jennie S. MacDonald Professor, and he retained the title until 1992, when

he became the inaugural holder of the Paul A. Samuelson chair, named for the MIT professor who is sometimes called the "father of modern economics." In 1997, Diamond stepped down from the prestigious chair to accept the title of institute professor, the highest possible professorship available at the school. MIT's institute professors are granted exceptional freedom to pursue their own research interests and are not required to teach, although Diamond has continued to do so, citing his love for imparting knowledge to his students and his belief that teaching complements and enriches his research.

In addition to his appointments at MIT, Diamond has been a visiting professor at several other schools, including University College in Nairobi (1968–69), Hebrew University in Jerusalem (1969), the University of Oxford's Nuffield College (1969) and Balliol College (1973–74), Harvard University (several times), the European University Institute (1992), and the University of Siena (2000).

MORE THAN AN ACADEMIC

Over the course of his career, Diamond has often focused on policy analysis rather than purely theoretical research. He has a particular interest in the subject of pensions. "Key to my work in this realm has been a series of enjoyable collaborations," he explained in an essay posted on the official Nobel Prize website. "This started serendipitously when, at the recommendation of Paul Samuelson, Bill [Hsiao] invited me to join the Panel on Social Security Financing consulting to the U.S. Senate Finance Committee, and I accepted. Pensions have been a perfect topic for me. They fit well in my public finance theory interests and with my social concerns. I have given many talks on Social Security, and ended some of them with a quote from Franklin Roosevelt, which I saw at his memorial in DC: 'The test of our progress is not whether we add more to the abundance of those who have much; it is whether we provide enough for those who have too little.'"

The work for which Diamond has won the greatest recognition is his research on "markets with search frictions"—markets in which buyers and sellers can have difficulty connecting with one another: those with used cars to sell and those needing reasonably priced transportation; landlords with apartments to rent and those seeking housing; and men looking for women to date and vice versa, for example.

In a piece for the *New York Times* (11 Oct. 2010), Harvard professor Edward Glaeser explained that Diamond's thoughts on the labor market—employers with jobs to fill and those searching for employment—were of great significance: "The most traditional economic model of the labor market assumes a labor supply schedule, which reflects the number of workers willing to work at a given wage, and a labor demand schedule, which describes the number of workers that companies are willing to hire at a given wage. At some wage, supply equals demand and that's the market equilibrium, which is where traditional economics predicts the world will end up. In markets with undifferentiated products—like copper or winter wheat—that model works pretty well, but it has some pretty obvious failings when it comes to labor or housing markets.

"In particular, the Economics 101 model does an awful job explaining an American civilian labor force where nearly one-tenth say they want a job and can't find one. . . . New paradigms emerge when reality crashes against theory, and that's what brought us [Diamond's] . . . search theory." Glaeser continued, "[Diamond's] work was distinguished both by elegant modeling—building the theoretical tools needed to make sense of labor turnover—and important insights. Perhaps the key idea is . . . that each 'additional worker makes it easier for vacancies to find workers and harder for other workers to find jobs.'" Diamond thus reasoned that the unemployed could congest the labor market, much as drivers congest a highway.

THE NOBEL PRIZE
In October 2010, it was announced that the Sveriges Riksbank Prize in Economic Sciences in Memory of Alfred Nobel was being awarded to Diamond, Dale T. Mortensen of Northwestern University, and Christopher A. Pissarides of the London School of Economics. Like Diamond, Mortensen and Pissarides had been researching markets with search frictions for decades. The three shared a cash prize of 10 million Swedish kroner (about $1.5 million). Glaeser echoed the sentiments of many observers when he wrote, "The prize manages both to honor timeless research on core economic questions and to highlight the ways in which economics addresses a most timely global problem. . . .

"The work of these economists does not tell us how to fix our current high unemployment levels, but it does help us to make some sense of our current distress. . . ."

In addition to the Nobel, Diamond's many other honors include Guggenheim Fellowships (1966 and 1982), several National Science Foundation Research Grants (from 1965 to 2011), the Mahalanobis Memorial Award (1980), the Nemmers Prize (1994), a Fulbright Fellowship (2000), MIT's Killian Award (2003), the Jean-Jacques Laffont Prize (2005), the Robert M. Ball Award (2008), and an honorary doctoral degree from Hebrew University (2010). Additionally, he is a longtime fellow of both the Econometric Society and the American Academy of Arts and Sciences, as well as a founding member of the National Academy of Social Insurance, which is a nonpartisan, nonprofit organization devoted to educating the public about such programs as Social Security, Medicare, and workers' compensation.

THE FEDERAL RESERVE
In April 2010, President Obama nominated Diamond for a seat on the board of governors of the Federal Reserve, the central bank of the United States, which has as its mission "to provide the nation with a safer, more flexible, and more stable monetary and financial system." The Federal Reserve is chaired by Ben Bernanke, a former student of Diamond, and many political observers pointed out that the two would have a good working relationship.

In August of that year, however, Republican lawmakers took advantage of a little-used procedural rule and returned Diamond's nomination to the executive branch before summarily taking a summer recess. Political insiders in Washington, DC, posited that the nomination had been blocked in retaliation for the Democrats' treatment of Randall S. Kroszner, a George W. Bush appointee who stepped in to fill an unexpired term on the Federal Reserve board from 2006 to 2009 but was then denied a full fourteen-year term.

Leading the charge against Diamond was Senator Richard Shelby, the top-ranking Republican on the Senate Banking Committee, who was widely quoted as saying, "I do not believe he's ready to be a member of the Federal Reserve Board. I do not believe that the current environment of uncertainty would benefit from monetary policy decisions made by board members who are learning on the job" (qtd. in Klein).

In September 2010, Obama renominated Diamond for the post. The following month, when the Nobel Prize announcements were made, most political observers assumed that the prestigious award would sway Diamond's opponents and allow him to sail through the confirmation process. They did not count on the Republican's intransigence; Shelby and his compatriots, in a stance some journalists characterized as "anti-intellectual," asserted that winning the Nobel Prize was no qualification for holding one of the few coveted spots on the Federal Reserve's seven-member board of governors.

There was an understandable outcry from many quarters. In a June 6, 2011, article for the *Atlantic*, James Fallows expressed an opinion echoed in several other major outlets, writing, "Let's be serious. A career politician with a law degree from the University of Alabama. . . . [v]ersus the economist who has just been recognized with the highest international lifetime-achievement honor that exists in his field—and whose specialty is studying America's worst economic problem of the moment, chronic unemployment. Hmmm, I wonder which of them might be in a better position to judge the other's street-cred about Fed policy. Yet Senate rules let one willful politician say: No." Fallows continued, "Here's the real question. America is rich and re-silient. But is it resilient enough to permit folly and self-destruction of this sort?"

In June 2011, Diamond informed the White House that he wanted his nomination with-drawn. In October 2011, Sarah Bloom Raskin, a former commissioner of financial regulation for Maryland, was appointed to the board in Dia-mond's stead.

DIAMOND'S BOOKS AND OTHER ACCOMPLISHMENTS

Diamond is the author and/or editor of several books, including: *Uncertainty in Economics, Readings, and Exercises* (1978); *Growth, Pro-ductivity, Unemployment: Essays to Celebrate Bob Solow's Birthday* (1990); *On Time: Lectures on Models of Equilibrium* (1994); *Social Secu-rity: What Role for the Future?* (1996); *Issues in Privatizing Social Security* (1999); *Social Secu-rity Reform* (2002); *Taxation, Incomplete Mar-kets, and Social Security* (2002); *Saving Social Security: A Balanced Approach* (2004); *Behav-ioral Economics and Its Applications* (2007); *Re-forming Pensions: Principles and Policy Choices* (2008); and *Pension Reform: A Short Guide* (2010).

From 1969 to 1971, Diamond was an asso-ciate editor of the *Journal of Economic Theory*, and he has held several editorial positions at the *Journal of Public Economics* and the *American Economic Review*. He chaired a study group for Kenya's Ministry of Planning in the late 1960s, and during the 1970s, he sat on advisory panels for the US Senate Finance Committee, the Con-gressional Research Service, and the National Commission on Social Security. He has held leadership posts with such groups as the Econo-metric Society and the American Economic Council and has been an associate of National Bureau of Economic Research since 1991.

PERSONAL LIFE

Diamond met his wife, Kate, while in Berkeley. They married in 1966, just ten days after he pro-posed. They have two sons: Matt, born in 1972, and Andy, born in 1979. The entire family ac-companied Diamond to Stockholm on Decem-ber 10, 2010, to witness his acceptance of the Nobel Prize.

The year 2010 also marked Diamond's sev-entieth birthday, which he celebrated by throw-ing out the ceremonial first pitch at Fenway Park, during a Boston Red Sox game. Kate had arranged the event, fulfilling one of her hus-band's long-held dreams. She also commissioned John Harbison to compose a piece of music in his honor titled "Diamond Watch: Double Play for Two Pianos."

SUGGESTED READING

Adams, Richard. "Peter Diamond's Nobel Prize in Economics Is All about Hard Work." *Guardian* [London]. Guardian News and Me-dia, 11 Oct. 2010. Web. 10 Aug. 2012.

Diamond, Peter. "When a Nobel Prize Isn't Enough." *New York Times*. New York Times, 5 June 2011. Web. 10 Aug. 2012.

Fallows, James. "What's Wrong with America, Chapter 817: Sen. Richard Shelby." *Atlantic*. Atlantic Monthly Group, 6 June 2011. Web. 10 Aug. 2012.

Glaeser, Edward L. "The Work behind the Nobel Prize." *New York Times*. New York Times, 11 Oct. 2010. Web. 10 Aug. 2012.

Klein, Ezra. "Fourteen Reasons Why This Is the Worst Congress Ever." *Washington Post*. Washington Post, 13 July 2012. Web. 17 Sep. 2012.

—Mari Rich

Rocco DiSpirito

Born: Nov. 19, 1966
Occupation: Chef

The chef, television personality, and cookbook writer Rocco DiSpirito has "come to embody the Faustian bargain of celebrity in the restaurant business," Jeff Gordinier wrote for the *New York Times* (December 17, 2008). "He is portrayed, and often satirized, as a supernaturally talented chef who squandered his gifts in the scattershot pursuit of fame, fortune and pink ruffled shirts." An alumnus of the Culinary Institute of America and protégé of such noted chefs as Dominique Cecillon and Gray Kunz, DiSpirito made his mark on the food world in the late 1990s as the executive chef and co-owner of the fusion restaurant Union Pacific in New York City's Gramercy Park neighborhood. The restaurant earned a coveted three-star rating from the *New York Times* and helped DiSpirito become one of the most talked-about chefs in the nation.

After winning a number of culinary hon-ors—including three consecutive James Beard Award nominations for best chef in New York (1999–01)—and launching his television career with appearances on the Food Network pro-gram *The Melting Pot*, in 2003 DiSpirito opened Rocco's 22nd Street, an Italian eatery in New York's Flatiron District inspired by his mother's home cooking. The venture was the subject of an NBC reality series, *The Restaurant*, which chronicled the travails of founding and running a new restaurant in a high-pressure locale. While the show, which aired for two seasons, drew high ratings, Rocco's 22nd Street proved to be a financial failure, and DiSpirito soon became

Courtesy of Mike Coppola/Getty Images

embroiled in a lawsuit with the enterprise's financier, Jeffrey Chodorow; the restaurant closed in September 2004. Since then, as Gordinier pointed out, DiSpirito has become better known for his appearances on various reality television shows (some of them, such as *Dancing with the Stars*, unrelated to the food world), and for marketing a line of kitchenware, than for his actual cooking. DiSpirito has maintained, however, that his passion remains the same. "I am a chef first and foremost," he told Kristen Browning-Blas for the *Denver Post* (September 12, 2011), "and the thing that makes me happiest is to cook for people."

EARLY LIFE AND EDUCATION

The youngest of three children, Rocco DiSpirito was born on November 19, 1966, in the New York City borough of Queens. His parents, Nicolina and Rafaelle, had come to New York in the 1950s from San Nicola Baronia, a town in the Campania region of southern Italy. They raised Rocco and his older siblings, Maria and Michael, in a multiethnic section of Queens called Jamaica. DiSpirito's parents did not speak English, and both had left school after the fourth grade, but they worked hard to provide for the family. Rafaelle toiled six days a week as a cabinetmaker, and Nicolina worked at a deli and in the cafeteria of a Jamaica public school. Although they sometimes struggled to make ends meet, the family always ate well. "Food was the one and only thing my parents were willing to splurge on," DiSpirito recalled in *Rocco's Italian-American* (2004), which

he co-wrote with his mother and the freelance writer Nina Lalli. "We never went on vacation, we always wore hand-me-downs and often played with makeshift toys, but we had more than enough food to eat all the time." DiSpirito fondly remembers bringing artisanal Italian lunches to school at a time when all of his classmates were bringing "peanut butter and jelly on spongy Wonder Bread with the crusts cut off, neatly wrapped in tight plastic with a juice box and, for dessert, Twinkies, Yodels, or individual pudding cups," as he wrote in the book.

DiSpirito developed "his single-minded obsession with food when other kids were in little league," as Sarah Bernard wrote for *New York* magazine (September 17, 2001, online), and he spent part of his childhood observing and helping his mother cook. Nicolina taught him how to make regional Italian specialties and nurtured his desire to try other cuisines; though his father disapproved, she often accompanied him on clandestine trips to McDonald's. DiSpirito was also greatly influenced by his grandmother, Anna Maria Iacoviello, who hosted enormous family dinners every Sunday at her rustic home in West Hempstead, Long Island. In *Rocco's Italian-American*, he described the home, which featured a rabbit hutch and chicken coop as well as a garden with more than 40 kinds of produce, as "a magical place, a piece of Italian soil in New York." He recalled to Maria Laurino for *Newsweek* (July 17, 2003) that his grandmother "had an orchard of apple, pear, cherry and blackberry trees. She made her own wine, preserved her own tomatoes. She made bread every day, as well as ricotta cheese and sausages. You know, she lived life the way she lived it in Campania. Amazing, really."

DiSpirito began working before he was 10 years old, shopping for groceries for a German-American neighbor. He spent the five dollars she paid him on pork-fried rice at a Chinese takeout restaurant. He also earned cash as a bag boy at a nearby supermarket and used his earnings to buy jumbo shrimp to eat. At age 11 DiSpirito found a job at a local pizzeria, where he "became obsessed with perfectly calibrating the balance between the ice and the bubbles in a fountain soda," as Gordinier wrote. With his $30 weekly pay, he took his mother out to eat in restaurants around the neighborhood. DiSpirito has cited his culturally diverse surroundings as a major influence on his food sensibilities. "I don't think there is more cultural diversity [anywhere] than in Queens," he told Gordinier. "I think in many ways my worldview on flavor was formed here."

DiSpirito has recalled that he was mugged repeatedly while growing up in Jamaica and that his home was burglarized, and in 1980 the family moved to New Hyde Park, a village located on Long Island in Nassau County, New York, to escape the violence and crime that had become prevalent in some areas of Queens. While attending high school in New Hyde Park, DiSpirito began working at a local German restaurant called the New Hyde Park Inn. (Prior to that job, he had gained some formal cooking experience in a hotel kitchen in Israel while participating in a work-study program.) There, he honed his cooking skills under chef Bernhard Breiter. In an interview for *Newsweek* (July 28, 1999), DiSpirito described Breiter to Jay Weinstein as "a real tough, old-fashioned German chef, who disciplined you with a stalk of celery as needed." Karl Rueck, the owner of the New Hyde Park Inn, remembered DiSpirito as "a happy young fellow who wanted to learn," as he told Sylvia Carter for *Newsday* (June 18, 2003). "He had a good attitude. He knew what he wanted, and he went out and got it."

In 1982, after graduating high school a year early, DiSpirito enrolled at the Culinary Institute of America in the town of Hyde Park, New York. Despite being just 16 years old, he stood out among his peers in the kitchen. Tim Ryan, one of his instructors and now the president of the school, recalled to Gordinier, "You could tell when he diced vegetables versus somebody else. You could pick his out of a group." DiSpirito graduated with honors in 1986 and then spent a year studying classical technique in France. He arrived in Paris without proper working papers but was able to secure an unpaid *stagiaire*, or internship, at the Michelin-rated restaurant Jardin de Cygne, where he studied under the renowned chefs Dominique Cecillon and Gray Kunz. DiSpirito earned money by working at an American restaurant in Paris called Cactus Charlie's. That income, however, sometimes proved to be insufficient. "I slept in the basement of [Jardin de Cygne], and a few times in the subway," DiSpirito recalled to Weinstein.

RESTAURANT CAREER

After returning to New York in 1988, DiSpirito found work at Adrienne, a French restaurant in the Peninsula Hotel, where he worked under Jean-Michel Diot and Jacques Chibois. He then spent two years at Boston University's School of Hospitality Administration, where he earned a bachelor's degree in 1990. After graduating, he worked briefly as a line cook at Aujourd'hui in Boston's Four Seasons Hotel, before returning to New York to work with a series of notable chefs, including Charlie Palmer, David Bouley, and Gilbert Le Coze. In 1994 he was hired by Gray Kunz to help with the relaunch of the four-star French restaurant Lespinasse, at the St. Regis Hotel, in midtown Manhattan. "I looked at his resume and felt he had the enthusiasm," Kunz recalled to Sarah Bernard. "I don't know if you can say angry, but he was so driven already, he had the ambition to succeed." Under Kunz, who was by then renowned for his Asian-fusion

cooking, DiSpirito honed the innovative cooking style for which he would eventually become known.

In 1995 DiSpirito left Lespinasse to open his own restaurant, Dava, on 39th Street and Lexington Avenue in Manhattan. The restaurant served inventive fare inspired by the creations at Lespinasse. Six weeks after Dava opened, the *New York Times* food critic Ruth Reichl declared (October 13, 1995, online), "Rocco DiSpirito isn't a name you are likely to forget. But you are bound to be hearing a lot of it." Reichl, who described DiSpirito's food as "complex," "imaginative," and "brilliantly original," later recalled to Sarah Bernard, "Nothing about [Dava] looked wonderful. Then the first dish brought out was brilliant. They brought out the next dish, and *it* was brilliant. Not copycat dishes, imitations of somebody else's, but really well-thought-out, well-executed, exciting food. There were flavors I had to struggle to identify—it was thrilling." Despite rave reviews, Dava closed after only six months. (Dava's owner, Joseph Lucin, allegedly fired DiSpirito for squandering the restaurant's budget on lavish food items; according to DiSpirito, the restaurant was already deep in debt by the time he arrived.)

In 1997 DiSpirito teamed up with several partners to open Union Pacific, an innovative fusion restaurant in the upscale Gramercy Park section of Manhattan. Featuring highly original dishes characterized by French and Asian influences, such as fois gras with wild strawberries and bay scallops with sea urchin, Union Pacific opened to wildly enthusiastic reviews, with the *New York Times* awarding it two stars in 1997 and three stars in 1998. In her three-star review for that publication (August 5, 1998, online), Ruth Reichl wrote, "DiSpirito has an interesting mind; he seems to think about flavor in ways that ordinary people don't," and declared, "I have yet to taste anything on [his] menu that is not wonderful." Union Pacific soon became a New York culinary hotspot and helped DiSpirito rise to national prominence.

TELEVISION CAREER

In 1999 DiSpirito was named one of America's best new chefs by *Food & Wine* magazine, and he received the first of his three consecutive James Beard Award nominations for best chef in New York. In October 2000 he appeared on the cover of *Gourmet* magazine's annual restaurant issue and was heralded by that publication as "America's Most Exciting Young Chef." Also that year he made his television debut as a co-host of the Food Network program *The Melting Pot*. DiSpirito's boyish good looks soon led to appearances on other television programs, including *Good Morning America*, as well as attention from such publications as *People* magazine, which named him "Sexiest Chef Alive" in 2002.

In 2003, after receiving yet another James Beard Award nomination as best New York chef, DiSpirito partnered with Jeffrey Chodorow to open Rocco's 22nd Street, an Italian restaurant in the Flatiron section of Manhattan. It specialized in dishes inspired by the southern Italian cooking of his childhood, including fresh pastas and meatballs made by his mother, Nicolina, who was housed in an apartment directly above the restaurant. DiSpirito's opening of Rocco's became the subject of a six-part NBC reality series called *The Restaurant*, which was produced by Mark Burnett (best known as the creator of CBS's hit reality series *Survivor*). DiSpirito told Sylvia Carter that the show was "like a writer writing an autobiography, or a movie maker making a movie about himself. This is my life. It is about treasuring and cherishing my childhood."

Premiering in July 2003, one month after Rocco's official opening, the series became an immediate hit; viewers got an inside look at everything from the construction of the restaurant to the hiring and training of staff to the creation of the menu. The opening night of the venue found DiSpirito dealing with kitchen fires, angry customers, an oblivious wait staff, and a lawsuit from a similarly named Manhattan restaurant. (Rocco's 22nd Street was originally named simply Rocco's before the Greenwich Village eatery Rocco Restaurant slapped DiSpirito with a lawsuit over trademark infringement.) In an assessment of the series for the *New York Times* (July 20, 2003), William Grimes wrote that the show "falls somewhere between a documentary and a stunt," but described it as "thoroughly gripping" entertainment that "goes down like a good dessert." He continued, "*The Restaurant*, despite its manipulations, opens a window that even professional food writers rarely get to look through. It makes clear, whether consciously or unconsciously, the unholy alliance of creativity, money and public relations that dominates New York's restaurant economy." Many of the show's 12 episodes, which aired over two seasons, from July 2003 until June 2004, centered on DiSpirito's tempestuous relationship with Chodorow, who officially closed Rocco's 22nd Street in September 2004 because of financial problems. DiSpirito and Chodorow subsequently filed a series of lawsuits against each other before settling their differences in 2005. (In 2005 Chodorow opened a Brazilian steakhouse called Caviar and Bananas in the same space that had housed Rocco's, but that venture has since closed.)

OTHER WORK

One month after the closure of Rocco's 22nd Street, DiSpirito stepped down as executive chef at Union Pacific to focus on endeavors outside of the restaurant business. Those endeavors have included hosting an hour-long morning show called *Food Talk* on the New York radio station WOR-AM, from 2004 to 2005; promoting his own line of cookware; and making guest appearances on numerous television shows. He has been featured as a guest chef on such talk shows as *The View*, *The Tony Danza Show*, and *The Ellen DeGeneres Show*, and on such reality-television programs as *The Biggest Loser* and *Top Chef*. In 2008 he appeared as a contestant on the popular *Dancing with the Stars*, finishing in ninth place overall. That year he also hosted a cooking program on the A&E Network called *Rocco Gets Real*, in which he offered tips to the home cook. His latest television series, *Rocco's Dinner Party*, debuted on the Bravo channel in 2011.

DiSpirito's first cookbook, *Flavor* (2003, with Kris Sherer), won a 2004 James Beard Award in the category "Best Cookbook: Cooking from a Professional Point of View." His other books include *Rocco's Five Minute Flavor: Fabulous Meals with 5 Ingredients in 5 Minutes* (2005), *Rocco's Real Life Recipes: Fast Flavor for Everyday* (2007), *Rocco Gets Real: Cook at Home, Every Day* (2008), *Now Eat This!: 150 of America's Favorite Comfort Foods, All Under 350 Calories* (2010), and *Now Eat This! Diet: Lose Up to 10 Pounds in Just 2 Weeks Eating 6 Meals a Day!* (2011). In 2011 DiSpirito began writing a weekly food column for the Associated Press titled "Now Eat This!"

While DiSpirito has endured harsh criticism for his some of his more recent career choices, he now considers himself a strong advocate for the home cook. "The vast majority of what I hear from the people who appreciate what I do—which is I think more of the general public, more of America, versus [those in the media], is that they love what I do," he told Gordinier, "and they feel like there is someone from the professional world advocating for them." He explained to Michael Hill for the Associated Press (September 11, 2009), "My feeling is that chefs have done a great job over the last 15 years of getting everyone all frothy at the mouth about the subject of food and wine and cooking and entertaining at home. I think the next level of this is getting them to actually participate."

DiSpirito, who has no children, is divorced from his college sweetheart, Natalie David. He has been romantically linked to a number of women over the last decade. An avid runner, he has competed in several triathlons.

SUGGESTED READING

Bernard, Sarah. "The Food Networker." *New York*. New York Media, 17 Sep. 1993. Web. 19 Dec. 2011.

DiSpirito, Rocco, Nicolina DiSpirito, and Nina Lalli. *Rocco's Italian-American*. New York: Hyperion, 2004. Print.

Gordinier, Jeff. "Taking Heat for Not Cooking." *New York Times*. New York Times, 16 Dec. 2008. Web. 19 Dec. 2011.

Hill, Michael. "Chef Rocco Cooks with a Little Help from His Fans." *Newsday*. Newsday, 11 Sep. 2009. Web. 19 Dec. 2011.

Laurino, Maria. "Is Rocco Really Italian?" *Daily Beast*. Newsweek/Daily Beast, 17 July 2003. Web. 19 Dec. 2011.

Reichl, Ruth. "Restaurants." *New York Times*. New York Times, 13 Oct. 1995. Web. 19 Dec. 2011.

—*Christopher Cullen*

Getty Images

Novak Djokovic

Born: May 22, 1987
Occupation: Professional tennis player

INTRODUCTION

In a *Sports Illustrated* profile about the Serbian tennis champion (23 May 2011, online), S. L. Price recounted an appearance by Djokovic on a national television show when he was just seven years old. Price wrote, "A child host asked the prodigy if his tennis was work or play. 'Tennis is my job,' [Djokovic] said. 'My goal in tennis is to become number one.'" Following a breakthrough 2007 season, Djokovic was consistently ranked among the world's top five male tennis players. He fulfilled his childhood dream in 2011, when he ascended to the top spot in the rankings.

EARLY LIFE AND EDUCATION

Novak Djokovic (pronounced NOH-vok DJO-koh-vihch) was born on May 22, 1987, in Belgrade, the capital city of the Republic of Serbia, which at the time was still part of Yugoslavia. The oldest of three sons born to Srdjan and Dijana Djokovic, he hails from a family of athletes; his father, uncle, and aunt were all members of the Yugoslavian national ski team, and his father also excelled at soccer. Djokovic's parents met when they were both serving as ski instructors at Mount Kopaonik, the country's largest and most popular tourist resort, where they would later open a pizza-and-pancake restaurant together. Djokovic's two brothers, Marko and Djordje, would also go on to pursue professional tennis careers.

Djokovic was first introduced to tennis at the age of four, when Genex, the state-owned enterprise responsible for developing the Kopaonik ski resort, built three municipal tennis courts not far from his parents' restaurant. He would often bring beers and pizzas to the employees at the tennis courts in exchange for several hours of free court time. Djokovic harbored a dream of one day becoming a tennis champion like his idol, Pete Sampras. "I saw Sampras, when I was three or four years old, and he was lifting up one of his seven trophies," he told Courtney Walsh for the *Australian* (1 Feb. 2011, online). "I was a very passionate kid, like every kid is when he dreams of something big."

Djokovic was six years old when he first met fellow Serbian and future mentor Jelena Genčić, a former national tennis player and renowned coach who had just launched a summer clinic at the ski resort. "It was the first day of my first year in Kopaonik, and I was doing a tennis camp. And he was just standing outside the tennis courts and watching all morning, and I said: 'Hey, little boy, do you like it? Do you know what this is?'" Genčić told Christopher Clarey for the *New York Times* (1 Dec. 2010, online). After she invited him to join her tennis camp, Genčić, who had discovered the nine-time Grand Slam champion Monica Seles, immediately took notice of Djokovic's raw talent. On his third day at the camp, she met with his parents and made a bold declaration regarding his potential for greatness. "I told them they had a golden child," Genčić said to Maik Grossekathöfer for the German weekly news magazine *Der Spiegel* (10 July 2011, online). "I was convinced he would be among the top five players in the world by seventeen. They were speechless."

Subsequently, Djokovic began training with Genčić. However, with no funding available from the Serbian Tennis Federation and no sponsors, he was forced to completely rely on his parents for financial support. He soon began making a name for himself as one of the camp's best players. "I used to divide the players into three groups according to their ability and Novak was so good I put him in the top group straight away, even though he'd only started playing a month earlier," Genčić told Paul Newman for the London *Independent* (9 June 2008, online). "I organized a tournament for the children every weekend and I made the semi-finals and final like a proper competition, with ballboys and ballgirls, line judges, everything. Novak got into the semi-finals and then the final. Word had already gone round about how good he was and quite a few people came to watch. He was only just six years old and he was playing a fourteen-year-old girl in the final. He won 6–0, 6–1."

Under Genčić's tutelage, Djokovic honed his skills at the Partizan Tennis Club in Belgrade. During the winters, he would have to train in an empty swimming pool, as the club did not have any indoor courts. Away from the court, Genčić exposed Djokovic to classical music to improve his focus and showed him footage of several top tennis players, including Pete Sampras and Andre Agassi, in an effort to instill in him a winning attitude.

Another influential factor in Djokovic's life was the ongoing and escalating violence between Serbians and Albanians following Kosovo's secession from Serbia in the early 1990s and the 1999 military intervention in Kosovo by NATO forces. On March 24, 1999, the first day of the NATO air strikes, Djokovic, along with his parents and his younger brothers, hid in the basement of their apartment building for two days before returning home. "We decided to go on living our lives as normal," Djokovic told Grossekathöfer. "If something happened, it would just happen." Although he resumed training with Genčić, their practices were not strictly limited to the Partizan Tennis Club. Every morning, as a precautionary measure, Genčić would closely monitor via radio where the NATO bombs fell in Belgrade and then schedule the practices at nearby courts, believing there was little likelihood that an area would be bombed twice in close succession.

In late 1999, several months after the end of the NATO air raids, Genčić encouraged Djokovic's parents to take advantage of the more advanced training techniques and facilities available abroad. She contacted Nikola "Niki" Pilić, a formerly top-ranked Croatian-born player in Yugoslavia and the founder of a renowned tennis school near Munich, Germany. After she convinced Pilić to take on Djokovic, the twelve-year-old left home to attend the elite Pilić Academy, a costly tennis school that his father funded with high-interest loans after failing to find sponsors or investors. Under Pilić's tutelage, which lasted for four years, Djokovic refined his serve and delivery.

CAREER

At the age of fourteen, Djokovic started competing in the Tennis Europe Junior Tour. In 2001, he captured the boys' fourteen-and-under title at the European Junior Championships in both the singles and the doubles categories. Djokovic was also part of the Yugoslavian national team that reached the finals in the boys' fourteen-and-under category at the 2001 International Tennis Federation (ITF) World Junior Tennis championships in the Czech Republic, where they came in second to Germany. Following victories at the prestigious Prince's Cup in Miami, Florida, two junior tournaments in France, and an eighteen-and-under title at an ITF tournament in Pančevo, Serbia, Djokovic ended 2002 ranked as the best under-sixteen player in Europe.

In 2003, Djokovic made his professional debut, playing mostly on the Association of Tennis Professionals (ATP) Challenger circuit and the ITF Futures circuit. His only singles victory was at his third Futures event, in Serbia and Montenegro, where he defeated Cesar Ferrer-Victoria of Spain in straight sets. Djokovic made semifinals appearances at two other Futures tournaments, also held in Serbia and Montenegro. Additionally, he was a boys' singles finalist at the International Bavarian Junior Challenge in Nuremberg, Germany, where he won the first set but retired early in the second set due to a back injury. He finished the year ranked 676 in the ATP singles rankings. Djokovic's best doubles showing came at his second Futures competition, where he and partner Ilija Bozoljac reached the quarterfinals.

Djokovic continued to compete in Futures and Challenger tournaments in 2004. As a singles player, he won titles at two Futures events, one in Hungary and another in Serbia and Montenegro, and also captured the men's doubles title with partner Dejan Petrović at the latter competition. Djokovic also claimed Challenger singles titles at the Aachen Challenger in Germany, also called the Lambertz Open by STAWAG, and the Budapest Challenger in Hungary. In doubles play, he reached the semifinals in two tournaments, a Challenger match in Helsinki, Finland (with Petrović), and a Futures match in Croatia (with Vladimir Pavićević), in the latter of which he was a singles semifinalist as well. Djokovic was also a member of the team that represented Serbia and Montenegro at the Davis Cup. By year's end, Djokovic was ranked number 187 in the world in men's singles and 381 in men's doubles.

In 2005, Djokovic made his debut at all four Grand Slam tournaments. After qualifying for the men's draw at the Australian Open, he suffered a first-round defeat to Marat Safin of Russia, who went on to capture the men's singles title. Djokovic improved on this performance at the French Open, where he was forced to retire from his second-round match due to breathing problems, as well as at Wimbledon and the US Open, advancing to the third round of both events. His only singles victory came in Italy, where he defeated Francesco Aldi at the San Remo Tennis Cup, part of the ATP Challenger Tour. His best result in doubles play was a quarterfinals appearance at the ATP Studena Croatia Open with fellow Serbian Janko Tipsarević. Djokovic and Tipsarević were also part of the Serbia and Montenegro team that competed against Belgium at the Davis Cup. By September of that year, Djokovic had hired a new trainer, veteran coach Riccardo Piatti, who was already coaching Ivan Ljubičić of Croatia at the time. Djokovic ended 2005 ranked number 83 in men's singles, making him the youngest player in the top one hundred; his doubles ranking fell to 694.

In early 2006, Djokovic's parents, who were still receiving no financial help from the Serbian Tennis Federation, contacted the Lawn Tennis Association (LTA), the sport's governing body in Great Britain, to inquire about their three children changing their nationalities and competing for England. Ultimately, they decided not to follow through. "The decision in the end was mine," Djokovic explained to Price. "I never wanted to change countries; it's something that is part of me. We are all really proud of where we come from. And though we've been through tough times, it makes us stronger."

By June 2006, Djokovic had parted ways with Piatti and started training with Marián Vajda, a former professional tennis player from Slovakia. Despite the coaching shakeup, Djokovic finished the year ranked in the top twenty in men's singles, following victories at the Dutch Open in Amersfoort, Netherlands, and the Open de Moselle in Metz, France—his first ATP titles. In Grand Slam tournaments, he had his best showing at the French Open, where he reached the quarterfinals; he also advanced to the fourth round of Wimbledon and the third round of the US Open. Djokovic significantly improved his doubles ranking, from 694 to 303, after reaching the quarterfinals of the Zagreb Indoors in Croatia and the prequarterfinals round of six different competitions: the Dutch Open, the Barcelona Open, the Studena Croatia Open, the Madrid Masters, the ABN AMRO World Tennis Tournament in Rotterdam, Netherlands, and the BA-CA-Tennis Trophy (later the Erste Bank Open) in Vienna, Austria.

Djokovic's breakthrough year came in 2007. After winning a singles title in January at the Next Generation Adelaide International (an ATP Tour event in Australia that later became part of the Brisbane International), Djokovic made headlines two months later at the Pacific Life Open in Indian Wells, California, where he reached the finals against Spain's Rafael Nadal,

then the world's second-ranked player. Despite his straight-set loss to Nadal, Djokovic's poise and skill impressed observers. He went on to win singles titles at the Miami Masters in Florida, where he defeated Nadal in the quarterfinals, as well as at the Estoril Open in Portugal and the BA-CA-Tennis Trophy in Vienna. In his most impressive win, Djokovic bested Switzerland's Roger Federer, then the top-ranked men's player, in three sets at the Rogers Cup (also called the Canada Masters, part of the ATP Masters Series) in Montreal, Canada.

Djokovic also performed well in Grand Slam tournaments in 2007, reaching the semifinals of both the French Open and Wimbledon. However, his best Grand Slam showing of the year came at the US Open, where he reached the finals but lost to Federer in three straight sets. Djokovic also played on the Serbian Davis Cup team that defeated Australia in the World Group playoffs, thereby advancing to the World Group for the first time. He achieved his best doubles results at the Cincinnati Masters, partnered with fellow Serbian Nenad Zimonjić, and the Open 13 in Marseille, France, with Tipsarević. By the end of 2007, Djokovic had broken into the top 10 for the first time in his career, climbing from 16 to number 3 in the ATP singles rankings; he also cracked the top 150 in doubles, finishing the year ranked 145.

Djokovic had an impressive start to the 2008 season. He faced Federer again at another Grand Slam tournament, the Australian Open in Melbourne, defeating him in the semifinals and then advancing to the finals, where he bested Jo-Wilfried Tsonga of France. With that victory, he became the first Serbian-born player to win a Grand Slam title, the sixth-youngest man in Australian Open history to reach the finals of the tournament, and the fourth-youngest champion ever. Djokovic also played against Federer in the semifinals of the US Open, but there Federer was victorious.

Over the course of the year, Djokovic added three more singles titles to his collection: the Pacific Life Open in Indian Wells; the Internazionali BNL d'Italia in Rome, Italy, also known as the Italian Open; and the Tennis Masters Cup in Shanghai, China. He was also a finalist at the Cincinnati Masters, the Thailand Open, and the Queen's Club Championships, as well as a semifinalist at the German Open Hamburg, the Dubai Tennis Championships, and the Monte-Carlo Masters. In addition, Djokovic had a strong showing at the Summer Olympics in Beijing, China, where he defeated American opponent James Blake to win the bronze medal. For the second consecutive year, he ranked as the third-best player in the world. His doubles ranking, however, fell dramatically to 586.

Djokovic's success in singles continued in 2009. He captured titles at five ATP events: the

Dubai Tennis Championships; the inaugural Serbia Open in Belgrade, hosted by Djokovic's family, who bought the license from the organizers of the Dutch Open event; the China Open in Beijing; the BNP Paribas Masters in France, also known as the Paris Masters; and the Swiss Indoors in Basel, Switzerland. Djokovic made finals appearances at the Cincinnati Masters, where he suffered a straight-set loss to Federer; the Gerry Weber Open in Halle, Germany; the Italian Open, where he defeated Federer in the semifinals before losing to Nadal in straight sets; the Monte-Carlo Masters, newly dubbed the Monte-Carlo Rolex Masters, where Nadal was once again victorious; and the Miami Masters, where he lost in straight sets to Andy Murray of Britain.

Djokovic's 2009 results in Grand Slam tournaments were equally strong. In addition to reaching the quarterfinals at Wimbledon, he was also a quarterfinalist at the Australian Open but retired early in his match against Andy Roddick of the United States due to the heat. Djokovic's best showing came at the US Open, where he advanced to the semifinals; for the third straight year, he went head-to-head with Federer, who claimed the match in a hard-fought three-set victory. Djokovic was also a semifinalist at the Shanghai Masters, the Open 13, the Rogers Cup, the Medibank International in Sydney, Australia, and the Madrid Open in Spain—the latter a grueling four-hour marathon in which Nadal fought off three match points.

In an effort to improve his fitness and serve, Djokovic hired a physical trainer and another coach, former top-ranked US player Todd Martin, who joined his coaching team in August. Djokovic reached a milestone in 2009, becoming the first men's tennis player since Mats Wilander of Australia to achieve a year-end number-three ranking for three consecutive years. In doubles, he fought his way back into the top 150, with a semifinals appearance at the Monte-Carlo Rolex Masters and quarterfinals appearances at the Madrid Open and the Gerry Weber Open. At the end of 2009, Djokovic agreed to a ten-year sponsorship deal with Sergio Tacchini, an Italian apparel company, after former sponsor Adidas failed to re-sign him.

In 2010, Djokovic retained his number-three singles ranking for a fourth consecutive year while claiming his second straight title at two events, the Dubai Tennis Championships and the China Open. His other highlights as a singles player included reaching the finals of the Swiss Indoors, where he lost to Federer in three sets, and advancing to the semifinals of the ABN AMRO World Tennis Tournament, the Monte-Carlo Rolex Masters, the Rogers Cup, the Shanghai Rolex Masters, and the Barclays ATP World Tour Finals, an end-of-season event held in London. He was a quarterfinalist at the Italian

Open and the Serbia Open, losing in the latter to fellow Serbian Filip Krajinović when breathing difficulties forced him to retire in the second set.

Djokovic also had his greatest success thus far in Grand Slam tournaments, reaching the finals of the US Open, the Wimbledon semifinals, and the quarterfinals of the Australian Open and the French Open, holding a two-set lead in the latter before being defeated. His lone doubles victory came at the Queen's Club Championships, with Jonathan Erlich of Israel, and he ended the year ranked 163 in doubles. Djokovic also won two of the three singles matches that helped Serbia defeat France and win its first-ever Davis Cup victory. However, Djokovic was experiencing problems with his serve, committing a greater amount of unforced errors and losing velocity on his second serve. As a result, he parted ways with Martin in April 2010. On the advice of his nutritionist, he also adopted a gluten-free diet.

In 2011, Djokovic had a dream season, winning a career-best ten titles, which included three of the four Grand Slam tournaments: the Australian Open (against Murray), the US Open (against Nadal), and Wimbledon (against Nadal). With his appearance in the Wimbledon finals, Djokovic achieved his childhood wish to become the number-one men's player in the world. In addition to the Grand Slam events, Djokovic prevailed against Nadal in the finals of four other events: the BNP Paribas Open in Indian Wells (formerly the Pacific Life Open), the Miami Masters, the Italian Open, and the Madrid Open. He also had significant victories against Federer in the finals of the Dubai Tennis Championships (his third consecutive title at that competition) and the semifinals of the Australian Open, the US Open, and the BNP Paribas Open. In addition, Djokovic opened the season with an impressive streak of forty-one winning matches.

At the start of the 2012 tennis season, Djokovic continued his dominance over Nadal, prevailing at the finals of the Australian Open, a physically and emotionally grueling five-set grudge match that lasted for five hours and fifty-three minutes. The contest, which broke the record for the longest singles final in Grand Slam history, was billed by many as one of the best finals ever. As of spring 2012, Djokovic, who was named the 2012 Laureus Sportsman of the Year, remains atop the ATP rankings, ahead of Nadal and Federer.

PERSONAL LIFE

Djokovic heads a business empire, Family Sport, which is run by his parents and other relatives. It includes the Novak Café and Restaurant, which has four branches in Serbia—two in Belgrade, one in Novi Sad, and one in Kragujevac—as well as a tennis school. The multilingual Djokovic, who speaks fluent Serbian, German, Italian, and English, has become well known for his impersonations of fellow tennis players, including Nadal, Roddick, Australia's Lleyton Hewitt, and Russia's Maria Sharapova. He lives in Monte Carlo with his longtime girlfriend, Jelena Ristić, whom he began dating in 2005. As of January 2012, the two were planning to marry later in the year.

SUGGESTED READING

Bishop, Greg. "Serbian Boom Defies an Easy Explanation." *New York Times*. New York Times, 7 Sep. 2011. Web. 12 Feb. 2012.

Clarey, Christopher. "Behind Serbia's Rise in Tennis, a Star and His Family." *New York Times*. New York Times, 1 Dec. 2010. Web. 12 Feb. 2012.

Dickson, Mike. "Djokovic Is the Court Jester Planning to Dethrone Kings Rafa and Roger at SW19." *Mail Online*. Associated Newspapers, 17 June 2011. Web. 12 Feb. 2012.

Grossekathöfer, Maik. "Street Fighter, Artist and Patriot: Tennis Star Djokovic Is the Pride of New Serbia." *Spiegel Online*. Spiegel Group, 10 July 2011. Web. 12 Feb. 2012.

McLernan, Neil. "Novak Djokovic Takes Wimbledon 2011 Title to End Rafael Nadal and Roger Federer Dominance." *Mirror*. MGN, 4 July 2011. Web. 12 Feb. 2012.

Price, S. L. "Staring Down History." *SI.com*. Turner Sports, 23 May 2011. Web. 12 Feb. 2012.

—*Bertha Muteba*

Nancy Dubuc

Born: 1969
Occupation: Television network executive

Nancy Dubuc has made a career of revitalizing network television by injecting it with nonfiction programming. "She could look at and articulate what an audience would respond to," Abbe Raven, president and CEO of A+E Television Networks, told Linda Haugsted for *Multichannel News* (29 Jan. 2007). Her approach worked at the A&E Network, where she succeeded in attracting a younger and broader audience with the creation and development of several reality series, including *Dog the Bounty Hunter* and *Growing Up Gotti*. She had similar success at the History Channel, where she significantly improved the network's ratings with the launch of testosterone-driven reality shows such as *Ice Road Truckers* and *Ax Men*. In 2010, Dubuc was appointed to head Lifetime Networks in the hopes of broadening its viewership beyond its largely female audience.

AP Photo

EARLY LIFE AND EDUCATION

Nancy Jean Dubuc was born in 1969 in the dormitories of Fordham University, a New York City–based private institution, to Carol D. Smith and Robert H. Dubuc, then a student at the school. She spent much of her childhood and adolescence growing up in Bristol, Rhode Island, where her mother worked as a nurse anesthetist and her father was a teacher, and received her primary- and high-school education at the Lincoln School, an all-girls college preparatory school in nearby Providence. After graduating in 1987, Dubuc attended Boston University's College of Communication, where she developed an interest in television. "I read a magazine article about a booker at [ABC late-night news program] *Nightline*, and I thought, 'That sounds really cool—you'd get to meet really interesting people!'" she told Leslie Bennetts for *Marie Claire* (14 Nov. 2011, online).

At the age of nineteen, Dubuc accepted an internship with NBC News, where she had a memorable encounter with Tom Brokaw, one of the network's well-known anchors. "I had to deliver something to Mr. Brokaw personally and he was in an animated conversation, which I realized was with his daughter. He waved me into his office as he hung up," Dubuc recalled to Jack Myers for *MediaBizBloggers.com* (23 Apr. 2007, online). "He looked at me seeing someone who was about the same age as his daughter and he asked, rhetorically, 'Are you all like this with your mothers?' Here I was all business and in the presence of an icon, but he was just really human and like my dad."

EARLY TELEVISION CAREER

After receiving a bachelor of arts degree in mass communication in 1991, Dubuc launched her television career, remaining in Boston to serve as a desk assistant for the daily half-hour news program *World Monitor*, a joint production between the *Christian Science Monitor* and the Discovery Channel. "I loved the adrenaline rush of live TV and within a year, I was a line producer," she told Chris Davison for *HRTS Society Views* (13 Nov. 2008, online). In 1992, after *World Monitor* had folded due to financial problems, Dubuc joined the Boston-based public broadcasting affiliate station WGBH-TV.

At WGBH, Dubuc worked on the popular, long-running home-improvement show *This Old House*. She credits her three-year stint at WGBH for providing her with a valuable learning opportunity: "It was actually the era of the last economic downturn which meant staffs were very lean, so I got firsthand experience in virtually every aspect of production," she told Davison. Dubuc then landed a job at *Discover Magazine*, a documentary television program that aired on the Discovery Channel from 1996 to 2000. During her tenure, she served as both the coordinating producer and the series producer. Dubuc earned two Emmy Award nominations for her work on the show: one in 1997, in the category of outstanding informational series for the episode "Immortality," and another in 1998 for an outstanding nonfiction series.

THE HISTORY CHANNEL

In 1999, Dubuc moved from Boston to New York City, where she had a fateful encounter with the woman who would become her mentor. "The major turning point of my career was meeting Abbe Raven, then head of programming for History [an A+E Networks cable channel]," Dubuc said to Davison. "She hired me as a program supervisor." In her new role as the History Channel's director of historical programming, Dubuc was responsible for overseeing a number of the network's shows, including *This Week in History*, an hour-long series highlighting key events of the past; *The Color of War*, a documentary program recounting the Second World War through the use of exclusive unseen footage and archived images, all in color; and *History IQ*, a game show in which contestants competed by answering trivia questions related to US and world history.

As program supervisor, Dubuc oversaw the network's first live program, *Live from Pearl Harbor*. This was the first of her unscripted programs for the A+E Networks. Another noteworthy credit was the four-part documentary *Egypt: Beyond the Pyramids*, on which Dubuc served as an executive producer. In 2001, the program received an Emmy Award nomination in the category of outstanding nonfiction special.

A&E NETWORK

Dubuc's tenure at the History Channel ended in 2002. She was recruited to work at *A&E* Network, the flagship channel of A+E Networks and the History Channel's sister station, in January of the following year. "When Abbe [Raven] was named general manager of the A&E network, I went with her as the VP of development," Dubuc told Davison. Almost immediately after taking the reins, Dubuc, who was in charge of creating and producing nonfiction programs and specials for the network, had to contend with several challenges. "It was trial by fire, I had no experience," she recalled.

At the time, A&E was struggling to retain its audience. One issue was that the average age of the channel's core viewers was sixty-one. Since its launch in 1984, A&E had been positioned as a more commercial version of PBS, focusing heavily on programming that consisted primarily of highbrow cultural fare aimed at an older, more upscale audience. Industry experts suggested that the network needed to broaden its programming offerings.

In what was viewed as a bold, unpopular move to reposition the network and attract a broader and younger audience, Dubuc supervised the creation and production of several reality-based programs for A&E. In July 2003, four of these shows made their debut, with mixed results: *All Year Round with Katie Brown*, a weekly series offering advice on interior design and cooking; *Sell this House*, an interior-design show devoted to helping homeowners affordably decorate their houses in preparation for sale; *The Well-Seasoned Traveler*, a culinary travel program hosted by chef Doug Duda; and *Makeover Mamas*, in which a married couple receives a two-day room makeover by an interior decorator and both mothers-in-law, using a $1,500 budget. Other shows under Dubuc's supervision included *City Confidential*, *American Justice*, *Cold Case Files*, and a revamped version of the franchise series *Biography*, which had expanded to include pop-culture subjects—another maneuver that was met with criticism.

Despite the complaints, A&E continued to provide its viewers with unscripted reality-television programs, a strategy that soon began to pay off. Dubuc's production credits in 2004 included the hit prime-time program *Dog, the Bounty Hunter*, a fast-paced show that follows Duane "Dog" Chapman and his family in their relentless pursuit of fugitives; *Growing Up Gotti*, a glimpse into the lives of Victoria Gotti, daughter of the late mobster John Gotti, and her three sons; *The First 48 Hours*, a behind-the-scenes look at homicide investigations; *Family Plots*, a groundbreaking program providing viewers with an inside look at a family-run mortuary business; and *Airline*, a series examining a day in the life of certain passengers and crew members of Southwest Airlines. That same year, following the success of *Sell this House*, Dubuc came up with the idea to launch a block of A&E's nonfiction fare that would be exclusively devoted to lifestyle or home-themed shows. The network's nonfiction programming department was also garnering recognition from the industry; both *Biography* and *Cold Case Files* earned nominations in the outstanding nonfiction series category at the 2004 prime-time Emmy Awards.

In February 2005, Dubuc was promoted to senior vice president of nonfiction and alternative programming at A&E. While overseeing the network's newly launched feature documentary production unit, A&E Indie Films, she continued to manage the crime documentaries *Cold Case Files*, *City Confidential*, and *American Justice*, as well as the network's lifestyle programming block. Dubuc also remained in charge of developing and creating reality shows, such as the popular prime-time hit *Intervention*, a gritty documentary program focusing on the struggle of addiction; *Inked*, a series set at a Las Vegas tattoo parlor; *Criss Angel: Mindfreak*, a show highlighting magic stunts performed by the illusionist Criss Angel; and *Knievel's Wild Ride*, featuring Robbie Knievel, son of pioneering stuntman Evel Knievel. Thanks to A&E's new approach to programming, the network began to make greater inroads with younger viewers. According to Nielsen Media Research, the average age of the network's viewers had dropped to forty-nine, as reported by Jon Lafayette for *Television Week* (19 Sep. 2005, online).

Dubuc assumed the title of senior vice president of nonfiction programming and new media content for parent company A+E Networks in June 2006. In addition to her previous duties, she was responsible for overseeing the development of nonfiction programs for the History Channel and the Biography Channel. Dubuc continued to develop reality shows for A&E, most notably one chronicling the personal life of the bassist of the rock group Kiss (*Gene Simmons: Family Jewels*) and another offering an inside look at a tactical police unit (*Dallas SWAT*). Her other production credits include *Rollergirls*, which follows the exploits of members of an all-female roller-derby league in Texas, and *Driving Force*, about competitive drag racer John Force and his three younger daughters. These new shows joined returning favorites.

RETURNING TO THE HISTORY CHANNEL

Coming full circle in December 2006, Dubuc accepted a position as executive vice president and general manager of the History Channel, which was seeking to overhaul its image from that of a dull, stodgy network whose programming consisted mostly of military-themed specials and documentaries to an engaging and exciting channel with more contemporary fare. "We want to communicate that history is not all about rote recitation of dates and timelines and facts and dead people," Dubuc told Anthony Crupi for *Mediaweek* (25 Feb. 2008, online). Soon after taking the reins in January 2007, Dubuc gave the approval to develop a series about ice truckers in Alaska.

Dubuc approved a number of other ambitious—and diverse—television projects. These included *The Universe*, a groundbreaking documentary series using computer-generated imagery (CGI) to explain the cosmos; *Jurassic Fight Club*, another series that uses CGI, as well as forensic methods, to recreate battles between prehistoric creatures; *Star Wars: Legacy Revealed*, a documentary special that examines the impact of the *Star Wars* film series on today's society; *Tougher in Alaska*, a reality program that provides viewers with a glimpse of the extreme everyday challenges faced by Alaskans; and *Human Weapon*, a show in which two hosts travel around the world to learn the origins and techniques of various martial-arts disciplines.

The decision to focus on shows that pushed the boundaries of historical and documentary programming quickly paid off. The first-ever episode of *The Universe*, which debuted in May 2007, became the network's most-watched premiere, especially among the key twenty-five-to-fifty-four and eighteen-to-forty-nine demographics. That same month, the *Star Wars* special became the History Channel's most-watched original telecast among the same demographics. Those achievements were soon eclipsed by the debut of *Ice Road Truckers* on June 17, 2007; the series was an instant hit, attracting 3.4 million overall viewers. The season finale in August 2007 drew 4.8 million, outperforming the premiere and helping *Ice Road Truckers* become the highest-rated show in the network's history.

As part of the rebranding strategy, Dubuc also focused on redesigning the network's online presence, making its website more user friendly and offering original video content. One such example, *Band of Bloggers*, featured video blogs from soldiers on the front lines of Iraq. The network underwent an additional makeover in March 2008, changing its name from the History Channel to simply History and adopting a new logo, a capital H. Building on the success of *Ice Road Truckers*, Dubuc spent the next three years championing unscripted programs that explored the lives and unconventional careers of blue-collar workers. Among them were *Ax Men*, a series that documents various logging crews working in remote forests in Oregon; *Pawn Stars*, a show that offers viewers a behind-the-scenes look at a family-operated pawn business; *American Pickers*, which follows two working-class men from Iowa as they travel across the United States in search of antiques and collectibles; and *Swamp People*, a program that focuses on alligator hunters.

During this period, the network achieved several notable highlights. Since its debut, *Pawn Stars* has become History's highest-rated program and has led to two spin-offs, *American Restoration* and *Cajun Pawn Stars*. In December 2011, History announced in a press release that it had finished in the top five of several key demographics: adults ages twenty-five to fifty-four, adults ages eighteen to forty-nine, males ages twenty-five to fifty-four, and males ages eighteen to forty-nine. From 2009 to 2011, the network experienced its highest growth over a two-year period—a 52 percent increase among adults ages twenty-five to fifty-four and adults ages eighteen to forty-nine.

Dubuc's career accomplishments were equally noteworthy. In August 2009, she was promoted to president of History. That same month, A+E Networks acquired Lifetime Entertainment, and in May 2010, Dubuc also became president of Lifetime Network, a channel whose programming has been overwhelmingly aimed at the female population. She had success in 2011 with the reality series *Dance Moms* and approved a spin-off of the show set in Miami. However, attempts at scripted fare—the female police dramas *Against the Wall* and *The Protector*, as well as *Five*, a short-film anthology dealing with breast cancer—did not achieve as much success. In an effort to reverse that trend, Dubuc approved the drama *The Client List*, starring Jennifer Love Hewitt, and a miniseries about the Hatfields and the McCoys, starring Kevin Costner.

HONORS AND PERSONAL LIFE

Dubuc sits on the nominating committee of the International Academy of Television Arts and Sciences, as well as on the boards of the National Association of Television Program Executives (NATPE) and the New York Television Festival. She also serves as cochair of the Realscreen Summit. Since 2008, she has appeared annually on *The Hollywood Reporter*'s Power 100 list of women in entertainment, and *Variety* magazine has featured her in their annual Women's Impact Report. Dubuc has been honored by *Multichannel News* and Women in Cable Telecommunications (WICT) as a 2007 Wonder Woman. She was the recipient of the Preserve America Presidential Award in 2007, the highest national award for achievement in historic preservation, for History's Save Our History initiative. Dubuc, who lives in New York City, has two children with her husband, advertising executive Michael Kizilbash.

SUGGESTED READING

Bennetts, Leslie. "The View from the Top." *Marie Claire*. Hearst, 14 Nov. 2011. Web. 21 Mar. 2012.

Davison, Chris. "Profile: Nancy Dubuc." *HRTS Society Views*. Hollywood Radio and Television Soc., 13 Nov. 2008. Web. 21 Mar. 2012.

Haugsted, Linda. "A Work of Non-Fiction: Dubuc Makes History Her Way." *Multichannel News* 29 Jan. 2007: 10. Print.

Myers, Jack. "Nancy Dubuc: Bringing History to Life at the History Channel." *MediaBizBloggers.com*. MediaBizBloggers, 23 Apr. 2007. Web. 21 Mar. 2012.

Rose, Lacey. "Can History Repeat Itself?" *Hollywood Reporter* 8 Apr. 2011: 60–64. Print.

—Bertha Muteba

David Eagleman

Born: April 25, 1971
Occupation: Neuroscientist, educator, writer

The neuroscientist David Eagleman is always involved in multiple scientific projects simultaneously, most of them investigations of people's perceptions of time and the workings of our unconscious minds. He is the director of the Eagleman Laboratory for Perception and Action at the Baylor College of Medicine, in Houston, Texas, where he is an assistant professor in the Departments of Neuroscience and Psychiatry. He also directs the Baylor College of Medicine Initiative on Neuroscience and Law, which addresses ways in which discoveries in neuroscience might affect existing or prospective laws; shed light on the effectiveness of punishments for criminal acts; and help determine methods of rehabilitation.

With the neurologist Richard E. Cytowic, Eagleman wrote *Wednesday Is Indigo Blue: Discovering the Brain of Synesthesia* (2009), which discusses the genetics and neuroscience of synesthesia, a condition in which people experience the world "across" senses, so that they may "hear" colors or "see," in particular colors, music, numbers, letters of the alphabet, or days of the week. In *Incognito: The Secret Lives of the Brain* (2011), Eagleman used evidence from neuroscience and psychology to argue that most of what we do, think, and believe is generated by parts of the brain to which we have no conscious access; he also explored the implications of neuroscientific discoveries for our legal system. His book *Sum: Forty Tales from the Afterlives* (2009) is a work of literary fiction that won him recognition for his wit and imagination. He is also the author of an e-book, *Why the Net Matters: Six Easy Ways to Avert the Collapse of Civilization* (2010).

EARLY LIFE AND EDUCATION

David Morris Eagleman was born into a secular Jewish family on April 25, 1971, in Albuquerque,

Getty Images

New Mexico, where he and his older brother, Joel, grew up. His mother, Cirel, was a high-school biology teacher. His father, Arthur, practiced forensic psychiatry, a field in which psychiatric knowledge "is applied to questions posed by the legal system," according to the website *Forensic-Psych*, and objective evaluations are provided to attorneys, courts, institutions, and other interested parties. When Eagleman was eight years old, he had an accident that powerfully affected the course of his life: while playing at a construction site one day, he fell off the roof of an unfinished house. Although he fell at a normal speed, he felt as if everything was happening in slow motion. That perception, or his memory of it, fascinated him. He told *Current Biography* (the source of all quotes in this article unless otherwise noted) that he later wondered, "Does that mean time is not what I thought it was?" (His nose was smashed when he landed; it healed well, and he suffered no other serious injuries.)

Eagleman's mother told Burkhard Bilger for the *New Yorker* (25 Apr. 2011) that at age twelve David understood enough about Einstein's theory of relativity to explain it to her and her husband. He had a phenomenal memory, too: he could remember lists of as many as four hundred nouns recited to him, "in reverse order, if people wished," Bilger reported. In high school Eagleman's greatest interests were in math and physics, and he did well in both. On his own he read books about space physics. As an undergraduate at Rice University, in Houston, he double-majored in British and American literature and space physics, thinking he would combine his love of writing and science. He ultimately abandoned space physics: "It was beautiful and wonderful—but very abstract, because everything was so far away." Meanwhile, Eagleman was obsessively reading many books and articles about the brain. He fondly remembers Judith Hooper and Dick Teresi's book *The Three Pound Universe: Revolutionary Discoveries about the Brain* (1986). In 1993 he earned a bachelor's degree in British and American literature.

Eagleman then decided that he wanted to study neuroscience at the Graduate School of Biomedical Science at the Baylor College of Medicine, a division of the Texas Medical Center. He has recalled saying in a telephone call to a school administrator, "I know I missed the [application] deadline and I don't have any biology on my transcript, but I read this whole stack of books on neuroscience. I know that this is what I want to do, so why don't you ask me any questions, and I'll tell you what I know." Eagleman thus secured not only a chance to apply but also, soon afterward, acceptance to the school, thanks to his strong background in math and physics, impressive fund of knowledge about the brain, and a forty-five-page paper, written for a Rice philosophy course, about the epistemological limits of information derived from brain-lesion studies. Because he lacked a solid grounding in biology, Eagleman relied heavily on his math skills in planning his doctoral research project: he created a computer simulation of a piece of neural tissue to analyze how certain chemicals travel in the brain. (The program was so complex that it tied up the Texas Medical Center's supercomputer for several days.) Eagleman received a PhD degree in 1998. He next pursued a postdoctoral fellowship at the Salk Institute for Biological Studies, in La Jolla, California, where he focused on questions related to biophysics—in particular, as he put it, "How do humans actually see the world and what does that tell us?" (Biophysics uses the principles of math and physics to investigate biological phenomena.)

EARLY CAREER

One of Eagleman's earliest papers is also among his most cited. Called "Motion Integration and Postdiction in Visual Awareness," it was written with Terrence J. Sejnowski and included in the March 17, 2000, issue of *Science*—the journal "all young post-docs hope to publish in," Eagleman said. The paper introduced a new explanation for the so-called flash-lag effect, a visual illusion in which, on a computer screen, a flash of light precisely aligned with (or atop) a moving object appears to the viewer not at the same location but lagging slightly behind the object. The brain, Eagleman believes, presents us with something like a "delayed video feed," giving us the story of what happened a fraction of a second after the actual event. In 2003 Eagleman became the director of his own lab, at the University of Texas, in Houston; in 2006 he moved on to Baylor.

In an experiment that Eagleman conducted in 2006, people sat at a table and repeatedly pushed a button that caused a light to flash immediately. Unbeknownst to the subjects, Eagleman next rigged the device so that each flash was delayed by 100 milliseconds—a difference too small for people to notice. Then Eagleman (again without telling the subjects) returned the device to its original setup, so that the light flashed instantly when the button was pushed. During that third part of the experiment, the subjects—with some amazement—reported that the light appeared to be flashing before they pressed the button. "This was a really stunning finding," Eagleman said, because, in addition to providing further evidence for the relatively sluggish speed at which humans process sensory inputs, it led him to wonder whether the improper perception of the timing of two events is one of the hallmarks of schizophrenia. Some schizophrenics perform actions but refuse to take credit or blame for them because they are certain that they did not act. "So as soon as I saw my subjects say, 'Oh, it wasn't me. The flash happened before I pressed the button,' I thought, 'Wait a minute! That's the kind of credit misattribution that schizophrenics do,'" Eagleman recalled. For the past three years, Eagleman has investigated the hypothesis that schizophrenia may in part be a disorder of time perception. He noted that the study of time perception is "completely missing from the clinical landscape"—that is, currently psychologists and others who examine schizophrenics or study mental illnesses rarely include tests of time perception.

TIME PERCEPTION IN LIFE-THREATENING SITUATIONS

One of Eagleman's most-talked-about experiments addresses the question of why time appears to slow down in life-threatening situations (as it did for him when he fell from the roof as a boy). In that experiment Eagleman made use of a ride in an amusement park in which subjects dropped (with their backs to the ground) from a height of 110 feet and then landed safely on a net above the ground. Predictably, because free fall is scary for nearly everyone, time appeared to slow down for those people: although the fall always took a certain number of seconds, they thought they had been falling for a greater number of seconds, usually about 30 percent more. Eagleman theorized that there might be two possible explanations: one could be that in life-threatening situations, brain processes accelerate, thereby making external events appear to be slower than they really are. The other is that the

discrepancy results from some aspect of memory. To find out if the former is true, Eagleman had his volunteers outfitted with wrist-worn devices that flashed numbers too quickly to permit humans to distinguish one from another; if, as they fell, they actually perceived the world in slow motion, they should have been able to see each number as it flashed. During the more than four years that Eagleman repeated that experiment, none of his subjects were able to make out the numbers, which led Eagleman to conclude that the apparent slowness of the fall is a function of how the subjects remembered it afterward. He believes that they remembered the fall that way because in life-threatening situations people get bombarded with sensory details—significantly more than they would normally be aware of—and their brains later interpret that to mean that the experience took longer than it actually did.

SYNESTHESIA

Eagleman's overarching interest in neuroscience stems from questions connected to the phenomenon of consciousness. He recognized synesthesia as a disorder that might help answer such questions, because people with synesthesia (called synesthetes) experience certain aspects of reality differently from people who do not have that condition. For example, during a bingo game certain synesthetes will "see" a number called out as purple or some other color. There appears to be a genetic basis for synesthesia—that is, its occurrence among family members is statistically greater than it is among nonrelated people. Eagleman is trying to establish a genetic explanation for why people experience reality differently, a field he calls "perceptual genomics." Scientists have determined that the difference in perception stems from differences in synaptic connections between nearby areas of the brain and/or slight differences in chemical balance. (The latter is evident from artificially induced synesthesia, which may occur, for example, when people take hallucinogenic drugs, such as LSD.) Approximately one in twenty-three people have some form of synesthesia, but it is present up to seven times more often among artistic people, such as painters, novelists, and composers. With Richard E. Cytowic, a pioneer in the study of synesthesia, Eagleman wrote *Wednesday Is Indigo Blue: Discovering the Brain of Synesthesia* (2009). In it the authors argued that the difference between a person with synesthesia and one without it is a matter of degree: "crosstalk" between different brain regions exists in both groups but is more intense in the synesthete. In a review for the *New Scientist* (30 May 2009), Liz Else wrote that she is "one of millions of people worldwide who see days as colors, which is the most common form of synesthesia," and she praised *Wednesday Is Indigo Blue* as "brimming with well-explained facts and cogently argued theories." She concluded, "This is a clear, clever book that will appeal to synesthetes in search of explanations, and to all with a passion for neurology's wild territory."

SUM: FORTY TALES FROM THE AFTERLIVES

Also in 2009 Eagleman published *Sum: Forty Tales from the Afterlives*, a work of fiction about life after death and the role of humans in the cosmos. The book contains forty very short stories, each offering a possible scenario for the afterlife. In one, God is the size of a microbe and is unconcerned with our existence; in another a team of dimwits have created humans in an experiment to figure out what they do not understand; in still another the afterlife is populated only by people we remember, and there is no chance of ever meeting a stranger. In other scenarios, after death we go to a cosmic waiting room and can move on to the next stage only when somebody refers to us (in the living world) for the last time, so that famous people are trapped in the waiting room indefinitely; or we are forced to relive our lives not in chronological order but by clumps of experience, so that we spend six days clipping our nails, twenty-seven hours in intense pain, seven months having sex, eighteen months waiting in line, thirty years sleeping, and so on. In another scenario Eagleman imagines the afterlife to be a place from which people can watch their enduring influences on the real world—children, inventions, businesses, recipes—until those influences disappear. "Most of these future options are extremely amusing, highlighting our self-importance and subjecting us to an astonishing range of humiliations, disappointments and surprises," Alexander McCall Smith wrote for the *New York Times Book Review* (14 June 2009). In a review for the London *Observer* (7 June 2009), Geoff Dyer called *Sum* "stunningly original" and added that it has "the unaccountable, jaw-dropping quality of genius." Dyer wrote that the book is greater than the sum of its parts, because it is really about "how to live." "Its success depends on a combination of exquisitely rendered detail and the massive implications that result," he declared. A popular as well as a critical success, *Sum* has been translated into twenty-three languages. Eagleman and Brian Eno read excerpts from *Sum* to music composed by Eno at the Sydney Opera House, in Australia, in 2009 and the Brighton Dome, in England, in 2010. In May 2012 a chamber opera based on *Sum*, by the German pianist and composer Max Richter, will debut at the Royal Opera House Linbury Studio, in London, England.

INCOGNITO: THE SECRET LIVES OF THE BRAIN

In the first chapter of *Incognito: The Secret Lives of the Brain* (2011), which is excerpted on his website, Eagleman wrote that the brain is "the most complex material we've discovered in the universe": a neuron usually has about 10,000 connections to nearby neurons, and there are approximately 100 billion neurons in an adult brain. "The brain is a complex system, but that doesn't mean it's incomprehensible," he wrote. "Our neural circuits were carved by natural selection to solve problems that our ancestors faced during our species' evolutionary history. Your brain is carved by evolutionary pressures just as your spleen and eyes are. And so is your consciousness. Consciousness developed because it was advantageous, but advantageous only in limited amounts. Our conscious minds are limited representations of the activity in our heads. Consciousness is the lowest man on the totem pole in the power structure of the brain. Most of what we do and think and feel is not under conscious control." In one of the many experiments Eagleman described to support his argument, researchers asked male subjects to judge the attractiveness of individual women's faces in a series of large photos. In half the photos the women's pupils were dilated, and in the other half they were not—a difference the scientists did not mention to the subjects. The men consistently ranked photos of the former group as more attractive than those in the latter group, but none of them could explain why. "Their choices weren't accidental," Eagleman wrote. "In the largely inaccessible workings of the brain, something knew that a woman's dilated eyes correlates with sexual excitement and readiness. Their brains knew this, but the men didn't—at least not explicitly. Presumably, the men also didn't know that their sense of beauty and attraction is deeply hardwired, steered in the right direction by programs carved by millions of years of natural selection." "Brains are in the business of gathering information and steering behavior appropriately," he continued. "It doesn't matter whether consciousness is involved in the decision making. And most of the time it's not. Whether we're talking about dilated eyes, jealousy, attraction, the love of fatty foods, or the great idea you had last week, consciousness is the smallest player in the operations of the brain."

Incognito became a *New York Times* nonfiction best seller. Most early reviews of *Incognito* praised the book. In the *New York Times* (19 June 2011), Jennifer Schuessler wrote that Eagleman "engagingly sums up recent discoveries about the unconscious processes that dominate our mental life, including his own pioneering work in time perception." Laura Sanders wrote for *ScienceNews* (16 July 2001), "In fresh, clear prose unencumbered by neuro-jargon, Eagleman weaves descriptions of simple, relatable experiments and compelling case studies . . . , convincing the reader that deep, mysterious machinations of the brain are calling the shots. . . . The book's pithy observations, breezy language and wow-inducing anecdotes provide temporary pleasure, but the book's real strength is in its staying power. A reader will be left to mull over Eagleman's provocative ideas about 'biologically informed jurisprudence.'" By contrast, *Incognito* struck Alexander Linklater, writing for the London *Guardian* (23 Apr. 2011), as "a breathless account of possible implications opened up by the rise of neuroscience as a way of looking at the world" and maintained that it "belongs to a popular trend of neuro-hubris—wildly overstating the ramifications of a science that is still in its infancy. The true fascination of neuroscience lies not in bombastic philosophical claims but in the fine details of brain function, illustrations of the mind-brain problem, and the human interest of case studies. There isn't even that much actual neuroscience in *Incognito*. Its illustrations are drawn just as much from the annals of evolutionary psychology, behavioural economics and more traditional forms of psychology."

Like some other critics, Josh Rothman, the *Boston Globe* (1 June 2011) reviewer, was strongly impressed by the chapter in *Incognito* titled "Why Blameworthiness Is the Wrong Question," which discusses the implications of neuroscience for society's beliefs about crime and punishment and the justice system in general. "Many of us," Eagleman wrote in that chapter, "like to believe that all adults possess the same capacity to make sound choices. It's a nice idea, but it's wrong. People's brains can be vastly different—influenced not only by genetics but by the environment in which they grew up." Children's brains can be affected by substance abuse by mothers during pregnancy, neglect or physical or psychological abuse, exposure to toxins such as lead, and head injuries; later in life substance abuse by individuals changes their brains. Many other environmental and genetic factors also affect people's brains. "The goal is to have a much more tailored legal system," Eagleman told *Current Biography*. "Some jurisdictions already have separate courts for juveniles, drug addicts, and those with mental-health issues." In Eagleman's view the focus should not be on blame or retribution but on predicting recidivism and helping criminals learn how to control their impulses.

In an essay on the same topic for the *Atlantic Monthly* (July/Aug. 2011), which was essentially an excerpt of the chapter on neurolaw in *Incognito*, Eagleman wrote, "Beyond customized sentencing, a forward-thinking legal system informed by scientific insights into the brain will enable us to stop treating prison as a one-size-fits-all solution. To be clear, I'm not opposed to incarceration, and its purpose is not limited to the removal of dangerous people from the streets. The prospect of incarceration deters many crimes, and time actually spent in prison can steer some people away from further criminal acts upon their release. But that works only for those whose brains function normally. The problem is that prisons have become our de facto mental-healthcare institutions—and inflicting punishment on the mentally ill usually has little influence on their future behavior."

OTHER PROJECTS

Eagleman is also the author of a digital book for the iPad, *Why the Net Matters: Six Easy Ways to Avert the Collapse of Civilization* (2010). According to Eagleman, the Internet can save humankind from six dangers that have destroyed civilizations in the past: natural disasters, resource depletion, economic meltdown, infectious disease epidemics, inadequate spread of information (including poor systems of education and censorship), and corruption.

Currently, Eagleman is working on at least four books. One is about brain plasticity—the brain's nonstop reconfiguring of its wiring; another is a cognitive-neuroscience textbook for undergraduates; a third, inspired by Steven D. Levitt and Stephen J. Dubner's best seller *Freakonomics: A Rogue Economist Explores the Hidden Side of Everything* (2005), is tentatively titled "Brainfood," which Eagleman calls "*Freakonomics* for neuroscience—all the really cool stuff that hasn't been asked about or written about anywhere else." He is also writing a book on neurolaw.

Eagleman spends most of his time working in his lab, carrying on various side projects, and writing. By his own account, he has no hobbies or free time. He married Sarah Alwin, who is also a neuroscientist, in 2010. The couple, who live in Houston, are expecting their first child, a boy, in February 2012.

SUGGESTED READING

Bilger, Burkhard. "The Possibilian." *New Yorker* 25 Apr. 2011: 54.

Chabris, Christopher F. "The Stranger Within." *Wall Street Journal*. Dow Jones, 15 June 2011. Web. Jan. 2012.

Dyer, Geoff. "Do You Really Want to Come Back as a Horse?" *Observer* [London] 7 June 2009: 23.

Eagleman. David Eagleman, n.d. Web. Jan. 2012.

Lewis, Jim. "Mind Games." *Texas Monthly* June 2011: 132.

Richards, Julian. "Brain Scientist vs. Novelist: What Use Is an Afterlife?" *New Scientist* 30 May 2009: 44.

—*Dmitry Kiper*

Kathleen Edwards

Born: July 11, 1978
Occupation: Singer-songwriter

The Canadian-born singer-songwriter Kathleen Edwards first brought her alternative country music—greatly influenced by Bob Dylan, Neil Young, Whiskeytown, and The Band—to American audiences in 2002, at the South by Southwest (SXSW) music festival, in Austin, Texas. The following year saw the American release of her debut album, *Failer* (2003), which featured songs such as "Hockey Skates" and "Six O' Clock News." She continued to make her own brand of alternative country—with tight instrumentation and sharp, witty lyrics—on her second and third albums, *Back to Me* (2005) and *Asking for Flowers* (2008), respectively. Edwards noticeably changed direction (more toward indie rock) on her fourth album, *Voyageur* (2012), which was coproduced by singer Justin Vernon, best known by his stage name Bon Iver.

Getty Images

EARLY LIFE

Kathleen Margaret Edwards was born on July 11, 1978 in Ottawa, Ontario, Canada. Because her father, Leonard, was a diplomat, the family occasionally lived abroad, particularly in Switzerland and South Korea. They moved to the latter country when Edwards was thirteen years old, and that experience had a profound impact on her as a teenager. Speaking to David Langness for *Paste Magazine* (1 Mar. 2008), Edwards recalled that time in her life: "I felt very alone and within myself, and I also got to see so much— cultures, lifestyles. I got to connect with a lot of older people who taught me a lot. I actually don't think I dated anyone my age. Seoul, Korea, at 13 is hard on a Canadian girl . . . I was thrust into an Asian culture where I was very unhappy . . . I spent those years alone and experiencing things, writing poetry and looking inward."

Edwards started playing music at a young age, but it took about a decade for her to embrace and fall in love with the country-influenced rock sound she would later start playing as an artist in her own right. She began taking classical violin lessons at the age of five, continuing with that instrument until she was seventeen. As a child she mostly listened to pop music. However, her musical taste eventually changed. Some key moments in her musical development included learning to play her older brother's guitar at summer camp, and receiving her own guitar as a gift when she was fifteen years old. Her musical aesthetic changed most significantly through listening to her brother's record collection, particularly his many Bob Dylan and Neil Young albums. Edwards would also listen to Tom Petty, Creedence Clearwater Revival, and more contemporary acts including Indigo Girls and Ani DiFranco.

Edwards returned with her family to her native Canada in 1997. She spent her last two years in high school becoming more and more engrossed in music, playing a lot of guitar in her room, and not devoting much time to studying. According to the biography that appears on her official website, it was upon her return to Canada that Edwards moved away from listening to "mainstream pop" and toward the singer-songwriters and country-influenced bands cited above.

EARLY MUSIC CAREER

During high school, Edwards had started playing cover songs on her acoustic guitar in neighborhood music venues, and she wanted to keep going with her music. She also wanted to write her own songs. Edwards was inspired by the music of such alternative country groups as Whiskeytown and singer-songwriters including Ryan Adams. Deciding to stick with music instead of going to college, Edwards moved out of her parents' place to an apartment in Ottawa. She supported herself by waitressing and started writing more of her own material. She recorded *Building 55* (1999), a seven-song EP of which she made five hundred copies. The following year she went on a kind of do-it-yourself tour of Canada in her old Chevy Suburban truck. She booked her own gigs (almost a dozen), sold her own records, found her own accommodations, and paid for food, gas, and shelter with the money she had made playing at shows.

That year, 2000, Edwards also started recording what would become her official first album. She was twenty-two years old when she left her busy lifestyle in Ottawa for a few months and moved to a farmhouse outside of Ottawa, in Wakefield, Quebec. Here she wrote the songs that would make up her full-length album debut *Failer*, which she would later record at Little Bullhorn Studios, in Ottawa. The majority of the album's songs deal in some way with her relatively recent breakup with her boyfriend. Although the songs were originally written using only her voice and an acoustic guitar, Edwards had in-studio help from some well-established country-rock musicians who played such instruments as the banjo, organ, saxophones, electric guitar, slide guitar, and lap-steel guitar. She released the album independently in early 2002. It was soon picked up by Maple- Music, an online Canadian music-promotion company. That led to a big break for Edwards: In 2002 she played the SXSW music festival in Austin, Texas. Soon she was signed by the Massachusetts-based record label Rounder Records, with whom she is still associated.

FAILER (2002)
In the United States, *Failer* was released in January 2003. It was primarily influenced by American roots music, country, and country rock. The album was full of songs about heartbreak, expressed in many different moods. On the song "Mercury," Edwards sings about searching for a good time. On the country-rock-pop number "Hockey Skates," she sings, "I'm so tired of playing defense / And I don't even have hockey skates." And the mellow number "Sweet Little Duck" features such lyrics as, "I sleep through most days / So the time goes by / And I think I drink now more than ever." The album also featured other songs about good times gone bad and troubled women, such as "Maria" and "One More Song the Radio Won't Like." Edwards's work shows influences from Bob Dylan, The Band, Tom Petty, Whiskeytown, and Lucinda Williams. Many reviewers have cited these influences, and the comparisons between Edwards and Williams have been most frequent. Accompanying the album's release, Edwards appeared on the *Late Show with David Letterman*, the *Tonight Show with Jay Leno*, and a concert tour of Europe.

The reviews for the album were mostly very positive. Despite her many influences and the fact that she was only twenty-two when she wrote the songs, reviewers praised her as an original—a young woman with her own voice, both musically and lyrically. In a review for *Paste Magazine* (1 Jan. 2003), John Schacht wrote, "The throaty Edwards sounds like Lucinda Williams with far fewer miles on the odometer, and she mines similar veins of hard living and love gone

wrong for her lyrics. But Edwards doesn't sound like an acolyte. She's got moxie, but a refreshingly fragile honesty in her writing tones down the bravado." Schacht went on to describe the songs on the album as "straight-ahead rockers" and "country and folk-tinged tunes," noting that Edwards "sounds like she's been at it for decades."

In his review for the Onion, Inc. website *A.V. Club* (27 Jan. 2003), Keith Phipps called *Failer* "[t]he kind of album made when heartbreak and whiskey combine with raw talent." Phipps also noted Edwards's similarities to Williams, but he concluded "there's no suggestion that Edwards is anything other than an original talent, and a formidable one at that."

BACK TO ME (2005)
Edwards's second studio album, *Back to Me* (2005), continued to explore the topics of romance and heartbreak. The album was produced by guitarist Colin Cripps, whom she had met the previous year. (Cripps and Edwards later got married, but their marriage would end in divorce five years later.) In addition to producing the album, Cripps cowrote two songs with Edwards, "Back to Me" and "Summerlong." The album featured similar instruments as *Failer*. On the attitude-filled title track, Edwards sings the following chorus, "I've got lights you've never seen / I've got moves I've never used / I've got ways to make you come / back to me." On "In State" she plays a tough woman who sends her law-breaking lover to jail; and she evokes much sadness in her listener on such tracks as "Old Time Sake" and "Pink Emerson Radio." With her sophomore album, Edwards reached the Billboard 200 charts: the album peaked at 173.

As with her previous record, the album received primarily glowing reviews. In another review for *A.V. Club* (1 Mar. 2005), Phipps offered praise for Edwards's second album: "Edwards has a suggestively melancholy voice, a gift for well-turned phrases, and an uncanny knack for making up-tempo tracks like 'In State' sound as intimate and raw as her ballads. She may not write the sort of songs that radio likes, but, then again, she's not really trying. Nor should she. Edwards' songs have a lived-in quality and an emotional specificity that's tough to achieve, much less sustain." Stephen M. Deusner, reviewing *Back to Me* for *Pitchfork.com* (13 Mar. 2005), considered Edwards's second album even better than her first, both in terms of its attitude and sonic dimensions. "*Back to Me* is a bolder album," Deusner wrote, "with Edwards figuring more prominently and actively in the more personal songs. Nowhere does she sound more brazen than on the title track, in which she promises no escape for an errant lover . . . Fittingly, her band on *Back to Me* sounds tighter and more dynamic than the one on *Failer*. This type of country music is not especially notable for its innovation, but there are flourishes of sound that elevate Back to Me above similar efforts by Tift Merritt and Kasey Chambers."

ASKING FOR FLOWERS (2008)

Three years later, Edwards released a new album, for which she learned to play the piano and hired new studio musicians. *Asking for Flowers* (2008) features eleven tracks and a bonus song. Some considered it her best album to date. Just as before, her music featured smart and witty song lyrics. On the title track Edwards sings, "Asking for flowers / Is like asking you to be nice / Don't tell me you're too tired / Ten years I've been working nights." Other such biting songs include "The Cheapest Key" and "I Make the Dough, You Get the Glory." But the album also contained sad musical narratives, such as "Scared at Night" and "Alicia Ross." The latter is based on a true story about a teenage girl who was murdered by her neighbor.

Whereas wit and sensitivity had been commonplace on Edwards's earlier records, political themes had not. *Asking for Flowers* features two politically and socially conscious songs, namely "Oh Canada" and "Oil Man's War." In the former Edwards takes aim at her native Canada, criticizing what she believes to be its flaws. She toured Europe and North America to promote *Asking for Flowers*. In addition to receiving a good deal of praise, the album peaked at 102 on the Billboard 200 chart.

In his review of the album for *Slant Magazine* (10 Mar. 2008), Jonathan Keefe praised Edwards's lyrics: "What distinguishes Kathleen Edwards from so many of the other female singer-songwriters on the roots-rock scene is her willingness to write lines of biting, vicious wit that transform otherwise straightforward narratives into stories with a bit more meat. It's a talent that gives her work a unique, engaging voice in an increasingly tired genre, and Edwards's pen is at its sharpest on her third album, *Asking for Flowers*." Keefe declared that the album is Edwards's "most accomplished work." In addition to praising her lyrics, Deusner, in a review for *Pitchfork.com* (9 Apr. 2008), applauded the singer's attitude: "There's a combativeness to Edwards' singing and songwriting, as if she knows she's working in a genre that favors tasteful decorum and too often churns out sonic wallpaper. On *Asking for Flowers*, she sounds better than her peers for being so much braver."

VOYAGEUR (2012)

Four years passed until the release of Edwards's fourth album, *Voyageur* (2012). Prior to recording it, Edwards decided to drastically change her musical direction and move away from Americana and country rock and more toward indie rock. To help her achieve this, she contacted US musician Justin Vernon, who is better known by the stage name Bon Iver. By 2011 Edwards and her husband had divorced; and she became involved in a romantic—and ongoing musical—relationship with Vernon. The two toured together in 2011, with Edwards performing as the opening act. As the coproducer of *Voyageur*, Vernon had significant influence on the sound of Edwards's new album, which featured personal tales, such as "Pink Champagne," about a former bride's regrets. Vernon contributed his vocals and played some instruments (such as guitar, piano, and banjo) on the album; and it was his indie-rock star power that attracted a few guests to the album, including Phil Cook (of Megafaun) and Norah Jones. The album rose to number 39 on the Billboard 200 chart, Edwards's highest place yet.

In a review for *Paste Magazine* (17 Jan. 2012), Ryan Reed observed that the "aptly-named *Voyageur* nonetheless finds Edwards in a state of transit—chronicling the mental, emotional and literal geographies that separate her narrators from their desires." He went on to discuss Edwards's musical exploration on the album: "Her freshly colored arrangements simply explode with sonic possibilities, expanding upon her previously straightforward Americana palette with layers of painstakingly crafted overdub dreaminess, dipping lavishly into jazz and lightly psychedelic textures." Yet not all reviewers were as impressed with Edwards's embrace of a new musical style. Some admired her willingness to experiment and be adventurous but criticized the new album for not being as consistently good as Edwards's first three releases. In a review for *A.V. Club* (17 Jan. 2012), Marcus Gilmer called the results "uneven."

In addition to the studio albums cited above, Edwards has also released a five-song live album, *Live from the Bowery* (2004); appearing one year after the American release of her debut album, *Live from the Bowery* features such songs as "Hockey Skates," "National Steel," and "Money Talks."

After a brief, health-related hiatus beginning in April 2012, Edwards has continued to tour and perform her material in Canada, the United States, and Europe. As reported on her official website, Edwards's tour schedule also includes concert appearances slated for December 2012 in the United Kingdom.

SUGGESTED READING

Deusner, Stephen M. "Kathleen Edwards: *Asking for Flowers*." *Pitchfork.com*. Pitchfork Media Inc., 9 Apr. 2008. Web. 10 Aug. 2012.

Gilmer, Marcus. "Kathleen Edwards: *Voyageur*." *A.V. Club*. Onion Inc., 17 Jan. 2012. Web. 10 Aug. 2012.

Phipps, Keith. "Kathleen Edwards: *Back to Me*." *A.V. Club*. Onion Inc., 1 Mar. 2005. Web. 10 Aug. 2012.

Schacht, John. "Kathleen Edwards: *Failer.*" *Paste Magazine*. Paste Media Group, 1 Jan. 2003. Web. 10 Aug. 2012.

—*Dmitry Kiper*

Daniel Ek

Born: February 21, 1983
Occupation: CEO and founder of Spotify

Getty Images

To those old enough to remember rushing to the record store to buy a coveted album on vinyl or waiting eagerly by the radio until a favorite track was played, Spotify, the music-streaming service cofounded by Swedish entrepreneur Daniel Ek in 2006, might seem like something from a science-fiction novel. Spotify's aim, according to its website, is "to help people to listen to whatever music they want, whenever they want, wherever they want." Spotify's users have access, on demand, to a library of more than 15 million tracks. Currently, Spotify boasts some 10 million registered users, with 2.5 million of those paying for ad-free, premium services. Echoing sentiments expressed by many other industry observers, tech reporter Krishnan Guru-Murthy, who interviewed the entrepreneur for the United Kingdom's Channel 4 News on March 7, 2009, asserted, "Ek will earn himself a place in music history alongside the inventors of vinyl, CD and the download," as quoted on the Spotify site. In 2010, the editors of *Time* magazine online listed Spotify as among its 10 Start-Ups That Will Change Your Life.

EARLY LIFE AND EDUCATION

Most reporters who profile Ek seize upon the fact that he started his first business at the age of fourteen, during the height of the technology boom in the 1990s. However, it is also interesting to note Ek's lifelong commitment to both music and technology—two passions that led him through various business ventures to the creation of Spotify. Born in Sweden on February 21, 1983, Ek was raised in Ragsved, a crime-plagued area of Stockholm, in a family with musical roots. After being presented with a guitar at the age of five, Ek quickly became proficient and went on to play multiple instruments, including bass, drums, harmonica, and piano. At some points in his life, he even considered pursuing a career as a musician. Ek's passion for technology emerged around the same time as he began to play music: His stepfather who worked in information technology (IT) granted him access to a Commodore VIC–20, a rudimentary eight-bit personal computer that had been introduced to the market in 1980. Ek took to computing as readily as he had taken to playing the guitar,

and by the age of seven, he could write basic computer code. As a teenager, he used his high school's computer lab to build commercial websites. By pricing them at $5,000, a fraction of their usual cost of $50,000, Ek attracted a large client base in the corporate world.

After Google turned down his application to work for the still-young company as an engineer, the sixteen-year-old Ek focused his after-school hours on improving his home business and eventually landed a job at the search engine optimization (SEO) company called Jajja. There, he worked to boost websites' ranking and visibility during Internet searches. As a high school graduate, Ek entered Sweden's Royal Institute of Technology with the intent of studying engineering. However, once he discovered how many of his courses involved the use of dry, theoretical mathematics, he left the institute.

GETTING A START IN BUSINESS

Since his early teens Ek had followed his curiosity and drive to understand aspects of the Internet world. Using the pay from his website company and later his employment at Jajja, he had purchased Internet servers to learn how they worked. In addition to creating websites, he had used his new servers to offer hosting services to his clients. Working with additional servers in later years, Ek had performed experiments with the simultaneous recording of television programs, much as the recording device TiVo does. Clearly, Ek's years of self-motivated technological experimentation gave him the edge for his first majorly lucrative achievement. After he had dropped out of the Royal Institute of Technology, the advertising company TradeDoubler hired him to provide information about their contracted websites. Ek quickly made $2 million with the program he created for TradeDoubler and the related patents he sold soon afterward.

Flexing the entrepreneurial muscles he had first used in high school when he organized his friends to help with his website design business, Ek went on to act as chief technical officer (CTO) of StarDoll, a website service aimed at preteen girls that allowed users to dress virtual paper dolls in a wide variety of fashions. Ek's other business ventures from this time period included a leadership position at Tradera, a Swedish online commerce service eventually bought by eBay, and the founding of the Internet advertising enterprise Advertigo, which was later acquired by TradeDoubler. By this point, Ek had amassed a fortune.

A CRUCIAL PARTNERSHIP

Martin Lorentzon, the cofounder of TradeDoubler, proved to be Ek's ride to even greater wealth and fame. More significant, the partnership the two would soon begin helped Ek through a period of identity crisis. After realizing that his luxurious lifestyle in Stockholm was leaving him dissatisfied, Ek had moved to a cabin in the woods near his parents' home, where he braved a harsh winter, practicing the guitar and meditating. As Ek told Steven Bertoni for *Forbes* (Jan. 4, 2012, online), "I was deeply uncertain of who I was and who I wanted to be." Around the same time that twenty-three-year-old Ek was struggling with depression and discontentment, TradeDoubler executive Lorentzon was also going through an aimless period. The two, fans of *The Godfather* and other gangster movies, began to spend time together, watching countless films and dreaming of starting a business that would combine Ek's two passions of music and technology. "I got a very strong feeling when I met Daniel," Lorentzon recalled to Bertoni. "To partner up I have to like the person like a brother, because we'll face so many problems. The value of a company is the sum of the problems you solve together."

Lorentzon resigned from the chairmanship of TradeDoubler and provided the seed money to cement his partnership with Ek. The two agreed to pursue Ek's ideas about technology and music. Ek has told reporters that the idea for what would become Spotify had originally come to him in 2002, when Napster, a peer-to-peer file-sharing website, went bankrupt and ceased operations in the wake of controversy over copyright infringement and illegal downloads. "I realized that you can never legislate away from piracy," Ek told Rupert Neate for the London *Telegraph* (Feb. 17, 2010, online). "Laws can definitely help, but it doesn't take

away the problem. The only way to solve the problem was to create a service that was better than piracy and at the same time compensates the music industry." While he admits that Spotify does not generate as much revenue for record labels as downloads do, he observes that without his service, piracy would run rampant. "For every play, are they getting as much as if someone paid to download? No, but on the other hand there are many more transactions happening on Spotify," he explained to Neate. "We are now one of [the record labels'] biggest partners in terms of digital music. We are a substantial revenue source for the whole of the music industry."

Ek and Lorentzon settled on the name Spotify, a combination of the words "spot" and "identify," because when they entered it into Google's search engine during a brainstorming session, no hits were returned, confirming that it was not associated with another product or concept. Still lacking a firm idea of the final shape their new enterprise would take, they hired a team of engineers and built a model "based on the interface of Apple's iTunes and the sleek black styling of Ek's Samsung flat-screen TV," as Bertoni described it.

A NEW KIND OF MUSIC SERVICE

Although Ek had been a big fan of Napster as a teen, discovering the music of rock bands such as the Beatles and Led Zeppelin through the service, he was hesitant to engage in the type of piracy condoned by Napster's founders. He also shunned the philosophy of Sina Simantob, the chief executive officer (CEO) of the music-sharing start-up Grooveshark, who once famously wrote in an internal company e-mail, "The only thing that I want to add is this: we are achieving all this growth without paying a dime to any of the labels," as quoted by Greg Sandoval for *CNET* (Nov. 28, 2011, online).

Ek instead set about encouraging record executives to share his vision for a new ad-supported, legal method for accessing music. Stymied in his attempts to get them to assign him worldwide rights to their music, he focused on winning European rights, assuming that the process would be quicker. Still, record executives remained reluctant. "They'd say, 'Yeah, this sounds really interesting' or 'Send me over some stats,' which really means 'There's no way in hell we're going to do this,'" Ek quipped to Bertoni. "But I was 23 at the time, and I thought, Wow, this is great, we're going to get this done." In the end, Ek and his engineers buckled and presented major record label heads with pirated music they had uploaded on Spotify. This was the only way they could show off the speed and ease of finding songs that characterized the application.

RECEPTION IN EUROPE

In late 2008 Spotify became available in Scandinavia, France, the United Kingdom, and Spain. The service functioned "as a celestial jukebox," media reporter Ben Sisario told Ben Ratliff, the host of the *New York Times* Popcast (July 14, 2011, online), explaining that unlike with iTunes and such music-sharing competitors as Rhapsody and MOG, users do not download the tracks or own them. Sisario said, "If you can listen to any song you want, either for free or for $10 a month. There's really no reason for you to be buying downloads anymore." Spotify's most basic services are supported by advertisements; listeners must listen to a brief ad for every hour of music they access. For a small fee, they can use an ad-free version of the service, and some subscribers chose to pay $10 a month, which allows them to use Spotify on their mobile devices.

Ek's business plan also included a strong social media component; those who sign up to use the service on their mobile devices are required to link their accounts to Facebook, enabling them to share playlists and favorite tracks. (Several Spotify engineers worked at Facebook headquarters for a year to perfect the app.) Some industry observers found the social component exciting. In a June 6, 2010, entry on Louis Gray's popular tech blog, for example, Gray wrote, "A near-immediate Spotify convert back in August when I first got my hands on the application, I have also enjoyed its iPhone app, and can now leverage the preferences and playlists from friends who I am connected to on Facebook, to see what songs they recommend. . . . The social elements of Spotify are great for finding shared musical preferences between friends you may [never] have known existed." Others found the Facebook connection intrusive. "Many Spotify prospects and customers reject the idea of mandatory social media participation to listen to music. Others have security and policy concerns with Facebook in particular, and there's the underlying reality that social media is essentially permanent," Chris Bucholtz wrote for the British publication *Business Computing World* (May 10, 2011, online). He continued, "Spotify forgot to remember that while social media is, well, social, it's also a personal choice."

Despite any such quibbles Spotify immediately became immensely popular. In Ek's native Sweden, fully one-third of the citizens now use the service, and a large percentage of those pay for premium service. By 2011 Spotify accounted for 50 percent of all Swedish music-industry revenue, particularly notable in a country long known for music piracy. "Spotify has had the biggest impact on the Scandinavian music market since the launch of the CD," Johan Lagerlöf, CEO of the European digital-download company X5 Music Group, told Bruce Houghton for *Hypebot* (July 7, 2011, online). He explained, "It

has eradicated music piracy almost on its own. Sweden was the home of [the] Pirate Bay [file-sharing website]. . . . Three years later, the Pirate Bay is not mentioned by anyone anymore. Spotify is, on the other hand, mentioned by almost everyone—including the old Pirate Bay fans. . . . It all happened simply because the users found a new legal service that they actually thought was much better than the old Piracy one."

NEW ARENAS FOR SPOTIFY

Ek was hailed as a savior of the music industry outside his native land as well; in 2009 the editors of the London *Guardian* (July 13, 2009, online) named Ek among the MediaGuardian 100, a list of the most powerful media figures of the year, declaring, "He is changing the music business as we know it." In mid-2011 Spotify made its much-heralded arrival in the United States. Although paid services were rolled out right away, the free version was made available by invitation only, mainly to the thousands of eager fans who had put in a request through the company website or on Twitter. (Ek maintains a popular Twitter feed under the name @eldsjal.) A press release posted on the company website announced the launch, declaring, "We're massively excited to be here," and adding, "More than 10 million Europeans can't be wrong, surely? OK, so they are wrong when it comes to spelling 'favourite' and 'doughnut.' But they know a great music service when they see it."

In late 2011 Spotify began adding to its functionality by offering various apps, including one that displays the lyrics to a song as it plays and another that lists music groups' upcoming concerts and links to buy tickets. The company also announced that it was opening its platform to those who wanted to develop their own apps.

INDUSTRY CHALLENGES

Some reporters questioned whether Spotify, which had attracted hundreds of millions of dollars in venture capital, would prove to be a viable concern in the long run. "Spotify faces a number of challenges in the American market," Ben Sisario wrote for the *New York Times* (July 13, 2011, online). "While the company had relatively little competition in Europe as a subscription service, in the United States a number of similar companies have gotten a head start, including Rhapsody, Rdio and MOG." Sisario went on to explain that, similar to Spotify, these types of services also allow paying users to save songs to their mobile devices. What is more, Sisario added, Spotify must contend with cloud-service offers from major companies such as Amazon, Apple, or Google. Bertoni also weighed in, writing, "The real threat to Ek, ultimately, isn't his product—it's the industry Spotify purports to save. Spotify will only be as successful as its music library,

and some bands—notably his two favorites, the Beatles and Led Zeppelin—aren't playing ball."

Recently the bands Coldplay and the Black Keys denied Spotify access to their new albums. Bertoni observed, "More ominously, the initial music licenses expire in two years, and Ek must deliver enough cash flow to prevent the labels from demanding higher royalties—or pulling out all together." He elaborated, "Right now the labels have the leverage, and Ek has wisely brought the big players into the tent—as part of the licensing deals, Spotify granted equity stakes to the four largest music labels (Warner, Universal, EMI, and Sony) and Merlin. . . . He has two years to make Spotify the world's dominant music source, a hitmaker so big no label or artist can afford to opt out."

PERSONAL LIFE

Ek, who is said to be worth at least $300 million, reportedly leads a quiet life in Stockholm, working long hours and then returning home to read or play the guitar. With the advent of Spotify in the United States during the summer of 2011, however, the entrepreneur's schedule filled up with extensive promotional tours and presentations about the music-sharing service. Somehow Ek manages to stay abreast of his company's technological growth, funding, and strategies for development, all the while projecting calm determination. As Spotify board member Sean Parker confided to Bertoni, "He's the only tech entrepreneur who's had the patience to achieve what he has with the record business. . . . He has this Zen-like patience and an ability not to crack under pressure or get frustrated."

SUGGESTED READING

Bertoni, Steven. "The Most Important Man in Music." *Forbes*. Forbes, 4 Jan. 2012. Web. 17 Jan. 2012.

Bucholtz, Chris. "Lessons Learned from Spotify's Social Media Strategy." *BCW IT Leadership*. Business Computing World, 10 May 2011. Web. 2 Jan. 2012.

Gray, Louis. "Spotify Social Is Close to a Music Utopia (If You Can Get It)." *LouisGray*. N.p., 6 June 2010. Web. 2 Jan. 2012.

Houghton, Bruce. "Top Swedish Music Exec Shares What to Expect as Spotify Launches in U.S." *Hypebot*. Skyline Music, 7 July 2011. Web. 2 Jan. 2012.

Moskowitz, Gary. "10 Start-Ups That Will Change Your Life." *Time*. Time Inc., 2010. Web. 2 Jan. 2012.

Neate, Rupert. "Daniel Ek Profile: 'Spotify Will Be Worth Tens of Billions.'" *Telegraph* [London]. Telegraph Media Group, 17 Feb. 2010. Web. 31 Dec. 2011.

Ratliff, Ben. "Popcast: Spotify Is Here; Which Services Might Suffer?" *New York Times*. New York Times, 14 July 2010. Web. 4 Jan. 2012.

Sandoval, Greg. "Grooveshark Email: How We Built a Music Service without, Um, Paying for Music." *CNET*. CBS Interactive, 28 Nov. 2011. Web. 31 Dec. 2011.

Sisario, Ben. "New Service Offers Music in Quantity, Not by Song." *New York Times*. New York Times, 13 July 2011. Web. 2 Jan. 2012.

Spotify.com. Spotify, 2011. Web. 29 Dec. 2012.

—*Mari Rich*

Steve Ells

Born: September 12, 1965
Occupation: Founder, co-CEO, and chairman of Chipotle Mexican Grill

In 1993, when Steve Ells had an idea for a casual restaurant that would serve overstuffed burritos and tacos, many of those he spoke to tried to dissuade him. "Friends said Mexican food is cheap—you can't charge five dollars for a burrito. But I said this is real food, the highest-quality food," Ells told Margaret Heffernan for *Reader's Digest* (Oct. 2008, online). "*Friends said you can't have an open kitchen, but I wanted the restaurant to be like a dinner party, where everyone's in the kitchen watching what's going on. They said people have to order their meal by number. But I said no, you have to go through the line and select your ingredients. And everyone gave me grief over the name: Nobody'll be able to pronounce it.*"

Proving those naysayers wrong, Chipotle Mexican Grill, Inc., as Ells dubbed his enterprise, currently has more than 1,200 locations in the United States, Canada, and England. In 2011, the company earned $2.27 billion in revenues. Ells is now considered a visionary who pioneered the category of "fast-casual" eateries, which serve higher-quality fare than typical fast-food franchises while retaining the speedy counter service of those places, and Chipotle is often held up as proof that environmentally friendly, humane practices can be implemented successfully in the competitive world of chain restaurants.

EARLY LIFE AND EDUCATION

M. Steven Ells was born on September 12, 1965, in Indianapolis, Indiana. He is the oldest of four siblings. His father, Bob Ells, was a pharmaceutical executive, and Ells's family lived in comfort and financial stability in Boulder, Colorado. Even as a child, Ells was interested in food. He was happy to sit in the kitchen and watch his mother and grandmother cook, and when he was seven years old, he learned to make scrambled eggs and toast for himself. By the time he was nine, he had graduated to eggs benedict, which he whipped up before the school bus came. Ells

Getty Images

Together, Tower and Waters had introduced what came to be known as "California cuisine," which placed an emphasis on fresh, locally grown ingredients. By 1990, when Ells joined him as a line cook, Tower's own restaurant, Stars, had become a beloved institution in San Francisco.

Because he did not earn a large salary as a line cook, Ells sought out reasonably priced places to eat when not working in the kitchen at Stars. He discovered that San Francisco's Mission District was home to several taquerias, tiny Mexican food stands that sold cheap but delicious meals. While eating at Zona Rosa on the corner of Haight and Stanyan Streets, Ells had the idea of opening up a restaurant of his own. "I was just sort of noticing how many people were going through the line and getting their burritos," he recalled to Bret Thorn for *Nation's Restaurant News* (27 Jan. 2003), "and all of a sudden I thought, 'If I could really sex up this burrito, do something different with the ingredients and open a little place, this could be a lot of fun.'" Ells also reasoned that he would earn enough from the burrito spot to start his own fine-dining establishment.

CHIPOTLE IS BORN

Ells's father, Bob, had always been supportive of his children, but he was nonetheless surprised when his son approached him for a loan in 1992. A burrito joint did not seem like a natural next step for a CIA-trained chef who had been working at one of the most respected restaurants in the country. Nonetheless, Bob lent his son $85,000, working out a five-year repayment plan with 7 percent interest. The pair figured that the new establishment would need to sell just over one hundred burritos a day to make a decent profit, and so Ells could pay back the loan to his father in a timely manner.

Ells found an 850-square-foot space on Evans Avenue in Denver, Colorado, near the University of Denver campus. The building, which dated back to the 1920s, had been an old Dolly Madison ice-cream store. Ells agreed to pay $200 a month in rent and repainted the building. On July 13, 1993, the first Chipotle Mexican Grill opened its doors.

Ells explained to Kristin Dizon for the *Seattle Post-Intelligencer* (6 Apr. 2004, online) why he chose to name his new venture after a type of smoked jalapeño with which few American diners were familiar: "I knew that I wanted to use chipotle peppers for the chicken and steak marinade. It's also in the barbacoa [shredded beef]. I love the flavor. It's used modestly—too much of it is too smoky and hot. But if used right, it gives a nuance and a flavor to the food. Everyone told me that it was a bad name to use, because no one knew what it was or could pronounce it. And now everyone knows what it is."

told Ron Ruggless for *Nation's Restaurant News* (25 Jan. 1999), "When other kids were watching television cartoons while growing up, I was watching cooking shows like Julia Child."

As a teenager, Ells worked flipping hamburgers at a fast-food restaurant, but he disliked the job and quit after a short time. After graduating from Boulder High School in 1984, he enrolled at the University of Colorado Boulder. With no particular career plan in mind, he studied art history. Ells was known among his friends at school for his culinary skills, and his dorm mates often served as test subjects for his experiments in the kitchen. Even then, he was fussy about ingredients, buying multiple heads of lettuce, for example, in order to get enough perfect leaves for a salad.

Upon graduating with a bachelor's degree in 1988, Ells applied to the Culinary Institute of America in New York. One of the most prestigious and competitive cooking schools in the country, the CIA, as it is known, counts among its graduates such cooking luminaries as Grant Achatz, Anthony Bourdain, Todd English, and Charlie Palmer. After earning admission to the school, Ells completed an intensive two-year course, and in 1990 he earned a coveted CIA degree.

A COOKING CAREER

After graduation, Ells found work with the celebrated chef Jeremiah Tower, who had gotten his own start at Chez Panisse in Berkeley, California, alongside owner Alice Waters.

There were mistakes made at the first location. "We didn't even have a menu board up, so people didn't know what to order," a company executive told Bonnie Brewer Cavanaugh for *Nation's Restaurant News* (4 Oct. 2004). "There was a line of customers outside the door, and we were yelling out [to them]. . . . There was a lot of 'What do you want?' with replies of 'What do you got?' It was a very uninviting environment . . . very chaotic." Still, by the end of the first month, Ells was selling a thousand burritos a day.

EXPANSION

Within eighteen months, Ells had opened a second Chipotle Mexican Grill, on Colorado Boulevard and Eighth Avenue in Denver. A third, in the town of Littleton, soon followed. By this time, Ells had refined the ordering system. Chipotle serves a limited menu consisting of overstuffed burritos, tacos, burrito "bols" (made without the tortilla wrapper), and salads. Customers progress along a counter, informing the staff exactly which ingredients they would like in their meal. Protein choices include chopped grilled chicken; sliced grilled steak; marinated and shredded beef, called barbacoa; and shredded pork, known as carnitas. Available toppings include cheese, sour cream, romaine lettuce, and an array of salsas, including one made of roasted corn. Pinto beans or vegetarian black beans are available, as is a cilantro-and-lime rice that has become a signature item. Freshly prepared guacamole and lime-infused tortilla chips are on the menu, but Ells has always ignored advice to serve desserts or other such extras—despite the fact that doing so would undoubtedly increase revenues—because he feels that the chain should stick with what it does best. With more than fifteen fresh ingredients arrayed in clear view behind the counter, each patron can assemble a custom creation. By one calculation, more than 65,500 different combinations are possible.

As his business grew, Ells also made changes to the look of Chipotle restaurants. Each Chipotle location has distinctive but recognizable design elements, conceived in collaboration with sculptor Bruce Gueswel. The restaurants feature a down-to-earth but hip setting that employs affordable materials. "Chipotle today has an unmistakable look. The layout and some details have evolved, but the basic materials—plywood, corrugated metal, stainless steel, exposed ductwork—are the same," Ells wrote in an essay for *Time* magazine (21 Sep. 2007, online). "These simple materials are elevated to something extraordinary through great design and architecture. And it's a design that is sympathetic to the food. The food is simple; the raw ingredients are very identifiable: chicken, steak, tomatoes, avocados, rice, and beans. But we elevate those very simple things through great cooking techniques."

Ells continued to expand his business, and customers continued to flock to Chipotle. By 1998, Ells owned fourteen restaurants, thirteen in Colorado and one in Kansas City. Value is an important part of the Chipotle business model; industry insiders have estimated that a meal that costs in the five- to seven-dollar range at Chipotle would command at least twelve dollars at a sit-down restaurant. However, Chipotle patrons are not primarily attracted by exceptionally low prices or specials. Instead, customer surveys have indicated that the exceptional freshness of the food and the attention to detail are major factors in its appeal.

Freshness has been of paramount importance to Ells from the moment he opened Chipotle. He feels that it is vital that customers can watch the lettuce being chopped in the prep area, the chips fried and doused with lime juice, and the guacamole mixed. Mats Lederhausen, a company executive, told Alex Markels for *US News & World Report* (21 Jan. 2008) that once Ells had called him out of a meeting: "He was screaming on the other end of the phone, 'I've found it! I've found it!' . . . 'They're not cutting the oregano in the right sizes!'" He explained that Ells had then launched into a rant about "how the size of the oregano, when it mixes with the water, oil, and salt, doesn't embed the right taste layers in the [black] beans." Lederhausen admitted, "Sure enough, the next time I tasted the beans, they were better."

A FAST-FOOD GIANT GETS INVOLVED

By 1998, Ells had raised $3 million for further expansion, $1.5 million from his proud father and $1.5 million in a private stock offering. Additional funds came from a surprising—and seemingly unlikely—source: McDonald's. "Suddenly . . . a $33-billion-a-year multinational had turned itself into a minority owner of a four-year-old Mexican chain that had yet to venture outside its home base of Denver," Ralph Raffio wrote for *Restaurant Business* (Apr. 1998). "The extraordinary deal raised as many questions as eyebrows, but perhaps none more pointed than this one: How did a guy like Steve Ells, an entrepreneur virtually unknown outside the Mile High City . . . become the most envied entrepreneur in the restaurant business? What magic enabled him to pull off what presumably hundreds of dreamers and schemers had failed to do?"

Some industry insiders theorized that because McDonald's had recently restructured its management, the time was right for the company to take some calculated risks. Others felt that the move provided a learning opportunity for the burger giant, in terms of food freshness and meal customization. The benefits for Chipotle were more obvious. Ells now had the capital to expand at an increased pace, access to bigger suppliers, and the industrial clout to get the best possible products for the best prices. McDonald's partnered with Ells until 2006, by which time there were almost five hundred Chipotles across the country. "We learned from each other," Ells told Margaret Heffernan, "but we use different kinds of food, and we aim for a different kind of experience and culture altogether. So we ended up going our separate ways."

In 2006, Chipotle's initial public offering (IPO) raised over $170 million during its first day, with shares going for $44 at the close of the market—up 100 percent from a $22 starting price. Ells's own shares were said to be worth more than $45 million, and industry observers estimated that McDonald's had earned $1 billion. Chipotle recorded the second-highest opening day of any restaurant IPO in American history, defeated only by Boston Chicken's 143-percent gain in 1993. (Boston Chicken was later rebranded as Boston Market and is currently owned by McDonald's.)

FOOD WITH INTEGRITY

In 1999, Ells came across an article in *The Art of Eating*, a quarterly newsletter, about how factory farming had adversely affected the taste of pork. He wrote in a piece for *Time* magazine, "I had a revelation about what makes for good-quality raw ingredients. Where the ingredients come from, how the animals were raised and how the produce was grown not only affect the flavor but also the environment, animal welfare and the preservation of family farms. Like most people, we were buying pork that was raised in confinement operations—big plants squeezing out the independent family farmer and making the rural landscape in Iowa uninhabitable. We switched suppliers, and our pork now comes from farmers who raise pigs humanely, according to protocols such as no growth hormones, no antibiotics and vegetarian feed."

Chipotle's pork is now supplied by Niman Ranch, a cooperative of small family farmers. Free-range pork costs considerably more than factory-farmed meat, and Ells was forced to raise the price of carnitas by a full dollar. Patrons proved willing to pay the premium, and carnitas sales ultimately doubled. Chipotle now also sources humanely raised, hormone-free chicken and beef and is beginning to seek out organically grown beans.

Although Chipotle advertises much less than most fast-food outlets, Ells adopted the motto "Food with Integrity" to trumpet his association with Niman Ranch and other organic food initiatives. "Freshness is no longer enough," he told several journalists. His vision resulted in several firsts. "Chipotle was the first national restaurant company to commit to serving naturally raised meat (from animals that are raised in a humane way, never given antibiotics or added hormone and fed a pure

vegetarian diet), the first to commit to local and organically grown produce, and the first to serve dairy (cheese and sour cream) made with milk from cows that are not treated with the synthetic hormone rBGH (recombinant bovine growth hormone)," a reporter wrote for Business Wire (23 June 2010). In 2010, the year he opened his thousandth restaurant, Ells spoke before the United States Senate in support of the Preservation of Antibiotics for Medical Treatment Act (PAMTA), which called for banning the unnecessary use of antibiotics in farm animals. Antibiotics are often used on factory farms to promote growth and compensate for unsanitary conditions, leading to the emergence of antibiotic-resistant strains of bacteria. Although the legislation did not pass Congress, efforts to reintroduce the bill have continued.

LABOR

Ells had an unwelcome encounter with the US government in 2011 when immigrations and customs officials performed a so-called silent raid, examining Chipotle's employment records. They found more than five hundred undocumented workers and forced the company to fire them. In response, Chipotle executives have vowed to work for immigration reform, and the company continues to maintain a good reputation among its predominantly Latino employees, who are given English-language education if they request it and ample opportunity for promotion.

OTHER VENTURES

In 2011, Ells served as a judge on the reality television show *America's Next Great Restaurant*, hosted by chef Bobby Flay. The program, which ran for one season, allowed competitors to present their original restaurant concepts, with the winner receiving start-up capital and professional guidance. From a field that included a meatball shop, quick-casual Indian cuisine, and gourmet grilled-cheese sandwiches, the winner was a health-conscious soul-food eatery called Soul Daddy.

Also in 2011, Ells himself experimented with a new concept, opening ShopHouse Southeast Asian Kitchen in Washington, DC. Similar to the Chipotle concept, patrons build their own custom meals, choosing among beef, pork, chicken, and tofu with a variety of Asian toppings. The Washington location has proved popular, but no definite expansion plans have been made yet.

Further increasing his profile, Ells mounted a food-and-music festival in Chicago in October 2011, the proceeds of which he donated to a nonprofit group called FamilyFarmed. He also released an animated promotional video that played in thousands of movie theaters before the main feature. Set to a tune sung by Willie Nelson, the video follows a hog farmer who dabbles with factory farming before returning to his gentler, healthier roots.

In an interview for the December 2007 issue of *ColoradoBiz* magazine, which named him 2007 CEO of the Year, Ells quoted a friend, the scientist Wes Jackson: "He says if your life's work can be accomplished in your lifetime, you're not thinking big enough. So I don't know that we can change the way people think about eating fast food in my lifetime. But I hope so."

SUGGESTED READING

Cavanaugh, Bonnie Brewer. "2004 Golden Chain." *Nation's Restaurant News* 4 Oct. 2004: 114. Print.

Dizon, Kristin. "A Moment with Steve Ells." *Seattle Post-Intelligencer*. Hearst, 6 Apr. 2004. Web. 15 Feb. 2012.

Ells, Steve. "Fine Fast Food." *Time*. Time, 21 Sep. 2007. Web. 15 Feb. 2012.

Heffernan, Margaret. "Dreamers: Chipotle Founder Steve Ells." *Reader's Digest*. Reader's Digest, Oct. 2008. Web. 15 Feb. 2012.

Hesser, Amanda. "Tex Macs." *New York Times Magazine* 27 Feb. 2005: 85. Print.

Horovitz, Bruce. "It's Like Chipotle on Chopsticks." *USA Today* 30 Sep. 2011: B01. Print.

Ruggless, Ron. "Steve Ells." *Nation's Restaurant News* 25 Jan. 1999: 68. Print.

—*Mari Rich*

Getty Images for AOL

Todd English

Born: August 29, 1960
Occupation: Chef, restaurateur, television personality, cookbook writer

The chef and restaurateur Todd English is "known for being perpetually in motion . . . ," Jeff Gordinier wrote for the *New York Times* (1 June 2011). "Compulsively entrepreneurial, he has helped create so many restaurants over the course of 20 years that it can be difficult to track them all." English graduated from the prestigious Culinary Institute of America in 1982, in his early twenties, and trained with a series of notable chefs in the United States and Italy. He polished his skills and conceived his own approach to cooking as the executive chef of Michela's, an award-winning Italian restaurant in Cambridge, Massachusetts, near Boston. In 1989 he opened his first restaurant, Olives, in Charlestown, a Boston neighborhood. Enthusiastic reviews greeted Olives, which specialized in a rustic Mediterranean cuisine; the restaurant became enormously popular and was widely credited with resuscitating Boston's culinary culture. "The food he was cooking was so unlike anything else in this city at the time," Barbara Lynch, a Boston chef who worked at Olives, told Gordinier. "Nobody else was doing fig pizza with prosciutto, or a nice, simple olive tart." In 1991 the James Beard Foundation named English "Rising Star Chef of the Year."

English later opened Olives restaurants in several other cities. He also launched Figs, an upscale pizza and pasta chain, which earned a Hot Concept Award from *Nation's Restaurant News*. The Beard Foundation named him best chef in the Northeast in 1994, and he won *Bon Appetit* magazine's Restaurateur of the Year Award in 2001. As of mid-October 2011, according to his website, the properties of Todd English Enterprises included a bakery and restaurants in five US states (including, in New York, locations in two airports) and on two Cunard Line cruise ships: the *Queen Mary 2* and the *Queen Victoria*. Of the total—about twenty—he fully owns only six of them, he told Jeff Gordinier; the others are "consulting, licensing deals." His restaurants have catered events held in connection with the Tony Awards, the MTV Music Video Awards, and the Sundance Film Festival, and their many catering-service clients include the singer John Legend, the violinist Joshua Bell, the fashion designer Vera Wang, and such companies as Victoria's Secret, Louis Vuitton, and Maserati. English has published four cookbooks, is marketing a line of cookware and other kitchen products, and sporadically since 2007, he has hosted the travel and cooking show *Food Trip* with Todd English, which airs on PBS TV stations and won the

James Beard Foundation Award for best television special in 2010.

A dozen of the restaurants that English has opened on his own or with others have failed, among them an Olives in Tokyo, Japan, and Olives branches in Washington, DC, Aspen, Colorado, and Biloxi, Mississippi; Rustic Kitchen and Bonfire in Boston; and English Is Italian, in New York. The original Charlestown Olives has remained closed since a kitchen fire in May 2010. English has often been criticized, in mainstream publications as well as in the blogosphere, for taking on too many projects at once and neglecting to maintain standards at his restaurants. Regarding his failed ventures, English told Gordinier, "It's like losing a big game. You've got to look at what you did wrong and make it better, and not do it that way the next time. But you're out there playing, man. You tried." English told Kim Atkinson for *Boston* magazine (Jan. 2003), "This is a trial-and-error thing. There's no 101 course on how to expand a restaurant business." As for his detractors, some of whom have published scathing ad-hominem attacks on him, Gordinier wrote, "It seems as though he dodges the slings and arrows in classic Todd English fashion: just keep moving." "Look, it's uncalled for," English said. "If I were molesting babies, I get it. But I'm not. I'm a guy with a dream trying to make it all happen." In an article for *Boston* magazine (Apr. 2009) titled "Reconsidering Todd English," Amy Traverso wrote, "If you think about his actual ambitions—as opposed to what we assume they should be—maybe he is misunderstood. . . . According to him, the critics never grasped what he was after. He had no intention of sacrificing himself on the altar of haute cuisine. . . . What he wanted was to be famous, to build an empire. And by that measure, certainly, things are exactly where he wants them."

EARLY LIFE AND EDUCATION

The first of two children, William Todd English was born on August 29, 1960, in Amarillo, Texas. The name of his father, who descended from German and Irish immigrants to the United States, is not readily available. His mother, born Patrizia Arcuni, is of Italian ancestry; at one time her family owned a large olive grove in Calabria, in southern Italy. English's parents divorced when he was about eight; his mother later remarried, but reportedly neither his biological father nor his stepfather played more than a peripheral role in his life. His sister, Wendy, who was born in 1962, worked for him in a marketing job; she died of breast cancer in 2006. According to Juliette Rossant in her book *Super Chef*, when English was three the family moved to Nebraska, where his mother catered affairs for friends. They next lived in Sandy Springs, Georgia, in the Atlanta metropolitan area, where English attended elementary school. As a boy he

loved to play baseball. "I slept with my glove as a kid," he told Sarah Rosenberg and Tom McCarthy on the ABC-TV program *Nightline* (12 Feb. 2010). "That was what I wanted to do and be." When English was in his teens, he and his family settled in Branford, Connecticut, near New Haven. He graduated from Branford High School in 1978.

English has described his mother and his maternal grandmother as excellent cooks. As a child he liked to watch his grandmother make pasta from scratch; he himself liked to make ice cream with the machine his mother bought him at his request. As a teenager he maintained a vegetable garden in the family's backyard. At fourteen he got a job as a dishwasher at a local Mexican restaurant. "There was a family feeling [there] that I liked," he told Sally Sampson, the coauthor of three of his cookbooks. "There was energy and camaraderie and at the end of the night, a great sense of accomplishment." When English was fifteen he began helping the restaurant's chef to prepare meals.

English earned a baseball scholarship to Guilford College, in Greensboro, North Carolina. Injuries (or poor grades, according to one source) forced him to leave the team. In 1980 he dropped out of Guilford and enrolled at the Culinary Institute of America in Hyde Park, New York. He completed the course there in 1982. Soon afterward he got a job at Jean-Jacques Rachou's acclaimed French restaurant La Côte Basque, in Manhattan. "I have never been so nervous in my life," he told Sampson. "I used to wake up sick to my stomach. I was terrified I couldn't perform. I had never stepped foot into a kitchen quite like it. Either you ran and jumped on the fast train or you got off. So I ran and ran." After about two years at La Côte Basque (which is no longer in business), English worked briefly at Bradley Ogden's Campton Place, a Mediterranean-style restaurant in a luxury hotel in San Francisco, California. Then, for half a year or so, he served a series of apprenticeships in Italy at restaurants whose owners were dedicated to maintaining Italian cooking traditions. In January 1986 English returned to the United States, and for the next three years, he worked as the executive chef at Michela's, Michela Larson's well-regarded Italian restaurant in Cambridge, Massachusetts, which he helped to launch.

OPENING OLIVES AND FIGS

In 1989, with financing from Jack Sidell, who owned the United Trust Corp. (and became famous for lending to upstart Boston-area restaurateurs), English opened his first restaurant, Olives, in Charlestown. It was named for English's then wife, Olivia, whom he had met when both were students at the Culinary Institute of America and who played a major role in his early restaurant business. "English's food was big, both in portion and in flavor," Amy Traverso wrote. "A single dish would contain elements sweet, sour, salty, bitter, crunchy, and soft (smoked duck breast lacquered with sweet ginger-orange glaze sitting atop a crispy-salty scallion pancake, the signature fig and prosciutto pizza). He had an uncanny ability to pull it all together into something transcendent—at least most of the time. He could just as easily go off the rails, but what mattered was that this was food that Boston had never tasted before. And that was thrilling." *Boston* magazine voted Olives the city's best new restaurant, and Olives soon became one of Boston's most popular mealtime destinations. It has been credited with spearheading the revitalization of the city's long-dormant culinary scene.

In 1992 English moved Olives to a larger space, also in Charlestown. It contained an expanded version of English's signature open kitchen, in which chefs and their assistants are visible to diners. Later that year English opened his first Figs, at the original Olives location. An immediate hit, the restaurant offered a wide variety of traditional and unusual pizza toppings and handmade pastas. In 1993 the hockey star Cam Neely and the Hollywood stars Glenn Close and Michael J. Fox recruited English to save their struggling, two-year-old restaurant on Martha's Vineyard, Massachusetts. English's efforts came to naught, and the restaurant soon folded. "I got wooed by the whole celebrity thing," English told Jay Cheshes for the *New York Observer* (25 Dec. 2000). "I jumped in without first finding out that there were some really serious problems." That incident notwithstanding, English was named best chef in the Northeast at the James Beard Awards ceremony in 1994.

OLIVE GROUP CORPORATION

In 1996 English opened two additional Figs outlets, one in Boston's Beacon Hill section and the other in Wellesley, a Boston suburb; a fourth debuted in Brookline, another Boston suburb, the next year. In 1998 English went into partnership with the restaurant developer James Cafarelli to form the Olive Group Corporation, with the goal of opening restaurants with the Todd English imprimatur further afield. English owned 75 percent of the company, while Cafarelli owned 25 percent and served as president. Their first venture, another Olives, opened that year at the brand-new Bellagio Hotel and Casino in Las Vegas, Nevada. While English chose the chefs and contributed to the restaurant's design and menu, Bellagio employees managed Olives Las Vegas. That arrangement prevailed in English's subsequent licensing and consulting projects, which allowed him to expand his empire without having to show up in person with any regularity at his restaurants.

In late 1999 English opened two more Olives restaurants, in Washington, DC, and at

the St. Regis Hotel in Aspen, Colorado. The following summer he launched KingFish Hall, a seafood restaurant in Boston's Faneuil Hall Marketplace; it was named "Best of Boston" by *Travel and Leisure Magazine* in 2000. English next set his sights on New York, opening the first of two Figs restaurants in La Guardia Airport's central terminal, in September 2000, and debuting Olives New York, at the W Hotel in Union Square, two months later. The 175-seat Olives New York, which has a swanky lounge and bar designed by David Rockwell (a Tony Award–winning set designer), immediately attracted a young, upscale clientele. In an assessment for the *New York Times* (15 Dec. 2000), William Grimes wrote, "Olives offers full-throttle, big-flavored Mediterranean food. . . . A small dish of olives and tapenade, served with hunks of focaccia and country bread, sets the tone, but the menu makes it clear that Olives has more than osso buco and polenta on its mind." In an undated "Critic's Pick" review of that Olives for *New York* magazine, Rob Patronite and Robin Raisfeld called English "a genius for artful, HungryMan dishes. He deftly stuffs his pastas with delectable fillings (like spring peas and sweet chestnuts) and slathers them with creamy cheeses. He molds cupolas of fois gras flan, builds pagodas of hanger steak, constructs pillboxes of tuna tartare with crunchy shrimps buried at the base. It's easy to get carried away, but save room for thrombotic desserts like warm chocolate pudding cake." English described Olives New York to Kim Atkinson as his "Mount Everest," adding, "I had to see if I could reach the top."

REACHING THE TOP

In 2001 *Bon Appetit* magazine named English the Restaurateur of the Year, and *People* listed him among the world's fifty most beautiful people. That year also marked the arrival of English's Bonfire, a steak house, at the Park Plaza Hotel in Boston, and Tuscany, an Italian restaurant at the Mohegan Sun Hotel and Casino, in Uncasville, Connecticut. His seafood restaurant Fish Club, in the Seattle, Washington, Marriott Waterfront Hotel, and a Tokyo branch of Olives began operating in 2003, and in 2004 he opened his eponymous restaurant on the *Queen Mary 2*, BlueZoo at Walt Disney World Resort's Dolphin Hotel, in Florida, and Ozone-Bos at Boston Logan International Airport. Also in 2004 English was inducted into the James Beard Foundation's Who's Who of Food and Beverage in America; analogous to a hall of fame in other fields, the who's who includes professionals ranging "from chefs to journalists to farmers to business executives to scholars," each of whom "has been identified by his or her peers as having displayed remarkable talent and achievement," according to the Beard foundation's website.

OTHER VENTURES

In 2005 English teamed with the restaurateur Jeffrey Chodorow to open English Is Italian, a short-lived venture in Midtown Manhattan. Restaurants of his that opened since then and remain in business include the Bonfire steakhouse at JFK International Airport, in New York; the Todd English restaurant on the *Queen Victoria*; the Plaza Food Hall, at the Plaza Hotel, in New York, which "offers dine-in and take-away options from more than eight culinary stations," according to its website; Ça Va, a brasserie in the InterContinental Hotel in Midtown Manhattan; the English Tap and Beer Garden (formerly called Wild Olives), in Boca Raton, Florida; the Todd English P.U.B., in Las Vegas; and CrossBar, in Midtown Manhattan, which is categorized as a gastropub—a pub that offers a more varied and sophisticated menu than the traditional British pub. English joined the Thompson Hotel Group to open two dining places—the gastropub Libertine in the Gild Hall, a hotel in Manhattan's Financial District, and the Asian-fusion restaurant Cha in Donovan House, a hotel in Washington, DC—but their partnership dissolved within a year. English teamed with the actress Eva Longoria to open Tex-Mex-style steakhouses, called Beso, in Hollywood, California, and Las Vegas; the latter filed for bankruptcy in 2011, and its fate remains uncertain.

English has cowritten four cookbooks: *The Olives Table: Over 160 Recipes from the Critically Acclaimed Restaurant and Home Kitchen of Todd English* (1997, with Sally Sampson); *The Figs Table: More Than 100 Recipes for Pizzas, Pastas, Salads, and Desserts* (1998, with Sally Sampson); *The Olives Dessert Table: Spectacular Restaurant Desserts You Can Make at Home* (2000, with Paige Retus and Sally Sampson); and *Cooking in Everyday English: The ABCs of Great Flavor at Home* (2011, with Amanda Haas). Along with the chef Ming Tsai and the writer and trained cook Michael Ruhlman, he served as a judge on the PBS cooking-competition series *Cooking Under Fire*, whose twelve installments ran in 2005. He currently hosts the international travel and cooking series *Food Trip with Todd English*, which debuted on PBS in 2007 and is now in its third season. The first season of the show won a James Beard Award and an Emmy nomination, as did a 2010 installment.

NEWS MEDIA CRITICISM

"From the standpoint of presence and productivity, Mr. English is one of the most successful chefs in the country," Jeff Gordinier wrote. "From a news media perspective, he is one of the most mocked and hounded, often portrayed as a party-hopping Casanova who has sacrificed his skill at the stove in a compulsive and compromise-ready hustle for brand expansion." One particularly harsh example of such criticism appeared in the February 2010 issue of *Esquire*, in which John Mariano suggested that one way to detect a bad restaurant is if "it is one of Todd English's." Another was in the May 2011 issue of *Boston*, in an anonymous article entitled "Dear Todd English; It's Not Us. It's You." Describing itself as a "breakup letter," the article castigated him for everything from ignoring the deteriorating quality of his restaurants to owing large amounts of money to landlords, publicists, contractors, and others, several of whom have sued him. "I don't get it," Jasper White, a multi-award-winning Massachusetts chef and restaurateur, said to Gordinier. "There's something about Todd that people take as arrogant, for some reason. Is it his look? But he's not arrogant. He's a down-to-earth, sweet man."

PERSONAL LIFE

From his marriage to the former Olivia Disch, which ended in divorce, English has three children: Oliver, Isabelle, and Simon. In 2008 he reportedly ended his engagement to Erica Wang, who had been working as an assistant of his for two years, a day or two before their scheduled wedding day. English owns homes in Beacon Hill and Manhattan.

SUGGESTED READING

Atkinson, Kim. "Being Todd English." *Boston Magazine*. Metrocorp, Jan. 2003. Web. Jan. 2012.

Cheshes, Jay. "Glamour-Hunk Chef Todd English Brings His Hormonal Act to Town." *New York Observer* 25 Dec. 2000: 4.

Gordiner, Jeff. "Todd English, the Chef in Motion." *New York Times* 1 June 2011: D1.

Spartos, Carla. "NYC's Tasty Dish! After Being Burned by Love, Sexy Celebrity Chef Todd English Is Back Fanning the Flames." *New York Post* 11 Aug. 2010: 35.

Todd English Enterprises. Todd English Enterprises, n.d. Web. Jan. 2012.

Traverso, Amy. "Reconsidering Todd English." *Boston Magazine*. Metrocorp, Apr. 2009. Web. Jan. 2012.

—*Christopher Cullen*

Jeff Fager

Born: December 10, 1954
Occupation: Television executive

Jeff Fager (FAY-ger) has served since June 2004 as the executive producer (the top post) of the Sunday-night CBS television program *60 Minutes*, which began its forty-fourth year on the air on September 25, 2011. Fager succeeded Don Hewitt, the legendary creator of *60 Minutes*, which is the oldest and most lauded newsmagazine in the history of American television. Fager has worked in broadcast journalism since he graduated from college, in 1977. He has been with the national CBS network since 1982, when he landed a job as a producer for CBS News. For various periods he was a producer for *CBS Evening News*, *48 Hours*, and *60 Minutes*; for the last-named show, his responsibilities included finding unique, little-explored, or particularly newsworthy stories and helping to transform them into what amounted to mini-documentaries of fifteen minutes or so, designed to grab viewers' attention. He held the title of executive producer for *CBS Evening News with Dan Rather* and then for *60 Minutes II*. As the executive producer of *60 Minutes*, he said in an interview for the PBS program *Frontline* (29 Nov. 2006), he is guided by a "traditional definition of news, which is anything somebody's trying to hide." "I think that's important, because when we stop thinking about uncovering information that's going to be useful to the viewer, to the American public, that's when we're not in the news business anymore," he said. "What's nice about a magazine is that we can mix it with a nice profile of a Hollywood celebrity; we can mix it with a story about a writer, about an adventure into Africa. But the bread and butter of what we do is news, and that is working on a story that someone doesn't want us to tell."

At *60 Minutes* Fager heads a staff that includes ten correspondents—Anderson Cooper, Steve Kroft, Lesley Stahl, and seven other on-air reporters and interviewers who (like Mike Wallace, Harry Reasoner, and Roger Mudd, to name a few from earlier decades) are the faces of the show. Currently, the *60 Minutes* staff also includes two senior producers, thirty-two producers, and thirty-one associate producers; an executive editor, an executive story editor, and nineteen editors; a broadcast manager; and many assistants. Under Fager's leadership in the last few years, *60 Minutes* has provided in-depth coverage of the wars in Iraq and Afghanistan, presidential and congressional elections, the worldwide economic downturn that began in December 2007, and the popular uprisings in Egypt, Libya, and other Muslim-majority nations in 2011. Fager has played a leading role in bringing *60 Minutes* into the digital age, by posting online its stories, commentaries, and—on *60 Minutes Overtime*—behind-the-scenes and other footage. Most recently he guided the creation of the *60 Minutes* iPad application. During the years that Fager served as the executive producer of *60 Minutes II* (1998–2004) and the seven and a half years that he has led *60 Minutes*, the two programs have won a total of thirty-three Emmy Awards, eight Peabody Awards, eight Edward R. Murrow Awards from the Radio Television Digital News Association, four

Getty Images

Alfred I. DuPont–Columbia University batons, and three Sigma Delta Chi Awards from the Society of Professional Journalists. The Producers Guild of America named Fager himself the best producer in nonfiction television in 2006, 2007, 2009, and 2010. In February 2011 Fager took on a second, newly created title, that of chairman of CBS News. According to a CBS press release (28 Feb. 2011), his mission in that position is to "transfer" the success of *60 Minutes* "to all of the news division's platforms, on television, radio and the Internet."

EARLY LIFE AND CAREER

Jeffrey B. Fager was born on December 10, 1954, in Wellesley, Massachusetts. He attended Colgate University, in the upstate New York town of Hamilton. After graduating, with a BA degree in English, in 1977, he moved to Boston, Massachusetts, where he worked as a production assistant at the local CBS station, WBZ-TV. Next, in 1978, he became a news writer at WEII, a Boston radio station, and later that year he took the job of assignment editor at WGBH-TV, the local public-television station. In 1979 he moved to San Francisco, California, where for three years he served as the broadcast producer at KPIX-TV, the local CBS affiliate. In 1982 he joined the national CBS network, in New York City, as a producer for the weekend edition of *CBS Evening News* and for *Nightwatch*, a news program that ran from 2:00 a.m. to 7:00 a.m. He was then promoted to producer at the weekday *CBS Evening News*, a position he held in 1984 and 1985. For the next several years, until 1988, he held the same title but worked out of CBS's London, England, office. He produced segments on many high-profile international matters, such as the Israeli-Palestinian conflict in Lebanon, Syria, and Jordan; the US bombing of Libya in 1986; the summit meetings held by President Ronald Reagan and the Soviet Union's leader, Mikhail Gorbachev, in Switzerland and Iceland; and events in the years leading up to the fall of communism in Eastern Europe and the demise of the Soviet Union. Speaking of violent confrontations within and between nations, he told Elizabeth Jensen for the *Los Angeles Times* (3 Feb. 2011), "You get to like it too much. It gets the blood going. It's addictive." Unwilling to be away from his family so much, he returned to the States. Fager told Jensen, "Family comes first."

ADVANCING AT CBS NEWS

Back in New York, in 1988, Fager was part of the CBS team that developed and launched *48 Hours*, the primetime CBS News magazine. The following year he became a producer at *60 Minutes*, which at that point had been on the air for twenty years. He worked mainly with the correspondents Steve Kroft and Morley Safer, covering such important international news stories as the United States–led military campaign against Iraq in 1991 (known as the first Persian Gulf war).

In 1994 Fager was promoted to the post of senior broadcast producer (second in command) at *CBS Evening News with Dan Rather*, where he oversaw the coverage of events including the war in Bosnia and the assassination of the Israeli prime minister Yitzhak Rabin, on November 4, 1995. Fifteen months after joining *CBS Evening News with Dan Rather*, Fager was promoted to executive producer. Writing for the Associated Press (24 Mar. 1997), Frazier Moore observed that under Fager the program had gotten "maybe better than ever" and seemed to have "recovered a sense of itself and what it stands for. Hard news!" Moore added that while *NBC Nightly News* had decreased coverage of foreign and domestic news, and ABC's *World News Tonight* had followed suit, *CBS Evening News with Dan Rather* was presenting substantial news reports. "Sometimes what's interesting is important, but that's not always the case," Rather told Moore. "And sometimes the most important thing, at least at first glance, is not very interesting. That means one of our jobs is to make the important as interesting as possible, and to report to people why they should care about it, even if at first glance they don't. Increasingly over the past year or so, I think the difference between us and our principal competitors has begun to be more apparent. And this is where Jeff [Fager] comes in."

60 MINUTES II

During his time working with Rather, Fager played a crucial role in creating *60 Minutes II*, a television newsmagazine modeled on *60 Minutes*. In an interview with Bill Carter for the *New York Times* (16 July 1998), Rather said, "I don't think there could be a *60 Minutes II* without Jeff and the credentials he brings to the table." Don Hewitt, the creator and executive producer of *60 Minutes*, also played a central role in the show's creation. Hewitt had been asked over the course of several years to expand *60 Minutes*, but he had resisted that idea, as had the *60 Minutes* correspondents Mike Wallace, Morley Safer, and Ed Bradley, because they feared diluting the impact of the original. But CBS administrators—among them the CBS Television president, Les Moonves; the CBS News president, Andrew Heyward; and the chief executive officer of CBS Inc., Mel Karmazin—wanted a *60 Minutes* offshoot, one that would offer the same high-quality programming as the original and the same ability to attract advertisers. Safer recalled to Lawrie Mifflin for the *New York Times* (21 Dec. 1998), "I told Andrew it was a rotten idea, an attempt simply to use the logo. Then, almost as an afterthought, I said, 'Unless you're going to take Jeff Fager off the *Evening News*, and put someone like Rather or [the journalist Bob] Simon and the very best correspondents in the company on it. Well, if they did that, how could I be anything but for it?'" Rather was very supportive of the idea from the start—before there was any talk of his becoming a *60 Minutes II* correspondent—and he gave Fager his blessing to leave his show and executive produce *60 Minutes II*. After awhile all the *60 Minutes* correspondents came around, in large part because Fager was to be executive producer. Initially broadcasting on Wednesday nights, *60 Minutes II* premiered in January 1999. In addition to Rather and Simon, its correspondents included such CBS News personalities as Vicki Mabrey and Scott Pelley; Charlie Rose, who had hosted *CBS Nightwatch* in the 1980s and had become the host and executive producer of his own interview program on PBS, also served as a *60 Minutes II* correspondent.

60 MINUTES

In 2003 CBS announced that Fager would replace Don Hewitt as executive producer of *60 Minutes* in June 2004. As news analysts made clear, Fager was going to inherit not only an institution but also a challenge. At the time of the announcement, the show had lost a million viewers since the previous season, and some of the show's best-known contributors—Safer, Wallace, and the commentator Andy Rooney—were in the process of cutting back their workloads or talking about doing so. Nevertheless, Fager did not waver in his view of what a newsmagazine program should deliver. He acknowledged the need for variety—balancing hard news with lighter fare—but insisted that the foundation of *60 Minutes* was news reports that dug deep and intrigued and stimulated viewers. In the 2006 *Frontline* interview, he said, "It's hard and it's expensive to do what we do. You send a team into Iraq to do a story on the war, and you pay a lot of money to cover that story. It's risky and it's difficult." He also said, "There is a conventional wisdom in the television business that you can't make that interesting to the American public, which is, I think, astonishing. . . . We're at war in the Middle East; we need to be covering that story. . . . It's easy to go the other way. It's easy to go tabloid, to be interview-driven, to be celebrity-driven. . . . What we're proud of is that we can still do the kind of reporting that we do and put it on 7:00 on Sunday night and do as well as we're doing."

Three years later, with the show's ratings up by about 10 percent from those for the previous season, Fager repeated that argument. Speaking to Valerie Block for *Crain's New York Business* (2 Mar. 2009), he said that the public had a high level of interest in hard-news stories about the wars in Iraq and Afghanistan, the congressional elections of 2010, and the ongoing financial crisis. Furthermore, because *60 Minutes* had remained profitable, the show had to lay off only two people from its staff of 120—far fewer than the number cut at many other media outlets. Fager also played a crucial role in having *60 Minutes* installments and clips posted on the CBS website. As he had told the PBS interviewer, getting the show to have an online presence was not his idea, "but as soon as I heard it, I was pushing it very hard." One compelling reason for doing so, he said, was that many people in their twenties and thirties no longer viewed evening television news programs to find out what was happening in the world; they turned to the Internet instead.

CHAIRMAN OF CBS NEWS

While maintaining his position as the executive producer of *60 Minutes*, in February 2011 Fager took on the newly created post of chairman of CBS News. That month Lara Logan, the chief CBS News foreign-affairs correspondent and a *60 Minutes* correspondent, became a subject of news stories herself. Logan had been in Egypt, covering the revolution that toppled the country's longtime dictator, Hosni Mubarak, and on February 11, along with a CBS producer, she was in Tahrir Square, in Cairo, the Egyptian capital, where thousands were celebrating his overthrow. Suddenly, a mob of up to three hundred men surrounded her; some of them pulled her away from her bodyguard and others ripped off her clothes, beat her, and sexually assaulted her. She was saved by other civilians and soldiers and

then flown back to the United States. During the four days she spent in a hospital, she and Fager released a statement to the press about what had happened to her. In an interview with Brian Stelter for the *New York Times* (29 Apr. 2011), Logan said that thanks to that statement, she had not been left "to carry the burden alone, like my dirty little secret, something that I had to be ashamed of." Fager told Stelter that he supported Logan's decision to speak out about her experience so openly: "There's a code of silence" about assaults of female journalists in some countries overseas "that I think is in Lara's interest and in our interest to break." On the May 1, 2011, edition of *60 Minutes*, Logan discussed the violent incident.

Headlines about the veteran journalist and CBS News anchor Katie Couric also appeared in 2011. In 2006 Couric had left NBC's *Today Show* to become the anchor of *CBS Evening News*. As the first woman to serve as the sole anchor of a major network's evening-news program, she carried a heavy burden of expectations. When she arrived at CBS, *CBS Evening News* was behind the evening-news programs of both ABC and NBC in number of viewers, and CBS executives hoped that she would attract a larger audience. Couric, in turn, hoped that in addition to her anchor duties, she would serve as an occasional contributor to *60 Minutes*, as her contract stipulated. Both Couric and CBS executives became disappointed: Couric failed to significantly improve the ratings of *CBS Evening News*, and she made only a few appearances on *60 Minutes*. Fager, by all accounts, had been lukewarm about having her on the show. In May 2011 Couric ended her tenure at CBS. Scott Pelley of *60 Minutes* replaced her as the anchor of *CBS Evening News*.

AWARDS AND PERSONAL LIFE

In 2007 Fager won the Gerald Loeb Award for Distinguished Business and Financial Journalism, which is presented by the Anderson School of Management of the University of California at Los Angeles. Fager and his wife, Melinda, live in New Canaan, Connecticut. The couple have three children. Melinda Fager is the owner of the Red Barn Applesauce Company. She is also a photographer; her pictures have often appeared in the *New Canaan Patch*, a local newspaper.

SUGGESTED READING
Carter, Bill. "It's Official: '60 Minutes' Gets Double." *New York Times* 16 July 1998: D6.
"CBS News promotes *60 Minutes* boss." Associated Press. *Crain's New York Business*. Crain Communications, 8 Feb. 2011. Web. Jan. 2012.
"Interviews: Jeff Fager." *Frontline*. 29 Nov. 2006. WGBH Educational Foundation, 27 Feb. 2007. Web. Jan. 2012.

Mifflin, Lawrie. "The Countdown to '60 Minutes II'; CBS Executives Ready a Clone of Their Golden Brand. *New York Times* 21 Dec. 1998: C1.

Rosenthal, Phil. "'60 Minutes' boss Fager takes over a CBS News in need of more than minute changes." *Chicago Tribune* 9 Feb. 2011: C20.

—*Dmitry Kiper*

Niall Ferguson

Born: April 18, 1964
Occupation: Historian

Scots-born historian Niall Ferguson is as prolific as he is controversial. His early work explores the history of European finance, though Ferguson has since expanded his studies to encompass the larger interactions of money and power throughout the world. Currently, Ferguson has more than ten hefty volumes to his name, with an expansive biography of Henry Kissinger, the former US secretary of state, in the works.

The upcoming Kissinger story may or may not follow suit with Ferguson's famous counterfactual interpretations of historical events, in which he explores potential alternate outcomes in history. For example, in his writings, Ferguson has questioned what would have happened if the British had not entered World War I. If there had been no Hitler, would World War II ever have occurred? Ferguson touts this "what if" approach as a way of understanding the uncertainties and options of history. "[W]e have a fundamental problem with historical philosophy," he told Alan Riding for the *New York Times* (6 Mar. 1999). "Some people just don't think the past could be any different. And that leads to the belief that history repeats itself. I think there's nothing more dangerous than people who exercise the power of prophecy on the basis of a deterministic theory of history."

Some of Ferguson's contemporaries have referred to him derisively as a revisionist historian. They argue that his counterfactual arguments are simply a gimmick meant to appeal to the masses, yielding little more than historical fiction. Other critics object to Ferguson's economist-like approach to history and his harshly quantitative assertions. For example, some have criticized his numerical arguments in support of old imperial Britain, saying that they perpetuate a dangerous "ends-justify-the-means" mentality. Ferguson's demeanor—often described as combative yet charming—has led to further accusations that he is all style and no substance. However, Ferguson is credited with making several important historical discoveries including, as cited by

Getty Images

Riding, that the banker Nathan Rothschild was nearly bankrupted after Napoleon's defeat at Waterloo, and that Scottish soldiers killed their German prisoners of war during World War I as a matter of routine. His expansive knowledge of financial history has also allowed him to make many prescient observations. He was warning American bankers of uncalculated risks as early as 2004—nearly four years before the collapse of the subprime mortgage market and the financial crisis in the United States.

Currently, Ferguson is the Laurence A. Tisch Professor of History at Harvard University, as well as a Senior Fellow of the Hoover Institution at Stanford University and a Senior Research Fellow of Jesus College, Oxford. He has written and hosted five documentary television programs, presented in tandem with his publications; one of which, *The Ascent of Money*, won the 2009 International Emmy for Best Documentary. During the 2008 US presidential campaign, he briefly served as a foreign policy advisor to Senator John McCain; he resigned the day former Alaska governor Sarah Palin was drafted as McCain's running mate. He also advises the large European hedge fund GLG Partners. In 2004, he was named one of *Time* magazine's 100 Most Influential People in the World.

SCOTTISH CHILDHOOD

Ferguson was born Niall (pronounced "Neel") Campbell Douglas Ferguson in Glasgow, Scotland on April 18, 1964. His father, Campbell Ferguson, is a physician who accepted a position at a Nairobi hospital when Ferguson was a toddler. The family lived there for two years before returning to Glasgow. Ferguson also has a younger sister. Ferguson's mother, Molly Ferguson, is a physicist. From a young age, his intellectual parents pushed him to excel in his studies. Ferguson happily obliged, and cites his parents as an inspiration for his career; still, he credits his maternal grandfather, former Glasgow *Herald* editor Tom Hamilton, with sparking his early enthusiasm for writing.

Ferguson's family moved to the city of Ayr when he was twelve, when his father took a medical position there. His mother taught physics at Wellington School. Despite the distance, Ferguson continued to commute to school at Glasgow Academy. Ferguson spent much of his time reading, sometimes consuming as many as five books a week. (He read Adam Smith's *The Wealth of Nations* at the age of eleven.) In his sixth year at Glasgow Academy, Ferguson recalls that he read both Shakespeare's *Hamlet* and Friedrich von Schiller's historical account of the Thirty Years' War. Still unsure whether to pursue fiction or nonfiction in his own writing, Ferguson found an answer in what he describes as his "Schiller versus Shakespeare" moment. "I was just enthralled by the sheer quantity of material [in Schiller's account]," he told Alf Young for the Glasgow *Herald* (1 Nov. 2008). "*Hamlet* was one text. You could read it 30 times or read a shelf of commentaries on it. But at some level there was less there. Much of it was the construction of one man's imagination whereas the Thirty Years [sic] War was the construction of tens of thousands of human beings and it can be viewed from multiple vantage points and constantly re-explored."

STUDENT AT OXFORD

Ferguson won a scholarship to Oxford University's Magdalen College, where he chose to study history. In his first years at Oxford he developed seemingly divergent interests in the punk rock band known as the Sex Pistols, along with Thatcherism, a political perspective named after British conservative politician Margaret Thatcher. "Being a Thatcherite was the political equivalent of being a punk," he told Nigel Farndale for the *Sunday Telegraph* (25 Mar. 2001); "a wonderful way to shock and outrage." Ferguson also explored the more creative aspects of his personality while at Oxford; he played double bass in a jazz quintet, edited a student magazine, and even appeared as the hookah-toting caterpillar in a student production of *Alice in Wonderland*. But artistic pursuits did not capture Ferguson's imagination for long. He soon returned to the library where he doubled down in his studies for the remainder of his academic career. Though he graduated with a degree in history in 1985, Ferguson also spent time under the tutelage of

the economist Gerald Harris, with whom he studied medieval financial history.

Ferguson was accepted into Magdalen's postgraduate program where he was a demy, or foundation scholar, until 1989. He chose the British historian and author Norman Stone as his thesis advisor. Stone was considered a "media don" who popularized his scholarly pursuits for the masses. It has also been noted that Stone bore a strong resemblance to Ferguson's early hero, the historian A. J. P. Taylor, who was famous for the television broadcasts of his lectures. This type of academic career—free from the bonds of academia and planted firmly in the larger cultural spotlight—would prove to be tremendously appealing to Ferguson. Stone, also a Scots-born Thatcherite, encouraged his young protégé to study finance and tax laws to gain a more grounded perspective on history.

After Stone rejected his first thesis proposal—the life of Viennese satirist Karl Kraus—Ferguson completed his dissertation on the German economy between 1914 and 1924. Ferguson bolstered his previous research at Oxford by spending a year and a half in Hamburg and Berlin perusing the Warburg Archives for information on the bout of hyperinflation that brought Germany to its knees after World War I. The fruit of this labor was his first book, *Paper and Iron: Hamburg Business and German Politics in the Era of Inflation, 1897–1927*, which was published by the Cambridge University Press in 1995.

COUNTERFACTUALS AND THE ROTHSCHILDS

Ferguson's next books were published by Penguin Press; his academic audience was expanding to include lay readers. In 1997 and 1998, Ferguson published *Virtual History: Alternatives and Counterfactuals* and *The Pity of War: Explaining World War I*, respectively. *Virtual History* is a collection of essays by a number of respected professors and historians that illustrates the heart of Ferguson's counterfactual approach to history. Indeed, it has been noted that Ferguson's long introduction to the book is mostly dedicated to the defense of this approach. Ferguson makes clear that all the hypothesized historical outcomes in the book were once "viable alternatives," as he puts it, in British history. The possibilities explored in *Virtual History* are featured in chapter titles such as "What if Charles I had avoided the Civil War?" and "What if Germany had invaded Britain in May 1940?"

The Pity of War, inspired by Ferguson's grandfather's service on the Western Front, received critical skepticism similarly to his earlier works, but it became a bestseller. In the book, Ferguson argues that Britain should not have entered World War I, a move that would have allowed the British to preserve their empire and might have prevented the rise of the Third Reich. Germany's aims in 1914 were modest, he writes, and Britain should have remained neutral and allowed Germany to win a limited continental war. Ferguson concludes that the blame for the war's astronomical death toll lies squarely on the shoulders of British politicians. The book ran counter to pervading historical views of the war, prompting historian R. W. Johnson to write for the *London Review of Books* (as quoted by Farndale) of Ferguson: "There is something of the clever-silly about his over-determined contrarianism."

British publishers Weidenfeld & Nicholson released Ferguson's extraordinary history of the Rothschild banking dynasty in 1998 as a single 1,309-page tome. In the United States, the history was divided into two volumes: *The House of Rothschild: Volume 1: Money's Prophets, 1798–1848* (1998) and *The House of Rothschild: Volume 2: The World's Banker, 1849–1999* (2000). The book was a product of five years of research, financed in part by the British branch of the Rothschild family. To perform the research, Ferguson was granted entry to the Rothschilds' extensive archives as the first person outside of the family to be admitted to their personal documents. For almost a century, the Jewish-German Rothchilds were known as the world's richest and most powerful family. They are credited with creating the first global bond market, lending money to the pope, and bailing out the Bank of England. Ferguson's detailed history of their saga was well received. In a book review for the *New York Times*, author Sylvia Nasar wrote that Ferguson's two volumes had "all the grandeur and sweep of a 19th-century three-decker novel" (23 Jan. 2000).

ARGUMENTS FOR AN AMERICAN EMPIRE

After signing a $1.4 million three-book deal with his publisher, the fast-working Ferguson found time to write and publish an "extra" history called *The Cash Nexus: Money and Power in the Modern World 1700–2000* (2001). The book was the first of Ferguson's oeuvre that encouraged the United States to pursue a global empire—a sentiment that is echoed in his later work. Published mere months after the inauguration of President George W. Bush, the book was critical of US foreign policy. "The greatest disappointment facing the world in the 21st century," Ferguson wrote in *The Cash Nexus*, is that "the leaders of the one state with the economic resources to make the world a better place lack the guts to do it." Ferguson later supported the war in Iraq as a remedy to this "disappointment." Like all of Ferguson's work, *The Cash Nexus* found its roots in finance. He argued that financial globalization could not occur without "imperial" guidance.

Continuing the themes he explored in *The Cash Nexus*, Ferguson published *Empire: The Rise and Demise of the British World Order and the Lessons for Global Power* in 2003, followed

by *Colossus: The Rise and Fall of the American Empire* in 2004. *Empire* provides a comprehensive history of British imperialism and takes the controversial stance that the British Empire did more good than it did harm. Ferguson does not gloss over Britain's faults—indeed he spends a majority of the book painting racism, slavery, and the condescending colonial mindset in great detail—but comes to the conclusion, after calculating cost and benefit, that Britain effectively changed the world for the better. (He argues that today's world could benefit from the "liberal empire" of the United States in the same way.) Ferguson has been criticized for aspects of his reasoning, including his argument that, had it not been for the well-intentioned Brits, the world might have fallen under a worse empire; essentially, the transgresses of the British Empire were bad, but not as bad as they might have been, according to a counterfactual interpretation. But the book also details the rise of Western culture and the early triumph of the British Empire over the burgeoning empire of Spain. The British were not only skilled conquerors but also skilled administrators, Ferguson argues, and thus their influence was felt throughout the world.

In *Colossus* (2004), Ferguson argues that the United States is indeed an empire, but that it is of the anti-imperialist variety; he cites the Cold War doctrine of containment as a perfect demonstration of the United States acting on its own long-term interests under an anti-imperialist guise. Ferguson writes that the United States must recognize its role as a global empire to assume the responsibilities it has hitherto been neglecting. At a time when the American public was critical of the war in Iraq, Ferguson criticized the Bush administration for not doing more, calling their poorly managed policies "imperialism lite." It was also in *Colossus* that Ferguson first warned of the United States' increasing financial dependence on China.

FINANCIAL HISTORIES AND THE WEST VERSUS THE "REST"

In his book *The Ascent of Money: A Financial History of the World* (2008), Ferguson anticipated aspects of the financial crisis that occurred months after its publication. The book is a sweeping economic history of the world, in which Ferguson recalls a lecture he gave at a banker's conference in 2006. He had concluded his lecture by observing how little it would take to initiate a decline in liquidity that would negatively affect the entire global financial system; he had been widely dismissed by the crowd. Ferguson cites his own natural contrarianism for his foresight. "If a majority of people subscribe to a particular view, it pays to question it," he told Young. "It pays to think: maybe this is wrong." In the *Ascent of Money*, Ferguson also continues his argument that the United States depends too heavily on Chinese money. The United States is so deeply in debt, Ferguson writes, that it has become a "dual country," which he dubs "Chimerica." As he writes in *The Ascent of Money*, the downfall of great powers can most often be attributed to unsound finances, and he effectively warns that the United States is in danger of making the same mistake.

Ferguson's book *High Financier: The Lives and Time of Siegmund Warburg* was published in 2010 after over a decade of research. Warburg, a wealthy German Jew who left his country in the early 1930s to make a name for himself in British finance, is little remembered outside of financial circles today. By all accounts he is a minor figure who never made the fortunes that can be attributed to his counterparts. But as Ferguson recognized, Warburg's unusual rise and—to today's Wall Street perspective—anachronistic policy of ethics provide an interesting glimpse into the early aspirations of finance.

Ferguson's most recent book, *Civilization: The West and the Rest*, was published in 2011. Just like *Empire*, *Colossus*, and *The Ascent of Money*, it was adapted into a television documentary series hosted by Ferguson on Britain's Channel 4 and the US Public Broadcasting Service (PBS). In the book, Ferguson attempts to answer how, around 1500 CE, the West, or what he describes as "a few small polities on the western end of the Eurasian landmass," came essentially to rule the rest of the world. Ferguson writes that Western ascendency was due largely to what he calls six "killer apps"—competition, science, democracy, medicine, consumerism, and work ethic. In a nod to modern technology, he argues that these apps are currently being "downloaded" by other countries. The book was criticized for its gimmicky structure, as was Ferguson for his reductive "Westerners" versus "Resterners" dichotomy.

LIFE AS A JOURNALIST AND PROFESSOR

Ferguson began his career in journalism while completing his doctorate at Oxford. During his brief stint in Hamburg, Ferguson partially supported himself (along with a German fellowship) by writing for London's *Daily Mail* and *Daily Telegraph*. He recalls long days of research for his own work concluded with a hastily penned news story called in to his editors. Still, Ferguson credits his experience as a journalist for making him a better writer and self-editor. To protect his burgeoning academic career, Ferguson wrote his more opinionated columns under the pseudonyms "Alec Campbell" and "F. F. Gillespie." (When an editor insisted on a running a picture of Ferguson beside his columns, he donned a pair of thick glasses as a disguise.) Ferguson has also contributed to the *Sunday Telegraph* (London), *Newsweek*, and *Bloomberg News*.

Ferguson returned from Germany in the early 1990s to take a research fellowship at Cambridge University's Christ's College, followed by a lectureship at Peterhouse, Cambridge. In 1992, he began lecturing at Jesus College in Oxford. In 2000, he became a professor of political and financial history. In 2002, he accepted the Herzog Chair in Financial History at the Stern School of Business of New York University, where he was voted "Professor of the Year" in 2003. In 2004, he accepted his current position at Harvard University. He has also held a one-year post at the prestigious London School of Economics.

PERSONAL LIFE

Ferguson is said to have been the inspiration for the character of Irwin, a contrarian teacher and television historian in Alan Bennett's play *The History Boys* (2004).

Ferguson was married to Sue Douglas, the former editor of the *Sunday Express*, for sixteen years. The two met in 1987, when Douglas was Ferguson's editor at the *Daily Mail*. The couple has three children, but separated in 2009 and later divorced.

Ferguson is now married to Ayaan Hirsi Ali, a Somali-born activist and former Dutch member of Parliament. The two met at a gala for *Time* magazine's 100 Most Influential People in the World, a list on which Ali also appeared, in 2009. Raised as a fundamentalist Muslim, Ali is now an atheist, feminist, and strident critic of Islam. She has lived under constant police protection since Islamic extremists issued a fatwa, or legal pronouncement, against her. Ali gave birth to the couple's son in 2011.

SUGGESTED READING
Farndale, Nigel. "The History Man." *Ottawa Citizen*. 25 Mar. 2001, final ed.: C4.

Nasar, Sylvia. "Masters of the Universe." *New York Times*. 23 Jan. 2000, final ed.: Book Review 8.

Riding, Alan. "An Oxford Historian Whose Vox Is Populi." *New York Times*. 6 Mar. 1999, final ed.: B9.

Young, Alf. "Money Maketh the Man." *Herald* (Glasgow). 1 Nov. 2008, final ed.: 12.

SELECTED BOOKS
Virtual History: Alternatives and Counterfactuals, 1997; *The Pity of War: Explaining World War I*, 1998; *The House of Rothschild*, 1999; *The Cash Nexus: Money and Power in the Modern World, 1700–2000*, 2001; *Empire: The Rise and Demise of the British World Order and the Lessons for Global Power*, 2003; *Colossus: The Rise and Fall of the American Empire*, 2004; *The War of the World: Twentieth-Century Conflict and the War of the West*, 2006; *The Ascent of Money: A*

Financial History of the World, 2008; *High Financier: The Lives and Time of Siegmund Warburg*, 2010; *Civilization: The West and the Rest*, 2011

SELECTED TELEVISION PROGRAMS

Empire: How Britain Made the Modern World, 2003; *American Colossus*, 2004; *The Ascent of Money: A Financial History of the World*, 2009; *The War of the World*, 2009; *Civilization: Is the West History?*, 2011

—Molly Hagan

Tyler Florence

Born: March 3, 1971
Occupation: Chef and television personality

"I try to boil it down to what matters," chef, television personality, and entrepreneur Tyler Florence explained to David Plotnikoff for the San Jose *Mercury News* (21 Oct. 2008). "To me it's all about starting out with great quality ingredients and then showing you a technique or two or three to get a masterpiece out of that." For over fifteen years, Florence has used that kind of simple, straightforward approach to teach millions of Americans how to cook.

A graduate of the prestigious College of Culinary Arts at Johnson & Wales University, he trained under a series of premier chefs in Charleston, South Carolina, and New York City before establishing his culinary reputation in the mid-1990s as executive chef of the acclaimed Manhattan restaurants Cibo and Cafeteria. Florence was propelled to national fame in 1999, when he became the host of his own Food Network television series, *Food 911*, where he travelled to people's homes to solve food dilemmas. Florence immediately attracted a large fan base—including a high percentage of women—with his good looks, charming personality, enthusiastic demeanor, and down-to-earth cooking style. He eventually became a mainstay on the Food Network; he has since hosted other specials and series, including *Tyler's Ultimate, How to Boil Water*, and *The Great Food Truck Race*.

In more recent years, Florence, who relocated from New York to the San Francisco Bay Area in 2007, has, in the tradition of other enterprising celebrity chefs, expanded his brand beyond the realm of television. Since then, he has created an empire worth $50 million, according to *Forbes* magazine. That empire, properties of which fall under his company, the Florence Group, includes a kitchen retail chain, four restaurants in the Bay Area, high-end culinary products, an eponymous wine label, lines of gourmet

FilmMagic

food products and organic baby food, and an iPhone app. Florence has also published seven cookbooks and launched a children's book series called *Tyler Makes*. He told Paolo Lucchesi for the *San Francisco Chronicle* (22 Apr. 2010), "The food community expects their chefs to be poor, little humble guys that hunt mushrooms by the third moonlight of the third full moon of the month. I've set myself up to have a vertically integrated, multi-tiered company."

EARLY LIFE AND EDUCATION

Kevin Tyler Florence was born on March 3, 1971 in Greenville, South Carolina. His father, Winston Florence, was a magazine publisher, and his mother, Phyllis Olson, was a businesswoman. Florence's parents divorced when he was about eight. His older brother, Warren, is a professional tennis instructor and a nationally published writer and editor who formerly served as editor in chief of *Tennis Industry* magazine; he is now the tennis director of the Palmetto Bluff Resort in Bluffon, South Carolina. Florence grew up as a self-described "latchkey kid" in a "suburban skateboard" culture, as he told Kay Rentschler for *Charleston* magazine (Dec. 2005, online). He was often left to fend for himself due to the busy schedules of his working parents, who were rarely at home. As a result he started cooking his own meals at an early age. "My parents didn't leave me at home because they didn't care, nor because they didn't want to be with me," he wrote in his book *Tyler Florence Family Meal: Bringing People Together Never Tasted*

Better (2010). "They had to work to give me a place to come home to and to keep that food in the fridge. In hindsight, who knows if I would ever even have found my calling if I hadn't been left alone to figure out how to put food on the table."

Aside from cooking out of necessity, Florence gained an appreciation and passion for food from his Southern roots. As a child he frequently visited his grandparents at their home in Georgia, where he was introduced to the pleasures of Southern home cooking. He enjoyed watching his grandmother make biscuits and gravy, collard greens, country ham, and fried chicken; he also fondly recalls taking in the aromas of his grandfather's smokehouse. He told Rentschler, "Going to see my grandparents was like going back fifty years. Every weekend was a history lesson in Southern food." Florence would later use his grandparents' influence to create what would become his signature: an honest, no-nonsense approach to cooking. "Most of the great food in the world is peasant food that's been reinvented," as he put it to Teresa Taylor for the Charleston *Post and Courier* (9 Apr. 2003).

Florence was diagnosed with attention deficit/hyperactivity disorder as a child, a disorder that severely affected his performance in school, so much so that he failed out of the third grade. His inability to concentrate and focus also led to him to "getting in trouble all the time," as he recalled in the Food Network series *Chefography* (21 Mar. 2007). Florence's passion for food, however, ultimately helped him find his focus. At fifteen, his parents told him that he would be responsible for all of his expenses from that point forward. So, he bought a car—a 1965 Comet Capri—and got a job as a dishwasher and busboy at a French restaurant in Greenville called the Fishmarket. Recalling his experience working at the restaurant, which was owned by his then girlfriend's parents, he told Jennifer V. Cole for *Travel and Leisure* magazine (Aug. 2004, online), "The chef was a god to me: he drove a Harley and women stopped by to see him every night. I thought, 'That's what I want to do.'" A few years later Florence started working as a line cook.

In 1989 Florence enrolled at the College of Culinary Arts at Johnson & Wales University (JWU) in Charleston, South Carolina. (The college has since moved to JWU's campus in Charlotte, North Carolina.) He graduated with honors with an associate's degree in culinary arts from JWU in 1991, and received a bachelor's degree in hospitality management from there in 1994. While attending JWU, Florence honed his culinary skills at some of Charleston's most respected restaurants, including Chef Donald Barickman's Magnolias and Chef Louis Osteen's Charleston Grill. Barickman remembered him as "an energetic powerhouse of a line cook who

went at it from every direction," as he told Kay Rentschler, while Osteen told the same writer that he "was always after something bigger, something better, something new." Florence has cited both chefs, who specialized in different styles of Southern regional cooking, as culinary influences. He noted to Tara Dooley for the *Houston Chronicle* (14 May 2003), "My influences have definitely been culinary school, but more than that, the school of hot stoves."

CAREER

After completing his studies, Florence moved to New York City, where he established himself as a chef. He worked with a series of world-renowned chefs, including Charlie Palmer, Marta Pulini, and Rick Laakonen, at Aureole, Mad 61, and the River Cafe, respectively, before becoming executive chef at the Italian restaurant Cibo, in the Murray Hill section of Manhattan, in 1995. At Cibo, which means "food" in Italian, Florence and his contemporary fare received acclaim in such publications as *New York* magazine, the *New York Times*, and *Time Out New York*. That buzz helped bring him to the attention of the then-fledgling Food Network, and in 1996, he made his television debut. Over the next several years, he would make guest appearances on such Food Network programs as *Ready Set Cook*, *Chef du Jour*, and *In Food Today*.

In 1998 Florence became executive chef and a founding partner of Cafeteria, a casual twenty-four-hour eatery in the Chelsea section of Manhattan. The restaurant, which serves inventive comfort food, achieved instant popularity and was nominated for best new restaurant in *Time Out New York*. "It was sort of a hyper-modern restaurant that served diner food," Florence told Jennifer Baldwin for the *Alameda Times-Star* (23 Apr. 2003). "But it was really great diner food. It was fried chicken and waffles and meatloaf and macaroni and cheese and collard greens. It was a really fun place." Florence remained executive chef of Cafeteria until 1999, when he joined the Food Network full-time for the launch of his kitchen emergency show *Food 911*. The thirty-minute show followed Florence as he traveled around the country solving various cooking dilemmas; on the show he taught home cooks how to cook everything from fried chicken to foie gras. "When I walk out of a house and a light bulb goes off in their head, 'I can do this, I can cook this,' it's the greatest feeling," he told Teresa Taylor.

Food 911, which aired more than three hundred episodes, helped Florence rise to celebrity chef status, as viewers fell in love with his energy, enthusiasm, and culinary flair. Commenting on the chef's widespread appeal, Kay Rentschler wrote, "On *Food 911*, Florence comes off as a hip neighborhood guy who teaches weekly guests to cook. . . . Fired-up and energetic, but always in control, Florence treats his guests as equals. He doesn't get all segment-rushed and frantic like a lot of TV chefs, and he keeps his message clear, uncomplicated, and free from technical chefspeak. . . . Ultimately, Florence's appeal lies somewhere in the mix between his cool, uncluttered TV shtick and the energy of a commercial kitchen he carries in his presence. You know he could slam out a couple of hundred covers and not even blink. But, at this instant, he's cooking with you, and promising mac and cheese that's 'absolutely off the hook.'"

The success of *Food 911* led to Florence hosting other Food Network series and specials, including *Planet Food, My Country, My Kitchen,* and *All American Festivals.* In April 2003 he started hosting *Tyler's Ultimate,* a weekly series in which he traveled around the world in search of the historical and culinary origins of popular dishes. Each installment of the series, which ran for eight seasons until 2010, featured Florence creating an "ultimate" version of a particular dish based on knowledge he gained about that dish from his travels. He explained to Phyllis Speidell for the Norfolk, Virginia, *Virginian-Pilot* (10 Dec. 2003) that the show was "not about creating the newest flavor combinations but about investigating traditional foods." Also in 2003 Florence began cohosting the Food Network cooking show *How to Boil Water,* with the comedienne Jack Hourigan. One of the network's flagship programs, debuting in 1993 with Emeril Lagasse as host, the thirty-minute show is premised around teaching novices how to cook. Florence's latest Food Network series, *The Great Food Truck Race,* premiered in August 2010. The series, which has aired for two seasons, features teams of specialty food trucks competing in weekly challenges across the country for a $100,000 grand prize. It has since been renewed for a third season.

In addition to hosting multiple Food Network series, Florence has added cookbook author, radio host, and a handful of other titles to his resume. His first cookbook, *Tyler Florence's Real Kitchen,* was published by Clarkson Potter in March 2003. Partly inspired by his experiences on *Food 911,* the book includes recipes for a mix of ethnic and domestic dishes and is structured into six specific dining situations (such as "Table for Two," "Weekend Brunch," and "The Cocktail Party"), with additional chapters for sides and desserts. Florence told Jennifer Baldwin that the book is "not about foie gras and truffles. It's really about what you want to cook at home." He followed up *Real Kitchen* with the *Eat This Book: Cooking with Global Fresh Flavors* (2005) and *Tyler's Ultimate: Brilliant Simple Food to Make Any Time* (2006), both of which were published by Clarkson Potter, in 2005. In an assessment of the former, Jennifer Olvera wrote for the *Chicago Sun-Times* (25 May 2005), "In his latest foray

into food, Florence divvies up helpings of devourable little bites, improvisational, nosh-worthy eats, impressive, consumable meals, summer wonders and lick-the-plate-clean desserts. His approach is conversational and down-to-earth, and the dishes, while largely straightforward, shoot for dazzling results."

In 2006 Florence replaced celebrity chef Rocco Dispirito as host of the popular morning show *Food Talk* on the New York radio station WOR-AM. He served as host of the show, which aired weekdays from 11:00 A.M. to noon, until September of that year. Also in 2006 he partnered with Applebee's International, Inc. to develop creative new menu items for the company's Applebee's Neighborhood Grill & Bar restaurant chain. He served as a spokesman for the chain and introduced the new items in a series of television and radio advertisements. While receiving flak from some of his food industry colleagues for "selling out," Florence has said that the money he earned from the endorsement partnership (around $3 million) allowed him to embark on other career ventures in an otherwise down economy. He told Paolo Lucchesi, "I wouldn't be here now if it wasn't for that opportunity."

In 2007 Florence moved from New York's Lower East Side to Mill Valley, California, after his second wife, Tolan, a Mill Valley native, convinced him that the Marin County city would be a better place to raise a family. (The two had first met at the 2004 Sundance Film Festival, after being introduced by Rocco Dispirito; they married in December 2006.) Describing the decision as "life-changing," he explained to Kym McNicholas for *Forbes* (18 May 2011, online), "We had money set aside from TV and endorsements. And we said, 'Let's just reinvent ourselves here—it's time.' And I thought let's make products that really come from our heart that we really want to use." The roots of Florence's company, the Florence Group, were officially planted in July 2008, when he and his wife opened their first kitchen retail shop, The Tyler Florence Shop, in Mill Valley. Housed in the first Banana Republic retail store, which had closed, the shop sells everything "from the finest antique chopping blocks to local Marin County preserves, the world's finest culinary tools, accessories, cookbooks and local artisan products," according to its website. In 2010 Florence opened two more retail outposts, one in San Francisco International Airport's Terminal One and another in Napa. He told David Plotnikoff that he sees his stores becoming "a third player in between [high-end cookware retailers] Williams Sonoma and Sur la Table."

In addition to his retail stores, Florence has expanded his brand to a wide range of other business ventures, including four restaurants in the San Francisco Bay Area. In June 2010 he opened his flagship restaurant, Wayfare Tavern, in San Francisco's Financial District. The three-level restaurant, which occupies the space that had housed the legendary San Francisco eatery Rubicon, features a rustic, turn-of-the-century look and offers traditional American specialties and an extensive wine list containing predominantly California wines. Florence's next restaurant concept, the Southern-inspired Rotisserie & Wine, opened in Napa in December 2010, and in March 2011, he teamed up with the Hall of Fame rocker Sammy Hager to open El Paseo, a classic "House of Chops" in Mill Valley. A second Rotisserie & Wine restaurant opened in San Francisco International Airport's Terminal Two, in May 2011.

Florence has lent his name to a line of cutlery and cookware sold by the Canadian entertainment company Outset; launched a signature brand of red and white wines in partnership with the Michael Mondavi family; released a collection of gourmet sauces, glazes, rubs, marinades, and seasonings called West Coast Cooking Essentials; cocreated Sprout Organic Baby Food; and introduced a cooking and recipe app for the iPhone. Florence, who serves as a contributing editor at *House Beautiful* magazine, has also ventured into the realm of kitchen design and created that publication's annual Kitchen of the Year at New York's Rockefeller Center in 2011.

Florence's other books include *Tyler Florence: Stirring the Pot* (2008), *Dinner at My Place* (2008), and *Start Fresh: Your Child's Jump Start to Lifelong Healthy Eating* (2011). In 2012 he released the first installment of a children's book series, titled *Tyler Makes Pancakes!* Florence has made regular guest appearances on such television shows as *The Today Show*, *The View*, *Good Morning America*, *The Oprah Winfrey Show*, and *The Tonight Show with Jay Leno*. He was named "Sexiest Chef Alive" by *People* magazine in 2003, received an honorary doctorate degree from JWU in 2004, and was named the Restaurateur of the Year by *Wine Enthusiast* magazine in 2011. He is a member of Macy's Culinary Council and has served as dean of culinary studies at COPIA: The American Center for Wine, Food, and the Arts in Napa since 2008. Florence is one of the most popular celebrity chefs on the social-networking service Twitter, with over 380,000 followers.

PERSONAL LIFE

Florence lives in Mill Valley with his wife, Tolan, their son, Hayden (born in 2007), and daughter, Dorothy (born in 2008). He has another son, Miles (born in 1996), from his previous marriage to Christie Leer. Florence has credited his wife with playing a major role in the creation of his culinary empire, which is now worth an estimated $50 million. He told Paolo Lucchesi that he ultimately wants "to have a winery up in Sonoma where my wife and I can just kick back, play with our grandchildren, and watch the grapes grow. And I'm starting that process now."

SUGGESTED READING

Florence, Tyler. *Tyler Florence Family Meal: Bringing People Together Never Tasted Better.* New York: Rodale, 2010.

Florence, Tyler. *Tyler Florence: Stirring the Pot.* De Moines: Meredith, 2008.

Hu, Janny. "Sunday Profile: Tolan and Tyler Florence." *SFGate.com*. Hearst Communications Inc., 29 Jan. 2012. Web. 16 Apr. 2012.

Lucchesi, Paolo. "A Tyler Triple Play; RESTAURANTS; Food Network Star's New Restaurants to Open in S.F., Mill Valley, Napa." *San Francisco Chronicle* 22 Apr. 2010: E1.

McNicholas, Kym. "Tyler Florence Is Cooking Up An Entrepreneurial Empire." *Forbes.com*. Forbes.com LLC, 18 May 2011. Web. 16 Apr. 2012.

Olvera, Jennifer. "Simply Dazzling; Down-to-Earth Dishes That Sparkle Are Florence's Forte." *Chicago Sun-Times* 25 May 2005: 1.

Plotnikoff, David. "Food Network's Tyler Florence, At Full Speed." *San Jose Mercury News* 21 Oct. 2008: NEWS.

—*Chris Cullen*

Dennis Fong

Born: March 11, 1977
Occupation: Entrepreneur and pro gamer

Dennis Fong has been referred to as the "Michael Jordan of video games" for his playing prowess at such popular games as Quake and Doom. "The emergence of a cyberspace celebrity reflects the evolution rapidly taking place in computer gaming," Joseph Pereira wrote for the *Wall Street Journal* (27 Aug. 1996), reporting on Fong's triumphs at several high-profile gaming competitions. "The Nintendo generation is no longer content to sit in front of a screen and blast a kid brother or the boy next door. With the advent of computer networks and faster modems and telephone links, a gamer can go online and challenge an opponent across the street or across the planet." Jordan famously parlayed his skill on the basketball court into a lucrative career as a product spokesperson and entrepreneur, and Fong has followed a similar trajectory. He is currently the CEO of Raptr, a social network and web portal for gamers.

EARLY LIFE

Fong was born in Hong Kong on March 11, 1977. The second of three boys, his father worked in information technology and his mother was a teacher. When Fong was eleven years

Time & Life Pictures/Getty Images

system to handle. Shortening it to "Threshold" seemed to drain it of much of its evocative power. Fong finally settled upon "Thresh." Aside from referring to the process of mechanically separating seeds from a harvested plant, the term is also defined as the act of "striking repeatedly," which fit the violent fantasy world of Doom.

Fong found that playing against real opponents, albeit remotely, made Doom seem more like an actual sport. Soon, he was squaring off against other players for several hours a day. Because Internet usage had not yet become widespread, he used Bulletin Board Systems (BBSs) to facilitate his gaming competitions. Users dialed into the BBS using a phone line, making the hobby a potentially expensive one, but Fong has told interviewers that the highest monthly bill his parents ever received was $150. Because challengers assumed the cost of competing against him, Fong found that he was able to sit back and wait until challenged. This happened with increasing frequency as his fame spread among avid gamers. Fong quickly added other games to his repertoire, including those in the now-popular Warcraft franchise. He also became adept at Multi-User Dungeon (MUD) games, which combine role-playing, interactivity, and chat. A MUD game generally employed text descriptions of the setting (often derived from fantasy or science fiction tropes), listed the other players and objects in the area, and detailed the goals (slaying a space alien or rescuing a damsel, for example). To complete a task—such as "pick up sword" or "follow path north"—the player enters a text command using the keyboard.

In the early 1990s, Fong began entering gaming tournaments. The first of these were sponsored by a service called DWANGO, which stood for Doom Wide-Area Network Game Operation, which allowed players to pay a set fee of about $10 per month in order to log in, chat, and find opponents. Later, as the roster of games expanded, the acronym was changed to Dial-Up Wide-Area Network Game Operation. The company eventually expanded to allow franchisees to set up servers across the country. Fong became a celebrity at DWANGO tournaments, trouncing anyone who challenged him.

old, the family immigrated to the United States and settled in Los Altos, California, where his father took a position as a manager at the computer giant Hewlett-Packard. Fong had attended American-run schools in his native Hong Kong, so his move to the United States was not an extreme culture change. Exhibiting their father's aptitude for technology, Fong's brothers, Lyle and Bryant, became fascinated by computers. "I was not," Fong admitted to David Kushner for *Salon* (5 Sep. 2000). "In fact, I hated computers and was much more into sports." Fong started a roller-hockey club at his high school, and played football, tennis, and volleyball. His attitude changed the day Lyle and Bryant introduced him to Doom. First released in 1993, Doom is a "first-person shooter" game, meaning that the player experiences the action from the perspective of a character moving through a three-dimensional world. In the case of Doom, the player assumes the role of a "space marine" inhabiting a military base on a distant moon beset by demonic creatures. Doom has been widely credited with popularizing the first-person-shooter genre, setting a new standard for 3D graphics, and pioneering network-enabled multiplayer gaming. Fong was hooked.

THRESH IS BORN
Logging in to play a multiplayer game required a screen name, and Fong initially chose "Threshold of Pain," liking the connotations of machismo and strength. He found, however, that the moniker contained too many letters for the computer

DEATHMATCH '95
When Fong was eighteen, he competed with gamers from around the world in an international tournament known as Deathmatch '95. The event was sponsored by id Software (the makers of Doom), GT Interactive Software (a now-defunct distributor), DWANGO, and Microsoft. Microsoft surprised many opting to venture into the world of competitive gaming and choosing to become involved in Deathmatch '95. "[For a long time] the software giant was an afterthought in the computer-games business. [But] today, Microsoft plays with the big boys," Jay Greene

wrote a few years after that tournament for the *Buffalo News* (19 Jan. 1999). "In many ways, the games business is a classic Microsoft tale: a story of how the company elbowed its way into a business, produced uninspired products early on, learned from its mistakes, and became a force in the industry. And it's also an example of how determined Microsoft can be when it sees an opportunity to win a piece of a $1.8 billion-a-year business."

Deathmatch players initially competed on DWANGO's twenty-two franchised servers to determine the best competitor from that server's region. On October 30, in an event dubbed Judgment Day, the regional champions, plus two European contestants, were flown to Redmond, Washington, home of Microsoft's main campus, to play the final rounds face-to-face. Comedian Jay Leno entertained the audience, and Microsoft CEO Bill Gates made a well-received speech, but many of the gamers were most excited to meet Fong. In person, he is unassuming and polite for someone who goes by Thresh online. "People expect me to be some whacked-out dude with long hair and tattoos, but I'm just a normal-looking, peaceful guy," Fong told Patti Hartigan for the *Boston Globe* (21 Jan. 2000).

On the gaming website TeamLiquid.net, Fong described Deathmatch '95 as "probably the biggest gaming tournament ever up to that point in gaming history. The tournament coincided with the launch of Microsoft Game Studios. . . . As you can imagine, Microsoft doesn't do anything small, so the event was a huge extravaganza, with the competition being one of the highlights of the launch party." "By virtue of having already played most of the top players around the country and beaten them," Fong told TeamLiquid.net, "I was considered one of the favorites to win the tournament. Another player who went by the handle 'Merlock' was considered the other favorite. Due to a random draw, we ended up facing each other in the semi-finals. I ended up beating him something like 10–5. Merlock got so upset he slammed the keyboard and threw his chair off-stage. It was quite the scene, particularly since LAN [Local Area Network] tournaments weren't all that common back then." Fong easily triumphed in the competition, winning VIP status on DWANGO for a year, a lifetime supply of id Software products, and a new computer—prizes with a reported value of almost $10,000.

Stories began circulating that Fong had almost supernatural abilities. "I always approached competitive gaming like speed chess. Chess is not a strategic game, but you're always thinking fast—two or three steps ahead of your opponent," he explained to Kushner. "You're always placing yourself in the other person's perspective. I got a reputation for doing that so well

that people starting calling it 'Thresh ESP.' But I was just anticipating my opponent's move."

BUSINESS CAREER

As the tournament circuit made more demands on his time, Fong dropped out of college to focus on gaming. His parents were not happy about his decision to leave school. Nonetheless, Fong was steadily earning prize money and small endorsement deals, and he beginning to mull over the idea of starting a business.

"My brothers and I decided to start Gamers.com back in 1996," he recalled to Kushner. "We had a huge passion for gaming, and believed that it would be a 'big deal' down the road. So one night, we logged onto the Internet, registered 'gamers.com' for seventy-five bucks, and off we went." "The first two years of our business were essentially a makeshift business school for us," Fong explained, "[W]e made every possible mistake entrepreneurs could make, but it was great because we learned how to be profitable without needing outside funding." Fong explained to Kushner the thinking behind creating the new Web portal: "We saw a need in the industry for something like this. There are literally thousands of Web sites dedicated to games on the Net, but no single, comprehensive source."

RED ANNIHILATION

In May 1997, Fong took part in Red Annihilation, a Quake competition. Quake, like Doom, is a first-person shooter game developed by id Software. Introduced in 1996, it had quickly become immensely popular. The game's protagonist travels through "slipgates," government-developed teleportation devices, in pursuit of an enemy code-named "Quake." In a review posted on the website of the retailer Game Spot (22 June 1996), Trent C. Ward enthused, "Quake is a masterpiece on every level, with its ominous atmosphere, silky-smooth animation, incredibly well-balanced gameplay and level design, and unparalleled soundtrack. Once again, the team at id Software has created a no-apologies, ultra-violent gorefest sure to be the new battleground of choice for single and multi-player combatants worldwide."

The 1997 Red Annihilation finals took place at the Electronic Entertainment Expo, an annual event commonly known as E3, which was held that year in Atlanta, Georgia. The top prize had the gaming world abuzz; John Carmack, a cofounder of id Software, was signing over his own red Ferrari 328 GTS, worth some $70,000, to the winner. To no one's surprise, Fong beat out fifteen other finalists and won the car. His parents, he told journalists, quickly stopped asking him to return to college and actually began urging him to practice his gaming more. In the weeks leading up to a major tournament, Fong played from four to eight hours a day. He was also extremely careful about his diet, eating sushi and drinking hot water with lemon juice.

Because the mainstream media had covered Red Annihilation extensively, Fong found himself the subject of several news stories, many of them breathlessly predicting a future in which gamers were as idolized as football and basketball stars. "Parents of computer game addicts, meet Thresh," Greg Miller wrote for the *Los Angeles Times* (3 Nov. 1997). "And think twice before you snatch that joystick out of your child's hand again." Joe Perez, an executive at the Total Entertainment Network, explained to Miller that he had founded a Professional Gamers League (PGL), hoping that it would one day attain the prestige of the NFL, NBA, or PGA. "Why can't somebody like Thresh get the same kinds of endorsements and sponsorships as [golfer] Tiger Woods?" Perez asked Miller. To those in the gaming world, Fong was undeniably compiling a record as impressive as that of Woods. Over the course of the next few years, he won every tournament he entered. The PGL produced a trading card with his picture, and fans regularly lined up to obtain his autograph.

AN INFUSION OF CAPITAL

In the fall of 1999, Fong was hired to give a speech to hundreds of technology executives at a conference in Monte Carlo. Afterwards, David Wetherell, the head of the Internet holding company CMGI, approached him to offer financial backing for Gamers.com. The website, which Fong and his brother were running under an umbrella company called GX Media (also referred to as Gamers Extreme), received $11 million from CMGI's investment arm.

By the following year, Fong, who had largely withdrawn from the tournament circuit, had hired a staff of 150 employees, each possessing a deep knowledge of the gaming world. They were responsible for indexing links to every game made, aggregating game reviews and ratings, and combing the web for industry news. Gamers.com became widely acknowledged as the most comprehensive website of its kind. Fong had, in effect, gone "from Master of the Virtual Universe to Master of a Corporation," as Mark Leibovich wrote for the *Washington Post* (23 Dec. 1999). The red Ferrari Fong had won was put on display in the lobby of the company's California headquarters. In 2001, the Internet company Ziff Davis Inc. acquired Gamers.com.

That same year, Fong and his brother Lyle founded Lithium Technologies, which specializes in an area known as Customer Relationship Management (CRM). Lithium builds online forums, blogs, and other such social applications that allow consumers to interact with brands. Among Lithium's many clients are such major companies as Sony, AT&T, Sephora, Lenovo, and Home Depot.

In 2003, Fong founded Xfire, a service that facilitated the sharing of game screen shots and videos and allowed for the live streaming of game play. The company, which had attracted almost 20 million users, was acquired by Viacom for a reported $102 million in 2008.

Fong currently heads Raptr, a company he founded after Viacom purchased Xfire. Raptr software streamlines the software used by computer gamers and helps gamers build their own user networks. In addition, Fong has written extensively about gaming and game strategy. For several years, he penned a popular column for *PC Gamer* magazine. He is also the coauthor of *Official Quake II: Strategies & Secrets* (1997), among other such guides.

GAMING: WHERE ANYTHING IS POSSIBLE

"According to PricewaterhouseCoopers (PwC), a consulting firm, the global video-game market was worth around $56 billion [in 2010]," Tim Cross wrote for the *Economist* (10 Dec. 2011). "That is more than twice the size of the recorded-music industry, nearly a quarter more than the magazine business and about three-fifths the size of the film industry." Cross also wrote that video game sales are expected to surpass $80 billion annually by 2015. There are now several companies running regular gaming events. Among the largest operations in the United States is Major League Gaming (MLG), which organizes competitions for a wide array of newer games, including StarCraft 2, Halo: Reach, and Call of Duty: Black Ops. The events attract thousands of spectators. Top players can easily earn six-figure annual incomes. The terms *electronic sports* and *e-sports* are now regularly applied to gaming. "Some critics are bothered by the absence of physical exertion, but that never held back chess," asserted Cross.

Fong believes that much of the popularity of video games stems from its inclusiveness. He sometimes tells interviewers about a friend who was in a motorcycle accident that left him paralyzed. Despite his disability, he remained an avid gamer. "There are no gender barriers, no physical limitations," he told Benjamin King for *Asian-Week* (3 Apr. 2002). "It doesn't matter if you're two feet tall or six feet tall. And there are no geographic barriers—you can play against someone across the world. The fact that my friend can be one of the top gamers in the world and be a paraplegic, that is the epitome of what gaming can be."

SUGGESTED READING

King, Benjamin. "The Gaming Revolution." *AsianWeek*. 03 Apr. 2002: 17.
Leibovich, Mark. "King of the Gamers." *Washington Post*. 23 Dec. 1999: A01.

Pereira, Joseph. "Cyberstar: Cyber Celebrity Teen's Game Skills Bring Fame, Endorsement." *Wall Street Journal*. 27 Aug. 1996: B01.

Zito, Kelly. "Caught Up In the Web." *San Francisco Chronicle*. 15 Dec. 1999: C01.

—*Mari Rich*

Kinky Friedman

Born: November 1 (some sources say October 31), 1944

Occupation: Musician, author, politician, social commentator

As a musician, author, politician, and social commentator, Richard "Kinky" Friedman wears many hats—including the signature Stetson that has made him a Texas icon. Friedman, who bills himself as a Jewish cowboy, has a taste for satire; he first gained notice as a country singer with his cheekily named band, Kinky Friedman and the Texas Jewboys, and later became a best-selling crime novelist in the 1980s, publishing over 19 mystery novels featuring himself as the lead detective. These endeavors have made him both the favorite songwriter of Bob Dylan (with whom Friedman toured in the 1970s) and the preferred novelist of former President Bill Clinton. Irreverent in attitude, he has been compared to the writer Mark Twain. In interviews he is always ready with a clever quip, and his songs bear titles like "They Ain't Makin' Jews Like Jesus Anymore" and "Get Your Biscuits in the Ovens and Your Buns in My Bed."

Not everyone sees the humor in Friedman's profane and often controversial style, however. A Jewish record producer refused to sign him, and Friedman's parents were none too pleased with his band's name, a spoof of the Depression-era country band Bob Willis and His Texas Playboys. His song "Get Your Biscuits in the Ovens and Your Buns in My Bed," enraged feminists and earned Friedman the "Male Chauvinist Pig of the Year Award" from the National Organization for Women in 1974, though the song was written as a send-up of the behavior of which he was being accused. Despite his critics, Friedman has a surprisingly wide fan base, and behind his outrageous titles, many of Friedman's songs strike a poignant note. For instance, "Ride 'Em Jewboy"—one of Friedman's most famous tunes—is a haunting meditation on the Holocaust. Sheldon Teitelbaum for the *Los Angeles Times* (October 15, 1989) wrote: "Friedman still meets Orthodox rabbis, Jewish Defense League alumni and American-born Israeli Army vets who say 'Ride 'Em Jewboy' became a personal anthem akin, in some respects, to the civil rights movement's 'We Shall Overcome.'" Still,

Courtesy of Brian Harkin/Getty Images

Friedman told Teitelbaum of his time with the Jewboys, "Many people could never get past the title of the song or, for that matter, the name of the band. It got a lot of people's backs up." Friedman maintains the band's legitimacy. "I wouldn't see us as a novelty act," he told a reporter for the *Grand Rapids (Michigan) Press* (January 30, 2005). "I would see us more as a combination of Lenny Bruce and Hank Williams. But it's all in the eyes of the beerholder."

Other songs in Friedman's repertoire—the band broke up in 1976, but he continued to write and perform solo—are overtly political. "We Reserve the Right to Refuse Service to You," released on the 1973 album *Sold American*, ridiculed racism, and the aforementioned "They Ain't Makin' Jews Like Jesus Anymore," satirized organized religion. In the 1980s, Friedman decided to enter Texas politics. In 1986, he ran for justice of the peace in his hometown of Kerrville, and in 2006, he ran for governor, pulling 12.6 percent of the vote, with the campaign slogans like "Why the Hell Not?" and "How Hard Can It Be?" While Friedman's political campaigns have been unsuccessful, Friedman remains popular for his particular brand of social commentary. He continues to talk about the death penalty, political corruption, and animal cruelty, to name a few issues, but swore off politics after running for agricultural commissioner in 2010. (He had announced his bid—as a Democrat—for governor in the 2010 election, but withdrew.) "It's finally dawned on me that it's a far better thing to be a musician than it is to be a politician," he told Daniel Taub for *Bloomberg News* (June 28, 2010, online). "If you've ever been in a room with a bunch of musicians, they're decent people. And you can't say that about politicians."

EARLY LIFE AND EDUCATION

Friedman was born Richard S. Friedman on October 31, 1944, in Chicago, Illinois, to Jewish parents. Of his birthplace, Friedman quipped to Adam Garfinkle for the *American Interest Magazine* (Summer 2006, online), "I lived there six months, and I couldn't find work—so I came down here to Texas." His father, Dr. Thomas Friedman, was a professor of educational psychology at the University of Texas, Austin, after the family moved to the Lone Star State. Friedman's mother, Minnie (Samet) Friedman, was a speech therapist. Friedman has two younger siblings, Roger and Macie. In 1953, his parents founded Echo Hill Ranch, a Jewish summer camp for children ages 7 to 13, near Kerrville in the West Texas Hill Country. The Friedmans ran the camp for over 50 years, and it now belongs to Friedman's brother, Roger.

Friedman spent most of his childhood in Austin and Houston. After his father taught him to play chess, Friedman became a prodigy at the age of seven. He even played against Polish grandmaster Samuel Reshevsky. "[Reshevsky] was playing fifty people at one time, of which I was the youngest," Friedman told Garfinkle. "He beat everybody, but I did better than a lot of the other players, and he told my dad afterwards that he's really got to watch this seven-year-old." One of Friedman's early heroes was singer-songwriter Slim Whitman. Friedman developed a love for country music during his summers at Echo Hill Ranch and wrote his first song, "Make My Coffee Blue," at 13. Talking with Kaye Northcott for *Texas Monthly* (May 1973, online), Friedman recalled performing for campers as a child. "I'd sing them to sleep in the bunkhouse," he said. "It was just like bedding down cattle for the night."

Friedman attended Austin High School, where he formed his first band, Three Rejects. He graduated in 1962 and enrolled in the University of Texas, Austin's Plan II Honors program, a liberal arts curriculum comparable to an Ivy League education. As a freshman, Friedman's friend Nick "Chinga" Chavin gave him the nickname "Kinky" because of his wild curly hair. In college, Friedman formed his second band, King Arthur and the Carrots, which lampooned the surfer sound of the rock duo Jan and Dean. King Arthur and the Carrots were a moderate local success, recording "Schwinn 24" and "Beach Party Boo Boo" in 1966. Friedman also became an activist in college; he spearheaded the protest (and eventual integration) of a local restaurant called The Plantation, and helped change the policy at a local drugstore that refused to accept

checks from blacks. He also tried, though unsuccessfully, to integrate his Jewish fraternity.

Friedman graduated in 1966 and, inspired by the late President John F. Kennedy, decided to join the Peace Corps. Though he trained for a project in Tanzania, Friedman was ultimately deselected; in his book, *What Would Kinky Do?: How to Unscrew a Screwed-Up World* (2008), he writes that the deselection was due to the attitude of "a supercilious, pipe-smoking psychologist who felt that I might not be fully committed to the goals of the Peace Corps because I had a band back in Texas called King Arthur and the Carrots." Friedman was later assigned to an agricultural post in Borneo. As an agricultural extension worker, he wrote in *'Scuse Me While I Whip This Out: Reflections on Country Singers, Presidents and Other Troublemakers* (2004) as quoted by the *Grand Rapids Press*, "my job was to help people who'd been farming successfully for 2,000 years improve their agricultural methods." However, he recalled, monsoons made it impossible to travel upriver, and little work was accomplished. In *'Scuse Me While I Whip This Out*, Friedman claims to have written several of his most popular songs during this time: "The songs I had written while in Borneo, including 'Ride 'Em Jewboy,' 'We Reserve the Right to Refuse Service to You,' and 'They Ain't Makin' Jews Like Jesus Anymore,' had a little something to offend almost everyone." Before heading back to the United States, Friedman visited Israel in 1968, and the following year returned to his family's Texas ranch, Rio Duckworth, located down the road from Echo Hill.

MUSIC CAREER

Friedman and his brother Roger remained at Rio Duckworth through the early 1970s; Roger promoted his brother while Friedman worked on his songs with his new band, Kinky Friedman and the Texas Jewboys. The original Texas Jewboys included Kenneth "Snakebite" Jacobs, Jeff "Little Jewford" Shelby, Billy Swan, Willie "The Singing Chinaman" Fong Young, and Thomas "Wichita" Culpepper. In 1971, Friedman tried unsuccessfully to get a recording deal in Los Angeles. He spent eight quiet months in the city—he performed in public only twice—but managed to impress Chuck Glaser of Nashville's Glaser Brothers recording studio. Glaser invited Friedman to Tennessee, and Friedman, eager to leave the West Coast, accepted. He later wrote the song "Flying Down the Freeway" with the lyrics: "Jettin' outta L.A. really set me free/ Goin' back to nature in my Chrysler car/ Flyin' down the freeway—gonna be a star." The Glaser Brothers, best known for recording John Hartford's hit "Gentle on My Mind," recorded with Friedman in 1972 after he signed with the small folk label, Vanguard Records. Friedman's first album, *Sold American*, was released in 1973; Northcott described the record's "genuine" and "sometimes innovative country-western sound." She added, "The album includes some stellar fiddle-playing by John Hartford, a somber church organ in 'The Top Ten Commandments,' a fine rumbling and whistling effect for 'Silver Eagle Express,' and a manic conversation sequence in 'Highway Café,' featuring Roger Friedman and Tompall Glaser as highway patrolmen describing an accident in which a semi-driver was squashed 'slicker 'en owlsh*t.'"

The album featured some of Friedman's most famous songs, including "Ride 'Em Jewboy," "We Reserve the Right to Refuse Service to You," "Get Your Biscuits in the Ovens and Your Buns in My Bed," and "The Ballad of Charles Whitman," about a former Marine known as the Texas Tower Sniper who killed 16 students on the University of Texas, Austin campus and wounded 32 others in 1966. Michael Andrews of the *Flagpole* (Athens, Georgia, October 11, 2006) later described the song "Sold American," the only Jewboys track to break the top ten on the country western singles chart, as a "wry stab at 1970s Nashville released during an era when purists of the country music hub were deadly serious about their industry connections." The album received popular and critical acclaim, and prompted Kinky Friedman and the Jewboys to release a second record, *Kinky Friedman*, in 1974. Produced by Willie Nelson, the album featured Waylon Jennings, and included the songs "They Ain't Makin' Jews Like Jesus Anymore," and "Wild Man from Borneo." A third and final album, *Lasso from El Paso* (1976), featured guest appearances by Bob Dylan, Ringo Starr, Dr. John, and Eric Clapton.

That year, 1976, marked the height of Friedman's musical career. He performed at Nashville's famed Grand Ole Opry, where he was announced, as quoted by Teitelbaum for the *Jerusalem Report* (September 9, 1993), as "the first full-blooded Jew ever to play the Opry." (The Jewboys were also one of the first bands at the Opry to have a black member.) The band was also invited to join Dylan's Rolling Thunder Revue concert tour with Clapton, Nelson, and Dylan. They traveled with other celebrities of the era, like poet Allen Ginsberg and songwriter Joan Baez. Friedman's friends from that time also included activist Abbie Hoffman, who spent time on Friedman's ranch during his years as a fugitive, and radio host Don Imus.

Thus, Friedman was no stranger to the rock-star lifestyle, and he often tells interviewers, as he did Teitelbaum, "the distance between the limousine and the gutter is a short one." The Texas Jewboys disbanded around 1976, and Friedman later wrote that he had developed an addiction to cocaine. He decided to begin a solo career, and moved to a converted loft on Vandam Street in the Greenwich Village neighborhood of New York City. Friedman made a living as a regular player at the Lone Star Café, a Texas-themed club on the corner of Fifth Avenue and 13th Street, and in 1983 he released an album, *Under the Double Ego*, which included the song "People Who Read People Magazine." Among the artists living in the Village, Friedman expanded his circle of friends to include *National Lampoon* editor Larry "Ratso" Sloman, *Daily News* reporter Mike McGovern, private investigator Steve Rambam, and the Englishmen Pete Myers and Mike Brennan. Collectively referred to as the "Village Irregulars," Friedman would use his friends as characters in his mystery novels.

WRITING CAREER

A longtime fan of the British mystery novelist Agatha Christie, Friedman didn't write his own fiction until he experienced a brush with real crime in 1984. While walking to the store to buy cigars—another Friedman trademark—he saved a woman who was being mugged. Friedman was celebrated in the press as a crime fighter, which in turn inspired him to write mysteries featuring a detective named for that local Greenwich Village hero—Kinky Friedman. The mugging marked the near-end of what Friedman referred to in his book *What Would Kinky Do?* (2008) as his "seven years of bad luck." His music career was past its peak. His close friend, Tom Baker, had died of an overdose a few years earlier in 1982, and Kacey Cohen, his first love, died in an automobile accident. When his mother got sick in 1985, Friedman decided to quit using drugs "cold turkey" and move back to Texas. His mother died soon after that, but, he told R. G. Ratcliffe for the *Houston Chronicle* (September 8, 2006, online), "I like to say it was the Hill Country, the Texas Hill Country that healed me." He has lived in Texas ever since.

Friedman's first novel, written while he was living in New York, was called *Greenwich Killing Time*. Its familiar hero, Kinky Friedman, Wayne Slater wrote for the *Chicago Tribune* (October 9, 1986), is a "cigar-smoking, cappuccino-drinking . . . contemporary private eye with a gift for understatement and wry allusion." The novel was rejected by 17 publishers before it was accepted by William Morrow & Co. in 1986. *Greenwich Killing Time* was well received; the late mystery writer Robert Parker said, according to Teitelbaum, "[Friedman] has a wonderful eye for detail, a good grasp of irony, the same kind of sense of humor I have, and a nice social conscience." Slater described Friedman's prose as "Raymond Chandler meets Talking Heads." In 1987, Friedman published a second novel, *A Case of Lone Star*, in which private investigator Kinky must stop a murderer who thinks he is Hank Williams from killing musicians who perform at the Lone Star Café. Much like the rest of Friedman's canon, *A Case of Lone Star* features the author's real-life friends. "They are flattered to pass into fiction," Friedman told Jim Lewis for United Press International (July 31, 1987, online). He added, "If you get a good plot from a Kinky book, I consider that gravy. Most of my writing is about people, life and death and style, I guess. I write about humor and insight into things I see or think I see. So it's not crucial who places the arsenic into the teacup. I'm writing with the same type of literary epilepsy that I used when I was in Nashville. Only now I'm writing in a little larger casino."

Through the 1980s and 1990s, Friedman wrote at a feverish pace, sometimes publishing two or three books in a year when he began writing nonfiction. His novels include: *When the Cat's Away* (1988); *Frequent Flyer* (1989); *Musical Chairs* (1991); *Elvis, Jesus and Coca-Cola* (1993); *Armadillos and Old Lace* (1994); *God Bless John Wayne* (1995); *The Love Song of J. Edgar Hoover* (1996); *Roadkill* (1997), which features the disappearance of Willie Nelson; *Blast from the Past* (1998); *Spanking Watson* (1999); *The Mile High Club* (2000); *Steppin' on a Rainbow* (2001); *Meanwhile Back at the Ranch* (2002); *Curse of the Missing Puppet Head* (2003); *Kill Two Birds & Get Stoned* (2003); *The Prisoner of Vandam Street* (2004), a spoof of Alfred Hitchcock's *Rear Window*, in which Kinky is bedridden with malaria; *Ten Little New Yorkers* (2005), in which Kinky dies and his obituary is written by former *New York Times* journalist and notorious plagiarist Jayson Blair; and a holiday novel called *The Christmas Pig: A Fable* (2006). Friedman's friend Evan Smith asked Friedman to write a back-page humor column for the magazine *Texas Monthly* in 2000. Friedman continues to write for the magazine, though he briefly left his post in 2006 when he decided to run for governor.

After publishing a book of recipes with Mike McGovern called *Eat, Drink and Be Kinky: A Feast of Wit and Fabulous Recipes for Fans of Kinky Friedman* in 1999—in the introduction, Friedman refers to the book as "a sort of culinary version of James Joyce's *Ulysses*"—Friedman published *Kinky Friedman's Guide to Texas Etiquette: Or How to Get to Heaven or Hell Without Going Through Dallas-Fort Worth* (2003), made up in part of writing that had appeared in *Rolling Stone* and *High Times*. The book celebrates everything Texas, solidifying Friedman's status as a state icon. In 2004, Friedman published a book of satirical portraits called *'Scuse Me While I Whip This Out: Reflections on Country Singers, Presidents and Other Troublemakers*. The book was followed by the Texas travelogue *The Great Psychedelic Armadillo Picnic: A "Walk" in Austin* (2004); *Texas Hold 'Em: How I Was Born in a Manger, Died in the Saddle, and Came Back as a Horny Toad* (2005); and *Cowboy Logic: The Wit and Wisdom of Kinky Friedman (And Some of His*

Friends) (2006), a book of one-liners ("I support gay marriage. I think they have every right to be just as miserable as the rest of us.") published during his gubernatorial campaign. *You Can Lead a Politician to Water, But You Can't Make Him Think: Ten Commandments for Texas Politics* was released in 2007, followed by the more autobiographical books *What Would Kinky Do?: How to Unscrew a Screwed-Up World* (2008) and *Heroes of a Texas Childhood* (2009), as well as *Kinky's Celebrity Pet Files* (2009), which profiled pets belonging to everyone from Johnny Cash and Brian Wilson to Phyllis Diller, Joseph Heller, and Bill Clinton.

POLITICAL CAMPAIGNS AND RECENT WORK

In 1986, Friedman ran unsuccessfully for justice of the peace of Kerrville. His two campaign slogans were: "I'll Keep Us out of War with Fredericksburg," referring to a neighboring city, and "I'd Be a Fine Judge if I'm Any Judge at All." The small race attracted national media attention. "Kinky won the election in New York, Chicago, Houston, Dallas, San Francisco and Los Angeles," his late father told Slater, "He just didn't win Kerr County." In 2006, Friedman ran as an independent for governor of Texas. He declared his candidacy at the Alamo in February 2005, and the announcement was broadcast on Don Imus's morning radio show. Fellow candidates and the media refused to take him seriously, and he was dismayed when they chastised him for his offensive song lyrics. "That's called social commentary, that's called satire," a frustrated Friedman told Janet Elliott for the *Houston Chronicle* (October 25, 2006, online). "I didn't expect the media to be so low," he added. "I thought they would go after the guy who's really stuffing money in his pants. That's (Governor Rick) Perry." Friedman hired Dean Barkley—the man who managed professional wrestler Jesse Ventura's successful 1998 gubernatorial campaign in Minnesota—as his campaign manager, but Barkley's savvy wasn't enough for Friedman to win the race. Despite Friedman's popularity with Texans, Perry was reelected, though Friedman garnered a respectable 12.6 percent of the vote, placing him fourth in the six-candidate race.

He was more successful in his 2010 run for agricultural commissioner (with the slogan "No Cow Left Behind"), in which he garnered 48 percent of the vote, but he later regretted the run. He has since given up politics in favor of writing and a return to music. In recent years, Friedman has released several albums, including, *From One Good American to Another* (1995); *Classic Snatches from Europe* (2003); *Mayhem Aforethought* (2005); *They Ain't Making Jews Like Jesus Anymore* (2005); *The Last of the Jewish Cowboys: The Best of Kinky Friedman* (2006); and *Live from Austin TX* (2007). In 2006, a tribute album called *Why the Hell Not* was released to benefit Friedman's political campaign; the album featured country singers Willie Nelson, Lyle Lovett, Dwight Yoakam, and others singing Friedman's songs. A similar tribute, *Pearls in the Snow: The Songs of Kinky Friedman*, was released in 1998. A documentary about Friedman's life, *Kinky Friedman: Proud to Be an A**hole from El Paso*, was released in 2001; the title is taken from one of Friedman's songs, a spoof of the Merle Haggard song "Okie from Muskogee."

In addition to his books and music, Friedman owns Kinky Friedman Cigars and hawks several food products, including olive oil marketed with his Palestinian hairdresser, Farouk Shami. Proceeds from the sale of Farouk & Friedman's Oil from the Holy Land benefit children in Israel and Palestine. Friedman also holds the distinction of having been invited to the White House by both President Bill Clinton and President George W. Bush. Former First Lady Laura Bush and Friedman were childhood friends.

When not on tour, Friedman lives down the street from Echo Hill Ranch, where he maintains Utopia Animal Rescue Ranch for homeless animals and enjoys playing chess with longtime friend Willie Nelson. Friedman, who has never been married, lives alone with his two dogs, Brownie and Chumley, whom he calls the Friedmans. He continues to write about politics and at the end of 2011 was working on a book with actor Billy Bob Thornton.

SUGGESTED READING

Andrews, Michael. "Reissues: New Then, New Again." *Flagpole* [Athens, Georgia] 11 Oct. 2006: 34. Print.

Elliott, Janet. "Governor's Race; Friedman Feels Sting of Political Attacks; He Contends His Track Record of Compassion Is Lost amid Debate about His Satirical Past." *Houston Chronicle* 25 Oct. 2006: A1. Print.

Garfinkle, Adam. "A Conversation with Kinky Friedman." *American Interest*. American Interest, Summer 2006. Web. 23 Dec. 2011.

Ratcliffe, R. G. "Friedman Has Personal Insight into Drug Problems; Candidate Admits He Was on Cocaine as a Musician." *Houston Chronicle* 8 Sep. 2006: B3. Print.

Schleier, Curt. "Read Kinky Friedman with a Heap of Salt; Country-Western Mystery Writer/Political Essayist Is a Mine of Irreverent Humor." *Grand Rapids Press*. 30 Jan. 2005: J8. Print.

Taub, Daniel. "Kinky Friedman, Texas Troubadour, Boots Politics for Music Tour." *Bloomberg*. Bloomberg, 28 June 2010. Web. 23 Dec. 2011.

SELECTED FICTION

Greenwich Killing Time, 1986; *A Case of Lone Star*, 1987; *The Mile High Club*, 2000; *Ten Little New Yorkers*, 2004; *The Prisoner of Vandam Street*, 2004; *The Christmas Pig: A Fable*, 2006

SELECTED NONFICTION

Eat, Drink and Be Kinky, 1999; *Kinky Friedman's Guide to Texas Etiquette*, 2003; *'Scuse Me While I Whip This Out*, 2004; *Cowboy Logic*, 2006; *You Can Lead a Politician to Water, But You Can't Make Him Think*, 2007; *What Would Kinky Do?*, 2008; *Kinky's Celebrity Pet Files*, 2009

SELECTED RECORDINGS

Sold American, 1973; *Kinky Friedman*, 1974; *Lasso from El Paso*, 1976; *Under the Double Ego*, 1983; *The Last of the Jewish Cowboys: The Best of Kinky Friedman*, 2006; *Live from Austin TX*, 2007

—Molly Hagan

Roland Fryer

Born: June 4, 1977
Occupation: Economist, educator

The economist Roland Fryer takes a multidisciplinary approach in seeking out answers to tough questions concerning the relationship between race and socioeconomic conditions. Fryer's work looks at the connection between poverty and low-quality education. Since 2003, when he was awarded a three-year fellowship at Harvard University, he has been writing papers on such topics as the racial achievement gap, the causes and consequences of distinctively black names, affirmative action, historically black colleges and universities, and a sociological phenomenon known as "acting white." He has worked with public schools in New York, Chicago, Boston, Dallas, Houston, Washington, DC, and other cities, incorporating experimental methods in the search for effective motivating factors. Fryer prides himself on putting facts and data first and works to avoid preconceived notions of what the solution to a problem should be. His research on black names was featured in a chapter of the best seller *Freakonomics: A Rogue Economist Explores the Hidden Side of Everything* (2005), by Steven D. Levitt and Stephen J. Dubner.

Fryer began teaching at Harvard University in 2006 and became one of the school's youngest tenured professors in 2008. His research and experiments have received recognition by a variety of media outlets and foundations. *Esquire* magazine profiled his work in its December 2005 "Best and Brightest" issue. *The Economist* named Fryer one of the eight top young economists in the world in December 2008. The

Courtesy the John D. & Catherine T. MacArthur Foundation

up going to prison. This did not deter Fryer from getting into criminal activity himself. By the following year, in his hometown of Lewisville, he was dealing marijuana and carrying a handgun. Around this time his father lost his job and began to gamble and drink heavily. Later Fryer had to bail his father out of jail after his arrest on rape charges. Everything appeared to be going downhill.

At the age of fifteen Fryer had an encounter with the police that would change his life. The police pulled him over after mistaking him for a crack-cocaine dealer. According to Dubner's profile, the officers drew their guns and made Fryer lie down on the ground. They then took him to the police station and interrogated him for several hours. After he was let go, Fryer got a call from some friends who wanted to pull a burglary that very night. Fryer said he would not be joining them. This turned out to be a very good decision because they all ended up being arrested and going to jail. Fryer's encounter with the police and with his friends going to jail led him to reconsider the direction of his life. He decided that he did not want to go to prison or end up dead because of drug dealing or other criminal activity.

After graduating from Lewisville High School, Fryer enrolled in the University of Texas at Arlington. His football and basketball skills earned him an athletic scholarship. In college, for the first time in his life, Fryer began to take his education very seriously. He served as vice president of the Philosophy Club and was a member of the Honor Student Advisory Council. In 1998, just two-and-a-half years after enrolling, he graduated with a bachelor of arts degree in economics. Fryer went on to attend graduate school at Pennsylvania State University in University Park, Pennsylvania. There Fryer realized that his work in math and economics could help him to understand the relationship between race and inequality. His doctoral dissertation was titled "Mathematical Models of Discrimination and Inequality." Fryer received his PhD in 2002. From 2001 to 2003 he served as a doctoral fellow at the American Bar Foundation.

following year *Time* magazine included Fryer on its list of the world's most influential people. In 2011 he received a $500,000 MacArthur Fellowship, commonly referred to as the MacArthur Genius Grant. Fryer is the director and founder of the Education Innovation Laboratory at Harvard University and a research associate at the National Bureau of Economic Research.

EARLY LIFE AND EDUCATION

Roland Gerhard Fryer Jr. was born on June 4, 1977, in Daytona Beach, Florida. Around 1980, his mother, Rita, left him in the care of his father, Roland. The following year Fryer and his father moved to Lewisville, Texas, not far from Dallas. Fryer was raised in Lewisville, where his father found work as a copier salesperson. Fryer spent his summers with his grandmother Farrise in Daytona Beach. Farrise's sister Ernestine and her husband, Lacey, also lived in the area, and Fryer often spent time at their house. "Lacey and Ernestine and some of their children were running one of the biggest crack gangs in the area," wrote *Freakonomics* coauthor Stephen J. Dubner in a profile of Fryer for the *New York Times Magazine* (20 Mar. 2005). "They would drive down to Miami to buy cocaine and then turn it into crack in their kitchen. As a boy, Fryer used to watch. . . . The family processed and sold as much as two kilograms of cocaine a week."

One day, when Fryer was twelve, he arrived at Ernestine and Lacey's house and saw them arrested by federal agents on drug charges. Two of his cousins were also arrested. All four ended

RELATING RACE AND ECONOMICS

In 2003, at the age of twenty-five, Fryer accepted an offer from Harvard University to join its Society of Fellows for three years. That fellowship, a very prestigious position, gave Fryer the freedom to research and write without any teaching obligations. During his time as a junior fellow, he developed a reputation both within his field and beyond as one of the youngest, brightest, most daring economists in the nation. In 2005 the well-known Harvard University labor economist Lawrence Katz, speaking of Fryer, said, "[A]s a pure technical economic theorist, he's of the first rate. But what's really incredible is that he's also much more of a broad social theorist—talking to psychologists, sociologists, behavioral geneticists—and the ideas he comes up with aren't the 'let's take the standard economic model and push a little harder' ideas."

Fryer's approach was to ask hard questions about race and inequality. He wanted the data to speak for itself. The jumping-off point for his research was what he deemed the plight of black Americans, who, on average, are still behind whites in standardized testing scores, life expectancy, income, and various other socioeconomic factors. Fryer sought to find out why this is the case and what can be done about it. He was looking for not only the diagnosis but also the cure.

During his Harvard fellowship Fryer authored and coauthored many notable papers. He wrote some of his first with the prominent economist Steven D. Levitt, the recipient of the John Bates Clark Medal, which is awarded every two years to the best American economist under the age of forty. Their first paper, "Understanding the Black–White Test Score Gap in the First Two Years of School," which appeared in the May 2004 issue of the *Review of Economics and Statistics*, argued that the reason that test scores of black American first and second graders are lower is because they attend worse schools. The authors cited the fact that black children of that age do better in private schools than in poor-quality public ones. Levitt and Fryer's third paper, "The Causes and Consequences of Distinctly Black Names," which appeared in the *Quarterly Journal of Economics* in August 2004, analyzed whether having a "distinctly black" first name, such as Shanice (for a female) or DeShawn (for a male), could have negative social or economic consequences. Prior to his analysis of a vast amount of data, Fryer wanted to know whether the relationship between having a distinctly black name and being poor was correlative or causal. The authors used data on all California births from 1961 to 2000 and noticed that starting in the early 1970s the gap in naming practices began to grow. For example, in California between 1989 and 2000, out of 277 girls named Shanice, 274 were black and, likewise, out of 457 boys named Tyrone, 445 were black. The authors found that distinctly black names were often chosen by poor, unmarried, uneducated mothers living in zip codes with a low per-capita income level. The name itself, the authors concluded, was not the cause but the outcome of economic disparities. That is, a child's name makes relatively little difference compared to the difference made by his parents' level of education and income. The following year this study was prominently featured in a book written by Levitt and Dubner entitled *Freakonomics: A Rogue Economist Explores the Hidden Side of Everything* (2005). The popularity of *Freakonomics*, which became a best seller, made Fryer's name known to a general reading audience and the mainstream media. When the book came out in May 2005, Fryer was twenty-seven years old.

POPULARITY AND PERFORMANCE

In the same month that *Freakonomics* came out, Fryer coauthored yet another eye-catching article, "An Economic Analysis of 'Acting White,'" which appeared in the *Quarterly Journal of Economics*. In the 1980s, sociologists theorized that some black high school students dismissed (and hence avoided) certain academic behaviors, such as getting good grades or taking advanced-placement courses, because they would be perceived as "acting white." Although the idea had been around for about two decades, the evidence was largely anecdotal—no one had done a large, statistically rigorous study of the theory. This is what Fryer set out to do. He took a sample of more than ninety thousand students in grades seven through twelve. The study asked them to list their friends and rank their popularity.

Instead of accepting a student's self-ranked level of popularity, Fryer counted two students as friends only if they both listed one another as such. He rated students with less-popular friends as generally less popular than someone with more-popular friends, even if there were slightly fewer of them. Fryer then compared the student's popularity ranking with their grade-point average (GPA). He found that for white students, having good grades, even a 4.0 GPA, did not result in them having fewer friends. In fact it often resulted in them having more friends. However, black students whose GPA was higher than 3.5 declined in popularity (had fewer friends and/or less-popular friends). For Hispanic students this pattern of decline started around a 2.5 GPA. Additionally Fryer found that black students in private schools or predominantly black schools did not generally lose popularity if they had high grades. Thus he concluded the stigma of acting white was mostly a problem for black students attending integrated schools. The study was discussed widely in the media including by the *New York Times*, the *Washington Post*, and National Public Radio. Fryer's studies and ideas continued to generate attention and controversy.

EDUCATION REFORM

In light of his growing popularity and unique ability to attract the attention of funders and public officials, Fryer decided to put some of his ideas to practice. He ran an experiment on third graders in the Bronx to see if their grades would improve by the promise of a reward, such as a pizza party. The data turned out to be inconclusive, but Fryer decided to expand the scope of the experiment to offer cash instead of prizes. Fryer's thinking, which he has stated many times in interviews, went as follows: Giving poor students a small cash incentive for getting good grades is not very different from the practice some parents have of giving their children a certain allowance for good academic performance. This got the attention of both New York City mayor Michael Bloomberg and the city's schools chancellor Joel I. Klein. In 2007, Mayor Bloomberg appointed Fryer the chief equality officer of the New York City Department of Education, a part-time position. Beginning with the 2007–08 academic year, forty mostly minority New York City public schools in Manhattan, Brooklyn, and the Bronx took part in a program designed by Fryer. Fourth-grade students took ten standardized tests throughout the year and could receive as much as twenty-five dollars for a perfect score and five dollars just for taking the test. Seventh-grade students could earn up to fifty dollars for a perfect score and ten dollars just for taking the test.

Late in 2007 Fryer left his post as chief equality officer, becoming the founder and CEO of the Educational Innovation Laboratory at Harvard, which focuses on education research. Fourteen public middle and elementary schools in Washington, DC, started a version of the cash incentives program, which offered small cash rewards for completing homework, getting good grades, good behavior, and good attendance. Although some were critical of the cash incentive strategy, Fryer argued that many families, if they have the means, partake in this practice privately. In 2010 the results were out; Fryer's experiment with cash incentives for academic performance was unsuccessful. Compared to control schools (where students did not receive cash incentives), the schools that paid students did not improve in performance. However, according to the *Economist*, there was a lesson learned nonetheless: "If students do not know how to improve their own performance, the best strategy may be to pick a simple task, reward pupils for doing it, and hope that this translates into higher grades. This was the approach Fryer took in Dallas, where second-grade students were simply given two dollars for every book they read if they passed a computerized comprehension test on it. Predictably this spurred them to read more books and improved their vocabularies. But it also improved their school grades substantially, although this is not what they were paid for."

Beginning in the fall of 2010, Fryer and public school officials in Houston, Texas, launched a three-year program, Apollo 20, which applied the principles of charter schools (publically financed, independently operated schools) to some Houston public schools. The five principles include extensive tutoring, high expectations, selective hiring of teachers and principals, longer school days and academic years, and frequent testing. Although some of the public schools in the Apollo 20 program have not seen improvements, some have seen substantial improvements. Fryer has been studying the data from both.

SUGGESTED READING

Chesler, Caren. "No Hesitations." *America* 16 July 2007: n. pag. Print.

Cook, Gareth. "Education's Coconut Cake Problem." *Boston Globe*. New York Times, 18 Dec. 2011. Web. 7 Feb. 2012.

Dubner, Stephen J. "Toward a Unified Theory of Black America." *New York Times Magazine* 20 Mar. 2005: 54. Print.

Tierney, John. "Computing the Cost of 'Acting White.'" *New York Times*. New York Times, 19 Nov. 2005. Web. 7 Feb. 2012.

—*Dmitry Kiper*

Jeanne Gang

Born: 1964
Occupation: Architect, educator

Jeanne Gang is the principal architect behind the award-winning Studio Gang, the architecture firm she founded in 1997. She is perhaps most famous for designing the high-rise Aqua Tower, so named for its undulating appearance, in her hometown of Chicago. The eighty-two-story building, the tallest building in the world designed by a woman, emphasizes Gang's passion for economy, sustainability, and utility. "Her building is most compelling as an example of architecture that is practical and affordable enough to please real-estate developers and stirring enough to please critics," Paul Goldberger wrote for the *New Yorker* (1 Feb. 2010). "Not many buildings like that get made at any height, or by architects of either gender."

Due to the influence of her grandmother, a seamstress and quilter, Gang is fascinated by patterns, construction, and how different materials fit together. Her passion has manifested itself in nearly all of her projects, including Aqua Tower, which required eighty-two separate floor plans to achieve its dancing façade, as well as Gang's early work Marble Curtain, which features interlocking puzzle pieces made of wafer-thin, translucent marble. Studio Gang's website touts the firm as "a collective of architects, designers, and thinkers," which speaks to Gang's holistic approach to construction. She and her small team are creative problem solvers who seek to apply their love of design to problems both local, such as wind patterns and bird migration, and global, such as sustainability and energy efficiency.

Gang's work has been honored and exhibited in many locations, including the International

Courtesy the John D. & Catherine T. MacArthur Foundation

Venice Biennale, the Modern Museum of Art (MoMA), the National Building Museum, and the Art Institute of Chicago. Since 1998, Gang has been an adjunct professor at the Illinois Institute of Technology (IIT), focusing on megacities and material technologies. In 2004, she was a visiting professor at her alma mater, Harvard's Graduate School of Design, and in 2005, she was the Louis I. Kahn Visiting Professor at the Yale School of Architecture. In 2007, she was a visiting lecturer at the Princeton University School of Architecture.

Gang received the coveted MacArthur Fellowship from the John D. and Catherine T. MacArthur Foundation in 2011. Known as the "genius" grant, the MacArthur is given each year to visionaries working in a variety of disciplines and comes with a $500,000 no-strings-attached stipend to be awarded over the course of five years. Gang also won an Academy Award in Architecture from the Academy of Arts and Letters in 2006 and was named a fellow of the American Institute of Architects (AIA) in 2009.

EARLY LIFE AND EDUCATION

Jeanne Gang was born in 1964 and grew up in Belvidere, Illinois. She was the third of four sisters and a self-described tomboy. Gang picked up the interests of her father, a civil engineer for Boone County. Her mother was a librarian and a seamstress.

Gang's childhood vacations influenced her work. With her father, she traveled across the country to see man-made structures like the Hoover Dam and the Golden Gate Bridge, as well as ancient wonders such as Mesa Verde in Colorado, where Pueblo Indians built dwellings into the canyon walls. The experience of the latter, Gang told Lynn Becker for her blog *Repeat* (21 Sep. 2011), left a lasting impression. "You don't even see that it's there," she said of the canyon. "You come over this top of the mesa and it reveals itself—the total integration of the landscape and this dwelling."

A love of animals almost led Gang to veterinary school, but physics and engineering were ultimately a bigger draw. She attended the University of Illinois Urbana–Champaign, and in 1984, she participated in the school's Versailles study-abroad program. While touring the cathedrals of Europe, Gang realized that in architecture, she could combine her love of fine art with her love of mathematics. She was captivated by the spatial aspects of Gothic architecture in cathedrals like Notre Dame and Chartres. After that, she told Becker of her chosen career path, "there was no going back."

Gang graduated from the University of Illinois in 1986. She received a Rotary Foundation Ambassadorial Scholarship and traveled to Zurich, Switzerland, to attend the prestigious Swiss Federal University of Technical Studies. She described the program to Becker as both "material-based and construction-based," much like IIT. While in Zurich, Gang was accepted into the Harvard University Graduate School of Design. At Harvard, Gang worked with Persian architect Homa Farjadi, with whom she studied feminist and identity theories and how they relate to architecture. She has cited Farjadi as an important influence on her work.

Gang's biggest influence, however, is Dutch architect and theorist Rem Koolhaas, who teaches at Harvard. Though Gang never had him as an instructor, she hoped to work with him and his firm, the Office of Metropolitan Architecture (OMA) in Rotterdam, upon her graduation in 1993. It took some maneuvering, but Gang finally landed an interview with Koolhaas. He was impressed by her thesis—a park with a parking area that uses water to filter river water—and assigned her to work on a project for a railroad station in the Hague. The project never came to fruition, and Gang was moved to two projects in France: a convention center called the Grand Palais in Lille and a private home for a newspaper publisher in Bordeaux.

The latter project took an unexpected turn when the publisher was paralyzed in an automobile accident. Despite his injury, he did not want his house to be one level, so Koolhaas designed the center room of the house as a giant elevator. The massive project was not completed until 1998, after Gang and her partner, Mark Schendel, were already working back in the United States. Though OMA was grueling, with employees often working eighty-hour weeks, Gang admired Koolhaas for his obsession with function and the types of buildings that are central to modern life, such as hotels and shopping malls. Referring to these types of structures, Gang told Becker, "There's so much building that goes on that no architect is involved with. [Koolhaas] was interested in getting that back."

Gang and Schendel's first project outside of OMA was for Rotterdam's Kunstpark in 1994. The two worked with artists Joep van Lieshout and Klaar van der Lippe to repurpose old shipping containers, which they used to create spaces to serve drinks and store rollerblades in the park. The project had a miniscule budget of $20,000, but Gang and Schendel were able to give their clients much more than they bargained for: the containers could be kept open all through the summer months, and during the winter, they could be closed up and stored away.

After two years with OMA, Gang returned to Chicago to work with the firm Booth Hansen and Associates. There, she worked on a project for Moraine Valley Community College in Palos Hills and a private home in Telluride.

STUDIO GANG

In 1997, Gang founded the Chicago-based Studio Gang/O'Donnell with partner Kathy O'Donnell, whom she met through Booth Hansen. The two women had both started out working on their own but decided to team up to take on bigger projects. Studio Gang/O'Donnell landed what would become Gang's breakthrough commission: the Bengt Sjostrom Starlight Theatre at Rock Valley College in Rockford, Illinois, an outdoor community theater. Director Mike Webb hoped to improve the size and function of the space while finding a way to shield his audience from the elements. The theater had a budget of $8.5 million, so Gang proposed implementing the renovations in three parts.

In 2001, around the time that Gang and O'Donnell went their separate ways, Gang and her team expanded the theater from 600 to 1,050 seats. They built a concrete structure at the back of the house for restrooms and a ticket booth, and the outside of the structure features a constellation of portholes that can be lit from the inside like a marquee. The first phase of Gang's plan also included an outdoor plaza in which patrons could gather. In 2002, Gang improved the function of the theater by expanding the fly space and installing translucent, weatherproof sliding doors in lieu of curtains. The sliding doors, adapted from airplane hangars, create an indoor space that can be used for rehearsals.

But it was the third and final phase of the project, completed in 2003, that made the Starlight Theatre one of Studio Gang's crowning achievements. Gang designed a retractable roof that opens, she told Becker, "like a helix," or, as it has been described by viewers, like an origami flower. In good weather, six petal-shaped stainless-steel panels with Douglas fir inlays open in sequence. With a direct connection to an Internet weather service, these panels automatically close in response to the threat of rain or high winds. The roof is visually breathtaking, economical (each panel was built off-site to cut scaffolding costs), and, perhaps most remarkably, silent; Gang was adamant that the roof's electric motors be completely hidden.

Gang's design for the Starlight Theatre won a host of awards, including the 2003 Award of Honor from the Society of American Registered Architects (SARA), the 2003 Gold Medal/President's Award from the Association of Licensed Architects (ALA), the 2004 Scholarship Prize/ Best Overall Design Award from the Metal Construction Association (MCA), the 2004 Honor Award for Distinguished Building from the Chicago chapter of the AIA, and the 2005 Merit Award from the United States Institute for Theatre Technology (USITT). Pulitzer Prize–winning architecture critic Blair Kamin for the *Architectural Record* (Oct. 2003) called it "powerfully sculptural" and "almost otherworldly."

In 2003, Gang completed a project she called the Marble Curtain for display in an exhibit called *Masonry Variations*, cosponsored by the International Masonry Institute, at the National Building Museum in Washington, DC. The free-standing cylindrical "curtain," assembled from 622 interlocking slices of marble and weighing 1,600 pounds, married Gang's love for patterns with her love for material construction. She fit the pieces together using regular glue. "As an architect, I've always been interested in finding out what a material can do: what is it good at, but also what are some of the unexpected qualities of it that haven't been explored?" Gang told Sara Goldsmith for *Slate Magazine* (16 Aug. 2011). "[You need] experimentation and a willingness to fail—not for someone's final building, obviously, but in the design process. If you have that attitude you always learn something. With the Marble Curtain, we learned more about that material from breaking it—from taking it down into a lab and pulling it apart—than if you just used it as it was always used before." The curtain moves outward and glows from an internal light source, giving it a cascading effect. The Marble Curtain won two awards, the 2004 PRISM Award Grand Prize from the *Architectural Record* and the Marble Institute of America and the 2004 Special Recognition Award for Interior Architecture from AIA Chicago.

Gang completed two very different projects in 2008. The first, which she often cites as her favorite, is the SOS Children's Villages Lavezzorio Community Center, which offers foster care and neighborhood family services in Chicago. Gang created the building using only donated materials; when a brick donation fell through, she changed her design to incorporate several different donations of concrete, building a "strata-wall" that patterns the differently colored mixes in waves. Inside, the building boasts large gathering spaces for classrooms, performances, and meetings. The design won several awards, including the 2008 Best Building Award from the Building Congress of Chicago.

The other project Gang completed in 2008 is a private residence in Chicago's West Town neighborhood. For the Brick Weave House, as it is known, Gang built a patterned, two-story brick "veil" around the front of the house that limits visibility from the outside but allows in sunlight. At night, the veil lights up like lantern.

In 2010, Gang and her studio completed the Nature Boardwalk at Lincoln Park Zoo in Chicago. Like some of her other projects, the site is both functional and educational, integrating the habitats in the pond over which it is built. The curved open-air pavilion, its design inspired by a tortoise's shell, features several bent-wood techniques used in furniture making to achieve a honeycomb-like diamond pattern. This design also won several awards, including the 2011 Best Small Structure Award from the Structural Engineers Association of Illinois. The same year, Gang completed a commission for the Media Production Center at Columbia College Chicago. She applied green solutions to the building's various soundstages and designed its exterior with blocks of colored glass based on the pattern of a television test screen.

For a 2012 exhibit at MoMA called *Foreclosed: Rehousing the American Dream*, Gang developed a proposal called "The Garden in the Machine," in which she suggested transforming the suburb and former factory town of Cicero, Illinois, into a vibrant green community to address the area's rampant unemployment and skyrocketing foreclosure rate. She collaborated with a housing advocate, a landscape designer, a writer, and a financial specialist to envision Cicero's rebirth. Calling the city an "inner-ring suburb" ripe for economic growth, Gang told Hedy Weiss for the *Chicago Sun-Times* (20 Sep. 2011), "Our ideal of urbanism is constantly changing. Architecture can provide the spark of recovery." Of the ambitious Cicero plans, she added, "But my job, even more than building things, is to be one step ahead, and to imagine what might come next."

AQUA TOWER

Gang's best-known and most celebrated project to date is Chicago's Aqua Tower, completed in 2010. The structure won the coveted Emporis Skyscraper Award, awarded annually in recognition of the best new skyscraper, in 2009. Gang had always hoped to build a skyscraper, though she did not expect to receive such a commission so early in her career. Studio Gang landed the project almost entirely by happenstance; at a 2006 dinner following a Frank Gehry architecture lecture in Chicago, Gang was seated next to a real-estate developer and architect named James Loewenberg, who asked her to take a look at preliminary plans for a project he was overseeing called Aqua Tower. He knew of her work and was hoping that she could take the rough design and, according to Jonathan Glancey for the London *Guardian* (21 Oct. 2009), "make it sing." Gang eagerly accepted the challenge.

Gang began with the familiar rectangular shape of a skyscraper and manipulated it according to Aqua Tower's unique environment. She and her team took into account wind patterns, bird flight paths, and even views of local landmarks. As always, Gang wanted the building to be sustainable. The resulting design features concrete balconies climbing up the eighty-two-story building in a swirling pattern, so that the building almost appears to dance. The balconies are not merely cosmetic, however, but grew out of utility and serve several purposes. The rippling effect, for instance, confuses the strong Chicago winds, breaking and weakening them so that each apartment in the residential building can have a balcony—a unique feature in a skyscraper as tall as Aqua Tower. The balconies, each different in shape and offering strategically placed views of the city, also offer solar shading, which reduces the need for ventilation in the summer. The tower also has one of Chicago's largest green roofs. Goldberger praised Aqua Tower for, as he wrote, "reclaim[ing] the notion that thrilling and beautiful form can still emerge out of the realm of the practical."

PERSONAL LIFE

Gang is the author of two books, both published in 2011. The first, called *Reveal: Studio Gang Architects*, is a collection of drawings, sketches, diagrams, and photographs that chronicles the young firm's projects and ideological evolution. The second book, *Reverse Effect: Renewing Chicago's Waterways*, features a design plan to rejuvenate the Chicago River using reclamation and green infrastructure to support and restore natural systems. The plan offers solutions to problems such as the threat of invasive species in the water system from the Great Lakes to the Mississippi River.

Gang married her partner, Mark Schendel, in 1998. The two met while they were both working for Koolhaas in the 1990s, and Schendel joined Studio Gang shortly after its founding in 1997. Gang and Schendel live in Chicago, where they serve as the only two principal architects for the firm.

SUGGESTED READING

Becker, Lynn. "Jeanne Gang: Before Aqua—an Early Portrait." *Repeat: Observations and*

Images on Architecture, Culture and More, in Chicago and the World. Lynn Becker, 21 Sep. 2011. Web. 21 June 2012.

Glancey, Jonathan. "Aqua Tower—the Tower that Jeanne Gang Built." *Guardian.* Guardian News and Media, 20 Oct. 2009. Web. 21 June 2012.

Goldberger, Paul. "Wave Effect: Jeanne Gang and Architecture's Anti-Divas." *New Yorker.* Condé Nast, 1 Feb. 2010. Web. 21 June 2012.

Goldsmith, Sara. "Material Interests: Studio Gang's Most Inventive Projects." *Slate Magazine.* Slate Group, 16 Aug. 2011. Web. 21 June 2012.

Kamin, Blair. "Bengt Sjostrom / Starlight Theatre: Studio/Gang Architects." *Architectural Record.* McGraw-Hill, Oct. 2003. Web. 21 June 2012.

Weiss, Hedy. "'Genius' Grant Winner Plots Rebirth of Cities. Architect Celebrates 'Vote of Confidence.'" *Chicago Sun-Times* 20 Sep. 2011: 5. Print.

SELECTED WORKS
Reveal: Studio Gang Architects, 2011; *Reverse Effect: Renewing Chicago's Waterways,* 2011

—*Molly Hagan*

Michelle Gass

Born: 1968
Occupation: President of Starbucks Europe, Middle East, and Africa

Chair and chief executive officer (CEO) Howard Schultz may be the driving force behind the Seattle-based Starbucks Corporation, the world's largest coffeehouse company, but Michelle Gass is perhaps the coffee juggernaut's greatest asset. During her fifteen years there, Gass has been responsible for orchestrating some of Starbucks's most successful ventures and for leading the company through sweeping changes. Describing her to Jenna Goudreau for *Forbes* (21 Nov. 2011), Schultz called Gass "a courageous leader with a rare combination of business and interpersonal skills," and one of her collaborators, Jack Anderson, CEO of the brand-design agency Hornall Anderson, stated that she is the company's "greatest kept secret."

Gass is a graduate of the Worcester Polytechnic Institute (WPI) and the University of Washington's Michael G. Foster School of Business. She worked with the consumer-goods company Proctor & Gamble before joining Starbucks in 1996 as the marketing manager for the Frappuccino line of blended coffee beverages.

After turning Frappuccino into a $2 billion-plus brand and one of Starbucks's most popular and successful products, Gass served in a variety of leadership positions at the company, during which she helped introduce other innovations to the coffee chain.

In January 2008 Gass was appointed to serve a special assignment in the office of the CEO as senior vice president of global strategy. In that role she served as Schultz's chief strategist and worked with him to create restructuring plans for the company in the wake of dwindling sales caused by the 2008 global financial crisis. After leading Starbucks back to profitability with the launch of such successful new products as Starbucks VIA Ready Brew instant coffee and the implementation of such initiatives as the company's loyalty-rewards program, Gass was assigned by Schultz to overhaul another company-owned brand, Seattle's Best Coffee, in 2009. As president of that company, she was credited with revamping the brand's image and for leading major expansion efforts.

In October 2011 Gass stepped into the role of president of Starbucks Europe, Middle East, and Africa (EMEA), one of four international operations divisions. Her appointment comes as part of Schultz's plans to grow Starbucks's international business. Known for her amicable demeanor, detail-oriented nature, innovative marketing sense, and uncanny understanding of customer needs and wants, Gass explained to Kathryn Skelton for the Lewiston, Maine, *Sun Journal* (28 Nov. 2011), "One of the things

I strive to be is a very approachable leader, a real person. I want everybody to feel very comfortable that they can talk to me about everything."

EARLY LIFE AND EDUCATION

Michelle Gass, born Michelle Petkers in 1968, grew up in Lewiston, Maine. Her parents, Bob and Claire Petkers, raised her with traditional Maine values and taught her the importance of hard work and humility. "The Maine work ethic is still deep inside me," Gass recalled to Skelton. After graduating from Lewiston High School as class valedictorian in 1986, she attended Worcester Polytechnic Institute (WPI) in Worcester, Massachusetts, where she studied chemical engineering.

During her time at WPI, Gass interned at Proctor & Gamble (P&G), a Fortune 500 company based in Cincinnati, Ohio, that specializes in the manufacturing of consumer goods. Her experience working in the research and development group of the company's health-care products group ultimately helped her discover her passion for working with people and her interest in consumer behavior. Gass, who had originally planned on a technical career in research and development, told Eileen McCluskey for *Transformations* (Spring 2005), WPI's quarterly magazine, "I was introduced to the world of the consumer and loved it."

FROM TOOTHPASTE TO COFFEE

After receiving a degree in chemical engineering from WPI in 1990, Gass moved to Cincinnati to accept a full-time position with P&G's health-care products group. She held a variety of roles in marketing and product development over the next six years, during which she observed consumer trends and helped launch several varieties of Crest toothpaste including Baking Soda Crest and Crest for Kids. Gass has said that P&G allowed her to utilize both her analytical and creative skills. "P&G really sparked my curiosity—that there are real people who create real insights around better laundry detergent and toothpaste and products that people interact with every day," she explained in an interview with *Foster Business Magazine* (Fall 2008), the biannual magazine of the University of Washington's Michael G. Foster School of Business. "It took my engineer's analytical bent and problem-solving mind and applied that to the customer. That's where I found my passion. And there was no turning back."

In 1996 Gass left P&G and relocated to Seattle, Washington, after her husband, engineer Scott Gass, received a business opportunity there. That year, Gass returned to school, enrolling at the University of Washington, where she received her MBA in 1999. It was during her first year at the school that she starting working for Starbucks. A classmate who worked at the rapidly growing coffeehouse chain had persuaded Gass to apply for a job there, and in September 1996 she was hired as the marketing manager for the company's line of Frappuccino blended beverages. Commenting on her decision to work for the company, Gass told Kathryn Skelton, "Even though I was in a very safe place at P&G, it felt like there was something else bigger out there calling. And surely there was, little did I know, a coffee company called Starbucks."

FRAPPUCCINO REVAMPED

As marketing manager for Starbucks's Frappuccino line, a position she held until 2001, Gass was charged with developing a growth strategy for the new product. First launched in 1995 in two flavors as part of Starbucks's efforts to expand into nontraditional coffee beverages, the Frappuccino—a creamy, frozen concoction of coffee, milk, and ice—had won instant popularity among customers but had yet to tap into its growth potential. In order to realize that potential, Gass began talking with customers in Starbucks stores to understand why they were buying the drink. In her interview with *Foster Business Magazine*, she said, "The big insight was that people were not just drinking it for the coffee. They were drinking it as an indulgence."

Working with a team of three, Gass overhauled the marketing of the Frappuccino brand to reflect its perception as an indulgent novelty treat. She introduced new flavors such as caramel and made the drink more visually attractive to customers by adding green straws, a domed clear-plastic lid, whipped cream, and caramel-syrup drizzles. Although those changes were initially met with resistance from baristas and top-level executives who were concerned the added accoutrements would hinder operations and service, Gass refused to relaunch the product without all of the modifications. She explained to Kate Macarthur for *Advertising Age* (1 June 2007), "If you don't do it in its full concept, then you can't have it." She added, "I'm a quantitative person, but when it comes to decisions and conviction, I'm more about passion and gut. If you take the easy road all the time, if you go with 'Squirt a little bit of syrup in it,' it might be a hit but won't be a big innovation. If we had not done that, I don't know if we'd have the Frappuccino business we have today."

Gass's instincts proved to pay off in grand fashion. Since Frappuccino's makeover the product has become one of Starbucks's most successful products. The Frappuccino brand, which also includes a line of bottled coffee beverages sold in retail stores and vending machines, brings in more than $2.5 billion in annual sales and makes up nearly a quarter of Starbucks's total annual revenue. Frappuccinos are offered in numerous flavors and versions, from basic coffee, mocha, and caramel, to a wide variety of coffee-free crème and juice blends, including green tea, vanilla bean, and strawberries and cream, among others. In July 2008 the company added a healthier alternative to the Frappuccino family, Vivanno Nourishing Blends smoothies, which include protein powder and real fruit among their ingredients. In May 2010 it launched the However-You-Want-It Frappuccino, which allows customers to create their own drink from thousands of possible combinations.

In addition to developing and expanding the Frappuccino brand, Gass has helped launch numerous other Starbucks products, including seasonal and holiday drinks such as the pumpkin spice latte, Black Apron Exclusives coffees, Tazo tea beverages, Ethos bottled water, and breakfast and lunch sandwiches.

CLIMBING THE CORPORATE LADDER

Gass meanwhile earned a series of promotions, rising from vice president of the company's beverage category in 2001 to senior vice president of its category management division in 2004. In the latter role, which she held for four years, she supervised a 150-person department that was responsible for developing many of the retail offerings at Starbucks. Although some of those were flops, including a chocolate beverage called Chantico launched in 2005 but discontinued just one year later, Gass became known for her willingness to work closely with members of her team to understand the reasons behind such failures.

That kind of urgency led Starbucks Corporation founder, chair, and CEO Howard Schultz to appoint Gass in January 2008 as senior vice president of global strategy. Responsible for much of Starbucks's global expansion, Schultz had returned to the helm that month, replacing Jim Donald, in response to falling stock prices and sales due to a dwindling economy and increased competition. Gass was brought on board to serve as Schultz's chief strategist in a special two-person office of the CEO and began working with him on restructuring plans for the company. "Howard set the agenda, drove the vision," she told *Foster Business Magazine*. "I was there to shape the narrative, bring the entire organization around it. It was an exhilarating challenge." As part of the "Starbucks Transformation Agenda," which was highlighted by seven major initiatives, Gass and Schultz closed nine hundred Starbucks shops worldwide and reduced costs by nearly $600 million. They also launched a new advertising campaign that focused on the quality of Starbucks coffee, and in late February 2008, closed down every shop in the United States for three hours to retrain baristas as part of efforts to recreate an emotional attachment with customers. "We were courageous and disruptive," Gass told Melissa Allison for the *Seattle Times* (22 May 2011). "I felt unleashed, with [Schultz's]

energy and vision and willingness to be courageous. For someone like me who thrives on that, it was like, 'Wow! This is going to be a ride.'"

In July 2008 Gass was named executive vice president of Starbucks's marketing and category division. In that role she was in charge of overseeing the implementation of the company's other transformation initiatives, one of which was the chain's bold move into instant coffee with the launch of Starbucks VIA Ready Brew. Gass organized and led the team that helped develop the product, which underwent months of test marketing before its launch on September 12, 2009. Although the very idea of the company tapping into the instant coffee market caused skepticism, stemming from instant coffee's widespread reputation for tasting bad, Starbucks VIA Ready Brew proved to be a great success and generated $100 million in sales within ten months of its launch.

Many credited Gass, who was responsible for coming up with the more marketable "Ready Brew" name, with playing a vital role in that success. Chris Bruzzo, former online-marketing executive for Starbucks, told Jenna Goudreau, "It was audacious. It got people nervous. But it took someone like Michelle to see the opportunity and then bring an entire organization through the curve of believing." By the end of March 2011, sales of Starbucks VIA Ready Brew had exceeded $200 million. Gass hopes the product will turn into another billion-dollar brand like Frappuccino in the future.

IMPROVING SEATTLE'S BEST COFFEE

After driving other reorganization efforts—including overhauling the company's food menu, launching its loyalty-rewards program, and strengthening its online presence—Gass was called upon by Schultz to lead Seattle's Best Coffee, a chain that had failed to gain much market traction since being acquired by Starbucks in 2003. She recalled to Goudreau, "I was drawn to it. There were no rules here. With a smaller brand in a nascent stage, I had the opportunity to create everything."

As president of Seattle's Best, a role she held from September 2009 to July 2011, Gass helped expand the chain by creating partnerships with fast-food chains such as Burger King and Subway, AMC Theaters, and Delta Airlines, thus increasing its distribution network from three thousand to more than fifty thousand locations in the United States and Canada. Gass developed a new logo and identity for the brand. She also simplified its packaged coffee business with the unveiling of Seattle's Best Coffee Levels System. Introduced in early 2011, the Levels line, which consists of five roasts differentiated by numbers and colors, proved to be a major success; by August of that year, it had experienced a double-digit increase in sales. Seattle's Best meanwhile also experienced double-digit sales growth under Gass, who expects the brand to reach $1 billion in sales in the next several years. She explained to *Seattle Times* reporter Melissa Allison that one of her main goals at Seattle's Best was to "create an emotional connection around fun and optimism and a level of approachability and simplicity," in efforts to help the chain distinguish itself as a separate entity from Starbucks. Commenting on Gass's motivational influence, Chris Bruzzo told Allison, "She gets people to work stronger, harder, to be more committed and have an 'everything matters' mentality."

GOING GLOBAL

In June 2011 Gass was named president of Starbucks's Europe, Middle East, and Africa (EMEA) division, as part of Schultz's reorganization of top-level executives to focus on international growth. She officially stepped into the role in October 2011. As head of Starbucks EMEA, Gass oversees twenty thousand employees and seventeen hundred stores in more than thirty countries where she is responsible for developing the Starbucks brand. The division makes up one of four entities of Starbucks's foreign operations (the others are Asia Pacific, Greater China, and the Americas), which bring in roughly a quarter of Starbucks's $10 billion-plus annual revenue. Starbucks executives plan to double those international revenues. In late 2011 Starbucks had over seventeen thousand stores worldwide, making it the largest coffeehouse chain in the world. Gass told Kathryn Skelton, "No matter where you go, there's a level of awareness and love of this brand. People are waiting for Starbucks to arrive." And, as quoted by Eileen McCluskey, Gass said, "I feel very proud to be associated with Starbucks. If I didn't feel absolutely impassioned about my work, I wouldn't be here."

PERSONAL LIFE

Gass was a recipient of the 2005 Ichabod Washburn Young Alumni Award for Professional Achievement from the Worcester Polytechnic Institute and in 2007 was named among *Advertising Age*'s Women to Watch, a list of thirty rising female marketing executives. She joined the board of directors of the women's clothing company Ann Taylor in 2008.

Gass lives in London with her husband Scott, a full-time homemaker, and their two children, Megan and Will. In her spare time, Gass, who typically wakes up at around 4:30 a.m. and works twelve-hour days, enjoys running and spending time with her family. "Scott and our children are the light of my life," she told McCluskey. "Starbucks has been very supportive of my family life. We're all thriving—my family, the company, it all fits together so well. I really feel this job has been my destiny."

SUGGESTED READING

Adamy, Janet. "At Starbucks, Low-key Vet Plots Course." *Wall Street Journal* 18 Mar. 2008: B1. Print.

Allison, Melissa. "She's Giving Seattle's Best Coffee a Jolt; Starbucks' Michelle Gass." *Seattle Times* 22 May 2011: D1. Print.

Goudreau, Jenna. "Starbucks' Secret Weapon." *Forbes* 21 Nov. 2011: 32. Print.

McCluskey, Eileen. "Life in the Espresso Lane." *Transformations* Spring 2005: n. pag. Print.

"Passion Play." *Foster Business Magazine* Fall 2008: 27. Print.

—*Christopher Cullen*

Leymah Gbowee

Born: February 1, 1972
Occupation: Peace activist

Leymah Gbowee received the 2011 Nobel Peace Prize for her work as a peace activist in Liberia, where two civil wars between 1989 and 2003 resulted in an estimated 250,000 deaths and caused the destruction of the country's infrastructure. The civil wars were rooted in conflicts between opposing tribal groups, backed by either the Liberian army or rebel militias. The tactics of rebel groups and government armies during Liberia's civil war were ruthless. When advancing on a village populated by supporters of an opposing tribe, soldiers indiscriminately tortured, murdered, and raped civilians. Gbowee was seventeen when the first civil war began. After being trained as a trauma counselor and a social worker, she worked with former child soldiers and victims of sexual violence. She became involved in the West Africa Network for Peacebuilding and, in 2001, cofounded the Women in Peacebuilding Network (WIPNET), which helps train and mobilize women to build peace in their communities. As fighting spread across the country for a second time in the late 1990s, Gbowee formed the Women of Liberia Mass Action for Peace, a group of Christian and Muslim women that demonstrated against the war. In the spring of 2003, Women of Liberia held weeks-long protests in Liberia's capital, Monrovia. The demonstrations received global media attention. Gbowee also held demonstrations in Accra, Ghana, during 2003 peace talks between Liberian President Charles Taylor and rebel group leaders. Thanks in part to Gbowee's efforts, the Accra Peace Accord was signed in August 2003. Two years later, Ellen Sirleaf—one of two co-recipients to share the Nobel Peace Prize with Gbowee—was elected president.

Getty Images

EARLY LIFE

Leymah Gbowee was raised with her four sisters—Geneva, Mala, Josephine, and Fata—in Monrovia. Gbowee's mother, a pharmacist, was seventeen years old when she had her first child. Gbowee's father, who was ten years older than her mother, rose through the ranks of Liberia's National Security Agency, becoming its chief radio technician and liaison to the United States. He worked under Liberian president William Tolbert in 1980, when Samuel K. Doe, a military leader and a member of the indigenous Krahn tribe, led an overthrow of the government. Gbowee's father was imprisoned for nine months for his association with Tolbert. Doe's government was the first in the country's history to be run by someone who was not a member of the country's Americo-Liberian elite. Plagued by corruption and human rights abuses, Doe proved unpopular as a leader and faced regular uprisings.

During her childhood, Gbowee's neighborhood included several family members, including her great aunt, a member of Liberia's powerful Sande secret society for women. Though Gbowee's family was more privileged than many others in Monrovia, they faced challenges; her parents had a strained relationship, and her father was adulterous and sometimes abusive. Her mother also punished her children with regular beatings. Nonetheless, Gbowee excelled in school and dreamed of becoming a pediatrician. She recalled in her 2011 memoir, *Mighty Be Our Powers: How Sisterhood, Prayer, and Sex Changed a Nation at War*, that her childhood was generally happy.

LIFE IN LIBERIA

In December 1989, Charles Taylor, a former colleague of Doe, invaded Liberia with a band of rebels from Cote d'Ivoire, Liberia's eastern neighbor. Gbowee began taking classes at the University of Liberia in March 1990 and moved with her family to the Monrovia suburb of Paynesville. In the early days of the war, the fighting seemed distant to Gbowee and her family. "Each night when we turned on BBC's World Service Focus on Africa, we heard reports about Charles Taylor and his rebel soldiers," she writes in her memoir. "They were attacking, capturing territory, moving south toward us. A kind of denial kept my parents complacent."

Both Taylor's rebels and the government armies opposing them were engaging in brutal tactics, such as the indiscriminate rape and murder of members of opposing tribes. Both armies recruited young boys to their ranks (often after their parents had been killed), often coercing them with drugs. Because Gbowee and her family were associated with Doe's government, they were transported by the United States Marines to Monrovia just before Taylor's rebels captured Paynesville in the spring of 1990. The family lived there only briefly before evacuating, along with thousands of others, to the Buduburam refugee camp in Ghana, just outside Accra. For several months, they lived in a shelter with no furniture, and struggled to find food. In September 1990, Doe was tortured and executed by Prince Johnson, the leader of the Independent National Patriotic Front of Liberia (INPFL), a rebel group that had splintered off from Taylor's.

Despite Doe's death, war raged on for years in Liberia between supporters of Doe, Johnson's INPFL, and Taylor's National Patriotic Front (NPF). The NPF gained the support of many of the Liberian people, and Taylor took control of much of the country, including Monrovia and the country's major industries. International peacekeeping forces installed a transitional government in 1991. However, Taylor refused to agree to a peace deal until 1997. All the while, the civil war continued, resulting in thousands of deaths and the displacement of millions of Liberians.

In July 1997, Taylor was elected president of Liberia, but he did little to improve the country's political situation, or the lives of its citizens. Instead, he focused on lending support to the Revolutionary United Front in Sierra Leone, which was fighting its own civil war.

EARLY CAREER

Gbowee began her career as a social worker at the UNICEF program rehabilitating refugees from Liberia and Sierra Leone in the 1990s.

At the time, she was living in Monrovia and had become romantically involved with a man whom she refers to in her memoir as Daniel, who worked at the United States Embassy. He fathered four children with Gbowee. In the spring of 1996, Gbowee's studies were interrupted when violence erupted after Taylor broke a treaty he had signed the year before. Gbowee evacuated the city with Daniel and her children and moved to Ghana to live with Daniel's family. In Ghana, Gbowee's relationship with Daniel, which had long been abusive, became more strained.

When Gbowee got the courage to leave Daniel, she returned to Paynesville and stayed with her parents, where she fell into a deep depression and struggled with alcoholism. With the encouragement of her friend and former colleague from the Monrovia relief agency, referred to as Tunde in her memoir, Gbowee applied to an associate's degree program in social work at the Mother Patern College of Health Sciences. Before she could be accepted, however, she had to gain more practical social work experience. She began volunteering at the Lutheran Church of Liberia/Lutheran World Federation's Trauma Healing and Reconciliation Program (THRP), conducting conflict resolution and peace-building workshops with villagers affected by the war. Gbowee served as a counselor to former child soldiers, helping them to reintegrate back into civil society.

In 1999, Gbowee began earning a salary and moved back to Monrovia with her children. She shared an apartment with her sister Geneva, as well as Geneva's daughter and other family members. Gbowee earned money working while Geneva cared for the children. As she learned more about conflict resolution strategies, Gbowee began to take part in conferences held by the West Africa Network for Peacebuilding (WANEP), a peace organization founded by Sam Doe in 1998.

In late 1999, fighting broke out again in Liberia as the anti-Taylor rebel group the Liberians United for Reconciliation and Democracy (LURD) began attacking towns and villages that supported Taylor. Gbowee and members of WANEP held workshops for security personnel in villages across Liberia, in an effort to ensure they would protect rather than exploit the community during the conflict. Gbowee noticed that the women often refrained from speaking up when men were present. Gbowee began holding special women-only sessions late at night, where women spoke about their experiences with sexual violence and exploitation. "In Africa, few mothers talked even to their daughters about sex," she writes in her memoir. "Many women who were raped never told their family members; the stigma would make everyone look at them differently. Everyone was alone with her

pain." Gbowee realized that women bore a significant amount of pain during wartime, and if change were to happen in Liberian society, women would need to become leaders.

WOMEN IN PEACEBUILDING NETWORK

Gbowee received an associate of arts degree from the THRP in 2001. That same year, she teamed up with fellow women's rights activist Thelma Ekiyor to found the Women in Peacebuilding Network (WIPNET), an organization funded by WANEP aimed at helping women from West African nations become a voice in peace building and conflict resolution in their communities. As Gbowee and Ekiyor began training Liberian women, fighting between government armies and rebels advanced toward Monrovia, and President Taylor declared a state of emergency. Gbowee helped her family relocate to Ghana, while she remained in Monrovia to continue her peace-building work.

In the spring of 2002 the violence in Liberia was growing into a full-blown civil war. In her memoir Gbowee recalls a dream she had: "I couldn't see a face, but I heard a voice, and it was talking to me—commanding me: 'Gather the women to pray for peace.'" Working with the leaders from WIPNET, she founded the Christian Women's Peace Initiative (WPI), a group of Lutheran women from local churches who met once a week to pray for the fighting to stop. Over the next several months the group attracted more women who were both Christian and Muslim and became known as the Women of Liberia Mass Action for Peace. In late 2002 and early 2003, Gbowee organized a series of women's peace marches that attracted more and more women. At a rally in April 2003, Gbowee read a statement demanding peace and announcing the beginning of a sit-in if Taylor did not respond within three days.

When Taylor did not respond, Gbowee led over two thousand women, dressed in white to show solidarity, to a soccer field in Monrovia. The group—which included workers from non-governmental organizations, members of local women's groups, university students and professors, and displaced women from refugee camps—chanted, sang songs, prayed, and held signs calling for peace. Three days later, the women moved their demonstration to a space just outside the parliament building. Following a week of protests, Gbowee and other leaders of the group received an invitation to the president's mansion to state their demands. Taylor responded by expressing his willingness to take part in peace talks, but also challenged the women to demand the same from the rebels.

PROTESTS

As the war raged on, the women of the Mass Action organized protests in villages and refugee camps all over Liberia. Gbowee also encouraged Liberian women to withhold sex from their husbands and male partners until a peace agreement was negotiated. Though the sex strike, which lasted just a few months, served little practical purpose, it attracted international media attention, and the women began receiving funding from sources all over the world.

After weeks of protests, peace talks between Taylor and rebel leaders were scheduled for June 4, 2003, in Accra. Though the Women in Liberia Mass Action were not formally invited to participate, Gbowee travelled with a delegation of about five hundred women to Accra. Dressed in white, they held a demonstration outside of the hotel where the meetings were held. On June 16, the parties signed a cease-fire agreement that included a promise by Taylor that he would step down from power. When Taylor quickly retracted that promise, rebels launched a series of attacks on Monrovia and elsewhere. As the surrounding regions descended again into violence and chaos, Gbowee sensed that the rebel leaders were not taking the negotiation process seriously.

In July 2003, Gbowee led a protest at the entryway of the negotiating hall. Linking their arms, Gbowee and other women demonstrators sat at the door and refused to let the men exit the building until they had reached a peace agreement. When security guards accused her of obstructing justice, a hysterical Gbowee threatened to strip naked, a bold act that represented a significant affront to accepted laws of behavior in Liberia. The threat worked, and the women continued their protests. Gbowee and some of the other women's leaders were invited into the negotiating hall to explain their frustration. From then on, the tone of the peace talks changed, and the international community threatened to cut off aid unless an agreement was reached. The women returned every day to pressure the leaders, and on August 11, Taylor resigned the presidency. On August 17, the Accra Comprehensive Peace Agreement was signed by rebel group leaders and Taylor supporters, establishing a transitional government headed by businessman Gyude Bryant.

POSTWAR REBUILDING

Following the signing of the peace agreement, Gbowee returned to WIPNET and became engaged in the postwar rebuilding process. She also travelled to conferences, promoting the work of WIPNET and the Women's Mass Action. In 2004, she spoke at a United States Agency for International Development (USAID) conference in New York about the role of women in disarmament and peace building. In May 2004, she attended a four-week peace-building conference at Eastern Mennonite University (EMU) in Harrisonburg, Virginia. In 2005, presidential elections were held in Liberia, and

Gbowee lent her support to Ellen Sirleaf, believing that a government run by a woman president was more likely to address the needs of women. Sirleaf won the runoff election in August with 59 percent of the vote, defeating the frontrunner, popular soccer player George Weah. With her victory in the election, Sirleaf became the first woman head of state in modern African history.

In December 2005, Gbowee stepped down as head of WIPNET, and in 2006, she co-founded the Women in Peace and Security Network (WIPSEN), a new women's organization independent from the oversight of WANEP. The organization works to unite women's movements throughout Africa. In 2006, Gbowee enrolled in a master's program in conflict transformation studies at EMU. Her coursework at EMU helped her to understand conflict negotiation tactics.

RECOGNITION

While completing her master's program, Gbowee was contacted by filmmaker Abigail Disney, who wanted to make a documentary about Gbowee and the role of women in ending the Liberian civil war. Gbowee and other women involved in the movement contributed much to the film, including many interviews. Directed by Gini Reticker and produced by Disney, *Pray the Devil Back to Hell* was named best documentary at the 2008 Tribeca Film Festival. Gbowee has received numerous awards for her work as a peacemaker, including the Blue Ribbon for Peace from Harvard University's John F. Kennedy School of Government (2007), the Gruber Prize for Women's Rights (2009), and the John F. Kennedy Profile in Courage Award (2009).

Gbowee's memoir, *Mighty Be Our Powers*, was published in September 2011. In October 2011, it was announced that Gbowee was one of three winners of the 2011 Nobel Peace Prize. The co-recipients of the prize were also women. Gbowee shared the prize with President Ellen Sirleaf and Yemeni peace activist Tawakkul Karman. The Nobel Prize committee noted in its press release that it was honoring the three women "for their non-violent struggle for the safety of women and for women's rights to full participation in peace-building work." In her acceptance speech, Gbowee recognized women fighting for peace in Zimbabwe, Congo, Uganda, and Afghanistan.

After winning reelection in November 2011, Sirleaf created a peace and reconciliation initiative and named Gbowee as its director. Gbowee continues to serve as the executive director of WIPSEN. In February 2012, she unveiled plans for a foundation to provide educational scholarships to African girls, called the Gbowee Peace Foundation Africa. Gbowee, who is a Lutheran, lives in Accra with her children. Her fifth child, Jaydyn Thelma Abigail, was born in June 2009.

SUGGESTED READING

Dargis, Manohla. "Unsung Heroines of Liberia, Making Guns Yield to Words." *New York Times* 7 Nov. 2008: C12. Print.

Gbowee, Leymah, with Carol Mithers. *Mighty Be Our Powers: How Sisterhood, Prayer, and Sex Changed a Nation at War.* New York: Beast, 2011. Print.

Pesta, Abigail. "All Hail, Leymah!" *Newsweek* 24 Oct. 2011: 10–11. Print.

—*Margaret Roush Mead*

Gabrielle Giffords

Born: June 8, 1970
Occupation: Former US representative from Arizona (Democrat)

Gabrielle Giffords represented Arizona's Eighth Congressional District in the US House of Representatives from January 2007 through January 2012. Giffords is a moderate Democrat who supports a woman's right to choose, strong security at the US–Mexico border, gun rights, tax relief for small businesses, and national healthcare reform.

At a public event in Arizona in January 2011, Giffords was shot in the head by an antigovernment radical. She was rushed into surgery and since then has made an impressive recovery, undergoing further surgery and rehabilitation, including having to relearn how to walk and speak. In November 2011 Giffords and her husband, astronaut Mark Kelly, published the book *Gabby: A Story of Courage and Hope* telling the story of her recovery. In January 2012 Giffords announced her resignation from office in order to focus on completing her recovery.

EARLY LIFE, EDUCATION, AND BUSINESS EXPERIENCE

A third-generation Arizonan, Gabrielle Giffords was born on June 8, 1970, in Tucson, Arizona. Giffords grew up in Tucson and attended Scripps College, a small liberal-arts college in Los Angeles County, California. She majored in sociology and Latin American history, receiving her BA in 1993, after which she studied for a year in Chihuahua, Mexico, on a Fulbright Scholarship. She then went on to attend Cornell University in Ithaca, New York, earning a master's degree in urban planning in 1996.

After a brief stint as a regional economic development associate at Price Waterhouse LLP in New York City, Giffords returned to her hometown to take over her family's business, El Campo Tire Warehouses, Inc. Giffords served as president and chief executive of El Campo Tires from 1996 to 2000. In 2000 she founded

P.K. Weis/Giffords Campaign - P.K. Weis via Getty Images

Giffords Capital Management LLC, a commercial property management firm, where she served as a managing partner until 2007.

LOCAL POLITICS

Also in 2000 Giffords switched her political affiliation from Republican to Democrat and ran a successful campaign for the 13th District seat in the Arizona House of Representatives, where she served from 2001 to 2003. During her term in the Arizona House, Giffords ran for the state senate seat in the same district against Libertarian Kimberly Swanson (as a result of redistricting, what was formerly the 13th District had become the 28th District). In 2002, at the age of thirty-two, Giffords became the youngest woman ever elected to the Arizona State Senate. In 2004 she was elected to her second two-year term in the state senate, but did not complete her term: In November 2005, Jim Kolbe, an eleven-term Republican representing Arizona's Eighth District in the US House, announced plans to retire, and Giffords became a very eligible contender for the seat. Kolbe was a moderate, openly gay Republican, and to many voters and political pundits it did not seem like a stretch that Giffords, a moderate Democrat, could succeed him.

NATIONAL POLITICS

In December 2005 Giffords resigned her seat in the Arizona State Senate to run for the US House to represent her state's Eighth District. In the Democratic primaries Giffords faced Tucson news anchor Patty Weiss, among other candidates. According to the *Almanac of American Politics* (2008), Giffords had several advantages over her Democratic rivals: She had raised more money and had gained the support of the pro-choice political action committee EMILY's List, the Sierra Club, and organized labor. After winning in the primaries, Giffords took on Republican Randy Graf in the general election. Graf focused mainly on one issue—immigration—and had a significant level of support in southern Arizona for his very tough stance on border patrol and illegal immigration from Mexico.

By October 2006 it appeared that Giffords would win the race. That month she received strong endorsements from two Arizona newspapers. An editorial in the *Arizona Republic* (Oct. 13, 2006) read, "[Giffords] is intelligent, articulate, has a track record as an effective lawmaker and a keen understanding of the needs and challenges of a southern Arizona district that shares a border with Mexico. What's more, her experience running her family's small business gives her insights into the issues that face residents of an urban district. . . . A former Republican, Giffords has a voting record in the state Legislature that shows her willingness to cross party lines and seek solutions that will work. That approach will be critical when a new Congress takes up the unfinished job of reforming immigration laws so flawed they have produced a crisis along the border." An editorial in the *Tucson Citizen* (Oct. 18, 2006) took on the issue of illegal immigration in some detail: "[Giffords] understands that illegal immigration cannot be stopped with a fence, just as 12 million or more illegal immigrants cannot be rounded up and deported or will not self-deport. . . . Giffords notes, we need myriad solutions, including high-tech border enforcement, economic development for Mexico and tamperproof IDs in a secure guest worker program so employers can hire legally— and be sanctioned if they do not." As expected, Giffords won the election in November 2006. She received 54 percent of the vote to Graf's 42 percent. This congressional election took place in the middle of President George W. Bush's second term, and Giffords, along with other Democrats, benefited from the Republican president's declining popularity and the decreasing public support for the Iraq War, which the Bush administration had launched in March 2003.

MAJOR POLITICAL ISSUES

When Giffords took office in early January 2007, she became part of a new Democratic majority in the US House. Even though she was a freshman member of Congress, she was assigned to serve on the House Armed Services Committee, the Foreign Affairs Committee, and the Science and Technology Committee. After only about two weeks on the job, she spoke with the editorial board of the *Arizona Daily Star* (Jan. 21, 2007). When asked about the legislative situation, Giffords already had a lot to discuss, commenting, "Democrats campaigned on a message that talked about change. And we specified a variety of issues that we were going to move within the first 100 legislative hours of the year." She went on to discuss the endeavors then underway, including making reforms to ethics, lobbying, and earmarks, increasing the national minimum wage, and employing the 9/11 Commission's recommendations. Giffords made a particular point of highlighting the bipartisan nature of these efforts.

In this interview, Giffords also expressed concern over potential problems with President Bush over legislation for stem-cell research and Medicare prescription drugs. Giffords saw the president as differing in opinion from the American people on both issues, saying of stem-cell research, "President Bush vetoed this legislation before; it was his first and only presidential veto. It's something that 70 percent of Americans support." Regarding Medicare Part D, she observed, "Philosophically, the majority of Americans support the idea that we can negotiate with the drug companies, that they can't dictate to us what the cost of these drugs should be." She then added, "Of course, the president has certain ideas on certain issues that may not necessarily reflect what Americans want or certainly what Congress wants."

Giffords was then asked about No Child Left Behind. Passed in 2001 this law created unified standards for public school students; opponents argued that it focused too much on standardized testing. Giffords explained the situation, saying, "First of all, it was underfunded by about $40 billion. So funding, or the lack of funding, was one of the biggest things that you could point to as to why this program has not been successful. . . . Sometimes we see the dumbing down of the test just to have more students pass. But overwhelmingly, what you hear from teachers, administrators, parents, even students is that there's such a focus on teaching to the test that other forms of the educational process, which are really critical, are completely pushed aside."

Giffords also discussed her first speech on the House floor, which dealt with the hot-button topic of immigration, particularly illegal immigration from Mexico into the United States. Michael Chertoff, then head of the Department of Homeland Security, supported the building of a fence on the Barry M. Goldwater Air Force Range, which is located in southern Arizona and runs along the US–Mexico border. When asked about Chertoff's support for the fence, which conflicts with environmental regulations, Giffords said, "I've always said that building a wall is not the solution to an immigration crisis—that we need to instead focus on high-tech security, on use of drones and radar, infrared technology. I think that when it comes to the environment or national security, the national security comes first. Whether or not the proposal that Chertoff has put forward actually deals with keeping us safer, again, I do not support the building of a wall." A few weeks later, in an interview with the *Arizona Capitol Times* (Feb. 2, 2007), Giffords stated that immigration is a "top priority" for her district, which is "one of 10 US–Mexico border districts." Illegal immigration from Mexico, she said, has a significant impact on her district, particularly its public schools, law enforcement, and hospitals. Two other local issues of great importance, she said, are the high veteran population in southern Arizona and the University of Arizona, which she called "our economic driver, in terms of keeping global competitiveness at the forefront."

REELECTION
Giffords went on to win both the 2008 and the 2010 elections for her seat in the US House. In the latter election, she narrowly defeated ultra-conservative Republican (and darling of the populist-conservative Tea Party movement) Jesse Kelly, who was a major proponent of Arizona's new immigration law, which sought to identify and deport illegal immigrants by means that were questioned by civil libertarians. Although Giffords opposed that law, she also opposed the numerous boycotts of her state by various organizations and cities around the country. Among those boycotters were the American Immigration Lawyers Association, the National Association for the Advancement of Colored People (NAACP), Sociologists Without Borders, and the National Urban League, as well as the cities of Boston, Seattle, San Francisco, St. Paul, Austin, and Columbus. Giffords argued that the boycott would hurt all Arizona workers.

Also in 2010 Giffords cast one of the most politically controversial votes of her career when she voted, along with a majority of House Democrats, for President Barack Obama's national health-care reform bill. Soon after that vote, someone broke the glass door of Giffords's office. The previous year, when Giffords had held a public event to discuss President Obama's health-care bill, the police were called when one of the attendees dropped a gun. Although no one was hurt at that time, another such public event would end in tragedy.

TUCSON SHOOTING
On the morning of January 8, 2011, Giffords held a Congress on Your Corner event, a public meeting near a Safeway grocery store in Tucson, Arizona. The goal was for Giffords to hear from her constituents. Shortly after ten o'clock in the morning, twenty-two-year-old Jared Lee Loughner shot Giffords in the head at close range. He then continued to shoot indiscriminately, leaving twelve more people wounded and another six dead. He was eventually stopped by bystanders and taken into police custody. Giffords was airlifted to the University of Arizona Medical Center in Tucson, where she underwent brain surgery. Following the operation, her condition was listed as critical.

Almost immediately after the shooting, politics was brought into the discussion. Particular scrutiny was given to the actions of former Alaska governor Sarah Palin, a conservative Republican whose website in March 2010 featured a "target map" with crosshairs aimed at members of Congress with whom Palin strongly disagreed, particularly regarding the issue of national health care. Frank Rich for the *New York Times* (Jan. 16, 2011) cited an interview Giffords gave soon after Palin had put up what Giffords called the "crosshairs of a gun sight over our district," adding that "when people do that, they've got to realize there's consequence to that action." Rich acknowledged that although both Democrats and Republicans in the past two years have used "violent" rhetoric, the argument constructs a "false equivalency." Rich then added, "This isn't about angry blog posts or verbal fisticuffs. Since Obama's ascension, we've seen repeated incidents of political violence. . . . Obama said, correctly, on Wednesday that 'a simple lack of civility' didn't cause the Tucson tragedy. It didn't cause these other incidents either. What did inform the earlier violence—including the vandalism at Giffords's office—was an antigovernment radicalism as rabid on the right now as it was on the left in the late 1960s."

A REMARKABLE RECOVERY
The day after the shooting, more details began to emerge about the nature of the injury and Giffords's condition. According to a report by Thomas H. Maugh II and Seema Mehta for the *Los Angeles Times* (Jan. 9, 2010), the bullet Loughner fired at Giffords did not lodge itself in her brain but rather passed through it from back to front, "missing the crucial central parts of the brain that control most bodily and cognitive functions," as Dr. Michael Lemole, the chief of neurosurgery described it. Maugh and Mehta detailed Giffords's injuries and the medical procedures and treatments she was receiving. They also related her doctors' hope for recovery, documenting that although she was being kept comatose and could not yet speak, "when she is periodically awakened, she is able to respond to simple commands, such as squeezing her hand and showing two fingers."

Throughout the month of January, Giffords continued to make progress; her condition was upgraded from critical to serious and then to good. In March she began to speak, and in May she watched her husband, Mark Kelly, take off in command of the space shuttle *Endeavour* from the Kennedy Space Center in Florida. Giffords then continued her recovery at a Houston, Texas, hospital. In August, in what was a surprise to many, Giffords returned to the floor of the House to cast a yes vote to raise the ceiling on the US national debt. Although the House had been involved in bitter partisan debates in the weeks prior, Giffords received a standing ovation when she entered. After casting the vote she returned to Houston to resume physical and speech therapy.

In November 2011 Giffords and Kelly appeared on an ABC News special that included footage of her recovery and an interview with news anchor Diane Sawyer. That month also saw the publication of *Gabby: A Story of Courage and Hope*, the story of Giffords's recovery, mostly written by Kelly with journalist Jeffrey Zaslow. The final, page-long chapter was written by Giffords herself. In it, she states that she will return to Congress despite some continuing impairment of both her language production and vision. According to a January 6, 2012, article on the CBS News website, Kelly told CBS correspondent Ben Tracy that despite his wife's ongoing speech difficulties, she "understands everything" and was in regular contact with both her district and Washington office, thanks to the efforts of her dedicated staff.

On January 8, 2012, Giffords and Kelly attended a memorial commemorating the one-year anniversary of the shooting. Two weeks later, on January 22, 2012, Giffords publicly announced that she was resigning from office and would not seek reelection that fall, citing a need to focus on her ongoing recovery and a desire to act in the best interests of her state. In the video posted on her website, she remained optimistic for her personal future as well as that of the country and once again emphasized cooperation, saying, "We can do so much more by working together."

PERSONAL LIFE

Giffords married Kelly in November 2007 after a yearlong engagement. At the time, she was thirty-eight and he was forty-three. Prior to the shooting, Giffords was an avid motorcycle rider. She is Jewish—Arizona's first Jewish representative in the US Congress—and belongs to a synagogue in Tucson.

SUGGESTED READING

"A Conversation with Gabrielle Giffords." *Arizona Daily Star* [Tucson] 21 Jan. 2007: H1. Print.

"Experience, Wisdom, Trust: Giffords in CD8." *Tucson Citizen* 18 Oct. 2006: A14. Print.

Maugh, Thomas H., II, and Seema Mehta. "Doctors Remain Hopeful for Gabrielle Giffords." *Los Angeles Times*. Los Angeles Times, 9 Jan. 2011. Web. 18 Jan. 2012.

"Profile: Gabrielle Giffords." *BBC News*. BBC, 2 Aug. 2011. Web. 18 Jan. 2012.

Rich, Frank. "No One Listened to Gabrielle Giffords." *New York Times* 16 Jan. 2011: WK10. Print.

Stolberg, Sheryl Gay, and William Yardley. "For Giffords, Tucson Roots Shaped Views." *New York Times* 14 Jan. 2011: A1+. Print.

—*Dmitry Kiper*

John Gimlette

Born: March 19, 1963
Occupation: Travel writer

The British travel writer John Gimlette, as Tom Fort wrote in a review for the London *Sunday Telegraph* (20 Apr. 2008), "is something of an absurdist among travel writers." Fort continued, "He has a nose for the incongruous and the nonsensical. He glories in tracking down rogues, fantasists and eccentrics, and delights in preposterous sights and improbable juxtapositions. He is a dazzling, if occasionally exhausting, entertainer."

Over the course of a decade, Gimlette has authored four critically acclaimed and wildly entertaining travel books: *At the Tomb of the Inflatable Pig: Travels through Paraguay* (2003), *Theatre of Fish: Travels through Newfoundland and Labrador* (2005), *Panther Soup: Travels through Europe in War and Peace* (2008), and *Wild Coast: Travels on South America's Untamed Edge* (2011). Both *At the Tomb of the Inflatable Pig* and *Theatre of Fish* were listed among the *New York Times'* hundred most notable books of the year, in 2004 and 2005 respectively, and all four of his books have been featured on the popular British radio station BBC Radio 4. Proclaimed by *Salon* online magazine as "the world's best living travel writer," Gimlette, who won the prestigious Shiva Naipaul Memorial Prize for travel writing in 1997, has been known for his vivid prose and untamed wit and for his ability to paint enthralling portraits of some of the world's most inhospitable and unforgiving places. In his books, he has used personal experience, exhaustive research, and colorful anecdotes to capture the true essence of the people and places he has encountered. He has traveled to over sixty countries, his destinations ranging from the jungles of Central and South America to the frozen tundras of Canada and Siberia.

While he is primarily known for his travel writing, which includes numerous articles for newspapers and magazines, Gimlette has also managed to balance a successful career as a barrister and has practiced law in London for over twenty-five years. He has drawn strong parallels between the two professions. "I couldn't do

© Colin McPherson/Corbis

who were stationed all over Asia. They were also accomplished authors; George Gimlette wrote a chronicle of the Nepali royal family in the 1890s, and John D. Gimlette wrote the influential handbook *Malay Poisons and Charm Cures* (1915), both of which remain in print. Gimlette's parents were also avid travelers and helped nurture his wanderlust.

When he was twelve years old, Gimlette traveled alone for the first time; his parents put him on a plane to Ireland, where he spent school summer holidays on a family friend's farm. At seventeen, he accompanied his mother on a trip to Hong Kong, traveling there and back via the famous Trans-Siberian Railway, the longest railway in the world. Following that trip, which took eight days each way, Gimlette "felt anything was possible," as he told travel writer Rolf Potts for the blog *Vagabonding* (Jan. 2008, online). "During a single journey I'd been spied on, admonished (for talking to the locals), half-pickled by the Soviet soldiers, and had neither washed nor eaten hot food. Despite that, it was one of the most enjoyable experiences imaginable." By that time, Gimlette had followed in the tradition of his forebears by recording accounts of his travels in diaries.

one without the other," he told Melanie Stern for *Legal Week* (17 Nov. 2011, online). "Both jobs involve the assimilation of huge amounts of information. In my clinical negligence work I might get many lever arch files of documents; somehow, I've got to work out from that what the crux of a case is. . . . Likewise with travel writing, I might read seventy books, record twenty hours of interviews, and take a couple of thousand photos on one three-month trip. That all has to be meaningfully whittled down into 130,000 words."

A FAMILY OF ADVENTURERS

John Gimlette was born on March 19, 1963, in London, England, to Dr. T. M. D. Gimlette and Ruth Curwen Gimlette. He has a sister, Philippa, and two brothers, Matthew and Edward. Gimlette comes from a family of distinguished explorers and writers; both his maternal great-grandfather, Dr. Eliot Curwen, and his maternal grandfather, Dr. Cecil Curwen, were respected amateur archaeologists whose various findings produced several important works. Eliot Curwen's work as a medical missionary in the far-flung reaches of Newfoundland and Labrador would later serve as the inspiration for Gimlette's second book. During that expedition, Curwen worked with Wilfred Grenfell, a medical missionary whose family ran the Mostyn House School in Parkgate, England, which Gimlette attended as a boy. Two of Gimlette's paternal great-uncles, George Gimlette and John D. Gimlette, were military surgeons

EDUCATION AND EARLY CAREER

Gimlette received his secondary education at the prestigious Rugby School in the town of Rugby in Warwickshire County, England. (Founded in 1567, the school is one of the oldest educational institutions in England and has produced a long line of prominent figures, including Prime Minister Neville Chamberlain, author and mathematician Lewis Carroll, and the Booker Prize–winning novelist Salman Rushdie.) After graduating in 1981, Gimlette spent some time traveling and working abroad. In 1982, he worked as a ranch hand on a farm in northern Argentina, and during the summer of that year, he traveled to the country of Paraguay for the first time. Initially ending up in Paraguay as a result of the Falklands War between the United Kingdom and Argentina, Gimlette became fascinated by the landlocked country's turbulent history and wide mix of inhabitants, and he kept detailed accounts of his observations.

After returning to England, Gimlette attended Jesus College, a constituent college of the University of Cambridge. While pursuing a law degree, he continued to travel extensively. One of his university summer holidays was spent in northern Pakistan, where he wrote a legal article about the country's refugee population. Though the article went unpublished, Gimlette told Stern, "it was a good experience in how law and travel can interface—probably the only time when the two have really meshed. Though the effect was to raise my interest in writing." Gimlette earned both his bachelor's and his master's degree at Jesus College and completed his law degree there in 1985.

In 1986, following the completion of his studies, Gimlette started working as a barrister at One Crown Office Row in London. During his legal career, he has practiced in a wide range of areas. Although his early practice consisted mostly of common-law work, including everything from criminal and civil cases to commercial and contract disputes, Gimlette has since developed a practice that mainly specializes in the areas of medical negligence, personal injury (including brain injury), and public funding. In those areas, he has brought four cases before the London Court of Appeal and one before the Supreme Court.

As a barrister, Gimlette has been known for his close attention to detail and expertise in handling complex scientific matters. "Generally, I spent my time advising on claims and their prospects of success," he told Cole Moreton for the London *Financial Times* (12 Aug. 2011, online). "There's also a lot of work connected with inquests, often representing doctors."

WRITING DEBUT

Gimlette did not consider writing professionally until 1997, when he saw an advertisement for the Shiva Naipaul Memorial Prize travel-writing competition while on his way home from work on the London Underground. (The Shiva Naipaul Memorial Prize is awarded annually for the best unconventional travel piece written by an English-language author thirty-five years or younger.) Off from court the next day, he wrote a story about his travels in Paraguay and then, as he told Moreton, hurried it across London in order to submit it in time for the competition's midnight deadline. The story, titled "Pink Pigs in Paraguay," won the 1997 Shiva Naipaul Memorial Prize and was published in the London *Spectator* in May of that year. The following year, Gimlette won a travel-writing competition sponsored by the British travel magazine *Wanderlust*. Soon afterward, he started writing travel features for newspapers and magazines. "People who write have always known they want to write," he explained to Potts. "It's usually just a question of opportunity."

Gimlette's rising profile as a writer ultimately helped him land a book deal, and in 2003, Alfred A. Knopf published his first travelogue, *At the Tomb of the Inflatable Pig: Travels through Paraguay*. (Knopf would also publish Gimlette's three subsequent books.) In the book, Gimlette recounts his adventures in Paraguay, from his first visit to the country as a teenager to his multiple return trips there as an adult, and chronicles the nation's riotous history. His travels took him from Paraguay's capital of Asunción through the country's vast frontiers and jungles, as he encountered indigenous tribes, arms dealers, fugitive Nazis, and other bizarre characters.

Gimlette intersperses those episodes with in-depth passages about bloody moments in Paraguayan history, including the oppressive dictatorships of Francisco Solano López and General Alfredo Stroessner and a number of destructive wars, most notably the War of the Triple Alliance, which lasted from 1864 to 1870 and reportedly wiped out 80 percent of the Paraguayan population. Gimlette, who originally intended to write a novel about Paraguay, further discusses how the country's mysterious exoticism has enticed the likes of such writers as Joseph Conrad, Voltaire, G. K. Chesterton, and Graham Greene.

At the Tomb of the Inflatable Pig received widespread praise from critics. Ben Macintyre, in a review for the *New York Times* (29 Feb. 2004), called the book "colorful and meandering, by turns hilarious and horrifying, often delightful, occasionally infuriating and very, very odd . . . an entirely faithful reflection of its subject, since, measured in terms of eccentric history per square foot, Paraguay is probably the strangest country on the planet." In another assessment for that publication (2 Mar. 2004), Michiko Kakutani described the book as "absorbing" and commented that Gimlette "writes with enormous wit, indignation, and a heightened sense of the absurd" and "gives us a cast of characters as vivid as any by Dickens or Waugh." Michael Upchurch further noted for the *Seattle Times* (8 Feb. 2004) that the book "blends travelogue, history and flights of descriptive whimsy to highly tonic effect. Gimlette's prose is such a vivid, hyperbolic affair that, as you read it, you may well find yourself checking your limbs for mosquito bites and heavy-duty chigger infestation." *At the Tomb of the Inflatable Pig* received several honors, including being named by Matthew Parris in the London *Sunday Telegraph*'s Books of the Year roundup in 2003 and listed among the *New York Times*' 100 Notable Books of the Year in 2004.

CLOSER TO HOME

Gimlette's second book, *Theatre of Fish: Travels through Newfoundland and Labrador* (2005), is inspired by his own ancestral history. In it, he tries to retrace the steps of his great-grandfather, Dr. Eliot Curwen, who traveled to Newfoundland and Labrador in 1893 to work as a medical missionary to inhabitants of those regions alongside Dr. Wilfred Grenfell. Having been fascinated by his great-grandfather's expedition since childhood, Gimlette decided to write the book after experiencing the region firsthand during a series of trips there in 2002. The resultant *Theatre of Fish*, the title of which refers to Newfoundland's abundance of cod, is structured into six literary acts and draws heavily from Curwen's journals and photographs, which Gimlette used to map out his own expedition.

Like Gimlette's first book, *Theatre of Fish* was well received by critics. In a representative review for the *Library Journal* (15 Sep. 2005), Lee Arnold wrote, "Witty author Gimlette here does for Newfoundland what he did for Paraguay in *At the Tomb of the Inflatable Pig*. He approaches his topics with a combination of respect and good-natured ribbing, shedding light on a previously obscure land." He later added, "As with Paraguay, the light Gimlette shines here reveals both paradise and perdition. We find aboriginal peoples nearly destroyed by disease and addictions. There are murderers, philanderers, cads galore, and, of course, the ever-present moose. But there's also the rugged beauty of Newfoundland and the richness of its natural resources (like the once ubiquitous codfish—a source of boom and bust)." *Theatre of Fish* was listed among the *New York Times'* 100 Notable Books of the Year for 2005.

In 2008, Gimlette published his third book, *Panther Soup: Travels through Europe in War and Peace*, which follows the path of an octogenarian US Army veteran, Second Lieutenant Putnam Flint, as he travels back to Europe for the first time in sixty years to recollect his experiences from World War II. (The book's title refers to the mud Flint's 824th Tank Destroyer Battalion, nicknamed the Panthers, stirred up as it went.) Flint served as Gimlette's guide, leading him on a journey through battle sites from southern France to Germany and the Austrian Alps and offering up musings about the war. As in his previous books, Gimlette explores little-known sites and encounters an assorted mix of characters along the way.

Panther Soup ultimately received mixed reviews from critics. Craig R. Whitney wrote in his review for the *New York Times* (25 May 2008), "The people, castles, vineyards, hotels, and restaurants in this travelogue are not those most travelers would come across. Many are in seedy neighborhoods only a young battle-fatigued lieutenant, or a writer determined to retrace his steps, would find attractive. . . . Gimlette tells a good story, though there's not much sustained digging below the surface to find deeper meaning, and when there is, sometimes it seems oversimplified and glib." In a positive review for *Booklist* (15 May 2008), Jay Freedman praised the work, calling it "a moving, often humorous, and thoroughly enjoyable account that works as both a wartime recollection and travelogue" and adding that the author "strikes just the right notes in juxtaposing the past and present."

RETURN TO SOUTH AMERICA

Gimlette's fourth book, *Wild Coast: Travels on South America's Untamed Edge*, was published in 2011. The book offers an account of his three-and-half-month-long expedition through the South American countries of Guyana,

Suriname, and French Guiana, known collectively as the Guianas region, in 2008. His journey took him through the region's lush jungles and remote villages, as well as to places such as the Devil's Island penal colony off the coast of French Guiana and the site of the infamous 1978 Jonestown massacre in Guyana. Despite having visited some of the most dangerous and least-known places in the world, Gimlette told Melanie Stern, "I still get culture shock. I find it hard adjusting where there are high levels of poverty, where people have really big health issues, and where there is a lot of crime. There have been times when I've thought, 'I just want to go home'—then I get used to it."

Gimlette splits his time between writing and practicing law. In order to write his books, he follows an exhaustive three-year planning cycle, which consists of one year of research, another of writing and traveling, and a third finishing the book. "Being a lawyer, I am not dependent on my earnings as a writer," he told Rolf Potts. "That's quite liberating. I can write what I want, when I want—and writing is therefore (for all its hardships) still a joy for me."

PERSONAL LIFE

Gimlette and his wife, BBC television presenter and writer Jayne Constantinis, live in London with their daughter, Lucy. He is a fellow of the Royal Geographical Society and a member of the Anglo-Paraguayan Society.

Gimlette regularly contributes articles to a number of London newspapers, including the *Guardian*, the *Independent*, the *Daily Telegraph*, and the *Times*. He also contributes travel articles and photographs to the magazines *Condé Nast Traveler* and *Wanderlust*.

SUGGESTED READING

Gimlette, John. "First Person: John Gimlette." Interview by Cole Moreton. *FT.com*. Financial Times, 12 Aug. 2011. Web. 3 Feb. 2012.

"John Gimlette: A Biography." *JohnGimlette.com*. John Gimlette, 2011. Web. 16 Dec. 2011.

Potts, Rolf. "Travel Writers: John Gimlette." *Rolf Potts' Vagabonding*. Rolf Potts, Jan. 2008. Web. 16 Dec. 2011.

Stern, Melanie. "The Wandering Wig." *Legal Week*. Incisive Financial, 17 Nov. 2011. Web. 15 Feb. 2012.

SELECTED WORKS

At the Tomb of the Inflatable Pig: Travels through Paraguay, 2004; *Theatre of Fish: Travels through Newfoundland and Labrador*, 2005; *Panther Soup: Travels through Europe in War and Peace*, 2008; *Wild Coast: Travels on South America's Untamed Edge*, 2011

—*Chris Cullen*

Michelle Goldberg

Born: September 23, 1975
Occupation: Journalist, writer

The award-winning journalist Michelle Goldberg is the author of the nonfiction books *Kingdom Coming: The Rise of Christian Nationalism* (2006) and *The Means of Reproduction: Sex, Power, and the Future of the World* (2009). In *Kingdom Coming* Goldberg argued that the Christian nationalist movement in the United States poses a danger to the country through its attempts to remove the separation of church and state and through a lack of regard for the concept of a pluralistic society. In *The Means of Reproduction*, she maintained that women's control over their own bodies is an essential human right and that some of the world's most pressing problems—among them overpopulation, environmental instability, sex-ratio imbalances in Asia, and the AIDS epidemic in Africa—can be effectively addressed by increasing the freedoms of women around the world. Goldberg, a former senior political writer for the online magazine *Salon*, continues to write about religion, feminism, and politics as a senior contributor to *Newsweek* magazine and the *Daily Beast* website. She also writes a column, "The Diasporist," for the online Jewish magazine *Tablet*.

EARLY LIFE AND EDUCATION

Michelle Helene Goldberg was born on September 23, 1975, and raised in Williamsville, New York, near Buffalo. At one time her father was an editor at the *Buffalo News*. In an essay she wrote for *Salon* (6 May 2003), Goldberg described her childhood as "mortifyingly provincial," and she longed from an early age to live in a big city. Her activism also began early. As a young teen she once collected classmates' lunch money to help pay for an abortion for a friend who was thirteen. "I was probably 14 when I realized there were people who were anti-choice," she told Nicole Peradotto in an interview for the *Buffalo News* (17 Mar. 1996).

In 1992, when she was a high school senior, representatives of the antiabortion group Operation Rescue came to Buffalo to try to shut down abortion clinics in the city. "I used to go to clinic defense before homeroom," she told the *Gothamist* (16 June 2006), adding that she and others would form a human chain in front of the clinic's doors in counterprotest. Goldberg got the wind knocked out of her when Operation Rescue activists, judging her to be the weakest "link" in the chain, charged in her direction. She told the *Gothamist* that the protest marked the first time she "encountered militant Christian fundamentalism face to face," though she admitted that in some ways the experience "gave me a distorted view of politicized Christianity," a subject

Matt Ipcar, courtesy of Penguin Press

she addressed in *Kingdom Coming*. "Hating high school," as she told the *Gothamist*, Goldberg graduated early, at sixteen, then earned a scholarship to attend the State University of New York (SUNY) at Purchase. During that period she also landed an internship at the music magazine *Spin*.

COLLEGE JOURNALIST

After two years at SUNY–Purchase, she transferred to SUNY–Buffalo, having "realized . . . that I couldn't get a better education at any other state school," as she told the *Gothamist*. In 1996 Goldberg—a pop-culture major—grabbed national headlines as a result of an editorial she wrote for *Spectrum*, the school's student newspaper, called "Rant for Choice." She wrote the piece in response to a campus display of 4,400 small white crosses, erected by the school's antiabortion group to symbolize the number of abortions performed daily in the United States. Goldberg was infuriated by the display. In "Rant for Choice," as quoted by Peradotto, she wrote: "To me, those crosses stand for desperate women, forced by religious lunatics into a horrifying death by knitting needle or Lysol"—that is, death brought on by self-administered abortions in times or places in which the procedure was illegal. She also wrote, "Anti-choicers have declared war on women. Now it's up to us to fight back. If that means guarding the clinic doors with Uzis, then that's what will have to be done. Just once, I'd like to see someone blow up one of their churches"—suggestions she later claimed to have meant not literally but as tongue-in-cheek polemic.

Within hours of the article's publication, the crosses had been vandalized. "It's understandable why people took her seriously," the University of Buffalo law professor Lucinda Finley told Peradotto. "Having been involved in the [pro-choice] struggle for a while, I could have predicted that would happen. It was counterproductive in advancing her viewpoint." The SUNY–Buffalo student antiabortion group sought disciplinary action against Goldberg, but the school maintained that "Rant for Choice" fell within her right to freedom of speech. The Reverend Rob Schenck even called, unsuccessfully, for a legal investigation into the matter. (Rob Schenck is the twin brother of Paul Schenck, a well-known Catholic priest and antiabortion activist, who organized the 1992 protest in which Goldberg was knocked to the ground.)

GRADUATE SCHOOL AND EARLY CAREER

Goldberg graduated from SUNY–Buffalo in 1996. She earned a scholarship to attend the Graduate School of Journalism at the University of California–Berkeley. "I'm one of the few journalists I know who is purely a product of public universities," she told the *Gothamist*. During her time at Berkeley, she began writing for the newly launched arts-and-culture magazine *Salon*. She also became a contributor to print journals including *Wired*, *Bust*, the *Buffalo News*, the *San Francisco Bay Guardian*, and several alternative weekly papers. After graduating in 1998, Goldberg settled in San Francisco as a freelance journalist and contributor to *Salon*. In the early 2000s she spent a year abroad, living in and reporting from such places as Jordan, Egypt, Iraq, Israel, and India. She returned to the United States to settle in the Cobble Hill neighborhood of Brooklyn, in New York City, where she was a senior political writer for *Salon* before becoming a senior contributing writer for *Newsweek*/the *Daily Beast* in 2009.

KINGDOM COMING

In 2000 Goldberg again encountered the most militant sector of the Christian right while writing a piece for the Silicon Valley weekly newspaper *Metro* on the "ex-gay" movement, which purports to "cure" homosexual men and women through religion. She was surprised by what she learned. "I found I had a lot of sympathy for the people I met—they were good, earnest men and women in a hellish situation, believing their only choices were trying to will themselves straight or exiling themselves from their families, communities and religion," she told the *Gothamist*. Later, she was surprised to learn that the movement— specifically, an umbrella ex-gay ministry called Exodus—was supported by the George W. Bush administration; Goldberg reported for

the *Huffington Post* (5 June 2006) that as president, Bush had invited two Exodus leaders to the White House in 2006, when he announced his endorsement of a constitutional amendment to ban same-sex marriage. Goldberg's interest in the role of theology in politics became the inspiration for her first book, *Kingdom Coming: The Rise of Christian Nationalism* (2006).

Christian nationalism, Goldberg explained, is not the same as evangelical Christianity. She estimated that as of 2006, 30 percent of Americans defined themselves as evangelical Christians, while less than 15 percent called themselves Christian nationalists, a group in favor of making Christianity the official religion of the United States. The Christian-nationalist movement began in the 1970s, as conservative Republicans sought to woo white conservatives away from the Democratic Party. Toward that end the televangelist Jerry Falwell was recruited to head the now defunct Moral Majority, and the Christian Coalition, a grassroots political organization, was founded by Pat Robertson in 1989. In *Kingdom Coming* Goldberg argued that that religious fringe had organized itself with growing success under the belief that the "separation of church and state is a fraud that needs to be eradicated so the nation can reach its fulfillment," as she explained to Marilyn H. Karfield for the *Cleveland Jewish News* (10 Nov. 2006).

Goldberg, who described herself as a "secular Jew and ardent urbanite," according to Dave Denison, writing for the *Texas Observer* (6 Oct. 2006), was aware that her view of Christian nationalism's influence on society might appear at the outset to be alarmist. To prove her point she offered examples of the reach and scope of that influence. Goldberg cited billions of dollars in government grants to overtly religious institutions (Robertson and the Christian Coalition alone have received over $24 million from the government for social-service programs allowed to discriminate against non-Christians in hiring); she also pointed to the Bush administration's systematic appointment of hard-line Christian conservatives as delegates to the United Nations, where they worked to ban abortion and access to contraceptives abroad. In addition, Goldberg noted that Christian nationalists had been very active—sometimes successfully—in trying to eradicate gay rights, espouse the teaching of creationism or "intelligent design" rather than evolution, and put taxpayer dollars toward the promotion of less-than-effective abstinence programs instead of contraception. "The case she makes," Denison wrote in his review of *Kingdom Coming*, "which is never shrill and only occasionally hyperbolic, is that there are a lot of influential Christians involved in politics who do not believe in democracy as we have come to know it."

Through her research Goldberg also encountered what she called the mainstream Christian right, which she found to have "an all-encompassing parallel reality with its own pop culture, revisionist history, news media, education system and pseudo-scientific infrastructure," as she told the *Gothamist*, with all aspects of those elements dictated by biblical scripture. She traveled across the country, attending conferences and prayer meetings and interviewing hundreds of people. She wrote about the popularity of David Barton, an author, revisionist historian, and former cochair of the Texas Republican Party, who argued that conservative Christianity played a core role in the founding of the United States. She also wrote about Janice Crouse of the group Concerned Women for America, who gave a presentation at the United Nations in which she compared feminism to communism.

Goldberg told the *Gothamist* that her extensive contact with Christian nationalists "left me more sympathetic to some of the individuals in the movement, and more alarmed about the movement as a whole." She added, "The anxieties people are dealing with, and that people like James Dobson [of the group Focus on the Family] speak to, are very valid. A lot of people are in despair. Our culture is crass and vulgar and nihilistic. Families are falling apart—especially in the most right-wing states, where divorce rates tend to be highest. Many long for a country in which it would be unthinkable for their husband or wife to leave them, so rhetoric about 'defending marriage' resonates." Goldberg warned that secularists do not take the Christian nationalist movement seriously enough. "[Christian nationalists are] not simply a mob of ignorant rubes," she told Harper. "The people at the forefront of the movement are often very smart. They've developed a rich, self-reinforcing parallel world and a powerful political ideology, and even if they lose a few elections, I don't see them giving up any time soon." *Kingdom Coming* was a finalist for the 2007 New York Public Library Helen Bernstein Award for Excellence in Journalism.

THE MEANS OF REPRODUCTION

Goldberg's second book, *The Means of Reproduction: Sex, Power, and the Future of the World*, was published in 2009. After finishing *Kingdom Coming*, Goldberg traveled the world studying reproductive rights, public health, and gender inequality. In the resulting book Goldberg argued, as paraphrased by Terry Gross for the National Public Radio program *Fresh Air* (13 Apr. 2009), that "reproductive rights are the place where many of the crucial forces shaping and changing women's lives intersect: religious authority, globalization, patriarchal tradition, international law, feminism, and American foreign policy."

Goldberg was inspired to broaden the scope of her book—which spans half a century and tells the stories of women across four continents—when she saw the Christian nationalist movement taking an increasing interest in global issues and influencing policy. She cited the highly contentious Global Gag Rule as an example; the rule, established in 1984 by President Ronald Reagan, denied aid to international groups "which perform or actively promote abortion as a method of family planning," as quoted by a reporter for the website *RH Reality Check* (19 Mar. 2009). The rule was repealed by President Bill Clinton, reinstated by President George W. Bush, and then repealed again by President Barack Obama. "In a way," Goldberg told the website, "the American antiabortion movement has had more of an impact abroad than at home." Among Goldberg's arguments in the book are that, as Katharine P. Jose put it in the *New York Observer* (31 Mar. 2009), "giving women control over their bodies is a basic human right." Goldberg maintained as well that the right to abortion is not a political issue but a health issue; she cited, for example, high numbers of deaths in regions around the world resulting from abortions performed illegally.

Goldberg spent over two years researching the book, and in 2008 she won the J. Anthony Lukas Work-in-Progress Award from the Nieman Foundation for Journalism at Harvard University. The judges described *The Means of Reproduction*, as quoted on Goldberg's website, as "a book of vaulting ambition and intellectual passion. Michelle Goldberg looks at literally the entire world through the prism of women's issues and women's rights. From abortion to female circumcision, from sexual trafficking to abstinence-only programs, from Poland to Ethiopia to Nicaragua, she examines the conflict between self-determination and patriarchal tradition." The book was also the recipient of the Ernesta Drinker Ballard Book Prize, which honors a female author for "advancing the dialogue about women's rights." The breadth of *The Means of Reproduction* was considered groundbreaking; Nicholas Kristof wrote about the book in his *New York Times* column (12 Apr. 2009), praising its "wonderful insight" and adding that Goldberg's arguments about the relationship between the world's ills and gender issues were "exactly right." Katharine P. Jose wrote that *The Means of Reproduction* "defies expectations by making an argument that stands outside of traditional liberal thinking about reproductive rights." She added, "The book reads like a history of the reproductive rights movements, from the 1960s through the Bush administration, giving a fluid sense of how international politics have deeply affected access to reproductive health services." Jose's conclusion was that "what *The Means of Reproduction* boils down to is that women should have the free will to make choices about their own reproductive health. It's a supremely reasonable idea."

CURRENT PROJECTS AND PERSONAL LIFE

Goldberg told an interviewer for *Powell's Books* about writing, "I like to be alone a lot of the time, authority makes me indignant, and I'm addicted to traveling—how else could I get by in the world?" Her book about Indra Devi, a famous actress and yogi who died in 2002, is scheduled for publication in 2012. Goldberg has been a contributor to many publications, including *Glamour, Rolling Stone,* the *Nation, New York,* the London *Guardian,* the *New Republic,* and *American Prospect.* In 2010 she began writing a column, "The Diasporist," focusing on aspects of Judaism, for the online publication *Tablet.* In 2007 Goldberg's essay "To Breed or Not to Breed," about her decision not to have children, was published in the collection *Maybe Baby: 28 Writers Tell the Truth About Skepticism, Infertility, Baby Lust, Childlessness, Ambivalence, and How They Made the Biggest Decision of Their Lives,* edited by Lori Leibovich.

Goldberg and her husband, Matt Ipcar, a designer, live in Brooklyn.

Getty Images

SUGGESTED READING

Goldberg, Michelle. "Controlling the Means of Reproduction: An Interview with Michelle Goldberg." Interview by Mandy Van Deven. *RH Reality Check.* RH Reality Check, 23 Mar. 2009. Web. Jan. 2012.

---. "Michelle Goldberg, Author." Interview by M. Harper. *Gothamist.* Gothamist LLC. 16 June 2006. Web. Jan. 2012.

---. "To Breed or Not to Breed." *Salon.* Salon Media Group, 6 May 2003. Web. Jan. 2012.

Kristof, Nicholas D. "Women and Development." New *York Times Opinion Pages: On the Ground.* New York Times, Apr. 12, 2009. Web. Jan 2012.

"Sex, Power, Women and 'The Future of the World.'" *Fresh Air.* Narr. Terry Gross. Natl. Public Radio. WHYY, n. p., 13 Apr. 2009. Transcript.

—*Molly M. Hagan*

Seth Grahame-Smith

Born: January 4, 1976
Occupation: Writer and producer

Seth Grahame-Smith first came to widespread attention with the publication of *Pride and Prejudice and Zombies* (2009), a best-selling book that is credited with kicking off the craze for literary "mash-ups," which combine two disparate elements or genres, often for comic effect. *Pride and Prejudice and Zombies,* for example, blends Jane Austen's formal prose style with that of pulp horror fiction. "It is a truth universally acknowledged, that a zombie in possession of brains must be in want of more brains," Grahame-Smith's book begins, echoing Austen's famed opening line about single men in possession of good fortunes being in want of wives. The comic effect goes deeper, however, than mere syntax. "In the original book, England could be burning to the ground and all they would care about is who has the nicest silverware," Grahame-Smith told Oliver Good for the Abu Dhabi *National* (9 June 2009). "In this version, the country literally is falling apart around them, so it becomes that much more ridiculous and funny that they continue to obsess about gossip and relationships, even in the midst of a zombie uprising."

Grahame-Smith followed *Pride and Prejudice and Zombies* with *Abraham Lincoln: Vampire Hunter* (2010), a historical biography and horror hybrid that proved as popular as his Austen mash-up. "Grahame-Smith wasn't the first writer to put a bizarre spin on a classic tale (arguably, Shakespeare was a skilled practitioner of genre remixing). But he's become the mash-up movement's modern avatar," Alexandra Alter wrote for the *Wall Street Journal* (5 Apr. 2012). "His irreverent literary reboot landed at precisely the right cultural moment. In recent years, digital remixing and sampling—once viewed as derivative at best and illegal at worst—has grown widespread. . . . A zombie-infused Regency romance doesn't sound so ludicrous in today's mash-up rich environment."

In the wake of his literary success, Grahame-Smith has found himself much in demand in Hollywood—in the early part of 2012 alone his film adaptation of *Abraham Lincoln: Vampire Hunter* was released for the big screen, as was Tim Burton's *Dark Shadows*, the script for which he helped pen. In 2011, Grahame-Smith co-founded his own production company with partner David Katzenberg. He has few illusions that he is producing high art. "I understand exactly what I am," he told Alter. "I'm a big, bombastic novelist and thrill-ride guy. I'm never going to win the National Book Award."

EARLY LIFE AND EDUCATION

Grahame-Smith was born Seth Jared Greenberg on January 4, 1976, in Rockville Center, New York, though he was raised mainly in Connecticut. His father is Barry M. Greenberg, the founder of a company that facilitates celebrity participation in philanthropic or corporate events. His parents divorced when he was three. After the divorce, his mother, who worked as an editor at Connecticut-based publisher Marshall Cavendish, changed their last name to Grahame. According to most sources, she did so in homage to her favorite author, Kenneth Grahame, who is best known for the children's classic *The Wind in the Willows* (1908). Later, after she remarried, she adopted a hyphenated surname that incorporated her new husband's surname.

Grahame-Smith's stepfather was a dealer in used and rare books; the basement of the family home was filled with thousands of horror, fantasy, and science-fiction titles that he had collected. At an early age, Grahame-Smith became familiar with such writers as Robert Heinlein, Ray Bradbury, and Isaac Asimov. "But the real turning point for me came when I was 12, and [my stepfather] said, 'Okay, you're old enough for [Dean] Koontz and [Stephen] King,'" he told Ed Symkus for the *Boston Phoenix* (11 May 2002). "I worshipped at the altar of King, and have since then."

In 1994, Grahame-Smith graduated from Connecticut's Bethel High School, where he had been involved in the theater department. He subsequently studied at Emerson College in Boston, Massachusetts, where he participated in a film-production group called Frames Per Second and co-executive-produced the student awards show known as the EVVYs during his junior year.

AFTER GRADUATION

Upon earning his bachelor's degree in film in 1998, Grahame-Smith moved to Los Angeles, California, where he found work as a production assistant. His initial duties, according to some sources, consisted of fetching coffee and delivering dry cleaning for his employers. Eventually, he began writing narration and voice-over scripts for History Channel and Discovery Channel programming.

Concurrently, Grahame-Smith was writing in other formats away from the office. "I wrote one terrible manuscript after another for a decade and I guess they gradually got a little less terrible," he told Alix Sharkey for the London *Telegraph* (30 Apr. 2010). "But there were many, many unpublished short stories, abandoned screenplays and novels . . . a Library of Congress worth of awful literature." Given the responsibility of approving potential script ideas, he found himself listening to a seemingly endless stream of hopeful writers. It occurred to him that he belonged with them, on the more creative side of the process.

FIRST BOOKS

After quitting his job, Grahame-Smith began trying to cobble together a living as a freelance writer. He found regular work with Quirk Books, a Philadelphia-based publisher specializing in pop culture, humor, horror, and a category the company calls "irreference." His first assignment for the company was *The Big Book of Porn: A Penetrating Look at the World of Dirty Movies* (2005). He explained to Brad Moon for *Wired* magazine's "Geek Dad" column (17 Mar. 2010) that he was not embarrassed about working on the title. "If you were a struggling freelance writer and somebody said: 'We'll pay you to hang out on porn sets for six months, travel to conventions, go clubbing with the world's biggest porn starlets, watch a bunch of DVDs and write a funny book about it,' what would YOU say?"

Grahame-Smith published *The Spider-Man Handbook: The Ultimate Training Manual* in 2006, which includes chapters on how to treat a radioactive spider bite, take on a gang of henchmen, and crawl up a wall. Following that publication was another tongue-in-cheek instruction manual called *How to Survive a Horror Movie: All the Skills to Dodge the Kills* (2007), which covers such topics as how to perform an exorcism, survive a night of babysitting, persuade a skeptical local sheriff, and vanquish a murderous doll or possessed pet.

In 2008, Grahame-Smith published the novelty book *Pardon My President: Ready-to-Mail Apologies for 8 Years of George W. Bush: Just Tear and Send!*; the pages take the form of letters a reader could ostensibly rip out, sign, and send. For example, one missive, addressed to "the People of France," describes Republican congressman Bob Ney's 2003 call for all French fries sold in the US Capitol to be rebranded as "freedom fries," to express Ney's displeasure with France's opposition to the invasion of Iraq. The letter reads, "I apologize. You see, Mr. Ney is an idiot.

If it's any consolation, a few years later he was sent to federal prison for corruption."

PRIDE AND PREJUDICE AND ZOMBIES

In 2009, Grahame-Smith heard from Jason Rekulak, an editor at Quirk Books. Rekulak had thought of a title for a book—*Pride and Prejudice and Zombies*—and needed a writer to take on the assignment. Grahame-Smith agreed and spent six weeks rereading Austen's 1813 novel, which is in the public domain, and revising it. "Austen wasn't very helpful," he joked to Carol Memmott for *USA Today* (5 Mar. 2010). "All she left me was the complete manuscript of one of the most beloved novels in the English language. I had to start on Page 1 and edit her work and weave in the zombie subplot that she had so carelessly forgotten."

Quirk initially published ten thousand copies of the book, expecting it to be only a modest success, but it debuted at number three on the *New York Times* best-seller list and quickly sold more than a million copies. Even many of Austen's most ardent fans and rigorous academicians were supportive. "I expected to be burnt at the stake; even to me it seemed slightly sacrilegious to rework one of the English language's greatest authors, but Austen lovers seem to have embraced it," Grahame-Smith told Sharkey. "I've had a lot of them tell me it's a great way to bring people into the Austen tent." *Pride and Prejudice and Zombies* has been optioned by Lionsgate Entertainment to be adapted into a film.

Not wanting to pigeonhole himself, Grahame-Smith turned down the chance to write another Austen mash-up; Quirk instead hired other writers to pen both a prequel to *Pride and Prejudice and Zombies* (*Dawn of the Dreadfuls*, 2010) and a sequel (*Dreadfully Ever After*, 2011).

ABRAHAM LINCOLN: VAMPIRE HUNTER

During his publicity tour for *Pride and Prejudice and Zombies*, Grahame-Smith noticed that several bookstores had set up displays for the upcoming two-hundredth anniversary of Abraham Lincoln's birth. Stephenie Meyer's *Twilight* book series (2005 to 2008), which focuses on a vampire and his human girlfriend, were at the height of their popularity at the time. "So next to every Lincoln table there would be a vampire table. Lincoln table, vampire table. Vampire table, Lincoln table," Grahame-Smith told Sharkey. The idea for his next mash-up presented itself to him immediately. "[Lincoln] didn't need vampires to make his life incredible, he was already an incredible guy. But if you add vampires, it's exponentially cooler," he explained. *Abraham Lincoln: Vampire Hunter* was published in 2010, earning its author a reported advance of $560,000, and landed quickly on the best-seller list.

Many historians and reviewers were impressed by the care that Grahame-Smith had taken with his subject matter and the sensitive way he had incorporated the themes of slavery and vampirism. "[T]his guy's on Mt. Rushmore, OK? He's on the $5 bill. He literally saved our nation from self-destruction," Grahame-Smith told Moon, explaining that during the course of his research, he had developed an even deeper respect for the nation's sixteenth president. "I intended vampire-hunting Abe to be the same brilliant, honest, idealistic self-made man he was in real life." Grahame-Smith was invited to give a reading at the Lincoln Presidential Museum in Springfield, Illinois; afterward, the state historian escorted him into a temperature-controlled vault, lent him a pair of gloves, and allowed him to hold the handwritten manuscript of the "Gettysburg Address"—an honor very few people are ever accorded.

Grahame-Smith wrote the screenplay for a big-budget film version of his book, which premiered in June 2012. The film stars Benjamin Walker as an ax-wielding Lincoln, intent on ridding the nation of its scourge of vampires. In a review whose sentiments were echoed by many critics, Marc Savlov wrote for the *Austin Chronicle* (22 June 2012), "Set aside any preconceived notions you may have and let this inspired reworking of American history wash over you in all its gory, blood-red, exsanguinated-white, and bruised-blue glory."

UNHOLY NIGHT

Grahame-Smith's book *Unholy Night*, which was published in 2012, is a revisionist look at the three wise men present at the birth of Jesus. As he had done before starting his Lincoln book, the writer—who was born into a Jewish household and attended an Episcopalian church after his mother's remarriage—did intensive research. "That meant going back and reading the New Testament, reading the Gospel of Luke and Matthew . . . and researching the traditions that sprung up around the Wise Men in the ensuing centuries," he told Andy Lewis for the *Hollywood Reporter* (7 Apr. 2012). "It's interesting how there's . . . just a handful of lines [about them] really. They come from the East, they show up at Herod's, they burn incense and myrrh, they show up at the manger, and they leave never to be heard from again. Looking at the most famous birth story of all time: What if I could tell that through an unknown lens?"

Grahame-Smith imagines Balthazar, Melchyor, and Gaspar as fugitive thieves, who are forced to go on the run from Herod after burgling his palace. Happening upon Joseph, Mary, and their infant in a stable, the trio helps the young family escape to Egypt, as Herod's soldiers begin to slaughter each firstborn son in Judea.

While there was a minor outcry from the religious right, most critics appreciated the book. In a review for *Entertainment Weekly* (13 Apr.

2012), for example, Anthony Breznican praised Grahame-Smith's imagination and thought-provoking characterizations. "It's risky to turn a holy birth into a bloody sword-and-sandal yarn," he wrote, "but if you can forgive that, I bet you-know-who would." Grahame-Smith has also worked on a screenplay for a film version of the book.

OTHER SCREEN AND TELEVISION WORK

In 2010 Grahame-Smith and David Katzenberg created *The Hard Times of RJ Berger*, a raunchy teen sitcom that aired on MTV for two seasons. Grahame-Smith and Katzenberg discovered that they shared a comic sensibility and worked exceedingly well together. "I'm a juvenile 34, and David's a mature 27," Grahame-Smith told Dave Itzkoff for the *New York Times* (20 May 2010). "We kind of meet at 30 1/2."

The pair joined forces in 2011 to found Katz-Smith Productions. The fledgling company signed a two-year deal that September with Warner Bros., and one of their first projects is reported to be a sequel to *Beetlejuice*, the 1988 Tim Burton hit about a ghost trying to drive a young couple out of their new home. Among their other possible projects are *Night of the Living*, an animated tale of monsters besieged by regular people; *Alive in Necropolis*, a supernatural crime thriller set in the real-life California town of Colma, which is home to a multitude of cemeteries; and *From Mia With Love*, a comedy about a group of awkward teenage boys who send for a Russian mail-order bride.

In addition to adapting his own books for the screen, in 2012 Grahame-Smith collaborated with director Tim Burton on *Dark Shadows*, which is based on a gothic soap opera of the same name. That program originally aired from 1966 to 1971 and has since enjoyed a loyal cult following. Although most reviewers found much to complain about, and the film was not the box-office success that had been predicted, Grahame-Smith was praised for his clever idea of setting the remake in the 1970s, a move that gave the recently resurrected vampire Barnabas Collins (played by Johnny Depp) several amusing lines and sight gags.

Grahame-Smith has been married since 2004 to Erin Stickle, a fellow Emerson College graduate. They have one son, Joshua, who was born in 2008. The family lives in Los Angeles.

SUGGESTED READING

Alter, Alexandra. "The Master of the Mash-Up." *Wall Street Journal*. Dow Jones & Co., 5 Apr. 2012. Web. 16 Aug. 2012.

Babayan, Siran. "Seth Grahame-Smith's New Book *Unholy Night* Asks: What the Hell Were the Three Wise Doing There?" *LA Weekly*. LA Weekly, 6 Apr. 2012. Web. 20 June 2012.

Good, Oliver. "Corpse Pride." *National* [Abu Dhabi]. Abu Dhabi Media, 9 June 2009. Web. 16 Aug. 2012.

Itzkoff, Dave. "A Standout Student at Ribald High." *New York Times*. New York Times Co., 20 May 2010. Web. 16 Aug. 2012.

Lewis, Andy. "Seth Grahame-Smith Touts New Novel 'Unholy Night,' Discusses Movie Schedule and Collaborating With Tim Burton (Q&A)." *Hollywood Reporter*. Hollywood Reporter, 7 Apr. 2012. Web. 16 Aug. 2012.

Memmott, Carol. "Q&A with Seth Grahame-Smith, Master of the Mashup." *USA Today*. Gannett Co. Inc., 5 Mar. 2010. Web. 16 Aug. 2012.

Sharkey, Alix. "Seth Grahame-Smith Interview." *Telegraph* [London]. Telegraph Media Group, 30 Apr. 2010. Web. 16 Aug. 2012.

Symkus, Ed. "Interview: Seth Grahame-Smith Emerges from the Shadows." *Boston Phoenix*. Phoenix Media/Communications Group, 11 May 2012. Web. 16 Aug. 2012.

—*Mari Rich*

LZ Granderson

Born: March 11, 1972
Occupation: Journalist and online columnist

A columnist and commentator for ESPN since 2003 and for the Cable News Network (CNN) since 2011, LZ Granderson offers a unique perspective that is informed in large measure by his singular personal and professional background. "I'm a black gay dude from [Detroit] who used to sell drugs and now listens to country music and snowboards on the weekend," he told Pardeep Toor for the *Flint Journal* (6 Jan. 2009). "I gave up trying to categorize or label myself years ago. I let other people do that while I just do me. I'm not a print guy, a TV guy, old media, new media, I'm just a journalist. A storyteller. I don't care which medium I tell the story, I just want the opportunity to share it." The recipient of the National Lesbian and Gay Journalists Association's 2008 Excellence in Journalism Award for opinion writing and the 2009 Gay and Lesbian Alliance Against Defamation (GLAAD) Award for online journalism, among other honors, Granderson often tackles difficult and divisive topics, whether concerning gay rights, racial relations, or other social issues. "If you're not uncomfortable with what you're saying," he commented in an interview with Max Tcheyan for the *Bleacher Report* (18 Nov. 2008), "maybe you're not digging deep enough."

Wirelmage

"MADE IN DETROIT"

Elzie "LZ" Granderson was born on March 11, 1972, in Detroit, Michigan, the third of five children born to his mother, Alma Miller. Elzie is a family name going back several generations. His mother had been a civil rights activist, registering voters in her native rural Mississippi, but moved north following some encounters with the Ku Klux Klan and in the hopes that her children would have better opportunities than she had growing up in the South. Still, she kept her ties to the region after moving to Detroit and Granderson spent many summers in Mississippi as a child. Granderson's father was largely absent during his youth. "I wasn't in his plans," Granderson told Terri Finch Hamilton for the *Grand Rapids Press* (8 Jan. 2012). Despite his mother's aspirations, Granderson's upbringing in Detroit was an impoverished one, he recalled in a column for ESPN's Page 2 website (20 Oct. 2006), but it shaped his identity and defined his character. "I was made in Detroit," he commented. "Government cheese in the morning. Canned pork at night . . . It wasn't always pretty but it was always home." Reflecting on coming of age in the city, he added, "I've stood in the cold outside of welfare lines, waited for buses an hour late, done homework without electricity and played the numbers. That's life in [Detroit]—down but never out."

Poverty was not the only difficulty Granderson encountered as a child. Up until he entered his mid-teens, or "once I got big," as Granderson recalled to Terri Finch Hamilton, he was regularly beaten by his abusive stepfather. The years of mistreatment had a lasting effect, both on Granderson's self-esteem and on his relationship with his family, especially his mother. "We had a difficult period where we didn't talk, during my 20s and 30s," he commented to Finch Hamilton. "It took me a long time to heal. Not from the abuse, but to heal from everybody's silence." With his problematic home life, Granderson looked elsewhere for acceptance and soon fell in with a street gang and began selling drugs. "I tried to sabotage my success," he told Finch Hamilton. "The abuse had given me a sense of unworthiness."

OBSESSED WITH SPORTS

Though he appeared to be headed down the wrong path, there were bright spots in Granderson's life. He was talented, creative, and driven. He developed a passion for sports as a youth, especially the Red Wings and the Pistons, Detroit's professional hockey and basketball franchises. "I grew up watching the Pistons, I grew up reading everything about the Pistons," he explained to Max Tcheyan. "When they won their first championship [in 1989], I remember camping out in Detroit outside to make sure I had the perfect parade spot. And I did it both years because they repeated." As he endured his stepfather's abuse, Granderson would turn to sports as an escape. "I'd be bleeding from being whipped and go to sleep reading the NBA [National Basketball Association] Almanac," he told Finch Hamilton. "It was my blanket that helped me heal. I read every line about every player." His family was too poor to attend the games, but Granderson loved to read about them in the paper. "I used to read [*Detroit Free Press* columnist] Mitch Albom as often as I could," he recollected to Pardeep Toor. "We were pretty poor so we didn't always have the change lying around for me to buy a paper and I would dig around trash cans looking for bottles to return. We couldn't afford to go to games but with Mitch, I didn't have to. He brought the game to me." Another influential writer for Granderson growing up was Nathan McCall, a reporter for the *Atlanta Journal-Constitution* and the *Washington Post*, among other publications. McCall's autobiography *Makes Me Wanna Holler* (1994) describes an African American journey very similar to Granderson's.

Along with sports obsessions, Granderson was also a gifted dancer and choreographer. He even received a scholarship offer from the Alvin Ailey American Dance Theatre in New York City but turned it down because his mother worried about him moving across the country.

COLLEGE AND GRADUATE SCHOOL

After graduating from high school, Granderson went to college at Western Michigan University in Kalamazoo, Michigan. There he majored in communications with a minor in journalism. Though he wrote for the school newspaper, covering the football and basketball teams, and interned at the *Kalamazoo Gazette*, journalism was not his career focus. After he completed his degree he began work as a model and actor, but, as he told Max Tcheyan, "once I got tired of picking up jobs once every few months and getting rejected most of the time, I decided to go to graduate school."

Intent on becoming a college or university president, Granderson entered the college administration program at Grand Valley State University in Allendale, Michigan. As his studies progressed, however, Granderson reevaluated the path he had chosen. He came to the conclusion that colleges and universities were increasingly hiring from the business community and thus studying education would not help him reach his goals. In the late 1990s, he left the program and returned to journalism as a higher education reporter for the *Grand Rapids Free Press*. Instead of studying at Grand Valley State, it was now his job to cover the university as a reporter.

COMING OUT

As Granderson was in the midst of the transition from graduate school to embracing his calling as a journalist, he was struggling with other realizations. Though he had become a devout Christian in college, had married at twenty-one, and become a father soon after, he had long wrestled with his sexual identity. In his youth, he found he was attracted to male characters on television. As he aged, he did not grow out of such sentiments, yet he had trouble characterizing himself as homosexual. "I didn't see anyone who was gay who liked sports who had been in a gang," he explained to Finch Hamilton. "Because of that, I didn't think I was gay." "I didn't have a vocabulary for it," he continued. "I didn't say 'I am gay' until graduate school. Unfortunately, I was married at the time." Before making that declaration, he had gone through years of denial, attempting to tamp down his feelings through prayer and his Christian faith. "I was not living an authentic life," Granderson said to Nardy Baeza Bickel for the *Grand Rapids Press* (15 Apr. 2009). "I thought I could 'pray the gay away.' Let's just say it didn't work."

In coming to terms with his sexuality, Granderson, at twenty-five, divorced his wife, whom he had known since his sophomore year of high school. Upset at how the denial of his sexuality had affected his family, Granderson remained intent on fulfilling his commitment as a father and setting a good example for his son.

CREATING HIS OWN OPPORTUNITIES

As his career in journalism got under way, Granderson's interest in sports journalism grew stronger. Obsessed with sports since childhood and seasoned by his sports reporting stint at Western Michigan, he looked for any opportunity to break into the field at the *Grand Rapids Press*. Unfortunately, his superiors had other ideas and held off on assigning him sports pieces. Reflecting on his difficulties in this regard, Granderson told Max Tcheyan that sports journalism "still is a profession that is dominated by straight, white males. So again, I don't want to make excuses, but certainly being a gay, black male in a straight, white male environment can be seen as an obstacle for some people who have preconceived notions about people who are different." For example, when he applied for a job to cover the Detroit Pistons, a team he had followed his whole life, the sports editor asked him, "What does a gay guy know about the Pistons?"

Under such circumstances, Granderson had to create his own opportunities. In the summer of 1995, he played pickup basketball with Shawn Respert, a recent graduate of Michigan State University and a standout player on the school's basketball team. At the time, Respert had just decided on a professional career and was soon to enter the 1995 NBA draft. He had yet to talk to the press, and Granderson convinced him to sit for a short interview after their game. Granderson subsequently wrote up the piece and submitted it to his *Grand Rapids Press* editors. "So the paper was kind of forced to run the interview because I was the only one that had one," he recalled to Tcheyan. "It wasn't assigned, but they were at least appreciative of my ingenuity and me taking advantage of the situation."

LESSONS LEARNED

Even with his Respert story, Granderson was not given a sports beat. Instead, he covered just about everything else, including religion, food and movie reviews, pop culture, and even homicides. Writing on such a broad array of topics helped Granderson grow into his craft. He picked up other lessons as well. Under the tutelage of *Grand Rapids Press* editor Gary Bond, he learned that getting the story right was more important than getting it first.

Early in his tenure at the *Grand Rapids Press*, Granderson was assigned to the night desk, covering late breaking news. A fatal car collision occurred, and in his rush to get out the story, Granderson laid the blame on the wrong driver in his article. Once his mistake came to light, Granderson's editor had him personally apologize to the driver's family. "It was more than an hour drive there and I cried all the way back," Granderson remarked in an interview with Jeff Pearlman on Pearlman's website (10 May 2012). "It was then I understood the responsibility of journalism and took the job a lot more seriously."

THE ATLANTA JOURNAL-CONSTITUTION

Several years into his tenure at the *Grand Rapids Press,* unable to break into sports writing, Granderson looked elsewhere for the next step in his career and accepted a position at the *Atlanta Journal-Constitution* as the newspaper's home design writer. "I had absolutely no background in home design whatsoever," he told Tcheyan. "But because I was gay, it was kind of assumed that I could figure it out."

Though it was not his ideal position, Granderson moved down to Atlanta and made the most of it, eventually transitioning from home design to entertainment and from there to sports, all the while showing a farsighted grasp of how the Internet was reshaping journalism. The shift to sports writing was facilitated by several allies at the *Journal-Constitution,* though the main catalyst was Granderson's single-minded persistence. "One of the things I developed as part of the entertainment section was a sports tab which I justified by saying that people go to sporting events as a source of entertainment," he told Tcheyan. "So I could write for that tab, which was considered a feature, and that way the sports department couldn't do anything about it. And eventually that led to me becoming a columnist for the sports department."

ESPN AND CNN

The quality of Granderson's writing and editing at the *Journal-Constitution* attracted the attention of ESPN. According to Granderson, the company was also impressed with how he "created ways in which the website and the print were able to interact with each other," he said to Tcheyan. Hired as a freelance writer for *ESPN The Magazine* in 2003, Granderson became the NBA editor the following year and soon the tennis editor as well. He eventually became an on-air commentator, serving on panel discussions for ESPN360's *Game Night,* among other network programming.

Still, Granderson's main task was writing columns for ESPN's Page 2 website (relaunched in 2012 as ESPN Playbook) and ESPN.com, where he often took on such difficult subjects as racism and homophobia in sports. Among the major stories he landed was one in 2005 involving the professional women's basketball player Sheryl Swoopes of the Houston Comets. At the time a three-time Olympic gold medalist and the most valuable player (MVP) of the WNBA, Swoopes chose an interview with Granderson to announce to the world that she was gay. In a 2008 column about his experience at the NBA All-Star Game in New Orleans, Louisiana, Granderson described enduring homophobic slurs in an encounter with would-be gay bashers. The article earned Granderson the 2008 Excellence in Journalism Award from the National Gay and Lesbian Journalism Association.

Based on his output for ESPN, CNN asked Granderson to write several guest columns for its website. Tackling such topics as the actor Charlie Sheen and the vice-presidential candidate Sarah Palin, his contributions generated an extraordinary amount of interest and were among the most widely read pieces on the site at the time. Richard Galent, an editor at CNN, told Finch Hamilton, "We started looking at the most popular pieces on the site, and his jumped out as already having gone viral." CNN subsequently offered Granderson a weekly CNN Opinion website column focusing on social and cultural issues and their impact on American society; he began posting on April 12, 2011. Along with his work for CNN, Granderson has continued to provide regular commentary for ESPN, where he is a columnist and senior writer for ESPN.com and *ESPN The Magazine.*

The enormous response elicited by his early CNN guest columns foreshadowed the impact of his regular contributions. His April 19, 2011, piece, entitled "Parents, Don't Dress Your Girls Like Tramps" became one of the most popular stories on the Internet at the time, and the year's fourth most shared story on the social networking site Facebook. Another of Granderson's columns, "Permissive Parents: Curb Your Brats" (5 July 2011), was twenty-eighth on the list.

FAST AND FURIOUS

Not all of the response to Granderson's work has been positive, however. His column about the Fast and Furious scandal, in particular, generated harsh criticism. Fast and Furious was a federal law enforcement operation that allowed American guns to fall into the hands of Mexican drug cartels for the purpose of tracking the weapons. Officials subsequently lost track of the guns, some of which ended up being used in crimes, including the murder of a federal agent. While the investigation of the scandal has become politicized, Granderson's take on the matter was seen by some as overly cavalier and irresponsible, especially coming from a journalist. In "Don't Be Nosy About Fast and Furious" (26 June 2012), Granderson declared, "there comes a point where the public's right to know needs to take a back seat to matters like national security and diplomacy." Glenn Greenwald, writing for *Salon* (27 June 2012), was incredulous: "I suppose the only thing surprising about [Granderson's column] is that someone who works in journalism, and a media corporation that claims to do journalism, would publish something that admits to thinking this way." Such criticism notwithstanding, Granderson is among the most popular columnists on both CNN and ESPN.

PERSONAL LIFE

Granderson lives in the suburbs of Grand Rapids with his teenage son, Isaiah. He is a member of the National Association of Black Journalists and was a Hechinger Institute Fellow at Columbia University. A dedicated athlete, he enjoys playing basketball and tennis. When not writing from his office studio in Grand Rapids, Michigan, or appearing on CNN and ESPN, Granderson frequently gives speeches on behalf of gay, lesbian, and transgender rights as part of the OUTmedia team. "There are not a lot of openly gay black men in the public eye and so I feel obligated to share my story in hopes of making things easier for those behind me," he remarked to Pardeep Toor.

SUGGESTED READING

Baeza Bickel, Nardy. "ESPN Columnist Speaks About Being Honest About Gender Preferences at End of GVSU's 'Day of Silence.'" *Grand Rapids Press*. Michigan Live LLC, 15 Apr. 2009. Web. 11 July 2012.

Finch Hamilton, Terri. "Profile: ESPN, CNN Journalist LZ Granderson." *Grand Rapids Press*. Michigan Live LLC, 8 Jan. 2012. Web. 11 July 2012.

Granderson, LZ. "Don't Be Nosy About Fast and Furious." *CNN*. Turner Broadcasting System Inc., 26 June 2012. Web. 11 July 2012.

---. "Parents, Don't Dress Your Girls Like Tramps." *CNN*. Turner Broadcasting System Inc., 19 Apr. 2011. Web. 11 July 2012.

---. "The Late Gary Bond, Friend and Mentor." *ESPN*. ESPN Internet Ventures, 15 May 2010. Web. 11 July 2012.

---. "Bless You Boys." *ESPN Page 2*. ESPN Internet Ventures, 20 Oct. 2006. Web. 11 July 2012.

Tcheyan, Max. "The B/R Interview: LZ Granderson." *Bleacher Report*. Bleacher Report, 18 Nov. 2008. Web. 11 July 2012.

Toor, Pardeep. "Interviews: Detroit Native and *ESPN Page 2*'s LZ Granderson Talks About Socials Ills, Detroit Pistons, Michael Jordan and Gay Athletes." *Flint Journal*. Michigan Live, 6 Jan. 2009. Web. 11 July 2012.

—*Paul McCaffrey*

Markus Greiner

Born: August 20, 1973–
Occupation: Physicist, educator

The German-born experimental physicist Markus Greiner has conducted pioneering research that is helping to illuminate characteristics of atoms apparent only when the particles are at temperatures near absolute zero, an artificially induced state in which their motion slows to a minuscule fraction of the speeds at which they move at ordinary room temperatures. By

Courtesy the John D. & Catherine T. MacArthur Foundation

producing an environment in which atoms are nearly motionless and by inventing a revolutionary kind of microscope with which to observe them, Greiner has enabled researchers who study ultracold atoms to examine, control, and manipulate them to an unprecedented extent.

In 2004, Greiner received the William L. McMillan Award from the Department of Physics of the University of Illinois at Urbana–Champaign for his groundbreaking contributions in the field of condensed-matter physics. In 2011, the John D. and Catherine T. MacArthur Foundation honored him with a $500,000 fellowship—commonly referred to as the MacArthur "genius award." The foundation recognized Greiner for "advancing our capacity to control the spatial organization of ultra-cold atoms with the aim of revealing basic principles of condensed matter physics," according to a post on its website (Sep. 2011). "Still early in his career, Greiner has already demonstrated the ability to develop techniques that open new avenues for [the] exploration of physics and to apply these advances to both fundamental physics and technology."

Absolute zero—zero degrees on the Kelvin scale—is equivalent to minus 273.15 degrees Celsius or minus 459.67 degrees Fahrenheit. The lowest temperature ever recorded measured less than one one-billionth of a Kelvin degree above absolute zero; reached in a laboratory at Harvard University, where Greiner works, it is lower than that of any temperature ever recorded under natural conditions anywhere in the universe. At temperatures near absolute zero, atoms enter what is called the quantum realm, in which their behavior is radically different from their behavior at room temperatures. In particular, they may coalesce to form a single "superatom," known as a Bose-Einstein condensate—an entity that does not exist in the natural world. Einstein-Bose condensates behave like waves as well as particles. They exhibit other properties that are counterintuitive and virtually impossible for most people to visualize or accept as real. "It's pretty cool stuff," Greiner told Marlene Cimons for the *National Science Foundation* (4 Nov. 2011, online). "But it is far from the everyday world, and hard to grasp for the public."

EDUCATION AND EARLY RESEARCH

Markus B. Greiner was born in Germany on August 20, 1973. From January 1999 to February 2000, he worked toward his diploma—equivalent in the United States to a master's degree—in experimental physics at the Ludwig Maximilians University (LMU) in Munich. He conducted research as a member of Theodor W. Hänsch's team. Hänsch later won the 2005 Nobel Prize in Physics; he has credited Greiner with helping him with his research into the quantum theory of optical coherence. Hänsch's team engaged in joint studies with the team of renowned physicist Immanuel Bloch, who had earned his PhD under Hänsch at the Max-Planck Institute for Quantum Optics in Garching, Germany. Their research centered on ultracold quantum gases.

Greiner's diploma thesis, entitled "Transport of Magnetically Trapped Atoms: A Simple Approach to Bose-Einstein Condensation" (2000), discusses the "development of a new scheme for a Bose-Einstein condensate apparatus for optical lattice experiments" and includes descriptions of the theory behind, design, and operation of the equipment. Optical lattices are made with laser beams—or, specifically, "a standing wave laser light field," as Greiner wrote. In a paper published in the science journal *Nature* (5 June 2008) and cowritten by his Harvard laboratory partner Simon Fölling, Greiner explains that optical lattices "have rapidly become a favored tool of atomic and condensed-matter physicists. These crystals made of light can be used to trap atoms at very low temperatures, creating a workshop in which to pore over and tinker with fundamental properties of matter." The Greiner Lab website notes that "the behavior of ultracold atoms in optical lattices is similar to that of electrons in solids." According to the MacArthur Foundation post, "Because optical lattices offer high-resolution control over the quantum state of hundreds or thousands of individual elements, they may also represent an important platform for investigating quantum computing or high-density information storage."

Greiner remained at LMU to pursue a PhD degree under Hänsch. "Quantum Phase Transition from a Superfluid to a Mott Insulator in a Gas of Ultracold Atoms," a paper that appeared in *Nature* (3 Jan. 2002) with Greiner, Hänsch, Bloch, and two others as authors, described the never-before achieved results of their principal experiments. A superfluid is a liquid that flows without friction; a Mott insulator, according to *Science 2.0* (27 Sep. 2009, online), is "a special phase of matter, usually formed at very low temperatures, in which certain materials that should conduct electricity act as electrical insulators, due to unusual interactions between electrons." The transition to which the title of the paper refers was triggered by variations in potential energy. These variations went from high, meaning that mostly positive electrical charges were present, to low, in which mostly negative electrical charges were present. The transition was measured in ultracold atoms loaded onto an optical lattice. "For low potential depths, the atoms form a superfluid phase, where each atom is spread out over the entire lattice, with long-range phase coherence across the lattice," Greiner and his associates wrote. "For high potential depths the repulsive interactions between the atoms cause a transition to a Mott insulator phase. In this phase the atoms are localized at the lattice sites with an exactly defined atom number, but no phase coherence throughout the lattice. The Mott insulator phase is characterized by a gap in the excitation spectrum, which is detected in the experiment. We also demonstrate that it is possible to reversibly change between the two ground states of the system."

DISSERTATION AND RESEARCH WITH DEBORAH JIN

Greiner's 2003 doctoral dissertation is entitled *Ultracold Quantum Gases in Three-Dimensional Optical Lattice Potentials.* In the dissertation abstract, Greiner states that the experiments he conducted under the supervision of Hänsch and Bloch had opened the door to "a new field of physics with ultracold gases." This new field was one in which a "novel quantum system offers the unique possibility to experimentally address fundamental questions of modern solid state physics, atomic physics, quantum optics, and quantum information." Greiner's dissertation earned him the American Physical Society's thesis award in 2004.

After Greiner completed his PhD, he settled in Colorado in 2003. There, as a postgraduate researcher, he worked with a group led by the celebrated physicist Deborah Jin at the Joint Institute for Laboratory Astrophysics (JILA) in Boulder, Colorado, which is operated by the University of Colorado at Boulder and the National Institute of Standards and Technology. In *Nature* (4 Dec. 2003), Greiner, Jin, and Cindy A. Regal, one of Jin's graduate students, reported that they had successfully synthesized the world's first "molecular Bose-Einstein condensate from a fermi gas,"—an extraordinary accomplishment that made headlines in the scientific press internationally.

At a press conference held at the University of Colorado on January 24, 2004, Jin, a 2003 MacArthur fellow, announced that she, Greiner, and Regal had created a "new form of matter" called a fermionic condensate. "Our fermionic condensate is not a Bose-Einstein condensate and not a superconductor but . . . may link these two behaviors," Jin explained to reporters. As explained in the April 2004 *Current Biography* profile of Jin, all elementary particles are either fermions or bosons. Einstein-Bose condensates are made up only of bosons. Jin's group created "a condensate in a gas of fermionic atoms" by creating an ultracold gas of potassium atoms in which, for the first time, the scientists paired fermions to make bosons. Their creation of a "new example of dramatic quantum behavior," Jin said, "gives the scientific community a new tool for understanding the basic physics behind superconductivity." That knowledge may provide clues to what is necessary to construct supercomputers that will operate at room temperatures. In a University of Colorado press release issued on the same day, Carl Wieman, the cowinner with Eric Cornell of the 2001 Nobel Prize in physics, praised the JILA trio's work as "a spectacular piece of physics." As a member of Jin's team, Greiner coauthored eight journal articles about fermi condensates.

INVENTION OF QUANTUM GAS MICROSCOPE

In 2005, Greiner joined the faculty of Harvard University in Cambridge, Massachusetts, as an assistant professor in the Department of Physics and the head of his own laboratory, where he has mentored the doctoral students and postdoctoral fellows who work with him. He was promoted to full professor in early 2012. Greiner conducts research that, according to the Greiner Lab's website, "focuses on studying ultracold gases loaded into artificial crystals of light known as optical lattices." Their development of the quantum gas microscope was announced publicly in 2009. Greiner told a reporter for *Science Daily* (17 June 2010, online), "Much of modern technology is driven by engineering materials with novel properties, and the bizarre world of quantum mechanics can contribute to this engineering toolbox. For example, quantum materials could be used to turn heat into electricity, or in cables that transport electricity very efficiently in a power grid. The challenge in understanding the behavior of such materials is that although we have many ideas about how they might work, we lack the tools to verify these theories by looking at and manipulating these materials at the most basic

atomic level. This is the problem we have set out to tackle."

Greiner has conducted research in his laboratory at Harvard and at the Center for Ultracold Atoms, the latter of which is operated jointly by Harvard and the Massachusetts Institute of Technology (MIT). He attracted wide attention among physicists with his report "A Quantum Gas Microscope for Detecting Single Atoms in a Hubbard Regime Optical Lattice," published in *Nature* (5 Nov. 2009). The report describes his group's construction of a new type of microscope with which they had detected single atoms of the element rubidium that had been cooled to five one-billionths of a Kelvin degree above absolute zero. In the *Harvard Gazette* (5 Nov. 2009, online), Steve Bradt wrote that Greiner and his colleagues had observed the rubidium atoms "in a crystalline structure made solely of light, called a Bose Hubbard optical lattice." Waseem S. Bakr, a graduate student who coauthored the report, told Bradt, "At such low temperatures, atoms follow the rules of quantum mechanics, causing them to behave in very unexpected ways. Quantum mechanics allows atoms to quickly tunnel around within the lattice, move around with no resistance, and even be 'delocalized' over the entire lattice. With our microscope we can individually observe tens of thousands of atoms working together to perform these amazing feats." The Greiner Lab's research was supported by the National Science Foundation, the US Army and Air Forces offices of scientific research, the Defense Advanced Research Projects Agency, and the Alfred P. Sloan Foundation.

RESEARCH INTO QUANTUM PHASE TRANSITIONS

The following year, Greiner announced that he and his group had "succeeded in coaxing ultracold atoms trapped in an optical lattice to self-organize into a magnet, using only the minute perturbations resulting from quantum mechanics," according to a press release issued by his laboratory (12 Apr. 2011, online). The press release states that by means of their "quantum simulator," the Greiner Lab researchers "found that when they applied a force to a crystal formed by ultracold atoms trapped in an optical lattice . . . the atoms behaved like a chain of little magnets that repelled one another, in the presence of an external magnetic field which sought to align them." According to Greiner, "Quantum fluctuations can make the magnets point in multiple directions simultaneously. This 'quantum weirdness' gives rise to many of the fascinating properties of quantum magnets." He added, "There remain many exciting questions to answer, and we have only just scratched the surface. By studying the bizarre and wonderful ways that quantum mechanics works, we open new perspectives not only for developing novel high tech materials, but also for quantum information processing and computation."

The article "Probing the Superfluid-to-Mott Insulator Transition at the Single-Atom Level," published in *Science* (17 June 2010, online), earned Greiner and the members of his laboratory team the Newcomb Cleveland Prize of the American Association for the Advancement of Science (AAAS), the oldest award bestowed by that organization. In December 2010, *Science*, which is an AAAS publication, included the article in its list of "breakthroughs of the year."

"BEYOND SUPERCOOL"

A paper entitled "Orbital Excitation Blockade and Algorithmic Cooling in Quantum Gases," written by the same Greiner Lab researchers, appeared in the December 22, 2011, issue of *Nature*. The paper described what a reporter for *R&D Magazine* (22 Dec. 2011) labeled a "proof-of-principle experiment." The experiment provided a new way to bring atoms in quantum gases to temperatures lower than ever before—"beyond supercool," in Greiner's words. "Ultracold atoms are the coldest objects in the known universe," Greiner told *R&D*. "Their temperature is only a billionth of a degree above absolute zero temperature, but we will need to make them even colder if we are to harness their unique properties to learn about quantum mechanics." A phenomenon called "orbital excitation blockade" makes this possible, according to a 2011 press release issued by the Greiner Lab. "When two atoms occupy the same lattice site, the excitation of one of them to a higher energy level (orbital) suppresses the excitation of the other. Excited atoms can then be removed from the system, taking [heat] entropy with them. This ability to control the number of atoms occupying each lattice site is also of interest for quantum computing, as it should allow the creation of quantum registers with thousands of lattice-trapped atoms, and, in principle, the implementation of two quantum-bit gates for generalized computing."

In its discussion of Greiner's "beyond supercool" experiment, *R&D* states: "The Harvard team has demonstrated that they can actively remove the fluctuations that constitute temperature, rather than merely waiting for hot particles to leave as in evaporative cooling. Akin to preparing precisely one egg per dimple in a carton, this 'orbital excitation blockade' process removes excess atoms from a crystal until there is precisely one atom per site." Greiner emphasized the importance of his laboratory's findings. "The collective behaviors of atoms at these temperatures remain an important open question, and the breathtaking control we now exert over individual atoms will be a powerful tool for answering it." He added, "We are glimpsing a mysterious and

wonderful world that has never been seen in this way before."

OUTSIDE OF THE LABORATORY

In an article for the *Harvard Crimson* (28 Sep. 2011, online) Shengxi Li wrote, "Despite his fame in the physics world, Greiner's greatest appeal to students seems to come from his down-to-earth attitude. At the end of a class, he takes his undergraduates out to ice cream. He also invites his graduate students to lunch on a regular basis." M. Eric Tai, a graduate student who has coauthored several of Greiner's journal articles, told Li, "He [Greiner] is so laid-back [that] you wouldn't expect him to be so good." He added: "Every year, the American Physical Society holds a conference for Atomic Molecular Optical Physics. When [Greiner] speaks . . . he fills the room, even at an 8 a.m. talk." Greiner told Li, "My approach [to] teaching is as much hands-on as possible, as much intuitive as possible, as much to foster creativity as possible . . . so students can explore how exciting physics can be."

MACARTHUR FELLOWSHIP

A week earlier, Samuel Y. Weinstock had reported in the *Harvard Crimson* (21 Sep. 2011, online) that Greiner had won a five-year, no-strings-attached, $500,000 MacArthur fellowship. "Although he is still deciding exactly how he will put the grant to use," Weinstock wrote, "Greiner is thinking about installing an exploration lab that would give physics students the chance to try out new things and retain what he described as their 'play spirit.'" According to Greiner, "That's how innovation in the long run comes along." Greiner and his wife live in Belmont, Massachusetts.

SUGGESTED READING

Bradt, Steve. "Insights on Quantum Mechanics: Harvard Physicists Create Simulative Process to Gauge Unseen Forces." *Harvard Gazette*. Harvard University, 17 June 2010. Web. 28 Mar. 2012.

___. "Quantum Gas Microscope Created: Offers Glimpse of Quirky Ultracold Atoms. Research Creates a Readout System for Quantum Simulation and Computation." *Harvard Gazette*. Harvard University, 5 Nov. 2009. Web. 28 Mar. 2012.

Cimons, Marlene. "Creating Quantum Matter: MacArthur Fellow Sees Endless Possibilities." *National Science Foundation*. *U.S. News & World Report*. U.S. News & World Report, 4 Nov. 2011. Web. 28 Mar. 2012.

Greiner, Markus. *Greiner Lab*. Department of Physics, Harvard University, n.d. Web. 28. Mar. 2012.

Li, Shengxi. "Genius Bar: Markus Greiner." *Harvard Crimson*. Harvard University, 28 Sep. 2011. Web. 28 Mar. 2012.

"Markus Greiner: Condensed Matter Physicist." *2011 MacArthur Fellows*. MacArthur Foundation, Sep. 2011. Web. 28 Mar. 2012.

"Research Probing a Quantum Phase Transition Wins the 2011 AAAS Newcomb Cleveland Prize." *Eurekalert!* American Association for the Advancement of Science, 15 Feb. 2012. Web 28 Mar. 2012.

—*Miriam Helbok*

Blake Griffin

Born: March 16, 1989
Occupation: Basketball player

In the history of the National Basketball Association (NBA), there have been players known for their extraordinary dunking ability—Julius "Dr. J" Erving, Michael Jordan, Shaquille O'Neal, Kobe Bryant, and Vince Carter among them—but never before has a player made such an immediate impact on the league with his gravity-defying aerial feats as the Los Angeles Clippers' power forward Blake Griffin. After only one season in the NBA, Griffin can already make a strong case for being the league's best dunker as well as one of its brightest all-around young talents. While the 2010–11 NBA season was largely dominated by discussion of the Miami Heat and the astronomically high expectations surrounding the team, given the newly assembled superstar trio of Dwyane Wade, Chris Bosh, and LeBron James, Griffin often challenged the Heat's so-called "Big Three" as the league's top new story with his jaw-dropping dunks—214 in total—and consistently exciting play. "He's a highlight at any second of the game, but he's also smart enough to know that the fundamentals are the part that will make him better and help this team," Vinny Del Negro, the Clippers' coach and a former NBA player, told Greg Beacham for the Associated Press (5 May 2011). "He handles it very well. He has great humility and great character." After being selected by the Clippers as the first overall pick in the 2009 NBA draft, Griffin missed the entire 2009–10 season with a knee injury. He returned in 2010–11 to lead all rookies in average number of points per game (22.5) and rebounds per game (12.1) and in number of double-doubles (67)—that is, contests in which he reached double digits in two statistical categories—while playing in all eighty-two games for the Clippers; he became the first rookie since Elton Brand in 1999–2000 to average at least 20 points and 10 rebounds per game. He was also the first rookie to be selected for an NBA All-Star Game since the Houston Rockets' Yao Ming in 2003, and he won the NBA Sprite

Getty Images

Slam Dunk Contest during the 2011 NBA All-Star Weekend, after jumping over a car to make a dunk. After sweeping the six Western Conference Rookie of the Month honors during the season, Griffin was the unanimous choice for 2011 NBA Rookie of the Year. Referring to his talent for highlight-reel dunks, he told John Branch for the *New York Times* (11 Dec. 2010), "I take pride in being able to finish"—that is, make a basket, particularly by dunking. He added, "There's a lot of great finishers that don't dunk that much. But I take pride in finishing."

EARLY LIFE AND EDUCATION

Blake Austin Griffin was born on March 16, 1989, in Oklahoma City, Oklahoma, to an African American father and a white mother. His father, Tommy, a high school basketball coach and math teacher, met his mother, Gail, a high school business teacher, while both taught at Oklahoma City's Classen High School in the early 1980s. His parents also owned a trophy business, which they ran out of the family's garage. Griffin became drawn to sports through his father, who had been a basketball player and a track star at Northwestern Oklahoma State University, and his brother, Taylor, who is nearly three years his senior. He started playing basketball in the first grade. "I wanted to do everything that my dad and my brother did," Griffin recalled to Kevin Baxter for the *Los Angeles Times* (9 Jan. 2011). "So with them being involved in basketball so much, that just came naturally to me. And I grew to love it."

Growing up, Griffin played in youth leagues for football, basketball, and baseball. While standing out among his peers, he was most competitive with his brother, who normally got the upper hand in sports. "I was bigger and stronger for most of our childhood, so I'd win at most things we'd do and he didn't like that," his brother told Blair Kerkhoff for the *Kansas City Star* (15 Mar. 2008). He added, "There was a point where everything we did—whether it was basketball, football, video games, no matter what it was—would end in a fight. For two years, my mom told us we couldn't even play together because it was going to end in a fight no matter what happened." Griffin and his brother were both homeschooled by their mother until seventh grade. Among their childhood friends was the future quarterback and 2008 Heisman Trophy winner Sam Bradford, a top pick in the 2010 National Football League draft.

Griffin's leaping ability was apparent early on, and by the time he was thirteen years old, he was already able to dunk a basketball. He attended Oklahoma Christian School, in Edmond, an affluent suburb north of Oklahoma City; there, he played with his brother on the school's varsity basketball team, which was coached by their father. In daily practices their father helped them master the basketball fundamentals of passing and dribbling. The Griffins led the Oklahoma Christian Saints to back-to-back state championships during the 2003–04 and 2004–05 basketball seasons, in which the team posted records of 29–0 and 24–2, respectively. Griffin began leading the Saints after his sophomore year, when his brother, who was named Oklahoma's High School Player of the Year for the 2004–05 season, accepted a basketball scholarship at the University of Oklahoma (OU). During the summer before his junior season, Blake Griffin played on an Amateur Athletic Union (AAU) team that competed in tournaments throughout Oklahoma, which helped strengthen his game. His play was nothing short of dominant during his junior season, when he averaged 21 points and 12.5 rebounds per game and helped take the Saints to a third consecutive state title. He was named the state tournament's Most Valuable Player (MVP) and was also named Player of the Year by the Oklahoma City Oklahoman. By that time Griffin had become one of the most sought-after recruits in the country. His play particularly won the attention of OU's new head coach, Jeff Capel. "I was blown away," Capel told Berry Tramel for the *Oklahoman* (8 Apr. 2009). "I hadn't seen a guy with that size and that strength and that incredible athleticism."

HIGH SCHOOL PLAYER OF THE YEAR ATTENDS OU

After some coaxing from his brother, Griffin, who also received scholarship offers from such college-basketball powerhouses as Duke University, the University of Kansas, the University of North Carolina at Chapel Hill, and the University of Florida, agreed to play for OU and committed to the school before his senior season. As a senior he averaged 26.8 points and 15.1 rebounds per game and led the Saints to a record of 26–3, en route to their fourth consecutive state title. He received state-tournament MVP honors for the second straight year and was again named Player of the Year by the Oklahoman, as well as by the newspaper Tulsa World. He was also named the Gatorade Oklahoma Player of the Year and was selected as a McDonald's All-American. After being ranked among the top twenty-five players in the nation, Griffin fulfilled his commitment to OU, joining his brother at the university. As a freshman he made an immediate impact on a Sooners' team that had posted a lackluster 16–15 record during the previous year; he averaged 14.7 points and 9.1 rebounds per game and ranked among the Big 12 Conference's leaders in scoring, rebounding, and field-goal percentage. Griffin received First-Team All-Big 12 Conference honors and was named to the conference's All-Rookie team. The Sooners improved their regular-season record to 21–10 and advanced to the second round of the National Collegiate Athletic Association (NCAA) tournament, where they lost to the University of Louisville, 78–48.

During his sophomore season Griffin distinguished himself as arguably the best college player in the nation. He started thirty-five games for the Sooners and averaged 22.7 points, 14.4 rebounds, 2.3 assists, and 1.1 steals per game. Griffin led the nation in rebounding and double-doubles (30) and led the Big 12 in scoring, rebounding, and field-goal percentage (.654). He also set both Big 12 and Sooners records for most rebounds (504) and double-doubles (30) in a single season; his 504 rebounds were the highest total for a college player since Larry Bird's 505 in 1979, and his rebound average was the highest since Tim Duncan's 14.7 in 1997. He also ranked among the nation's leaders in other statistical categories, finishing second in field-goal percentage and eleventh in scoring. Griffin's season was highlighted by his performance in a game against Texas Tech on February 14, 2009, in which he scored 40 points and pulled down 23 rebounds, both career highs. He became just the third player in Sooners' history to record at least 40 points and 20 rebounds in a game (the others are Wayman Tisdale and Alvan Adams). Earlier that season he also became the only player in Big 12 history to score at least 20 points and make at least 20 rebounds in consecutive games, accomplishing the feat in games against Davidson College and Gardner-Webb University. The Sooners, meanwhile, finished the regular season with a record of 27–4 and returned to the NCAA tournament. In four tournament games Griffin averaged 28.5 points, 15 rebounds, and 2.3 assists and posted an astonishing .780 field-goal percentage. Those numbers helped the Sooners advance to the tournament's Elite Eight; they were eliminated from the competition, losing to the University of North Carolina Tar Heels, 72–60, in the south regional final. Griffin's dominating play resulted in his winning virtually every major college-basketball award at the end of the 2008–09 season. He was a unanimous selection to the First-Team All-Big 12 team and was the consensus college player of the year. His honors also included the Naismith Award, the Oscar Robertson Trophy, the Rupp Trophy, the John R. Wooden Award, and the Associated Press (AP) Player of the Year Award.

FIRST OVERALL PICK IN 2009 NBA DRAFT

Following his sophomore year at Oklahoma, Griffin announced that he would forgo his final two years of college to enter the 2009 NBA draft. He finished his college career at OU ranked first of all time in field-goal percentage (.618), second in rebounds per game (11.8), third in double-doubles (40), sixth in points per game (18.8), ninth in rebounds (805), and seventeenth in points (1,278). Griffin is only the third player in school history (after Wayman Tisdale and Alvan Adams) to reach one thousand points in his first two seasons. He is widely credited with transforming Oklahoma's previously unheralded basketball program into a national powerhouse. Commenting on Griffin's influence in luring other highly touted recruits to the school, Jeff Capel told Thayer Evans for the *New York Times* (9 Mar. 2009), "When you're trying to rebuild a program, sometimes all it takes is one guy and then that one guy allows you to get other guys, especially if it's a guy like Blake."

As was widely expected, Griffin was selected with the first overall pick in the 2009 draft, by the Los Angeles Clippers. In the process he became the first Oklahoma native ever to be taken with the top pick in the draft. In July of that year, he signed a three-year, $16 million contract with the team. (The Clippers recently picked up a fourth-year option on his contract.) Griffin wasted little time living up to expectations. During the Clippers' 2009 Summer League, he averaged 19.2 points, 10.8 rebounds, and 3.2 assists in five games and was named Summer League MVP. He continued to play well in the 2009 NBA preseason, averaging 13.7 points, 8.1 rebounds, 2.1 assists, and 1.7 steals in seven games. Griffin's NBA debut, however, was postponed indefinitely after he injured his left kneecap during a dunk in the Clippers' final preseason game, against the New Orleans Hornets; the stress fracture forced him to undergo season-ending surgery. In Griffin's absence the Clippers finished third in the Pacific Division with a record of 29–53. Meanwhile, their eight-year head coach, Mike Dunleavy, was fired midway through the season and replaced on an interim basis by Kim Hughes. At season's end Hughes was replaced by Vinny Del Negro, a former NBA player who had spent the previous three seasons coaching the Chicago Bulls.

NBA DEBUT WITH THE CLIPPERS

After dedicating the entire 2010–11 off-season to improving his overall game through an intensive regimen of rehabilitation, weightlifting, and practicing, Griffin returned to the court. "When I got injured," he recalled to Greg Beacham, "I just decided I had to come back even better. I had to keep improving even while I couldn't play, and I dedicated myself to that." He went on to have one of the most electrifying rookie campaigns in recent memory. After sitting out the Clippers' Summer League play while recovering from his knee surgery, Griffin returned to action during the 2010 NBA preseason, in which he averaged an impressive 17.3 and 12.3 rebounds in six games. He then made his long-awaited NBA debut, on October 27, 2010, in a game against the Portland Trail Blazers, held at the Staples Center in Los Angeles. Griffin scored the first points of his pro career with a spectacular dunk. Though the Clippers lost the game, 98–88, he finished with a double-double, scoring 20 points and grabbing 14 rebounds.

While the Clippers went on to lose forty-nine more games during the 2010–11 season, finishing with a record of 32–50, Griffin emerged as an NBA star. He played in all eighty-two regular-season games and led all rookies in average number of points (22.5) and rebounds (12.1) per game, which were good for twelfth and fourth places in the league, respectively; he became the first rookie to average at least 20 points and 10 rebounds since Elton Brand did so as a member of the Chicago Bulls during the 1999–2000 season. He also led all rookies with 67 double-doubles and finished second among rookies in average number of assists per game (3.8). Griffin additionally set a Clippers' franchise record for most consecutive double-doubles (27), which he recorded over a two-month span, from November 20, 2010, to January 19, 2011; it was the longest rookie double-double streak since 1968. He also set a Clippers' rookie record for most points in a game, scoring a career-high 47 points in a January contest against the Indiana Pacers. That effort marked his second game of the season with at least 40 points (the other occurring against the New York Knicks, on November 20, 2010), making him the first rookie with two 40-point games since Allen Iverson in 1997.

ALL-STAR NOD

Griffin's play during the first half of the 2010–11 NBA season led coaches to select him as a reserve for the 2011 All-Star Game. He became the first rookie All-Star since the Houston Rockets' Yao Ming in 2003 and just the tenth Clipper to earn an All-Star nod. (Griffin was the first rookie to be voted in as an All-Star reserve by coaches since the San Antonio Spurs' Tim Duncan in 1998.) During the 2011 NBA All-Star Weekend, he competed in the Rookie Challenge and the NBA Sprite Slam Dunk Contest. He won the latter event in dramatic fashion, after jumping over the hood of a 2011 Kia Optima while a surrounding gospel choir sang the R&B star R. Kelly's "I Believe I Can Fly." (Griffin dedicated the winning dunk to his childhood friend and high school teammate Wilson Holloway, who had died of Hodgkins lymphoma in the week leading up to the event. He gave his slam-dunk trophy to Holloway's family.) In total, Griffin finished the 2010–11 season with 214 dunks, the second-highest total in the league behind the Orlando Magic's Dwight Howard, who had 227. Many of those dunks appeared on nightly highlight reels and went viral on the Internet, including one in which he jumped out of reach of the New York Knicks' seven-foot one-inch center Timofey Mozgov, and another in which he slammed his head against the backboard after jumping too high on a dunk attempt against the Minnesota Timberwolves. "His highlights are sick," the Lakers forward Ron Artest said, as quoted by Kevin Baxter. "I hope he dunks on me. Would you buy that poster? I'd buy it and tell him to sign it."

2011 ROOKIE OF THE YEAR

After garnering all six of the Western Conference Rookie of the Month honors during the season, a feat matched only by the New Orleans Hornets' Chris Paul (who swept all monthly honors as a rookie during the 2005–06 season), Griffin was a virtual shoo-in for the 2011 NBA Rookie of the Year Award. He received all 118 first-place votes, making him the first unanimous selection since San Antonio's David Robinson in 1990 and just the third in NBA history (the first was Ralph Sampson, in 1984). He was also the lone unanimous selection to the NBA All-Rookie First Team. Considered by many to be "a once-in-a-generation talent and the most electrifying combination of size, strength, and power to enter the league in more than a decade," as Kevin Baxter wrote, the six-foot-ten, 251-pound Griffin has already helped renew interest in a Clippers' franchise long known for personifying futility in the NBA, with losing records in eighteen of the last nineteen seasons. "He's definitely going to transcend the game," his Clippers teammate Baron Davis, a point guard, told Baxter. "His only fight is chasing the Hall of Fame."

PERSONAL LIFE

Griffin lives in Manhattan Beach, California. He has signed endorsement deals with the trading-card company Panini and the consumer-electronics company Vizio, and he has appeared in commercials for the Subway restaurant chain, AT&T, Nike, and Kia Motors. He is known for being a "gym rat," as he dedicates much of his free time to working out. At times he has even clashed with coaches and trainers over his tendency to push himself too hard in workouts. He is also known for his wit and has a reputation among his teammates and family members as a jokester. His older brother, Taylor, was a member of the NBA's Phoenix Suns for two seasons (2009–10) before signing with the Belgacom Liege, a professional basketball club in Belgium, in 2010.

SUGGESTED READING

Baxter, Kevin. "A Rising Superstar Lifts Downtrodden Clippers." *Los Angeles Times* 9 Jan. 2011: A1.

Branch, John. "Rookie's Dunks Earn Online Views and On-Court Smiles." *New York Times.* New York Times Co., 10 Dec. 2010. Web. Jan. 2012.

Helsley, John. "March Is Why Blake Griffin, Taylor Griffin Stayed at OU." *NewsOK.* Oklahoman NewsOK, 18 Mar. 2009. Web. Jan. 2012.

Holmes, Baxter. "Blake Griffin Stands as Oklahoma's Tower of Strength." *Los Angeles Times* 24 Mar. 2009: C1.

—*Christopher Cullen*

Parisa Hafezi

Born: February 4, 1970
Occupation: Journalist and bureau chief for Reuters in Iran

Many people ask reporter Parisa Hafezi why she continues to do her job in the wake of being kidnapped and beaten by Iranian security forces and facing continual government harassment and surveillance. She has a ready answer. As she explained to Maria Sanminiatelli for an Associated Press article that appeared in the London *Guardian* (27 Oct. 2011), "This is not my job—this is my life."

Hafezi, who remained in Iran to report on the violent 2009 uprising while other news agency employees were fleeing to safety, received a Courage in Journalism Award from the International Women's Media Foundation (IWMF) for her work. "I need[ed] to stay in the field," she told Lesley Kennedy for *More* magazine (24 Oct. 2011). "Without witnessing events like protests, how can you report it properly? . . . Being beaten or detained is part of our job, particularly for those who cover

Getty Images

government workers were ordered to adhere to Islamic dress codes, and public amenities, such as beaches and recreation facilities, were segregated by gender. Any public physical contact between the sexes could be grounds for whipping, and adultery could earn a woman the death penalty. Single women could also be subjected to tests of their virginity if found alone with an unmarried man, and the minimum age at which girls could be married was reduced to nine.

Despite a cultural atmosphere in which women were routinely considered secondclass citizens or worse, Hafezi's parents continued to stress that her education was as important as that of her younger brother and that they valued her accomplishments highly. Both Hafezi's mother and father were politically minded and intellectual. The family home was filled with books—including many that had been banned by the ayatollah—and Hafezi was an avid reader, finishing books that were well above her grade level, even as she struggled to comprehend the material.

CHOOSING A FIELD OF STUDY

When Hafezi was thirteen, she was required to choose a field of study—one focused on either science or the humanities. Because she greatly admired her father, she initially chose the latter, so that she could become a lawyer like him. She recalled to *Current Biography*, "My father convinced me not to, because after the revolution, women were banned from practicing some professions, including becoming a judge, and female lawyers were almost jobless at that time." (Even Shirin Ebadi, who in 2003 became the first Iranian and the first Muslim woman ever to win the Nobel Peace Prize, had been stripped of her judgeship and demoted to an administrative post after the revolution.)

Hafezi decided to pursue dentistry instead of law, and after finishing high school at the age of seventeen, she took the national university entrance exam. Despite passing the test with an impressive score, she was rejected because of her family's reputation as liberal. Gravely disappointed by the rejection, she traveled instead to neighboring Turkey, where other young Iranians were then pursuing degrees in medicine. In just two months she had learned the local language and taken the university entrance exams for foreign students. Once again, however, she was denied, despite being a top student.

Ever pragmatic, she abandoned her goal of becoming a dentist and instead learned metallurgical engineering at Ankara's Middle East Technical University. There, she was a stellar student, although she has admitted that she sometimes studied to the exclusion of everything else, making it difficult to participate in extracurricular activities or socialize.

stories in hostile environments. You cannot sit in an office in the United States or Europe or anywhere else and write about protests in Iran."

EARLY LIFE AND EDUCATION

Hafezi was born on February 4, 1970, in Orūmīyeh (also written Urmia or Urūmiyeh), the capital of Iran's Azerbayjan-e Gharbi province. Located in a fertile agricultural region surrounded by numerous bodies of water (including Lake Urmia, one of the largest salt-water lakes in the world), Orūmīyeh is home to an Azeri Turkish majority, as well as Kurdish and Armenian minorities.

Hafezi's mother was a psychologist, and her father was a lawyer. When Hafezi was a year old, she and her family moved to the Iranian capital, Tehran, because of the educational opportunities there. "As long as I [can] remember, my father wanted me to be an educated and independent woman," Hafezi told *Current Biography*. "I went to [the] best schools in Tehran." When Hafezi was nine years old, the Iranian Revolution, also known as the Islamic Revolution, took place. Iran's Westernized monarch, Shah Mohammad Reza Pahlavi, was deposed, and an Islamic republic was instituted, under the repressive leadership of Ayatollah Ruhollah Khomeini.

While poverty and illiteracy undeniably decreased in the wake of the revolution, Khomeini opposed equal rights for women. Within just months of his rise to power, female

GETTING STARTED IN JOURNALISM

Further disappointment awaited Hafezi upon her graduation. Returning home to Iran, she found no engineering jobs available to her and soon began to feel desperate. In an attempt to help, a family friend introduced her to the Turkish ambassador to Iran. He in turn helped her to find a job as a correspondent at Turkey's Anatolian News Agency, which hired her in 1993. Despite having no previous interest or experience in journalism, Hafezi found that she enjoyed the work and was proud to be the first female journalist working for a foreign media company in postrevolutionary Iran. Initially, because of her youth and inexperience, she found that she had to prove herself to officials and colleagues alike.

In 1995 Hafezi next joined ANSA, an Italian news agency, which had a small office in Tehran. By this time she had earned the respect and trust of her fellow journalists. Whenever the ANSA bureau chief went on vacation, she stepped in, and she discovered that the added responsibility suited her well. She gradually built a wide network of analysts, diplomats, and other sources, and her reputation as a skilled and savvy journalist spread.

During the 1999 pro-democracy student protests in Iran, international news organizations were looking for journalists to provide on-the-ground coverage of the unrest. NTV, a major Turkish news channel, approached Hafezi, and although she had never worked for a television station, she agreed to take a behind-the-scenes role.

The following year, a group of senior NTV journalists traveled to Iran to report on the 2000 parliamentary elections. On the day of their arrival, Hafezi accompanied them to a live taping. Moments before the program was due to start, someone noticed that the senior reporter wearing a blue jacket could not be taped in the station's blue room because of the technical difficulties the coordinated colors would pose. Hafezi was quickly ordered to stand in front of the camera and handle the live program herself, despite never having been on air before. "Surprisingly, my editors liked my natural behavior," she recalled to *Current Biography*. "I became well known in Turkey because I was a woman reporting from an Islamic country and spoke the language fluently. . . . I learned a lesson [then]: Always be yourself and believe in yourself."

THE SITUATION IN IRAN

Since the 1979 revolution, Iran had been widely considered a pariah by the Western world because of its repressive policies. In 2002 President George W. Bush went so far as to refer to the country as part of an "axis of evil," along with Iraq and North Korea, because of its nuclear ambitions, which were presumed to be nefarious. In 2005 Mahmoud Ahmadinejad, the ultraconservative mayor of Tehran, assumed the presidency, and international censure intensified even further. (Ahmadinejad, firm in his resolve that Iran had the right to develop nuclear technology, also frequently spouted anti-Israel rhetoric, and in 2006 Iran hosted a highly controversial conference that featured a contingent of Holocaust deniers.) The UN Security Council imposed strict sanctions on the country in 2006, and the following year the United States followed suit, calling for the most severe and sweeping sanctions it had imposed on that nation since the revolution. Ahmadinejad, however, had no inclination to soften either his domestic or international policies.

As a result, Iran remained a difficult country in which to work—perhaps especially for women journalists. "Let's just start with shaking hands," Hafezi explained to Tabby Biddle for the *Huffington Post* (24 Oct. 2011). "When you see someone, the first thing that you do is shake hands to establish contact. As a woman, you cannot do that in Iran. It's forbidden. And then when you're meeting with an official, you have to take care of your head scarf because if anything happens, you will lose your press card." She continued, "We are in a country where your husband can ban you from leaving the house or from leaving the country. So imagine if you are a journalist and you have to travel to cover stories, and your husband bans you from [doing so]." Censorship has also been a major issue for reporters of both genders; following the adoption of a new press law in 2000, for example, the government banned the publication of more than a dozen reform-minded newspapers, and in subsequent years more news outlets have met the same fate.

REUTERS

In 2005, while still working at NTV, Hafezi became a senior correspondent with Reuters, a major international news agency. The company has a storied history, which began in 1851, when Paul Julius Reuter, a German-born immigrant, settled in London. In his native land he had founded a news service that employed a combination of telegraph technology and carrier pigeons, and once settled in his adopted city, he opened an office in the financial district. Transmitting stock-market quotes and news between London and Paris, he enjoyed great success and soon opened branches throughout Europe. The company continually expanded, making inroads into the United States and Far East and acquiring numerous newspapers and publishing firms. In 2008 Reuters affiliate Thomson Corporation and Reuters Group PLC merged, creating Thomson Reuters, as the organization is now officially known.

In 2006 Hafezi, who was mentored at Reuters by veteran Lebanese-born reporter Samia

Nakhoul, was named deputy chief of the agency's bureau in Tehran. She held that post until 2009, when she was promoted to bureau chief. She received her promotion just a month before mass uprisings broke out in the wake of a contested election.

THE 2009 PROTESTS

In June 2009 Ahmadinejad was declared to have triumphed in the presidential election. The rival candidates immediately challenged the results, alleging that Ahmadinejad had engaged in vote-rigging. Their supporters took to the streets to demonstrate. When Hafezi ventured among them to provide an eyewitness account of the events, she was beaten by riot police wielding electric batons. Officials had banned members of the foreign media from leaving their offices during the street protests, and they were summarily considered to be risks to national security. Despite that, Hafezi remained undeterred, and she and her staff filed regular reports for Reuters, which was branded a "Zionist news agency" by the Iranian government.

A few days after the election, the Reuters office was raided by plainclothes agents, who questioned Hafezi and her staff, seized recording equipment, and ransacked their desks. Hafezi—who was both mildly humiliated and somewhat amused when the interlopers did not believe that a woman was in charge of the office—was able to notify a London-based colleague on the sly so that Reuters would be aware of the raid. Shortly after that, as hundreds of activists, reporters, and opposition leaders were seized and detained, Hafezi herself was snatched from her home by four men, who took her to an unmarked building where they interrogated and beat her for hours. The most disturbing part, she recalls, was being falsely accused of engaging in illicit sexual relationships with former government officials. How else, her interrogators asked, could she have obtained the information she was reporting.

In 2010 Hafezi's press credentials were revoked for a month and a half, and she now works under the assumption that her phone lines and e-mail accounts are being constantly monitored. She must periodically remind herself, as she told Tabby Biddle, "I'm not a spy. I'm not a political activist. I'm just doing my job." She continued, "You think, 'Okay, whoever wants to listen, let them listen. Let them watch me. Let them control my telephones, my house, whatever. I'm not doing anything wrong.'"

THE INTERNATIONAL WOMEN'S MEDIA FOUNDATION

In 2011 the IWMF, a group devoted to promoting the role of women in the media and advocating for freedom of the press, gave Hafezi a Courage in Journalism Award for her work in Iran. Joining her on the podium were three fellow award recipients: Chiranuch Premchaiporn, who may face a twenty-year prison sentence for criticizing the Thai monarchy on the Internet; Adela Navarro Bello, who refuses to stop reporting on Mexican drug cartels despite repeated death threats; and Kate Adie, a forty-year veteran of journalism long known for reporting from war zones for the British Broadcasting Company (BBC).

Hafezi has said that the award signals to her that she was right to remain in Iran in 2009, despite the fact that some observers, including members of her own family, have questioned that choice. She believes that the media attention she has gotten in the wake of receiving the prize may have a positive impact on Iranian women as a whole. "As women in the Middle East, we are under more pressure compared to [those in] other countries," she said to Biddle. "It helps all of us because our work is being acknowledged."

PERSONAL LIFE

Hafezi's brother died several years ago, and her mother often expresses anxiety about the dangers facing her only surviving child. On occasion, Hafezi also feels pressure from her own children; she has two teenage daughters, Melory and Goltane, who witnessed her travails in 2009 and worry deeply that she will be detained or beaten again. (Despite those fears, Goltane has recently expressed some interest in becoming an investigative reporter.)

Hafezi is divorced from the girls' father and has implied to interviewers that the split was an acrimonious one. In October 2011, when she traveled to IWMF ceremonies in New York and Los Angeles to receive her Courage in Journalism Award, he denied their daughters permission to leave the country to accompany her.

She explained to *Current Biography* that she advises aspiring journalists, "If you are telling the truth, then don't be afraid of anyone [or] anything"—advice she puts to use on a continual basis. Asked by Lesley Kennedy if she could foresee ever leaving her country, Hafezi replied, "There are [still] many stories to be covered in Iran."

SUGGESTED READING

Biddle, Tabby. "Courage in Journalism." *Huffington Post.* Huffington Post, 24 Oct. 2011. Web. 24 June 2012.

Derr, Holly L. "Kate Adie and Parisa Hafezi: Profiles of Courage in Journalism." *Ms. Magazine.* Liberty Media for Women, 28 Oct. 2011. Web. 24 June 2012.

Kennedy, Lesley. "Meet Courage in Journalism Award Winner Parisa Hafezi, Reuters Bureau Chief, Iran." *More Magazine.* Meredith Corporation, 24 Oct. 2011. Web. 24 June 2012.

Sanminiatelli, Maria. "Iranian, Mexican, Thai Women Win Journalism Award." *Guardian* [London]. Guardian News & Media, 27 Oct. 2011. Web. 24 June 2012.

—*Mari Rich*

Chris Hardwick

Born: November 23, 1971
Occupation: Comedian, actor, writer, podcaster

Television and Internet podcast host and producer Christopher Ryan Hardwick is also an actor, comedian, musician, and writer. "For me, I go about my career like it's a game of *Warcraft*," Hardwick told Erik Leijon for the *Montreal Mirror* (28 July 2011, online). "I build up resources and then I branch out into different things, while continuing to have my resources feed my nerd empire." Hardwick, who rose to fame in the mid-1990s as one of the cohosts of MTV's zeitgeist-defining dating game show *Singled Out* (1995), has come to be known as "a Renaissance man among geeks," as Nicole Campos wrote for *LA Weekly* (19 May 2011, online), for his prolific output in a wide number of entertainment mediums. Since 2008, he has run and operated the popular technology and culture website *Nerdist*. He has also hosted the highly acclaimed weekly *Nerdist* podcast since 2010. Both of those ventures have served as the springboard for Hardwick's own multimedia "nerd empire," properties of which fall under the umbrella corporation of Nerdist Industries.

A man of many hats, Hardwick serves as a contributing writer for *Wired* magazine; makes up one half of the comedic musical duo Hard 'n Phirm, with his friend Mike Phirman; and hosts two television shows: G4 network's *Web Soup* (2009), a spin-off of E! Entertainment Television's *The Soup* (2004); and AMC's *Talking Dead* (2011), a live half-hour talk show that airs after that channel's hit horror series *The Walking Dead*. Additionally, he travels the country as a stand-up comedian and occasionally acts in television sitcoms and feature films. Hardwick has approached his multifaceted career with the intention of "getting as many side projects as possible, keeping as many balls in the air as you can," as he told Kevin Purdy for *Lifehacker* (29 Apr. 2009, online). "What you're doing, basically, is diversifying your portfolio." He added, "I don't know how it happened, exactly, but I've been lucky enough to amass a full-time career out of a series of independent projects."

EARLY LIFE AND EDUCATION

Hardwick was born on November 23, 1971, in Louisville, Kentucky. His father, Billy Hardwick,

FilmMagic

was a world-class professional bowler, and his mother, Sharon Hills, was a real estate agent. Because of his father's profession, Hardwick had a peripatetic childhood, moving from city to city until his father retired from the professional bowling circuit. When he was in the third grade, his family settled in Memphis, Tennessee, where his father ran and operated a bowling center. In his book *The Nerdist Way: How to Reach the Next Level (In Real Life)* (2011), Hardwick says that he "was a spoiled nerd at the dawn of the digital revolution" and that he was essentially "grown in a bowling center" at a time "when bowling alleys figured out the addictive, quarter-munching qualities of videogames."

During his youth, Hardwick developed a penchant for such pursuits as video games, chess, and the classic fantasy role-playing game *Dungeons & Dragons*. He also followed in his father's footsteps by taking up bowling and was talented enough to shoot a 289 out of a perfect three hundred at the age of ten. Hardwick participated in several bowling exhibition matches on television at a young age, thanks to his father's celebrity in the bowling world, and made appearances on *The Mike Douglas Show*, *The Richard Simmons Show*, and *Captain Kangaroo* in the early 1980s. Despite his bowling talent, he considered comedy his true passion and fostered dreams of becoming a stand-up comedian. He was a huge fan of the comedian Steve Martin and had every one of his comedy records growing up. In an interview with Jessica Gardner for *Backstage*, (22 Sep. 2011, online), Hardwick called Martin "a gateway to every comic" in the late 1970s and 1980s. He added: "All I did when I was a kid was watch comedy—standup, any kind of British comedy I could get, *Monty Python*, *The Young Ones*, any of that stuff. That was really my childhood."

Hardwick attended St. Benedict at Auburndale High School, a private Catholic school in Cordova, Tennessee. Midway through his freshman year, he transferred to Regis Jesuit High School, in Aurora, Colorado, after moving with his mother and stepfather to Denver—Hardwick's parents had divorced in 1982. Hardwick spent his freshman through junior years at Regis before moving again with his mother and stepfather to Los Angeles, California, where he attended another Jesuit preparatory school, Loyola High School, for his senior year. He recalled to Leijon, "In high school I got good grades, was in chess club, computer camp—I was very active in all things nerdy." After graduating from Loyola in 1989, Hardwick enrolled at the University of California, Los Angeles (UCLA), where he majored in philosophy. He had originally intended on majoring in mathematics and then art before settling on philosophy. He thought that philosophy "would be good for comedy," as he told Christopher Cobb for *University Wire* (5 Nov. 2001, online). While attending UCLA, Hardwick met Mike Phirman. The two were both members of the school's stand-up comedy club and began singing musical parodies together under the name Hard 'n Phirm. In 1995, they entered and won UCLA's annual Spring Sing talent competition, but broke up shortly afterwards. They would reform eight years later.

BREAKING INTO TELEVISION AND SINGLED OUT

During his time at UCLA, Hardwick launched his television career. In 1991, he made his acting debut with a small part on the ABC drama series *thirtysomething*, which helped him get into the Screen Actors Guild (SAG). He next appeared as a contestant on the USA Network dating game show *Studs* (1991). Hardwick told Caleb Bacon for *LAist* (30 June 2009, online) that his friends had "wrangled" him into auditioning for the show with them "because I had a car and the other people didn't." He added: "I ended up getting on this show and I had to go out with these girls. They made it seem like all of this stuff happened on the dates and nothing remotely happened." After turning down an opportunity to appear as a contestant on another dating game show, Hardwick auditioned for and landed a gig as the host of an MTV game show called *Trashed* (1993). He left UCLA two quarters away from graduating in 1994 to host the show, which featured contestants wagering prized possessions to answer pop culture trivia questions. Despite having a stable of budding comedy writers that

included Doug Benson, Janeane Garofalo, Joel Hodgson, Bob Odenkirk, and Brian Posehn, *Trashed* was cancelled after only five months. Former MTV executive Lisa Berger told Stephen M. Silverman for *People* (30 Sep. 1996), "The end result of *Trashed* is that everyone loved Chris." Soon afterward, Hardwick was offered a job to cohost the MTV dating game show *Singled Out* with the 1994 Playboy Playmate of the Year, Jenny McCarthy.

Singled Out would prove to be Hardwick's breakthrough. The show debuted on MTV on June 5, 1995, and it became an immediate success. It aired thirty minutes a day, five days a week, and featured male and female contestants separately picking from a pool of fifty members of the opposite sex for a date. Contestants, called "Pickers," would be escorted onto the show's set blindfolded and would then be required to pare down the field of potential dates through a series of questions and stunts over several rounds. Hardwick hosted *Singled Out* during its entire four-season run. He shared hosting duties with McCarthy for the show's first three-and-a-half seasons and then with another Playboy Playmate, Carmen Electra, for the last season and a half. Hardwick has referred to his work on the show as "bad," and he told Gardner that he focused more on "trying to be a host and not just be myself." Nevertheless, he became known for his trademark cynical demeanor, which served as a perfect complement to McCarthy's zany personality, and was credited with helping the show become one of the most popular on MTV in the 1990s. The show was cancelled in May of 1998.

Concurrently with *Singled Out*, Hardwick served as a disc jockey for the Los Angeles alternative rock station KROQ/106.7 FM. He hosted the station's late-night show, which aired from midnight to five o'clock in the morning. He also landed several television and feature film roles, appearing in two episodes of the Fox series *Married with Children* in 1996 and in the comedy films *Courting Courtney* (1997) and *Art House* (1998). Around the time *Singled Out* was cancelled, Hardwick left KROQ to co-host a drive-time radio show with Courtland Cox, called *The Untitled Hardwick/Cox Project*, on the Los Angeles modern rock station KLYY/Y-107.1 FM. While co-hosting the show, he landed a starring role on the short-lived UPN sitcom *Guys Like Us* (1998). On the show, which only ran for thirteen episodes, Hardwick played an aspiring musician whose bachelor lifestyle is altered when his roommate's six-year-old brother comes to live with them.

In 1999, after both his radio show and sitcom were cancelled, Hardwick returned to the stand-up circuit and started performing at comedy clubs and comedy festivals all over the United States. Two years later, he returned to television to host the reality-based dating show, *Shipmates*

(2001), which followed blind daters on a Carnival cruise ship. The show aired for two seasons in syndication. During this time, Hardwick's life began to unravel as a result of a growing dependence on alcohol and video games. He wrote in *The Nerdist Way*: "I was doing stand-up full-time and unwittingly tripped over my thirtieth birthday. It was at this first mortality mile-marker that I began to look around at my life: I was consuming a baby elephant's weight in alcohol *every day* . . . my apartment was always a mess, I had ruined my credit, and I had no real work prospects. I had become what I'd always dreaded being—the fat, drunk guy who used to be on television." Hardwick hit rock bottom in 2002 while working as an intern on *The Daily Show with Jon Stewart*. Stewart was interviewing guest McCarthy, when he joked that her former *Single Out* co-host had been reduced to the show's coffee boy. "I had just gotten called out on one of my favorite shows for being a loser," Hardwick says in *The Nerdist Way*. "And the worst part was, *Stewart was right*."

HARD 'N PHIRM AND OTHER PROJECTS

In 2003, after seeking help from a therapist, Hardwick decided to give up alcohol for good. He told Bacon: "Ultimately, it's the best decision I've ever made in my life. There's an economy of energy that you have in your life. You just have to devote it to things that are good for you, for the most part." Now focusing all of his energies toward work, Hardwick, who also gave up gaming about a year later, landed a supporting role in Rob Zombie's horror feature and directorial debut, *House of 1000 Corpses* (2003), and in the highly anticipated *Terminator* sequel, *Terminator 3: Rise of the Machines* (2003). He also reformed the musical comedy duo Hard 'n Phirm with his friend Mike Phirman.

Following in the tradition of such musical parodists as Weird Al Yankovic, Stephen Lynch, and Tenacious D, Hard 'n Phirm specializes in songs about mathematics, science, and other geeky endeavors. Hardwick sings and plays the melodica and Phirman sings and plays the guitar. In 2005, the duo released the album, *Horses and Grasses*, which features the hit songs "Rodeohead" and "Pi." The former song is comprised of a medley of Radiohead songs sung in a bluegrass style, and the latter is about the mathematical ratio of the same name. "Pi" featured a popular accompanying music video directed by Keith Schofield and has received over one million Internet downloads. In 2008, Hard 'n Phirm appeared in a half-hour special for *Comedy Central Presents*, where they performed several unreleased songs, some of which they planned to add to a second studio album. Hard 'n Phirm contributed songs to Rob Zombie's animated horror-comedy film *The Haunted World of El Superbeasto* (2009). They have also recorded songs for television series and podcasts, and they frequently perform at comedy clubs, colleges, and music venues around the country. In an interview with Ryan McKe and Ron Babcock for the comedy magazine *Modest Proposal* (Feb. 2006, online), Hardwick described Hard 'n Phirm as "the *Blade* of music and comedy," referring to their hybrid musical style and the actor Wesley Snipes' eponymous human-vampire character in the action film *Blade* (1998) and its two sequels, *Blade II* (2002) and *Blade: Trinity* (2004).

In addition to Hard 'n Phirm, Hardwick has since carved out "a snug little niche for all of the things I'm passionate about," as he states in *The Nerdist Way*. In 2007, he hosted a weekly science program for PBS called *Wired Science*, which was made in collaboration with *Wired* magazine. That program led to him becoming a contributing writer at *Wired* in 2007 and landing a gig as a technology and gadget correspondent for the G4 cable channel's flagship program *Attack of the Show!* in 2008. In June 2009, he became the host of another G4 program, *Web Soup*, a weekly series about trending videos on the Internet. *Web Soup* is a spin-off of the E! Channel's long-running celebrity pop culture series *The Soup* (2004). Hardwick has also voiced characters in several animated television series, most notably Otis the Cow on Nickelodeon's *Back at the Barnyard*, from 2007 to 2011. Since 2009, he has appeared as a regular guest on such shows as *Chelsea Lately*, *The Late Late Show with Craig Ferguson*, and *Late Night with Jimmy Fallon*. In 2011, Hardwick began hosting a live half-hour talk show on the AMC network called *Talking Dead*, in which he interviews celebrity fans and cast and crew members of AMC's hit horror series *The Walking Dead*. Later that year, he had a small role in the Oscar-nominated drama *Extremely Loud & Incredibly Close* (2011), which starred Tom Hanks and Sandra Bullock.

NERDIST INDUSTRIES

Along with his many acting and hosting "side" jobs, Hardwick is the founder and chief creative officer (CCO) of the Los Angeles based multimedia company Nerdist Industries, which was formed in partnership with the newsletter *GeekChicDaily* in 2011. The company's flagship properties include the popular tech-culture website *Nerdist* and the weekly *Nerdist* podcast, which Hardwick produces and co-hosts with the comedians Jonah Ray and Matt Nira. Since debuting in February 2010, the podcast, which typically runs one hour in length and occasionally airs live, has featured a wide array of celebrity guests, including actors, musicians, and comedians. The podcast has consistently ranked among the top ten comedy podcasts on iTunes. It has also been named one of the best comedy podcasts by the *A.V. Club* and *Rolling Stone*. In a round-up of the best podcasts of 2010, a writer for the *A.V. Club* (29 Dec. 2010, online) commented that "the *Nerdist* podcast embraces minutiae as it relates to comedy, film, television, the Internet, and other nerdy pop-culture pursuits. A freewheeling, hour-long conversation presided over by TV/stand-up vet Chris Hardwick, the *Nerdist* is more like a laid-back conversation with friends than an interview show—probably because most of the guests are Hardwick's friends/acquaintances from the comedy world (though non-comic guests like Stan Lee, Ozzy Osbourne, and even the Muppets have also appeared)."

Thanks to the popularity of his podcast, Hardwick has been able to considerably expand the Nerdist brand. The brand now includes a talk show for BBC America, a Nerdist channel on the video-sharing website YouTube, the Nerd-Melt theater at Meltdown Comics in Hollywood, a social network called NODE, and numerous other Nerdist-sponsored podcasts. In November 2011, Hardwick published the self-help book *The Nerdist Way: How to Reach the Next Level (In Real Life)*, which offers a humorous chronicle of his journey from washed-up television host to nerd cult hero. Commenting on the characteristics of "nerddom," he told Leijon; "Being a nerd is about obsessing unnaturally over something. If you obsess about and endlessly deconstruct something at the expense of everything else in your life, that's nerdy. It just so happens nerds often gravitate towards more imagination-driven vehicles. . . . Ultimately, I started all of my other projects to get my nerd point-of-view out to the world, with the hope that it would direct people to my live comedy, which is what I really care about. But everything I do is with the same voice—I always talk about nerdy stuff."

Hardwick lives in Los Angeles, California. He was once engaged to the model and actress Jacinda Barrett and also had a long-term relationship with the comic actress Jane Varney. He is an inveterate user of the social networking service Twitter and has 1.5 million "followers."

SUGGESTED READING

Bacon, Caleb. "Chris Hardwick: Nerdism for Fun and Profit." *LAist*. Gothamist, 30 June 2009. Web. 4 Apr. 2012.

Campos, Nicole. "Chris Hardwick: Funny, You Don't Look Nerdist." *LA Weekly*. LA Weekly, 19 May 2011. Web. 4 Apr. 2012.

Hardwick, Chris. "Self-Help for Nerds: Advice from Comedian Chris Hardwick." *Wired*. Condé Nast, 21 Oct. 2011. Web. 1 Mar. 2012.

Leijon, Erik. "The Dean of Dweebs: Chris Hardwick Fine-Tunes His Nerd-Dar at Just for Laughs." *Montreal Mirror*. Communications Gratte-Ciel Ltée, 28 July 2011. Web. 4 Apr. 2012.

Purdy, Kevin. "How Nerdist Chris Hardwick Gets Things Done." *Lifehacker*. Gawker Media, 29 Apr. 2009. Web. 4 Apr. 2012.

— *Chris Cullen*

Naomie Harris

Born: September 6, 1976
Occupation: Actor

"Star quality is a hoary old phrase, but Naomie [Harris] has it to spare," British motion picture director Danny Boyle told Stuart Husband for the London *Observer* (2 July 2006). Harris first captivated American audiences in 2002, when she was cast as the female lead in Boyle's low-budget thriller *28 Days Later*. Four years later she garnered greater recognition for her memorable turn as a voodoo priestess in the second and third installments of the *Pirates of the Caribbean* movies. In 2011 she made headlines when she was cast as Miss Moneypenny—the first woman of color to play the part—in the latest James Bond film. Some sources suggest that Harris's character will not be called "Miss Moneypenny," and that she will have a more active role in *Skyfall* than the Moneypenny character has had in the Bond series.

EARLY LIFE AND CAREER

Naomie Melanie Harris was born on September 6, 1976 in London, England and grew up in Finsbury Park, an ethnically diverse area of north London. Harris was raised by her mother, Liselle Kayla, an immigrant from Jamaica whose family moved to England when she was five years old. After obtaining a degree in sociology from the University of London, Kayla went on to pursue a career as a journalist, playwright, and television scriptwriter. She eventually married an arts teacher, with whom she has a son and another daughter. Harris barely knew her Trinidad-born father, a property developer. "He came up and introduced himself when I was about seven and walking home from school but I don't have anything to do with him," Harris told Husband.

Harris was two years old when she was first bitten by the performing bug. "I don't know where it came from," she recalled to Husband. "I used to spend hours in front of the mirror with a hairbrush, singing and dancing and making myself cry." When she was seven years old, Harris joined a weekly after-school drama club at the renowned Anna Scher Theatre School, located in the north London borough of Islington. She showed a talent for performing, winning an award for the most promising actress of the year. "I have such fond memories of going to that club. I loved Anna Scher. She was an incredibly inspirational teacher," she said to Anne Joseph in an interview for the *Times Educational Supplement* (8 Apr. 2011).

With the encouragement of Scher, Harris eventually began auditioning for roles. In 1987 the eleven-year-old made her small-screen debut, with a guest appearance on the series adaptation of the children's book *Simon and the*

Witch, which aired on the British Broadcasting Corporation (BBC). However, the aspiring actress struggled to fit in with her classmates at St. Marylebone Church of England School, an all-girls school in central London. "I was bullied at St. Marylebone, so secondary school wasn't the greatest experience," she confided to Joseph. "The Anna Scher after-school club was also an escape. . . . I was with like-minded people and it was a supportive and caring environment. And I was doing something that I was really passionate about."

Harris continued to pursue acting while attending secondary school. Two years after her television debut, Harris had a minor part in *Erasmus Microman*, an educational children's series that was shown on ITV, a public service station based in the United Kingdom. Harris landed her first regular series role in 1992, when she was cast as Shuku in another ITV children's program, *Runaway Bay*, a weekly show that chronicled the adventures of a group of friends living on the Caribbean island of Martinique. (It lasted two seasons until its cancellation in 1993.)

Upon completing her compulsory education, the sixteen-year-old had strongly considered abandoning school to pursue a full-time acting career, but her mother convinced her to attend sixth-form college and study for the A-levels, which are the standard entrance examinations for public universities in the United Kingdom. Harris's experience as a student at Woodhouse College, in the Finchley district of north London, proved to be remarkably different from her

stint in secondary school. "I met a lot of cool people at sixth-form college who remain my friends to this day," she shared with Husband. "I also had this inspirational teacher called Mr. Murdoch who made me fall in love with sociology. He said I had the potential for Cambridge [University], which got me so excited." Harris was eventually accepted at Pembroke College, one of the University of Cambridge's oldest colleges, where she studied social and political science with a specialization in psychology. "For me it was all about, what forms the individual? What makes a person tick? In life you usually play one role," she said to Johanna Schneller for the Canadian *Globe and Mail* (3 June 2011). "But I think we all have many other sides. What's great about acting is, you get to air out all those sides."

In 1994, while attending Cambridge, Harris had a costarring role in a revival of the British science fiction television series *The Tomorrow People*, which aired on ITV until 1995. Following her 1998 graduation from Cambridge, Harris trained for two years at the renowned Bristol Old Vic Theatre School, which counts Academy Award recipients Daniel Day-Lewis and Jeremy Irons among its alumni. She put herself through school with scholarships. However, Harris struggled to find acting work. "I'd go to dinner parties with friends, and people would say: 'What do you do?' I just felt I had no right to call myself an actor as I wasn't working," she told Lisa Sewards for the London *Daily Mail* (28 Mar. 2008).

FROM CHILD STAR TO ADULT ACTRESS

Nine months after completing her studies at Bristol, Harris tried out for the female lead in *28 Days Later*, a film directed by Danny Boyle, whose previous credits included the 1996 cult classic *Trainspotting* and the Leonardo DiCaprio drama *The Beach*. "When she came in, it was clear she was very intelligent and very beautiful, but she had a bit of a Princess Anne hairdo, and an accent to match," Boyle recalled in an interview with Dee O'Connell for the London *Observer* (19 Oct. 2002). "But then she read the part and, as soon as she read it, you knew she had the balls to do it."

After Harris was cast in Boyle's postapocalyptic movie, she embarked on a grueling nine-month shoot that began on September 1, 2001—less than two weeks prior to the terrorist attacks in the United States. "Because we did a month of night shoots, we were trying to sleep during the day, and not having any sunlight for a month does weird things to you," she said in an interview posted on the Cinema Blend website. "It was really physically demanding as well. . . . There is no way of being thrown on the floor without getting some bruises. And then we were filming in November, at night, with rain machines, wind machines, rats, and covered in blood, so all of it was really grueling."

Next came costarring roles in the coming-of-age film *Living In Hope* (2002), which explores the friendship between five male college students; and the independent drama *Anansi* (2002), which chronicles the tribulations of a group of West Africans who immigrate illegally to Germany. Harris also appeared in a minor role in *Crust* (2003), a low-budget British comedy about a pub owner who discovers a seven-foot-long shrimp on the beach and teaches the crustacean to box, as part of a get-rich-quick-scheme.

Harris garnered attention on the small screen for her leading role in the 2002 adaptation of Zadie Smith's award-winning novel *White Teeth* (2000). In the four-part multigenerational and multiethnic series, which first aired in September on Channel Four and was broadcast in the United States the following year, Harris portrayed Clara, a Jamaican-born resident of London who is estranged from her mother, a devout Jehovah's Witness. She also appeared as the female lead in the two-part BBC political docudrama *The Project*, a behind-the-scenes look at Britain's Labour Party. Other TV credits in 2002 included guest appearances in the British crime drama *Trial & Retribution* and the short-lived adventure series *Dinotopia*, which aired on ABC.

GARNERS ATTENTION IN THE UNITED STATES

American audiences became better acquainted with Harris in 2003, after the release of Boyle's thriller *28 Days Later*, which deals with the aftermath of a deadly virus outbreak in the UK that has turned most of the population into homicidal zombies. The film made its unofficial debut at the Sundance Film Festival in January and had its official US premiere five months later. Although the film earned mixed reviews, Harris was singled out by a number of critics for her performance as Selena, who is among four remaining survivors of the epidemic. "Naomie Harris, a newcomer, is convincing as Selena, the rock at the center of the storm," Roger Ebert wrote in a critique of the film that is posted on his personal website (27 June 2003). Owen Gleiberman was equally complementary: "In Boyle's film . . . the thin characters are effective at the start but take you only so far (though the beautiful Naomie Harris has a no-nonsense allure)," he wrote for *Entertainment Weekly* (27 June 2003). Shot mostly on digital video with a budget of nearly $10 million, *28 Days Later* was an unexpected commercial success. Despite a limited release, the film grossed $45 million domestically and more than $82 million worldwide, aided by an online promotional campaign that included banner ads posted on AOL and Yahoo, as well as a preview of the movie featured on the Apple movie trailer website.

Harris's next film, the British psychological thriller *Trauma*, also had its premiere at the 2004 Sundance Film Festival. Harris costarred as Elisa, a car crash victim whose surviving husband, played by Colin Firth, awakens from a coma but is haunted by visions of his deceased wife. Later that year she appeared opposite Pierce Brosnan and Woody Harrelson in the comedy caper *After the Sunset*, in which she played a Bahamian police constable who teams up with an FBI agent (Harrelson) to track down a jewel thief (Brosnan). She followed that up with a costarring role in *A Cock and Bull Story* (2006), Michael Winterbottom's adaptation of Laurence Sterne's eighteenth-century novel. The critically acclaimed British ensemble comedy received a limited US release the following January.

SUCCESS AT THE BOX OFFICE

Harris gained further recognition in the United States, with a supporting role in *Pirates of the Caribbean: Dead Man's Chest*. "Gore [Verbinski] didn't actually want me for the part because he said that I was actually too pretty. . . . He wanted an older actress," Harris revealed to Hanh Nguyen in an interview posted on Zap2it.com (6 July 2006). "The casting director, Denise Chamian . . . persuaded Gore to audition me. When I walked into the room, he said, 'You're going to have to do this . . . three [or] maybe four times so . . . let's just have a go.' And so I read it once and then he [asked], 'How would you like to come to the Bahamas?'"

To embody the role of Tia Dalma, Harris underwent a complete physical transformation. In addition to the black makeup she wore around her eyes and lips, she donned a dreadlocked wig, fake tribal tattoos, and prosthetic teeth; she also adopted a thick Jamaican accent. Released in early July 2006, *Pirates of the Caribbean: Dead Man's Chest* was met with mixed reviews but went on to gross more than $423 million domestically; with a worldwide box-office gross of $1.066 billion, *Dead Man's Chest* became the highest grossing film of 2006.

That summer Harris also had another hit with the film version of the 1980s hit police drama *Miami Vice*, in which she costarred opposite Colin Farrell, Jamie Foxx, and the world-renowned Chinese actress Gong Li. For her role as Trudy Joplin, a Bronx-born undercover detective and the love interest of Ricardo Tubbs (played by Foxx), Harris had to learn to speak with a Bronx accent. As part of her research, she met with Drug Enforcement Agency (DEA) agents in New York City and accompanied them on actual raids; she also visited a shooting range, where she learned to fire machine guns. On July 28, 2006, Michael Mann's big-screen adaptation of *Miami Vice* had its theatrical release in the United States. Reviewing the film for the *New York Times* (28 July 2006), A. O. Scott wrote:

"In the movie version . . . only real movie stars, who command attention simply by allowing the camera to behold them, will do. Mr. Foxx, sly, taciturn and effortlessly charismatic, certainly fulfills the requirement, as does Ms. Gong, a goddess of global cinema whose every word you hang on even when you can't understand a single one. If there is any justice in the world, Ms. Harris . . . will join their ranks before long." Despite lukewarm reviews from the critics, the film proved a hit with audiences, grossing more than $63 million at the domestic box office and nearly $164 million worldwide.

In 2007 Harris reprised her role as Tia Dalma in *Pirates of the Caribbean: At World's End*, the third film in the *Pirates of the Caribbean* series. Her character's role was greatly expanded in this latest sequel. Like its predecessor, *Pirates of the Caribbean: At World's End* received a mixed response but managed to become the top-grossing film of the year. Harris was nominated for a British Academy of Film and Television Arts (BAFTA) Award in the rising star category but lost to Eva Green.

AWAY FROM THE MAINSTREAM

Over the next several years, Harris moved away from the big-budget productions and decided instead to focus on smaller, less mainstream fare. She next appeared opposite Josh Hartnett in *August* (2008), playing the former girlfriend of a dot-com entrepreneur who attempts to rekindle their relationship while struggling to keep his company afloat during the 2001 stock-market crash. The film, which also costarred the musician David Bowie, made its debut at the January 2008 Sundance Film Festival and went into limited release six months later. Harris followed that up with a costarring turn in another independent drama, *Explicit Ills* (2008), which premiered at the South by Southwest Festival in early March before its limited US release a year later.

For her next role Harris played Poppy Shakespeare, an outpatient at a mental health facility, in the television adaptation of Clare Allan's best-selling 2006 novel of the same name. After it was first aired on Channel Four in late March 2008, *Poppy Shakespeare* spent the following year on the international festival circuit, including the Santa Barbara and Gothenburg Film Festivals, as well as the Seattle International Film Festival. In April 2008 Harris returned to the big screen as part of the largely male ensemble cast for *Street Kings*, an action thriller starring Keanu Reeves, Forest Whitaker, and Hugh Laurie. A year later Harris appeared in the British romantic comedy *My Last Five Girlfriends*, which had its premiere at the Tribeca Film Festival. She then had a costarring role in *Morris: A Life with Bells On*, a comedy about a fictional avant-garde folk dancing troupe in England. In the critically acclaimed mockumentary, which

was released in September 2009, Harris plays Sonja, the romantic interest of the troupe's eccentric leader. In November 2009, she appeared opposite the Korean-born entertainer Rain as a forensic researcher in the martial-arts thriller *Ninja Assassin*.

Her next project was the two-part miniseries *Small Island*, a television adaptation of Andrea Levy's prizewinning 2004 novel. The historical drama aired in December 2009 on the BBC One channel and was also broadcast on the Public Broadcasting Service (PBS) in April of the following year. Harris earned critical raves for her portrayal of a Jamaican immigrant who experiences racism while living in postwar London with her husband (played by David Oyelowo). In a review for the London *Guardian* (6 Dec. 2009), Sam Wollaston wrote: "It's . . . sumptuous to look at, with fine performances, especially from Naomie Harris, haughty, awkward Hortense, who finds the postwar motherland she arrives in isn't quite as she'd imagined it." Harris won Best Actress honors at the 2010 Royal Television Society Programme Awards.

Harris learned to play the guitar for her role as Denise Roudette, the girlfriend of 1970s British punk singer Ian Dury in *Sex & Drugs & Rock & Roll* (2010). She subsequently reteamed with Oyelowo in *Blood and Oil*, in which she starred as a British-born Nigerian public relations executive who is dispatched by her oil firm to the Niger Delta region to handle a hostage crisis involving several kidnapped workers. Filmed in South Africa, the two-part television drama aired on the BBC Two network in March 2010. Later that year Harris also made a guest appearance in the British anthology series *Accused*. In early 2011 she reunited with Boyle when she appeared in his stage adaptation of Mary Shelley's *Frankenstein*, during a three-month run at London's National Theatre.

Her next starring role was in *The First Grader*, in which she played Jane Obinchu, a real-life first-grade instructor in rural Kenya who teaches Kimani N'gan'ga Maruge, an eighty-year-old villager and former soldier, to read and write. Harris committed to the project after reading the script. "I'd just done *Ninja Assassin*, a big Hollywood movie that was shot in Berlin, and I wanted something that was going to be more fulfilling creatively," she told Leah Rozen in an interview for BBC America (17 May 2011). The movie, which was shot on location in Kenya, was officially screened at several festivals. During the press tour for *The First Grader*, which had a limited US release in May 2011, it was announced that Harris had been cast in the latest installment in the James Bond film series, scheduled to be released in late 2012. To prepare for her role, she frequented a gun range for several weeks and also learned to stunt drive. It is rumored that Harris is set to portray Winnie

Mandela in a big-screen adaptation of South African politician Nelson Mandela's 1995 autobiography, *Long Walk to Freedom*.

Harris, a practicing Buddhist, lives in Finsbury Park, just down the street from her mother.

SUGGESTED READING

Husband, Stuart. "Miami Nice." *Observer* [London]. Guardian News and Media Ltd., 1 July 2006. Web. 18 June 2012.

Joseph, Anne. "My Best Teacher—Naomie Harris." *Times Educational Supplement*. TSL Education Ltd., 8 Apr. 2011. Web. 18 June 2012.

O'Connell, Dee. "Naomie That Girl." *Observer* [London]. Guardian News and Media Ltd., 19 Oct. 2002. Web. 18 June 2012.

Rozen, Leah. "Actress Naomie Harris: From First Grade to Frankenstein." *BBCAmerica*. BBC Worldwide Americas Inc., 17 May 2011. Web. 18 June 2012.

Schneller, Johanna. "Naomie Harris: I Think We All Have Many Sides." *Globe and Mail* [Toronto]. The Globe and Mail Inc., 3 June 2011. Web. 18 June 2012.

Sewards, Lisa. "Poppy Dazzle: The Actress Who Conquered Hollywood but Remains Unknown Here." *Daily Mail* [London]. Associated Newspapers Ltd., 28 Mar. 2008. Web. 18 June 2012.

Wollaston, Sam. "Being Alan Bennett and Small Island." *Guardian* [London]. Guardian News and Media Ltd., 6 Dec. 2009. Web. 18 June 2012.

—*Bertha Muteba*

Jennifer Roper, courtesy of Simon & Schuster

Sam Harris

Born: April 9, 1967
Occupation: Neuroscientist, writer, activist

With the publication of his first and second books, *The End of Faith: Religion, Terror, and the Future of Reason* (2004) and *Letter to a Christian Nation* (2006), the neuroscientist, writer, and activist Sam Harris inspired heated debate about religion, its roles in the lives of individuals, and its impacts on communities and nations. *The End of Faith* won the 2005 PEN/Martha Albrand Award for Nonfiction, which "recognizes an American author's first published book of general nonfiction, distinguished by qualities of literary and stylistic excellence," according to the PEN website. The book was a best seller, as was *Letter to a Christian Nation*, a slim version of its predecessor. The controversies the books stirred up placed Harris alongside such contemporary thinkers as the evolutionary biologist Richard Dawkins, the Darwinist philosopher Daniel C.

Dennett, and the journalist and author Christopher Hitchens, all of whom are highly vocal in their conviction that religions have no basis in scientific fact—that is, none of them can produce evidence to back up their tenets. Those who believe in any religion do so only because they assume or have faith that it is true, not because they can point to scientific knowledge demonstrating its veracity, according to those thinkers. Harris has maintained that while the fundamentalists of the major religions have caused enormous harm around the world and are likely to continue to do so, they are not the only ones who pose a danger to others. Religious liberals or moderates do so as well, he has argued, because, in the name of religious tolerance, they have glossed over facets of various religions that have led to terrible violence time and again, thus providing "cover" for extremists, as he has put it. "It is of course taboo to criticize a person's religious beliefs," Harris wrote in an essay for *Newsweek* (13 Nov. 2006). "The problem, however, is that much of what people believe in the name of religion is intrinsically divisive, unreasonable and incompatible with genuine morality."

For more than a decade beginning when he was about nineteen, Harris engaged full-time in a study of Eastern and Western religions and philosophies. During that period, in Asia and the US, he devoted hundreds of hours to meditation and silent contemplation. In his third book, *The Moral Landscape: How Science Can Determine Human Values* (2010), he wrote, "I see nothing irrational about seeking the states of mind that lie at the core of many religions. Compassion, awe, devotion and feelings of oneness are surely among the most valuable experiences a person can have." "Ecstasy, rapture, bliss, concentration, a sense of the sacred—I'm comfortable with all of that," he told Lisa Miller for *Newsweek* (25 Oct. 2010). "I think all of that is indispensable." In 2009 Harris earned a PhD degree in neuroscience. He believes that while history has shown that religions cannot inspire most people to be moral, someday neurologists and other scientists will provide evidence that "genuine morality" can be traced to activities of particular areas of the brain. That is the theme of *The Moral Landscape*.

Like Dawkins, Dennett, and Hitchens, Harris has been called an atheist, but he does not apply that label to himself. That is because, in his view, the term suggests that atheism itself is a religion. In "An Atheist Manifesto," written for the online magazine *Truthdig* (7 Dec. 2005)—the word "atheist" in the title being used as the quickest way to indicate the contents of the piece—Harris wrote, "Atheism is not a philosophy; it is not even a view of the world; it is simply a refusal to deny the obvious. . . . It is worth noting that no one ever needs to identify himself as a non-astrologer or a non-alchemist. Consequently, we do not have words for people who deny the validity of these pseudo-disciplines. Likewise, atheism is a term that should not even exist. . . . The atheist is merely a person who believes that the 260 million Americans (87% of the population) who claim to never doubt the existence of God should be obliged to present evidence for his existence. . . . Atheism is nothing more than a commitment to the most basic standard of intellectual honesty: One's convictions should be proportional to one's evidence. Pretending to be certain when one isn't—indeed, pretending to be certain about propositions for which no evidence is even conceivable—is both an intellectual and a moral failing. . . . The atheist is simply a person who has perceived the lies of religion and refused to make them his own."

In 2007, with his wife, Annaka Harris, Harris founded the nonprofit foundation Project Reason, which, according to its website, is "devoted to spreading scientific knowledge and secular values in society. The foundation draws on the talents of prominent and creative thinkers in a wide range of disciplines to encourage critical thinking and erode the influence of dogmatism, superstition, and bigotry in our world." "In a world brimming with increasingly destructive technology, our infatuation with religious myths now poses a tremendous danger," Harris wrote for his *Newsweek* essay. "And it is not a danger for which more religious faith is a remedy." In addition to Dawkins, Dennett, and Hitchens, Project Reason's twenty-two-member advisory board includes the cognitive scientist Steven

Pinker, the biochemist J. Craig Venter, the theoretical physicist Steven Weinberg, the writer Salman Rushdie, and the writer and filmmaker Ayaan Hirsi Ali.

EARLY LIFE AND EDUCATION

Sam Harris was born on April 9, 1967, in Los Angeles, California, to a mother who is of Jewish descent and a father (now deceased) who was a Quaker. His mother, Carolyn, who remarried, "has always been a most extraordinary friend" to him, he wrote in the acknowledgements in *The Moral Landscape*; she has also served as a careful reader of his manuscripts. On November 18, 2006, Harris told an interviewer for the PBS TV series *Religion & Ethics Newsweekly* (5 Jan. 2007), "I have an unremarkable history. I had a totally secular upbringing and was just encouraged to explore things as I saw fit. I was never raised an atheist as opposed to religious. It just was not an issue. In my teens I just got interested in spiritual experience and what happens after death and just began to see that religion is really the discourse that treats these phenomena and started exploring meditation and other specifically Eastern brands of religious thinking." He added that his interest in religions extended to Western faiths, too.

After high school Harris enrolled at Stanford University, in Palo Alto, California. Taking the drug ecstasy when he was eighteen led him to consider "the possibility that the human mind—his own mind—might be able to achieve a state of loving unselfishness without the help of drugs," Lisa Miller wrote. That idea led Harris to leave Stanford in 1986, before his junior year, and to embark on his own program of study in religion and philosophy. While traveling in India and Nepal, he practiced meditation and studied with Hindu and Buddhist teachers. In the United States one of his instructors was Sharon Salzberg, a cofounder of the Insight Meditation Society and the Barre Center for Buddhist Studies. "His passion was for deep philosophical questions, and he could talk for hours and hours," Salzberg recalled to David Segal for the *Washington Post* (26 Oct. 2006). "Sometimes you'd want to say to him, 'What about the Yankees?' or 'Look at the leaves, they're changing color!'" Harris repeatedly spent weeks or months at a stretch (a total of about two years) without speaking, in what is known as silent meditation or silent retreat. He also read hundreds of books. During those eleven years of self-study, Harris was financially supported almost entirely by his mother.

STANFORD AND UCLA

Harris returned to Stanford in 1997 and in 2000 completed a BA degree in philosophy. He then entered the University of California at Los Angeles (UCLA) to pursue a doctorate in neuroscience. His dissertation adviser was Mark S. Cohen, an expert in the use of magnetic resonance imaging (MRI), including functional MRI, which indicates how various external stimuli affect the flow of blood in particular areas of the brain. For his research Harris scanned the brains of adults when they were considering the truth or falsehood of particular written statements. He focused on changes in blood flow in the brains of religious people when they were thinking about religious tenets or propositions that they believed were true. Then he compared those scans with the brain scans of people who thought that such tenets or propositions were false or who felt uncertain regarding their truth or falsity. Harris also studied the effects on the brain of nonreligious thoughts about the truth or falsity of statements in the areas of geography, mathematics, ethics, or semantics, among others.

The MRI scans produced for his research have "no relevance to the question of whether or not there is a God," Harris told Brad A. Greenberg for *UCLA Magazine* (1 Apr. 2008). "Even if we had a perfect belief detector, we still can't tell you what is true in the world. You put somebody in the scanner who believes Elvis is still alive, and all we will be able to tell you is, 'Yes, he does believe Elvis is still alive.'" He concluded: "If you are given a proposition you truly don't believe, it is just mere words. The moment you give them credence, a complete transformation of your neurology and psychology and physiology occurs. Belief is the hinge upon which the door to behavior and emotion swings." The results of his research, in which Cohen and others collaborated, were the subject of Harris's PhD dissertation. They were also published in the *Annals of Neurology* in February 2008 and, online, in the Public Library of Science publication *PLoS One* in October 2009. The latter paper concluded, "Our study compares religious thinking with ordinary cognition and, as such, constitutes a step toward developing a neuropsychology of religion. However, these findings may also further our understanding of how the brain accepts statements of all kinds to be valid descriptions of the world." Harris earned a Ph. degree in 2009.

SEPTEMBER 11 AND THE END OF FAITH

The terrorist attacks of September 11, 2001, led Harris to abandon his graduate research almost entirely for more than five years and begin work on the book that became *The End of Faith*. "It was my immediate reaction to Sep. 11—the moment it became clear" ("and it became clear in about 24 hours") "that we were meandering into a global, theologically inspired conflict with the Muslim world, and were going to tell ourselves otherwise, based on the respect we pay to faith," he told Blair Golson for *Truthdig* (3 Apr. 2006). "The last thing we were going to admit was

that people were flying planes into our buildings because of what they believed about God. We came up with euphemisms about this being a war on terror, and Islam being a religion of peace, and we were pushed even further into our own religiosity as a nation." In *The End of Faith*, Harris wrote that both the Bible and the Koran contain statements in which God condemns to death those who reject him or behave in other ways that he deems unacceptable, and that both works have been invoked to justify violent conflicts within and between communities and nations. But the Koran, said to be a transcription by the prophet Muhammad of the word of God, focuses far more heavily on the punishments awaiting those who do not believe in God. "The basic thrust" of Islam, Harris wrote, "is undeniable: convert, subjugate, or kill unbelievers; kill apostates; and conquer the world." The September 11 attackers were well educated and came from middle-class families; they were driven not by poverty and lack of opportunity but apparently by their faith in Islam, including the conviction that those who martyr themselves in the name of religion will be rewarded in heaven.

In examples of American public policy whose roots may be found in religion, Harris cited the ban on marijuana use, including for medical purposes, and on mind-altering drugs—a prohibition that he believes stems from religious concepts of sin and has led to the imprisonment of thousands of people who hurt nobody. He also noted the belief of President George W. Bush, a born-again Christian, that a human egg becomes a person the moment it is fertilized. That belief led Bush to bar the use of federal funds for research using human embryonic stem cells, a resource that many scientists believe might be enormously useful in understanding many diseases and thereby finding cures for them. In another example, many legislators' opposition to abortion led Congress to withdraw federal funds from organizations, such as International Planned Parenthood Federation, that make birth control available to people in developing countries, on the ground that those organizations might be providing or advising women about abortions; by cutting off those funds, the United States was thus greatly increasing the occurrences of unwanted pregnancies (and, consequently, abortions) in those countries and, by limiting the distribution of condoms, contributing to the spread of AIDS.

In *The End of Faith*, Harris also wrote, "People of faith fall on a continuum: some draw solace and inspiration from a specific spiritual tradition, and yet remain fully committed to tolerance and diversity, while others would burn the earth to cinders if it would put an end to heresy." He noted that in public discourse, most aspects of religion cannot be questioned the way people question assertions connected with the hard and soft sciences, history, and virtually every other discipline; few challenge religious beliefs and practices, however dangerous. In that connection he wrote, "The problem that religious moderation poses for all of us is that it does not permit anything very critical to be said about religious literalism. We cannot say that fundamentalists are crazy, because they are merely practicing their freedom of belief; we cannot even say that they are mistaken in religious terms, because their knowledge of scripture is generally unrivaled. All we can say, as religious moderates, is that we don't like the personal and social costs that a full embrace of scripture imposes on us. . . . Moderates do not want to kill anyone in the name of God, but they want us to keep using the word 'God' as though we knew what we were talking about. And they do not want anything too critical said about people who really believe in the God of their fathers, because tolerance, perhaps above all else, is sacred. To speak plainly and truthfully about the state of our world—to say, for instance, that the Bible and the Koran both contain mountains of life-destroying gibberish—is antithetical to tolerance as moderates currently conceive it. But we can no longer afford the luxury of such political correctness. We must finally recognize the price we are paying to maintain the iconography of our ignorance."

"*The End of Faith* and *Letter to a Christian Nation* contain plenty to outrage just about everyone," David Segal wrote. "Harris assails political correctness, evangelicals, liberals, right-wingers and even Judaism, which often gets a pass in such debates." Few reviews of *The End of Faith* (or *Letter to a Christian Nation*) praised the book wholeheartedly; most were decidedly mixed, and some disparaged it entirely. Among the most enthusiastic readers was Natalie Angier, who wrote for the *New York Times* (5 Sep. 2004), "The End of Faith articulates the dangers and absurdities of organized religion so fiercely and so fearlessly that I felt relieved as I read it, vindicated, almost personally understood." Angier was taken aback, though, by Harris's assertion that it was "time for us to admit that not all cultures are at the same stage of moral development" and by what she termed his "strained defense for the use of torture in wartime." In the *Humanist* (1 May 2005), David A. Niose described *The End of Faith* as "a call to arms: an energetic and persuasive argument in favor of assertively fighting irrationality," but he predicted that it was "unlikely to get a fair hearing in the marketplace of ideas; the title alone is too extreme for the average person." "Harris opines that religion has become so outdated and dangerous that those inclined toward reason-based beliefs and values should make a concerted effort to toss all faith-based religious thinking—not just fundamentalist but moderate religion as well—into the trash heap of history," Niose wrote. "This kind of talk is controversial even within the secular community, where many believe that nontheists should stand together with moderate religionists to confront fundamentalism." In addition, Niose wrote, "Harris' passion sometimes rises to the level of obsession, leaving him with arguments that seem too pointedly directed at religion alone, to the exclusion of other targets. While certainly religious faith has a long track record of perpetuating ignorance, stunting scientific inquiry, and affirmatively causing unimaginable pain and horror, Harris seems to suggest that religion is just about the only cause of such misfortunes. In his rant against religion, Harris almost completely ignores other forces—imperialism, colonialism, nationalism, militarism, economics, politics, as well as social and psychological factors—in bringing about the ills of the world. As such, many of his arguments smack of oversimplification and imbalance." Niose also noted, "Harris' exuberance sometimes results in his making statements that are just plain shocking," such as that "some propositions are so dangerous that it may even be ethical to kill people for believing them."

In the *Progressive Christian* (Mar./Apr. 2007), Gilbert Viera offered criticism of *The End of Faith* on another front: "Harris charges that all religious beliefs lack evidential truth. What he means, of course, is that they do not fall within the grid of truth as defined by science. This is the perennial controversy between religion and science. One side argues there is a single standard for deciding objective truth on all matters, that belonging to science. The other asserts that knowledge takes different forms and requires different paradigms for their discernment." Noting "life's astounding wonders and mysteries," Viera added, "We who affirm both faith and reason contend that we are facing here, as in the whole realm of human imagination and creativity, realities that cannot be made subject to the language of science and its protocols of proof." In the *Nation* (16 May 2011), Jackson Lears, too, questioned Harris's certainty that science will produce "a total explanation of the nature of things" and is "the only repository of truth." In addition, he charged, "Harris is not interested in religious experience. He displays an astonishing lack of knowledge or even curiosity about the actual content of religious belief or practice." In the *Harvard Law & Policy Review* (Sum. 2007), Ryan Spear faulted Harris for discussing religion as resulting from the irrational or pathological states of individuals and ignoring "the social character of religious practice." "Religious belief may live, in some sense, in the individual conscience, but religious practice lives in the public sphere. Thus, an individual's religion is inevitably bound up with the entire matrix of human culture: history, language, tribal codes, familial relationships, political ideology, art, science, commerce."

THE MORAL LANDSCAPE

In *The Moral Landscape* Harris declared that "questions about values—about meaning, morality, and life's larger purpose—are really questions about the well-being of conscious creatures. Values, therefore, translate into facts that can be scientifically understood." From that it follows, Jonathan Derbyshire wrote for the *New Statesman* (18 Apr. 2011), that "well-being is something that is measurable."

"The 'science of human flourishing' that [Harris] lays out in the book is an updated version of utilitarianism," Derbyshire continued, "in which well-being replaces pleasure as the source of moral value. Crudely put, in the view that Harris defends, an action is right to the extent that it promotes well-being." "It's odd that one can share so many of Harris's views and yet find his project largely unsuccessful," H. Allen Orr wrote for the *New York Review of Books* (12 May 2011). "I certainly share his vision of the well-being of conscious creatures as a sensible end for ethics. And I agree that science can and should help us to attain this end. And I certainly agree that religion has no monopoly on morals. The problem—and it's one that Harris never faces up to— is that one can agree with all these things and yet not think that morality should be 'considered an undeveloped branch of science.'" Similarly, in the *Skeptic* (2011), Massimo Pigliucci wrote, "There is much about which Harris and I agree. We are both moral realists, i.e., we believe that moral questions do have non-arbitrary answers. . . . We both agree that religion has absolutely nothing to do with morality, though I don't think of it as the root of all evil, which seems to be a good summary of Harris' view of it. Finally, both Harris and I think that moral relativism is . . . downright pernicious in its effects on individuals and society. Here is where the two of us disagree: I do not think that science amounts to the sum total of rational inquiry . . . , which he seems to (implicitly) assume. I do think that science should inform the specifics of our ethical discussions, . . . but I maintain that ethical questions are inherently philosophical in nature, not scientific. Ignoring this distinction, I think, does a disservice to both science and philosophy. . . . I think that a combination of these two disciplines . . . is our best hope for a more rational and compassionate humanity."

Harris's essay "Lying" appeared as an e-book in 2011.

PERSONAL LIFE

"My writing is angrier than I am," Harris told David Segal. "The maniac comes out a bit when I get behind the keyboard." Harris and his wife, Annaka, married in 2004. The couple have a daughter, Emma. For security reasons, Harris does not divulge where they live.

SUGGESTED READING

Greenberg, Brad A. "Making Belief." *UCLA Magazine.* UC Regents, 1 Apr. 2008. Web. Jan. 2012.

Harris, Sam. "Sam Harris Extended Interview." *PBS: Religion & Ethics* Newsweekly. Educational Broadcasting Corp., 5 Jan. 2007 Web. Jan. 2012.

---. "Sam Harris: The Truthdig Interview." Interview by Blair Golson. *Truthdig.* Truthdig, LLC. 3 Apr. 2006. Web. Jan. 2012.

Segal, David. "Atheist Evangelist." *Washington Post* 26 Oct. 2006: C1.

—*Molly M. Hagan*

Katharine Hayhoe

Born: 1972
Occupation: Climate scientist

Katharine Hayhoe is the director of the Climate Science Center at Texas Tech University, as well as the head of a consulting company called AT-MOS Research, which provides climate projections to clients in both the public and private sectors. She is also the co-author, along with her husband, evangelical pastor Andrew Farley, of *A Climate for Change: Global Warming Facts for Faith-Based Decisions* (2009). Hayhoe, also an evangelical Christian, told Tom Miller for the PBS show *Nova* (April 27, 2011), "There's often a perceived conflict between science and faith. It's a little bit like coming out of the closet, admitting to people that you are a Christian and you are a scientist." Although many religious and political conservatives profess doubt about the reality of global warming, Hayhoe has stated that human-driven climate change is as certain a phenomenon as the law of gravity or Einstein's theory of relativity; she attributes skepticism about the topic to media coverage that misleadingly portrays climate change as a two-sided issue. "The most recent survey I've seen found that almost 98 percent of scientists in related or relevant fields to climate science agreed that human production of heat-trapping gases was the main or most important influence on climate change today, and was responsible for much of the climate change that we've seen over the last 50 years," Hayhoe told Kate Galbraith for the *Texas Tribune* (September 22, 2011).

Hayhoe explained to a journalist for the Christian environmental Web site Restoring Eden, "I firmly believe there is no conflict at all between faith in an all-powerful God and understanding that humans are radically altering the

Courtesy of Mark Umstot, courtesy of Katharine Hayhoe

face of our planet. In fact, they are completely compatible." She continued, "We already know that bad things happen in our world. Poor choices have consequences. We live this out in our own lives, and now we see the same principle at work at the global scale. Climate change is already affecting our planet and its inhabitants. The greatest impacts are already being felt by the poor and the disadvantaged, who lack the resources to adapt. This is true both here in the United States, as well as in developing nations around the world. As Christians, we are called to love God and love others. Recognizing the reality of climate change and reaching out to help our global neighbors is a tangible expression of this love." Hayhoe, who was an important contributor to the Nobel Prize-winning Intergovernmental Panel on Climate Change (IPCC), believes that everyone can help combat global warming by making simple changes in their daily lives. To further that cause, she gives countless interviews and works to raise public awareness, devoting so much of her free time to lecturing that she has been called the "Climate Evangelist."

EARLY LIFE AND EDUCATION

Hayhoe was born in 1972 in Etobicoke, a municipality within the city limits of Toronto, Ontario. Both of her parents were teachers. Her earliest memory, she has told journalists, is of stretching out on a blanket in the park at age four and learning to find the Andromeda galaxy in the night sky. "As far back as I can remember,

my father was teaching me about the world around us," Hayhoe told Tom Miller, "whether it was memorizing all of the birds that we would see in our backyard, or keeping an eye out for all of the rare wild flowers that there are in Ontario, or the giant telescope that we dragged with us on most of our family vacations. But at the same time, from the very beginning, as he taught me about the world, he also taught me that it was the result of a God who created it. And the more I study the world, the more it seems to me that that is the case."

Hayhoe spent many of her childhood summers at a vacation cottage in the Canadian Shield, an area also known as the Laurentian Plateau. When she was nine, her family moved to the South American nation of Colombia, where her parents worked as missionaries and taught in a bilingual school. Hayhoe spent a lot of her time hiking through the Colombian mountains to visit remote villages and examining the unusual flowers and fruits growing alongside the roads. She returned to Ontario to attend the University of Toronto, where she studied physics and astronomy. As an undergraduate student, she worked in the university's research labs, operating a telescope that studied variable stars and testing satellite instruments that measured the earth's atmosphere. She told Kate Galbraith, "It became apparent [to me] fairly quickly that one of the greatest issues related to atmospheric physics was the fact that humans are actually altering the content of our atmosphere, putting more heat-trapping gases into our atmosphere than would normally be there, and those heat-trapping gases are affecting the climate of our planet." After earning her BS degree in 1994, Hayhoe spent a year backpacking through Europe. She then pursued her graduate degree in atmospheric science under the mentorship of Donald Wuebbles at the University of Illinois at Urbana-Champaign, choosing the school, in part, because it hosted a large and active chapter of the Intervarsity Christian Fellowship. She soon became a leader in the group, and through its activities she met her future husband, Andrew Farley. Hayhoe graduated with an MS degree in atmospheric sciences in 1997 and married Farley in 2000. (Later, in 2010, she received her PhD degree from the school.)

CAREER

By 2004 Hayhoe had begun region-specific impact studies with ATMOS Research & Consulting in South Bend, Indiana, while Farley taught at the University of Notre Dame. That year she appeared as a guest on the National Public Radio program *Talk of the Nation* (August 27, 2004), discussing a paper she had authored for the *Proceedings of the National Academy of Sciences* (*PNAS*) that described how climate change might affect the people, industries, and ecology of California. "We chose California because it is a challenging case," she told the show's host, Ira Flatow. Hayhoe and her team had envisioned two hypothetical scenarios for the study. In the first, the world does not alter its current behavior and continues to liberally use fossil fuels. In the second scenario, scientists look for alternate sources of energy but do not, as Hayhoe noted, take "specific actions to reduce . . . emissions of greenhouse gases." She discovered that neither scenario yielded particularly optimistic results. "We found the impacts [of continued fossil fuel emissions] were widespread over almost every sector that we looked at," she told Flatow. "We found that with higher temperatures, you get more frequent and severe periods of extreme heat. As you can imagine, that affects human health in both the urban and rural areas. We found reductions in snowpack in the mountains, impacts on water supply in California, impaired quality of wine grapes. . . . [There would be major damage to] the vegetation and the ecosystems that make California such a unique place." She continued, "The Central Valley might feel more like Death Valley." In response to skeptics, including the National Center for Policy Analysis, which described Hayhoe's study as "a doomsday prediction by climate alarmists," Hayhoe defended her figures. "From the science side, I would say that our study is actually rather conservative," she told Flatow. "The whole point of the study is to show that we have the potential to determine the outcome of our own future. The choices that we make today are going to have huge impacts on the amount of change that we see in the future."

Hayhoe has conducted similar region-specific studies in other parts of the country. Her midrange climate predictions indicate that summers in West Virginia will soon feel more like those in Arkansas or Kansas. "The West Virginia that people are used to, that they grew up in, that their parents grew up in, it's not going to be the same place their children grow up in," she told Pam Kasey for the (West Virginia) *State Journal* (February 2007). "We are seeing all kinds of signatures of [climate] change [in West Virginia and] all over the country. For example, trees and flowers are blooming earlier in the year, and we're seeing new species growing where they didn't grow before because it was too cold." By the end of the century, she predicts that Cincinnati, Ohio—which now gets 18 days per year of temperatures over 90 degrees—could be subject to 85 days of such extreme heat. "In addition," as Bob Downing reported for the *Akron (Ohio) Beacon Journal* (July 29, 2009), "Ohio will get more heavy rains that would trigger flooding; winters would be shorter; smog would continue to be a problem in Northeast Ohio and Cincinnati; and the water level on Lake Erie will fall about 18 inches. Ohio farmers will also be

heavily impacted. Crops and livestock will face substantially more heat stress, decreasing crop yields and livestock productivity. The growing season will become up to six weeks longer but crop pests like the corn earworm are likely to spread."

Hayhoe has also addressed the recent outbreak of extreme weather in Texas, which experienced a crippling drought and record-breaking temperatures in 2011. She told Galbraith, "We have already altered the background conditions of our atmosphere, through increasing our production of these heat-trapping gases and increasing the average temperature of the atmosphere. . . . We have changed the background conditions in terms of not just the temperature but the humidity and also the weather patterns that we've experienced. So in that sense, every event that happens—snowstorm, heat wave, drought, flood—every event that happens has some contribution or component of climate change in it, because we've changed the background conditions."

Citing the drought in Texas and other such extreme events that have occurred over the past decade, Hayhoe has deemed strange weather patterns to be the products of "global weirding," a concept broader than simple global warming, which reflects only one aspect of climate change. "It's certainly true that we have an enormous diversity of weather on our planet and that's why we have to be careful not to immediately jump to conclusions about what could be causing a specific weather event," Hayhoe told Daniela Minicucci for the Canwest News Service (May 26, 2011). She used an analogy to describe the new and disturbing weather trends. "When we throw a pair of dice, we always have a chance of rolling two sixes," she told Minicucci. "That's the natural variability. What climate change is doing, however, is slowly, one by one, removing one other number at a time and replacing it with an identical six. So our chances of rolling double sixes for many extreme events have slowly been increasing,"

Hayhoe began teaching at Texas Tech University in 2005, and she became director of the Climate Science Center at the university in 2011. In 2007, as an associate professor in the Department of Geosciences, she contributed to the United Nations Intergovernmental Panel on Climate Change (IPCC). The study included scientists from 130 countries who reached a nearly unanimous conclusion about human-driven climate change. "The further we go the more evidence we see that our predictions are right," Hayhoe told Caleb Hooper for the Texas Tech *Daily Toreador* (February 16, 2007, online). "If we wait more than 10 or 20 years before taking action on climate change, extreme measures could be required to prevent what scientists call 'dangerous human-driven change.'" The IPCC shared the 2007 Nobel Peace Prize with former US vice president and environmental activist Al Gore "for their efforts to build up and disseminate greater knowledge about man-made climate change, and to lay the foundations for the measures that are needed to counteract such change," as noted on the Nobel Foundation's Web site.

FAMILY AND FAITH

In 2009 Hayhoe and her husband, Andrew Farley, co-authored *A Climate for Change: Global Warming Facts for Faith-Based Decisions*. Farley is a pastor at Ecclesia Church in Lubbock, Texas, as well as a tenured professor of linguistics at Texas Tech. The two decided to write the book because they were concerned that evangelical Christians were being misinformed about climate change. (While other religious groups have called for action to prevent climate change, evangelicals remain divided.) "This book came from conversations with friends who wanted to know the truth about climate change from a fellow Christian—someone they could trust," Hayhoe stated, as quoted in a Texas Tech press release (October 29, 2009, online). "We realized we had an incredible opportunity to speak out on one of the most pressing issues facing our generation. Most Christians are not scientists, and it's hard to say how many scientists are Christians. In our family, we have both."

Hayhoe and Farley stress the importance of separating science and politics. "Many Christians may feel like they've been burned by scientists in the past, perhaps on issues related to the sanctity of life, or the creation-evolution debate. Complicating the issue is the fact that climate change has become so politicized, albeit falsely so. The result is that conservatives, and many Christians, tend to view climate change as yet another environmental issue driven by a liberal agenda with ulterior motives," Hayhoe told the writer for the Restoring Eden Web site. "The science of climate change has nothing to do with red politics, or blue politics, or any kind of politics. It's a simple matter of temperature readings and long-term trends that have been happening over the last few centuries."

Hayhoe recalled that Farley had once been a "climate change skeptic" because of the misinformation perpetuated by conservative pundits. They spent many late nights together, she said, verifying each piece of evidence in support of climate change until he was convinced. The couple hopes to convince others with their book, which addresses the issue from both a scientific and theological standpoint. Hayhoe and Farley conclude with a biblical call to action. "As we say in the book," Hayhoe told Jim DiPeso for the Republicans for Environmental Protection Web site, "God may have given us the ostrich, but it wasn't as a mythical example to imitate when confronted with unpleasant facts we'd rather ignore. Instead of burying our heads in the sand, we should take Gideon as our model, who examined all possible options and then when he'd had his questions answered, took action."

Hayhoe served as the lead author on the United States Global Change Research Program report "Global Climate Change Impacts in the United States" (2009) and the National Research Council report "Climate Stabilization Targets: Emissions, Concentrations, and Impacts Over Decades to Millennia" (2010). She recently won funding from the United States Geological Survey (USGS) to develop a national database of climate-change projections and is a principal investigator with the Department of the Interior's South-Central Climate Science Center.

Hayhoe lives in Lubbock, Texas, with her family.

SUGGESTED READING

Downing, Bob. "Scorching Summers a Definite Possibility." *Ohio.com*. Akron Beacon Journal, 29 July 2009. Web. 19 Dec. 2011.

"Dr. Katharine Hayhoe Talks About California's Climate Change." *Talk of the Nation*. NPR. 27 Aug. 2004. Radio.

Hayhoe, Katharine. "Thermometers Don't Lie: An Interview with Author Katharine Hayhoe." *Restoring Eden*. Restoring Eden, 2010. Web. 19 Dec. 2011.

Kasey, Pam. "Atmospheric Scientist Offers View of a Changed West Virginia." *State Journal* [West Virginia] 9 Feb. 2007: 6. Print.

"Katharine Hayhoe." *The Secret Life of Scientists and Engineers* (*Nova* web video series). PBS, 2011. Web. 19 Dec. 2011.

Minicucci, Daniela. "Spree of Deadly Storms Points to 'Global Weirding.'" *Global Toronto*. Shaw Media, 26 May 2011. Web. 19 Dec. 2011.

—*Molly Hagan*

Chris Hedges

Born: September 18, 1956
Occupation: War correspondent, author

Prior to becoming a prolific book author, Chris Hedges covered war and conflict in Central America, the Middle East, the Balkans, and Africa, primarily reporting for the *New York Times*. As part of a team of reporters who covered global terrorism for the *New York Times*, Hedges won the 2002 Pulitzer Prize for Explanatory Reporting. That year he also published his first book, *War Is a Force That Gives Us Meaning*, which became a best-seller. Hedges is the author of

Getty Images

many other books, including *What Every Person Should Know About War* (2003), *Losing Moses on the Freeway: The 10 Commandments in America* (2005), *American Fascists: The Christian Right and the War on America* (2007), *I Don't Believe in Atheists* (2008), and *Death of the Liberal Class* (2010). Hedges is a senior fellow at the Nation Institute in New York City and a weekly columnist for Truthdig.com, a news and reporting website. He has also written for *Harper's Magazine*, the *New York Review of Books*, the *Christian Science Monitor*, *Foreign Affairs*, and other publications. In addition to his native English, Hedges speaks Arabic, French, and Spanish.

EARLY LIFE AND EDUCATION

Christopher Lynn Hedges was born on September 18, 1956, in St. Johnsbury, Vermont, and grew up in Schoharie County, New York. He learned religion and liberal values from his parents, particularly his father. His mother was a seminary graduate who worked as a professor, and his father was a Presbyterian minister. In a comment for the website *Americans Who Tell the Truth* (undated), Hedges wrote of his father: "He was an early and vocal supporter of the civil rights movement at a time when Dr. Martin Luther King was, in rural white enclaves like ours, one of the most hated men in America. He opposed, although a veteran of World War II, the Vietnam War and told me when I was about twelve that if the war was still being fought when I was eighteen and I was drafted he would go to jail with me." Alongside his support for the civil

rights and antiwar movements, his father also supported gay rights. This in part was because his brother, Hedges' uncle, was gay. "I have always sought to meet the moral and ethical standards my father set," Hedges added.

In the mid-1970s, Hedges enrolled at Colgate University, a liberal arts college in Hamilton, New York. During Hedges' time at the university, his father worked as a minister at a church in Syracuse, New York. He asked his son to found a gay and lesbian alliance at the university, because many of those students were afraid to come out. Hedges, who is not gay, founded the alliance. The alliance functioned, but Hedges did not attend. In 1979, he received a BA in English literature and then went on to attend Harvard Divinity School in Cambridge, Massachusetts. During his time at the divinity school, which he attended on a full scholarship, Hedges ran a church: he preached, ran a youth group, and did funeral services. Although he was pleased with what he was doing, his grades suffered as a result. He was also different from most of the students at the school, Hedges told Jonathan Beasley for the Harvard Divinity School website (14 Mar. 2008), because he did not go there to "find himself." His was not a quest for personal spiritual growth. So why did he attend? "Because I came out of an activist household," he told Beasley. "Issues of justice were paramount in terms of what it is we were called to do as Christians. This notion of a spirituality being 'how is it with me,' was sort of an anathema. And I think there was a heavy residue of that at Harvard, as there probably was at most divinity schools when I was in seminary." Hedges received his master of divinity degree in 1983.

WAR CORRESPONDENT

Hedges began his journalism career reporting on the civil war in El Salvador, a conflict that lasted throughout the 1980s into the early 1990s. He spent about five years in Latin America. After studying Arabic, he went to Jerusalem, Israel, and then to Cairo, Egypt. He spent seven years reporting in the Middle East, primarily for the *New York Times*. He initially worked for the *Dallas Morning News* but around 1990 joined the *New York Times*. In February 1991, while reporting on the Persian Gulf War, Hedges was detained for several hours by US military officials in Saudi Arabia. He had been interviewing local shopkeepers and American soldiers fifty miles from the Kuwaiti border when he was detained for being on the "front line" without a public affairs officer; as a result, his credentials were temporarily confiscated. The incident received a good deal of press. For the *Washington Post* (11 Feb. 1991) Howard Kurtz wrote, "(Hedges') brief detention points up the growing frustration among journalists who say the Pentagon is choking off coverage of the war by refusing to dispatch more than a handful of military-escorted pools with US ground forces, and by barring those who venture into the desert on their own. At stake, in the view of these critical journalists, is whether reporters have any hope of penetrating the fog that continues to hang over the war effort."

The following month, Hedges and several dozen Western journalists were captured by Iraqi army forces after they crossed over from Kuwait into Iraq. They were held for five days before being released, to the relief of family members and colleagues. The incident served as yet another reminder of the dangerous nature of being a war correspondent. A year later, in February 1992, Hedges reported from northern Iraq. The Kurdish people there were experiencing a humanitarian crisis, including escalating crime and a serious lack of food and medicine. In November of the following year, Hedges reported that the Iraqi government—still under the rule of Saddam Hussein—was attacking Shiite Muslims in the country's southern marshlands. In 1995, Hedges left the Middle East to cover the war in Bosnia for the *New York Times*. Three years later, he covered the war in Kosovo, which was then part of Yugoslavia. During his time reporting in the Middle East and the Balkans, Hedges was frequently interviewed by various Western media outlets, especially National Public Radio, for his on-the-ground perspective and expertise.

TERRORISM COVERAGE AND LEAVING THE TIMES

Hedges next joined the *New York Times* investigative team, for which he covered the terrorist group al-Qaida while based in Paris, France. In 2002, Hedges' team of reporters won the Pulitzer Prize for Explanatory Reporting for their coverage of global terrorism. Hedges also won the 2002 Amnesty International Global Award for Human Rights Journalism. In May 2003, he delivered a commencement address at Rockford College in Rockford, Illinois. In his speech, Hedges spoke out against the US invasion of Iraq, which had been launched in March of that year. Some audience members reacted to the speech by booing and heckling him. The speech became a talking point. Soon after, Hedges was called into the offices of the *New York Times* and told that he would have to stop his antiwar activism, as it conflicted with his duty to impartiality as a reporter. Hedges had no intention of stopping his activism, so he quit the *New York Times*, after reporting there for almost fifteen years.

BOOK AUTHOR

Hedges' first book, *War Is a Force That Gives Us Meaning* (2002), makes the case—using the author's extensive experience covering war and conflict—that war, to those who take part in it, is addictive and provides a sense of purpose. In

the book, Hedges does not make a case either for or against war. Rather, his point is descriptive. In the opening pages, Hedges writes: "War and conflict have marked most of my adult life. I have been in ambushes on desolate stretches of Central American roads, locked in unnerving firefights in the marshes in southern Iraq, imprisoned in the Sudan, beaten by Saudi military police. . . . And yet there is a part of me that remains nostalgic for war's simplicity and high. The enduring attraction of war is this: Even with its destruction and carnage it gives us what we all long for in life. It gives us purpose, meaning, a reason for living." Hedges comments on the psychological consequences of war in a forthright manner. With regard to the dangerous and addictive nature of war, he writes: "The rush of battle is a potent and often lethal addiction, for war is a drug, one I ingested for many years. It is peddled by mythmakers—historians, war correspondents, filmmakers, novelists, and the state—all of whom endow it with qualities it often does possess: excitement, exoticism, power, chances to rise above our small stations in life, and a bizarre and fantastic universe that has a grotesque and dark beauty. . . . Fundamental questions about the meaning, or meaninglessness, of our place on the planet are laid bare when we watch those around us sink to the lowest depths. War exposes the capacity for evil that lurks just below the surface within all of us."

War Is a Force That Gives Us Meaning received generally positive reviews. Hedges' extensive experience as a war reporter gave him a good deal of credibility. Since he was so forthcoming and open about how he felt about war—saying things many would not dare admit—he received even more praise. Most critics admired his fearless honesty. In a review for the *New York Times* (29 Sep. 2002), Abraham Verghese wrote that *War Is a Force That Gives Us Meaning* is a "brilliant, thoughtful, timely and unsettling book whose greatest merit is that it will rattle jingoists, pacifists, moralists, nihilists, politicians and professional soldiers equally." The book was released about a year after the September 11, 2001 terrorist attacks, as the United States was on the path to war with Iraq, making it all the more timely; it became a best seller.

Hedges' second book, *What Every Person Should Know about War* (2003), was released a few months after the US invasion of Iraq, and soon after his controversial commencement speech at Rockford College. Hedges once again used his many years as a war and conflict correspondent, combined with military, medical, and psychological research, to compile an on-the-ground guide to war. The book is composed of a wide variety of questions and answers, such as: "Will I make friends during combat?"; "What is a dirty bomb?"; "Will I become more religious?"; and "What are the most common forms of physical torture?" Hedges used the question-and-answer rhetorical device to educate and subtly demonstrate how many questions, myths, and uncertainties there are about war. In a review for the *New York Times* (6 July 2003), Robert Pinsky described the book as a "noble, flawed effort to deepen our American understanding of war by making facts personal." Like several other critics who gave the book mixed reviews, Pinsky called it at times "too eccentric, too self-parodic" to live up to its goal.

Hedges' next three books focus on themes of religion and fundamentalism. At the beginning of *Losing Moses on the Freeway: The 10 Commandments in America* (2005), Hedges presents the Ten Commandments as they appear in the Bible. He spends the rest of the book incorporating stories on the theme of the commandments—based either on his personal experience or the experience and stories of people he met on the road. He writes of an Episcopal bishop who served in Vietnam, the Central American immigrant regulars at a bar on Long Island, and others. Although some reviewers praised the book in its entirety, most observed that the best parts are Hedges' autobiographical details, to which Peter Temes for the *New York Times* (6 June 2005) referred as the "buried memoir."

American Fascists: The Christian Right and the War on America (2007) followed. In it, Hedges makes the case that the religious right—ultraconservative Christians, namely the "dominionist movement"—want to transform America from a democracy into a Christian state. This movement, he wrote, is embodied by such Christian leaders as James Dobson, Pat Robertson, and Jerry Falwell. Hedges' research for the book included attending an Evangelical seminar and a religious broadcasters' convention. The "dominionists," he wrote, want to replace constitutional law in America with biblical law. The book received mixed reviews. *I Don't Believe in Atheists* (2008) came next. While promoting *American Fascists*, Hedges came across such intellectual figures as Christopher Hitchens and Sam Harris, the so-called New Atheists. Hedges took issue with their demonizing of religion. Like Hedges' previous two books, *I Don't Believe in Atheists* received mixed reviews. In particular, some reviewers took issue with his mischaracterizations or simplifications of the positions of the New Atheists. In a review for the *Boston Globe* (19 Mar. 2008), Rich Barlow wrote, "What I've read of the atheist writers leaves me unpersuaded that they're chasing utopia, but Hedges' main point that they're often intolerant cranks is dead-on. Still, his book is a cascade of invective that, coming in such a slender volume, makes it surprisingly and tediously repetitive. Nevertheless, atheists and believers should read Hedges, if only to better inform their theologies with appropriate humility."

Collateral Damage: America's War against Iraqi Civilians (2008), which Hedges coauthored with Laila Al-Arian, is a collection of fifty interviews with Iraq War veterans who spoke honestly about the horror and violence they witnessed in the war. The following year saw the publication of *Empire of Illusion: The End of Literacy and the Triumph of Spectacle* (2009), in which Hedges makes the case that corporations have too much power, which they use to reshape people's sense of self-worth. *Death of the Liberal Class* (2010) paints a gloomy scenario for the American working class as well as Western civilization as a whole. In 2011, a collection of Hedges' columns for Truthdig.com were published in a book called *The World As It Is: Dispatches on the Myth of Human Progress* (2011). The columns address the decline of America's status in the world from multiple angles, such as politics, the environment, foreign policy, and economics.

Chris Hedges and his wife, actor Eunice Wong, live in Princeton, New Jersey. They have one child, Konrad. Hedges also has two children, Noelle and Thomas, from a previous marriage.

SUGGESTED READING

Barlow, Rich. "Harsh Words for Atheists, and a Search for Common Ground." *Boston Globe* 19 Mar. 2008: F3. Print.

Beasley, Jonathan. "A Conversation with Chris Hedges." *Harvard Divinity School*. Harvard University, 14 Mar. 2008. Web. 14 Mar. 2012.

"Chris Hedges, Columnist." *Truthdig*. Truthdig, 2012. Web. 5 Mar. 2012.

Derakhshani, Tirdad. "On a Dream Deferred to Capitalism." *Philadelphia Inquirer* 28 July 2009: E1. Print.

Goodman, Amy. "Chris Hedges on *American Fascists: The Christian Right and the War on America*." *Democracy Now!* 19 Feb. 2007. Web. 5 Mar. 2012.

Hedges, Chris. *War Is a Force That Gives Us Meaning*. New York: Anchor, 2002. Print.

Shetterley, Robert. "Chris Hedges." *Americans Who Tell the Truth*. Web. 5 Mar. 2012.

Verghese, Abraham. "Wars Are Made, Not Born." *New York Times* 29 Sep. 2002: BR21. Print.

Wilder, Charly. "I Don't Believe in Atheists." *Salon*. Salon Media Group, 13 Mar. 2008. Web. 5 Mar. 2012.

— *Dmitry Kiper*

Matthew Herbert

Born: 1972
Occupation: Electronic musician, producer, and composer

British electronic music artist Matthew Herbert "has done more for the possibilities of sampling culture than any other artist currently at work," Dimitri Nasrallah wrote for the monthly Canadian music magazine *Exclaim!* (Nov. 2008). "Whether he's chopping up food for sound, leading big bands, writing manifestos, railing against globalization, or simply making dance music out of bodily functions," Nasrallah noted, "Matthew Herbert has consistently taken his music into corners other people couldn't even imagine. Like Brian Eno, he's eclectic, wildly creative, and eager to collaborate with a wide range of musicians and musical styles." Herbert, the founder of the independent label Accidental Records and creator of an influential manifesto called the "Personal Contract for the Composition of Music (Incorporating the Manifesto of Mistakes)," or PCCOM manifesto, has been recording and performing professionally under a variety of aliases, including Wishmountain, Doctor Rockit, Herbert, Radio Boy, and the Matthew Herbert Big Band, since the mid-1990s. Under those aliases Herbert has released nearly two dozen full-length albums and countless other EPs and singles covering a diverse range of styles, including house, techno, pop, classical, big band, jazz, and funk. He is known particularly for his sampling prowess and pioneering use of found sounds in electronic dance music, which have helped him become one of the most in-demand remixers and producers in the music industry. He is also known for his strong political views, which have inspired many of his musical compositions.

EARLY LIFE AND EDUCATION

Herbert was born in 1972 and grew up in the village of Five Oak Green, in Kent, a county in southeastern England. His father worked as a sound engineer for the British Broadcasting Corporation (BBC) and his mother was a teacher; he has a sister, whose name has not been publicized. Herbert developed a fascination with music at an early age, largely through the influence of his father, who started him on piano and violin lessons when he was four years old. "He would always be taking something apart," he said of his father to Dimitri Nasrallah, adding, "Seeing the insides of a radio was just as much of influence as what came out of it." Herbert was raised in a strict Methodist household and grew up without a television. As a result he spent much of his childhood playing various instruments, listening to the radio, and leading other isolated

Redferns via Getty Images

pursuits. Early on Herbert developed alternative musical tastes through the radio, becoming a fan of such artists as the groundbreaking German electronic-music band Kraftwerk and the American avant-garde singer-songwriter Tom Waits. He told Larry Fitzmaurice for the music website Pitchfork (13 Feb. 2012), "For me, music was a little window into an alternative world. And when your diet is mainstream music, you become very receptive to anything that deviates from that."

Naturally musically gifted, Herbert started playing in school orchestras and choirs when he was seven years old. By the time he reached his teens, he was playing a variety of instruments in different bands, among which included a twenty-five-piece, Glenn Miller–style big band jazz ensemble. At sixteen, Herbert toured Europe for the first time with one of the orchestras he was involved with. During this time his musical interests expanded to include psychedelic rock, hip-hop, and aleatoric music, or music in which some elements are left to chance. Herbert was greatly influenced by a school music teacher, Pete Stollery. Stollery introduced Herbert to the work of the American composer Steve Reich, whose 1966 piece "Come Out to Show Them," about the 1964 Harlem riots, made innovative use of found sounds and tape loops. After listening to "Come Out," Herbert explained to Nasrallah, "That's when I realized that music wasn't just scales or something you did for an hour a week with a slightly scary violin teacher. It was political, it was electronic, futuristic somehow, if that's the appropriate word, it's challenging, beautiful, airy, and it's unique as well. It was something I'd never heard before in that way."

UNIVERSITY AND THE RAVE SCENE

Herbert studied drama at England's Exeter University in the early 1990s. By that time he had accumulated enough electronics equipment to set up his own home recording studio. At Exeter Herbert became fascinated by the relationship between music and performance and started recording and sampling everyday sounds from his surroundings to include in his drama compositions. It was during this time that he discovered the burgeoning British rave scene, which spawned different genres and subgenres of electronic dance music. Growing fond of house music, Herbert started deejaying at raves and other venues around England. He soon developed a following and began creating dance music assembled from his growing catalog of found sounds under the moniker Wishmountain. Herbert's original and forward-thinking musical style helped him catch the attention of the now-defunct dance music label Mighty Force, which was best known for releasing works by the electronic music performer Aphex Twin (the stage name of Richard D. James). According to Herbert's website, the label released his first production credit, a collaborative EP called *Monster Magnet* (under the guise of Fog City), in 1993. Herbert went on to collaborate with other artists, including the British production duo Global Communication. By the time he graduated from Exeter University, in 1994, he was recording and performing diverse styles of music under an array of aliases.

EARLY CAREER

After college, Herbert moved to London to pursue his career in music full-time, a decision inspired by the death of a close friend in 1994. He told David Stubbs, in a biography posted on Herbert's website, "This death was the impetus to push on with my music. It's the silent powerplant at the heart of my work." Herbert gave his first major public performance as Wishmountain in January 1995, at the Arches nightclub in Glasgow, Scotland, for which he performed a live deejay set using only a sampler and a bag of potato chips. The set was well received and prompted him to sample and rework numerous other everyday objects during subsequent live sets. (Herbert has published a sonography on his website detailing all of the sounds he has recorded over the course of his career.) Also in 1995 Herbert released his first full-length album—*Ready to Rockit*—as Doctor Rockit, on the Clear label. The album featured an "electro-jazzy sound with vocal snippets," as was noted in *The Rough Guide to Rock* (2003), which was edited by Peter Buckley. Herbert's profile rose

considerably in 1996, with the release of a number of projects under his Wishmountain, Doctor Rockit, and Herbert monikers. That year saw him release his first Wishmountain EP, Radio, on Universal Language Productions; his second full-length effort as Doctor Rockit, The Music of Sound, on Clear; and debut album as Herbert, 100lbs, on Phono Records, which featured material compiled from a series of EPs. As Herbert, his music was rooted largely in the house genre, characterized by the heavy use of samples and repetitive four-to-the-floor, or 4/4, rhythms, which stood in contrast to the sonic experimentalism of Wishmountain and electro-based sound of Doctor Rockit. David Stubbs wrote that 100lbs "feels very much a Herbert album . . . self-consciously assembled, precisely weighted, sleek, sending micro-fragments showering and skittering across its own, silvery surfaces yet plumbing Moog House depths." Herbert would record under yet another alias—Radio Boy—in 1997, when he released the album Long Live Radio Boy on the Antiphon label.

RADIO BOY AND HERBERT

In 1998, Herbert released the album *Wishmountain is Dead—Long Live Radio Boy*, on Antiphon, marking his last effort under the name Wishmountain, which he abandoned in favor of Radio Boy. As Dimitri Nasrallah puts it, "The Radio Boy alias pursues the same experimental sampling ethos of Wishmountain, but with a more direct political stance in mind, reflecting the rising importance of politics in Herbert's views and the continued influence of the early sampling politics embedded in Steve Reich's compositions." In the same year, Herbert released another album under the Herbert moniker, *Around the House,* on the Phonography label. For that album, which was critically well received, Herbert turned away from using samples of other people's music in favor of sounds of everyday, household objects such as kitchen sinks and washing machines, which he sampled into accessible house rhythms. The album featured vocals by his then-girlfriend and eventual first wife, the jazz singer Dani Siciliano (whom he had met while touring in San Francisco), who sang on such tracks as "So Now" and "We Still Have (The Music)." In a review of *Around the House* for the AllMusic website, John Bush made note of Herbert's "deep liquid basslines and staccato kitchen-sink percussion" and praised Siciliano's "languorous vocals." (*Around the House* was rereleased on the !K7 label in 2002.)

By the late 1990s Herbert had started contributing music to film soundtracks, including director Justin Kerrigan's comedy *Human Traffic* (1999). He had also become an in-demand remixer working on songs for a wide range of artists, including Spacetime Continuum, Agent

Blue, Moloko, Atom Heart, Motorbass, Furry Phreaks, Sven Vath, Presence, and Visit Venus.

HERBERT'S MANIFESTO

In 2000 Herbert released a mix album of his own called *Let's All Make Mistakes*, which included songs by such techno artists as Plastikman, Theo Parrish, and Green Velvet, as well as five original productions. That same year he founded the independent label Accidental Records and wrote a manifesto, titled "Personal Contract for the Composition of Music (Incorporating the Manifesto of Mistakes)"—or PCCOM manifesto—which featured a list of eleven artistic principles that would provide a template for much of his subsequent work. Herbert's manifesto forbids the use of drum machines, synthesizers, prerecorded sounds, and the sampling of other people's work, while encouraging accidents and randomness in the recording process. Calling his decision to create the manifesto "entirely sudden," Herbert, who by that time had become fed up with the ideologically vacant house music scene, explained to Stubbs, "It was an exciting realisation—that the artistic agenda in electronic music was there for the taking. I don't mean that in an arrogant way, but in a practical way. There has never been any magazine or place for people to talk about music in the way I was brought up to talk about art, literature, film, etc." Herbert's PCCOM manifesto has drawn comparisons to the Danish filmmaker Lars von Trier's Dogme 95 Manifesto, which features a set of rules about filmmaking.

THE MECHANICS OF DESTRUCTION AND BODILY FUNCTIONS

In 2001 Herbert released two of his most overtly political albums, *The Mechanics of Destruction* and *Bodily Functions*, under his Radio Boy and Herbert monikers, respectively. The former tackled the theme of globalization and corporate greed through the use of sounds culled entirely from wasteful consumer products, featuring samples of everything from a McDonald's Big Mac ("McDonalds") to Rupert Murdoch's the *Sun* newspaper ("Rupert Murdoch"). Herbert gave away *The Mechanics of Destruction* for free via download on his website, as a way to further drive home the album's message. Meanwhile, for *Bodily Functions*, he centered on the theme of human relationships by using samples taken mostly from the human body, which were set "against a jazzy house backdrop," as Jonathan Wingfield noted for the *New York Times* (10 Mar. 2010). This album again featured Dani Siciliano on vocals. Herbert described *Bodily Functions* to Nasrallah as "a political album about relationships and feeling alienated from the state, about the alienation that begins to crop up in personal lives once corporations begin popping up everywhere."

THE MATTHEW HERBERT BIG BAND

Herbert next reinvented himself as the leader of the Matthew Herbert Big Band, with the album *Goodbye Swingtime*, which was released on Accidental in 2003. For the album, which was recorded at the famous Abbey Road Studios, he assembled a full swing orchestra made up of sixteen British jazz musicians, including trombonist Gordon Campbell, saxophonist Nigel Hitchcock, bassist Dave Green, and pianist Phil Parnell; the band was rounded out by Dani Siciliano and other performers. Like *The Mechanics of Destruction* and *Bodily Functions*, *Goodbye Swingtime* was made under the guidelines set forth in the PCCOM manifesto and carried a political message. It featured elaborate big band orchestrations (all written by Herbert) set to politically inspired sounds, such as percussive beats made by dropping phonebooks or paging through political books written by Noam Chomsky and Michael Moore, as a way to criticize the 2003 invasion of Iraq. The Matthew Herbert Big Band would subsequently perform at jazz festivals all over the world. In 2008 Herbert reconvened the band for a follow-up album—*There's Me and There's You*—which featured the London-based session singer Eska and dealt with the theme of overconsumption.

PLAT DU JOUR

Herbert concentrated on the subject of food for 2005's *Plat du Jour*—released as Matthew Herbert—which was assembled from a large collection of sounds related to food preparation, production, and consumption. Among its tracks included "The Truncated Life of a Modern Industrialised Chicken," which had a recording of thirty thousand broiler chickens in a barn; "An Empire of Coffee," which incorporated the thud of sixty Vietnamese coffee beans being dropped into a can of weedkiller; "Sugar," which included the sound of a can of Coca-Cola; and "An Apple a Day . . .," which featured an audio sample of more than three thousand people eating an apple. In conjunction with the release of *Plat du Jour*, Herbert launched the website Plat du Jour, which provided in-depth information about the two-and-a-half-year making of the album. For his accompanying live show, he performed alongside a brigade of chefs. As noted on the Accidental Records website, a writer for the London *Guardian* called the resultant live shows "a wild stimulation of senses, feet, and intellect."

SCALE

In 2006 Herbert released the album *Scale* (as Herbert) on the !K7 label. Inspired by funk and disco, the album featured eleven tracks that incorporated the sounds of more than six hundred objects, among which included bells, coffins, and petrol pumps. It was both a critical and commercial success and was Herbert's first album to reach the Top 20 on *Billboard*'s electronic music album chart. *Scale* also marked his last collaboration with Dani Siciliano, who sang on ten of the album's eleven tracks. (The two would separate following the recording of the album.) Andy Kellman, in a review of the album on the website AllMusic, commented, "Herbert is more upset about the state of the planet than ever, especially when it comes to the actions and inactions of Bush and Blair, but he has also made it known that he aimed to make an enjoyable, richly musical album full of melodies and multi-part harmonies." He added that its songs "are unmistakably his and Siciliano's, sounding like no one else, twisting and swinging and drifting with optimum vibrancy. Some of them are big and bold enough to be used in a stage production. All of them are 100 percent heavenly, even when they're dealing with loss."

THE "ONE" TRILOGY

Score, compilation of Herbert's unreleased film scores, was released on !K7 in 2007. He has since recorded a trilogy of albums—*One One*, *One Club*, and *One Pig*—the first two of which were released in 2010 and the third in 2011. All three albums, known as the "One" trilogy, were released on Accidental Records under the name Matthew Herbert. For the first installment, which tracks a day in the life of a single man, Herbert wrote and performed every piece of music himself, and for the second, he used samples taken from one night at the Robert Johnson club in Frankfurt, Germany. The third is based on the life and eventual slaughter of a pig on a farm in the British countryside. Although *One Pig* began drawing complaints from the animal rights organization People for the Ethical Treatment of Animals (PETA) more than a year before its release, Herbert has said that the album is meant to reflect on the harsher realities in everyday life. "The pig is simply the most divisive of all animals," he told Ben Sisario for the *New York Times* (17 Oct. 2011). "You probably come into contact with a pig product 10 or 20 times in one day, from ink jet paper to a glass of milk. And yet they're the subject of so much scorn and contempt. I think it's strange that we've built a society that's so dependent on something, and yet we rarely give it a voice of its own." He added, "The most important message of a lot of my projects is that I would like us to listen to the world a little more carefully."

MOST RECENT ALBUMS AND COLLABORATIONS

Herbert's other recordings include *Mahler Symphony X*, a reinterpretation of the Austrian composer Gustav Mahler's tenth symphony. The album was released on the Deutsche Grammophon label in 2010, and the score to the 2011 YouTube documentary film *Life in a Day*, which he made in collaboration with the British composer Harry Gregson-Williams. In addition to remixing hundreds of songs, Herbert has produced albums for several artists, including the Irish singer-songwriter Róisín Murphy's solo debut *Ruby Blue* (2005), the British band the Invisible's Mercury Prize–nominated self-titled debut (2008), the British singer-songwriter Micachu's debut *Jewelry* (2008), and the British pop artist Rowdy Superstar's debut *Battery* (2010). He worked as a programmer on the Icelandic singer-songwriter Björk's album *Vespertine* (2001), and has collaborated with the likes of such high-profile musicians as Quincy Jones, Dizzee Rascal, Ennio Morricone, R.E.M., Perry Farrell, Yoko Ono, and John Cale of the Velvet Underground. He has also composed music for various dance companies and theaters. To date, he has performed numerous sold-out shows at venues on four continents around the world.

Herbert is divorced from his longtime collaborator Dani Siciliano. He has since remarried and has a son.

SUGGESTED READING

Birchmeier, Jason. "Matthew Herbert: Biography." *AllMusic*. Rovi Corp., 2012. Web. 18 July 2012.

Fitzmaurice, Larry. "Matthew Herbert: The Avant-Electronic Explorer on Kraftwerk, Tom Waits, De La Soul, and More." *Pitchfork*. Pitchfork Media Inc., 13 Feb. 2012. Web. 18 July 2012.

Hodgkinson, Will. "Big Bang." *Guardian* 30 Oct. 2003: 26. Web. 18 July 2012.

Nasrallah, Dimitri. "Herbert: Pitch Control." *Exclaim.ca*. Exclaim! Magazine, Nov. 2008. Web. 18 July 2012.

Richardson, Mark. "Interviews: Matthew Herbert." *Pitchfork*. Pitchfork Media Inc., 10 July 2006. Web. 18 July 2012.

Sisario, Ben. "Raising an Album, from Pigpen to Studio." *New York Times*. New York Times Co., 17 Oct. 2011. Web. 18 July 2012.

Stubbs, David. "Matthew Herbert Biography." *Matthew Herbert*. Matthew Herbert, 2011. Web. 18 July 2012.

Welsh, April. "Matthew Herbert's One Pig Project." *Independent*. independent.co.uk, 22 Aug. 2011. Web. 18 July 2012.

Wingfield, Jonathan. "Bring in Da Noise." *New York Times*. New York Times Co., 10 Mar. 2010. Web. 18 July 2012.

—*Chris Cullen*

Félix Hernández

Born: April 8, 1986
Occupation: Baseball player with the Seattle Mariners

Seattle Mariners pitcher Félix Hernández has been known by the nickname "King Félix" ever since making his major-league debut in August 2005 at the age of nineteen. Given the moniker by national sports pundits and fans for his ability to win games single-handedly, the Venezuelan-born Hernández has since lived up to his status as baseball's "next big thing," and in six full seasons with the Mariners, he has established himself as one of the most dominant pitchers in Major League Baseball (MLB). After overcoming adversity in his first three full major-league seasons, in which he posted a win-loss record of 35–32 under three different managers, Hernández enjoyed a breakout year in 2009, earning his first career All-Star selection. The following year, he was awarded the American League (AL) Cy Young Award for his performance in the 2010 season, making him only the second Mariners pitcher and second Venezuelan to receive the honor. In 2011, Hernández earned his second career All-Star selection and recorded more than two hundred strikeouts for the third consecutive year.

Blessed since his early teens with a ninety-mile-per-hour fastball, Hernández has been known to keep hitters constantly off balance with a repertoire that also includes a nasty curveball, a deceptive changeup, and an occasional slider, all of which vary in speed and movement. Texas Rangers outfielder and 2010 AL Championship Series Most Valuable Player Josh Hamilton told Larry LaRue for the Tacoma, Washington, *News Tribune* (1 Apr. 2011), "He's scary good. You can't sit on any pitch because if you guess wrong you're just helpless up there." Former Mariners manager Don Wakamatsu, now the bench coach for the Toronto Blue Jays, told LaRue, "If he's not the best pitcher in our league, he's in the argument. The way he competes, the way he battles, may be as impressive as what he throws."

EARLY LIFE AND EDUCATION

Félix Abraham Hernández Jr. was born on April 8, 1986, in Valencia, the capital of the northern state of Carabobo and the third-largest city in Venezuela. He was raised in the neighborhood of Fundación Valencia, in a middle-class family that stressed the importance of hard work. His father, Félix Sr., worked around-the-clock shifts as a truck driver in order to make ends meet for the family; he later owned and operated his own fleet of trucks before retiring. Hernández inherited his baseball talent from his father, who was reportedly an accomplished player in his youth.

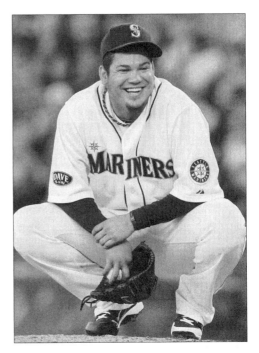

Getty Images

He started playing the sport as a child and grew up idolizing the Venezuelan right-handed pitcher Freddy García, a two-time All-Star who debuted with the Mariners in 1999 and later joined the New York Yankees.

As a boy, Hernández also took a liking to basketball and initially harbored dreams of playing professionally. His mother, Mirian, joked to Geoff Baker for the *Seattle Times* (26 Nov. 2006), "He was terrible as a child. He skipped school all the time to play basketball. I was the one who told him, 'You're going to play baseball because it's what I want you to do.'" Hernández's talent in baseball was evident early on, and he soon found himself playing on squads with children much older than him. His older brother, Moises, began to play the sport as well; he signed a minor-league contract with the Mariners in 2011.

Hernández first came to the attention of major-league scouts while competing in a baseball tournament in the city of Maracaibo, Venezuela, at age fourteen. His ninety-mile-per-hour fastball caught the attention of Luis Fuenmayor, then a scout in the Mariners organization. Amazed by Hernández's skills not only as a pitcher but also as a hitter, Fuenmayor quickly passed word along to Seattle scouts Pedro Avila and Emilio Carrasquel, who subsequently recommended Hernández to Bob Engle, the team's director of international relations. "He was a big kid with a good arm and good velocity, but the separator physically was his breaking ball," Engle told Mike Dodd for *USA Today* (25 Aug. 2005).

"He had a very advanced curveball for a young man."

The scouts would keep Hernández on their radar over the next two years, during which a bidding war began among a handful of other major-league teams, including the New York Yankees, Atlanta Braves, Houston Astros, and Los Angeles Dodgers. With his father leading negotiations, Hernández ultimately chose the Mariners, and in July 2002, shortly after graduating from high school in Valencia, he signed as a non-drafted free agent with the team and was awarded a signing bonus of $710,000. Impressed with the Mariners' persistence, Hernández's father, who ordered him to stay off the pitcher's mound for a brief period in order to protect his arm, recalled to Baker, "We felt very comfortable putting Félix in their hands."

CAREER

Hernández spent three years in the Mariners farm system, first pitching for the Washington-based Everett AquaSox, the organization's short-season single-A affiliate. In eleven games with the AquaSox, he compiled a record of seven wins and two losses, with a 2.29 earned run average (ERA) and seventy-three strikeouts in fifty-five innings. He finished the 2003 season with the single-A Wisconsin Timber Rattlers, striking out eighteen batters in two starts. Hernández began the 2004 season with the San Bernardino, California, Inland Empire 66ers, an advanced single-A affiliate, and went on to play with the double-A San Antonio Missions. After compiling a combined win-loss record of 14–4 and a 2.95 ERA for the San Bernardino and San Antonio clubs, Hernández was named the Mariners' Minor League Pitcher of the Year.

Hernández entered the 2005 season rated by *Baseball America* as the number-two prospect and opened the year playing with the Tacoma Rainiers in the triple-A Pacific Coast League. Despite being sidelined for a month due to shoulder bursitis, he achieved a win-loss record of 9–4, along with a 2.25 ERA and one hundred strikeouts in eighty-eight innings. For his performance, he earned league Rookie of the Year and Pitcher of the Year honors.

After seeing Hernández dominate triple-A competition and post a career minor-league win-loss record of 30–10 with a 2.59 ERA, Mariners leadership felt he was ready to play in the major leagues. Hernández made his major-league debut on August 4, 2005, in a game against the Detroit Tigers. He pitched five innings, allowing one earned run on three hits before suffering a 3–1 loss. Hernández attained his first career win on August 9, in a contest against the Minnesota Twins. In that game, his second start, he pitched eight scoreless innings and allowed just five hits. Hernández finished his rookie campaign with a win-loss record of 4–4 and a 2.67 ERA

in twelve starts, nine of which were "quality starts"—starts in which he pitched at least six innings and allowed no more than three earned runs. Despite his remarkable debut, the Mariners finished fourth out of the four teams in the AL West division for the second straight year, with a record of 69–93. Nonetheless, Hernández's arrival immediately offered hope to the Seattle franchise, which had been yearning for a dominant starting pitcher ever since the departure of Randy Johnson during the 1998 season.

With extremely high expectations surrounding him in 2006, his first full year in the majors, Hernández struggled. He pitched erratically throughout much of the season, posting a win-loss record of 12–14 with a subpar 4.52 ERA and 176 strikeouts in 191 innings. His struggles were attributed to pressure as well as poor conditioning—he had gained a significant amount of weight during the 2006 off-season—and bad mechanics. The Mariners finished the season with a 78–84 record, placing fourth in the AL West.

After overhauling his diet and workout regimen during the 2007 off-season, Hernández arrived at 2007 spring training twenty pounds lighter and entered the season determined to exceed expectations. The Mariners rewarded his hard work by naming him starting pitcher for the first game of the season, in which the Mariners faced the Oakland Athletics. Hernández struck out a career high of twelve batters and allowed no runs and just three hits in eight innings, resulting in a 4–0 Mariners victory. He became one of very few opening-day pitchers in major-league history to record at least twelve strikeouts and only the fourth pitcher since 1900 to start and win a game on opening day before reaching the age of twenty-one. He fared even better in his second outing of the season, on April 11, when he posted a one-hit complete game shutout against the Boston Red Sox.

Hernández's scorching start to the 2007 season came to a standstill after he strained his elbow in his third start of the season, which forced him to miss a significant number of games. Upon returning to the rotation, he was unable to regain his momentum, despite finishing the year with a career high of fourteen wins and a team-leading 165 strikeouts. The Mariners, meanwhile, finished second in the AL West with an 88–74 record. The team enjoyed success despite the abrupt midseason resignation of manager Mike Hargrove, who was replaced by bench coach John McLaren.

Hernández's inconsistent pitching led the Mariners to focus on strengthening the team's starting rotation during the 2008 off-season, which resulted in the acquisition of pitchers Erik Bedard and Carlos Silva from the Baltimore Orioles and Minnesota Twins, respectively. With those signings, Hernández was moved back in the pitching rotation. Despite that setback, he enjoyed a solid season, starting at least thirty games for the third consecutive year and pitching more than two hundred innings for the first time in his career. He led the Mariners in both of those categories as well as in strikeouts (175), despite finishing the season with a win-loss record of 9–11. The majority of Hernández's losses were widely attributed to the lack of run support he received from his team. The Mariners finished last in the AL West for the fourth time in five seasons, with a 61–101 record. Consequently, both manager John McLaren and general manager Bill Bavasi were replaced by Jim Riggleman and Lee Pelekoudas, respectively, before the end of the season

Despite the Mariners' poor overall performance, Hernández's 2008 season was highlighted by three impressive feats that occurred during consecutive games in June. The first came in a June 11 game against the Toronto Blue Jays, during which Hernández recorded his five hundredth career strikeout and became, at twenty-two, one of the youngest pitchers to reach that milestone. In the fourth inning of his next start, on June 17, he became the thirteenth AL pitcher in history to record an "immaculate inning," an inning in which a pitcher throws only strikes. Hernández then followed that up by hitting a grand slam off of fellow Venezuelan pitcher Johan Santana during an interleague game against the New York Mets on June 23, becoming the first Mariners pitcher in history to hit a grand slam. At the end of the season, Hernández was named the Mariners' Pitcher of the Year by the Seattle chapter of the Baseball Writers Association of America. In January 2009, he signed a one-year, $3.8 million deal with the team.

After showing glimpses of his potential in his first three seasons, in 2009 Hernández finally emerged as a Cy Young Award–caliber talent. That season he led the major leagues and set a franchise record with twenty-nine quality starts, also tying for the major-league lead in wins (nineteen) and leading the AL in win-loss percentage (.792, with a record of 19–5). He also finished among the AL leaders in a number of other statistical categories, ranking second in ERA (2.49) and starts (thirty-four), third in innings pitched (238.2), and fourth in strikeouts (217), all of which marked career highs. He earned AL Pitcher of the Month honors for June and September and was selected to his first career All-Star team.

Hernández's excellent performance in 2009 was largely credited to first-year manager Don Wakamatsu, who had replaced Riggleman prior to the season and publicly chastised Hernández after a poor performance in a May game against the Los Angeles Angels of Anaheim. Following that game, Hernández increased his focus, resulting in a 15–2 win-loss record over his last

twenty-five starts of the season. Rick Adair, who served as pitching coach in 2009, told Baker for the *Seattle Times* (18 Nov. 2009), "He showed a willingness to make some adjustments and just take things a little more serious." Hernández finished second to Kansas City Royals pitcher Zack Greinke in the voting for the 2009 AL Cy Young Award and was named the Mariners' Pitcher of the Year for the second consecutive year. Under Wakamatsu, the Mariners enjoyed a twenty-four-game improvement from the previous year, going 85–77 and finishing third in the AL West.

In January 2010, Hernández and the Mariners agreed to a five-year, $78 million contract extension. While the Mariners once again had a 101-loss season, Hernández posted stellar numbers for the second consecutive year. During the 2010 season, Hernández led the AL and set a franchise record with a 2.27 ERA and also led the league in starts (thirty-four), quality starts (thirty), innings pitched (249.2), and opponent batting average (.212). He also finished second in the league with a career high of 232 strikeouts. Despite those numbers, Hernández finished the season with a win-loss record of 13–12. As in his 2008 season, he was the recipient of poor run support and finished with the worst run support average in the AL. The Mariners scored one or fewer runs in ten of his thirty-four starts, and the team's total of 513 runs was the lowest in the major leagues in nearly forty years.

Baseball writers ultimately chose to reward Hernández for his performance in the 2010 season. He was named AL Pitcher of the Year by the magazine *Sporting News* and named the Mariners' Pitcher of the Year for the third straight year. He also won that year's AL Cy Young Award, receiving twenty-one of a possible twenty-eight first-place votes. In the process, he became only the second Mariners pitcher (after Randy Johnson in 1995) and second Venezuelan (after Johan Santana in 2004 and 2006) to receive the honor. While Hernández's win record was the lowest posted by a Cy Young Award–winning starter in a full season, he said after receiving the award, "This confirms the Cy Young is an award not only for the pitcher with the most wins but the most dominant," as quoted by the Associated Press (19 Nov. 2010).

Prior to the 2011 season, Eric Wedge, a former MLB player who had previously managed the Cleveland Indians, was named the Mariners' sixth manager in six seasons. Wedge replaced Daren Brown, who had served as the team's interim manager after the firing of Wakamatsu midway through the 2010 season. Under Wedge, the Mariners enjoyed only modest improvement in 2011, as the team finished last in the AL West with a 67–95 record. That season saw Hernández earn his second career All-Star selection after going 14–14 with a 3.47 ERA. He started at least thirty games for the sixth consecutive season and pitched at least two hundred innings for the fourth straight year. He also amassed more than two hundred strikeouts for the third consecutive year, becoming one of the few pitchers to achieve that feat by the age of twenty-five.

Despite his age, Hernández has begun to take on a more active leadership role in the clubhouse. He has also willingly embraced his role in the team's plans for the future. "He's handled all of it very well," Mariners general manager Jack Zduriencik told Larry Stone for the *Seattle Times* (31 Mar. 2011). "Félix is a very genuine person. He's fun to be around. He's got a fantastic future—and he's got a great career going right now. He has a good relationship with an awful lot of people here. He signed when he was sixteen. For eight years, the guy has been here. I think he sincerely wants us to win. That's a great element to have out of your number-one starter, and obviously an All-Star and Cy Young winner. We hope we can put all this together, and he leads the charge."

PERSONAL LIFE

Hernández, who represented Venezuela in the 2009 World Baseball Classic, spends his offseasons in Valencia with his wife, Sandra, and his two children, Mia and Abraham. A dog lover, he serves as a spokesperson for the Humane Society for Seattle/King County.

SUGGESTED READING

Baker, Geoff. "At Home with Félix Hernández." *Seattle Times* 26 Nov. 2006: C1. Print.

Dodd, Mike. "Mariners' Dream Teen: The Next Great Pitcher?" *USA Today* 25 Aug. 2005: 1C. Print.

LaRue, Larry. "It's All About Félix." *News Tribune* [Tacoma] 1 Apr. 2011: B1. Print.

Morosi, John Paul. "Big Cast Was Involved in Courtship of Félix: Mariners Struck All the Right Chords in Serenade of Venezuelan Youngster." *Seattle Post-Intelligencer* 31 Aug. 2005: D1. Print.

Stone, Larry. "Hard Work, Great Talent Propelled Félix Hernández." *Seattle Times*. Seattle Times, 31 Mar. 2011. Web. 6 Mar. 2012.

—*Chris Cullen*

Hugh Herr

Born: October 25, 1964
Occupation: Biophysicist, engineer

The biophysicist and mechanical engineer Hugh Herr was a highly skilled, experienced mountaineer when, at age seventeen, he got lost during a storm while climbing with a friend on New Hampshire's Mount Washington. By

Christian Science Monitor/Getty Images

the time the two were rescued, their long exposure to frigid temperatures had caused severe frostbite—in Herr's case, in his lower legs. The tissue damage proved to be irreparable, and Herr's legs were amputated below his knees. More agonizing to him than the extreme pain he suffered physically for many months was the knowledge that a volunteer rescuer, Albert Dow, had died in an avalanche while searching for him on Mount Washington. His anger at himself for his mistakes on the mountain and his shame regarding Dow's fate inspired in him an "extraordinary swelling of energy and a desire to not wallow in self-pity but to do something worthwhile with my life," he told Terry Gross for the National Public Radio program *Fresh Air* (10 Aug. 2011, online). That energy and desire led Herr, who had valued climbing over school, to become a fiercely dedicated undergraduate and graduate student. He went on to become a leading researcher in the biological and physical aspects of human movement and a pioneering designer of state-of-the-art artificial knees, ankles, and limbs for amputees and aids for people with limited mobility. Herr told Logan Ward for *Popular Mechanics* (29 Sep. 2005, online) that his work focuses on the "difficult problem of using modern synthetic materials to replace the extraordinary systems nature has given us." He told Andy Greenberg for *Forbes* magazine (29 Nov. 2009, online), "I feel a responsibility to use my intellect and resources to do as much as I can to help people. That's Albert Dow's legacy for me."

Herr is the director and principal investigator of the Biomechatronics Research Group at the Media Lab of the Massachusetts Institute of Technology (MIT), where he is an associate professor in the Department of Media Arts and Sciences and the MIT-Harvard Division of Health Sciences and Technology. Biomechatronics is a field in which biology, mechanics, and electronics intersect. Herr and his team have created devices that have benefited amputees and others both physically and emotionally, helping them to "recover not just their bodily movements but the quality of life they enjoyed before their need for prostheses," Herr said in a press release distributed by PR Newswire (1 Sep. 2011, online). People who have had legs amputated because of accidents or war-related injuries constitute only a small percentage of amputees in the United States; far more have lost legs because of diabetes. In part because of the growing incidence of obesity-triggered diabetes, the number of amputations is expected to increase greatly.

The bionic knees, ankles, and limbs invented in Herr's lab embody major advances in the comfort, durability, energy efficiency, safety, flexibility, adaptability, mobility, and even aesthetics of prosthetics. "We want the bionic limb to have a humanlike shape, but we don't want the bionic limb to look human," Herr told Gross. "We want it to look like a beautiful machine, to express machine beauty as opposed to human beauty. . . . We don't want the user of these prosthetic limbs to be ashamed of their body, ashamed of the fact that part of their body is artificial. We want them to celebrate it. So to do that, we need to put forth synthetic structures that are elegant." Herr is the founder and chief technology officer of iWalk, which markets inventions such as the PowerFoot motorized ankle-foot prosthesis.

"Below the knee . . . down to the floor, I'm artificial," Herr told Gross. "I'm titanium, carbon, silicon, a bunch of nuts and bolts. My limbs that I wear have five computers, twelve sensors, and muscle-like actuator systems that enable me to move throughout my day." Herr owns many pairs of limbs, with feet designed for walking, jogging, running, and climbing on different surfaces. His climbing prostheses have enabled him to climb more efficiently than he did with his own legs. "In the very near future," he said in the press release, "as we continue to learn how to efficiently connect prostheses to the human body, both electrically and mechanically, we will expand controllability and feeling of the artificial limb."

Herr's honors include the Boy Scouts of America's Young American Award in 1990, the Next Wave: Best of 2003 Award from *Science* magazine, the 2005 Breakthrough Leadership Award from *Popular Mechanics*, the 2007 Heinz Award in Technology, the Economy and Employment, and the Spirit of da Vinci Award from the

National Multiple Sclerosis Society's Michigan chapter in 2008.

EARLY LIFE

The youngest child of John and Martha Herr, Hugh Miller Herr was born in Lancaster, Pennsylvania, on October 25, 1964. On his father's side, Herr is descended from a Mennonite minister who immigrated to Lancaster from Switzerland in 1710 to escape religious persecution. He grew up on the family farm in Lancaster with his siblings, Hans, Beth, Ellen, and Tony. The Herr siblings assisted with farm chores from an early age and helped their father with his work building houses. In his acceptance speech for the Heinz Award, Herr said that his parents had impressed upon him "the simple idea that there's no obstacle too great when confronted with the power of the human spirit."

During the summers the Herrs traveled west to mountainous areas of the United States and Canada to camp and hike. Herr's brothers Tony and Hans became avid climbers, and by age seven, Herr was accompanying them. He became particularly interested in mountaineering, which encompasses activities including rock climbing, ice climbing, and bouldering, each with or without ropes or other specialized equipment. Succeeding at difficult climbs requires an enormous amount of knowledge about the environment, safety hazards and precautions, proper use of equipment and techniques, and human physiology.

By age seventeen Herr had become well known as one of the boldest and most skilled young climbers on the East Coast, having conquered a number of the most difficult climbs at a younger age than anyone else. Little interested in academic subjects, he had enrolled in a vocational program at Penn Manor High School, a local public school. He worked mostly in the machine shop, where he learned to make things with metal and wood.

In January 1981 Herr and an older friend from Lancaster, Jeff Batzer, climbed Pinnacle Gully in Huntington Ravine on Mount Washington. Rising 6,288 feet, the mountain is the highest peak east of the Mississippi River. According to the Mount Washington Observatory website, its climate is akin to "that of Northern Labrador, hundreds of miles further north. Three major storm tracks converge over the mountain, forming harsh and turbulent weather conditions." Furthermore, its "combination of the extreme wind, fog, wet, and cold" has led Mount Washington to be called Home of World's Worst Weather. Describing the trail Herr and Batzer took, the observatory website states, "During the snow-free months the Huntington Ravine Trail is regarded as the most exposed and intimidating hiking path in the White Mountains. Add a little bit of snow and making your way through the Ravine automatically becomes a full-blown mountaineering challenge."

NEAR-DEATH EXPERIENCE

In January 1982 Herr, then a junior in high school, and Batzer returned to Mount Washington. Although it was snowing the observatory had detected no danger of avalanches in Odell Gully, a seven-hundred-foot ice face in the Huntington Ravine, so Herr and Batzer decided to climb there. Warmly dressed and well equipped, they started out on the morning of Saturday January 23, 1982. Soon, to lighten their load, they abandoned their sleeping bag and other camping provisions. When they reached the top of the gully, they decided to continue on to the mountain's summit. Before long, blowing snow caused visibility to plummet to less than thirty feet, and gusts of wind buffeted them. With an inadequate map and no compass, Herr and Batzer became lost. During the next three days and nights, they became increasingly disoriented and incapacitated by the cold, suffering from frostbite, exhaustion, and thirst.

The failure of Herr and Batzer to return on Saturday to the climbers' facility where they had stayed Friday night triggered the formation of search teams by the Appalachian Mountain Club (AMC), the Mountain Rescue Service, the New Hampshire Fish and Game Department, and the US Forest Service. On Sunday morning employees and volunteers began to look for them, knowing only that Herr and Batzer had intended to climb Odell Gully, not that they had extended their climb. The teams searched for three days, despite inclement weather and the death of one volunteer rescuer, twenty-eight-year-old Albert Dow, in an avalanche. On the afternoon of January 26, Melissa "Cam" Bradshaw, an AMC member, found Herr and Batzer by chance while snowshoeing. Bradshaw had no radio or other means of communication; neither did a pair of hikers she came upon and directed to the men. Several hours passed before Herr and Batzer were taken by helicopter to a nearby hospital. Herr was later transferred to a Philadelphia medical center. There, in March, after repeated efforts to save Herr's legs failed, both legs were amputated below the knee. "I was told by my doctor that I would never climb again," he told Frank Moss, the author of a book about MIT's Media Lab, *The Sorcerers and Their Apprentices* (2011).

After leaving the hospital Herr used a wheelchair for a month before he was fitted for his first pair of artificial limbs. Made of plaster of paris, they were heavy, clumsy, and uncomfortable and designed for very slow walking on horizontal surfaces, not for rapid walking, running, or rock climbing. Nevertheless, by the summer of 1982, Herr had resumed climbing. Having completed his junior year of high school with

home tutors, he returned to Penn Manor. He soon began to design his own prostheses in the school's machine shop, using metals and acrylic resin laminates. "Building and testing every prosthetic model he dreamed up, he became his own guinea pig, as unafraid of pain and failure as he was unbothered by the countless falls he took as a climber," Eric Adelson wrote for *Boston* magazine (Mar. 2009, online). Herr told Charles J. Murray for *Design News* (Dec. 2010), "I realized that the artificial part of my body is a blank slate from which to create. The limitations were really limitations of technology. My biological body was not disabled. My artificial limbs were disabled." In the spring of 1983, a feature article about him appeared in *Outside* magazine. The cover photo showed him sitting on a boulder, equipped with prosthetic legs and seated next to feet of his own design.

EDUCATION

Herr graduated from high school in 1983. During the next two years, he spent much of his time climbing. In 1985 he enrolled at Millersville University, a state university near Lancaster. He immediately discovered that he loved his courses, particularly mathematics; he later chose to major in physics. He excelled academically, later telling Adelson that his "intellectual birth was in college." Herr also worked with Barry Gosthnian, a prostheticist in Mechanicsburg, Pennsylvania, with whom he collaborated on a design for a socket that cushions an amputee's stump at the points of contact with the prosthesis; theirs incorporated fluid-filled bladders. In May 1990, just before Herr earned a bachelor's degree in physics, he and Gosthnian were awarded a patent, the first of many for Herr, for their "inflatable limb prosthesis with preformed inner surface." In 1993 Herr earned a master's degree in mechanical engineering from MIT. He completed a PhD in biophysics from Harvard University in 1998. His dissertation was entitled "A Model of Mammalian Quadrupedal Running."

RESEARCH AND INVENTION

Herr has worked in MIT's Media Lab since 1998, beginning as a postdoctoral fellow. He taught at Harvard Medical School, as a member of the Department of Physical Medicine and Rehabilitation, from 1999 to 2004; he became a professor at MIT in 2004. He has supervised the preparation of many undergraduate and graduate theses and doctoral dissertations. As the head of the Biomechatronics Group, he guides research aimed at understanding the neurological, muscular, and other elements involved in balance and mobility. The lab then uses such knowledge to create devices that mimic the body's musculoskeletal design, muscle behavior, range of motion, and mechanisms that enable it to respond instantaneously and continuously to such external conditions as a bumpy sidewalk.

Devices designed in Herr's lab include a microprocessor-controlled prosthetic knee—formally, the variable-damper knee prosthesis—that "automatically adapts to an individual's walking style and environment," according to Össur, the Icelandic-based company that markets it as the Rheo Knee. In 2001 Herr unveiled a robotic fish that swam by means of electronically activated frog muscles. A "low-cost, body orientation sensor" followed three years later. According to Charles J. Murray, the lab's PowerFoot prosthesis enables below-knee amputees "to climb stairs, traverse ramps, walk fast, and exert a level of force that's comparable to that of a biological ankle. And it does it all while enabling users to walk with a normal gait." The PowerFoot has "a small [direct-current] motor, a transmission, and a series spring," Murray explained. "Together, the three elements work with a carbon composite spring foot to provide the power that would otherwise be missing from an amputee's step." *Time* magazine ranked the Rheo Knee and the PowerFoot among the best inventions of 2004 and 2007, respectively.

Herr envisions that within the foreseeable future, "the artificial prosthesis will become more intimate with the biological human body," as he told Terry Gross. One way of accomplishing this will involve attaching a prosthesis "mechanically, by a titanium shaft that goes right into the residual bone, where you can't take the artificial limb off," he said. An electrical interface between the body and prosthesis may provide another means for this; as Herr explained, "the nervous system of the human will be able to communicate directly with the synthetic nervous system on the artificial limb."

Herr and his team have also designed an ankle-foot orthosis for people with intact limbs who suffer from foot-drop gait, a consequence of certain types of strokes. To help those whose legs are paralyzed or whose leg muscles are impaired, the team is working on exoskeletal robotic structures. "That's a robot that wraps around a biological limb," Herr explained to Gross. The robot will push on "the impaired biological limb in just the right way to allow a person to stand, walk, and even run." He and his colleagues are also constructing "exoskeletal structures that [augment] human capability beyond what nature intended." In the future Herr envisions, "when a person, for example, goes jogging, they'll routinely wear robots . . . to protect their joints."

Herr is optimistic about his own future as well. He told Gross, "My biological body will degrade in time due to normal, age-related degeneration. But the artificial part of my body improves in time because I can upgrade. I can get the best computer, the best motor system, the best artificial intelligence." He continued,

"So I predict that when I'm eighty years old, I'll be able to walk with less energy than is required of a person that has biological legs. I'll be more stable. I'll probably be able to run faster than a person with biological limbs. . . . In fact the artificial part of my body is in some sense immortal."

PERSONAL LIFE

Herr and his wife, Patricia Ellis Herr, have two daughters, Alexandra and Sage, both of whom are veteran hikers and climbers. Patricia Herr is the author of *Up: A Mother and Daughter's Peakbagging Adventure* (2012).

SUGGESTED READING

Adelson, Eric. "Best Foot Forward." *Boston*. Metrocorp, Mar. 2009. Web. 27 Jan. 2012.

"The Double Amputee Who Designs Better Limbs." *Fresh Air*. Natl. Public Radio, 10 Aug. 2011. Web. 26 Jan. 2012.

Greenberg, Andy. "A Step beyond Human." *Forbes*. Forbes.com, 25 Nov. 2009. Web. 25 Jan. 2012.

"Hugh Herr." *Biomechatronics Group*. Massachusetts Institute of Technology, n.d. Web. 26 Jan. 2012.

McCarthy, Alice. "Hugh Herr: Back on Top." *Science Careers*. Amer. Assn. for the Advancement of Science, 20 June 2003. Web. 29 Jan. 2012.

Moss, Frank. *The Sorcerers and Their Apprentices: How the Digital Magicians of the MIT Media Lab Are Creating the Innovative Technologies That Will Transform Our Lives*. New York: Crown, 2011. Print.

Murray, Charles J. "Bionic Engineer." *Design News* Dec. 2010: 38–41. Print.

Osius, Alison. *Second Ascent: The Story of Hugh Herr*. Harrisburg: Stackpole, 1991. Print.

Ward, Logan. "2005 Popular Mechanics Breakthrough Awards." *Popular Mechanics*. Hearst Communication, 29 Sep. 2005. Web. 26 Jan. 2012.

—*Miriam Helbok*

Rolf-Dieter Heuer

Born: 1948
Occupation: Particle physicist, director-general of CERN

For most of his life, Rolf-Dieter Heuer has dedicated himself to advancing the field of particle physics. Heuer once said, "I was always motivated to work at the energy frontier—wherever that was," as quoted by Virginia Gewin in *Nature* (Jan. 2008, online). Heuer spent fourteen years with the European Organization for Nuclear Research (CERN), a renowned particle-physics

AFP/Getty Images

laboratory on the Swiss-French border, where he climbed through the ranks to serve as spokesperson of a project involving the design and construction of a detector for the lab's flagship accelerator. After leaving CERN in the late 1990s, Heuer returned to his native Germany after accepting a faculty position at the University of Hamburg. There Heuer was among a group of researchers responsible for gathering data for an experiment involving the largest particle accelerator at Deutsches Elektronen-Synchrotron (DESY), the country's foremost research facility for high-energy particle physics. By the early 2000s he had joined the staff at DESY, serving as its director of research for particle physics. Heuer's career came full circle in 2009 when he was appointed director-general of CERN. Since taking the reins he has overseen the repair of the Large Hadron Collider (LHC) and the ongoing search for new phenomena such as the Higgs boson.

EARLY LIFE AND EDUCATION
Rolf-Dieter Heuer was born in 1948 in the municipality of Boll, which is located in the district of Göppingen in Baden-Württemberg, Germany. His father worked as a clerk, and his mother was a homemaker.

In 1969 Heuer attended the University of Stuttgart, where he studied nuclear physics before earning his degree in 1974. He then pursued his doctoral studies at the University of Heidelberg, where he was supervised by Professor Joachim Heintze.

EARLY RESEARCH
In 1977, after earning his PhD, Heuer accepted a faculty position as a research scientist at the University of Heidelberg. There Heuer immediately became involved with the approved JADE experiment, which was a scientific collaboration between participating universities from three countries—Japan, Deutschland (Germany), and England—lending their names to the acronym. Heuer was responsible for managing the building of the particle detector, also called JADE, whose research was subsequently performed at the Positron-Electron Tandem Ring Accelerator (PETRA) housed at the Hamburg-headquarters of DESY, Germany's biggest research center for particle physics. (An accelerator stimulates subatomic particles to a high velocity and then initiates a high-impact collision with other particles in order to gain a better understanding of the structure of the universe.)

During his five-year tenure at the University of Heidelberg, Heuer narrowly avoided a maximum critical accident (MCA) following the breakdown of one of the conductors at DESY just as an experiment was about to be conducted, resulting in dangerous, high-risk conditions. He told Anna-Cathrin Loll for the *Asia Pacific Times* (Sep. 2009, online), "This made me understand the importance of continuous quality controls."

WORK AT CERN
In January 1984 Heuer left Heidelberg and moved to Geneva, Switzerland, where he joined the staff of CERN, the largest particle-physics lab in the world. Heuer was entrusted with the high-risk responsibility of supervising the design and construction of another particle detector during the experimental phase. The detector in question was the Omni-Purpose Apparatus for the LEP (more commonly known as OPAL), one of four particle detectors constructed at CERN; the three others were ALEPH, DELPHI, and L3. "If only one of the conductors rips, the whole thing won't work anymore," he said in his interview with *Asia Pacific Times*. "With 20,000 conductors, you can imagine that you do lose some sleep over it."

When the biggest electron-positron accelerator, the Large Electron-Positron (LEP), first entered the startup phase in 1989, Heuer served as the run coordinator, a role he held for three years. According to the CERN website, the Large Electron Positron collider "was the accelerator that put the Standard Model of particle physics through its paces. The numerous data taken by the four experiments well and truly tested the model to an incredible level of precision. The experimental results agreed with the theoretical predictions and helped to establish the Standard Model's validity."

In 1994 Heuer was named spokesperson for OPAL, which was among the more renowned investigations in particle physics, and he was charged with overseeing everything that involved the collaborative effort, including a staff of more than three hundred physicists. His duties also included analyzing the data from LEP1 and the energy-upgrade program of LEP1, which converted it into a new accelerator named LEP2. Heuer remained in the post as OPAL's spokesperson until August 1998, leaving after four years because he no longer felt challenged.

RESEARCH IN GERMANY

That same year Heuer returned to Germany and joined the faculty of the University of Hamburg, where he held a professorship. During this period Heuer was among a group of scientists conducting research on the H1 experiment at the Hadron Electron Ring Accelerator (HERA). According to the website for DESY, "HERA was the only storage ring facility in the world in which two different types of particle were accelerated and then collided head-on. This concept required two different accelerators . . . in which the two kinds of particle were accelerated separately and then brought to collision at highest energies using sophisticated beam guidance systems. No one had ever tried to build such a facility before." Another notable achievement was Heuer's establishment of Forschung mit Leptoncollidern (Research with Lepton Colliders), a group comprised of young physics students from German universities.

In December 2004 Heuer was hired by DESY to work for their lab as a director of research for their national particle-physics program. (The DESY lab was a member of the Helmholtz Association of German Research Centres, Germany's biggest scientific institution.) In an effort to bolster DESY's standing as Germany's main lab for particle physics and reinforce its ties to CERN, Heuer participated in two experiments, ATLAS and CMS. Both were conducted at the most powerful particle accelerator in the world, the Large Hadron Collider (LHC), whose experiments, according to the LHC website, "are expected to address questions such as what gives matter its mass, why nature prefers matter to anti-matter, and how matter evolved from the first instants of the universe's existence." Following is a description of both experiments according to the LHC website: "Designed to see a wide range of particles and phenomena produced in LHC collisions, each involves approximately 2,000 physicists from some 35 countries. These scientists use the data collected from the complex ATLAS and CMS detectors to search for new phenomena. . . . They also measure the properties of previously-discovered quarks [matter particles] and bosons [force-carrying particles] with unprecedented precision, and are on the lookout for completely new, unpredicted phenomena." Additionally, Heuer was responsible for fostering the lab's involvement in research and development for the International Linear Collider (ILC), an electron-positron collider that has yet to be built, as well as upgrading the luminosity for the LHC.

RETURN TO CERN

Heuer's profile in the world of particle physics was considerably heightened in December 2007 when he was selected to replace Robert Aymar as director-general of CERN. Following the end of Aymar's tenure in 2008, Heuer took over the five-year post on January 1, 2009, in the midst of a worldwide financial crisis. He also inherited another immediate challenge: The previous September, the LHC—which had ended its experimental phase and was weeks away from its highly anticipated startup on October 21, 2008—experienced an electrical issue. In an article for *Nature* (Feb. 23, 2010, online), Geoff Brumfiel explained, "A connection between two superconducting cables developed a small amount of resistance, which warmed the connection until the cables—cooled by liquid helium to superconducting temperatures—lost their ability to carry current. Thousands of amps arced through the machine, blowing a hole in its side and releasing several [tons] of liquid helium. The expanding helium gas created havoc, spewing soot into the machine's ultraclean beamline and ripping magnets from their stands." As a result, the LHC was forced to shut down while extensive and necessary repairs were being made.

With increasing media interest in the LHC, CERN was thrust into the global spotlight. The lab was featured in a scene in producer Ron Howard's 2009 thriller, *Angels and Demons*, starring Tom Hanks. Heuer sought to capitalize on this attention by repositioning CERN as more than just a European particle-physics laboratory, but rather as a renowned international hub for scientific research.

A few months into his term as director-general, Heuer promoted a corporate culture that encouraged open communication and sought to bridge the gap between management and employees. To that end Heuer kept the staff informed, communicating major news via e-mail messages and including regular updates regarding the repairs of the LHC in the company's weekly bulletin; he also became more of a fixture at the CERN lab.

Heuer became equally concerned about establishing and maintaining clear and open lines of communication with laboratories, institutes, and governments around the world. Those external parties included the governments of CERN's twenty member countries, who are responsible for financing its programs and managing activities at its facilities, as well as other nonmember nations with whom CERN has cooperation agreements to use the CERN lab for experiments and research. For this reason Heuer created an external relations office to serve as liaison. With the express goal of promoting the open exchange of ideas and information, Heuer launched the CERN Global Network; he also began traveling around the world and giving lectures about particle physics. Another project involved establishing a new center at CERN to analyze and interpret the data output from the LHC.

SETTING RECORDS

Once again all eyes were on CERN on November 20, 2009, with the successful restarting of the LHC, and three days later the data from the first collisions were recorded in all four of its detectors—ATLAS, CMS, ALICE, and LHCb. On November 30, 2009, the LHC set a new record; it became the highest-energy particle accelerator in the world by circulating protons to 1.18 TeV (trillion electron volts), surpassing the previous eight-year record of 0.98 TeV set by the Tevatron, a particle accelerator located at the Fermi National Accelerator Laboratory outside of Batavia, Illinois. In early December the LHC set another world record when the intensity of the beam was increased and the high-impact collision between the two proton beams was documented at 2.36 TeV. Following a shutdown of the LHC in mid-December, the accelerator started up again in February, operating at less than half of its full capacity. Yet another record was set in March 2010 when collisions between two proton beams were recorded at 3.5 TeV per beam (a total energy level of 7 TeV); at the time this was the highest level of energy that had been achieved in a particle accelerator. This event, which was covered by more than a hundred journalists, marked the official start of the LHC research program. Although no discoveries had yet been made with the LHC, Heuer expressed hope that the LHC would be able to locate dark matter, which is invisible and accounts for about 90 percent of the mass of the universe.

In July 2010 CERN found itself in the spotlight again when initial results from the LHC were presented at the thirty-fifth International Conference on High-Energy Physics, which was attended by French president Nicolas Sarkozy. In September 2010 scientists at CERN observing CMS, one of the detectors of the LHC, reported that they had detected a foreign, ridge-like formation produced by the proton collisions. Although these scientists have not yet been able to determine what it is, they published their findings in an effort to promote discussion within the scientific community. CERN scientists continued to observe proton-proton collisions with the CMS detector until the end of October 2010. This was followed by a switch from protons to lead ions for the rest of the year in an effort to more closely mimic conditions similar to the Big Bang.

In 2011 Heuer's staff reported observing what they believed to be Higgs boson, a theoretical, invisible particle (sometimes referred to as the "God particle") at two of the LHC's detectors, ATLAS and CMS. The Higgs boson is thought to give mass to everything in the universe. "It is responsible for the mass of fundamental particles," Michael Barnett, senior physicist at the Lawrence Berkeley National Laboratory and coordinator of education and outreach at CERN, told Jenny Marder for the blog *Rundown News* (Dec. 13, 2011, online). He explained, "Without that, you don't get the stars and the planets and the universe that we see today. In that sense, it's responsible for our existence. . . . Without it, you'd have this cold, dark universe." Despite the lack of definitive evidence, Heuer is encouraged by the findings and believes that his lab will have an answer regarding the existence of the Higgs boson at some point.

PERSONAL LIFE

Heuer lives in the Pays de Gex, France, with his wife, Brigitte. He provided the foreword to the 2009 book *LEP: The Lord of the Collider Rings at CERN, 1980–2000*, written by Herwig Schopper.

SUGGESTED READING

Brumfiel, Geoff. "Did Design Flaws Doom the LHC?" *Nature*. Nature Publishing Group, 23 Feb. 2010. Web. 17 Jan. 2012.

Cookson, Clive. "Domestic Science." *Financial Times*. Financial Times, 23 Sep. 2011. Web. 17 Jan. 2011.

Gewin, Virginia. "Movers: Rolf-Dieter Heuer, Director-General, CERN, Geneva, Switzerland." *Nature* 451.7178 (2008): 602. Web. 17 Jan. 2012.

Loll, Anna-Cathrin. "Lord of the Particles." *Asia Pacific Times*. Asia Pacific Times, Sep. 2009. Web. 18 Jan. 2012.

Marder, Jenny. "Hunt for Higgs Continues; Scientists Work to Separate the 'Signal from the Noise.'" *The Rundown*. MacNeil/Lehrer Productions, 13 Dec. 2011. Web. 18 Jan. 2012.

Sopova, Jasmina. "UNESCO and CERN: Like Hooked Atoms." *UNESCO Courier* (Jan.–Mar. 2011): 48–49.Web. 17 Jan. 2011.

Yurkewicz, Katie. "A New Leader for CERN." *Symmetry Magazine* 6.2 (2009): n. pag. Web. 17 Jan. 2011.

—*Bertha Muteba*

Carsten Höller

Born: 1961
Occupation: Artist

The Belgian-born artist Carsten Höller began his career as a scientist, and just as the content of his work has changed since he earned his doctorate in biology, so too has his approach to it. Though Höller was once concerned with arriving at new and definite conclusions, the focus of his art leads viewers to question what they take for granted: the evidence of their own eyes.

Many of Höller's frequently large-scale works are aimed at disorientation, from his exhibit of giant re-creations of mushrooms hanging from a ceiling to his room of simultaneously flashing lightbulbs and his signature creation of slides that pass through several floors and invite viewers to go down them. Playfulness animates his work, which has been displayed at some of the most prestigious museums and galleries in the world. "The impressive thing about Höller," Jonathan Jones wrote for the *Guardian* (12 Oct. 2006, online), "is how many fans of contemporary art rate him one of the leading figures of the new millennium."

Getty Images

EARLY LIFE AND EDUCATION

The younger of two brothers, Carsten Höller was born in 1961 in Brussels, Belgium. His father, who worked for the European Union, was from what was then West Berlin, Germany; his mother came from Communist-controlled East Berlin. Speaking of the multilingual and multicultural nature of the environment in which he grew up, Höller said to Elizabeth Day for the *Observer* (25 July 2009, online), "I could go out of the house and hear Flemish and English spoken in the same community." He added, "I don't think unity is necessarily a thing to strive for."

The seeds of Höller's artistic proclivities were perhaps planted when he was a boy; in the *Observer* (7 Oct. 2006, online), Lynn Barber reported that en route to school, Höller used to pass an elderly person's residence with four fire-escape slides jutting from the top, and he always had the urge to slide down them himself—an act art patrons would later perform as part of Höller's exhibits. Nonetheless, at age eighteen, he left Brussels for Germany with the aim of becoming a scientist.

In Germany, Höller enrolled at the University of Kiel, where he studied biology. He earned his doctorate in the early 1990s. In his thesis, which he wrote on plants and aphids, he argued that plants beleaguered by insects can emit what amount to SOS signals: scents that attract aphid predators. Höller became an important entomologist in Germany, where he was in charge of a research lab. Despite his success, it was at that time that he began to feel disenchanted with his

field. "I could see it all in front of me," he said to Cate McQuaid for the *Boston Globe* (22 Jan. 2006), referring to his future. "My mentor at university, I could see his life: teaching, writing, not really science anymore. The research part becomes less and less."

Meanwhile, Höller had met a group of artists and was impressed with them and their work. He began visiting galleries and reading magazines related to art. He contemplated the idea of creating his own works, but "I didn't just want to express myself," he explained to Day. "I don't think that's very interesting." Instead, he considered ways to play with art viewers' perceptions, causing them to question what they were seeing. "While [Höller's] work as a scientist was devoted to solving problems and narrowing down the field of uncertainty," Day noted, "his work as an artist became a prolonged meditation on the quality of doubt and possibility."

ART CAREER

Höller's debut work was a sentence, "Together to the future," put on scaffolding in Hamburg, West Germany, in 1989; done in black letters against a white background, the sentence was seventy feet long end-to-end. During the time that the work was on display, the Berlin Wall came down. With that politically charged event, Höller's art piece, the significance of which had been unclear and open to interpretation, took on new meaning. Many East Germans coming to West Germany saw the work and took pictures of it. The experience strengthened Höller's desire to create works that would examine the relationship between art and its viewers' perceptions and expectations.

In the early 1990s, Höller drew a great deal of attention through an exhibit that challenged viewers' expectations with regard to its subject matter: it displayed creations said to be for catching and killing children. One of the pieces included was a swing attached to the edge of a roof of a high-rise building. "I never hated children," the artist explained to Barber, "but I hated the idea of making children, the whole reproductive process. There's no freedom if you cannot get rid of the biological machinery that makes us decide to do this thing and not that thing. I thought very much about how you could break that chain." He added, "But I think once you have really explored a certain conviction, it is time to give it up. I don't think you should go on holding it for the rest of your life."

With his art career taking off, Höller left the field of science in 1994 to pursue art full time. He told Day that his father "took a while" to become reconciled to that decision and that his mother "didn't embrace it." In the 1990s, Höller became associated with a group of artists— among them Andrea Zittel, Maurizio Cattelan, Rirkrit Tiravanija, Pierre Huyghe, and Philippe Parreno—whose multimedia interdisciplinary work sought to redefine notions of art and the spaces it occupies. In 1998, Höller teamed up with artist Rosemarie Trockel on an installation that appeared at the Donald Young Gallery in Seattle, Washington. That multimedia work included a two-minute looping video, *Atma & Shobbha*, in which a man and woman run through winding streets in Palermo, Italy. The work also featured five aluminum columns, each over ten feet tall, with portholes containing either colorful glass circles or gargoyle-like dolls. Upstairs from those objects were drawings of the dolls. "That's the show," Regina Hackett wrote for the *Seattle Post-Intelligencer* (30 Jan. 1998). "Seen repeatedly, it exercises a strange hold."

In 2000, at the Prada Foundation in Venice, Italy, which houses the art collection of the fashion designer Miuccia Prada, Höller mounted "Upside Down Mushroom Room," made up of large representations of mushrooms that rotate while suspended from the ceiling. That same year, at the Contemporary Arts Center in Cincinnati, Ohio, Höller took part in an eleven-person show, to which he contributed his 1996 creation *Flying Machine*—a participatory work into which viewers could strap themselves.

Höller's next major exhibit was also a participatory one, the type for which he would become well known. The centerpiece was a sixty-two-foot steel slide going down through a three-story stairwell. That exhibit, advertised as Höller's first major museum show in the United States, was mounted at the Institute of Contemporary Art

in Boston, Massachusetts, in 2003. Höller also designed a slide for Prada's office in Milan, Italy. "It goes right through the building," Höller explained to Barber, "so as she goes down she has a very quick glimpse of what everyone is working on. Then it makes a big curve outside the building and lands exactly where her driver is waiting to drive her home." Asked by Barber if the slide had changed Prada's life, Höller responded that the change was visible in the fashions Prada had produced since she began using the slide.

Another work from 2003, *Sliding Doors*, appeared at the Musée d'Art Contemporain in Marseille, France, as well as the Tate Modern in London, England. Viewers approached a series of sliding doors that opened as they drew near and closed when they went through. The doors gave a reflection of each viewer, until finally a set of doors opened and someone else appeared.

In January 2006, at the Massachusetts Museum of Contemporary Art (Mass MoCA) in Boston, Höller opened the exhibit *Amusement Park*. Contained in Mass MoCA's large Building 5 Gallery, the work consisted of re-creations of amusement park rides. In keeping with his aim of challenging perceptions, the flying-saucer rides moved at an extremely slow pace, appearing to be still or moving depending on whether the viewer was stationary or walking. Riderless bumper cars charged along and crashed into other cars as if driven by invisible beings. McQuaid described the work as "deeply soothing" and "also downright spooky," saying that the "contradictions within the work make one's head spin." Höller explained to McQuaid, "Many of my works have to do with confusion, and surrendering yourself to confusion in order to get more out of yourself."

In the fall of that year, the Tate Modern, as part of its Unilever exhibition, displayed *Test Site*. This work by Höller consisted of five very large stainless-steel slides, one of which descended from the top floor and went down five stories. "I think slides would make everyone happy," Höller said to Barber. "It's virtually impossible to go down a slide without smiling. . . . I think a slide can change our perception of space and speed. Our brain structure is obviously affected by this vertigo effect and things that seem to be organized in a certain way can be reorganized and experienced in another order." People going down the slides would scream, he concluded, "not because they're scared, but because they are let loose. They are finally free."

In 2007, the Shawinigan Space of the National Gallery of Canada hosted Höller's *One, Some, Many*, a three-part exhibit. *The Belgian Problem*, whose title alludes to the political conflict in Belgium between French-speaking and Flemish-speaking groups, was the first part of the exhibit. It consisted of two enormous aviaries facing each other, one containing starlings from Ontario, Canada, the other starlings from Quebec. *The History of the Laboratory of Doubt* included two labyrinths through which viewers moved in the dark, ending in larger spaces. In one of those spaces, what appeared to be the ceiling hung from wires and swung gently, disorienting viewers; in another, 2,688 lightbulbs flashed repeatedly and simultaneously. The third part of the exhibit was *Amusement Park*.

Jon Davies, writing for *C Magazine*, an international quarterly about contemporary art, gave *One, Some, Many* an almost wholly negative review. Referring to *The Belgian Problem*, he noted, "Of course, the birds were not buying any of this, and remained almost silent, the unpredictability of creaturely life sabotaging the actual experience of the work, if not the mildly clever concept behind it" (22 Mar. 2008). About *The History of the Laboratory of Doubt*, he wrote, "There is a cold and sterile quality to the interactions he seeks from participants, which makes one wonder if Höller sees his audience as mere rats in a maze. . . . If Höller wants to claim that these experiments are designed to foster 'radical doubt' in us, he has to accept that this doubt could be turned against him and the excesses of the art world." Davies concluded, "Sadly, it seems that Höller's jumbo-sized artworks have trapped him in a Catch-22: when they work, they seem no more than superficial if awe-inspiring diversions, and when they malfunction, one can only focus on the huge expenditure that went into their failure."

In 2008, Höller was one of a group of artists, all of whom had come to prominence in the early 1990s, whose works were shown at what was called *theanyspacewhatever* at the Guggenheim Museum in New York City. Höller's contribution to the show was a rotating hotel room. In November of that year, the Höller-designed Double Club opened in London. Financed by the Prada Foundation and located in an abandoned former warehouse, the Double Club was aimed at mixing Western and Congolese culture. One side of its bar provided Congolese beer under a roof of corrugated iron, while on the other side, champagne was served from behind a shining semicircle of copper.

At the Hamburger Bahnhof Museum für Gegenwart in Berlin, in the fall of 2010, Höller introduced a work called *Soma*, named for a mythic healing drink sought by nomads in northern India in the second millennium BCE. The exhibit contained objects familiar to followers of Höller's work, including a representation of a hotel room on a mushroom-shaped structure.

The New Museum in New York City hosted a retrospective of Höller's work, *Carsten Höller: Experience*, in the fall of 2011. In addition to a slide, a sensory-deprivation tank, and a slow-motion carousel, the exhibit's purposely disorienting items included the *Pinocchio Effect*, which called for participants to hold their noses with their fingers while placing a vibrating device on their arms, bringing on the sensation that their noses were growing. There were also pairs of goggles that allowed viewers to see objects as their retinas actually perceive them: backward and upside-down. Randy Kennedy reported for the *New York Times* (26 Oct. 2011) that when he tried on a pair, he took one step and was forced to hold a table to stay upright. Another device employed a tiny video screen in front of the viewer's eye to create the sensation of walking through a forest; at a certain moment, one's eyes seemed to move in separate directions, around both sides of a tree. "Mr. Höller's works . . . set out to induce a general kind of madness: a troubling, anti-Enlightenment awareness that despite the certainties won by science over the past three or four hundred years, human beings still know relatively little about the world around them and have no good reason even to trust their senses," Kennedy wrote. "While such a state may seem disturbing, Mr. Höller views it instead as 'truly productive,' an existential means of throwing off the bonds of determinism and treating human experience, if only for a little while, as a kind of artwork to be shaped and played with."

In late 2011, Höller won the Enel Contemporanea Award, sponsored by the Italian energy company Enel and given annually to an original work embracing the theme of energy. Höller's winning work was *Double Carousel with Zöllner Stripes*. Its carousels turned slowly in opposite directions, allowing riders to board and step off with ease; the stripes on the carousel gave an illusion of even slower speed. The work was on display in the Museo d'Arte Contemporanea Roma, or MACRO, in Rome, Italy.

PERSONAL LIFE

Carsten Höller was described by Barber as "bespectacled and geeky, with a bulging forehead," looking "like the sort of boy who was always called Brains at school." Among Höller's hobbies is breeding birds. He is married to the Swedish artist Miriam Bäckström, with whom he has a daughter. The family lives in Stockholm, Sweden.

SUGGESTED READING

Barber, Lynn. "Go Down the Slippery Slope." *Observer*. Guardian News and Media, 7 Oct. 2006. Web. 16 Mar. 2012.

Davies, Jon. "One, Some, Many: 3 Shows by Carsten Höller." *C Magazine* 22 Mar. 2008: 45. Print.

Day, Elizabeth. "Top of the Pop-Ups." *Observer*. Guardian News and Media, 25 July 2009. Web. 16 Mar. 2012.

Hackett, Regina. "Two Artists Join Forces in Unsettling Installation and Video at Donald

Young." *Seattle Post-Intelligencer* 30 Jan. 1998, "What's Happening" sec.: 16. Print.

Jones, Jonathan. "Artist's New Installation Induces a Sense of Vertigo, Literally and Otherwise." *Guardian*. Guardian News and Media, 12 Oct. 2006. Web. 16 Mar. 2012.

Kennedy, Randy. "Is It Art, Science or a Test of the People?" *New York Times* 26 Oct. 2011: C1. Print.

McQuaid, Cate. "Ghosts at the Carnival: At Carsten Höller's Installation at Mass MoCA, Step Right Up and Rattle Your Mind." *Boston Globe* 22 Jan. 2006: N1. Print.

—*Cliff Thompson*

Cheri Honkala

Born: circa 1963
Occupation: Human rights activist, executive director of Kensington Welfare Rights Union

For twenty-five years, Cheri Honkala has been an antipoverty crusader and advocate for Philadelphia's low-income and homeless population. She is the executive director of the nonprofit Kensington Welfare Rights Union (KWRU), which she founded in 1991, as well as the Poor People's Economic Human Rights Campaign, which she founded in 1997. That same year, she was named *Philadelphia Weekly*'s "Woman of the Year." To support her causes and, often, to put food on the table, Honkala has danced at topless bars and accepted annual Thanksgiving donations from well-known mobsters. Details such as these have made Honkala famous as an antipoverty maverick. Her family-led protests—she was "occupying" vacant buildings and city landmarks long before the Occupy Wall Street movement—have made her a media darling.

As of 2011, Honkala has been arrested more than two hundred times for various offenses. Former Philadelphia mayor Ed Rendell once called Honkala and her rabble-rousing "a constant pebble in my shoe." In 2011, Honkala ran for sheriff of Philadelphia on the Green Party ticket; her platform was a promise to end all evictions in the city of Philadelphia. Some have argued that Honkala's press-grabbing tactics harm the very groups she is trying to help, but she and her many supporters have disagreed. "The city wants the poor and powerless to be invisible," Honkala said at a 2000 protest in Philadelphia, as quoted by Karen Abbott for *Salon* (31 July 2000, online). "And we're not gonna be invisible."

Honkala has amassed a fiercely loyal following among low-income people spanning age, race, and gender. "One of the important things that I've learned is that if you're inside the boxing ring, you shouldn't have someone outside

Getty Images

telling you how to punch," she explained to Cole Stangler for *Counterpoint* (4 Nov. 2011, online). "I think, for low-income people, for most of our lives, people have been writing from academia and other walks of life about what our experience is like—I think if we look at history, people that have actually been in that [disadvantaged] situation have always played the biggest part in changing history."

A ROUGH START

Honkala was born in Minneapolis, Minnesota, in 1963, to a mother of five on welfare. Her birth father left the family shortly after Honkala was born. Her stepfather abused her and her mother, who was classified as an unfit parent when Honkala was in her early teens. After turning thirteen, Honkala was placed in nine different institutions for juveniles; at the age of sixteen, she married and became pregnant as a way to avoid further placements. Her husband, a heroin addict, left her after a month.

Finding herself homeless, Honkala convinced a car dealer to sell her a car, which she lived in while pregnant. When Honkala lost the car, she sought shelter in abandoned houses. "They had no room in any of the shelters," she told Kathleen Hayes for CNN's the *Flipside* (22 Aug. 2003). "And so that's when I began to notice that they keep heat on in abandoned houses in the north so that the pipes don't freeze. And it was one night that I thought I was going to freeze to death that I decided to break the law and move myself into a government-owned abandoned property and to stay there until I could find some way to pull my life back together and to secure affordable housing for myself and my son." Her son Mark was born in 1980 when Honkala was seventeen.

To find housing on vacant properties, Honkala joined forces with other women she met through welfare. She also joined groups to advocate for the homeless and protest for social services. Despite her situation, Honkala managed to graduate from South High School in Minneapolis and attend three years of college classes at the University of Minnesota, where she studied to be a teacher. Money troubles and accusations of misappropriated student grants forced her to withdraw in the mid-1980s. Honkala and her son found themselves homeless once again, until her second marriage took them both to Philadelphia in 1989.

KWRU AND THE POOR PEOPLE'S ECONOMIC HUMAN RIGHTS CAMPAIGN

Although Honkala's second marriage, to a union official, later ended in divorce, she remained in Philadelphia. She settled in the poor Kensington neighborhood in North Philadelphia. To help mothers and low-income people like herself, Honkala founded the Kensington Welfare Rights Union in 1991. The KWRU office was located in an old row house in a section of Kensington known as the Badlands. The nonprofit organization aimed to help poor and homeless families keep their housing and possessions, and, if need be, take over one of the city's numerous abandoned properties for shelter. The group was founded in the spirit of reframing the debate about social services and welfare. According to KWRU, the proper debate is not about government assistance or charitable donations, but about human rights.

The KWRU receives no public funding and offers a seemingly practical solution to the homeless—if the government refuses to provide you housing, you can take it yourself. Honkala has claimed that no one has ever permanently settled on a vacant property; the KWRU-driven "takeovers," as they call them, have most often ended in arrest. However, the tactic has attracted enough attention to place over five hundred of Honkala's followers in permanent housing. Among other services, the group operates several "Human Rights Houses" for homeless families and individuals.

The KWRU has faced criticism from government officials, including those from the Department of Housing and Urban Development (HUD), for not playing by the rules. Homeless people face long waiting lists for public housing—it is not uncommon for the process to take several years—and officials have said that it is unfair for Honkala and the KWRU to "cut the line," so to speak, using illegal tactics. Honkala,

pointing to the thousands of empty city properties, overflowing shelters, and families on the streets, has said that the rules are not the point when it comes to survival. "Certainly, no one has a lease to go into these properties," she told Jeff Gelles for the *Philadelphia Inquirer* (12 Dec. 1995). "But there's a moral right. Let's put it that way."

In 1997, the KWRU decided to bring its cause to the national stage. The group sponsored an event called the "March of Our Lives." The march began at the Liberty Bell in Philadelphia and culminated in a mass protest at the United Nations in New York City. The KWRU was protesting the 1996 Welfare Reform Act, which they claimed was a human rights violation for mandating drastic cuts in social services to the poor. The March of Our Lives served as a launching pad for Honkala's next endeavor, the Poor People's Economic Human Rights Campaign.

In 1999, in an effort to address the dearth of affordable housing in Philadelphia, the KWRU organized a series of takeovers and encampments, including a tent city named "Clintonville," for President Bill Clinton—a nod to the Depression-era Hoovervilles, named after Herbert Hoover—and a camp settled on Independence Mall near the Liberty Bell. The protests resulted in numerous arrests, including Honkala's. For her sentence, Honkala was banned from the Liberty Bell. In the following years, the KWRU and the Poor People's Economic Human Rights Campaign continued to expand their efforts. In 1999, they led organizations from across the United States, Canada, and Latin America in a "March of the Americas" from Washington, DC, to the United Nations. In July 2000, the groups drew a crowd of nearly ten thousand homeless and poor people in the "March for Economic Human Rights." They were protesting the 2000 Republican National Convention in Philadelphia, and were the only group denied a permit by city authorities. Cross-country bus tours, organized by the Poor People's Economic Human Rights Campaign, followed in 2002 and 2003.

After a disrupted protest in Philadelphia in 2003, Honkala organized a march from Marks, Mississippi, to Washington, DC. The march commemorated Dr. Martin Luther King Jr.'s unfulfilled Poor People's Campaign on the anniversary of his "I Have A Dream" speech. As a part of the protest, Honkala and her followers set up a "Bushville," named for President George W. Bush, on the National Mall in Washington. As a result, the National Mall was added to the growing list of American landmarks from which Honkala, the KWRU, and the Poor People's Economic Human Rights Campaign have been permanently banned.

A SENSE OF PURPOSE

A formerly homeless mother named Tara Colon told Randy LoBasso for *Philadelphia Weekly* (23 Mar. 2011): "She's [Honkala] taught us that being poor isn't something to be ashamed of. . . . She's done things that are looked upon as immoral, but she makes them moral choices by saying, 'Everything around me is wrong. It's wrong that children are hungry and it's wrong that children are homeless.'" Honkala has been arrested more than two hundred times for offenses such as trespassing. At the 2002 World Trade Organization meeting in Seattle, she was arrested for assaulting a police officer. The charge was later dropped when a video emerged proving her innocence in the encounter.

Honkala has garnered criticism for the ways she funds her organizations. The KWRU is run exclusively on private donations, and when donations are low, Honkala has been known to dance topless to keep the group running. Beginning in the mid-1990s, she accepted donations from notorious Philadelphia mob boss "Skinny" Joey Merlino. Merlino offered to donate turkeys for Thanksgiving, cater a Christmas dinner for sixty guests, and buy Christmas presents for Honkala's homeless families. Honkala readily accepted. The tradition was continued even after Merlino himself was put in jail. Such stories have made people wonder why Honkala has not taken a job in social work to help her causes. She lived on welfare until the late 1990s and has received offers for work, once even for a Democratic Philadelphia mayor. She refused. "I say 'no,'" she told Abbott, "because the number-one thing I need to be doing is using my skills to build a movement . . . a massive movement to end poverty in this country."

In 1997, Honkala was one of two women featured in the book *The Myth of the Welfare Queen* by David Zucchino. Zucchino, a Pulitzer Prize–winning journalist, is also a former editor of the *Philadelphia Inquirer*. The book sought to challenge the stereotype that women on welfare were somehow playing the system or living big on government handouts. *The Myth of the Welfare Queen* was praised for its precise reporting. Honkala and Odessa Williams, the disabled mother and grandmother who was profiled along with her, were not depicted as sinners or saints, but rather as women struggling to provide for their children, even through imperfect means. The same year, Honkala was the subject of the documentary film *Poverty Outlaw*, which premiered at the 1997 Sundance Film Festival. Directed by Peter Kinoy and Pamela Yates, the film featured Honkala but made a broader point about how poverty disproportionately affects women and children. Both *The Myth of the Welfare Queen* and *Poverty Outlaw* illustrated a battle, familiar to many American women, with the degrading cycle of poverty and an eroding social safety net.

In 2004, a documentary film crew followed Honkala and a band of protesters from Jersey City, New Jersey, to New York City, where they were planning to protest that year's Republican National Convention. The group consisted predominantly of homeless women and children who made encampments or slept in churches and pooled their food stamps along the way. The film, released in 2006, was called *August in the Empire State*. Directed by Gabriel Rhodes and Keefe Murren, the film also chronicled the story of a young Latino businessman and Republican named Paul Rodriguez who was running for Congress. Journalist Michelle Goldberg was featured as well, as she followed Honkala's group to New York. Goldberg reported on the surveillance crews that trailed the protestors across New Jersey. Often the number of undercover police officers was greater than the group that they were watching. Goldberg tried to interview a couple of officers sitting in their car watching Honkala, but the officers rolled up their tinted windows when she approached.

The protest was slated to be one of the largest in the history of the Poor People's Economic Human Rights Campaign. The film crew was on hand to capture the raw emotion in Honkala's voice as she pleaded with police not to tear down the group's encampment when they reached the city. Though Honkala and her followers were forced to abandon their makeshift "Bushville," they completed a peaceful and successful march from the United Nations to Madison Square Garden the next day, which was featured as a part of the film's triumphant conclusion.

CAMPAIGN FOR SHERIFF OF PHILADELPHIA

In 2011, Honkala ran for sheriff of Philadelphia on the Green Party ticket. With the campaign slogan "Keeping Families in Their Homes," she promised that if elected she would put a freeze on foreclosures and evictions. Honkala considered her campaign to be part of a larger statement on the political predominance of banks and corporations over families and communities. She chose to run with the Green Party specifically because it does not accept money from banks and corporations, but also in order to formally distance herself from the Democratic Party. "I've been in too many fights in my life where I thought I was separate from the machine and the corporate money, only to find out later on that I was being used as a pawn for the Democratic Party," she told LoBasso.

During her campaign, Honkala supported the creation of community-based land trusts with which communities could control the appropriation of vacant properties for the public good. She hoped to push this legislation through with the help of the City Council. She also embraced the nascent Occupy Wall Street movement and won the endorsement of the National Organization of Women (NOW). Still, many saw Honkala's run as a publicity stunt, and she was not considered a formidable opponent to her more politically-established counterparts. The eventual winner of the five-candidate race was Democrat and former state representative Jewell Williams.

Honkala lives with her younger son, Guillermo, in Philadelphia. Her older son, Mark Webber, is a Hollywood actor and director. Webber continues to appear with his mother at events and marches, and he contributes financially to her causes.

SUGGESTED READING

Abbott, Karen. "Unwelcome in America." *Salon.* Salon Media Group, 31 July 2000. Web. 26 Mar. 2012.

Gelles, Jeff. "Occupants of Church Finding New Homes for the Holidays." *Philadelphia Inquirer* 12 Dec. 1995 final ed.: B1. Print.

Hays, Kathleen. "March on Washington: Confronting Poverty in America Head-on." *Flipside.* CNNfn, 22 Aug. 2003. Television.

Stangler, Cole. "Interview with Cheri Honkala." *Counterpoint.* Counterpoint Magazine, 4 Nov. 2011. Web. 26 Mar. 2012.

—*Molly Hagan*

Getty Images

Drew Houston

Born: March 4, 1983
Occupation: Internet entrepreneur, CEO of Dropbox, Inc.

By late 2006, the MIT graduate and then budding entrepreneur Drew Houston had grown tired of the cumbersome process of having to e-mail himself files and carrying around USB thumb drives in order to retrieve all of his work, so he started writing code for a software program that would enable him to access his files from anywhere. "I knew there had to be a better way," he explained to Victoria Barret for *Forbes* (28 June 2010). "The USB is really no better than a floppy disk." What materialized from those coding sessions was Dropbox, a free online storage service that allows people to access and share their documents, photos, and videos from virtually any computer or phone. Dropbox's company slogan is "Simplify your life."

Founded in 2007 by Houston and his business partner, Arash Ferdowsi, with funding from the start-up incubator Y Combinator, Dropbox has revolutionized the way many people work. It has become one of the fastest growing companies in the world, thanks in part to the astronomical rise in the use of smartphones, tablets, and other mobile devices, and the attendant increase in people wanting to access and share their information. Since launching in 2008, Dropbox has experienced dramatic growth, rising from one hundred thousand users to more than fifty million in 175 countries; 325 million files are now saved on the service daily, and a new user is added every second. As the company's founder and chief executive officer (CEO), Houston has led much of that growth, going so far as to turn down acquisition overtures from the late Apple mastermind Steve Jobs and Google cofounder Sergey Brin, in efforts to build it into a major company. In doing so, he has won over investors and become "the tech world's equivalent of a rock star," Jessica Guynn wrote for the *Los Angeles Times* (15 Jan. 2012, online).

Houston came closer to realizing his far-reaching vision for Dropbox in September 2011, when he helped raise more than $250 million from some of Silicon Valley's leading venture capital firms, which set the company's valuation at $4 billion. While Dropbox faces heavy competition from rival storage services such as Apple's iCloud, Houston has focused on making the company stand out for its simplicity and by expanding its presence across a wide range of devices. He told Casey Newton for the *San Francisco Chronicle* (19 Apr. 2011), "What we're about is simplifying millions of people's lives by allowing them for the first time to have all your stuff in front of you, wherever you are, on any device. As this world gets more complicated, there are billions of devices and apps and services that all don't talk to each other—Dropbox is really the fabric that ties all these things together. . . . If we can make someone's life better, or save them an hour of time—multiplied by a billion people—there's nothing else you can do and have that level of impact."

EARLY LIFE AND EDUCATION

Andrew W. "Drew" Houston (pronounced HOW-stuhn) was born on March 4, 1983, in the Boston suburb of Acton, Massachusetts, to an electrical engineer and a high school librarian. His interest in technology began as a toddler. He started toying with computers at the age of three and learned how to program when he was five. Houston would consequently spend much of his youth in front of a computer, learning how to write code, despite his mother's efforts to involve him in other extracurricular activities. "She was subtle about making me normal, I guess, and I can appreciate it now," he told Victoria Barret, in another article for *Forbes* (7 Nov. 2011), referring to the family summers he spent in New Hampshire without his computer.

By the time he entered his freshman year at Acton-Boxborough Regional High School, Houston had parlayed his coding skills into a paying job as a computer programmer for an online game. He would land other programming-related jobs throughout high school, during which he became dead set on pursuing a career as an Internet entrepreneur. In high school, Houston stood out among his peers not only with his Bill Gates–like understanding of computers but also for his extreme precociousness in mathematics. That kind of intelligence helped him score a perfect 1600 on the SAT and win acceptance to the Massachusetts Institute of Technology (MIT), in Cambridge, Massachusetts.

While majoring in computer science at MIT, Houston spent his spare time coding and reading business books. He read books on everything from sales and finance to management and negotiations, in efforts to learn about the process behind running a successful start-up company. In an interview with Andrew Warner for Warner's blog, Mixergy.com (21 Dec. 2011), Houston explained, "I realized that there's a lot more to starting a business or to understanding how the world works beyond just the engineering." He would increase his business knowledge even further after joining the MIT fraternity Phi Delta Theta, for which he served as rush and social chair. Surrounding himself with a group of like-minded aspiring entrepreneurs, Houston has credited his fraternity experience with providing him with "a crash course in project management and getting people to do stuff for you," as he told Victoria Barret.

Houston's entrepreneurial aspirations led him to take a one-year leave from MIT in 2004 to form Accolade, an online SAT prep company. He would develop the company over the next three years, during which he learned about the inner workings of Internet start-ups. Despite failing to secure adequate funding, the company enjoyed moderate success. In his interview with Warner, Houston called Accolade "a really great experience," but acknowledged that the company "was really much more of a marketing challenge," as it competed with bigger, more established SAT brands. While continuing to work on Accolade, Houston returned to MIT to complete his degree. He received his BS in electrical engineering and computer science from MIT in January 2006, after graduating a semester early.

CAREER

After graduating from MIT, Houston started working as a software engineer for Bit9, a privately held company based in Waltham, Massachusetts. There, he worked on a series of projects for the company's security software. Concurrently with that job, which paid him $85,000 a year, Houston continued to develop Accolade. His frustration increased, however, as that company failed to take off, and by the fall of 2006, he had grown even more frustrated after seeing several of his friends leave Massachusetts for California to launch start-ups of their own.

It was around this time that Houston began seeing the problems with constantly having to carry around USB thumb drives and having to send copious numbers of e-mail attachments to share his files. This stood in stark contrast to his experiences at MIT, whose state-of-the-art Athena computer system allowed him to access and share his files across thousands of interconnected campus workstations. The final straw for Houston came in November 2006, while waiting for a bus to New York at Boston's South Station. Initially wanting to use the four-hour bus ride to work on a coding project, he discovered that he had left the USB thumb drive with his work at his apartment. He immediately started coding the software for what would eventually become Dropbox. Commenting on the lack of Internet storage services available to meet his needs at the time, Houston explained to Jon Ying, in an interview posted on the Dropbox blog (5 Feb. 2009, online), "I tried everything I could find but each product inevitably suffered problems with Internet latency, large files, bugs, or just made me think too much. Nothing just worked, so I started hacking something together for myself and then realized it could solve these problems for a lot of other people."

In April 2007, following months of coding and planning, Houston travelled to San Francisco, California, to pitch Dropbox to Paul Graham of the influential start-up funding firm Y Combinator, which had previously rejected his proposal for Accolade. Graham told Houston he needed a cofounder, and a friend introduced him to

Arash Ferdowsi, a third-year MIT computer science student and son of Iranian immigrants who shared similar interests and ambition. Ferdowsi quickly signed on as the company's chief technology officer, and soon afterward Dropbox received $15,000 in seed funding from Y Combinator. Houston and Ferdowsi used part of the money to rent an apartment in Cambridge, where they holed up for the next four months, coding for up to twenty hours a day. Recalling his initial meeting with Ferdowsi, who dropped out of MIT one semester shy of graduating to join Dropbox, Houston told Andrew Warner, "We both sort of shared that desire to do something important, and do it soon, because there was a very limited window of time."

In August 2007, at Y Combinator's biannual demo day, held at their offices in Mountain View, California, Houston announced his intentions for Dropbox. Presenting Dropbox as a tool that "just works," he explained how the storage service would effectively sync and backup users' files across the web, thus allowing them to access and share them from anywhere. Houston's presentation helped woo investors, and in September he and Ferdowsi moved to San Francisco; shortly after, Dropbox landed another $1.2 million in funding from the prominent venture capital firm Sequoia Capital, located in Silicon Valley, California. Michael Moritz, one of the firm's senior partners, told Victoria Barret (7 Nov. 2011), "Big companies would go after this, I knew. I was betting they have the stamina and intellect to beat everyone else."

Houston and Ferdowsi spent the next year developing the technology that would enable Dropbox to work on all operating systems (Microsoft, Apple, and Linux). During this time, word of mouth about Dropbox spread, and after Houston and Ferdowsi submitted a demonstration video to the social news website Digg, in March 2008, Dropbox landed seventy thousand users overnight. "Arash and I were sitting across from each other doing database queries, and there were hundreds of people signing up per minute," Houston recalled to Rachel Swaby for *Wired* (22 Dec. 2011, online). "We watched it hit the front page of Digg. Then the top 10. We were thinking . . . what did we do here?"

In September 2008, Houston officially launched Dropbox to the public; at that time it had one hundred thousand users. Dropbox offers up to two gigabytes of free storage, with the option of adding more through premium accounts, including 50 gigabytes for $10 per month and 100 gigabytes for $20 per month. In October 2011, Dropbox added a new premium service for businesses called Dropbox for Teams, which costs $795 per year for five users and offers 1,000 gigabytes of storage. Available in five languages—English, Spanish, French, German, and Japanese—Dropbox is known for its simplicity of use. Users download the Dropbox software to their computer and then add any file they want to a special Dropbox folder, which then automatically saves to the computer, while being backed up safely on the Dropbox website. Once files are saved, users are able to access and share those files on any computer or mobile device connected to the Internet. Any changes made to files are also saved to Dropbox simultaneously. "We're building the fabric for a new, different kind of web, where your files follow you to whichever device you happen to be working on," Houston explained to Victoria Barret (28 June 2010).

Dropbox immediately attracted a large following among people who had been looking for a better way to access files from a plethora of new mobile devices, such as smartphones and tablets. Instead of using traditional marketing or advertising, Houston and Ferdowsi began offering free storage to existing users in return for referrals. That system paid off, with the number of users rising from two hundred thousand in 2008 to three million in 2009. Dropbox's unprecedented growth, meanwhile, not only attracted more investors but also potential bidders, including none other than the late Apple CEO Steve Jobs, who, in December 2009, unsuccessfully tried to acquire the company for an undisclosed nine-digit sum. Despite other tempting acquisition offers, including one by Google cofounder Sergey Brin, Houston has remained steadfast in his desire to turn Dropbox into a major company. He told Jessica Guynn, "People may know us today as the magic folder on their desktop or the app on their phone. But we see ourselves as building the Internet's file system."

Houston's insistence on developing Dropbox to its full potential has resulted in one of the fastest growing companies in the world. Since its launch in 2008, Dropbox has amassed more than fifty million users in 175 countries, and it welcomes a new user about every second. More than one million files are saved to the service every five minutes, as the phrase "Dropbox me" has entered many people's vocabularies. Dropbox's users include college students, professors, filmmakers, musical artists, professional sports teams, and a wide range of retail and commercial businesses. While more than 95 percent of those users are nonpaying customers, Dropbox has proven profitable, with company revenues of roughly $240 million in 2011, according to *Forbes*.

In September 2011, Houston received more than $250 million in funding from seven of Silicon Valley's top venture capital firms. The firms, which included Index Ventures, Goldman Sachs, Sequoia, and RIT Capital Partners, set Dropbox's value at $4 billion; Houston's 15-percent stake in Dropbox is thus worth an estimated

$600 million. Dropbox board member and Sequoia Capital partner Bryan Schreier told Casey Newton, in another article for the *San Francisco Chronicle* (19 Oct. 2011), "What Dropbox is becoming is a foundation that underlies our computers, our phones, our tablets, and whatever else comes next. It's very rare that any company can come in and essentially change the entire landscape." Dropbox plans to use most of the money for expansion, as it faces serious competition from some of the world's biggest technology companies. One of the company's stoutest rivals is Apple's iCloud, a storage service released in October 2011. Another rival storage service tool, Google's Drive, is expected to launch sometime in 2012. Houston has already begun combating such competition through partnerships with a number of phone manufacturers, including HTC, which now features a preinstalled Dropbox app on all of its Android phones. He also hopes to increase Dropbox's presence through deals with camera makers and television manufacturers. Houston told *Wired*'s Rachel Swaby, "Soon you'll walk into a Best Buy or Fry's and you'll see that little box everywhere. This is the first time I will see my photos or play my music in my little room and it's not going to be a science project."

In February 2012 Dropbox moved into new headquarters in San Francisco's China Basin neighborhood. The 85,000-square-foot space features its own café and gym and will accommodate a Dropbox staff that is expected to rise from seventy to more than two hundred by 2013.

PERSONAL LIFE

Houston ranked tenth on Reuters and Klout's listing of the fifty most influential executives on the web in 2012. He has also been named by *BusinessWeek* as one the best young entrepreneurs in the tech industry, and has been listed by *Inc.com* among the "30 Under 30" top young entrepreneurs in America. Houston, a diehard fan of the band Pearl Jam who enjoys playing guitar in his spare time, lives in a downtown San Francisco apartment building that houses eleven of his friends and fellow entrepreneurs.

SUGGESTED READING

Barret, Victoria. "Dropbox: The Inside Story of Tech's Hottest Startup." *Forbes* 7 Nov. 2011: 82. Print.

Guynn, Jessica. "Dropbox Inventor Determined to Build the Next Apple or Google." *Latimes. com.* Los Angeles Times, 15 Jan. 2012. Web. 20 Feb. 2012.

Houston, Drew. "How Dropbox Became the Startup Steve Jobs Wished to Own— with Drew Houston." *Mixergy.com.* Mixergy, 21 Dec. 2011. Web. 20 Feb. 2012.

Newton, Casey. "Saving Time, Saving Files; 25 Million Use Dropbox to Synchronize in the Cloud." *San Francisco Chronicle* 19 Apr. 2011: D1. Print.

Swaby, Rachel. "With Sync Solved, Dropbox Squares Off With Apple's iCloud." *Wired. com.* Conde Nast Digital, 22 Dec. 2011. Web. 20 Feb. 2012.

—*Chris Cullen*

Robin Hunicke

Born: March 15, 1973
Occupation: Video game designer and producer

Robin Hunicke, a doctoral candidate in computer science at Northwestern University who specializes in artificial intelligence (AI) and game design, is better known for her work on several highly popular video games. After meeting Will Wright, the creator of *The Sims* (a game that allows users to create and populate virtual domestic scenarios), Hunicke began work in 2005 on follow-up versions of that game, *Sims 2: Open for Business* and *MySims*. She also worked on *Boom Blox*, a puzzle game brought out jointly by the filmmaker Steven Spielberg and the company Electronic Arts (EA), before becoming a producer at the Los Angeles–based Thatgamecompany in 2009; there, she has designed the highly anticipated game *Journey*, which is scheduled to go on sale in the spring of 2012. Hunicke has been a role model for many women in an industry long seen as a male domain.

EARLY LIFE AND EDUCATION

Robin Hunicke, called "Birdie" as a child because of her first name, was born in Albany, New York, on March 15, 1973. She was raised in Saratoga Springs. "My dad was Homer Simpson," Hunicke said to Jamin Warren for the website Kill Screen, referring to the suburban father on the long-running animated sitcom *The Simpsons*. Her father, an engineer who had served in the Merchant Marine, worked on the reactor at a nuclear power plant outside Schenectady, New York. According to Hunicke, her father "was a quality nerd, and spent a lot of time thinking about process and making sure things were safe. It is similar to what I do!" Her mother was a teacher. Hunicke's parents "were into colonial arts," as she told Warren, describing how they operated a loom in their home and made their own paper. Her grandmother sewed most of her clothes.

Saratoga Springs is well known for its horse-racing track, and as a girl, Hunicke often went to races. She also enjoyed riding her bicycle in the town, which had "old buildings" and "was really very idyllic," she recalled to Warren. In addition, she liked painting in watercolors,

and meaning. Suddenly the seed sprouted—branches reaching to touch almost everything I was interested in!" At the university, as Hunicke explained to Kevin Kelly for *G4* (Sep. 25, 2011, online), her work "was essentially in narrative and storytelling and the ways in which humans share information." Her thesis for her bachelor's degree was a computer program designed to tell a story that changed as it was read. While working on her thesis, she began to spend time at the university's AI laboratory and to read books related to that subject, including *Scripts, Plans, Goals, and Understanding: An Inquiry into Human Knowledge Structures* (1977) by Roger C. Schank and Robert P. Abelson, and she was "hooked," as she told Hong-Porretta. She added that her "heroes" tend to be artists or designers, mentioning in particular game designers Will Wright and Keita Takahashi, musicians Jeb Bishop and Aphex Twin, comic-book creator Chris Ware, and sculptor Lee Bontecou, whose work she says "transformed my sight, hearing, and playing. I admire their ability to communicate through design—which I aspire to do as well."

Hunicke told Kevin Kelly that when she enrolled in a graduate program at Northwestern University in Chicago, she "thought about whether machines could express thoughts and feelings." At an AI conference during those years, she met Will Wright, who told her that with her skills and interests, she should consider working in game design. "That really was what I wanted to do, I just didn't know it," she said to Kelly, recalling, "Back then, there weren't any schools for gaming, there weren't programs."

GAMING CAREER DEBUT

At Maxis, the company Wright had cofounded with Jeff Braun and sold to the Redwood City, California–based EA in 1997, Wright had designed *The Sims*, a game in which players create and direct the lives of virtual people. The players decide on their characters' appearances and character traits, choose their careers and homes, and make them interact and form relationships with others; the characters' daily needs are the responsibility of the players, who must see to it that, for example, the Sims have regular meals and use the bathroom. The characters speak a language called Simlish.

Sims 2 debuted in 2004. The following year Hunicke, who told Hong-Porretta that she has "had a few jobs here and there" as a "waitress, shopgirl, teacher, freelance web monkey, writer, photographer," joined Maxis and helped design additional versions of *The Sims*. She designed objects that appeared in *Sims 2: Open for Business*, which went on sale in March 2006. While *Sims* characters had jobs in the earlier versions of the game, they were never seen at work; this changed in *Open for Business*, which allows

taking photographs, and woodworking, and she dreamed of being an artist. At the same time, she had an aptitude for math and science and an affinity for activities that required logic and technical skill, such as her brother's video games. Hunicke "was branded as 'gifted' and given a lot of opportunities," Liz Lawley wrote for the blog *Mamamusings* (July 29, 2005). "But the opportunities were in a creative and expressive context, not in the context of procedural learning. Never tied to programming or math or problem-solving." For that reason, Lawley wrote, Hunicke's "overall enthusiasm for school waned" during her junior high and high school years.

A bright spot during that period came during the summer when she was sixteen. Her parents sent her to Cambridge University in England to participate in an art-related program. While there, she saw work by the English poet and artist William Blake (1757–1827), who had created illustrations to accompany his own poems. Hunicke took photos of the illustrations and then used a computer to alter the images. "This planted a tiny seed," she told Souris Hong-Porretta in an interview for the *Hustler of Culture* blog (Oct. 31, 2004, online), "the idea that I could use machines to communicate or create new things—combine efforts, as Blake had done."

Hunicke enrolled at the University of Chicago, where she took a course titled Computer Programming as a Liberal Art. The class, she recalled to Hong-Porretta, covered "programming, architecture, poetry, philosophy . . . all the ways that our daily lives are rich with structure players to have their characters sell merchandise or offer services by setting up beauty salons or restaurants, for example. Players are also responsible for characters' skills, which will determine the success of failure of the enterprises; positive interactions with customers are crucial, and businesses run more smoothly when characters fire lazy employees. The player can measure customer satisfaction, and the success of a business, by the number of stars the business receives. In *Open for Business*, characters can operate their businesses while keeping other jobs.

After working on *Open for Business*, Hunicke "was very hungry to do design," as she told Aaron R. Conklin for the website Get in Media. "I wanted to do original design, not just work on objects for a system that had already been designed." Accordingly, she was made the lead designer for *MySims*, which debuted in 2008. The setting of that game is not suburbia but rather a fantasy world that has gone awry. The premise is that that world's builders have left, followed by most of its other citizens; the character the player creates is a builder who must restore a place to which others will return. Discussing the process of designing *MySims*, Hunicke told Conklin, "I'll be totally honest—I was not ready for that job. I thought I was, and I wasn't. And it was probably the lowest point of my career. . . . The structure wasn't in place at EA to take a grad student with good ideas and turn her into a strong, confident leader. The one thing I'm really proud of is that the core mechanic of building things and giving them away stayed through the entire game. I still think that's great."

The year 2008 also saw the release of *Boom Blox*, a game Hunicke designed for EA, based on an idea by filmmaker Steven Spielberg. "I really wanted to create a video game that I could play with my kids," the filmmaker said, as quoted by Aaron Thomas for *GameSpot* (May 7, 2008, online). The game contains more than three hundred puzzles that involve very high towers of blocks; through various methods, players try to extract blocks without having the towers come crashing down. As the game progresses, players move through many levels, earning scores that bring gold, silver, or bronze medals.

A TURNING POINT

After working on *MySims*, *Boom Blox*, and *Boom Blox Bash Party*, Hunicke took a vacation in the Himalayan nation of Bhutan, where she climbed a sixteen-thousand-foot mountain. It "was pretty insane," she told Conklin. "I trained hard, but I wasn't ready. When I got over the mountain and started walking down back to my life, I realized I needed to make a change." She broke up with her boyfriend and moved out of the apartment they shared. At the same time, she thought about her next career move. During that period, she got to know Kellee Santiago, cofounder of

Thatgamecompany (TGC), who suggested that Hunicke join their game-developing business. There, Hunicke began work on *Journey*. She told Conklin, "I saw [*Journey*] and knew it was the next game for me—it's a game where you go over a mountain."

With the online *Journey*, Hunicke and her associates at the dozen-member TGC sought to create a playing experience different from that found in other games. An oft-discussed aspect of Hunicke's approach to game design is that she begins with an emotion she wants to evoke, then creates a game with that emotion in mind. *Journey* de-emphasizes structure in order to facilitate a feeling of collaboration between players, who may not know each other. The game is set in a desert, with one character seeking others. Hunicke explained to Keith Stuart for the London *Guardian* (Dec. 6, 2011, online), "The narrative of *Journey* is about what *you* do in it." She added, "If you want to follow someone you may, if you want to lead, you can lead. These things create the narrative of your own journey. That's what we wanted—we wanted to leave it up to the player, the individual."

In addition to her work for TGC, Hunicke participates in the annual Game Developers Conference, where she has helped organize such events as the Game Design Workshop and the Experimental Gameplay sessions, and speaks at game festivals all over the world. She also helped establish the education committee of the ten-thousand-plus-member International Game Developers Association; the committee's curriculum guide has been used around the world to teach game development.

PERSONAL LIFE

Hunicke writes a blog, *Gewgaw*, on the Northwestern University website. Her posts have addressed topics beyond games. In her entry for June 9, 2010, for example, she wrote, "Because of my work on games for children and families, I became very interested in climbing childhood obesity rates." She went on to say that she was "thrilled" to take part in First Lady Michelle Obama's campaign, Let's Move, which according to its website is "dedicated to solving the challenge of childhood obesity within a generation." Specifically, Hunicke reviewed apps for the campaign's program Apps for Healthy Kids, which awarded prizes to those who created "innovative, fun and engaging software tools and games that encourage children . . . to make more nutritious food choices and be more physically active." In another post (Apr. 2, 2010), she wrote about her participation in the 2010 Game Design Workshop, saying, "More than anything—I wanted people to take away one very important message: YOU ARE RESPONSIBLE FOR THE DIVERSITY OF YOUR TEAM/PROJECT/COMPANY. . . . Every time you hire someone, you should be trying to build a more diverse, robust and creative team. That comes from diversity of thought, experience, interests, gender, sexuality and race—just to name a few."

Selene Emad-Syring, writing for *New Moon* (July–Aug. 2007, online), a magazine aimed at young girls, asked Hunicke, "What advice would you give to a girl who wants to be a video game designer?" Hunicke replied, "Game designers are curious—they read a lot, they travel, they learn new things. They watch how people learn, have fun, and grow so they can make fun games that help people learn and grow." She also emphasized the collaborative and creative aspects of the job, saying, "You should be good with people, because making a game isn't just about you, but about your whole team. And you need to be a gamer. You need to play—not necessarily video games, but board games, tennis, sports, acting—any group activities that are playful. Anything creative or playful is good for a game designer."

Hunicke is married to Ben Smith, a software engineer for the game company Blizzard Entertainment.

SUGGESTED READING

Conklin, Aaron R. "Lead Producer Robin Hunicke: Don't Stop Believin.'" *Get in Media*. Full Sail University, n.d. Web. 17 Jan. 2012.

Emad-Syring, Selene. "Gamegirl: We Asked a Video Game Designer Some SIM-ple Questions." *New Moon*. New Moon, July–Aug. 2007. Web. 17 Jan. 2012.

Grayson, Nathan. "Adventure Time: Thatgamecompany on *Journey*." *VG247*. Videogaming247, 10 Oct. 2011. Web. 17 Jan. 2012.

Hong-Porretta, Souris. "Interview: Robin Hunicke." *Hustler of Culture*. TypePad, 31 Oct. 2004. Web. 17 Jan. 2012.

Kelly, Kevin. "Journey: Robin Hunicke Talks Sand, Indie Games, and Thatgamecompany." *G4*. G4 Media, 25 Sep. 2011. Web. 17 Jan. 2012.

Stuart, Keith. "Robin Hunicke on *Journey*, AI and Games That Know They're Games." *Guardian* [London]. Guardian, 6 Dec. 2011. Web. 17 Jan. 2012.

—*Clifford Thompson*

Getty Images

Jon Huntsman Jr.

Born: March 26, 1960
Occupation: Politician, businessman, diplomat

A former Utah governor and US ambassador to China, Jon Huntsman Jr. is a moderate politician and businessman who briefly entered the 2012 Republican presidential primary. Huntsman was twice elected governor of his very conservative home state of Utah and enjoyed a whopping 90-percent approval rating when he left office to serve as ambassador to China in 2009. He announced his presidential campaign on June 21, 2011, at Liberty State Park, New Jersey, the same place where Ronald Reagan announced his 1980 run. However, Huntsman's stances on key Republican issues, such as climate change and same-sex civil unions, seemed out of step with his more conservative fellow candidates. He decided to end his campaign in January 2012.

Huntsman's life story, much like his politics, breaks the current Republican mold. He is a Mormon and former rock-and-roll musician. His father is a billionaire philanthropist whose aim is to give away all of his fortune before his death. He is fluent in Mandarin Chinese and Taiwanese; not to mention that, in a politically divided landscape, Huntsman is a moderate whose policies have won support from both sides of the aisle. During his tenure as governor, Utah was named one of the three best-managed states in the country by the Pew Center for the States. As chairman of the Western Governors' Association, Huntsman spearheaded efforts to address climate change with public policy—though he famously distanced himself from this work during his 2012 primary run.

After suspending his presidential campaign, Huntsman was named a member of the board of directors for Ford Motor Company and for Huntsman Corporation, founded by his father. He has also become an outspoken advocate for reform within the Republican Party and the formation of a third party. Though he vehemently denies any speculation that he will run for political office again, Huntsman told Joe Scarborough for MSNBC's "Morning Joe," as reported by *The Hill*'s Justin Sink (23 Feb. 2012), that the party was lacking in "big, bold, visionary" ideas, instead choosing to pander to social conservatives. "I see zero evidence of people getting out there and addressing the economic deficit—which is a national-security problem, for heaven's sake," he said. "I think we're going to have problems politically until we get some sort of third-party movement or some alternative voice out there that can put forward new ideas."

EARLY LIFE

Huntsman is a seventh-generation resident of Utah. Raised in the Church of Jesus Christ of Latter Day Saints, he is a descendant of David Haight, a member of the Quorum of Twelve Apostles, a governing body in the Mormon Church. Huntsman was born Jon Meade Huntsman Jr. on March 26, 1960, in Palo Alto, California. He is the eldest of nine children. His mother Karen was a homemaker. His father, Jon Huntsman Sr., was in the United States Navy when his son was born, and Huntsman spent his early years living in the basement of an apartment building in San Diego. When Huntsman was seven years old, his father became president of a joint venture company with Dow Chemical. Three years later, in 1970, the elder Huntsman founded a packaging company called the Huntsman Container Corporation; within the first few years of its existence, the company developed the clamshell container that McDonald's uses to package its hamburgers. He sold the company for millions when Huntsman was in his teens, although the elder Huntsman stayed on as CEO of the business. Huntsman Sr., now a billionaire and well-known philanthropist, also worked for the Nixon administration, and Huntsman lived in Washington, DC, as a young boy. "We certainly had a lot more than most other average families, and I plead guilty to that," Huntsman told Dan Harrie for the *Salt Lake Tribune* (29 Apr. 2004). "But my upbringing was a lot more normal and grounded in reality than a lot of people would probably think."

By all accounts, the Huntsman family was well known in Salt Lake City for both their wealth and what can only be described as royal status within the ubiquitous Mormon Church. Still, Huntsman didn't flaunt his family's good fortune; as a teenager, he worked an entry-level job as a dishwasher at Marie Callender's pie shop and a Japanese restaurant called Mikado. In 1978, just short of graduation, Huntsman, a classically trained pianist, dropped out of Highland High School to play keyboard in a progressive rock band called Wizard. He wore his hair long and shaggy like popular musician Rod Stewart, and thought that Wizard would be his ticket to fame. The band mixed songs by 70s and 80s rock bands such as REO Speedwagon and Led Zepplin with their own music. Huntsman was best known for his solo on the Speedwagon cover, "Roll with the Changes." A man named Jimmy Pitman, a Los Angeles music producer and former member of the band Strawberry Alarm Clock, took on Wizard, and the band spent months in the recording studio, though no record ever materialized. The bandmates went their separate ways after about eighteen months, and Huntsman was sent on a two-year mission trip (a rite of passage for Mormons) to Taiwan.

MISSIONARY AND AMBASSADOR

Huntsman's mission was considered a hardship post. He lived in a cockroach-infested apartment and awoke early each morning to learn the language, teach English, and attempt to bring converts to the Mormon faith. Huntsman says that the mission had a profound effect on him. He learned Mandarin and the Taiwanese dialect Hokkien (he can also speak Cantonese), but he also learned to look at his birth country from a new perspective. "I got to Taiwan and wondered why people hated Americans," he told Jacob Weisberg for *Vogue* (18 Aug. 2011), "why we were yelled at and spat upon. Nobody stopped to mention that America had just withdrawn diplomatic relations with Taiwan. It left an indelible impression. For the first time you could see the power of the US at work overseas. It left me hungry to learn all I could." Huntsman finished his education when he returned to the United States. He took his GED and enrolled in several classes at the University of Utah before transferring to the University of Pennsylvania. He graduated with a bachelor's degree in international politics in 1987. During that time, he also worked on the advance team in the Reagan White House.

In 1992, President George H. W. Bush nominated the thirty-two-year-old Huntsman to become the US ambassador to Singapore—the youngest head of an American diplomatic mission in over a century. He also served as deputy assistant secretary for Asian and Pacific affairs in the Department of Commerce during the first Bush administration and was appointed as one of two US deputy trade representatives by President George W. Bush on Huntsman's forty-first birthday on March 26, 2001.

GOVERNOR OF UTAH

Huntsman says that his decision to run for governor of Utah came when he decided that he needed to be closer to his family. In 2004, after winning a Republican primary saturated with candidates, he ran against Democrat Scott Matheson Jr. and won. He made jobs and economic growth a priority during his terms and took more liberal stands on immigration and the environment than others in the Republican Party might have. In an effort to cut costs and save energy, Huntsman instituted a controversial four-day workweek for state employees in 2008. He hypothesized that by working four ten-hour days (with a three-day weekend) as opposed to five eight-hour days, the state would save $3 million in energy costs. While the number ended up being closer to $1 million, the temporary program (which ended in 2011) was well received, with an 85-percent approval rating.

In 2006, Huntsman formed the Blue Ribbon Advisory Council on Climate Change (BRAC), to bring together representatives from both the public and private sectors to address climate change; and in 2007, Huntsman signed Utah onto the Western Climate Initiative, pledging that the state would lower its carbon emissions through a cap-and-trade system. He set a goal to reduce greenhouse gases in Utah by 20 percent by 2015, and noted during his reelection the following year that few other Republicans would have taken such a step to address man-made climate change. As chairman of the Western Governors' Association (WGA), Huntsman worked with governors of both parties to develop a sustainable energy plan to present to President Barack Obama in 2008. Huntsman also signed the Energy Independence Pledge, penned by Salt Lake City billionaire and oilman T. Boone Pickens. The Pickens plan called for the United States to invest in wind power energy. "There are three things that must drive our nation's energy policy: affordability, energy independence and sustainability," Huntsman said in a statement, as quoted by Patty Henetz for the *Salt Lake Tribune* (4 Oct. 2008). "The Pickens plan and the WGA efforts are aimed at finding innovative solutions that are right for our country." He was awarded the Leadership in Energy Efficiency Award by the Southwest Energy Efficiency Project in 2006.

For his moderate positions on hot-button issues, Huntsman was able to win the support of both Republicans and Democrats, and his approval ratings often passed 90 percent. In 2008, he passed market-based health care reform in Utah, which extended benefits to children. He cut the state income tax and, in 2007, brought Utah's jobless rate down to 2.3 percent—the lowest in state history. He opposed teaching "intelligent design" in Utah's public school science classes, and he was the first Utah governor to openly support same-sex civil unions—contrary to the Republican Party in the state and most citizens of Utah. He also endorsed Equality Utah's Common Ground Initiative. In 2009, Huntsman was reelected, running against Democrat Bob Springmeyer, with 78 percent of the vote.

AMBASSADOR TO CHINA

Going into his second term as governor, Huntsman enjoyed an incredible 90-percent approval rating when he was nominated by President Obama to serve as ambassador to China on May 16, 2009. Many speculated that the appointment was a shrewd political move on the part of the Obama administration—an attempt to move a plausible Republican presidential challenger in 2012 out of the country. But others pointed out that Huntsman was more than qualified for the position and that his appointment was a part of Obama's larger bipartisan policy—more of a show of good will across the aisle than political angling. In any case, Huntsman eagerly accepted the post. Congress unanimously approved his appointment, and he was sworn in on August 11, 2009.

It was Huntsman's fourth time living in Asia, and he purposely pursued a more outspoken course than during his previous diplomatic missions, in an effort to pressure China toward more liberal and democratic policies, particularly with regard to social networking and the Internet. Huntsman realized that his actions, he told Weisberg, "would carry with it some pain—but also . . . that it was the United States laying down a marker." In the months leading up to his resignation, Huntsman found himself at an Arab Spring–inspired public protest in Beijing, and later invited Han Han, China's famous blogger and racecar driver, to ride motorcycles with him in Shanghai. The Chinese government forbade Han Han from accepting the invitation.

Huntsman left his post in the spring of 2011, but during his service, he recognized more than ever the need for fundamental change in the domestic politics of the United States. Huntsman had been living in China during the rise of the Tea Party and was highly critical of the movement as well as of the congressional squabbling that ensued. "With a weak and rotting core, you don't have much of a foreign policy," he told Weisberg. "You're discounted at the negotiating table, economically and militarily. So when people ask what's the best course of action for the US-China relationship, I can give you ten academic responses. But the reality is we need to rebuild our core."

A PREASSEMBLED CAMPAIGN

Huntsman met John McCain's former campaign strategist John Weaver while he was governor. Weaver was impressed with Huntsman, and saw, perhaps before Huntsman, a possible presidential candidate. He began introducing Huntsman to influential Republican donors in early 2009; thus, Huntsman's decision to accept the diplomatic post in China blindsided him. However, when Huntsman agreed to the ambassador appointment, he said publicly that he would resign after two years; then, in a 2011 *Newsweek* article, he alluded to the possibility of another political campaign. Weaver took this as a signal, and began to quietly assemble the makings of a presidential campaign while Huntsman was in China. As an active member of the Obama administration, Huntsman was unable to be involved in this process or, he claims, even know of it until his resignation on April 30, 2011. The campaign began in earnest the next day.

During Huntsman's brief time on the primary campaign trail, he caught the attention of many moderates, but he failed to take off in the way many of his more conservative fellow candidates did. In numerous speeches, Huntsman called for a "new industrial revolution"; he said that as president, he would rebuild the economy to generate the excitement of prosperity that he said exists in China. He focused on jobs and foreign policy while the Republican campaign debates devolved into arguments about who was more socially conservative. He even, as quoted by *New York Times* columnist Paul Krugman (29 Aug. 2011), worried aloud that the Republican Party was quickly and disturbingly becoming the "anti-science party" for its views on climate change. But his more moderate positions did not win him much support in the Republican race. As the race wore on, he tried to contort his views to appeal to the party base. He changed his position on cap-and-trade, stating that such a program was an economic unreality. He also softened his views on man-made climate change; when asked about his own views on the environment during the primary, Huntsman intimated that there was strong evidence for global warming but that he remained unsure. But after a poor showing in New Hampshire, where he had been concentrating his efforts, Huntsman dropped out of the race on January 15, 2012.

While Huntsman failed to rouse the Republican base, three of his daughters achieved celebrity for their witty Twitter and video commentary on the primary at @Jon2012girls. The telegenic twenty-something trio, consisting of Mary Anne, Liddy, and Abby Huntsman, amassed a following for their send-ups of other candidates and support for their father. Many saw the girls' efforts as refreshing amid one of the most negative primaries in recent memory. Though Huntsman is no longer in the running for Republican nominee, his daughters continue to appear on news programs calling for a more moderate Republican Party.

BUSINESS EXPERIENCE AND FAMILY

Huntsman went to work for his family's manufacturing business, Huntsman Chemical Corporation, in 1987. He oversaw the company's expansion into China, where they currently run several plants, and was later named chairman. He also served as an executive for the Huntsman Cancer Foundation and chief executive of the Huntsman Family Holdings Co. He has also served on the boards of the Utah Opera and KSL-TV's Family Now campaign, which offers information and support for Salt Lake City families. He was appointed the chairman of the Quality Growth Commission's "Envision Utah," a joint public-private initiative organized by the Coalition for Utah's Future in 1997. He resigned to accept his second diplomatic post.

Huntsman met his wife, Mary Kaye, in high school. They crossed paths at their part-time jobs at the Levi's store and Marie Callender's. They began dating years later. The two married in 1983. Mary Kaye is heavily involved in the decision-making process of her husband's political career; some analysts have said that her political skills rival those of her husband.

The couple has seven children: Mary Anne, Liddy, Abby (Livingston), Jon Huntsman III, and Will are his biological children. His youngest children, grade-schoolers Gracie Mei and Asha Bharati, are both adopted. His two sons are both training to be naval officers, and his eldest daughter, Mary Anne, is a concert pianist. Abby, recently married, worked as a public relations consultant on Huntsman's campaign. Liddy attends the University of Pennsylvania.

Huntsman identifies himself as spiritual rather than religious. Though he and his family are members of the Mormon faith, he often says that he is inspired by different faiths and philosophies as well; he has also stressed the importance of raising his adopted daughters with a strong grounding in the respective cultures of their birthplaces: China and India.

Huntsman is a motorcyclist and motocross enthusiast; he rode his Harley-Davidson to work in China. Still an avid music fan, he kept a keyboard in a room adjacent to his office while he was governor, and jammed with REO Speedwagon and Styx at the Utah State Fair in 2005. He still has a band called Politically Incorrect; they practice in Huntsman's basement. Huntsman and his family live in the Kalorama neighborhood of Washington, DC.

SUGGESTED READING

Bai, Matt. "Huntsman Steps into the Republican Vacuum." *New York Times*. New York Times, 20 Jun. 2011. Web. 5 Mar. 2012.

Harrie, Dan. "Silver Spooner or Dishwasher?" *Salt Lake Tribune* 29 Apr. 2004, final ed.: C1. Print.

Henetz, Patty. "Huntsman Backs Energy Pledge." *Salt Lake Tribune*. Salt Lake Tribune, 4 Oct. 2008. Web. 5 Mar. 2012.

Krugman, Paul. "Republicans Against Science." *New York Times* 29 Aug. 2011, late ed.: A23. Print.

Sink, Justin. "Huntsman Calls for Third Party, Says GOP '12 Field Lacks Big Ideas." *The*

Hill. Capitol Hill Publishing, 23 Feb. 2012. Web. 5 March 2012.

Weisberg, Jacob. "Jon Huntsman: The Outsider." *Vogue.* Condé Nast Digital, 18 Aug. 2011. Web. 5 Mar. 2012.

—Molly Hagan

Brian David Johnson

Born: c. 1972
Occupation: Futurist and author

We live in an age in which companies employ social-media gurus and product evangelists—titles unheard of just decades ago. Computer-chip manufacturer Intel has on its staff a futurist, Brian David Johnson. "Johnson is hardly the world's first futurist—a vocation of prognosticating scientists and social scientists dating back to the likes of Jules Verne and H. G. Wells. But he is the first to hold that title at Intel," Larry Greenemeier wrote for *Scientific American* (8 Nov. 2011, online). Greenemeier continued, "Far from just imagining a future whose fate depends largely on the actions of others, Johnson has the resources at his disposal to transform his future-casting into reality." Johnson stresses the practical nature of his work to journalists. "It sounds science-fictiony," he admitted to Alex Knapp for *Forbes* (13 Oct. 2011, online). "But it's ultimately pragmatic. Chip designs have lead times of five to ten years, so it's important to have an understanding of how people will *want* to interact with computers. I'm literally working on chips for 2020 right now."

EARLY LIFE AND EDUCATION

Perhaps befitting a person whose job description is based upon looking to the future, Johnson, born in the early 1970s, has publicized few biographical details about his early years. He has told interviewers that he grew up in a world steeped in technology: His mother worked in the field of information technology (IT), and his father was a radar-tracking engineer. On occasion, his father would bring home schematic drawings of radar systems from the office. At other times, he came bearing actual mechanical pieces of a system, which he allowed Johnson to dismantle and reassemble. "I was learning to read schematics [at] the same time I was learning to read [books]," he recalled to Greenemeier.

As a youth, Johnson—who is not to be confused with the now-retired major-league baseball player of the same name—owned an Atari 2600 video-game console. Released in the late 1970s, it was the first system to use microprocessor-based hardware and removable game cartridges. He has credited his hours of

playing Bezerk—a game in which the player must shoot marauding robots—for showing him the "magic" of interactive technology. The family also owned a Texas Instruments TI99/4A, among the first 16-bit computers manufactured for home use. Released in 1981, it was priced at a few hundred dollars, a figure that made it attractive to enthusiastic hobbyists. Johnson used the machine to play such rudimentary games as Munch Man and TI Invaders and also taught himself programming in BASIC (Beginner's All-purpose Symbolic Instruction Code), a computer language that had been developed in the early 1960s at Dartmouth College by John George Kemeny and Thomas Eugene Kurtz. "One of the really neat things about the TI99/4A was that you could save your programs to the Texas Instruments Program Recorder," Johnson wrote in his book *Screen Future: The Future of Entertainment, Computing, and the Devices We Love* (2010). "At night when I was done saving off my newest BASIC programming masterpiece, I would take the cassette tape up to my room and listen to it on my cassette player. As the tape screeched and bleeped along I used to imagine the code I had just written, trying to see if I could recognize the lines and commands in the noise. . . . It was almost as if I could see the glowing 1s and 0s [of binary code] floating in the air of my darkened bedroom." When he was not working on the TI99/4A, Johnson could often be found reading. He particularly enjoyed science fiction by such authors as Isaac Asimov, Ray Bradbury, and Robert Heinlein. Later, as his tastes expanded, he added Philip K. Dick and J. G. Ballard to his list of favorites.

Johnson attended the New School for Social Research in New York City. Affiliated with New York University (NYU), the school had been among the first in the country to offer courses in futurism, some taught by famed futurist Alvin Toffler as early as the mid-1960s. (Toffler's best-known book is arguably the 1970 volume *Future Shock*, which argued that technological change was occurring at such an accelerated pace that many people were unable to adapt and were suffering from extreme stress as a result; he drew upon the concept of culture shock for his title.) The New School provided Johnson with an education ideally suited for his current position. "That's the lovely thing about the New School when I went," he explained to Greenemeier. "You could take whatever you wanted. I studied a lot of computer science, but . . . [there] was this great mix where I could study sociology, I could study economics, I could study film and I could go down to [New York University] and take classes." He continued, "As a futurist I need the technical chops to understand what we're talking about. But I also need the research chops to be able to go out and pull all this together and then have the ability to express it. . . . That's one of the things I took away from the New School."

Upon graduating from the New School with a BA degree in 1993, Johnson began his career in interactive television (ITV), a field in which applications and programming allow a viewer to control content delivered through a television set, including interactive program guides, video on demand, and digital video recording. Johnson served as the executive producer for international projects for the Discovery Channel and British Airways, among other companies.

INTEL

Johnson joined Intel in 2002. The company was launched in 1968 by engineers Bob Noyce and Gordon Moore. Its first product was the highly successful 3101 Schottky bipolar random access memory (RAM), a high-speed, 64-bit innovation that easily beat its competitors to the market. By the mid-1970s, Intel technology could be found in such ubiquitous products as traffic lights and cash registers. In 1993 the tech giant introduced the Pentium processor, which contained more than three million transistors and was three hundred times faster than its predecessors; Intel cofounder Gordon Moore had famously predicted in 1965 that the number of transistors on a chip would double every two years. By the mid-1990s, more than 85 percent of all desktop computers were being powered by Intel chips. It is now the largest maker of semiconductor chips in the world, reporting revenue of almost $13 billion in the first fiscal quarter of 2012 alone.

Johnson still holds the first title that was assigned to him at Intel: consumer-experience architect. In that capacity he researches and maps the public's experience with the company's products and services. In addition to Johnson, Intel's user-experience group includes ethnographers and cultural anthropologists, who travel all over the world to study cultural practices that shape how people relate to and use new technologies. How people use consumer electronics—watching television, sharing personal videos on a cell phone—varies widely according to the cultural setting in which they find themselves. "To understand what technologies people will want in the future you have to understand what they are doing today," Johnson wrote in *Screen Future*, explaining why such research is vital.

Those findings are then conveyed to the group's engineers and research designers, who use the data to determine platform requirements and specifications for new products. "When you combine this [type of cultural] understanding with a knowledge of technological innovations then you can come away with a fair approximation of possible products, technologies, and services that people might actually want to buy, set up, and use on a daily basis," Johnson continued. "In brief, consumer experience architecture allows you to take multiple inputs and sources of information such as ethnographic research, emerging scientific theory, technology and infrastructure trends, innovation, even public opinion or science fiction, and gather them into a holistic description of the technical and experiential requirements that are needed to deliver a product or service that consumers would want to use."

BECOMING A FUTURIST

As a consumer-experience architect, Johnson had always used the process of future casting—which combined computer science, social science, and trend spotting. He explained to Greenemeier that Intel's chief technology officer, Justin Rattner, had approached him about adding the title of futurist to his job description: "And I said, 'No way.' That's a huge responsibility, especially for a place like Intel." He continued, "At the time Justin wanted me to get out there and start talking to people about the future. We had such discussions internally, but we hadn't been talking about it with others outside the company. The next week [June 30, 2010], we released the book *Screen Future*, which was this work about technology in 2015. I sat down and talked to the press. Almost everyone said, 'So you're Intel's futurist.' At that point I realized that I already had the job."

Johnson is looking ahead to 2020. He calls one theme he is exploring "the secret life of data." He explained to Alex Knapp, "Algorithms will talk to algorithms, machines will talk to machines, and humans won't be involved. When data takes on a life of its own, what will that do? How will we remember that when that data comes back, it's ultimately meant for humans? It has to make our lives better. We can't forget that." He is also pondering the implications of what he has termed "the ghost of computing"—the end result of a process by which computers become so small, efficient, and ubiquitous that they pervade all aspects of our lives without us being overtly aware of them. "What happens when it's embedded in the wall?" he asked news anchor Emily Chang for Bloomberg West (16 Aug. 2011). "What happens when it's in your shoe and in your TV?"

Johnson finds distressing the climate of fear that often arises when discussing new technologies. The issue crystallized for him one night when he was lecturing in San Francisco. A man in his fifties began discussing his teenage daughters and what he perceived as their dependence on their electronic devices. How, he wondered, would they ever learn to maintain relationships with real humans, hold down jobs, and be functioning members of society? He became so visibly agitated that the venue's security guards were wary.

"I understood why he was fearful," Johnson wrote for *Slate* (17 Jan. 2012, online), "because he loves his daughters and wants them to have a good future. The fact is his daughters' smartphones just haven't been around as long as TV; we haven't yet established norms, or language, for what's socially acceptable and what's off limits. . . . We are currently in the middle of coming to grips with what these devices mean to us. This isn't a technology problem; it's a broader cultural conversation about what kind of future we want to live in." Johnson has explained that any new technology is feared initially. Even after that fear dissipates, a certain segment of the population will reject the innovation, believing it to be frivolous or useless. (Johnson has cited an episode of the popular sitcom *Seinfeld*, in which an elderly character is given a costly personal electronic organizer but will use it only to calculate tips in restaurants.) The final stage, as Johnson describes, occurs after the technology has become mundane and fully incorporated into everyone's lives. "Though their representatives might deny it, Google and Apple actually strive to be dull, not cutting-edge," he wrote for *Slate*. "Once a company's product becomes ordinary, it has been knit into our lives and history."

THE TOMORROW PROJECT

Johnson is also responsible for overseeing Intel's Tomorrow Project, which involves talking with a wide variety of scientists, entertainers, and ordinary consumers. The conversations are then posted as videos or podcasts on Intel's website in order to spark further discussion. (Some of the most-watched episodes feature will.i.am of the band Black Eyed Peas, who explains how digital technology has changed the recording industry and talks about how he foresees making music in the future.) In addition to viewing the clips, those interested can follow Johnson on Twitter, where his account name is @IntelFuturist.

As part of the Tomorrow Project, he also approached a group of science-fiction authors, including Douglas Rushkoff and Ray Hammond, to write short pieces that were then collected in *The Tomorrow Project: Bestselling Authors Describe Daily Life in the Future* (2011). "There's a great symbiotic history between science fiction and science fact—fiction informs fact," Johnson told Greenemeier. "I go out and I do a lot of lectures on AI [artificial intelligence] and robotics . . . and every time people come to me, pull me aside and say, 'You do know the reason why I got into robotics was C3PO [a character from *Star Wars*].'" Intel Press later published *The Tomorrow Project Anthology* (2011), a larger volume that includes a novella by Cory Doctorow and an essay by will.i.am in addition to several pieces of short fiction.

OTHER BOOKS

Johnson is himself a writer of science fiction. Among his books is *Fake Plastic Love* (2007), a novel involving a robotic sex doll, Ann-Mar, crafted in the likeness of Ann Margaret, a curvaceous Swedish American actor. Ann-Mar, who is found abandoned in a junk shop by the novel's hero, Rem Kang, holds the key to unraveling a web of political conspiracy, blackmail, and betrayal. The book has not been widely reviewed.

In addition to *Screen Future*, Johnson's nonfiction work includes *Science Fiction Prototyping: Designing the Future with Science Fiction* (2011), which offers a guide to using fiction as a way of exploring the future in practical terms. He cites as one example of an influential sci-fi prototype the 1983 film *WarGames*, which combined excitement over the advent of personal computers (such as his TI99/4A) with the imagined possibility of a nuclear war precipitated by unchecked technology. "The most famous line from the movie is when the [computer] asks [the young protagonist], 'Shall we play a game?' crudely vocalized through a make-believe voice synthesizer. But those words . . . captured everything that was exciting and amazing about the movie. Yes! I wanted to play a game," Johnson wrote in *Science Fiction Prototyping*.

WHAT THE FUTURE HOLDS

Johnson estimated in *Science Fiction Prototyping* that by 2015 there will be more than 500 billion hours of content available and that people will own more than fifteen billion devices with which to access that material—"more content than is humanly knowable available on more devices than there are people on the planet," as he described it to Emily Chang.

He continually stresses to journalists that he is optimistic about humanity's prospects and believes that his mission is to help Intel's consumers achieve the future they desire. "So many people think the future is something that is set," he told Greenemeier. "They say, 'You're a futurist, make a prediction.' The future is much more complicated than that. . . . The fact of the matter is, the future is made every day by the actions of people." He concluded, "The biggest way you can affect the future is to talk about it with your family, your friends, your government."

SUGGESTED READING

Emily, Chang. "Brian David Johnson, Futurist, Intel, Talks about Technology at Bloomberg TV." *Bloomberg Transcripts* 16 Aug. 2011: n. pag. *Newspaper Source Plus*. Web. 15 May 2012.

Greenemeier, Larry. "Prescient Processing: A Q&A with Intel Futurist Brian Johnson, and Why We Shouldn't Fear the Future." *Scientific American*. Scientific American, 8 Nov. 2011. Web. 11 May 2012.

Johnson, Brian David. "The Four Stages of Introducing New Technologies." *Slate*. Slate Group, 17 Jan. 2012. Web. 11 May 2012.

Johnson, Brian David. *Screen Future: The Future of Entertainment, Computing, and the Devices We Love*. Santa Clara: Intel Press, 2010. PDF file.

Knapp, Alex. "Intel's Guide to the Future." *Forbes*. Forbes.com, 13 Oct. 2011. Web. 11 May 2012.

—*Mari Rich*

FilmMagic

Mindy Kaling

Born: June 24, 1979
Occupation: Actress, writer, producer

"There is the extra little 'smile' that infuses her scripts, which is hard to quantify." Emmy-nominated writer and actress Mindy Kaling is most recognizable for her role as Kelly Kapoor on the popular NBC sitcom *The Office*. Less known are her roles behind the scenes, where she heads a staff of eighteen writers and serves as an executive producer of the show. "Mindy has long been considered the best writer on *The Office*, and every actor on the show thinks she writes for them the best. There is the extra little 'smile' that infuses her scripts, which is hard to quantify," costar and fellow writer/producer B. J. Novak told Emma Rosenblum for *New York Magazine* (27 Sep. 2010, online). Speaking of how Kaling treats each character, he added, "Characters aren't joke machines to her, or types to satirize. As a person, she's incredibly sentimental, more than anyone I've met, but she's also incredibly sharp. . . . That allows her to express real emotions without shyness, but also without clichés."

The Office premiered on NBC in 2005 and was inspired by the British sitcom of the same name, which starred comedian Ricky Gervais as the hopelessly awkward boss of a fictitious paper company in the United Kingdom. The comedy was styled as a fictional documentary, or mockumentary, in which a host of oddball characters regularly acknowledged the cameras that captured daily interactions at the office. The show aired from 2001 to 2003 and became one of the BBC's most popular shows of all time. "It was really scary because the original version is pretty much the perfect show," Kaling told Zach Swiss for the *Dartmouth* (23 Mar. 2006, online). "It was such a daunting task to have to adapt it, so I feel really lucky," she said of the show's American success. In 2004, American television writer Greg Daniels, a former staff writer for *Saturday Night Live* and *The Simpsons* and creator of *King of the Hill*, decided to bring the comedy to the United States, setting the office of the similarly fictitious Dunder Mifflin paper company in Scranton, Pennsylvania. Actor Steve Carell, who has since left the show, was cast as well-meaning yet bumbling manager Michael Scott. The show was nearly identical to the British version, with Rainn Wilson as Carell's eccentric sidekick and actors John Krasinski and Jenna Fischer playing the show's love interests, but its subtle style of humor was tailored to an American audience. Kaling, hired in 2004, was the show's first female writer. She was promoted to executive producer in 2011. The show's first season attracted favorable reviews from critics and a respectable viewing audience, though it was not considered a hit. However, by the second season, viewership skyrocketed. The show became an enormous success and began its eighth season in September 2011.

In addition to her work onscreen, Kaling published a book of comedic essays titled *Is Everybody Hanging Out without Me? And Other Concerns* in 2011. As an actress, she has also appeared in the big-screen comedies *The 40-Year-Old Virgin* (2005), *Unaccompanied Minors* (2006), *License to Wed* (2007), *Night at the Museum: Battle of the Smithsonian* (2009), *Despicable Me* (2010), and *No Strings Attached* (2011). She also served as a guest writer for *Saturday Night Live* in 2006.

A YOUNG COMEDY NERD

Kaling was born Vera Mindy Chokalingham on June 24, 1979, in Boston, Massachusetts. Her father, Avu Chokalingham, is an architect from Chennai, India, and her mother, Swati, is a gynecologist from Mumbai. (Her parents appeared in a 2006 episode of *The Office*, written by Kaling and titled "Diwali" after the Hindu festival of lights, as the parents of Kaling's character, Kelly Kapoor.) The Chokalinghams met in Lagos, Nigeria, where Swati was working as a gynecologist. The couple's only language in common is English; Avu speaks Tamil, while Swati speaks Bengali and Hindi. They moved to the United States in 1979, the same year Kaling was born. Her middle name, Mindy, is taken from the television show *Mork and Mindy*, which was, according to Kaling, the only American show available on Nigerian television while her parents were living there.

Kaling and her older brother, Vijay, were raised in Cambridge. When Kaling was three years old, her mother was finishing her residency and working nights at a hospital in Boston, while her father, who was working in New Haven, drove nearly three hours home each day to watch Kaling and her brother. Unsurprisingly Kaling inherited her parents' ambitious work ethic early. She attended the prestigious Cambridge day school Buckingham Browne & Nichols, where she excelled in Latin. In her downtime, beginning in junior high, Kaling began studying sketch-comedy shows, including *The Kids in the Hall*, *In Living Color*, and *Saturday Night Live*, with "attentive nerdiness," she told Curtis Sittenfeld for the *New York Times* (25 Sep. 2011). "I could tell you who the line producer on *Saturday Night Live* was when I was twelve years old." She graduated from high school with honors in 1997 and attended Dartmouth College.

By her own account, Kaling blossomed at Dartmouth, joining an improvisational comedy troupe called the Dog Day Players and an a cappella group called the Rockapellas. She also created a comic strip in the school newspaper, the *Dartmouth*, called "Badly Drawn Girl," which won her a major following. Though Kaling began her college career as a Latin major, she graduated with a degree in playwriting in 2001. At eighteen, she had interned at the television show *Late Night with Conan O'Brien* in New York, and she decided to move to the city the summer after her graduation. Kaling, fellow Dartmouth alum and close friend Brenda Withers, and Withers's brother shared a small apartment in the Astoria neighborhood of Queens.

BIG BREAK: PLAYING BEN AFFLECK

By her own exacting standards, Kaling characterizes her start in New York as a failure. She auditioned unsuccessfully for several Broadway musicals while working as a production assistant on the daytime television show *Crossing Over with John Edward*, featuring the popular psychic. She also started doing stand-up comedy and shortened her last name from Chokalingham to Kaling because she was frustrated with club emcees making jokes about how difficult her name was to pronounce.

Unhappy with their lack of theatrical opportunities, Kaling and Withers, whom Kaling had met while singing with the Rockapellas, wrote a play together inspired by the tabloid coverage of then "it" actors Matt Damon and Ben Affleck. Hot off their 1998 Oscar win for writing the movie *Good Will Hunting* (1997), it seemed, Kaling recalled, as if their faces were on the cover of every magazine that came into her apartment. As a joke, Kaling and Withers began impersonating the two men. "A lot of it was just 'what if,'" Kaling told Karin Lipson for *Newsday* (31 Aug. 2003). "We started doing improvisations with different scenarios." The improvisations, featuring the tall, blond Withers as Damon and the dark, petite Kaling as Affleck, soon became the play *Matt & Ben*, which made its debut at the 2002 New York International Fringe Festival. *Matt & Ben* is a fantastical take on the creation of Damon and Affleck's much-lauded screenplay; in Kaling and Withers's telling, the manuscript for *Good Will Hunting* falls from the sky while the two are trying to pen a screen adaptation of J. D. Salinger's novel *The Catcher in the Rye* (1951).

Kaling and Withers's play featured imagined flashbacks of Damon and Affleck as teenagers as well as cameo appearances from Salinger and actress Gwyneth Paltrow, both also played by Withers and Kaling. *Matt & Ben* was named Best Overall Production of the Fringe and moved to Performance Space 122 in Manhattan's East Village for an Off-Broadway run. As a publicity stunt, Kaling and Withers posted a fake cease-and-desist letter from Damon and Affleck's lawyers on their website. The show continued to play to sold-out crowds and won a highly favorable review from the *New York Times* (12 Aug. 2003), despite the bit of stage business gone awry the night critic Bruce Weber attended the show. "This is a sharp script," Weber wrote, "and it delivers its cleverness mostly without nudging you in the ribs. And in the end it's unsentimental and smart about long friendships, too; when you're not looking they tend to tiptoe right up to enmity." He added of the play's "climactic fight scene": "In it, Ben takes a swing at Matt and knocks him out, but on Friday evening's performance, Ms. Kaling's right hook was a little too realistic. It connected and broke Ms. Withers's nose." Withers was taken to the hospital after the show and was ready to perform again the next night.

KALING AND KAPOOR
After a sold-out New York run, *Matt & Ben* moved to Los Angeles in 2004, where Greg Daniels saw it with his wife. Daniels was impressed with the construction of the show and with Kaling's performance. Two months later Kaling gave him a spec script she had written for the television show *Arrested Development*. Daniels hired her as a staff writer on *The Office*; her contract also contained a performance clause, though she did not fully realize it until later. For her new job Kaling moved to small apartment in West Hollywood. She was twenty-four and the only female writer on a staff of eight. She did not make her acting debut in the show, as the Valley Girl–esque customer-service representative Kelly Kapoor, until *The Office*'s second episode, "Diversity Day," written by fellow writer/performer B. J. Novak. The conceit of the episode—office manager Michael Scott offends his ethnically diverse coworkers in an effort to promote racial tolerance—provided the perfect opportunity to introduce Kaling's Indian character as a foil. Yet speaking of Kapoor's ethnicity, Kaling told Lisa Tsering for *India-West* (27 Oct. 2006), "The great thing about playing Kelly is that her being Indian is maybe the fifth thing you'd say about her. She's such a character; girly, chatty, teenager-y and gossipy, and then you remember, oh yeah, and she's Indian too."

As *The Office* skyrocketed in popularity, Kaling began to take a more active role in the show's production. To date she has written twenty of the show's episodes, many of which are considered classics by fans. "The Dundies," the season two premiere, introduced the annual Dundie awards Michael bestows on his staff; in the episode, Pam (Fischer) gets drunk, kisses Jim (Krasinski), and finds herself banned from the local Chili's restaurant for life. Another season two episode, "The Injury," features one of Kaling's

favorite lines, after Michael burns his foot on a George Foreman grill after getting out of bed: "I like waking up to the smell of bacon. So sue me." Perhaps Kaling's most celebrated episode is the one she cowrote with Daniels, called "Niagara," in which Pam and Jim get married. The two-part show, which takes place in Niagara Falls, aired in 2009 and was praised for its comedic yet tender rendering of the couple's seasons-long romance. Both Kaling and Daniels were nominated for an Emmy for "Niagara" in 2010.

DEEP THOUGHTS
Kaling's ability to balance laughs and poignant moments on *The Office* might come from her love of romantic comedies. Her favorite is *You've Got Mail* (1998), starring Tom Hanks and Meg Ryan, which she first saw when she was interning at *Conan* as a teenager. Kaling talks about the genre extensively in her book *Is Everyone Hanging Out without Me? And Other Concerns*, published in 2011. An excerpt describing "rom com" female stereotypes—including "The Klutz," "The Ethereal Weirdo," "The Woman Who Is Obsessed with Her Career and Is No Fun at All," and "The Woman Who Works in an Art Gallery"—was published in the *New Yorker*. "Why do all the women have to be klutzes?" she asked Rosenblum. "All these pretty women with no discernable flaws, so let's make them a klutz! Or what about all the skinny women shoving food in their mouth on dates? It would be so much funnier if the women weren't skinny." Referring to the satirical newspaper the *Onion*, she added, "That's a great *Onion* headline: 'Actual Fat Woman Shoves Food in Her Mouth in Romantic Comedy.'"

Is Everyone Hanging Out without Me? And Other Concerns, which is part memoir, also includes humorous comparisons between Kaling and her *Office* character; their differences are noted in a list titled "Things Kelly Would Do That I Would Not," which includes faking a pregnancy and writing a letter of support to actress Jennifer Aniston. The book was well received despite its lack of intimate details about her life, a conscious decision made by Kaling. She told Hadley Freeman for the London *Guardian* (9 Nov. 2011) that she thinks female comedians often overshare in their books, detailing sexual exploits and addictions for laughs. She remarked, "Tina Fey's book [*Bossypants*, 2011] actually came as a huge relief to me because she showed that you can tell stories but also be private and, actually, being a little discreet now feels almost fresh."

Reviewers have praised Kaling's pithy observations on everything from Hollywood gossip to her feelings about one-night stands to the androgyny of her childhood haircuts, but they accuse the book of containing little more substance. Kaling declines to wade into the absurd-yet-consuming "Are women funny?" debate in the comedy world but makes pointed observations about how all female comedians are always compared to one another, a phenomenon that does not occur among her male cohorts. She jokes that when *Saturday Night Live* comedian Kristen Wiig is successful, people lament the fall of Tina Fey, as if, she has told numerous sources, "there can only be one" female comedian on top.

CONQUERING THE WEB AND OTHER ENDEAVORS

Offscreen and off the page, Kaling has also become somewhat of an Internet sensation. In 2008, she closed down her popular blog *Things I've Bought That I Love*, which chronicled her passion for shopping (a trait that she and Kapoor share) with signature wit. She has since started a new blog called *The Concerns of Mindy Kaling*. On Twitter, a forum fast becoming the measure of comedians in 140 words or less, Kaling has garnered over 1.6 million followers. Her tweets include riffs such as "My heart wants white jeans but my head says no. Kidney says go for it, spleen is ambivalent. Ovaries say no comment, rather rudely actually," as quoted by Sittenfeld. Kaling maintains that she spends no longer than a minute composing each tweet. She also chronicles life on the set of *The Office*, a boon for devoted fans, of which the show has many. Kaling, a self-described workaholic, often puts in twelve- to eighteen-hour days on the show. When not in the writer's room, she can be found on set playing Kapoor; she has even directed two episodes.

As of 2009, Kaling's NBC contract includes a development deal for her to create her own sitcom. She is currently working on a show in which she will play a gynecologist, inspired by her mother. Vijay, Kaling's brother, told Sittenfeld that his mother is "a professional gossip who does Pap smears." Kaling has alluded to portraying a character who might be similarly described.

In 2010, Kaling cowrote a romantic-comedy script with *Office* producer Brent Forrester called *The Low Self-Esteem of Lizzie Gillespie*, about a woman with low self-esteem who is pursued by an incredibly attractive man. As of early 2012, it remains in development.

Kaling is in a relationship with web analyst and improvisational actor David Harris. She lives in West Hollywood, California.

SUGGESTED READING

Freeman, Hadley. "G2: Girly Power." *Guardian* 9 Nov. 2011, final ed.: 6. Print.
Lipson, Karin. "Riffing on Two Regular Guys." *Newsday* 31 Aug. 2003: D15. Print.
Rosenblum, Emma. "The Funny Side of Love: *The Office*'s Star Writer Could Be the Future of Romantic Comedy." *New York Magazine*. New York Magazine, 27 Sep. 2010. Web. 29 Dec. 2011.
Sittenfeld, Curtis. "I Want It Both Ways." *New York Times* 25 Sep. 2011, late ed.: 40. Print.
Swiss, Zach. "Dartmouth Alum Embarks on Acting, Writing Career for *The Office*." *TheDartmouth.com*. Dartmouth, 23 May 2006. Web. 29 Dec. 2011.
Tsering, Lisa. "NBC Hit *The Office* to Celebrate Diwali." *India-West* 27 Oct. 2006: C1. Print.
Weber, Bruce. "Bad Will Hunting, Armed with Venom Darts." *New York Times* 12 Aug. 2003, late ed.: E1. Print.

SELECTED BOOKS AND PLAYS

Matt & Ben, 2004; *Is Everyone Hanging Out Without Me?*, 2011

SELECTED FILMS AND TELEVISION SHOWS

The 40-Year-Old Virgin, 2005; *The Office*, 2005–2012; *Unaccompanied Minors*, 2006; *License to Wed*, 2007; *Night at the Museum: Battle of the Smithsonian*, 2009; *Despicable Me*, 2010; *No Strings Attached*, 2011

—Molly Hagan

Jim Koch

Born: May 27, 1949
Occupation: Brewmaster, founder of the Boston Beer Company

"In a craft-beer world populated by the likes of Pete's Wicked Ale, Rogue, Ruffian, and Rhino Chasers, it can come as a shock to recognize that the outstanding success story continues to be a brand with a portrait of a politically incorrect two-centuries-dead, white Anglo male on the package," Gerry Kermouch wrote for *Brandweek* (9 Sep. 1996). Kermouch was referring to Samuel Adams beer, brewed by the Boston Beer Company, currently the largest craft brewery in the country. Founded in 1984 by sixth-generation brewmaster Jim Koch, the company was the first in the United States to pose serious competition to the established German and Dutch breweries. Koch has been widely credited with fomenting a revolution in the beer industry, introducing Americans—who had by the 1980s become accustomed to weak, industrially brewed products—to full-bodied, flavorful beers.

EARLY LIFE AND EDUCATION

Charles James Koch, known as Jim, was born on May 27, 1949, in Cincinnati, Ohio, to Dorothy and Charles Koch. His father had graduated from the oldest brewing school in the nation, the

Bloomberg via Getty Images

Siebel Institute of Technology, and had apprenticed at several venerable Cincinnati breweries, including Burger, Hudepohl, Schoenling, and Wiedemann. The fifth generation of eldest Koch sons to enter the profession, Charles Koch subsequently became a brewmaster at the Wooden Shoe Brewery in Minster, Ohio.

Jim Koch exhibited an entrepreneurial spirit from an early age, mowing lawns, tarring driveways, and delivering newspapers to earn pocket money as a teenager. He continued working to help pay his tuition after entering Harvard in the late 1960s. Koch graduated with a bachelor's degree in government studies in 1971. Unsure of his future career path, he remained at Harvard to undertake a combined graduate program in business and law. He gradually became discontent, however, and in 1973 dropped out of the program, reasoning that he could always return when he had a firmer sense of his career goals.

Koch enjoyed mountain climbing, and once out of Harvard he found a job as a mountaineering instructor with Outward Bound, an organization that takes groups of business professionals, at-risk youths, and other individuals on wilderness excursions. Koch remained with Outward Bound for about three years before returning to Harvard. In preparation for reentering school, he interviewed for a summer job at the prestigious consulting firm Bain & Company. His interviewer was a former graduate school classmate, Mitt Romney. "He flushed me," Koch told Todd Hyten for the *Boston Business Journal* (9 Dec. 1994). "It was probably the right decision. I'd just come

from living in the woods for three years, I wasn't exactly dressed for success either." Koch completed his graduate program in 1978, earning a dual degree in business and law.

As a Harvard graduate, Koch found himself in great demand on the job market. He accepted a post with the Boston Consulting Group (BCG), one of the largest and most respected consulting firms in the region, and was soon earning a quarter-million dollars a year. Despite his enviable salary and the power his job commanded, Koch found himself discontented once again. In 1984, with no firm long-term plan, he gave his employers notice that he would be leaving.

THE BEER BUSINESS

Koch's thoughts turned to the traditional family business, and he approached his father about starting a small brewery. "[He] thought I was crazy," Koch recalled in 2011 at the Beverage Forum, an annual executive conference. "'We've spent twenty years trying to get the smell of a brewery out of our clothes,' [he] said. [But] I believed that it wasn't in the clothes, it was in the blood."

Despite his misgivings, Charles passed on to his son the recipe for Louis Koch Lager, the original family recipe, which had been stored in a trunk in the attic. He also provided a small amount of start-up funding, as did several other family members, friends, and former clients. "[They] were at that time, gosh, paying $3,000 a day to listen to my advice," Koch explained to Beverly Schuch for *CNN Business News* (4 Dec. 1994). "So it was easy to get them to put in $5,000 or $10,000 with the promise of free beer." Koch supplemented that capital with $100,000 of his own money, saved from his earnings at BCG.

Koch saw himself filling an important niche. "In 1984, the beer industry was in what I call the Blue Nun stage," he explained to Greg W. Prince for *Beverage World* (Dec. 1994), making reference to a once-popular brand of very inexpensive wine. "It was where the wine business was in 1968. It was divided into domestic beers which were lighter and less flavorful, consistent and relatively inexpensive, and imports which came in green bottles and had more flavor, sometimes not good flavor. . . . You went to a bar, they had domestic, they had import and that was it." Small domestic breweries, which had numbered more than one thousand when his father was starting out, had by then dwindled down to a mere handful, bought out or crushed by large conglomerates.

Koch brewed his first batch of beer in his kitchen. He called it Samuel Adams Boston Lager, naming it after one of America's Founding Fathers. "I wanted to have an American beer with an American name and sell it as an American beer; not pretend to be something coming from Europe," he told Paul Solman for the *Mac-Neil/Lehrer NewsHour* (26 Aug. 1986). "Samuel Adams was the perfect figure. He was a patriot who instigated and nurtured the American Revolution. He was the man who, more than anyone else, threw the foreigners out. And on top of it, he was a brewer." (The Adams family owned a malt house next to their home in Boston.) Additionally, Koch told journalists, he did not want to put his own German surname on the bottle, because it was so likely to be mispronounced.

With the help of Rhonda Kallman, his former BCG secretary, who had once worked as a bartender, Koch tried to get large distributors to agree to carry the beer. When they were unsuccessful at convincing the distributors to take on such a small account, they began toting around individual bottles in a briefcase lined with cold packs, encouraging bartenders to try it for themselves. Slowly, they met with success. When the first bartender agreed to place an order, Koch was so excited that he left the bar without finding out how many cases the man wanted. Koch rented a warehouse and a truck, making deliveries himself. "Try schlepping five cases of beer down the steps of one of those Faneuil Hall restaurants—you're talking 160 pounds! It gave me an appreciation of who does the hard work in the company," Koch told Robert A. Mamis for *Inc.* (Dec. 1994).

When the beer brewing outgrew Koch's kitchen, he made the decision to use a contract brewer with state-of-the-art equipment, rather than immediately investing in a brewery of his own. This tactic saved Koch millions of dollars. He chose the Pittsburgh Brewing Company in Pennsylvania. The move raised the ire of other craft brewers, most of whom had started out as home brewers and then purchased enough equipment to expand in a minor way. They felt that Koch was being dishonest by portraying himself as an artisan beer maker when others were doing the actual brewing. Koch was not swayed by their arguments, however. As demand increased, he made additional contract agreements with City Brewing in La Crosse, Wisconsin; High Falls Brewing in Rochester, New York; FX Matt Brewery in Utica, New York; Blitz-Weinhart, in Portland, Oregon; and other facilities. By the end of the decade, the Boston Beer Company had become the largest contract brewer in the United States, making some seventy thousand barrels per year. "If a beer is good it doesn't matter where it's made," he pointed out to Peter V. K. Reid for *Modern Brewery Age* (10 Sep. 1990). "People drink the beer not the label. Only an idiot would drink a beer just because it's local, and I can't build a business for my children by selling beer to idiots." He continued, "Beer can't just be local, it has to be fresh and good. Unfortunately, just because a beer is brewed locally doesn't guarantee freshness—I think Miller and Budweiser are fresher than most micro[brews] on the shelves."

Avoiding the use of his start-up funds to build a brewery allowed Koch to invest heavily in advertising. He was determined to create ads very different from those of the conglomerates, which typically featured women in bikinis or handsome, young men drinking. Instead, he used the opportunity to educate consumers about how premium beer is made and why they should be willing to pay more for a high-quality brew. He also liberally gave away patio umbrellas, cocktail napkins, and other branded items for Boston-area restaurants and bars to use, so the name Sam Adams became a ubiquitous presence around town. "You used to go into a bar and ask for a Sam Adams, and they'd say, 'What's that?' Now they say, 'We don't carry that beer.' That's progress," he joked to Reid in 1990.

Early on, Koch named Kallman vice president of marketing. He felt that it was important she have an impressive title so that everyone in the male-dominated industry would take her seriously. The Boston Beer Company's corporate culture has always been unusual; from the beginning, almost half of its sales representatives have been female. "I'm often asked why I hire so many women," Koch told Mamis. "The answer is, I don't; I hire talented, resourceful, intelligent, energetic people. It happens that God made half of them women."

The company's advertising also featured what some saw as unfair potshots at foreign brews. One slogan stated: "When America asked for Europe's tired and poor, we didn't mean their beer." Koch maintained that such premium foreign beers as Beck's and St. Pauli Girl would not even be permitted for sale in Germany. The country's strict regulations allow beers to contain only four ingredients: water, yeast, malt, and hops. Using independent testers, he discovered that some of the beers were prepared for the US market by adding refined sugar and processed corn, which lighten the beer to suit American palates and stabilize it for shipping. It was an undeniable feather in his cap when Sam Adams passed a rigorous purity test to become the first American beer ever to be allowed to be sold in Germany.

Some within the industry began referring to Koch as the "P.T. Barnum of brewing," because of his boastfulness and showmanship. Many pointed out that the picture on his labels bore little resemblance to the historic Samuel Adams. Furthermore, they pointed out, the real Samuel Adams was a failure as a brewer; his business collapsed in 1764.

However, even Koch's direct competitors have admitted that Sam Adams is an exceptionally high-quality beer. In 1985, just six weeks after it made its April debut—on Patriot's Day, a civic holiday in Massachusetts that commemorates the anniversary of the Battles of Lexington and Concord—Sam Adams took home top honors at the annual Great American Beer Festival. It has been a perennial favorite at the event ever since. After Bill Clinton requested that it be served at his inauguration, Koch's beer was regularly stocked at the White House.

Koch credits his success to his careful attention to the quality of his ingredients; some of his television ads feature footage of him hand-selecting hops in Bavaria. He also considers freshness a major factor and was a pioneer in stamping a sell-by date on each of his products. He is known for going into restaurants and bars unannounced to make sure no one is selling his beer beyond its expiration date. In one radio ad, Koch discussed the importance of freshness, with the sound of breaking bottles in the background. It was not an artificial sound effect—workers were actually destroying bottles of stale beer.

In 1988, Koch renovated the abandoned Haffenreffer Brewery in Jamaica Plain, an old brewing neighborhood in Boston. Critics called the tiny facility nothing more than a tourist attraction, rather than a serious brewery. Nevertheless, it allowed the Boston Beer Company to justify its name, giving it a manufacturing base in the city for the first time. In the mid-1990s, Koch took over Cincinnati's Hudepohl-Schoenling Brewery, which had been created by the merger of two companies at which his father had apprenticed a half-century before. Boston Beer thus shed its former reputation as a contract brewer, and Koch family history came full circle. In 2008, the company also acquired a large facility in Pennsylvania's Lehigh Valley.

Koch, who took the company public in 1995, has introduced several varieties of beer in addition to the original Sam Adams. One particularly fraught venture was his introduction of a fuller-bodied reduced-calorie beer, which gradually found fans. He has also pioneered a category of "extreme beers," with complex flavors and exceptionally high alcohol content (25 percent, as compared to the usual 4 or 5 percent). "I wanted to prove that beer had all the quality and dignity and wonderfulness of any alcoholic beverage," he told a reporter for *Brandweek* (8 Aug. 2005, online). "The idea that there is a beer out there that is as good as the best port or the best cognac or the best sherry ever made is stunning to people until they taste it. And even then they say this can't be beer. I say 'Hey dude, we made it in a brewery, in a brew kettle, and with our brewing ingredients. It's beer.'" Koch continued, "Here's this little brewery that is making the strongest fermented beverage in human history . . . and putting it alongside great sherries, cognacs, and ports in blind taste tests and winning."

Koch is intent on proving that his beers, while much more affordable than good wine, pair just as well with food. He has pointed out,

for example, that his seasonal summer ale is brewed with lemon zest and West African pepper and makes a wonderful marinade or accompaniment for grilled shrimp and chicken. His black lager, he says, pairs especially well with strong cheeses.

Boston Beer, which trades on the New York Stock Exchange under the symbol SAM, records gross revenues of more than $500 million a year. Koch stepped down as CEO in 2001 and now holds the title of chairman. In 2008, he created a microloan program called Brewing the American Dream, which provides capital to small businesses in the food, beverage, or hospitality industries.

Koch's wife, Cynthia Fisher, heads a biotechnology firm. They have two children. Koch also has two children from his first marriage.

SUGGESTED READING

Beach, Patrick. "If You Really Like Craft Beer, Thank Pioneer Jim Koch." *Austin American-Statesman*. 20 May 2009: D1. Print.

Hyten, Todd. "Pour Man." *Boston Business Journal* 9 Dec. 1994: 17. Print.

Kermouch, Gerry. "A Dead American Patriot with Plenty of Life Left Yet." *Brandweek* 9 Sep. 1996: 42. Print.

Mamis, Robert A. "Market Maker." *Inc.* Dec. 1995: 54. Print.

Prince, Greg W. "Little Giants." *Beverage World* Dec. 1994: 26. Print.

Reid, Peter V. K. "The Dark Prince: Master of the 'Unholy' Art of Contract Brewing." *Modern Brewery Age* 10 Sep. 1990: 38. Print.

—*Mari Rich*

Robert K. Kraft

Born: June 5, 1941
Occupation: Chairman and CEO of the Kraft Group, owner of the New England Patriots

Though not as widely recognized as Jerry Jones, the high-profile owner and general manager of the Dallas Cowboys, Robert K. Kraft has established himself as one of the most influential figures in the National Football League (NFL). In 1994, against the wishes of several close advisors, Kraft acquired the New England Patriots for $172 million, then the highest sum ever paid for a professional sports franchise. Prior to the purchase, the Patriots had been considered one of the NFL's worst teams and one of the league's least profitable franchises: during the four seasons leading up to the acquisition, they had compiled a league-worst 14–50 record and had finished dead last in revenue and attendance during that time. Undaunted, Kraft vowed

Courtesy of Rob Carr/Getty Images

to bring home a championship to New England, and, using the business acumen he had developed while building the Kraft Group, his paper-and-packaging empire, he made good on that pledge. The Patriots reached their second Super Bowl in his third year of ownership—their first appearance had occurred in 1985, when they were trounced by the Chicago Bears. The franchise captured its first-ever Super Bowl title in 2001 and then added back-to-back Super Bowl victories in 2003 and 2004.

Since Kraft became the owner of the Patriots, the team has won more Super Bowl titles (3) and made more Super Bowl appearances (5) than any other NFL team. They have also won more regular-season games (180, entering the 2011 season), playoff games (17), division championships (10), and conference championships (5) than any other team in the league. Now one of the most valuable sports franchises in the world, with an estimated value of $1.4 billion, the Patriots are the crown jewel of Kraft's business empire. The Kraft Group, his Massachusetts-based diversified holding company, was founded in 1998 and also includes the paper-and-packaging giant Rand-Whitney, the wood-products manufacturer International Forest Products, the New England Revolution soccer team, and Gillette Stadium. Bob McNair, the owner of the NFL's Houston Texans, told Bob Hohler for the *Boston Globe* (January 30, 2005), "The thing about Bob's success is, he's a long-term thinker who is able to maintain an objective viewpoint in a very emotional business. He has the discipline to not get carried away by the emotion of chasing a short-term fix and hurting the long-term position of his team or the league. A lot of people don't have that discipline." Kraft has attributed much of his success to his employees. He explained to Leonard Shapiro for the *Washington Post* (January 27, 2004), "You hire the best people you can find, hold them accountable, be available for big picture things and let them do it day to day. I always try to find people who are smarter than I am and let them do their job."

EARLY LIFE AND EDUCATION

Robert Kenneth Kraft was born on June 5, 1941 in the Boston suburb of Brookline, Massachusetts. The middle of three children, he was raised in an Orthodox Jewish family. Kraft's father, Harry, owned a small dressmaking business in the Chinatown section of Boston and was a lay leader at the Kehillath Israel synagogue in Brookline. The family struggled financially because of Harry's insistence on giving more than he could afford to charity, coupled with his unwillingness to press those who owed him money. Still, Kraft feels that his parents provided him with a strong foundation in life. "I was blessed to have a strongly spiritual and loving family," he told Richard Kindleberger for the *Boston Globe* (December 19, 1993). "Money can't buy it, nothing can buy it, that sense of family love, and also discipline."

Kraft grew up just three blocks from Braves Field, then the home of baseball's Boston Braves. An avid fan, he sold programs at the ballpark and collected money for the Jimmy Fund for pediatric cancer care before the games. In 1953 the Braves moved to Milwaukee, Wisconsin, and Kraft, then 12 years old, was heartbroken. "A piece of me died that day," he recalled to Jill Lieber for *USA Today* (January 21, 1997). "I cried forever."

While attending Brookline High School, Kraft considered trying out for the school's football team but was discouraged from doing so by his father, who believed sports would interfere with his Hebrew studies and prevent him from observing the Sabbath. Kraft complied with his father's wishes. "My father was the most important person in my life," he told Lieber. "He'd say, 'Whenever you get too high on yourself, go down to the beach and look out over the vast ocean. Then, pick up a handful of sand and realize that one grain is all you are in the space of time. Then, he'd say, 'When you go to bed at night, make sure the people you came in contact with are richer for it.'"

The president of his senior class, Kraft graduated from Brookline in 1959 and received an academic scholarship to Columbia University in New York City. There, he finally found his way onto the football field, joining the school's lightweight intramural league. He proved to be a standout and lettered as a running back and safety. He also remained active in student politics and served as president of his class. Upon graduating in 1963, he entered Harvard Business School in Boston. In June of that year he married the former Myra Hiatt, the daughter of the prominent Worcester industrialist and philanthropist Jacob Hiatt. In 1965 the newly-wed Kraft earned a master's degree in business administration and began a brief stint on Wall Street.

CAREER

Kraft, however, was quickly persuaded by his wife to join Rand-Whitney, her father's paper-and-packaging company. Despite initially butting heads with his father-in-law over business matters, Kraft ultimately developed a good relationship with the older man. In 1968 he acquired half of the company from Jacob Hiatt in a leveraged buyout, and four years later, he bought the remaining half. Kraft subsequently founded International Forest Products, which manufactures, markets, and distributes such commodities as containerboard, pulp, lumber, specialty papers, and biofuel. Collectively, Rand-Whitney and International Forest Products now comprise the nation's largest privately held paper-and-packaging company. Both fall under the umbrella of the Kraft Group, a diversified holding company that Kraft founded in 1998; the group has more than 5,000 employees and conducts business in more than 80 countries. In addition to its paper and packaging enterprises, the group focuses on real estate and private equity investment, sports and entertainment, and philanthropy.

Kraft's history with the New England Patriots dates back to 1971, the year the team changed its name from the Boston Patriots and found a permanent home at Schaefer Stadium in Foxboro, Massachusetts. (The Boston Patriots had been founded in 1959 as part of the American Football League and had played in various venues, including Nickerson Field, Fenway Park, Alumni Stadium, and Harvard Stadium.) In 1971 Kraft, although not yet enjoying great financial success, began purchasing season tickets for himself and his sons at Schaefer Stadium. (The venue was renamed Sullivan Stadium in 1983 and then Foxboro Stadium in 1990.) Sometimes they snuck in friends to accompany them, cramming eight or nine boys into six seats. While the Patriots were perennial losers during those early years, Kraft remained a diehard fan. "I used to sit on those benches," he recalled to Monte Burke for *Forbes* (September 19, 2005), "and dream about what I would do if I owned the team."

In 1975 Kraft purchased the Boston Lobsters of World Team Tennis (WTT), a nascent professional tennis league founded by the legendary player Billie Jean King. The co-ed organization enjoyed modest success, thanks to Kraft's heavy investment in such international stars as Martina Navratilova, but folded after only a few years. (It reformed in 1981.) Kraft later made unsuccessful bids to buy both the Boston Red Sox and the Boston Celtics. Nevertheless, his "first love was always the Patriots," as he told Burke. "I knew it would be a long shot. I mean, what are the odds of owning a team in your hometown?" Although it seemed a far-fetched dream, even to him, Kraft began positioning himself to own the team in 1985, when he bought a 10-year option on the property surrounding Foxboro Stadium. Then, in 1988, he and a partner, the mall developer Steve Karp, purchased the stadium itself and its lease agreement for $25 million in bankruptcy court. (Kraft would buy out Karp five years later.)

The Remington razor tycoon Victor Kiam also made headlines in 1988, when he bought the Patriots for $87 million from the team's original owner, the Boston businessman Billy Sullivan. Financial difficulties forced Kiam to sell the team in 1992 to St. Louis businessman James Busch Orthwein, the great-grandson of Anheuser-Busch founder Adolphus Busch.

PATRIOTS OWNER

In January 1994 Kraft purchased the Patriots from Orthwein for a then-record sum of $172 million. (That record was surpassed only months later, when former Hollywood producer Jeffrey Lurie purchased the Philadelphia Eagles for $194 million.) Many observers, including members of his own family, thought the purchase was a foolish one, particularly because Orthwein, who had toyed with the idea of moving the team to St. Louis, had offered him a $75 million buy-out to abandon his bid shortly before the deal closed. But, Kraft recalled to Bob Hohler, "This was my dream, my roots. If your family is important to you, then community assets are important to you, and I've always believed that sports teams bind a community together like nothing else."

The steep price Kraft paid for the Patriots puzzled many NFL insiders, as the team was just finishing one of the worst four-year stretches in its already dismal history, with a league-worst 14–50 record and a lackluster .219 winning percentage. One of Kraft's first moves was to spearhead a marketing campaign that promised to bring home a championship to New England. Fans immediately responded to the new owner's optimism and enthusiasm. Season ticket sales rose dramatically, and by the first game of the 1994 season, every game had been sold out, marking the first time in franchise history that such a feat had been accomplished.

Kraft became a regular presence at the stadium, often riding a golf cart before home games to interact with fans. The Patriots have sold out every home game since the 1994 season, and currently have one of the longest waiting lists for season tickets among all NFL teams, with approximately 60,000 names and a projected 50-year wait time.

In addition to a rejuvenated fan base, under Kraft's leadership the Patriots experienced one of the most dominating runs in sports history. During his first year of ownership, the team earned their first playoff berth in seven years; they reached their second-ever Super Bowl in his third year before losing to the Green Bay Packers, 35–21, in Super Bowl XXXI (1996). Following that loss, Bill Parcells, then the team's head coach, left to coach the New York Jets. (It has been reported that Kraft often clashed with Parcells, a legendary yet cantankerous two-time Super Bowl-winning coach, over player decisions.) Kraft then hired Pete Carroll, who had spent the previous two seasons as defensive coordinator of the San Francisco 49ers. Carroll spent three seasons coaching the Patriots, helping the team win an AFC East title (1997) and earn two playoff berths (1997 and 1998).

In 2000 Kraft took one of the biggest risks of his career when he replaced Carroll with Bill Belichick, a longtime assistant of Parcells who had formerly served as head coach of the Cleveland Browns. Belichick, who had earned a reputation for being a difficult but brilliant coach, had been slotted to succeed Parcells as head coach of the New York Jets but resigned from the team only one day into his tenure to accept the Patriots' offer. (Belichick famously scrawled his resignation on a sheet of paper right before he was supposed to be introduced at a press conference as the Jets' coach.) In return for Belichick, the Patriots gave up their first-round draft choice to the Jets. For Kraft, the move proved to be one of the most fruitful of his career. On February 3, 2002 the team won Super Bowl XXXVI with an upset victory over the high-flying St. Louis Rams, 20–17. The season was also notable for the emergence of second-year quarterback Tom Brady, an otherwise unheralded sixth-round draft pick who had stepped in to replace injured starting quarterback Drew Bledsoe. Brady went on to lead the Patriots to an 11–5 record and AFC East title, en route to the Super Bowl, in which he was named the game's Most Valuable Player (MVP). At the end of the season Foxboro Stadium was demolished and replaced by a new state-of-the-art facility, Gillette Stadium. (The Boston-based Gillette Company had purchased the naming rights.)

Since the 2001 season, the Patriots have enjoyed unprecedented success, and Bill Belichick and Tom Brady have formed one of the greatest coach-quarterback tandems in league history. Entering the 2011 season, the Patriots had won more games (135, including the postseason), more conference championships (4), and more

Super Bowl titles (3) than any other team in the NFL during that span. The Patriots added back-to-back Super Bowl titles in 2003 and 2004, with victories over the Carolina Panthers and Philadelphia Eagles, in Super Bowls XXXVIII and XXXIX, respectively. In 2007 they returned to the Super Bowl for the fourth time in seven seasons but were upset by the New York Giants, 17–14. Still, that year the Patriots won a franchise-record fifth consecutive AFC East title after becoming the first team in league history to compile a perfect 16–0 record during the regular season.

From 2003 to 2007 the Patriots won an impressive 77 games, the most by any team during a five-year span in league history. They also set several records for consecutive wins, including the record for the longest winning streak in league history—21 consecutive games (including three playoff games) from October 2003 to October 2004. In November 2011 Bill Belichick and Tom Brady surpassed Hall of Famers Don Shula and Dan Marino of the Miami Dolphins for the most regular-season wins (117) of any coach-quarterback duo in history.

Much of the Patriots' success has been attributed to Kraft's leadership and his business model for the franchise. The team is now worth nearly $1.4 billion, making it one of the most valuable sports franchises in the world. Kraft belongs to several of the league's most important committees, including the NFL Network committee and the finance committee, and he chairs the broadcast committee. As a member of the NFL's labor committee, he was recently lauded for helping to settle the 2011 NFL lockout.

OTHER VENTURES

In addition to the Patriots, Kraft owns the New England Revolution, a team with Major League Soccer (MLS), a top-flight professional league consisting of teams from both the United States and Canada. He has owned the team since MLS's inception in 1996. He also sponsors the Israeli Football League (IFL), an American-style league that was founded in the summer of 2005. Both the Patriots and Revolution play their home games at Gillette Stadium, a privately financed $325 million sports facility that opened in 2002, after the demolition of the Foxboro Stadium. The first major real estate project of the Kraft Group, the high-tech stadium has a seating capacity of 68,756 and features 6,000 club seats and 87 luxury suites. In 2007 the Kraft Group developed the area surrounding the stadium into a "lifestyle and entertainment center" called Patriot Place. The 1.3 million-square-foot space includes several boutiques and restaurants, a four-star hotel, and a movie theater.

Kraft holds board memberships with Viacom, the Federal Reserve Bank of Boston, and the Dana-Farber Cancer Institute, and he also serves as a trustee emeritus of Columbia University and as a trustee of Boston College. He has received honorary degrees from a number of academic institutions, and in October 2011 he was inducted into the American Academy of Arts and Sciences. A dedicated philanthropist, he supports the Boys & Girls Clubs of Boston, the Boston Symphony Orchestra, Children's Hospital Boston, and the United Way of Massachusetts, among many other such causes.

On July 20, 2011, Kraft's wife of nearly 48 years, Myra, who was also known for her philanthropic activities, died after a long battle with cancer. The couple had four sons: Jonathan, Daniel, Josh, and David.

SUGGESTED READING

Burke, Monte. "Unlikely Dynasty." *Forbes* 17 Sep. 2005: 122. Print.

Hohler, Bob. "Patriots' Kraft Has Led Winning Drive." *Boston Globe* 30 Jan. 2005: A01. Print.

Kindleberger, Richard. "The Family Man." *Boston Globe* 19 Dec. 1993: A01. Print.

Lieber, Jill. "Kraft's Loyalty Pays Off for Patriots, Fans." *USA Today* 21 Jan. 1997: C01. Print.

Shapiro, Leonard. "Owners Put Great Deal into Super Bowl Run." *Washington Post* 27 Jan. 2004: D03. Print.

—*Christopher Cullen*

Getty Images

Petra Kvitova

Born: March 8, 1990
Occupation: Tennis player

On July 2, 2011 the twenty-one-year-old Czech tennis player Petra Kvitova (kuh-VIT-uh-vah) defeated the celebrated Maria Sharapova of Russia in a 6–3, 6–4 upset at Wimbledon to win her first Grand Slam title. Kvitova is only the third left-handed female player to triumph in that contest since the first women's singles competition was held at Wimbledon, in 1884. (The second woman was the Czech-born Martina Navratilova—Kvitova's idol since childhood—who won the first of her nine Wimbledon championships in 1978 and the last in 1990, a few months after Kvitova's birth.) The six-foot-tall Kvitova "found the near-perfect mix of power, spin and patience to blow Maria Sharapova off Centre Court in a curiously uneven Wimbledon final, and announce what might be a new age in women's tennis," Kevin Mitchell wrote for the *London Observer* (3 July 2011). "She is not an elegant player, but she hits with purpose." "There's no secret to Petra Kvitova's powerful serve, which is one of the best on the tour," Katrina Adams wrote for *Tennis* (July/Aug. 2011). "Her motion is simple and her mechanics straightforward—and

that's all you need for a great serve. Her stance is wide and relaxed, and her balance is excellent."

Kvitova was coached only by her father, a recreational tennis player, until 2006, the year she turned professional. On October 16 of that year, she ranked 778th in the world. A year later, her rank had jumped to 214th. She was seeded 57th on October 13, 2008; 55th on October 12, 2009; 31st on October 11, 2010; and eighth when she faced Sharapova at Wimbledon. According to Kevin Mitchell, writing for the *London Guardian* (3 July 2011), she is "getting better faster than anyone in the game." As of October 24, 2011, the Women's Tennis Association (WTA) ranked Kvitova third, behind Caroline Wozniacki of Denmark and Sharapova. On that date she ranked first among women in prize money for the year, with $3,395,943.

EARLY LIFE

The daughter of Jiří Kvita and his wife, Pavla Kvitová, Petra Kvitova was born on March 8, 1990, in Bilovec, in the Moravian-Silesian region of eastern Czech Republic. (Her surname appears without an accent in English-language sources.) She grew up with her two brothers, Jiří and Libor, in the nearby town of Fulvek, which has about six thousand residents and four tennis courts. Her father, a former schoolteacher who is now Fulvek's deputy mayor, began to play tennis with her when she was of preschool age. Later she often practiced after school for an hour or two with her brothers and on weekends with her parents. "Until I was nine I was probably the best but then I was third or fourth in my age group," she told an interviewer for the *Liverpool (UK) Daily Echo* (4 July 2011). When she was sixteen she moved to Prostejov, a small city about two hours distant from Fulvek by car, whose facilities include a national Czech tennis center and a well-known hotel tennis club. "My parents encouraged me to move, because I didn't have any sparring partners" except for members of her family, Kvitova told Kevin Mitchell for the *London Guardian*. In Prostejov she has sometimes volleyed with the Czech champion Tomas Berdych.

TURNING PRO

After Kvitova won several championships in the Czech Republic, an instructor encouraged her to pursue tennis as a career. She turned professional in 2006. That year she won two singles titles on the International Tennis Federation (ITF) circuit, which holds tournaments for young tennis players. In 2007 she won four singles titles on the ITF circuit and played her first WTA main draw, at the Nordea Nordic Light Open, where she lost in the first round to Marta Domachowska. In 2008 Kvitova defeated Anabel Medina Garrigues in the first round of the WTA Tour Open Gaz de France; she lost to Elena Dementieva in the second round. In the first round of the 2008 WTA Cellular South Cup, she triumphed against the four-time Wimbledon champion Venus Williams in a 2–6, 6–4, 6–3 upset. "In the first set, I didn't believe [I could win]," Kvitova told Ron Higgins for the Memphis, Tennessee, *Commercial Appeal* (27 Feb. 2008). "I was very nervous. [Williams] is a great champion." "She hit some really good shots," Williams said of Kvitova to Higgins. "Her serve kept me off-balance. I missed on a lot of shots that I normally hit. She's a good young player." During the second round of that tournament, Kvitova was defeated by Alla Kudryavtseva.

Later in 2008 Kvitova won a singles set against Kateryna Bondarenko during the first round of WTA Internationaux de Strasbourg. She lost in the second round to Ai Sugiyama. During that year's French Open, she beat Akiko Morigami, Samantha Stosur, and Agnes Szavay in the first, second, and third rounds, respectively; Kaia Kanepi defeated her in the fourth round. She beat Sorana-Mihaela Cirstea and Martina Müller in the first and second rounds, respectively, of the WTA Budapest Grand Prix, where she lost to Andreja Klepac in the quarterfinals. She won against Alisa Kleybanova in the first round of the WTA East West Bank Classic before losing to Melanie South in the second round. After defeating Aiko Nakamura in the first round of the WTA Rogers Cup, Kvitova lost to Ana Ivanovic in the second round. In the WTA Zurich Open she was victorious against Patty Schnyder and Sofia Arvidsson in the first and second rounds,

respectively; she then lost to Ana Ivanovic in the quarterfinals. During the WTA Generali Ladies Linz, Kvitova defeated Tamira Paszek in the first round and lost to Marion Bartoli in the second round. She earned $218,750 in prize money in 2008. Since that year David Kotyza has coached her, and Jozef Ivanko has served as her fitness trainer.

WINS FIRST CAREER TITLE

In 2009 Kvitova won her first career title, at the WTA Tour Moorilla Hobart International, where she topped Iveta Benesova, 7–5, 6–1. Benesova, too, is Czech, and her coach is Kotyza; Kvitova and Benesova are friends and roomed together during the Hobart competitions. In the 2009 WTA BNP Paribas Open, Kvitova defeated Pauline Parmentier and Benesova in the first and second rounds, respectively, then lost to Vera Zvonareva in the third round. She beat Sybille Bammer in the first round of the 2009 WTA Mutua Madrilena Madrid Open, then lost in the second round to Francesca Schiavone. Also in 2009 Kvitova advanced to the second rounds of three WTA events: the Tour Collector Swedish Open, the ECM Prague Open, and the Banka Koper Slovenia Open. She progressed to the fourth round of the 2009 U.S. Open, where she was defeated by Yanina Wickmayer. In the 2009 WTA Generali Ladies Linz, she advanced to the finals, where she again lost to Wickmayer. During the 2009 season she earned $259,301 in prize money.

2010

During the 2010 Australian Open, Kvitova defeated Jill Craybas in the first round, then lost to Serena Williams in the second round. In the 2010 Fed Cup World Group First Round, she defeated Andrea Petkovic and then lost to Anna-Lena Groenefeld in the second round. She later advanced to the semifinals of the 2010 WTA Regions Morgan Keegan Championships & the Cellular South Cup, where she lost to Maria Sharapova. Also in 2010 Kvitova made it to the second rounds of the WTA BNP Paribas Open, the WTA Sony Ericsson Open, and the WTA Internazionali BNL d'Italia. After winning against Sorana Cirstea, Jie Zheng, Victoria Azarenka, Caroline Wozniacki, and Kaia Kanepi, she advanced to the semifinals at the 2010 Wimbledon tournament, where she was defeated once again by Serena Williams. "I didn't have many chances to win," Kvitova recalled to Kate Battersby for the website *Wimbledon* (2 July 2011). "Serena played so well. I was young and I didn't think that I could beat her." At the 2010 US Open, Kvitova lost to Kim Clijsters in the third round. She was defeated by Caroline Wozniacki in the third round of the 2010 WTA Tour China Open. During the 2010 season she won the

WTA Newcomer of the Year Award and earned $647,508 in prize money.

2011

In 2011 Kvitova won her second career title, when she defeated Andrea Petkovic in the final round of the WTA Brisbane International. At that year's Australian Open, she advanced to the quarterfinals, where she was defeated by Vera Zvonareva. In the second round of the women's doubles at that competition, she and her partner, Michaella Krajicek, lost to Nathalie Grandin and Vladimira Uhlirova. Kvitova earned her third career title by defeating Kim Clijsters in the final round of the WTA Open GDF Suez; along the way, in the quarterfinals, she bested Yanina Wickmayer. At the WTA Mutua Madrilena Madrid Open, Kvitova won her fourth career title, beating Victoria Azarenka of Belarus in the final round, 6–1, 3–6, 6–2. Kvitova, Christopher Clarey wrote for the *New York Times* (30 June 2011), "was an irresistible force" against Azarenka. "With the net on Centre Court dividing them, the left-handed Kvitova and the right-handed Azarenka were like 21-year-old mirror images with their long legs, bare shoulders, braided ponytails and all-white ensembles. But Kvitova, with more natural power and the bigger serve, is better on grass. She simply had too much for the fourth-seeded Azarenka, who was repeatedly left lunging for shots in the corners and sometimes missing completely as her visage darkened. . . . Kvitova made good use of her left hand to slice wide serves into Azarenka's two-handed backhand and generate— in her hot moments—brutally effective depth. . . . Kvitova was relentless once she took command of a rally from inside the baseline." Clarey also noted that Martina Navratilova, who congratulated Kvitova after the match, "has been one of Kvitova's strongest advocates." As a result of that win, Kvitova made it into the top ten of the WTA Tour ranking for the first time. During the 2011 French Open, she advanced to the fourth round, where she was defeated by Li Na. She advanced to the final round of the 2011 WTA Aegon International, where she lost to Marion Bartoli.

In 2011 Kvitova became the first left-handed player to reach a Wimbledon women's singles final since Navratilova, in 1990. (The British lefty Ann Jones won that event in 1969.) At that competition, held at London's All England Lawn Tennis and Croquet Club from June 20 to July 3, 2011, Kvitova won her first Grand Slam title, by defeating Maria Sharapova in the final round. "Competing in her first Grand Slam final, the twenty-one-year-old Kvitova didn't play her best tennis of the Wimbledon fortnight," Liz Clarke wrote for the *Washington Post* (2 July 2011). "But she didn't have to against Sharapova, whose quest for a fourth major title, and her first since undergoing shoulder surgery in 2008, was undercut by her erratic serve. . . . But what was more notable about the match than the standard of play was Kvitova's emergence as a steely challenger with the mental strength that women's tennis has lacked in recent years, apart from Venus and Serena Williams and Sharapova." In her contest with Sharapova (who was the Wimbledon winner in 2004, when she was seventeen), Kvitova recalled to Kate Battersby, "I was like I am before a normal match. I was surprised how I was feeling on court because I was focused only on each point and each game, and not on the final and the medal. Sometimes my serve wasn't so good, so I had to keep mentally good. I knew I had to be the first one to play hard, and I had to make the points. I did that." Sharapova said of Kvitova to Christine Brennan for *USA Today* (2 July 2011), "She was hitting really powerful and hitting winners from all over the court. She made a defensive shot into an offensive one. . . . I think she was just more aggressive than I was, hit deeper and harder, and got the advantage in the points."

"Kvitova's game is mature beyond her 21 years, but off the court, she is innocence personified," Karen Crouse wrote for the *New York Times* (2 July 2011). "She giggled and blushed her way through" the news conference held after her Wimbledon victory "while absently twirling strands of her long hair around her index finger." "Some human qualities shine through language barriers," Kate Battersby wrote for the Wimbledon website article. "Petra Kvitova's English may not yet quite be the equal of her tennis, but no matter—sweetness is her first language." "I don't think I'm a star, I just want to stay normal," Kvitova said, according to the *Liverpool Daily Echo* (4 July 2011). "I don't want to change."

Kvitova lost in five tournaments in August and September 2011: the US Open, the Western and Southern Financial Group, the Rogers Cup, the Toray Pan Pacific, and the China Open. According to Douglas Robson, writing for *ESPN Go* (29 Aug. 2011), "Players rarely follow up their maiden major with immediate Slam hardware." "When I won Wimbledon I felt a sort of pressure, of course," Kvitova told him. "Yeah, maybe it's a little bit of this." She also said, "Everything [is in] the head. If you are thinking on the court negatively, it's bad." On October 16, 2011, Kvitova won her fifth title of the year, at the Generali Ladies Linz, by defeating Dominika Cibulkova, 6–4, 6–1. "I was fighting for every point this week," she said, as quoted on the website *WTA Tennis* (16 Oct. 2011). "The semifinal with Jelena [Jankovic] was tough, but it was very nice tennis from both of us. I played my best at the end of it—it was a very good match. And the first set with Dominika was very close. I know how well she plays and I knew I had to play well to beat her." Kvitova's coach did not accompany her to the Linz competition. "I came here alone,"

Kvitova told the WTA interviewer. "I just wanted to enjoy every match and get some practice on indoor courts—that's it. I just wanted to have a free mind."

In her leisure time Kvitova enjoys watching movies and reading crime novels. She lives with her family in Fulvek and also maintains an apartment in Prostejov.

SUGGESTED READING

Crouse, Karen. "Crowning of Champion Is Changing of the Guard." *New York Times*. New York Times Co., 2 July 2011. Web. Jan. 2012.

Pucin, Diane. "Petra Kvitova Beats Maria Sharapova, Wins First Wimbledon Title." *Los Angeles Times: Sports*. Los Angeles Times, 2 July 2011. Web. Jan. 2012.

Robson, Douglas. "Kvitova Looks Like a Grass-Court Natural in Capturing Wimbledon." *USA Today: Tennis*. Gannett Co., 4 July 2011. Web. Jan. 2012.

White, Jim. "Wimbledon 2011: Victory for Petra Kvitova over Maria Sharapova in Final Is All Too Much for Father Jiri." *Telegraph* [London]. Telegraph Media Group, 3 July 2011. Web. Jan. 2012.

—Joanna Padovano

Getty Images for Park City Live

Talib Kweli

Born: October 3, 1975
Occupation: Musician and poet

Talib Kweli came into the underground hip-hop scene in a major way in 1998 with the release of the self-titled debut album of the hip-hop duo Black Star, which consisted of Kweli and the rapper Mos Def. This album was a big hit with critics and fans of "conscious" hip-hop, a subgenre of rap that strives to send out thoughtful life messages and intentionally does not partake in the objectification of women and worship of wealth that is commonplace in much mainstream rap. After Mos Def went solo the following year, Kweli released an album in collaboration with DJ Hi-Tek, titled *Reflection Eternal* (2000). His true solo debut came in 2002, with the release of the album *Quality* (2002). The following year Kweli got a big boost to his career and reputation when world-famous rapper Jay-Z referenced him in the song "Moment of Clarity" on *The Black Album* (2003). Kweli's next album, *The Beautiful Struggle* (2004), caught some off guard because it featured more pop-sounding songs than his fans had grown to expect. Kweli went back to his "conscious" roots with the albums *Right About Now* (2005) and *Eardrum* (2007). In 2011 he released the album *Gutter Rainbows*, which, like most of his efforts, was popular with music critics and loyal fans but did not get him a gold record or mainstream recognition. Kweli has continued to attract more praise and respect than mass popularity. Also in 2011, for the first time in more than a decade, he started collaborating with Mos Def (Yasiin Bey) as Black Star. The duo's first live-televised appearance was on the comedy-news show *The Colbert Report*. Throughout his career, Kweli has featured a variety of guest musicians and producers on his albums, including Kanye West, Just Blaze, will.i.am, Norah Jones, Faith Evans, Mary J. Blidge, and the Neptunes.

EARLY LIFE AND EDUCATION

Talib Kweli Greene was born on October 3, 1975, in Brooklyn, New York, into a family of academics: His father taught sociology and his mother taught English. Talib (pronounced ta-LIB in Arabic or ta-LEEB in American English) means "seeker" or "student" in Arabic, and Kweli means "of truth" in Ghanian. Kweli has a younger brother, Jamal, who is a law professor. Before developing an interest in becoming a hip-hop performer, Kweli was drawn to acting and the written word. Starting in elementary school, he wrote poems, stories, and short plays. He was also passionate about baseball and set his sights on becoming a professional baseball player. In junior high school, he began writing hip-hop rhymes, primarily to make an impression on the "cool kids" in school.

In high school, at the age of fourteen, Kweli met Mos Def (born Dante Terrell Smith-Bey; known as Yasiin Bey as of 2011). By this point Mos Def was on his way to becoming a television actor, but he too was developing a passion for hip-hop. In an interview with Tavis Smiley on his National Public Radio show (19 Feb. 2003), Kweli recalled doing poetry readings with Mos Def: "We would be the only ones rapping. . . . We would be making rhymes and [moms would] be doing poems, but the content of our rhymes would always go with the poetry scene. And so we just started to gravitate toward each other, because we were both young poets/rappers."

STARTING OUT IN HIP-HOP

After graduating from high school, Kweli went on to study experimental theater at New York University (NYU). But before completing the program, he decided that he wanted to pursue music full time. After getting a job at Nkiru Books, the oldest African American–owned bookstore in Kweli's home borough of Brooklyn, Kweli dropped out of NYU and started steering his artistic efforts toward making hip-hop. Kweli and Mos Def would walk around the Greenwich Village neighborhood in Manhattan. In Washington Square Park they would watch and take part in impromptu rap sessions on the street.

In 1994 Kweli met DJ Hi-Tek (born Tony Cottrell). Hi-Tek, then a member of the rap group Mood, was very impressed with Kweli's skills and talent and asked him to appear on a few tracks on Mood's album *Doom* (1997). Also in 1997 Kweli and DJ Hi-Tek recorded the song "Fortified Love," which the Rawkus music label released on its compilation *Soundbombing* (1997). The song became somewhat of a hit in the underground hip-hop scene. The following year Kweli appeared on another compilation, the *Lyricist Lounge, Vol. 1* (1998).

ALBUMS AND GROWING RECOGNITION

In 1998 Kweli and DJ Hi-Tek asked Mos Def to join their group—they called it Black Star—and later that year they released their first album, *Mos Def and Talib Kweli are Black Star* (1998), on Rawkus records. The album soon gained acclaim from music fans, critics, and fellow hip-hop artists. In a review for *Entertainment Weekly* (23 Oct. 1998), Matt Diehl wrote, "This East Coast rap duo . . . makes its ties to hip-hop's roots clear by reinterpreting old-school classics. . . . [I]ts new-school energy, however, is anything but retro." In fact, most critics and fans saw so much promise in the album that they began to anticipate the next one. Writing for Allmusic.com, Jason Kaufman reflected that sentiment: "There's no slack evident in the tight wordplays of Def and Kweli as they twist and turn through sparse, jazz-rooted rhythms calling out for awareness and freedom of the mind. . . . Their wisdom-first

philosophy hits hard when played off their lyrical intensity, a bass-first production, and stellar scratching. . . . flawless tracks like the cool bop of 'K.O.S. (Determination)' and 'Definition' hint that Black Star is only the first of many brilliantly executed positive statements for these two street poets." But by the following year, Black Star was no more. Mos Def, perceived to be the more charming member of the group, released a solo album, *Black on Both Sides* (1999), and then went on to pursue his burgeoning acting career.

These circumstances led to the release of *Reflection Eternal* (2000), which Kweli made with DJ Hi-Tek under the group name Reflection Eternal. The name, as Kweli has explained in many interviews, comes from the book *Monument Eternal*, written by Alice Coltrane, the widow of the jazz legend John Coltrane. Kweli had read the book when he was in high school, and it made quite an impression on him. The group's name, Reflection Eternal, alludes to the fact that people are both a reflection of their ancestors and of their social and cultural environment. The album featured such songs as "Move Somethin'" and "The Blast," both of which became underground hits. The album generally received good notices, but what attracted even more attention were Kweli's live shows, where he got back to hip-hop basics, rapping songs from the album over straightforward beats and improvising some lines.

Kweli's first full-length solo album was *Quality* (2002), which featured many young rising stars of the hip-hop genre, most notably the up-and-coming rapper and producer Kanye West. Their collaboration spawned the song "Get By," which would become Kweli's biggest hit to date. Other producers who contributed to the album include Jay Dee, DJ Quik, Ayatollah, DJ Scratch, and Megahertz. Despite the variety of contributors, Kweli stayed on message, emphasizing the importance of a higher consciousness and social awareness. In the song "Stand to the Side," for example, he proclaims, "I wanna write the songs that right the wrongs." Mos Def appeared with Kweli on the song "Joy," about their children, and Black Thought, the lead emcee of the hip-hop group The Roots, appeared on the track "Guerilla Monsoon." Although the album did not sell exceptionally well, it was a big success with music critics and fans. It peaked at number six on the R & B Albums chart and at number twenty-one on the Billboard 200 chart. Writing for the *New York Times* (25 Nov. 2002), Kelefa Sanneh called the album a "great success."

It was the following year, in 2003, that Kweli got one of the greatest reviews of his career from the world-famous rapper Jay-Z. In a track on *The Black Album* (2003), Jay-Z rapped, "If skills sold, truth be told / I'd probably be, lyrically, Talib Kweli," suggesting that Jay-Z himself feels pressure to cater to the masses but admires

Kweli's abilities. Fans, rappers, and critics took note. And it was in this climate, soon after a great compliment from one of the best-known rappers of his generation, that Kweli released his sophomore record, *The Beautiful Struggle* (2004). The album was generally perceived as a mixed bag—full of successful beats and rhymes but also occasionally aimed at a wider audience in a way that was not entirely convincing. It appeared that, more than ever, Kweli had his eyes on the charts. The album featured such popular guest stars as Faith Evans, Mary J. Blidge, the Neptunes, and Kanye West. A reviewer for *Time Out* (29 Sep. 2004) pointed out that Kweli's second solo album "showcases more of his deeply conscious fare." Writing for the *Chicago Tribune* (11 Oct. 2004), Joshua Klein noted that some of Kweli's best lines on the album are "self conscious enough of Kweli's role as hip-hop's perpetual savior but plenty confident enough to deliver." With regard to the self-conscious lyrics, however, Rashod D. Ollison for the *Baltimore Sun* (11 Nov. 2004) observed: "Despite the interesting subject range, *Beautiful Struggle*, at times, feels a little calculated as Kweli goes out of his way to thwart preconceived notions about who he really is." In an interview with Ken Capobianco for the *Boston Globe* (8 Oct. 2004), Kweli explained the name of the album: "I disagree with people who say that the struggle is something that is ugly or bad because what makes it beautiful is the light at the end of it. And there always is a light, a way out, something for people to reach out for and hold on to, and that's what makes us appreciate the struggle more. Of course, it's hard, but there's a level of dignity that I see goes in with that hard work, and that's what makes everything all the more rewarding." *The Beautiful Struggle* peaked at number three on the R & B Albums chart and at number fourteen on the Billboard 200 chart.

Although Kweli's next album, *Right About Now* (2005), was dubbed a "mixed tape," it featured well-produced songs. There were some attempts at more radio play, like on the tracks "Rock On" and "Fly That Knot," but most were of the consciousness-raising sort Kweli was best known for: "Drugs, Basketball & Rap" took on those popular rappers who proudly sing about drugs and violence; "Supreme, Supreme," which features Mos Def, sent a positive message about taking charge of your life; and "Ms. Hill," about the former Fugees rapper/singer Lauryn Hill, asked Hill to come back to the music world. In a review that appeared in the *Chicago Tribune* (13 Dec. 2005), *Los Angeles Times* writer Soren Baker observed, "Talib Kweli extends his impressive credentials with another strong batch of songs that are as entertaining as they are thought-provoking." Ken Capobianco, in a review for the *Boston Globe* (30 Dec. 2005), pointed out that *Right About Now* is an improvement over Kweli's previous attempts at radio-friendly fare: "There's none of the overworked slickness that marred his last couple of works." Some tracks, Capobianco noted positively, "mix Kweli's cerebral word wizardry with party instincts." The praise from critics was nearly unanimous. In *New York* magazine (12 Dec. 2005), a young reviewer sang the album's praises: "There's no point in quoting one verse or chorus; they're all amazing. It's like grad school for rappers." Kweli's hard-core fans were also pleased, but the album did not sell as well as the previous one. *Right About Now*, according to Gail Mitchell writing for *Billboard* magazine (14 Jan. 2006), sold 40,000 copies in the first few weeks after its release, whereas his previous album, *The Beautiful Struggle*, sold 288,000 units by this time. Later that year Kweli released *Liberation* (2007), a nine-song, half-hour-long album released online and made available for free download. It features such tracks as "Engine Running," "What Can I Do," and "Over the Counter."

The year 2007 saw the release of two Kweli albums, *Eardrum* and *Focus*. Whereas *Focus* contained previously released songs and some rare tracks, *Eardrum* was a full, proper album of new material—and it was very well received. Most critics agreed that on *Eardrum* Kweli did not try to force his way into the mainstream and that his new effort was a strong one. For the album Kweli worked with such hip-hoppers as Madlib, Just Blaze, and will.i.am. He also featured the singer Norah Jones on the track "Soon the New Day," a sultry, soulful number. In a review for the *Baltimore Sun* (16 Aug. 2007), Rashod D. Ollison called the album "excellent." In an interview with Ollison, Kweli said, "Hip-hop's in a great place. . . . But so many people only pay attention to what's in the top 10, and there's much more than that. Hip-hop artists have much more to say than what you hear all day on the radio." When asked whether he anticipated *Eardrum* would be his long-awaited commercial breakthrough, he replied, "I never feel like that with my records, you know . . . I make music I want to hear. When it's out there, I have no control over how it's perceived." With regard to *Eardrum* in particular, Kweli added, "I want people to focus on the musicality as opposed to just focusing on the lyrics. . . . The record is more mature. I hope people get that." Wyclef Jean, who, like Lauryn Hill, was a member of the Fugees and later went on to have a solo career, praised the album in the pages of the *New York Times* (9 Dec. 2007). "Talib Kweli to me is hip-hop," he said. "'Eardrum' . . . is one of the most eclectic [albums] in hip-hop. The native tongue styles, the conscious rap, it's all there in Talib Kweli." His focus on the music paid off in terms of chart topping as well: *Eardrum* hit second on both the R & B Albums and Billboard 200 charts.

Following the release of *The Mceo Mixtape* (2008), Kweli put out yet another solid album, *Gutter Rainbows* (2011). The name, according to a statement on the artist's official webpage, comes from his childhood days, when he saw gutters in his native Brooklyn that were full of dirt, oil, and water—the combination of which made for a shining, beautiful rainbow. The title also serves as a kind of metaphor that combines both beautiful and grimy parts of childhood and life in general. The album features such tracks as "After the Rain," "So Low," "Wait for You," and the title track, "Gutter Rainbows." Writing for the *Chicago Tribune* (4 Feb. 2011), Allison Stewart observed that despite his many years in hip-hop, Kweli is "more influential than he is famous." Kweli made an effort to focus on live instrumentation for *Gutter Rainbows*, an album Stewart observed "has a rich, almost retro feel to it." In an interview with Stewart, Kweli reflected on the current state of hip-hop, particularly that of "conscious" or "progressive" hip-hop, and how it is both like and unlike the old days: "I feel like progressive hip-hop is actually at the forefront, way more popular than fake gangsta rap. It is not as culturally nationalistic as it was when I came in the business, though. It is more about defining a value system for a new hip-hop culture, rather than celebrating our parents' ideals. . . . The new generation of artists [is] more open-minded with their approach to music."

In 2011 Kweli and Mos Def (Yasiin Bey)announced that they would reunite as Black Star to release a mix-tape album inspired by the soul singer Aretha Franklin sometime in 2012. In 2011 Black Star performed several concerts and made a notable appearance on the Comedy Central television show *The Colbert Report*. Their songs "Fix Up" and "You Already Knew" were released as singles in 2011. Black Star performed the latter in January 2012 on *Late Night with Jimmy Fallon*.

PERSONAL LIFE

Kweli and his wife, DJ Eque, married in 2009. Kweli has two children from a previous relationship: Amani, a son, and Diyani, a younger daughter. In interviews Kweli has stated that although he no longer belongs to any particular religion, he considers himself a spiritual person and that, although some worthwhile lessons can come from religious teachings, he said he opposes the fundamentalist and divisive nature of religion.

SUGGESTED READING

Capobianco, Ken. "Kweli Takes on His Critics." *Boston Globe* 8 Oct. 2004, Arts sec.: C12.

Jean, Wyclef. "A Little Bit Country, a Little Bit Everything Else." *New York Times* 9 Dec. 2007, sec. 2: 37.

Kweli, Talib. "Rapper Talib Kweli Discusses His Career and New CD." *The Tavis Smiley Show*. Natl. Public Radio, 19 Feb. 2003. Print. Transcript.

Pareles, Jon. "Talib Kweli and Madlib." *New York Times* 8 Jan. 2007: E3.

Stewart, Allison. "You Might Not Know Talib Kweli—But You Should." *Chicago Tribune* 4 Feb. 2011: 9.

"Talib Kweli." *Year of the Blacksmith*. Blacksmith Music Company, n.d. Web. 11 May 2012.

—*Dmitry Kiper*

Mariusz Kwiecień

Born: November 4, 1972
Occupation: Operatic baritone

Mariusz Kwiecień is a leading baritone opera singer known not only for his powerful, captivating voice but also for his naturalistic acting and handsome features. He has performed the title roles in the operas *Eugene Onegin* and *Don Giovanni* and portrayed Marcello in *La bohème*, Almaviva in *The Marriage of Figaro*, and Malatesta in *Don Pasquale*, among other notable roles. After joining the youth training program of New York's Metropolitan Opera in 1999, he began to gain recognition for both his voice and his subtle acting ability, eventually receiving widespread critical attention. In addition to the Metropolitan Opera, he has performed with the Paris Opera, the Vienna State Opera, the San Francisco Opera, and various others. His first solo album, *Slavic Heroes*, was released in January 2012 to enthusiastic reviews.

EARLY LIFE AND EDUCATION

Mariusz Kwiecień was born on November 4, 1972, in Kraków, Poland, one of two children. His father sold auto parts and then became a taxi driver, and his mother worked as a nurse. Kwiecień's love of music developed early in life. He sang in a church choir, and his passion for Renaissance and baroque sacred music led him to compose madrigals for the group. Kwiecień also enjoyed dancing and writing poetry. Because of his promising vocal talent, friends and a music teacher encouraged him to apply to the conservatory in Kraków. He did, and he was accepted to its vocal program at the age of eighteen. His first passion for singing was not opera; he loved lieder, nineteenth-century German and Austrian classical songs typically accompanied by piano. However, hearing classmate Daniel Borowski perform opera proved to be a life-changing experience. "The color, power, and beauty of Borowski's voice just amazed me," Kwiecień told John von Rhein for the *Chicago Tribune* (23 Mar. 2008). "I thought that if a real operatic voice sounds like that, I wanted to have it." Following

Wirelmage

this revelation, Kwiecień moved to Warsaw to study opera at the Warsaw Academy.

In 1993 Kwiecień made his debut in the Kraków Opera's production of Henry Purcell's *Dido and Aeneas*. The following year he won first prize in the Duszniki-Zdrój International Competition in Poland. He won the Vienna State Opera and Hamburg State Opera prizes in the Hans Gabor/Belvedere Competition in Austria in 1996 and went on to win the Mozart Interpretation Prize and Audience Choice Award at the 1998 Francisco Viñas Competition in Barcelona, Spain. In 1999 Kwiecień was selected to represent Poland at the Singer of the World competition in Cardiff, Wales.

CAREER

In 1999 Kwiecień was invited to audition for New York City's Metropolitan Opera. At the audition, it became apparent that he was not going to receive an offer to join the company; he had difficulty understanding instructions due to his poor English, and his singing technique, though impressive, was still unpolished. He was instead offered a place in the Met's Lindemann Young Artist Development Program, in which he studied and sang for two years. "I came to America to show that I was ready for anything," Kwiecień told Matthew Gurewitsch for the *New York Sun* (18 July 2006), "and I discovered that I wasn't exactly what I thought. I didn't have the technique I thought I had. I didn't have the knowledge of styles. . . . And the Met protected me from singing too much too soon, as well as from roles that

would have been too heavy." From 1999 to 2003, he performed with the Metropolitan Opera more than thirty times, albeit in minor parts.

During the 2003 Met Chamber Ensemble series at Weill Recital Hall in New York, the largely unknown Kwiecień performed Maurice Ravel's Don Quixote song cycle, and New York opera critics began to take notice. A few days later he sang the role of Marcello in Giacomo Puccini's opera *La bohème*, and he returned to the role the following year in his debut with the San Francisco Opera. Writing for the *San Francisco Chronicle* (8 Jan. 2004), critic Steven Winn described the young baritone's performance: "Kwiecień commands attention whenever he's onstage. His lustrous, virile tone and rugged, wide-eyed good looks provide immediate appeal. But it's his instinct for the moment, a fine-tuned responsiveness and transparency, that makes his Marcello so real." At the end of 2004 Kwiecień performed Johann Sebastian Bach's *Ich habe genug* at the Weill Recital Hall, accompanied by a violinist and oboist, as part of a concert by the Met Chamber Ensemble.

The following year he sang the role of Count Almaviva in Wolfgang Amadeus Mozart's opera *The Marriage of Figaro*. In a review for the *New York Times* (5 Feb. 2005), Allan Kozinn noted that Kwiecień carried his role with a "balance of courtly gracefulness and earthiness." Kwiecień also played the part of Guglielmo in Mozart's *Così fan tutte*. Some critics considered those two Mozart opera performances to be his breakthrough, as they gained him more widespread attention among opera enthusiasts. In 2006 he sang the lead in Mozart's *Don Giovanni*, accompanied by the Boston Symphony Orchestra, and portrayed Dr. Malatesta in the Metropolitan Opera's production of Gaetano Donizetti's *Don Pasquale*, appearing alongside Russian soprano Anna Netrebko. The following year Kwiecień sang the role of Don Giovanni at the San Francisco Opera. Like some other opera critics, Joshua Kosman of the *San Francisco Chronicle* (4 June 2007) considered the production to be inconsistent, noting that it "kept shifting in and out of focus." The major exceptions to the inconsistency, however, were Kwiecień and the music director Donald Runnicles, "who alone seemed to have fully internalized the unholy energy that pulses through this opera."

Kwiecień opened the Met's 2007–08 season with his portrayal of Enrico in Donizetti's opera *Lucia di Lammermoor*. Reviews of the production were somewhat mixed, yet there was little debate about Kwiecień's performance, which was generally deemed superb. In a review for *Variety* (25 Sep. 2007), Eric Myers observed that Kwiecień's "incisive acting skills, rich voice, and attractive presence have turned him into a bit of a matinee idol among opera buffs." In December of 2007, Kwiecień returned to the

San Francisco Bay Area to perform a solo recital, which included a variety of songs by Ravel, Robert Schumann, and the Polish composer Mieczyslaw Karlowicz, at the University of California Berkeley's Hertz Hall. In an interview with Kosman for the *San Francisco Chronicle* (2 Dec. 2007), Kwiecień' described the challenges of a solo recital as opposed to a role in a big production: "In *Don Giovanni*, I come, I seduce, I go to my dressing room, I have a drink of water, I call a friend. Then I go back, I kill, I seduce. I only need this energy for short periods. . . . But in a recital, you start to give, and two hours later you're still giving. You have to be able to sell not only yourself but also the music and the poetry, all the time. It's very challenging to create this special energy between you and the audience."

When, in the spring of 2008, Russian baritone Dmitri Hvorostovsky had to leave a Lyric Opera of Chicago production of Pyotr Ilyich Tchaikovsky's opera *Eugene Onegin* halfway through the run, the company asked if Kwiecień' could take over the title role. Although he was also performing in Donizetti's *Lucia di Lammermoor* at the Metropolitan Opera and Vincenzo Bellini's *I puritani* at the Seattle Opera that season, Kwiecień' took on the part. Throughout 2009 and 2010, he performed in the United States and appeared in numerous productions in Europe.

In the fall of 2011 Kwiecień' took on one of the most prominent roles of his singing career, the lead in a production of *Don Giovanni* directed by the Tony Award–winning director Michael Grandage. By this point Kwiecień' was well known for his excellent portrayal of Don Giovanni, and with experience and age he had gained a deeper understanding of the role. "I did it for the first time nine years ago," he told Zachary Woolfe for the *New York Times* (9 Oct. 2011). "I thought then that Don Giovanni was a young, happy, powerful, strong guy with great looks, and basically he's going to hell because of his really great life. And that's half true. But now I come at it from an older point of view. He is young and full of energy, but not necessarily happy energy. He is really searching for excitement in his life. And excitement comes as death. The whole thing from the beginning is preparation for this death. Now it is not only youth but age and resignation and lots of looks behind: how it was and where I am going."

During a dress rehearsal on October 10, Kwiecień' was injured while performing a sword fight scene. It was not the first time he had been injured onstage; he had previously injured himself during a performance of *La bohème* in June 2011. Kwiecień' was taken to a nearby hospital, where he underwent surgery for a herniated disc in his back. Swedish baritone Peter Mattei took over the role for opening night and two subsequent performances, but

Kwiecień' returned to the stage two weeks after undergoing surgery. In a review for the *New York Times* (27 Oct. 2011), Anthony Tommasini wrote that Kwiecień''s "performance was a triumph of physical rehabilitation and artistic determination." Although Tommasini observed that Kwiecień''s voice was not fully recovered, he praised Kwiecień' for his performance and noted, "In rejoining the cast Mr. Kwiecień' brought the concept behind Mr. Grandage's tame, visually dreary production into better focus." His second performance, on October 29, was transmitted in high definition to movie theaters in more than forty countries, reaching an audience of more than two hundred thousand. Kwiecień' went on to perform the role of Belcore in the Metropolitan Opera production of Donizetti's *L'elisir d'amore* and appear in operas in Tokyo, Japan; Los Angeles, California; Santa Fe, New Mexico; and his native Kraków.

In addition to appearing onstage, Kwiecień' has recorded performances for a number of albums, including *A Night at the Opera* (2004), *Brahms: Ein Deutsches Requiem* (2008), and *Bel Canto Spectacular* (2009), and appeared in filmed productions of *Eugene Onegin* and several other operas. He released his first solo album, *Slavic Heroes*, in January 2012. The album features Kwiecień''s performances of operatic works by Eastern European composers such as Stanislaw Moniuszko, Tchaikovsky, and Bedřich Smetana. The Polish Radio Symphony Orchestra, conducted by Łukasz Borowicz, accompanies Kwiecień' on the album. *Slavic Heroes* received a great deal of praise, with critic Tim Ashley observing, in a review for the London *Guardian* (5 Jan. 2012), that the acting ability for which Kwiecień' is renowned comes through in the sound of his voice: "He has a remarkable ability to color his voice to suit each character, so that Borodin's Prince Igor, thinking of his wife on the eve of battle, sounds very different from Rachmaninov's Byronic Aleko, teetering on the edge of self-destruction." David Shengold, in a review for *Opera News* (1 Apr. 2012), noted the "impressive phrasing and beautiful tone" of Kwiecień''s voice, which "takes well to recording."

Kwiecień' resides in New York City and Kraków and also owns a house in the mountains outside Kraków. His hobbies include international travel and nature photography.

SUGGESTED READING

Kosman, Joshua. "Baritone Mariusz Kwiecień', 100 Percent Heart, to Sing in Berkeley." *San Francisco Chronicle* 2 Dec. 2007: N24.
___. "Splendor of *Giovanni* Too Short." *San Francisco Chronicle* 4 June 2007: E1.
Tommasini, Anthony. "Delayed By Injury, Giovanni Still Arrives." *New York Times* 27 Oct. 2011: C1.

___. "A Polish Prince Seizes the Stage." *New York Times* 2 Mar. 2008: AR27.

Von Rhein, John. "Kwiecien´ Brings Energy, Confidence to Onegin." *Chicago Tribune* 23 Mar. 2008: C6.

—*Dmitry Kiper*

Mourad Lahlou

Born: 1968
Occupation: Chef, restaurateur

Yearning for the traditional family meals he enjoyed while growing up in his native Morocco, chef Mourad Lahlou started cooking after traveling to the United States to attend college. In 1996, Lahlou and his brother Khalid opened a Moroccan restaurant called Kasbah in San Rafael, California. Despite a lack of formal culinary training, Lahlou became head chef of the restaurant. Kasbah featured standard Moroccan fare and decor and became an immediate success, earning a coveted three-star rating from the *San Francisco Chronicle*.

In 2001, after the lease for Kasbah expired, Lahlou and his brother closed down the restaurant to open Aziza, a modern Moroccan establishment named after their mother, in San Francisco's Richmond District. Like Kasbah, Aziza was quickly awarded a three-star rating by the *Chronicle*. The restaurant has also been awarded a Michelin star and has come to be regarded as one of the best Moroccan restaurants in North America.

Lahlou has risen to international prominence as an innovator of contemporary Moroccan cuisine. He is known for recreating traditional Moroccan recipes with the fresh local and seasonal ingredients of Northern California, as well as for a sensual cooking style that maximizes the distinct flavors and textures of each dish. Lahlou has constantly worked to adapt his style, experimenting with new modern techniques and ingredients in his efforts to evolve Moroccan cuisine and its often-misperceived food culture. His close friend Daniel Patterson, a celebrated chef and restaurateur who owns the two-Michelin-star-rated San Francisco restaurant Coi, told Samantha Schoech for *SF State Magazine* (Spring/Summer 2010, online), "What he has done brilliantly is bring his personal experience and cultural background together with a California sensibility."

An appearance on the Food Network's popular cooking competition show *Iron Chef America* in 2009 helped Lahlou rise to fame. He released his first cookbook, *Mourad: New Moroccan*, in the fall of 2011. Commenting on his philosophy on food and dining, he explained to

© Russell Yip/San Francisco Chronicle/Corbis

Antoinette Bruno for food magazine *StarChefs. com* (June 2007, online), "I think a chef should make people experience something they haven't experienced before. I want people who eat my food to taste the familiar and the foreign all at once. Dining isn't just about the food, it's about the entire experience."

EARLY LIFE AND EDUCATION

Mourad Lahlou was born in 1968 in Casablanca, the largest city in the North African country of Morocco. His mother, Aziza, originally from the ancient Moroccan city of Marrakech, had moved to Casablanca to marry his father. Lahlou's parents divorced just months after he was born, at which point his mother took him and his older brother, Khalid, back to her family home in Marrakech. He and his brother were raised in a sprawling twenty-room building in the old, walled part of the city known as the medina quarter. (Medina quarters are highly populated, car-free areas characterized by their narrow, winding streets, often featuring merchant shops and historical sites.)

Though Lahlou never saw his father again, he has recalled being spoiled with attention as a boy. "In Morocco, family is everything," he explains in *Mourad: New Moroccan*. "The idea of a kid growing up with only one parent isn't just a sad matter to cluck your tongue at. It's thought of as a tragedy, and when it happens people tend to overcompensate. I lost a dad, but when we moved into that beehive of a house, I gained a dozen parents—my uncles, aunts, great-grandmother, grandmother, and grandfather—who showered me with attention, love, and praise. And food."

Lahlou grew up immersed in Moroccan food culture and spent nearly every day of his childhood in the family kitchen. There, he watched and listened as his mother and other female family members meticulously prepared the day's meals while discussing the minutiae of everyday life. Although Moroccan men traditionally left the cooking to the women, Lahlou learned how to cook through observation. One of his biggest culinary influences was his mother, who fostered his love of food and taught him how to make traditional Moroccan specialties, recipes he would later recreate from memory.

Lahlou has cited his parents' divorce as a major factor in his learning how to cook. "Without the divorce, I truly believe I would be a failure as far as the cooking is concerned because I would not have spent that much time with my mom," he told Vicki Larson for the Marin County, California, *Marin Independent Journal* (14 Nov. 2011). "I would not have been able to rewind in my head and figure out what she was doing when she was cooking. I would not have had that perspective of how important making food was, even more important than actually eating food."

Growing up, Lahlou learned other valuable lessons about food from his grandfather, Hajj Ben Seddiq, a successful and well-respected textile business owner whom Lahlou has referred to as his lifelong idol. As a child, Lahlou accompanied his grandfather on trips to the local markets, where the two picked out fruits, vegetables, and spices to use in the family's midday meal—the biggest event of the day in Moroccan culture. Lahlou has said that his family would spend all of breakfast discussing the day's lunch menu, but that his grandfather would always be the one who determined it. In *Mourad: New Moroccan*, he describes his grandfather as "an executive chef" and says that their "treasure hunts in the market added up to a lifelong appreciation of raw materials and their possibilities." Later, as a chef, Lahlou became a strong proponent of local farmers' markets, visiting several Bay Area markets every week to hand select fresh organic produce.

Once Lahlou graduated high school, he planned to attend university in the Bordeaux region of France, where one of his aunts lived. He scored so well on the *baccalauréat*, the French academic qualification exam, that when he instead decided to study in the United States, he was immediately able to secure a student visa. In 1985, he traveled from Marrakech to San Francisco, California, to attend San Francisco State University (SF State), where his brother was already studying. "I was seventeen years old, I didn't speak a word of English, and, though I didn't realize it at the time, the first chapter of my life had ended," he recalls in *Mourad: New Moroccan.*

After taking six months of English classes, Lahlou enrolled at SF State to study economics. He shared an apartment with his brother in San Francisco's Richmond District and earned his half of the rent by working as a waiter at a nearby Moroccan restaurant called Mamounia, which had been established in the 1970s by the Moroccan food pioneers Mehdi and Said Ziani. One of the first Moroccan restaurants of its kind in the United States, Mamounia offered a basic five-course tasting menu and featured all the clichés of Moroccan food culture, from tented ceilings and cushioned seats to costumed waiters and scantily clad belly dancers. The restaurant helped usher in a wave of similarly themed Moroccan establishments across the country. Lahlou worked nights at Mamounia throughout college, and he ate there either before or after his shifts to help alleviate feelings of homesickness. However, he notes in *Mourad: New Moroccan* that the authentic flavors he grew homesick for "were nowhere to be found in that kitchen."

Lahlou's unsatisfying experiences eating at Mamounia eventually inspired him to start cooking for the first time. Frustrated with the substandard copycat dishes served there and at other Moroccan establishments and longing for the multicourse family lunches of his childhood, he started experimenting in the kitchen and working from memory to recreate his mother's traditional Moroccan recipes. "I was very homesick so I started cooking to feel more connected to home," he told Bruno. "It was cheap and a way for me to survive." By the time he completed his master's degree in economics from SF State in 1995, Lahlou had developed his culinary skills enough to host Moroccan dinner parties for his friends and professors, many of whom encouraged him to pursue a culinary career. Nonetheless, despite his growing seriousness about cooking, he still harbored plans to earn a doctorate in economics and ultimately hoped to return to Morocco to work as an economist for the World Bank or the International Monetary Fund (IMF).

CAREER

Lahlou's cooking career was largely set in motion by his brother, who persuaded him to put his doctoral plans on hold in order to help out with a Moroccan restaurant Khalid was opening in the San Francisco suburb of San Rafael. The two were forced to borrow money on twelve credit cards after turning away financiers who had hoped to perpetuate the same stereotypical Arabian theme of other Moroccan establishments. "I wasn't going to open a Moroccan Disneyland," Lahlou told Julia Moskin for the *New York Times* (5 Oct. 2011), "and I wasn't going to make Moroccan '70s hotel food."

After receiving some assistance from Mamounia's Said Ziani, the two brothers opened Kasbah in July 1996, with Mourad serving as head chef and Khalid running the front of the house. Situated in a pink freestanding building surrounded by palm trees, Kasbah featured many of the typical Middle Eastern trappings—tented rooms, Oriental rugs, low tables, and the occasional belly dancer—but with a modern, chic look. The restaurant also featured a menu of classic Moroccan dishes, most of which were made with newer local ingredients and a lighter touch. Guests, meanwhile, were provided with tableside hand washing before and after their meals and were encouraged to follow Moroccan tradition by eating everything with their hands.

Two months after Kasbah opened, *San Francisco Chronicle* food critic Michael Bauer awarded it three stars for excellence. In his review for the *Chronicle* (1 Sep. 1996), Bauer declared, "Kasbah is the type of restaurant that forces diners to put away all pretense and revel in the sensual aspects of dining." Kasbah received a flurry of other positive reviews, instantly becoming one of the most popular Moroccan restaurants in the San Francisco Bay Area. Bauer praised Lahlou for his "rich and rustic but clean" style of cooking, and in 1998, the *Chronicle* named him a "Rising Star Chef." Referring to his initial decision to take just a semester off before returning to school to pursue his PhD, Lahlou told Schoech, "The first day we opened we were so packed. And it just never let up. All the reviews were so good, I thought, OK, maybe I'll take two semesters off."

In 2001, following a successful five-year run, Lahlou and his brother closed Kasbah after their lease for the restaurant ran out. In November of that year, they opened another incarnation of the restaurant in San Francisco's Richmond District. Though the new restaurant was originally called Mosaic, the Lahlou brothers decided to change the name to Aziza as a way to honor their mother, who had suffered a minor heart attack just days before the restaurant's grand opening. At Aziza, Lahlou hoped to develop the innovative cooking style he had honed at Kasbah and planned to create a contemporary restaurant that would help evolve Moroccan cuisine—a vision that differed from that of his brother, who left the venture after a year.

The resultant menu for Aziza featured creative riffs on traditional Moroccan specialties, with a strong emphasis on lighter flavors brought out by the fresh, local ingredients of Northern California. The menu was complemented by an extensive wine list featuring bottles from around the world. Aziza opened to rave reviews and has since evolved from a casual Moroccan restaurant to an upscale fine dining establishment that specializes in modern, innovative cuisine. It has become one of the most renowned restaurants in the Bay Area. Among its most enthusiastic supporters is Bauer, who awarded the restaurant three stars in 2002 and then three and a half stars in 2009; every year since the restaurant's opening, Bauer has listed it in the *Chronicle*'s annual list of the top one hundred restaurants in the Bay Area. He wrote in his initial assessment of Aziza for the *Chronicle* (17 Feb. 2002), "A warm feeling infuses Aziza that can't be duplicated by most restaurants," and in another blurb about the restaurant called it "by far the best Moroccan restaurant in the city" (13 Apr. 2003).

Aziza offers a wide array of starters and entrees, as well as a multicourse tasting menu. It also features a list of artisan cocktails and a dessert menu designed by the award-winning pastry chef Melissa Chou. Nearly all of Aziza's offerings, from its breads and couscous to its condiments, spreads, and dips, are made in house. Lahlou has been known to make many of those offerings using cutting-edge culinary techniques, such as the sous-vide method, in which food is cooked in a vacuum-packed bag.

In March 2009, Lahlou put his culinary skills on full display when he appeared on the popular Food Network cooking show *Iron Chef America*. The show pits world-class guest chefs against resident "Iron Chefs" in a one-hour cooking competition centered on a secret ingredient. On the show, he defeated Greek American chef Cat Cora by a record-breaking margin. Lahlou, whose secret ingredient was redfish, recalled to Vicki Larson on another occasion, "It was really intense. It was hard. It's not something for everybody. You have to have a certain style and demeanor to be able to do it" (24 Feb. 2009, online).

The *Iron Chef* victory helped bring national attention to Aziza. In 2009, it was named one of the top ten Bay Area restaurants of the decade by the *Zagat* guide, and in 2010, it became the first Moroccan restaurant in North America to receive a star in the prestigious *Michelin Guide*. Aziza maintained its rating in 2011 and 2012. Lahlou himself has also received a number of culinary honors, including being named a *StarChefs.com* "Rising Star Chef" in 2007 and being selected as a semifinalist for the James Beard Award for Best Chef in the Pacific region in 2010, 2011, and 2012.

Lahlou's first cookbook, *Mourad: New Moroccan*, was published by Artisan Books in October 2011. The 389-page book, written in collaboration with food writers Susie Heller, Steve Siegelman, and Amy Vogler and featuring photography by Deborah Jones, chronicles Lahlou's journey as a chef and provides an overview of Moroccan cuisine and culture. It also includes detailed recipes for many of the inventive dishes served at Aziza. Moskin called Lahlou's book a "personal, idiosyncratic work that flows mostly from two small rooms: his family's kitchen in

Marrakesh and his own in San Francisco." Lahlou explained to Larson that in writing the book, he did not "want to dumb down the food. Once you just do it and try to understand it, then it becomes second nature. This is food for the family. They're not there to judge you. It's the journey that matters." He has filmed a PBS companion series to the book that focuses on both traditional and modern Moroccan cuisine. He told Schoech, "It's a bridge between Morocco and what I'm doing at Aziza, showing there is a link, it's not arbitrary."

PERSONAL LIFE
Lahlou lives in the Bay Area and has been romantically linked to Farnoush Deylamian, an SF State alumna and the general manager of Aziza. Thin and fit, he sports a signature shaved head to honor his grandfather, who passed away in 1999, and is covered in jet-black tattoos, all of which signify important moments in his life. He is fluent in Arabic, French, Moroccan, and English and semi-fluent in Spanish.

SUGGESTED READING
Bruno, Antoinette. "Chef Mourad Lahlou." *StarChefs.com.* StarChefs, June 2007. Web. 19 Dec. 2011.

Gold, Amanda. "Aziza's Chef Has Always Carved a Unique Path." *San Francisco Chronicle* 25 Oct. 2009: A1. Print.

Lahlou, Mourad, et al. *Mourad: New Moroccan.* New York: Artisan, 2011. Print.

Larson, Vicki. "Marin's Iron Chef: Sausalito's Mourad Lahlou Challenges Cat Cora on Food Network Show." *Marin Independent Journal.* MediaNews Group, 24 Feb. 2009. Web. 20 Mar. 2012.

---. "Memories of Youth Inspire Sausalito's Mourad Lahlou." *Marin Independent Journal* 14 Nov. 2011: Food section. Print.

Moskin, Julia. "One Pot, Two Directions." *New York Times* 5 Oct. 2011: D1. Print.

Schoech, Samantha. "Star Chef." *SF State Magazine.* San Francisco State University, Spring/Summer 2010. Web. 19 Dec. 2011.

—*Chris Cullen*

Miranda Lambert

Born: November 10, 1983
Occupation: Country-music singer, songwriter

By her early 20s, with such songs as "Kerosene" and "Gunpowder & Lead," Miranda Lambert had developed a reputation for writing and performing country songs about strong, tough-talking women who don't take kindly to being cheated on, abused, or otherwise disrespected.

Courtesy of Ethan Miller/Getty Images

Her first three albums—*Kerosene* (2005), *Crazy Ex-Girlfriend* (2007), and *Revolution* (2009)—have all reached platinum status, each selling a million or more copies. Lambert is also adored by many critics, who appreciate her mixing of pop and rock with country. She plays between 80 and 100 shows a year, all over the United States, and has opened for such country luminaries as Keith Urban, George Strait, Dierks Bentley, and Toby Keith. In 2011 Lambert married the country-music star Blake Shelton; released an album with her new group, Pistol Annies, called *Hell on Heels*; and brought out her fourth solo album, *Four the Record*. Will Hermes, writing for *Rolling Stone* (July 18, 2011, online), called Lambert "the most gifted woman to hit country's mainstream in a decade."

EARLY LIFE AND FAMILY
Lambert's father, Richard Lee ("Rick") Lambert, was serving as an officer with the Dallas Police Department and singing in a country-music group called Contraband when he met Lambert's mother, Beverly June ("Bev") Hughes, who was then a fitness instructor. Miranda Leigh Lambert was born on November 10, 1983, in Longview, Texas. She has a brother. Shortly after her birth the family moved to Van Alstyne, Texas, where her parents opened a detective agency, specializing in collecting evidence on cheating spouses. Unable to keep the business afloat, the Lamberts relocated again, to Lindale, Texas, a town of roughly three thousand people, when Miranda was six. There, living in a shabby house

and raising pigs, rabbits, goats, and chickens, they were "flat-out poor," as Rick Lambert recalled to Skip Hollandsworth for *Texas Monthly* (October 2011). Rick and Bev Lambert got a big break in 1997, when they were hired as detectives by the lawyers of Paula Jones, who had accused President Bill Clinton of having sexually harassed her when he was the governor of Arkansas. The Lamberts soon moved into a large home in Lindale, where, at the suggestion of a local minister, they began to take in battered women. Miranda Lambert, who was in her early teens at the time, occasionally listened to the women's tales of violence and verbal abuse. She was also present at the family's dinner table as her parents talked openly about their detective work—stories of cheating spouses, alcohol abuse, and domestic violence. Those stories provided her with a wealth of material for country songs, which she began writing as a teenager.

Starting when she was very young, Lambert's father played guitar and sang for her, and they would often listen to albums together. "I remember my parents swearing that when I was 3 years old, I was harmonizing," Lambert told Mario Tarradell for the *Dallas Morning News* (April 29, 2007). "My mom was like, 'Is she singing harmony?' And my dad said, 'I think she is.' As far back as I can remember I've loved music. . . . I just grew up with it. It's in my blood." At the age of 16, she entered her first country-music talent contest, and she soon had a small band backing her up, playing with her in honky-tonk bars in Texas. She played mainly covers of songs by country singers such as Rusty Weir, and by the age of 17, she was singing professionally. Less than a year later, with financing from her father, she put out an independently produced album, *Miranda Lambert* (2001), which featured the songs "Texas Pride" and "Somebody Else." (An indifferent student eager to start her career, she had finished school early by participating in a program called Operation Graduation, which, she told Hollandsworth, was "made up of a bunch of pregnant girls and druggies and me.")

CAREER

In 2003 Lambert got the break that would launch her career. For nine weeks she appeared on the USA cable-television network's program *Nashville Star*, a country-music answer to Fox's highly popular singing-contest show *American Idol*. Lambert placed third, gaining a lot of media exposure in the process. As a result, at 20 years of age, she landed a record deal with Sony. At Sony's offices in Nashville, Tennessee, she met with many executives, "and they started going through their thing, saying, 'We need you to write with this person and work with this producer so that we can produce a great record,'" Lambert's agent, Joey Lee, recalled to Hollandsworth. "And Miranda basically stopped

everyone in their tracks and said, 'Have y'all listened to my songs? Because that's who I am and that's what I'm going to keep doing, and if I can't do it my way, I'll go home and come back when you're ready for me.' She was eighteen years old and walking away from a major record deal. And right then, to his credit, the president of the label said, 'Okay, Miranda, go make your record.'"

Lambert wrote or co-wrote 11 of the 12 songs on her major-label debut, *Kerosene* (2005). Even though her singles, such as the title track, did not receive much radio play, the album went platinum, selling more than one million copies. And while *Kerosene* included a few gentle numbers, music fans and the press focused on the tougher material: songs about cheating boyfriends and women who take justice into their own hands. "Her long blond hair and Playmate looks may have helped make her first album this year's biggest-selling solo country debut," Sasha Frere-Jones wrote for the *New Yorker* (November 14, 2005), "but she's no novelty—the title track, 'Kerosene,' is one of the year's best songs. Lambert wrote it herself, an anomaly in Nashville. It's anomalous in structure, too, closer to rock in its repetitive form: one nagging guitar figure and pounding drums relieved every eight bars by a three-chord turnaround. Lambert has a strong twang, but she's not a belter like last year's rookie sensation Gretchen Wilson—she lets her verses cruise." Lambert got even more recognition and press after she performed "Kerosene" at the 2005 Country Music Association Awards ceremony. The record reached number one on the Country Albums chart and number 18 on the *Billboard* 200 chart. In 2007 Lambert was named the top new female vocalist by the Academy of Country Music.

Lambert's sophomore release, *Crazy Ex-Girlfriend* (2007), also went platinum, despite the fact that Lambert was still not getting much radio play. (By way of explanation, Lon Helton, the publisher of *Country Aircheck*, told Jon Caramanica for the April 29, 2007 edition of the *New York Times*, "[Lambert is] a little harder-edged than what you're going to hear from most female artists in this format. It might be closer to what some men sing, and to radio programmers it might make it a hair uncomfortable.") Lambert wrote or co-wrote most of the songs on the album, which also included covers, such as Patty Griffin's "Getting Ready" and Gillian Welch's "Dry Town." Alongside ballads such as "More Like Her" and "Desperation" were the "tough-chick" songs for which Lambert was becoming increasingly famous: in the title track the singer takes revenge on an ex-boyfriend's new lover, and in "Gunpowder & Lead" she shoots an abusive boyfriend. Hollandsworth reported that such songs struck a chord with many female listeners, quoting one as saying, "Miranda puts into words what we're all thinking." He quoted the country singer Kenny Chesney as observing that Lambert was "singing to an audience that wasn't being sung to."

Crazy Ex-Girlfriend received a lot of critical praise and was named album of the year by the Academy of Country Music. "Backed by ragged, loud guitar work and production that is full but not slick, Ms. Lambert sounds like a brash rabble-rouser, an emotionally insightful spark plug," Jon Caramanica wrote. "And in the context of the current country mainstream, safe as it is, she sounds very much like an outsider." Like her previous record, *Crazy Ex-Girlfriend* reached number one on the Country Albums chart and did even better than her first album on the *Billboard* 200 chart, peaking at number six. In a review for Allmusic.com, Stephen Thomas Erlewine wrote, "*Crazy Ex-Girlfriend* would have been impressive if it was just a showcase of her strengths as a singer or as a songwriter, but since it is both, it's simply stunning, a breakthrough for Lambert and one of the best albums of 2007, regardless of genre."

Expectations were high for the release of Lambert's third album, *Revolution* (2009). The album's first track, "White Liar," about a cheating boyfriend, became Lambert's most successful single to date, going to number 38 on the *Billboard* Hot 100 chart. As with Lambert's previous record, there were rowdy and humorous revenge tales as well as mellow ballads, such as the nostalgic "The House That Built Me." (That song climbed to number 28 on the *Billboard* Hot 100 chart.) The record, with 15 songs of varying mood and sensibility, was Lambert's longest and most musically diverse to date, featuring more nods to classic rock and country rock. "I hope I've been able to break open some doors for more open-mindedness in country. People have told me I have," she is quoted as saying on her Web site. "But it's been a lot of work, and it's been a lot of putting my feet in the dirt and saying, here's the line I won't cross. I may have lost a lot of things for it or I may have gained a lot of things. But I know that I sleep great at night." In addition to gaining Lambert a growing audience, the album was fairly popular with critics. "Lambert has crafted a style perfectly in tune with a trend toward a less-sanitized, rougher-edged sound in contemporary country exemplified by Jamey Johnson, Dierks Bentley and Jason Aldean," Ray Waddell wrote for Billboard.com (December 4, 2010). "Lambert believes *Revolution* is the most representative album so far of who she wants to be as an artist." Lambert told Waddell: "I feel like I'll always keep moving forward, and I'll change, not only as a woman but as an artist. But *Revolution* represented exactly who I was at 26 years old, who I had become. It was one of those records where, for the first time, I could say, in all truth, 'I want to hand this record to my heroes. I feel confident enough about it.'"

In 2010 Lambert won a Grammy Award for best female country vocal performance; several Country Music Association (CMA) awards, including female vocalist of the year; and several Academy of Country Music awards, including top new female vocalist. Lambert made history when she was nominated for nine CMA awards, the most ever for a female country musician; the only other musicians nominated for nine or more CMA awards are Merle Haggard and Alan Jackson.

Lambert's fourth studio album, *Four the Record*, came out in November 2011. She wrote or co-wrote six of the 14 songs, including "Baggage Claim"—about a woman who destroys her no-good boyfriend's possessions—which features Josh Kelley on background vocals and Steve Winwood on the B-3 organ. On the song "Better in the Long Run," Lambert sings a duet with her husband, the country singer Blake Shelton. The song is about a couple breaking up. "What can I tell you? It's a heck of a good song," Lambert told Hollandsworth. "And let's face it, isn't the dark side a lot more interesting? Seriously, if all I did was sing about all the really nice things that happen to women, I'd be bored to death." The album was mostly well-received. "Like a shard of glass hiding in shag carpet, Miranda Lambert has a voice that's small and dangerous," Chris Richards wrote for the *Washington Post* (October 31, 2011). "And the shag is contemporary country—it's the genre of pop music most ready to absorb disparate sounds into its fibers without compromising its uniform appearance. Spend an hour dialed in to country radio and you'll hear the influence of the Cars, Southern rap and U2 all whiz past without much of a fuss. Lambert, Nashville's most beloved tough-talker, is up to something similar on her new album. . . . After her 2009 disc *Revolution* cleaned house at just about every major awards show last year, she's decided to try on a few different styles—often making them sound like her own. With 'Fine Tune,' the 27-year-old sings about heartbreak and defibrillation as her backing musicians wilt into a fog of distortion like a deflated Led Zeppelin. Despite its adventurous spirit, *Four the Record* remains only the second-best album Lambert minted this year. Her new group, the Pistol Annies, stunned the industry last summer by topping the country album chart with very little promotion and some very compelling tunes. . . . Her voice has never been big, but Lambert knows how to use its clarity and bite to inhabit every corner of a song. And as a songwriter, her gifts are numerous—one of which is her ability to transpose rage into laughs."

The other 2011 album Richards was referring to was *Hell on Heels*, by the Pistol Annies, an all-female country-music trio Lambert had formed in 2010. The album features such songs as "The Hunter's Wife," "Takin' Pills,"

"Bad Example," and "Hell on Heels." Genevieve Koski, in a review for the *A.V. Club* (August 30, 2011), observed that "dwelling on the trio's gender means overlooking the real merit of Pistol Annies, which is the skilled, lively interplay between the songwriting and vocal talents of Ashley Monroe, Angaleena Presley, and Miranda Lambert. Monroe's classic Tennessee country, Presley's twangy Kentucky bluegrass, and Lambert's rebellious Texas honky-tonk combine into a colorful portrait of a modern Southern woman who's vivacious, independent, and vulnerable in equal measure. In terms of spirit and songwriting, Pistol Annies slot in nicely alongside touchstones like Dolly Parton, The Judds, and Dixie Chicks, though Lambert, Monroe, and Presley have a youthful tendency to sacrifice sincerity in favor of cleverness. At a lean 30 minutes, *Hell On Heels* is too slight to deliver completely on the trio's promise, but the sense of fun and sisterly affection that pervades the album makes it a winning opening salvo from an intriguing new group."

PERSONAL LIFE

Hollandsworth wrote that Lambert is "utterly unpretentious." Lambert's parents operate the Miranda Lambert Store & Headquarters, in Lindale, which houses news clippings and other items connected to the singer and sells merchandise such as T-shirts. For protection from attacks related to their former line of work, Rick and Bev Lambert taught their children to use firearms, and Miranda Lambert carries a pistol. She also enjoys hunting. The five-foot four-inch Lambert and the six-foot five-inch Blake Shelton had been dating for five years when they got engaged, in May 2010. They married a year later. At home the couple often sing together, trying to outperform each other. "I try to outsing her and make her sound sucky," Shelton told Hollandsworth, "and she does everything she can to make me look bad, and this goes on, all night long, like two dogs fighting for a bone."

SUGGESTED READING

Caramanica, Jon. "Mess with This Texan, You'll Pay in a Song." *New York Times* 29 Apr. 2007, nat. ed., sec. 2: 27. Print.

Frere-Jones, Sasha. "Goings On About Town." *New Yorker* 14 Nov. 2005: 28. Print.

Hollandsworth, Skip. "The Girl Who Played with Firearms." *Texas Monthly* Oct. 2011, Features: 102. Print.

Tarradell, Mario. "On Her Own Country Music: Miranda Lambert Succeeds on Talent and Grit." *Dallas Morning News* 29 Apr. 2007: E1. Print.

Waddell, Ray. "Miranda Lambert: The Billboard Cover Story." *Billboard.com*. Billboard, 29 Nov. 2010. Web. 21 Dec. 2011.

SELECTED WORKS

Kerosene, 2005; *Crazy Ex-Girlfriend*, 2007; *Revolution*, 2009; *Four the Record*, 2011; *Hell on Heels*, 2011

—*Dmitry Kiper*

Jeffrey M. Landry

Born: December 23, 1970
Occupation: US representative from Louisiana (Republican)

On November 2, 2010, in his first successful run for elective office, the Republican Jeff Landry won the seat representing Louisiana's Third Congressional District in the US House. Ever since he announced his candidacy for that post, Landry has had the backing of supporters of the Tea Party movement; in the House he is a member of the Tea Party Caucus. Like those far-right members of the GOP and many other Republicans, Landry favors such measures as a constitutional amendment to require a balanced federal budget, oil exploration in the Arctic National Wildlife Refuge and an end to restrictions on offshore drilling, and the repeal of the Obama administration's health-care-reform initiative (known as the Patient Protection and Affordable Care Act of 2010). He opposes any increases in federal taxes, the federal debt ceiling, and spending for federal-government activities not connected with defense.

EARLY LIFE

Jeffrey Martin Landry was born on December 23, 1970, in St. Martinville, Louisiana, to Edna, a teacher, and Al, a business owner. Although he grew up with many friends and neighbors who were Democrats, Landry was drawn to a more conservative point of view when he heard President Ronald Reagan discuss his fiscal policies. After graduating from high school, Landry worked in his state's sugarcane fields and served for almost a dozen years in the Louisiana National Guard. During that time he trained for deployment in Operation Desert Storm. Although he is considered a veteran because he was on active duty, he was never sent to Iraq—a fact that would become a campaign issue in 2010. Landry was discharged from the US Army with the rank of sergeant. He has also worked as a sheriff's deputy in St. Martin Parish and as a police officer in the village of Parks.

Landry attended the University of Louisiana at Lafayette (then the University of Southwestern Louisiana), where he earned a BS degree in environmental and sustainable resources in 1999. He then enrolled at the Loyola University College of Law, in New Orleans, Louisiana, and

Office of Congressman Jeff Landry

received a JD degree in 2004. He subsequently began practicing as an attorney and cofounded a small business that "supported the oil and gas industry," according to his official website.

ENTERS POLITICS

In 2007 Landry ran for a seat in the State Senate but lost to the Democrat Troy Hebert. In 2010 he made a bid for the US House seat being vacated by Charlie Melancon, a Democrat who was running for the US Senate. Landry was endorsed by the far-right Tea Party and attended several of the group's rallies.

Landry and the former State House Speaker Hunt Downer (who had been a Democrat until 2001) opposed each other in a runoff election for the Republican nomination. Landry attacked Downer for his former party affiliation, and the Tea Party spearheaded a "Down with Downer" campaign. Thanks in large part to those efforts, Landry clinched the nomination. In the general election he faced the Democrat Ravi Sangisetty, an attorney of Indian descent. The national Democratic Party ignored the race for the most part, due to the district's heavily conservative history, and Landry—armed with a war chest significantly larger than Sangisetty's—won the election with 64 percent of the vote.

Landry's victory was not completely free of problems, however. On several occasions he was criticized for his claim that he was a veteran of Desert Storm. He explained that although he had not set foot in Iraq, he was still considered a veteran. "I have never claimed to have served in Iraq," Landry said, as quoted by Jeremy Alford for the Lafourche Parish, Louisiana, *Daily Comet* (24 Aug. 2010). "The only reason I didn't go is because the war ended so quickly. I certainly never tried not to go."

WORK IN CONGRESS

Landry sits on the House Committees on Natural Resources, Transportation and Infrastructure, and Small Business. He is also a member of the Republican Study Committee, the Congressional Sportsmen's Caucus, the National Guard and Reserve Components Caucus, the Coast Guard Caucus, and the Tea Party Caucus, among other such groups.

Landry opposed the creation of the Joint Select Committee on Deficit Reduction, as called for in the Budget Control Act of 2011. Known informally as the Super Committee, it was composed of six members of the House and six members of the Senate and was evenly divided between Republicans and Democrats. In a letter sent to the committee on November 17, 2011, Landry and seventy-one other Republican signatories urged the committee not to include any tax increases in their recommendations. "Increasing taxes on Americans would destroy jobs, erase all hope of an economic recovery, and simply serve to feed out-of-control spending in Washington," the letter declared. (The committee disbanded several days later, after concluding that the Republican and Democratic members' differences of opinion could not be bridged before the mandatory November 23 deadline.)

Landry made headlines when, in the Capitol on September 8, 2011, he sat holding a sign reading "Drilling = Jobs" while President Barack Obama delivered a speech about job creation during a joint session of Congress. While Landry's supporters applauded his action, others denounced it as disrespectful.

In his leisure time Landry enjoys hunting and fishing. He and his wife, Sharon, have one son and live in New Iberia, Louisiana.

SUGGESTED READING

Alford, Jeremy. "Congressional GOP Race Hits Boiling Point." *DailyComet.com* [Lafourche Parish, Louisiana]. DailyComet.com, Aug. 24, 2010. Web. Jan. 2012.

Grace, Stephanie. "U.S. Rep. Jeff Landry Isn't Helping His Constituents: Stephanie Grace." *Nola (Times-Picayune): Greater New Orleans.* New Orleans Net, 22 Sep. 2011. Web. Jan. 2012.

U.S. Congressman Jeff Landry. Landry.House. gov, n.d. Web. Jan. 2012.

—William Dvorak

Kalle Lasn

Born: March 24, 1942
Occupation: Author, activist

Estonian-born anticonsumer activist and author Kalle Lasn is the founder of the Vancouver, British Columbia–based nonprofit Adbusters Media Foundation and the editor of *Adbusters Quarterly* magazine. Known for its striking visual commentary, the magazine features no advertisements—it relies entirely on newsstand and subscriber sales as well as donations to fund its production. In 2011 Lasn and Adbusters spearheaded the Occupy Wall Street movement that swept cities worldwide in an effort to draw attention to global political unrest, corporate greed, and the ill effects of the 2008 financial crisis. In the summer of 2011, Lasn was walking his dog when he came up with the image of a ballerina holding a pose atop *Charging Bull*, a well-known sculpture near Wall Street in New York City. He was attracted to the image, he told Mattathias Schwartz for the *New Yorker* (28 Nov. 2011), because of the "juxtaposition of the capitalist dynamism of the bull with the Zen stillness of the ballerina." From the image, the idea of a protest formed quickly. When the image was published, protesters being teargassed were shown in the background. The text on the image read, "What is our one demand? #OccupyWallStreet. September 17th. Bring tent." Lasn chose the date of September 17, 2011, his mother's birthday, to begin the proposed occupation.

Lasn is the author of two books. *Culture Jam: The Uncooling of America* was published in 1999. (A later edition was published under the title *Culture Jam: How to Reverse America's Suicidal Consumer Binge—And Why We Must* in 2000.) Lasn's second book, *Design Anarchy*, about the complacency of artists and designers in a consumer-centric culture, was published in 2006.

Lasn is also no stranger to controversy as demonstrated by the 2004 *Adbusters Quarterly* article "Why Won't Anyone Say They Are Jewish?" The piece, signed by Lasn, listed the names of fifty influential neoconservatives in the administration of President George W. Bush, denoting those that are Jewish with a black dot; Lasn wrote that neoconservative pro-Israel sentiments may have pushed Bush to war with Iraq in 2003. Many readers canceled their magazine subscription after the piece was published. Still Lasn defended the article and strongly denied charges of anti-Semitism. He wrote, as quoted by Drew Grant in the *New York Observer* (20 Oct. 2011, online), that though the article was admittedly a "provocation," the neoconservatives were "no ordinary group—they are the most influential political/intellectual force in the world right now." He added, "They have the power to

© Christopher J. Morris/Corbis

start wars and to stop them. They are the prime architects of America's foreign policy since 9/11—a policy that is heavily weighed in favor of Israel and a key source of anti-Americanism in the world. . . . Is it not just as valid to comment on the Jewishness of neocons as it is to point out that the majority of them are male or white or wealthy or from the Western world or have studied at a particular university?"

Lasn has also been criticized for his various hypocrisies, not the least of which being his strategy of using mass-marketing techniques to warn people about mass-marketing techniques. In 2003 Lasn and the Adbusters Media Foundation even began selling their own product: an ethically produced sneaker called the Blackspot to compete with shoe giant Nike. Some reasoned that the so-called antibrand was just another form of branding, marketed to ethically conscious consumers. But Lasn, a regular contributor to the conservative and corporately owned Toronto *Globe and Mail* newspaper, does not deny his inconsistencies and instead admits his flaws and notes that he is simply trying to make a difference.

EARLY LIFE AND CAREER

Kalle Lasn was born in Tallinn, Estonia, on March 24, 1942, seven months after the Nazi occupation during World War II. Lasn's father, a tennis champion, buried his trophies in the backyard before rushing his family onto one of the last boats to Germany after the Russian Army's advance into Estonia in 1944. Lasn spent his early childhood in German refugee camps, where he recalls falling asleep on a cot as his uncles discussed politics. He maintains that his tumultuous early life instilled in him a belief in the world's capacity for change. "World wars, revolutions—from time to time, big things actually happen," he told Matthias Schwartz, adding, "When the moment is right, all it takes is a spark."

Lasn's family immigrated to Australia in 1949 and settled in Adelaide. Lasn told Fergus Shiel for the Melbourne *Age* (21 Nov. 2000), "I must admit I had a pretty hard time of it when I was in Australia. . . . I was made to feel like I wasn't quite up to snuff in some sense. Like I wasn't quite a bona fide member of society." Lasn stayed close to home for college and attended the University of Adelaide, where he received a bachelor of science degree in mathematics in 1961. Lasn moved to Melbourne, where he did aeronautics research for the Australian Government Department of Defence, working with computer-simulated war games.

On a trip to Europe, Lasn's boat stopped at the Japanese port city of Yokohama. The twenty-three-year-old Lasn was so taken by the country that he remained in Japan and moved to Tokyo, where he founded a market-research firm in 1965. The firm created consumer reports for alcohol and tobacco companies through feeding punch cards into an IBM mainframe. Despite his participation in an industry that he would later come to despise, Lasn called his years in Japan some of the best of his life. "I was struck by how well Japanese society and culture worked in those days. It was so much better than anything I had experienced up to that point in my life," he told Gabriele Hadl for the *Kyoto Journal* (2001, online). "People were intelligent and accessible, and the whole culture seemed not just safe, but well grounded and spiritually robust." Lasn became a successful businessman, making enough money to travel the world for three years. When he returned to Japan, he married Masako Tominaga.

ACTIVISM IN CANADA

After selling his research firm for a substantial amount of money in 1967, Lasn moved to Canada and began his career as a documentary filmmaker. With Psychomedia Productions, the Public Broadcasting Service (PBS) affiliate KCTS Seattle, and the National Film Board of Canada (NFB), Lasn directed a series of films, most of which were about his years of Japan. The documentaries were broadcast on PBS and the Canadian Broadcasting Corporation (CBC) and earned Lasn over fifteen international awards. Lasn's films include the shorts *Ritual* (1977), *Children of the Tribe* (1980), *Japan Inc: Lessons for North America?* (1981), *Satori in the Right Cortex* (1985), and *The Autumn Rain: Crime in*

Japan (1990), as well as the feature-length films *Japanese Women* (1984) and *The Rise and Fall of American Business Culture* (1987).

Lasn and his wife were settled in Vancouver, British Columbia, the home of a thriving environmental movement, when, in 1989, the Canadian foresting industry first aired a commercial on CBC called "Forests Forever." The spot lauded Canada's lumber companies for responsibly managing timberlands for environmental preservation. Angered by the promotion, Lasn argued, with supporting statistics from the University of British Columbia, that loggers were cutting down forests at a rate that did not promote regrowth and that the Canadian government supported their endeavor because of the industry's powerful role in the economy. Lasn approached CBC for a thirty-second slot to air his own counteradvertisement, but he was turned away. He told Mary Williams Walsh for the *Los Angeles Times* (23 June 1992), "Television is the most powerful medium of our time, and if they won't take your money for your thirty-second slot, then you're excluded. That skews the democratic process."

Not to be deterred, Lasn and a small group of environmentalists produced a newsletter to tell other groups about their thwarted efforts against the CBC policy. He was surprised to find that others had similar stories to tell. "It started to grow. People started coming in with their own stories, about how ten years ago they couldn't get a [labor] union ad on TV," he told Walsh. "It was like a groundswell of frustrated media suppression." Eventually, CBC stopped airing "Forests Forever" to remain consistent with its issue-advertising policy—the same policy that it had used against Lasn. Meanwhile, Lasn and his colleagues, including Lasn's long-time cameraman Bill Schmalz, decided to expand their newsletter into a magazine that would offer eye-catching layouts and thoughtful commentary on consumer culture, advertising, and the decline of the environment. They founded Adbusters Media Foundation and named the new bimonthly magazine *Adbusters Quarterly*.

ADBUSTERS

Adbusters Quarterly touts itself as the Journal of the Mental Environment. It also became an early proponent of culture jamming by launching bold, attention-grabbing public attacks against their corporate targets. The well-funded Canadian logging industry may have been Adbuster's first opponent, but the foundation soon launched media campaigns against such corporate monoliths as McDonald's, Benetton, Calvin Klein, and Absolut Vodka. Their satirical strategy was both sophisticated and effective. One advertisement—a take on advertisements for Calvin Klein perfume—shows the naked back of a female model and is accompanied by a sexually suggestive soundtrack. When the camera zooms in closer it becomes apparent that the woman is vomiting as a voice-over asks, "Why do nine out of ten women feel dissatisfied with some aspect of their own bodies?" In 1992, the vodka producer Absolut threatened to sue Adbusters over their parody advertisement "Absolut Nonsense," which implied that drinking alcohol causes impotence in consumers. Lasn issued a press release challenging Absolut executives to publicly debate the campaign, but the company dropped the potential suit after the *Los Angeles Times* and the *Washington Post* covered the story.

Lasn's first book, *Culture Jam: The Uncooling of America*, was published in 1999. The book received mixed reviews, but *Culture Jam* has become required reading in many university sociology and marketing classes. Reviewer Sparkle Hayter for the Toronto *Globe and Mail* (13 Nov. 1999) wrote, "Most convincing is his case for the way the media is subtly and not-so-subtly manipulating and brainwashing the consumer. Instead of actual rebellion, he writes, which would be threatening to the Establishment, we are fed the idea that rebellion can be obtained by buying a snazzy car, wearing the 'coolest' athletic shoes, drinking a particular beer, buying our clothes from a particular chain store—in other words, by following the crowd."

In 2003, inspired by his dislike of former Nike chief executive Phil Knight, Lasn developed the Blackspot sneaker. The shoe was produced with natural materials, including hemp, recycled tires, and vegan leather, and manufactured in a fair-trade factory chosen by Lasn. In the London *Independent* (15 Dec. 2003), reporter Iain Aitch described the product as a "dead ringer" for the Nike-owned Converse Chuck Taylor shoe. Converse, Aitch wrote, was once considered a "rebel" brand before the Nike Corporation acquired it in 2001. Despite its familiar appearance, the Blackspot features a black circle in the place one might expect to see a Nike logo. Lasn told Aitch, "I think that if we are successful with our sneaker, other people will repeat the experiment against other corporations. And if we can prove that it works, it will be a prototype to use in other industries and could well be a movement that leads capitalism into that bottom-up direction." Blackspot has yet to become a strong competitor to the Nike brand, but the sneakers continue to be sold on the Adbusters website and by independent retailers worldwide.

Lasn's second book, *Design Anarchy*, was published in 2006. The book, which claims that the integration of design and commerce has engendered a consumerist culture, was inspired by British designer Ken Garland's 1964 manifesto *First Things First*. (In 2000, Lasn, Garland, *Adbusters* designer Chris Dixon, and graphic designer Tibor Kalman reworked *First Things First* and published it under the title *First Things First*

2000.) In *Design Anarchy*, Lasn worries that the current generation of designers has been taught to use their skills exclusively for selling products. The "old-school designers," he argues, as quoted by Laurel Saville for *Step inside Design* (Nov. 2007), "have forgotten that we [designers] are very powerful people, and we are the creators of this culture." Nonetheless, Lasn believes that the status quo can be reversed. "I think designers are starting to realize that they're creating the slickness of this culture, the tone, the ambience," he wrote. "The medium is the message, and we designers control the media itself. We have incredible power, and over the next ten, twenty, thirty years, we can play a huge part in solving this crisis we find ourselves in."

OCCUPY WALL STREET

After the 2008 financial crisis, Adbusters' longtime fight against corporate dominance and greed found new resonance. In 2011 *Adbusters* called for a "Tahrir moment"—a reference to the Egyptian protests in Cairo's Tahrir Square earlier that spring. Lasn envisioned a movement that combined the approach of the *acampadas* (campers) in Spain and the successful youth-driven movement in Cairo. On July 13, 2011, Lasn posted a message on the Adbusters website suggesting that protestors "flood into lower Manhattan, set up tents, kitchens, peaceful barricades and occupy Wall Street." The directive spurred over a thousand encampments worldwide, including the one in Manhattan's Zuccotti Park near Wall Street.

Much like the protests of the Arab Spring, the Occupy movement was largely directed through social media. It seemed as though Lasn, who had once lamented the undemocratic policies of television, had found a new medium for his message.

The movement was criticized for lacking specific demands, however. Protestors came with their own lists of grievances, which included the skyrocketing unemployment rate, the rising cost of tuition and health care, and the bank bailout. Lasn himself proposed demands, including a Robin Hood tax, which would impose a 1 percent tax on all financial transactions; restoration of the 1932 Glass-Steagall Act, which placed restrictions on the comingling of commercial banking and investing; and the reversal of the 2010 US Supreme Court ruling in *Citizens United v. Federal Election Commission*, which declared that corporations were considered legal citizens and thus able to contribute freely to political campaigns. Still none of these were officially recognized as demands by the Occupy movement, which functioned according to a populist, direct-democracy model. In the same vein Lasn is careful not to present himself as the face of the movement, which adopted the slogan We Are the 99 Percent—a reference to the inequality of wealth distribution in the United States, where 1 percent of people have more income than the remaining 99 percent.

The Occupy encampments gained attention as the fall of 2011 progressed. In Zuccotti Park, run-ins with New York City police officers wielding pepper spray only increased Occupy's momentum. In the early morning of November 15, New York City mayor Michael Bloomberg ordered the police to forcefully clear the encampment because, he later announced, conditions among the campers had become unsanitary. The raid—ironically coming days before the date *Adbusters* had encouraged protestors to "declare victory" and evacuate the park—sparked enough outrage to fuel the November 17 Day of Action, a mass protest that put Occupy Wall Street back in the headlines. Though most of the encampments were abandoned for the winter, Lasn is optimistic for the movement's future. He told Robert Seigel for National Public Radio's *All Things Considered* (6 Dec. 2011), "I predict a myriad of [Occupy] projects next spring."

PERSONAL LIFE

Shortly after moving to Canada, Lasn and his wife were involved in a serious car accident in which they lost their six-month-old child. "It's one of those things that puts your life on a whole new plane," he told Ian Mulgrew for the *Vancouver Sun* (12 Feb. 2000). "After that, there were no more babies. Maybe that's why I'm in activism. If I had a couple of teenagers on my hands, I don't know if I'd have time."

Lasn and his wife live on a five-acre farm in Aldergrove, British Columbia, just outside of Vancouver.

SUGGESTED READING

Frazier, Mya. "When a Brand Buster Becomes a Brand." *Advertising Age* 26 Nov. 2007: 1–29. Print.

Hadl, Gabriele. "Culture Jammer's Guide to Enlightenment: A Talk with Adbusters' Kalle Lasn." *Kyoto Journal* 46 (2001): n. pag. Web. 18 Jan. 2012.

Harkin, James. "The Logos Fight Back." *New Statesman* 18 June 2001: 25. Print.

Schwartz, Mattathias. "Pre-Occupied." *New Yorker* 28 Nov. 2011: 28–35. Print.

Yardley, William. "The Branding of the Occupy Movement." *New York Times* 28 Nov. 2011, late ed.: 1. Print.

SELECTED BOOKS

Culture Jam: The Uncooling of America, 1999; *Culture Jam: How to Reverse America's Suicidal Consumer Binge—And Why We Must*, 2000; *First Things First 2000* (with Ken Garland, Chris Dixon, and Tibor Kalman), 2000; *Design Anarchy*, 2006

SELECTED FILMS

Ritual, 1977; *Children of the Tribe*, 1980; *Japan Inc: Lessons for North America?*, 1981; *Japanese Women*, 1984; *Satori in the Right Cortex*, 1985; *The Rise and Fall of American Business Culture*, 1987; *The Autumn Rain: Crime in Japan*, 1990

—*Molly Hagen*

Jim Lee

Born: August 11, 1964
Occupation: Artist and copublisher of DC Comics

"If you want to understand the history of mainstream American comics from the 1990s to present day, you need to know about Jim Lee," Alex Biese wrote for the *Asbury Park Press* (23 Jan. 2011). Lee, who is no relation to that other comic-world icon Stan Lee, helped create a new *X-Men* series with longtime writer Chris Claremont. The first comic in the newly revamped series, known to fans as *X-Men #1*, became the best-selling comic book of all time, according to the *Guinness Book of World Records*, shipping more than eight million copies. (The issue was printed with five different covers from which readers could choose, and many collectors purchased a copy of each, which dramatically increased sales.)

Widely celebrated for his crucial role in founding the groundbreaking company Image Comics, Lee is currently copublisher of DC Comics, a subsidiary of the Time Warner conglomerate. Despite his increased corporate duties, Lee remains a working artist, and as the executive creative director for DC Universe Online, he created much of the visual environment for the massive multiplayer online role-playing game that was released to great fanfare in early 2011. No matter his professional titles and responsibilities, Lee is a legendary figure to fans of superheroes and comics. "From commercial cover artist to rogue to video game director, Jim Lee's signature is synonymous with modern comics' culture," Zac Turgeon wrote for the online magazine *Blast* (13 Feb. 2009).

Lee has been very clear about what the comics culture does and does not encompass. "I lean more toward the entertaining aspects in comics," he told Skylar Browning for the *Missoula Independent* (29 June 2006). "I think there are some comics that are more literary or try to be more culturally influential. . . . We're dealing with superheroes here—we're not dealing with *My Dinner with Andre*-type books. Our characters are traveling through solar systems and picking up buildings or flying through the core of the sun. I try to make that believable and to pull that reader into the experience."

Wirelmage

EARLY LIFE AND EDUCATION

Lee was born on August 11, 1964, in Seoul, South Korea. His father was a respected anesthesiologist, and his mother, as Peter Rowe wrote for the *San Diego Union-Tribune* (18 July 2010), was "an avowed enemy of comics."

When Lee was five years old, he moved with his family to the United States. They settled in St. Louis, Missouri, where his father continued to practice medicine. Both parents assumed that Lee would be following in his father's footsteps. "This is a very common Asian story," Lee told Rowe. "You meet any Korean kid who emigrated when young or was born here and they all have exactly the same story of parents being so pushy." Early on, he discovered a love for comics, although, as Rowe wrote, "[He] lost several collections to [his mother's] diligent housekeeping, and neither parent encouraged his passion for these disreputable publications." Still, when he traveled out of town with his father for medical conventions, he would peruse the hotel-room Yellow Pages for the local comic shop and ask to be taken there.

Lee found a compatriot in a fellow immigrant named Brandon Choi who also loved comics; their parents had known one another in Korea, and the families attended church together on Sundays. The Lees and Chois were among the few Korean families then living in St. Louis, which further strengthened their bond.

Bowing to parental pressure, Lee entered Princeton University where he majored in psychology with the intent to enter medical school after he graduated. Permitted to select a few electives, he chose art classes, remembering how he had loved to draw comics when he was younger. (Lee had been voted "best artist" in his second-grade class, and later, many of his high-school friends had assumed that he would choose some type of career in the arts.) The classes rekindled his interest, and despite spending one successful summer as a nurse's intern at a hospital in Germany, he began reconsidering his plans for medical school.

After graduating from Princeton in 1986, Lee convinced his parents to give him one year to try to break into the world of professional comic book artists. He promised them that if it didn't work out, he would enter medical school immediately. When they agreed, he returned to St. Louis and set up a drawing table in his childhood bedroom. "I'm sure my parents thought I was crazy," Lee recalled to Rowe. "They had dropped sixty-five grand on my education and I'm in the house, drawing in my underwear."

CAREER AT MARVEL

Lee drew a twenty-page comic book, made color photocopies, and mailed them to forty-five comic book publishers. The vast majority did not respond since many companies make a practice of ignoring unsolicited manuscripts. Three publishers responded with bland, standardized rejection slips. One of the form letters, however, was signed by Dick Giordano, the head of DC's editorial department, and it contained a few handwritten lines of encouragement.

Invigorated by Giordano's sentiments, Lee toted his portfolio to New York City for a comics convention in 1987. He tirelessly made the rounds, showing his work to fellow artists and editors. Fortuitously, he met Archie Goodwin, a Marvel executive, who was willing to talk to the aspiring artist. The man recognized Lee's talent. He was hired by Marvel, and his career was launched.

Although Lee's parents had held onto the hope that he would decide to go to medical school, they were happy for him. Later, when he began enjoying some measure of financial stability, he paid to send them on a cruise for their anniversary. Lee's success in the comic book industry had also proved undeniably to his parents that there are many paths to success in the United States: Lee reimbursed them for his college tuition.

At Marvel, Lee was assigned to work as a penciller (the artist who does the initial sketches based on a script or a concept) on *Alpha Flight*, which featured a Canadian team of superheroes, and in 1989, on *The Punisher War Journal*, a violent tale with a vigilante protagonist. Working on the latter series sharply honed Lee's skills at drawing weapons; readers would write letters of complaint if he got even a small detail wrong.

Lee also served as a guest artist for *Uncanny X-Men*, a series featuring a band of mutant heroes who had made their first appearance in 1963 as the creation of writer Stan Lee and artist Jack Kirby. The original series featured the characters of Angel, who had wings sprouting from his back; the Beast, who possessed superhuman strength and agility; Cyclops, who could emit a powerful beam of energy from his eyes; Iceman, who could freeze anything around him; Marvel Girl, who had telepathic and telekinetic powers; and their teacher and leader, the scientific genius known as Professor X. The original series ceased publication in 1970 after sixty-six issues, but it was later brought back into print in 1975 and introduced several new and international heroes, changing from time to time as new members were introduced and old ones retired.

In 1991, Marvel launched the series' second volume, which was a spinoff of the original *Uncanny X-Men*. Called *X-Men*, it was written by Marvel veteran Chris Claremont. Claremont was already an undisputed icon at Marvel, where he had worked for more than fifteen years on *Uncanny X-Men*. Lee was assigned to work with him as artist and co-plotter.

Marvel expected the first issue to be in great demand with collectors and speculators, and it was printed with several covers in the hope that many would want to own each cover. An added marketing strategy allowed four of the covers to be combined in order to form a large panoramic image, while a fifth was an elaborate gatefold arrangement that opened to reveal the same large picture. As predicted, retailers ordered more than eight million copies of the title. At the 2010 Comic-Con convention in San Diego, California, the *Guinness Book of World Records* announced that Marvel Comics was being added to its latest edition as the publisher of the best-selling comic book of all time.

Despite their shared success, the professional relationship between Lee and Claremont was not good. Their work habits and creative vision differed widely, and ultimately, when pressed, the title's editor, Bob Harras, sided with Lee. Claremont left his job after the third issue, setting off a firestorm of debate and recrimination in the fan press. "What happened with *X-Men* was . . . a different type of situation in that Chris was a veteran and had been working on the book for sixteen, seventeen years and I was just a young punk," Lee told Skylar Browning. "It's not as conducive to working things out."

Lee remained at Marvel, but working conditions were difficult despite Claremont's absence; issues of creative control were increasingly coming to the forefront for Lee and for several of his fellow artists. Although the popularity of comics had fluctuated over the past decades, a new generation of fans helped to ensure that series were often selling out as fast as they were released.

Many were becoming fans of specific artists. Lee—who had founded his own fledgling studio, Homage, while still at Marvel—had an exceptionally large and appreciative following. "Lee took a secondary *X-Men* character, Psylocke, and made her a star," Rizal Solomon enthused for the *Malay Mail* (30 Oct. 2002). "Before he came along, she was stuck in a stuffy costume. Lee got rid of that and gave her a slick and sexy Ninja look, which meshed well with her powers. He put in a whole lot of martial arts into the action sequences . . . and made Asians cool in mainstream American comics."

IMAGE COMICS

Lee and many of his fellow artists at Marvel realized they should be wielding more creative clout; they had grown weary of being pulled off projects they had worked on for years, seemingly at the whim of company executives, and they felt subject to sometimes illogical censorship. Lee has pointed out, for example, that they were not allowed to use the phrase "Oh my God," because of a prohibition at Marvel against the word *God*.

The industry was rocked when Lee and several other Marvel artists, including Marc Silvestri, Rob Liefeld, Todd McFarlane, Erik Larsen, Whilce Portacio, and Jim Valentino, all with stellar reputations among fans, abandoned Marvel to form their own company in 1992. "I think I was very fortunate to hit my stride in an environment where you had the Batman movies being very successful, the Ninja Turtles, the Power Rangers, all [that] stuff," Lee told George Johnston for the now-defunct quarterly magazine *Yolk* (30 Sep. 1997). "I remember taking an econ[omics] class in college and learning to put in a certain amount of time, then make a decision and stick by it rather than agonizing about it. There's risk involved but it's not gonna break you."

The artists called their new venture Image Comics and structured it in an unusual "creator-owned" manner. Each of the founding members established his own studio and produced his own comic books, thus ensuring that each artist would fully own and control his characters and work. (Portacio ultimately opted not to become a full partner, which causes some confusion when sources refer to the "gang of six," rather than seven, when discussing those who left Marvel.)

Lee called upon his old friend Brandon Choi, who had graduated from law school and was contemplating going to film school, to join him as a writer. Lee dubbed his new company WildStorm Productions after two of the main titles in his line: *WildC.A.T.s: Covert Action Teams* and *StormWatch*. *StormWatch* was based on the premise that the United Nations had gathered a group of soldiers and superheroes to act as a global crisis-intervention team, whereas the plotlines in *WildC.A.T.s* stories revolved around a centuries-long war between two tribes of aliens with exceptional powers. A *WildC.A.T.s* animated television series was created in 1994 and ran through 1995, which added to the company's financial success.

Among other titles released by WildStorm were *WetWorks*, *Team 7*, and *Gen 13*. *Gen 13*, which featured a cast of teenagers with superhuman powers, went on to become one of the best-selling series of the era and generated a line of popular videos.

By the mid-1990s, Image was a multimillion dollar company and had become direct competition for Marvel and DC. WildStorm alone was adding several new imprints to its roster, including Cliffhanger Comics, which was intended to showcase the work of emerging young artists. Many in the industry were thus surprised when Marvel approached Lee in 1996 with a proposal. Hoping to boost sales on some of their most revered titles and recognizing the power that Lee's name held for fans, they asked him to take over creative duties on the *Fantastic Four* and *Iron Man* series under a program they dubbed Heroes Reborn. (Another studio took on similar responsibilities for *The Avengers* and the *Captain America* series.) The new venture put increased scheduling demands on Lee who hired a large, in-house creative team, including cutting-edge computer colorists, to handle the load.

A NEW CHAPTER

In 1998, DC, Image Comics's other main rival, acquired Lee's company. Lee remained onboard to manage it, but after being relieved of many business-related obligations, he was able to devote more time to creating artwork. The collaboration proved to be a fruitful one. Of particular note to fans were the comics Lee created featuring the iconic characters of Batman and Superman. He was involved in a well-received 2002–2003 story arc in which Batman fights a mysterious villain named Hush, and the following year Lee illustrated *For Tomorrow*, a twelve-issue Superman series. In 2005, Lee teamed with Frank Miller, one of his idols, on the new series *All Star Batman and Robin, The Boy Wonder*, which reimagines Robin's origins and more fully examines the relationship between the boyish sidekick and the hero. Although the series met with great critical acclaim, it was plagued by delays, which sometimes frustrated fans.

In 2006, Lee began creating the art for DC Universe Online, a massive multiplayer online role-playing game, which was eagerly anticipated in the comics and gaming communities. Released in 2011, it allows players to create their own heroes or villains and interact with existing DC characters.

Meanwhile, in 2010, as Time Warner, DC's parent company, reorganized its various divisions and executives, Lee was named a copublisher of DC Comics. In this capacity, as Peter Rowe wrote, "Lee is expected to superheroically leverage comic book characters and story lines throughout the Time Warner empire, for everything from feature films to mobile phone applications." This new role also puts Lee at the forefront of important decision making regarding DC's digital comic campaigns and its online games, which further adds to his status within the company. As Rowe explained, "Converse wants to make Superman sneakers? Call Lee. Pottery Barn crafts comics-inspired furniture for kids? Sounds like another job for Super Artist."

Lee sometimes draws the ire of fans and industry observers, however, as when he oversaw a design of Wonder Woman. Finding her tight red top and spangled shorts dated, he drew her with less-revealing black leggings and a biker jacket. Although many male comic-book fans decried the new look, some mainstream pundits, including Tim Gunn, the cohost of the popular television show *Project Runway*, and Robin Givhan, the influential fashion critic for the *Washington Post*, applauded Lee's decision.

PERSONAL LIFE

Lee has been the subject of several books, including *The Art of Jim Lee*, 2007; *Image Comics: The Road to Independence*, 2007; and *Icons: The DC Comics and WildStorm Art of Jim Lee*, 2010. He has told journalists that he is comfortable with his level of fame. "I get recognized sometimes when I go out, but no one follows me around, no one cares where I eat. It's not real celebrity-ism," he explained to Skylar Browning. "When I go to a show, yeah, people will wait in line for hours for your signature or follow you into the bathroom or want to take pictures of you. But I get the best of both worlds because for a couple days each month when I'm at a show or make an appearance I get treated like a king and the rest of the time I can just go about my daily life."

Lee stands five feet four inches tall, and many fans speculate that whenever slightly built Asian men are depicted in the background of Lee's drawings, he has inserted a self-portrait into his work.

Lee has three daughters from his first marriage. He currently lives in La Jolla, California, with his second wife, Carla Michelle.

SUGGESTED READING

Biese, Alex. "Comic Genius: Art of DC Comics Chief Explored in Visual Essays." *Asbury Park Press*. 23 Jan. 2011: 27. Print.

Browning, Skylar. "Drawn to Success: Superhero Comic Artist Jim Lee Walks a Fine Line." *Missoula Independent*. 29 June 2006: 36. Print.

Johnston, George. "Jim Lee and Brandon Choi." *Yolk*. 30 Sep. 1997: 40. Print.

Rowe, Peter. "Superhero Superstar: La Jolla Resident Jim Lee Has Risen to the Top of the

Comics World." *San Diego Union-Tribune*. 18 July 2010: 1. Print.

Solomon, Rizal. "Marvellous Comeback." *Malay Mail*. 30 Oct. 2002: 28. Print.

Turgeon, Zac. "Time Well Spent: Jim Lee and Marv Wolfman." *Blast*. B Media Ventures LLC, 13 Feb. 2009. Web. 15 Jan. 2012.

—*Mari Rich*

Philip Levine

Born: January 10, 1928
Occupation: US poet laureate

Pulitzer Prize–winning poet Philip Levine writes in a straightforward style about his childhood in Detroit during the Great Depression, his Russian Jewish roots, his time in Spain in the mid-1960s, racial and social injustices, and his four years working different (and difficult) industrial jobs in Detroit after the end of World War II. Although he has an impressive oeuvre, Levine is best known for his poems about the latter, and he is often referred to as a "poet of the working class" or a "poet of industrial America." He is the author of twenty books of poetry, including *Not This Pig* (1968), *They Feed They Lion* (1972), *What Work Is* (1991), *Breath* (2004), and *News of the World* (2009), and has received many awards for his poetry throughout his long career. Levine achieved greater name recognition in America in 2011, when he was named poet laureate of the United States.

EARLY LIFE

The son of Russian Jewish immigrants, Philip Levine was born on January 10, 1928, in Detroit, Michigan. Levine's father died when he was five years old, after which Levine and his identical twin brother, Edward, were raised solely by their mother. Levine grew up during the Great Depression in Detroit and its outskirts, where he encountered violence, unemployment, and poverty. He began writing poetry during his teen years. Sometimes he would stand outside near his house, in the dark, and compose poems in his head. "What I found was a voice within myself that I didn't know was there," Levine recalled in an interview with Jessica Goldstein for the *Washington Post* (10 Aug. 2011). "A joy in my being, in creation, in the physical world that surrounded me." He added, "It began with a love of just the language. There was nothing that I had ever read that moved me as powerfully as some of the poetry I read. . . . Poems were something I could memorize and carry with me, and recite them in my head, and live with them."

AP Photo

STUDY AND WORK

After graduating from high school in 1946, Levine attended Wayne University (later Wayne State University) in Detroit, where he also worked a variety of industrial jobs to make ends meet. Years later, that experience of long, hard work would continue to provide him with material and inspiration for his poetry: he worked with chrome plates in a plumbing-parts factory, drove a truck for Railway Express, built transmissions for Cadillac, and worked in a Chevrolet plant. He received his bachelor's degree in 1950.

In 1953, Levine left Detroit for the University of Iowa, where he studied at the renowned Iowa Writers' Workshop with the poets Robert Lowell and John Berryman. The latter made a great impression on Levine; in an interview with Robert Taylor for the *Boston Globe* (2 Feb. 1994), Levine recalled, "No matter what you hear about his drinking, his madness, his unreliability as a person, I am here to tell you that in the winter and spring of 1954, living in isolation and loneliness in one of the bleakest towns of our difficult Midwest, John Berryman never failed his obligations as a teacher." Levine earned his MFA in 1957 from the University of Iowa, where he also taught writing. At the age of twenty-six, he decided with absolute certainty that he was going to become a poet. "I had immense confidence," Levine told Goldstein. "I don't know where the [expletive] it came from. I knew I could do this thing. I didn't know what the [expletive] it would be or where it would go."

After receiving the coveted Stegner Fellowship at Stanford University and studying for a year with the poet and critic Yvor Winters, Levine and his wife and two children settled in Fresno, California, in 1958. He taught writing and literature at California State University, Fresno from 1958 until 1975. He then continued to teach at the university part time until 1992, when he retired. In addition to Fresno State, Levine has had temporary stints as a teacher at a variety of colleges and universities, including Tufts University, Columbia University, Vassar College, Princeton University, New York University, and University of California, Berkeley.

BOOKS

About five years after moving to Fresno, Levine published his first book of poetry, *On the Edge* (1963). In that slim volume, Levine's work experience and skepticism with regard to the "American dream" are palpably reflected. His second book of poetry, *Not This Pig* (1968), explores this theme in a more lyrical and passionate manner. In the poem "Animals Are Passing from Our Lives," Levine hints at the working-class struggle by telling a story about a pig that does not want to be butchered from the pig's point of view; the pig cries, "No. Not this pig."

After the release of *Pili's Wall* (1971) and *Red Dust* (1971), Levine put out what some considered his strongest collection of poetry to date, *They Feed They Lion* (1972). Levine was fascinated with Spain, and he visited the country during an academic sabbatical in the 1960s. Like his working-class days, the trip provided him with plenty of writing material and inspiration, and it also deepened his love and appreciation for Spanish-language poets. *They Feed They Lion*, for example, contains a poem titled "To P.L., 1916–1937," which is about a Republican soldier fighting in the Spanish Civil War. Like his previous collections, the book also addresses themes of industrial America and social injustice.

Next came the book of poetry titled *1933*, published in 1974. The book, which includes such poems as "1933," "Uncle," and "Letters for the Dead," was perhaps the poet's most autobiographical work to date; Levine's father had died in 1933. The collection includes many often-surreal poems about family members and his native Detroit. Levine's surrealism can reasonably be attributed at least in part to his time in Spain and the influence of such Spanish-language poets as Cesar Vallejo and Pablo Neruda.

Levine's surrealism also surfaces in *The Names of the Lost* (1976), which includes such noteworthy poems as "Belle Isle, 1949," about a young couple bathing in the grimy Detroit River. The Spanish Civil War remained a source of inspiration, as is evident in the poem "On the Murder of Lieutenant José del Castillo by the Falangist Bravo Martinez, July 12, 1936." Many poems in the book are elegies to Levine's family members.

The year 1979 saw the publication of two works of poetry, *Seven Years from Somewhere* and *Ashes: Poems New and Old*, the latter being Levine's first career-spanning collection. The new poems in both collections maintain Levine's themes of work, everyday life, the Spanish Civil War, and familial memories. Levine also continued to use down-to-earth (by poetry standards) language. His goal was to tell stories and evoke feelings, not to dazzle the reader with clever wordplay or complex metaphors. As Levine gained more acclaim for his poetry, he faced both criticism and praise for his straightforward style.

Three years after the publication of *One for the Rose* (1981), Levine published his second comprehensive collection, titled *Selected Poems* (1984), which includes poems from all his previously published ten books. In a review of *Selected Poems* for the *Washington Post Book World* (5 Aug. 1984), Joel Conarroe observed a subtle yet noticeable thematic and emotional transition from Levine's early poetry to his more recent work. Reading from *On the Edge* to *One for the Rose*, Conarroe wrote, "is like stumbling through a forbidding woods finally to emerge in a sun-dappled field. Levine seems to have gone through the reverse of a mid-life crisis; I would describe it as a renaissance except I'm not sure about the 're.' Call it a mid-life emergence. His early books are grim, documenting a sensibility accustomed to failure, loss, bigotry, and violence. Examples of the latter are especially chilling." Conarroe then elaborated on the latter-day Levine, writing that the poet in his middle age had turned somewhat more hopeful without being naive and seemed to have resolved events that had haunted him for years, including his father's death.

Not all reviewers, however, wrote so enthusiastically about Levine's transformation as a poet. After the publication of his next collection, *Sweet Will* (1985), Levine was criticized in the pages of the *New York Times* (29 May 1985) by Michiko Kakutani, who observed that Levine's early works, such as *Not This Pig* and *They Feed They Lion*, were full of "moral urgency that the reader found hard to resist." The use of colloquial language then was quite effective, wrote Kakutani; however, she did not think that Levine's new outlook, in which anger was replaced at least in part by acceptance, was well served by his conversational verse.

After the release of *A Walk with Thomas Jefferson* (1988), Levine put out yet another comprehensive collection, *New Selected Poems* (1991), which presents the poems in chronological order. That same year also saw the publication of a new book of poetry, titled *What Work Is* (1991), which won both the National Book

Award for Poetry and the Los Angeles Times Book Award. Some reviewers pointed out that the biographical note in *What Work Is* had been revised; while the notes in Levine's previous books referred to his time in Detroit as having "a succession of stupid jobs," the one in *What Work Is* read "a succession of industrial jobs."

This change, as well as the softening of his anger and the increased use of humor in his poems, led some reviewers again to point to a change in Levine's perspective. In a review for the *Washington Post* (14 July 1991), Alfred Corn observed that "the opening poems are suffused by a chastened tone that contrasts with the sarcasm of some of the earlier poems. It didn't seem possible that Levine could improve on his first working-class portraits, yet I feel that these new poems are an improvement: An extra dimension of dignity has been conferred on his characters. We sense their conviction that there is nothing 'stupid' about the prospect of earning one's living, even in harsh and exploitative circumstances. The poems 'Fear and Fame,' 'Coming Close,' 'Every Blessed Day,' and the title poem are perhaps the most moving that Levine has written—tender without being sentimental, calm but not lacking in passion, written in a diction as clear and lucid as spring water."

The poem "Fear and Fame" describes how Levine, during his days working at "Feinberg and Breslin's / First-Rate Plumbing and Plating," would put on his helmet, protective boots, and respirator. *What Work Is* also contains "Burned," Levine's longest poem to date. Toward the end of the poem, Levine writes, "The earth's own sighs, / the day's last breath going out, / my own silent cry of denial. They're / all asleep, all the windows from here / to the end of the world are open, / I can hear the even breathing / of all that is wordless and final." In his enthusiastic review of *What Work Is*, Jan Herman of the *Los Angeles Times* (3 Nov. 1991) observed that the book's "twenty-five poems, though dense with life's debris, are a passionate affirmation." Herman also pointed out that Levine was not only older and wiser but also warmer, even when dealing with tough subject matter such as survival, urban decay, love, and death. Yet in many instances the "sardonic temperament" that was very common in his earlier poetry still comes through, though in subtler ways.

In 1994, Levine released *The Simple Truth*. Featuring poems that mine his past experiences in his newly (somewhat) triumphant style, the collection won the Pulitzer Prize for poetry in April of the following year. Also published in 1994 was an essay collection called *The Bread of Time: Toward an Autobiography*, a collection of nine autobiographical and literary essays. Some are dedicated to Levine's mentors, such as John Berryman in Iowa and Yvor Winters in California; some refer to his Russian Jewish roots and

his years spent in working-class Detroit doing manual labor; others tell the story of living in Spain in the mid-1960s, working there as a tutor, and discovering the Spanish poet and playwright Garcia Lorca. Readers also learn that one of the people Levine most admired in his childhood was a pants presser in a tailor shop, in whose movements Levine saw that "all work was worth doing with elegance and precision and that necessary work granted dignity to the worker."

Reviewing one of Levine's subsequent books of poetry, *The Mercy* (1999), for the *New York Times* (18 Apr. 1999), Adam Kirsch observed that Levine's projection of himself as "a common man" is a persona that is most likely a reflection of Levine as a person; however, Kirsch added, "it is also a literary creation, with antecedents in Whitman and Hemingway: masculine, sentimental, fraternal, sensual." Although Kirsch called *The Mercy* "one of Levine's finest books," he criticized the poet's insistence on writing about real experiences in a nonliterary way, which he thought Levine was doing to try to avoid sounding artificial.

Five years later, Levine published the poetry collection *Breath* (2004), so titled because he noticed that the word "breath" often comes up in the poems. The epigraph, taken from a line in the last poem in the book, "Call It Music," reads as follows: "Some days I catch a rhythm, almost a song / in my own breath." Music, particularly jazz, has played an important part in the poet's life and has proved to be an inspiration, and the book is full of references to jazz greats such as Lester Young, Charlie Parker, Clifford Brown, Miles Davis, and Bud Powell. In a glowing review of *Breath* for the *New York Times* (21 Nov. 2004), Terrence Rafferty observed, "What gives Levine's work its urgency is that impulse to commemorate, the need to restore to life people who were never, despite their deadening work, dead things themselves, and who deserve to be rescued from the longer death of being forgotten." Five years after *Breath* came *News of the World* (2009). The title of this collection is appropriate, as many of the poems are set in Cuba, Spain, Portugal, and other countries outside of the United States. The book was, for the most part, positively received.

In August 2011, Levine was selected to be the poet laureate of the United States. Librarian of Congress James Billington hailed Levine as the laureate "of the industrial heartland," as quoted by Charles McGrath in the *New York Times* (9 Aug. 2011, online). Soon after the announcement, sales of Levine's books increased significantly. Particularly in demand were *The Simple Truth* and *What Work Is*. Of his appointment, Levine said to Andrew Goldman for the *New York Times* (4 Nov. 2011, online) that he has been surprised by the attention. "People like my doctor or the guy who sells me wine or the people in my gym come up to me and say, 'Oh, Phil, this is marvelous.' Some of them didn't even know I was a poet. Now there are mobs of people when I give readings." While pleased with the honor, Levine also said that he did not seek it out, nor does he take it too seriously.

AWARDS AND MILESTONES

Throughout his long career, Levine has received many honors and awards, including a Guggenheim Foundation fellowship (1973), the Frank O'Hara Prize (1973), an American Academy of Arts and Letters Award (1973), the National Book Critics Circle Award (1980), the Ruth Lilly Poetry Prize (1987), two National Book Awards (1980, 1991), and the Pulitzer Prize for poetry (1995).

Levine married his wife, Fran, a painter, in the mid-1950s. He is a father and a grandfather. He lives with his wife in Fresno, California.

SUGGESTED READING

Buckley, Christopher, ed. *On the Poetry of Philip Levine: Stranger to Nothing*. Ann Arbor: U of Michigan P, 1991.

Corn, Alfred. "Songs of Innocence and Experience." *Washington Post Book World* 14 July 1991: 3.

Dirda, Michael. "A Life Lived Poetically." *Washington Post* 14 Feb. 1994: D2.

Herman, Jan. "Philip Levine's Factory Stiffs, Society's Throw-Aways." *Huffington Post.* TheHuffingtonPost.com, 11 Aug. 2011. Web. 11 May 2012.

McGrath, Charles. "Voice of the Workingman to Be Poet Laureate." *New York Times*. New York Times, 9 Aug. 2011. Web. 11 May 2012.

Rafferty, Terrence. "Can't Forget the Motor City." *New York Times Book Review* 21 Nov. 2004: 19.

—*Dmitry Kiper*

Michael Lewis

Born: October 15, 1960
Occupation: Nonfiction writer

Beginning with his first book, *Liar's Poker* (1989), about the greed of Wall Street, bestselling nonfiction author Michael Lewis has developed a reputation as an insightful and witty writer with an ability to make any subject entertaining. His books *Moneyball* (2003), about the new use of statistics in baseball, and *The Blind Side* (2006), about an uneducated, impoverished youth who makes it big in college football, were big hits with reviewers and readers, and later made into major motion pictures. He is the author of many other books, including *The Big Short* (2010) and

WireImage

Boomerang (2011). Lewis joined *Vanity Fair* as a contributing editor in February 2009. He has also written for such publications as the *New York Times Magazine*, the *New Yorker*, *Gourmet*, *Sports Illustrated*, the *New Republic*.

EARLY LIFE AND EDUCATION

Michael Monroe Lewis was born on October 15, 1960 in New Orleans, Louisiana. His father, J. Thomas, worked as a corporate lawyer, and his mother, Diana, was a community activist. Lewis grew up in New Orleans, where he attended the private Isidore Newman School, graduating from its high school in 1978. Both of his parents graduated from Isidore in 1955. After graduation, Lewis enrolled at Princeton University, in New Jersey. At Princeton, he focused on art history, and in 1982, earned his bachelor's degree in art and archeology. Lewis then moved to the United Kingdom, where he pursued a master's degree at the London School of Economics (LSE). In 1984, while still in school, he received an invitation from a distant cousin to a dinner given by Queen Elizabeth II. At the dinner, Lewis, in a rented tuxedo, found himself sitting next to a woman who turned out to be the wife of a managing partner at Salomon Brothers, a big Wall Street investment bank. Lewis made such an impression on the woman that she asked her husband to find the young man a job.

A BRIEF CAREER IN FINANCE

Lewis graduated from the LSE with a master's degree in economics in 1985. Because of the connection he had made at the Queen's dinner, he was hired at Salomon Brothers as a junior bond salesman. Lewis worked in New York and later in the Solomon Brothers office in London. Initially, as a trainee, Lewis made $48,000 a year. However, by 1987, working as an institutional bond salesman at the London office, he was earning an annual salary of $225,000. Lewis could have stayed at his position and made a substantial amount of money, but he was turned off by the aggressive and unethical nature of the job—for example, selling bonds to investors that the Salomon bond salesmen knew would soon decrease substantially in value. In early 1988, he resigned, deciding instead to become a financial journalist.

WORK AS A FINANCIAL JOURNALIST

The three years Lewis spent at Salomon Brothers provided him with the material for his first book, *Liar's Poker: Rising Through the Wreckage on Wall Street* (1989). The book describes Lewis's work at Salomon Brothers—where he advised investors on what bonds to purchase, knowing that Salomon could not unload those bonds to anyone else. The book also describes the atmosphere of greed in the culture of Wall Street. Lewis writes about how the traders not only gambled the firm's money, figuratively speaking, but also how they literally gambled with each other. In the book, he describes how the firm's top traders would play a few hands of liar's poker—the game of the title—for a few hundred dollars, each trying to guess the numbers on dollar bills. Lewis alleges that John Gutfreund, chair of Salomon Brothers, challenged John Meriwether, one of the company's top traders, to a game of liar's poker worth $1 million. According to Lewis, Meriwether turned around and challenged Gutfreund to a $10 million game. Salomon Brothers officially denies the story. Although the game did not occur, Lewis uses the story to portray the reckless approach to large sums of money by many Wall Street investment bankers. *Liar's Poker* also describes the excessive spending that occurred at Salomon Brothers before the 1987 stock market crash. As a result of the crash, the company made significant personnel cuts, but Lewis kept his job because he was making a good deal of money for the firm.

The success of *Liar's Poker* served as a testament to Lewis's ability to draw readers into subject matter that might seem, upon first consideration, uninteresting or dry. Critics worldwide praised the book. In a review for the *New York Times* (29 Oct. 1989), Richard L. Stern called Lewis's account of his time at Salomon "very funny." Stern concludes that Lewis was "as good a writer as he was a bond salesman. Perhaps that's because both jobs involve being able to tell a good story." John Schwartz, writing for *Newsweek* (20 Nov. 1989), said that the "the hilarious incidents [in the book] combine to form a dismal picture [of] a culture driven solely by greed, with traders 'jamming' poor investments into the portfolios of much-maligned customers." On a similar note, a review published in the *Economist* (18 Nov. 1989) states that Lewis's "impressionistic but thoroughly readable book catches the hypocrisy and arrogance of financiers over the last decade. Since banks started their insane lending to Latin America, financiers everywhere have been eager to emphasize that banking is a vocation as much as a business." The review continues: "But *Liar's Poker* strongly suggests that the gambling element has eclipsed the grand old business of investment banking; matching borrowers with lenders, and steering wealth towards investments that will create still more."

Lewis continued to produce his own unique brand of financial journalism. In 1991, he published two books. In *Pacific Rift: Adventures in the Fault Zone Between the U.S. and Japan*, he describes the differences and similarities between the way business is done in the United States and Japan. *The Money Culture*, a collection of Lewis's essays and articles, profiles big financial players such as Ivan Boesky, Leona Helmsley, and Donald Trump. Lewis's next book, *Trail Fever: Spin Doctors, Rented Strangers, Thumb Wrestlers, Toe Suckers, Grizzly Bears, and Other Creatures on the Road to the White House* (1997), represented his first venture into political writing. The material in the book is from Lewis's coverage of the 1996 US presidential campaign for the *New Republic*. "This book is not the usual insider account of how Mr. Clinton won and Mr. Dole lost, as told by the candidates and their 'rented strangers,' the aides, consultants and spin doctors who write the campaign script," wrote Phil Gailey for the *New York Times* (8 June 1997). "It is deeper, funnier and more edifying than that. It is about the almost farcical demands of politics in the television age and about how little an indifferent and cynical electorate asks of candidates who manipulate the issues instead of addressing them, who ignore the great questions before the country instead of honestly debating them." In *Trail Fever*, Lewis argues that neither Bill Clinton, the Democratic candidate, nor Bob Dole, the Republican candidate, talked openly and honestly about the issues. Their campaigns, according to Lewis, were well-oiled machines meant to guide their respective candidates through debates and public appearances and avoid honest discussion of the issues. Lewis found that the less popular candidates, such as Pat Buchanan, Steve Forbes, Alan Keys, and Morry Taylor were more forthcoming with the American public. Although their views were often extreme or provocative, Lewis believed they had a candor that Clinton and Dole did not. Lewis's conclusion, which many reviewers agreed with but some found too cynical, was that speaking one's mind was a sure way to endanger a presidential candidacy.

EXPLORING SILICON VALLEY

For his next book, *The New New Thing: A Silicon Valley Story* (1999), Lewis again ventured into new territory. He approached it in his recognized style: smart, entertaining writing that is full of engaging dialogue and descriptions. *The New New Thing* focuses on the story of entrepreneur and engineer Jim Clark, the founder of Healtheon, Silicon Graphics, and Netscape. The introduction of Netscape made the Internet less chaotic and more approachable for computer users. After the company went public, its stock price rose rapidly, creating an atmosphere of speculation around other technology companies. Lewis's book explores Clark's way of thinking, and examines his view of technology and the future.

Next: The Future Just Happened, published in the summer of 2001, picked up where Lewis's previous book had left off. By this time, the dotcom bubble, which had grown as a result of speculation and over-valuation of technology companies, had burst. Lewis chose to focus on a new narrative: the Internet has destroyed many previously entrenched business hierarchies. Lewis selected several examples to make his point. Perhaps most prominently, Lewis profiled Jonathan Lebed, who as a thirteen-year-old started selling obscure stocks that he had hyped up in online chat rooms—and made a few hundred thousand dollars in the process. He eventually gained the attention of the Securities and Exchange Commission (SEC). Other teenagers Lewis profiled include the fourteen-year-old Daniel Sheldon of the United Kingdom who created a file-sharing program, and Marcus Arnold, a fifteen-year-old California kid who posed online as a legal expert whose "expertise" was the result of watching TV shows about the law.

Next received mixed reviews. The reviews that were generally positive opined that Lewis's storytelling ability is superior to his economic or sociological thinking. In a review for the *New York Times* (29 July 2001), Walter Kirn pointed out that Lewis "writes best when he's personalizing, not analyzing, economic change." *Newsweek*'s David Brooks (20 Aug. 2001) observed, "Lewis's mistake is to take these fantastic psychological sketches and try to hold them up as representative sociological nuggets. When he is analyzing personalities, he is fresh and original; when he is practicing sociology, he is the victim of dead philosophers. He shoehorns every tale into the stereotypical conflict between the noble child and the corrupt adult civilization." In early August 2011, a four-hour BBC documentary based on the book aired on A&E. Like the book, it received mixed reviews.

MONEYBALL AND THE BLIND SIDE

Lewis's next book, *Moneyball: The Art of Winning an Unfair Game* (2003), received generally excellent reviews and was beloved just the same by baseball fans and those who cared little for the sport. At its core, the book is not just about baseball, but something bigger: working against traditional thinking and turning a generally accepted system of analysis on its head. *Moneyball* details the work of Oakland Athletics general manager Billy Beane and his unique, statistics-driven method for acquiring new players. With help from a young statistician by the name of Paul DePodesta, Beane recruited players using statistics ignored by other teams, such as on-base percentage (as opposed to batting average). A film version of the book, starring Brad Pitt and Jonah Hill, was released in 2011.

Lewis's 2005 book *Coach: Lessons on the Game of Life* (2005), details his high school baseball career and his coach's lessons about the sport and life in general. Lewis published *The Blind Side: Evolution of a Game* in 2006. Just as he did in *Moneyball*, Lewis used one central character to illustrate the evolution of a sport. The hero of *The Blind Side* is Michael Oher, an African American child born in Memphis to a poor, crack-addicted mother who was looking after as many as ten young children. Oher did poorly in school, had to repeat several grades, barely spoke, and was living in miserable surroundings. His life changed after meeting Sean and Leigh Anne Tuohy, white Evangelical Christians who became his legal guardians. In his mid-teens Oher was six feet five inches tall and weighed approximately 340 pounds. *The Blind Side* tells how Oher became a successful high school and collegiate athlete. The book is also about the trend in college and professional football in recruiting strong, agile offensive linemen to protect the quarterback, particularly his blind side (the side his back is facing). In a review for the *New York Times* (12 Nov. 2006), George F. Will concluded, "Oher's story is not pretty, but Lewis tells it well." And Janet Maslin of the *New York Times* (5 Oct. 2006) observed, "[The book's] dialogue is sharp and its anecdotes well chosen. Its aim for both the heartstrings and the funny bone is right on the mark." A film version of the book, staring Sandra Bullock and Quinton Aaron, was released in 2009.

OTHER WORKS

In 2008, Lewis edited *The Real Price of Everything: Rediscovering the Six Classics of Economics*, a large compilation of classic works by such economists as Adam Smith and Thomas Malthus. He also edited *Panic: The Story of Modern Financial Insanity*, a collection of newspaper articles, magazine stories, and academic works about major financial collapses by such economists as Paul Krugman, John Cassidy, and Lewis himself.

For *Home Game: An Accidental Guide to Fatherhood* (2009), Lewis turned to himself and his family for material. The book focuses on his three young children, two girls and a boy, and the process of learning Lewis experiences in raising them. The book is a compilation of stories Lewis wrote for the online magazine *Slate*. Lewis returned to financial matters in his next two books. *The Big Short* (2010) is the story of investors who made money by trading on predictions related to the US housing market before its collapse in 2008. The book explored one of Lewis's favorite topics: the outsider and out-of-the-box thinker who does not go with the flow of popular opinion. A reviewer for the *Economist* (20 Mar. 2010) called the book "hugely entertaining." In *Boomerang: Travels in the New Third World* (2011), Lewis explores how the 2008 global financial crisis affected countries like Ireland, Iceland, and Greece. Michiko Kakutani, in a review for the *New York Times* (27 Sep. 2011), wrote, "Mr. Lewis's ability to find people who can see what is obvious to others only in retrospect, or who somehow embody something larger going on in the financial world, is uncanny. [I]n this book, he weaves their stories into a sharp-edged narrative that leaves readers with a visceral understanding of the fiscal recklessness that lies behind [the] headlines." Like most of his other books, *Boomerang* became a bestseller.

Lewis and his wife, former television personality Tabitha Soren, live in Berkeley, California. They have three children: daughters Quinn and Dixie, and a son, Walker.

SUGGESTED READING

Maslin, Janet. "Three Strikes You're Out at the New Ballgame." *New York Times* 12 May 2003: 6.

Queenan, Joe. "There Goes the Bonus." *Forbes* 30 Oct. 1989: 14.

Stern, Richard L. "Overpaid and Guilt-ridden." *New York Times* 29 Oct. 1989: 39.

—*Dmitry Kiper*

Antony Garrett Lisi

Born: January 24, 1968
Occupation: Theoretical physicist and adventurer

Antony Garrett Lisi, who goes by the first name Garrett, is a theoretical physicist as well as a surfing and snowboarding enthusiast. The latter description is notable because Lisi, whose life is dictated by the seasons of the surf and slopes, claims to have discovered the elusive "theory of

© Ron Haviv/VII/Corbis

everything" in his spare time. The theory of everything, or TOE, is the decades-long quest of theoretical physicists to link Einstein's general theory of relativity, which describes large and/ or tangible things, like snowflakes and stars, to quantum mechanics, which describes very small things, like subatomic particles. The theory would also mathematically explain how the four governing forces of nature—electromagnetic force, gravity, and strong and weak nuclear forces—are able to coexist.

In the 1960s, physicists began developing the standard model of particle physics, an incomplete if not important theory that describes how fundamental particles interact. The theory incorporates three of the forces but not gravity. The most popular candidate for a working TOE, which includes gravity, is string theory. String theory, developed in the late 1960s and early 1970s, describes particles as vibrating strings, as opposed to zero-dimensional points; the vibrations of these strings create different particles. There are five variations on string theory that are collectively referred to as M-theory. The theory is complex (it requires the existence of several compacted dimensions beyond the four that are known to humans), though the mathematics are aesthetically seductive to most theoretical physicists—most physicists that is, except for Lisi. Lisi believes that there is a much simpler way to describe the known universe. He set forth his own idea, based on a mathematical super structure called E_8, in a 2007 paper titled, "An Exceptionally Simple Theory of Everything."

EARLY LIFE

Lisi was born on January 24, 1968, in San Diego, California. His mother died when he was a baby. His father, who later remarried, is a probate attorney and former Navy fighter pilot. Lisi was playing in the ocean before he learned to walk. As a child, he also took an interest in computers. Using an Apple II, Lisi programmed and designed video games in his bedroom. At the age of sixteen, his father gave him an old VW microbus. Lisi used it to search the California coastline for waves as he learned to surf.

Lisi enrolled at the University of California, Los Angeles (UCLA), where he became obsessed with applying mathematics to the secrets of the universe. He graduated summa cum laude and first in his class in 1991 with dual degrees in mathematics and physics. Additionally, he received the Kinsey Prize for Outstanding Graduating Senior in Physics. Lisi was accepted to several PhD physics programs, including one of the world's best at UC Berkeley. He ultimately chose UC San Diego, where he could live on the beach.

As a doctoral student, Lisi worked with theoretical physicist Roger Dashen, to whom he expressed an interest in spinor fields, which are mathematical representations of electrons. He wanted to focus on a particular mathematical anomaly that he thought might explain certain properties of an electron. Four years into Lisi's doctorate, Dashen died of a heart attack while teaching a seminar. Lisi, who was in the class that day, was devastated. He decided to set aside his research on spinor fields and pursue a more conventional track. Lisi finished his doctorate in 1999. He completed his dissertation on the physics of the movement of water over a swimming dolphin.

Lisi first encountered string theory as a graduate student. He told Benjamin Wallace-Wells for the *New Yorker* (21 July 2008) his reaction upon hearing for the first time about a new string theory development called the Maldacena conjecture: "It was very interesting mathematics," Lisi said. "But I remember walking out of this office and wondering what it had to do with any physical reality. And, as far as I could tell, it didn't." Lisi realized that for a theoretical physicist, his post-doctoral options would be limited to studying the intricacies of string theory. Academia had settled around the theory as the best bet for a working TOE, but Lisi was unconvinced. "If you share an office next to a guy for twenty years, and you like him and you're friends with him, it's hard to tell him that you think that his whole idea of how the universe works is completely wrong," Lisi said of his colleagues. He decided he would rather leave academia altogether than conform.

NOMADIC PHYSICIST

After earning his PhD, Lisi moved to Hawaii with computer scientist and friend Brandyn Webb. Lisi had saved up some cash from his investment in Apple as a grad student. He lived on the grounds of the Sudbury Maui School and encouraged one of the students, who chart their own course of study, to study the physics of baseball. Lisi and Webb spent their time surfing and thinking about physics. In fact, Lisi's surfboard is covered in mathematical equations that describe the movement and proliferation of waves.

In 2002, Lisi moved to Breckenridge, Colorado, to teach snowboarding. There he came across the revival of an obscure description of gravity in a paper by theoretical physicist Lee Smolin. Smolin is one of the developers of the theory of loop quantum gravity. Begun in the 1980s, the loop quantum gravity theory challenges string theory. In his paper, Smolin describes gravity as the connection between two moving shapes; Lisi combined the description with the standard model on a geometric structure known as a Clifford bundle. The result was crude, but the number of coincidences between the shapes and the theories suggested to Lisi that he might be on to something.

In 2004, Lisi bought a white utility van and moved back to Maui. He remodeled the vehicle as a makeshift residence, though it lacked a toilet, and parked it on the beach. Lisi and his girlfriend Crystal Baranyk, whom he had recently met online, lived there for nearly a year. For income, Lisi relied on Baranyk, who is an artist and worked as a consultant on a Hollywood science fiction movie. Computer scientist Reichart Von Wolfsheild hired him to create probability tables in order to predict payout rates for Las Vegas poker machines (the two would later co-host a season of the History Channel television show *Invention USA* in 2011), and he taught a few introductory physics courses at a branch of the University of Hawaii.

By 2006, Lisi's meager finances were wearing thin. He applied for a grant through the Foundational Questions Institute, a group that provides funds for theoretical physicists. Lisi was awarded a stipend of $38,640 per year for two years; he was the only physicist of the thirty selected who was not working out of a major university or institute. With his first check, he bought a mountain bike. Lisi's friends loaned them their house on Lake Tahoe, in California, for the season. It was there, perusing mathematics blogs in the early morning, that Lisi saw the possibility for a mathematical coincidence that he found very enticing.

THE E8 STRUCTURE

On the blog Lisi had been reading, he saw a post by John Baez, another proponent of loop quantum gravity, about a structure called E_8. E_8 is considered one of the most elegant symmetrical structures in mathematics and boasts 248 dimensions. It was discovered in 1887 by the Norwegian mathematician Sophus Lie. Lie applied group theory, a concept used in abstract algebra, to geometry. The result is what is known as a Lie group, which refers to an underlying symmetry between an algebraic structure and a geometric structure. E_8 is considered an exceptional Lie group, as opposed to a simple one. It was not until 2007 that a group of physicists, with the aid of a supercomputer, were able to map the interworkings of E_8. In other words, they were able to solve the equation set forth by Lie over one hundred years ago. It took the computer four years to complete the task; many sources have written that the equation typed in small print would cover an area roughly the size of Manhattan. The work toward solving E_8 was the subject of Baez's blog post that Lisi read in 2006.

Lisi noticed that the E_8 structure was a rough match with the geometrical structure he had been building for several years with the Clifford bundles. "It was the most stunning thing I could ever ask for," Lisi told Evan Ratcliff for *Outside* magazine (5 May 2008). "I walked around with my brain tickling, thinking, This is going to work."

Lisi mapped the contents of the standard model directly onto E_8. The mathematics seemed to work for the first generation particles, or particles that appear in everyday life. The standard model accounts for second- and third-generation particles that are variations on their first-generation counterparts in extraordinary circumstances or high energy. When Lisi finished, there were twenty points on E_8 left without a corresponding particle. Lisi hypothesizes that these points represent particles that have yet to be discovered. If one of these unknown particles were to be discovered, Lisi reasons, his TOE would hold.

Lisi published his paper "An Exceptionally Simple Theory of Everything" online in 2007. The cheeky title also refers to the classification of E_8 as an exceptional Lie group. Earlier, Lisi had attended a conference where he met Smolin, who expressed an interest in Lisi's work. Lisi valued the encouragement of other physicists. As he told Wallace-Wells of his independent working life: "Ninety-five percent of my time is virtually wasted. If I were in a university, one of my colleagues would say, 'No, that direction makes no sense—other people have looked into it, and it doesn't go anywhere.' Here no one stops me."

Lisi's paper generated a lot of public excitement very quickly. Newspapers touted him as a maverick genius that had shirked the stuffy world of academia for a bohemian existence scribbling equations in his van. The fact that Lisi appeared in the press at all was unusual for a theoretical physicist. He was juggling interviews and crafting a lecture for a TED conference

(TED, or Technology, Entertainment, Design, is a nonprofit that promotes the spreading of ideas) months after an abstract of "An Exceptionally Simple Theory of Everything" appeared in *Scientific American*. Others, like Smolin, saw in Lisi a possibility for clarity in a field increasingly dominated by impenetrable and untestable theories. "There's a dream that underlying the physical universe is some beautiful mathematical structure, and that the job of physics is to discover that," Smolin told Wallace-Wells. "The dream is in bad shape." Smolin compared his longing for that dream to a recovering alcoholic. Hearing Lisi for the first time, Smolin said, "was like being offered a drink."

BACKLASH AND DEBATE

Despite his personal celebrity, Lisi has experienced bitter criticism for his E_8 theory, particularly among leading string theorists. By publishing his theory, he stepped into a raging scientific debate. Lisi, a long-time critic of string theory, aligned himself with physicists like Smolin, who in 2006 published a book called *The Trouble with Physics: The Rise of String Theory, the Fall of a Science, and What Comes Next*.

Lisi and Smolin argue that the trouble with string theory is that it has become permanently divorced from the real world. The mathematics of the theory are seen as beautiful, but the theory itself relies on the existence of ten to eleven dimensions that are too small to be detected by humans. Furthermore, using the latest technology, it is impossible to test string theory. This is because the vibrations of the strings operate at too high a frequency. Physicists like Smolin, Wallace-Wells wrote, worry that the mathematics part of string theory, which continues to grow, has become "an exercise in its own complexity."

Still, there are problems with Lisi's E_8 theory, some of which Lisi's paper cites. For instance, Lisi's structure does not account for second- and third-generation particles, and there are several other aspects of the theory that remain unfinished or undefined. Lisi admits that the E_8 theory is a work in progress, and it could very well be wrong. Nevertheless, he has staked his career on this not being the case. John Donoghue, a physicist at the University of Massachusetts at Amherst, told Ratcliff of Lisi, "No one has come up with a theory that works yet. It's the same for all of us. It's premature to canonize him but premature to say he's barking up the wrong tree."

THE FUTURE

The world's most powerful particle accelerator, the Large Hadron Collider (LHC), began operations in Switzerland in 2008. The LHC is one of the world's largest scientific instruments created to study the universe's smallest particles. Scientists hope the speed of the particles and the conditions of their resulting collision will recreate the conditions they hypothesize followed the Big Bang, the cosmological model many scientists theorize that created the universe.

The beginning of the LHC was a significant event for theoretical physicists because it marked the first time that a number of theories could be tested. In 2012, physicists found evidence for the elusive Higgs boson using the LHC. More accurately, they found a particle that behaved in a way that they expected the Higgs to behave according to the standard model. The Higgs boson, physicists believe, gives other particles mass. The boson is a part of a larger Higgs field; scientists believe the boson "chipped" off a piece of this field post-collision. The discovery, revealed with a high degree of certainty, was a milestone because it gave a tantalizing glimpse into other parts of the universe that the LHC might be capable of revealing.

Since his 2007 publication, Lisi, and others who have taken an interest in his theory, has been working on incorporating the second- and third-generation particles onto the E_8 structure. He has also been working on finding properties that might describe the twenty missing particles suggested by the E_8 structure. If he can predict these properties, the LHC could ultimately prove or disprove his entire theory by finding a particle that matches the properties he describes.

PERSONAL LIFE

Outside of physics, Lisi has kept himself busy as a thrill-seeker. He once broke his board in an especially rough wave; the surf carried him so far down the coast that he had to hitchhike home with a bloody face. He has been known to wear a laboratory coat on the ski slopes. "I've tried to make the rest of my life good enough that even if the physics theories don't work out," he told Ratcliff, "it wasn't a waste of time."

Lisi hosted one season of the television show *Invention USA* on the History Channel in 2011. On the show, Lisi and Von Wolfsheild searched the country for the next great inventors.

Lisi and Baranyk have lived on the island of Maui and on Lake Tahoe. They continue to relocate at their whim.

SUGGESTED READING

Farrar, Steve. "Einstein on a Snowboard." *Sunday Times* [London]. Times Newspapers Ltd., 18 Nov. 2007. Web. 11 July 2012.

Highfield, Roger. "Surfer Dude's Theory of Everything: The Magic of Garrett Lisi." *Telegraph* [London]. Telegraph Media Group Ltd., 10 Nov. 2009. Web. 11 July 2012.

Lisi, A. Garrett, and James Owen Weatherall. "A Geometric Theory of Everything." *Scientific American*. Nature American, Inc., 29 Nov. 2010. Web. 18 July 2012.

Merali, Zeeya. "Is Mathematical Pattern the Theory of Everything?" *New Scientist*. Reed Business Information Ltd., 15 Nov. 2007. Web. 11 July 2012.

Ratcliff, Evan. "Has a Surfer/Snowboarder Who Lives in a Van Rewritten Physics? Maybe." *Outside*. Mariah Media Network, LLC., 5 May 2008. Web. 11 July 2012.

Wallace-Wells, Benjamin. "Surfing the Universe: An Academic Dropout and the Search for a Theory of Everything." *New Yorker*. Condé Nast. 21 July 2008. Web. 11 July 2012.

—*Molly Hagan*

Jonah Lomu

Born: May 12, 1975
Occupation: Rugby player

Jonah Lomu, a former winger for New Zealand's All Blacks national rugby union team, was one of the most feared and devastating forces ever to step on the rugby pitch. Lomu, who is of Tongan descent, emerged from a troubled and violent upbringing in a tough South Auckland neighborhood to become one of New Zealand's most beloved sports icons. In 1994, at age nineteen, he became the youngest player ever to play in an All Blacks test match (a sanctioned international contest between two teams).

After appearing in several other international competitions, Lomu achieved his breakthrough at the 1995 Rugby World Cup in South Africa, where he delivered "one of the most destructive solo performances ever witnessed," Tim Gow declared in the *Daily Express* (28 May 2004). He scored seven tries in five matches (a try being the equivalent of a touchdown in American and Canadian football), including four in a semifinal match against England. While New Zealand lost to host nation South Africa in the World Cup final, Lomu was named player of the tournament and rose to become the sport's first true global superstar and its first millionaire. He went on to star for the All Blacks at the 1999 Rugby World Cup in Wales, where he scored a record eight tries, becoming the all-time World Cup top try scorer with fifteen in total. Altogether, he amassed thirty-seven tries in sixty-three career test matches for the All Blacks.

Standing at an imposing six feet five inches and weighing around 280 pounds, Lomu is credited with revolutionizing the game of rugby with his rare combination of blazing speed and brute strength. His ability to punish and steamroll multiple defenders at a time led the esteemed rugby commentator Ian Robertson to call him a "colossus, who has bestrode the world of rugby,"

AFP/Getty Images

as Fraser Thomson noted for the *Birmingham (England) Post* (15 Dec. 2001).

Lomu's career, which also included stints playing for several New Zealand regional teams, was cut short in 2002 by a degenerative kidney disease called nephrotic syndrome, which forced him to undergo a kidney transplant in 2004. Following a successful recovery, Lomu returned to make his rugby comeback the following year, moving to Wales to sign with the Cardiff Blues of the Celtic League (now known as the RaboDirect Pro 12), where he played for just one injury-plagued season. Subsequent injuries and diminished ability led to his retirement from rugby in 2007, though he made another short-lived comeback two years later.

While Lomu's debilitating condition prevented him from living up to what was viewed as astronomical potential, with people remembering him "as a rugby supernova, a player who once lit up the sport's firmament, oh-so-brightly but all-too-briefly," as Alasdair Reid wrote for the Glasgow *Sunday Herald* (8 Jan. 2006), he remains one of the most legendary rugby players of all time.

EARLY LIFE AND EDUCATION

Jonah Tali Lomu was born on May 12, 1975, in Auckland, the largest and most populous city in New Zealand. When he was very young, his parents, Semisi and Hepi Lomu, sent him back to their native Tonga to live with his maternal aunt and uncle, "perhaps so he could see and understand the world through their eyes," Chris

Hewett wrote for the *Independent* (9 Oct. 1999). He was raised there until he reached school age.

While being sent to live with other family members was common in Polynesian tradition, Lomu recalled to Tim Gow, "Usually the eldest is taken by the father's side but I wasn't because I wasn't named after my grandfather. They sent me to my mother's family." As a result, he grew up thinking his aunt and uncle were his parents. In contrast, Lomu's younger brother, John, who is one year his junior, was brought up by his father's family and named after his grandfather. Lomu has said that he was disowned by his father's side of the family because of his name and that he has no idea why his brother was named after his grandfather instead.

At around the age of seven, Lomu returned to Auckland to live with his parents. He grew up in a modest state house in Mangere, a poverty-ridden, gang-infested neighborhood on the city's south side. Lomu endured a difficult childhood, plagued by pent-up anger and aggression and a strained relationship with his father, who was described by Abigail Wild for the Glasgow *Herald* (4 June 2004) as "a hard-working but heavy-drinking, heavy-handed mechanic." Lomu's father often physically abused him and his deeply religious mother during alcohol-related episodes.

Lomu would channel a growing hatred for his father into a life of petty crime and violence. It has been noted that as a youth, he routinely got into fights, stole cars, and was occasionally brought home by the police. Like many of his friends in South Auckland, Lomu hung out with local street gangs, one of which was led by his uncle David Fuko. Impressed with Lomu's natural strength and size, Fuko expressed interest in recruiting him into his gang to carry out criminal assignments. While many apocryphal stories surround Lomu's childhood and adolescence, there is one that has been widely publicized: when Lomu was thirteen, a would-be mugger decided against stealing Lomu's shoes when he stood up to reveal how big he was.

A turning point for Lomu came in 1988, when his uncle and a cousin were murdered by a rival Samoan gang in a mall in the nearby suburb of Otara. Fearing a similar fate for himself, he decided to leave his burgeoning life of crime behind him. He told M. Colman for the Queensland, Australia, *Courier Mail* (22 May 1999), "When I lost my uncle I knew I was either going to end up like him or behind bars." Not long after the murders of his uncle and cousin, Lomu's mother sent him away to Methodist Wesley College, a strict boarding school in the town of Pukekohe, located approximately thirty-five miles south of Auckland.

It was at Wesley College, one of the oldest schools in New Zealand, that Lomu first became involved in rugby union. He had previously competed in track and field and played rugby league while a student at Auckland Primary School; Wesley's headmaster and rugby union coach, Chris Grinter, convinced Lomu to switch sporting codes after recognizing his enormous athletic potential. In contrast to rugby league, where two teams of thirteen players compete against each other, rugby union features fifteen players per team. Rugby union is considered the national sport of New Zealand, where it has been "elevated to religious status," as Fraser Thomson noted.

At Wesley, Lomu became a loose forward, one of three forwards in the back row of the scrum, for the school's rugby union squad. With his above-average size and speed, he quickly stood out among his peers. Under Grinter, who stepped in as a father figure, Lomu learned discipline and how to control and harness his anger. "When I first started playing rugby I was very angry," he recalled to Tim Gow. "If someone hurt me I would chase them around the field for the rest of the game." Lomu's anger with his father, however, boiled over while on holiday during his second year at Wesley, when the two got into a violent exchange. After throwing his father across a room in retaliation for another alcohol-induced beating, he was banished from his parents' home for good. Undaunted, Lomu spent future school holidays with friends and girlfriends; he would not make amends with his father until years later.

During his final year at Wesley, in 1993, Lomu was made head boy and served as captain of the rugby team. Throughout his time at the school, he also played on a county development rugby union squad, where he was regularly the top try scorer, and excelled in track and field. He reportedly set records in sprint, hurdle, and discus events, completing the 100-meter dash in a lightning-fast 10.8 seconds. "I have no doubt rugby saved me," Lomu told Gow. "The majority of my friends of the time before rugby are now either six feet under or behind bars. I often think about how lucky I was."

CAREER

In 1993, after rising rapidly through New Zealand's rugby union system, Lomu started playing for the Counties Manukau Steelers in the National Provincial Championship (NPC), New Zealand's top domestic rugby competition. Since 2006, the NPC has consisted of two major provincial competitions, the professional ITM Cup and the amateur Heartland Championship. The Steelers are one of fourteen teams who participate in the ITM Cup competition, which is held every year from late July to October. Lomu played with the Steelers for approximately five years, during which time he earned twenty-nine caps (for international appearances with the team) and scored ninety-five points (amassed from four different scoring methods).

Meanwhile, in 1994, he made his debut with New Zealand's national sevens team at that year's Hong Kong Sevens tournament, where he showcased his phenomenal abilities. (Rugby sevens is a variation of rugby union with seven players on each side.) In June of that year, Lomu won a spot on New Zealand's All Blacks national rugby union team, making his test-match debut at the left-wing position in a match against France in Christchurch, New Zealand. At the age of nineteen years and forty-five days, he became the youngest All Blacks player in history.

After playing in a second All Blacks test match in the summer of 1994, also against France, and appearing in several other sevens tournaments, Lomu was selected to New Zealand's national squad for the 1995 Rugby World Cup in South Africa, which propelled him to international rugby superstar status. In five matches at the tournament, he scored seven tries, four of which came in a career-defining semifinal match against England that is "still considered to be the single most extraordinary individual performance in the . . . history of international rugby union," according to Chris Hewett.

Lomu helped lead New Zealand to the World Cup final, where they lost to South Africa's national rugby union team, the Springboks, 15–12. Despite the loss, he was named player of the tournament and soon afterward became one of the most feared and recognizable rugby players in the world. "Lomu combined pace and power," Alasdair Reid noted, "as no player had combined them before . . . [Rugby's] scales had traditionally balanced speed against size, but Lomu added them together in a devastating package. The wider game watched on in awestruck disbelief; experienced players wondered aloud whether it was within the power of another human being to stop Lomu in his tracks."

Two months after the World Cup, rugby turned professional, and Lomu became the face of the sport, leading to him receiving multi-million-dollar contracts and endorsement deals. According to sources, Lomu subsequently turned down several offers to play other sports, including a lucrative contract to play with the American National Football League's (NFL) Dallas Cowboys, in order to remain with New Zealand's national team.

Lomu continued to play on All Blacks squads until 2002, when he was forced to leave the team due to weakened health caused by an energy-depleting kidney disease called nephrotic syndrome, which he was first diagnosed with in 1996. In all, Lomu played sixty-three test matches and scored thirty-seven tries in seventy-three career matches for the All Blacks. More than half of those tries came during the 1995 season and the 1999 Rugby World Cup in Wales. At the latter, he again dominated the competition with eight tries, setting a tournament record and becoming the all-time Rugby World Cup top try scorer, with fifteen in total. Although New Zealand was upset by France in the semifinals 43–31, Lomu scored two tries in the match, which "has been described as the greatest game of rugby ever played and the most colossal upset in the history of the sport," Fraser Thomson noted. Lomu made his last appearance for New Zealand's national team in a match against Wales at Millennium Stadium in Cardiff in November 2002.

In addition to his appearances for New Zealand's All Blacks, Lomu led his country's sevens team to a gold medal at the 1998 Commonwealth Games in Kuala Lumpur, Malaysia, which he described to Thomson as "one of the most emotional nights of my life." He also helped New Zealand win the title at the 2001 Rugby World Cup Sevens, the top international rugby sevens tournament, in Argentina, defeating Australia 31–12.

Lomu further competed for provincial teams in the Super Rugby competition, which was launched in 1996 and is regarded as the leading professional rugby union competition in the southern hemisphere. He played for the Auckland Blues from 1996 to 1998 and won consecutive Super Rugby titles with that club in 1996 and 1997. He then spent the 1999 Super Rugby season with the Waikato Chiefs before joining the Wellington Hurricanes, with whom he played from 2000 to 2003. Meanwhile, he continued to play on the NPC circuit, and after leaving Counties Manukau in 1999, he became a member of the Wellington Lions. He played for the Lions from 2000 to 2002 and led the club to the NPC title in 2000.

Lomu had to leave all levels of rugby union play in early 2003, when his debilitating kidney condition forced him to undergo daily dialysis. He started receiving dialysis treatment for up to eight hours a day, five times a week, the effects of which caused severe nerve damage to his legs and feet. "Eight hours on dialysis. Or kick the bucket? That was no option," he explained to Alex Brown for the Melbourne *Age* (23 Apr. 2005). "You have two choices in life when your kidneys fail. You either do dialysis or you die. And dying is not in my vocabulary." After facing possible paralysis, Lomu underwent a kidney transplant in July 2004, receiving a kidney donated by one of his friends, the Wellington radio personality and disc jockey Grant Kereama. Soon afterward he underwent an intense training and rehabilitation program in efforts to return to the rugby pitch.

Lomu officially made his comeback in June 2005, when he led a team against former English rugby captain Martin Johnson's invitational XV squad at a match in Twickenham, England. He scored a try in the first half of the match but suffered a shoulder injury that prevented from returning in the second half. After being forced to undergo shoulder surgery, Lomu sat out the remainder of the 2005 NPC season. That season he had a signed a contract to play for New Zealand's provincial NPC team North Harbour, but his injury resulted in him serving as a coach with the team instead. From late 2005 to 2006, he played with the Welsh professional rugby union club the Cardiff Blues, where he enjoyed limited success before being sidelined again due to an ankle injury. Afterward, he returned to New Zealand to play for Massey Rugby Club and then North Harbour in the NPC competition.

In 2007 Lomu announced his retirement from professional rugby due to his kidney condition and persistent injuries, which prevented him from achieving the same level of play he had enjoyed in his heyday. Nonetheless, he attempted another comeback in 2009, when he signed with the French rugby union club Marseilles Vitrolles of the Fédérale 1 league.

Despite having his career shortened by illness and injury, Lomu continues to be regarded with awe in rugby circles, with many ranking him among the best players of all time. He has received a number of honors for his contributions to rugby, including a Special Merit Award from the International Rugby Board (IRB) in 2003 and appointment as a member of the New Zealand Order of Merit in 2007, the same year he was inducted into the International Rugby Hall of Fame (IRHOF). In 2011 he was inducted into the IRB Hall of Fame and served as an ambassador for the seventh Rugby World Cup, which was hosted and won by New Zealand. "I want to be remembered as a person who loved what he did," Lomu said to Tim Gow. "I don't want to be remembered as a great or anything like that, just someone who enjoyed playing rugby, who played it because he loved it."

In 2012 Lomu announced that he would need a second kidney transplant following the failure of his first donated kidney. He returned to receiving daily dialysis and began looking for a compatible donor.

PERSONAL LIFE

Lomu married his third wife, Nadene Quirk, in a cliff-top ceremony in Wellington, New Zealand, in 2011. Lomu's once-estranged father was among the wedding guests. The couple live in the south of France with their two sons, Brayley and Dhyreille, born in 2009 and 2010, respectively. Lomu, whose personal life has provided fodder for the tabloids, was previously married to South African Tanya Rutter from 1996 to 2000 and to New Zealander Fiona Taylor, who served as his personal manager, from 2003 to 2008. He is involved in many charitable activities through his association with such organizations as UNICEF New Zealand, Monaco Peace and Sport, the Special Olympics, the National Kidney

Research Foundation, and the Ronald McDonald House.

SUGGESTED READING

Brown, Alex. "Lomu's Impossible Dream." *Age* [Melbourne] 23 Apr. 2005, Sport sec.: 7.

Cain, Nick. "Stopping the Juggernaut." *Sunday Times* 20 May 2007, Sport sec.: 19.

Colman, M. "Escape from the Streets." *Courier-Mail* [Queensland] 22 May 1999, Weekend sec.: 3.

Gow, Tim. "How the World's Greatest Rugby Star Is Facing the Battle of His Life: Jonah's Trying Times." *Daily Express* 28 May 2004, News sec.: 38.

Hewett, Chris. "On the Wing and a Prayer; Profile: Jonah Lomu." *Independent* 9 Oct. 1999, Comment sec.: 5.

Reid, Alasdair. "Lomu: Faded Glory; Borders v. Cardiff: World's Most Famous Player Arrives at Netherdale." *Sunday Herald* [Glasgow] 8 Jan. 2006: Sport 24.

Taylor, Phil. "Secret of Jonah's Family Bust-Up." *NZ Herald*. APN Holdings NZ, 1 May 2004. Web. 22 June 2012.

Thomson, Fraser. "The Saturday Interview: Jonah Lomu—Man in Black." *Birmingham Post* 15 Dec. 2001, Sport sec.: 34–35.

Wild, Abigail. "I Used to Be Wild, I Used to Be Crazy. But I've Learned to Control It: Jonah Lomu's Health Worries Helped Him Reassess His Priorities." *Herald* [Glasgow] 4 June 2004: 19.

—*Chris Cullen*

Ki Longfellow

Born: December 9, 1944
Occupation: Novelist, playwright, and theater producer and director

When Ki Longfellow published her first novel, *China Blues* (1989), the work was praised for its depiction of 1920s America. Longfellow enjoyed moderate success with readers and critics throughout the early nineties for her subsequent novel *Chasing Women* (1993). After the death of her husband—British comedian Vivian Stanshall—in 1995, Longfellow, who had formerly published under her given name Pamela Longfellow, became Ki (rhymes with "sky") Longfellow, after the name the eccentric Stanshall had envisioned for his wife in a dream. There followed almost ten years without a novel from Longfellow until she published *The Secret Magdalene*, arguably her most popular work, in 2005. The book is a fictitious—though factually based—account of the life of Mary Magdalene. It became so popular that Longfellow decided to complete

Courtesy of Ki Longfellow

a trilogy of novels about the lives of famous ancient women called the Divine Feminine. The second book in the series was *Flow Down Like Silver: Hypatia of Alexandria* (2009) and the final installment is tentatively titled *The Time of the Bee*. Longfellow prides herself on following her muse wherever it may lead her; in 1985, she and her husband wrote and composed a comic opera called *Stinkfoot* that became a cult classic. Her most recent work is a supernatural horror novel called *Houdini Heart* (2011). Longfellow has also contributed writing to publications including *Ms. Magazine*, *Cream Magazine*, and *Rolling Stone*.

EARLY LIFE

Longfellow was born on Staten Island in New York City on December 9, 1944, to a French-Irish mother and an Iroquois father. Longfellow's mother was a teenager and the author spent periods of her childhood in foster care and with family. Her mother later married a member of the United States Navy. Despite the fact that she never saw her mother or stepfather with a book in their hands, Longfellow knew she wanted to be a writer at the age of four when she wrote a five-page piece she called "The Red Pony." Longfellow grew up on naval bases in Hawaii and Marin County, California, and graduated from Redwood High School in Larkspur, California, in 1962.

At the age of nineteen, Longfellow had what she believed was a divine experience of self-actualization that would inform her later novel,

The Secret Magdalene (2005). In 1963 Longfellow gave birth to a daughter, Sydney Longfellow.

VIVIAN STANSHALL AND THE OLD PROFANITY SHOWBOAT

Longfellow lived in England from 1972 to 1975. She returned to California briefly, only to move back to England in 1977. That same year, Longfellow met British comedian and musician Vivian Stanshall on a blind date set up through a mutual friend. Longfellow had never heard of him, though Stanshall had already gained quite a following as a musician by that time. As their relationship progressed, the two lived on a houseboat called the *Searchlight* near the Thames River for the next five years. Longfellow gave birth to their daughter, Silky Longfellow-Stanshall, in 1979. Longfellow and Stanshall were married on September 9, 1980.

In 1983, Longfellow took the first step in realizing her lifelong dream of owning an operating showboat. Along with Stanshall, Longfellow purchased a twenty-eight-year-old Baltic coaster. The vessel was known as the *Thekla*, but the Stanshalls christened it the *Old Profanity Showboat* and docked in Bristol's harbor. In 1984, the *Old Profanity Showboat* opened as Bristol's first floating theater venue and bar. It became a home to a host of artists, musicians, and actors. To accommodate their various talents, Longfellow and Stanshall decided to write a comedic opera that would be performed on the boat. Longfellow and Stanshall wrote and scored the surreal musical that came to be known as *Stinkfoot*.

Stinkfoot, for which Stanshall wrote twenty-seven songs, debuted at the *Old Profanity Showboat* in 1985. The plot was based on a series of children's tales Longfellow had written about a New York City alley cat in the 1970s. A literary agent turned down the series, but it became popular among Longfellow and Stanshall's children as a set of bedtime stories. The musical also features an aging music hall artist named Soliquisto; other characters in the sprawling show include the Persian Moll, Elma the Electrifying Elver, The Left Half of Screwy the Ocean Liner's Brain, the Partly Cooked Shrimp, the Balanced Nose, and Mrs. Bag Bag.

The making of the show was filmed as a BBC *Arena* documentary that aired in 1984. The show was well received by *Old Profanity* fans but failed to gain traction with a West End audience, where it debuted in the late 1980s. The story was published by Sea Urchin Press in 2003 and enjoyed an anniversary production in 2010, featuring Longfellow and Stanshall's daughter, Silky, as Elma the Electrifying Elver. The *Old Profanity Showboat* closed for financial reasons in 1986, though it reopened as a nightclub called the Thekla a few years later.

Stanshall was formerly a member of the successful Bonzo Dog Doo-Dah Band. His later comedy recordings drew a wildly loyal fan base diverse enough to include comedian Gilda Radner and musician John Lennon. Longfellow has often referred to Stanshall as a British national treasure. Stanshall was capable of breathtaking creativity—many thought he was a genius—but he had an even greater capacity for self-destruction. Longfellow and her daughters left Stanshall, who suffered from drug and alcohol addictions, in the mid-1980s. Longfellow settled in Vermont but frequently visited her husband. He died in a house fire in 1995.

WRITING CAREER

Longfellow's debut novel, *China Blues*, is set in San Francisco and follows its characters from the 1906 earthquake through Prohibition. Though it was only her first novel, it ignited a bidding war when Longfellow approached publishers with the manuscript. The novel was published by Doubleday (in the United States) and HarperCollins (in the United Kingdom) in 1989; it was later translated into Spanish, Hebrew, Swedish, Czech, and German. *China Blues* was optioned for a film by Richard Zanuck and David Brown, but the project never came to fruition. The novel was re-released by Eio Books in January 2012.

Longfellow published her second novel, *Chasing Women*, in 1993. The novel was also historical fiction, and took place in New York City in the 1930s. Longfellow published both *China Blues* and *Chasing Women* under the name Pamela Longfellow.

After Stanshall's death in 1995, Longfellow stopped writing and spent most of her time on a farm in Vermont. She began studying Gnosticism and the biblical figure Mary Magdalene in early Gnostic gospels. For seven years, Longfellow devoured scholarly information on Magdalene, but told *Solander: The Magazine of the Historical Novel Society* (May 2007) that the journey of her resulting novel was "pure magic."

After years of exhaustive research—though the novel is fictional, each detail is rooted in fact—Longfellow told *Solander* that *The Secret Magdalene* languished on her agent's desk. Frustrated, she approached an independent Vermont publishing company called Eio Books. The company was small and could only sell the book online and in local bookstores. Still, *The Secret Magdalene* was published (under the name Ki Longfellow) in 2005 to popular and critical success.

Soon after publication, Longfellow was asked to contribute an essay to the fourth installment of writer Dan Burstein's *Secrets* series, called *Secrets of Mary Magdalene: The Untold Story of History's Most Misunderstood Woman* (2006). Around that time, a woman named Susan Lee Cohen purchased Longfellow's novel in a Vermont bookstore and read it in one sitting. Cohen was a longtime literary agent with the Riverside

Literary Agency and contacted Longfellow upon finishing the book. She signed Longfellow in a matter of weeks and was able to arrange a publication deal with the Crown Publishing Group, a division of Random House. *The Secret Magdalene* was then re-released across the country in 2007.

Longfellow credits much of the novel's success to timing; *The Secret Magdalene* was introduced to readers shortly after the release of Dan Brown's 2003 novel *The Da Vinci Code*. But she also insists that the world was ripe for Mary's story. Longfellow refers to Magdalene as "our Goddess," or the missing piece of the Christian religion as it is currently understood. "[T]he world psyche is now ready for the return of the Feminine, and this is especially true for the Western World bereft of the Goddess for so long, and in desperate psychological disarray because of it," she told *Solander*, adding that ancient women need to be restored to their proper (and prominent) role in Christianity. *The Secret Magdalene* was optioned by Sundance Award-winner, Nancy Savoca, and a film is currently in pre-production.

Longfellow became so attached to her subject that she decided to make *The Secret Magdalene* the first in a trilogy called the Divine Feminine. Longfellow's next novel, and the second novel of the trilogy, was called *Flow Down Like Silver: Hypatia of Alexandria*. The novel told the story of Hypatia, a Roman philosopher and noted mathematician who was murdered by a Christian mob. The book was published by Eio Books in 2007. Hypatia is also recognized as one of the last pagan teachers. The third book in Longfellow's trilogy, tentatively title *The Time of the Bee*, has yet to be published.

"Writers may think they know what they're going to say, but they can be very wrong," Longfellow wrote in the short biography on her blog. Perhaps she is referring to her most recent publication, titled *Houdini Heart* and published in 2011. Longfellow says she felt compelled to write the supernatural horror story while trying to finish *The Time of the Bee*. Inspired by the works of Edgar Allan Poe, H. P. Lovecraft, and Shirley Jackson, Longfellow sets her story at the once-glamorous River House Hotel in Vermont. The book was considered for the 2011 Horror Writer's Association Bram Stoker Award.

SUGGESTED READING

"Incredible Voyage of the Boat which Became a Theatre." *Bristol Evening Post* 8 Aug. 2006: 38. Print.

Gortner, Christopher. "Seeking the Divine." *Solander: The Magazine of the Historical Novel Society* 11.1 (2007): 29–31. Print.

Longfellow, Pamela. *China Blues*. New York: Doubleday, 1989. Print.

Longfellow, Ki. *The Secret Magdalene*. Brattleboro, VT: Eio, 2005. Print.

---. *Houdini Heart*. Brattleboro, VT: Eio, 2011. Print.

Stanshall, Vivian, and Ki Longfellow-Stanshall. *Stinkfoot: An English Comic Opera*. Rotterdam, the Netherlands: Sea Urchin, 2003. Print.

"The Secret Magdalene." *Publishers Weekly* 253.45 (13 Nov. 2006): 30. Print.

—Molly Hagan

Caroline Lucas

Born: December 9, 1960
Occupation: British politician

On May 6, 2010, British politician Caroline Lucas was the first member of England's Green Party to be elected a Member of Parliament (MP). She represents the Brighton Pavilion constituency. Lucas joined the Green Party in 1986 at a time when, as she told Sophie Morris for the *Independent Extra* (25 May 2010), "there was a new awareness of the seriousness of the climate change crisis but also the benefits that could be gained by tackling it in a fair and effective way." Though it took her twenty-four years to win an office in the House of Commons, Lucas warns that time is of the essence. "There's a real urgency to what the Green Party's about," she told Morris. "Climate scientists say that we have eight-to-ten years to get our emissions down, and if we miss that window of opportunity it will be a lot more difficult logistically to avoid the worst of climate change. That makes the next few years absolutely crucial."

Prior to her election to the Commons in 2010, Lucas served as a Green Party Member of the European Parliament (MEP) for southeast England for nearly a decade, and in 1993, Lucas was the second member of the Green Party to win a county council seat in Oxfordshire. England's Green Party has been fielding parliamentary candidates since 1979, though Lucas, head of the party from 2008 to 2012, was the first to succeed with an adapted manifesto relating the environmental issues at the party's core to the economic and social issues of the 2010 election. The party, once hostile to economic growth, now embraces what they call the Green New Deal, arguing that environmental industries will create new jobs and a more stable economy.

Lucas is credited for the shift in the party's environmental focus as well as for the party's growing viability; indeed, she was considered the frontrunner of her three-way race against candidates from two of England's largest political factions: the Labour Party and the Conservative

John Stillwell/PA Photos /Landov

with the Campaign for Nuclear Disarmament (CND) as a teenager. She went on to attend the University of Exeter where she received a BA degree with honors in English literature in 1983. As an undergraduate, Lucas frequently traveled to the military bases at Molesworth and Greenham Common to protest the use of nuclear weapons. In 1986, while pursuing her doctorate in English and women's studies at Exeter, Lucas came across a book called *Seeing Green* (1984) by British environmentalist and Green Party advocate Jonathon Porritt. Lucas says that reading the book changed her life. "Until then, I'd been interested in the women's movement and I'd been interested in the environment and I'd been very active in CND but I hadn't made the connections between these different things," she told Huw Spanner for the online magazine *Third Way* in 2005. "What I discovered from *Seeing Green* was that all these things are connected." Lucas sought out the Green Party headquarters to volunteer and found that it was located down the street from where she lived on Clapham High Road in South London. She spent several years as a volunteer before becoming the party's first national press officer from 1987 to 1989. Some sources have reported that she also earned a diploma in journalism at this time. Lucas earned her PhD in English and women's studies in 1989.

Lucas left her position as Green Party press officer when she decided she wanted to run for office. In the early 1990s, she began work as the national press officer for Oxfam International, which seeks solutions to poverty and social injustice worldwide. She remained a part of Oxfam for ten years, working also as a communications officer at the organization's Asia desk in 1991 and as a policy advisor on trade and the environment in 1994. From 1997 to 1998, Lucas worked as a team leader for trade and investment and advised the UK Department for International Development.

THE GREEN PARTY AND BRITISH POLITICS

Lucas served as cochair of the Green Party of England and Wales from 1989 to 1990. In 1993, she became only the second Green to win a county council seat in the United Kingdom. She served on the Oxfordshire County Council until 1997.

Despite a few minor successes, the Green Party failed to make a significant impact in England in the 1980s and 1990s. Many argued that the Green Party's disdain for orthodox leadership was to blame; the party favored a system in which two senior figures were chosen—one male and one female—but several more figures served as the party's voice. The result was chaotic, and the decisions were permanently split. In addition to mismanagement, the English Green Party—the only European Green Party without

Party (also known as the Tory Party). Her success, due in part to the votes of disillusioned liberal Labour voters, served as a tipping point for the party. During the campaign, Lucas noted to Peter Walker for the London *Guardian* (15 Apr. 2010), "It's massively important for people to know that we can win. We find [while campaigning] on the doorsteps that so many people want to vote Green. They just want to know that a Green vote has a chance of getting someone elected."

Lucas was named the United Kingdom's "Most Ethical Politician" by readers of the London *Observer* in 2007, 2009, and 2010; she is also one of the Environment Agency's one hundred eco-heroes. Lucas was named Newcomer of the Year in the London *Spectator*'s 2010 Parliamentarian Awards and MP of the Year in the Scottish Widows and Dods Women in Public Life Awards in 2011.

EDUCATION AND ACTIVISM

Lucas was born on December 9, 1960 in Malvern, Worcestershire, England. She grew up in a conservative, middle-class home. Her father was a businessman who ran a small central-heating company in Malvern. Her mother was a homemaker who raised Lucas and Lucas's two siblings. Lucas attended Malvern Girls' College in Worcestershire and spent most of her childhood adhering to the conservative political views with which she was raised.

After the Falklands War in 1982, Lucas's worldview changed, and she began volunteering parliamentary representation at the time—suffered from an image problem. (Lucas recalls getting into arguments with party officials who were going to appear on television while she was serving as the Green Party's national press officer; the officials were offended when she asked them what they were planning to wear.) Still, remnants of the old Green Party stereotype, which many characterize as an angry sandal-wearing hippie who is more concerned with protecting wildlife than with protecting humankind, remain. It is a stereotype that Lucas has spent her career trying to eradicate. When the party finally elected a single leader, they chose Lucas in 2008. In 2012, she chose not to run for reelection so that a new leadership voice might be heard.

Under the current British electoral system, known as "first past the post," the candidate with the most votes in their constituency is elected MP. The system has proven problematic under Britain's multiple party system, and it is widely blamed for the poor representation of Greens in public positions as compared to other European countries. Several alternatives to the first-past-the-post system have been presented in recent years including Alternative Voting (AV), a system in which voters rank candidates in order of preference. A referendum for AV appeared on the ballot in 2011, but lost. Lucas has strongly advocated for Proportional Representation (PR), in which each party would be allotted a number of parliamentary seats proportional to the number of votes it received in the general election. The PR system, Lucas argues, would give smaller parties such as the Greens a fighting chance against larger parties. Until the system changes, Lucas remains focused on relating the principals of the Greens to a wider pool of voters as an assurance to her constituents that a vote for the Green Party is not, as was once believed, a vote wasted. For this reason, Lucas is wary of examples like the American presidential election in 2000, when Green Party candidate Ralph Nader contributed to the victory of Republican George W. Bush by splitting the democratic vote with Vice President Al Gore in the state of Florida. Lucas told Geoffrey Lean for the *Independent on Sunday* (17 May 2009) that she is seeking to change the paradigm by breaking through what she calls the "credibility barrier."

MEMBER OF EUROPEAN PARLIAMENT

In 1999, Lucas was elected as a Member of the European Parliament (MEP), located in Brussels, Belgium, representing South East England. The same year, the United Kingdom adopted a system of proportional representation in accordance with participating European countries, and Lucas became one of the first two British Green MEPs (the other was Jean Lambert, who continues to represent the London region). She won by 256 votes. The dual win represented the

first time any British Green was elected to a position above the level of local council. Lucas was subsequently reelected to her post in 2004 and 2009. She was replaced by Keith Taylor in 2010, when she was elected MP.

Though Lucas and Lambert represented a minority in the European Parliament, they became fairly influential. Lucas served as a member of the International Trade Committee; the Environment, Public Health and Food Safety Committee; and the Women's Rights and Gender Equality Committee. She also served as the president of the Animal Welfare Intergroup, the copresident of the Peace Initiatives Intergroup, and the vice president of the Parliament's Permanent Delegation to Palestine. As an MEP, Lucas drafted a Commission Communication on the negative impact of air travel on the environment, and she persuaded the European Parliament to initiate changes and enforce noise restrictions on airlines. She also commissioned research demonstrating the inadequacy of safety guidelines regarding mobile phones and electromagnetic technologies and amended legislation to strengthen the case against genetically modified crops. She worked hard to put animal protection issues on the agenda; her efforts in this regard earned her the Michael Kay Award from the Royal Society for the Prevention of Cruelty to Animals (RSPCA) in 2006.

As a member of the Trade and Energy Committee from 1999 to 2004, Lucas forced the European Commission to legally investigate the British nuclear industry and promote green energy as a viable alternative. She was also a vocal opponent of the Iraq war and the production and use of depleted uranium weapons. Throughout her career, Lucas has participated in many nonviolent protests and has been arrested several times. Speaking of a particular demonstration when she ran into the street and lay down in front of a police car, Lucas told Aida Edemariam for the London *Guardian* (15 May 2010), "It's not something I do lightly—it's not some sort of joke. I think there is a role for nonviolent direct action when democratic channels have failed." In 2008, Lucas was voted MEP of the Year in the *Parliament* magazine awards for her work on trade.

MEMBER OF PARLIAMENT AND A GREEN NEW DEAL

In 2008, as the leader of the Green Party of England and Wales, Lucas introduced a platform that she called the Green New Deal. (The name was inspired by US president Franklin D. Roosevelt's series of economic programs in the 1930s known as the "New Deal.") The program grew out of the most pressing concerns of the day and proposed to create jobs, "beat" the recession, and create an environmentally sustainable economy. Lucas successfully blended Green ideals (reduce greenhouse gas emissions, promote renewable energy, offer free home insulation, and conduct bans on genetically modified food and animal testing) with liberal ideals such as a nationalized railway system, universal dental care, pensions increased above the poverty line, and a basic citizen's income. She became an active voice in the Green New Deal Group, which allied experts in finance, energy, and the environment. She told a reporter for the online environmental news service ENDS Europe (10 Sep. 2009) that her ultimate goal was not just "green growth," but that she hoped the initiatives would "act as a bridge helping to build a transition towards a steady state economy."

Lucas became such a popular figure that she was already the favorite when she entered the MP race in Brighton Pavilion in 2010. (A popular Labour MP was retiring.) It certainly helped that the Brighton constituency was friendly with the Green Party, though a Green candidate had never won a parliamentary election there. (Indeed, until Lucas, there had never been a Green MP in the United Kingdom.) Still, the race was close. Lucas's victory was announced the morning after election day; she won Brighton Pavilion with a majority of 1,252 votes over the Labour Party's Nancy Platts.

In the Commons, Lucas is cochair of the All Party Parliamentary Group on Fuel Poverty, and she is vice-chair of the Public and Commercial Services as well as the Sustainable Housing, Animal Welfare, and CND All Party Parliamentary Groups. She is also a member of the Parliament's Environmental Audit Committee.

Despite her historic victory, Lucas is not resting on her laurels. She has very publicly criticized the British Parliament for its archaic and ineffective practices. "I never thought I would say the European Parliament is a beacon of transparency but compared to Westminster it is," she told Tanya Gold for the London *Telegraph* (3 Sep. 2010). Lucas has also condemned Parliament's recent austerity measures, criticizing the current government for cutting the budget instead of investing in jobs, and she continues to demand a massive investment in green industry and training for "green collar" jobs. Lucas is known as an extremely vocal MP, participating in over seventy-six debates in 2011 alone.

PERSONAL LIFE AND FAMILY
Lucas is coauthor, with Mike Woodin, of the book *Green Alternatives to Globalisation: A Manifesto* (2004). She has also authored numerous leaflets that outline her extensive work on trade, the environment, animal protection, peace, and human rights. Lucas is an Honorary Fellow of the Institution of Environmental Sciences and Patron of the Westminster Social Policy Forum.

Lucas has also served as vice president of the RSPCA (the Royal Society for the Prevention of Cruelty to Animals), the Stop the War Coalition, and the Campaign Against Climate Change and Environmental Protection UK (formerly National Society for Clean Air); she has also served as a director of the International Forum on Globalization.

Lucas is an advisory board member of the think tanks Protect the Local, Globally; the Centre for a Social Europe, Radiation Research Trust, the Transitions Towns Network, and the Council of the Constitution Unit.

Lucas met her husband, Richard Savage, while working for Oxfam in Oxford. The couple has two sons and lives in Brighton.

SUGGESTED READING
Edemariam, Aida. "Caroline Lucas: 'We Could Have Had a New Politics. This Isn't It.'" *Guardian* [London] 17 May 2010: 38. Print.

Gold, Tanya. "Caroline Lucas: The Green in Beige Who Could be Nick Clegg's Nemesis." *Telegraph* [London]. Telegraph Media Group, 3 Sep. 2010. Web. 13 June 2012.

Morgan, Andrew. "Caroline Lucas: Leading the Charge for UK's Greens." *ENDS Europe Report* 10 Sep. 2009: 13. Print.

Morris, Sophie. "'You can do politics without selling out.'" *Independent Extra* 25 May 2010: 16. Print.

Spanner, Huw. "High Profile: Green Shift." *Third Way*. Third Way, 4 Feb. 2005. Web. 12 June 2012.

Lean, Geoffrey. "There's a Light at the End of the Tunnel." *Independent on Sunday* 17 May 2009: 30. Print.

SELECTED WORKS
Green Alternatives to Globalisation: A Manifesto, 2004

—*Molly Hagan*

Fabio Luisi

Born: 1959
Occupation: Principal conductor of the Metropolitan Opera

"Why certain conductors rise to the top and others don't isn't always clear," music critic Zachary Lewis wrote for the Cleveland, Ohio, *Plain Dealer* (Nov. 29, 2011). "In the case of Fabio Luisi, however, the hype appears to be justified." Internationally acclaimed conductor Fabio Luisi was named principal conductor of New York's prestigious Metropolitan Opera in September 2011. Though Italian-born, Luisi has spent much of his career in Austria and Germany; he is also chief conductor of the Vienna Symphony

Orchestra, a post that he assumed in 2005. Luisi took a traditional path to the podium, moving from his early studies in piano to coaching opera singers in Graz, Austria, before pursuing conducting. He is equally comfortable with musicians and vocalists and, perhaps because of his varied musical background, is known as an extremely versatile director. Luisi's repertoire spans European classical music tradition, including works by Wolfgang Amadeus Mozart, Richard Strauss, Giuseppe Verdi, Richard Wagner, and Gustav Mahler. He believes that the musical styles of various composers inform one another; for example, alternating between Mozart and Wagner, he told Andrew Patner for the *Chicago Sun-Times* (Nov. 6, 2011), is a reminder "that we can play Wagner's music as music. You can take all of this 'pan-Germanic' pathos out of these operas, drop this very slow and heavy pace and find the music there, which is Wagner's great gift."

Luisi is known as an exacting conductor who works hard to bring out the subtleties of the music he directs, but he is careful not to overstep the bounds of what he sees as a delicately defined role. He told Ronni Reich for the Newark, New Jersey, *Star-Ledger* (Nov. 6, 2011), "I don't like the word interpretation, actually. It puts me on the same level as the composer." Luisi's few critics point out that he is an impersonal presence at the podium, but conversely, Luisi accuses many of his colleagues of being "too personal" with the works they conduct. "I consider my job [to be] trying to understand what the composer wanted and translating it into sounds," he told Reich. "We advocate for these composers, I think this needs a lot of modesty, a lot of experience, a lot of study, which doesn't stop. It never stops."

In his position at the Metropolitan Opera, Luisi is poised to one day assume the role of musical director. The job, which is held by James Levine (who has been in the position for more than forty seasons), is considered one of the most important in opera. Luisi assumed his role as principal director when Levine, who suffered a debilitating fall in 2011, canceled his engagements for the Met's 2012–13 season. Luisi has substituted for Levine on countless occasions—even to the detriment of his relationship with other opera houses—and will continue to do so for the foreseeable future. Despite what some insiders describe as a delicate situation (there has been no talk of Levine's resignation), Luisi is happy working with the Met and considers New York his new artistic home.

EARLY LIFE AND EDUCATION

Luisi was born in Genoa, Italy, in 1959. His father, a saxophone player in a jazz band, led Luisi to study music beginning at the age of four. "At that age you can't decide for yourself

AP Photo

so it was my parents who decided that I should have piano lessons and that proved to be a very good move," Luisi told Mansel Stimpson for the website Classical Source (Mar.–Apr. 2011). He added, "I liked it from the very first moment." Luisi was the private student of Professor Memi Schiavina at the Niccolò Pagani Conservatory in Genoa and received his diploma in 1978. As a teenager Luisi was invited to study in Paris with the Italian pianist Aldo Ciccolini. He also studied with Antonio Bacchelli in Italy, but toward the end of his training as a pianist, he began to consider a career as a conductor. He told Stimpson, "Initially conducting was only a very remote possibility and one which I didn't take seriously."

At seventeen Luisi began working as an accompanist for young opera singers, but he later came into contact with renowned Turkish soprano Leyla Gencer and the Italian music critic and vocal coach Rodolfo Celletti. Luisi developed a friendship with Celletti, who invited him to coach at the Festival della Valle d'Itria, a summer festival in southeastern Italy. "I still felt that piano was wonderful and wanted to continue it, [but] I became aware also of its limitations," Luisi told Stimpson. "In contrast the orchestra provides so many more possibilities, be it in opera or in the concert hall; there's the chance to work on the sound of the different instruments and to do so with a huge repertoire." Luisi coached singers and worked as a part-time lecturer, teaching music theory and chamber music at the conservatory in La Spezia for two years before making the decision to pursue conducting.

Luisi was fascinated with Croatian conductor Milan Horvat, who was working in Genoa at the time. After Luisi approached him at a performance, Horvat told him that he taught a class at the Musikhochschule in Graz, Austria. "So that was where I went," Luisi told Stimpson, "and he is the only one with whom I have studied." To pay for his education Luisi worked as an accompanist, even though he could not speak German when he arrived in Graz. Luisi became well acquainted with the works of Austrian and German symphonists and opera composers, including Mahler, Strauss, Wagner, and Anton Bruckner. "I could not have conducted such composers without living there and speaking the language," he told Heidi Waleson for the *Wall Street Journal* (Sep. 27, 2011, online). In 1983 Luisi received a diploma with high honors and began his position as an opera coach at the Graz Opera.

EARLY CONDUCTING CAREER
Luisi's is a classic—and some say old-fashioned—career path for a conductor. "It was usual in the 1930s, '40s, '50s that opera conductors were first coaches for years and years in some small theater," Luisi explained to Zachary Woolfe for the *International Herald Tribune* (Oct. 12, 2011). "I've played a lot of recitative with harpsichord in my life. You feel so connected to what's happening onstage. It's a way to be in the action with the singers, and you have the possibility of accelerating the action or slowing it down. I know where the singers breathe; I know where they need help; I know where I have to push them; I know where I have to help them. That's an experience you cannot have if you don't do this type of career, but younger conductors now are not doing it."

Luisi made his debut in 1984 in Martina Franca, Italy, conducting Domenico Cimarosa's Requiem. The same year, he conducted Gioachino Rossini's *Il Turco in Italia* at the Teatro dell'Opera Giocosa in Genoa and Gaetano Donizetti's *Viva la Mamma* at the Graz Opera, where he spent the next four years conducting operas in both German and Italian.

In Graz, he encountered conductors who inspired his later work, including American Leonard Bernstein, Austrian Herbert von Karajan, and Romanian Sergiu Celibidache. "Bernstein I admired for his energy and for being constantly in the music," Luisi explained to Stimpson. "With Karajan it was his mind that appealed: his was a very, very clear and intellectual kind of conducting. As for Celibidache, he paid such attention to the sound of the orchestra and showed how important it could be to play slowly in order to bring out things that normally we don't hear."

INTERNATIONAL CAREER
In 1987 Luisi began his international career, making debuts in and across Europe—from Berlin, Frankfurt, Bordeaux, and Leipzig to the Stuttgart State Theater, the Mannheim State Theater, and the Vienna State Opera, at which he became a regular presence. From early on Vienna was a welcoming artistic home for Luisi. As reported by Daniel J. Wakin for the *New York Times* (Apr. 24, 2011), local Viennese music critic Wilhelm Sinkovicz for the *Die Presse* once wrote, "If a conductor like Luisi enters the pit, you really feel something special is going on."

In 1989 Luisi received his big break as a substitute for Italian conductor Giuseppe Patanè at the Munich Opera in a performance of Rossini's opera *The Barber of Seville*. The same year he made his debut with the Vienna State Opera. Luisi spent much of his early career conducting operas because, as he explained to Stimpson, "everybody thinks of an Italian conductor as one who conducts opera." He estimated that he was working with operas 80 percent of the time and symphonies 20 percent of the time, though he acknowledged that prior to 2007 all of his musical-director and chief-conductor positions were held with symphony orchestras. In 1990 Luisi founded the Grazer Symphonisches Orchester. He remained its artistic director until 1995.

In 1995 Luisi became the artistic director and chief conductor of the Tonkünstlerorchester in Vienna, where he conducted over 250 concerts before leaving his post in 2000. He even won over local audiences performing Sunday afternoon concerts at Vienna's famous concert hall, the Musikverein. Working with the Tonkünstlerorchester introduced Luisi to Japan; his Japanese tour with the orchestra was so successful that Luisi continues to make regular appearances in the country. In 1996 Luisi was appointed, with the late Swiss conductor Marcello Viotti and Austrian Manfred Honeck, as artistic director of the MDR Symphony Orchestra in Leipzig; Luisi took over sole directorship in 1999. He also served as the musical director of the Orchestre de la Suisse Romande based in Geneva, Switzerland, from 1997 to 2002.

MAKING WAVES IN GERMANY
With the MDR, Luisi made several highly acclaimed recordings, including symphonies by Mahler and Austrian composer Franz Schmidt. "I am musically curious and like to explore: what I don't know, I want to know. Sometimes I discover that something is not my thing, but at other times it very definitely is," Luisi told Stimpson. "The symphonies of Franz Schmidt were a case in point." Luisi has conducted Schmidt's Symphony no. 4 with the MDR, the Philadelphia Orchestra, the San Francisco Symphony, and the Concertgebouw in Amsterdam. He even programmed Schmidt's opera *Notre Dame* in Dresden, Germany. Schmidt was a little-known rival of Mahler, but his reputation has been marked by his association with the Nazi Party.

(Wagner and Strauss—who held an official position in Nazi Germany—are also considered, Wakin wrote, "politically or morally tainted artists.") These facts do not escape Luisi, who encourages discussions of composers' music and politics: He told Wakin, "[These composers' associations with the Nazis is] a very, very ugly thing."

Luisi left the MDR in 2007. That same year Luisi became the general music director of the Saxon State Opera and its orchestra, the Dresden Staatskapelle, one of Europe's oldest and most prestigious orchestras. His position there ended somewhat abruptly, however, when Luisi resigned in 2010. Luisi accused the orchestra's management of going behind his back to arrange a deal with ZDF, a German broadcasting network. (As musical director, Luisi would typically be consulted in business decisions.) The deal involved what Wakin, writing for the *New York Times* (Feb. 5, 2010), described as "a high-profile and potentially lucrative" contract to televise a special New Year's Eve performance with the Staatskapelle. The orchestra arranged the broadcast and hired conductor Christian Thielemann to appear in it; Luisi was informed two weeks later. Disappointed with the Staatskapelle's actions, Luisi resigned. Thielemann, toward whom Luisi maintains he harbors no ill will, succeeded him as general music director. "I told everybody [he] was a very good choice," Luisi told Wakin. "I gave my congratulations personally to [him]."

NEW YORK METROPOLITAN OPERA

Luisi made his US debut in 2000, conducting the New York Philharmonic, and traveled to Chicago's Lyric Theater to conduct Verdi's opera *Rigoletto* the same year. He made his Metropolitan Opera debut in 2005, conducting Verdi's opera *Don Carlo*. Luisi began devoting more time to the Met and became its principal guest conductor in 2010. That season he conducted twenty performances, including well-received productions of Mozart's *The Marriage of Figaro*, Engelbert Humperdinck's *Hansel and Gretel*, and Strauss's *Elektra*. He won further acclaim when he stepped in for music director James Levine to conduct Giacomo Puccini's *Tosca* and, a few weeks later, the revival of Alban Berg's *Lulu*. The latter, long considered a Levine specialty, endeared Luisi to audiences and critics alike. By 2011 Luisi was considered not only the Met's top "pinch-hitter," as Anthony Tommasini for the *New York Times* (May 9, 2011) put it, because of Levine's health problems, but also an increasingly essential part of the company.

In the spring he conducted, with avant-garde theater director Robert Lepage, a production of Wagner's *Das Rheingold*. Luisi brought his signature, clear-minded efficiency to the piece. "Mr. Luisi went for a leaner, though still robust, sound," wrote Tommasini for the *New York Times* (Apr. 1, 2011). "And rather than stepping in like some dynamo to show off and shake things up, Mr. Luisi built here not by pumping up the volume or opting for quick tempos, but by coaxing no-nonsense, vibrant and clean playing from the orchestra." Luisi followed the production with two performances originally scheduled to be conducted by Levine: Mozart's *Don Giovanni*, which Luisi conducted from the harpsichord, and Wagner's *Siegfried*, a cycle of the composer's four-part *Der Ring des Nibelungen*.

In September 2011 Levine suffered a fall that required emergency surgery and was forced to cancel his 2012–13 engagements. Luisi was immediately promoted from principal guest conductor to principal conductor and was called to take over many of the maestro's performances. The effects of the substitution, Wakin reported for the *New York Times* (Sep. 22, 2011), "rippled across two continents," as Luisi canceled numerous engagements in the United States and abroad. The Teatro dell'Opera in Rome, with which Luisi was scheduled to conduct a new production of *Elektra*, threatened legal action. There was a canceled performance of Mahler's Symphony no. 7 with Luisi's own Vienna Symphony and a canceled engagement at the Teatro Carlo Felice in his hometown of Genoa. Further complications arose in Essen, Germany, and San Francisco; in some cases even Luisi's substitutes required substitutes, Wakin reported. Though some theaters were understanding, the situation did not cast the Met or Luisi in a positive light within the classical-music world.

With his schedule back on track, Luisi is expected to conduct two more cycles of Wagner's *Der Ring des Nibelungen* in the spring of 2012. Luisi has declined to extend his contract with the Vienna Orchestra past the 2012–13 season, though he is still slated to become music director of the Zurich Opera in 2012, with an initial contract lasting five years. Luisi anticipates work on several operas by composer Leŏs Janáˇcek, for which he is learning to speak Czech.

PERSONAL LIFE

Luisi has received the Austrian Cross of Honor for Science and Art. In 2006 he was named a Cavaliere Ufficiale of the Italian Republic.

Luisi and his wife, a photographer and former professional violinist, have three sons. The family moved from Vienna to the Upper West Side of Manhattan in New York City in 2011.

SUGGESTED READING

Lewis, Zachary. "Conductor Luisi Turns an Uneven Program into Gold." *Plain Dealer* [Cleveland] 29 Nov. 2011: E6. Print.

Patner, Andrew. "Fabio Luisi a Good Bet for the Met." *Chicago Sun-Times* 6 Nov. 2011: 1. Print.

Reich, Ronni. "Stepping up to the Podium: The Met's Principal Conductor Also Leads the

Vienna Symphony Orchestra." *Star-Ledger* [Newark] 6 Nov. 2011: 3. Print.

Wakin, Daniel J. "Awaiting the Heir Apparent." *International Herald Tribune* 12 Oct. 2011: 16. Print.

---. "Maestro's Injury Ignites Game of Musical Chairs." *New York Times* 22 Sep. 2011: C1. Print.

Waleson, Heidi. "Next in Line at the Opera." *Wall Street Journal*. Wall Street Journal, 27 Sep. 2011. Web. 18 Jan. 2012.

SELECTED WORKS

Sinfonie Nr. 2 Es-Dur, 2006; *Sinfonie Nr. 3 A-Dur.*, 2006; *Sinfonie Nr. 4*, 2006; *Sinfonie Nr. 4 G-Dur.*, 2006; *Sinfonie No. 6 A-moll*, 2006; *Sinfonie No. 2*, 2007; *Concertante Variations/Concerto for the Left Hand*, 2007; *Don Juan, Aus Italien & Don Quixote*, 2009; *I Capuleti e I Montecchi*, 2009

—*Molly Hagan*

Susanne Bakken

Lise Lunge-Larsen

Born: October 15, 1955
Occupation: Writer

Lise Lunge-Larsen came to the United States as a college freshman, and she brought with her a great love and appreciation for the folklore of her native Norway. Much of that folklore inhabits her children's stories. Starting in the mid-1970s in Minneapolis, Minnesota, while still in college, Lunge-Larsen became well known in the local children's literature circle as an exciting, engaging storyteller. But it would take more than two decades for her to write her first illustrated children's book, *The Legend of the Lady Slipper* (1999). Nevertheless, the years she spent telling stories proved a great benefit to her writing.

Since the publication of her first book, Lunge-Larsen has gone on to write such children's books as *The Troll with No Heart in His Body and Other Tales of Trolls, from Norway* (1999), *The Race of the Birkebeiners* (2001), *The Hidden Folk: Stories of Fairies, Gnomes, Selkies, and Other Secret Beings* (2004), *Noah's Mittens* (2006), *The Adventures of Thor the Thunder God* (2007), and *Gifts from the Gods: Ancient Words and Wisdom from Greek and Roman Mythology* (2011). Her books have received many awards and honors, including ones from the New York Public Library.

GROWING UP: A LOVE FOR BOOKS

Lise Lunge-Larsen was born on October 15, 1955, in Oslo, Norway. According to Lunge-Larsen, she saw her first troll when she was three years old. She was walking in a forest with her mother, who pointed to a "troll"—the root of an overturned tree. In an essay titled "Why Do Children Love Troll Stories?" that appears in the introduction to *The Troll with No Heart in His Body*, Lunge-Larsen recalls finding the troll with her mother and described the impact this made on her: "Together we examined the troll, found his nose, arms, and even his eye sockets. It was a magical moment, and to this day I point out all the dead trolls in the landscape to my children and their friends: A huge rock pile is a troll that burst, a tree root lying on its side is an ancient troll, an oddly shaped rock may be part of a nose." Lunge-Larsen, from a very young age, began to see the real world as one that is full of mysteries and wonder. Her imagination was also helped by the fact that her house was full of books.

Lunge-Larsen's father was in charge of the old and rare books division at a publishing house, but in 1961 he left that job to start his own business. In a brief autobiography on Lunge-Larsen's personal website, she stated that her house soon became an antiquarian bookstore, meaning the books her father sold were old, rare, or collectable. Lunge-Larsen was around the age of five at the time, and she loved "living among the huge stacks of musty old books and the wall-to-wall book cases." She and her brother also polished leather-bound books. In 1962, Lunge-Larsen started elementary school, where a "heartless teacher" scolded her for her poor handwriting, which the teacher believed to be a reflection of a lack of intelligence. In addition to that, Lunge-Larsen was also a slow reader.

By middle school, however, Lunge-Larsen appeared to have a talent for foreign languages, namely English, French, and German. In her autobiography, Lunge-Larsen recounted her parents' reaction to her newly discovered talent: "My parents excitedly discuss the possibility of me becoming a secretary to a boss who does international business and will need language expertise. He will surely fall in love and marry me. I fail typing class to prevent such a fate." Soon, however, her language skills came in handy for her parents: her father let her take telephone orders from international customers. By the time she was in high school, Lunge-Larsen had become a fairly good student.

Aside from her passion for reading, Lunge-Larsen was also in love with the theater. Her first "acting role" came when she was about seven years old. At the school health fair, she was so disgusted with having to eat a yellow-cheese sandwich that she pretended to faint. Everyone bought her act, even the school nurse, so she was sent home. She later started to take part in school skits and, once she was in high school, joined the drama club. According to Lunge-Larsen, "Finally my loud voice and love of an audience [were] appreciated."

LATER EDUCATION AND LOCAL ACCLAIM

In 1973, Lunge-Larsen traveled to Minneapolis, Minnesota, to visit her parents' friends. She also got a chance to stay with their daughter, Jackie, at Augsburg College in Minneapolis. It was then that she met a student by the name of Steve Kuross and, she remembers in her autobiography, "fell madly in love." The following year, Lunge-Larsen won a Crown Prince Harald Scholarship from the Norway-America Association, enabling her to attend Augsburg College for one year. After her year at Augsburg College came to an end, she did not want to leave the college or Kuross. To stay in Minneapolis, she began working at the Augsburg College children's library, where she became familiar with American children's literature.

Around this time, Lunge-Larsen wrote her first story for a children's literature class. Titled "The Three Billy Goats Gruff" (1974), it was an adaptation based on a Norwegian folktale of the same name. The story became a local favorite, which led to Lunge-Larsen reading it to children all over the city. In 1976, her storytelling career "took off," she states in her autobiography, when Swedish author Maria Gripe could not make a reading and Lunge-Larsen was asked to take her place. As a result of telling Norwegian folktales to an audience of librarians and lovers of children's literature, Lunge-Larsen became an in-demand reader and acquired more local fame in children's literature circles. She read to children throughout the Twin Cities of Minneapolis and St. Paul, Minnesota.

After receiving her bachelor's degree in 1977, Lunge-Larsen began graduate school at the University of Minnesota. After a year of studying theoretical linguistics, she changed direction after realizing how much she disliked the subject. Instead, she switched her major to applied linguistics with a minor in children's literature. She wrote her master's thesis on the uses of folktales and storytelling as a tool in teaching English to students whose native language is not English. Lunge-Larsen got her master's degree in 1980. That year, she also married Steve Kuross in a ceremony in her native Norway. After studying folklore at the University of Oslo, in Norway, Lunge-Larsen received a grant to study the use of folklore and storytelling as tools for teaching English as a Second Language (ESL)—the topic of her master's thesis. She also taught storytelling at Hamline University, in St. Paul.

Throughout the 1980s, Lunge-Larsen continued to be fascinated by stories and folklore, and she even thought about going for a PhD in folklore. A paper she wrote about folklore led to appearances on local television and the cover of the local *TV Guide*. By the time her third child was born, in December 1988—her first two were born in July 1983 and March 1986—she decided that she would not pursue a doctorate in folklore and would instead "spend [her] time telling stories to [her] children and anyone who will listen" (*Lise Lunge-Larsen*).

BOOKS AND FOLKLORE

Lunge-Larsen began working on her first book in 1997. In a piece she wrote for the Children's Literature Network website, she offered some insight into her process and motivation with regard to writing children's books. "I find that my writing process has been shaped by my experience as a storyteller. When I work on a story, I spend a lot of time telling it out loud to find the right rhythm and pacing. I even record myself so I can hear different versions. And when I feel stuck, I always tell my story to groups of children. Somehow, with all those faces looking up at me, I seem to know exactly what it is I need to say, what can be shortened or cut, and what needs to be played up. It's like magic."

For her first book, *Legend of the Lady Slipper* (1999), Lunge-Larsen and her coauthor, Margi Preus, adapted an Ojibwe tale. (The Ojibwe are an American Indian nation of North America.) The story tells of a young girl who puts on warm moccasins and walks across a frozen lake in a snowstorm. She travels from her village to a nearby village in order to obtain a special herb that is supposed to save her people. To immerse the reader in the story's roots, the authors use certain Ojibwe words, such as *ma-ki-sin waa-big-waan*, which is the name of the flower the girl seeks to find, and *mashkiki*, which means "medi-cine." The book, which is illustrated by Andrea Arroyo, was named a Notable Social Studies Trade Book for Young People and was a finalist for the 1999 Great Lakes Book Award.

Later in 1999, Lunge-Larsen published her second book, *The Troll with No Heart in His Body and Other Tales of Trolls, from Norway*, which is illustrated with woodcuts by Betsy Bowen. The book was inspired by the folktales of the author's native country. *The Troll with No Heart in His Body* is made up of nine stories, including "The Boy and the North Wind," "The Handshake," and "The Three Billy Goats Gruff." A reviewer for *Kirkus Reviews* (15 July 1999) wrote, "It's an appealing collection: varied but not too long, spiced with danger, heroism, humorous moments, and violence that's toned—not watered—down." The book received the Minnesota Book Award, the Riverbank Review Book of Distinction honor, and the Anne Izard Storyteller's Choice Award, among others.

In an essay that appears in *The Troll with No Heart in His Body*, Lunge-Larsen wrote in detail about the importance of troll stories: "Telling or reading folktales is one way to cultivate a child's soul and humanity. With their ancient symbolic images, such stories reach deep inside children to connect them with their essential nature. Troll stories do this better than many folktales because the troll acts as such a clear foil to the hero or heroine." Furthermore, "everything about the troll is contradictory to human nature: they are enormous, grotesque creatures with super-human strength. They are full of treachery and falseness and stand for all that is base and evil. To fight trolls, you can't be like them or use their weapons. Thus, battling trolls brings out the very best in those who dare confront them: intelligence and ingenuity, courage and persistence, kindness and pluck, and the ability of men and women to rely on what each has to offer. To do battle with a troll is to learn to draw the best of our humanity."

Lunge-Larsen continued to draw inspiration from Norway with her next children's book, *Race of the Birkebeiners* (2001), with woodcut illustrations by Mary Azarian. Set in 1206 in Norway's snowy mountains, the story is of a group of warriors who travel on skis across cold, treacherous terrain to bring baby Prince Hakon to a safe destination, away from the nobles who are trying to kill the boy. The name *Birkenbeiner* refers to the bark of birch wood—instead of armor, which the poor men could not afford—that is wrapped around the warriors' legs. The story is in fact a historical tale that is still widely told in Norway. *Race of the Birkebeiners* received the Minnesota Book Award and the Children's Folklore Society of the American Folklore Society Award, as well as others.

The author returned to telling tales of mythical creatures with *The Hidden Folk: Stories of Fairies, Gnomes, Selkies, and Other Secret Beings* (2004), which features illustrations by Beth Krommes. The book, full of very short stories of the supernatural, received a good deal of honors and awards, including the Minnesota Book Award, the honor of Best Illustrated Book from *USA Today*, and the honor of being placed on the "100 Titles for Reading and Sharing" children's book list by the New York Public Library. Two years later, Lunge-Larsen followed *The Hidden Folk* with *Noah's Mittens* (2006), with illustrations by Matthew Trueman. *Noah's Mittens* is a retelling of the biblical story of Noah's Ark, but with a twist: in the book, Noah learns how to make wool felt from the sheep on board his arc—so it is not just about what Noah did for the animals but what they did for him. Like her previous book, *Noah's Mittens* was put on the New York Public Library's "100 Titles for Reading and Sharing" list.

The Adventures of Thor the Thunder God (2007), with illustrations by Jim Madsen, was Lunge-Larsen's next project. *The Adventures of Thor* is the story of the "biggest, strongest, and bravest" of the gods. Lunge-Larsen adapts five Thor stories and retells the Viking myths in her own unique way. One story tells of Thor impersonating the goddess Freya. In another, Thor continuously feeds a family on only two goats. Lunge-Larsen infuses these action-packed stories with humor and wit.

Lunge-Larsen turned back to her interest in linguistics for her next project, *Gifts from the Gods: Ancient Words and Wisdom from Greek and Roman Mythology* (2011). Illustrated by Gareth Hinds, the book explains the etymology of English words that have roots in Greek and Roman mythology. *Gifts from the Gods* takes a close look at seventeen words—such as *panic, echo, genius, janitor,* and *museum*—and for each one there is a story. The word *janitor*, for example, comes from Janus, the god of hallways and doorways; the word *museum* has its roots in the name of temples for worshiping muses. In a review for the *New York Times* (1 Nov. 2011), Pamela Paul stated that the book is "an inventive blend of glossary and anthology" and "provides a fine introduction to one of the Greeks' enduring legacies: their impact on the English language." Paul went on to say that "while American children are being introduced to foreign languages at increasingly young ages (Mandarin for toddlers being all the rage), they spend little time examining the etymological intricacies of their mother tongue, native or adopted. With stories that explain the Greek and Roman origins of certain words and expressions, the book gives children something different."

In addition to her children's books, Lunge-Larsen has contributed two pieces to the book

Celebrating Birch: The Lore, Art, and Craft of an Ancient Tree (2007). She has also published several articles in *New Moon*, a magazine for young girls. She blogs about folklore on the Children's Literature Network website.

Lunge-Larsen lives in Minnesota with her husband. They have three children: Emily, Even Christian, and Erik.

SUGGESTED READING

"Lise Lunge-Larsen." *Kirkus Reviews*. Kirkus, 2012. Web. 8 June 2012.

Lise Lunge-Larsen. Lise Lunge-Larsen, 2012. Web. 8 June 2012.

Lunge-Larsen, Lise. "Lise Lunge-Larsen." *Children's Literature Network*. Children's Literature Network, 2012. Web. 8 June 2012.

Paul, Pamela. "The Power of Myth, Kid-Lit Version." *New York Times*. New York Times Co., 1 Nov. 2011. Web. 8 June 2012.

Van Hoesen, Lori. "An Interview with Lise Lunge-Larsen." *Quill Inc*. Lori Van Hoesen, 15 Apr. 2012. Web. 8 June 2012.

SELECTED WORKS

Legend of the Lady Slipper, 1999; *The Troll with No Heart in His Body and Other Tales of Trolls, from Norway*, 1999; *Race of the Birkebeiners*, 2001; *The Hidden Folk: Stories of Fairies, Dwarves, Selkies, and Other Secret Beings*, 2004; *Noah's Mittens*, 2006; *The Adventures of Thor the Thunder God*, 2007; *Gifts from the Gods: Ancient Words and Wisdom from Greek and Roman Mythology*, 2011

—Dmitry Kiper

Susan Lyne

Born: April 30, 1950
Occupation: Chairman of Gilt Groupe

Reviewing the long career of Susan Lyne, one might be forgiven for thinking that her résumé belongs to several different people. Over the past three-plus decades, her leadership style has been in demand, regardless of the industry in which she works. For four years, starting in 1978, she served as the managing editor of the New York alternative weekly paper the *Village Voice*. For the next three years, she had a high-level post at a film-production company founded by actress Jane Fonda. In 1987 Lyne founded the film magazine *Premiere*, where she served as editor in chief for nearly a decade. Beginning in the late 1990s, she held several top positions at ABC Television, serving during her last two years at the network as president in charge of

entertainment; in that capacity she developed such popular, critically acclaimed shows as *Desperate Housewives* and *Lost*. Then, in late 2004, she became president and chief executive officer (CEO) of Martha Stewart Living Omnimedia (MSLO), where she remained for four years, helping the company expand its product line and return to profitability in the wake of Stewart's imprisonment. In 2008 she became CEO of Gilt Groupe, a members-only luxury-goods shopping Web site, where, in September 2010, she was named chairman.

EARLY LIFE AND EDUCATION

The oldest of five children in an Irish-Catholic family—one son and four daughters—Susan Markham Lyne was born on April 30, 1950, in Boston, Massachusetts, to Eugene and Ruth Lyne. Her father was a lawyer and entrepreneur, and the family was raised in comfortable circumstances. After graduating from high school, Lyne attended, in succession, art school, George Washington University, and the University of California at Berkeley, leaving each without graduating. (Lyne still does not hold a college degree.) In a conversation with Jennifer Reingold for the CNN Money Web site (October 3, 2011), Lyne suggested that her dropping out did not reflect a lack of seriousness or ambition but, rather, the revolutionary spirit of the times. "I never really thought twice about leaving school," she said. "It was a moment when we felt we were going to change history." In Berkley in the late 1960s, she lived in a house run by associates of the leftist activist Tom Hayden, a co-founder of Students for a Democratic Society. Lyne herself did not fully take part in the scene; she made silk-screen art and found work at the Blue Fairyland preschool, helping with candlemaking. It was then that she met Jane Fonda, whose daughter attended the preschool. (Fonda later married Hayden.)

CAREER IN JOURNALISM

In 1975 Lyne moved to San Francisco, California, across the bay from Berkeley. That year she became an associate editor at *City* magazine, where she discovered her talent as an editor. "I could write a piece and it would be fine," Lyne told Jennifer Reingold, "but I could assign a piece and it would be brilliant. I could make another person's work that much better by the questions I asked." In 1976 she joined the *New Times*, a San Francisco–based bi-weekly publication, where she worked as the West Coast editor. During her time there she got an interview with Bill and Emily Harris, imprisoned members of the Symbionese Liberation Army (SLA), a radical group that, between 1973 and 1975, committed a series of bank robberies and various violent acts, including murder. The group gained notoriety when its members kidnapped the newspaper heiress Patty Hearst, who ultimately joined the SLA for a period of time and participated in several bank robberies. A detail from the interview that Lyne conducted, cited in court by the prosecutor in the Hearst case, helped lead to Hearst's conviction.

Lyne left the *New Times* in 1978 and moved to New York City. That year she became the managing editor of the *Village Voice*, owned at the time by the media mogul Rupert Murdoch. Next Lyne joined IPC Films, a film-production company founded by Jane Fonda and Bruce Gilbert. In her capacity as vice president in charge of creative development, Lyne looked for stories and articles that could be made into films. In 1984 Lyne married George Crile III, a reporter and producer with the long-running CBS newsmagazine *60 Minutes*. The following year she left IPC Films. She had become impatient with how long movies took to develop; at the same time, the new popularity of the videocassette recorder (VCR) convinced her of the importance of film in people's lives. Around that time she approached Rupert Murdoch with the idea of publishing a quality magazine focusing on the film world, with her as editor. Murdoch agreed, and *Premiere*, inspired by a French magazine, launched in 1987, quickly becoming very popular with the general public.

Lyne served as the magazine's editor for nine years. On several occasions during that time, Joe Roth, president of the Walt Disney Co., tried to recruit her. In January 1996 Disney announced that Lyne would be its executive vice president for acquisitions and development of intellectual material and new opportunities—a newly created post. Writing for the *New York Times* (January 3, 1996), Deirdre Carmody paraphrased Roth as saying that Lyne "would be the most senior creative person in the motion picture group in New York and would be looking for opportunities to acquire screen plays and stage plays, as well as dealing with agents and publishers about books that might be made into films." Discussing his decision to hire Lyne, Roth told Reingold, "In my 40 years in the business, I've rarely asked anyone [out of the business] to come in. But she had great business skills and great people skills and great taste." Two years later Lyne was promoted to executive vice-president in charge of movies and miniseries for the ABC television network, which Disney owns. In that capacity she oversaw the airing of such biographical films as *The Three Stooges*, *The Audrey Hepburn Story*, *Anne Frank: The Whole Story*, and the Emmy Award–winning *Me and My Shadows*, about the actress Judy Garland; she also launched the six-part miniseries *Rose Red*, written by the novelist Stephen King, the premiere of which was watched in 20 million households.

MEDIA EXECUTIVE

In January 2002, as ABC was experiencing declining prime-time ratings, the company announced that Lyne would replace its creative executive Stu Bloomberg, making her president of ABC's entertainment division. Lyne thus took on the biggest challenge of her wide-ranging career up to that time. By then ABC had had four presidents of entertainment in five years (including Lyne), and the network lagged behind NBC and CBS in the ratings. By May 2002 Lyne and her team had looked over 110 scripts and screened 29 pilots. From those she chose eight series for the coming TV season, including *Legally Blond*, based on the hit movie. Meanwhile, ABC finished the present season without a show among TV's 25 top-rated programs. Making matters worse, ABC was in last place among the major networks in winning viewers between the ages of 18 and 49, a highly sought-after demographic.

Then, early that summer, Lyne inadvertently caused some minor controversy by proclaiming that ABC's main goal was not to create innovative shows but to provide good entertainment. In explaining her comments, Lyne said to Michael Freeman for *Electronic Media* (September 9, 2002), "I was really speaking more to the fact that all of us in the business—critics and executives alike—can get into a tunnel-like mentality because [of] all of the material we have to review for TV. We can sometimes miss the fact [that] an engaging show is an engaging show, even if it does not break any new ground. We are going to do great programming at this network, but I don't measure the quality of a show or the value of a show by whether it is different than anything that has been done before." In January 2003, after the ratings collapse of *Who Wants to Be a Millionaire*, ABC announced that it would air five reality-TV shows, including *Extreme Makeover*, about people undergoing plastic surgery. By the end of that year, ABC's ratings had improved, and the network was attracting more viewers between the ages of 18 and 49. Lyne also developed such shows as the drama *Lost* and the drama-comedy *Desperate Housewives*, which were set to air in the new TV season, starting in the fall of 2004. Prior to that, however, in April of that year, Lyne was fired from ABC—as were several other executives in the network's entertainment division. As recently as a week before the firing, Lyne had been assured that she was going to keep her job. (*Desperate Housewives*, a ratings hit, went on to win six Emmy Awards for its first season.)

In a conversation with Adam Bryant for the *New York Times* (October 3, 2009), Lyne called the firing a "defining moment" for her. "I was totally shocked," she said. "But it was also one of those moments where I couldn't hide. There was no, 'She's leaving to explore other opportunities,' or all the niceties of job changes in the corporate world. And the fact that it was as public and as sudden actually turned out to be liberating, because I didn't have to make things up or try to put a nicer face on it." She added, "And it gave me an ability to really look honestly at my tenure there, and to think really clearly about what I wanted to do next. And I had never in my life taken time off. So I had gone from one job to another, always because someone offered me a job. But I had never been able to direct my own career. It was the first time in my life I was able to do that. So what I thought was the worst thing that could have happened to me actually turned out to be a real opportunity."

As she had done before, Lyne moved on to an entirely new industry. In 2004 she joined the board of directors of Martha Stewart Living Omnimedia, the publishing, broadcasting, and merchandising company founded and owned—via a majority of shares—by the home-enhancement icon Martha Stewart. In October 2004 Stewart was sent to a minimum-security prison for five months for conspiracy, obstruction of justice, and two counts of making false statements in a case that originated with allegations of insider trading. In November 2004 Lyne was appointed president and CEO of MSLO. That year the company had lost $60 million, so Lyne had a hard road ahead of her. Lyne made trips to the prison in West Virginia where Stewart was held; because Stewart was legally forbidden to discuss company business in detail, "I could report in to her on what we had done, but I couldn't ask her opinion about something, or get her desires going forward," Lyne told Laura Rich for the *New York Times* (April 24, 2005). "It had to be far more general than a typical business conversation. But we talked a lot about how and why she formed the company and how she looked at the brand, and the things that she loved about the magazines, and just her whole point of view on why this was important. I just got a very clear sense of what drove her and what was important to her." As the head of the company, Lyne "cut costs and boosted morale," according to Reingold, "both inside MSLO and with advertisers." By the end of 2006, she could proclaim that MSLO was gaining momentum. In 2007 a line of Martha Stewart home furnishings debuted at Macy's department store. That year *Crain's New York Business* (September 16, 2007) declared Lyne to be one of the "most powerful women in New York." (In April 2005 Stewart had returned to the company, but she was still not legally permitted to be involved in it full time.)

In the summer of 2008 Lyne stepped down from her post as president and CEO of MSLO. A few months later she took on the job of CEO at Gilt Groupe, an online startup that sells high-end luxury goods at a discount. The timing of her arrival, with regard to the global economy, was less than propitious: Lyne started her new job in September 2008, which coincided with the beginning of the worldwide financial crisis. Another hurdle was her lack of familiarity with the world of Internet startups. But as before, Lyne unselfconsciously asked about everything she did not understand. By the end of 2010, the company had made around $400 million in revenue, and in September of that year she was made chairman. According to the company's Web site, Gilt Groupe has expanded to include business lines in home décor (Gilt Home), items for children and infants (Gilt Kids), men's apparel and gear (Gilt Man), artisanal foods and wines (Gilt Taste), an online retail store for men's apparel and accessories (Park & Bond), vacation travel (Jetsetter), and local services (Gilt City); the company has also founded the leading flash-sale site in Japan (Gilt Japan). (A flash sale is a limited-time online offer of large discounts on goods.)

PERSONAL LIFE

In late 2005 Lyne's husband was diagnosed with pancreatic cancer; he died in May 2006. During his illness Lyne continued to work full time. Although, as Reingold reported, Lyne "suffered along with her husband," Lyne told Reingold, "I needed a thread to the future, something that would connect me to life after George. Work was an antidote to the sadness. I can't tell you it was the right decision, but it felt like salvation at the time."

In her interview with Adam Bryant, Lyne talked about her leadership style: "My biggest challenge as a manager overall has always been moving from the nice to the 'this is what we're going to do.' And I still always like to get input, listen to what people have to say. But it's really clear that the decision has to be made at some point, and I'm a whole lot more comfortable with that now than I was 25 years ago." Later in the interview Lyne added: "One of the things I do more of is to make sure I can carve out a certain period of time every week to step back and think about the big picture. I think early in my career I was constantly looking at what was coming next week, next month, but rarely carving out time to really think about the future. It's useful on so many levels, not just because it does give you long-term focus, but because it forces you to re-assess all those short-term decisions, too. I need time alone, quiet time alone, to do my job well."

Lyne is a member of the board of AOL and a trustee of two New York City–based institutions of higher learning, Rockefeller University and the New School. She lives in New York City and has two children, Susan and Jane, from her marriage to George Crile, and two stepchildren, Katherine and Elizabeth, from Crile's previous marriage.

SUGGESTED READING

Bryant, Adam. "Want to Talk to the Chief? Book Your Half-Hour." *New York Times*. New York Times, 3 Oct. 2009. Web. 21 Dec. 2011.

Carmody, Deirdre. "The Median Business; Film Magazine Editor to Lead Disney's Development Effort." *New York Times* 3 Jan. 1996, nat. ed.: D5. Print.

Freeman, Michael. "ABC: Conservative Talk, Bold Actions." *Electronic Media* 9 Sep. 2002: 28. Print.

Reingold, Jennifer. "The Many Lives of Susan Lyne." *CNN Money*. Cable News Network, 3 Oct. 2011. Web. 21 Dec. 2011.

Rich, Laura. "C.E.O, If Not The Star." *New York Times* 24 Apr. 2005, nat. ed.: 4.

—*Dmitry Kiper*

Joe Maddon

Born: February 8, 1954
Occupation: Manager of the Tampa Bay Rays

In November 2005, after more than three decades spent working at both the minor- and major-league levels for the Los Angeles Angels of Anaheim organization, Joe Maddon was appointed manager of the Tampa Bay Rays, the youngest team in Major League Baseball (MLB). He beat out several candidates, despite having had no previous major-league managerial experience. "From the beginning, we felt our ideal candidate would have infectious energy and optimism,

Getty Images

strong communication skills, [an] extensive player development background, and [a] willingness to embrace new ideas," Andrew Friedman, the Rays' executive vice president of baseball operations said in an interview for the Associated Press (15 Nov. 2005). "He is a teacher, a leader, and a strong communicator. . . . He understands what it takes for a team to be successful."

Since taking the reins at Tampa Bay, Maddon has more than met expectations, employing an unconventional coaching philosophy that uses statistics to analyze game strategies. "I like numbers. I like instincts. I like trusting your gut," he remarked in the Associated Press interview. "I think you think with your brain, your heart, and your stomach." After three losing seasons (2005–07), Maddon led his team to American League (AL) East Division titles in 2008 and 2010, as well as a World Series appearance in 2008 and a wild-card berth in 2011. For his effort he was twice voted AL Manager of the Year, in 2008 and 2010.

EARLY LIFE AND EDUCATION

Joseph John Maddon was born on February 8, 1954 to Albina "Beanie" (Klocek) and Joseph Anthony Maddon in Hazleton, a small coal-mining town in northeastern Pennsylvania with a population of about twenty-five thousand people. Growing up, Maddon lived with his parents, his younger sister Carmine (pronounced CAR-mean), and his younger brother Mark in a modest apartment overlooking C. Maddon & Sons Plumbing and Heating. The family enterprise was founded in the 1930s by Maddon's grandfather, Carmen, an Italian immigrant who had shortened his surname from Maddoni to Maddon after his arrival in America. Maddon's father, a plumber, eventually operated the company with his four brothers, whose families also lived in the same four-story apartment building. Maddon's mother, who is of Polish descent, has worked as a waitress and bookkeeper at the nearby Third Base Luncheonette, another family-owned business that was started by her sister and brother-in-law.

Maddon developed a passion for sports at an early age. He grew up playing Little League baseball and demonstrated natural leadership skills while serving as quarterback for the State Trooper Eagles, a local youth football team. "By the time I was [ten] I was learning plays and assignments, not only for myself but everyone else on the team," he told Marc Topkin for the *Tampa Bay Times* (2 Apr. 2006). "And I was calling audibles. So maybe that motivated me to look into things a little more deeply." Maddon's father also encouraged his son's athletic pursuits. "He knew how much I loved to play ball, all the sports. And he encouraged me not to go into [the plumbing business]," Maddon told Bill Chastain in an interview for *MLB.com* (15 June 2007).

A STANDOUT HIGH SCHOOL ATHLETE

By the time he had reached his teens, Maddon was a standout athlete at Hazleton Area High School (now Hazleton Elementary/Middle School), where he lettered for three years playing for the Mountaineers' varsity football and the baseball squads. As a junior, Maddon helped lead his team to the 1971 Hughie McGeehan League Championship and the District Eleven title, and as Hazleton High's quarterback, nicknamed "Broad Street Joe," Maddon also set school records in three offensive categories: pass attempts (185), pass completions (93), and yards passing (1,290).

After graduating from high school in 1972, Maddon turned down offers from two Ivy League institutions: Princeton University and the University of Pennsylvania. Instead, he accepted an athletic scholarship to Lafayette College, a liberal arts school in Easton, Pennsylvania. However, with the freshman season under his belt, Maddon, an economics major, made the choice to quit playing football, in large part due to his undersized five-foot-eleven frame. The decision greatly disappointed his father. "That was the only time he was ever upset with me in our lives together," Maddon revealed to Chastain. "He stayed mad at me for about six weeks."

Under the guidance of Norm Gigon, the baseball coach at Lafayette, an undaunted Maddon, who had pitched and played shortstop during high school, made the transition to catcher, with the intention of pursuing a baseball career.

"Joe had a strong drive to be a baseball player. . . . I told him the only way he had a chance [at pro ball] was to try catching," Gigon told Paul Reinhard for the *Morning Call* (22 Oct. 2008). "He wasn't a big kid, but he had intestinal fortitude and drive. . . . He had a good arm . . . and had good power, too." Maddon was the catcher for the Lafayette Leopards from 1973 until 1975, when the California Angels offered him a minor-league, free-agent deal prior to his senior year. "They offered me absolutely nothing," Maddon said to Reinhard in another interview for the *Morning Call* (3 Sep. 2010). "I got zero bonus; I had an incentive bonus which I never collected on. . . . There was no way I was coming back to school if I had a chance to play baseball. I wanted it that badly, and I was not to be denied."

MINOR-LEAGUE PLAYING CAREER

Maddon was assigned to the Quad Cities Angels, the team's Class-A affiliate in the Midwest League. In 1976, his first professional season, the twenty-two-year-old appeared in fifty games and batted .294, with forty-eight hits, eighteen runs scored, twenty-two runs batted in (RBIs), eighteen walks, and nine doubles. After finishing the regular season with seventy-two wins and fifty-nine losses (the league's third best record), the Quad Cities Angels won the Southern Division title, following their one-game playoff victory over the Cedar Rapids Giants. The Angels subsequently advanced to the Midwest League Championship but lost to the defending champion Waterloo Royals.

Maddon then spent the next two seasons (1977–78) playing for the Salinas Angels, the team's Class-A affiliate in the California League. In his first year he made fifty-eight game appearances and ended the season with a .250 batting average, forty-five hits, twenty-four RBIs, twenty-three runs scored, six doubles, and three home runs. His team finished third with a regular-season record of seventy-nine wins and sixty-one losses, behind the first-place Fresno Giants and the Lodi Dodgers, the runners-up and 1977 California League champions. In 1978 Maddon batted .261 with two home runs, ten doubles, fifteen runs scored, and sixteen RBIs in forty-two games for the Salinas Angels, who repeated as third-place finishers, with eighty-four regular-season wins—thirteen-and-a-half games behind the first-place Visalia Oaks, also winners of the 1978 California League pennant.

Maddon ended his playing career with another Class-A affiliate of the California Angels—the Santa Clara Padres—for whom he hit .250 with fifteen hits, eight runs scored, two doubles, and seven RBIs in twenty game appearances. The team finished last in the league, winning only forty-seven games and losing ninety-three.

ASCENDING THROUGH THE COACHING RANKS

In 1980, a year after being released by the Angels, Maddon accepted an offer from the organization to become a scout. He joined their minor-league managerial ranks the following year as the manager for the Idaho Falls Angels, the team's affiliate in the Pioneer League, which is an advanced rookie league with a shortened schedule. Under Maddon's watch, the team amassed twenty-seven victories and forty-three losses—the league's second-worst record.

After spending one season with the Idaho Falls Angels, Maddon was appointed manager of the Salem Angels, the team's Class-A affiliate in the Northwest League, during Salem's inaugural 1982 season. In only his second year as a manager, he helped the Salem Angels capture the Northern Division pennant, despite a disappointing record of thirty-four wins and thirty-six losses. Maddon subsequently led his squad to the Northwest League championship title, earning Northwest League Manager of the Year honors. A year later he resumed managerial duties for the Salem Angels, but the team failed to make the playoffs, coming in last in their division and with a mediocre record of thirty-one wins and thirty-nine losses.

In 1984, Maddon took over as manager of the Peoria Chiefs, the Angels' Single-A affiliate in the Midwest League, while also serving as the coordinator of their Arizona Instructional League. The team notched sixty-six victories and seventy-three losses to finish second in their division (behind the Springfield Cardinals) and eighth in the Midwest League. Maddon's work in the instructional league attracted the attention of Gene Mauch, then manager of the major-league club whom Maddon cites as a mentor. "He told me I had created a great atmosphere," he said to Hal Bodley in an interview posted on *MLB.com* (23 Oct. 2008). "I had no idea what he was talking about, but he made me stop and think about it. He was talking about relationship building, organizational skills—all the other outside peripheral things I was doing but didn't realize how important they were."

The following year the Angels promoted Maddon to manage the Midland RockHounds, their Double-A affiliate in the Texas League. During his first season in Double-A, the team amassed the league's worst record, winning only fifty-nine games while losing a league-high seventy-seven. The RockHounds also had the highest earned run average (ERA) in the league, at 5.42. In 1986, the club had slightly better results, with sixty-two victories and seventy-one losses; however, the team finished with the league's highest ERA (5.19) for the second consecutive year.

Despite two consecutive losing seasons with the RockHounds, Maddon remained with the Angels as a roving hitting instructor, a position he held for six years (1987–93). During the early 1990s he also worked in the front office as the team's minor-league field coordinator.

PROMOTED TO THE MAJORS

In May 1994, after a brief stint as the director of player development, Maddon, who was also in his third year as a field coordinator, accepted an invitation to join the Angels' major-league staff as a bench coach under manager Marcel Lachemann. In his new position, Maddon adopted an unconventional approach, relying heavily on computer research and statistical analysis to evaluate game strategies. "I used to be made fun of for carrying a computer. . . . It was met with a lot of resistance at first. Like anything new, it takes a while to catch on," he recalled to Ian Browne for *MLB.com* (12 Nov. 2003). "I've always been an organization freak. When computers came along, I found it a better way to organize my stuff. I started using computer programs to track the opposition, whether it was a spray chart or a manager's tendencies." Following a strike-shortened 1994 season, the team amassed a record of forty-seven victories and sixty-eight losses to finish fourth in the American League (AL) Western Division.

Maddon served as the first base coach in 1995, during which the Angels invested in developing a computer program that would allow them to quickly generate various statistics of opposing hitters. Despite ending the regular-season with seventy-eight wins and sixty-seven losses—the second-best record in the AL West—the Angels, who were still being managed by Lachemann, endured a late-season collapse, squandering a twelve-game lead with thirty-eight games remaining. They failed to advance to the playoffs, finishing one game behind the Seattle Mariners.

In August 1996, after his team had compiled a disappointing record of fifty-two victories and fifty-nine defeats, Lachemann resigned as manager and was succeeded by John McNamara, a former Angels player with eighteen years of major-league managing experience; Maddon, who had resumed his bench coach duties, retained his position on the coaching staff. When interim manager McNamara was temporarily sidelined by a calf injury, Maddon took over, amassing eight wins and fourteen losses for the Angels, who finished fourth in the AL West, with an overall record of seventy wins and ninety-one losses.

In November 1996, the team changed their franchise name from the California Angels to the Anaheim Angels and appointed Terry Collins as the permanent manager. Maddon remained the bench coach under Collins, who guided his team to consecutive second-place finishes in the division during his first two seasons (1997–98). In June 1998, Maddon filled in for Collins while he served an eight-game suspension. After the Angels managed only fifty-one wins while losing eighty-two games in 1999, Collins stepped down, and Maddon was named the interim coach for the rest of the season. Anaheim won nineteen of its remaining twenty-nine games but finished last in its division.

THE SCIOSCIA ERA

Although Maddon interviewed for the permanent job, the Angels hired former Dodgers catcher Mike Scioscia, who retained Maddon as his bench coach. In his first year, Scioscia led the team to eighty-two wins and eighty losses, as well as a third-place finish in the AL West. After another third-place result in 2001, the Angels ended the 2002 season as winners of the AL Wild Card; their regular-season record of ninety-nine wins and sixty-three losses was also third best in the league behind the New York Yankees and the Oakland Athletics.

After defeating the Yankees in the best-of-five American League Division Series (ALDS), the Angels, who were making their first playoff appearance since 1986, advanced to the best-of-seven American League Championship Series (ALCS). Anaheim prevailed over the Minnesota Twins in five games to reach the World Series against the San Francisco Giants, winners of the National League Wild Card. The Angels won the series, four games to three, and captured their first-ever World Series title in franchise history. The championship victory marked a bittersweet moment for Maddon, whose father had passed away only six months before.

In 2003, the Walt Disney Company sold the Angels franchise to Arturo "Arte" Moreno, who became Major League Baseball's first Hispanic team owner. The club failed in their bid to make the playoffs and repeat as World Series champions after compiling seventy-seven wins and eighty-five losses, which put the team in third place in their division. In November, after the baseball season had ended, Maddon traveled to Boston, Massachusetts, to interview for the Red Sox managerial vacancy. "You could tell he was innovative, thoughts he had about handling players in the clubhouse. He was very smart and very organized, which impressed us," Theo Epstein, the Red Sox general manager, told Bill Burt for the *Eagle-Tribune* (16 Oct. 2008). "But I wasn't sure if he was a good fit here, as [this was] his first major league job." Terry Francona, who had previously managed the Philadelphia Phillies for three years (1997–2000), was ultimately named the Red Sox manager.

The next season Maddon returned as the bench coach for the Angels, whose ninety-two wins and seventy losses helped them capture their first division title since 1986. In the ALDS, the team proved to be no match against the eventual World Series champion Red Sox, who completed a three-game sweep to advance to the ALCS. In 2005, the Angels, now renamed the Los Angeles Angels of Anaheim, claimed their second consecutive AL West division, after winning ninety-five games and went on to win the ALDS three games to two. They faltered in the ALCS, however, losing to the Chicago White Sox, the eventual World Series winners that year.

MANAGER OF THE TAMPA BAY RAYS

Maddon's dream of running a major-league team finally came true on November 15, 2005, when he was appointed to replace the temperamental Lou Piniella as manager of Florida's Tampa Bay Devil Rays. One of Maddon's first moves involved adopting the mantra "Attitude Is a Decision," in an effort to change the mindset of his young team, who were perennial last-place finishers in their division. Although the Devil Rays amassed the worst record in the American League and in the majors (with sixty-one wins and one hundred and one losses), in 2006 the team won forty-one out of eighty-one home games—the franchise's first-ever winning record at Tropicana Field, whose attendance increased by 200,000.

With the infusion of talented young hitters (Carl Crawford, B. J. Upton, and Delmon Young), key free-agent signings (Carlos Peña and Akinori Iwamura), as well as strong starting pitching from Scott Kazmir and James Shields, the Devil Rays slightly improved their 2007 record to sixty-six wins and ninety-six losses. Peña's performance (forty-six home runs and one hundred twenty-one RBIs) earned him AL Comeback Player of the Year and Silver Slugger Award honors. Although the team was last in the league and in the majors for the second consecutive year, home attendance at Tropicana Field increased for the second straight season, marking another franchise milestone.

During the offseason the team changed its name to the Tampa Bay Rays and also made notable acquisitions, including starting pitcher Matt Garza, longtime reliever Troy Percival, and veteran outfielder Cliff Floyd. In spring training, Maddon had T-shirts printed with the message "9 = 8," preaching the idea that if the nine players on the field competed hard for nine innings, the Rays would be one of eight teams to advance to the postseason.

In his third season, Maddon also made several bold moves. He not only moved pitcher J. P. Howell to the bullpen but also kept pitcher Edwin Jackson in the starting rotation even though he had only won five games and had lost fifteen in 2007; Maddon placed rookie third baseman Evan Longoria in the middle of the batting order, usually occupied by the team's top run producers. He also stressed accountability with his players, even going so far as to bench B. J. Upton on several occasions for a lack of effort.

STRATEGY PAYS OFF

Maddon's strategy paid off. Despite injuries to several key players, including Kazmir, Peña, Longoria, and Floyd, the Rays won ninety-seven games and captured their first-ever AL East division title, fulfilling their goal of making the playoffs. After beating the Chicago White Sox in the ALDS and the Boston Red Sox in the ALCS, the Rays earned their first trip to the World Series, where the Phillies defeated them in five games. Maddon was named AL Manager of the Year after obtaining twenty-seven out of twenty-eight first-place votes from the Baseball Writers' Association of America. In addition to receiving similar honors from the *Sporting News* and *USA Today*, he was the recipient of the Chuck Tanner Baseball Manager of the Year Award.

In May 2009, Maddon signed a three-year extension to remain in Tampa. Although the Rays failed to defend their division title, he guided his team to an overall record of eighty-four wins and seventy-eight losses, as well as a third-place finish in the AL East. The following year the Rays regained their 2008 form. Despite posting the second-lowest team batting average, the Rays had the league's second-lowest ERA and were en route to winning a league-best ninety-six games and capturing the division for the second time in three years. However, the team failed to advance past the ALDS, losing to the Texas Rangers. Maddon finished third in the AL Manager of the Year voting.

After losing their first six games of the 2011 season, the Rays still managed to win ninety-one games and earn the AL wild-card berth—their third consecutive postseason appearance. They accomplished this feat by overcoming a nine-game deficit in September to overtake the Boston Red Sox. Maddon's efforts won him his second AL Manager of the Year award. For the second straight season, the Rays faced the Rangers in the ALDS with a similar outcome. In February 2012, Maddon received another three-year contract extension reportedly worth $6 million. More than a third of the way through the 2012 season, the Rays are third in their division.

PERSONAL LIFE

Two weeks after the last game of the 2008 World Series, Maddon married long-time fiancée Jaye Sousoures. He has two children, Sarah and Joey, from his first marriage to Bette Stanton, as well as two grandchildren. Maddon is a cycling enthusiast who loves classic cars and wine. Each year he hosts a holiday dinner (held between Thanksgiving and Christmas), during which he prepares an Italian/Polish meal for the homeless in his native Hazleton, Pennsylvania.

SUGGESTED READING

Barancik, Scott. "Business: Devil Rays Exec Calls Business Outlook Bright." *Tampa Bay Times*. Times Publishing Co., 4 Oct. 2006. Web. 26 June 2012.

Bodley, Hal. "Maddon Had Great Mentor in Mauch." *MLB.com*. Major League Baseball Advanced Media, L.P., 23 Oct. 2008. Web. 23 June 2012.

Browne, Ian. "Epstein Interviews Angels' Maddon." *MLB.com*. Major League Baseball Advanced Media, L.P., 12 Nov. 2003. Web. 26 June 2012.

Burt, Bill. "Crazy Like a Fox." *Eagle-Tribune*. Community Newspaper Holdings, Inc., 16 Oct. 2008. Web. 26 June 2012.

Chastain, Bill. "Maddon Reflects Fondly on Father." *MLB.com*. Major League Baseball Advanced Media, L.P., 15 June 2007. Web. 21 June 2012.

"Devil Rays Hires Angels Coach Maddon as Manager." *ESPN MLB*. ESPN Internet Ventures, 15 Nov. 2005. Web. 11 July 2012.

Reilly, Mike. "Angels Coaches Learning to Play Hardball with Software." *Los Angeles Times*. Tribune Co., 26 Sep. 1995. Web. 25 June 2012.

Reinhard, Paul. "Lafayette Honors Joe Maddon, Manager of the Rays." *The Morning Call*. Tribune Co., 3 Sep. 2010. Web. 21 June 2012.

---. "Still The Same Ol' Joe: His Coach and a Former Teammate at Lafayette Knew Joe Maddon Would Be a Success." *The Morning Call*. Tribune Co., 22 Oct. 2008. Web. 21 June 2012.

Topkin, Mark. "A Man with a Multitrack Mind." *Tampa Bay Times*. Times Publishing Co., 2 Apr. 2006. Web. 27 June 2012.

---. "Joey's Home." *Tampa Bay Times*. Times Publishing Co., 14 May 2006. Web. 21 June 2012.

—*Bertha Muteba*

Rooney Mara

Born: April 17, 1985
Occupation: Actress

Nominated in 2012 for both a Golden Globe and an Academy Award in the best actress category for her portrayal of Lisbeth Salander, the title character in the David Fincher–directed blockbuster *The Girl with the Dragon Tattoo* (2011), Rooney Mara is one of the most promising American actors of her generation. In addition to *The Girl with the Dragon Tattoo*, she has starred in the independent film *Tanner Hall* (2009) and the 2010 remake of the horror classic *A Nightmare on Elm Street*, and she has earned near universal praise for her small but integral part in the critical smash *The Social Network* (2010).

WireImage

Mara's career-defining role thus far remains Lisbeth Salander. Describing her performance, David Denby observed for the *New Yorker* (12 Dec. 2011), "Mara . . . cuts through scene after scene like a swift, dark blade." Starring alongside the larger-than-life cinematic presence of British actor Daniel Craig of James Bond fame, she nevertheless carries the film, Denby contends. Craig's performance "is modest, quiet, even rather recessive. It's Mara's shot at stardom, and he lets her have it."

EARLY LIFE AND EDUCATION

Patricia Rooney Mara was born on April 17, 1985, in Bedford, New York, and is one of four children of Timothy Christopher "Chris" Mara and the former Kathleen McNulty Rooney. Mara has two brothers, Daniel and Conor, and an older sister, Kate. Mara's paternal great grandfather, Timothy James "Tim" Mara, founded the National Football League New York Giants in 1925. Her maternal great grandfather, Arthur Joseph "Art" Rooney, Sr., established the Pittsburgh Steelers professional football team in 1933. Mara's father is an executive with the Giants. Her mother works as a part-time real estate agent and journalist.

Hailing from two of the foremost families of American sports, Mara is often assumed to have enjoyed an exceptionally privileged upbringing, but she insists such reports are overblown. "I don't have a trust fund," Mara told Jonathan Van Meter for *Vogue* (17 Oct. 2011). "I grew up in a little cul-de-sac in the suburbs and went to

public school. I went to Costco on the weekends." As she explained to Jake Coyle for the Associated Press (28 Dec. 2011), "I had a normal childhood. I wasn't like some spoiled little football brat." Still, she could not avoid her football heritage and attended every Giants Sunday home game with her family, going directly from church to Giants Stadium in East Rutherford, New Jersey. "I was dragged to football games every week," she recalled to Peter Davis for *Paper Magazine* (4 Jan. 2010). "I just started liking it a few years ago, but I really hated it growing up."

Thanks to their mother's love of Broadway and classic films, both Mara and her sister were drawn to acting from an early age. Though Kate committed to acting at the age of twelve, Mara decided she'd go to college first. "I don't know when I decided to act," she explained to Cindy Pearlman for the *Chicago Sun-Times* (15 Dec. 2011). "I grew up going to different plays. And I always loved watching old movies with my mom. I guess that's where it sprang from for me. I don't know if I ever decided that acting was something I wanted to try. It's not like it's something I ever really decided." Though she took acting classes at Bedford's Fox Lane High School, Mara appeared in only one school play, starring as Juliet in a production of Shakespeare's *Romeo and Juliet*.

After graduating in 2003, Mara spent four months visiting South America, stopping in Bolivia, Peru, and Ecuador as part of the Traveling School, which is a high school study-abroad program for young women. Upon her return to the United States, she entered George Washington University in Washington, DC, but after her freshman year she transferred to the Gallatin School for Individualized Study at New York University (NYU), in New York City. While at Gallatin, Mara devised her own curriculum, focusing on psychology, international social policy, and the nonprofit sector, which gave her ample opportunities to receive college credit for overseas volunteer work. Spending time at an orphanage in the disadvantaged Kibera district of Nairobi, Kenya, would later lead to the formation of her own charity.

BREAKING INTO ACTING

In addition to her studies, Mara made some appearances in student films, which helped revive her interest in acting. At nineteen she began to test the waters by auditioning for various professional roles, and the following year she made her screen debut with a minor part in the direct-to-video supernatural thriller *Urban Legends: Bloody Mary* in which her sister Kate played the lead. During her early career, Mara was often credited as either Tricia or Patricia Mara. She later opted to use Rooney: Her family has a long tradition of members going by their middle names, and, as she explained to Peter Davis, "I never really liked my first name. . . . I never felt like a Tricia. And Rooney is more memorable."

Mara next surfaced the following year in an episode of the television series *Law and Order: Special Victims Unit* and several other small parts in television and film followed over the next two years. In 2007, she appeared in an episode of the television series *Women's Murder Club*, starring Angie Harmon. In 2008, Mara landed a role in the James Bolton–directed *Dream Boy*, an independent film about the surreptitious love affair between two gay southern teenagers, and she appeared in an episode of the television program *The Cleaner* starring Benjamin Bratt.

The pace of Mara's screen and television work picked up considerably in 2009. In addition to appearances in two episodes of the television drama *ER*, she had small parts in several films, chief among them *The Winning Season* and *Youth in Revolt*. Mara also landed her first starring role in the Tatiana von Furstenberg-directed prep-school drama *Tanner Hall*.

Set at an all-girls boarding school in New England, *Tanner Hall* centers on four students. Mara played Fernanda, a senior whose affair with a much older man, Tom Everett Scott's Gio, fuels the movie's plot. Though reviews for the film were mixed, with Andy Webster for the *New York Times* (8 Sep. 2011) describing it as an "uneven drama . . . [that] rarely rises above the generic," Mara's performance earned praise. Webster commented, "Despite her misjudged affair, Fernanda is unwaveringly noble and blemish free." Betsy Sharkey for the *Los Angeles Times* (9 Sep. 2011) observed, "Mara's chemistry with Scott gives the film some spark."

A NIGHTMARE ON ELM STREET

Though her acting career was picking up, Mara managed to complete her studies at NYU receiving her diploma in 2010. After graduation, she moved to Los Angeles, where she scored her next major film role in the 2010 remake of the horror classic *A Nightmare on Elm Street*, playing Nancy Holbrooke, the female lead, opposite Jackie Earle Haley and Kyle Gallner. The *Nightmare on Elm Street* movie franchise debuted in 1984 under the direction of Wes Craven, and the 2010 rendition did not break much new ground by adhering to the conventions of the franchise. It drew mixed reviews from critics such as A. O. Scott for the *New York Times* (29 Apr. 2010) who wrote, "the movie traffics in overly familiar scare tactics, setting up predictable false alarms and telegraphing in advance just when Freddy will pop into the frame and utter one of his labored witticisms." Still, Scott did reserve some tepid praise for the actors, commenting, "The cast—notably Rooney Mara and Kyle Gallner as Freddy's longest-surviving prey—are reasonably adept at screaming, crying, looking sleepy and earnestly delivering expository information

they glean from research on the Internet and at the local bookstore." Working on *A Nightmare on Elm Street* was not a great experience for Mara. "I hated it," she declared to Van Meter. "It left me thinking, if this is what is available to me, then I don't necessarily want to be an actress. And then I got the script for *The Social Network*."

THE SOCIAL NETWORK

The Social Network (2010) is a fictionalized account of the creation of the social-networking website Facebook. Directed by David Fincher and scripted by Aaron Sorkin, the film starred Jesse Eisenberg as Mark Zuckerberg, Facebook's college-age creator, with Justin Timberlake and Andrew Garfield in supporting roles. Mara plays Mark's girlfriend, Erica Albright, who, in what Ann Hornaday for the *Washington Post* (1 Oct. 2010) described as "the film's small masterpiece of an opening scene," unceremoniously dumps Zuckerberg after his insensitivity and unwitting insults go too far. A critical triumph, the film was nominated for eight Academy Awards, winning three (best editing, best adapted screenplay, and best film score), and winning four Golden Globes for best picture, best director, best screenplay, and best score.

LISBETH SALANDER

Though her role in *The Social Network* was a minor one, Mara left a lasting impression. Fincher was especially taken with her performance. "I knew that Rooney had something special," he explained to Will Lawrence for the *Telegraph* (15 Dec. 2011). "Finding somebody who can take on Jesse Eisenberg, with an Aaron Sorkin script, is not an easy thing to do, but that's what Rooney did in *The Social Network*." Fincher started to consider Mara for the role of Lisbeth Salander, the lead in his next movie, *The Girl with the Dragon Tattoo*, a film adaptation of Stieg Larsson's bestselling book by the same name.

In the meantime, following her memorable showing in *The Social Network* and with her passion for acting rekindled, Mara grew more selective in her choice of roles. "I got really picky," she told Jake Coyle. "I didn't work for a year. I didn't work until I got this part [Lisbeth Salander] because I was just trying to find something that I was really passionate about."

For Mara, the casting process for *The Girl with the Dragon Tattoo* was long and difficult, taking the better part of three months. Lisbeth Salander, an "androgynous, bisexual computer hacker with multiple piercings and a distinctive tattoo on her back," as described by Hirschberg, for *W* (Feb. 2011) was one of the most sought-after roles in Hollywood. Scarlett Johansson and Natalie Portman, among others, were all in the running. Fincher settled on Mara early on, but the studio was hesitant. With a budget approaching $100 million, a comparatively unknown and untested lead actor could result in disappointing box office sales. Weeks of screen tests and auditions followed. To get into character, Mara took up smoking. She read all the Stieg Larsson books and went on a diet to achieve Salander's waifish frame. "They did one test, then another a week later," Mara recalled to Hirschberg. "They shot me in the subway in L.A. in full hair and makeup with a motorcycle. Every day they had a new request. On a Monday morning, David called me in, and I said, 'What do you want me to do to my hair now?' I was at the end of my rope. He told me I had the part. I hadn't even read the script yet."

Later that week, Mara moved to Stockholm, Sweden, where she would spend much of the next year, and began her metamorphosis into Salander. Her eyebrows were bleached and most of her hair was cut off, and what was left was dyed black. She was coated with piercings in her lip, nose, eyebrows, and four in each ear. She took kickboxing and motorcycle lessons as well as dialect classes. As she studied the role, Mara felt a certain kinship with the antisocial Salander. "I am very slow to warm," she remarked to Van Meter. "I've always been sort of a loner."

The film costarred Daniel Craig as Mikael Blomkvist, a disgraced left-wing journalist who accepts a job investigating a long-ago crime. Hired by a member of the wealthy Vanger family, whose ranks include a sordid selection of deranged sadists, Blomkvist enlists the computer-hacking talents of the troubled Salander to help him uncover the truth and an unusual romance soon blossoms. "Lisbeth can hack any machine, crack any code and, when necessary, mete out righteous punitive violence, but she is also (to an extent fully revealed in subsequent episodes) a lost and abused child," A. O. Scott remarked for the *New York Times* (19 Dec. 2011). "And Ms. Mara captures her volatile and fascinating essence beautifully." The role of Lisbeth was not an easy one with its physically taxing stunt work and emotionally difficult sequences. Nevertheless, *The Girl with the Dragon Tattoo* earned a positive reception, though its box office numbers, while in excess of $100 million, were somewhat disappointing. In a typical review, David Denby declared, "This is a bleak but mesmerizing piece of filmmaking; it offers a glancing, chilled view of a world in which brief moments of loyalty flicker between repeated acts of betrayal." Mara was singled out everywhere for praise. "Mara makes every scene that she appears in jump," Denby wrote.

Though she did not win the best actress Golden Globe or Oscar awards in 2012, Mara's performance as Salander, coupled with her earlier triumph in *The Social Network*, transformed her into one of Hollywood's most sought-after stars. In the aftermath of these career-defining roles, Mara signed on with acclaimed directors Terrence Malick, Spike Jonze, and Steven Soderbergh, and in 2013 she is slated to star alongside Christian Bale and Ryan Gosling in the Malick film *Lawless*; with Olivia Wilde, Joaquin Phoenix, and Amy Adams in an as-yet untitled Jonze film; and with Channing Tatum and Jude Law in Soderbergh's *The Bitter Pill*. Additionally, Mara has agreed to reprise her role as Salander in *The Girl Who Played with Fire*, though a release date has not yet been announced.

PHILANTHROPY AND PERSONAL LIFE

A committed philanthropist, Mara founded her own charity in 2009 called Faces of Kibera, which seeks to provide food, shelter, and medicine to orphaned children in Kibera, a slum in Nairobi, Kenya. The impetus for starting it was her disappointment with the efforts of other organizations. "It's frustrating because there are so many nonprofits sprouting up everywhere, it's become a business opportunity," Mara told Michael Martin for *Interview* (June 2009). "The people who need help aren't really getting it. So I started my own." She has been romantically linked to Charlie McDowell, an aspiring director and the son of the actors Malcolm McDowell and Mary Steenburgen. Though her portrayal of Salander brought her international stardom, Mara admits to some ambivalence about her renown. "That kind of fame is not something I ever wanted for myself," she told Van Meter. "It just so happens that this huge, gigantic monster of a film came around that also happens to have the most incredible character that I ever could have dreamed up."

SUGGESTED READING

Hornaday, Ann. "The Social Network: A Universal Story That's Hard Not to Like." *Washington Post*. Washington Post, 1 Oct. 2010. Web. 20 Aug. 2012.

Lawrence, Will. "Rooney Mara: The Girl Who Nearly Walked Away from a Dream Role." *Telegraph*. Telegraph Media Group Ltd., 15 Dec. 2011. Web. 16 Aug. 2012.

Van Meter, Jonathan. "Rooney Mara: Playing with Fire." *Vogue*. Condé Nast, 17 Oct. 2011. Web. 15 Aug. 2012.

Webster, Andy. "Rich Girls Have All Kind of Drama." *New York Times*. New York Times, 8 Sep. 2011. Web. 20 Aug. 2012.

—*Paul McCaffrey*

Max McCalman

Born: February 18, 1953
Occupation: Maître fromager

The renowned cheese expert, author, and educator Max McCalman "brings a passion to his job bordering on obsession," Scott A. Johnson wrote for the Little Rock *Arkansas Democrat-Gazette* (July 9, 2006). McCalman, he continued, "thinks about and eats cheese constantly. He has suffered something he calls 'cheese elbow' (stiffness in his left, cutting arm). And sometimes, he admits he has even smelled like cheese." One of the leading authorities on cheese in the United States, McCalman has spent nearly two decades observing, studying, smelling, tasting, preparing, serving, and nurturing some of the world's finest cheeses. He told Ashley Chapman for the *Christian Science Monitor* (June 4, 2003), "I'm pretty much 24/7 cheese." McCalman, who is also known for his expertise in pairing wine with cheese, worked various jobs in the food and hospitality industries before finding his professional calling in 1994, when he was appointed *maître fromager*, or cheese master, at chef and restaurateur Terrance Brennan's highly acclaimed New York restaurant Picholine (pronounced peesh-oh-LEEN).

As the first restaurant-based "cheese sommelier" in the United States, McCalman oversaw the development of Picholine's lauded cheese program and the construction and design of the restaurant's own cheese cave, the first of its kind in the country. Picholine quickly earned raves from New York's food critics for its groundbreaking cheese service and was credited with inspiring the creation of cheese programs and cheese caves in other dining establishments across the country. McCalman has since created cheese programs for two other Brennan-led establishments, the Artisanal Fromagerie, Bistro, and Wine Bar and the Artisanal Premium Cheese Center, which opened in New York in 2001 and 2003, respectively. He has also coauthored, with freelance writer David Gibbons, three books about cheese: *The Cheese Plate* (2002), the James Beard Award–winning *Cheese: A Connoisseur's Guide to the World's Best* (2005), and *Mastering Cheese: Lessons for Connoisseurship from a Maître Fromager* (2009). McCalman is currently the maître fromager, dean of curriculum, and director of affinage at the Artisanal Premium Cheese Center, for which he oversees five cheese caves.

EARLY LIFE AND EDUCATION

Mark Allen "Max" McCalman was born on February 18, 1953, in Louisville, Kentucky, to Glynn and Sally McCalman. He has three brothers—Clyde, David, and Scott, all of whom have worked in the restaurant business—as well as a

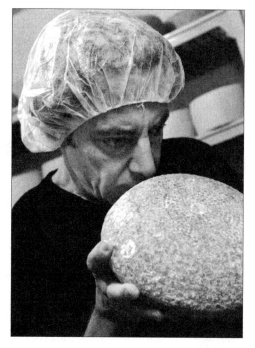

AP Photo

half-sister on his father's side. McCalman was raised mostly in Arkansas but spent parts of his childhood living in other areas of the world as a result of his parents' work as missionaries. Four and a half years of his childhood were spent in Brazil, where his father served as director of an American school. It was there that McCalman experienced the pleasures of fine dining and food service for the first time. He has admitted that the country's delectable food and picturesque surroundings made it hard to return to the United States. "I didn't want to leave Brazil because we had a very nice lifestyle down there," he told Johnson. "We had a house right on the beach, one of the prettiest beaches in the world."

When McCalman was eleven years old, his family moved back to the United States and settled in Little Rock, Arkansas. He went on to attend Little Rock's Parkview High School, graduating in 1971. Afterward he remained in his home state and enrolled at Hendrix College in Conway, Arkansas. He displayed early signs of his meticulous nature while working at the college's radio station, where as station manager he became known for his penchant for playing a wide variety of music.

McCalman began his first restaurant job during the summer after his junior year, becoming a waiter at a T.G.I. Friday's. He later confessed to Johnson that he had taken the job because "girls were really impressed with the waiters there." McCalman majored in developmental psychology at Hendrix College but dropped out shortly before graduating. Nonetheless, he has cited his field of study as helping him in his development as a maître fromager.

RESTAURANT CAREER

After leaving college, McCalman continued to work in the restaurant industry. In the late 1970s he began to work as a *chef de rang*, or assistant headwaiter, at Restaurant Jacques and Suzanne, an upscale Swiss-French restaurant in Little Rock. The restaurant's *maître d'hôtel* (headwaiter) at the time, Louis Petit, described McCalman to Johnson as "extremely talented," and Petit noted, "He wanted to learn this business the real way." McCalman soon became a maître d'hôtel himself, leaving Restaurant Jacques and Suzanne to work at La Petit Roche, another fine-dining establishment in Little Rock. He then left Little Rock for Dallas, Texas, where he took a job with the Sheraton Corporation. It was while designing that company's wine list that he experienced proper cheese tastings for the first time.

McCalman has stated that his interest in cheese dates back to childhood. In the introduction to his book *Mastering Cheese: Lessons for Connoisseurship from a Maître Fromager* (2009), he recalled, "One of my earliest childhood memories is of sitting at my mother's kitchen counter one day when I had a cold. A piece of cheese beckoned. Yet Mom told me not to touch it, no doubt because she thought I might transmit my germs to it. This was pretty much what we were all taught in the United States during the cold war—that we should be afraid of *all* bacteria. Hovering near the top of the list of foods to be avoided was cheese. . . . After that early incident in the kitchen, I don't remember seeing any cheese on my family's table for the rest of my formative years." Reflecting on his passion for cheese as an adult, he mused, "You might say I was essentially drawn to cheese because I was denied it when I was young. Having been cheese starved early in life, I've been trying to get my hands on it ever since—for nutrition and also for enjoyment and pleasure."

McCalman spent several years working for the Sheraton Corporation, first in Dallas and then in New Jersey, and served in a variety of roles, ranging from maître d'hôtel to sommelier. He then worked briefly at a Hilton Hotel in New York's midtown Manhattan before leaving to accept a position as general manager of the Water Club, a scenic waterfront restaurant on Manhattan's East Side. Throughout this time McCalman deepened and broadened his knowledge of cheese and the cheese-making process, and as he stated in an online interview with *Behind the Burner*, by the early 1990s, "cheese became [his] mission." That single-minded pursuit was realized in 1994 when McCalman was charged with helming the cheese program at Picholine, which opened in the previous year on Manhattan's West Side. Picholine proprietor Brennan

recalled to Johnson that McCalman "was a quick study and became the expert." Brennan relied upon to "pick the right cheeses and keep growing the cheese list with high quality examples."

CHEESE MASTER

As the maître fromager at Picholine, which specializes in French-Mediterranean cuisine, McCalman was responsible for sourcing, selecting, preparing, and serving more than fifty artisanal cheeses from around the world. He was also charged with supervising the development of those cheeses in a special temperature- and humidity-controlled cheese cave, described by Jane Gross for the *New York Times* (May 11, 1999) as "a mere walk-in closet, sheathed in Italian stone and outfitted with a compressor that keeps the temperature below 50 degrees and the humidity at 85 percent." Each night McCalman served his cheese selections on a cheese trolley, preparing custom-made cheese plates based on diners' preferences. That kind of bespoke food service helped Picholine earn rave reviews from critics and become one of the most respected fine-dining establishments in New York. Most critics made special note of the restaurant's inventive cheese service, which Gross likened to a form of performance art. "I dare anyone to listen to the maître de fromage, Max McCalman, talk about his cheese and not order something," the esteemed food critic Ruth Reichl wrote in her three-star review for the *New York Times* (Mar. 15, 1996). "He speaks so lovingly, and with such knowledge that I long to taste each cheese that he describes. Personally, I've given up on dessert at Picholine."

Picholine has consistently earned high ratings from Zagat Survey and is one of the few restaurants in New York to receive two stars in the prestigious *Michelin Guide*. It has since been credited with revitalizing the European-style cheese plate in American restaurants and prompting the construction of cheese caves in other eateries around the country. McCalman, meanwhile, has been recognized as having significant influence on the modern artisanal cheese movement in the United States. "I would say, more than anyone else he led to the way for the serious appreciation of cheese as a separate course in American restaurants," the *New York Times* food columnist Florence Fabricant told Johnson. "He brought ceremony to it. He brought connoisseurship. And he helped people know what to look for when they are ordering cheeses."

The popularity and success of Picholine's cheese program led Brennan to open a second restaurant, Artisanal Fromagerie, Bistro, and Wine Bar, in 2001. Located in the Murray Hill neighborhood of Manhattan, the restaurant features an extensive selection of award-winning wines and cheeses and includes a retail cheese counter. In 2002 it was awarded Best Brasserie Cuisine by the Zagat Survey. During the following spring, McCalman helped Brennan open a third establishment, Artisanal Premium Cheese Center, a ten-thousand-square-foot cheese emporium in the Hell's Kitchen section of Manhattan. The center houses five state-of-the-art cheese caves and includes a restaurant, online store, and cheese-education program. McCalman currently serves as the center's dean of curriculum, director of affinage, and maître fromager. In those roles he is responsible for overseeing the center's cheese caves, training fromagers, and designing the curriculum for the center's educational programs. He told Jeff Gordinier for the *New York Times* (Oct. 5, 2011), "I like to think of our facility here as a day school for cheese. As soon as the obstetrician is O.K. with releasing the baby cheese into our care, then we'll put it through day school here, and we'll nurture the cheese until it's ready to go out into the real world."

WRITER AND CHEESE ADVOCATE

McCalman has coauthored three books about cheese with the New York–based freelance writer David Gibbons. His first, *The Cheese Plate*, was published by Clarkson Potter in 2002. The book chronicles the history of cheese and cheese making and offers a guide to enjoying some of the world's best cheeses; it received nominations for awards by the International Association of Cooking Professionals (IACP) and the James Beard Foundation. In 2005 McCalman published his second book, *Cheese: A Connoisseur's Guide to the World's Best*, which features in-depth descriptions of two hundred of the world's best cheeses. In its introduction, he wrote, "If our first book was a useful introduction to the world's finest cheeses, this one aims to be a standard-bearer. It is not intended to be encyclopedic, but rather a Hall of Fame." The book, which also includes recommended wine pairings, enjoyed strong commercial sales and won the 2006 James Beard Award for best reference book. McCalman's third book, *Mastering Cheese: Lessons for Connoisseurship from a Maître Fromager*, was published in 2009 and is based on courses taught at the Artisanal Premium Cheese Center. In 2011 the book was named the world's best book on cheese for the previous year at the Gourmand International World Cookbook Awards and was a finalist in the food and beverage reference/technical category at the annual IACP Cookbook Awards.

McCalman has served as a contributing editor for such publications as *Cheese Connoisseur* and *Culture* and been profiled in *Food and Wine* magazine and the *New York Times*, among other publications. He has been featured as a guest on television shows such as *Queer Eye for the Straight Guy* and *The Daily Show*. McCalman is also in demand as a food-industry consultant and has lectured and taught at a number of academic institutions, including the Culinary Institute of America, the Institute of Culinary Education, the New School, and New York University. He has also conducted workshops for the Epcot International Food and Wine Festival at Walt Disney World and served as a judge at national and international cheese competitions.

The commercial consumption of cheese in the United States has increased significantly since the early 1990s, and McCalman has worked to continue that trend by advocating on behalf of artisanal-cheese producers around the world. "Americans are becoming more aware of what they're putting in their mouths," he explained to Rachel Vessey for the Minneapolis *Star Tribune* (Oct. 27, 2005). "I think it stems from a grass-roots movement that has been slowly building. More and more people are seeking out organic foods and products that are really good for them." He added to Johnson, "It's not just a passing fad. I see this as here to stay. That being said, I do worry about the future of artisanal cheese making. The move to globalization and industrialization, the use of pesticides and herbicides, these are very sinister things, and I feel ultimately that these 'real' foods won't be around one day—or at least fewer and fewer will be around. I feel like right now we're in the golden age of cheese, but I've already seen more than a few drop off the radar screen."

McCalman has also worked tirelessly to raise awareness about the nutritional values of cheese, which he has frequently referred to as a "near-perfect food." Some of the common misperceptions about cheese that he has tried to dispel include its reputation among the general population as cholesterol raising and fattening. "Gram for gram there is more nutrition available in cheese than in any other foodstuff," he explained to Chapman. McCalman himself has sampled hundreds of cheeses, but he names Sbrinz, a hard cow's milk cheese made in Switzerland, as his favorite. He has also spoken of his preference for cheeses made with "uncompromised," or unpasteurized, milk.

For his expertise in all aspects of cheese making, McCalman has earned the rare distinction of being named a Garde et jure (guard and judge) by France's Guilde Internationale des Fromagers, and in January 2011 he was one of four people chosen from a group of nearly two hundred candidates to receive a French Food Spirit Award.

"Cheese is preserved milk and as such it is our first food," he explained in his interview with *Behind the Burner*. "I want to demystify cheese by talking and writing about it. I want to take care of and support cheese, for a long time it has had a bad rap and part of my mission is to set the record straight on behalf of cheese." He told

Vessey at the *Star Tribune*: "Cheese has been good to me in so many ways but most especially for my health."

McCalman lives in the Park Slope neighborhood of Brooklyn, New York. He has a daughter, Scarlett, from his second marriage.

SUGGESTED READING

Chapman, Ashley. "For 'Happy' Cheese, Here's Your Man." *Christian Science Monitor* 4 June 2003: 15. Print.

Cole, Katherine. "On the Northwest Vine the Prince of Pairing Wines, Cheeses." *Oregonian* [Portland] 14 Mar. 2004: L9. Print.

"Expert Interview: Max McCalman." *Behind the Burner*. Behind the Burner, n.d. Web. 22 Dec. 2011.

Gordinier, Jeff. "Cheese: A Coming-of-Age Story." *New York Times* 5 Oct. 2011: D1. Print.

Gross, Jane. "Public Lives: The Pungent Passion of a Maestro of Cheese." *New York Times* 11 May 1999: B2. Print.

Johnson, Scott A. "Mark Allen McCalman." *Arkansas Democrat-Gazette* [Little Rock] 9 July 2006: n. pag. Print.

McCalman, Max, and David Gibbons. *Cheese: A Connoisseur's Guide to the World's Best*. New York: Clarkson Potter, 2005. Print.

---. *Mastering Cheese: Lessons for Connoisseurship from a Maître Fromager*. New York: Clarkson Potter, 2009. Print.

Reichl, Ruth. "Restaurants." *New York Times* 15 Mar. 1996: C26. Print.

Shephard, Sherry P. "Cork Wine Tasting Festival to Feature Seminars with Cheese Expert." *Times* [Shreveport, LA] 31 Mar. 2010: n. pag. Print.

Vessey, Rachel. "Connoisseur Serves Cheese and Advice: Choose Your Cheese as Carefully as You Do Your Wine, Says This Expert." *Star Tribune* [Minneapolis] 27 Oct. 2005: 1T. Print.

—*Christopher Cullen*

Larry Busacca/Getty Images for Sundance Film Festival

Thomas McCarthy

Born: January 30, 1966
Occupation: Filmmaker, screenwriter, actor

The three feature films that Thomas McCarthy has written and directed sprang from some of his real-life experiences. They all have elements of drama and comedy; they all involve chance meetings of strangers that lead to friendships or unusual alliances; and they are "all about men facing pivotal moments in their lives," Ann Hornaday noted for the *Washington Post* (25 Mar. 2011). "The ability to tell believably human stories has helped make McCarthy a Sundance [Film Festival] darling," Steven Zeitchik wrote for the *Los Angeles Times* (22. Jan. 2011). McCarthy's first film as a writer/director was *The Station Agent* (2003), about the unlikely connections that develop among a lonely dwarf, a naïve, talkative Cuban American food vendor, and a woman whose marriage has disintegrated and whose young son has recently died. McCarthy followed that with *The Visitor* (2008), whose leading characters are an emotionally numb New England college professor, a couple (a man from Syria and a woman from Senegal) who are living in the United States illegally, and the Syrian man's mother. McCarthy's latest film is *Win Win* (2011), about a struggling lawyer and volunteer high school wrestling coach and the teenager who unexpectedly comes to live with his family in suburbia. "Like *The Station Agent* and *The Visitor* before it, *Win Win* bears the familiar, deeply gratifying earmarks of a Tom McCarthy picture, featuring fully rounded characters who are wholly original without being self-consciously quirky, observed by McCarthy with compassion and a sense of humor that's never patronizing or glib," Hornaday wrote.

McCarthy is also an accomplished actor. He has had parts in plays, among them the Broadway production of *Noises Off* (2001–02), and in many television series and films. After making one-time appearances on such TV shows as *New York Undercover* (1996), *Spin City* (1998), and *Law & Order: Special Victims Unit* (2000), he starred in the short-lived TV series *Boston Public* (2000–01). One of his best-known roles was that of the newspaper reporter Scott Templeton in the critically acclaimed HBO series *The Wire*, in 2008. He was cast, most often in minor roles, in major motion pictures including *Meet the Parents* (2000), *Good Night, and Good Luck* (2005), *Syriana* (2005), *Flags of Our Fathers* (2006), and *The Lovely Bones* (2009). McCarthy cowrote the story for the Disney-Pixar animated film *Up*, which attracted moviegoers of all ages and received an Oscar nomination for best original screenplay.

EARLY LIFE AND EDUCATION
One of the five children of Gene and Carol McCarthy, Thomas Joseph McCarthy was born on January 30, 1966. (He has sometimes used "Tom McCarthy" as his professional name.) He grew up with one sister and three brothers in New Providence, New Jersey. His father worked in the textile industry; his mother was a homemaker. "I don't come from a family of artists," he told Ruthe Stein for *SFGate* (20 Mar. 2011). "In fact, most of them are in the corporate or financial world. But they are all great storytellers. They will tell me a story about their day—something I really don't care about—but the way they spin it, it becomes really interesting to me and very funny and dramatic." McCarthy attended New Providence High School, where he was a "mediocre" member of the wrestling team, he told Loren King for the *Boston Globe* (20 Mar. 2011). He then enrolled at Boston College, in Massachusetts, where he studied management before switching to philosophy. A classmate of his encouraged him to try acting, and after a successful audition, he joined My Mother's Fleabag, a local comedy improv group. After he completed his bachelor's degree, in 1988, he decided to pursue acting as a career. He and other members of Fleabag rented a house on Cape Cod, Massachusetts, for the summer and performed in small theaters and bars. After the summer the troupe moved to Minneapolis, Minnesota, where they performed under the new name Every Mother's Nightmare.

After a year McCarthy, having tired of a steady diet of improv comedy, moved to Chicago, Illinois, to take part in more serious theater productions. He won a few roles but came to feel that he was not adequately prepared for the stage. In 1992 he enrolled in the master's degree program at the Yale School of Drama, in New Haven, Connecticut. While there he cowrote and directed the burlesque *The Napoleonade*, about Napoleon. Well-received (and, in 1996, mounted in Chicago by the Eclipse Theater Company), the spoof led to a writing fellowship for McCarthy. His next work was *The Killing Act*, a two-act play about the circus impresario P. T. Barnum, which he directed

Off-Broadway. The four foot five Peter Dinklage, who is a dwarf, starred as Tom Thumb (the stage name of Charles Stratton, who was a midget, not a dwarf). McCarthy was impressed by the ways in which, in real life, Dinklage handled the rude reactions of passersby to his diminutive stature, and he and Dinklage became friends. After McCarthy graduated from the Yale School of Drama, in 1995, he secured parts in television programs and films. "I was doing a lot of acting, but I wanted to work on the kinds of movies I like to see, and I wasn't finding them," he told Tim Townsend for *Boston College Magazine* (Fall 2003).

THE STATION AGENT
"It's always difficult to point to the exact inspiration for a film," McCarthy told an interviewer for *Cinema Review* in 2008. "I collect a lot of different ideas and keep them in one big file, and then I pull out the ones that are most resonant for me." One day, while driving through a rural part of New Jersey, McCarthy noticed an old, abandoned train depot. Intrigued, he took photos of it and left a note for its owner. The owner turned out to be a railfan (or railroad buff), one of an estimated 250,000 people in the United States whose interest in the history, culture, rolling stock, or other aspects of railroads has become a hobby. At the owner's invitation McCarthy attended a meeting of a railfan group and then embarked on intensive research about railfans and railroading. Inspired by what he learned, as well as by the appearance of the old depot, he started writing the script of *The Station Agent*, with parts created specifically for Dinklage, the actress Patricia Clarkson, and the actor Bobby Cannavale, a friend whom he had met in regional theater ten years earlier. From 1994 to 2003 Cannavale was married to a daughter of the prolific Hollywood director Sidney Lumet, and through Cannavale McCarthy met with Lumet and got advice on scriptwriting and the day-to-day tasks of moviemaking. *The Station Agent* was shot in three weeks during the summer of 2002 for $500,000—a small sum by Hollywood standards. McCarthy, who had never before made a film of any length, "was barely holding it together," he recalled to Townsend. "Working with the actors is where I felt the most comfortable, but I was learning the technical stuff on the fly. You're the captain of this ship and you don't know how 80 percent of the ship works."

McCarthy proved to be a quick study: *The Station Agent* was accepted for screening at the Sundance Film Festival, where it was enthusiastically greeted and won the Audience Award, the Waldo Salt Screenwriting Award, and the Special Jury Prize for Outstanding Performance (for Clarkson). In an interview with Stephen Whitty for the Newark, New Jersey, *Star-Ledger* (12 Jan. 2003), John Cooper, the festival's director of programming, said, "I hate to say it's a near-perfect movie, but it sort of is." He added, "It's a little film, but it's just so precisely written and conceived. And then there are these beautiful, flawless performances." *The Station Agent* begins with Dinklage portraying Finbar McBride, a loner with a passion for trains who works in a hobby shop, repairing model trains. When a friend of his dies, Fin inherits an old train depot (in the film, the one McCarthy had happened upon earlier) and moves into it, with the expectation and hope of remaining solitary. A young Cuban American man named Joe (Cannavale), who is lonely but not by choice, takes over his father's lunch truck while the father is ill and parks it near the depot during the day. One of Joe's regular customers is Olivia, an artist who is grieving for her son, who has recently died, and for her marriage, which is ending. The film follows Fin, Joe, and Olivia as they slowly develop ties to one another. "That may make the film sound intolerably cute, even cloying, but it's neither," Manohla Dargis wrote for the *Los Angeles Times* (12 Jan. 2003). "*The Station Agent* avoids cliché, principally by refusing to make a fetish out of either its characters' hurt or its star's height. In this sense, the film isn't about a dwarf but a brooding, darkly handsome outsider who happens to be a dwarf. The wonder of the performance is that as the story evolves, Fin's height matters less and less."

Released in theaters nationwide later that year, *The Station Agent* received overwhelmingly positive reviews. "The key accomplishment of writer-director McCarthy and his actors is how finely these people are drawn," Kenneth Turan wrote for the *Los Angeles Times* (3 Oct. 2003). "McCarthy has the best ear and eye for what makes people individual as well as an exact sense of how far he can go without jeopardizing empathy and believability. He knows how messy other people's lives turn out to be when you get involved with them, and he understands not only the risks to yourself when you do, but the cost to yourself when you don't." The cast of *The Station Agent* (which also included Michelle Williams, Paul Benjamin, and Raven Goodwin) won many honors; in addition to an Independent Spirit Award, best-screenplay awards came from BAFTA (the British Academy of Film and Television Arts), the Las Vegas Film Critics Society, and a half-dozen film festivals. The film won the Audience Award or Special Jury Award at several other festivals.

Following the success of *The Station Agent*, McCarthy introduced the film to audiences in Oman and Lebanon at the invitation of the US State Department, which had organized a cultural outreach program in the Middle East. "I was struck by how little I knew about the region, about the people, about the culture," he told the *Cinema Review* interviewer. "Our country is so involved politically and militarily there, but with all the news and the headlines and the drama, we can forget that there are human beings on both sides of this. How can I eliminate that a little bit? That always is my call to arms." McCarthy later returned to Lebanon's capital, Beirut, to work with young filmmakers, and afterward he met members of New York City's Arab community. Interested in how the United States deals with illegal immigrants, he started visiting immigrant detention centers and talking to illegal immigrants detained in them. According to Tina Daunt, writing for the *Los Angeles Times* (11 Apr. 2008), McCarthy was surprised to learn that on any given day at that time, more than 27,000 people were detained at more than 330 detention centers, and that whereas in 2001 there were about 95,200 illegal immigrants detained in the United States, in 2006 there were more than 283,100, of whom 85 percent had no legal representation. At a detention center in Elizabeth, New Jersey, McCarthy met a Nigerian man who had been held there for more than three years. Part of *The Visitor* (2008), McCarthy's second film, grew out of that relationship.

THE VISITOR

The Visitor is told from the point of view of sixty-two-year-old Walter Vale (Richard Jenkins, in his first leading role in a feature film), a widowed Connecticut economics professor who seems to have lost all interest in life, as well as the ability to experience or express any emotions. Walter reluctantly travels to New York City to attend a conference, only to discover that, as the result of a rental scam, two illegal immigrants who are strangers to him have moved into his Manhattan apartment: Tarek (Haaz Sleiman), a drummer from Syria, and his Senegalese girlfriend, Zainab (Danai Gurira), a jewelry maker who sells her wares on the street. Although he is completely taken aback, Walter agrees to let them remain in the apartment. "Many of the choices that send us in a completely different direction in life are arbitrary," McCarthy told the *Cinema Review* interviewer. "I think that's the magic of life, isn't it? It makes us realize, as much as we like to imagine we have control over our fate and destiny, we really don't. That's something that happens in this movie." As Walter's friendship with the couple grows, Tarek persuades Walter to try his hand at playing African drums. A turning point comes when Tarek is arrested by Homeland Security agents and taken to an immigrant detention center in the city. The professor decides to help him. Soon afterward Walter meets Tarek's mother, Mouna (Hiam Abbass), who comes to New York from Michigan after growing increasingly fearful over her son's unusual silence.

"It is possible," A. O. Scott wrote for the *New York Times* (11 Apr. 2008), "to imagine a version of this story—the tale of a square, middle-aged white man liberated from his uptightness by an infusion of Third World soulfulness, attached to an exposé of the cruelty of post-9/11 immigration policies—that would be obvious and sentimental, an exercise in cultural condescension and liberal masochism. Indeed, it's nearly impossible to imagine it any other way. And yet, astonishingly enough, Mr. McCarthy has. Much as *The Station Agent* nimbly evaded the obstacles of cuteness and willful eccentricity it had strewn in its own path, so does *The Visitor*, with impressive grace and understatement, resist potential triteness and phony uplift." Ann Hornday for the *Washington Post* (18 Apr. 2008) observed that McCarthy directed the film with "sensitivity and exquisite tonal control." Juan-Carlos Selznick, writing for the *Chico News & Review* (29 May 2008), described the portrait of Walter as "smart" and "moving" and wrote that Tarek, Zainab, and Mouna each made "an appealing and significant impression in the film and on its central portrait." "But McCarthy has designed these roles in ways that raise issues too large and insoluble for the fragile story of Walter to bear," he complained. "Immigration issues, post-9/11 anxieties and hysteria, New York-style multiculturalism, the injustices of an age of terror—that great stew of hot-button topics adds both currency and urgency to the film, but it also leaves you wishing McCarthy had done more to make the immigrant characters more three-dimensional and less reduced to functions of dramatic convenience in the story of one man's tentative, bittersweet renewal." Tom Huddleston, in a review for *Time Out: London* (3 July 2008), offered harsher criticism: "Implausibly warm and logically fuzzy, [McCarthy's] treatment of his immigrant protagonists smacks of crude political correctness. These figures are essentially perfect: polite, fun-loving and affectionate, model citizens pitted against a faceless, repressive state. While elements of this may ring true, it feels distinctly underwhelming as drama, drowning McCarthy's subtle, searching dialogue and incisive, humanist character development in a morass of right thinking, left-leaning platitudes." Richard Jenkins's bevy of honors for his work in *The Visitor* included an Academy Award nomination, while McCarthy earned an array of awards and nominations for his direction and screenwriting.

WIN WIN

The seeds of McCarthy's next film included a phone conversation in which he and Joseph "Joe" Tiboni, a friend of his since fourth grade, reminisced about their high school wrestling days. Tiboni, an elder-care lawyer who lives with his wife and two daughters in New Providence, New Jersey, became the inspiration for Mike, the hero of *Win Win*, and he agreed to join McCarthy in writing the script. Mike (played by Paul

Giamatti) is an elder-care lawyer who volunteers as a wrestling coach at the local suburban high school, whose team has been notably unsuccessful. In many ways an average American Joe and family man, Mike is financially strapped. Desperate to supplement his income, he becomes the court-appointed guardian of Leo, an old man who is one of his clients, and has Leo moved to a nursing home—an arrangement that provides Mike with a monthly stipend and places Leo in a safe environment but skirts the law. Without warning, Leo's teenage grandson Kyle (Alex Shaffer, making his motion-picture debut) appears; having run away from home and finding that his grandfather can no longer provide him with a place to stay, he moves in with Mike's family, enrolls at the local high school, and joins the wrestling team, where he shines. In real life Shaffer is a state champion in wrestling, and the other students McCarthy cast for the team are also real wrestlers. The film was shot in New Providence, with Amy Ryan in the role of Mike's wife.

Many critics praised *Win Win* for presenting a warm, touching story in an original way, while its plot and details struck others as bordering on cliché. "Mr. McCarthy neatly sets up the elements that will bring about Mike's self-deluding rise, his near-calamitous fall and his eventual redemption," A. O. Scott wrote for the *New York Times* (18 Mar. 2011). "There are no real surprises, but this is not to say that *Win Win* is rote or formulaic. Quite the opposite. Mr. McCarthy, who has written and directed two other features—and who is a first-rate character actor specializing in second-rate characters—has a deep and nuanced understanding of the rules of comedy, which is at once the most rigorous and the most elastic of narrative genres. He also possesses a sharp wit and a generous spirit, mocking his characters without meanness and lampooning their social circumstances without condescension." Michael Sragow for the *Baltimore Sun* (3 Apr. 2011) found the film "deeply funny and moving," and Peter Travers, writing for *Rolling Stone* (10 Mar. 2011), described it as "hilarious and heartfelt with a tough core that repels all things sappy." "This movie wins you over, head and heart, without cheating," he declared. The dissenters included Connie Ogle, the *Miami Herald* (6 Apr. 2011) reviewer, who acknowledged that "*Win Win* has plenty of things going for it—a gentle sense of humor, a mostly understated use of sports that never becomes too overwrought and the always-terrific Paul Giamatti." "But in the end," she complained, "the film stacks up just this side of twee, as the sort of quirky fare that's passably entertaining without ever offering anything real or remarkable," and she concluded that it is "the sort of easygoing, shrug-it-off film in which complicated legal matters are quickly and easily solved, [and] problems are never totally insurmountable."

CURRENT PROJECT AND PERSONAL LIFE
McCarthy wrote the screenplay for *Million-Dollar Arm*, a Walt Disney motion picture inspired by the sequence of events that led two baseball players from India, Rinku Singh and Dinesh Patel, to sign contracts with the Pittsburgh Pirates in 2008. The film is scheduled for release in 2013.

McCarthy has an apartment in Manhattan. He remains close to his parents, who still live in New Providence, and his siblings. One of his nephews was named for him.

SUGGESTED READING
Angelo, Megan. "Just Like the Good Old Days in the Ring." *New York Times: Movies*. New York Times Co., 18 Mar. 2011. Web. Jan. 2012.

Dargis, Manohla. "Rising Up to Play First Starring Role." Los Angeles Times: Sundance Film Festival. Los Angeles Times, 21 Jan. 2003. Web. Jan. 2012.

Hornaday, Ann. "*Win Win*: Wrestling to Find a Life of Integrity." *Washington Post: Movies*. Washington Post, 25 Mar. 2011. Web. Jan. 2012.

Townsend, Tim. "The Independent." *Boston College Magazine*. Trustees of Boston College, Fall 2003. Web. Jan. 2012.

—*Dmitry Kiper*

AP Photo

Dakota Meyer

Born: June 26, 1988
Occupation: US soldier and Medal of Honor recipient

In the nearly 150 years that have passed since Jacob Parrott, a private in the Union Army during the Civil War, earned the first Congressional Medal of Honor on March 25, 1863, more than 40 million people have served in the United States Armed Forces. By the end of 2011, only 3,458 of those men and women had ever received the Medal of Honor, "the highest award for valor in action against an enemy force which can be bestowed upon an individual serving in the Armed Services of the United States," as the website of the Congressional Medal of Honor Society states. The most recent winner is Dakota Meyer, who received the medal from President Barack Obama in a ceremony at the White House on September 15, 2011.

Meyer is only the sixth person to have won the award for actions in the war in Afghanistan, which began on October 7, 2001. He was recognized for his actions on September 8, 2009, when he was a twenty-one-year-old Marine Corps corporal. During a battle in the Ganjgal Valley of Afghanistan that started as a surprise enemy attack and raged for six hours, Meyer rescued three dozen American and Afghan fighters and helped to retrieve the bodies of four other Americans, despite heavy enemy fire and the failure of US commanders off-site to approve repeated requests for backup until late in the fighting. In addition, Meyer killed "at least eight enemy fighters," according to Bing West in a *Wall Street Journal* article (Sep. 15, 2011, online) and accounts in many other sources, and there is little doubt that he helped to prevent an unknown number of American and Afghan forces from being injured or killed.

For some time Meyer thought about building a career in the Marine Corps, but when his second tour of duty ended, he returned to civilian life. Since winning the Medal of Honor, he has engaged in many media interviews, given talks to schoolchildren, and participated in an array of events and ceremonies nationwide, all despite his feelings of discomfort at being given accolades or made the center of attention. As he has often said, he believes it is more important to honor the memories of his fellow Americans who perished that day and to pay tribute to all those who have served and are serving in Afghanistan and Iraq. Meyer told Dan Lamothe for the *Marine Corps Times* (Nov. 23, 2010, online), "A lot of people call me a hero, and it kills me. I feel like the furthest thing from that because I let those guys down," referring to the

Americans who died during the fighting in Ganjgal. He added, "Anything that comes out of it, it's not for me. It's for those guys because they are the true heroes." Meyer has earned numerous other awards in addition to the Medal of Honor, among them a Purple Heart and a Navy and Marine Corps Achievement Medal.

EARLY LIFE

An only child, Dakota L. Meyer was born on June 26, 1988, in Columbia, Kentucky. His mother left when he was young, and he was brought up by his father, Michael Meyer, on a three-hundred-acre farm outside Greensburg, a town near Columbia. His paternal grandparents, who owned an adjacent farm, helped raise him. According to Fox News (Dec. 16, 2011, online), his grandmother, Jean Meyer, told a reporter that Dakota Meyer had "never done anything that we had to get on him about or punish him for—nothing. You couldn't have asked for a better boy growing up and he still is. He would do anything in the world for anybody."

In his *Wall Street Journal* article, Bing West wrote that as a four-year-old Meyer was so determined to drive his father's tractor, he was not deterred when his father told him he would have to wait until he was strong enough to turn its crank to start it. Within an hour the boy had managed to "repeatedly [jump] from the tractor hood onto the crank until it turned over." "When he was five," West wrote, "he solemnly assured his grandmother that he would guard her against robbers." Meyer learned how to shoot at a young age, and he became an expert marksman; according to a transcript of his interview with David Martin for the news magazine *60 Minutes* (Sep. 18, 2011), he "can hit a squirrel at 750 yards."

According to Jim Michaels for *USA Today* (Sep. 7, 2011), the teenage Meyer was "smart but also irrepressible" and irreverent; he liked to play jokes on his father and teachers. He attended Green County High School in Greensburg, where, he told Michaels, "I definitely wasn't the model student." He was a running back and a linebacker for the school's football team, and he became a "popular jock," Michaels wrote. As a senior he volunteered to tutor members of a class of special-needs students. Their teacher, Tana Rattliff, told Michaels that the students became extremely fond of Meyer and would cheer for him at football games. Thanks to Meyer, Rattliff said, it was "the best year of teaching I ever had. We became like a family." Meyer's father told Bing West, as quoted in West's book *The Wrong War: Grit, Strategy, and the Way Out of Afghanistan* (2011), "The thing about Dakota is his determination. He's just plain goal-oriented. Once he gets something into his mind, he'll stick at it until he does it."

MILITARY TRAINING

Meyer abandoned his plan to attend college when a Marine Corps recruiter visited his high school during his senior year. After classes ended that day, he brought the recruiter home to get his father's permission to enlist, as he was still seventeen years old. Meyer signed a contract for a four-year stint in the Marines. He turned eighteen during the thirteen weeks he spent at Parris Island, South Carolina, the Marine Corps Recruit Depot. According to the facility's website, Marines are trained in three phases: "Basic Learning," which is "physical and mental"; instruction in the use of rifles; and field exercises. Training culminates with the Crucible, fifty-four hours during which recruits travel forty-eight miles on foot, negotiating obstacles ("29 problem-solving exercises") while carrying forty-five pounds of equipment, enduring sleep deprivation, and subsisting on a total of three meals. "Without doubt," the website asserts, "Marine boot camp is more challenging—both physically and mentally—than the basic training programs of any of the other military services." After his basic training, Meyer joined the infantry and chose to specialize in sniping, saying, "I don't want to join the Marine Corps and have a job that I could have as a civilian," as quoted by Michaels.

HEROIC ACTIONS

Meyer spent his first tour of duty in Iraq in 2007–08. For his second tour he chose an assignment in Afghanistan, where he believed he would see more action. On September 8, 2009, he was one of a small group of Marines and US Army and Navy advisers working with a battalion of several dozen Afghan troops and border policemen. The Americans' assignment that day was to accompany the Afghans to a village in Kunar Province in the Ganjgal (or Ganjigal) Valley of eastern Afghanistan, near the border with Pakistan. Members of the Afghan military had scheduled a meeting with village elders who, at an earlier meeting, had expressed a willingness to switch their allegiance and that of the other villagers from the Taliban to the Afghan government and its army. During the meeting Meyer and others in his team were to station their armored vehicles outside the village, but within sight and sniping distance of it, to prepare for possible attacks. Neither the Americans nor the Afghan soldiers anticipated trouble, believing that the elders had decided to reach out to them with friendly intentions; nevertheless the Americans were told that in the event of an enemy attack, they could call a nearby US command center for air cover and help would arrive within ten minutes.

At about 2:00 a.m., Meyer, his team, and members of the Afghan battalion set out on their mission. Meyer was driving a Humvee equipped with a turret gun. When they arrived at the observation post within the valley, those assigned to meet with the elders began to walk toward the village. Although the sky was still dark as the men approached, lights were already on in many homes; September 8 that year fell during Ramadan, the holiest thirty days in the Muslim calendar, when observant Muslims eat breakfast before sunrise and fast during the day. As Meyer waited alongside his truck, he was disconcerted to see women, children, and a few old men leaving the village. As one old man came near, Meyer tried to ask him where they were going, but "the man refused to shake his hand and hurried past," Bing West reported in his book.

Suddenly, at 5:30 a.m., moments after dawn, all the lights went out, and between fifty and two hundred Taliban snipers—the estimated number of snipers varies greatly in different sources, as does precisely what happened during the ensuing battle—began shooting from the high ground on either side of the valley and the fields surrounding the village. It was obviously an ambush. "They had mortars, rockets, rocket-propelled grenades, and small-arms fire," Meyer told David Martin. "We were set up."

Soon, three Marines and a navy corpsman had become trapped inside the village. One of them, First Lieutenant Michael Johnson, radioed the command center, informing the officers of their location and those of the insurgents and calling for immediate air support, but his request was denied because "it was too close to the village," as Meyer told Martin. He added, "The response was basically, 'Try your best.'"

During the next forty-five minutes, the command center rejected several more calls for air support, as well as Meyer's requests for permission to move from his position and attempt to help his comrades. After he was turned down a fourth time, Meyer decided to disregard his superiors' orders and enter the so-called kill zone. "Those were my brothers, and I couldn't just sit back and watch," he explained, as quoted by President Obama at the Medal of Honor ceremony. With Staff Sergeant Juan Rodriguez-Chavez, who agreed to serve as his driver, Meyer rode toward the village atop his Humvee, firing the turret gun amid flying bullets, mortars, and rocket-propelled grenades. They soon came upon several wounded Afghan infantrymen, and Meyer left the truck to bring them inside. Within a few minutes he had brought two other wounded Afghans to safety in the Humvee. He and Rodriguez-Chavez then turned around and drove to a safe location behind a small hill, where they left the injured men. According to West, when Meyer asked members of an army platoon at the site to accompany them back into the battle zone, no one stepped forward, as their commanding officers had forbidden them to do so. At that point

Meyer's Afghan translator, Fazel, volunteered to join Meyer and Rodriguez-Chavez.

During their second foray into the fighting, Meyer repeatedly left the truck to rescue Afghan infantrymen; Fazel took his place at the turret gun each time. Their Humvee was so damaged by the time they brought the wounded to safety that they needed another truck for their third trip into the kill zone. When its turret gun jammed, Meyer used his rifle instead. "Up ahead, a group of Americans, some wounded, were desperately trying to escape the bullets raining down," President Obama said in his White House remarks, referring to a group led by Lieutenant Ademola Fabayo. "[Rodriguez-Chavez] wedged the Humvee right into the line of fire, using the vehicle as a shield. With [Meyer] on the guns, they helped those Americans back to safety as well."

During the rescue Meyer's right arm was hit by shrapnel, but he ignored the wound. One of those rescued was Sergeant First Class Kenneth Westbrook, who had been shot in the neck; he died in the hospital a week later. His wife, Charlene Westbrook, told David Martin that before his death, her husband said, "We were surrounded, we were ambushed, and we called for help. No one came. They kept telling us fifteen minutes, fifteen minutes, and no one showed and we were just sitting ducks."

Meyer, Rodriguez-Chavez, and Fazel went back for the fourth time, still looking for Johnson's team, rescuing still more injured Afghan fighters. Meyer later recalled to interviewers, "I didn't think I was going to die. I knew I was." During a fifth attempt, the three men were accompanied by Lieutenant Fabayo, Captain William Swenson, and Swenson's Afghan interpreter, Ahmad Shafi. The pilot of a Black Hawk helicopter radioed to them that he had spied some bodies and had dropped a purple-smoke grenade to mark the spot, as it was not safe for him to land to attempt a rescue. Instead Rodriguez-Chavez drove as near to the spot as he could. Meyer left the truck by himself and, despite the bullets raining down around him, raced toward the smoke. "I just took off running and it was probably the longest run of my life," Meyer told David Martin. "I felt like I couldn't move fast enough because it's wide open. Rounds are hitting everywhere around me. I jumped into this trench, and when I did, I landed on Gunnery Sergeant Johnson." In addition to Edwin Johnson, Meyer found the bodies of Lieutenant Michael Johnson, Staff Sergeant Aaron Kenefick, and Hospitalman Third Class James Layton. At his signal the other men joined him, and they all "knelt down, picked up their comrades and—through all those bullets, all the smoke, all the chaos—carried them out, one by one," President Obama reported. "Because, as [Meyer] says, 'That's what you do for a brother.'"

The US Army later conducted an investigation of the events at Ganjgal. According to the army's final report, as quoted by David Martin, lead investigator Colonel Richard Hooker determined that "key leaders" at the command center had been "clearly negligent" and that their actions had been "inadequate and ineffective, contributing directly to the loss of life which ensued." The report attributed their failure to take proper action to "an atmosphere of complacency." Hooker told Martin, "If we'd gotten supporting aviation . . . early in the fight, we . . . wouldn't be sitting here having this conversation. That's my firm belief." An army major and an army captain received letters of reprimand for their unacceptable performance, a punishment that, while not as severe as a court martial, effectively ended their careers in the military, Hooker told Martin. He added, "It means professional disgrace and ruin." In his *Wall Street Journal* article, Bing West wrote that there were two investigations and three letters of reprimand.

MEDAL OF HONOR

When Meyer completed his four years with the Marines, he chose not to reenlist. Instead, he found work with Ausgar, a military subcontractor. On November 8, 2010, Dan Lamothe reported in the *Marine Corps Times* that Meyer's actions in Ganjgal had led the Marine Corps to recommend him for the Congressional Medal of Honor. After gathering extensive sworn testimony from men who had witnessed his heroism in the field of battle, the White House approved the award. More than 150 of Meyer's relatives and friends attended the ceremony at the White House on September 15, 2011, at which President Obama placed the medal around his neck.

Staff Sergeant Juan Rodriguez-Chavez and Lieutenant Ademola Fabayo each received a Navy Cross, a distinction one notch below the Medal of Honor, for their actions on September 8, 2009. In response to complaints that they too deserved the Medal of Honor, military sources said that Meyer had been singled out because of his extraordinary solo effort to reach the bodies of the four trapped Americans. Some observers also questioned why Captain William Swenson has received no honors; Meyer himself told Dan Lamothe for the *Marine Corps Times* (Sep. 13, 2011, online) that the military's failure to recognize Swenson's actions with a medal was "ridiculous," and said, "If it wasn't for him, I wouldn't be alive today."

In November 2011 Meyer filed a lawsuit against BAE Systems, a Department of Defense contractor that had hired him in March of that year. According to the suit, soon after he joined BAE, he had complained to his supervisor about BAE's intention to sell to Pakistan a weapon component that was superior to what he and his fellow Marines had been issued. The supervisor "began berating and belittling" him, the suit charged, as quoted by Amy Davidson in the *New Yorker* (Dec. 7, 2011, online). When Meyer tried to return to Ausgar, he learned from an Ausgar representative that his BAE supervisor had told a Defense Department official that Meyer was "mentally unstable," had a drinking problem, and had failed to finish tasks. In December 2011 Meyer and BAE Systems reportedly reached an amicable agreement, and the suit was dropped.

As of January 2012 Meyer was working for the construction company McDan in Kentucky, near where he grew up, and held the rank of sergeant in the Individual Ready Reserve of the US Marine Corps Reserve. He maintains a personal website and has completed some undergraduate courses.

SUGGESTED READING

Curtis, Colleen. "President Obama Awards Medal of Honor to Dakota Meyer." *White House Blog*. WhiteHouse.gov, 15 Sep. 2011. Web. 1 Jan. 2012.

Davidson, Amy. "The Case of Dakota Meyer." *New Yorker*. New Yorker, 7 Dec. 2011. Web. 1 Jan. 2012.

Lamothe, Dan. "Ambush Survivor up for Medal of Honor." *Marine Corps Times*. Marine Corps Times, 8 Nov. 2010. Web. 1 Jan. 2012.

---. "MoH Nominee Says He Does Not Feel Like a Hero." *Marine Corps Times*. Marine Corps Times, 23 Nov. 2010. Web. 1 Jan. 2012.

Michaels, Jim. "In an Afghanistan Firefight, the Making of a Hero." *USA Today* 7 Sep. 2011: A1. Print.

West, Bing. "The Afghan Rescue Mission behind Today's Medal of Honor." *Wall Street Journal*. Wall Street Journal, 15 Sep. 2011. Web. 1 Jan. 2012.

---. *The Wrong War: Grit, Strategy, and the Way Out of Afghanistan*. New York: Random, 2011. Print.

—*Miriam Helbok*

Tiya Miles

Born: January 17, 1970
Occupation: Historian and educator

Tiya Miles, a professor at the University of Michigan, is an expert on the interactions between African Americans and American Indians during the nineteenth century. The recipient of a John D. and Catherine T. MacArthur Foundation Fellowship, or the "genius grant," she has written two critically acclaimed books on the topic—*Ties That Bind: The Story of an Afro-Cherokee Family in Slavery and Freedom* (2005) and *The House on Diamond Hill: A Cherokee*

Courtesy the John D. & Catherine T. MacArthur Foundation

Plantation Story (2010)—and has contributed to numerous other volumes.

Miles has found that despite the commonly held notions about the affinity between the two groups, the reality was much bleaker and more complex. American Indians routinely enslaved African Americans, and although many Afro-Indian children were born during the colonial era, the Cherokee Nation later fought to exclude former slaves and their children from tribal membership and consequently denied them a share of the financial compensation granted by the US government after 1866. "My heart was broken [as I conducted my research]," Miles told Elizabeth Atkins for the Detroit-based arts-and-culture magazine *B.L.A.C.* (March 2012). "I felt like, 'How could an oppressed group of people of color disavow their historical ties with black people when they have people of African ancestry in their tribal nation? And what does that mean about how far we have or have not come?'" Her scholarship is now dedicated, as she told Atkins, to "help[ing] people who stand on opposite sides of this line to find a bridge."

EARLY LIFE

Tiya Alicia Miles, whose first name is pronounced TIE-ya, was born on January 17, 1970, in Cincinnati, Ohio. Her father, Benny, taught in the Cincinnati public schools and later became a principal; her mother, Patricia, worked in a downtown department store and later earned

a law degree. The couple divorced when Miles was two years old.

A gifted student who loved to write, Miles attended elementary and junior high school in Cincinnati. One day Miles's mother saw an advertisement for a philanthropic organization called A Better Chance, which provides scholarships to bright, low-income individuals of color to attend preparatory schools. At her mother's urging, Miles took the required test, and to her surprise, she was granted a full scholarship to the Middlesex School in Concord, Massachusetts. She was intensely reluctant to leave her friends, family, and familiar surroundings. "I was a fifteen-year-old, African American girl from urban Ohio, and I was living in the country with wealthy, white New Englanders, for the most part," Miles recalled to Patricia Montemurri for the *Detroit Free Press* (31 Oct. 2011). "In so many ways, I didn't fit in." Although Miles longed to return to Ohio, her parents convinced her not to give up the scholarship. Her perseverance paid off; when she graduated in 1988, she was ranked first in her class.

HIGHER EDUCATION

After graduating from the Middlesex School, Miles enrolled in Harvard University, where she majored in Afro-American studies. There, she met her future husband, Joseph Gone, a clinical psychology student and a citizen of the Gros Ventre tribal nation with family ties to the Fort Belknap Indian Reservation in Montana.

Miles had long been interested in the shared history of African Americans and American Indians. When Miles was a child, her grandmother had related to her a colorful oral history of the family's Afro-Indian roots, spinning particularly exciting tales about the strength and bravery of Miles's female ancestors. Although she was fascinated by the stories, Miles focused instead on African American literature while at Harvard, earning a bachelor's degree in 1992. She next attended Emory University in Atlanta, Georgia, from which she earned a master's degree in women's studies in 1995. One of her mentors at Emory was American Studies professor Rudolph Byrd. "One of the first novels we read [in his class] was Toni Morrison's *Beloved*," Miles reminisced to Tom Nugent for *Emory Magazine* (winter 2012). "With the help of Professor Byrd, I began to see the intimate ways that slavery had affected the lives of Morrison's characters. Now I was seeing the inside of a person's being, as well as the outside. And that was extremely important for my later work as a historian who became determined to catch the texture, the inner feeling, and the lived experiences of my historical subjects." On the subject of mentors, she told Keosha Johnson for *TheGrio* (31 Jan. 2012), "I have benefitted from the generosity of more good people than I could possibly name from a range of racial and gender backgrounds. Mentors do not always come in the external packaging that one might expect."

It was while pursuing her doctorate at the University of Minnesota that Miles turned her academic focus to the shared history of Indians and African Americans. She took a class on American Indian history during which she read about the relationships between the South Carolina–based Catawba Indians and the African Americans of the region. "That changed my whole trajectory," Miles told Kenneth Cooper for *Diverse: Issues in Higher Education* (9 Dec. 2010).

DISSERTATION RESEARCH

In 1998 Miles became a Ford Foundation dissertation fellow, and the following year she was awarded a Thurgood Marshall dissertation fellowship at Dartmouth College in New Hampshire. Despite the academic prestige and recognition accorded by the fellowships, Miles did not find completing her dissertation an easy task. Distressingly, she discovered during the course of her research that her grandmother's tales were in all likelihood highly embroidered and that the real history of African-Indian relations was a deeply troubled one. "In black American culture, a lot of families have stories about ancestors running away to the Indians for safety. So to hear about Native Americans actually owning black slaves, it really punctures that story—that notion about native spaces being safe havens," Miles explained to Cooper. Miles was far from alone in believing long-cherished but probably unauthentic family histories. Even after reading her work or hearing her lectures, people regularly approach her in public forums to discuss their own Afro-Indian origins. She added to Cooper, "I personally feel that one needs to be very careful and conscientious about making claims having to do with Native American ancestry or identity."

In one especially disturbing incident during her dissertation research, Miles contacted an archivist to try to find information on a little-known woman named Doll, a slave and wife of a Cherokee farmer whose life would later form the basis of *Ties That Bind*. "I said my real interest was looking at black and native women. The archivist laughed out loud!" she told Atkins. "He said black women were not important enough to be remembered and native women were not important enough to be remembered, let alone together." Miles continued digging, however, and found the needed documents on her own. In 2000 she earned her doctorate from the University of Minnesota.

ACADEMIC CAREER

While serving as a fellow at Dartmouth, Miles worked as the coordinator of the Shabazz Center, a residential facility affiliated with the school's African and African American Studies Program. She also coorganized the first national conference on relations between African Americans and American Indians.

After earning her PhD, Miles joined the faculty of the University of California, Berkeley, as an assistant professor of ethnic studies. She remained there until 2002, when she was hired by the University of Michigan. She now chairs the school's Department of Afroamerican and African Studies and also serves as a professor in the Program in American Culture and the Department of Women's Studies. In one of her courses—Blacks, Indians, and the Making of America—her students prepared research papers about the slaves on a Georgia plantation owned by a wealthy Cherokee leader and businessman. The students' papers were incorporated into a booklet and made available to visitors to the plantation's main house, the Chief Vann House, which had become a historic site. The family and home later became the subjects of Miles's *The House on Diamond Hill*.

Miles also holds a position in the school's Native American Studies Program. In that capacity, she has been involved in addressing controversies regarding the dioramas of American Indian scenes at the university's Museum of Natural History, which some observers found inaccurate and offensive, and the ethics of holding indigenous human remains in the Museum of Anthropology's collection. The dioramas were ultimately dismantled, although the debate as to whether the human remains should be returned to their place of origin for reburial continues.

BOOKS

In 2005 the University of California Press published *Ties That Bind: The Story of an Afro-Cherokee Family in Slavery and Freedom*. In the book, Miles traces the story of a celebrated Cherokee warrior and wealthy farmer named Tarsekayahke, more commonly called Shoe Boots, and the African slave, Doll, who became his wife and bore him five children. She wrote in her preface, "The Shoeboots family story opened up an entire history that I, growing up in an African American family, majoring in Afro-American Studies in college, and studying Native American history in graduate school, had never heard. And yet this story seemed vital to gaining a full understanding of the American past, since it moved through and encompassed key moments, issues, and struggles both in African American and American Indian histories."

Miles admits to feeling great ambivalence about Shoe Boots. While he was undeniably a slave owner and sometimes trader, he did at one point successfully petition the Cherokee Nation to have three of his children with Doll made his legal heirs. Doll could never belong to a Cherokee clan, however, and the tribal council ordered Shoe Boots to "cease begetting any more Children by his said slave woman." Thus, the two children born to them after the petition was settled were not granted citizenship.

Critics hailed the book for its unique perspective and depth of research. In one representative assessment, Joshua Piker, a history professor at the University of Oklahoma, wrote for *H-Net Reviews* (July 2006), "This is, then, a wide-ranging and ambitious book [that] offers a challenging narrative, one that succeeds in speaking to issues fundamental to Native and American history without losing track of its obligations to the individuals and families at its center." *Ties That Bind* garnered a Frederick Jackson Turner Award from the Organization of American Historians and a Lora Romero Distinguished First Book Award from the American Studies Association. The year after the book's publication, Miles was named a "top young historian" by the History News Network.

In 2010 the University of North Carolina Press published *The House on Diamond Hill: A Cherokee Plantation Story*. The book traces the history of James Vann, a Cherokee chief who established the Diamond Hill Plantation in Georgia early in the nineteenth century. In the 1830s, when the Cherokee Nation was forced by the US government to migrate westward on the infamous Trail of Tears, the Vann family left Georgia and resettled in Oklahoma, and their former home was given to white men who had won a land lottery. Like Miles's first book, *The House on Diamond Hill* received a slew of awards, including the Erminie Wheeler-Voegelin Prize from the American Society for Ethnohistory, the National Council on Public History Book Award, and the Lilla M. Hawes Award from the Georgia Historical Society. Daniel B. Thorp echoed the sentiments of many other reviewers when he wrote for the *Journal of Southern History* (Feb. 2012), "Miles's research is solid; her writing is clear, and the story she tells is both important and compelling. *The House on Diamond Hill* is an exemplary book."

Miles has also contributed chapters or essays to such collections as *Testimony: Young African Americans on Self-Discovery and Black Identity* (1995), *Confounding the Color Line: Indian-Black Relations in Multidisciplinary Perspective* (2002), and *IndiVisible, African-Native American Lives in the Americas* (2009). In 2006 she co-edited the anthology *Crossing Waters, Crossing Worlds: The African Diaspora in Indian Country*. She has also contributed to periodicals such as the *Journal of Social History*, *Ms.*, the *Michigan Quarterly Review*, and *Women and Language*.

OTHER ACTIVITIES AND HONORS

In 2011 Miles was named a fellow of the John D. and Catherine T. MacArthur Foundation, which cited her efforts in "reframing the history of colonial America in works that illuminate the complex relationship between African and Cherokee peoples." The prestigious fellowship includes a $500,000 cash award, and Miles is using the windfall to fund ECO Girls, an organization she founded to provide environmental and cultural opportunities for girls living in urban areas of Michigan. "I really want to . . . broaden the girls' horizons," Miles told Danny LaChance for the University of Minnesota's alumni publication, *Minnesota Magazine* (Winter 2012). "We'll be trying to get them to recognize that who they are is connected to where they are and the natural world around them." To that end, the girls learn gardening, go on field trips to apple orchards and recycling plants, and engage in discussions of black history, among other activities. Although the group operates predominantly in the southeast part of the state, Miles envisions expanding it to other areas and founding chapters for boys as well.

PERSONAL LIFE

Miles and her husband, who also teaches at the University of Michigan, have three children: twin daughters, Nali and Noa, and a son, Sylvan. When Miles and Joseph Gone announced their impending wedding, their families were not instantly supportive. "We learned that our families—both families of color—were not very well-equipped to relate with one another," she told James Tobin for the University of Michigan's *MLSA Magazine* (Fall 2007). "I had a fantasy that people of color would have a natural affinity and support each other. We learned in a very personal way that that was not necessarily the case."

Despite these difficulties, Miles has noted that the extended families have reached a stage of loving acceptance. Her children visit Gone's home reservation in Montana during the summers, and they also attend the Milk River Powwow, an annual gathering for people of mixed Indian descent. They also make frequent trips to Cincinnati, where, as Miles told Atkins, they experience "a slice of what [she] had growing up as a black girl." Miles continued, "They do things with my relatives, attend a black Baptist church, and go to vacation bible school."

Miles lives with her family in Ann Arbor, Michigan. Among the most prized possessions in their home is a multicolored quilt made by Miles's great-aunt as a girl in Mississippi. In her free time, Miles enjoys hiking and reading mysteries.

SUGGESTED READING

Atkins, Elizabeth. "The Genius of Dr. Tiya Miles." *B.L.A.C.* Metro Parent Publishing, Mar. 2012. Web. 3 July 2012.
Cooper, Kenneth. "Scholar Documents Historic Ties between African-Americans and Native Americans." *Diverse: Issues in Higher*

Education. Cox, Matthews, and Associates, 9 Dec. 2010. Web. 3 July 2012.

LaChance, Danny. "A Natural Scholar." *Minnesota.* University of Minnesota Alumni Association, Winter 2012. Web. 3 July 2012.

Montemurri, Patricia. "What These 3 MacArthur Foundation Winners Do Is Genius." *Detroit Free Press.* Gannett, 31 Oct. 2011. Web. 3 July 2012.

Nugent, Tom. "The Memory Keeper." *Emory Magazine.* Emory University, Winter 2012. Web. 3 July 2012.

Tobin, James. "Ties That Bind: Tiya Miles Confronts Misconceptions in Her Work and Life." *MLSA Magazine.* University of Michigan, Fall 2007. Web. 3 July 2012.

—*Mari Rich*

WireImage

Shala Monroque

Born: July 25, 1979
Occupation: Fashion editor

A former editor-at-large for *Pop* magazine and the current creative director of *Garage*, a new fashion and arts publication, Shala Monroque (SHAH-la MON-rok) was described by Vanessa Grigoriadis for *New York* magazine (22 Aug. 2011) as a "very modern kind of style icon." Monroque, Grigoriadis wrote, "has the distinction of being a central inspiration for two of this era's most powerful visual tastemakers. . . . She's a friend of [the designer] Miuccia Prada, for whom she functions as a kind of muse and unofficial ambassador, hosting a salon called Miu Miu Musings at the stores around the world. And she's the girlfriend of art-world impresario Larry Gagosian, the foremost gallerist on the planet." In a piece for the *New York Times* (30 Dec. 2010), Edward Barsamian named Monroque one of the best-dressed women of the year and praised her "youthful blend of whimsy and sophistication." "Whether craning necks in an urban turban at the CFDA [Council of Fashion Designers of America] dinner or in prim 1950s silhouettes from Prada, Miu Miu, and Chanel, Monroque stood out from the repeat step-and-repeat offenders this year," he wrote. Monroque told an interviewer for the *Ladies Room TV Vlog,* "When I think of icons or people . . . I don't think of what they were wearing but more about their confidence or their soul or what they give back and I'm attracted to that."

EARLY LIFE

Monroque was born on July 25, 1979, in Saint Lucia, an island in the Caribbean Sea. She told Natasha Inchley for *Vogue Australia* (8 Aug. 2011), "[My] love of color came from growing up in Saint Lucia and being surrounded by tropical flowers and a mesmerizing ocean. I now feel as though vivid color is saturated in my mind." Monroque's mother, who shared with her daughter a love of fashion, ran a hotel gift shop. She often brought her daughter unsold copies of *Vogue* and *Tatler.* "My mother didn't make that much money but she spent a lot of it, by her own standards, on clothes," Monroque told Inchley. "She also took a lot of care with her appearance and consequently I did, too. I learned to appreciate nice things." Monroque's aunt, who owned a clothing boutique called Trendy's, made frequent trips to the garment district in New York City for merchandise to bring back to Saint Lucia.

Growing up, Monroque watched broadcasts of such iconic American television shows as Leave It to Beaver. "I always knew as a kid that I wanted to live in America," she told Grigoriadis. "Life [there] just seemed better, and freer. I couldn't believe that on TV, kids would just open the fridge, pull out a box of orange juice, and drink from it." The shows also influenced her taste in clothing. "I always loved dressing and had the newest things," she explained to Grigoriadis, "but I always had the fifties ideas."

As a teenager Monroque became a high school track star and budding poet. When she came in second in a local beauty pageant, she won a trip to Miami, Florida. That trip marked her first time outside Saint Lucia. "I had always had this romantic idea about taking a Greyhound bus," she told Grigoriadis, "so I thought I'd take the 30 hour trip [from Florida] to New York." There, Monroque stayed with an uncle who lived in the borough of Queens and visited an aunt who worked as a dresser at fashion shows. "The moment I knew I wanted to live here is when I got to go to a Jean Paul Gaultier party, and there were red knee-high feathers throughout the whole floor," she recalled to Grigoriadis, referring to a famous French fashion designer.

MOVES TO NEW YORK

Determined to remain in the city, Monroque initially looked for a job as a nanny—a common position for women from the Caribbean— but her uncle convinced her that the work would be demeaning. Instead, she found a job at a photo studio for $200 a week. Soon she discovered a more lucrative position as a hostess at the upscale New York City restaurant Man Ray, and she later held a similar post at the exclusive Japanese restaurant Nobu. With her increased income Monroque moved into a tiny apartment with a shared bathroom in the predominantly black neighborhood of Harlem.

In 2003 Monroque, then twenty-four, read a Craigslist ad for a *Seventeen* magazine photo spread centered on the changing image of the "typical" American girl. Photographed by Mary Ellen Mark, Monroque appeared in the November issue of the magazine, which quoted her as saying, "I was raised in St. Lucia, which has produced two Nobel laureates. This forces me to dream extravagantly. I want to be an important writer and tell my stories. New York is a good place to do that. When I finally stood in Times Square, I was the happiest person alive."

Monroque later accepted a job as the maître d' at Kittichai, a Thai restaurant on Thompson Street, in downtown Manhattan. To celebrate, she purchased a pair of dark wraparound sunglasses that cost her more than a week's pay. She described them to Grigoriadis as "very intense, like something guys from St. Lucia would wear." Her romance with the enigmatic art dealer and gallery owner Larry Gagosian began at about that time, although in interviews Monroque has declined to describe their first meeting.

SHALA'S RABBIT HOLE AND MIU MIU MUSINGS

Monroque began to write a blog, *Shala's Rabbit Hole*, in 2010. She posts about a range of subjects, including the frustrations of seasonal shopping, her style icons Josephine Baker and Katharine Hepburn, and the joys of Caribbean culture. Having befriended the designer Miuccia Prada, Monroque also conducts regular salons called "Miu Miu Musings" (named for one of Prada's lines) at which she invites fashion insiders and bloggers to discuss current trends in the industry. The first gathering took place on December 10, 2010, at the Miu Miu store in New York City. The event was hosted by Monroque and André Leon Talley, the former editor-at-large for *Vogue* magazine. Talley wrote of the salons for the *Vogue* website (10 Feb. 2011), "Informal, stream-of-consciousness conversational evenings have always been easy for me, and it seems Shala's get-togethers are going to be de rigueur for a lot of fashion passionistas. . . . As pretentious as it sounds, the point of the evening is to inspire thought and dialogue about the current fashion climate." Prada told Anne Monoky for *Harper's Bazaar* (13 Aug. 2010), "[Monroque] has such an incredible sense of fashion, and, more importantly, it's all very instinctive and natural. It's really a gift." The admiration is mutual: Monroque told Inchley, "I love Miuccia's mind. I like the fact that she has a provocative and a political side. I see how her education in political science influences what she does and I love the way she translates that into fashion."

POP AND GARAGE

Another of Monroque's friends, Dasha Zhukova, widely known as the girlfriend of the Russian oligarch Roman Abramovich, had taken over the off-beat luxury publication *Pop* in 2009, with the aim of broadening its content to include arts and culture. Monroque became *Pop's* editor-at-large. The pair next began planning a new magazine called *Garage*, named after the art center Zhukova had opened in Moscow. The debut issue, which listed Monroque on the masthead as creative director, was published in September 2011 and featured—among other provocative content—photos of racy tattoos designed by the artists Richard Prince and Damien Hirst, an Alexander McQueen dress made of lettuce, and an eerie dollhouse in which a puppet-like model donned high-end garments. In a review for the *New York Times* (24 Aug. 2011), Eric Wilson deemed it "one of the most intriguing magazines to come along in years" and wrote, "It is not entirely clear whether this is a fashion magazine that takes more than a passing interest in art, or an art magazine that knows its stuff about fashion."

Monroque, an avid traveler, lives for about six months of the year in a townhouse on the Upper East Side of New York City with Gagosian, who is thirty-four years her senior.

SUGGESTED READING

Grigoriadis, Vanessa. "Ms. Muse." *New York.* New York Media LLC., 14 Aug. 2011. Web. Jan. 2012.

Monroque, Shala. *Shala's Rabbit Hole.* Shala Monroque, Oct. 2011–Sep. 2012. Web. Jan. 2012.

"Spotlight On: Shala Monroque." *Vogue: Vogue Black TV.* Edizione Condé Nast S.p. A., n. d. Web. Jan. 2012.

—*Molly M. Hagan*

Beth Mooney

Born: ca. 1955
Occupation: CEO of KeyCorp

When Beth Mooney became the chair and chief executive officer (CEO) of KeyCorp in May 2011, she also became the first female CEO of one of the top twenty independent banks in the United States. That year she was also named among the most powerful women in business by *Forbes* magazine. Prior to that, starting in 2006, Mooney was KeyCorp's chair of community banking. According to the company's website, the Cleveland-based bank is "one of the nation's largest bank-based financial services companies, with assets of approximately $89 billion. Key companies provide investment management, retail and commercial banking, consumer finance, and investment banking products and services to individuals and companies throughout the United States as well as—for certain businesses—other countries."

Mooney's road to the top involved a great deal of determination and hard work. After nearly a decade working as a bank manager for First Republic Bank in Dallas, Texas, in the 1980s, Mooney worked for Bank One Corporation in Ohio in the 1990s as a senior vice president and chief financial officer (CFO), then as regional president and chief operating officer (COO), and finally as its president, chair, and CEO. Her next significant long-term affiliation was with AmSouth Bancorp, also a top-twenty national bank, first in Tennessee and then Alabama. She served as the bank's CFO from 2004 to 2006, after which she joined KeyCorp. In addition to honors and recognition from the financial press, Mooney received the YWCA Women of Achievement Award in 2008. Teresa Dixon Murray, in a profile for the Cleveland, Ohio, *Plain Dealer* (20 Feb. 2011), wrote of Mooney: "Colleagues, employees and former bosses said the fifty-six-year-old Mooney possesses an unusual combination of talents: incredible leadership ability that makes people want to work hard for her; a scary knack for numbers; genuine compassion for people; no-nonsense bluntness; and an intelligence that she doesn't flaunt, but you know is there."

EARLY LIFE AND EDUCATION

The youngest of three children, Beth Elaine Mooney was raised in Midland, Michigan, by her mother, an English teacher, and her father, a chemist for the Dow Chemical Company. When Mooney was in high school, the family moved three times, ending up in Texas, where she also attended the University of Texas. There she studied history and received a BA in 1977. Prior to graduation she decided that she would be a teacher, but after less than a year of teaching American history to high school students,

Courtesy of KeyCorp

she decided that she was not suited for that profession. In 1978 she found work as a secretary at the First City Bank in Houston, Texas. The following year she moved to Dallas, Texas. (She was married at that time, but by the mid-1980s, the relationship would end in divorce.)

Mooney desperately searched for work in the banking industry, but being a woman and having no banking experience made the task very difficult. In an interview with Murray, Mooney recalled, "I went to every bank in Dallas. I informed the [human resources] departments that I was there to apply for their management training program. I got laughed out of every place in town." She then tried one more place, the First Republic Bank, the largest bank in Texas. She was so persistent that the human resources office finally sent her to Keith Schmidt, the man in charge of the management-training program. They ended up talking for hours, and Schmidt accepted her into the program—so long as she took MBA classes at night. Mooney would go on to earn her MBA degree from Southern Methodist University in Dallas in 1983.

Mooney eventually worked her way up from the position of manager at First Republic to the post of senior vice president in 1985—at the age of thirty, the bank's youngest. Being a woman, she still encountered open sexism from what she has called the "good ol' boys" network. After walking into one particularly important meeting with a group of developers, she noticed that the men—there were only men—looked at her condescendingly. Unfazed, she took out her compact mirror and asked, "Do I look stupid?" The men took her seriously after that. Mooney remained at the bank until 1987. The following year she joined Citicorp Real Estate, a subsidiary of Citibank, as the company's vice president and area director in both Dallas and Washington, DC. It was her first nonbanking position in nearly a decade; however, she soon returned to banking when the opportunity arose.

CAREER IN BANKING

In 1993 Banc One Corporation asked Mooney to join the company's holding company for its Ohio banks. Mooney agreed, and starting in March 1993, she became the senior vice president and CFO of Bank One Ohio, then an affiliate of Banc One. In September of the following year, she took over as president and CFO of Bank One in Akron, Ohio—the first woman to do so in the bank's history. Mooney told Abe Zaidan for the Cleveland, Ohio, *Plain Dealer* (23 Aug. 1994), "I believe that being a leader requires effective communication." She continued, "I also think it's important to find a consensus when looking for solutions to problems. But in the end, when a decision is required, you have to be willing to take a risk, knowing that if this or that solution doesn't work, I'll be held accountable. That's the way it has to be. Others [who are involved in the decision] must know that if there is a problem, you'll support them. The buck stops with me." Within a year Mooney helped expand the bank's twenty-four-hour phone-banking system and oversaw a program that offers checking accounts and direct deposit for all employees at a company. In 1995 she was elected chair and CEO of Bank One, and starting in January of the following year, she was also the company's president.

In 1997 Mooney stepped down from all her posts and moved to Columbus, Ohio, where she continued her work for Bank One, this time as regional executive in charge of Bank One's commercial real estate lending for Ohio and Kentucky. After only six months she left her post and took on a new position in Dayton, Ohio, at DP&L, a holding company for the Dayton Power and Light Company, where in June 1998 she became a chief operating officer (COO). As the company's COO, she was in charge of financial relations and operations, the treasury, fuel procurement, purchasing, and information systems. Mooney left after less than a year with DP&L, however, and early in 2000, facts emerged in the financial press about the reasons for her departure: the company had apparently planned to make her its next CEO but then decided against it; Mooney later sued DP&L for damages exceeding $1 million, and the suit was settled out of court. Landing on her feet, however, Mooney returned to Bank One in June 1999, this time as chair, president, and CEO of Bank One NA, a company with assets of more than $30 billion.

Her second stint with Bank One did not last long. In June 2000 she moved to Nashville, Tennessee, to work for AmSouth Bancorp, the country's twentieth-largest bank at the time, where she served as head of AmSouth's Tennessee operations. Writing for the Nashville *Tennessean* (6 Sep. 2000), Getahn Ward stated, "Mooney's stint with AmSouth in Tennessee comes at a critical stage for the Birmingham, Alabama–based bank." Ward explained, "After gaining the largest market share in the Midstate and doubling its size overall through acquiring First American Bank of Nashville, AmSouth now faces the dual task of guarding newly gained ground while continuing to grow deposits in a tough bank environment. Banks making such large acquisitions normally can expect to lose a certain percentage of the acquired bank's customers. Analysts said AmSouth so far has done well with the operational conversion, but other challenges such as melding different cultures of the two banks remain." In 2004 Mooney was promoted to CFO, for which she had to move to AmSouth's headquarters in Birmingham, Alabama. The following year *USBanker* magazine named her one of the twenty-five most powerful women in banking; in 2006 the magazine ranked Mooney fifth among the nation's top ten bank CFOs.

CEO OF KEYCORP

In April 2006 Mooney left AmSouth to join KeyCorp in Cleveland, Ohio, as the chair of the company's thirteen-state community banking unit, where her initial responsibilities included retail and commercial banking. Three regional presidents and four business-segment strategists reported to her directly. After federal regulators, in the summer of 2007, gave permission for KeyCorp to make acquisitions, the company set out to improve the strength of its presence in the West and Northeast. The company soon set out to acquire the New York–based USB Holding for $575 million. However, the following year proved to be a difficult one. After two straight quarterly losses for KeyCorp and the worldwide financial collapse, which began around September 2008, the company was struggling—yet it was still working to upgrade its branches with new technology and trying to make acquisitions in the West and Northeast.

In May 2011 Mooney took over as the chair and CEO of KeyCorp, which was planning to focus more on increasing its fee-based revenue in capital markets, private banking, and investment banking. By that point KeyCorp had already opened seventy-seven new branches in the two preceding years and was planning on opening forty new branches in 2011. By July of that year the company announced that it had had five consecutive profitable quarters. In a third-quarter conference call transcript posted by *Morningstar.com* (20 Oct. 2011), Mooney said,

"Our third-quarter results demonstrate consistent positive momentum for Key as we continue executing our relationship strategy. Despite the uneven pace of the recovery and regulatory changes, we are gaining traction in both the Community Bank and the Corporate Bank and we believe we have the right business model to compete and win in the marketplace. With the strong foundation of our strong balance sheet in place, we are well-positioned to organically grow our franchise and remain disciplined with respect to expense and capital management."

Dubbed the "velvet hammer" for her quiet but firm leadership style, Mooney's rise has come as no surprise to those who know her. Upon her appointment as KeyCorp CEO, Thomas Hoaglin, a former CEO of Ohio's Huntington Bank who has worked with Mooney, told the Cleveland, Ohio, *Plain Dealer*, "I always had a conviction that she would run a bank."

PERSONAL LIFE
Divorced with no children, Mooney lives in Bratenahl, Ohio, where she enjoys reading, golfing, and dining out.

SUGGESTED READING
Monks, Matthew. "New KeyCorp CEO Product of Old-School Grooming." *American Banker* 22 Nov. 2010: 1+. Print.

Mooney, Beth. "Key Executive Believes in Setting the Tone." *Plain Dealer* [Cleveland] 10 Jan. 2010: D1. Print.

Murray, Teresa Dixon. "KeyCorp's New CEO Sets High Standards, Gets Others to Buy In." *Plain Dealer* [Cleveland] 20 Feb. 2011, National: A1+. Print.

Ward, Getahn. "Ambitious at AmSouth." *Tennessean* [Nashville] 6 Sep. 2000, Business: 1E+. Print.

Zaidan, Abe. "New Bank Chief Brings Skills as Communicator." *Plain Dealer* [Cleveland] 23 Aug. 1994, Metro: 2B. Print.

—*Dmitry Kiper*

Piers Morgan
Born: March 30, 1965
Occupation: Journalist and television personality

Piers Morgan was virtually unknown to US audiences until 2006, when television host Simon Cowell selected him to serve as cohost for the show *America's Got Talent*. Morgan was already familiar to tabloid audiences in his native Britain, where he became the youngest editor of the now-defunct tabloid newspaper *News of the World*, followed by a nearly decade-long stint at the *Daily Mirror*, another tabloid newspaper,

Getty Images for Extra

until he was fired in 2004 as a result of a photo scandal. Since then he has carved out a respectable television career as a judge on *America's Got Talent* and its British counterpart, and as the host of several interview shows in the UK.

In 2011 Morgan was selected by the Cable News Network (CNN) to replace Larry King, who was retiring from his eponymous primetime talk show after twenty-five years. Discussing his new gig with Richard Huff for the *New York Daily News* (8 Sep. 2010, online), Morgan confided, "I'm not interested in doing one of these politically partisan shows. What I want to do is extricate the truth from public figures and famous people. I see myself as the receptacle of getting the real story."

EARLY LIFE AND EDUCATION
Piers Morgan was born Piers Stefan O'Meara on March 30, 1965, in the village of Newick in East Sussex (though other sources list his birthplace as Guildford, a town in the county of Surrey, in South East England.) Piers, who was reportedly named after the British racecar driver Piers Courage, hails from a creative family: his mother, Gabrielle, was an artist, and his father, Vincent, briefly worked as a journalist before changing careers. "His mother persuaded him to become a dentist because there was more money and security and all that but it was interesting to find . . . out that it's obviously in the blood," Morgan told Ginny Dougary in an interview for London's *Times Magazine* (7 Apr. 2007, online) that was posted on Dougary's personal website.

Morgan's father died when he was a year old, after which he was raised by his mother and his grandmother. His mother was eventually remarried to Glynne Pughe-Morgan, a Welshman, whose surname Morgan adopted. The family settled in the village of Fletching in East Sussex, where Gabrielle and Glynne ran the Griffin Inn pub. Morgan first developed a love of journalism at an early age, while attending the Fletching Church of England Primary School: "I was really into newspapers at five or six [years old], and used to point out the headlines that grabbed me. I learnt to read through the papers," he recalled to Jonathan Sale for the London *Independent* (8 May 2008, online).

When Morgan was seven years old, his parents enrolled him at Cumnor House, a preparatory day and boarding school in East Sussex, where he was a boarder from age eleven to thirteen. Morgan later transferred to the Chailey School, a secondary institution in the rural East Sussex district of Lewes. Upon completing his compulsory education at age sixteen, he spent the next two years at Lewes Priory Sixth Form College, preparing for the standard entrance examinations for public universities in the United Kingdom. After disappointing results, Morgan, who would have had to retake certain exams in order to gain admission to Warwick University, took a yearlong sabbatical from school. He accepted a position as an insurance clerk at Lloyd's of London. "It was good money . . . 150 [pounds] a week, but after nine months I was in tears with boredom," Morgan told Hunter Davies for the London *Independent* (13 Dec. 1994, online). He successfully applied for one of the nearly sixty spots in the competitive one-year journalism training course being taught at Harlow College's Journalism Centre, the oldest journalism school in Britain.

CAREER

Once Morgan had completed the intensive year-long program, he took his time before launching a career in journalism. "Everyone on that course got a job on a local newspaper. I was the last, because I insisted on London; I'd been told the stories were juiciest in London and could be sold to the national papers," he explained to Sale. In 1985 Morgan served as a reporter with the Surrey and South London Newspaper Group. While he was a writer for the *Wimbledon News* and the *South London Press*, Morgan also carried out freelance duties for the *Sun*, a British tabloid newspaper known for its sensational style of journalism, published by Rupert Murdoch's News Corporation. His freelance work attracted the attention of the *Sun's* editor Kelvin MacKenzie, who recruited Morgan to write and act as a de facto editor of Bizarre, the paper's daily entertainment news and gossip column.

Upon assuming his new position in 1989, Morgan shortened his surname from Pughe-Morgan to Morgan for byline purposes, becoming professionally known as Piers Morgan. With the Bizarre column, which featured photos of Morgan posing alongside high-profile entertainers, Morgan managed to achieve quasi-celebrity status in his native country. "I became the Friend of the Stars, a rampant egomaniac, pictured all the time with famous people—Madonna, [Sylvester] Stallone, [David] Bowie, Paul McCartney, hundreds of them. It was shameless, as they didn't know me from Adam," he told Davies. The success of the Bizarre column made quite an impression on upper management. "I got a call one day, asking me to see Rupert Murdoch in Miami. I suspected it must be something good," Morgan recalled to Davies. Morgan, who had previously turned down a promotion as features editor of the *Sun*, was offered the opportunity to serve as editor of *News of the World*, a weekly sister publication of the *Sun*.

In 1994, despite having no prior executive experience, the twenty-eight-year-old Morgan took over the editorship of *News of the World*, becoming the youngest head of a national newspaper in the United Kingdom in more than half a century. Under his leadership, *News of the World* quickly gained notoriety for its intrusive and sensationalistic style of journalism. Morgan came under fire on April 2, 1995, for the paper's coverage of fashion model Victoria Spencer's stay at Farm Place, a private rehabilitation clinic in Surrey, where she was receiving treatment for alcohol and eating disorder issues. The article detailed her marital problems with Charles Spencer, her then-husband and Princess Diana's younger brother, who filed a grievance with the Press Complaints Commission (PPC), an independent watchdog organization for the British press. It was determined that Morgan was in violation of the editor's code of practice. After being contacted by Lord John Wakeham, then chairman of the PCC, Murdoch issued a public apology in which he sternly reprimanded Morgan for his actions.

In August 1995 Morgan resigned from his post as editor of *News of the World*, and two months later he stepped into a new role as editor of the *Daily Mirror*, a rival British tabloid newspaper. He denied that his decision was influenced in any way by Murdoch's public rebuke. However, it was not long before Morgan found himself under the microscope once again. He drew intense criticism for the front-page headline "Achtung! Surrender: For you Fritz, ze Euro 96 Championship is over," on the eve of England's semifinal soccer match against Germany at the 1996 European Football Championship, held at London's Wembley Stadium on June 26. Equally controversial was the *Daily Mirror's* accompanying front-page photo of English teammates Paul

Gascoigne and Stuart Pearce wearing superimposed World War II soldiers' helmets, as well as a letter from the editor parodying Prime Minister Neville Chamberlain's 1939 declaration of war against Germany. In response to the backlash, Morgan issued a public apology. "It was intended as a joke, but anyone who was offended by it must have taken it seriously, and to those people I say sorry," Morgan told Ian Thomsen for the *New York Times* (26 June 1996, online).

In April 1998, the staff of Morgan's paper was approached by Anna Ferretti, the fiancée of James Hewitt, a former British Army officer who had carried on a five-year affair with the late Princess Diana. Ferretti unveiled sixty-four handwritten love letters that she had secretly taken from Hewitt's safe. (Diana had written the letters to Hewitt while he was serving in the Persian Gulf from December 1990 to March 1991.) The staff at the *Mirror* paid Ferretti £1,000, but instead of photographing the letters to determine their authenticity, they turned them over to officials at Kensington Palace, Diana's official residence. Hewitt successfully sued to have the letters returned to him in February 1999.

Morgan incurred the wrath of the British royal family in November 1998, when his paper ran a front-page story regarding a minor sports injury sustained by Prince Harry, Diana's younger son, during a rugby game. Although no specific details of the injury were published, Prince Charles, Harry's father, filed a complaint with the PCC, charging that the *Mirror* had breached the commission's code of practice regarding the right to privacy. Morgan found himself once again under the scrutiny of the PCC in February 2000, when an exposé in the *Daily Telegraph* disclosed that Morgan had acquired £20,000 worth of shares in the UK-based electronics firm Viglen on January 17, 2000—a day before Viglen was recommended as a stock tip to readers of the *Mirror*'s City Slickers financial advice column. Morgan denied allegations that he had knowingly and purposely driven up the stock's price in order to sell it at a profit, a process known in the United Kingdom as share ramping. Instead, he attributed the situation to coincidence. Although an investigation by the Department of Trade and Industry (DTI) uncovered that Morgan had spent £67,000 and not £20,000, as he had previously reported, Morgan was cleared of any wrongdoing. However, he was heavily censured by the PPC, who ordered him to publish a four-page apology.

Despite the negative publicity, Morgan managed to retain his job as the *Mirror*'s editor, but found himself in legal trouble again in February 2001, after the paper published photos of the British supermodel Naomi Campbell attending a Narcotics Anonymous meeting in London. The following year Campbell filed an invasion-of-privacy lawsuit against the *Mirror* and was awarded £3,500 in damages.

In the wake of the September 11, 2001, terrorist attacks, Morgan sought to adopt a less sensational style for his newspaper, which had been experiencing a gradual decline in circulation. He made notable changes, such as replacing its red masthead, characteristic of British tabloids, with a black one; focusing more on serious news; and hiring several reputable journalists, including Christopher Hitchens, Matthew Norman, Jonathan Freedland, and Miranda Sawyer. "[The changes] are about becoming a serious paper with serious news, serious sport, serious gossip, and serious entertainment," Morgan told Matt Wells for the London *Guardian* (16 Apr. 2002, online). At the 2002 British Press Awards, held in March at London's Hilton Hotel, the *Daily Mirror* garnered prizes for newspaper of the year and team of the year for its coverage of the September 11 attacks.

Morgan's tenure as the *Daily Mirror*'s editor came to an abrupt end on May 14, 2004, after the newspaper's front-page photos of British Army soldiers allegedly mistreating Iraqi prisoners were later identified as fakes. Subsequent to his firing, Morgan, who had previously hosted the 2003 British Broadcasting Corporation (BBC) television documentaries *Tabloid Tales* and *The Importance of Being Famous*, launched a career on the small screen. He teamed up with Amanda Platell, the former editor of the *Sunday Mirror* (the *Daily Mirror*'s sister publication), to host *Morgan and Platell*, a weekly political talk show. The series, which premiered in November 2004, aired on Channel Four for three seasons before being cancelled in November 2005.

In December 2005 Morgan announced that he would serve as a celebrity judge on *Got Talent*, a variety show being developed and produced by fellow Brit Simon Cowell, a popular judge on the Fox reality singing competition *American Idol* and the UK talent show *The X Factor*. In early December 2005 Morgan was tapped by Cowell to appear on *America's Got Talent* as one of the judges on the three-person panel, alongside pop singer Brandy Norwood and television actor David Hasselhoff. The show, hosted by Regis Philbin, made its television debut in June 2006 and was an instant hit for NBC, garnering high viewer ratings.

Morgan also served as the presenter of the television documentary series *You Can't Fire Me, I'm Famous*, which profiled celebrities who have been famously fired. The series aired for two seasons on the BBC One channel, from June 2006 to October of the following year. Also in 2007, Morgan was among the celebrities featured on the first season of *Comic Relief Does The Apprentice*, a show featuring participants performing various tasks to raise funds for Comic Relief, a British charity devoted to tackling famine. That summer Morgan and Hasselhoff were invited back as judges for the second season of *America's Got Talent*, which aired from June 2007 to August 2007. Norwood, who had been involved in a car collision and lawsuit, was replaced by Sharon Osbourne, while television celebrity Jerry Springer took over hosting duties. During this period Morgan also reprised his judge's role on the British version of the series, *Britain's Got Talent*, whose condensed, first-season format consisted of nine daily broadcasts, from early to mid-June. Morgan was a member of a judging panel that included Cowell and Amanda Holden.

Over the next several years, Morgan remained a television fixture in both the United States and his native country. In January 2008 he appeared in the first season of *Celebrity Apprentice*, during which the all-male and all-female celebrity squads competed against each other, with each celebrity raising money for their designated charities. Morgan, who had frequent and memorable run-ins with female contestant Omarosa Manigault-Stallworth, avoided elimination and was eventually named the winner at the season finale, which aired on NBC on March 27, 2008.

While *Celebrity Apprentice* was being broadcast in the United States, Morgan was serving as the host of the Independent Television (ITV) documentary show *Piers Morgan on Sandbanks*, a three-part series exploring the lifestyles of the rich that aired from early to mid-January. In May 2008, Morgan agreed to a two-year contract with ITV to remain a judge on the second, third, and fourth seasons of *Britain's Got Talent*. His 2008 TV credits also included the BBC interview series *The Dark Side of Fame with Piers Morgan*. As part of the ITV deal, Morgan also hosted two series: *Piers Morgan On . . .* (2009–10), in which he traveled to various exotic locales, and *Piers Morgan's Life Stories* (2009–), in which he conducts one-on-one celebrity interviews with guests such as television personality Sharon Osbourne, tennis player Boris Becker, and mezzo-soprano Katherine Jenkins. During this period Morgan appeared on three more seasons of *America's Got Talent*.

In September 2010, after announcing that he was leaving *Britain's Got Talent*, Morgan agreed to a four-year deal with CNN to take over the prime-time slot of the veteran television and radio host Larry King, headlining his own US prime-time talk show. He also signed another two-year contract with ITV to host new episodes of *Life Stories*. *Piers Morgan Tonight* made its CNN debut on January 17, 2011, with Oprah Winfrey as its first guest. Other notable first-season guests included Newt Gingrich, Simon Cowell, Beyoncé, Charlize Theron, Deepak Chopra, Sean Penn, Corey Booker, Tom Brokaw, Donald Rumsfeld, and Condoleezza Rice.

In July 2011, Morgan found himself one of the people at the center of a scandal involving allegations that News Corporation (publisher of the *Sun* and *News of the World*, among others) had illegally accessed personal bank, medical, and tax information via bribery, as well as hacking into the voicemail and computers of celebrities, the royal family, and crime victims. In December 2011, Morgan testified by videoconference at a British government hearing to deny allegations that he engaged in these illegal measures when he was an editor at the *Daily Mirror* and at *News of the World*.

In addition to his journalism career, Morgan has also written several books, including *Secret Lives* (1991) and *Private Files of the Stars* (1992), both coauthored with John Sachs, as well as the biographies *To Dream a Dream: The Amazing Life of Phillip Schofield* (1992), *Take That: Our Story* (1993), and *Take That: On the Road* (1994). He is also the author of *Va Va Voom! A Fan Diary of Arsenal's Invincible Season* (2005), as well as the autobiographies *The Insider: The Private Diaries of a Scandalous Decade* (2005), *Don't You Know Who I Am?* (2007), and *God Bless America: Misadventures of a Big Mouth Brit* (2009). Morgan has also teamed up with Nicky Cox, a BBC reporter he met during his tenure at the *Sun*, to launch *First News*, the UK's only weekly national newspaper for preteens.

PERSONAL LIFE

Since June 2010 Morgan has been married to fellow journalist Celia Walden. Their daughter, Elise, was born in November 2011. Morgan also has three sons, Spencer William, Stanley Christopher, and Albert Douglas, from his first marriage, to Marion Shalloe, which lasted from 1991 to 2008. Morgan, a cricket fan and admirer of the Arsenal Football Club, is also a co-owner of the Kensington pub The Hansom Cab.

SUGGESTED READING

Dougary, Ginny. "Educating Piers." *Times* [London]. Times Newspapers, 7 Apr. 2007. Web. 19 Apr. 2012.

Huff, Richard. "It's Official: Piers Morgan to Replace Larry King on CNN in January." *New York Daily News*. NYDailyNews.com, 8 Sep. 2010. Web. 19 Apr. 2012.

Sale, Jonathan. "An Education in the Life of Piers Morgan." *Independent*. Independent. co.uk, 8 May 2008. Web. 19 Apr. 2012.

Thomsen, Ian. "Oh, Sorry—Tabloids Lose the Soccer War." *New York Times*. New York Times, 26 June 1996. Web. 19 Apr. 2012.

Wells, Matt. "£20m New Look for 'Serious' Mirror." *Guardian*. Guardian News and Media, 16 Apr. 2002. Web. 19 Apr. 2012.

—Bertha Muteba

Denise Morrison

Born: January 13, 1954
Occupation: CEO of Campbell Soup Company

In August 2011 Denise Morrison realized her lifelong goal of becoming a chief executive officer (CEO) of a Fortune 500 company when she succeeded Douglas Conant as president and CEO of the Campbell Soup Company, the world's largest soup maker. In the process she became the first woman and the twelfth person overall to head the packaged goods behemoth, which was founded by fruit merchant Joseph A. Campbell and icebox manufacturer Abraham Anderson in 1869.

Among the first generation of women to pursue top-level positions in corporate America and part of an exclusive group of women who head Fortune 500 companies, the Boston College–educated Morrison began her career in the consumer packaged goods industry in the mid-1970s. She started working in the sales organization at Proctor & Gamble and then held various positions of increasing responsibility at the food and beverage giants PepsiCo and Nestlé USA over the following two decades. In 1995 Morrison joined Nabisco Foods, where she led the company's sales organization and helped introduce innovations such as its line of single-serving snacks. After Kraft Foods acquired Nabisco in 2000, she was named executive vice president and general manager of the company's snacks and confections divisions.

Morrison's tenure at Campbell began in 2003, when she was hired by Conant to serve as president of global sales and chief customer officer (CCO). Since then, she has enjoyed a rapid ascension at the company, rising to president of its US soup, sauces, and beverages division in 2005 and president of its North American soup, sauces, and beverages division in 2007. Morrison was named Campbell's executive vice president and chief operating officer (COO) and joined the company's board of directors in October 2010 as part of her transition to president and CEO. Known as a customer- and results-oriented leader who is "tough on the issues and tender on people," as noted by Diane Brady and Matthew Boyle for *Bloomberg Businessweek* (23 June 2011, online), Morrison has been regularly listed by *Fortune* magazine in its annual survey of the fifty most powerful women in business.

EARLY LIFE AND EDUCATION

Morrison was born Denise Sullivan on January 13, 1954, and grew up in Elberon, New Jersey. Her father, Dennis, was a Korean War veteran who held executive roles at several phone companies, and her mother, Connie, was a home-maker who later became a successful real estate agent. Morrison has three younger sisters,

AP Photo

Maggie Wilderotter, Colleen Bastkowski, and Andrea Doelling, all of whom have launched successful business careers. Wilderotter is the chair and CEO of Frontier Communications; like her sister, she has been consistently named by *Fortune* magazine as one of the fifty most powerful women in business. Bastkowski is a regional vice president of sales at Blackboard Mobile. Doelling, an accomplished horse jumper who competes on the professional equestrian circuit, was formerly a senior vice president of sales at AT&T Wireless.

With her sisters Morrison was raised in a business-oriented and disciplined household. Her parents taught her the value of hard work, commitment, and personal responsibility from an early age and provided her with a blueprint that would ensure success later in life. Morrison's father began schooling Morrison and her sisters in the principles of business not long after they entered grade school. He reportedly even made them formulate a business plan for getting their ears pierced. Morrison's mother instilled in her the importance of family and education and encouraged her to follow her ambitions. Morrison has often said that her parents made her and her sisters feel part of a team through family activities such as daily morning workouts, weekly oral reports on books unrelated to school, and weekly chores assigned to each sister using "job jars" from which they could choose and trade tasks. Morrison told Barbara Turvett for *Working Mother* (May 2008) that the daily workouts taught her discipline, the oral reports helped develop her oral communication skills, and the job jars taught her how to negotiate successfully.

Morrison also learned the importance of giving back to the community. During her youth she and her sister Maggie, with whom she was extremely close, organized neighborhood carnivals to raise money for muscular dystrophy and other causes. She told Turvett, "We learned you could work hard, make a profit, and then share it with the community." Though they engaged in healthy competition with each other at times, Morrison and Maggie always provided a support network for one another, and they both acted as mentors to their two younger sisters, who often sought career advice. The four Sullivan sisters maintain constant contact with each other and refer to themselves as "the network," supporting each other by drawing on their unique skills and strengths. "Denise is the strategist, Maggie the networker, Andrea the communicator, and I'm the competitive one," Morrison's sister Colleen told Carol Hymowitz for the *Wall Street Journal* (12 Feb. 2007).

Morrison attended Long Branch High School in Long Branch, New Jersey, where she was a standout student and member of the school marching band. She had joined the marching band as a baton twirler after trying out unsuccessfully for the school's cheerleading squad. Heeding her parents' advice to carve out a strategic plan for everything she was involved in, she eventually rose to become captain of Long Branch's baton-twirling team and became the school's first fire twirler. Morrison would later use that same approach in her business career. She told *Knowledge@Wharton* (2 Mar. 2011), the online journal of the Wharton School of Business, "I say that good work and positive results are a given, but you need to also have a plan. And you need to be the author and controller of that plan."

After graduating from high school, Morrison attended Boston College (BC) in Chestnut Hill, Massachusetts. There, she continued to excel academically and remained involved in extracurricular activities as a majorette in the BC marching band. During her senior year she was inducted into BC's prestigious Order of the Cross and Crown Honor Society, which recognizes students who have achieved distinction both inside and outside the classroom. In 1975 she graduated magna cum laude with a bachelor's degree in economics and psychology.

CAREER

After graduating from BC, Morrison joined Proctor & Gamble's paper products division in Boston, Massachusetts, becoming the first woman to work in the company's sales organization. Morrison went on to spend about seven years with the company, during which she held various sales roles. She was forced to overcome numerous obstacles as a woman working in what was then a largely male-dominated industry. Because of her gender, Morrison often had to convince clients to do business with her and was also forced to assert herself more in business meetings; she had to appease one of her bosses when she became pregnant and was granted only six weeks of maternity leave. Those early experiences led her to map out a strategic plan for her career—a plan that would ultimately help her achieve her goal of becoming a CEO. Morrison told *Knowledge@Wharton*, "Don't just let your career happen to you. You need to be strategic about how you define your leadership journey and where that takes you."

Morrison moved to New York when her first husband received a job offer there in the early 1980s. Due to her relocation, she was told that she would have to take a lower-level sales job at Proctor & Gamble; she instead left the company to accept a better position at PepsiCo, becoming a manager of business and project development. Morrison told Hymowitz, "I learned then to manage my own career—and that loyalty to people counts more than loyalty to any one company." In 1984, after working for Pepsi for two years, she joined Nestlé USA, where over the next decade she held various senior marketing and sales roles. During this time Morrison divorced, remarried, and moved to Bakersfield, California, after her second husband expressed the desire to run a fruit farm there. In Bakersfield, where Nestlé owned and operated an ice cream plant, she helped establish the company's national sales office for chilled and frozen foods. She served as national sales manager of that division and later served as vice president of marketing and sales for the Bakersfield-based Nestlé Ice Cream Company.

Morrison's professional relationship with Conant began in 1995, when she requested a meeting with him after being faced with the dilemma of moving her Nestlé division to Cleveland, Ohio. Looking to remain in California while one of her daughters finished high school, she sought out career advice from Conant, then the president of Nabisco Foods, and the two met at a coffee shop in Palm Springs. Impressed by her passion, preparedness, and willingness to expand her career, Conant offered her a job with Nabisco's sales organization. Morrison left Nestlé to work for Nabisco's sales force in California until her daughter graduated and then moved east to the company's headquarters in Camden, New Jersey, where she was named a senior vice president. Morrison has said that a work-life integration approach allowed her to balance the demands of career and family. She recalled to Caroline Cox for the women's business website *Little Pink Book* (July 2011), "I vividly remember faxing term papers back to [my daughters] from various hotels when I traveled. . . . I got many strange looks from the hotel managers, but it was my way to stay connected to my daughters."

As head of Nabisco's sales organization, a position she held until the late 1990s, Morrison helped develop a business plan for a line of single-serving snacks that included different assortments of cookies and crackers. Her plan impressed Nabisco CEO Jim Kilts, who named her general manager of the company's single-serving snack division. When Kraft Foods acquired Nabisco in December 2000, Morrison became executive vice president and general manager of the company's snacks and confections divisions, overseeing and developing many of the company's well-known brands. Around this time she began to explore other career options outside of Kraft and again sought the counsel of Conant, who left Nabisco/Kraft in January 2001 to become president and CEO of Campbell. Morrison, who considers Conant one of her mentors, recalled to *Knowledge@Wharton*, "I called him and said, 'I think I'm ready to change careers and I'd like some advice.' And he said, 'My advice is that you come here.'"

Conant appointed Morrison president of global sales and chief customer officer (CCO) of Campbell in April 2003. Morrison, who had agreed to join the company under the condition that she would eventually be able to head one of its larger divisions, was hired to oversee all of Campbell's sales and serve as an executive voice for the customer, reporting directly to Conant. During her two years as president of global sales and CCO, she led initiatives to strengthen Campbell's relationship with its customers and retail partners. "We are in an era of fragmented consumers and consolidated retailers, so the degree [to which] we can collaborate with our customers at multiple levels in the company is really important," Morrison told Vicki Powers for *CRM* magazine (Nov. 2004). "Having a CCO puts you in a better position to set that in motion."

In June 2005 Morrison was named president of Campbell's US soup, sauces, and beverages division. In that role she began spearheading efforts to lower the sodium content of the company's wide range of soups. "We were always the poster child for salt," she told *Knowledge@Wharton*. "I can remember sitting around a table with a small group of people, and I said, 'I'm tired of this. We need to be the poster child for wellness.' And they all looked at me like I had two heads." Despite that skepticism, Morrison's wellness campaign was set in motion in 2006, when Campbell launched low-sodium versions of its top-selling soups as well as reduced-sodium versions of its popular Healthy Request and children's condensed soup lines. The new offerings, which featured natural sea salt, enjoyed solid sales figures and received a relatively positive response from consumers.

In October 2007 Morrison was promoted to president of Campbell's North American soup, sauces, and beverages division. She continued to lead the company's health and wellness charge in this role, and in 2008 Campbell introduced another line of reduced-sodium soups, Campbell's Select Harvest (formerly Campbell's Select), and expanded its wellness offerings by acquiring the celebrity chef and restaurateur Wolfgang Puck's organic soup business. Campbell further reduced sodium in varieties of its soups and other products in 2009 and 2010. During that time Morrison initiated an aggressive advertising campaign against the General Mills–owned soup maker Progresso. She also combated falling sales caused by the 2008 global financial crisis by introducing promotions and temporary price discounts on select Campbell products.

In October 2010 Morrison was named executive vice president and COO and elected to Campbell's board of directors after it was announced that she would succeed Conant as CEO following his retirement in 2011. Morrison's appointment was generally applauded on Wall Street, though some questioned whether she would be a good leader for Campbell due to her insider status and central role in the company's low-sodium push, which ultimately failed to increase sales and attract new customers. Morrison nonetheless called her promotion "the achievement of a lifelong dream," as quoted by Sarah Skidmore for the Associated Press (28 Sep. 2010). As COO she led all of Campbell's global businesses and oversaw corporate strategy, marketing, and research and development. She also began working with a new senior leadership team to develop a strategic plan for Campbell's future growth.

On August 1, 2011, Morrison officially succeeded Conant as Campbell's president and CEO, becoming the first female chief executive and the twelfth leader in the company's history. Since stepping into her role, Morrison has focused heavily on boosting Campbell's sales and increasing its global presence through brand building and innovation in the wake of declining soup sales and increased competition from other food companies. She has launched an overhaul of Campbell's soup products in efforts to improve flavor and has focused on targeting a younger consumer demographic by introducing dozens of new products. "Sodium reduction is important," she explained to Martinne Geller for Reuters (12 July 2011, online), "but we have to do other things, like taste and more culinary credentials."

Morrison ultimately hopes to develop Campbell into one of the greatest companies in the world. She explained to *Knowledge@Wharton*, "I love what I do. I get up every day wanting to go to work. There was a dawning on me a couple of years ago, that it wasn't about just getting to be CEO, it was about building a great company and bringing the people of Campbell's to a whole different level. That was enormously exciting. It was a turning point for me [to realize] that it wasn't just about me, it was about the company."

In addition to serving on Campbell's board, Morrison is a member of the boards of the Consumer Goods Forum, the Grocery Manufacturers Association, and Students in Free Enterprise (SIFE), a nonprofit organization dedicated to making a positive impact on communities through the application of business concepts and principles. She is also a cofounder and board member of the Healthy Weight Commitment Foundation and serves as chair of the Grocery Manufacturers Association's health and wellness committee. Morrison has been named to *Fortune* magazine's annual list of the fifty most powerful women in business every year since 1999, ranking twenty-first in 2011, and is a regular participant in the women's mentoring program run by the magazine and the US State Department. She was named *Snack Food & Wholesale Bakery* magazine's Executive of the Year (2003) and has received the Legal Momentum Aiming High Award (2007) and *Philadelphia* magazine's Trailblazer Award (2010), among others. In 2001 she was inducted into the Academy of Women Achievers of the YWCA of New York.

PERSONAL LIFE

Morrison resides in Princeton, New Jersey, with her husband, Tom, an investment banker. She has two grown daughters, Michelle and Kelly. She has publicly expressed gratitude for the sacrifices her family has made to accommodate her career. A voracious reader, she tries to read at least one book per week.

SUGGESTED READING

Brady, Diane, and Matthew Boyle. "Campbell's Recipe for a CEO Yields Denise Morrison." *Bloomberg Businessweek*. Bloomberg, 23 June 2011. Web. 3 Apr. 2012.

Cox, Caroline. "Denise Morrison—Campbell Soup Company's First Female CEO." *Little Pink Book*. Pink Street, July 2011. Web. 3 Apr. 2012.

"From Soup to Negligee: Success According to Victoria Secret's Lori Greeley and Campbell Soup's Denise Morrison." *Knowledge@Wharton*. Wharton School of the University of Pennsylvania, 2 Mar. 2011. Web. 3 Apr. 2012.

Hymowitz, Carol. "Raising Women to Be Leaders: The Four Sullivan Sisters Learned to Work Early, Aim High, and Try Again." *Wall Street Journal* 12 Feb. 2007: B1–3.

Turvett, Barbara. "Get Ready for Work." *Working Mother* May 2008: 83.

—*Chris Cullen*

Dustin Moskovitz

Born: May 22, 1984
Occupation: Cofounder of Facebook and Asana

In 2004, at the age of nineteen, Dustin Moskovitz—along with Mark Zuckerberg and a handful of other Harvard University students—cofounded Facebook, the social-networking site that now has 500 million active users worldwide. In September 2011 *Forbes* valued Moskovitz's net worth at $3.5 billion, making him the world's youngest billionaire. (Zuckerberg, whose net worth is $17.5 billion, is eight days older than Moskovitz.) The story of Facebook's creation was dramatized in the film *The Social Network* (2010), which starred Jesse Eisenberg as Zuckerberg and Joseph Mazzello as Moskovitz. Moskovitz served as Facebook's vice president of engineering until 2008, when he cofounded Asana, a company that seeks to improve the efficiency with which people work together. "Asana wants people to live in this app throughout their work day . . . ," Sarah Lacy wrote for the website *TechCrunch*. "Like Facebook, Asana sees its eventual customer base as, well, everyone."

EARLY LIFE

Dustin Aaron Moskovitz was born on May 22, 1984 to Richard A. Moskovitz, a psychiatrist, and Nancy Siegel. He grew up in Ocala, Florida, where he attended Vanguard High School, graduating in 2002. At Vanguard he was in the International Baccalaureate (IB) program, which at the time was directed by Sara Dassance. In an e-mail message to Bill Thompson for the *Ocala Star-Banner* (21 Mar. 2011), Dassance recalled the young Moskovitz: "Dustin was obviously very bright, but I would not have predicted his fame and fortune based on the 17-year-old I knew. Some students put a lot of pressure and stress on themselves—usually needlessly—to succeed and get the top grades. Dustin appeared more relaxed and balanced, enjoying his life and his friends."

DEVELOPING FACEBOOK AT HARVARD

In 2002 Moskovitz entered Harvard University, in Cambridge, Massachusetts. In November 2003 his roommate and fellow sophomore Mark Zuckerberg, in a prank that brought him much notoriety on campus, created Facemash—a website that displayed photos of two Harvard students at a time and allowed visitors to click on the photo they found more attractive. Harvard officials quickly summoned Zuckerberg, accusing him of illegally using Harvard's student ID photos and violating students' privacy. Zuckerberg, who was let off with a warning, instantly acquired a reputation at Harvard as a programming genius. That month he was approached by three Harvard students—Divya Narendra

Araya Diaz/Getty Images for TechCrunch

and the twin brothers Cameron and Tyler Win-klevoss—who asked him to join their project, HarvardConnection, which was to be a social-networking website for the school's students. While Zuckerberg worked on that, he also de-voted time to his own project: putting the fresh-man directory (called "the facebook") online. "I just thought that being able to have access to different people's profiles would be interesting," Zuckerberg told John Cassidy for the *New Yorker* (15 May 2006). "Obviously, there's no way you can get access to that stuff unless people are throwing up profiles, so I wanted to make an ap-plication that would allow people to do that, to share as much information as they wanted while having control over what they put up." After a week of nearly nonstop work, Zuckerberg put up the site, Thefacebook.com, on February 4, 2004. (The following year the site dropped "the" and became known simply as "Facebook.") "It was a normal night in the dorm," Moskovitz told Cassi-dy. "When Mark finished the site, we told a cou-ple of friends. And then one of them suggested putting it on the Kirkland House [undergraduate residence] online mailing list, which was, like, three hundred people. And, once they did that, several dozen people joined, and then they were telling people at the other houses. By the end of the night, we were, like, actively watching the registration process. Within twenty-four hours, we had somewhere between twelve hundred and fifteen hundred registrants." Before the month was up, Zuckerberg was getting e-mails from students at other universities who wanted access

to Facebook. Zuckerberg recruited Moskovitz, an economics major who had worked part-time at a Harvard computer lab, to help him expand the site, first to Columbia, Stanford, and Yale Universities, and then, within months, to dozens of other schools nationwide.

FACEBOOK MOVES TO SILICON VALLEY

After the end of Moskovitz's sophomore year, in June 2004, when Facebook had 150,000 regis-tered student users, Moskovitz, Zuckerberg, and their roommate Andrew McCollum moved to Silicon Valley, in California, the nation's tech-nology mecca. Renting a house in Palo Alto that they called "Casa Facebook," they worked as long as sixteen hours per day on maintaining the website. During the summer—when most stu-dents were not even in school—Facebook con-tinued to grow rapidly, and by September the site had 250,000 registered users. Moskovitz and his housemates, who were twenty years old or so at the time, decided not to return to Harvard and to focus instead on expanding Facebook to include more colleges. That would require a lot of their time, a great deal of space on computer serv-ers—and a considerable amount of money. In 2004, while still on the East Coast, Zuckerberg had a meeting with Sean Parker, the cofounder of Napster, a highly popular (and illegal) music-sharing website. In Palo Alto the two met again, on the street, by chance. Soon Parker began in-troducing Zuckerberg to major venture capital-ists. The first significant investment in the site was $500,000 from Peter Thiel, the founder of the online payment service PayPal; the second, which came in May 2005 from Jim Breyer of the firm Accel Partners, was $12.7 million. By that time eight hundred colleges were on Facebook. By the end of the year, the site—after permitting those as young as thirteen to join and allowing users to put up as many photos as they liked—had more than five million registered users.

In two years, by the end of 2007, that num-ber had grown nearly tenfold, with Facebook now providing its services to 50 million users. Report-edly, Viacom offered to buy Facebook for $750 million, and Yahoo! made a bid of $1 billion, but both offers were rejected. To Zuckerberg and his partners—Moskovitz, Chief Technology Officer Adam D'Angelo, and others—money was less important than the long-term development of what they saw as an increasingly indispensable social network with tentacles in nearly every as-pect of its users' lives. In October 2007 Moskov-itz, in his capacity as Facebook's vice president of engineering, made an announcement at a cell-phone convention in San Francisco, California: his company was introducing a mobile version of Facebook for BlackBerry users. In most technol-ogy circles, that development was seen as a "win-win" scenario: Research in Motion, the company that manufactures the BlackBerry Smartphone, would see its product become more appealing to younger people, and Facebook would get millions of older members. Speaking at the conference, as quoted by Ryan Kim in the *San Francisco Chronicle* (25 Oct. 2007), the twenty-three-year-old Moskovitz said, "I believe mobile is the next frontier in social networking." (The iPhone, Apple's version of the "smartphone," had come on the market only a few months earlier.) By the second half of 2008, Facebook was available in two dozen languages and had 100 million active users, and the company itself had grown to seven hundred employees.

STARTING ASANA

Meanwhile, by early 2008 the relationship between Zuckerberg and Moskovitz, according to some reports, had become severely strained. As a result Moskovitz no longer wanted to be affiliated with Facebook and asked that his title of vice president be dropped and his official company biography and photo be removed from the Facebook site. While Zuckerberg and Moskovitz had been known to argue—sometimes passionately—with each other, the latest disagreement was seen as unprecedented. *Valley Wag* (23 Apr. 2008), a Silicon Valley gossip and news blog, speculated that one clue about the rift could be found in a 2005 Denver University newspaper article in which Moskovitz was referred to as Facebook's "No Longer Expendable Programmer." That mock title, an inside joke, seemed to allude to Zuckerberg's having referred to Moskovitz as "expendable" and as "a soldier" during Facebook's legal battles with the Winklevoss twins, the founders of the rival social-network site ConnectU. "Here's a theory: Back in 2005, Zuckerberg must have convinced Moskovitz to laugh off the slight," the *Valley Wag* reporter wrote. "Could the final stages of the legal process [have] turned up evidence that persuaded Moskovitz Zuckerberg wasn't joking?" Speculation aside, Moskovitz and another Facebook officer, Justin Rosenstein, had been planning to form a start-up company, Asana, and in October 2008 Moskovitz announced that he was leaving Facebook. (Moskovitz's $3.5 billion net worth comes principally from his 6 percent stake in Facebook.)

It did not take long for Moskovitz and Rosenstein to raise funds for Asana—$1.2 million to start—from an impressive list of investors: Ron Conway, Peter Thiel, Mitch Kapor, Owen van Natta, Sean Parker, and Jed Stremel, a former director for mobile technology at Facebook. Then, in November 2009, Moskovitz closed talks with other investors, from whom he raised $9 million. In addition to Rosenstein, two other Asana staffers, S. Alex Smith and David Braginsky, came from Facebook. Speaking to Scott Duke Harris for the *San Jose (California) Mercury News* (25 Nov. 2009), Rosenstein said that at Facebook

he and Moskovitz, as team leaders, had struggled—sometimes unsuccessfully—with "keeping everyone on the same page." Although e-mail, wikis, meetings, and other such tools and methods were helpful, "not a day went by when there wasn't some miscommunication or misunderstanding that slowed down production." The expressed goal of Asana is to minimize or eliminate such problems by allowing individuals and companies to collaborate more effectively. (Harris reported that "asana" is "a Sanskrit word for a yoga posture to enhance well-being.") After much anticipation, in February 2011 Asana unveiled a video on its website to demonstrate the basic ideas and functionality of its product—which was in an early, so-called "private beta" test stage. Sarah Lacy wrote, "You can tell Asana was cocreated by one of the founders of Facebook. There's that almost hubristic mission: To fix how people work together and make the global work place a better, more efficient, less frustrating place. . . . It's about helping people work together more efficiently—cutting out reliance on email, cutting down on the need for those endless meetings, easily assigning and tracking tasks in one instance that is always up to date. . . . Moskovitz and Rosenstein are clear: If they don't accomplish that, they have failed." *Forbes* magazine (Mar. 2011) reported that Moskovitz had declared the "values" of the new company to be "pragmatism," "being a mensch," "admitting when you're wrong," and "chill-ness." In November 2011 Asana launched its product, "a web application that connects everyone with what's going on, their shared priorities, and who owns each part of the effort," according to the Asana website, on which customers can sign up for the application.

THE SOCIAL NETWORK

David Fincher's 2010 film, *The Social Network*, which was nominated for an Academy Award for best picture, reconstructed the events surrounding Facebook's founding and the resulting legal entanglements. On the website *Quora* (16 July 2010), Moskovitz gave his thoughts on the movie: "It is interesting to see my past rewritten in a way that emphasizes things that didn't matter (like the Winklevosses, who I've still never even met and had no part in the work we did to create the site over the past 6 years) and leaves out things that really did (like the many other people in our lives at the time, who supported us in innumerable ways). Other than that, it's just cool to see a dramatization of history. A lot of exciting things happened in 2004, but mostly we just worked a lot and stressed out about things."

PERSONAL LIFE AND PHILANTHROPY

Moskovitz lives in San Francisco with his girlfriend, Cari Tuna, a Yale University graduate and former *Wall Street Journal* reporter. Moskovitz has signed on, along with sixty-eight other billionaires (including Zuckerberg), with the Giving Pledge. Started in 2010 by Warren Buffett and Bill and Melinda Gates, that project calls on billionaires to give at least 50 percent of their wealth to charity during their lifetimes or to arrange for that amount to be donated after their deaths. Moskovitz has called Tuna his "partner" in philanthropy.

SUGGESTED READING

Asana. Asana, n. d. Web. Jan. 2012.

Cassidy, John. "The Online Life: Me Media." *New Yorker*. Condé Nast, 15 May 2006. Web. Jan. 2012.

"Dustin Moskvitz." *Forbes: Forbes 400 Richest Americans*. Forbes.com LLC, 2012. Web. Jan. 2012.

Schonfeld, Erick. "Facebook Co-Founder Dustin Moskovitz Raises $9 Million for New Collaboration Startup, Asana." *TechCrunch*. AOL Inc. 24 Nov. 2009. Web. Jan. 2012.

—*Dmitry Kiper*

Courtesy of Helen Jones Photography

Dambisa Moyo

Born: September 15, 1969
Occupation: Economist, author

The African-born economist Dambisa Moyo quickly gained both popularity and notoriety with the publication of her first book, *Dead Aid: Why Aid Is Not Working and How There Is a Better Way for Africa* (2009). That year *Time* magazine placed Moyo on its list of the "100 Most Influential People in the World," and the World Economic Forum named Moyo, who turned 40 in 2009, among its Forum of Young Global Leaders. In her book, to the delight of some and the disapproval of others, Moyo proposed cutting off government-to-government aid to Africa within five years. She proposed replacing aid—which she saw as promoting a cycle of dependency, governmental corruption, and the very poverty it is intended to eradicate—with free-market solutions, such as fewer trade restrictions and more "microloans," or small loans given directly to entrepreneurs. Not least significant in Moyo's argument was the fact—brought up by everyone who wrote about her—that the case against aid to Africa was being made by an African. Moyo's second book, *How the West Was Lost: Fifty Years of Economic Folly—And the Stark Choices Ahead* (2011), analyzed the ways in which Europe and the United States had lost ground economically. In addition to her books, Moyo has written for publications including the *Wall Street Journal* and the London *Independent*.

EARLY LIFE AND EDUCATION

Dambisa Moyo was born on September 15, 1969, in Lusaka, the capital of Zambia, a landlocked nation in southern Africa. Her father, who obtained a doctorate in linguistics, founded and ran the Integrity Foundation, an organization aimed at fighting governmental corruption in Africa. Her mother later chaired the Indo-Zambia Bank, a financial partnership between Zambia and India. In the pages of the Canadian newspaper *National Post* (June 2, 2009), in a piece excerpted from *Dead Aid*, Moyo shed light on her family's history and conditions in Zambia: "In July, 1970, 90 students graduated from the University of Zambia, in the country's capital, Lusaka. Among them were the university's first black graduates, and my parents were two of them. They were both studying for undergraduate degrees—my father reading linguistics, and my mother English. They came from different tribes, from different parts of rural colonial Africa: my father, the son of a miner in apartheid South Africa; my mother, the daughter of a man who would later train to be a teacher. My mother did not speak my father's language, and hence they mainly conversed in English. They met and married while still students. Zambia had been independent from British colonial rule for just six years, and the excitement at the prospect of what amazing things lay ahead was palpable. Although, upon graduation, my mother had 11 job offers, my father wished to continue his studies. He was offered a scholarship at the University of California at Los Angeles, and very soon afterwards my parents packed up my sister and me and decamped to America. Our move was all planned. My parents' goal was for my father to further his education, and then return to Africa. The 1970s were an exciting time to be African. Many of our nations had just achieved independence, and with that came a deep sense of dignity, self-respect and hope for the future. My parents lived, worked and studied in the United States for eight years, and upon my father's PhD graduation in 1978, they promptly moved back to Zambia, convinced that their future, and the futures of their children, lay in their homeland."

Although neither of her parents was an economist, the economics of Africa was a frequent topic of discussion at the family's dinner table. There was also lighter fare in the household: according to Mary Ann Sieghart, writing for *Newsweek* (February 21, 2011), Moyo recalled that while growing up she "watched all the most amazing American and British TV—*Dallas, Dynasty, Fawlty Towers*." After earning a BS degree in chemistry in Lusaka (some sources state that she earned it in the United States), Moyo left Zambia after the summer of 1990, when an attempted coup against then-president Kenneth Kaunda temporarily closed the university. Moyo then got a scholarship to American University, in Washington, DC, and left her native country, thinking that she would return eventually. Upon receiving an MBA degree from American, she worked as a consultant in the Washington, DC, office of the World Bank, from 1993 to 1995. She then enrolled in the Kennedy School of Government at Harvard University, in Massachusetts, where she earned a master's degree in public administration in 1997. Next she moved to England to attend Oxford University. "While away, I missed key moments in my country's history—our political move from one-party state to multiparty democracy in 1991, the overhaul of our economy from socialism to capitalism and the tragic advent of the HIV-AIDS epidemic," Moyo wrote in the Canadian *National Post* essay. "Although pulled by family and cultural ties in Zambia, every time I looked, prospects for my personal development appeared to diminish. There seemed to be fewer and fewer reasons for me to return, and more and more reasons for me to stay away. I could not help feeling that job opportunities commensurate with my education and experience lay not at home, but abroad. Those jobs that did exist at home were in an environment laden with creaking bureaucracy." Moyo, "like many other educated Africans," she wrote, felt that her "country continues to flounder in a seemingly never-ending cycle of corruption, disease, poverty and aid-dependency."

CAREER

In 2001, after receiving a doctorate in economics from Oxford University, Moyo joined the London, England, office of the investment-banking and securities firm Goldman Sachs, where she was put in charge of economic research and strategy for sub-Saharan Africa. One of her primary responsibilities was to help developing nations in Africa issue bonds so that they could raise funds. (She also worked with the governments of Israel and Turkey.) African national leaders and financial ministers, Moyo concluded, were not interested in lobbying investors to buy bonds so long as those leaders had the option of acquiring foreign aid. In 2008 Moyo attended the World Economic Forum, in Davos, Switzerland, an invitation-only conference for highly influential business, political, academic, and other leaders; that event inspired her to speak out about her views. "It was at a party to raise money for Africans," she told Deborah Solomon for the *New York Times* (February 22, 2009), "and there were no Africans in the room, except for me." Talking to Solomon just before the publication of her first book, Moyo was asked what she thought had prevented Africans from obtaining economic stability. "I believe it's largely aid," she said. "You get the corruption—historically, leaders have stolen the [aid] money without penalty—and you get the dependency [on aid], which kills entrepreneurship. You also disenfranchise African citizens, because the government is beholden to foreign donors and not accountable to its people."

In *Dead Aid: Why Aid Is Not Working and How There Is a Better Way for Africa* (2009), Moyo pointed out that the more than $1 trillion in development-related aid transferred since the end of World War II from wealthy nations to poor countries in Africa has not raised Africans' standard of living. Not only has the aid not helped, she argued, but in many cases it has made the situation much worse; and countries that have accepted aid are in a vicious circle of dependency, corruption, market distortion, and more poverty. Moyo noted that between 1970 and 1998, when an extraordinary amount of aid money went to Africa, the continent's poverty rate increased from 11 percent to 66 percent. "While her analysis of the history of aid is very compelling," a reviewer wrote for the London *Guardian* (February 5, 2009), "it's the practical solutions . . . which mark her book out." The reviewer highlighted Moyo's proposed solutions: that African countries issue debt bonds on the international markets and thereby boost their credit ratings; that trade barriers be relaxed, thereby making it easier for African nations to trade; that African countries reach out to more large nations to seek investments of the kind China has made in Africa; and that the entrepreneurial spirit be encouraged in Africa through such modern efforts as microfinance. (Moyo did not criticize humanitarian or emergency aid; her concern is primarily with government-to-government aid.)

Moyo also took aim at celebrity champions of aid to Africa, with the singer Bono prominent among them; the book's title is an answer to Live Aid, the high-profile, celebrity-driven 1985 music concert whose proceeds went to famine relief in Africa. Moyo asked rhetorically, as quoted by Aida Edermariam in the London *Guardian* (February 19, 2009), "How would British people feel if tomorrow Michael Jackson started telling them how they should get out of the housing crisis? Or if Amy Winehouse started to give the US government advice about the credit crunch? And was listened to?"

A reviewer for the *Economist* (March 14, 2009) pointed out that much of what Moyo wrote had already been argued by writers and thinkers including William Easterly, Paul Collier, and Robert Calderisi. "Yet," the reviewer continued, "the intellectual arguments about aid are still conducted largely within a small circle of Western white men. So it is good to welcome a new voice to the debate, and a black African woman too. . . . It is remarkable that so few voices have been raised in Africa, supposedly the main beneficiary of the world's largesse, about how the aid money should be spent, or even whether it should be received at all. Unfortunately, Ms. Moyo's contribution ends there, for *Dead Aid* does not move the debate along much. Yes, she has joined the chorus of disapproval—and that in itself might surprise a few diehards who think that Africans should just be grateful for the aid and shut up. But her arguments are scarcely original and her plodding prose makes her the least stylish of the critics. Moreover, she overstates her case, almost to the point of caricature. There is almost nobody left, even in the aid lobby, who seriously thinks that bilateral (government-to-government) aid is the sole answer to world poverty, as she suggests. 'Trade not aid' is only one of several newish mantras among aidniks that seem to have passed her by. Nonetheless, Ms. Moyo is right to argue that the rich world—and Africa—should now focus on other ways of helping poor countries. Ms. Moyo shows how some countries, such as Ghana, have successfully tapped the bond markets for funds. She also has good discussions on the virtues of microfinance, venture capital and liberalising trade. By concentrating on these three, African governments might well raise more money on their own; some might even lessen their dependency on aid."

If the review in the *Economist* was mixed, other assessments were almost purely negative. Madeleine Bunting wrote for the London *Guardian* (February 14, 2009) that the book is "poorly argued," particularly the sections having to do with the political economy of Africa: unlike the many Asian countries to which Moyo looked as models, Bunting maintained, many African countries did not have "a strong, interventionist

state that nurtured industry and an elite who invested in their own country." According to Bunting, Moyo was too optimistic about the power of the private sector and free market but was right in saying that there are aspects of aid that are not helpful, such as the continued protectionism of both the United States and the European Union. Like many other reviewers, Bunting pronounced Moyo's call to end aid to Africa in five years "irresponsible."

Moyo's second book, *How the West Was Lost: Fifty Years of Economic Folly—And the Stark Choices Ahead* (2011), was less controversial than her first but also less popular, both with critics and the public. The book focuses on the economic failures of the West and successes of China. Consumer culture, Moyo argued in the book, has led Westerners down the wrong path, to overborrowing, overspending, overinvestment in unaffordable state-run pension plans, and too great an emphasis on investing in homes, which Moyo deems unproductive. In addition, she wrote, Western nations have failed to encourage young people to study math and science in college and pursue careers in those fields, which are needed to advance a nation as a whole. By contrast, Moyo expressed admiration for China's spirit of hard work and entrepreneurialism and its leaders' ability to make tough decisions quickly—the latter mostly a result of the fact that China is not a democratic country, as pointed out by many reviewers. Perhaps most strikingly, the book concludes with Moyo imagining possible scenarios in which the United States would become a "socialist welfare state" or default on its debt.

Most reviewers found plenty to disagree with in *How the West Was Lost*. Sean O'Grady pointed out for the London *Independent* (February 6, 2011) that 25 years ago there was a similar buzz surrounding Japan and its supposedly inevitable economic takeover of the West. Soon, however, Japan found itself mired in economic stagnation. "An absurd real estate boom, dodgy banks and unproductive over-investment were features of Japan in the 1980s and 1990s," O'Grady wrote, "and are features of China now, to a greater or lesser degree. Of course, the Japanese still boast world-leading companies, they are rich and have an enviably orderly society. But world domination? No, reader-san." Then O'Grady addressed the China issue directly: "Unlike Moyo, I suspect that the Chinese economy is not as formidable as it seems; it is too remote from market signals, still semi-command in structure and has no free press or political parties to deal with shortcomings and corruptions. In other words it is not the West that is too democratic, but China that's not democratic enough to be economically efficient."

Perhaps the harshest criticism of the book was issued by the *Economist* (January 22, 2011).

A reviewer for that magazine attacked Moyo's economic analysis: "In comparing America's economy with China's, for instance, whether you convert yuan into dollars at market exchange rates or after adjusting for purchasing power matters a lot. Measuring at purchasing-power parity makes the gap in GDP [gross domestic product] and living standards look narrower. This explains a great deal of the difference between two sets of figures that Ms. Moyo cites. Yet she does not mention it. This is basic stuff. Much else in elementary economics also gets mangled here." Furthermore, the reviewer argued, Moyo made gross factual errors. For example, she wrote that General Motors had been bought by the Italian car company Fiat, which in actuality had acquired a 25 percent stake in Chrysler.

PERSONAL LIFE

Sieghart acknowledged that Moyo had sometimes faced condescension in her field because of her gender and origin. When asked if that bothered her, Moyo laughed and told Sieghart, "My parents just didn't get the memo because they've always raised us to be color, gender, and country-blind, and so if people are going to address my arguments based on where I'm from or because I happen to come in the packaging I come in, that's not my issue, that's their issue. Address the point; don't be patronizing." She went on to say, "My parents could have been like, 'Woe is me'; instead they just forged on, and that's how we were raised. They could have given us a lot of reasons: you're a girl child; you're in Africa; you're in one of the world's poorest economies; forget it, you're never going to go to Harvard; you're never going to go to Oxford; you're never going to write books."

Moyo sits on the board of directors of the Swedish oil company Lundin Petroleum, the beer company SABMiller, and the financial-services provider Barclays. Moyo, who travels frequently, has apartments in both London and New York City. She is at work on a third book.

SUGGESTED READING

Bunting, Madeleine. "The Road to Ruin." *Guardian*. Guardian News and Media, 13 Feb. 2009. Web. 21 Dec. 2011.

Clarke-Jones, Joanna. "A Gift that Keeps on Giving." *Guardian*. Guardian News and Media, 5 Feb. 2009. Web. 21 Dec. 2011.

"How the Reader Was Lost; Economic Folly." *Economist* 22 Jan. 2011, Books & Art. Print.

Moyo, Dambisa. "How to Fix Africa." *National Post* 2 June 2009: A14. Print.

Solomon, Deborah. "The Anti-Bono." *New York Times*, New York Times, Feb. 22 2009. Web. 21 Dec. 2011.

"Voice of Disenchantment: Foreign Aid." *Economist* 14 Mar. 2009, Books & Art. Print.

SELECTED WORKS

Dead Aid: Why Aid Is Not Working and How There Is a Better Way for Africa, 2009; *How the West Was Lost: Fifty Years of Economic Folly—And the Stark Choices Ahead*, 2011

—*Dmitry Kiper*

Kate and Laura Mulleavy

Born: Kate, February 11, 1979; Laura, August 31, 1980
Occupation: Founders of fashion label Rodarte

Sisters Kate and Laura Mulleavy are the founders of the Los Angeles–based fashion label Rodarte. The avant-garde Rodarte (pronounced "ro-DAR-tay," based on their mother's maiden name) was once described by Meredith Bryan for the *New York Observer* (18 Feb. 2009) as "the fashion equivalent of a Basquiat: people in the know really love it, but to everyone else it's inscrutable or a little bit ugly." Without any formal training in fashion design, the sisters built one of the most sought-after names in the fashion business in just a few short years, mounting their first show in the fall of 2005, while they were both still in their twenties.

Described by Susan Morgan for the *New York Times* (7 Sep. 2008) as "gifted and indefatigable cultural hunter-gatherers," the Mulleavy sisters draw inspiration from a multitude of sources, including the landscape of their home state of California, Japanese horror films, apocalyptic fantasies, and the novels of John Steinbeck. Fittingly, they prize layers in their materials as well, and they have been known to develop new and creative ways of manipulating textiles to serve their vision. For their spring 2010 collection, presented in the fall of 2009, the sisters developed an elaborate story line in which a live woman is incinerated before being born again as a California condor, a large vulture native to the state; one particularly noted detail among the ravaged textiles in the collection was shoes with claws that served as stiletto heels.

But the Mulleavys' appeal has grown far beyond the fashion world. Their roving aesthetic has captured the imaginations of filmmaker Darren Aronofsky, for whom they designed costumes for the 2010 Academy Award–winning film *Black Swan*, and celebrated architect Frank Gehry, with whom they collaborated on a space-age production of the opera *Don Giovanni* at the Los Angeles Philharmonic in 2012, among others. Their fans include *Star Wars* director George Lucas, and their gowns have been worn by such women as actors Cate Blanchett and Natalie Portman (an early admirer), musician Joanna Newsom, and the First Lady of the United States, Michelle Obama.

Getty Images

EARLY LIFE

The Mulleavy sisters were born in Pasadena, California, Kate on February 11, 1979, and Laura on August 31, 1980. Their mother, Victoria, who is of Mexican-Italian descent, is an artist; their father, William, is a botanist who is credited with discovering a new species of fungus. The free-spirited Mulleavys, who lived in a cabin in a redwood forest after they were first married, have had a significant influence on their daughters' work. Victoria taught them to sew and introduced them to cinema (the sisters cite the 1938 Katherine Hepburn film *Bringing Up Baby* and the 1939 classic *Gone with the Wind* as inspirations for their early interest in clothes), while William instilled in them a love of the natural world.

The sisters spent most of their childhood in Aptos, California, outside the city of Santa Cruz, though they spent two years in Alabama when their father was hired to develop a new method for growing morels there. In high school, the Mulleavys devoured fashion magazines like *Vogue* and *Harper's Bazaar* but never considered fashion a viable career. "Fashion didn't seem like a reality," Laura told Amanda Fortini for the *New Yorker* (18 Jan. 2010). "It didn't seem like an attainable job, like something you could do." At her high-school graduation, Laura was named valedictorian of her class, and Kate wrote her commencement address.

Both Mulleavys attended the University of California, Berkeley, where Kate studied art history and Laura began in a premedical program, though she later switched her major to English literature. The sisters, who had learned to sew at an early age, signed up for a costume-design course together, but both later dropped it. They graduated together, Kate staying a semester longer and Laura leaving a semester early, in January 2002. Unsure of their next step, the Mulleavys moved back to their family home in Pasadena.

For a little over a year, Kate and Laura cycled through various creative obsessions. Later, the Mulleavys would tell reporters that all they did was watch horror movies.

FASHION "FAIRY TALE"

In 2004, the Mulleavy sisters decided to pool their resources and create their first fashion line. Kate contributed the money she had made from selling her record-album collection, and Laura chipped in her earnings from waitressing at a local restaurant. (Laura would continue to waitress for the next several years.) In total, they had a little under $17,000. Over the next six months, working at their kitchen table, the Mulleavys created seven dresses and three coats.

For their first line, the Mulleavys drew inspiration from their California home. The dresses were flowing and delicate, featuring classical lines with artistic flourishes; one gown was modeled after a redwood tree, with intricately folded pleats and frayed edges that resembled bark. The Mulleavys made paper miniatures of each piece that fit inside a paper armoire and sent one such set of "paper dolls" to Cameron Silver, the owner of Decades, a vintage couture retailer in Los Angeles. Impressed, Silver agreed to meet with the Mulleavys and was soon on the phone with his various contacts in New York. With Silver's blessing, the Mulleavys packed up their collection in a cardboard box and flew to the East Coast in early 2005. They brought their dresses to the offices of *Women's Wear Daily* and, with unprecedented good fortune, found their designs featured on the cover of the magazine three days later.

After returning to Los Angeles, the Mulleavys received a visit from the high priestess of fashion herself, *Vogue* editor in chief Anna Wintour. Wintour, who would become one of their earliest (and certainly most influential) champions, gave the Mulleavys a piece of advice that they held dear. "What you are doing is very personal," the characteristically stoic Wintour told them, as the Mulleavys have recalled to various sources. "You should keep it that way."

RISE OF RODARTE

In the next five years, the name Rodarte appeared in *Vogue* dozens of times, though the collections often spoke for themselves. The Mulleavys mounted their first show—their spring 2006 collection—in the fall of 2005, drawing inspiration from tree-bark formations and the youth of Northern California in the 1960s. Their fall 2006 collection featured soft waves of organza and chiffon, as well as expertly constructed pleated trousers. The illusion of floating did not come easily; one gown alone took over 150 hours to complete. Laird Borrelli, a fashion critic for *Style* (8 Feb. 2006), called the collection "poetry in motion." Pieces from the fall 2006 collection were featured at a pop-up store housed by the chic Parisian boutique Colette on the Rue Saint-Honoré, where Karl Lagerfeld, fashion icon and creative director at Chanel, bought a Rodarte gown for his "muse" Amanda Harlech. Lagerfeld was so impressed with the Mulleavy sisters that he invited them to an exclusive gathering at his apartment that night, where they were photographed by fashion editor Suzy Menkes. The party and the photograph were of great significance in the fashion world; the Mulleavys had been anointed.

The Rodarte spring 2007 collection was a departure from the Mulleavys' previous designs. Inspired by the bold art of the late Robert Rauschenberg, the sisters sought to create maximum visual impact with their work. The collection featured exaggerated bows and collars, variations on the eighteenth-century fashions depicted in the portraits of Thomas Gainsborough. The Rodarte fall 2007 collection saw the sisters' further experimentation with shape and volume as well as material. They collaborated with crystal manufacturer Swarovski and molded fake leather into a tailored pair of pants. While the workmanship was widely admired, some editors criticized the designs as unwearable.

For their spring 2008 collection, the Mulleavys were inspired by a trip to Japan and the films of director Yasujirō Ozu. They then turned to Japanese and South Korean horror films for their fall 2008 collection, pieces from which have been on display at the Museum of Contemporary Art in Los Angeles. For the dark designs, the sisters looked for textiles that resembled bandages covering an open wound. Laird Borrelli-Persson described for *Style* (5 Feb. 2008) what would become one of Rodarte's signature collections: "the gothic knitwear had a torn-web quality, and the tortuous, sadomasochistic shoes (a reworking of last season's) wrung winces from the audience, but the show was bigger than just that, more ambitious. String sculptures by the German-American artist Eva Hesse gave birth to the shaggy pieces with a primitive rag-doll look. Romantic, full-skirted cocktail numbers looked like they could have been painted by the Impressionist Edgar Degas."

The Rodarte spring 2009 collection boasted a more apocalyptic theme. The Mulleavys cited inspirations such as landscape paintings, the sculptor Olafur Eliasson, and photographs of the earth from space; the latter holds particular significance for the sisters, as they grew up near the famous Mount Wilson Observatory. While building their fall 2009 collection, the sisters worked with shoe designer Nicholas Kirkwood to design wrapped leather boots that would reach far up the thigh. The collection was architectural, evoking materials one might use to build a house—granite, slate, marble, concrete. The Mulleavys cited the dilapidated houses

alongside the California freeway as an inspiration. The pieces reflected the sisters' love of layering and manipulating materials; they have often expressed a desire to submit their designs to various natural processes, including sun bleaching, burning, and even burial.

This "ruined" notion was more fully explored in the Rodarte spring 2010 collection, in which the textiles used in the pieces were destroyed in a number of ways before they hit the runway. After being warped and wrapped, the finished pieces bore only a passing resemblance to what they once were. The sisters had worked with a film costumer to "age" the pieces. Inspired by the landscape of Death Valley, the Mulleavys created a narrative for their collection, featuring a woman who had been burned alive and then reborn as a California condor.

Rodarte's fall 2010 collection struck a much different note. After several collections of darkness, the Mulleavys ventured into the world of dreams. In an effort to explore their Mexican heritage, the sisters patched together textiles of various designs for a free-flowing arts-and-crafts effect. Inspired by a drive from El Paso to Marfa, Texas, near the Mexican border, the sisters wanted to pay homage to the country of their grandparents, but also to the horrors of the raging drug wars that loom large in the nearby city of Juárez. The Mulleavys used the word *sleepwalking* to describe the collection, and the effect was ghostly as models walked the runway by the flickering light of candles, their shoes (designed by Kirkwood) crafted to look like melting wax.

In 2011, Rodarte abandoned the more idiosyncratic dishevelment of past collections in favor of more classic silhouettes. Their spring 2011 collection featured dresses with cutaway shoulders and flattering, high-waisted trousers. The color palette reflected their memories of growing up in 1970s California; with a characteristic flourish, textiles and platforms were made to look like the faux-wood paneling that was popular during the era. For the fall 2011 collection, the sisters looked to the colors and landscape of the American Great Plains and the stunning visuals of Terence Malick's 1978 film masterpiece *Days of Heaven*.

While the previous Rodarte collection had featured predominantly muted tones, the spring 2012 collection was a vast departure. The sisters focused on colors drawn from the paintings of Vincent van Gogh and, as they told sources, from the forest depicted in Disney's 1959 animated film *Sleeping Beauty*; vibrant gold, deep purple, blue, and green dominated their well-received show. For their fall 2012 collection, the Mulleavys continued to experiment with more commercial wear. Their inspiration was the Australian outback, which Nicole Phelps noted for *Style* (14 Feb. 2012) "wasn't so far removed in spirit from last fall's homage to Terence Malick."

Critics cheered the duo's focus on retail-friendly sweaters and jackets, and fans of Rodarte's more eccentric pieces were satisfied with a new shoe design that featured sand inside a Plexiglas heel.

NOTABLE COLLABORATIONS, EXHIBITIONS, AND AWARDS

The Mulleavys, recommended by actress Natalie Portman, also designed the costumes for Darren Aronofsky's 2010 movie *Black Swan*. The sisters delved into ballet history to construct a tutu for Portman, the film's star, that many described as sculptural. *Black Swan*'s dark premise, a reworking of the classic *Swan Lake* alongside the gritty inner workings of the ballet world, seemed in line with the Mulleavys' interests, but uncharacteristically, the sisters did not turn to their favorite horror films for inspiration; instead, they studied Eva Hesse's "Accession II" sculpture, a metal cube with an open top that reveals an interior bristling with sharp teeth. "That in and of itself describes the ballet world to us perfectly," Laura told Venessa Lau for *Women's Wear Daily* (2 Dec. 2010). "It's perfect and beautiful and, yet, terrifying inside." Portman, who won an Oscar for her role in the film, wore a Rodarte gown to the Academy Awards that year.

In 2010, the Mulleavys worked with the composer Nico Muhly and the choreographer Benjamin Millipied to design costumes for a ballet called *Two Hearts*, which premiered with the New York City Ballet. They have also teamed up with clothing retailers, including Target, Gap, and Opening Ceremony, the latter collaboration in 2011 marking their first foray into menswear. Rodarte designs have been exhibited by several prestigious museums and galleries, including the Museum of Contemporary Art (MOCA) in Los Angeles, the Smithsonian Cooper-Hewitt National Design Museum in New York, the Fashion Institute of Technology Museum, and the Metropolitan Museum of Art's Costume Institute.

The Mulleavys have won a host of awards and honors for their work, including the Ecco Domani Fashion Foundation Award for emerging designers and the Council of Fashion Designers of America (CFDA) Award in 2009. In 2006, they were named runners-up in the CFDA/Vogue Fashion Fund competition, for which they were awarded $50,000. In 2008, Rodarte was the first American fashion house to be awarded the coveted Swiss Textiles Award. *Artforum* magazine reviewed their 2010 show *Quicktake: Rodarte* at the Cooper Hewitt Museum.

PERSONAL LIFE

The Mulleavy sisters are uncommonly close, sharing an e-mail address as well as a cell phone, and are known to finish each other's sentences. They are also notorious homebodies. Though they name Hollywood starlets such as Natalie Portman and Elle Fanning as close friends, the sisters rarely involve themselves in the goings-on of fashion's elite. Notably among fashion designers, the Mulleavys are not physical ambassadors of their own creations; in other words, they do not wear what they make, preferring T-shirts and jeans.

Their unusual creative process is visually captured in the book *Rodarte, Catherine Opie, Alec Soth* (2011), which features portraits of people wearing Rodarte designs as well as photographs of the California landscape, including a California condor, by photographers Opie and Soth. The Mulleavy sisters live with their parents in Pasadena and work out of a studio loft in downtown Los Angeles.

SUGGESTED READING

Borrelli, Laird. "Rodarte, Fall 2006: New York." *Style*. Condé Nast, 8 Feb. 2006. Web. 11 June 2012.

Borrelli-Persson, Laird. "Rodarte, Fall 2008: New York." *Style*. Condé Nast, 5 Feb. 2008. Web. 11 June 2012.

Bryan, Meredith. "Elijah Wood Gets Spurred at Rodarte! It's 'Artistic.'" *New York Observer*. New York Observer, 18 Feb. 2009. Web. 15 June 2012.

Fortini, Amanda. "Twisted Sisters: The Designers behind Rodarte." *New Yorker* 18 Jan. 2010: 32.

Lau, Venessa. "Kate and Laura Mulleavy's 'Swan' Song." *Women's Wear Daily* 2 Dec. 2010: 4.

Morgan, Susan. "Double Vision." *New York Times* 7 Sep. 2008: 74.

Phelps, Nicole. "Rodarte, Fall 2012: New York." *Style*. Condé Nast, 14 Feb. 2012. Web. 11 June 2012.

SELECTED WORKS

Rodarte, Catherine Opie, Alec Soth, 2011

—*Molly Hagan*

Mark Murphy

Born: July 13, 1955
Occupation: CEO for the Green Bay Packers

When Mark Hodge Murphy assumed his post as president and chief executive officer (CEO) of the National Football League's (NFL's) Green Bay Packers, in January 2008, he took over the reins of one of the unique franchises in all of sports. Unlike sports teams with high-profile owners, the Packers are owned by their fans, making them the only publicly owned major professional sports team in the United States. They also play in the smallest market of any US sports team and remain the last of the so-called small-town teams in the NFL. Despite those distinctions, the Packers have enjoyed more success than any other franchise in professional football history, with a record thirteen NFL league championships (including four Super Bowl titles), and have thrived economically, thanks to their unique ownership structure and one of the most rabid and passionate fan bases in professional sports. Packers fans are commonly called "cheese-heads," referring both to the foam "cheese" hats they wear on game day and to the high volume of cheese production in the state of Wisconsin.

Since arriving in Green Bay, Murphy, a former All-Pro safety for the Washington Redskins and a member of the National Football League Players Association (NFLPA) who previously served as the athletic director at Colgate University (1992–2003) and Northwestern University (2003–07), has worked to build on the Packers' longstanding success on and off the field by launching initiatives aimed at carrying the franchise into the future. In 2010, Murphy, who played on the Redskins' 1983 Super Bowl–winning team, became the first person to be a member of Super Bowl–winning franchises as both a player and a CEO, when the Packers defeated the Pittsburgh Steelers, 31–25, in Super Bowl XLV. Bob Harlan, Murphy's predecessor as Packers president and CEO, said about Murphy, as quoted by Jason Wilde for the *Wisconsin State Journal* (4 Dec. 2007), "He has a great understanding of the culture of the Green Bay Packers, the city, the fans, the corporate structure, the ownership . . . He's down to earth. . . . He doesn't bring an attitude with him. He's a calming influence."

EARLY LIFE AND EDUCATION

The older of two children, Murphy was born on July 13, 1955, in Fulton, New York. He moved several times growing up, spending part of his youth in Texas and New Jersey, before settling with his family in the Buffalo, New York, area, in 1970. Murphy's father, Hugh (known as "Big Murph"), worked as the director of labor relations for the Buffalo-based Roblin Steel Company, and his mother, Nancy, taught elementary school. Early on, Murphy learned the art of negotiating and the importance of building strong personal relationships from his father, who spent much of his time traveling around the country making compromises with unions on labor contracts. "I grew up around labor relations," he told Jerry Sullivan for the *Buffalo (New York) News* (18 Sep. 2010). "I remember thinking this was something I would like to do. My father understood both sides. He was the type who was respected by everybody. I remember talking to union people who said how much they appreciated my father and they felt he was fair to them."

Getty Images

Murphy developed a fondness for sports as a boy and grew up a fan of the NFL's Buffalo Bills. His father purchased Bills' season tickets, and Murphy frequently watched games at War Memorial Stadium, where the team played its home games until 1973. That year the Bills moved into Ralph Wilson Stadium, located in the Buffalo suburb of Orchard Park. Murphy attended Clarence High School, a public school outside of Buffalo, where he was a standout on the football, basketball, and baseball teams. His athletic talents were such that he was honored as the top all-around athlete in western New York by the *Buffalo Courier-Express* newspaper during his senior year. Coming out of high school, Murphy was courted to play professional baseball by several major-league teams, including the New York Mets and Pittsburgh Pirates, but he turned down those offers to attend Colgate University, a small, private liberal-arts college in Hamilton, New York, with a strong academic reputation.

At Colgate, Murphy was a four-year starter and a captain of the football and baseball teams. He also played on the basketball team during his freshman year before playing in Colgate's Noontime Hoops League for the rest of his college career. Despite being a multisport talent, Murphy made his collegiate mark in football. As a defensive back he became known for his toughness, intelligence, and competitiveness. During his junior season he established himself as one of the best defensive backs in the Eastern Collegiate Athletic Conference (ECAC) and was honored with Colgate's Hal W. Lahar Trophy, awarded annually to the team's most valuable defensive player. As a senior he helped lead Colgate to an 8–2 record under first-year head coach Fred Dunlap, and was selected to the All-ECAC First Team at defensive back. Former Colgate sports-information director Bob Cornell remembered Murphy as a "big, big defensive back," as he told John Pitarresi for the Utica, New York, *Observer-Dispatch* (4 Feb. 2011). "He was a tough . . . hard-nosed football player." During his time at Colgate, Murphy established the Hamilton Youth Basketball League and served for a time as its commissioner. He graduated from Colgate with an economics degree in 1977.

PLAYING CAREER

Standing six feet four and weighing 210 pounds, Murphy had the size, combined with toughness and smarts, to succeed in the NFL, but he lacked the prototypical speed for a player at his position. As a result, he was not taken in the 1977 NFL Draft. Eventually, the Redskins signed him as an undrafted rookie free agent, reportedly after the team's head coach George Allen "hid" him in a hotel room on draft day to prevent him from signing with other teams. Murphy signed a two-year contract with the Redskins that paid him $21,000 per year. Though Allen famously disdained rookies and was known to trade away many of his draft picks for veteran players, Murphy impressed the Redskins' coaching staff with his grit and intellect and was one of two rookies to be kept on the team's 1977 roster. Murphy spent the first two seasons of his NFL career in a backup role, serving as the Redskins' nickelback, or fifth defensive back, before earning a starting spot as a free safety in the 1979 season, when he replaced Jake Scott, a five-time All-Pro, a member of the undefeated 1972 Miami Dolphins team, and a player widely considered to be among the finest safeties in NFL history.

From 1979 to 1984, Murphy emerged as one of the leaders and standouts on a Redskins defense that consistently ranked among the best in the league. In 1980, he was elected a team captain and served in that role for the following four seasons, during which the Redskins reached two Super Bowls, winning Super Bowl XVII over the Miami Dolphins in 1983 and losing Super Bowl XVIII to the Los Angeles (now Oakland) Raiders in 1984. Murphy's best season came in 1983, when he led the NFL with nine interceptions and earned All-Pro and Pro Bowl honors. He retired following the 1984 season, in which he missed nine games with a knee injury, after getting cut from the Redskins on his thirtieth birthday. In eight seasons with the Redskins, Murphy made a total of twenty-seven interceptions in 109 games and led the team in tackles on four occasions. Commenting on Murphy's leadership qualities and football intelligence, the Pro Football Hall of Fame coach Joe Gibbs,

who served as head coach of the Redskins on two separate occasions, from 1981 to 1992 and from 2004 to 2007, told Jeff Bercovici for *Forbes* (26 Sep. 2011), "He was somebody I could go and talk to if we were having problems. . . . He was so smart. He made the absolute most of his abilities."

THE NFLPA AND A LAW CAREER

In each of his last five seasons as a player, Murphy served as the Redskins' player representative to the NFLPA, during which he was exposed to the inner workings of the league. He became one of the union's most active members and was part of its bargaining committee during the 1982 players' strike. The strike lasted for fifty-seven days and resulted in a shortened nine-game season, in which the Redskins went 8–1 and won the franchise's first Super Bowl title.

Murphy was eventually promoted to vice president of the union, a role he held from 1983 to 1984. At that time, Murphy recalled to Jerry Sullivan, "If you were involved in the union, the owners didn't like you. . . . We were pushing to change the system and the owners were adamantly against it. There just wasn't a good working relationship." That contentiousness was exemplified by Murphy's own boss, former Redskins owner Jack Kent Cooke, who went so far as to call Murphy a "communist" for his union activities. Murphy has told many sources that he believes he was ultimately forced into early retirement by Cooke after the 1984 season as payback for his role within the NFLPA. Nonetheless, he has maintained that getting cut was the best thing that ever happened to him. Calling his experience as a player representative "invaluable," Murphy told Gary Myers for the New York *Daily News* (3 Feb. 2011), "What I learned about business and negotiations and the NFL, I owe an awful lot to that experience."

During his tenure with the Redskins, Murphy attended American University's Kogod School of Business in Washington, DC, where he earned a master's degree in finance in 1983. After retiring as a player, in 1985, he remained in Washington to work full time for the NFLPA as an assistant executive director. He held that role for the next three years, during which time he oversaw agent-certification, degree-completion, and career-planning programs for players. He also worked closely with the union's longtime executive director Gene Upshaw, a Pro Football Hall of Fame lineman for the Oakland Raiders who was instrumental in securing free agency for NFL players. Along with Upshaw, Murphy served on the union's bargaining committee and played an active role in negotiations during the 1987 players' strike, which lasted for twenty-seven days and resulted in one week of games being canceled. That year, three weeks of replacement players played for three weeks before NFL players agreed to return to work. During his time as assistant executive director, Murphy attended Georgetown University Law School, where he received his JD degree in 1988.

Following his stint with the NFLPA, Murphy went to work for the Washington, DC, law firm Bredhoff and Kaiser. He worked there for a brief time before becoming a trial attorney for the US Department of Justice, in 1989. He spent four years working in the Department of Justice's Federal Programs Branch of the Civil Division, where he handled a number of big cases involving government agencies, including one in which the US Bureau of the Census was sued by the state of Montana, which challenged the constitutionality of the agency's methods of apportionment. Montana lost the case in an appeal to the US Supreme Court, which ruled in favor of Murphy and the Bureau of the Census. Murphy has pointed out similarities between being a lawyer and an athlete. "In some ways it [being a lawyer] helped me get my competitive fix," he told Mike Unger for *American* (15 Apr. 2008), the alumni magazine of American University. "Especially if it's a trial where you're working together with a group of attorneys, there are a lot of similarities to getting ready for a game."

RETURN TO COLGATE
In 1992, Murphy left the Department of Justice to become the athletic director at his alma mater, Colgate University. He succeeded his former coach, Dunlap, who retired after serving in the role for four years. As Colgate's athletic director, a position he held for eleven years, Murphy helped overhaul the school's football program, turning a perennial losing team into a playoff team. After the 1995 season, in which the Colgate Raiders posted a disastrous 0–11 record, Murphy fired head coach Edward Sweeney and replaced him with Dick Biddle, who led the team to its first-ever Patriot League titles in 1997 and 1999 and to three consecutive appearances in the National Collegiate Athletic Association (NCAA) Division I-AA playoffs, from 1997 to 1999. During that time Murphy was credited with playing a major role in persuading the NCAA to allow Patriot League teams to compete in the Division I-AA playoffs. Biddle continues to serve as Colgate's head football coach and has since become the winningest coach in school history, leading the Raiders to league titles in 2002, 2003, 2005, and 2008. In 2003, the Raiders posted a perfect 7–0 conference record and a 15–1 record overall en route to advancing to the Division I-AA Championship Game, becoming the first Patriot League team to do so.

Murphy not only helped transform Colgate's football program but also strengthened many of the university's other sports programs. Colgate's men's basketball team earned consecutive NCAA tournament appearances in 1995 and 1996, while men's ice hockey and women's soccer, softball, and volleyball teams also made NCAA tournament appearances. As athletic director Murphy became known as a strong proponent of the student-athlete, with Colgate student-athletes having one of the highest graduation rates among all Division I-AA schools. He also was known for keeping an unflappable demeanor in times of crisis. Former Colgate basketball coach and current University of Tulsa assistant Emmett Davis, whom Murphy hired in 1997 to replace the school's beloved head coach Jack Bruen (who had died suddenly from pancreatic cancer) told Rob Demovsky for the Green Bay, Wisconsin, *Press-Gazette* (16 Dec. 2007), "The best way to describe Mark is he's very even keeled. He's not an alarmist. Sometimes, when crisis arrives, people fly off the handle. But he's very even tempered and relies on common sense."

During his tenure at Colgate, Murphy continued to stay connected to the NFL by joining the league's Player Advisory and Youth Football committees, where he served under his friend and mentor, former NFL commissioner Paul Tagliabue. He served on the Player Advisory committee from 1994 to 2002 and has served on the Youth Football committee since 2002. In an interview with Lori Nickel and Don Walker for the Milwaukee, Wisconsin *Journal Sentinel* (3 Jan. 2010), Tagliabue, whom Murphy first met and worked with as a Redskins player representative, praised Murphy's "ability to reach across the divide and talk with people who also understand both perspectives that can essentially lead to sensible compromises and consensus."

MOVE TO NORTHWESTERN UNIVERSITY
Murphy left Colgate in June 2003, when he was hired as the athletic director at Northwestern University, in Evanston, Illinois. He turned down job offers from such Ivy League schools as Cornell, Harvard, and Princeton to accept the position in charge of directing a nineteen-sport program with 160 full-time employees and a $40 million budget. In his four and a half years as athletic director, Murphy helped Northwestern, a Division I-A school and member of the highly competitive Big Ten athletic conference, enjoy some of the best athletic success in its 150-plus year history. During that span, Northwestern captured three NCAA team championships, nine conference team championships, eight individual national championships, and thirty-four individual Big Ten titles, and it produced forty-nine first-team all-Americans.

Meanwhile, the Wildcats football team earned two berths in bowl games, the 2003 Motor City Bowl and 2005 Sun Bowl, which were only the fifth and sixth bowl appearances in school history. In each of Murphy's last three years as athletic director, Northwestern finished in the top thirty of the annual US Sports Academy Directors' Cup competition, which ranks colleges and universities based on their on-field athletic success. (The competition is now known as the National Association of Collegiate Directors of Athletics [NACDA] Learfield Sports Directors' Cup.) Under Murphy's guidance Northwestern also consistently had one of the highest student-athlete graduation rates in the nation, with a rate of 98 percent in 2007, tying for best in the nation. That year, Murphy was honored as one of the one hundred most influential educators in the United States by the Institute for International Sport and was named NACDA Central Region Athletic Director of the Year.

PRESIDENT AND CEO OF THE GREEN BAY PACKERS

On December 3, 2007, Murphy resigned as athletic director at Northwestern to become the tenth president and CEO of the Packers. He was hired to replace Bob Harlan, who retired after nearly two decades at the helm, during which he guided the Packers through a period of unprecedented success and led a major renovation of the team's historic Lambeau Field. Now the Packers' chairman emeritus, Harlan felt Murphy, who was selected from a field of nearly sixty candidates, stood out because of his extensive experience in the NFL. "We needed someone who knew the National Football League," Harlan said, as quoted by Wilde on December 4, 2007. "You need someone who can walk into an owners meeting and not be startled by what he's going to hear. He's met the owners, he's met the commissioner, he knows the National Football League and the problems (it has). And as I looked at the other candidates we had from the National Football League, I had to come back to Mark. He's got the experience. He brought an element that they did not." Murphy officially succeeded Harlan as the Packers' president and CEO on January 28, 2008, one week after the Packers lost to the eventual Super Bowl champion New York Giants, 23–20, in the National Football Conference (NFC) Championship Game.

Founded in 1919 by Earl "Curly" Lambeau (the first Packers coach and the namesake of Lambeau Field) and George Whitney Calhoun, the Packers are the third oldest franchise in the NFL and the only publicly owned major US sports team, with more than 112,000 individual shareholders. Unlike typical shareholders, Packers shareholders receive no dividend on their original investment and are limited to owning no more than 200,000 shares, thus preventing any one individual from gaining majority control over the team. They do, however, have voting rights and the freedom to attend annual shareholder meetings. All profits, meanwhile, are invested back into the team. While the Packers' ownership structure violates current NFL ownership

rules, which require teams to have a principal owner, the Packers are exempt because they were publicly owned before such rules went into effect in the 1980s. As president and CEO of the Packers, Murphy represents the team at NFL owners meetings and other league functions, and sits on a seven-member executive committee (elected from a forty-five-member board of directors) responsible for overseeing all team operations and business. Shortly after arriving in Green Bay, he assembled an executive leadership team made up of several new vice president positions, including vice president of sales and marketing and vice president of organizational and staff development, in efforts to strengthen the franchise's upper-management structure. Commenting on his business philosophy, Murphy explained to Nickel and Walker for the *Journal Sentinel* (3 Jan. 2010) "My philosophy of management is that you don't micromanage; you hire good people and allow them to do their jobs. You also hold them accountable to success. If we're not having success, then it's my job to look at a situation and determine what changes are needed to allow us to be successful."

PACKERS TRANSITION: FROM FAVRE TO RODGERS

One of Murphy's biggest moves since taking over as Packers president and CEO was making the difficult decision to part ways with the team's beloved franchise quarterback and three-time NFL most valuable player (MVP) Brett Favre, who had formally announced his retirement in March 2008, only to return later that July. Though Favre had led the Packers to the NFC Championship Game during the previous season, Murphy, along with Packers general manager Ted Thompson and Packers coach Mike McCarthy, entered the 2008 NFL season committed to former number-one draft pick Aaron Rodgers as the team's quarterback. After much back and forth, Murphy went ahead with the Packers' long-term plans and released Favre, who subsequently signed with the New York Jets. (Favre retired and unretired several more times, spending the 2008 season with the Jets and the 2009–10 seasons with the Minnesota Vikings, before officially retiring in January 2011.)

For Murphy, the Favre decision, albeit controversial among Packers fans at the time, proved to be one of the most rewarding of his career. After finishing the 2008 season with a 6–10 record, the Rodgers-led Packers made the playoffs in 2009, finishing second in the NFC North Division with an 11–5 record. They lost to the Arizona Cardinals, 51–45, in the NFL wildcard playoff round. Then, in 2010, in Murphy's third year at the helm, the Packers returned to the top of the NFL, winning Super Bowl XLV by defeating the Pittsburgh Steelers, 31–25, to secure their fourth Super Bowl title and record thirteenth NFL championship. In the process, Murphy became the first person in history to earn Super Bowl rings as both a player and a CEO.

The Packers enjoyed another dominant run in the 2011 season, when they posted a franchise-best 15–1 record and notched the top seed in the NFC playoffs. Though the Packers failed to defend their title, losing to the New York Giants, 37–20, in the NFC divisional playoff round, the team's season was considered a success, and Rodgers, who had been named MVP of Super Bowl XLV, was awarded the NFL MVP award, after setting a single-season NFL record with a passer rating of 122.5.

PACKERS' FINANCIAL SUCCESS

In addition to steering the Packers toward the pinnacle of success on the field, Murphy has been credited with helping the team enjoy unprecedented economic growth. In 2011, the Packers generated record profits, achieving a net income of $42.7 million and team revenues of $302 million, up from $17.1 million and $282.6 million the previous year. The team also set records for profit from operations and local revenue, earning $43 million and $130.4 million, respectively.

Murphy's initiatives to improve the Packers' marketing and retail operations have contributed to the organization's financial success, including the enhancement of the Packers Pro Shop and Packers.com businesses, both of which achieved record sales in 2011. Other plans Murphy has set in motion to increase Packers revenue and to improve the overall fan experience include a $143 million expansion project at Lambeau Field. As part of the project, a new high-tech sound system was installed at the stadium in 2011 and new scoreboards with high-definition video boards were installed in 2012. The last phase of the project, which will add around seventy-five hundred additional seats to the stadium's south end-zone area, is scheduled to be completed before the start of the 2013 season. Murphy hopes to attract new fans and boost local tourism through the launch of future real estate development projects around Lambeau Field and the Green Bay area.

Since 2008, Murphy has served as a member of the powerful NFL Management Council Executive Committee, which serves as the bargaining team for negotiations with the NFLPA. As a member of the committee he was lauded for helping players and owners come to terms on a new collective bargaining agreement during the contentious 2011 NFL lockout.

PERSONAL LIFE

Nickel and Walker described Murphy as "tall and broad-shouldered" and as looking "like a golfer straight off the links of Ireland and hardly like the onetime safety who led the National Football League in interceptions in 1983." Murphy and his wife, the former Laurie Young, whom he met while attending Colgate University, live in the Green Bay area. They have four children: Katie, Emily, Brian, and Anna. Murphy is actively involved in a number of charitable organizations, including Big Brothers Big Sisters of America, and serves on the National Advisory Board of the Positive Coaching Alliance, which aims to improve the culture of youth sports. He was inducted into the Colgate Athletics Hall of Honor in 1985 and into the Greater Buffalo Sports Hall of Fame in 2002. In his spare time, Murphy enjoys fishing, playing golf, and working out.

SUGGESTED READING

Bercovici, Jeff. "The Power of the Packers." *Forbes* 26 Sep. 2011: 86–90. Print.

Demovsky, Rob. "Murphy's Long Journey: From Colgate to Packers." *Press-Gazette* [Green Bay, Wisconsin] 16 Dec. 2007: 2. Print.

Goessling, Ben. "New Leader of the Pack." *Washington Times* [DC] 3 Sep. 2008: E14. Print.

Greenfeld, Karl Taro. "The Green Bay Packers Have the Best Owners in Football." *Bloomberg Businessweek.* Bloomberg L.P., 20 Oct. 2011. Web. 16 July 2012. Print.

Myers, Gary. "Packers Exec Can See Fruits of Labor." *Daily News* [New York] 3 Feb. 2011: 59. Print.

Myslenski, Skip. "A True Believer." *Chicago Tribune.* Chicago Tribune, 24 Aug. 2003. Web. 16 July 2012.

Nickel, Lori, and Don Walker. "The Man behind the Pack." *Journal Sentinel* [Milwaukee, Wisconsin] 3 Jan. 2010: A1. Print.

—*Chris Cullen*

Naif Al-Mutawa

Born: 1971
Occupation: Comic-book creator and entrepreneur

Naif Al-Mutawa "is changing the world, one comic book at a time," Jahanzeb Aslam wrote for the Pakistani edition of *Newsweek* (18 and 25 Apr. 2011). A US-educated native of Kuwait, Al-Mutawa is the creator and developer of *The 99,* a comic-book series that features what he calls on his website "the first group of comic superheroes born of an Islamic archetype." The characters who comprise the 99 are crime-fighting young people from all over the world, each of whom embodies one or another of the ninety-nine attributes of Allah ("God" in Arabic) in Islam. Those characters, men and women who range in age

AP Photo/Teshkeel Media Group, Cara Hromada Photography

from eight to their early twenties, are mentored by Dr. Ramzi Razem, a Spaniard who is described on *The 99*'s official website, The99.org, as a psychologist, historian, and lecturer. Dr. Razem, who in some ways represents Al-Mutawa's alter ego, has dedicated himself to overcoming the evil Rughal, who is bent on gaining control of the 99 and their powers.

THE PHILOSOPHY BEHIND *THE 99*

Al-Mutawa is a clinical psychologist, writer, educator, and entrepreneur. He is the founder and chief executive officer of the Teshkeel Media Group, which was started in 2004 and publishes *The 99*. Al-Mutawa designed *The 99* as a way to combat negative views of Islam and the widely held stereotype of Muslims as treacherous villains. At the same time, Al-Mutawa is trying to illustrate a positive model of heroism for young Muslims who have been exposed to glorifications of violence and extreme interpretations of the Qur'an, the sacred text of Islam.

The 99 conveys its messages indirectly. The series does not make overt references to God, religious beliefs or laws, prayer, or houses of worship; rather, the stories emphasize the importance of treating one another with courtesy and respect, which is a basic tenet of Islam, as well as other religions worldwide. The series also demonstrates the importance of diversity and such universally prized virtues as mercy, wisdom, and generosity. Each installment of *The 99* tries to show youngsters that people everywhere are similar in terms of their needs, feelings, and

aspirations, and that despite differences in circumstances, religions, and cultures, all people can work together to battle evil and injustice, solve problems, and improve their communities.

"As a culture, we Muslims don't have any heroes," Al-Mutawa told Aslam. "We have historical figures that are revered, but we don't have any modern-day heroes." Following the terrorist attacks of September 11, 2011, Al-Mutawa, the father of five sons, "started thinking about role models for my children. I wasn't happy with how the West saw Islam, and I wasn't happy with how Islam saw itself." In an opinion piece for CNN. com (22 Aug. 2010), he wrote, "It is finally time that all of us became more accountable for that which our children will be hearing. . . . If we allow small-minded men to spout fear and hate in the name of our religion, we will enable them to brainwash another generation as they did our own. And soon, the next generation will fall into a pit of dissonance. To sit by silently makes us all complicit."

In stressing the need for a series like *The 99*, Al-Mutawa has mentioned to journalists and potential investors a book of stickers made for children on the West Bank whose illustrations, according to George Gene Gustines for the *New York Times* (12 Oct. 2011), "championed suicide bombers and martyrdom while depicting bloody scenes of the Israeli occupation of Palestinian territories." When Henry Elliman, in an interview for Haverford College, posed the question "How do you fight extremism with *The 99*?" (21 Feb. 2012), Al-Mutawa responded, "The idea is to crowd it out. Deliver more messages that kids can identify with. I firmly believe that the only way to beat extremism is through arts and culture. That's what happened in Europe with the Reformation and the Renaissance, and that's what has to happen in the Muslim world. No guns, no bombs, no war is going to work. This is the only way that will."

In 2008, *Forbes* magazine included *The 99* on its list of "the top twenty trends sweeping the globe," and in 2009, at the World Economic Forum on the Middle East, Al-Mutawa received the Schwab Foundation Social Entrepreneurship Award. In 2010, President Barack Obama made special mention of *The 99* in his introductory remarks at the first Presidential Summit on Entrepreneurship, which was launched in the wake of Obama's speech in Cairo that called for new respect and cooperation between the United States and the Muslim world. At the summit, nearly three hundred participants from fifty nations heard President Obama say that "the most innovative response" to his appeal for improving relations between the United States and predominantly Muslim countries "was from Dr. Naif Al-Mutawa. . . . His comic books have captured the imagination of so many young people with superheroes who embody the teachings and tolerance of Islam" (26 Apr. 2010).

Discussing the animated series based on *The 99*, Al-Mutawa wrote in "A Letter to My Sons," posted on his website, Al-Mutawa.com (2 July 2009), "I told the writers of the animation that [it is] only when Jewish kids think that *The 99* characters are Jewish, and Christian kids think they're Christian, and Muslim kids think they're Muslim, and Hindu kids think they're Hindu, that I will consider my vision as having been fully executed."

AL-MUTAWA'S EARLY YEARS

Naif Al-Mutawa, who turned forty in 2011, was born in Kuwait City to parents whom he has described as conservative Muslims. As a boy, he rejected the belief that the Qur'an could be interpreted in only one way and that there was only one way to practice Islam. "While I didn't know much when I was young, I knew that I could not live in a black or white, either-or world," he wrote in "Let the Qur'an Define Itself," posted on his website. A talk by Talal Eid, a young imam who had been studying at the Harvard Divinity School, reassured him that he could be "the judge of [his] own actions" and that he was free to "make [his] own rules using the lessons [he] learned with the heart and mind that God gave [him]."

The imam, he recalled, gave a compelling example: "If you ask me whether charging interest is haram (forbidden) in Islam, I would say yes and I would quote chapter and verse from the Qur'an for you. But if I didn't pay for my car with an installment loan, I wouldn't be able to come here to talk to you about Islam." In "Art, the Universal Language of Religion," an essay written for the Common Ground News Service (22 Jan. 2008), Al-Mutawa declared, "It is an absolute shame that the Qur'an continues to be held hostage by those who favour the idolatry of words over the depth of their meaning and the elasticity of the human intellect."

For many summers starting in 1979, Al-Mutawa attended Camp Robin Hood in New Hampshire, a traditional camp for boys and girls, where he made many Jewish friends. (According to some sources, his parents at first had a mistaken impression about the type of camp it was, perhaps thinking that it focused on weight reduction.) As a camper, Al-Mutawa was introduced to *Superman*, *Archie*, and other American comic books; he enjoyed reading them, but they never became a big interest of his. "My love for reading is a staple part of my identity but as I grew up I became a novel junkie," he told Richard Vasseur for the website Jazma Online (26 Mar. 2006), in an interview later posted on The99.org.

EDUCATION

Al-Mutawa began his formal education at the American School of Kuwait. He transferred to Al-Bayan Bilingual School at the end of fourth grade and remained there throughout high school. Then he enrolled at Tufts University in Medford, Massachusetts, where he accumulated many more credits than were required because he had resolved to complete four majors. (Upon his graduation in 1994, the school recognized three: clinical psychology, English literature, and history.) As an undergraduate, according to the Global Experts website, Al-Mutawa served as an intern at the United Nations Convention of Human Rights in Geneva, Switzerland, and "wrote widely read columns for both the Arab and American press that focused on social and political commentary."

During the next decade, Al-Mutawa earned an MA in organizational psychology from the Teachers College of Columbia University, an MBA from Columbia, and an MA and a PhD in clinical psychology from Long Island University in Brooklyn. His dissertation was entitled "The Influence of Religion upon the Development of Post-Traumatic Stress Disorder among Kuwaiti Prisoners of War." During that period, he worked as a clinical psychologist at Bellevue Medical Center, where he treated people who had been prisoners of war during the Gulf War and citizens of countries who had been tortured in their native lands for political reasons.

Al-Mutawa also wrote three children's books on the theme of tolerance. The first, *To Bounce or Not to Bounce*, which he self-published in 1996, is about Bouncy Jr., who is born a half-sphere in Bouncyland, where everyone is perfectly round. "The inhabitants of Bouncyland are judged by how high they can bounce and how fast they can roll," Al-Mutawa told Vasseur. Bouncy "is unable to do either. Thus, he becomes the subject of ridicule until his difference serves as the basis of a new, more equitable society." The book won a UNESCO Prize for literature in the service of tolerance in 1997. Al-Mutawa's other children's books are *What's in a Color?* and *Get Your Ties out of Your Eyes*, the latter of which was "banned in Kuwait because censors felt it was commenting on the Qur'an," Fahmida Rashid wrote for *Islamic Horizons* (July/August 2006).

THE BEGINNING OF *THE 99*

Starting in 1997, Al-Mutawa tried his hand at various entrepreneurial endeavors, doing little writing that was not related to school. He has traced the seed of the project that grew into *The 99* to a conversation that he had with his sister, Samar, during a taxi ride in London, in which she urged him to write for children again. As the story of *The 99* took shape in his imagination, he realized that he was drawing upon his college and graduate-school educations. In the speech he gave at the American University of Kuwait graduation ceremony in 2011, later posted on his website, Al-Mutawa explained, "*The 99* is English literature, as it took an ability to analyze heroes already in existence to be able to create new ones. *The 99* is history, with a rich backstory rooted in the fall of Baghdad in the thirteenth century and the fall of Granada in the fifteenth century. *The 99* is psychology because it involved creating over one hundred characters. . . . And *The 99* is a business."

As Al-Mutawa told Faiza Saleh Ambah for the *Washington Post* (11 June 2008), he "wanted to create something that would be a classic, not another made-in-the-fifth-world product." He envisioned a series whose quality would rival that of the Spider-Man or Superman comics or the Japanese cartoon *Pokémon*. In 2004, with $7 million in start-up funds acquired from fifty-four investors in eight countries, including $1 million from former Columbia classmates, Al-Mutawa launched the Teshkeel Media Group. He then began to develop *The 99* in collaboration with highly accomplished writers and illustrators, most of them veterans of Marvel Comics and DC Comics; the team has included Fabian Nicieza, Stuart Moore, Josef "Joe" Rubinstein, Ron Wagner, Roy Richardson, and June Brigman.

By April 2011, Al-Mutawa had raised a total of $40 million from "sixty-one institutional and individual investors," according to Aslam. *The 99* attracted unexpected interest in late 2005 and early 2006 after the Danish newspaper *Jyllands-Posten* printed twelve cartoons depicting the prophet Muhammad, whom Muslims credit with bringing to earth the message of Allah. A huge controversy erupted over the cartoons, which many Muslims denounced as defamatory. As a result, Al-Mutawa has recalled in interviews, people who Googled "Muslim" and "cartoons" to learn more about the controversy often reached sites discussing *The 99*. In 2006, the Unicorn Investment Bank of Bahrain bought a 30 percent share in Teshkeel, a move that expanded support for *The 99* among Muslims. "The bank has been amazing," Al-Mutawa told Aslam. "They have never rejected a single idea."

THE 99: STORY AND CHARACTERS

According to the "Origins" installment of *The 99*, the adventures depicted in the series resulted from actual historical events. The first was the 1258 destruction of the Dar Al Hikma library in Baghdad, a repository of books by both Muslim and non-Muslim scholars, during a Mongol invasion. The second event was the 1492 surrender of Granada, a Moorish refuge, to forces led by King Ferdinand and Queen Isabella of Spain, which ended Moorish domination of that part of the Iberian Peninsula. The subsequent expedition of Christopher Columbus to the New World was significant as well. In *The 99*'s fictionalized

account, these events led to the dissemination of ninety-nine magical gemstones in Asia, the Middle East, Africa, Europe, and the New World. Each of the stones embodies, in a reduced form, an attribute of Allah—a special power that is transferred to the character who possesses it. Each stone also contains a mechanism that enables its powers to "self-update."

As of early 2012, the series had introduced twenty characters in addition to Dr. Razem, the founder and director of The 99 Steps Foundation, and Rughal, the villain. The characters are "modern, secular and spiritual, moving seamlessly between East and West," Ambah wrote. Examples include Widal the Loving, a twenty-one-year-old Filipina named Hope Mendoza; Bari the Healer, a nineteen-year-old South African named Haroun Ahrens; Wassi the Vast, an eleven-year-old Indian boy named Ashok Mohan; Noora the Light, eighteen-year-old Dana Ibrahim, a native of the United Arab Emirates; and Darr the Afflictor, the twenty-two-year-old American John Weller. According to The99.org, "While each of our heroes has their own power, each of their powers is enhanced by working in teams of three. Our characters must decide which three heroes and sets of powers are best suited to solve the problem at hand." As he explained at the 2010 TED Global conference, Al-Mutawa places three characters on each team to avoid dealing with Muslim restrictions on extramarital relationships between men and women.

The 99, which debuted in 2006 and appears in four installments annually, is aimed at children ranging from six to twelve years of age. It is currently available in Arabic, English, Chinese, Turkish, Portuguese, and half a dozen other languages, and is popular in nations such as Egypt, Saudi Arabia, Brazil, France, and Indonesia. In late 2011, annual sales of the comic books totaled about one million. An animated cartoon based on the series is airing on television in several countries, and a film adaptation, *The 99 Unbound*, premiered at the New York Film Festival in 2011. A theme park based on *The 99*'s characters opened in Kuwait in 2009.

The 99 has been criticized by both Muslims and non-Muslims. Some Muslim critics of the series object to the idea of imbuing humans with Allah's attributes; others have complained that by focusing on three-character teams, *The 99* is subtly planting the Christian notion of the trinity in the minds of young readers. Critics of *The 99* in the West include Pamela Geller, who in her blog *Atlas Shrugs* and in an interview with CNN has condemned the series as a weapon in "the ongoing onslaught of cultural jihad." The Hub, a children's cable network that is a joint venture of Discovery Communications and Hasbro, acquired the rights to *The 99* animated television series in 2010, but because of complaints from Geller and others, its owners decided that airing the animated series in the United States carried too many risks for a fledgling company. Also in 2010 came the first of a special six-installment comic-book series with DC Comics in which members of the 99 join with Superman, Batman, and Wonder Woman to fight crime. This rare comic-book crossover "thrilled" Al-Mutawa, Carole Cadwalladr wrote for the *Observer* (23 Oct. 2010). "It is pretty amazing," Al-Mutawa said to her; "our characters are going to be hanging out with Batman and Superman!"

ADDITIONAL ACTIVITIES AND HONORS

In 2009, Al-Mutawa cofounded the Soor Center for Cognitive Behavioral Psychotherapy in Kuwait. He has taught clinical psychology at the Kuwait University and served as an associate editor of *The Encyclopedia of Positive Psychology* (2008). In 2010, he won the Intersector for Business and Religion Award from Intersections International, and in 2011 he earned an Ecademy Award from the Columbia Business School, which honors alumni who have become successful entrepreneurs. Also in 2011, *Wham! Bam! Islam!*, Isaac Solotaroff's documentary about Al-Mutawa and *The 99*, aired on the PBS television network.

In the *New York Times* (22 Jan. 2006), Hassan M. Fattah described Al-Mutawa as "burly" and "fast-talking," with "a dry wit." Al-Mutawa and his second wife, Rola Banaja, maintain homes in Kuwait City and New York City. His five sons, Hamad, Faisal, Khalid, Rayan, and Rakan, are US citizens, and the older ones attend Camp Robin Hood during summers.

SUGGESTED READING

Aslam, Jahanzeb. "New Age, New Heroes." *Newsweek Pakistan*. AG Publications, 18 and 25 Apr. 2011. Web. 10 Mar. 2012.

Fattah, Hassan M. "Comics to Battle for Truth, Justice and the Islamic Way." *New York Times*. New York Times, 22 Jan. 2006. Web. 10 Mar. 2012.

Gustines, George Gene. "Along the Heated Trail of the Man Who Created Muslim Superheroes." *New York Times*. New York Times, 12 Oct. 2011. Web. 10 Mar. 2012.

Hamdan, Sara. "Comic-Book Heroes Help Change Image of Islam." *New York Times*. New York Times, 27 July 2011. Web. 10 Mar. 2012.

Mutawa, Naif Al-. "Islam-inspired Comic Superheroes Fight for Peace." *CNN.com*. Cable News Network, 22 Aug. 2010. Web. 18 Mar. 2012.

Truitt, Brian. "*The 99* Aspires to Teach Muslim Principles." *USA Today*. Gannett, 20 Sep. 2011. Web. 10 Mar. 2012.

Villeminot, Florence. "Muslims Fighting Evil." *Newsweek International* 5 Mar. 2007: 58. Print.

—*Miriam Helbok*

Chouchou Namegabe

Born: ca. 1980
Occupation: Anti-rape activist

Award-winning Congolese journalist Chouchou Namegabe (SHEW-shew nahm-ah-GAH-bay) is a founding member of the South Kivu Women's Media Association. Namegabe, who is also known as Chouchou Namegabe Nabintu and Chouchou Namegabe Dubuisson, has worked as a radio journalist in the Democratic Republic of the Congo's dangerous South Kivu province since the late 1990s, during the height of the Second Congo War. The conflict, also called the Great War of Africa, was the deadliest conflict in Africa's modern history. It began in 1998 and involved over twenty armed militias and eight nations.

During the war, Namegabe's radio station, Radio Maendeleo, shut down from 1999 until 2001. When Namegabe returned to the airwaves in 2002, she began broadcasting her opinions about the conflict. Although a peace treaty officially ended the conflict in Congo in 2003, villages throughout Africa's largest country, including in Namegabe's own South Kivu, continued to be razed by rebel forces. The Enough Project, founded by American activist John Prendergast, estimates that the war killed over 5 million people and displaced 1.7 million. The war centered on control of Congo's valuable mineral resources, including deposits of cobalt, copper, gold, and uranium, which are sold to electronics companies and manufacturers of cell phones and computers.

Violence related to the war has significantly affected Congolese women. In May 2008, Major General Patrick Cammaert, a former UN deputy force commander, told the Enough Project, "It is more dangerous to be a woman than to be a soldier right now." The United Nations estimates that over fifteen thousand sexual attacks took place in the Congo in 2010 alone. In 2011, Danielle Shapiro for the *Daily Beast* (11 May 2011) reported that the women of the DRC were raped at twenty-six times the rate previously reported by the UN, with four women attacked every five minutes. Her report cited a study by the American Journal of Public Health.

Although there has been dispute about the statistics, all evidence points to a pandemic of violence taking place in Congo. Employing systematic rape and torture as weapons of war, rebel fighters and militias are destroying Congolese communities by targeting girls as young as three months and women as old as ninety. Before Namegabe's broadcasts, thousands of Congolese women suffered in silence. Congolese culture has historically viewed rape victims as adulterers, and throughout the conflict, victims have

Wirelmage

not reported attacks for fear they will be outcast by their families and communities.

In 2002, Namegabe began broadcasting the testimonies of rape victims in a campaign to end the silence surrounding the issue of rape. In Congo, radio is a major source of information, and radio broadcasts reach even the most remote villages. Local languages did not even have a word for "rape" when Namegabe began her broadcasts, further evidence of the stigma of rape in Congo. To circumvent this problem, she and her fellow journalists borrowed a word from a neighboring Tanzanian dialect: *ubakaji*.

"To break the silence helps first the victims; it's the first step to heal their internal wounds," Namegabe told Alison Walkley for the newsletter *Africa News* (17 Nov. 2009). "It helps those still hiding. They come to us, thinking that they were the only ones. . . . [The broadcast] helps the community. We touch everybody." Namegabe has brought her campaign to the international stage, testifying before the International Criminal Court at The Hague in the Netherlands in 2007 to classify rape as a weapon of war and before the Senate Foreign Relations Committee in the United States in 2009 to lobby for the rights of women. Also in 2009, Namegabe received the Vital Voices Global Partnership Fern Holland Award, as well as the Knight International Journalism Award for outstanding work in journalism. Despite the fact that the world community has applauded her work, Namegabe continues to face threats for airing the women's stories in the DRC.

EARLY LIFE

Namegabe was born in Bukavu, the capital city of the DRC's South Kivu province. She was born in about 1980, the eldest of ten siblings. The transistor radio in her house, she recalled, was the exclusive property of the men in her family, which included her unemployed father and five brothers. "I spent all my youth watching it from a distance," she told Delphine Minoui for the *Daily Beast* (28 June 2010, online).

As a young girl, Namegabe studied theater in secondary school. When she announced to her father that she wanted to become an actor, he was outraged. He told her that if she were to pursue a career, she should become a teacher so that she might educate her brothers and sisters. When she refused, he beat her. He finally told her that if she wanted to pursue acting, she needed to find a husband to support her. Namegabe, who recalls the story humorously, told her father she was too young to marry and found a job at the local radio station at the age of seventeen.

In 1997, Namegabe began working in the studio of Radio Maendeleo, where she voiced a character in a popular radio drama. One of Namegabe's neighbors, Clotilde Aziza Bangwene, happened to be a producer at Radio Maendeleo; Bangwene was looking for an actor to voice the character of an orphan boy named Fulushi in an educational broadcast, and Namegabe was given the part. She became a local celebrity before her twentieth birthday. "Chouchou was afraid and timid," Bangwene told Minoui. "But as soon as she started speaking in the microphone, she gained a lot of self-confidence." Namegabe then became a weekly contributor at Radio Maendeleo, lending her voice to children's programs and cooking shows and eventually becoming one of the station's eight full-time journalists. In a country where most of the female population remains illiterate, Namegabe's path was considered controversial. "People said, 'How can a lady talk on the radio? How can she speak in front of so many people, especially men?'" she recalled to Kelly Nuxoll for the *Huffington Post* (20 Mar. 2009, online). She added, "I am not someone who likes the status quo." Bangwene remains a close friend to Namegabe; Namegabe still calls her "Mummy."

SURVIVORS SHARE THEIR STORIES FOR THE FIRST TIME

When Namegabe first began investigating cases of rape in Congo, what she heard horrified her. Like many living in the DRC, she was aware that rapes were taking place but wrongly assumed that the driving force behind the crimes was sexual. The word *rape* (and the Tanzanian word, *ubakaji*, that Namegabe and her fellow journalists found to communicate it) does not accurately describe the atrocities that are taking place against the women of Congo. The aim, Namegabe soon discovered, was to destroy communities—not by killing, but by inflicting a level of suffering beyond human comprehension. Still, after Namegabe's first broadcast, she confronted widespread outrage. She told Minoui that people would yell at her on the street: "How dare you talk about sex on the airwaves?"

Yet that first broadcast, aired in 2001, provoked another unexpected response: an outpouring of support from rape survivors. Namegabe recalls that the next day, three women sought refuge at the offices of Radio Maendeleo, still limping in pain from the brutal attacks they had suffered. The women were so scared that they refused to give their names or the names of their villages, but they felt compelled to tell their stories. Namegabe reports that more women came each day, some walking for days just to reach South Kivu.

The first survivor Namegabe met, who gave the first testimony aired on Radio Maendeleo, was recovering at Panzi Hospital in Namegabe's birthplace, Bukavu. "The victim was lying down on a bed of blood," Namegabe recalled to Minoui. "She had been raped by seven different men in the village of Mwenga, who had eventually shot a gun into her vagina. She was half conscious." The woman told her story but refused to give her name. The early anonymous accounts Namegabe collected kept her awake at night, and she soon realized that simply collecting the stories was not enough. She and her colleagues launched radio-listening clubs for women. In Congo, it is traditional for men to gather in such clubs, but thanks to Namegabe's work, thousands of women are now able to do so as well.

SOUTH KIVU WOMEN'S MEDIA ASSOCIATION

In 2003, Namegabe founded the South Kivu Women's Media Association, or AFEM, an abbreviation of its French name (Association des Femmes des Médias du Sud-Kivu). Based in Bukavu, the association trains female journalists and creates programming for women that is broadcast on fifteen local radio stations. The group has collaborated with local radio clubs as well. In their first year, they worked with over fifty clubs in South Kivu alone, reaching over ten thousand women listeners. In 2008, AFEM recorded over one hundred testimonies on audiocassettes and CDs and distributed them to clubs in more rural villages. In addition to survivor testimonies, the group publicizes health and legal resources available for victims.

Namegabe and her colleagues risk their lives traveling across the country to record stories for the air. Julienne Baseke, a journalist with AFEM, told Dominique Soguel for *Women's eNews* (12 Nov. 2008), "There are no real safety guards. Rape is a risk. Death is a risk. Our hope is that if we go there and report the facts, then maybe justice will be delivered. Access is never the problem. It is the threats and the retractions that come afterward." Armed with few supplies—in 2008, it was reported that the forty journalists working with AFEM shared one video camera and used an outdated sound-editing program—the group's job was made even more difficult after their offices were robbed in 2008.

ACTIVISM ABROAD

In December 2007, Namegabe took her recorded testimonies to The Hague in an appeal to the International Criminal Court (ICC) to investigate sex crimes in the DRC. Although the ICC defines rape as a crime of war and a crime against humanity, militia chief Thomas Lubanga, the first person arrested on a warrant issued by the ICC, was not tried for rape before the court. The ICC claimed that they lacked proof to press such charges against Lubanga, which prompted Namegabe to arrive with four hundred testimonies documenting his abuses. Namegabe also called for international attention to the women of Congo and for medical personnel and investigators in an effort to stem the violent pandemic.

In front of the assembly, Namegabe gave the haunting testimony of one Bukavu woman who was raped by seven militiamen in front of her five children and husband. The militiamen killed her husband and forced her eldest son to rape her before killing each of her children and forcing her to eat their flesh. Though the woman begged to be killed herself, the militiamen kept her as a sex slave. Without any accountability for the crimes, Namegabe told the court, the violence would not end. Regarding sex crimes, "[t]he international community is silent on this issue," she said, as reported by a journalist for the South Africa *Star* (11 Dec. 2007), "and the Congolese government does nothing to end this crime against humanity."

In 2009, Namegabe was invited to speak before the United States Senate Committee on Foreign Relations. On May 13, Senators Barbara Boxer and Russ Feingold, along with the Subcommittee of African Affairs and the Subcommittee on International Operations and Organizations, Human Rights, Democracy and Global Women's Issues, held a hearing on sexual violence and rape as a tactic of war. The hearing was called "Confronting Rape and Other Forms of Violence against Women in Conflict Zones Spotlight: DRC and Sudan." Presenters included American playwright and activist Eve Ensler and Prendergast of the Enough Project, but it was Namegabe's testimony that received the most attention. In an emotional plea, she asked for pledges to help end the violence. "The women ask why? Why such atrocities? Why do they fight their war on women's bodies?" she said, as quoted by several sources, including the Inter Press Service

(IPS) website. "It is because there is a plan to put fear into the community through the woman, because she is the heart of the community. When she is pushed down, the whole community follows."

Senator Boxer, ambassador-at-large for global women's issues within the Department of State, and Melanne Verveer, cofounder of the group Vital Voices (a nongovernmental organization founded by Secretary of State Hillary Clinton that trains and empowers women leaders), pledged their support for a Congo task force to address Namegabe's concerns. These concerns include the lack of adequate medical assistance to deal with the spread of sexually transmitted diseases and the absence of appropriate legal sanctions available to bring perpetrators to justice. Perhaps most frustrating to Namegabe, though, was the lack of media attention to fuel international aid. She told the committee, as quoted in an interview for the *National Journal* (13 May 2009, online), "When a gorilla is killed in the mountains, there is an outcry, and people mobilize great resources to protect the animals. Yet more than five hundred thousand women have been raped, and there is silence. After all of this you will make memorials and say, 'never again.' But we don't need commemoration; we want you to act now."

THE UNITED STATES AND CONGO
The same year Namegabe testified before the US Senate, Secretary Clinton paid a historic visit to the war-torn eastern DRC in August 2009. Prior to the meeting, Clinton condemned violence against women in Congo, officially calling the attacks crimes against humanity. Namegabe was one of the representatives to meet with the secretary during her visit to Goma, the capital of the North Kivu province. Clinton, visibly moved by victims' stories, expressed a personal pledge to end the violence. Nonetheless, Aaron Hall and Sasha Lezhnev of the Enough Project filed a report called "US Congo Policy: Matching Deeds to Words to End the World's Deadliest War" (4 Oct. 2011) that criticized Clinton's efforts. "Clinton's personal commitment to addressing the underlying drivers of conflict in eastern Congo has translated into a series of ad hoc initiatives," they wrote, "but not yet a cohesive US policy." While conflict in the Congo has received unprecedented attention from senior US officials—the United States has begun several initiatives to aid victims in Congo and is the largest financial backer of the UN's peacekeeping mission there—the Enough Project asserts that the United States has failed to use the relationship it currently enjoys with DRC president Joseph Kabila to leverage its demands. The report quoted an unnamed women's rights activist from Bukavu: "The US can have such an impact here," she said. "It is the only country

that [neighboring country] Rwanda and Kabila will listen to."

Namegabe continues to raise awareness throughout the United States, speaking at summits such as "Informed Activism: Armed Conflict, Scarce Resources, and Congo" at Clark University in Worcester, Massachusetts, in 2011, in partnership with the nongovernmental organization Jewish World Watch.

AWARDS
In 2009, Vital Voices awarded Namegabe with the Vital Voices Global Partnership Fern Holland Award, which brought Namegabe to the United States to spread awareness about violence against women in the DRC. Actor, director, and activist Ben Affleck presented her the award at the Kennedy Center in Washington, DC. The same year, Namegabe received the prestigious Knight International Journalism Award for her outstanding work in South Kivu. She received the award on November 12, 2009, at the International Center for Journalists' twenty-fifth anniversary awards dinner in Washington, DC. In addition to her work protecting the rights of women, Namegabe has been incredibly vocal concerning freedom of expression and the press in the DRC. Many media outlets, including the radio station Radio Mudanga, have been banned in the country, and Namegabe's AFEM continues to receive death threats. In 2011, Namegabe was named one of the "100 Most Inspiring People Delivering for Girls and Women" by the women's advocacy group Women Deliver.

PERSONAL LIFE
Namegabe is married to Belgian humanitarian worker Jean-FranÇois Dubuisson, who is the head of the United Nations Development Program in the DRC. They have two children.

SUGGESTED READING
Hall, Aaron, and Sasha Lezhnev. "US Congo Policy: Matching Deeds to Words to End the World's Deadliest War." *Enough Project*. Center for American Progress, 4 Oct. 2011. Web. 30 Jan. 2012.

"Jail Term for Media Mogul." *Star* [South Africa] 11 Dec. 2007, early ed.: 4. Print.

Minoui, Delphine. "Congo's Anti-Rape Crusader." *Daily Beast*. Newsweek/Daily Beast, 28 June 2010. Web. 27 Jan. 2012.

Namegabe, Chouchou. "Congo Activist Presses Senators on Violence." Interview by David Herbert. *NationalJournal.com*. National Journal Group, 13 May 2009. Web. 29 Dec. 2011.

Nuxoll, Kelly. "One Congolese Woman Uses Radio as a Weapon against Rape." *Huffington Post*. HuffPost News, 20 Mar. 2009. Web. 27 Jan. 2012.

Shapiro, Danielle. "Congo Rape Crisis: Study Reveals Shocking New Numbers." *Daily*

Beast. Newsweek/Daily Beast, 11 May 2011. Web. 30 Jan. 2012.

Soguel, Domonique. "Band of Congo Radio Reporters Aid Rape Victims." *Women's eNews.* Women's eNews, 12 Nov. 2008. Web. 29 Dec. 2011.

Walkley, Alison. "Congolese Journalist Speaks about DRC Female Atrocities." *AllAfrica.com.* AllAfrica, 17 Nov. 2009. Web. 29 Dec. 2011.

—*Molly Hagan*

FilmMagic

Mohamed Nasheed

Born: May 17, 1967
Occupation: Maldivian politician, former president of the Maldives

"In politics in this country," Mohamed Nasheed, the deposed president of the Maldives, told a writer for the *Economist* (30 Oct. 2008), "you're either in government or in jail." A longtime political dissident and democratic activist, Nasheed—often called by his nickname, Anni—spent the better part of two decades resisting the dictatorship of President Maumoon Abdul Gayoom, who had ruled the tiny archipelago nation of around 330,000 people since 1978. While enduring torture, imprisonment, and exile, Nasheed set a moral example that earned him comparisons to former South African president Nelson Mandela and the moniker "the Mandela of the Maldives."

"I have personally experienced the worst that a malicious regime can contrive in order to suppress its people," he later said in a speech at a British Conservative Party conference in Manchester, England, as quoted by Robin McKie for the *Observer* (10 Oct. 2009). "I was imprisoned on sixteen different occasions and spent a total of six years in jail. Of these, I spent eighteen months in solitary confinement." The details of the government's treatment of Nasheed are severe. "Punishments included severe sleep and water deprivation, being fed food with crushed glass and being chained to a chair outside for twelve days," Olivia Lang wrote for *BBC News* (29 Oct. 2008). During his term of solitary confinement, Nasheed was imprisoned in a tiny metal shack. Due to beatings and torture, he developed a permanent limp. He also missed the births of his children during his imprisonment.

Nasheed's years of nonviolent activism paid off in October 2008, when, in the first multiparty elections in Maldivian history, he defeated Gayoom to secure the presidency. Thereafter, while working for reform at home, he also emerged on the international scene as an eloquent global-warming activist and the subject of the documentary *The Island President* (2011).

of any nation on the planet—poses an existential threat.

While he won recognition throughout the globe, Nasheed faced entrenched opposition at home, and in February 2012, he was forced from office at gunpoint, leaving the fate of democracy in the Maldives uncertain. Despite his many trials, however, Nasheed remains an idealist. "I'm not cynical about anything. I trust humanity, and I think we have an amazing capacity to do good," he told Ann Hornaday for the *Washington Post* (13 Apr. 2012). "No one's waking up to do bad. We all wake up and hope we're going to do some good."

EARLY LIFE
Mohamed Nasheed was born on May 17, 1967, in Malé, the capital of the Maldives. His father was a successful businessman. For his early education, Nasheed attended the all-male Majeediyya School in Malé from 1971 to 1981. He spent the next two years in Colombo, Sri Lanka, where he studied at the Overseas School. From Sri Lanka, Nasheed next moved to Wiltshire, England, completing his secondary education at Dauntsey's School and passing his university qualification exams, or A-levels, in 1984.

Nasheed's classmates at Dauntsey's remembered him fondly, recalling a well-liked and talented student who enjoyed tennis, rugby, and especially cricket. "He had the most amazing sense of humor, he was very charismatic," Jennifer Cole, a school friend of Nasheed's, told

Nick Britten, John Bingham, and Chris Irvine for the *Daily Telegraph* (30 Oct. 2008). "He had an opinion on everything, he used to play devil's advocate, I think he won a public speaking prize at school. . . . He also loved reading; he would just spend hours in bookshops." Nasheed stayed in England for his undergraduate degree, attending Liverpool John Moores University, where he earned a bachelor of arts degree in maritime studies in 1989.

POLITICAL DISSIDENT AND PRISONER OF CONSCIENCE

Following his graduation, Nasheed returned to the Maldives and, with some associates, founded the magazine *Sangu*. His writing for the publication soon attracted the attention of the ruling Gayoom regime. Over the first five issues of *Sangu*, Nasheed had emerged as a leading critic of the government, writing a series of exposés about political corruption and human-rights abuses. In response to one of Nasheed's articles alleging that the 1989 Maldivian presidential elections had been illegitimate, on November 24, 1990, the police raided *Sangu*'s offices. The magazine was outlawed, and Nasheed, twenty-three years old, was placed under arrest. His long career as a political dissident and democratic activist had begun.

Following his arrest, Nasheed was taken to the Dhoonidhoo detention facility, where he was kept in solitary confinement. On April 8, 1992, he was sentenced to over three years in jail for his alleged participation in a terrorist conspiracy. After he spoke with reporters about his treatment by the authorities, another ten months was added to his sentence for "endangering the peace and stability of the country," according to a report by Amnesty International (May 1996). Nasheed's appeal of the verdict was rejected in May 1993, but he did not serve the full sentence and received his release the following month.

Fresh out of prison, Nasheed took up his reporter's pen once again and continued to chronicle political developments in the Maldives. With an associate, Mohamed Latheef, Nasheed sought to register a new political party with the government in October 1994. Since political parties were not explicitly mentioned in the Maldivian constitution, they were denied. The following month, after returning to the Maldives from a trip to Nepal, Nasheed was arrested once again, this time for critical comments he had made in a Filipino publication about recent elections in the Maldives.

Nasheed was in and out of jail over the next two years. His passport was taken from him, his movements restricted, and his access to legal counsel curtailed. On April 3, 1996, following a questionable trial, Nasheed finally received his sentence: two years in the Gaamadhoo prison. His tribulations did not go unnoticed; Amnesty International declared him a "prisoner of conscience," drawing attention to his case and agitating for his release. Nasheed served three months and then was placed under house arrest for a time, only to be returned to Gaamadhoo for another three months. He was released in December 1996.

Once he was out of prison, Nasheed returned to politics. He successfully ran for the People's Majlis, the Maldivian parliament, in 1999, representing a district in Malé. An outspoken advocate of democracy and political reform, Nasheed once again tried to register a political party, the Maldivian Democratic Party (MDP), without success. His parliamentary career was short lived. Accused of stealing official documents—allegedly children's books—Nasheed was arrested on October 8, 2001, and detained for a number of weeks, at times in solitary confinement. Following another questionable trial, on November 8, 2001, he was sentenced to two-and-a-half years' banishment on the isolated island of Angolhitheemu. The sentence was upheld on appeal, and Nasheed was expelled from the parliament. After six months on Angolhitheemu, he was transferred to house arrest and released on August 29, 2002.

In September 2003, Hassan Evan Naseem, a nineteen-year-old inmate in a Maldivian prison, died while in custody. This sparked a prison riot, during which the authorities shot nineteen convicts, killing three. As news of these incidents leaked out to the public, popular demonstrations erupted. The scale of the "Black Friday" disturbances, as they came to be known, was unprecedented in Maldivian history, as mobs registered their disgust by setting fire to government buildings. Nasheed requested that a doctor take a look at Naseem's body to determine whether he had died of torture. A later investigation revealed that Naseem had been beaten to death by a number of security personnel. The widespread unrest was a pivotal moment in Maldivian resistance to the Gayoom regime, which declared a state of emergency, and calls for reform thereafter gathered momentum. Nevertheless, the following month, running unopposed, Gayoom was reelected president with over 90 percent of the vote.

Despite the growing opposition movement, Nasheed, unable to reclaim his parliamentary seat and still facing government persecution, went into voluntary exile in November 2003. He traveled first to Sri Lanka and then to Great Britain, where he was granted political asylum. While in exile, he and some fellow dissidents founded the MDP. During his stay in the United Kingdom, Nasheed developed a rapport with leaders of the British Conservative Party.

Meanwhile, on December 26, 2004, an enormous earthquake in the Indian Ocean set off a massive tidal wave that inundated the coastlines in its path. Indonesia and Sri Lanka were especially hard hit. Some estimates of the death toll exceed a quarter of a million people. In the Maldives, eighty-two people were killed and twenty-six were reported missing. Much of Malé was flooded, as were many of the country's other islands, inhabited or otherwise. A number of beach resorts—the country's chief economic engines—were completely submerged. For the Maldives, the economic cost of the disaster was estimated at $375 million. Many found the Gayoom government's response to the crisis wanting, and opposition to the regime continued to build.

Returning to Malé from exile in April 2005, Nasheed again dedicated himself to democratic activism. Two months later, Gayoom opened the door to constitutional reforms, legalizing political parties, among other measures, and Nasheed promptly registered the MDP. However, in August 2005, during a demonstration in advance of the anniversary of the Black Friday protests, the regime arrested Nasheed once again, charging him with sedition and terrorism. The charges were later dropped.

As Gayoom instituted reforms, paving the way for a new constitution and democratic elections, Nasheed organized a campaign of civil disobedience to speed up the process. Presidential elections were subsequently scheduled for 2008. In April 2008, the MDP chose Nasheed as its representative in the national elections. After securing 24 percent in the first round of voting, Nasheed faced Gayoom in the runoff election. During the campaign, Nasheed constructed a coalition of opposition parties to rally the anti-Gayoom vote. He also relied on political operatives from the British Conservative Party to help craft his campaign message. For this, despite being a Sunni Muslim, he was accused by Gayoom supporters of spreading Christianity.

THE ISLAND PRESIDENT

On October 28, 2008, Nasheed was elected president of the Maldives with 54 percent of the vote. He was sworn in the following month, pledging to build democracy and fight poverty and the drug epidemic. Upon assuming office, he did not seek to settle scores with the old regime. "I have forgiven my jailers, the torturers. They were following orders," he said, as quoted by Ben Doherty for the *Sydney Morning Herald* (7 Jan. 2012). "I ask people to follow my example and leave Gayoom to grow old here."

How to recover from the dictatorship was just one of the dilemmas confronting Nasheed as president. A heroin problem had ensnared much of the country's youth, with the United Nations estimating that four in ten young people abused hard drugs. The tourism-dependent economy, and with it the nation's finances, was deteriorating in the face of a global recession,

while fears of Islamic extremism and terrorism continued to grow. The threat of global warming also hung over the country.

Throughout his presidency, Nasheed worked to raise awareness about the dangers of global climate change. As temperatures increase, the polar ice caps melt, causing sea levels to rise. For the Maldives, the issue is one of survival. The nation's peak elevation is 2.4 meters above sea level, and 80 percent of the country lies at less than a meter; rising sea levels could erase the nation from the map. According to Doherty, "Fourteen of the country's two hundred inhabited islands are already gone, massive coastal erosion making their seaside villages unlivable. A further seventy islands rely on desalinated drinking water because groundwater aquifers have been overcome by seawater."

The documentary filmmaker Jon Shenk detailed Nasheed's early efforts as president to rally international support for limiting greenhouse-gas emissions in *The Island President*. The movie follows Nasheed in the Maldives and to international climate-change conferences at the UN in New York and in Copenhagen, Denmark. As part of his efforts to raise awareness, Nasheed staged an underwater cabinet meeting in scuba gear. In March 2009, he pledged that the Maldives would shift to renewable energy sources by 2020 to become the world's first carbon-neutral nation. He also started a fund to pay for the relocation of all Maldivian citizens should climate change make their nation unlivable. In her article on *The Island President*, Hornaday wrote, "If Nasheed's mission doesn't end with unqualified success in Copenhagen, what emerges is still an impressive portrait of a charismatic, compelling leader punching far above his weight and managing to land a few blows."

DOWNFALL

Just as *The Island President* received a wider theatrical release in early 2012, the domestic political situation in the Maldives reached a crisis point. During his presidency, Nasheed had difficulty managing his disparate coalition, especially with pro-Gayoom forces still a powerful and obstructionist presence throughout all sectors of government. Early in his tenure, cabinet members from other parties started to resign; soon these parties abandoned the coalition altogether. To protest corruption and obstructionism in parliament, Nasheed's entire cabinet stepped down in 2010. Replacing them led to clashes with parliament and the judiciary. Popular protests against Nasheed broke out in December 2011, and an opposition movement developed that included many of the Islamic political parties that had helped elect Nasheed in 2008.

The following month, Nasheed ordered the arrest of a criminal-court judge he believed was stalling on corruption cases involving members of the former regime. This set off even larger civil disturbances. Soon, elements of the police sided with the protesters, while the armed forces appeared to remain loyal to Nasheed. With his house surrounded by police, he went to army headquarters to complain. "But they said they were siding with the police, and they asked me to resign within one hour," Nasheed told Tad Friend for the *New Yorker* (27 Feb. 2012). "They said that if I did not resign they would use their arms on the people—and on me, for good measure."

Nasheed chose to announce his resignation at the president's office in Malé. He was escorted there and, on February 7, 2012, stepped down from office. His vice president, Mohamed Waheed Hassan—whom Nasheed suspected conspired in the plot to oust him—succeeded him. "I believe if I continue as the president of the Maldives, the people of the country would suffer more," Nasheed said in his resignation statement, as quoted by Jim Yardley for the *New York Times* (7 Feb. 2012). "I wish the Maldives would have a consolidated democracy. I wish for justice to be established. My wish is for the progress and prosperity of the people."

In the aftermath of his resignation, demonstrations by Nasheed's supporters were broken up with tear gas and batons, and a warrant was issued for his arrest. Despite Nasheed's claim that the power transfer was an illegitimate coup d'état, the United States and India quickly recognized the new government, while the United Nations stayed in the background. In a piece for the *New York Times* (8 Feb. 2012), Nasheed blamed his downfall on the remnants of the Gayoom dictatorship, stating that "long after the revolutions, powerful networks of regime loyalists can remain behind and can attempt to strangle their nascent democracies."

Since his resignation, Nasheed has traveled the world promoting *The Island President*. When at home in the Maldives, he is under constant government surveillance. On June 16, 2012, he secured the MDP's presidential nomination; however, it is unclear when the next presidential election will take place. Waheed has said that according to the constitution, the earliest possibility is in July 2013.

PERSONAL LIFE
Nasheed is married with two daughters. His wife works for the United Nations. Among the honors Nasheed has earned over the years are the 2009 Anna Lindh Prize for his contributions on behalf of human rights and a 2010 United Nations Champions of the Earth Award. In 2009, *Time* magazine declared Nasheed a "Hero of the Environment," and *Newsweek* named him to its 2010 "World's Ten Best Leaders" list. During his various stays in prison, Nasheed wrote several books on Maldivian history. A gifted speaker, he

is renowned for delivering eloquent addresses without the use of notes or teleprompters.

Despite all he has endured, Nasheed has never given in to despair or wavered in his commitment to the future. "You carry on; you keep going," he told Peter Howell for the *Toronto Star* (15 June 2012). "You take a step forward and then the next day, you wake up and take another step. If you fail, or if you are beaten back down, you never give up. You get back on your feet again and keep trying. One day, when we have run out of all of our failures, the only thing left will be success."

SUGGESTED READING
Britten, Nick, John Bingham, and Chris Irvine. "New Maldives President Mohamed Nasheed Is British Public Schoolboy with Tory Links." *Daily Telegraph*. Telegraph Media Group, 30 Oct. 2008. Web. 21 June 2012.

Burke, Jason, and James Melkie. "Mohamed Nasheed: Maldives Leader Who Has Been in Tighter Spots." *Guardian*. Guardian News and Media, 9 Feb. 2012. Web. 21 June 2012.

Doherty, Ben. "Maldives Faces Tides of Change." *Sydney Morning Herald*. Fairfax Media, 7 Jan. 2012. Web. 21 June 2012.

Hornaday, Ann. "Mohamed Nasheed Talks About 'The Island President,' Keeping Fragile Democracy Afloat." *Washington Post*. Washington Post, 13 April 2012. Web. 21 June 2012.

Howell, Peter. "Island Ex-President Mohamed Nasheed Still Making Waves." *Toronto Star*. Torstar Media Group, 15 June 2012. Web. 21 June 2012.

Lang, Olivia. "'Anni' Heralds New Era in Maldives." *BBC News*. British Broadcasting Company, 29 Oct. 2008. Web. 21 June 2012.

Nasheed, Mohamed. "The Dregs of Dictatorship." *New York Times*. New York Times, 8 Feb. 2012. Web. 21 June 2012.

Ramesh, Randeep. "Maldives Human Rights Activist Wins Presidential Election." *Guardian*. Guardian News and Media, 29 Oct. 2008. Web. 21 June 2012.

—*Paul McCaffrey*

Ory Okolloh
Born: 1977
Occupation: Activist, lawyer

Ory Okolloh is currently the policy manager for Africa at Google. She works with government leaders, regulators, industry groups, and technology specialists to increase the availability and utility of the Internet on her native continent. Before signing on with the online giant, Okolloh, a lawyer by training, maintained a popular political blog called *Kenyan Pundit*. She was also instrumental in founding both *Mzalendo*, a website that tracks the performance of Kenyan members of parliament (MPs), and Ushahidi, an innovative software platform that allows ordinary citizens to report on events they are witnessing in real time, using text messaging, e-mail, Twitter, and other online services. Ushahidi has proven a flexible and vital tool in situations of civil unrest or natural disaster and has been deployed all over the world. The software allows users to collect information through "crowdsourcing," gathering texts, video, pictures, and other posts written by those experiencing an event firsthand. "Ushahidi remixes have been used in India to monitor elections; in Africa to report medicine shortages; in the Middle East to collect reports of wartime violence; and in Washington, DC, where the *Washington Post* partnered to build a site to map road blockages and the location of available snowplows and blowers," Anand Giridharadas wrote for the *New York Times* (13 Mar. 2010).

Getty Images

EARLY LIFE AND EDUCATION

Okolloh was born in the east African nation of Kenya in 1977. Because of the African ethos that calls for helping all family members in need, a steady stream of aunts, uncles, cousins, and grandparents appeared on the Okollohs' doorstep seeking aid, regularly depleting her parents' coffers. Thus, while her mother and father were not desperately poor, money was continually in short supply. "The bellwether for whether our family was broke or not was breakfast," she explained at a talk held in Arusha, Tanzania, in June 2007, under the auspices of the nonprofit group TED (Technology, Entertainment, Design). "You know, when things were good, we had eggs and sausages. When things were bad, we had porridge."

Okolloh's intelligence became evident when she was a child, and her parents were determined that she should attend a more challenging private Catholic school instead of the free public school in their neighborhood. At the start of every term, an administrator entered the classroom, announced the names of students whose parents had not paid their tuition in a timely manner, and asked those students to leave the school until their debts were settled. Okolloh was frequently on the list, causing her great embarrassment. Although as an adult she came to appreciate their desire to see her receive a first-class education, as a girl she often wondered why her mother and father would not simply settle for sending her to the local elementary school.

Kenyan high schools are rigidly ranked, and students are admitted to top-tier national schools only if they score well enough on standardized entrance exams. Students with lower scores are relegated to second-tier provincial schools. Okolloh set her sights on one of the national institutions but missed the cut-off score by a single point. Dismayed by her obvious disappointment, her father set out to convince the school's headmistress to admit her, arguing that his daughter was obviously smart and would be a wonderful student, despite the one-point shortfall on her test. "Because we were nobodies, and because we didn't have privilege, and because my father didn't have the right last name, he was treated like dirt," Okolloh recalled during her TED talk. "And I sat and listened to the headmistress talk to him, saying, you know, 'Who do you think you are?' and, you know, 'You must be joking if you think you can get a slot.' And I had gone to school with other girls who were kids of politicians and who had done much, much worse than I did, and they had slots there. And there's nothing worse than seeing your parent being humiliated in front of you, you know?" When the school called a few weeks later, admitting that they had a slot to fill, Okolloh, who still felt stung, refused to attend, opting for a school that was considered somewhat less prestigious instead.

When it was time to choose a college, Okolloh did not consider Kenyan universities, believing that they stifled creativity and encouraged stale, formulaic thinking. "I never would have survived the University of Nairobi," she explained in a video posted on the website SavingAfrica.org. "I would have been in trouble [constantly] for talking out of turn or refusing to play by the rules."

It seemed to Okolloh that in the United States, things would be different. "They really know how to recognize talent there and to harness it," she said in the SavingAfrica.org video. She won admission to the University of Pittsburgh, graduating summa cum laude in 2000, with a bachelor's degree in political science. While there, she was active in the group Pittsburgh Action Against Rape (PAAR), which provides crisis intervention and counseling and lobbies against sexual violence. She also worked as an intern for both the American Civil Liberties Union (ACLU) and the Institute for Democracy in Kenya.

While Okolloh was still a student, her father became ill with AIDS. The medication he was on cost thirty dollars a day, and while it halted the symptoms of the disease, the family was soon unable to afford his treatment. A friend who traveled to India on occasion volunteered to bring back a supply of a more affordable, generic version of the pill, which helped for a time. Ultimately, even that solution grew too expensive. One Friday in 1999, he became desperately sick, and the family realized that he needed medical attention immediately. With no cash on hand to buy the needed drugs—ATMs were not common in Kenya—they took him to a public hospital, where the staffers started an ineffective course of intravenous fluids. He died before the banks opened on Monday.

HARVARD

Okolloh decided to attend law school after earning her BA, despite her professor's attempts to dissuade her. Professor Mitchell Seligson believed that it would be a waste of her talents to enter an already crowded field. After she explained, however, that many of the social activists she had encountered possessed legal training, Seligson relented. Disappointed that she intended to apply to law school only in Pittsburgh, which was familiar and comfortable to her, he convinced her to try for Harvard. It was a wise choice; not only was she accepted, but she quickly became one of the most accomplished students in her class.

In 2003 Okollah was awarded a Chayes International Public Service Fellowship, which she served at the World Bank's Department of Institutional Integrity. She also became actively involved with the *Harvard Human Rights Journal* and Advocates for Human Rights, a group that allowed Harvard law students to gain practical legal experience while earning academic credit. Additionally, she served as the vice president of the Harvard African Law Association, whose mission is to unite students of African descent, while spreading information about the legal, social, and economic issues facing Africa. In the midst of her many extracurricular activities, she also contributed to her family's financial well-being. She helped support her mother in the wake of her father's death, paid her sister's tuition bills, and chipped in for the care of an orphaned cousin. Okolloh earned her law degree in 2005.

EARLY CAREER

With a Harvard law degree in hand, Okolloh found herself in great demand. She had been a summer associate at the Washington, DC, office of the well-regarded firm Covington and Burling, and she was offered a six-figure salary to join the practice on a permanent basis. "With two paychecks, or three paychecks, I could have solved a lot of my family's problems," she said at the TED conference in Tanzania. "But I walked away from that, because my passion was here [in Africa]." Okolloh accepted a post as the legal and corporate-affairs manager for Enablis, a company that provides business-development services, capital, and support to emerging entrepreneurs in Africa. Vitally interested in the political situation in her native country, she also started a blog, *Kenyan Pundit*, which carried the tagline "Opinions, commentary, na kadhalika." (the Swahili phrase *na kadhalika* is translated by most sources as "et cetera" or "and so on.")

In 2006, working with a technically adept colleague, Okolloh initiated a web project tracking the performance of members of Kenya's parliament. Dubbed *Mzalendo,* meaning "patriot," the site includes biographies of all the Kenyan MPs, as well as their voting and attendance records. Administrators also post the content of relevant bills. Additionally, readers can submit questions, which are then posted for the politicians to answer. "We started this because we were tired," Okolloh explained in Tanzania. "I believe that accountability stems from demand. You're not just going to be accountable out of the goodness of your heart. And we as Africans need to start challenging our leaders. . . . Another thing is that these leaders are a reflection of our society. We talk about African governments like they've been dropped from Mars, you know? [But] they come from us. And what is it about our society that is generating leaders that we don't like? And how can we change that?"

USHAHIDI

In December 2007 Okolloh, who was then living in Johannesburg, South Africa, traveled back to Kenya to vote in the hotly contested presidential election between incumbent Mwai Kibaki, an ethnic Kikuyu, and the opposition leader, Raila Odinga, a member of the Luo tribe. The election, as Jeffrey Gettleman wrote for the *New York Times* (31 Dec. 2007), "seems to have tapped into an atavistic vein of tribal tension that always lay beneath the surface in Kenya but until now had not provoked widespread mayhem." When

Kibaki was declared the winner of an election deemed by international observers to be undeniably flawed, widespread rioting broke out, and martial law was declared. A total media blackout was announced, making it difficult for journalists to get information.

As Okolloh updated *Kenyan Pundit* with the little news she was able to glean from her sources in parliament and elsewhere, she was flooded with comments from worried readers, informing her of incidents of sectarian violence they had witnessed in their own villages and towns. She began posting new information every few minutes. "There was a realization that we're not that far from a civil war," she recalled to Josh Halliday for the London *Guardian* (16 Aug. 2010). "There was fear and anger, and a sense of community soon grew. It spiraled completely when people were struggling to find out what was going on, including journalists." Okolloh was force to return to Johannesburg on January 2, 2008, when she ran out of diapers and formula for her infant daughter, whom she had brought with her to Nairobi, Kenya's capital. However, she remained determined to continue her postings and to share the information she was receiving more effectively.

Counting on the power of social media, she wrote on her blog: "For the reconciliation process to occur at the local level the truth of what happened will first have to come out. Guys looking to do something—any techies out there willing to do a mashup of where the violence and destruction is using Google Maps?" Within just a few days, volunteer programmers, including David Kobia, a Kenyan computer expert living in Alabama, had written a software code that allowed anyone to send in information—including video and photos—via text message, phone, or e-mail. The information was then uploaded onto a map, providing a broad picture of what was happening, based on the amount of data originating from each location. The original site evolved into an open source platform that anyone could repurpose for their own needs. Okolloh subsequently wrote on her blog, "Last week, in between nightmares about where my country was going, I was dreaming of a Google mashup to document incidents of violence, looting, etc., that have occurred during the post-election crisis. Today, Ushahidi is born." (*Ushahidi* means "testimony" in Swahili.) In order to ensure some measure of reliability, Okolloh tried reaching some of those sending in initial reports and used secondary government sources, information from aid groups, and whatever press contacts she could muster to verify the submissions.

In late 2008, as a quarter-million refugees fled violent clashes in the Democratic Republic of Congo, several hundred miles away in Johannesburg, Okolloh coordinated on-the-ground reports of food and water shortages and medical emergencies. Ushahidi has since been used to track violence in Gaza, the availability of medicine in African pharmacies, and poll activity in India, among other situations.

The service became even more of a global phenomenon when a massive earthquake hit Haiti in mid-January 2010, killing an estimated fifty thousand people and leaving more than a million homeless. Within four days, Ushahidi had received some one hundred thousand urgent reports from the ground, such as, "No food or drinking water since 1/12, location Tabarre Port-au-Prince, Haiti, 01/28/2010" and "Still in need of food and water at the Carrefour sports centre, location Carrefour sports center Port-au-Prince Haiti, 23:51." While wrenching to read, the messages allowed rescue workers to find people buried in the rubble or get needed supplies to those in trouble. The following month, a similarly severe earthquake struck Chile, displacing a reported 1.5 million people, and Ushahidi once again came to widespread attention for its role in the disaster recovery.

On a more lighthearted note, American journalists took great delight in pointing out the irony of Ushahidi being used when severe snowstorms hit the mid-Atlantic region of the United States in the winter of 2010. "Think about that," Anand Giridharadas wrote. "The capital of the sole superpower is deluged with snow, and to whom does its local newspaper turn to help dig out? Kenya."

GOOGLE

At the end of 2010, Okolloh was hired by Internet behemoth Google to oversee company policy in Africa. She gave up leadership of Ushahidi to accept the post and wrote on her blog: "The role will involve developing policy [and] strategies on a number of areas of relevance to Google and the Internet in Africa and will involve working with different parties including government leaders, policy makers, regulators, industry groups, and so on. It is a huge opportunity to bring Google's resources to bear as far as the growth and development of the Internet in Africa (and hopefully a reminder of why I went to law school in the first place!)."

In 2010 the editors of *Foreign Policy* magazine placed Okolloh on their list of the world's one hundred top thinkers. The following year the editors of *Fast Company* named her one of the most influential women working in the field of technology; Chris Dannen wrote for the magazine that year, "It's [her] kind of technological creativity that can answer critics' insistence that Twitter is just for Ashton Kutcher to tell people what he had for lunch." Similarly, the editors of *Newsweek* placed her in the number-one spot on their 2011 list of the twenty most powerful women in Africa.

Giridharadas summed up Okolloh's contributions eloquently, writing, "They say that history is written by the victors. But now, before the victors win, there is a chance to scream out with a text message that will not vanish. What would we know about what passed between Turks and Armenians, between Germans and Jews, if every one of them had had the chance, before the darkness, to declare for all time: 'I was here, and this is what happened to me'?" Okolloh lives in Johannesburg with her three daughters.

SUGGESTED READING

Bahree, Megha. "Citizen Voices." *Forbes* 8 Dec. 2008: 83. Print.

Giridharadas, Anand. "Africa's Gift to Silicon Valley: How to Track a Crisis." *New York Times*. New York Times, 13 Mar. 2010. Web. 1 Mar. 2012.

Halliday, Josh. "Ushahidi: Giving Citizens the Power to Put News on the Map." (London) *Guardian*. 16 Aug. 2010: M1. Print.

Howard, Caroline. "Names You Need to Know in 2011: Ory Okolloh." *Forbes*. Forbes.com, 12 Nov. 2010. Web. 1 Mar. 2012.

Naidoo, Shanthini. "Tracking the Chaos." (South Africa) *Times*. 31 Aug. 2010: 23. Print.

—*Mari Rich*

Matthew Olsen

Born: February 21, 1962
Occupation: Director of the National Counterterrorism Center (NCTC)

Since he was sworn in as director of the National Counterterrorism Center (NCTC), on August 16, 2011, Matthew Olsen has been charged with one principle responsibility: "Doing everything [I] can to prevent an attack. That is my overriding mission here," he told Suzanne Kelly and Pam Benson for *CNN News* (14 Sep. 2011, online). "Beyond that, it is to continue to place the center on a footing where we can be the place where all threat and terrorism information is available for analysis." Though his role as the nation's top counterterrorism operative is often compared to that of Jack Bauer, the fictional protagonist of the Fox Network's series *24*, who single-handedly thwarts various spectacular terrorist attacks, Olsen's day-to-day responsibilities require a different skill set. Olsen's predecessor at the NCTC, Michael Leiter, told Kelly and Benson that "as director of NCTC you are charged with coordinating communications between organizations you don't control . . . so you have to be able to use the power of persuasion."

Olsen built those powers of persuasion over the course of a twenty-year career as a

Getty Images

government attorney. He has served at the US Department of Justice (DOJ) and the US attorney's office for the District of Columbia, headed President Barack Obama's Guantanamo Review Task Force, and has been the general counsel for the National Security Agency (NSA). Even before he joined the NCTC, Olsen was regarded as "one of the most powerful attorneys in the federal government," according to a writer for the *Washington Post's* online "WhoRunsGov" section (2012).

EARLY LIFE AND EDUCATION

Matthew Glen Olsen was born on February 21, 1962, in Fargo, North Dakota, one of three children and the only son of Van and Myrna Olsen. In 1965 Van Olsen moved the family to Washington, DC, where, for the next ten years, he served as chief of staff to Republican congressman Mark Andrews of North Dakota. Subsequently, he represented domestic sugar beet growers in dealings with Congress and helped negotiate trade agreements as a federal appointee to the Agricultural Technical Advisory Committee.

Olsen earned his bachelor's of arts degree from the University of Virginia in 1984. He spent the following year as a copy aide at the *Washington Post*. He then attended Harvard Law School from 1985 to 1988, where he was the executive editor of the *Harvard Civil Rights–Civil Liberties Law Review*. After graduating cum laude from Harvard Law, Olsen moved to Washington, DC, where from 1988 to 1990, he clerked for Judge Norma Holloway Johnson at the US District

Court for the District of Columbia. Following the conclusion of his clerkship, Olsen stayed in Washington, joining the law firm of Arnold & Porter as an associate.

A GOVERNMENT ATTORNEY

Olsen left Arnold & Porter in 1992 to begin his career in public service, accepting a position as a trial attorney at the DOJ's Civil Rights Division. Two years later, he became a federal prosecutor when he was appointed assistant US attorney for Washington, DC—a post he would hold for the next dozen years. During his tenure as a federal prosecutor, Olsen advanced to a supervisory role. Coinciding with his rise through the ranks, the focus of the US attorney's office and of national law enforcement shifted, as concerns about terrorism and domestic security increased in the late 1990s and became paramount following the September 11, 2001, terrorist attacks. Olsen adapted with the changing situation and took a leading role in many of the office's more sensitive cases, including some covering international terrorism and espionage. Commenting on his experience as a federal prosecutor in the questionnaire he submitted to the US Senate Select Committee on Intelligence as part of the confirmation process for his NCTC appointment, Olsen wrote, "I learned first-hand the value of working as a team with professionals in operational roles and of building coalitions with federal, state, and local partners" (12 July 2011, online).

From 2003 to 2004, Olsen was deputy chief of the organized crime and narcotics trafficking section of the Washington, DC, US attorney's office. From 2004 to 2005, he acted as special counsel to Robert F. Mueller III, the director of the Federal Bureau of Investigation (FBI). The FBI experience proved invaluable to Olsen, giving him insights into how to successfully conduct prosecutions related to national security. During his time reporting to Mueller, Olsen had "a front-row seat," as he told Carol D. Leonnig for the *Washington Post* (14 Aug. 2005, online). "What I saw at the FBI is that these [terrorism] cases take time to develop. And they end up in a prosecutor's office because of relationships with a law enforcement agency . . . trust that develops over years."

At the time Olsen's collaboration with the FBI ended, Kenneth L. Wainstein, the US attorney for Washington, DC, was positioning his office to take a lead role in investigating and prosecuting suspected terrorists. Wainstein tapped Olsen to set up and run the office's national security section, a team composed of around a dozen attorneys that would specialize in cases impacting national security. "The national security section will bring together prosecutors handling cases involving terrorism, terrorism hoaxes, espionage, leaks of classified information, and

other sensitive matters," wrote Leonnig. Olsen served as chief of the national security section from 2005 to 2006.

THE DEPARTMENT OF JUSTICE (DOJ)

In 2006, Olsen's twelve-year career at the US attorney's office came to a close when he accepted a position as deputy assistant attorney general at the DOJ. There, he helped establish the agency's national security division, which was created to facilitate and regulate the exchange of information between prosecutors and US intelligence services. He spent the next three years overseeing it, first as deputy assistant attorney general, then as acting assistant attorney general. Olsen described the unit's role to Robert Schmidt and James Rowley for *Bloomberg* (31 Jan. 2008, online): "We want to make sure that everyone knows what each other's doing. . . . make sure that we're taking full advantage of this [intelligence] information."

During his time at the national security division, Olsen dealt with a host of complicated dilemmas arising out of the George W. Bush administration's prosecution of the War on Terror. Following the 9/11 terrorist attacks, the administration implemented a series of surveillance measures to gather intelligence on potential terrorists. Some of these procedures involved wiretapping and collected data from domestic calls, in apparent violation of the law. When revelations regarding these practices were reported by the press in 2005, the administration revamped its approach, and Olsen carried out the changes the following year. "One of his responsibilities there was to oversee implementation of new legal procedures and rules that were introduced after the Bush administration's electronic-surveillance program was publicly exposed," Mark Hosenball reported for *Newsweek* (10 June 2006, online).

While at DOJ, Olsen argued before the Federal Intelligence Surveillance Court (FISC) on behalf of various federal agencies seeking approval to wiretap American nationals. Established by Congress in 1978 as part of the Federal Intelligence Surveillance Act (FISA), the FISC is a secret court that has jurisdiction over requests by the federal government to conduct surveillance on suspected foreign agents.

GUANTANAMO BAY REVIEW TASK FORCE

In January 2009, the newly inaugurated president Barack Obama established the Guantanamo Bay Review Task Force to examine issues with the Guantanamo Bay detention center for suspected terrorists at Guantanamo Bay Naval Base in Cuba, and to work toward closing the detention center. The new attorney general, Eric Holder, appointed Olsen as executive director of the task force in February 2009. Opened by the Bush administration in January 2002, the detention center at Guantanamo Bay, also called GTMO or Gitmo, has been used to house detainees captured on the battlefields of Afghanistan, Iraq, and elsewhere during the War on Terror. The location was chosen because it was outside of US legal jurisdiction, and thus, authorities maintained, GTMO prisoners did not have the legal rights afforded those on American soil, and they could be held without charge or trial and be subjected to more severe interrogation measures. Once opened, GTMO became a focus of criticism both in the United States and abroad, with many seeing it as an affront to human rights. GTMO defenders, on the other hand, argued that the facility was required to maintain national security and keep terrorists from once again conspiring to attack the United States.

By the time Olsen was selected to head the task force, around 240 terrorism suspects were held at GTMO. It was up to Olsen and the sixty-member task force—composed of attorneys, defense analysts, and intelligence agents—to decide whether to prosecute, transfer, release, or continue to hold GTMO prisoners, and to determine whether the facility could indeed be closed. Among Olsen's first tasks as executive director was to set up an intelligence database accessible to all members of the task force, which contained all known intelligence about the detainees. "There's no precedent for what we've done in terms of collecting this information in one place—it didn't exist in one place before we started this process," Olsen told a reporter for the *BBC* (17 Jan. 2010, online). From there, the task force set about analyzing the data and attempting to formulate a consensus on how to best handle each prisoner.

"We have a meeting every Wednesday," Olsen told the *BBC*, describing the task force's deliberations. "We review the cases of the detainees at Guantanamo and try to reach decisions about the appropriate disposition of each detainee." For each prisoner, a variety of issues had to be sorted through. "We look at the questions of transfer and we look at the questions involving the possible prosecution of detainees," Olsen stated. "What we are looking at is 'can this person be safely transferred out of the United States?' . . . 'Can they be transferred to a country that will be able to implement adequate mitigation measures to address any threat the detainee may pose?' It's a judgment on risk. . . . And then with respect to prosecution, there's the judgment on 'is there sufficient admissible evidence to pursue a prosecution?'"

One particular complication for the task force was how to handle detainees from the nation of Yemen. The al-Qaeda terrorist network had a strong presence in Yemen, and there had been instances of Saudi detainees being released from GTMO and resurfacing in Yemen

as terrorist operatives. Moreover, transferring Yemeni prisoners from GTMO to facilities in their home country carried an element of risk that they could escape, as central authority in large sectors of the country was not strong enough to prevent the possibility. Olsen understood that there would always be an element of risk. He told the *BBC* reporter, "No decision about any of these detainees is without some risk. We need to be clear about the fact that we're making predicted judgments at some level about whether somebody is going to pose a risk to us in the future if they are released. . . . But I do think that what we are doing is bringing to bear the right people and the right approach to make those decisions in the best possible way."

The task force completed its work in January 2010 and published its findings later that May. Based on its recommendations, GTMO remained open, though on a much smaller scale. Of the 240 detainees, many of whom had already been moved from the facility, the task force determined that most were low-level fighters and did not pose a serious threat to the United States. Yet around 10 percent were judged to be actively involved in some capacity in plots to attack the United States at the time they were captured. The status of another 5 percent of detainees could not be determined.

The task force concluded that 126 of the inmates should be transferred out of GTMO either to their home countries or to some other nation. Another thirty Yemeni detainees could be sent home once security conditions stabilized there. Additionally, the task force found there was sufficient evidence to prosecute thirty-six GTMO prisoners either in military tribunals or federal courts. And, according to the *Washington Post*'s "WhoRunsGov," forty-eight GTMO detainees were to remain in Cuba "because they were ruled too dangerous for release yet unprosecutable, either because a trial would compromise intelligence-gathering measures, or because evidence was obtained using force."

Though the task force's conclusions were a disappointment for many who had hoped to see GTMO closed, Olsen won plaudits for his stewardship of the task force. *Newsweek*'s Hosenball commented that "although six separate government agencies took part in the review, Olsen managed to get a unanimous decision from the participants on how to resolve each detainee's case." As a consequence, Olsen retained the confidence of the president, who soon appointed him to lead another important project.

THE NATIONAL SECURITY AGENCY (NSA) AND NATIONAL COUNTERTERRORISM CENTER (NCTC)

Following the completion of the task force's work in January 2010, President Obama named Olsen associate deputy attorney general in

March, and then, in July, chose him to serve as the National Security Agency (NSA)'s general counsel. After obtaining the necessary security clearances, Olsen took up his duties at the NSA the following month. As he had with the GTMO task force, Olsen would once again handle some of the nation's most sensitive intelligence matters. The NSA position, according to "WhoRunsGov," is "considered one of the most powerful, albeit secretive, legal positions in the federal government." Hosenball described the NSA as an "ultrasecret agency" that "uses some of the world's most powerful computer systems in a global electronic-eavesdropping network that civil-liberties advocates call the closest thing the US government has to [George] Orwell's Big Brother."

Olsen held his NSA post for the next year, until Obama nominated him for the NCTC post. In a White House press release announcing his nomination (1 July 2011, online), Obama stated: "Matt has a distinguished record of service in our intelligence community and I'm confident he will continue to build on our strong counterterrorism efforts. Matt will be a critical part of my national security team as we work tirelessly to thwart attacks against our nation and do everything in our power to protect the American people."

The NCTC was established by an act of Congress in 2004 to "Lead our nation's effort to combat terrorism at home and abroad by analyzing the threat, sharing that information with our partners, and integrating all instruments of national power to ensure unity of effort," according to the NCTC's website. The NCTC accomplishes this mission through a two-pronged strategy. First, it functions as a clearinghouse for all US terrorism-related intelligence by examining, correlating, and sharing data from and among various sources. Second, it plans counterterrorism operations. On the first responsibility, the NCTC director reports to the director of National Intelligence; on the second, he reports to the president.

Despite his credentials at the US Attorney's office in Washington, the DOJ, and the NSA, Olsen faced some opposition to his confirmation. Republican congressman Frank R. Wolf of Virginia wrote a letter voicing his concerns to the Senate committee debating his nomination. He claimed that Olsen was not forthright with Congress while heading the Guantanamo task force and recommended that the Senate reject him. Despite Wolf's objection, the Senate voted to confirm Olsen, and he officially began his post in August 2011.

Each day at the NCTC, Olsen begins his morning with a threat briefing compiled by intelligence analysts, which details potential plots that may be developing and how the NCTC is addressing them. Thereafter, he attends meetings, many of them management related. When Olsen came to the NCTC, Leiter told him to always keep two principles in mind. "The first thing was that the greatest asset of the center was the work force and to really pay close attention to the care and feeding of the work force," Olsen told Kelly and Benson. "The second was to be really mindful of the team effort and that we work largely as part of a broader team, as part of the counterterrorism community, and spend some part of every day thinking about collaborating."

PERSONAL LIFE

Olsen is married to Fern Louise Shepard, with whom he has three children. Over the years he has received various awards and honors, among them the Attorney General Distinguished Service Award in 2010, the Attorney General Award for Excellence in Furthering National Security in 2008, and the John Marshall Award for Trial Advocacy in 2006. From 2001 until he joined the NCTC, Olsen served as an adjunct professor at Georgetown University Law Center. Reflecting on his shift from practicing attorney to national security manager, Olsen told Kelly and Benson, "I definitely don't miss being a lawyer. I totally have embraced this role."

SUGGESTED READING

BBC News. "The Man Who Decides the Fate of Guantanamo Detainees." *BBC News.* The British Broadcasting Corp., 17 Jan. 2010. Web. 21 May 2012.

Finn, Peter. "Matthew Olsen Tapped as Next Head of NCTC." *Washington Post.* Washington Post Co., 1 July 2011. Web. 21 May 2012.

Hayden, Erik. "Getting to Know the Nominated Counterterrorism Chief." *Atlantic Wire.* Atlantic Monthly Group, 1 July 2011. Web. 21 May 2012.

Hosenball, Mark. "New Chief Lawyer for UltraSecret NSA." *Newsweek.* Newsweek/Daily Beast Co., LLC, 10 June 2010. Web. 21 May 2012.

Kelly, Suzanne, and Pam Benson. "The Man Who Would Keep You Safe: The Case File on Matthew Olsen." *CNN.* Cable News Network, 14 Sep. 2011. Web. 21 May 2012.

"WhoRunsGov: Matthew Olsen." *Washington Post.* Washington Post Co., Web. 21 May 2012.

—*Paul McCaffrey*

Amancio Ortega Gaona

Born: March 28, 1936
Occupation: Fashion entrepreneur

Amancio Ortega Gaona is the founder and long-time former chairman of the Inditex Group, the biggest clothing retailer by sales in the world. Inditex is best known for being the parent company of the global fashion juggernaut Zara (pronounced THAH-rah in Spain and ZAH-rah everywhere else), which has "become as much a symbol of Spain as paella and sangria," Dale Fuchs wrote for the London *Independent* (13 Jan. 2011). Ortega, who came from humble beginnings and received no formal education, started working in the fashion industry in his early teens and ran a successful clothing manufacturing business before opening his first Zara store in 1975 in the port city of La Coruña in northern Spain.

Instead of outsourcing his goods to external suppliers, like most other clothing retailers at the time, Ortega adopted a vertical integration model for his enterprise, which allowed him to control every aspect of the production and distribution process, from the sourcing of raw materials to the design, selection, and cutting of cloth, to wholesale and retail sales. Zara thus became known for offering trendy and high-quality haute couture clothing at affordable prices and for producing a wide range of ever-changing stock at a rapid rate—a revolutionary and now much-imitated strategy that has come to be referred to as "fast fashion," in which designs move from runway to store in a matter of weeks to satisfy the latest customer needs and preferences. Ortega's "fast fashion" model proved to be a major success and during the late 1970s and early 1980s he opened Zara stores all over Spain.

Ortega formed Inditex in 1985 to help with Zara's expansion into other countries, which began in the latter part of that decade with the opening of stores in Portugal, New York, and Paris; there are now over 1,600 Zara stores in more than eighty countries around the world. Remarkably, Ortega has steered Zara through rapid global expansion without any form of traditional advertising, instead relying on word of mouth and prime locations for his stores, all of which use eye-catching window displays and elegant in-store layouts to attract customers. This "democratization of fashion," as it has been called, prompted Daniel Piette, a member of the executive committee of the luxury goods group Moët Hennessy Louis Vuitton (also known as LVMH), to call Zara "possibly the most innovative and devastating retailer in the world," as Stephen Armstrong noted for the London *Telegraph* (13 Aug. 2008). Meanwhile, the Spanish press has famously nicknamed Zara "the Terminator" for its forceful presence in the textile world.

© Dusko Despotovic/Sygma/Corbis

Despite being the richest man in Spain and fifth richest man in the world, according to *Forbes* magazine, Ortega has earned a reputation for being notoriously protective of his private life, never granting interviews and shunning social and public events; there were no known photographs of him until the late 1990s, when several were released in the run-up to Inditex's initial public offering (IPO) on the Spanish Stock Exchange in 2001. Nevertheless, the profile of Zara and Inditex has continued to rise despite a slowdown in consumer spending and fluctuating economic conditions. In 2011 Ortega stepped down as chairman of Inditex to retire; he remains on the company's board. Inditex generates nearly $14 billion in annual worldwide sales and, in addition to its flagship chain Zara, owns a slew of other popular clothing brands, including Pull & Bear, Massimo Dutti, Bershka, and Stradivarius.

EARLY LIFE AND EDUCATION

Amancio Ortega Gaona—also known to family and close friends as "Cholo"—was born on March 28, 1936, in Busdongo de Arbas, a town in the León province in northwestern Spain. His father was a railway worker and his mother worked as a housemaid. Ortega's older brother, Antonio, was the first in his family to work in the fashion and textile industry and is credited with ushering Ortega's move into the business; Antonio died of bone cancer in 1987. His older sister, Josefina (known as "Pepita"), also played a major role in his early fashion career and worked at Inditex until her retirement. His other sister, Pilar, who died in 2000, was never involved in the activities of Ortega and his siblings. According to Enrique Badía's book *Zara and Her Sisters*, when Ortega was about nine years old his family moved to La Coruña (also known as A Coruña), a city in the region of Galicia on Spain's northwestern coast. There, he and his family lived in modest surroundings. There is no known information of Ortega receiving a formal higher education and Badía indicates that he left school as early as the age of eleven to start working.

Ortega's first foray into the fashion industry came at the age of thirteen, when he got a job as an unpaid apprentice and delivery boy for the high-end shirtmaker Gala. He worked for Gala for several years, during which he "learnt the importance of delivering your product directly to a customer without an outside distributor," Elizabeth Nash wrote for the London *Independent* (27 Oct. 1999). In the early 1950s Ortega joined Antonio and Josefina at a clothing retailer in La Coruña called La Maja, where he started working as a tailor's assistant. At La Maja, which was, like all other shops of its kind at the time, owned by a local family, he learned the ins and outs of the apparel business, including all facets of the production and distribution process. Ortega soon began to envision the idea of creating a vertically integrated fashion and textile business, after seeing the many disadvantages that retailers like La Maja faced with buying garments, most of which were expensive and uniformly designed, from outside distributors and wholesalers. Nearly all of the garments purchased by retailers at the time came from traditional supply channels in the northeastern region of Catalonia, leading him to think that if he could produce original high-quality garments at a lower cost and faster rate, retailers would start buying from him.

CAREER

Ortega began turning his ideas into reality in 1963, when he left La Maja to start manufacturing women's quilted bathrobes, which were then rising in popularity in Spain. With a paltry start-up capital of around 5,000 pesetas (the equivalent of $37 today), he teamed up with his brother, sister, sister-in-law, and soon-to-be first wife, Rosalía Mera (whom he married in 1966), and started working on various bathrobe designs in his brother's dining room, cutting out pieces of fabric by hand. He then secured consignments of cheaper fabric from raw material suppliers in Barcelona and started selling bathrobes of his own unique designs to local retailers, including Gala and La Maja, at half the price of suppliers from Catalonia. Ortega's bathrobes sold well and he soon expanded into other clothing lines, including men's shirts and sportswear. He eventually moved his production operation from his

brother's dining room to a rented garage near La Coruña, as demand for his garments increased; he would move to an even bigger space several years later. Meanwhile, he built strong relationships with wholesalers and retailers not only by offering lower prices for equal quality garments but also by guaranteeing on-time deliveries, which was then uncommon among suppliers.

In 1972, Ortega and his brother used their savings to establish a garment-making factory, Confecciones GOA, in the industrial town of Arteixo, on the outskirts of La Coruña. (GOA is the inverted acronym of the Ortega brothers' names.) The factory enabled them to further expand their production capacity as they began exporting their goods to other European countries. Ortega subsequently opened other clothing factories in and around Arteixo, which would ultimately come to serve as the home base for his fashion and textile empire. He moved into distribution and retailing in 1975, when he opened his first Zara shop in downtown La Coruña, on a street that faced one of the city's best-known department stores. Ortega had originally called the shop Zorba, after being inspired by the popular 1964 film *Zorba the Greek*, but decided to change its name after discovering that a bar of the same name existed only several blocks away. He settled on the now-iconic name Zara after working out a series of combinations from the letter molds that had already been cast for the original Zorba sign. At the time Ortega "could not have imagined that his company would one day become a gigantic conglomerate," an Inditex executive told Stryker McGuire for *Newsweek* (17 Sep. 2001).

With Zara, Ortega worked to forge close relationships with his customers by offering stylish, designer clothes at affordable prices and through a lightning-fast production and distribution system that allowed him to stock his stores with the latest trends in a matter of weeks. "Zara's aim was to democratise fashion," an Inditex annual report stated, as noted by Elizabeth Nash for the London *Independent* (27 Oct. 1999). "In contrast to the idea of fashion as a privilege, we offer accessible fashion that reaches the high street, inspired by the taste, desires and lifestyle of modern men and women." Ortega's unique approach of putting the customer at the center of his business proved successful and within the first decade of Zara's launch he was able to expand the chain to major cities all over Spain, with stores opening in Madrid, Barcelona, and Valencia. During this time Ortega became known for his uncanny ability to choose ideal locations for his stores, all of which featured elegant designs and served as the main publicity for the chain. A company spokesman explained to Fiona McCann for the *Irish Times* (16 Aug. 2008), "Inditex has renounced advertising its brands. Inditex does not take advantage of its commercial position, but allows the customer to form his own perception about the brand through the store itself. That's the reason why the stores are always in prime locations and very carefully designed."

In 1985 Ortega formed the umbrella corporation Industria de Diseño Textil, known as the Inditex Group, to act as the holding company for Zara and his many other textile entities. Around this time he hired José María Castellano, a computer and logistics expert and professor of economics at the School of Business Studies in La Coruña, to serve as Inditex's CEO and his right-hand man. Castellano, who would serve as the public face of Inditex for two decades before leaving the company in 2005 in acrimonious circumstances, developed the technology for Ortega's "fast fashion" concept and helped played a major role in Zara's rapid expansion into other countries. That expansion began in 1988, when the first Zara store outside of Spain opened in Oporto, Portugal. The following year the chain entered the US market for the first time with the opening of a store in New York, and in 1990, the first European branch outside of Iberia opened in Paris, France. By that time nearly one hundred Zara stores had opened in Spain. The Inditex executive told McGuire that these openings were "as clear a sign as any that he [Ortega] did not intend for his company to stay small."

During the 1990s Ortega continued to lead Inditex's global expansion while further growing the company with the launch of other clothing concepts and sister chains. In 1991 he founded the clothing retailer Pull & Bear, which offers casual clothing and accessories for men and women between the ages of fourteen and twenty-eight. Later that year he purchased a 65 percent stake in Massimo Dutti, a Spanish retailer that offers a wide range of contemporary clothing for men, women, and children. In 1992 Ortega opened the first Zara store in Mexico and over the following two years he added branches in Greece, Belgium, and Sweden. He acquired full control of Massimo Dutti in 1995, and in 1998 he launched a fourth clothing chain, Bershka, which targets young men and women. A fifth retailer, the young women's fashion brand Stradivarius, was acquired in 1999. By the end of the decade, Inditex-owned stores had entered numerous new markets in Europe, Asia, South America, and North America.

Despite helming one of the fastest growing companies in the world, Ortega remained relatively unknown until May 23, 2001, when the Inditex Group made its IPO on the Spanish Stock Exchange. With a 60 percent majority share in the company, he instantly became a billionaire and one of the wealthiest men in the world, thus considerably raising his international profile. Nonetheless, on the day Inditex stock debuted, Ortega, who had put off taking the company public for years due to his steadfast desire to keep his privacy, sent Castellano and another board member to Madrid to pose for the mandatory photograph. He reportedly celebrated the occasion by watching it on television for several minutes before following his normal routine of eating lunch in the cafeteria at Inditex headquarters. Meanwhile, requests for media interviews and photo opportunities were politely but quickly denied, leading the local newspaper La Voz de Galicia to write, as noted by Stryker McGuire, "Of Amancio Ortega, we know very little. We must be content with what we can learn from his empire sewn of such fine cloth." Since floating Inditex on the Spanish stock exchange, Ortega has grown the company to become the largest fashion retailer in the world, a title the company has held since 2008, when it overtook the American clothing retailer Gap for the top spot. The Inditex Group now has eight store formats, the latest three of which include Oysho, a lingerie chain that launched in 2001; Zara Home, a linens and home décor brand founded in 2003; and Uterqüe, an accessories retailer that debuted in 2008. The group is also comprised of more than one hundred companies involved in activities related to textile production. According to the company's official website, Inditex has more than 92,000 employees—80 percent of whom are female—and operates more than 5,500 stores in eighty-two countries on five continents. Zara alone has a network of more than 1,600 stores in more than four hundred cities worldwide and generates more than half of Inditex's nearly $14 billion in annual revenue. Since 2000 Inditex headquarters have been located in Arteixo, Spain, in an ultramodern, 55,000-square-meter space that employees have affectionately referred to as "the Cube."

While there is still little information known about Ortega, he has been widely credited with revolutionizing the fashion industry with his Inditex business model, which has been adopted by competitors and studied by prominent business schools around the world, including Harvard Business School, the Wharton School of the University of Pennsylvania, and the IESE Business School in Spain. Ortega's "model" uses vertical integration to achieve full control of a rapid production and distribution system "more akin to Dell Computer and Wal-Mart than to Gucci or Louis Vuitton," John Tagliabue wrote for the New York Times (30 May 2003). That system has allowed Ortega to respond quicker to customer needs and cut back significantly on inventory costs. For example, Zara stores are stocked with new designs on a twice-weekly basis and receive only small collections at a time, thus reducing the need for unnecessary markdowns. Because the majority of goods are produced at Inditex-owned factories in Spain and other nearby countries, like Portugal and Morocco, imitations of the latest catwalk fashions can make their way into stores in just several weeks, compared to several months for most other retailers, most of whom rely on inexpensive third-world labor for the manufacturing of their goods. Inditex also spends considerably less on advertising than competitors, relying almost exclusively on word of mouth and the prime locations and alluring designs of its stores to lure prospective customers. At "the Cube," designers test different window displays and layouts in a vast room that has been built to resemble a city shopping street. Those displays and layouts then make their way into stores every two weeks. "We try to always be attentive in stores to what our customers are demanding," the Inditex spokesman explained to McCann. "The information comes from the stores to the creation teams so that we can react and adapt our designs, our new models to what the consumers are demanding."

RETIREMENT

In January 2011 Ortega announced that he would be stepping down as chairman of Inditex at the company's annual meeting. He appointed Pablo Isla, the company's deputy chairman and CEO since 2005, to serve as his successor; Isla officially succeeded him in July 2011. Although retired, Ortega remains on Inditex's board and reportedly continues to play an active role in the company's day-to-day operations. In 2012 he was listed by *Forbes* magazine as the richest man in Spain and fifth richest man in the world in its annual survey of the world's richest people, with a net worth estimated at $37.5 billion. He is the second richest man in Europe behind fellow fashion tycoon Bernard Arnault, the chairman and CEO of LVMH. While Ortega's majority stake in Inditex makes up the bulk of his fortune, he has also made a number of real estate investments, with properties in Madrid, Paris, London, Miami, New York, Chicago, and Washington, DC, and invested in the gas, tourism, and banking industries. In addition, he owns a horse-jumping circuit and a stake in a professional soccer league and has founded an eponymous nonprofit philanthropic organization. Commenting on Ortega's alleged "retirement," José Luis Nueno, a marketing professor at IESE Business School in Barcelona, told Fuchs, "I don't think Mr. Ortega is about to go play golf. He is interested in the soul of the company. I don't think he'll leave this activity until the day he passes."

PERSONAL LIFE

Ortega is a "handsome, round-faced, jovial man whose commanding presence belies his diminutive stature," as Richard Heller wrote for *Forbes* (28 May 2001). He and his second wife, the former Flora Pérez, married in 2002 after living together for many years. Their daughter, Marta (born in 1983), has worked at Inditex since 2007 and is being groomed to take over the reins of the company. (In February 2012 she married the Spanish equestrian star Sergio Alvarez Moya.) From his marriage to Rosalía Mera (whose stake in Inditex has also made her a billionaire), which ended in divorce in 1986, Ortega has two other children: daughter Sandra (born in 1968) and son Marcos (1971). Despite his wealth, Ortega is said to live modestly with his wife in a house in La Coruña. However, he has enjoyed some of the spoils of his riches, owning a collection of sports cars, a luxury yacht, a private plane, and several other homes and apartments around the world. According to Badía, he does not use bodyguards and often walks through La Coruña's city center without being noticed.

SUGGESTED READING

Armstrong, Stephen. "The Son of a Railwayman Who Launched a Runaway Chain." *Telegraph.co.uk*. Telegraph Media Group Ltd, 13 Aug. 2008. Web. 15 June 2012.

Badía, Enrique. *Zara and Her Sisters: The Story of the World's Largest Clothing Retailer*. New York: Palgrave, 2009.

Berwin, Lisa. "Inside Inditex." *Retail Week*. EMAP Ltd., 20 Nov. 2009. Web. 7 June 2012.

Fuchs, Dale. "End of the Line for Zara Tsar Who Built a €9bn Empire." *Independent.co.uk*. Independent.co.uk, 13 Jan. 2011. Web. 7 June 2012.

"The Future of Fast Fashion." *Economist* 375.8431 (18 June 2005): 57–58.

McCann, Fiona. "How to Win the Retail Race in Style." *Irish Times* 5 Aug. 2008: News Features 5. Print.

McGuire, Stryker, et al. "Fast Fashion." *Newsweek* 17 Sep. 2001: Business 36.

Nash, Elizabeth. "Focus: The Discreet Mogul Fashioning an Empire." *Independent* [London, UK] 27 Oct. 1999: Business 2.

Rohwedder, Cecilie. "Zara Stores' Fast Fashion to Get Even Faster." Associated Press 20 Feb. 2008: Business News.

Tagliabue, John. "A Rival to Gap That Operates Like Dell." *New York Times* 30 May 2003: W1.

—*Chris Cullen*

Phedon Papamichael

Born: February 1962
Occupation: Cinematographer and director

Award-winning cinematographer Phedon Papamichael Jr. has participated in the production of over fifty films. Though born in Greece, Papamichael spent most of his childhood in

Germany, but his career has been centered in the United States. He has worked with several award-winning directors including Alexander Payne (*Sideways, The Descendants*), Kathryn Bigelow (*Wild Palms*), and Oliver Stone (*W.*). Papamichael has won several international awards including the Orpheus Career Achievement Award from the Los Angeles Greek Film Festival (LAGFF) in 2010. He became a member of the International Cinematographers Guild in 1995 and a member of the Academy of Motion Picture Arts and Sciences in 1997. Within the Academy, he served on the Cinematographers Branch Executive Committee for several years. Papamichael is also a member of the American Society of Cinematographers (ASC). He is the president of Diaspora Films, Inc. and co-owns the lighting company Bella Luce Entertainments Lighting with Rafael Sánchez.

Papamichael has worked on a range of films from popular romantic comedies (*While You Were Sleeping*, 1995, with Sandra Bullock; *America's Sweethearts*, 2001, with Julia Roberts and Catherine Zeta-Jones) to critically acclaimed dramas (*Sideways*, 2004, with Paul Giamatti; *Walk the Line*, 2005, with Joaquin Phoenix). For his work on the television miniseries *Wild Palms* (1993), Papamichael was nominated for the ASC Award for Outstanding Achievement in Cinematography for the episode "The Floating World, Part II." He was nominated for the same award in 1996 for his work on a television movie called *White Dwarf* (1995). Papamichael has directed several feature films including *Arcadia Lost* (2010) with Nick Nolte, but he relishes his role as a cinematographer. "We're very fortunate as cinematographers," he told Bob Fisher for an interview for the International Cinematographers Guild (13 May 2006), "because everybody thinks they can write; everybody thinks they can direct; everybody thinks they can edit; but nobody assumes that they can do what we do, which is tell the story visually with light and motion. It's a mystery to them. We still have this mystique about what we do."

EARLY LIFE

Papamichael was born in Athens, Greece, in 1962. His father, Phedon Papamichael Sr., was a painter and production designer who worked with the director John Cassavetes. His mother was from Germany. The family moved to the United States in 1966 when the elder Papamichael was working with Cassavetes on the film *Faces* (1968), starring Gena Rowlands (who was also Cassavetes's wife). While his father stayed to finish the film, Papamichael and his mother moved to Munich.

Papamichael initially thought he wanted to be a painter like his father, but he told Fisher that picking up his first Super 8 camera at the age of fourteen was like "an instant love affair."

Wirelmage

As a teenager, Papamichael began to shoot and edit his own movies. He loved the films of Luis Buñuel, François Truffaut, and the German director Wim Wenders. But he can pinpoint his love of cinematography to one film in particular. "It was the first time I wrote down a cinematographer's name," he told Fisher. The film was Jean-Luc Godard's *Le Mépris*—or, as it was released in English, *Contempt* (1963)—starring Brigitte Bardot. The cinematographer was Raoul Coutard. Papamichael was attracted to Coutard's wide, graphic shots. He had already taken up still photography at the time. He told Fisher that the film reminded him of one of his photographs in its style and use of primary colors. "Around that time I realized that there is someone who is in charge of telling stories visually," he said. He began watching the films of Italian director Bernardo Bertolucci who worked with the cinematographer Vittorio Storaro; Papamichael was especially drawn to their collaborations on *The Conformist* (1970) and *Last Tango in Paris* (1972) with Marlon Brando.

LEARNING BY MISTAKES

Papamichael completed his schooling in Germany. He attended the University of Munich where he received a degree in fine arts in 1982. At the time, he considered himself a photographer and a few of his photographs were published in European magazines. After he had completed his mandatory military service in Greece, he sent twenty of his photographs to his father, who was working in the United States with Cassavetes on the film *Love Streams*, which was released in 1984. Papamichael received a letter back from Cassavetes. It said, he recalled to Fisher, "Your photography captures the spirit of a new generation in a classical form." The letter also asked Papamichael to come to the United States and shoot Cassavetes's next film.

Cassavetes, who died in 1989, was known as a pioneer of American cinema. He was also known to be incredibly impulsive. When Fisher expressed disbelief at Cassavetes's offer, Papamichael simply replied, "John was like that." Still, Papamichael jumped at the opportunity. His mother wanted him to stay in Munich and study architecture, but he moved to New York City in 1983. He roomed with Liz Gazzara, the daughter of actor Ben Gazzara. Papamichael arrived as Cassavetes was cutting *Love Streams*.

Gazzara asked Papamichael to shoot a short film with her. He had never shot film before but understood composition and depth of field. Cassavetes gave them one of his old cameras, an Éclair NPR that he had used to shoot the film *Faces* when Papamichael was a child. For about five thousand dollars, they made a twenty-minute film starring their friends Nick and Xan Cassavetes. Papamichael told Fisher that the film was a "learn-by-mistake experience." In the screening room, he realized from the intermittent blue flashes on the screen that his camera was leaking light. The possibility of such a problem with a professional camera never occurred to Papamichael. For many other problems that he encountered, he felt he was "inventing" ingenious solutions that later turned out to already exist, such as spreaders to hold a camera's legs together or pulling focus by marking the floor. He made a few more short films with his friends. In order to support himself during this time, he worked briefly as a photojournalist, photographing celebrities and events for European magazines.

EARLY CAREER IN LOS ANGELES

In 1985, Papamichael and his friends moved to Los Angeles, California. He worked for the University of California, Los Angeles, (UCLA) shooting medical films for one hundred dollars a week. He tried to get work as an assistant cameraman and interviewed with Robby Müller, the cinematographer working on Barbet Schroeder's film *Barfly* (1987) and Theo van de Sande for the action film *Miracle Mile* (1988). He did not get either job. A friend recommended that Papamichael look at a newspaper called *Drama-Logue*, where student films were advertised, and he began making phone calls and was able to land a job. Though Papamichael never attended film school, he worked on a UCLA graduate film. On the set, he met his future collaborator, director Alexander Payne, who was working as the boom man.

In the late 1980s, Papamichael's friend, who was a graduate of the American Film Institute (AFI), asked him to work on a film called *Deadly Dreams* (1988). He was the director of photography in the second unit. The film was Papamichael's first collaboration with the prolific film producer Roger Corman. It was during this period that Papamichael was introduced to director Katt Shea. Papamichael would become the cinematographer on Shea's next three films: *Dance of the Damned* (1989), *Stripped to Kill II: Live Girls* (1989), and *Streets* (1990), starring a young Christina Applegate as a teenage prostitute running from a serial killer cop. The movies were shot in quick succession, with little more than fifteen days of shooting for each. Even though he was working sixteen- to eighteen-hour days, Papamichael told Fisher that the set-up was "fantastic training." He also recalls Corman's strange production demands. For instance, Corman didn't want the crew to use a dolly track, which allows for smoother camera movements. To work around this, the crew assigned one production assistant to watch the parking lot for Corman's Mercedes so they could then hide the dolly track if Corman dropped by the studio. Despite Corman's eccentricities, Papamichael enjoyed working on B movies because he was given a fair amount of creative leeway. "The bottom line was [Corman] didn't really care as long as the movie had full frontal nudity and people were getting killed," Papamichael told Fisher. His crew on the Corman films included Janusz Kaminski, Mauro Fiore, and Wally Pfister. Kaminski went on to direct, but Fiore and Pfister continued to work with Papamichael on a number of features.

Papamichael worked once as a gaffer (an electrician) during that period. It was the only time he worked as another member of the crew. He transitioned out of the Corman sphere and to high-budget movies when Shea asked him to work with her on *Poison Ivy* (1992) for New Line Cinema. The film starred Drew Barrymore (who Papamichael briefly dated) and had a four million dollar budget.

1990S

Papamichael had shot one studio film (Walt Disney Pictures' *Cool Runnings*, 1993, with the director Jon Turteltaub) when actress Diane Keaton asked him to shoot a film she was directing, also for Disney. His friend Kaminski, who had shot Keaton's earlier television film *Wildflower* (1991), had recommended him. Keaton was directing a movie called *Unstrung Heroes* (1995) with Andie MacDowell, John Turturro, and Michael Richards. The film marked Papamichael's entry into the Cinematographer's Guild, as well as the beginning of his longtime collaboration with gaffer, Rafael Sánchez.

Papamichael worked on a comedy with director Jon Turteltaub called *Driving Me Crazy*

(1991). He initially didn't want to take the project, but the Motion Picture Corporation of America (MPCA) offered him a chance to direct his own film if he accepted. Papamichael shot the movie, which led to an extended collaboration with Turteltaub. The two worked on the successful romantic comedy *While You Were Sleeping* with Sandra Bullock, Bill Pullman, and Peter Gallagher; and a fantasy-drama called *Phenomenon* (1996) about a man, played by John Travolta, who acquires super-intelligence and telekinesis. Papamichael's directorial debut was a television movie called *The Sketch Artist* (1992). He cast Drew Barrymore, Jeff Fahey, and Sean Young and hired Wally Pfister as the cinematographer. Pfister was nominated for a CableACE Award for Best Cinematography for *The Sketch Artist*. Papamichael then directed the film *Dark Side of Genius* for Pacific Shore Pictures in 1994.

In 1996, Papamichael collaborated with Nick Cassavetes who was directing a film called *Unhook the Stars*, featuring Gena Rowlands (Cassavetes's mother) and Marisa Tomei. The movie was well received and both Rowlands and Tomei were nominated for Screen Actors Guild (SAG) awards. Following the Cassavetes film, Papamichael shot two larger budget features, *Mousehunt* (1997), a family comedy starring Nathan Lane, and *Patch Adams* (1998) with Robin Williams. He also shot two features for director Wim Wenders, whom he had admired as a teenager. The two had met while working on commercials. The first film was a concert documentary featuring Willie Nelson and Emmylou Harris called *Willie Nelson at the Teatro* (1998). The second film was called *The Million Dollar Hotel* (2000).

2000S

Papamichael's work with Wenders earned him an international following. In 2000 he teamed up with Georgian director Nana Dzhordzhadze for the film *27 Missing Kisses*. The film earned Papamichael a cinematography award at the Avignon Film Festival. Despite his European success, Papamichael prefers the American system of making movies because he feels that it is more reliable. According to Papamichael, European directors can wait years to shoot a film due to scheduling problems.

In 2005, Papamichael shot director James Mangold's biopic *Walk the Line*, with Joaquin Phoenix playing the country musician Johnny Cash and Reese Witherspoon playing his wife and fellow country music star, June Carter. The film was well received and Papamichael would later count it among his favorites. It was especially important to Mangold that Phoenix and Witherspoon be able to sing. In other films about famous musicians, the actor's voices are dubbed; but Mangold insisted that the voices

heard in the film be those of the actors and not recordings of Cash and Carter. As a result, Papamichael was able to capture some electric performance footage for the film. In an interview for Panavision, Papamichael told Suzanne Lezotte (7 Oct. 2011) that filming Phoenix as he interacted with the crowd of extras as Cash was "inspirational."

The film *Sideways* was the first major collaboration between Papamichael and director Alexander Payne. It was a huge success for Payne, who favors intimate films and complicated characters. However, Payne did not make another feature until the 2011 film *The Descendants*, based on a novel by Kaui Hart Hemmings about an emotionally struggling family living in Hawaii. Payne asked Papamichael to shoot the film, a task that required capturing the majesty of the Hawaiian Islands and the minutiae of family life. "We were able to dive right in," Papamichael told Leo Adam Biga for his blog (5 Nov. 2011). "Sometimes the camera is not as intimate as I'd like to place it. [Payne is] very much an observer—he likes to stay a little wider, a little distant, and I pushed it a little bit and we got in tighter." Papamichael added, "We're still exploring our aesthetic as our collaboration continues. It's all very subjective, all very personal. Everybody sees things a little differently." In 2012 Papamichael began shooting a film with Payne called *Nebraska*.

As a director, Papamichael's credits include a horror film called *From Within* (2008) and a drama called *Arcadia Lost*, which is set in Greece. As a cinematographer, Papamichael's other films include: *The Pursuit of Happyness* (2006), starring Will Smith; the Western *3:10 to Yuma* (2007), starring Russell Crowe and Christian Bale; Oliver Stone's film *W.* (2008) about former President George W. Bush; and *The Ides of March* (2011), directed by George Clooney. Papamichael also worked on a Judd Apatow comedy called *This is 40*, which is set for release in late in 2012.

PERSONAL LIFE

Papamichael has worked on over one hundred commercials, and between films he continues to accept ads for numerous internationally known corporations headquartered in both the United States and Europe. Papamichael has also shot several music videos including U2's "The First Time," "Electrical Storm," and "Stuck in a Moment," as well as "All These Things I've Done" for the Killers.

"I have this rule where I don't want to do a feature film unless I would personally pay ten dollars to see in a movie theater," Papamichael told Fisher. "I've been lucky, because I work on movies that I like, and I'm in a position to wait for projects that I like."

Papamichael married Eka Chichua in 2006. They have homes in Los Angeles and Athens, Greece.

SUGGESTED READING

Biga, Leo Adam. "Phedon Papamichael, Jim Burke, and Shailene Woodley Discuss Working with Oscar-winner Alexander Payne on *The Descendants* and Kaui Hart Hemmings Comments on the Adaptation of her Novel." *Leo Adam Biga's Blog.* WordPress, 5 Nov. 2011. Web. 15 July 2012.

Fisher, Bob. "Interview: Phedon Papamichael." *Local 600: International Cinematographers Guild.* Local 600, 13 May 2006. Web. 13 July 2012.

---. "A Tale of Two Johns: John Cassavetes and Johnny Cash Have Helped Cement DP Phedon Papamichael's Place in Hollywood." *MovieMaker.* MovieMaker Magazine, 3 Feb. 2007. Web. 18 July 2012.

Lezotte, Suzanne. "Phedon Papamichael, ASC, Lenses 'The Ides of March.'" *Panavision.* Panavision, Inc., 7 Oct. 2011. Web. 15 July 2012.

"Phedon Papamichael." *IBDb.* IMDb.com, Inc., 2012. Web. 18 July 2012.

FilmMagic

SELECTED WORKS

Sketch Artist, 1992; *While You Were Sleeping*, 1995; *Unhook the Stars*, 1996; *Patch Adams*, 1998; *27 Missing Kisses*, 2000; *Sideways*, 2004; *Walk the Line*, 2005; *The Pursuit of Happyness*, 2006; *3:10 to Yuma*, 2007; *This Is 40*, 2012

—Molly Hagan

Jacques Pépin

Born: December 18, 1935
Occupation: French chef and author

In a career spanning more than six decades, the French chef Jacques Pépin has earned a reputation as one of the most distinguished and respected chefs in the world. Known as the quintessential French chef, Pépin has inspired generations of home cooks and celebrity chefs and played a major role in the United States' culinary revolution with his simple, elegant, and innovative approach to cooking. Beginning his cooking career in his early teens, Pépin worked at such acclaimed restaurants as the Plaza Athénée in Paris and Le Pavillon in New York before becoming the director of research and development for the Howard Johnson hotel and restaurant chain, where he spent nearly a decade developing upscale frozen food items. After being involved in a serious car accident in the 1970s, Pépin transitioned out of a life in the kitchen and into a career as a culinary teacher, writer, and television host. He has since written more than two dozen books, hosted more than a dozen public television cooking series, and taught at culinary schools around the world. Known particularly for his expert technique, Pépin has insisted that the key to good cooking lies in grasping basic fundamental skills. "I don't cook the way I cooked thirty-five years ago," he told Michele Kayal for the Associated Press (3 Aug. 2011), "but the way you make an omelet, the way you bone a chicken, that doesn't change."

EARLY LIFE

The second of the three sons of Jean-Victor and Jeanne Pépin, Jacques Pépin was born on December 18, 1935, in Bourg-en-Bresse, a town near the city of Lyon in the Rhône Alpes region of southeastern France. His father was a skilled cabinetmaker who specialized in period furniture, and his mother was a waitress and homemaker. Along with his brothers, Roland and Richard, Pépin grew up in a small apartment complex in Bourg-en-Bresse during the tough economic times of World War II. When Pépin was four years old, his father was drafted into the army, and his mother was left with the responsibility of taking care of the three children. Pépin's mother worked hard to support and feed the family, toiling six days a week as a waitress at a local hotel and then spending her only day off bicycling around the surrounding countryside on food-gathering expeditions. Some of Pépin's earliest memories revolve around food and his mother's ingenuity as a cook. He has fondly recalled his mother making do with unconventional recipes, such as using a cooked mixture of beets and water in place of sugar and making a version of French toast with eggs preserved in a mixture of lime and water. Pépin has also said that his father, who eventually joined the French Resistance, occasionally made trips back home during the war and left small gifts of food behind for him and his brothers.

Like many other French children during the war, Pépin spent his summers living on rural farms, where he performed chores in exchange for room and board. In his autobiography *The Apprentice: My Life in the Kitchen* (2003), he recalled that it was while tasting freshly squeezed cow's milk on a host's farm that he first realized that "food could be much more than mere sustenance." Pépin brought his growing fascination with food to Lycée Saint-Louis, a strict Jesuit-run boarding school in Bourg-en-Bresse, which he began attending as a young boy after his mother persuaded the school's director to grant him early admission. (Pépin's older brother, Roland, also attended the school.) He managed to cope with the school's unpalatable food offerings by bartering with other boarding students, many of whom came from rural areas and occasionally received packages of farm-produced delicacies. On one occasion, Pépin traded his prized pocketknife to a student for a saucisson, or dry sausage, which he gave to his brother Roland as a gift for his first Communion. Other edible luxuries of Pépin's youth included chewing gum and chocolate bars, which American soldiers tossed to the gathering crowds when Allied tanks passed through town following the liberation of Paris.

CULINARY EDUCATION

After the end of World War II, Pépin and his family left their Bourg-en-Bresse apartment, which had been bombed twice during the war, to move to the nearby town of Neyron. Much to Pépin's delight, he and his brother were subsequently enrolled in a new and much less strict school. In Neyron, his parents purchased a two-story building that housed a run-down eatery, Hôtel L'Amour, which they immediately set out to revive. Despite having no formal cooking experience, his mother became the restaurant's head chef while his father, who continued to work as a cabinetmaker, helped out as a sous-chef and maintained a basement wine cellar. Pépin and his brothers, meanwhile, were recruited to perform jobs such as peeling and dicing vegetables, preparing sandwiches, and foraging for ingredients. After turning Hôtel L'Amour into a success, Pépin's mother purchased and overhauled a second eatery, Le Restaurant de la Gare in the village of L'Arbresle. She opened a restaurant of her own, Chez Pépin, in the city of Lyon, in

1947 and eventually sold the establishment to open a larger, more sophisticated restaurant, Le Pélican.

By the time he reached his teens, Pépin had already worked in each of his mother's four kitchens and become fully determined to follow in her footsteps. "More than anything in the world," he wrote in *The Apprentice*, "I wanted to be a chef." At thirteen he received a dispensation to take an exam that would allow him to leave primary school a year early. After passing the exam, Pépin left school for good to accept a formal apprenticeship. He told Russ Parsons for the *Los Angeles Times* (24 Oct. 1996), "I didn't think about being a lawyer or a doctor or a professor." On the contrary, as he wrote in *The Apprentice*, Pépin loved the "hurly-burly noise of the kitchen. The heat. The sweat. The bumping of bodies. The raised voices. The constant rush of adrenaline."

EARLY CAREER

Pépin spent three years as an unpaid apprentice at Le Grand Hôtel de l'Europe in Bourg-en-Bresse, where he studied under chef Paul Jauget. During this time he worked up to fourteen hours a day, seven days a week, and learned invaluable cooking skills and techniques by observing and imitating Jauget. Pépin has said that Jauget taught him and his fellow apprentices how to cook by having them rely solely on their senses, instead of using formal textbooks and written recipes. After completing his apprenticeship in 1952, Pépin became a commis, or trainee, at L'Hôtel d'Albion in the resort town of Aix-les-Bains. There, he mastered new regional dishes and techniques and learned how to work quickly and efficiently as part of a small kitchen team that was responsible for turning out four hundred meals a day. Pépin worked at L'Hôtel d'Albion for a summer season before finding work at L'Hôtel Restaurant de la Paix in the village of Bellegarde, near Geneva, Switzerland, where he ran his own kitchen for the first time. He worked there during the winter of 1953 and left with what he has described as a newfound sense of confidence. Afterward he worked briefly at a prestigious restaurant in Lyon called La Coupole.

In 1953, at the age of seventeen, Pépin left Lyon to work in Paris, home to some of the best culinary talents and restaurants in the world. He recalled to Parsons, "I was young and I had a kind of yearning for adventure. To a certain extent, that was spurred by my mother. She would tell me stories about a chef she had worked for who had cooked on a boat and had gone around the world." Upon arriving in Paris, Pépin found a job as a second commis at La Maxéville, a brasserie in the Montmartre district of Paris, but left the establishment after just a few weeks due to his dissatisfaction with its uninspired food choices.

Shortly afterward, Pépin secured a job as a *commis entremetier*, or chef's assistant, at Le Meurice, one of the Paris's most prestigious hotel restaurants. There, he was introduced to the rigors of haute cuisine (high-end, sophisticated food). From Le Meurice, Pépin went to work for chef Lucian Diat at the Plaza Athénée. Under Diat, a perfectionist who demanded flawless execution on every dish, Pépin mastered his culinary skills and rose rapidly through the ranks.

Pépin's fast-rising cooking career was temporarily halted when he was drafted into the French navy during the Algerian War. As part of his military service, from 1956 to 1958, he worked as a cook at the French naval headquarters in Paris. Through a series of fortuitous circumstances, his service also included working as a personal chef to three French heads of state: Félix Gaillard, Pierre Pflimlin, and Charles de Gaulle. After receiving his military discharge, Pépin returned to work at the Plaza Athénée.

COMING TO NEW YORK
Having set his sights on exploring new career opportunities in the United States, in 1959, Pépin moved to New York. "I had always wanted to come to America," he told Parsons. "For me, it was El Dorado, what Paris was to me when I was seventeen. And from the first day, I loved it." On his first day in New York, Pépin, through the help of his sponsor, Ernest Lutringhauser, found a job as a *chef de partie*, or line cook, at restaurateur Henri Soulé's Le Pavillon, which was then regarded as the best French restaurant in the United States. There he worked under the esteemed French chef Pierre Franey, who would become his close friend and mentor.

Despite being well paid, Pépin left his job at Le Pavillon after only eight months due to his frustration over the way Soulé treated his kitchen staff. Soon afterward he received an offer to work as a personal chef to newly elected president John F. Kennedy, but he instead accepted an offer from businessman Howard Deering Johnson to lead research and development at his eponymous chain of restaurants. At the Howard Johnson Company, Pépin was reunited with Franey, who had left Le Pavillon under similar circumstances, and the two began to develop upscale frozen food concepts for the chain. "I had done state dinners and I didn't want to go back," he explained to Parsons. "Howard Johnson was perfect for me then. I wanted to work in a very American environment; I wanted to work with American food, and I wanted to work in the American language."

NOUVELLE CUISINE
Pépin remained with the company throughout the 1960s, during which he and Franey helped revolutionize mass food production techniques and became central figures in America's culinary revolution. The two became part of a group of culinary pioneers that helped change the way Americans cook, eat, and think about food through the popularization of nouvelle cuisine ("new cuisine") and other cooking innovations. The group's prominent figures included *New York Times* food critic Craig Claiborne, *House Beautiful* magazine editor and cookbook author Helen McCully, chef and food writer James Beard, and chef, author, and television personality Julia Child. Prior to the emergence of nouvelle cuisine, which is characterized by fresh, quality ingredients and light sauces, food was considered by most Americans as nothing more than mere "sustenance, full stop," as Pépin explained in *The Apprentice*. "Viewing it as something important, as integral to a nation's culture as its music, art, and literature, made you a member of a small, oddball minority."

COLUMBIA AND LA POTAGERIE
Seeking to continue his education and gain a better grasp of the English language, Pépin attended Columbia University's School of General Studies in New York. He earned his bachelor's and master's degrees from Columbia in 1970 and 1972, respectively. Pépin almost completed a PhD in French literature at Columbia before a disagreement with an advisor over his dissertation topic led him to leave school.

In 1970, after nearly a decade, Pépin left Howard Johnson's to open a French soup restaurant, La Potagerie, in Manhattan. Described in *The Apprentice* as "nothing more than a glorified cafeteria," La Potagerie served fresh, inventive soups at affordable prices and achieved considerable financial success, becoming one of the most popular destinations for soup in New York. The restaurant closed after only a few years, following a number of disagreements between Pépin and his business partners.

TEACHER
Pépin's life took a new direction in 1974, when he was involved in a near-fatal car accident. He lost control of his car while trying to avoid a deer and suffered multiple life-threatening injuries, including a broken back, a broken pelvis, and a severely broken left arm that was almost amputated. Pépin's injuries made it nearly impossible for him to work in a restaurant kitchen. His love of cooking remained, however, and he soon began a career as a cooking instructor, restaurant consultant, cookbook writer, and ultimately, television host. "I was in the right place at the right time," he told Parsons, referring to the trend of kitchen stores and affiliated cooking schools opening across the country in the 1970s. Seizing an opportunity to bring French cuisine to the American masses, Pépin initially gave cooking lessons to private clients and was later recruited to teach at cooking schools throughout

the United States and abroad. He was also hired as a consultant for various restaurants, including the famed Windows on the World restaurant at the World Trade Center, which opened in 1976. Pépin has been a part-time faculty member at Boston University's Metropolitan College since 1983 and has served as dean of special programs at the International Culinary Center (originally the French Culinary Institute) since 1988.

WRITER

Pépin's first experiences as a writer came in the 1970s, when he started writing cooking how-to columns for *House Beautiful* magazine. In addition to *House Beautiful* magazine, Pépin has served as a columnist for the *New York Times* and *Food & Wine* magazine.

Pépin's first cookbook, *A French Chef Cooks at Home*, was published in 1975 and included recipes for traditional French dishes. The following year he released *La Technique*, which featured fully illustrated guides to more than 150 basic cooking techniques. *La Technique* is considered a landmark in the cookbook genre and has since won several awards and influenced chefs such as Tom Colicchio, an award-winning chef and restaurateur and a cohost of television network Bravo's cooking competition series *Top Chef*, who told Kayal that he learned to cook after reading *La Technique* as a teenager. Pépin followed *La Technique* with the equally influential companion book, *La Methode*, in 1979. In the 1980s Pépin released what is considered to be his masterwork, *The Art of Cooking*, an ambitious two-volume guide to a wide-ranging assortment of classical cooking techniques featuring thousands of step-by-step color photographs.

TELEVISION HOST

In addition to publishing many influential cookbooks, Pépin influenced millions of home cooks as a host of numerous public television cooking series. In 1982 he taped his first Public Broadcasting Service (PBS) series, *Everyday Cooking with Jacques Pépin*, which showcased simple comfort food recipes, many of which were featured in a companion book that was released that same year. Pépin went on to host more than a dozen other cooking shows, becoming known for his friendly, down-to-earth demeanor, unpretentious approach, and unparalleled technical skills. Tina Salter, a producer at the PBS station KQED-TV, which has produced most of Pépin's shows, explained to Kayal, "He's about sharing good food, demonstrating good technique, and really educating the viewer. That's what separates him from everyone else. He's the consummate teacher."

Other notable cooking shows hosted by Pépin include the hit 1990s series *Jacques Pépin's Cooking Techniques*, which was based on his book *La Technique*, and *Julia and Jacques Cooking at Home*, which he cohosted with Child.

Julia and Jacques Cooking at Home received widespread critical acclaim and was honored with several awards, including an Emmy Award in 2001. Pépin has also cohosted several cooking series with his daughter, Claudine, including *Jacques Pépin Celebrates!* Many of his television series have been released in conjunction with companion cookbooks, as in the case of the television program and accompanying cookbook *Essential Pépin* (2011). The book, Pépin's twenty-sixth, features more than seven hundred recipes and is packaged with a searchable DVD. In a review of *Essential Pépin*, the chef, best-selling author, and television personality Anthony Bourdain commented, "Jacques Pépin is The Master. The undisputed authority on . . . well, just about everything relating to food. If Jacques Pépin tells you this is the way to make an omelet—or to roast a chicken, then for me, the matter is settled. . . . Nobody knows more or does it better."

HONORS AND PERSONAL LIFE

Pépin is a member of a number of industry organizations, including the International Association of Culinary Professionals. He has received numerous awards and honors for his contributions to the culinary arts, including the James Beard Foundation's Lifetime Achievement Award. Pépin was awarded France's highest civilian honor, the French Legion of Honor, in 2004.

Pépin and his wife, Gloria, whom he met while skiing in upstate New York, married in 1966. The couple live in Madison, Connecticut, in a house that was once a brick factory. Their daughter, Claudine, has cohosted television series with her father, appeared on numerous other television programs, and taught classes on food and wine pairing at such institutions as the International Culinary Center and the Sommelier Society in New York. Pépin enjoys painting in his spare time. His acclaimed, best-selling memoir, *The Apprentice: My Life in the Kitchen*, was published in 2003.

SUGGESTED READING

Gordinier, Jeff. "There's the Wrong Way and His Way." *New York Times* 19 Oct. 2011: D1.

Kayal, Michele. "For Pépin, Cooking Is about Technique, Not Stardom." *AP.org.* Associated Press, 3 Aug. 2011. Web. 16 July 2012.

Parsons, Russ. "Monsieur Technique." *Los Angeles Times* 24 Oct. 1996: H1.

Pépin, Jacques. *The Apprentice: My Life in the Kitchen.* Boston: Houghton, 2003.

Rozzo, Mark. "The Original Iron Chef Jacques Pépin." *Men's Vogue* Oct. 2008: 98.

Schiff, Stacy. "There's Always Room for Jell-O." *New York Times* 4 May 2003: BR11.

Weinraub, Judith. "In the Hot-Stove League, This Kid Was a Natural." *Washington Post* 22 Apr. 2003: C4.

—*Chris Cullen*

Katy Perry

Born: October 25, 1984
Occupation: Pop singer and songwriter

Until her mid-teens the phenomenally success-ful pop singer/songwriter Katy Perry heard pop, rock and roll, and other secular music only by chance or on the sly, because her parents allowed her to listen only to gospel and other Christian songs. Perry started singing in a church choir at age nine, and when she entered her teens, she began to write faith-based songs herself. Deter-mined to make it big in the music world, she quit school at fifteen and then, in Nashville, Ten-nessee, polished her skills in singing, songwrit-ing, and playing the guitar. She recorded ten of her religious songs for a Christian label, which released them on an album just before her six-teenth birthday. Called *Katy Hudson* (Perry's original name), the album attracted no notice, and Perry turned away from Christian themes in her songwriting. During the next half-dozen years, she teamed up with accomplished profes-sionals while under contract with Def Jam and then with Columbia, but both labels dropped her without marketing any of her work. In 2007 she signed with the newly formed Capitol Mu-sic Group, and the next year the label released her album *One of the Boys*. By that time she had become an international sensation, thanks to her hit song "I Kissed a Girl," which reached the number-one spot on charts in twenty countries and earned Perry a Grammy Award nomination.

With her next album, *Teenage Dream* (2010), which she made with A-list producers who had worked with artists including Beyoncé, Rihanna, and Britney Spears, Perry became the first wom-an—and only the second person, after Michael Jackson—to see five songs in succession from the same disk land at the top of the Billboard 200 chart. Although most professional review-ers have not greeted her work enthusiastically, to date sales of Perry's singles have surpassed 50 million digital downloads, and in total *One of the Boys* and *Teenage Dream* have sold upwards of 14 million copies. As of mid-November 2011, Perry had earned more than two hundred nominations for music awards worldwide and won more than sixty. Her honors include a total of six awards (in 2009, 2010, and 2011) from the American Society of Composers, Authors, and Publishers (ASCAP), three People's Choice Awards, three MTV Europe Music Awards, three MTV Music Video Awards, a BMI Award, and a Brit Award.

Writing for the *New York Times* (19 Aug. 2010) around the time of *Teenage Dream*'s re-lease, Melena Ryzik noted that in gaining fame, Perry has followed the "modern pop star play-book," which calls for "relentless promotion, cor-porate crossover, brand development and cheeky over-the-top persona." Perry, Ryzik continued,

Getty Images

has "proved adept at working those angles, mak-ing an unlikely turnaround from gospel singer to provocative starlet . . . and pop-culture personal-ity." During performances Perry typically chang-es into an array of flamboyant, one-of-a-kind out-fits, and she has posed topless or scantily clad for *Esquire, Rolling Stone*, and other national magazines. She is also known for using profane language and for her "cheeky sense of humour," "strong, throaty voice," and "ear for anthemic hooks," Sheryl Garratt wrote for the London *Observer* (10 Aug. 2008). In the *New York Times* (20 June 2011), the music critic Jon Pareles described Perry as "a bubblegum pop act for a raunchy era: not uncommercially wholesome, intermittently crude with a wink."

EARLY LIFE

The second of the three children of Keith and Mary (Perry) Hudson, Perry was born Kather-yn Elizabeth Hudson on October 25, 1984, in Santa Barbara, California. She adopted "Perry" as her surname after recording her first album, to prevent being confused with the actress Kate Hudson. Perry's sister, Angela, who is two years her senior, has sometimes assisted her on con-cert tours. Her brother, David, is three years her junior. Her father and mother have said that they were hippies during the 1960s. Before they be-came parents they rediscovered their Christian faith; after years as itinerant or storefront preach-ers, they founded the nondenominational Keith and Mary Hudson Ministries, based in Irvine, California. Their website, after noting that they are Katy Perry's parents, identifies Keith Hudson as an evangelist and "end-time messenger" for God. According to their posted itinerary, they preach widely in the United States and overseas; at some of their stops, Mary Hudson holds conferences designed specifically for women. The Hudsons have published two faith-centered books; a third is scheduled to appear in 2012.

CHRISTIAN UPBRINGING

During Perry's earliest years her parents were mostly on the road, and the family moved frequently; they later returned to Santa Barbara, where Perry attended Christian elementary and middle schools and Christian summer camps, among them a "surf camp where the kids prayed for big waves," Melena Ryzik wrote. According to Perry, the Bible was the only book her mother ever read aloud to her when she was a child, and her parents banned from their home most TV shows, all music videos, and virtually all recorded music except religious songs. Perry sometimes heard popular music at friends' houses, however, and according to Sheryl Garratt, writing for the *New York Post* (7 Dec. 2008), she "us[ed] a down comforter to seal up the cracks in her bedroom door—and muffle devil's music by the likes of Queen."

Freddie Mercury, Queen's lead vocalist, "became her idol," Garratt added, "and rock 'n' roll her mission." While Perry has remained a Christian—she was "born again" at thirteen and had the name "Jesus" tattooed on the inside of her left wrist at eighteen—she has described her beliefs as different from those she held as a child. "Though she says she doesn't take the Lord's name in vain, she regularly flouts many of the other commandments she grew up with," Melena Ryzik noted.

Interviewers have often asked Perry about her parents' reactions to her work, given the disparity between the messages of Christianity and Christian songs, on one hand, and Perry's song lyrics and decidedly immodest apparel and behavior, on the other. In a representative response Perry told Tamara Palmer for the Phoenix, Arizona, *Metromix* (27 Jan. 2009), "My family definitely are very supportive. I have pushed their envelope from the day I was born. I was always the kid at the dinner table who, if there was a line you shouldn't cross, I took a big leap over it. That kind of has always been me; there's never really been an edit button on my keyboard of life. And I guess my parents weren't ever so shocked when I was singing very frank or honest songs." Noting that her father has four tattoos that say "Jesus," she likened him to a "modern rock 'n' roll pastor." Keith Hudson told Colette

M. Jenkins for the Akron, Ohio, *Beacon Journal* (3 Sep. 2010), "Sometimes when you bring children up in a good environment, they want to try something different. We might

not always agree with what they're doing, but they're still our children." He also said that Perry "has a great deal of notoriety, but she's still our daughter. We have a great relationship with her, we love her and pray for her and want the best for her."

QUITTING SCHOOL TO PURSUE A CAREER IN MUSIC

When she was nine Perry became a choir girl at her parents' church. Around that time her sister began to take singing lessons, and "Katy insisted on joining in too," Leah Greenblatt wrote for *Entertainment Weekly* (1 Aug. 2008). By age thirteen she had become determined to pursue a career in music, and she started learning to play the guitar. After her freshman year at Dos Pueblos High School, a public school in Goleta, California, near Santa Barbara, she earned a General Equivalency Diploma (GED) and ended her formal education. "I left school because I knew who I was and what I wanted," she told Edna Gundersen for *USA Today* (19 Aug. 2010). She told Sheryl Garratt, "As much as I am cheeky and full of opinions, essentially I know what I'm doing. . . . I feel I've got a good head on my shoulders."

Her parents approved her decision to quit school, albeit with misgivings, and when she was fifteen, determined to launch her career, she began to travel frequently to Nashville, where her parents "had some connections in the gospel industry," she told Greenblatt. In Nashville she devoted many hours to improving her guitar playing, and with the help of veteran gospel musicians, she honed her songwriting skills. She landed a deal with a Christian music label called Red Hill Records, which released her first album, *Katy Hudson*, just before she turned sixteen. Its ten tracks, all with religious messages, included "Faith Won't Fail," whose refrain is, "He'll prevail / In the midst of all my trials and tribulations / And He'll prevail / In the midst of all my sin and temptations / He'll prevail / When I fail and He will pick me up / For time and time again my faith won't fail." Perry performed at a series of churches and other places to promote the album, but it received little attention and attracted few buyers. Described by Stefanie Cohen for the *New York Post* (15 Aug. 2010) as "a collision of gospel sentiment and Alanis Morissette angst" and by the *New York Times* (16 June 2008) critic Jon Caramanica as "a moody, eclectic collection of Christian contemporary music," it soon disappeared, as did Red Hill, which went bankrupt at the end of 2001. One of the album's coproducers, Tommy Collier, told Cohen, "Katy was kind of a diamond in the rough. You could tell she was gonna be an expensive race car, but she didn't know how to drive it yet." Earlier in 2001 Perry (as Katy Hudson) had performed as an opening act for Phil Joel, a New Zealander, who was touring to promote his album *Watching Over You* in the United States.

EARLY CAREER

With the aid of industry contacts, Perry met the music producer and songwriter Glen Ballard, who had collaborated with artists and groups including Michael Jackson, Van Halen, and Aerosmith and, perhaps most famously, had cowritten and produced Alanis Morissette's Grammy Award–winning album, *Jagged Little Pill* (1995). "I was first impressed by [Perry's] musicality and taste," Ballard told Lisa Robinson for *Vanity Fair* (June 2011), as quoted by Jeff Dedekker in the Regina, Saskatchewan, *Leader-Post* (27 June 2011). "The unusual way she played the guitar demonstrated that she was a seeker. Katy communicates fun and passion; her music sounds like a celebration but it's clearer to me that there's great intelligence behind it. Katy's emotional range and stylistic range are enormous." With her parents' reluctant permission, at seventeen Perry moved to Los Angeles, California, where for the next three years or so, she worked with Ballard and reinvented herself as a pop singer. After a string of rejections from record labels, Perry signed with Island Def Jam Records, but in 2005, for reasons never made public, Def Jam shelved the album she and Ballard had recorded, and soon afterward the label dropped Perry. One of her collaborations with Ballard, a song called "Simple," was included on the soundtrack for the film *The Sisterhood of the Traveling Pants* (2005).

Perry next signed with Columbia Records, which teamed her up with the Grammy-nominated writing and production group the Matrix (Lauren Christy, Graham Edwards, and Scott Spock), who had collaborated with musicians including Christina Aguilera, Avril Lavigne, Shakira, and Korn. Along with Adam Longlands, Perry provided vocals for a Matrix-produced rock album, but Columbia ended its association with her before the project was completed. In an interview with Monica Herrera for *Billboard* (31 July 2010), Perry compared her experiences with Def Jam and Columbia to "taking a kid to Disneyland and then making them wait outside. The people just wouldn't let me through the gates—what could I do?" During that period Perry supplemented money she borrowed from her parents by securing a few jobs. One involved critiquing demo tapes for Taxi Music, an independent artist-and-repertoire (A&R) company based in Calabasas, California.

BIG BREAK

Perry got her big break in 2007, when a record-industry publicist, Angelica Cob-Baehler, and an A&R executive, Chris Anokute, recommended her to Jason Flom, the chairman of the newly formed Capitol Music Group. Perry, having reclaimed the songs she had recorded for Def Jam and Columbia, now re-recorded them for Capitol with various producers under Flom's direction. In November 2007 Capitol released her debut single, "Ur So Gay," with an accompanying music video. Cowritten by Greg Wells, the song is about a "metrosexual" man (or such men in general); it starts with the lines "I hope you hang yourself with your H&M scarf / While jacking off listening to Mozart." Writing for the *New York Times* (7 Nov. 2010), Alex Hawgood described it as "a jab at image-conscious straight men that many critics said was homophobic." "Ur So Gay" failed to reach the Billboard Hot 100 chart, but it created a buzz on the Internet, and the superstar Madonna praised the song on Ryan Seacrest's morning radio show.

"I KISSED A GIRL"

Perry attracted a huge amount of attention worldwide with her next single, "I Kissed a Girl," which was produced by Dr. Luke. It contains the lyrics "It's not what I'm used to / Just wanna try you on / I'm curious, for you, / Caught my attention / I kissed a girl / And I liked it / The taste of her cherry chapstick / I kissed a girl / Just to try it / I hope my boyfriend don't mind it / . . . / You're my experimental game / Just human nature." "I Kissed a Girl" was extremely popular: it sold more than four million digital downloads, and it held the number-one spot on the Billboard Hot 100 chart for seven consecutive weeks and reached the top spot on charts in more than twenty countries. It was also widely condemned, both by those who interpreted it as promoting homosexuality or bisexuality and those in the lesbian and gay community who found it offensive or "felt used" by Perry, as Barry Walters, a music critic for *Spin* and *Rolling Stone*, told Alex Haywood. "I Kissed a Girl" was the lead song on Perry's album *One of the Boys* (2008), which spawned two additional Top 10 singles ("Hot N Cold" and "Waking Up in Vegas"). The album peaked at number nine on the Billboard 200 chart and has since sold more than seven million copies worldwide. "I Kissed a Girl" earned Perry a Grammy Award nomination for best female pop-vocal performance.

ONE OF THE BOYS

Its popular success notwithstanding, the reactions of most music critics to *One of the Boys* were lukewarm or negative. In an assessment for the *New York Times* (16 June 2008), Jon Caramanica wrote that Perry's "ideas about gender and sexuality seem as situational as her highly amalgamated style. Hers is a neatly commodified kind of rebellion: looks from Dita von Teese, production by way of Britney Spears and Alanis Morissette, vocals à la Ashlee Simpson and Avril Lavigne." He also wrote, "Ms. Perry . . . has an easy way with melody and is best served by producers who give her room to emote. Dave Stewart (of Eurythmics) takes the helm on 'I'm Still Breathing,' a calm and certain obituary for a dead relationship. And 'Thinking of You,' produced by the underappreciated Butch Walker, is gently and compellingly angry." Alex Miller, the reviewer for the British weekly *NME* (11 Sep. 2008), gave *One of the Boys* three stars out of ten and warned readers, "If you've got even a passing interest in actually enjoying a record, don't buy this one." In a scathing review for the *All Music Guide*, Stephen Thomas Erlewine wrote, "Given [Perry's] long line of botched starts, maybe it makes sense that the twenty-four-year-old trollop is singing with the desperation of a fading burlesque star twice her age, yet Perry's shameless pandering on *One of the Boys* is startling, particularly as it comes in the form of some ungodly hybrid of Alanis Morissette's caterwauling and the cold calculation of Britney Spears in her prime. . . . [Perry] sinks to crass, craven depths that turn *One of the Boys* into a grotesque emblem of all the wretched excesses of this decade."

TEENAGE DREAM

Perry's "California Gurls," an electropop song made for her third studio album, reached the number-one spot on the Billboard Hot 100 singles chart within four weeks of its release, in May 2010, making it the fastest-rising single by a Capitol Records artist since Bobbie Gentry's "Ode to Billie Joe" in 1967. The song, in which the rapper Snoop Dogg joined Perry, spent seven consecutive weeks atop the Billboard Hot 100 chart; it has since sold more than five million digital downloads. "California Gurls" is the first track on *Teenage Dream*, which arrived in stores on August 24, 2010. *Teenage Dream* debuted at number one on the Billboard 200 chart and sold 192,000 copies in its first week; it has since sold more than seven million copies worldwide. The disk produced four additional number-one singles ("Teenage Dream," "Firework," "E.T." [with Kanye West], and "Last Friday Night [T.G.I.F.]"), making Perry the first woman and only the second artist to have five number-one singles from the same album; Perry also became the first artist in the half-century history of the Billboard Hot 100 chart to have at least one song remain in the Top 10 for a complete calendar year. She launched a worldwide tour in support of the album in February 2011.

In a review of *Teenage Dream* for the Brisbane, Australia, *Courier Mail*, Cameron Adams wrote, "There is some fine pop here," citing in particular "Teenage Dream, " "Firework," and "Not Like the Movies," but also complained, "For a smart woman, Katy Perry makes some seriously dumb pop songs. Her unavoidable No. 1 'California Gurls' kills brain cells upon impact. . . . Perry is an adequate if unremarkable pop star, but she knows to surround herself with the right crew to dumb things down to bring sales up." "Give Katy Perry credit: She knows how to make a song that will totally rule on radio . . . ," Chuck Arnold and Jessica Herndon wrote for *People* (6 Sep. 2010). "Hitmakers like Dr. Luke, Max Martin, Christopher 'Tricky' Stewart and Stargate . . . help give *Teenage Dream* a youthful bounce and sheen on giddy pleasures like 'Peacock,' a strutting standout. But when things slow down and turn serious in the second half on dreary tunes like 'Who Am I Living For?' and 'E.T.,' it's a rude awakening from all the fun." Greg Kot, the *Chicago Tribune* (22 Aug. 2010) reviewer, found little to like in *Teenage Dream* and gave it one star out of four. "Katy Perry seems like a likable enough goofball, the kind of diva whose flashy trash fashions and offbeat humor promise something more interesting than formula pop. But formula pop is exactly what she dishes out, . . . split between girls-gone-wild cliches and melodramatic power ballads. The Frankenstein-like productions . . . sap the music of personality, presence, surprise. Too often she sounds robotic, like a wind-up toy incapable of singing with any elegance or nuance. She either stutters for effect . . . or lands on the beats so emphatically . . . that it's almost comical. . . . Singing ability is not a prerequisite for making great pop music, but original ideas and inventive presentation are—and both are lacking."

On October 23, 2010, Perry married the British comedian and actor Russell Brand. "It's beautiful to have a teammate," she told Edna Gunderson for the *Chicago Sun-Times* (14 Aug. 2011). "When you're single, you use so much energy looking for The One. When you find him, it's whew, you can turn that radar off and breathe."

SUGGESTED READING

Cohen, Stefanie. "Katy-clysmic!" *New York Post*. NYP Holdings Inc., 15 Aug. 2010. Web. Jan. 2012.

Friedlander, Noam. *Katy Perry*. New York: Sterling, 2012.

"Katy Perry on Her Religious Childhood, Her Career, and Her Marriage to Russell Brand." *Vanity Fair*. Condé Nast Digital, 3 May 2011. Web. Jan. 2012.

"Katy Perry Talks Body Image, Fame and Politics in Rolling Stone Cover Story." *Rolling Stone*. Rolling Stone, 22 June 2011. Web. Jan. 2012.

—*Christopher Cullen*

Adrian Peterson

Born: March 21, 1985
Occupation: Football player

Adrian Peterson of the Minnesota Vikings is considered one of the best running backs in the National Football League (NFL). Nicknamed "A. D." (short for "All Day") for his tireless energy both on and off the football field, the six-foot-two, 217-pound Peterson is known for his brute strength and breakaway speed. During his NFL career, he has demonstrated an uncanny ability to run over and elude defenders. "There's something unique about the way Peterson runs," Joe Wuebben wrote for *Muscle & Fitness* (Oct. 1, 2008). "It's hard to put a finger on exactly what it is, yet you can see it every time he carries the ball. . . . It's as though every time he touches the ball, he's in a hurry to get somewhere."

Peterson first showcased that powerful, explosive running style at the University of Oklahoma before making the jump to the NFL after his junior year in 2007, when he was selected by the Vikings in the first round of that year's draft. Peterson had a record-breaking rookie season—he broke the NFL single-game rushing mark with 296 yards and finished second in the league in rushing with 1,341 yards, en route to being named the 2007 Associated Press (AP) NFL Offensive Rookie of the Year. He returned in 2008 to become the first Vikings running back to lead the league in rushing with a franchise-best 1,760 rushing yards.

During the 2009 season Peterson set another Vikings record with eighteen rushing touchdowns and finished first in the league in scoring among non-kickers. In 2010 he eclipsed the thousand-yard rushing mark for the fourth consecutive year and finished tied for fourth in the NFL in rushing touchdowns with twelve. He has earned Pro Bowl selections in each of his four seasons and was named to the AP All-Pro first team in 2008 and 2009. Peterson, who endured his fair share of adversity and tragedy in his path to NFL superstardom, told Jim Corbett for *USA Today* (Apr. 18, 2007, online), "Resilience is what I'm all about. I run angry. Football allows me to take out some of my pain on the field. When I go out on the field, I just put it in my mind that I'm playing for my family."

EARLY LIFE

Adrian Lewis Peterson was born on March 21, 1985, in Palestine, Texas, a small town located forty miles east of Dallas. He is one of fifteen children born to Nelson Peterson and Bonita Brown, who never married and broke up shortly after Adrian was born.

Both parents were distinguished athletes. Peterson's father was a standout high school basketball player in Florida before going on

to star at Idaho State, where he holds the seventh-best single-season scoring mark, with 603 points during the 1984–85 season. Nelson Peterson had aspirations of playing professionally in the National Basketball Association (NBA) and had been invited to try out with the Philadelphia 76ers, but his basketball career ended prematurely after his brother accidentally shot him in the leg in a freak accident. Peterson's mother was a four-time state champion in track and field at Palestine's Westwood High School, which helped her win a track scholarship to the University of Houston. She had hoped to compete at the 1984 Summer Olympics in Los Angeles, California, but those plans were derailed after she became pregnant. Peterson also has an uncle, Ivory Lee Brown, who spent one season in the NFL as a running back with the Phoenix Cardinals (now known as the Arizona Cardinals).

When Peterson was a child, he was nicknamed "All Day" (later shortened to "A. D.") by his father for his hyperactive nature and tendency to go "all day," all the time. Unsurprisingly, given his athletic pedigree, he channeled much of that energy into sports and other physical activities. "Palestine was very small," he recalled, speaking to Sean Jensen for the *St. Paul Pioneer Press* (July 21, 2007). "You could basically get anywhere you had to get. That's something I definitely remember. I remember walking all the time or riding my bike—that's how I got my legs so strong—being a kid and going on adventures. Trying to discover something new."

FAMILY TRAGEDY

Growing up Adrian Peterson shared a close bond with his brother Brian, who was less than a year older than he was. The two were extremely competitive and often challenged each other to foot races, which Brian usually won. Brian's life ended tragically when he was struck and killed by a drunk driver while riding his bicycle. Adrian, who was barely eight years old at the time, witnessed the tragedy. "When Brian passed, there was a big part of him that was gone because they did everything together," his mother told John E. Hoover for the *Tulsa World* (Aug. 20, 2006). "A big part of his life was just gone, and that really hurt him bad." The drunk driver responsible for Brian Peterson's death was ultimately convicted and sent to prison.

Following his brother's death, Adrian found an escape from his grief in football. He began playing organized football around the age of eight. His father, who worked as a forklift operator at a local Wal-Mart warehouse, coached many of his youth-league teams and helped him develop his skills at the Palestine Athletic Complex. Adrian's outstanding athletic ability was apparent early on and throughout his youth he "dominated just about every game he played," as Blair Kerkhoff noted for the *Kansas City Star* (Oct. 22, 2004). When he was eleven years old, he was named the Most Valuable Player (MVP) at a state youth-football tournament after reportedly going the entire competition without being tackled. Peterson's youth-league coach at the time, Steve Eudey, told John E. Hoover, "That was kind of the first time that we began to realize he was pretty special. Because that was against kids we didn't know. We knew he was better than all the kids we had."

Despite his athletic promise, Adrian's life took another troubling turn when he was thirteen: His father was arrested and convicted for money laundering in connection with a major crack-cocaine distribution ring. His father, who had become involved in the drug trade largely to supplement his income, was sentenced to ten years in prison but was released after serving eight years. Adrian maintained a close relationship with his father throughout his time in prison. "He missed him, a whole lot," his mother told Blair Kerkhoff. His mother remarried to a local Baptist minister, Frankie Jackson. "[Adrian] grew up with his dad, and he was always there for him. He showed him how to play ball. Then all the sudden he's not there anymore," she said. "There was a lot of anger and a lot of hurt." During this time Jackson stepped in as a father figure for Adrian, who struggled academically for a time due to his emotional distress, which consequently slowed the development of his athletic career.

HIGH SCHOOL CAREER

Adrian Peterson attended Westwood High School for one year before transferring to Palestine High School, where he played football, basketball, and competed in track and field. He played several games on Westwood's varsity-football squad as a freshman, but his season was cut short by a knee injury. He was then limited to just three games on Palestine's junior varsity football squad during his sophomore season as a result of poor grades and state rules for transfer students. Peterson's full eligibility was restored for his junior season, and in his first varsity game at Palestine, he rushed for 212 yards. He followed that up with an astonishing 340 rushing yards in his next game and went on to finish his junior season with 2,051 yards and twenty-two touchdowns. He eclipsed the two-thousand-yard mark again as a senior, when he rushed for 2,960 yards and thirty-two touchdowns and was the consensus high school Player of the Year.

Peterson's final high school game was particularly noteworthy, when he rushed for a remarkable 350 yards and six touchdowns without playing in the second half. Jeff Harrell, who coached his football and track teams at Palestine, noted to Sean Jensen, "After handing him the ball a few times, it didn't take a brain surgeon to figure out that you should just keep giving him the ball. I was criticized for not throwing it enough. But he averaged over nine yards a carry." Peterson was reportedly so fast that his coaches had to line him up eight yards behind the quarterback to ensure that he would not beat him to the handoff.

COLLEGE FOOTBALL STAR

Peterson was recruited heavily by football powerhouses all over the country, particularly the University of Texas at Austin and Texas A&M University, but he chose to attend the University of Oklahoma (OU). Many scouts had rated Peterson the number-one high school football recruit in the nation. A football-recruiting analyst, Jeremy Crabtree, told Blair Kerkhoff, "In most years, there are three or four players who could be No. 1. But he was so far advanced in his game, he was as solid a No. 1 as maybe I've ever seen." Peterson decided on Oklahoma following a recruiting trip in which he observed how hard players on the football team worked. Despite his talent, he immediately impressed players and coaches with his humility and work ethic. Jerry Schmidt, the director of sports enhancement for OU, told Joe Wuebben, "At a young age, Adrian understood the importance of conditioning and keeping his body fine-tuned. He had a lot of God-given ability, but he worked his tail off."

In 2004 Peterson posted one of the best seasons for a freshman running back in National Collegiate Athletic Association (NCAA) history. He set a school record and the NCAA freshman rushing record, with 1,925 yards, breaking marks set by Billy Sims and Ron Daynes, respectively. He also set NCAA freshman records for rushing attempts (339), consecutive hundred-yard rushing games (9), and total hundred-yard rushing games (11). He became the first Oklahoma freshman to earn first-team All-American honors and finished second in the voting for the Heisman Trophy, which was the highest finish ever for a freshman. He helped lead Oklahoma to a perfect 12–0 record and an appearance in the 2004 national title game, which they lost to the University of Southern California (USC), 55–19. Peterson subsequently entered his sophomore campaign in 2005 as one of the Heisman favorites, but he was limited to 1,108 rushing yards after missing several games due to a leg injury. He then missed seven games during his junior year after suffering a broken collarbone, which slowed his production to 1,012 rushing yards. After returning to play in the 2007 Fiesta Bowl, in which he rushed for 77 yards and two touchdowns in a 43–42 loss to Boise State, Peterson announced that he would forgo his senior year to enter the NFL Draft. He finished his college career at OU ranked third in career rushing yards with 4,045 and fourth in career rushing touchdowns with forty-one, despite only having played in thirty-one games. Oklahoma's offensive coordinator Chuck Long told Blair Kerkhoff, "In my 10 years of coaching I've never seen anybody like him. He makes it look easy, but it's not easy."

Despite concerns about his durability, many analysts projected Peterson, who had already been deemed NFL-ready after his freshman year, to be a top ten pick in the 2007 NFL Draft. He silenced many of his detractors after participating in that year's NFL Scouting Combine, in which he achieved some of the best marks among running-back prospects, completing the forty-yard dash in 4.4 seconds and posting a 38-inch vertical jump. Peterson performed exceptionally at the event despite receiving the tragic news, on the eve of his workout, that his half-brother, Chris Paris, had been shot and killed in a carjacking in Houston. He told Jim Corbett, "Chris would have wanted me to go ahead and work out. I had just talked to him a couple of days before. He told me it was a once-in-a-lifetime opportunity and just take care of business." Impressed not only with his physical attributes but also with his mental strength, the Minnesota Vikings selected Peterson in the first round, with the seventh overall pick of the 2007 NFL Draft. The team signed the running back to a five-year contract worth approximately $40.5 million.

MINNESOTA VIKING

Peterson wasted little time living up to expectations. He made his professional debut on September 9, 2007, against the Atlanta Falcons. In the game, which the Vikings won 24–3, he rushed for 103 yards on nineteen carries and scored his first career touchdown after making a 60-yard reception. Over his next two games, he accrued 268 more yards from scrimmage (168 rushing and 100 receiving) and scored his first career rushing touchdown. His three-game total of 431 yards from scrimmage set a Vikings record. Peterson was named the Offensive Rookie of the Month for September, after amassing 549 yards from scrimmage and 383 rushing yards in his first four professional games.

Peterson enjoyed a breakout performance in his fifth career game, in a match against the Chicago Bears, when he rushed for 224 yards on twenty carries and scored three touchdowns, including one on a 73-yard run. Peterson also added 128 yards on four kickoff returns. His 224 rushing yards and 73-yard touchdown run were both franchise-bests, and his 361 all-purpose yards (224 rushing, 9 receiving, and 128 returning kicks) set an NFL rookie record. After totaling 133 rushing yards and 222 all-purpose yards in his next two games, he was named the NFL Offensive Rookie of the Month for October. Around this time, Hall of Fame cornerback Deion Sanders, an analyst for the NFL Network, said, "[Peterson] has the vision of a Marshall Faulk, the power of a Terrell Davis, and the speed of an Eric Dickerson. Let's pray he has the endurance of an Emmitt Smith," as quoted by Dave Campbell for the Associated Press (Oct. 21, 2007, online).

The highlight of Peterson's remarkable rookie campaign came during the ninth week of the season in a game against the San Diego Chargers, when he broke the NFL single-game rushing mark and his own Vikings' franchise record with 296 yards. This performance broke the previous single-game record of 295 set by Jamal Lewis during the 2003 season. Peterson ended the season with 1,341 rushing yards (in fourteen games, missing two due to injury), which led the National Football Conference (NFC) and placed him second in the NFL. He also had twelve rushing touchdowns, the second-highest single-season total in Vikings history. His average of 95.8 rushing yards per game led the league, and his average of 5.6 yards per carry set a Vikings record. He also set a Vikings record with four rushes of 50 or more yards and tied another franchise record with seven plays of 50 or more yards (four rushing, one receiving, and two returning kickoffs).

Peterson's record-breaking achievements helped the Vikings improve on their record from the previous year, as they finished with a record of 8–8, good for second in the NFC North Division. At the end of the season, Peterson was named the AP Offensive Rookie of the Year, earning 46.5 votes from a nationwide panel of fifty sportswriters, and was voted the Vikings offensive MVP. He was also selected to the AP All-Pro second team and earned his first Pro Bowl selection, as the starting running back for the NFC Pro Bowl squad. He subsequently earned MVP honors at the annual Pro Bowl game after rushing for 129 yards on sixteen carries and scoring two touchdowns.

RECORD-BREAKING SEASONS

During the 2008 season, Peterson picked up where he left off as a rookie and finished with 1,760 rushing yards, which led the NFL and broke a Vikings' single-season record. In the process he became the first Vikings running back ever to lead the league in rushing. Meanwhile, he led the league in rushing yards per game for the second consecutive year, averaging a career-high 110 yards in sixteen games. He also scored ten rushing touchdowns and set Vikings' single-season records for most rushing attempts (363) and most games with at least one hundred yards rushing (10). Peterson was voted the Vikings offensive MVP for the second straight year and earned his second career Pro Bowl selection; he was also named to the AP All-Pro first team for the first time. In addition, he finished second in the voting for the AP Offensive Player of the Year Award and fourth in the AP's voting for NFL MVP. The Vikings won the AFC North Division with a record of 10–6 and advanced to the postseason for the first time since the 2004 season. The Vikings were defeated by the Philadelphia Eagles in the wild-card playoff round, 26–14.

Peterson continued to solidify his status as the NFL's best running back in 2009, when he rushed for 1,383 yards and a franchise-best eighteen rushing touchdowns, which led the league and helped him finish first in scoring among all NFL non-kickers. The arrival of All-Pro quarterback Brett Favre during the 2009 off-season also helped Peterson reestablish himself as a pass-catching threat out of the backfield, and he finished with a career-high forty-three receptions for 436 yards. He was named a Pro Bowl starter for the third straight year and was named to his second straight AP All-Pro first team. Meanwhile, thanks to a vastly improved passing attack led by Favre, who enjoyed a career year, and a dominant rushing attack anchored by Peterson, the Vikings finished with a 12–4 record to successfully defend their NFC North title. The Vikings then advanced to the NFC Championship Game, where they lost to the eventual Super Bowl champion New Orleans Saints, 31–28, in an overtime thriller. In the game Peterson rushed for 122 yards and tied a team playoff record with three touchdowns.

The 2010 season saw Peterson surpass the thousand-yard rushing mark for the fourth straight season, with 1,298 yards, which was good for sixth in the league and second in the NFC. He also notched twelve rushing touchdowns, which placed him tied for fourth in the league and tied for first in the NFC. He earned his fourth straight selection to the Pro Bowl and was named to his second AP All-Pro second team. The Vikings, however, failed to defend their NFC North title and missed the playoffs with a record of 6–10. Their disappointing season was plagued by turmoil and a chaotic chain of events that included a Brett Favre sex scandal, the firing of head coach Brad Childress, and the collapse of the Hubert H. Humphrey Metrodome's inflatable roof as a result of a severe snowstorm. Childress was replaced by the team's defensive coordinator, Leslie Frazier, who was retained for the 2011 season.

On September 10, 2011, Peterson signed a seven-year contract extension with the Vikings worth a reported $100 million. The contract includes $36 million in guaranteed money and makes him the highest-paid running back in NFL history.

During the second week of the 2011 season, Peterson eclipsed 6,000 rushing yards for his career and became the Vikings' all-time leader in rushing touchdowns, after rushing for 120 yards and two touchdowns against the Tampa Bay Buccaneers. He also had two touchdown receptions in the game. He missed Weeks 12, 13, and 14 of the season due to a high-ankle sprain but returned for a Week 15 matchup against the New Orleans Saints, in which he carried the ball ten times for 60 yards in 42–20 Vikings' loss. Entering the last two games of the season, Peterson stood just 104 yards shy of Robert Smith's Vikings record for most rushing yards, and 68 yards away from reaching the thousand-yard plateau for the fifth straight year. He currently ranks fourth on the NFL's all-time list for rushing yards per game, with an average of 93.3.

PERSONAL LIFE

Peterson lives in Eden Prairie, a suburb of Minneapolis, Minnesota. He has a daughter, Adeja (born in 2004), from his past relationship with Ashley Brown. In 2008, Peterson established the All-Day Foundation, which is dedicated to enriching the lives of at-risk children.

SUGGESTED READING

Campbell, Dave. "Player of the Week: Rookie Peterson off to a Sensational Start for Vikings." *USA Today*. USA Today, 21 Oct. 2007. Web. 8 Dec. 2011.

Carlson, Jenni. "From Childhood Tragedy to Prize Recruit." *Oklahoman* [Oklahoma City] 1 Feb. 2004: D1. Print.

Corbett, Jim. "Adrian Peterson Runs through Anger to the NFL." *USA Today*. USA Today, 18 Apr. 2007. Web. 8 Dec. 2011.

Evans, Thayer. "The Pride of Palestine: Texas Town Follows Its Star." *New York Times* 23 Sep. 2007: 10. Print.

Isaacson, Melissa. "Oklahoma Running Back Channels Heartache into Huge Headaches for Opponents during a Record-Breaking Freshman Season." *Chicago Tribune* 29 Oct. 2004: C1. Print.

Kerkhoff, Blair. "Carrying a Load." *Kansas City Star* 22 Oct. 2004: D1. Print.

Moore, David. "Breakthrough Adrian Peterson Puts Himself on NFL Map with Sizzling Start." *Dallas Morning News* 21 Oct. 2007: C1. Print.

Thomas, David. "The Elusive One." *Fort Worth Star Telegram* 19 Oct. 2003: C12. Print.

Svrluga, Barry. "Peterson Is Delivering, Sooner Rather Than Later." *Washington Post* 29 Oct. 2004: D1. Print.

Wuebben, Joe. "Run Adrian Run: From the Dirt Roads of Texas, Minnesota Vikings Running Back Adrian Peterson Became the NFL's Brightest Young Talent—and Perhaps the League's Hardest Worker." *Muscle & Fitness* 1 Oct. 2008: 124. Print.

—*Christopher Cullen*

Getty Images

Rosamund Pike

Born: January 27, 1979
Occupation: Actress

Since her breakout movie debut as the beautiful and devious Miranda Frost in the James Bond film *Die Another Day* (2002), British stage and screen star Rosamund Pike has developed into one of the United Kingdom's more versatile and accomplished actresses. Pike fuses natural charisma with an acting talent that she has honed since childhood. Though Pike has played the lead in a number of theatrical productions on the British stage, depicting Alma in Tennessee Williams's *Summer and Smoke* and the title characters in Terry Johnson's *Hitchcock Blonde*, Yukio Mishima's *Madame de Sade*, and Henrik Ibsen's *Hedda Gabler*, she is known principally for her supporting roles in such films as *The Libertine* (2004), *Pride and Prejudice* (2005), *Fracture* (2007), *An Education* (2009), *Barney's Version* (2010), *Made in Dagenham* (2010), *Wrath of the Titans* (2012), and the forthcoming *Jack Reacher* (2013). As Ann Hornaday observed for the *Washington Post* (28 Jan. 2011), Pike "has become something of a best-kept secret among discerning viewers. General audiences may not know her name, but they may well have found themselves captivated by her un-showy but indelible supporting performances."

EARLY LIFE

Rosamund Mary Elizabeth Pike was born January 27, 1979, in London, England, the only child of Julian Pike, an opera singer (and now the head of vocal and operatic studies at the Birmingham Conservatoire, in Birmingham, England), and Caroline Friend Pike, an opera singer and concert violinist. Though raised in London, Pike spent much of her youth traveling with her parents whose musical careers took them all over Europe. Despite the apparent glamour, the Pikes were not wealthy. "We often didn't have much money, but [my parents] loved their work and that kind of made everything else worthwhile for them. I felt secure in every other way, though," Pike told Stuart Husband for the *Observer* (12 Oct. 2002).

The early introduction to the world of drama and the arts left an impression on Pike and steered her toward her future career. "I spent quite a lot of time in rehearsal rooms or in the wings, looking at [my parents] being the stars," she commented to Lynn Barber for the *Observer* (23 May 2009). "It was definitely what gave me the bug, seeing my mum playing the Merry Widow—it's a wonderful opera—and she had this boa and a big wig, and looked just gorgeous: like a film star, I thought. I was a bit of a frumpy child and she just looked incredibly glamorous and exciting."

Belying her youth, Pike displayed an early dedication to acting as a calling and, thanks in part to the artistic exposure she received as a child, developed a precocious perception that helped her grow into her craft. "I was weirdly serious about [acting] from very young, about 10 or something," she remarked to Barber. "And watching my parents, there was a real analytical interest in what made something believable and what made it not believable, or what made something moving or funny, or why these lines didn't ring true."

EDUCATION

In 1990, at the age of eleven, Pike earned herself a scholarship to the prestigious Badminton School, an all-girls boarding academy in Bristol, England. Throughout her time at Badminton, Pike found it difficult to fit in among her wealthy classmates. As a young teenager, she recalled herself as a bit of an ugly duckling, far from the glamorous beauty she would become. Nevertheless, Pike's commitment to acting did not diminish. She took part in a number of school plays and, due to her height, she often performed the male roles. At sixteen, she was accepted into the National Youth Theatre, a training ground for the United Kingdom's most promising young actors. Two years later, she played Juliet in the organization's production of William Shakespeare's *Romeo and Juliet*.

Pike did exceptionally well on her university entrance exams and after graduating from Badminton in 1997, went on to Wadham College, Oxford University. There she studied English and took part in various dramatic productions staged at the school. She also made her television debut, appearing in a supporting role in the film *A Rather English Marriage* (1998), which was broadcast by the British Broadcasting Corporation (BBC). The following year she appeared in several episodes of the BBC miniseries *Wives and Daughters*.

As her acting ambitions overshadowed her academic ones, Pike made the decision to focus exclusively on her passion. She dropped out of Wadham and applied to a number of drama schools. Despite her strong credentials, "I got rejected from them all," Pike informed Lucy Cavendish for the *Telegraph* (18 Mar. 2009). "It was very hard to take. I had to crawl back to Wadham and beg to be allowed to finish my degree." The overwhelming rejection was hard for her to reconcile. In hindsight, the reasons for her lack of success were complicated. As she explained to Judith Woods for the *Mail* (24 Sep. 2010), "Later I met someone who had been on one of the panels, and he admitted I'd done the best audition he'd ever seen but he'd been overruled because his colleagues felt I was born with a silver spoon in my mouth, which simply isn't true." Despite her relatively modest upbringing, Pike's private school education, upper-class accent, and stunning appearance led people to erroneous conclusions about her background. "There's this impression that I've somehow lived a charmed life," Pike explained to Woods. "I wouldn't mind being thought of as privileged if I'd had any of the wealth that's supposed to accompany it, but we weren't at all well off."

BOND GIRL

As she finished up her studies at Oxford, Pike landed several small roles on British television in 2000 and 2001. She graduated from Wadham in 2001, earning an upper second class honors degree, the equivalent of graduating magna cum laude in the United States. After completing school, she went on auditions while also looking for a job. She acted in an episode of the British police procedural *Foyle's War* in 2002, but a truly breakout role eluded her. As she weighed whether to accept a position at the Waterstones bookstore chain, she auditioned for *Die Another Day,* starring Pierce Brosnan, Halle Berry, and Judi Dench. Pike read for the role of Miranda Frost, an Olympic fencer and double agent who becomes romantically involved with Bond. Pike did not think she had a serious chance of landing the part and left the audition with few illusions, heading off to an isolated cottage in Lincolnshire. The house had no phone, so she had no idea that everyone on the film, including the director Lee Tamahori, was trying to get a hold of her for the first of many callbacks. After numerous screen tests, "They told me, you're the Bond girl," Pike recollected to Woods. "And I was completely speechless. It hit me: it's like becoming part of movie history."

Though *Die Another Day* received mixed reviews, the film was a box office smash, grossing over $400 million worldwide. For Pike, *Die Another Day* propelled her to international stardom. As Lucy Cavendish noted in the *Telegraph* (19 Mar. 2009), "She seemed to come from absolutely nowhere yet was received with rapturous attention by audiences worldwide." The role earned her a 2003 Empire Award for best newcomer from the British film magazine *Empire*.

After *Die Another Day*, rather than pursue more film work, Pike opted instead for the stage, accepting the title role in *Hitchcock Blonde*, which premiered on London's West End, at the Royal Court Theatre, in the spring of 2003. The play is set variously in the years 1999, 1959, and 1919 and explores the legendary filmmaker Alfred Hitchcock's on-screen obsession with blonde women. Pike played the body double of the actress Janet Leigh during the filming of Hitchcock's *Psycho* (1960) and its iconic shower sequence. The role was a difficult one, involving a prolonged nude scene, where for ten minutes Pike wore nothing except a pair of high heels.

FILM ROLES

Pike returned to the silver screen in 2004, appearing in two pictures, the Amos Gitai–directed *Promised Land* and *The Libertine*, starring Johnny Depp. A French-Israeli film, *Promised Land* depicted sex trafficking in Israel. While reviews for the film varied among the English-speaking press, *Promised Land* was honored at the 2004 Venice Film Festival with a special prize for its promotion of peace.

In *The Libertine*, directed by Laurence Dunmore, Pike played Elizabeth Malet, the long-suffering wife of John Wilmot, the Earl of Rochester, and the film's title character. A seventeenth-century poet and satirist with ties to England's King Charles II, Rochester was famous, too, for his drunken debauchery and early death. With few exceptions, *The Libertine* did not fare well critically. Pike's performance stood out, however. Alison Jane Reid, writing for the *Independent* (3 Dec. 2005), described Pike's Elizabeth as a "heart-breaking portrait of love and loyalty betrayed as the stoic consort of Johnny Depp's Rochester." At the 2005 British Independent Film Awards, Pike captured the best supporting actress honor.

Pike took the role of Jane Bennet in *Pride and Prejudice*, Joe Wright's adaptation of the 1813 Jane Austen novel. The film stars Keira Knightley as Elizabeth Bennet and Matthew Macfadyen as Mr. Darcy and centers on various efforts to see the five Bennet sisters successfully married off. The film, Stephen Holden wrote for the *New York Times* (11 Nov. 2005), "gathers you up on its white horse and gallops off into the sunset. Along the way, it serves a continuing banquet of high-end comfort food perfectly cooked and seasoned to Anglophilic tastes. In its final minutes, it makes you believe in true love, the union of soul mates, happily-ever-after and all the other stuff a romantic comedy promises but so seldom delivers." Alison Jane Reid described Pike performance as "supremely intelligent."

While working on the set of *Pride and Prejudice*, Pike was offered a role in *Doom* (2005), a science fiction film based on the video game of the same name. "When I got the call about *Doom*, I was in a bonnet in a field near Tunbridge Wells. I thought: 'My God, if they could see me—they would probably recast!'" Pike informed James Nottram for *Metro* (27 Oct. 2009). Pike played Dr. Samantha Grimm, a forensic archaeologist, stationed on Mars who meets up with a detachment of space marines sent to the planet to investigate strange happenings at a research lab where they encounter a host of deadly creatures. "*Doom* was a truly dreadful film," Pike told a writer for the *Scotsman* (2 Oct. 2009). "It was beset by certain problems. At one stage, we really thought it would be quite brilliant and edgy."

ON STAGE AND SCREEN
Following a return to the stage as Alma in Tennessee Williams's *Summer and Smoke,* which opened at London's Apollo Theatre in 2006, Pike appeared with Anthony Hopkins and Ryan Gosling in the legal suspense thriller *Fracture*. Playing corporate attorney Nikki Gardner, Pike

becomes romantically involved with Gosling's character, Willie Beachum, a district attorney looking to make a lucrative transition into private practice—if he can just put one puzzling murder case to rest.

Pike next played a supporting role in the Holocaust drama *Fugitive Pieces* (2007), adapted from the Anne Michaels novel. Pike's character, Alex, is the wife of Jakob Beer, portrayed by Stephen Dillane, a young Holocaust survivor who after seeing his family slaughtered by the Nazis in Poland escapes to Greece and then to Canada, where he becomes a writer and teacher. Haunted by his past, Jeannette Catsoulis observed for the *New York Times* (2 May 2008), "Jakob remains shackled to memories that draw him ever inward and repel his high-spirited young wife, Alex (a touching Rosamund Pike)." The role earned Pike a Genie Award nomination for best supporting actress by the Academy of Canadian Cinema and Television.

Set in London in the early 1960s, *An Education* follows Jenny, a sixteen-year-old girl, played by Carey Mulligan, as she is enticed into an affair with a much older man, portrayed by Peter Sarsgaard. Based on a memoir by Lynn Barber and adapted for the screen by Nick Hornby, the film was a critical smash. Kenneth Turan wrote for the *Los Angeles Times* (9 Oct. 2009), "*An Education* does so many things so well, it's difficult to know where to begin when cataloging its virtues." Regarding Pike's contributions, a writer for the *Scotsman* enthused, "Not only does [*An Education*] prove what a consummate scene-stealer she is, but it shows us a side of her we have never seen before: the comedienne par excellence." As an ensemble, the cast of *An Education* was nominated for a 2010 Screen Actors Guild (SAG) Award.

In March 2009, Pike played the lead in a London stage production of *Madame de Sade*. The role reunited Pike with her *Die Another Day* costar Judi Dench. Among Pike's other notable credits of 2009 is the film *Surrogates*, described by Robert Abele for the *Los Angeles Times* (25 Sep. 2009) as "a slick sci-fi number that presents a future in which flawless, hot-bodied, chicly dressed synthetic humans do the everyday living/working/playing, their every action neurally controlled by their real-human counterparts, a risk-averse population of shut-ins who've gone to seed." *Surrogates* starred Bruce Willis as a spiritually broken police officer unable to recover from the loss of his son and featured Pike as his surrogate-dependent wife.

RECENT WORK
In 2010, Pike took turns on both the stage and screen headlining a production of *Hedda Gabler*; costarring with Paul Giamatti and Dustin Hoffman in *Barney's Version*, a film adaptation of the Mordecai Richler novel; and playing a supporting

role in *Made in Dagenham*, a British film about a 1968 strike by female employees at a Ford plant over gender-based pay discrimination. In each effort, Pike garnered superlative reviews. Regarding her portrayal of Hedda Gabler, Lyn Gardner wrote for the *Guardian* (7 Mar. 2010), "It is often suggested that the role of Hedda Gabler is for actresses what Hamlet is for male actors, and I've seldom seen one quite so mad, bad and dangerous to know as the Hedda offered here by Rosamund Pike. She is genuinely thrilling and genuinely scary, fixing everyone with her icy, merciless gaze, before finally turning that fatal gaze upon herself." As Miriam, the romantic obsession of Paul Giamatti's Barney in *Barney's Version*, "Pike breathes welcome warmth and life into Miriam, a paragon of wisdom, self-possession and inaccessible sex appeal," Ann Hornaday wrote. In *Made in Dagenham*, the character of Rita O'Grady, played by Sally Hawkins, leads the striking women, and as Justin Change commented for *Variety Reviews* (11 Sep. 2010), "Pike, as an upper-crust housewife sympathetic to Rita's cause, nearly upstages Hawkins in their moving scenes together."

The years 2011 and 2012 were especially busy ones for Pike. She performed in the British television miniseries *Women in Love* (2011), which was based on two D. H. Lawrence books—*The Rainbow* (1915) and *Women in Love* (1920); the Rowan Atkinson spoof of James Bond movies, *Johnny English Reborn* (2011); and the bird-watching comedy *The Big Year* (2011), starring Steve Martin, Owen Wilson, and Jack Black. She also landed a supporting role in the thriller *The Devil You Know* (2012) and played the goddess Andromeda in the blockbuster sequel *Wrath of the Titans*. She also acted alongside screen legends Tom Cruise and Robert Duvall in *Jack Reacher*, which is scheduled to open in early 2013.

Despite the increasing film and television work, Pike remains committed to the stage and has spoken of wanting to do a play every year—even with the comparatively lower pay. "My agents look on in horror, because it doesn't bring any money in at all," Pike observed to a writer for the *Scotsman*. "But I never thought I'd make any money at all doing this business. Film was never even on the cards."

PERSONAL LIFE

In the spring of 2012, Pike gave birth to her first child, a son whom she and her partner, businessman Robie Uniacke, named Solo. Pike has been with Uniacke since December 2009, and previously she was romantically linked to actor Simon Woods and director Joe Wright, who helmed *Pride and Prejudice*.

As for her future as an actor, Pike told Lynn Barber, "I want to be respected, so that to have my name attached to a project means

something. Obviously it would be great to do some wonderful enriching roles, but I want to just carry on doing it all my life. Because it just keeps you so young, it keeps you so fulfilled—it's the most fulfilling job in the world, really."

SUGGESTED READING

Barber, Lynn. "I Don't Sleep Around, If That's What You Mean . . . Would You Like Some More Cake?" *Observer*. Guardian News and Media Ltd., 23 May 2009. Web. 12 July 2012.

Cavendish, Lucy. "Rosamund Pike Interview." *Telegraph*. Telegraph Media Group Ltd., 18 Mar. 2009. Web. 12 July 2012.

Hornaday, Ann. "Rosamund Pike Talks About 'Barney's Version' and Inching into the Spotlight." *Washington Post*. The Washington Post Co., 28 Jan. 2011. Web. 12 July 2012.

Husband, Stuart. "The Name's Pike, Rosamund Pike." *Observer*. Guardian News and Media Ltd., 12 Oct. 2002. Web. 12 July 2012.

"Interview: Actress Rosamund Pike." *Scotsman.com*. Johnson Publishing Ltd., 2 Oct. 2009. Web. 12 July 2012.

Vankin, Deborah. "Rosamund Pike Isn't Afraid to Mix It Up." *Los Angeles Times*. Los Angeles Times, 2 Dec. 2010. Web. 12 July 2012.

—*Paul McCaffrey*

John Popper

Born: March 29, 1967
Occupation: Harmonica player, singer, songwriter, member of Blues Traveler

The singer, songwriter, and world-class harmonica player John Popper is the front man of the jam band Blues Traveler, which he formed in the late 1980s. The group had its mainstream breakthrough in 1995, with the Grammy Award–winning single "Run-Around," which spent nearly a full year on the charts. Although Blues Traveler's success was periodically slowed by Popper's health issues—which included injuries sustained in a serious auto accident, an angioplasty, and gastric-bypass surgery—as well as by the death in 1999 of its bass player, the group has enjoyed a consistently loyal following and has released critically acclaimed albums including *Travelers & Thieves* (1991), *Save His Soul* (1993), *Four* (1994), *Live from the Fall* (1996), *Straight on Till Morning* (1997), *Bridge* (2001), *Truth Be Told* (2003), and *Bastardos!* (2005). Popper recently formed a side group, John Popper and the Duskray Troubadours, which he conceived, according to a band press release, as a "scrappy, roots-rock alter ego of Blues Traveler."

EARLY LIFE AND EDUCATION

John Popper was born on March 29, 1967, in Cleveland, Ohio. His father, Robert, was a native of Hungary who immigrated to the United States in the 1950s to escape his birth country's Communist regime. Popper, who studied the piano, guitar, and cello before settling on the harmonica, is reportedly related to David Popper (1843–1913), a noteworthy cellist and composer. When Popper was young his family moved to the East Coast, eventually settling in Princeton, New Jersey. While attending Princeton High School, Popper met the drummer Brendan Hill, and they began performing as a duo, mimicking the John Belushi/ Dan Aykroyd act known as the Blues Brothers. "I actually got into the blues because of the [1980 film] Blues Brothers, because what I really wanted to be was a comedian, just like John Belushi," Popper told Alan Niester for the Toronto, Ontario, *Globe and Mail* (9 July 1997). "That led me to Paul Butterfield, and that led to me to the old blues guys, and that led me to Jimi Hendrix. When I heard Hendrix, I knew I wanted to be a musician." (Years later Popper had a cameo in the 1998 Blues Brothers sequel.)

STARTS BLUES TRAVELER

Shortly after Popper graduated from high school, in 1986, he and Hill—along with the guitarist Chan Kinchla and the bassist Bobby Sheehan—formed Blues Traveler. The four moved to New York City, and Popper enrolled at the New School for Social Research. There, he told Niester, "the school band was jazz-oriented, it was a very big bebop school. They used to let me do the solos. Sure, rock 'n' roll was my vocabulary, but there's definitely a big bebop influence [in my harmonica playing]." Attending classes by day, Popper played local clubs with his bandmates at night. They quickly earned a reputation for lengthy improvisational shows that put them "at the forefront of an emerging movement of rootsy jam bands, a vibrant community that also produced Phish and the Spin Doctors," according to the band's website. Popper told Steve Hochman for the *Los Angeles Times* (20 Sep. 1991), "Here's our shtick line to describe our music: It's our garage band attempt at our appreciation of jazz improvisation through the reality of rock 'n' roll. Rock has its own vocabulary, but you can approach it with freedom."

Fans began following Blues Traveler from venue to venue. "They're bored, and I think they're fans of real music," Popper told Hochman. "I keep getting surprised everywhere we go how many there are." The band was signed by A&M Records in 1989, and Popper left the New School without earning his degree. An eponymous debut album was released in 1990 and included eleven original songs, all written or cowritten by Popper. "Blues Traveler's loose jam structures on basic blues riffs mark them as

Getty Images

a band in the tradition of such predecessors as the Grateful Dead," William Ruhlman wrote in a review of the recording for the *All Music Guide* website. "Unlike that communal effort, however, this group has a distinct focal point in virtuoso harmonica player and vocalist John Popper." In 1991 the band's sophomore effort, *Travelers & Thieves*, made an appearance on the Billboard 200 chart. Blues Traveler toured relentlessly, playing some 250 shows that year. "We've always been predominantly a live band," Popper told Scott Brodeur for *Billboard* (25 Jan. 1992). "Our studio albums are nice tries, but the live shows just totally blow them away." In the summer of 1992, when the band was three weeks into the recording of its third studio album, Popper crashed his motorcycle on the way to the studio, near New Orleans, Louisiana. Riding an estimated 70 miles per hour, he broke his arm and shattered his leg. After he recovered the band resumed recording and touring, with Popper playing some shows in a wheelchair for a while.

H.O.R.D.E. AND THE EARLY 1990S

That year Blues Traveler helped found the Horizons of Rock Developing Everywhere (H.O.R.D.E.) music festival, which also featured such bands as the Spin Doctors, Phish, and Widespread Panic. The festival became a popular annual event and was mounted until 1998. "Forget Woodstock: The '90s version of a Generational Celebration has gone mobile," Gina Arnold wrote about the phenomenon for the *San Francisco Chronicle* (1 Sep. 1995).

"Judging by the number of traveling multiact bills crossing the nation this summer, musical fun in the summer sun is also clean, well-organized, streamlined and financially successful—in short, everything Woodstock wasn't." Arnold continued, "Now in its fourth season, the 23-date H.O.R.D.E. tour is outselling Lollapalooza. Unlike the latter, which aims at 15- to 25-year-old alternayouth, H.O.R.D.E.—dubbed 'Hippiepalooza' by industry insiders—is meant to appeal to a cross-section of fans, particularly those with a penchant for '70s-sounding, Southern white, blues-rock jamming."

Blues Traveler released the album *Save His Soul* in 1993, followed by *Four* (1994), the recording that brought the band its first mainstream success. Thanks in large part to the infectious song "Run-Around," which spent forty-nine straight weeks on the singles chart, the album peaked at number eight on the Billboard 200, marking the first time a Blues Traveler album had made it into the top ten. The album ultimately sold more than six million copies, and the single earned Popper and his cohorts a Grammy Award for best rock vocal performance by a group or duo. In 1995 Popper played a small role in an episode of the popular sitcom *Roseanne*, and the following year Blues Traveler recorded the theme song that was played during the show's final season (1996–97). Reportedly hoping to ensure their fan base that the hit single, Grammy Award, and TV exposure had not altered their core values, the band next released *Live from the Fall* (1996), a double-disk live recording filled with lengthy jams.

STRAIGHT ON TILL MORNING AND *ZYGOTE*

Straight on Till Morning (1997), the group's next studio effort, was generally well received and reached number 11 on the album chart. In a review for the Newark, New Jersey, *Star-Ledger* (6 July 1997), Jay Lustig called the recording "positively infectious" and wrote, "Blues Traveler has gone in a more accessible direction, with Popper singing from the heart." In his review for the *All Music Guide* website, Stephen Thomas Erlewine wrote, "The commercial success of Four was a mixed blessing for Blues Traveler. It did give them a wider audience, but it also put them in the delicate position of pleasing their new, hook-happy fans while retaining their hardcore, jam-oriented cult following. They skillfully manage to do just that on *Straight on Till Morning*, the bluesy, ambitious follow-up to *Four*." He continued, "On the whole, *Straight on Till Morning* is a tougher album than any of its predecessors, boasting a gritty sound and several full-on jams. But the key to the album is its length and its sprawling collection of songs, which find Blues Traveler trying anything from country-rock to jangling pop/rock. They manage to be simultaneously succinct and eclectic, and they occasionally throw in a good pop hook or two. Blues Traveler are still too loose to be a true pop/rock band . . . but *Straight on Till Morning* is the first studio record that captures the essence of the band." Popper told Alan Niester, "On *Four*, I was very much aware of the fact that nobody had really heard me play harmonica before, and that was a kind of gimmick factor in my mind. So I was playing in a sort of 'Hey, look at me, look what I can do' mode. On this album [*Straight on Till Morning*], I didn't have to worry about that. I could play more melodically. I didn't have to show my chops off."

While on vacation in Hawaii in May 1999, Popper, who then weighed more than 400 pounds, felt crushing chest pain. He subsequently underwent an angioplasty to clear an artery that had been almost completely blocked. He spent the next few months recuperating and completing a solo album, *Zygote* (1999). While the album received little attention from anyone other than Blues Traveler's core fans, in a review for the *All Music Guide* website, Stephen Thomas Erlewine praised the "supple singing, elongated phrasing, affection for blues-rock, and astounding harmonica playing" and opined that *Zygote* "make[s] the case that Popper is a worthwhile solo artist in his own right."

TRAGEDY AND TRANSITIONS

On August 20, 1999, Bobby Sheehan was found dead of a drug overdose. Chan Kinchla's younger brother Tad joined the group to play bass in his stead, and a fifth member, the keyboardist Ben Wilson, was subsequently added. While working on a new studio album, the reconfigured group made available for download on its website a four-song EP, *Decisions of the Sky—A Traveler's Tale of Sun and Storm*.

In 2000 Popper had gastric-bypass surgery. By the time Blues Traveler's next studio album, *Bridge* (2001), was released, he had lost more than 100 pounds. The new album divided critics. A reviewer for *Entertainment Weekly* (1 June 2001), for example, wrote, "What's always lifted [the group] above their peers are Popper's percussive harmonica and those wonderfully melodic songs—both of which are abundant here," while a contributor to the music website *Sonic-Net* asserted, "On *Bridge*, they're still traveling down the long and winding improvisational road, with most of the tracks averaging around five minutes in length. . . . This time out, though, the songs feel like they're twice that."

After releasing another live album, *Live: What You and I Have Been Through*, in 2002, the group returned to the studio to record *Truth Be Told* (2003). In a review for the *Baltimore Sun* (24 July 2003), Rashod D. Ollison wrote, "The musicianship throughout is tighter than a pickle jar lid, more focused than on previous efforts." Eric Ward, reviewing *Truth*

Be Told for *Glide Magazine* (25 Aug. 2003), wrote, "It's easy to claim that life on the road, long tours and some struggling years together give a band some legitimacy, but when you've endured well over a decade that included a severe motorcycle accident, major surgery, creating your own touring festival, a Grammy, a founding member's death and over 10 million in album sales, you've pretty much seen it all. Though with a skewed line-up that for now seems solidified, the Blues Traveler story is apparently far from over." Ward continued, "*Truth Be Told* is Blues Traveler finally back to business, pushing forward rather than merely looking back. . . . [It's] vintage Blues Traveler, complete with self-disclosing lyrics, fiery harmonica, powerful solos and those Popper ballads that never fail to evoke emotion. Still far from a throwback, and miles from the repetitive-beat-bandwagon most [music groups] have succumbed to, it's the album you hoped they'd make once everything they've been through eventually settled down."

LATER WORK AND COLLABORATION

Bastardos! (2005) met with similar praise. Stephen Thomas Erlewine wrote for the *All Music Guide* website, "What makes it one of their best [albums] is how the band stretches from psychedelia to soulful pop and back toward their signature blues-rock, writing sturdy songs all the while. It's strong on a song-by-song basis, particularly since each track is sonically distinct, but all the moods complement each other, resulting in an album that might not be the most representative Blues Traveler album (although it isn't all that far removed from their trademark sound, either), but is certainly the richest, most diverse album they've ever done, and quite arguably their best."

In 2006 Popper released *The John Popper Project*, a collaborative effort that featured DJ Logic (a Bronx-born turntable artist), Tad Kinchla, and several other guest artists. "Forget everything you ever knew about John Popper and Blues Traveler. This is no jam band but they can play some," Thom Jurek wrote for the *All Music Guide.* "This is one steamy, groove-laden set that offers a view of Popper as not just a harmonica master who can play dozens of them through more effects that you can shake a speaker at, but as a serious funk and futuristic R&B vocalist."

In 2007 Blues Traveler recorded *Cover Yourself*, on which they reinterpreted or rearranged several songs in their catalog, including "Run-Around." They followed that with *North Hollywood Shootout* (2008), which received generally lukewarm reviews. Writing for *Slant Magazine* (24 Aug. 2008), Jonathan Keefe called it a "slightly over-reaching attempt at reclaiming some of their former commercial relevance," and Andrew Leahey, in a review for *Paste Magazine* (29 Aug. 2008), wrote that the album "lacks the cohesion of Blues Traveler's previous work." Most reviewers were particularly perplexed by a track that featured the actor Bruce Willis performing a rambling monologue, "a move that is either unexpectedly awesome or sadly misguided," Leahey wrote.

Popper's latest recording, *John Popper & the Duskray Troubadours* (2011), is the result of a side project separate from Blues Traveler. The Troubadours include the bassist Steve Lindsay, the drummer Mark Clark, the guitarists Kevin Trainor and Aaron Beavers, and the multi-instrumentalist Jono Manson, who also engineered and produced the recording. Stewart Oksenhorn wrote for the *Aspen (Colorado) Times Weekly* (6 Mar. 2011) that the new band is providing a chance for Popper, whom he described as a "superhuman musician [who takes] the harmonica places nobody could have imagined," to take artistic chances. Still, he wrote, "the Duskray Troubadours are not a huge gamble. For one thing, the group has already recorded a self-titled album that was released this past week. *John Popper and the Duskray Troubadours* is 12 songs that are a step away from Blues Traveler material—mellower, more focused on the songs and less so on the harmonica and guitar solos. And Popper's principal partner in the band, Jono Manson, is hardly an unknown quantity [in the music world]."

PERSONAL LIFE

An avid collector of firearms, Popper owns a reproduction of an 1858 cannon. Because the law prohibits him from firing actual cannon balls, he has been known to use it to launch cans of dog food up to one thousand yards. "If you ever see a guy with dog food in the trees, he probably owns a cannon," he quipped to Jeff Spevak for the *Rochester (New York) Democrat and Chronicle* (28 Apr. 2011).

In 2007 Popper, who had been arrested four years earlier for marijuana possession, was stopped while speeding in his SUV in Washington State. Police found several handguns and rifles, a set of brass knuckles, and a Taser, as well as a small quantity of marijuana. Because he had permits for the firearms and agreed to surrender the brass knuckles and Taser, he was charged only with drug possession.

Popper, who is unmarried, generally identifies himself as a libertarian, although he rarely expresses political opinions in his music. "All you do, when you talk about politics, is alienate people," he told Spevak. "The stuff I write about is beyond that. It's beyond people's opinions. I try to look for a basic idea that we can all relate to. Love being good, hearts being broken. I'm a uniter."

SUGGESTED READING

Oksenhorn, Stewart. "John Popper Brings Dusk-ray Troubadours to Aspen." *Aspen Times Weekly*. Aspen Times, 6 Mar. 2011. Web. Jan. 2012.

Ollison, Rashod D. "Blues Traveler Has Survived the Perils of Rock." *Baltimore Sun*. Baltimore Sun, 24 July 2003. Web. Jan. 2012.

Sessa, Sam. "Odd Pairing Clicks." *Baltimore Sun*. Baltimore Sun, 19 Oct. 2006. Web. Jan. 2012.

Ward, Eric. "Blues Traveler: *Truth Be Told*." *Glide Magazine*. Glide Publishing LLC, 25 Aug. 2003. Web. Jan. 2012.

—Dmitry Kiper

John Prendergast

Born: March 21, 1963
Occupation: Activist, organization official, writer

Getty Images

"I felt very early on an affinity with those who would stand up against things that are wrong," the human-rights activist John Prendergast said on the *Diane Rehm Show* (18 May 2011), which airs on National Public Radio. "I felt injustice acutely, at a cellular level for many complicated reasons. . . . When given an opportunity to fight against human rights abuses in Africa, I feel utterly compelled to do all I can." Prendergast has been working to end such abuses in Africa for more than twenty-five years. He has done so under the auspices of Human Rights Watch, UNICEF, and other humanitarian-aid and human-rights organizations and think tanks; as a special adviser to Susan Rice, the assistant secretary of state for African affairs during President Bill Clinton's second term; as the director of African affairs at the National Security Council, an arm of the US executive branch; as special adviser on African issues for the International Crisis Group; and as the cofounder, in 2007, and cochair of the Enough Project, whose stated goal is "to end genocide and crimes against humanity." Prendergast has focused mostly on atrocities that have occurred in Uganda, the Congo, and Sudan in the course of civil wars, which have often been abetted by outside governments that aid one side or another directly or indirectly. Those atrocities, which have affected many hundreds of millions of people, include killings and maimings, sometimes tantamount to genocide; sex slavery and the rapes of females of all ages; the starvation, malnutrition, and disease suffered by many refugees; and the conscription of child soldiers.

To stop and prevent such brutality and cruelty, Prendergast has traveled dozens of times to areas of conflict in Africa, on "fact-finding missions, peace-making initiatives, and awareness-raising trips," as he wrote for a widely quoted blurb about himself. He has held talks with politicians, military and rebel officers, and heads of various warring factions in African nations (at times finding himself in life-threatening situations) as well as with officials in the United States. To gain publicity for his missions and spur those in positions of power to act, he has teamed up with Hollywood stars including George Clooney, Javier Bardem, Ryan Gosling, Angelina Jolie, Brad Pitt, Mia Farrow, and Don Cheadle, all of whom have traveled with him in African trouble spots and accompanied him to congressional hearings and offices of American policy makers. He and Cheadle have cowritten two books: *Not on Our Watch: The Mission to End Genocide in Darfur and Beyond* (2007) and *The Enough Moment: Fighting to End Africa's Worst Human Rights Crimes* (2010). (The Democrat Barack Obama and the Republican Sam Brownback, both US senators at the time, cowrote the introduction to *Not on Our Watch*.) Prendergast has also written or cowritten hundreds of commissioned reports and articles for professional journals, national and regional newspapers, and popular magazines as well as eight other books. Those books include the dual memoir *Unlikely Brothers* (2011), written with Michael Mattocks; in it, in addition to his professional life, Prendergast discussed his experiences as an unofficial "big brother" to Mattocks, one of seven children raised by a single mother in Washington, DC. (*Unlikely Brothers* is the source for quotes in this article unless otherwise indicated.)

EARLY LIFE AND EDUCATION

The first of the two sons of John Prendergast (called Jack) and Claire Prendergast, John Prendergast was born on March 21, 1963, in Indianapolis, Indiana. His brother, Luke, is a high school teacher. The brothers were raised in a devoutly Roman Catholic family. Before their parents married their father considered doing good works by becoming a Catholic priest, and their mother by becoming a nun. Prendergast's mother, a trained social worker, volunteered with local Head Start classes and Catholic-run programs during her years as a homemaker. His father, a Korean War veteran, worked as a traveling salesman for a frozen-foods company and was often home only on weekends. In *Unlikely Brothers* Prendergast described his father as a brilliant storyteller who was ever-ready to help others and extraordinarily skilled at connecting with people of all ages.

During Prendergast's elementary-school years, he was a good student and excelled at sports, and he never engaged in serious mischief. Nevertheless, when he was about eight, his father began to subject him to "a new and growing impatience and anger . . . that I couldn't figure out." "Again and again, it seemed, Dad would single me out for a harsh, relentless, and unexpected scolding— often when I felt I was doing nothing wrong. The forcefulness of the anger was shocking and profoundly destabilizing to me." His father's rages continued through Prendergast's high school years, "making me feel like a worthless loser," even though Prendergast got good grades, participated in school sports, never drank, smoked, or tried drugs, and held after-school jobs. By his own account, as a child Prendergast also suffered because the family moved repeatedly, mostly within the Midwest, and in each new neighborhood and school, he would feel like an outsider. His unhappiness grew when, during puberty, he developed cystic acne—the most disfiguring form of acne— on his face and back; he feared that he looked like a monstrous lizard in the eyes of others. (In his freshman year at college, the acne abated, thanks to medication.) A series of injuries and other physical problems that ended his dream of becoming a professional basketball player compounded his misery when he was a teen.

After Prendergast completed eighth grade, his family moved to Berwyn, a suburb of Philadelphia, Pennsylvania. He attended a strict Catholic prep school for a year, then transferred, at his own insistence, to Archbishop Carroll High School, in Radnor, another Philadelphia suburb. At the school in Radnor, a more liberal Catholic institution that had a strong basketball program, three of his teachers influenced him greatly. One was Garrett Wiznicki, an English teacher who sparked his passion for the writings of authors including Jack Kerouac, James

Joyce, Jean-Paul Sartre, Søren Kierkegaard, and Samuel Beckett and who expressed genuine interest in Prendergast's ideas and opinions. The second was Joseph Stoutzenberger, a teacher of religion who was "very Buddhist in his outlook" and talked about "the centrality of compassion" in the major religions; Stoutzenberger's requirement that his students serve the community led Prendergast to volunteer in a homeless shelter. From the third teacher, Joan Kane, who taught Spanish, he learned about the organizations Amnesty International and Bread for the World.

COLLEGE YEARS INTERRUPTED

After high school Prendergast enrolled at Georgetown University, in Washington, DC. As a volunteer tutor of reading in children's homes in Washington, he witnessed firsthand the poverty-related problems that prevailed in the city's low-income housing projects. At the end of his freshman year, eager for "world knowledge and experience," he dropped out of college, equipped himself with a tent, sleeping bag, and backpack, and began to hitchhike across the country on what Steve Hendrix, writing for the *Washington Post* (16 May 2011), termed his "personal save-the-world tour." Money from his parents and earnings from odd jobs supported him. In several cities he helped in political campaigns; in Texas and Mexico he became acquainted with issues affecting manual and farm laborers. During his travels he met three social-justice activists who "eliminated any doubts I might have had about whether one person can make a difference": Patrick Goggins, who worked toward peace among Northern Ireland Protestants and Catholics; Paul Comiskey, a Jesuit priest fighting against the death penalty and for improved prison conditions in California; and John Maher, the cofounder of the Delancey Street Foundation, which provides shelter and rehabilitation services for former convicts, substance abusers, and others in need.

During the summer of 1983, Prendergast returned to Washington, DC, where he took courses at George Washington University and served as an intern at the Robert Kennedy Memorial Youth Policy Institute and as a volunteer coach for a boys' basketball team. That summer he met the Mattockses, a homeless African-American family headed by a single mother, who lived in a shelter supervised by a Georgetown friend of Prendergast's. He immediately became an informal "big brother" to Michael, the eldest boy, and James, who were seven and six years old then. On weekends the boys would stay with his parents in Berwyn while he worked for a landscaping firm. In the fall Prendergast moved to Philadelphia and was hired by the Democratic congressman William H. Gray, an African-American Baptist preacher who was serving his second term in the House of Representatives.

Prendergast's job entailed helping constituents, mostly with problems involving bureaucracies or landlords. Also, through the organization Big Brothers Big Sisters, he became involved with Khayree and Nazir Lane, brothers living in Philadelphia; on weekends he continued to visit Michael and James Mattocks or would have his parents take care of them. Later, Luke Prendergast took over as Khayree and Nazir's Big Brother.

LEARNING ABOUT AFRICA

While nursing a sprained ankle at home one day, Prendergast saw a television news story about the famine then gripping Ethiopia, which had been triggered by civil war and other human actions and exacerbated by drought. "Somehow for the first 21 years of my life, I'd missed the fact that such a level of human suffering could exist," he told Daniel Bergner for the *New York Times* (5 Dec. 2010). He immediately decided that he should go to Ethiopia to aid victims of the famine. Denied a visa both to Ethiopia and to its neighbor Sudan, Prendergast, who knew next to nothing about Africa, secured one to Mali, which is nearly three thousand miles west of Ethiopia. He bought a plane ticket to Bamako, Mali's capital, giving little thought to how his absence might affect Michael, James, Khayree, and Nazir. "I was a do-gooder . . . in the universal sense," he admitted to Gwen Ifill, who interviewed him for the weeknight TV show *PBS NewsHour* (17 June 2011), "but not necessarily in the interpersonal sense."

On the flight to Mali, Prendergast met a specialist in Mali's Agriculture Ministry who had studied at Georgetown and recognized him. Prendergast accepted the man's invitation to board at his compound in Bamako and accompany him on his travels around Mali, during which the man talked about the ways in which developed countries and the World Bank kept the prices of agricultural exports from Africa artificially low. "Millions of small-scale farmers in developing countries in Africa and elsewhere are impoverished, and their families are needlessly hungry and poor so that Americans and Europeans can pay a penny less for a cup of coffee or a dime less for a t-shirt . . . ," Prendergast learned. "Now that I knew all this, what was I going to do about it?"

After three months Prendergast returned to his job in Congressman Gray's office, but he realized that he would rather help Africans than people in the United States. "I hungered to figure out the bureaucracy of foreign aid the way I'd once yearned to understand the way services were delivered to poor folks in America." He offered his services to the organization Operation Crossroads Africa and "signed on without even asking where they'd send me or what I'd have to do when I was there. All I knew was, it was a way to get back" to Africa. The organization assigned him to a team that helped to build a school in Zanzibar, a semi-autonomous territory associated with Tanzania. Although he stayed to complete the project, he questioned the wisdom of spending so much money to send Americans to do a job that, given the necessary materials, the people who lived there could have accomplished.

While still in Africa Prendergast learned that the United Nations High Commissioner for Refugees and others had set up a camp in Hargeysa, in northwest Somalia, for refugees who had fled the famine in Ethiopia. He immediately traveled to Hargeysa, where he spent the next several months helping out in the camp. He soon learned that a substantial portion of the food and other supplies sent from overseas to aid the refugees wound up in the hands of the military and others loyal to the longtime dictator of Somalia, Siad (or Siyaad) Barre. Despite the well-known brutality of the Barre regime, during the Cold War the United States government considered him a reliable ally; hundreds of millions of dollars in U.S. aid to Somalia helped Barre to remain in power. Prendergast realized that "it wasn't going to be enough to visit every conflict-torn corner of Africa and understand each famine and war firsthand. . . . I was going to have to become equally expert in the politics of foreign policy in Washington, D.C."

In 1986, back in the United States, Prendergast earned a BA degree in geography and urban studies from Temple University, in Philadelphia. (By his own account, after he left Georgetown he had taken courses at three other colleges as well.) He spent one term in graduate school at the University of Pennsylvania before transferring to the School of International Service of American University, in Washington, D.C., where he received an MA degree in international relations in 1990. Meanwhile, he had become a consultant for the organization Bread for the World, which according to its website is "a collective Christian voice urging our nation's decision makers to end hunger at home and abroad." As one of those voices, Prendergast would talk to congressional aides about food shortages overseas. He also served as a live-in supervisor to seven mentally challenged adult residents of a group home.

WORKING FOR PEACE IN AFRICA

By then Prendergast was spending about two-thirds of the year outside the United States, in the Horn of Africa (Kenya, Somalia, Ethiopia, Eritrea, and Djibouti) and Central African countries including Angola, Congo, Liberia, Sierra Leone, and Rwanda. He worked at one time or another for many nongovernmental organizations, writing reports and popular articles about what he had observed. A turning point for him came in 1994, when, in Rwanda, over the course of three months, as many as 800,000 members of the minority Tutsi tribe perished at the hands of extremist members of the Hutu majority. The US government ignored what was happening, a White House official told him, because the American public expressed no interest in taking action. The failure of the United States to respond to the atrocities prompted Prendergast to expand his efforts to include ordinary Americans. Determined to build what he called "a popular constituency for peace in Africa," he began giving talks at colleges and conferences. "I had some pretty compelling material. . . . I'd seen, with my own eyes, the starvation in Ethiopia, the anarchic mayhem in Somalia, the child soldiers in Uganda, the slave raiding in Sudan, and the genocide in Rwanda."

In 1996 Prendergast won a fellowship from the US Institute for Peace and a job as an adviser to Susan Rice, who, as a State Department assistant secretary of state, advised President Bill Clinton on African affairs. The fellowship paid his salary at the White House for six months. Prendergast had met Rice earlier, at a conference at Princeton University at which Prendergast had condemned the United States for making no effort to end the violence in Rwanda. At the end of the six months, Rice created a permanent position for Prendergast, as the National Security Council's director for African affairs. "I was right in the thick of things," he recalled. He regularly conferred face to face with Rice and Joseph C. Wilson, who had served as an ambassador in Africa before being appointed the National Security Council's senior director for African affairs, and sometimes with President Clinton himself. Prendergast sensed that Clinton felt haunted by what had happened in Rwanda; the president "exuded a palpable hunger to do right by Africa," Prendergast wrote. Prendergast was with Clinton when, in Rwanda in 1998, the president publicly acknowledged, "We in the United States and the world community did not do as much as we could have and should have done to try to limit what occurred in Rwanda in 1994." During that period Prendergast was in Africa most of the time. "I was traveling from one conflict zone to the next as an advisor to President Clinton's high-level peace envoys. We were negotiating with presidents, rebel leaders, militia commanders, and warlords, and we were trying to find peaceful solutions to some of the deadliest wars in the world since World War II." One successful effort in which he played a large role was the ending, in 2000, of armed conflict between Ethiopia and Eritrea.

CODIRECTOR OF INTERNATIONAL CRISIS GROUP

In 2001, after Clinton left the White House, Prendergast became the codirector of the Africa program of the International Crisis Group (ICG). Based in Brussels, Belgium, the ICG is described on its website as "an independent, non-profit, non-governmental organisation committed to preventing and resolving deadly conflict"; toward that end the group advises governments, the United Nations, the European Union, and other such bodies. In that position Prendergast urged that economic sanctions be imposed against Zimbabwe, whose inhabitants had suffered decades of human-rights abuses and drastic economic deprivation under the rule of the nation's longtime dictator, Robert Mugabe. The European Union and the United States imposed such sanctions in 2002 and 2003, respectively; the sanctions remained in place as of late 2011. (The United States provides humanitarian aid to Zimbabwe.) Prendergast remained with the ICG until 2006. In the preceding years, in addition to Zimbabwe, he had investigated and reported on conditions in Somalia, Northern Uganda, and Sudan.

THE ENOUGH PROJECT

In 2007 Prendergast cofounded the Enough Project with Gayle Smith, with whom he had worked in the Clinton White House. The project was set up with funds from the foundation Humanity United and with the support of the Center for American Progress, with which Enough is closely affiliated. The goal of the project, according to its website, is to help "build a permanent constituency to prevent genocide and crimes against humanity." "Too often," the post continued, "the United States and the larger international community have taken a wait-and-see approach to crimes against humanity. This is unconscionable. Genocide and war crimes are not inevitable, and we at Enough want to create noise and action both to stop ongoing atrocities and to prevent their recurrence. Our mission is to help people from every walk of life understand the practical actions they can take to make a difference." "Enough's strategy papers and briefings provide sharp field analysis and targeted policy recommendations," the website states. "Enough is also working to develop the policies, tools, and investments that can best be applied to prevent crimes against humanity and genocide now and in the future." The Enough Project currently concentrates on the complex continuing conflicts, and attendant massive human suffering, in Sudan and South Sudan, the Congo, Uganda, and Somalia.

OTHER PROJECTS AND PERSONAL LIFE

With Tracy McGrady and other basketball stars, Prendergast cofounded the Darfur Dream Team Sister Schools Program, which links American schools to a dozen schools maintained for children from Darfur, a region in Sudan, who are living in refugee camps in Chad. He is a board member of and adviser to the organization Not on Our Watch, cofounded by George Clooney and four other Hollywood figures, which develops "advocacy campaigns that bring global attention to international crises and give voice to their victims," according to its website. "It's easy to see why celebrities are drawn to Prendergast," Christine Spines wrote for *Entertainment Weekly* (30 May 2008). "With his shaggy hippie-chic haircut and rugged road map of a face, he's exactly the sort of righteous, world-saving warrior that actors love playing on screen. . . . But Prendergast has earned his action-hero credentials."

In addition to the volumes he wrote with Cheadle and Maddocks, Prendergast's books include *Without Troops and Tanks: The Emergency Relief Desk and the Cross Border Operation into Eritrea and Tigray* (1994, written with Mark Duffield); *Civilian Devastation: Abuses by All Parties in the War of Southern Sudan* (1994, with Jemera Rone and Karen Sorenson); *Frontline Diplomacy: Humanitarian Aid and Conflict in Africa* (1996); *Crisis and Hope in Africa* (1996); and *Crisis Response: Humanitarian Band-Aids in Sudan and Somalia* (1997).

Prendergast's marriage to Jean, a nutritionist, in 1991 ended in divorce. In 2011 he married Sia Sanneh, a lawyer for the Equal Justice Initiative and a Yale Law School lecturer.

SUGGESTED READING

"John Prendergast and Michael Mattocks: 'Unlikely Brothers.'" *Diane Rehm Show.* Narr. Diane Rehm. American U Radio/NPR. WAMU 88.5, n. p. 30 May 2011. Transcript.

Leung, Rebecca. "Witnessing Genocide in Sudan." CBS News: 60 Minutes. CBS News Interactive Inc., 11 Feb. 2009. Web. Jan. 2012.

Prendergast, John, and Michael Mattocks. *Unlikely Brothers: Our Story of Adventure, Loss, and Redemption.* New York: Random, 2011.

Rosenberg, Amy S. "Old Bonds of Brotherhood Endure for Rights Activist Prendergast." *Philadelphia Inquirer* 17 May 2011: D1.

—*Molly M. Hagan*

Reince Priebus

Born: March 18, 1972
Occupation: Chairman of the Republican National Committee

Since January 2011, Reince Priebus has held the position of chairman of the Republican National Committee (RNC), a political organization that promotes and supports the Republican Party and hosts the annual Republican National Convention. In 2007, Priebus became chairman of the Wisconsin branch of the Republican National Committee. From 2009 to 2010, he served as the RNC's general counsel. Priebus, who holds

AP Photo

a law degree from the University of Miami, is a political conservative: pro-life, anti–gay marriage, pro–gun rights, and pro–tax cuts. He has garnered a substantial amount of support from the populist-conservative Tea Party. Priebus's term as RNC chairman ends in January 2013, but he is eligible to stand for reelection.

EARLY LIFE AND EDUCATION

Reince Priebus was born on March 18, 1972, in Kenosha, Wisconsin. It is worth noting that there are only a handful of people with the last name of Priebus living in the United States, and over the course of Priebus's career, many political journalists, pundits, and headline writers have made many references to his name's spelling, pronunciation, and rarity.

Priebus grew up in Kenosha and graduated from Tremper High School. He then attended the University of Wisconsin–Whitewater, where he became president of the student body. He graduated cum laude in 1994. Following graduation, he worked for a year at the Wisconsin state legislature as a legislative aide to three state lawmakers and served as committee clerk for the Assembly Education Committee.

Although he considered pursuing a career in politics at that time, Priebus chose instead to attend law school, enrolling in the University of Miami in Florida. During his time there, Priebus interned as a law clerk at the Wisconsin Court of Appeals, the US District Court in Florida's southern district, and the NAACP Legal Defense Fund. After receiving his law degree in

1998, Priebus joined the law firm of Michael Best & Friedrich in Milwaukee, Wisconsin. He was made partner in 2006.

POLITICAL CAREER

Priebus's first attempt to enter politics was a run for a seat in the Wisconsin state senate in 2004. Only thirty-two years old at the time, he was still working as a corporate litigation lawyer when he registered to run as a Republican in the district that includes most of Kenosha County and a part of Racine County. By October 2004, Priebus had raised around $164,000—three times as much as his opponent, incumbent Democrat Bob Wirch. Despite his fundraising advantage and promises to cut taxes, however, Priebus was at a disadvantage when it came to experience; Wirch, who was sixty years old at the time, had worked as a laborer and union leader and held county and state elected offices for eighteen years. Priebus lost the election in November.

REPUBLICAN PARTY OFFICIAL

In 2007, Priebus was named chairman of the Wisconsin Republican Party—the youngest chairman in its history. During the 2008 US presidential campaign, he praised the record of the Republican Party candidate, Senator John McCain of Arizona. In addition, he criticized the experience of Democratic Party candidate Senator Barack Obama of Illinois. After Priebus spoke to Greg J. Borowski of the *Milwaukee Journal Sentinel* (5 June 2008), Borowski wrote, "Priebus argued that McCain, a longtime US senator from Arizona, is well-positioned to win in November, in part because Democrats have nominated the weaker of the two finalists. He cited questions about Obama's experience and leadership, noting 'four years ago, he was a state senator.'" Borowski then quoted Priebus as saying, "I think the experience issue is the Achilles' heel of Barack Obama, going up against someone like John McCain. Our best ammunition in many cases comes from the Democrats. The Democrats have been questioning Barack Obama's experience and judgment for a very long period of time."

Priebus's time as chairman of the Wisconsin Republican Party was "not without controversy," according to Mark Guarino of the *Christian Science Monitor* (16 Jan. 2011). "During the 2008 presidential election," wrote Guarino, "local Democrats cited an e-mail leaked from Priebus's office that they said came close to advocating voter intimidation in some of Milwaukee's inner-city, and heavily Democratic, neighborhoods." He continued, "In September, a nonpartisan watchdog group called One Wisconsin Now filed complaints with the federal and state attorneys general, charging that state Republicans and tea party organizations had engaged in vote suppression, targeting minorities and college students."

CAMPAIGN FOR RNC CHAIRMAN

In January 2009, the Republican National Committee named Michael Steele as chairman. Priebus and Steele met in late 2008, and Priebus managed his chairman selection campaign. Steele told Craig Gilbert of the *Milwaukee Journal Sentinel* (15 Feb. 2009) that when he met Priebus, there was an "instantaneous click." Steele and Priebus held similar opinions about the future of the Republican Party and the RNC. Six candidates ran for the position, competing for the support of the 168 members of the Republican National Committee, and Priebus helped Steele court some of these members. "So many times, we've talked about minority outreach, outreach in the Northeast, the Midwest," Priebus told Gilbert. "But we just talk about it. At some point, we have to have a person in a leadership post that can do it." However, Steele was criticized for making too many television appearances and for making the gaffe of implying that US president Barack Obama began the war in Afghanistan, which actually began during the previous administration.

By the fall of 2010, it was clear that Steele's job as RNC chairman was in jeopardy. Despite pressure from some Republicans not to seek reelection to the chairmanship, Steele refused to bow out of the race. In early December 2010, Priebus announced his candidacy for the position of RNC chairman. During his campaign, he emphasized that he would take a behind-the-spotlight approach and focus on working hard for the GOP rather than making a name for himself. Priebus also touted his work with the conservative Tea Party groups in Wisconsin, his experience as a fundraiser, and his work with the campaign of US senator Ron Johnson.

In January 2011, all RNC chairman candidates took part in a well-publicized debate. At the debate, Priebus made the case that if an individual supports abortion rights and is in favor of the federal government's stimulus program and the bailout of the US auto industry, then he or she might not be a Republican. Priebus also discussed his favorite book, *The Reagan Diaries* (2007), and the fact that he is a gun owner.

Priebus's campaign for the RNC chairmanship also saw some controversy. In December, it was reported that he had helped clients obtain money from the federal stimulus plan—a program he openly opposed. Priebus denied the allegation. He won the vote to become RNC chairman and assumed office on January 20, 2011. At thirty-eight years old, Priebus became the youngest person to take on the position since Lee Atwater in 1988.

RNC CHAIRMAN

Writing for *Politico* (16 Jan. 2011), Kenneth P. Vogel observed that although Priebus will face many challenges in his new post, among his most difficult will be "building support from the anti-establishment tea party without offending big GOP donors or the independent voters the party needs in 2012." Some Wisconsin Tea Party leaders, wrote Vogel, had "misgivings about Priebus's handling of the party endorsement process, which they saw as emblematic of the clubby establishment politics that the tea party has railed against since the movement burst onto the scene in April 2009 in opposition to what its activists saw as a fiscally reckless agenda being pursued by President Barack Obama and the Democratic Congress." Among other concerns was his alleged involvement in his law firm's efforts to get federal stimulus funds, which did not sit well with many Tea Party supporters.

But Priebus also had plenty of support from other Tea Party leaders in his home state. "Some activists credited him with reaching out to the dozens of tea party groups in the state," wrote Vogel, "listening to activists' concerns about the party, trying to coax some into local and county parties and—above all—helping the GOP retake the governor's office, control of the state Legislature, two congressional seats and a US Senate seat."

After taking over as RNC chairman, Priebus fired the Michael Steele aides who were going to organize the Republican Party's 2012 national convention in Tampa, Florida, and hired former RNC chairman Ed Gillespie and former head of the Republican Governors Association Nick Ayers instead. Additionally, Priebus announced a minimum fundraising goal of $400 million to compete with President Obama, who is expected to raise $1 billion for his 2012 reelection campaign.

When Priebus took over as chairman, the RNC debt was approximately $24 million. By the end of March 2011, he succeeded in lowering the RNC's debt to $19.8 million. Although real-estate tycoon and Republican Party supporter Donald Trump and others continued to question the validity of President Obama's birth certificate, Priebus dismissed this as a nonissue. The president was born in the United States, he said, and the party should focus on issues that are more relevant to voters.

During an interview on NBC's *Today* show (5 Apr. 2011), Priebus criticized President Obama's economic policy. He stated that during the first term of the Obama administration, the United States had lost twenty-six million jobs. However, the fact-checking website Politifact (6 Apr. 2011) accused Priebus of grossly overstating the number. According to Politifact, "We arrived at these figures, as economists do, by comparing job gains with job losses to determine a net total.

It's theoretically possible that 26 million jobs were lost during the Obama presidency and that 23.2 million jobs were created, leaving a net of 2.8 million jobs lost. But even if that were the case, economists across the political spectrum say it would be highly misleading of Priebus to focus on the job losses without citing the offsetting job gains."

In July 2011, the RNC reported raising $6.7 million for the month and $37 million for the year. In November 2011, Priebus spoke at the University of Chicago's Harris School of Public Policy Studies. As quoted by Rick Pearson for the *Chicago Tribune* (17 Nov. 2011), Priebus said, "There's someone in charge of this country that promised a whole heck of a lot four years ago, right? He did it in a bigger way and it didn't work out. Everything's worse. You can get into, you want to argue all of the details, but everything is worse." Priebus went on to say that Obama "may have had good intentions, but the road to recovery isn't paved with good intentions. I think you understand that's a different road." In the second half of 2011, the RNC raised nearly $51 million, reaching a yearly total of $88 million. The organization also cut its debt down to $11.8 million. Reince Priebus and his wife, Sally, have two children, Jack and Grace.

SUGGESTED READING

Balz, Dan. "Under New Management, RNC Emerges from Tumult of Steele Era." *Washington Post* 17 Apr. 2011: A2. Print.

Gilbert, Craig. "GOP Makeover Gets Fresh Wisconsin Face." *Milwaukee Journal Sentinel* 15 Feb. 2009: A1. Print.

Guarino, Mark. "Republican Party Chair Reince Priebus: What's His Record in Wisconsin?" *Christian Science Monitor*. Christian Science Monitor, 16 Jan. 2011. Web. 23 Mar. 2012.

Pearson, Rick. "RNC Chief on Obama: 'A Fish Rots at the Head.'" *Chicago Tribune*. Tribune, 17 Nov. 2011. Web. 23 Mar. 2012.

Schouten, Frederika. "New RNC Chairman Begins Shake-up." *USA Today* 21 Jan. 2011: 5A. Print.

Vogel, Kenneth P. "Reince Priebus's Tea Party Tightrope." *Politico*. Politico, 17 Jan. 2011. Web. 23 Mar. 2012.

—*Dmitry Kiper*

Dafnis Prieto

Born: July 31, 1974
Occupation: Drummer and composer

Working with both modern kits and traditional percussion instrumentation, fusing the Afro-Cuban rhythms of his homeland with cutting-edge jazz and a host of other influences, the Cuban-born percussionist, bandleader, and composer Dafnis Prieto is one of the most technically accomplished and innovative drummers working today. His arrival in the United States in 1999 was compared to an asteroid strike by Ben Ratliff of the *New York Times* (17 Jan. 2002), and in the years since, he has played with a veritable who's who of contemporary musicians, both in the jazz world and beyond. Summing up his career, Chip Boaz for the *Latin Jazz Corner* (18 Oct. 2011) stated, "Prieto has shown himself to be a technically astounding drummer, an inspired bandleader, an edgy avant-garde musician, a supportive sideman, and a genre-bending composer that has contributed to jazz, Latin music, modern classical settings, and more."

Prieto has released four albums as a bandleader—*About the Monks* (2005), the Grammy-nominated *Absolute Quintet* (2006), *Taking the Soul for a Walk* (2008), and *Live at Jazz Standard NYC* (2009). In 2007, he was nominated for a Latin Grammy in the best new artist category. In recognition of Prieto's potential as an artist, he received in 2011 the so-called "genius grant," a MacArthur Fellowship from the John D. and Catherine T. MacArthur Foundation. "My style is based on the rich polyrhythmic foundation that developed in Cuba because of the immersion of African culture there," Prieto told Ted Drozdowski for Broadcast Music Inc.'s *MusicWorld* (6 Feb. 2012), reflecting on his influences and evolution as an artist. "As I gained experience I found the freedom within my playing to feel open enough to create much more within those rhythms."

EARLY LIFE AND EDUCATION

Dafnis Prieto was born on July 31, 1974, in Santa Clara, the capital of the province of Villa Clara in central Cuba. His father earned his living as an elevator mechanic. Trained as an accountant, his mother kept the books at a factory that produced equipment for sugarcane processing facilities. Prieto grew up in a largely Afro-Cuban neighborhood, an environment that helped inspire his lifelong passion for music. "I was surrounded by music," he told Tomas Pena for *All about Jazz* (22 Dec. 2004). "Music was everywhere; on the radio and in the streets." The young Prieto was especially fascinated by the *comparsas*, bands of musicians who perform in Cuban conga parades as part of the festival of Carnival. During the lead up to the celebration,

Courtesy the John D. & Catherine T. MacArthur Foundation

the *comparsas* would practice in Prieto's neighborhood, sometimes right in front of his family's home. Though only six or seven at the time, Prieto was enthralled by the sounds and rhythms. His mother recognized his growing obsession and, Prieto recalled to Pena, "Whenever the comparsas would rehearse in front of my house [she] would get very nervous. She knew I was about to get lost . . . . Invariably, I would always find a way to sneak out of the house and follow the comparsas."

Prieto's musical education commenced soon afterward. He joined a local social club that provided musical instruction. There, he learned *son*, *guaracha*, *rumba*, and other standard rhythms of Cuban music. For his musical instrument, he initially took up the Spanish guitar. Then, one of his instructors decided to form the social club's music students into a band. There were already half a dozen guitar players, so the teacher asked some of them to select other instruments. "As fate would have it," Prieto told Pena, "I picked the bongos." His choice was hardly surprising, given that his childhood was saturated with the percussive rhythms of Cuban music. "[E]verywhere—in the streets, coming out of open windows—I heard the sound of drums that captured Cuban music's African influence," Prieto told Drozdowski. "It was in the air every day." During one of the band's shows, the clave player failed to appear—the clave is a percussion instrument consisting of two short and thick wooden sticks that are rhythmically banged together. Without any prompting, the bongo-playing Prieto started making the sounds of the clave with his mouth. Impressed by this display, his music instructor spoke to Prieto's mother and recommended that she send him to the local music conservatory.

NATIONAL SCHOOL OF MUSIC

At the age of eleven, Prieto graduated to a full drum kit and began a four-year stint at the music conservatory of the Santa Clara School of Fine Arts, where he was trained as a classical percussionist. Several years later, he was accepted at the National School of Music in Havana and moved from Santa Clara to the Cuban capital to take up his studies. At the National School of Music, he continued his education in classical percussion. Living in Havana, Prieto was introduced to new forms of music; he quickly developed a passion for jazz and started experimenting with it in his spare time. Early on, he was drawn to such American jazz composers as the pianist Armando "Chick" Corea and the saxophonist John Coltrane, listening every day to the latter's 1964 studio album *A Love Supreme*. Elvin Jones, who drummed for Coltrane, was another influence. As Prieto immersed himself in the medium, he studied the saxophonist Michael Brecker, the drummer Steve Gadd, and the pioneering multi-instrumentalist Ornette Coleman. One of jazz's great innovators, Coleman played a key role in the emergence of both free jazz and avant-garde jazz.

Despite being introduced to the work of such luminaries, Prieto was isolated from much of the jazz world in Cuba, and his education in the medium was far from complete. Nevertheless, his capabilities as a musician were undeniable even as a teenager, and while still studying at the National School of Music, he went on his first overseas tour, performing at jazz festivals in Europe. As the artist grew more seasoned, he became enamored with avant-garde jazz, an especially unconventional and groundbreaking form that embraces unusual structures, rhythms, and instrumentation. In 1992, Prieto graduated from the National School of Music. For the commencement ceremonies, he put together a band and played an avant-garde jazz composition he had created. "The group," he recalled to Pena, "consisted of four horns, a bass, and myself on the traps, kettle drums, and whistle. It was a rather revolutionary concept."

PROFESSIONAL MUSICIAN STATUS

After completing his studies at the National School of Music, Prieto became a full-time professional musician. He went on tour in support of the pianists Ramon Valle and Carlos Maza, as well as the multi-instrumentalist Bobby Carcassés, joining his band Columna B. "It was fun, I learned a lot sharing the music with them," Prieto told Pena, "but I was also interested in playing with other musicians." The Cuban jazz scene, while vibrant, was not especially large, and it was cut off from the major jazz currents in the United States. Prieto started to feel constricted. It was not easy to support himself, either. "The avant-garde scene in Cuba is really small and it is very hard to make a living as a jazz musician," he told Pena. "To survive you have to travel out of Cuba, make money (American dollars), and spend it in Cuba. Besides, I didn't have a place to live in Havana because my family lived in Santa Clara, so I had to rent places all the time."

The year 1996 was a seminal one for Prieto. The American jazz saxophonist Steve Coleman visited Cuba, and he and Prieto embarked on a serendipitous collaboration. "With Steve, more than playing in his band, I did research," Prieto told Ben Ratliff for the *New York Times* (17 Jan. 2002). "I looked at South Indian music; we did a trio project about the sun, moon, and the Earth; and we did a thing about yin and yang." Prieto also traveled to Spain with Columna B. His wife, Judith Sanchez Ruiz, a professional dancer, had a two-year performance contract in Barcelona, and Prieto opted to stay with her for a year. "I decided then and there that I would not return to Cuba," Prieto told Pena. He soon received an offer to play with the Canadian jazz saxophonist Jane Bunnett and her band, Spirit of Havana, and subsequently went on tour in Canada and the United States. Visa troubles kept him from going back to Spain; he was forced to head home to Cuba, but only after giving serious thought to staying in New York City.

NEW YORK CITY

Three years later, in 1999, visa difficulties left Prieto stranded in Toronto, Canada. He headed to New York City, where he applied for residency. "I left Cuba because I felt suffocated professionally," he told Siddhartha Mitter for the *Boston Globe* (23 Feb. 2012). "I didn't have many options to do what I wanted to do musically." Elaborating further on his motivations to Ratliff, Prieto stated, "The kind of music I was doing there in Cuba was sort of on the side of jazz—avant-garde Latin music—and I didn't see myself in Cuba doing that for long. The only guys I saw playing that kind of music were the ones who were already playing with me, so there was nowhere to go."

Prieto received a warm welcome in New York and immersed himself in the local jazz scene. He played with dozens of musicians and fifteen different bands in just his first several years in the United States, including the avant-garde jazz great Henry Threadgill and his band Zooid, Eddie Palmieri's Latin jazz orchestra, and Claudia Acuña's South American–inflected jazz group. He also collaborated with his wife on some performances and studied American drumming traditions, exploring the work and styles of Max Roach, Billy Higgins, and Ed Blackwell.

Discussing Prieto's talents as a drummer, Brian Lynch, a trumpeter who played with him, observed to Ratliff, "He brings the intelligence level up. . . . He knows form, and he remembers things. He'll be swinging, he'll be in the clave rhythm, but he'll make these little shifts with it—just a little spurt, where there's an impossibly complex rhythm, but it's all precise."

Still, the transition was not an easy one. Raised in provincial Cuba, Prieto had found Havana overwhelming. New York City was even more intimidating. "I remember saying to myself, 'New York is the last place I ever want to live,' he told Pena. "Three years later I was not only living in New York but enjoying it." Soon, he was working again with Steve Coleman and teaming up with other jazz greats, such as the Cuban bandleader and pianist Chucho Valdés; he played drums on various live and studio recordings.

ABOUT THE MONKS AND ABSOLUTE QUINTET

As a bandleader, Prieto released his first album, *About the Monks*, on the Zoho label in 2005. The album, Prieto explained to Pena, "is dedicated to the many people and artists who have inspired my soul." Prieto put together a six-person band for *About the Monks*, which features trumpet, bass, saxophone, piano, violin, and percussion. Reviewing the work for *Latin Jazz Corner* (18 Oct. 2011), Chip Boaz described the music as "[moving] between hard-bop fire, modern play with time signatures, nods to Cuban tradition, and an inherent rhythmic complexity and drive that explodes from the speakers."

For *Absolute Quintet* (2006), Prieto's Grammy Award–nominated follow up to *About the Monks*, he included many of his bandmates from the first album. The eclectic lineup covers keyboard, percussion, saxophone, violin, and cello, with Threadgill playing alto saxophone on one track. Reviewing the release for *All about Jazz* (9 May 2006), Mark F. Turner wrote, "Like 2005's *About the Monks*, the new music has quirky rhythms and snaking patterns, matched with Prieto's ever-lively playing. But now he brushes his compositions with wider and more thoughtful strokes." Boaz wrote that "Prieto shatters all expectations with this album, plunging his musicianship in a completely new direction that edges on funky fusion." Despite such praise, *Absolute Quintet* did not capture the Grammy Award for best Latin jazz album, which went to the Brian Lynch/Eddie Palmieri Project for their record *Simpático*. Based on his output, Prieto was also recognized at the Latin Grammys with a 2007 nomination in the best new artist category, though he did not win that honor.

A SONG FOR CHICO AND OTHER WORKS

For his third album, *Taking the Soul for a Walk* (2008), Prieto employed a sextet lineup of bass, piano, trumpet, percussion, and two saxophones. Released on Prieto's own Dafnison label, the record earned a positive critical reception. "Never has the line between traditional Latin-jazz and twenty-first-century postbop been so wonderfully blurred as on *Taking the Soul for a Walk*," wrote Michael J. West for *JazzTimes* (June 2008). "Prieto and his gang are as tight as they come."

Collaborating with the New York Afro Latin Jazz Orchestra and its director, Arturo O'Farrill, Prieto composed the title track to their 2008 album, *A Song for Chico*, in tribute to Chico O'Farrill, Arturo's father. The following year, the record earned the Grammy Award for best Latin jazz album.

Since his arrival in the United States, Prieto has performed with many different lineups and has been a member of a number of different bands. There is no overlap from one project to the next, however. Each is distinct. "None of my bands play any of the same material," he told Drozdowski. "I write for the group, for individual players, and for the moment—not by formula. Music should always be about honest communication. If we're going to say something pure and honest, it can't be premeditated." One of his bands, the Si O Si Quartet, is featured on his fourth album as a bandleader, *Live at Jazz Standard NYC* (2009). In addition to Prieto on the drums, the lineup includes Peter Apfelbaum on the saxophone, Manuel Valera on the piano, and Charles Flores on the bass. "The drummer's writing sounds fresh and innovative, pulling colorful harmonies out of the group and constantly playing with rhythmic evolution," Boaz wrote in his review of *Live at Jazz Standard NYC* (18 Oct. 2011). "The most mature statement from Prieto that we've heard, this album overflows with intelligent risk taking, skillfully crafted drama, and masterful interplay that demands repeated listens."

MACARTHUR FELLOW

In September 2011, the MacArthur Foundation contacted Prieto and informed him that he had been named one of twenty-two 2011 MacArthur Fellows. MacArthur Fellowships are anonymously awarded to American residents "across all ages and fields who show exceptional merit and promise of continued creative work," according to the MacArthur Foundation's website. Each unrestricted fellowship is worth $500,000 paid out over five years. For Prieto, the honor was well-timed. "I'd been kind of struggling to get my projects moving," Prieto told Mitter. "The MacArthur will really help me get through a lot of barriers." He has planned to use the fellowship to finish an album with one of his bands, the Proverb Trio, which consists of Prieto, Jason Lindner on the keyboard, and the rapper Kokayi. Among other projects, he also plans to use the fellowship to help him publish a book about the art of drumming.

ADDITIONAL WORK

Since 2005, Prieto has served as an adjunct instructor in music at New York University (NYU), and as an educator he has led drum workshops throughout the country. In addition to his MacArthur Foundation Fellowship, Prieto is the recipient of a 2005 grant from Chamber Music America's New Works: Creation and Presentation Program and was named the up-and-coming musician of the year by the Jazz Journalists Association in 2006, among other awards and honors. He counts the Spanish surrealist painter Salvador Dali as one of his favorite artists and as someone who has had a deep influence on his perspective as a musician.

In addition to the artists mentioned above, Prieto has played with such jazz icons as Branford Marsalis, Arturo Sandoval, and Herbie Hancock. Though he has made his name in the genres of jazz and Latin music, Prieto does not like to confine himself to labels. "I don't look at myself as a jazz musician," he told Eric Fine for *JazzTimes* (August 2008). "I studied classical music in the conservatory. I did research on folkloric music because I actually grew up listening to folkloric music in Cuba. I don't even like that much the [idea] of being a jazz musician. I try to do the music that represents my life now."

When not touring, Prieto makes his home in the New York City neighborhood of Washington Heights in upper Manhattan. He is separated from his wife Judith Sanchez Ruiz, with whom he has a son, Lucian.

SUGGESTED READING

Chinen, Nate. "Meditation, and Time with the Sticks." *New York Times*. New York Times Co., 11 May 2012. Web. 21 Aug. 2012.

Drozdowski, Ted. "Catching Up with Dafnis Prieto, Winner of MacArthur Foundation Fellowship." *MusicWorld*. BMI, 6 Feb. 2012. Web. 21 Aug. 2012.

Fine, Eric. "Dafnis Prieto: Multilingual Rhythms." *JazzTimes*. JazzTimes Inc., Aug. 2008. Web. 21 Aug. 2012.

Mitter, Siddhartha. "Dafnis Prieto Plays More than Meets the Ear." *Boston Globe*. New York Times Co., 23 Feb. 2012. Web. 21 Aug. 2012.

Pena, Tomas. "Dafnis Prieto: About the Monks." *All about Jazz*. All about Jazz, 22 Dec. 2004. Web. 21 Aug. 2012.

"Prieto, Dafnis (Dafnis Prieto Rodriguez)." *Encyclopedia of Jazz Musicians*. Jazz.com, 2012. Web. 21 Aug. 2012.

Ratliff, Ben. "From Cuba, with Rhythm, Taking Jazz by Storm; Dafnis Prieto Makes His Mark in New York" *New York Times*. New York Times Co., 17 Jan. 2002. Web. 21 Aug. 2012.

—*Paul McCaffrey*

René Redzepi

Born: December 16, 1977
Occupation: Chef and restaurateur

The Danish chef René Redzepi is, in the eyes of many culinary observers, one of the most influential chefs in the world. He is the head chef and co-owner of Noma, a two-Michelin-star restaurant in the Christianshavn district of Copenhagen, Denmark. ("Noma" is a portmanteau of the Danish words "nordisk" and "mad," which translates as "Nordic food.") Since opening Noma in 2003 at the age of twenty-five, Redzepi has been credited with redefining Nordic cuisine and for transforming Denmark into a worldwide culinary destination. Dubbed the "master scavenger of the Nordic coast" by Jane Kramer for the *New Yorker* (21 Nov. 2011), he is known particularly for his use of foraging techniques to find local produce and wild food and for a style of cuisine that reflects a sense of time and place in the Nordic region—a region that includes Denmark, Norway, Sweden, Finland, Iceland, Greenland, and the Faroe Islands. Along with his staff of "gastronomic explorers," as he described them to John Walsh for the London *Independent* (25 Nov. 2010), Redzepi has created dishes that have wowed food critics and patrons alike. As a result, the restaurant, which seats only around forty at dinner, has earned considerable renown as a global culinary hotspot. Lydia Itoi, writing for *Time* magazine online (21 Sep. 2007), hailed Noma as "a visionary modern restaurant," and Frank Bruni, in an article for the *New York Times* (6 July. 2010), called it "an international sensation." Noma's reputation came full circle in 2010, when it was named the best restaurant in the world by the British trade magazine *Restaurant*, in its annual "World's 50 Best Restaurants" list; Noma maintained that title in 2011. Redzepi, meanwhile, has since risen to celebrity chef status: in 2010 he released his first cookbook, *Noma: Time and Place in Nordic Cuisine*, and he appeared on the British Broadcasting Corporation's (BBC) cooking competition series *MasterChef: The Professionals*. Despite his newfound fame, he insisted to Jasper Gerard for the London *Telegraph* (28 Apr. 2010), "Food is not about becoming famous. It really is about giving."

EARLY LIFE AND EDUCATION

Along with his twin brother, Kenneth, René Redzepi was born on December 16, 1977 in Copenhagen, Denmark, to a Macedonian father and a Danish mother. His father, a cab driver, had met his mother, a cleaning lady, while they were both working in Copenhagen. Redzepi and his brother were raised in Copenhagen but spent their summers in their father's homeland of

AFP/Getty Images

CAREER

Redzepi spent one year attending restaurant school, where he received training in cooking and other disciplines, such as baking, butchering, waitering, and restaurant management. He worked at a hotel restaurant for some years before landing an apprenticeship in 1996 at Copenhagen's Michelin-rated French restaurant Pierre André. He served as an apprentice under chef Philippe Houdet. "I still remember the first dish I got on the menu," Redzepi told Sabine Durrant for the London *Guardian* (6 Nov. 2010). "I took a piece of pineapple and I rubbed it with saffron and spices, roasted it, turning it caramel butter, like a piece of meat, and served it with ice cream."

In 1998 Redzepi left Copenhagen to accept a job at Jacques and Laurent Pourcel's Le Jardin des Sens ("The Garden of the Senses"), a three-Michelin-star restaurant in Montpellier, France. Despite accepting the position to be closer to French cuisine, he found the restaurant's rigid atmosphere uninspiring and stressful. "I didn't enjoy that period," he told Jay Rayner for the London *Observer* (23 May 2009). "A lot of shouting in the kitchen. A lot of aggression." Redzepi first heard about the Spanish chef Ferran Adria's world-renowned three-Michelin-star restaurant elBulli while working for the Pourcel brothers. Located in the Catalonian region of Spain, elBulli had become widely regarded as the best restaurant in the world, thanks to Adria's extremely influential and inventive "molecular cuisine"—a type of cooking characterized by culinary foams, gels, and other gastronomic innovations. After experiencing elBulli's food firsthand as a guest, Redzepi asked Adria for a job, and soon afterwards, he was offered a position at the restaurant as a *stagiare*, or unpaid apprentice. He worked there during the 1999 summer season and left with a new "sense of freedom," as he told Rayner.

After his stint at elBulli, Redzepi secured a *stagiare* position at another three-Michelin-star restaurant, Thomas Keller's French Laundry, in Yountville, in Napa Valley, California. He spent several months there before returning to Copenhagen to work at the French restaurant Kong Hans Kaelder under chef Thomas Rode Andersen. In late 2002, the Danish food television personality and entrepreneur Claus Meyer approached him with the proposition of opening and running his own restaurant in an old eighteenth-century warehouse formerly used by whalers and fishermen in Copenhagen's Christianshavn harbor district.

In November 2003, following nearly a year of preparation and planning, Redzepi, Meyer, and another partner teamed up to open the restaurant Noma on the ground floor of the warehouse, which had been converted into an arts and culture center called the North Atlantic House.

Macedonia, then a part of Yugoslavia. It was there where Redzepi's interest in and appreciation for food took shape. Redzepi continued to spend his summers in Macedonia until the outbreak of the Bosnian war in 1992.

While Redzepi grew up foraging for ingredients that would be used in his father's home-cooked meals, most of his Danish friends were stuck eating ready-made food. "It was the time of the microwave," he told Walsh, referring to the typical Danish cuisine of the 1980s. "You chucked a box of chicken and spices in the oven and cooked it." Redzepi enjoyed the benefit of a rich culinary upbringing, but his family lived by very modest means, and he grew up understanding the value of hard work. However, Redzepi's blue-collar work ethic did not carry over to the classroom, and he disregarded his studies in favor of other activities. He told Walsh, "I didn't have any standpoints, except girls, soccer, basketball and hanging out." Redzepi was homeschooled during the time his family lived in Macedonia, but he received the bulk of his formal education in Copenhagen.

When Redzepi was fifteen years old, he was declared ineligible for secondary school due to his poor grades. Directionless, Redzepi decided to follow a friend, named Michael Skotbo, into a local restaurant trade school. One of his first assignments there included finding a recipe and cooking it for a food competition. He settled on a roasted chicken with rice in cashew nut sauce, which placed first in presentation and second in flavor.

Redzepi, who had turned down more lucrative offers from several acclaimed Copenhagen establishments, designed a menu that aimed to reflect Nordic cuisine and was purposefully devoid of standard fine dining delicacies like fois gras and Iberico ham—a concept that was met with almost universal derision from the Danish food cognoscenti, who went so far as to give the restaurant offensive nicknames in the Danish press. Despite that kind of sentiment, Noma opened to positive reviews. Redzepi, however, remained unsatisfied. Tired of "taking recipes from other cultures, serving essentially the same 'Scandinavian French' food," as he put it to Kramer, he resolved to rethink his approach.

A turning point for Redzepi came during a trip to Greenland in March 2004, while hunting for musk oxen with one of Noma's game suppliers. Finding himself stranded at a Greenland airport due to a severe snowstorm, he recalled to Rayner, "It was very cold, minus 55, and I was suddenly struck by the enormity of where we were. We are a huge landmass with only 25 million people. Here, where we are, nature is as it wants to be, and I began thinking about how to reflect that nature, express it on the plate." Upon returning to Denmark, Redzepi decided to overhaul Noma's menu with the aim of creating a cuisine that evoked both the time and place of the Nordic region. He began foraging around Denmark to help deepen his knowledge of local and seasonal ingredients and started reading old recipe books and survival guides to gain a better understanding of what people in the region ate.

Redzepi's foraging expeditions and various brainstorming sessions resulted in a menu consisting of innovative dishes made only with ingredients indigenous to the Nordic region. Focusing strictly on local, sustainable fare, he helped reinvent Nordic cuisine while transforming Noma into one of the most influential and popular restaurants in the world. By 2012, the twelve-table, forty-seat restaurant serving multicourse meals at both lunch and dinner was booking up to three months in advance and receiving more than 100,000 reservations per month.

Patrons of Noma have been presented with an abundance of fresh coastal vegetation, such as beach cabbage, bulrushes, and sea buckthorn, along with a wide variety of herbs, fruits, and berries, from ramson leaves to wood sorrel to lingonberries. Some entrées are meant to be eaten without silverware, from plates fashioned out of local rocks and shells. A few of Noma's best-known dishes include chicken skins with roasted rye bread, smoked cheese, and lumpfish roe; Icelandic langoustine with oyster emulsion, seaweed powder, and rye bread crumbs served on a rock; radishes in a flowerpot of edible soil consisting of malt and hazelnut flour and an Icelandic sheep's milk yogurt called *skyr*; and a live fjord prawn served in a Mason jar of ice. Redzepi

told Anne Kingston for *Maclean's* (27 Oct. 2010), "The challenge for me is to telegraph the actual flavour of the field and sea, the narrative of the dish in your mouth."

Redzepi's forward-thinking ideas about food helped Noma earn a star in the prestigious Michelin Guide in 2005, along with a second star in 2007, a rating it has since retained. (Noma is the only restaurant in Denmark with two Michelin stars.) The restaurant has also won prestige among food critics, chefs, and restaurateurs around the world, enjoying a steady rise in *Restaurant* magazine's annual "World's 50 Best Restaurants" list, on which it ranked number 33, 15, 10, and 3, in 2006, 2007, 2008, and 2009, respectively. In April 2010, Noma made waves when it finished first on the highly influential list, dethroning Adria's elBulli, which had held the top spot the previous four years. ElBulli closed in July 2011; Noma went on to retain its number-one ranking that same year. Redzepi, meanwhile, has collected several culinary honors, including being named a rising star chef by Michelin in 2006 and named International Chef of the Year by the Spanish guide Lo Mejor de la Gastronomia in 2008, also receiving the Chef's Choice prize at the 2009 *Restaurant* magazine awards. He has called Noma's popularity a product of the times, explaining to Kingston, "I think our restaurant represents perfectly what the world wants right now in terms of sustainability, the footprint you leave behind you, what's good for mother Earth."

At Noma, Redzepi oversees a staff of roughly seventy people from more than a dozen countries, with English as the language of choice. His staff includes chefs, *stagiares*, and waiters, as well as network of professional foragers and local farmers. Most of Noma's chefs take on the roles of foragers and servers and most of the restaurant's crops are harvested on a nearby polycultural farm. In 2008, Redzepi and Meyer established a nonprofit organization and Noma test kitchen called the Nordic Food Lab, which works to explore new possibilities for Nordic cuisine. The lab is located on a houseboat near the restaurant.

In October 2010, Redzepi released his first cookbook, *Noma: Time and Place in Nordic Cuisine*, which was published by Phaidon Press. Featuring a foreword by the acclaimed Danish Icelandic artist Olafur Éliasson and other introductory passages by Rune Skyum-Nielsen, the book's 320 pages chronicle the history of Noma and include the recipes for many of Redzepi's signature dishes. In November 2010, Redzepi appeared as a guest on the BBC cooking competition series *MasterChef: The Professionals*. In August 2011, he appeared on the Australian version of the series. While these television appearances indicate the typical spoils of life as a celebrity chef, Redzepi has turned down numerous business offers to open other restaurants, choosing instead to remain focused on what he started with Noma. He confided to Anne Kingston, "This is something unique and I'm proud to be part of it. It gives me much more satisfaction than opening a place for the profit of it."

PERSONAL LIFE

Durrant described Redzepi as looking like a "film actor" with "floppy hair," "penetrating brown eyes," and a "surprisingly short" stature. He lives in an apartment in Copenhagen with his wife, Nadine, who is a former Noma waitress, and their two young daughters, Arwen and Genta, born in 2008 and 2011, respectively. An admitted workaholic, he told Durrant that he enjoys being "a devoted husband and a perfect father" on Sundays and Mondays, his only days off.

SUGGESTED READING

Aguirre, Abby. "Danish Modern." *New York Times* 4 Dec. 2011: 86. Print.

Bruni, Frank. "A Nordic Chef Explores His Backyard." *New York Times* 7 July 2010: D1. Print.

Kingston, Anne. "Nordic Obsession." *Maclean's* 1 Nov. 2010: 82–84. Print.

Kramer, Jane. "The Food at Our Feet; Why Is Foraging All the Rage?" *New Yorker* 21 Nov. 2011: 80–91. Print.

Redzepi, René, and Rune Skyum-Nielsen. *Noma: Time and Place in Nordic Cuisine*. London: Phaidon, 2010. Print.

—*Chris Cullen*

Getty Images

Andy Reid

Born: March 19, 1958
Occupation: Football coach with the Philadelphia Eagles

Philadelphia Eagles head coach and executive vice president of football operations Andy Reid has developed a reputation as one of the most admired and respected figures in the National Football League (NFL). Known for his even-tempered demeanor, meticulous organizational skills, and expert handling of players and coaches, Reid has achieved many distinctions and accolades since taking over as head coach of the Eagles in January 1999. Reid, a former offensive lineman who broke into the coaching profession as an assistant under such coaching legends as LaVell Edwards and Mike Holmgren, is the longest-tenured coach in the NFL and second-longest-tenured coach or manager in Philadelphia's professional sports history, behind Philadelphia Athletics manager Connie Mack.

Reid has also been the guiding force behind the most successful period in Eagles franchise history. Between 1999 and 2011, he led the team to six National Football Conference (NFC) East Division titles (2001–4, 2006, and 2010), five NFC Championship games (2001–4, 2008), one Super Bowl berth (2004), and 136 wins (including playoffs)—the most wins for a coach in franchise history, second only to the New England Patriots' three-time Super Bowl–winning coach Bill Belichick for most in the league since 1999. He also has the most playoff wins (10) and the highest winning percentage (.609) of any Eagles coach and is one of only five active NFL coaches with at least 100 wins. Reid's achievements have helped him earn NFL Coach of the Year honors on three occasions (2000, 2002, and 2010).

In addition to serving as head coach, Reid has also held the title of executive vice president of football operations with the Eagles since 2001, making him one of only a handful of NFL head coaches with the power of general manager and full autonomy over player personnel decisions. The Eagles' owner and chairman, Jeffrey Lurie, has described Reid as being "like a CEO on the field. He understands the big picture and the short-term picture. You have to always balance the two. Disciplined. Prepared. Smart. It's an awfully good combination."

EARLY LIFE

The younger of the two sons of Walter and Elizabeth Reid, Andrew Walter Reid was born on

March 19, 1958, in Los Angeles, California. He and his older brother, Reginald, were raised in a two-bedroom Spanish-style home in the Los Angeles neighborhood of Los Feliz, an affluent enclave known for its many celebrity inhabitants and cultural diversity. At an early age Reid learned the importance of a strong work ethic and education from his parents, who both hailed from the East Coast. His father was an artist who designed backdrops for theatrical productions and movie sets; his mother worked as a radiologist at a hospital in the nearby city of Burbank. Reid inherited his meticulous nature from his father, who often brought him along to sets and taught him how to make cabinets and other pieces of furniture. Meanwhile, he learned organizational skills and developed a love of sports from his mother, a diehard fan of the hometown Los Angeles Dodgers, which had moved from Brooklyn, New York, to Los Angeles the year Reid was born.

Like his mother, Reid rooted for the Dodgers and regularly attended games at Dodger Stadium, which opened in 1962 and was located less than ten minutes away from his home. He was also a fan of Los Angeles's NFL team, the Rams (which later moved to St. Louis), and grew up idolizing such Rams stars as defensive tackle Merlin Olsen and defensive end Deacon Jones. Reid began playing on youth-league sports teams as a boy and spent hours each day playing football and other sports with his older brother and other neighborhood children. He has cited his brother, then a distinguished athlete at John Marshall High School in Los Angeles, as his main athletic inspiration. Physically bigger than many of his peers, Reid held his own in street pick-up games with his brother and his friends, despite the ten-year age gap between them. He later said to Jeff McLane for the *Philadelphia Inquirer* (18 June 2012), "He and his buddies made sure I wasn't going to be the big, soft kid."

Reid's large size was evident in 1971, when, at thirteen years old, he won a nationally televised NFL Punt, Pass, and Kick competition against his much smaller peers. Like his older brother, he attended John Marshall High School, where he lettered in football, basketball, baseball, and track. Despite weighing in excess of 220 pounds as a freshman, Reid proved to be a nimble athlete and became a standout offensive and defensive lineman, kicker, and punter on the school's varsity football team. As a senior cocaptain, he kicked three game-winning field goals, leading John Marshall to a 7–3 record and a berth in the quarterfinal round of the city playoffs. That year he was voted the team's most inspirational player. John Marshall High has since honored Reid with a trophy named after him, the Andy Reid Trophy, which is awarded annually to the best lineman on the football team.

EDUCATION

Reid, who was also a star pitcher and an academic standout, was offered scholarships by a number of colleges, including the University of California, Los Angeles, but turned them down in hopes of fulfilling his dream of playing for the University of Southern California (USC). After being deemed unready to play there, Reid was advised by USC's coaching staff to enroll at Glendale Community College in Glendale, California, where he played for two seasons as a starting offensive lineman and kicker. There, he developed into a Division I-A–caliber player under head coach Jim Sartoris, a former USC All-American, and was named an honorable mention All-American as a sophomore.

Prior to his junior season, Reid transferred to Brigham Young University (BYU) in Provo, Utah, which competes in the National Collegiate Athletic Association (NCAA) Football Bowl Subdivision (previously Division I-A), the highest level of college football. Reid played as an offensive lineman under legendary BYU head coach LaVell Edwards, who would become his mentor. He sat out his first year at the school to recover from a serious knee injury, suffered in the final game of his sophomore season, then spent the remainder of his career there as a backup to All-American tackle Nick Eyre. During his time at BYU, Reid wrote a sports column for the Provo *Daily Herald* that was modeled after the writing style of the late, famed *Los Angeles Times* sportswriter Jim Murray. He also got married and converted to his wife's Mormon faith. He received a bachelor's degree in physical education from BYU in 1981.

EARLY CAREER

Though Reid had aspired to become a doctor after college, he decided instead to pursue a coaching career on the recommendation of Edwards, who believed he had a natural gift for it. He was subsequently hired by Edwards to work as a graduate assistant on BYU's coaching staff for the 1982 season. Edwards told Doug Robinson for the Salt Lake City, Utah, *Deseret Morning News* (5 Feb. 2005) that it was Reid's "temperament and his understanding of the game and his ability to work with people" that had convinced him he would make a good coach, adding, "He was a popular guy on the team, and he was a good student."

While working as a graduate assistant under Edwards at BYU, Reid met Mike Holmgren, then the school's quarterbacks coach. Impressed with Reid's strong work ethic and insatiable willingness to learn, Holmgren promised that if he ever landed an NFL head coaching job, he would hire Reid. During this time Reid began keeping daily detailed notes of his thoughts, experiences, and observations, a practice he would continue throughout his coaching career. He earned a master's degree in professional leadership in physical education and athletics from BYU in 1982.

In 1983 Reid, with the help of Edwards, landed a position as offensive coordinator at Division II San Francisco State University (SF State) in California, where he worked under renowned coach Vic Rowen. The position came with only a modest salary, so Reid took on multiple side jobs to make ends meet for his family. Those jobs included umpiring baseball games, teaching tennis and racquetball, and working as a limousine driver for such movie stars as Rock Hudson and Loni Anderson. He also sold hot dogs on SF State's campus twice a week to help raise funds for the school's cash-starved football program.

Financial struggles notwithstanding, during Reid's three-year tenure as offensive coordinator, SF State led the nation in both passing and total offense all three years. In 1986, Reid left SF State to become the offensive line coach at Northern Arizona University in Flagstaff, where he stayed for just one season. He then spent two seasons as offensive line coach at the University of Texas at El Paso, where he worked under coach Bob Stull. In 1989, he followed Stull to the University of Missouri in Columbia, where he served as offensive line coach for three seasons.

RISE TO THE NFL

When Mike Holmgren became head coach of the Green Bay Packers in 1992, Reid, as promised, was hired as the Packers' tight ends and assistant offensive line coach. Despite having little experience working with tight ends, Reid quickly picked up his new role, which helped him gain a better all-around grasp of the offense. He coached the Packers' tight ends and assisted with the offensive line for five seasons, during which he helped guide tight ends Keith Jackson and Mark Chmura to multiple Pro Bowl selections. The Packers posted winning seasons every year during that span, earning four consecutive playoff berths (1993–96) and two NFC Central Division titles (1995–96) and defeating the New England Patriots in Super Bowl XXXI, the franchise's third Super Bowl title and first since 1967.

Reid became known for putting in marathon work hours, often arriving at his office as early as three in the morning after getting just a couple hours of sleep. He would, however, return home each morning to eat breakfast and share a prayer with his family before going back to the office. He explained to Bob Ford for the *Philadelphia Inquirer* (24 Jan. 1999), "My family, my church, and my profession are the things I try to balance the best way I can. You have to have some priorities and know your life, or you spread yourself too thin. I'm constantly working at that."

After the Packers' Super Bowl–winning 1996 season, Holmgren promoted Reid to quarterbacks coach, a role he held for two seasons. In his new position Reid worked closely with Packers All-Pro quarterback Brett Favre and helped guide him to a third consecutive Associated Press (AP) NFL Most Valuable Player (MVP) Award during the 1997 season. That year the Packers finished with a 13–3 record and won a third consecutive NFC Central Division title. They advanced to the Super Bowl for the second year in a row but failed to defend their title, losing to the Denver Broncos in Super Bowl XXXII. The Packers would return to the playoffs for a sixth consecutive year in 1998, when they finished second in the NFC Central Division with a record of 11–5; however, they then lost to the San Francisco 49ers in the first round of the playoffs.

Shortly after that loss Holmgren resigned from the Packers to become head coach and general manager of the Seattle Seahawks. Under Reid's watch Favre finished the 1998 season as the NFL leader in completions, completion percentage, and passing yards. Favre described Reid to Paul Attner for *Sporting News* (23 Dec. 2002) as "a good guy, a good person," with "an ability to read players, to get them to follow him and play for him. They want to win for him; it's as simple as that."

MOVE TO PHILADELPHIA

On January 11, 1999, Reid became the twentieth head coach of the Philadelphia Eagles, hired to replace Ray Rhodes after the Eagles finished with a franchise- and league-worst 3–13 record in 1998. Reid was chosen over a number of other, more experienced candidates, many of whom had already served customary tenures as NFL offensive or defensive coordinators at the very least. In the process Reid became only the second position coach in ten years to go directly to a head-coaching job.

Despite Reid being a relatively unknown name around the league at the time and having no head-coaching experience at any level, Eagles executives were immediately blown away by his enthusiasm, intellect, and thorough preparation—he arrived at his interview with a thick binder containing detailed notes on everything from his coaching philosophies and schemes to practice and meeting schedules and even players' dress codes. Recalling his and his colleagues' first impression of Reid, Eagles owner and chairman Jeffrey Lurie told Doug Robinson, "We all looked at each other and said, 'Wow.' This guy really comes right out at you. . . . I remember how the 49ers picked Bill Walsh and the Redskins picked Joe Gibbs—out of the box." Lurie's "out of the box" hiring of Reid perplexed Philadelphia's sports media and angered much of the city's notoriously ruthless fan base, who had been expecting a more accomplished name to fill the role. Nonetheless, the risky move would prove to be one of the most rewarding of his career. Reid, who outlined his plans for rebuilding the Eagles franchise in his first news conference, was signed to a five-year deal worth approximately $5 million.

Reid's tenure with the Eagles got off to a rocky start. In one of his first major moves at the helm, he used the second overall pick in the 1999 NFL Draft to select quarterback Donovan McNabb, a choice that was famously met with a chorus of boos by Eagles fans on draft day. Though McNabb had amassed a decorated All-American career at Syracuse University, many fans—including Philadelphia's then mayor, former Pennsylvania governor Edward G. Rendell—had lobbied hard for the Eagles to draft Heisman Trophy–winning running back Ricky Williams of the University of Texas. Fans and critics became more incensed when the Eagles began the 1999 season by losing seven of their first nine games, while Reid kept McNabb on the bench to develop under veteran quarterback Doug Pederson. Although McNabb went on to start the last seven games of that season, the Eagles finished last in the NFC East Division for the second consecutive year, with a record of 5–11.

MASTER PLAN

Eagles fans saw the first glimpses of Reid's master plan for the franchise during the 2000 season, when he led the team to an 11–5 record and a second-place finish in NFC East Division, marking the greatest single-season turnaround in franchise history. That year saw McNabb emerge as the star franchise quarterback that Reid had originally envisioned he would become, as he accounted for nearly 75 percent of the Eagles' total offense, setting new team records for passing attempts and completions and leading all NFL quarterbacks with a career-high 629 rushing yards. He subsequently earned his first career Pro Bowl selection and finished second in the voting for the AP NFL MVP Award, beaten only by St. Louis Rams running back Marshall Faulk. On the strength of McNabb's play, the Eagles earned their first playoff berth since 1996 and advanced to the NFC divisional playoff round, where they lost to the New York Giants. The team's remarkable turnaround helped Reid earn NFL Coach of the Year honors from the Maxwell Football Club, *Football Digest*, and *Sporting News*.

Over the next four seasons, Reid would transform "the most cynical and frustrated of sports cities and teams from a perennial loser into a perennial contender," as Doug Robinson noted. The Eagles posted records of 11–5, 12–4, 12–4, and 13–3 from 2001 to 2004, winning four consecutive NFC East titles and advancing to four straight NFC Championship games. In

2002 Reid was named the AP NFL Coach of the Year and the Maxwell Football Club NFL Coach of the Year, having helped the Eagles tie for the best record in the league despite losing McNabb for the last six games of the season due to a broken ankle. The following season, Reid led the Eagles to the top record in the NFC for the second straight year, with the team winning twelve of their last fourteen games.

The Eagles carried that momentum into the 2004 season, winning thirteen of their first fourteen games and finishing with the number-one seed in the NFL playoffs. They would subsequently put behind them the agony of three straight defeats in the previous three NFC title games by defeating the Atlanta Falcons in the 2004 NFC Championship Game and advancing to the franchise's first Super Bowl since 1980. In Super Bowl XXXIX, the Eagles lost to the defending champion, the New England Patriots, in a dramatic game that was not determined until the final minutes. Despite the loss, Reid ended that season with seventy-one career wins—the most of any coach in Eagles history, surpassing Hall of Famer Earle "Greasy" Neale's previous record of sixty-six career wins with the club.

LATER SEASONS

Following a disappointing 2005 season in which the Eagles failed to qualify for the playoffs, Reid helped the team return to form in 2006 with their fifth NFC East title in six seasons. Despite sputtering to a 5–6 start and playing the last six games of the season without McNabb, who had gone down with a season-ending injury for the second consecutive year, the Eagles rattled off five consecutive wins to end the year under backup quarterback Jeff Garcia. They went on to defeat their NFC East rival, the New York Giants, in the NFC wild-card round of the playoffs before losing to the New Orleans Saints in the NFC divisional round.

Shortly after that loss, Reid took a five-week leave from the Eagles to tend to legal matters involving his two eldest sons, Garrett and Britt, both of whom were arrested on gun- and drug-related charges in separate incidents on January 30, 2007. He accompanied both of his sons to a rehabilitation facility in Florida. The two were later ordered to serve short prison sentences for their crimes.

After dealing with his family crisis, Reid returned to the Eagles for the 2007 season, hoping to build on his team's success from the previous year. The team, however, struggled to an 8–8 record and finished in last place in the NFC East. The Eagles bounced back and reestablished themselves among the NFL's elite in 2008, finishing second in the NFC East with a 9–6–1 record and advancing to their fifth NFC Championship game in eight seasons, where they lost to the Arizona Cardinals. That season

Reid became the thirty-seventh coach in NFL history to reach one hundred career wins and only the twenty-second to accomplish the feat with a single franchise.

Reid led the Eagles back to the playoffs in 2009 and 2010, where they finished second and first in the NFC East, with records of 11–5 and 10–6, respectively. In 2010, he also coached reborn quarterback Michael Vick, who had joined the team the previous year in a backup role after serving nearly two years in prison for running an illegal intrastate dogfighting ring, to a surprising Pro Bowl campaign, with Vick leading an explosive Eagles offense that finished second in the NFL in total offense. Though the Eagles lost to the eventual Super Bowl champion Green Bay Packers in the wild-card playoff round, Reid was named the Maxwell Football Club NFL Coach of the Year for the third time in his career, while Vick was named the NFL Comeback Player of the Year.

After making several notable free-agent acquisitions during the 2011 off-season, Reid's Eagles entered the 2011 season as legitimate Super Bowl contenders. They ultimately failed to live up to expectations, however, finishing second in the NFC East with an 8–8 record and missing the playoffs for the first time since 2007. The team entered the 2012 season with similar aspirations, and Reid came into the season with the second-highest winning percentage among active NFL coaches with at least one hundred games to their credit.

Reid is one of thirty-one coaches in NFL history to have coached two hundred or more regular-season games and is only the thirteenth to do so with one team. He is also one of just eleven coaches in league history to remain with his original team for twelve or more seasons. Reid has developed more first-time Pro Bowl players (nineteen) than any other coach in the league since becoming the Eagles' coach in 1999, and, like his mentor Mike Holmgren, he has overseen a number of assistants who have gone on to NFL head coaching careers, among them Baltimore Ravens coach John Harbaugh, Minnesota Vikings coach Leslie Frazier, Carolina Panthers coach Ron Rivera, and Cleveland Browns coach Pat Shurmur. Reid is signed with the Eagles through the 2013 season.

PERSONAL LIFE

Reid and his wife, Tammy, live in the affluent Philadelphia suburb of Villanova. They are devout Mormon and members of the Church of Jesus Christ of Latter-Day Saints. As part of his Mormon faith, Reid abstains from drinking alcohol, smoking, and swearing. He was inducted into the Glendale Community College Athletic Hall of Fame in 2003 and into the John Marshall Athletic Hall of Fame in 2012.

On August 5, 2012, Reid's eldest son, Garrett, was found dead in his dorm room at Lehigh University, where he had been working as an assistant to the Eagles' strength and conditioning coaches during the team's annual NFL training camp. While no official cause of death was released, Reid hinted in a statement to the media that his son's death may have been drug related. Among the more than nine hundred people who attended Garrett Reid's funeral were the entire Eagles organization, NFL commissioner Roger Goodell, Patriots coach Bill Belichick, Holmgren, Harbaugh, and numerous other current and former players, coaches, and officials. In the Eagles' 2012 preseason opener, Eagles players honored Garrett by wearing black helmet decals emblazoned with his initials.

Reid and his wife have two other sons, Britt and Spencer, and two daughters, Crosby and Drew Ann.

SUGGESTED READING

Attner, Paul. "A Bear of a Man, a Winner of a Plan." *Sporting News* 23 Dec. 2002: 22–25. Print.

Bowen, Les. *Philadelphia Eagles: The Complete Illustrated History*. Minneapolis: MVP, 2011. Print.

Didinger, Ray, and Robert S. Lyons. *The Eagles Encyclopedia*. Philadelphia: Temple UP, 2005. Print.

Ford, Bob. "The Eagles' New Coach Is the Man with the Plan." *Philly.com*. Philadelphia Media Network, 24 Jan. 1999. Web. 16 Aug. 2012.

Harmon, Dick. "Count on This: Reid Will Have Eagles Prepared." *HeraldExtra.com*. Daily Herald, 27 Jan. 2002. Web. 16 Aug. 2012.

McLane, Jeff. "Back to Coach Reid's Old Stomping Ground." *Philly.com*. Philadelphia Media Network, 18 June 2012. Web. 16 Aug. 2012.

Robinson, Doug. "Reid Soars: Eagles Coach Studied at Foot of LaVell Edwards." *Deseret-News.com*. Deseret News, 5 Feb. 2005. Web. 16 Aug. 2012.

—*Chris Cullen*

Carmen Reinhart

Born: October 7, 1955
Occupation: Economist

Carmen Reinhart is one of the most frequently cited female economists in the field. Reinhart's history-based, data-driven approach to analysis not only separates her from many economists who rely heavily on theory, it has also won her recognition from many respected economists and a great variety of media outlets. In an article

Bloomberg via Getty Images

In addition to having authored and coauthored a variety of articles in many economics journals, Reinhart has also written essays and editorials in mainstream publications such as the *Financial Times*, the *Washington Post*, and the *Wall Street Journal*. In 2011 Reinhart became a senior fellow at the Peterson Institute for International Economics, a nonpartisan research institution in Washington, DC. In an interview with Vivien Lou Chen, Morris Goldstein, who is also a senior fellow at the institute, said of Reinhart: "She's done very important work and looked at things other people didn't notice." In 2010 *Foreign Policy* magazine put Reinhart on its list of Top 100 Global Thinkers.

EARLY LIFE

Carmen M. Reinhart was born Carmen Castellanos on October 7, 1955, in Havana, Cuba. Her father, Luis Alfonso, worked as an accountant, and her mother, Julia Castellanos, was a homemaker. As a young girl Carmen was fascinated by the ships that centuries ago sailed in precise routes from South America to Spain with vast amounts of silver. It was an early indication of her future fascination with economics and its historical roots.

Not long after Carmen was born, the political situation in Cuba changed drastically. In 1959 Fidel Castro overthrew the Cuban leader Fulgencio Batista and became the country's new leader. Carmen and her parents, along with many other Cubans, experienced many changes and a great deal of turmoil during those times. In 1961, in what is known as the Bay of Pigs invasion, the American government tried to overthrow Castro with an army of Cuban exiles. The mission failed.

The following year, Soviet missiles were discovered en route to Cuba, bringing the United States and the Soviet Union to the brink of nuclear war. According to a profile of Castro on the BBC News website, "The superpowers stood eyeball to eyeball, but it was the Soviet leader who gave way, pulling his missiles out of Cuba in return for a secret withdrawal of US weapons from Turkey. Fidel Castro, though, had become America's enemy number one." According to a profile of Castro on biography.com, "On May 1, Castro announced an end to democratic elections in Cuba and denounced American imperialism. Then at year's end, Castro declared himself a Marxist-Leninist and announced the Cuban government was adopting communist economic and political policies." It was in this political climate that Carmen and her family left Havana for the United States in the mid-1960s. Carmen was ten years old at the time. In California her father worked as a carpenter and her mother as a seamstress.

for *Bloomberg News* (Aug. 27, 2010, online), Vivien Lou Chen wrote, "Reinhart's work in the past 20 years has proved prescient, which she says is her proudest accomplishment." Chen continued, "In 1992, as a researcher at the Washington-based International Monetary Fund (IMF), she and Columbia University economist Guillermo Calvo wrote about the likelihood of abrupt reversals of capital flows into Latin America. That was before the Mexican peso collapse of late 1994. In 1996, a year before the Asian financial meltdown, she co-wrote a paper documenting the links between banking and currency crises."

Since 2001 Reinhart has frequently collaborated with Harvard University economist Kenneth S. Rogoff. One of their most significant works is the book *This Time Is Different: Eight Centuries of Financial Folly* (2009), which true to Reinhart's style heavily relies on history and data and presents a detailed analysis of economic crises of the past eight hundred years. Jon Hilsenrath for the *Wall Street Journal* (Feb. 5, 2010, online) called it "one of the most important economic books of 2009," and Ezra Klein for the *Washington Post* (Aug. 6, 2011) made the case that the book is "perhaps the finest study of financial crises ever published." *This Time Is Different* became a best seller and has been translated into thirteen languages, including Chinese, Japanese, Russian, Spanish, Italian, Swedish, and Turkish.

EDUCATION

In her late teens, Carmen moved to Miami, Florida. After taking an economics course at a Miami community college, she decided to pursue the field further and enrolled at Florida International University in Miami to study economics. After receiving a bachelor's degree in 1978, Carmen attended Columbia University in New York City, where she studied with such prominent economists as Robert Mundell, who acted as her thesis adviser and would go on to win the Nobel Prize for economics two decades later in 1999. She received a master of arts degree in 1980 and a master of philosophy degree in 1981. At Columbia she met her future husband, economist Vincent Reinhart, with whom she would later go on to coauthor various economics papers. They married in August 1981.

After marrying and receiving her master's degrees, Carmen Reinhart decided to put a hold on her doctoral education and entered the business world. From 1982–86 she worked as an economist at Bear Stearns, which at the time was a large international financial institution. She spent her last year at Bear Stearns working as a chief economist after which she returned to Columbia University. She received her PhD in 1988.

CAREER

After graduating from Columbia, Reinhart joined the International Monetary Fund (IMF) in Washington, DC. The IMF is a part of the United Nations that assists member governments with economic development. According to its official website, the organization "provides policy advice and financing to members in economic difficulties and also works with developing nations to help them achieve macroeconomic stability and reduce poverty." Reinhart worked as an economist at the IMF until 1994, and in 1995 she was promoted to senior economist, a position she held until 1996. Writing for the *New York Times* (July 4, 2010), Catherine Rampell said of Reinhart's tenure at the IMF, "She honed her knack for economic archaeology at the I.M.F., spending several years performing 'checkups' on member countries to make sure they were in good economic health." Rampell also talked about Reinhart's collaboration with fellow female economist Graciela Kaminsky on the paper "The Twin Crises." She noted, "The article looked at the interaction between banking and currency crises, and why contemporary theory couldn't explain why those ugly events usually happened together. The paper bore one of Ms. Reinhart's hallmarks: a vast web of data, compiled from 20 countries over several decades."

In 1996 Reinhart left the IMF to join the teaching staff of the University of Maryland as an associate professor of economics. From 1998 to 2001 Reinhart served as the director of the university's International Security and Economic Policy program. In 2000 she was promoted to professor, and she held that post until 2009.

In 2001 Reinhart returned to the IMF for two more years. She was appointed deputy director and senior policy adviser by chief economist Kenneth S. Rogoff, who thought highly of her work. Speaking to Rampell, Rogoff explained why he wanted to work with Reinhart, "Carmen in many ways pioneered a bigger segment in economics, this push to look at history more. She was just so ahead of the curve."

In her profile of Rogoff and Reinhart for the *New York Times*, Rampell observed that although Reinhart has a big following among economists, "She says she feels that the heavyweights of her profession have looked down upon her research as useful but too simplistic." Reinhart explained, "You know, everything is simple when it's clearly explained. It's like with Sherlock Holmes. He goes through this incredible deductive process from Point A to Point B, and by the time he explains everything, it makes so much sense that it sounds obvious and simple." Although Reinhart left her post at the IMF in 2003, she continued to collaborate with Rogoff.

BOOKS AND PUBLICATIONS

In January 2008, at the American Economics Association annual conference in New Orleans, Reinhart and Rogoff presented a paper they had written, entitled "Is the 2007 US Sub-Prime Financial Crisis So Different? An International Comparison." The paper compared the United States' subprime mortgage crisis of 2007 to eighteen earlier crises in the developed world. According to an article in the *Economist* (Jan. 12, 2008), Reinhart and Rogoff demonstrate "that, although details may vary, banking crises follow the same broad script. Each blow-up is preceded by rising home and equity prices; an acceleration in capital inflows driven by optimistic foreign investors; a rapid build-up of debt; and—immediately before the storm hits—an inverted V-shaped path for the economy, with growth first picking up and then faltering." The review further observed, "The years just before the start of the subprime meltdown fit the Reinhart-Rogoff template remarkably well." Later that month, in an interview on National Public Radio's program *Morning Edition* (Jan. 23, 2008), Reinhart said that an economic slowdown was all but a certainty that year. "We would be incredibly lucky if we didn't have one," she said. Once again, Reinhart's prediction was accurate. Later that year, in September 2008, the world was shaken by a far-reaching financial crisis.

The same month of the following year saw the publication of Reinhart and Rogoff's book *This Time Is Different: Eight Centuries of Financial Folly* (2009), which had its roots in the subprime financial crisis paper they presented at the American Economics Association conference. The book, which was a great success with economists and a best seller, offered more data and historical analysis than is typical for most contemporary economists, whose publications tend to be heavy on theory. Speaking to Rampell, Rogoff said, "The mainstream of academic research in macroeconomics puts theoretical coherence and elegance first, and investigating the data second."

Rampell provided some context for the authors' approach, stating, "In the past, other economists often took the same empirical approach as the Reinhart-Rogoff team. But this approach fell into disfavor over the last few decades as economists glorified financial papers that were theory-rich and data-poor. Much of that theory-driven work, critics say, is built on the same disassembled and reassembled sets of data points—generally from just the last 25 years or so and from the same handful of rich countries." Rampell then made the case that Reinhart and Rogoff's book is having a palpable influence on economics and the study of financial crises. She noted, "In the wake of the recent crisis, a few economists—like Professors Reinhart and Rogoff, and other like-minded colleagues like Barry Eichengreen and Alan Taylor—have been encouraging others in their field to look beyond hermetically sealed theoretical models and into the historical record."

The book's historical examination is broad, covering eight hundred years and sixty-six countries. In fact, the book's title, *This Time Is Different*, is a reference to the belief of many investors who think that they have found a fail-proof investment approach and that "this time is really different." The book delves into such topics as sovereign and domestic debt, banking crises, inflation, currency, and subprime mortgage lending, as well as the relationships between them and their implications for the future. In a review for the *Cato Journal* (Winter 2011), Kurt Schuler praised the authors for having "written in a style accessible to a broad audience. . . . The narrative is clear and moves along well, without getting bogged down in trivialities even where the authors are discussing technical points of definition."

In the preface to *This Time Is Different*, the authors point out that although they examine a variety of financial crises over many centuries, there is a common theme to them all: "excessive debt accumulation, whether it be by the government, banks, corporations, or consumers, often poses greater systemic risks than it seems during a boom." In other words, during prosperous times it is usually hard for many to gauge how escalating debts will inevitably become harmful to the economy as a whole.

Schuler wrote, "As well as defaulting on external debt, many governments have defaulted on their domestic debt." He added, "Reinhart and Rogoff's work here is the most novel part of the book, because before their efforts, long-term international data on domestic debt were severely lacking. Especially valuable is their analysis of debt and inflation. . . . Although some countries have graduated from debt crises, banking crises are a recurring phenomenon in rich and poor countries alike." Even when Reinhart and Rogoff discuss topics that have been significantly covered by other economists, they still manage to offer important insights. According to Schuler, their examinations of currency crashes and subprime mortgage crisis in particular "break new ground by showing how frequently crises have been connected with booms and busts in housing markets."

In 2011 Reinhart was appointed the Dennis Weatherstone Senior Fellow at the Peterson Institute for International Economics, a research institute that studies international economic policy. The institute published Reinhart and Rogoff's second book, *A Decade of Debt* (2011), as part of its Policy Analyses in International Economics series. The institute's website states that the work "presents evidence that public debts in the advanced economies have surged in recent years to levels not recorded since the end of World War II, surpassing the heights reached during the First World War and the Great Depression. At the same time, private debt levels, particularly those of financial institutions and households, are in uncharted territory and are (in varying degrees) a contingent liability of the public sector in many countries."

In addition to the publications cited above, Reinhart has also coedited a number of economics books, including *Ratings, Rating Agencies and the Global Financial System* (2002), *Money, Crises, and Transition: Essays in Honor of Guillermo A. Calvo* (2008), *The First Global Financial Crisis of the 21st Century—Part I: August 2007–May 2008* (2011), and *The First Global Financial Crisis of the 21st Century—Part II, June–December, 2008* (2011). Along with Morris Goldstein and Graciela L. Kaminsky, Reinhart is the coauthor of the economics book *Assessing Financial Vulnerability: An Early Warning System for Emerging Markets* (2000). She has authored and coauthored many economics papers in a variety of journals, including *American Economic Review*, *Cato Journal*, *Economic Journal*, and *World Bank Economic Review*, among many others.

SUGGESTED READING

Chen, Vivien Lou. "Reinhart's Seven More Years of High Unemployment Hit Fed Today." *Bloomberg News*. Bloomberg, 27 Aug. 2010. Web. 12 Jan. 2012.

Hilsenrath, Jon. "Q & A: Carmen Reinhart on Greece, US Debt, and Other 'Scary Scenarios.'" *Wall Street Journal*. Dow Jones, 5 Feb. 2010. Web. 12 Jan. 2012.

Klein, Ezra. "Let's Call It the 'Great Contraction.'" *Washington Post* 6 Aug. 2011: A7. Print.

Rampell, Catherine. "They Did Their Homework (800 Years of It)." *New York Times* 4 July, 2010: BU1. Print.

Schuler, Kurt. *"This Time Is Different: Eight Centuries of Financial Folly."* Cato Journal 31.1 (Winter 2011): 151. Print.

—*Dmitry Kiper*

Getty Images

Manon Rhéaume

Born: February 24, 1972
Occupation: Hockey player

Manon Rhéaume was thrust into the spotlight in September 1992, when she received an invitation to attend training camp for the National Hockey League (NHL) team Tampa Bay Lightning. Although Phil Esposito, the Lightning's president and general manager, conceded that the invitation was a publicity stunt, Rhéaume capitalized on the opportunity. "When I started playing hockey I was the only girl and, often, I wasn't chosen for the top teams because I was a girl," she told Kristen Odland for the *Calgary Herald* (24 Jan. 2009). "Here and there, I [was] fortunate people didn't let that stop them from choosing me . . . they just wanted the best goaltender. . . . So, when I got invited to Tampa Bay—at that point, I didn't care why they invited me. I had an opportunity to play at the highest level possible. I didn't want to have any regrets." Rhéaume's appearance during an exhibition game marked the first time that a woman had played in a men's professional hockey league, thus elevating her to pioneer status. She has since played for various men's hockey teams, most recently the Flint Generals.

EARLY LIFE

Manon Rhéaume was born on February 24, 1972, to Nicole and Pierre Rhéaume in the tiny ski-resort town of Lac-Beauport, a suburb of Quebec City, Quebec. She is the middle of three children, with an older brother, Martin, and a younger one named Pascal. She first learned to skate as a three-year-old and started donning goalie pads at the age of five, after being introduced to the sport of ice hockey by her father, a contractor who managed the town's outdoor skating rink and also served as the coach of his sons' novice hockey team. Rhéaume would wear padded clothing and block shots during practice sessions in her family's backyard rink. "My mom thought I was crazy," she told Mark Johnson for the Milwaukee *Journal Sentinel* (8 Aug. 2005) "At the time, nobody was playing hockey if you were a girl."

At age five, Rhéaume made her competitive debut, patrolling the net for her brothers' team at a tournament. "I said to my father, 'I would like to be your goaltender.' He laughed. But then he said, 'Why not? You take shots from your brothers at home,'" she recalled to William Plummer for *People* (28 Sep. 1992). Growing up, Rhéaume often competed against boys while playing youth hockey in the Quebec City area. "Manon was always too strong for the girls," her mother told Christopher Sullivan for the Associated Press (22 Nov. 1992).

However, Rhéaume, who also participated in other sports for a time, including ballet, baseball, and skiing, faced discrimination and some backlash for playing on all-boys' teams. "So many parents think their boy should go into the National Hockey League," she said to Linda Kay for the *Chicago Tribune* (16 Dec. 1991). "When I would try out for a spot as a goalie, some parents thought I was taking a position that should have gone to their boy."

YOUTH PIONEER

The eleven-year-old Rhéaume made history in 1984, when she became the first girl ever to take part in the world's largest and most prestigious international youth-hockey event: the Quebec International Pee-Wee Hockey Tournament, an annual eleven-day competition held each

February in Quebec City. By the age of twelve, Rhéaume was playing pee-wee hockey on a year-round basis. "It was my passion," she told Plummer. Rhéaume achieved another milestone by becoming the first girl to play in the bantam division (for ages thirteen and fourteen) at the double-A level, also known as tier-two hockey, which is regarded as youth hockey's second-highest competitive skill level.

However, Rhéaume became discouraged when she was not given the opportunity to try out for any tier-one teams in the midget division (ages fifteen to seventeen), a step below the junior hockey level, the top players of which are recruited into the professional ranks. When she turned seventeen years old, she took a hiatus from her favorite sport and focused instead on her studies, enrolling at a junior college in Sainte-Foy, now part of Quebec City. However, after her first year of school, the eighteen-year-old Rhéaume resumed playing hockey and joined a women's team in Sherbrooke. In 1991, the competitive squad won a regional tournament to advance to the Esso Women's Nationals, where Rhéaume's team lost in the finals to the North York Aeros of Ontario.

Following the end of the 1991 season, Rhéaume received a surprise invitation to attend training camp with the Louisville Jaguars, an all-men's junior ice-hockey squad whose roster also included her younger brother, Pascal. (Founded in 1990 as the Saint-Antoine Rapidos, the Jaguars—since renamed the Saint-Jérôme Panthers—were at the time a farm team of the Trois-Rivières Draveurs, who competed in the Quebec Major Junior Hockey League, one of the three leagues that comprise the Canadian Hockey League.) Rhéaume beat out four other male candidates for the backup goalie position on the tier-two team.

In late November 1991 she received a call-up to the Draveurs squad due to an injury sustained by the starting goaltender. Rhéaume, who served as the backup to second-string goalie Jocelyn Thibault, made her debut against the Granby Bisons. Rhéaume made history with her appearance, becoming the first female goalie to play in the Quebec Major Junior Hockey League and the first female player to appear in a men's top-level hockey game. She played for seventeen minutes, allowing three goals, and was removed from the game after a puck hit her protective mask, leaving a gash over her right eye; the wound would later require stitches.

GOLD MEDAL FOR TEAM CANADA
In 1992, Rhéaume was named a member of the Canadian national women's hockey squad. She competed in the International Ice Hockey Federation (IIHF) World Women's Championships, a prestigious international women's tournament that was held in April in Tampere,

Finland. The Canadian team dominated the first-round competition, defeating China, Denmark, and Sweden to advance to the final round. After a decisive four-run semifinal victory over Finland, Team Canada defeated the US in the finals, scoring eight unanswered goals. During her team's dominating performance, Rhéaume earned three wins, including two shutouts, and only allowed two goals. She was named to the tournament's all-star squad.

TURNING PROFESSIONAL
In August 1992, Rhéaume accepted an invitation to training camp from the Tampa Bay Lightning. In doing so, she became not only the first woman to try out for a club in the National Hockey League (NHL) but also the first to sign a professional hockey deal. On September 23, 1992, Rhéaume achieved another milestone by becoming the first woman to play in an NHL exhibition game. She played for one period and allowed two goals while blocking seven of nine shots during a preseason loss to the St. Louis Blues. In the wake of her achievement, Rhéaume became an international phenomenon, appearing on several high-profile television shows, including Late Night with David Letterman, The Today Show, and Entertainment Tonight.

In November, after failing to make the team out of training camp, Rhéaume signed a three-year contract with the Atlanta Knights, Tampa Bay's top minor-league squad in the International Hockey League (IHL). On December 13, 1992, she became the first woman to play a regular-season game in the IHL. Rhéaume, who replaced starter David Littman during the second period, played for five minutes; she blocked three shots and gave up only one goal against the Salt Lake Golden Eagles, who won 4–1.

Rhéaume made headlines again on April 10, 1993, when she made her first start in goal for the Knights in front of a home crowd of twenty thousand people. The appearance marked the first time that a woman had started a regular-season professional hockey game. Although Rhéaume had twenty-five blocked shots, she allowed six goals to the visiting Cincinnati Cyclones before being removed during the third period for an extra skater. The Cyclones scored two more empty net goals to win 8–6.

Rhéaume's next appearance for the Knights came during a preseason game against the Boston Bruins in October 1993. Following a poor performance at the start of the 1993–94 regular season, during which Rhéaume surrendered three first-period goals en route to a 4–2 loss, the Knights demoted her to the now-defunct Knoxville Cherokees of the East Coast Hockey League (ECHL), another Tampa Bay Lightning affiliate. On November 6, 1993, Rhéaume, the third-string goalie, was designated to start against the Johnstown Chiefs. She played the entire game, blocking thirty-two out of thirty-eight shots for a 9–6 victory. This achievement earned Rhéaume the distinction of being the second female goalie to start and win a professional hockey game; Erin Whitten of the Toledo Storm was the first.

In February 26, 1994, Rhéaume, who had recorded another victory and a tie in three more games with the Cherokees, was traded to the Nashville Knights, a former affiliate of the Tampa Bay Lightning. As a member of the Nashville Knights (1993–94), she recorded three wins in four games while making 109 saves and surrendering twelve goals.

WINNING MORE MEDALS

In April 1994, Rhéaume was part of the Canadian women's national hockey team that traveled to Lake Placid, New York, to defend its 1992 gold medal at the IIHF Women's World Championships. Team Canada advanced to the final round of the tournament, following first-round victories against China, Norway, and Sweden. After defeating Finland in the semifinals, the Canadian squad faced off against Team USA in a finals rematch and captured their second consecutive IIHF World Championship gold medal. Rhéaume compiled a record of three wins in four games, with six goals allowed, during Team Canada's gold-medal run. For the second time in her career, she was voted to the tournament's all-star team.

During the summer Rhéaume played for the New Jersey Rockin Rollers, a squad that competed in Roller Hockey International (RHI), a now-defunct men's inline-hockey league. By November of that year, Rhéaume had returned to the IHL after a trade from the Nashville Knights to the Las Vegas Thunder; in 1994–95 she blocked fourteen shots and allowed three goals in two games. Following her brief stint with the Thunder, Rhéaume spent 1994–95 with another Las Vegas–based team: the Aces, a semiprofessional squad in the Pacific Southwest Hockey League (PSHL). That same season she also suited up for the Tallahassee Tiger Sharks of the ECHL, giving up four goals and making twelve saves in her only appearance with the team. Rhéaume continued to garner attention in 1995, when she appeared in an exhibition match, also known as a friendly game, with VEU Feldkirch, an Austrian men's ice-hockey club.

Between 1995 and 1997, Rhéaume played for two professional roller-hockey teams in the RHI, the Ottawa Loggers and the Sacramento River Rats. In October 1996, she traveled with the women's national hockey team to compete at the Pacific Rim Three Nations Cup, where Team Canada reached the finals against perennial rivals Team USA. Following her team's shutout victory, Rhéaume added another gold medal to her record. A month later, she signed a deal with the Nevada-based Reno Renegades, a now-defunct minor-league ice-hockey squad in the West Coast Hockey League (WCHL). During the 1996–97 regular season, Rhéaume appeared in eleven games, making 262 saves and allowing forty goals while amassing a record of two wins, three losses, and a tie.

In the summer of 1998, the first year that women's hockey made its Olympic debut, Rhéaume rejoined the national hockey squad for the Winter Games in Nagano, Japan. Team Canada, the gold-medal favorites, advanced to the medal round after compiling a first-round record of four wins and one loss to finish second behind the undefeated Team USA. The two teams went head-to-head in the finals, where the American squad finally triumphed over Rhéaume and her compatriots to claim the gold medal.

BLAZING NEW TRAILS

After winning silver at the 1998 Olympic Games, Rhéaume took a sabbatical from playing hockey in 1998. She spent the 1999–2000 season serving as goaltending coach for the University of Minnesota-Duluth (UMD) Bulldogs, the women's ice-hockey team. In 1999, Rhéaume was not selected to be part of the Canadian women's hockey team that captured gold at the 2000 IIHF World Women's Championships, hosted that year in Canada. She officially announced her decision to retire from international competition in July 2000, following an eight-year stint as the goaltender for the Canadian national women's squad.

In search of a new challenge, Rhéaume signed a contract in September 2000 to play forward for the Montreal Wingstars in the National Women's Hockey League (NWHL). After ending the 2000–2001 season with a record of thirty wins, six losses, and four ties to finish first in the Eastern Division, the Wingstars were eliminated in the first round of the playoffs by their division rivals, the Sainte-Julie Pantheres.

While playing for the Wingstars, Rhéaume was hired by Mission Hockey, an athletic equipment manufacturer in Irvine, California. As the company's head of global marketing, she spent three years helping to create and market the Betty Flyweight, a brand of skates specifically designed for women. In 2003 Rhéaume started working as the director of marketing and coordinator of girls' hockey programs at the Powerade Iceport, a five-rink sports facility in Cudahy, Wisconsin. Two years later, she accepted a position in Farmington Hills, Michigan, as the director of marketing and sales at the Central Collegiate Hockey Association (CCHA), one of the country's premier men's hockey conferences.

Rhéaume was a member of the Little Caesars senior women's amateur squad that won the 2008 USA Hockey Women's Senior A National Championships in West Chester,

Pennsylvania. That same year she created an eponymous foundation with the goal of granting scholarships to young female athletes. She also sought to kick start her playing career by attending the training camp of the Port Huron Icehawks, a Michigan-based minor-league team in the IHL. In 2009 Rhéaume was signed by the Minnesota Whitecaps of the Western Women's Hockey League (WWHL). She was the goaltender for the team, which reached the finals of the inaugural 2009 Clarkson Cup before losing to the Montreal Stars. Rhéaume made headlines again in April of that year when she played for the Flint Generals of the IHL, becoming the third woman to suit up for the men's team.

PERSONAL LIFE

Rhéaume, the founder of an eponymous international women's invitational hockey tournament, published her autobiography, *Manon: Alone in Front of the Net*, in 1993. She was also the subject of *Manon Rhéaume: Woman behind the Mask*, an hour-long documentary that aired on Canadian television in 2000. She has a son, Dylan, from her first marriage in 1998 to former hockey player Gerry St. Cyr, whom she later divorced. Since then, she has reportedly remarried and has a second son.

SUGGESTED READING

Brody, Susan. "100 Greatest Female Athletes." *Sports Illustrated Women*. CNN/Sports Illustrated, n.d. Web. 12 July 2012.

Caputo, Pat. "When in Rhéaume: Female Youth Players Follow in Pioneer's Footsteps." *Oakland Press*. Oakland Press, 12 Nov. 2009. Web. 12 July 2012.

Dillman, Lisa. "Manon Among Boys: Professional Hockey's First Female Players Makes First Start Tonight for Minor League Team." *Los Angeles Times*. Los Angeles Times, 10 Apr. 1993. Web. 12 July 2012.

Johnson, Mark. "Female Hockey Pioneer Calls the Shots Now: Manon Rhéaume Is Coaching and Directing Girls Hockey in the Milwaukee Area." *Madison.com*. Madison.com, 8 Aug. 2005. Web. 12 July 2012.

Odland, Kristen. "Rhéaume Helped Make Hockey a Girls' Game." *Canada.com*. Postmedia Network, 24 Jan. 2009. Web. 12 July 2012.

Plummer, William. "The Puck Stops Here." *People* 28 Sep. 1992: 85–88. Print.

Shine, T. M. "Girl With A Goal: The First Woman to Try Out for a Professional Hockey Team Seems Ready, Willing, Able and Coolly Confident." *Sun Sentinel* [South Florida]. Tribune, 22 Sep. 1992. Web. 12 July 2012.

Sullivan, Christopher. "On Ice and Off, 'a Lot of Pressure, a Lot of Action.'" *Los Angeles Times*. Los Angeles Times, 22 Nov. 1992. Web. 12 July 2012.

Villiers, Kelly. "Knights Goalie Adjusting to Male Sports World." *Seattle Times*. Seattle Times, 10 Jan. 1993. Web. 12 July 2012.

—*Bertha Muteba*

Adam Riess

Born: December 16, 1969
Occupation: Astrophysicist, educator

"The research that leads to a Nobel Prize in physics can sometimes be a little obscure," Michael D. Lemonick wrote for *Time* magazine (5 Oct. 2011). "In 1990, for example, three scientists got the nod 'for their pioneering investigations concerning deep inelastic scattering of electrons on protons and bound neutrons.' Got that? The next year, the prize went to a scientist 'for discovering that methods developed for studying order phenomena in simple systems can be generalized to more complex forms of matter.' But sometimes, you just can't help saying, 'Wow!' and maybe: 'What took the Nobel folks so long?'" The discovery that elicited a "Wow" from Lemonick was made, in part, by Nobel laureate Adam Riess, a physicist from Johns Hopkins University. Riess and his colleagues had found that the universe, contrary to previous beliefs, was expanding faster and faster as time went on, and that the phenomenon was probably due to a mysterious force known as dark energy, which is now thought to comprise fully three-quarters of the universe.

EARLY LIFE AND EDUCATION

Adam Riess was born on December 16, 1969, in Washington, DC. His father, Michael, was a US Navy engineer who served during the 1960s as chief scientist for antisubmarine warfare. He later moved the family to Warren, New Jersey, where he owned and operated a frozen food distributorship and pursued various other entrepreneurial ventures. Riess's mother, Doris, maintained a thriving practice as a clinical psychologist. Riess's paternal grandfather was the respected journalist Curt Riess, who was best known for his reporting during World War II, as well as for such books as *The Nazis Go Underground* (1944), about Germany's efforts at espionage, and *The Berlin Story* (1952), a cultural history of that city. Adam, the youngest of Doris and Michael's children, has two older sisters: Gail Saltz, a psychiatrist and media commentator, and Holly Hagerman, an artist who specializes in oil portraits.

As a child, Riess loved sports and was particularly enamored of soccer. In addition to his physical prowess, Riess exhibited great intellectual curiosity. "Besides pestering my family with questions," he wrote in a statement posted on

© The Nobel Foundation. Photo: Ulla Montan

the Shaw Prize website, "I conducted my own 'experiments' to learn about the world around me including sticking wires into electrical outlets, tasting everything in the spice rack and cutting earthworms in half—all to see what would happen." He was exceptionally interested in dinosaurs and toyed with the idea of becoming a paleontologist one day.

Along with his sisters, who were also precocious, Riess built a tree house when he was about eight years old. The difference between the Riess children's structure and others in their suburban neighborhood, however, was that they constructed a working telegraph line for theirs. Excited about the burgeoning computer technology of the day, Riess had learned programming by the time he was eleven and was teaching an adult education course in computer use by the time he was in his teens.

Although his children were undeniably bright, Riess's father nonetheless insisted that they learn the value of physical labor, and all three were made to work at a delicatessen he once owned. On one memorable day a customer became ill in the restroom. Sent to clean the mess, Riess balked. "[My father] lit into me later about that," he recalled to Michael Anft for *Johns Hopkins Magazine* (Feb. 2008). "He told me, 'You have to do what you have to do. You think you're better than everyone else there?' He let me know that there were people who had to do that kind of work for a living. What I took from all that was that I had to really work hard to do

the things I like. I was terrified of having to do something where I would just watch the clock."

Riess attended the Watchung Hills Regional High School, one of New Jersey's most highly ranked secondary schools. Designated both a National Merit Scholar and Garden State Distinguished Scholar, he served as president of the National Honor Society, and during his senior year he won prizes for outstanding performances in calculus and biology. In addition to his love of science, he maintained a deep interest in history, especially the American Civil War. He also worked on the school newspaper and was a valued member of the Watchung Hills Academic Team. When he graduated in 1988, he was named salutatorian.

Upon leaving Watchung Hills, Riess entered the Massachusetts Institute of Technology (MIT), where he majored in physics. He had maintained his love for history and chose it as his minor field of study; his final research paper, which drew upon his deep knowledge of sports, focused on the so-called Black Sox scandal of 1919. At MIT Riess was a member of Phi Delta Theta and roomed at a fraternity house overlooking the Charles River. As in high school, Riess excelled, earning a 4.94 grade point average (on a 5.0 scale) and being elected to the academic honors society Phi Beta Kappa. While at MIT he served during the summer as an intern at the Lawrence Livermore National Laboratory, a California-based government institution with a mission to use "science and technology in the national interest," particularly in regard to issues of national security. At Livermore Riess was involved in the search for Massive Compact Halo Objects (MACHOs)—bodies of matter that emit no light, such as neutron stars or red dwarf stars. In 1992 Riess graduated from MIT with a bachelor's degree and embarked on graduate studies.

A NEW CHAPTER AT HARVARD

Riess next enrolled at Harvard University, thinking that he might become involved in the search for extraterrestrial intelligence (SETI). After realizing that he might never gather enough data to support a thesis, he changed his focus. "I knew next to nothing about astronomy or astrophysics. But I was intrigued with ideas like, How will the universe end? and, How long has it been here? These were the big questions," he told Anft. "What I was amazed to find was that this wasn't just a subject for speculation. You could go out with a telescope and answer them. It may be difficult, but there's a methodology." Riess began studying under Robert Kirshner, a renowned physics professor who had earned a global reputation for his research on supernovae.

A supernova occurs when a star explodes at the end of its life, giving off an incredible burst of light that can be seen at distances of up to

10 billion light-years. This can happen in two ways. In the first case, a stars run out of fuel and cannot sustain itself against its own weight. The central part subsequently collapses, and the outer layers of the star fall in on the core and then rebound in a massive explosion. In the second set of circumstances, matter piling up on the compressed core of an already dead star reaches sufficient density to trigger the explosion. In an article for the *New York Times* (18 Feb. 2003), Dennis Overbye explained that "the exploding stars of choice are known as Type Ia. They originate on dense burned-out cinders about the size of Earth that are known to astronomers as white dwarfs." He added that "if a white dwarf has a companion star, it can have a violent, brief resurrection as a Type Ia supernova. In that case, the intense gravity of the white dwarf can steal material from its neighbor. When its mass exceeds a critical limit, about 1.4 times the mass of the sun, the star destroys itself in a fury as bright as four billion suns." The brightness of these Type Ia explosions can be used to help calculate their distance. Because they had exploded when the universe was young, the supernovae farthest away from the Earth could provide valuable information to scientists about conditions at that time.

Riess proved to be a talented graduate student. When assigned to teach undergraduates, he frequently structured his classes along the lines of a game show so that they would be encouraged to participate. He was especially adept at conveying complex concepts to laypeople; later, as a full professor at Johns Hopkins, he began regularly teaching a course dubbed Great Discoveries in Astronomy and Astrophysics, geared toward humanities majors. Working closely with Kirshner and another Harvard professor, William Press, he learned to make precise measurements with telescopes and analyze the data retrieved. His doctoral thesis, "The Multicolor Light Curve Shape Method," detailed a method by which scientists could account for the effect of variables—such as the presence of cosmic dust or differing luminosities and colors—when measuring supernovae. The paper later won him the annual Astronomical Society of the Pacific (ASP) Robert J. Trumpler Award, given for a thesis of great significance by a North American doctoral candidate. Riess earned his PhD from Harvard in 1996.

THE HIGH-Z SUPERNOVA TEAM
Upon earning his doctoral degree, Riess accepted a three-year Miller Research Fellowship from the University of California, Berkeley. He also joined the High-Z Supernova Team, a group of international scientists. High-Z is a reference to redshift (represented by a "z" in scientific equations) which is the Doppler effect observed when a celestial object is moving farther away

from Earth. A few years before, Saul Perlmutter, with whom Riess would eventually share many of the science world's top honors, had begun leading a team at the Lawrence Berkeley National Laboratory to meticulously search the cosmos for supernovae. Now, Schmidt's competing team, which also included Kirshner, tapped Riess to analyze data for a project titled "Measuring the Cosmic Deceleration and Global Geometry of the Universe with Type Ia Supernovae." Although the work was sure to be painstaking and unglamorous, Riess agreed. (Somewhat ironically, his office at the university was located only a short distance from that of Perlmutter at the national lab.)

Soon, both teams were collecting confusing data. The expansion of the universe that started with the big bang some thirteen million years ago had long been thought to be slowing, as the outward push of individual galaxies was affected by gravitational pull. New data, however, seemed to be showing that the expansion was instead speeding up. "The Universe is behaving like a driver who slows down approaching a red stoplight and then hits the accelerator when the light turns green," Riess explained to David Whitehouse for the BBC News (4 Apr. 2001), using one of the vivid metaphors for which he has become known. He has also compared the galaxies to raisins in a loaf of bread made with a lot of yeast, pushing vigorously away from each other as the loaf rises.

Although Riess was reassured somewhat when he found out that Perlmutter's team was attaining similar results, he still worried that he had made a mistake in his calculations. They were not the only scientists ever stymied by such an issue. "I liken it to if you took a pair of keys and threw them up in the air with the purpose of measuring how fast they fall back down, to measure how much the Earth tugs at your keys, and then they went up instead," Riess told Ira Flatow, the host of the National Public Radio program *Science Friday* (16 Mar. 2012). "You would be very confused, and that's the position my colleagues and I were in, in 1998, when we saw the universe not slowing down as we expected but actually speeding up, implying the existence of this very mysterious dark energy."

The dark energy to which he was referring was a source of much excitement in the scientific community. Physicists had long spoken of four basic forces: gravity, a strong force that holds atoms together, a weak force that keeps electrons in place, and electromagnetism. Now, suddenly, it seemed that a fifth force—dark energy—not only existed but made up the vast majority of the universe. "Dark energy is the name given to an unexplained force that is drawing galaxies away from each other, against the pull of gravity, at an accelerated pace," Clara Moskowitz wrote for Space.com (27 Apr. 2009). She added: "Dark energy is a bit like anti-gravity. Where gravity pulls things together at the more local level, dark energy tugs them apart on the grander scale." A few days after the High-Z Team announced their findings about the expansion of the universe, Perlmutter's team confirmed that they had reached the same conclusion. The editors of *Science* magazine deemed it 1998's "breakthrough of the year."

A MOVE TO BALTIMORE

Despite the accolades and excitement, Riess knew that further investigation was needed. He wanted to measure supernovae even farther away—from the era before dark energy began to exert its pull, roughly seven billion years ago. If the pace of expansion was truly accelerating, those supernovae would appear brighter than expected. The only telescope capable of helping was the powerful Hubble, and in 1999 Riess joined Baltimore's Space Telescope Science Institute, where it was housed. In 2001 Riess and his colleagues found a supernova 11 billion light-years away that was, indeed, twice as bright as expected. The Hubble telescope had recorded it two years earlier, but it had gone unnoticed until Riess reviewed the images. (He has described looking at such images as akin to viewing a television screen full of static.) Still, he continued to search for corroborating evidence, a task made easier when the Hubble was fitted with a new, more powerful camera. Within a few years Riess had measured the dozen most distant supernovae ever found, confirming his theory.

AWARDS

Riess has since received numerous prizes for his work. In 2006, the year he joined the faculty at Johns Hopkins University, he shared the prestigious Shaw Prize for Astronomy with Perlmutter and Schmidt. In 2008 he was awarded a fellowship from the John D. and Catherine T. MacArthur Foundation. The fellowship includes a $500,000 monetary award, nicknamed the Genius Grant. His biggest honor came in 2011, when he received a call from Sweden early one morning. The caller, from the Royal Swedish Academy of Sciences in Stockholm, informed him that he would be sharing that year's Nobel Prize in Physics with Perlmutter and Schmidt, for their "discovery of the accelerating expansion of the Universe through observations of distant supernovae." Perlmutter received half of the 10 million kroner prize (about $750,000), while Riess and Schmidt each received a quarter (about $325,000).

PERSONAL LIFE

Since 1998 Riess has been married to Nancy Joy Schondorf, an industrial designer whom he had met while at MIT. When Riess left for Harvard, the pair communicated by blinking flashlights across the Charles River. They have a daughter, Gabrielle, born in 2004, and a son, Noah, born in 2010. When Gabrielle was a toddler, Riess referred to her as "my favorite supernova."

Despite the sometimes cutthroat competition of the science world, Riess has been widely praised as a generous and gracious person. In his spare time he enjoys watching professional football and collecting historical coins. He has good-naturedly admitted that he cannot identify most constellations and is able to find only the Big Dipper with any degree of accuracy.

SUGGESTED READING

Anft, Michael. "Chasing the Great Beyond." *Johns Hopkins Magazine*. Johns Hopkins University, Feb. 2008. Web. 1 Mar. 2012.
Clark, Stuart. "Heart of Darkness." *New Scientist* 17 Feb. 2007: 28. Print.
Easterbrook, Gregg. "The Revolutionary Ideas of Nobelist Adam Riess." *TheAtlantic.com*. Atlantic Monthly Group, 4 Oct. 2010. Web. 1 Mar. 2012.
Lemonick, Michael D. "The Physics Nobel: Why Einstein Was Wrong About Being Wrong." *Time*. Time, 5 Oct. 2011. Web. 01 Mar. 2012.
Overbye, Dennis. "Scientist at Work: Adam Riess: His Prey: Dark Energy in the Cosmic Abyss." *New York Times* 18 Feb. 2003: F01. Print.

—*Mari Rich*

Mariano Rivera

Born: November 29, 1969
Occupation: Baseball player

"When you talk about the best starting pitchers of all time, there's a lot of different names thrown out. You probably have four or five guys always in the conversation," New York Yankees first baseman Mark Teixeira told Kevin Baxter about teammate Mariano Rivera in an interview for the *Los Angeles Times* (2 Oct. 2011). "When you talk about the greatest relievers of all time, there's only one guy. The conversation begins and ends with Mo." Rivera has been the linchpin of a Yankees dynasty that captured four World Series titles between 1996 and 2000. Over the next decade he withstood injuries and questions about his age to help lead his team to several postseason appearances, culminating in another World Series victory in 2009. Rivera, whom many project as a first-ballot Hall-of-Fame inductee, added to his legacy as the best closer of all time, with his record-setting 608th save in 2012.

EARLY LIFE AND AMATEUR CAREER

Mariano Rivera was born on November 29, 1969, in Panama City, Panama, and grew up in the fishing village of Puerto Caimito. His father, Mariano Rivera Sr., was a fishing boat captain, while Rivera's mother, Delia, stayed home and took care of Rivera and his siblings: an older sister named Delia, and two younger brothers, Alvaro and Giraldo. Rivera first showed an interest in baseball when he was seven. Like many children in Panama, he could not afford equipment, so he fashioned a glove from a cardboard box that he used until the age of twelve, when his father purchased one made of leather. He and his friends often played pick-up games on the beach, on the streets, or on an abandoned field, using tennis balls and bats made of tree branches. However, baseball was not Rivera's only sport. "My main game was soccer; my second game was baseball," Rivera said in an interview with actor Richard Gere for *Gotham* (April/May 2012). He *eventually gave up soccer due to injury and* turned his focus back to baseball. After graduating from Pedro *Pablo* Sanchez High *School when he was sixteen, he* spent the next three years working as a fisherman alongside his father and his uncle, until he was evacuated from a capsizing boat. "It was a job that was way too tough for me," he told Mel Antonen for *USA Today* (9 Oct. 2006).

Rivera subsequently pursued a baseball career, playing shortstop for Panamá Oeste, a local amateur team. While competing at a national tournament, the nineteen-year-old caught the attention of Herb Raybourn, a scout for the Kansas City Royals. "I saw that he could run, he had a good arm and he had good hands, but I didn't think he could be a major league shortstop. So I passed on him," Raybourn recalled to Jack Curry for the *New York Times* (5 July 2009). Rivera made more of an impression at the tournament the next year, when he replaced his team's struggling ace pitcher. Impressed by his pitching, two of Rivera's teammates contacted Chico Heron, a scout for the New York Yankees. Two weeks later Heron invited Rivera to attend a tryout in Panama City, where he again crossed paths with Raybourn, now the Yankees' director of Latin American operations. "The fluidity of his arm is what I liked," Raybourn told Curry. "Plus, his ball had a lot of movement. You could see him being a starter or a reliever."

MINOR LEAGUES WITH THE YANKEES

On February 17, 1990, Raybourn signed Rivera as an undrafted amateur free agent. Months later Rivera traveled to the Yankees' minor-league training facility in Tampa, Florida, to pitch for the Gulf Coast League (GCL) Yankees, the team's affiliate in the Rookie League. In twenty-two appearances (mostly as a reliever), he pitched a total of fifty-two innings, giving up an

Getty Images

earned run while striking out fifty-eight batters. He had an impressive six-win–one-loss record and finished with an earned-run average (ERA) of 0.17. In the last game of the season—Rivera's only appearance as a starting pitcher—he recorded a no-hitter. A year later Rivera was promoted to the Greensboro Hornets, the Yankees' single-A affiliate in the South Atlantic League. Rivera, whom the organization projected as a starting pitcher, made fifteen starts. Despite a disappointing four wins and nine losses, he gave up only thirty-six walks while registering 123 strikeouts in 114 2/3 innings—an impressive walk-to-strikeout ratio. However, the language barrier proved challenging. "My first year, when I was in Tampa, my second year in North Carolina, it was no English. I cried, because I couldn't communicate with my teammates, with my pitching coordinator, my manager—I was frustrated," he confided to Gere.

Undaunted, in 1992 Rivera pitched for the Fort Lauderdale Yankees, the Class A-Advanced affiliate in the Florida State League (FSL). He compiled five wins, three losses, and a 2.28 ERA before undergoing season-ending reconstructive elbow surgery. During the offseason Rivera was made available in the 1992 Major League Baseball (MLB) expansion draft, but neither of the expansion teams (the Colorado Rockies and the Florida Marlins) selected him. He returned to the mound in 1993, making twelve minor-league rehab starts—two for the Gulf Coast Yankees and ten for the Greensboro Hornets. Rivera spent the early part of 1994 with the Tampa Yankees during their first year in the FSL. After compiling three wins and a 2.21 ERA in seven starts to help lead the team's Class A-Advanced affiliate to its first FSL championship, he made the jump to the Double-A level, joining the Albany-Colonie Yankees in the Eastern League. His record of three wins and no losses, coupled with a 2.27 ERA in nine starts, earned him another promotion in 1994, this time to the Columbus Clippers, the team's triple-A affiliate in the International League, for whom he started six games. He struggled, finishing with four wins and two losses, a 5.81 ERA, and twenty-three strikeouts in thirty-one innings.

MAJOR-LEAGUE DEBUT

After starting the 1995 season at Columbus, Rivera made his major-league debut with the Yankees on May 23, when starting pitcher Jimmy Key was placed on the fifteen-day disabled list due to an inflamed tendon in his rotator cuff. Rivera had a forgettable outing, allowing eight hits and five runs before being removed after three and one-third innings; the Yankees lost to the California Angels (now called the Los Angeles Angels of Anaheim) 10–1. Rivera's first major-league victory came against the Oakland Athletics on May 28; he pitched five and one-third innings and gave up seven hits and an earned run in the Yankees' 4–1 win. On June 11 Rivera was demoted to the Yankees' triple-A club in Columbus, following a disappointing start in which he lasted only two and two-thirds innings while yielding seven hits and four earned runs to the Seattle Mariners in the Yankees 10–7 victory.

Rivera rested his sore shoulder for two weeks, and when he resumed throwing, the velocity on his fastball, which had previously registered in the eighty-eight- to ninety-mile-per-hour range, inexplicably experienced a sudden increase. His velocity reached ninety-six miles per hour during his five-inning, no-hit performance (shortened by rain) against the Rochester Red Wings on June 26. The outing caught the attention of Yankees management, who had considered including Rivera in a trade with the Detroit Tigers for the starting pitcher David Wells. "And right about that time, Mariano's velocity in the minors jumped to 95–96 [miles per hour]," Gene Michael, the team's general manager, told John Harper for the *New York Daily News* (30 June 2009). "I didn't believe it when I saw our report, but I checked it out with scouts from other teams who were there and it was true. At that point there was no way I was trading him."

On July 4 Rivera was recalled to the major leagues and started against the Chicago White Sox, giving up no earned runs and striking out eleven batters in eight innings while leading the Yankees to a 4–1 victory. After mixed results in his next three starts, Rivera was mostly used as a middle reliever for the remainder of his rookie

season and finished with a mediocre win-loss record of 5–3 and a 5.51 ERA. The Yankees, however, came in second to the Boston Red Sox in the American League East Division and earned a postseason berth—their first in fourteen years. Rivera was named to the roster for the best-of-five American League Division Series (ALDS) against the Seattle Mariners. His postseason debut came in game two—an extra-inning victory in which he threw three scoreless innings and was declared the winning pitcher. Rivera also held the opposition scoreless in game three, which the Yankees lost by three runs, and in the fifth and final game—an extra-inning loss for the Yankees.

FIRST WORLD SERIES CHAMPIONSHIP

In 1996, the Yankees' first season under manager Joe Torre (1996–2007), Rivera was designated as the set-up man for John Wetteland, the team's closer. His new role required him to come out of the bullpen and pitch the seventh and eighth innings of close games and then make way for Wetteland to face opposing batters in the ninth inning. Rivera quickly established himself as one of the more dominant relief pitchers in the American League, giving up only thirty-four walks, twenty-five runs, and seventy-three hits in 107 2/3 innings while posting eight wins and three losses, along with a 2.09 ERA. He also had 130 strikeouts, breaking the franchise's single-season record previously set by Rich "Goose" Gossage in 1978. Rivera's strong regular-season performance, which helped the Yankees capture the American League East pennant, did not go unheralded. He finished third in the American League (AL) Cy Young pitching award voting and came in twelfth in the voting for the American League's Most Valuable Player (MVP) award.

After besting the Texas Rangers three games to one in the ALDS and winning five games against the Baltimore Orioles in the best-of-seven American League Championship Series (ALCS), the Yankees advanced to the World Series, where they defeated the Atlanta Braves four games to two. Rivera's dominance was again on display during the postseason. He struck out ten and allowed only one earned run, ten hits, and five walks in 14 1/3 innings, earning a World Series ring in his first full season in the major leagues.

YANKEES' CLOSER AND WORLD SERIES MVP

When Wetteland, the World Series MVP, became a free agent after the 1996 season, the Yankees opted not to re-sign him, and instead promoted Rivera to closer in 1997. He initially struggled in his new role, failing to convert three of his first six save opportunities. "The harder I tried, the tougher it got. It was like moving in quicksand. I kept sinking," Rivera told Antonen. "Joe [Torre] told me that, 'As long as you are here, you'll be the closer.' That's exactly what I needed to hear." Rivera eventually found his footing and ended the season with forty-three saves and an ERA of 1.88; he was also named to his first All-Star Game, where he also earned a save. The Yankees placed second in the AL East and advanced to the ALDS. After recording his first save in game one of the series, Rivera surrendered the tying home run in the Yankees' game-four loss to the Cleveland Indians, who won the series in five games.

Rivera overcame this disappointing performance, and over the next several years, he mastered his signature pitch: a hard-breaking, high-velocity cut fastball, which is regarded as one of the best pitches in baseball. His thirty-six saves, along with a 1.91 ERA, during the 1998 regular season helped the Yankees to 114 wins—the most in baseball—and the AL East crown. Rivera gave up no postseason runs. He had two saves in his team's sweep of the Texas Rangers in the ALDS and added another (against the Indians) in the ALCS, which the Yankees won in five games to advance to the World Series, where Rivera recorded three more saves, including one in the Series-clinching fourth game.

In 1999, after three full years of major-league service, Rivera became eligible for salary arbitration and signed a one-year, $4.25 million deal. Rivera, who had adopted Metallica's "Enter Sandman" as his entrance music, was the major-league saves leader, converting forty-five of forty-nine to win his first AL Rolaids Relief Man Award and lead his team to their second consecutive AL East title. He also made his second consecutive All-Star Game appearance. In postseason play he remained scoreless, notching two saves in the Yankees' three-game sweep of the Rangers in the ALDS. He was the winning pitcher in game one of the ALCS, in which he also had saves in games two and four against the Boston Red Sox, whom the Yanks defeated to reach the 1999 World Series. After pitching his team to a game-three victory and recording saves in the first and fourth games, Rivera was named the MVP of the series, which the Yankees won after a four-game sweep of the Atlanta Braves. He also came in third in the Cy Young voting.

A year later, Rivera, who earned a $7.25 million contract in arbitration, appeared in his third All-Star Game and finished in the top ten in saves, with thirty-six. Rivera, whose team won their third straight AL East pennant, gave up no runs and saved three games to help the Yankees defeat the Athletics in the ALDS. During the ALCS his consecutive scoreless innings streak reached thirty-three and one-third, setting a new postseason record previously held by former Yankee Whitey Ford (1950, 1953–1967). After beating the Seattle Mariners in six games, the Yankees advanced to their third straight World Series, this time against their crosstown rivals,

the New York Mets. Rivera went on to record a save in game four and another in game five to capture his fourth World Series ring.

QUESTIONS ABOUT CONSISTENCY

In 2001 Rivera signed a four-year, $39.99 million contract. He was impressive, giving up only twenty-three runs and twelve walks, while notching a career-high fifty saves and eighty-three strikeouts in eighty and two-thirds innings. For the second time in his career, Rivera led the major leagues in saves and won the AL Rolaids Relief Man Award; he also made his fourth All-Star Game appearance. After another first-place finish in the AL East, the Yankees moved on to the ALDS, where Rivera earned two saves against the Oakland Athletics, who lost in five games. In the ALCS Rivera's two saves helped his team reach the World Series against the Arizona Diamondbacks. His save in game three, along with the scoreless tenth inning he pitched to secure the game four win, allowed the Yankees to even up the series. Rivera also made a game five appearance, throwing two more scoreless innings, en route to another extra-innings victory. However, in the seventh and deciding game, Rivera committed an uncharacteristic throwing error and eventually gave up the winning run in the bottom of the ninth inning for his first postseason loss. "The single didn't even leave the infield dirt. It was tough to get over. It took me a few days," he told Antonen. Following the World Series loss, the seemingly indomitable Rivera lost his aura of invincibility. In 2002 he only pitched forty-six innings and earned only twenty-eight saves—both career lows. He spent three separate stints on the disabled list—two for a shoulder strain and one for a groin injury. Despite this Rivera earned an AL roster spot in his fifth All-Star Game and his team placed first in the AL East, for the fifth straight time. However, he saw limited action in the postseason, recording a save in game one of the ALDS. For the first time in five years, the Yankees failed to advance to the World Series; they were defeated three games to one by the Angels, the eventual champions.

Over the next decade, as the Yankees struggled to reclaim the championship, Rivera defied the age barrier and remained productive. Despite missing most of the first month in 2003 with another groin injury, he recorded forty saves (sixth-best in the majors) and an ERA below two during the regular season, which concluded with the Yankees' sixth straight AL East title. After beating the Minnesota Twins in the ALDS, the Yankees advanced to the ALCS to face the Red Sox, their historic rivals. In game seven Rivera threw three scoreless innings in the Yankees' extra-inning, walk-off victory and was declared the winning pitcher and the series MVP. Although the Yankees lost to the

Florida Marlins in the World Series, Rivera finished the postseason with a total of five saves and only gave up an earned run in sixteen innings. He was rewarded with a two-year, $21 million extension to his contract, plus a third-year option, during the offseason. In 2004 the thirty-five-year-old Rivera had career highs with seventy-four appearances and a league-leading fifty-three saves; he also reached the three-hundred-save mark and pitched in his sixth All-Star Game.

He won his third Rolaids Relief Award and finished ninth in the MVP race while helping his team to a seventh consecutive AL East crown. The Yankees, who beat the Twins in an ALDS rematch, faced the Red Sox again in the ALCS. Rivera saved the first two games of the series but was scrutinized after he was unable to close out games four and five; the Red Sox overcame a three-games-to-none deficit to advance past the Yankees to the World Series. The scrutiny intensified after Rivera started off the 2005 season with two blown saves at Yankee Stadium against the Red Sox. He surmounted the rough start, garnering his second save in the All-Star Game (his seventh) and finishing third in the AL, with forty-three saves, along with a personal-best ERA (1.38). Other 2005 accolades included his fourth Rolaids prize, a second-place finish in the Cy Young voting, and ninth place in the AL MVP contest. The Yankees, winners of their eighth division title, failed to get past the Angels in the ALDS, despite saves by Rivera in the opening and fourth games of the series.

Rivera's save totals declined, from thirty-four in 2006 to thirty in 2007, while his ERA rose from 1.80 to 3.15, the highest of his career. He also earned a save (his third) at the 2006 All-Star Game. Both seasons the Yankees, who finished first and second respectively, failed to make it past the ALDS. During the offseason Rivera, a free agent, remained with the Yankees, signing a three-year, $45 million deal that made him the highest-paid relief pitcher in MLB history. He had a bounce-back season in 2008, his first year under new manager Joe Girardi (2007–present) and the Yankees' final year in the old Yankee Stadium. Despite suffering with season-long shoulder pain, Rivera saved thirty-nine games—seventh-best in the majors—and had an impressive walk-to-strike-out ratio, allowing only six walks while striking out seventy-seven batters in seventy and two-thirds innings. Rivera, who lowered his ERA to 1.40, was fifth in the AL Cy Young voting, and notched his ninth All-Star Game appearance. His team finished third in the AL East and did not advance to the postseason for the first time in twelve years. Rivera was diagnosed with bone spurs in his throwing shoulder and underwent offseason surgery.

RETURN TO THE WORLD SERIES

In 2009 there were questions surrounding the health of Rivera's shoulder. He reverted to form, converting forty-four saves (the third most in the majors) and appearing in his tenth All-Star Game, during which he had a record-setting fourth save. Rivera also claimed his fifth AL Rolaids Relief prize and the Sporting News Pro Athlete of the Year Award. After the Yankees won 103 to clinch the AL East division, Rivera had one goal in mind. He wanted to win another World Series title.

Following a sweep of the Minnesota Twins in the ALDS and the defeat of the Angels in the ALCS, the Yankees reached their first World Series since 2003. Rivera's wish became reality in game six, when he recorded the final out in the ninth inning against the Philadelphia Phillies. Notwithstanding a modest thirty-save season in 2010 and the Yankees' elimination in the ALCS, Rivera signed a two-year, $30 million contract to remain in New York. With his forty-four saves in 2011, the forty-one year old became the oldest player in major-league history to save forty (40) games and the leader in all-time career saves, with 608. Rivera, who missed the 2010 and 2011 All-Star games due to injury, also had the distinction of being the fifteenth pitcher in the history of the majors to appear in one thousand games and first hurler to do so with one team. After undergoing offseason vocal cord surgery, Rivera got off to a promising start, recording five saves in the first month of the 2012 season. His season was cut short on May 3, when he suffered a tear to his anterior cruciate ligament (ACL) in his right knee while catching fly balls in the outfield during batting practice. He was prescribed medication to treat a blood clot before undergoing surgery. Although he had been rumored to retire after the season, Rivera has announced plans to return to the mound in 2013.

PERSONAL LIFE

Rivera has been married to his childhood sweetheart, Clara, since November 1991. The couple live in Westchester County, New York, and have three sons: Mariano Jr., Jafet, and Jaziel. Rivera, a devout Christian, has established an eponymous charity and is the owner of Mo's New York Grill in New Rochelle, New York.

SUGGESTED READING

Antonen, Mel. "Yanks' Rivera continues to learn." *USA Today*. Gannett Company, 9 Oct. 2006. Web. 14 May 2012.

Baxter, Kevin. "To Many, Yankees' Mariano Rivera Has No Equal." *Los Angeles Times*. Tribune Company, 2 Oct. 2011. Web. 14 May 2011.

Curry, Jack. "Scout Saw Effortless Ability in Rivera." *New York Times*. New York Times Company, 5 July 2009. Web. 14 May 2012.

Gere, Richard. "Richard Gere Interviews Mariano Rivera." *Gotham*. Niche Media, April/May 2012. Web. 14 May 2012.

Harper, John. "At start of Mariano Rivera's Yankee career, Gene Michael almost traded him." *New York Daily News*. New York Daily News. 30 June 2009. Web. 14 May 2012.

—Bertha Muteba

Aaron Rodgers

Born: December 2, 1983
Occupation: Football player with the Green Bay Packers

Getty Images

"I want to be the best," Green Bay Packers quarterback Aaron Rodgers told Lori Nickel for the Milwaukee *Journal Sentinel* (24 Oct. 2010). "I've always wanted to be the best." In four full seasons as the Packers' starting quarterback, Rodgers has, in fact, established himself as arguably the best quarterback in the National Football League (NFL). In reaching such elite status, however, Rodgers has had to overcome significant obstacles: He was not recruited out of high school, and despite enjoying a decorated two-year college career at the University of California, Berkeley, he was only the twenty-fourth overall selection of the 2005 NFL Draft, in which he was taken by the Packers. Furthermore, he was relegated to the backup quarterback role for three years, deferring to the Packers' legendary quarterback Brett Favre.

Finally getting his chance to start during the 2008 season (when Favre, who had retired and then unretired, was traded to the New York Jets), Rodgers passed for more than four thousand yards and twenty-eight touchdowns and accumulated an impressive 93.8 passer rating. In 2009, he again compiled more than four thousand yards passing, becoming the first NFL quarterback to do so, and earned his first Pro Bowl selection. During the 2010 and 2011 seasons, Rodgers emerged as one of the premier quarterbacks in the league. In 2010, he guided the Packers to the team's fourth Super Bowl win and record thirteenth NFL championship, when they defeated the Pittsburgh Steelers, 31–25, in Super Bowl XLV; Rodgers was the game's most valuable player (MVP), passing for more than three hundred yards and three touchdowns.

In 2011, Rodgers earned his second Pro Bowl selection and was named to the Associated Press (AP) All-Pro First Team for the first time of his career, after becoming the first quarterback in league history to throw forty-five-plus touchdowns with six or fewer interceptions in a season. Rodgers helped the Packers record a league-best 15–1 record, and at the end of that season he was voted the AP NFL MVP and AP Male Athlete of the Year.

Known for his uncanny accuracy, superior arm strength, and cerebral approach to the game, Rodgers has refused to let outside influences disrupt his performance on the field. He explained to Nickel, "I have expectations of myself that are normally greater than the ones put on me and our team. . . . I just always felt there was more for me than what people expected of me." Packers head coach Mike McCarthy told Jim Corbett for *USA Today* (20 Jan. 2011), "He's definitely the quarterback we all hoped he would become. . . . He's definitely developed into a special player. He does it the right way. He's everything we hoped he'd be."

EARLY LIFE AND EDUCATION

The second of three sons, Aaron Charles Rodgers was born on December 2, 1983, in Chico, a city north of Sacramento, California. His older brother, Luke, is two years his senior, and his younger brother, Jordan, is five years his junior. Rodgers's father, Ed Jr., a chiropractor, met Rodgers's mother, Darla, a dancer who later became a homemaker, while attending California State University, Chico (better known as Chico State), where he was a standout offensive lineman for the school's football team. Rodgers developed a passion for football through his father, who had tried out unsuccessfully for several teams in the Canadian Football League before playing semi-professional football with the Twin City Cougars of the California Football League for three-plus seasons, in 1978 and then from 1979 to 1981.

Rodgers began watching NFL games at the age of two, and by five, he was updating statistics of NFL players on his football cards and formulating game plans. Rodgers athletic abilities were apparent early on, and when he was a boy, he was reportedly able to throw a football through a tire strung from a tree. He grew up rooting for the closest NFL team, the San Francisco 49ers (the Oakland Raiders called Los Angeles home at the time), and idolizing the 49ers' legendary quarterback Joe Montana, who captured four Super Bowl titles in the 1980s. Rodgers admired Montana's ability to thrive in high-pressure situations and dreamed of following in his footsteps one day.

Rodgers was raised mostly in the Chico area, but he spent part of his elementary and middle school years in Beaverton, Oregon, where his father attended chiropractic school for three years. He has credited his father, who had worked a variety of jobs to support the family before settling on a career as a chiropractor in his late thirties, for instilling in him and his brothers a strong work ethic and sense of responsibility. "I'd see him go into the garage and study for four hours," he said of his father to Nickel. "I did not realize at the time, but he was doing it all for us." Because of his father's frequent job changes, Rodgers reportedly attended nine different schools growing up. He attended Vose Elementary and Whitford Middle Schools, in Beaverton, before moving back to Chico with his family in 1997. That year, he attended eighth grade at Champion Christian School, where, during the admittance interview, he boldly responded to a question about what he would do to make the school better by declaring that he would make their sports teams "really good," as his father noted to Karen Crouse for the *New York Times* (30 Jan. 2011). By that time, Rodgers had already excelled in youth-league football, basketball, and baseball, as a quarterback, point guard, and pitcher, respectively.

HIGH SCHOOL AND COLLEGE CAREER

Rodgers attended Pleasant Valley High School in Chico, where he played football, basketball, and baseball. As a sophomore, he made the junior varsity football squad. Despite his size (he was five feet six and weighed 120 pounds), Rodgers, who had large hands and feet, made an immediate impression on his coaches with his strong arm, sound mechanics, intellect, and football acumen. As the starting junior varsity quarterback for Pleasant Valley during his sophomore season, he called many of his own plays based on his ability to dissect and manipulate opposing teams' defensive schemes. One of his high school football coaches, Ron Souza, told Brad Townsend for the *Dallas Morning News* (1 Feb. 2011), "If he were to be tested, Aaron probably

has a photographic memory. . . . Nine out of 10 of us are concrete learners. We have to learn motor movements by doing them over and over. Aaron could visualize what we wanted. You never had to doodle it up for him."

Rodgers made Pleasant Valley's varsity football team as a junior and, in his junior and senior seasons, passed for a combined 4,419 yards. He earned all-section accolades in both years (2000 and 2001) and set school records for touchdowns (six) and all-purpose yards (440) in a single game and passing yards (2,303) in a single season as a senior. Rodgers also pitched for Pleasant Valley's varsity baseball team as a senior; his fastball was reportedly clocked at 90 miles per hour. Along with his athletic achievements, he excelled academically, graduating with an A-minus grade point average and scoring a 1310 out of 1600 on his Scholastic Aptitude Test.

Despite a stellar high school football career, Rodgers did not receive any scholarship offers from NCAA Division I-A schools. Although he had helped Pleasant Valley's varsity team reach the sectional semifinals during both his junior and senior seasons, recruiters did not seriously recruit players from the school. Also, though he had almost grown to his adult height of six feet two, Rodgers had yet to fill out his frame, weighing under 200 pounds; he was deemed too small to play Division I-A football. As a result, he remained close to home and enrolled at Butte College, a junior college in Oroville, California.

Rodgers spent his freshman year at Butte and played on the school's football squad under head coach Craig Rigsbee, who lived in the same housing complex as his family. (Rigsbee literally walked over to Rodgers's home to offer him a scholarship to the school.) In his one season at Butte, Rodgers shined, throwing for 2,408 yards and twenty-eight touchdowns, with only four interceptions, and posting a completion percentage of 61.9. He also rushed for 294 yards and seven touchdowns. He led Butte to a 10–1 record, a NorCal Conference championship, and a number-two national ranking among community colleges. He was named both the NorCal Conference and region MVP and earned third-team all-America honors from JC Grid-Wire. Playing with a motley crew of castoffs, Rodgers recalled to Jarrett Bell for *USA Today* (7 Sep. 2008), "I was exposed to a ton of guys with different backgrounds and cultures. . . . Guys from Florida, Texas, and Canada. Guys at 25 and 26 years old, still trying to make it. My center was 25. Our free safety, the team leader, was 22 and had been to jail. To be, at a young age, able to get guys to play with you and raise their game, that was a huge lesson. Probably the best year of football for me, as far as personal development. I learned a lot about myself as a leader."

Because of his strong academic performance in high school, Rodgers was able to transfer to the University of California, Berkeley (Cal) after his freshman year. He was awarded a scholarship to play football by head coach Jeff Tedford, who had spotted him by accident while watching game film of his teammate, Butte tight end Garrett Cross. Rodgers, who had impressed Tedford with his arm strength and ability to read defenses, quickly learned Tedford's pass-oriented playbook and became the Golden Bear's starting quarterback in the fifth game of the 2003 season. He was soon named an offensive team captain and subsequently enjoyed one of the best seasons by a sophomore quarterback in the history of the Pacific-10 Conference (Pac-10, now the Pacific-12 Conference), passing for 2,903 yards and nineteen touchdowns, with only five interceptions, and amassing a completion percentage of 61.6 and 210 rushing yards. In his ten starts, he led Cal to a 7–3 record and helped Cal clinch its first bowl berth since 1996. In the 2003 Insight Bowl, Cal defeated Virginia Tech, 52–49. During the game, Rodgers threw for a collegiate-high 394 yards and compiled 424 yards of total offense, good for the third highest total in school history.

During his junior season at Cal, Rodgers again served as a team cocaptain and established himself as one of the best quarterbacks in American college football. He started in all twelve games and passed for 2,566 yards and twenty-four touchdowns, while posting a 66.1 percent completion percentage. He also had a passer rating of 154.4, which ranked second in the Pac-10 behind University of Southern California (USC) quarterback Matt Leinart.

Rodgers was selected as a quarterback for the All-Pac-10 First Team, finished ninth in the balloting for the Heisman Trophy as the top player in college football, and was named the Golden Bears' Co-Offensive MVP. In addition, he received all-America honors from the Associated Press and other organizations and earned Pac-10 All-Academic Second Team honors. Running an explosive offense that averaged more than thirty-seven points per game, Rodgers helped lead Cal to a 10–1 regular-season record (their only loss was to the USC Trojans, the eventual national champions), a number-four national ranking (the school's highest since 1952), and the 2004 Pac-10 championship. However, despite their record, the Golden Bears, lost out on a possible Bowl Championship Series berth to the University of Texas and were then upset by the Texas Tech Red Raiders, 45–31, in the 2004 Holiday Bowl.

Shortly after the disappointing bowl-game loss, Rodgers, who majored in American studies, decided to skip his senior season to make himself eligible for the NFL Draft. He finished his college career at Cal as the school's all-time

leader in passer rating (150.3) and interception percentage (1.95). Speaking with Jason Wilde for the *Wisconsin State Journal* (7 Sep. 2008), Tedford described Rodgers as a "student of the game. He loves it. He submerges himself in it. He doesn't just memorize things. He understands concepts."

PROFESSIONAL CAREER

Analysts and scouts projected Rodgers as a top-ten pick in the 2005 NFL Draft, with some even considering him a potential number-one overall pick. However, the San Francisco 49ers, who had the top pick in that year's draft, passed on Rodgers after deeming him not "athletic enough," as Nickel noted. Instead, they selected quarterback Alex Smith of the University of Utah. Rodgers slipped to the twenty-fourth overall pick; the Packers believed he would eventually replace Favre. Despite being disappointed with his draft placement, Rodgers welcomed the opportunity to serve as an understudy to one of the greatest and most durable quarterbacks in NFL history. "I think the first progression every quarterback makes is you come in being the guy, and if you're not the starter you realize that there's someone better in front of you, and that's a big step to take because when you're the guy you're confident," he explained to Tom Silverstein for the Milwaukee *Journal Sentinel* (7 Sep. 2008). "Second, figure out the things he does that are better than you and study it and work on those things and improve." During the summer of 2005, Rodgers signed a five-year deal with the Packers worth $7.7 million.

BACKING UP FAVRE

During the 2005–07 seasons, Rodgers played only occasionally while serving as Favre's backup. During that time, he headed the Packers' scout-team offense in practice every day, where he was responsible for running upcoming opponents' offensive plays to prepare the defense. The Packers veteran wide receiver Donald Driver told Tim Layden for *Sports Illustrated* (7 Nov. 2011) that Rodgers "took every scout-team possession like it was the last possession of his life." While Favre made little effort to serve as a mentor to him during that time, avowing that it was not part of his job description, Rodgers made a point to shadow Favre as much as possible in practices and on game days in efforts to learn all the nuances of quarterbacking. "I'd watch him like a hawk," he noted to Silverstein, adding, "Anytime he opened his mouth in meetings to talk to a receiver I listened. . . . I wrote it down."

In 2005, after performing poorly during the preseason, Rodgers made his NFL debut as quarterback for the Packers in a week-five matchup against the New Orleans Saints. Briefly replacing Favre in the fourth quarter of the game, which the Packers won 52–3, Rodgers completed his only pass attempt, to fullback Vonta Leach for no gain. That year, he played in two more games, in weeks fifteen and seventeen, against the Baltimore Ravens and Seattle Seahawks.

In the week-fifteen contest with the Ravens, in which the Packers lost handily, 48–3, Rodgers filled in for Favre near the end of the third quarter and completed eight of fifteen passes for sixty-five yards and one interception. In the game against the Seahawks, he entered for the game's final play in a 23–17 Packers victory. Despite winning the final game, the Packers ended the season with a disastrous 4–12 record, after entering the season having won three consecutive National Football Conference (NFC) North division titles. Packers head coach Mike Sherman, now the offensive coordinator for the Miami Dolphins, was consequently fired and replaced with McCarthy, who had spent the previous season as the offensive coordinator for the 49ers.

Rodgers developed further under McCarthy, a former quarterbacks coach, who required him to attend his mandatory quarterback school as part of the Packers' off-season program. During the school, which was held several days a week in six-hour sessions, Rodgers focused on improving his hand-eye coordination, his mechanics, and his physical conditioning. Despite his initial reluctance to make changes, Rodgers has said that the school helped him become a better all-around quarterback.

In 2006, Rodgers relieved Favre on two occasions (both times due to injury), appearing in games against the Philadelphia Eagles and the New England Patriots, in weeks four and eleven. In those games, he ran a total of thirty-six offensive plays, completing six of fifteen passes for forty-six yards, with no touchdowns or interceptions. After sustaining a broken left foot in the game against the Patriots, which the Packers lost 35–0, Rodgers did not play for the remainder of the 2006 season. The Packers improved their record from the previous year, going 8–8, but missed the playoffs for a second consecutive season.

Rodgers filled in for Favre on two more occasions during the 2007 season, in which he served as the Packers' primary backup quarterback for the third consecutive season. His duties included providing in-depth weekly reports to Favre and the team's coaches on upcoming opponents, which helped him gain superior knowledge of opposing teams' players and tendencies. During the season, Rodgers completed twenty of twenty-eight passes for 218 yards, throwing one touchdown. He had a passer rating of 106.0 and rushed seven times for twenty-nine yards. His first career touchdown pass came on an eleven-yard strike to wide receiver Greg Jennings in a week-thirteen game against the Dallas Cowboys. In that game, the Packers' rally, led by Rodgers, who completed eighteen of twenty-six passes for 201 yards, fell short, as the team lost to the Cowboys, 37–27.

Rodgers missed the final four weeks of the season because of a hamstring injury but returned to serve as Favre's backup during the postseason. The Packers finished the season with a conference-best 13–3 record and won their first NFC North division title since 2004. With home-field advantage throughout the playoffs, the Packers defeated the Seattle Seahawks in the NFC divisional playoff round, 42–20, the Packers played in the NFC Championship Game, losing to the eventual Super Bowl champions New York Giants, 23–20, in overtime. Rodgers played in the final series of the NFL divisional game against the Seahawks but did not play against the Giants in the NFC Championship Game.

RODGERS BECOMES THE PACKERS' STARTING QUARTERBACK

After Favre's long-delayed retirement before the 2008 season, Rodgers was named the Packers' starting quarterback. Although Favre abruptly unretired in training camp that year, the Packers ultimately settled on Rodgers as their quarterback; Favre was traded to the Jets. The decision to trade Favre, who had not only broken every major NFL passing record as a Packer but also appeared in a record 275 consecutive games (including the playoffs), greatly angered Packers fans, many of whom took out their frustration by heckling Rodgers in training-camp practices. Undaunted, Rodgers, who was also forced to deal with mass-media attention as a result of the Favre drama, handled the difficult situation—described by Silverstein as "arguably one of the hardest assignments in recent NFL history"—with poise and professionalism. McCarthy said of Rodgers to Wilde, "I think he grew up . . . I think he did a very good job of handling a challenge, handling a situation that there really wasn't a script for. It was unprecedented."

In his first season as a starter, Rodgers showed flashes of his potential to become an elite NFL quarterback. In his debut as a starter, in a game in which the Packers beat the Minnesota Vikings 24–19 on September 8, 2008, he completed eighteen of twenty-two passes, compiling 178 yards. Rodgers was the first quarterback other than Favre to start a Packers' game since 1992. The following week, he led the Packers to another victory, over the Detroit Lions, passing for more than three hundred yards for the first time in his career and throwing three touchdown passes; he was named the FedEx Air Player of the Week.

Rodgers suffered a partially separated shoulder early in the season but played through the injury, earning the respect of his teammates. He started in all sixteen regular-season games, passing for 4,038 yards and twenty-eight touchdowns with only thirteen interceptions. He became the fourth Packers quarterback to record four thousand or more passing yards in one season (after Favre, Don Majkowski, and Lynn Dickey) and only the second NFL quarterback to surpass the four-thousand-yard plateau in his first season as a starter (the first was Kurt Warner, who accomplished the feat as a member of the St. Louis Rams in 1999). Rodgers's numbers notwithstanding, the Packers finished with a losing 6–10 record and missed the playoffs. Seven of the losses were by seven points or fewer and included two overtime defeats. After signing a six-year, $65 million contract extension with the Packers in October 2008, Rodgers entered the 2009 off-season dedicated to improving his performance in come-from-behind situations.

ELITE STATUS AND THE PACKERS' RETURN TO THE SUPER BOWL

During the 2009 season, Rodgers became one of the top quarterbacks in the league. He started every game for the second consecutive year and threw for a then career-high 4,434 yards, thirty touchdowns, and only seven interceptions, while posting a remarkable 103.2 passer rating. He also rushed for 316 yards and five touchdowns. He was the first quarterback in NFL history to compile four-thousand-plus yards in each of his first two seasons as a starter and the first quarterback in league history with at least thirty touchdown passes, five rushing touchdowns, and seven or fewer interceptions in the same season. Early that season, Rodgers quickly put to rest any doubts about his ability to perform in high-pressure situations, when he led the Packers to a 21–15 opening-day, come-from-behind victory over the Chicago Bears. In the game he threw a fifty-yard touchdown pass to wide receiver Jennings. Rodgers was the NFC Offensive Player of the Month in October, passing for 988 yards and posting a completion percentage of 74.5 and passer rating of more than 110 for the month. He earned his first career Pro Bowl selection during the season. The Packers finished second in the NFC North division, at 11–5, and advanced to the postseason. In a 51–46 overtime loss to the Arizona Cardinals, Rodgers threw for a franchise playoff best 423 yards and tied a franchise playoff mark with four touchdown passes.

Rodgers confirmed his status as an elite quarterback in 2010. Despite missing one regular-season game because of a concussion, he finished the year with 3,922 passing yards, twenty-eight touchdown passes, and a 101.2 passer rating, while adding a career-high 356 rushing yards and four rushing touchdowns. He was selected as a first alternate to the NFC Pro Bowl squad and was named the FedEx Air NFL Player of the Year. Despite losing fifteen players to injuries during the course of the season, the Packers finished second in the NFC North and earned the NFC's sixth playoff seed.

After winning road playoff games against the Eagles, the Atlanta Falcons, and the Bears, the Packers faced the Steelers in Super Bowl XLV, which was held at Cowboys Stadium in Arlington, Texas, on February 6, 2011. The Packers defeated the Steelers, 31–25, and Rodgers was Super Bowl MVP, completing twenty-four of thirty-nine passes for 304 yards and three touchdowns. Leading up to the Super Bowl, he posted one of the most dominating postseason performances in NFL history while setting several postseason passing records. In the NFC divisional round against the Falcons, Rodgers completed thirty-one of thirty-six passes for 366 yards and three touchdowns. His passer rating was 136.8, the highest in league postseason history among quarterbacks with at least thirty-five pass attempts. He also tied a league record in that game for throwing at least three touchdown passes in three consecutive playoff games.

Rodgers carried his dominant play from the 2010–11 playoffs into the 2011 regular season, posting the best numbers of his career. He finished the year with a career-high 4,643 passing yards, forty-five touchdown passes, and only six interceptions, and he amassed a league-best 122.4 passer rating, which is the highest single-season quarterback rating in NFL history. He became the first quarterback in league history to throw forty-five or more touchdown passes with six or fewer interceptions in a single season.

Rodgers was named to his second career Pro Bowl and first as a starter and earned his first AP All-Pro First Team selection. He also garnered NFC Offensive Player of the Month honors for September, October, and November and FedEx Air Player of the Week honors on six occasions. Bolstered by Rodgers's record-breaking numbers, the Packers won the first thirteen games of the season, finishing with a league-best 15–1 record. They won their first NFC North title since 2007 and earned home-field advantage throughout the playoffs, but they lost to the eventual champion New York Giants, 37–20, in the NFC divisional playoff round.

Despite the Packers' disappointing finish, Rodgers was recognized for his efforts during the regular season and won the 2011 AP NFL MVP award, receiving forty-eight first-place votes (second-place finisher, Drew Brees of the New Orleans Saints, received two). He was the first Packers player to win the award since Favre, who won three consecutive from 1995 to 1997, and the fifth Packer overall (after Bart Starr, Jim Taylor, Paul Hornung, and Favre). He was also named the 2011 AP Male Athlete of the Year.

PERSONAL LIFE

During the off-season, Rodgers, who is single, lives in Del Mar, an affluent beach town located twenty miles north of San Diego, California. In 2011, he signed an endorsement deal to be a spokesman for State Farm Insurance and has since appeared in a series of popular State Farm commercials for the company's "Discount Double Check" program, in which he pokes fun at his signature "championship belt" touchdown celebration. He has been involved in numerous charitable activities and worked extensively with the Midwest Athletes Against Childhood Cancer Fund. He is an avid fan of indie rock and country music and enjoys playing golf and the guitar in his spare time. He cofounded his own independent record label, Suspended Sunrise Recordings, which signed a Chico, California-based indie rock band called The Make.

SUGGESTED READING

Bell, Jarrett. "Leader of the Pack? Shadow of Favre Looms Large for Rodgers." *USA Today* 7 Sep. 2008: Sports 1C. Print.

Brown, Daniel. "Going Back to Mr. Rodgers' Neighborhood." *Mercury News* [San Jose] 5 Feb. 2011: News. Print.

Corbett, Jim. "Aaron Rodgers Is a Superstar QB out to Join Super Bowl Club." *USA Today* 20 Jan. 2011: Sports 1C. Print.

Crouse, Karen. "Packers' Rodgers Has Deep Roots in Chico." *New York Times*. New York Times, 30 Jan. 2011. Web. 6 Aug. 2012.

"Green Bay Packers: Aaron Rodgers." *Packers*. Green Bay Packers, 2012. Web. 6 Aug. 2012.

Layden, Tim. "All for One, One for All." *SI.com*. Time Warner. 7 Nov. 2011. Web. 6 Aug. 2012.

Nickel, Lori. "Does Rodgers Have What It Takes to Lift Team in Big Games?" *Journal Sentinel* [Milwaukee] 23 Oct. 2010. Web. 6 Aug. 2012.

Pells, Eddie. "Rodgers Fights Off Favre Legacy to Build His Own." Associated Press 5 Feb. 2011. Print.

Silverstein, Tom. "The Education of Aaron Rodgers: Young QB Has Had Plenty of Time to Watch and Learn." *Journal Sentinel* [Milwaukee] 7 Sep. 2008: S3. Print.

Townsend, Brad. "Patience, Perseverance Key for Packers Passer Aaron Rodgers." *Dallas Morning News*. Dallas Morning News, 1 Feb. 2011. Web. 6 Aug. 2012.

Wilde, Jason. "A Torch Passed: Aaron Rodgers Hopes to Make His Legendary Succession a Success." *Wisconsin State Journal* [Madison] 7 Sep. 2008: 3. Print.

—*Chris Cullen*

Nile Rodgers

Born: September 19, 1952
Occupation: Guitarist, songwriter, music producer

Nile Rodgers may not be a household name, but for the past thirty-five years, his work has been familiar to nearly everyone who follows pop music. In the late 1970s and early 1980s, as the guitarist and coproducer for the disco-soul-funk band Chic—which he cofounded with his longtime collaborator, the late Bernard Edwards—he wrote such hits as "Le Freak," "Dance, Dance, Dance," and "Good Times." The last-named song is not only one of Chic's best-known works but also one of their most influential: as an example, for the groundbreaking song "Rapper's Delight," the hip-hop group Sugar Hill Gang sampled the bass line of "Good Times," which also inspired the art-rock group Queen's hit "Another One Bites the Dust." Beginning in the 1990s Rodgers's songs were also sampled by such hip-hop artists as the Notorious B.I.G. The songs Rodgers wrote for others in the 1970s and '80s include some of the most anthemic hits of modern times, among them Sister Sledge's "We Are Family" and Diana Ross's "I'm Coming Out"; he has also produced albums by such megastars as Ross, David Bowie, Madonna, Duran Duran, Mick Jagger, and Jeff Beck. For much of the 1990s and the first decade of the 2000s, Rodgers composed and produced music for high-profile films—*Beverly Hills Cop III*, *Rush Hour 2*, and others. In 2011 he published a memoir, *Le Freak: An Upside Down Story of Family, Disco, and Destiny*.

EARLY LIFE

Nile Gregory Rodgers was born on September 19, 1952, in New York City. He provided a detailed account of his childhood in an essay for the *New York Times* (11 Sep. 2011), which was adapted from his memoir. His mother, Beverly, conceived him when she was only thirteen years old; his father, Nile Rodgers Sr., was sixteen. A wedding was planned, but Beverly changed her mind at the last minute. Beverly, whom Rodgers described as smart and beautiful, later met Bobby Glanzrock, a white, Jewish man who became Rodgers's stepfather. With his mother and stepfather, Rodgers moved frequently around New York, settling in 1959 in an apartment in Greenwich Village, the bohemian center of Manhattan. That was when it occurred to Rodgers that his parents were "different," as he wrote. In that era, even on the progressive streets of Greenwich Village, the sight of a white man and a black woman walking together caused some people to stare. Beverly and Bobby, who listened to a lot of jazz, used the Beat slang of

Getty Images

the time and took many drugs—most devastatingly, heroin. "Beverly and Bobby may not have been model parents," Rodgers wrote, "but they were a really good fit for each other; art, literature and especially their love of music bonded them together. But as they spiraled deeper and deeper into addiction, they were also increasingly self-centered, not infrequently criminal and less and less interested in the responsibilities of raising a kid. On some level, it was great to be treated like a peer, to be on a first-name basis with my parents, but it wasn't exactly a substitute for the usual parental cocktail of nurturing and discipline. Respect? Yes, there was plenty of that. If I had a problem, we'd 'rap on it.' Then they'd ask me something like: 'Are we copacetic?' If I said, 'Yeah, I guess so,' the matter would be settled with a five slap or some other affirming gesture." Rodgers sometimes saw his biological father, a gifted percussionist drawn to Afro-Cuban rhythms. Nile Sr., who in his son's recollection was warm and kind—if mentally unstable and addicted to drugs— taught his young son to listen to rhythm patterns. Rodgers also studied music in public school, and by the time he was 14 years old, he was already fairly proficient on a number of musical instruments.

BEGINS MUSIC CAREER

While still in his teens, Rodgers began his music career in New York City as a session guitarist. He went on tour with the Sesame Street band and then played in the house band of the well-known Apollo Theater, in Harlem, backing such big-name acts as Aretha Franklin, Ben E. King, Parliament Funkadelic, and Screaming Jay Hawkins. In 1970 Rodgers met the bassist Bernard Edwards, and the two began a musical partnership that would last a quarter century. They formed the Big Apple Band, serving as backup musicians for an R&B group called New York City—which had a minor hit with "I'm Doing Fine Now," toured extensively, and in 1973 opened for the Jackson 5 on the US leg of that supergroup's first international tour. After New York City broke up, Rodgers and Edwards met the drummer Tony Thompson, with whom they formed a funk-rock band called the Boys. They had a hard time getting signed, because, they were told, a black rock band would be hard to promote. As a result Rodgers, Edwards, and Thompson toured often as the Big Apple Band, working alongside such renowned vocalists as Ashford & Simpson and Luther Vandross. Because there was another act called Big Apple Band, Rodgers and Edwards changed their band's name to Chic— which, in addition to Rodgers, Edwards, and Thompson, included the singers Alfa Anderson and Norma Jean Wright (who was later replaced by Luci Martin). Chic's first single was the demo "Dance, Dance, Dance (Yowsah, Yowsah, Yowsah)," which they pitched unsuccessfully to several big record labels. After a small record label, Buddha, released it in 1977, the song became a huge hit in dance clubs, which led to a major record deal with Atlantic. After Atlantic re-released "Dance, Dance, Dance," the song became a Top 10 hit. Chic's self-titled debut album, which came out in 1977, showcased the group's mix of the Euro-disco, R&B, funk, and soul genres. Despite being panned by most rock critics—who heard too much disco in Chic's music—the record was very popular, thanks in part to the group's second single, "Everybody Dance." Rodgers and Edwards cowrote all of the group's songs and served as Chic's leaders and producers, an arrangement that would continue with future Chic albums.

HITTING THE BIG TIME

Chic truly hit the big time with their second album, *C'est Chic* (1978), which featured the popular songs "I Want Your Love," "Chic Cheer," and "Le Freak." Robert A. Hull, writing for the *Washington Post* (23 Sep. 1979), called "Le Freak" one of the "goofiest and funniest singles of this dull decade—one can hear the song 50 times and not be able to pinpoint its hypnotic appeal." *C'est Chic* came out at the height of disco fever and climbed to number one on the Billboard R&B chart and number four on the Billboard 200 chart. In a review for *AllMusic*, Jason Birchmeier wrote about the significance of the album: "Producers Bernard Edwards and Nile Rodgers were quite a savvy pair and knew that disco was as much a formula as anything. As evidenced here, they definitely had their fingers on the pulse of the moment, and used their perceptive touch to craft one of the few truly great disco albums. In fact, you could even argue that *C'est Chic* very well may be the definitive disco album. After all, countless artists scored dance-floor hits, but few could deliver an album this solid, and nearly as few could deliver one this epochal as well. *C'est Chic* embodies everything wonderful and excessive about disco at its pixilated peak." Chic followed their sophomore album with another hit record, titled *Risque* (1979). Considered to be one of the group's quintessential albums, *Risque* featured such hits as "My Feet Keep Dancing," "My Forbidden Lover," and "Good Times." In his review Hull observed that has "an abundance of inspiring music guaranteed to motivate a veritable symphony of pelvic distortion on any dance floor. [One] quick listen, and it's easy to hear why all cuts from the album are currently climbing the disco charts. The key to Chic's entrancing sound is Nile Rodgers' guitar work and Rodgers/Bernard Edwards' sweeping production. This team's devotion to detail was not apparent on Chic's cliche-hit, 'Dance, Dance, Dance (Yowsah, Yowsah, Yowsah),' but with 'I Want Your Love,' possibly Chic's greatest tune, Edwards & Rodgers' craftsmanship hit its stride." The album peaked at number 5 on the Billboard 200 chart.

TRANSITIONS DURING 1980S

As the 1980s commenced, disco began to lose its grip on the public. Chic's *Real People* (1980) sold fairly well, peaking at number 30 on the Billboard 200 chart, but it was clear that the group's popularity was falling. The following year the group released *Take It Off* (1981), which clearly represented an attempt to reduce its Euro-disco feel; Chic's music had always contained elements of funk and soul, but those were more pronounced now, as were pop and rock sounds. The album, which peaked at number 124 on the Billboard 200 chart and number 36 on the R&B chart, impressed some notable critics, such as the music journalist and blues historian Robert Palmer. In his review of the album for the *New York Times* (23 Dec. 1981), Palmer wrote: "The key to Chic's new direction turned out to be the same Chic rhythm section that powered the group's disco hits. The new album, *Take It Off*, succeeds brilliantly because it throws the spotlight squarely on Mr. Rodgers's guitar, Mr. Edwards's bass and Tony Thompson's drums. The sweet, elegant string arrangements that figured so prominently in the earlier Chic hits have been scrapped, and the new album's group vocals are lean, almost percussive. The first single to be released from the album, 'So Fine,' uses Mr. Rodgers's guitar as its lead instrument. He picks tricky, clipped rhythm figures, sounding at times a little like the late jazz guitarist Wes

Montgomery, while the band punctuates with stop-time rhythms. The vocalists fill in like a horn section. On other numbers, Mr. Edwards's bass takes the lead, and the voices and other instruments fall into place around it, like iron filings around a magnet. The deliberately sparse production emphasizes that this is the sound of a few gifted musicians working closely together." Chic's last two albums of that era—*Tongue in Chic* (1982) and *Believer* (1983)—yielded no hit songs and were largely ignored, except by the band's die-hard fans.

Chic disbanded in 1983. That same year— before Chic officially broke up—Rodgers's debut solo album, *Adventures in the Land of the Good Groove*, came out. The album, which featured Edwards on bass, for the most part eschewed disco in favor of funk ("Yum-Yum") and R&B ("My Love Song for You"). Two years later Rodgers released *B-Movie Matinee*, which, full of synthesizer-driven pop and dance songs, was a departure from both his first solo album and his work with Chic. With the exception of the song "Let's Go Out Tonight," which reached number 88 on the Billboard Hot 100 chart, the album did not generate any hits.

More significantly during that decade, Rodgers was considered the "hottest record producer in the business," in the words of Dennis Hunt, writing for the *Los Angeles Times* (9 Nov. 1985). Initially, in working on songs for other acts, he shared songwriting responsibilities with Edwards. In 1979 Rodgers, while still with Chic, had produced and cowritten most of the tracks for the Sister Sledge album *We Are Family*, including the title song, which became a huge hit and one of the most recognizable songs of the 1970s. He also wrote and coproduced all the songs for the next Sister Sledge album, *Love Somebody Today* (1980). Rodgers performed the same services for *Diana* (1980), the Diana Ross album that included such hit singles as "Upside Down" and "I'm Coming Out." Then, in the same year that Chic's members went their separate ways, Rodgers coproduced David Bowie's *Let's Dance* (1983), Bowie's best-selling album to date, containing the hits "Let's Dance," "China Girl," and "Modern Love." Rodgers also contributed his guitar playing to that art-rock dance record. The following year he produced Madonna's album *Like a Virgin* (1984), among whose hits were the title song and "Material Girl." Also that year Rodgers mixed the Duran Duran single "The Reflex," which later hit number one on the Hot 100 chart, and "The Wild Boys," which reached number two on the chart. In a 1985 interview with Hunt, Rodgers conceded, "I work too much. I should learn to say no. I always bite off more than I can chew." Rodgers also produced Mick Jagger's *She's the Boss* (1985), Jeff Beck's *Flash* (1985), Duran Duran's *Notorious* (1986), Debbie Harry's *One More into the Bleach*

(1988), and *Family Style* (1990), by the blues-guitar-playing brothers Jimmie Vaughan and Stevie Ray Vaughan. In the 1990s Rodgers's work was frequently sampled by rappers such as MC Lyte, Puff Daddy, Notorious B.I.G., Faith Evans, and Will Smith.

CHIC REUNITES
In 1992 Chic reunited and released *Chic-Ism*, an album of new songs that recalled the band's glory days. The record, which made it to number 39 on the R&B chart, had no hit singles but included the critically successful tracks "Chic Mystique" and "Your Love." In an interview with Larry Flick for the *New York Times* (15 Feb. 1992), Edwards explained why he had gotten back together with Rodgers to re-form Chic: "I think we realized that we share a creative bond that we have not been able to match with other people. More than anything, we genuinely missed making music together." In 1996, in a series of commemorative concerts in Japan, Rodgers performed alongside Edwards, Sister Sledge, Steve Winwood, Simon Le Bon, and the Guns N' Roses guitarist Slash. During that trip, soon after one of the performances, Edwards died of pneumonia. Recalling the incident two years later in an interview with Neil Strauss for the *New York Times* (2 Apr. 1998), Rodgers said: "He died on the last night of the show, and being the kind of musician he is, there's no way he's just going to leave the stage or cancel the show. Midway through the concert, we were doing 'Let's Dance,' and all of a sudden, the bass dropped out at the beginning of the verse. I thought: 'Wow, that's clever. . . .' And I turned around and didn't see him. He had passed out, and the roadies had picked him up and placed him behind the stage, and he was sitting there playing. When we took a break in the middle of the show to change clothes, I realized how incredibly sick he was. This is a person I love closer than any family member, a person I know better than anyone who has ever walked this earth, and I knew there was no way he was leaving that stage. That's how we were brought up." Rodgers added: "I'll never forget his last speech to the people from Japan. He told them he was a little sick with the Tokyo flu, but he was still here. He told me how much he loved me and how we've been together a long time, and he would do anything for me. Then we went into 'Good Times' and everybody in the house started singing it with us: 10,000 people who didn't even speak English singing 'Good Times' at the top of their lungs. At the end of the show, Bernard was crying in my arms, and he just said: 'You know, man, we did it. This music is bigger than us.'"

FILM AND WRITING PROJECTS
In addition to composing and producing songs for his own groups and other artists, Rodgers has created soundtracks for several films, including *Coming to America* (1988), *Blue Chips* (1994), *Beverly Hills Cop III* (1994), and *Rush Hour 2* (2001). His songs—particularly those he wrote for Chic, Diana Ross, and Sister Sledge—have been used in more than one hundred films and TV shows.

Rodgers's memoir, *Le Freak: An Upside Down Story of Family, Disco, and Destiny*, was well-received by critics. A reviewer for *Publishers Weekly* (3 Oct. 2011) wrote, "Rodgers's page-turning memoir is packed with emotionally charged vignettes of a tumultuous childhood and equally dramatic adulthood that found him awash in cash, cars, and celebrities. . . . While the story of velvet ropes and addiction is a common one, Rodgers's version emphasizes the arc of his life, rather than relying on salacious details or name-dropping to provide a narrative. His storytelling skills propel the reader through the book. . . . Remarkable for its candor, this rags-to-riches story is on the year's shortlist of celebrity memoirs." Luke Bainbridge wrote for the *London Observer* (5 Nov. 2011), "This is a rich, warm tale of a fascinating life in the golden age of New York—and pop."

HONORS, ORGANIZATIONS, AND PERSONAL LIFE
Rodgers has received many honors, including the National Academy of Recording Arts and Sciences New York Chapter's Governor's Lifetime Achievement Award. In 2005 he was inducted (along with Edwards) into the Dance Music Hall of Fame, in New York. Chic has been nominated to the Rock and Roll Hall of Fame six times—in 2003, '06, '07, '08, '10, and '11. Rodgers served as co-musical director for the tribute concert to Ahmet Ertegun (the founder and president of Atlantic Records) at the Montreux Jazz Festival in the summer of 2006.

Rodgers is the founder of the We Are Family Foundation, a not-for-profit organization dedicated to the vision of a "global family," according to its website. The foundation's goal is to inspire and educate children and promote cultural understanding.

In 1998 Rodgers founded Sumthing Distribution, a nationwide record distributor and creative outlet for independent artists and record labels. Most notably, it has created soundtracks for such popular video-game franchises as Resident Evil and Halo.

In 2010 Rodgers had surgery to combat an aggressive form of cancer. In March 2011 he announced that, according to test results, he is "cancer-free."

SUGGESTED READING
Hunt, Dennis. "Producer Is Cuts Above the Field." *Los Angeles Times* 9 Nov. 1985: V1.

Palmer, Robert. "The Pop Life." *New York Times* 23 Dec. 1981: C12.

Rodgers, Nile. "Mr. Rodgers's Neighborhood." *New York Times T: Men's Fashion Magazine.* New York Times Co., 7 Sep. 2011. Web. Jan. 2012.

—*Dmitry Kiper*

Virginia M. Rometty

Born: 1958
Occupation: CEO of IBM

Bloomberg via Getty Images

On January 1, 2012, Virginia M. Rometty, a thirty-one-year veteran of International Business Machines Corporation (IBM) became the company's president and chief executive officer. Rometty is the ninth person, and the first woman, to assume the top post at IBM. The company, as described by the *New York Times* in March 2012, is "the largest single supplier of information technology to corporations worldwide, selling more than $100 billion a year in services, software and hardware to businesses and governments." Rometty started her career at IBM two years after graduating from college, where she was among very few women who majored in electrical engineering and computer science then. As she rose up the corporate ladder, Rometty became a skilled manager, adding to her technological expertise a deep knowledge of marketing, sales strategy, and finance. According to an article published in the *Ottawa (Canada) Citizen* (27 Oct. 2011), she earned a reputation as "a polished executive who can close a sale."

Rometty has played a major role in transforming IBM from a seller of goods into a highly innovative corporate consultant. She has helped the company increase its focus on gathering and analyzing data in order to provide technological solutions to problems in finance, insurance, health care, and transportation. Through Rometty's guidance, the company has also shifted from reliance on petroleum-based fuels to sources of green energy. In 2002, Rometty spearheaded IBM's acquisition of PricewaterhouseCoopers Consulting (PwC), and then led the assimilation within IBM of PwC's 30,000 consulting professionals, who had been working in 160 nations. Rometty—at that time the general manager of IBM's business and information technology consulting unit—told Hymowitz and Frier, "It was the first and only time a professional services firm of that size has been integrated into another large company."

Rometty has stated that soon after beginning her career in business, she "learned to always take on things I'd never done before." In a speech she gave at *Fortune* magazine's 2011 Most Powerful Women Summit, Rometty said, "Really early, early in my career, I can remember being offered a big job. Right away I said, 'You know what? I'm not ready for this job.'" That night, when she told her husband about the offer and her response, "he just looked at me and he said, 'Do you think a man would have ever answered that question that way?' What that taught me was you have to be very confident even though you're so self-critical inside. Growth and comfort do not coexist."

EARLY YEARS AND EDUCATION

The oldest of four children, Rometty was born Virginia Marie "Ginni" Nicosia in Chicago, Illinois, in 1958. After her parents divorced, her mother raised her. Rometty's brother, Joseph T. Nicosia, is the chief executive officer of the Allenberg Cotton Company, a major international cotton-trading firm. Her sister Darlene Nicosia is the director of procurement for the Europe Group of Coca-Cola. Annette Ripper, another sister, was a partner with the management-consultant company Accenture for eighteen years. In the *New York Times* (2 Nov. 2011, online), James B. Stewart wrote that Rometty "is described as especially close to her mother," and he noted that she brought her mother to an event celebrating IBM's 100th anniversary in 2011.

Rometty majored in computer science and electrical engineering at the McCormick School of Engineering and Applied Science of Northwestern University, in Evanston, Illinois. "When I look back on my time at Northwestern, and then through the course of my career, I recognize that the most valuable thing I learned here was how to solve problems," Rometty told a McCormick/Northwestern Alumni Association interviewer (25 June 2010, online). "Not just engineering and science problems, but how to apply myself to any type of problem. In a word, I learned how to step back and 'think.'" Graduating with high honors, Rometty earned a BS degree from Northwestern in 1979.

EARLY CAREER

After finishing college, Rometty undertook an internship with the General Motors Institute, in Detroit, Michigan. Known as Kettering University since 1998, the school specializes in engineering and management, and grants both bachelors and masters degrees. Rometty worked with the institute's applications and systems development group. While working at the institute, she met and married her husband, Mark Rometty.

In 1981, Rometty went to work for IBM as a systems engineer in Detroit. IBM was first known as the Computing Tabulating Recording Corporation when it was established in 1911, following the merger of four companies that were marketing products such as clocks and electric tabulators. It was renamed the International Business Machines Company in 1924, during the half-century that the company was led by Thomas J. Watson, who coined its motto, "Think." When Rometty joined IBM, the company was headed by John R. Opel. John F. Akers served as CEO from 1985 to 1993; he was succeeded by Louis V. Gerstner Jr., who was CEO until 2002. Gerstner's successor as CEO was Samuel J. Palmisano. During her early years at IBM, Rometty served in several positions. She worked as a business and information-technology consultant, and as a general manager in IBM's global insurance and financial services sector. In the later position, she set up a "lucrative consulting division for the insurance sector," according to an IBM press release (25 Oct. 2011, online). Rometty also served as general manager for IBM's global services in the Americas.

MANAGING NEW PARTNERSHIPS

Among many other accomplishments, Rometty was instrumental in the completion of the 2002 deal between IBM and American Express (AmEx). As Larry Greenemeier wrote for *Information Week* (25 Feb. 2002, online), the $4 billion, seven-year deal established IBM as the sole manager of AmEx's "Web site, network servers, data storage, and help-desk support." The business agreement was the largest such deal ever negotiated by IBM Global Services.

Rometty was the general manager for strategy, marketing, and sales opportunities in IBM's global services division when, in July 2002, IBM announced that it had concluded an agreement with PricewaterhouseCoopers to acquire PwC's consulting division. The deal was valued at approximately $3.5 billion. Rometty helped to negotiate many aspects of the deal, which many observers considered risky at that time. Later, she oversaw the integration of 30,000 PwC professionals into a new corporate consulting arm. Rometty also helped promote and explain the deal in the media. As Daniel Eisenberg wrote for *Time* (2 Dec. 2002, online), she "insisted on taking time to call a few of her major customers to assure them that she would stay involved in their accounts." "It was vintage Rometty," he noted, "whose people skills and relentless focus on the customer have some IBM insiders discussing her as future CEO material." "We're creating a new category of services," Rometty told Eisenberg, referring to IBM's goal of becoming a major consultant for corporate clients in the areas of finance, purchasing, human resources, and customer services. Douglas T. Elix, the head of IBM's global services division, told Eisenberg that Rometty "has a great ability to gain the confidence of executives, including CEOs."

IBM BUSINESS CONSULTING

Rometty became the general manager of the new IBM Business Consulting Services unit, which includes 100,000 business consultants and service experts. More than 90 percent of PwC professionals chose to join the IBM workforce, and Rometty was praised for their smooth assimilation to IBM's organizational structure. Tereza Nemessanyi, a PwC employee who had participated in the acquisition process, wrote for the website Women 2.0 (Oct. 2011) that on the day IBM announced its purchase of PwC Consulting, she and the thousands of other PwC consultants received a recorded phone message that began, "Hello, I'm Ginni Rometty." "In roughly two minutes," Nemessanyi continued, Rometty "welcome[d] us to the IBM family, [told] us we were very special, that we would retain the best of our culture, and—make no mistake—we'd very soon be part of IBM. . . . It was electric." Referring to the "cost-cutting culture" that prevailed at IBM, Hymowitz and Frier reported that "when [management] wanted to cut travel budgets" by making the former PwC employees and all other IBM consultants "stay at Holiday Inns" rather than more upscale accommodations, Rometty "helped them fight—and win."

In 2005, Rometty was promoted to senior vice president of IBM Global Business Services. In this role, she was instrumental in developing IBM's cloud computing capacity. In 2007, IBM teamed up with Google to develop a cloud-based system for students and educators. As Steve Lohr described for the *New York Times* (8 Oct. 2007, online), the project resulted in "large data centers that students can tap into over the Internet to program and research remotely." Using IBM's SmartCloud in early 2012, cancer researchers at the Freie Universität Berlin succeeded in analyzing 12,000 patient records 250 times faster than was previously possible. The municipal government of Wuxi, an industrial and commercial center in southeastern China, created a "virtual infrastructure" that benefited both new businesses and city planners and transformed [the city] into a "high-tech hub in less than four years."

Rometty also had a large hand in the commercialization of Watson, IBM's question-and-answer supercomputer, which, as Darryl K. Taft wrote for eWeek.com (2 Nov. 2011), "understands the meaning and context of human language, can analyze data, and learn correlations between data. When applied to the banking and finance industry," Taft continued, "Watson-like technologies can uncover hidden patterns in data that can rapidly identify market trends, and provide deep, integrated risk analysis." Watson made its debut before a national television audience in February 2011, when it participated on the quiz show *Jeopardy!* Watson was pitted between two human contestants: Ken Jennings, who won for seventy-four consecutive weeks on *Jeopardy!* in 2004, and Brad Rutter, whose dollar winnings are greater than those of any other *Jeopardy!* player. Watson won the three-day match by a margin of more than $50,000.

On October 31, 2011, IBM hosted a symposium at which company representatives introduced Watson to professors and students from the Sloan School of Management at the Massachusetts Institute of Technology and Harvard Business School. The participants discussed the ways in which such technology can be applied by researchers and entrepreneurs. They also discussed how teachers and students might, in Taft's words, "benefit from the ability to work with companies to create curricula that incorporate real-world case studies and [bring] breakthrough technology like Watson into the classroom." Taft quotes Bernard Meyerson, vice president of innovation and academic programs at IBM, as saying, "Watson will transform how the world works. Our goal in demonstrating Watson's capabilities and sharing our insights from its development is to challenge the leaders of tomorrow to leverage this new capability in ways we've yet to imagine."

CEO OF IBM

On October 25, 2011, IBM announced that its board of directors had chosen Rometty to succeed Samuel J. Palmisano as president and CEO of the company, effective on January 1, 2012. Rometty also earned a seat on the board. The press release announcing the decision explained how Rometty had been "accountable for revenue, profit, and client satisfaction in the 170 global markets in which IBM does business. She is responsible for IBM's worldwide results, which exceeded $99 billion in 2010. She also

is responsible for leading IBM's global strategy, marketing and communications functions." In a statement included in the press release, Palmisano, who remained IBM's chairman, described Rometty as "more than a superb operational executive. With every leadership role, she has strengthened our ability to integrate IBM's capabilities for our clients. She has spurred us to keep pace with the needs and aspirations of our clients by deepening our expertise and industry knowledge. . . . She brings to the role of CEO a unique combination of vision, client focus, unrelenting drive, and passion for IBMers and the company's future."

On January 1, 2012, IBM was listed eighteenth overall on *Fortune* magazine's annual ranking of the largest 500 corporations in the United States. On that date, when Rometty took over as IBM's head, she joined seventeen other women with the top position in a Fortune 500 company. In a talk she gave at Northwestern University in 2011 in conjunction with IBM's celebration of its centennial, Rometty said, according to a McCormick School news release (16 Mar. 2011, online), that as an IBM executive, she had always been guided by Thomas J. Watson's core principle. "We must never think what we have today," she said, "will satisfy demand ten years from now."

Along with many others, Rometty has attributed IBM's longevity to its continual reinvention of itself and its focus on meeting the needs of its customers. Rometty told the Northwestern University audience that success in business also requires "making big bets"—taking large but carefully considered risks. It is also vital, she said, to create within a corporation "a culture of working for a higher purpose."

As IBM's chief executive officer, Rometty has campaigned widely to publicize the company's "Smarter Cities" program, which has initiated nearly 2,500 municipal projects worldwide. According to IBM.com, "The IBM Intelligent Operations Center for Smarter Cities (also available for cloud) synchronizes and analyzes efforts among sectors and agencies as they happen, giving decision makers consolidated information that helps them anticipate—rather than just react to—problems. By using these tested approaches, cities can manage growth and development in a sustainable way that minimizes disruptions and helps increase prosperity for everyone." In a groundbreaking project described by Natasha Singer for the *New York Times* (3 Mar. 2012, online), IBM created, "a citywide system integrating data from some thirty agencies, all under a single roof" in Rio De Janeiro, Brazil. "City employees in white jumpsuits work quietly in front of a giant wall of screens—a sort of virtual Rio, rendered in real time," Singer wrote, after visiting the operations center. "Video streams in from subway stations and major intersections. A sophisticated weather program predicts rainfall across the city. A map glows with the locations of car accidents, power failures and other problems. . . . What is happening here reflects a bold and potentially lucrative experiment that could shape the future of cities around the world." In November 2011, IBM Social Media released a video recording of "How to Build a Smarter City," a talk that Rometty gave in Rio de Janeiro.

Martin Feldstein, the George F. Baker professor of economics at Harvard University and a former president of the National Bureau of Economic Research has called Rometty "a serious, no-nonsense thinker." Fred Amoroso, one of Rometty's supervisors in the 1990s, has described her as "an engaging woman—great with customers. Customers just love Ginni." In a profile for *McCormick Magazine* (Fall 2010, online), Rometty told Emily Ayshford, "I have a huge passion for clients. None of our businesses would exist without them. In my position, I'm responsible for those relationships across the company, and today that's all about how to change their businesses and make their businesses successful. It's not about technology. It's about how to drive outcomes for them in a world that's become very volatile and complex and full of opportunity."

From 2006 to 2009, Rometty was a member of the board of directors of the American International Group (AIG). She is a member of the Council on Foreign Relations; the board of overseers and board of managers of the Memorial Sloan-Kettering Cancer Center; the board of directors of APQC (the American Productivity & Quality Center); and the board of trustees of Northwestern University. As a participant in IBM's Women in Technology Council and Women's Leadership Council, she has actively promoted diversity within the company's workforce. She is also a "senior sponsor" of IBM's Women's Executive Council. Her honors include the 2006 Association of Management Consultants Firms' Carl S. Sloane Award for Excellence in Management Consulting, and the Northwestern Alumni Association's 2010 Alumni Merit Award.

PERSONAL LIFE

Rometty and her husband maintain homes in Bonita Springs, Florida; Bloomfield Hills, Michigan; and White Plains, New York, a few miles south of IBM's Armonk, New York, headquarters. According to thomaswhite.com, Mark Rometty "always kept a very low profile" as his wife gained ever-greater responsibilities at IBM. He works as the manager, treasurer, and principal investor in the Bam Oil Company, based in Bonita Springs. In their leisure time, the Romettys enjoy scuba diving.

SUGGESTED READING

Eisenberg, Daniel. "Ginni Rometty: Head of IBM Business Consulting Services." *Time*. Time, Inc., 2 Dec. 2012. Web. 4 Mar. 2012.

"Global Players: Virginia Rometty, CEO-designate, IBM." *Thomas White*. Thomas White Global Investing, 22 Nov. 2011. Web. 5 Mar. 2012.

Hymowitz, Carol, and Sarah Frier. "A New Boss at Big Blue; Virginia Rometty, a 'Serious, No-nonsense Thinker,' Becomes the First Female CEO of Behemoth IBM." *Ottawa (Canada) Citizen* 27 Oct. 2011: D6.

Krantz, Matt, and Jon Swartz. "IBM Joins Elite Group of 100-Year-Old Companies." *USA Today*. USA TODAY, Gannett Satellite Information Network, Inc., 16 June 2011. Web. 5 Mar. 2012.

Stewart, James B. "A C.E.O.'s Support System, a k a Husband." *The New York Times*. The New York Times Co., 4 Nov. 2011. Web. 5 Mar. 2012.

Waters, Richard. "More Than a Big Smile on Big Blue's Face." *Financial Times*. Financial Times LTD, 28 Oct. 2011. Web. 5 Mar. 2012.

—*Miriam Helbok*

Jon Ronson

Born: May 10, 1967
Occupation: Journalist, documentary filmmaker

The British journalist Jon Ronson is best known in the United States for his informative and amusing best sellers: *Them: Adventures with Extremists* (2001), for which he spent time with Muslim fundamentalists, Ku Klux Klan (KKK) members, and other extremists; *The Men Who Stare at Goats* (2004), the unbelievable yet true story of the US Army's attempt to teach paranormal powers to a select group of soldiers; and *The Psychopath Test: A Journey through the Madness Industry* (2011), in which Ronson examines the concept of madness in conversations with psychologists as well as people he suspects of being psychopaths. *The Men Who Stare at Goats* was made into a major motion picture, released in 2009, starring George Clooney, Jeff Bridges, Ewan McGregor, and Kevin Spacey. Most of the reporting for these three books had roots in Ronson's Channel 4 documentaries, such as *Tottenham Ayatollah* (1997), *New Klan* (1999), and *Secret Rulers of the World* (2001). Ronson is also a columnist for the London *Guardian* newspaper.

GROWING UP AND ROCKING OUT

Jon Ronson was born to Jewish parents, David and Paula Ronson, on May 10, 1967, in Cardiff, Wales. Some of his fondest and most vivid memories of growing up in Cardiff include listening to records, watching films, and reading books. In a 2005 interview with blogger Anthony Brockway that appears on Ronson's official website, Ronson recalled, "I remember seeing a double bill of Woody Allen's *Zelig* and Martin Scorsese's *King of Comedy* at Chapter [Arts Center]. I remember that better than pretty much anything that actually happened to me. Yes, the things I remember most clearly from my childhood are things I watched and listened to rather than things I experienced." Ronson also listened to the rock music of Tom Waits, David Bowie, and Lou Reed, read Kurt Vonnegut novels, and played keyboard.

After graduating from high school, Ronson moved to London, where he studied journalism at the Polytechnic of Central London. When he was around twenty years old, Ronson unexpectedly joined a pop/rock band, the Frank Sidebottom Oh Blimey! Big Band. Ronson had had no plans to join the band—until one night, at the very last minute, the band's keyboardist could not play and the band asked Ronson if he could join them on stage. Ronson recalled to Brockway that although he knew none of the songs, he was assured by the band's manager that he would be okay if he could play the "C, F, and G" chords. After the concert, Ronson stayed with the band, moved to Manchester, England, and dropped out of school. "Life on the road was a more glamorous prospect than journalism studies," he told Brockway.

Ronson stayed with the band for three years. During his time with the band, Ronson cohosted a late-night radio show in Stockport, England, about ten miles southeast of Manchester. Although Ronson did not hold onto that gig, it would ultimately lead him to his first writing job, which would then lead to television documentary work and ultimately to a career as a bestselling author.

TELEVISION DOCUMENTARIES

After Ronson was fired from the late-night radio show, Manchester newspapers campaigned to persuade the station to reinstate him and his cohost. As a result of the media attention, Ronson was contacted by an editor for *Time Out* magazine to write a weekly column. During his brief time as a columnist, he got a call from a former journalism teacher from his days at Polytechnic of Central London, who suggested that he do a television series. He eventually ended up meeting with higher-ups at the BBC, who provided him with substantial funds for a six-part, half-hour television series on BBC 2.

The show, titled *The Ronson Mission*, premiered in 1993 and was a series of documentary-style "comedy investigations" tailored for the youth market. Ronson was twenty-six years old at the time. The show had six "missions,"

Getty Images

which included satirical examinations of celebrity charity projects, cult leaders, and absurdist interviews, such as Ronson and his camera crew running up to Serbian dictator Radovan Karadžić at peace talks in Geneva, Switzerland, and asking him, "You're one of the world's most elegant dictators. How do you manage to keep so fit?"

Neil Crombie, the show's producer, told Louise Jury for the London *Guardian* (7 Sep. 1993) that the show was "screamingly funny," although "we think of what we are doing as journalism . . . . We try to explore dark subjects in a bleak, personal, and odd way." Most critics, however, were not amused. James Rampton wrote for the London *Independent* (9 Sep. 1993), "Ronson may be a dazzling ironist on the cutting edge of deconstructionism, fearlessly sending up exploitative investigative documentaries. But that doesn't make him funny." Rampton then pointed out that most of Ronson's "satirical punches . . . fail to find the target."

Ronson was critical of the show himself. Speaking to Brockway, Ronson recalled, "We basically made it up as we went along. . . . Actually, most of it was terrible. I was just in my mid-twenties. I had had no ambition whatsoever to be on TV. It was all quite surreal." He added, "I didn't enjoy making it, primarily because these were the days before [digital video] cameras, and so there was a huge crew . . . After *The Ronson Mission* I didn't make any more TV shows for at least three years. I was glad to have it behind me."

But opportunity came calling again when Ronson was contacted by Channel 4. Convinced that the newly available high-resolution eight-millimeter (hi-8) camcorders were much smaller and therefore less intrusive, Ronson set out to treat the camera as a kind of notebook in his next foray into documentary filmmaking. Ronson's second documentary for Channel 4, *Tottenham Ayatollah* (1997), was a major success. Will Self for the London *Observer* (13 Apr. 1997) called it "a funny, yet genuinely perceptive, fly-on-the-wall documentary."

For *Tottenham Ayatollah*, Ronson spent a year with Omar Bakri Muhammad, the titular "ayatollah," a radical Islamist who came to England after being exiled from Syria for his support of militant Muslim terrorist groups such as Hamas. He settled in Tottenham, a borough in the Greater London area. Omar Bakri believes in a very strict interpretation of the Qur'an and hates Jews, homosexuals, and generally most things Western, including popular music. Ronson did not initially tell Omar Bakri that he was Jewish, and when he did, Omar Bakri claimed to have known all along.

In his positive review of the documentary, Will Self pointed out its major theme, "While the majority of Muslims who live in Britain are far from being fundamentalists, there is nevertheless a great deal of mutual incomprehension between our communities. The British tradition of granting political asylum becomes that much more problematic when the asylum-seekers are on the face of it objecting precisely to the secular ethic that supports the tradition." Yet despite Omar Bakri's "bloodthirsty rhetoric," wrote Self, he turns out to be "a perversely likable man." Many more Channel 4 documentaries followed. *Tottenham Ayatollah* was the beginning of what would become Ronson's trademark: looking earnestly—with a kind of faux naïveté—into the lives of individuals whose beliefs most people would find objectionable, odd, unbelievable, or despicable. Ronson again employed that approach for *Dr. Paisley, I Presume* (1998). For the documentary Ronson followed Reverend Ian Paisley on an evangelical tour of Cameroon, a country in Western Africa, where Paisley preached his fundamentalist interpretation of the Bible. "The result," wrote Peter Bradshaw for the London *Evening Standard* (28 Apr. 1998), "was hilarious and surreal, with Dr. Paisley emerging from the shimmering heat-haze landscape like a bad dream coauthored by Joseph Conrad and Mo Mowlam."

Ronson next explored organized racism in the United States in *New Klan* (1999), which looked at KKK leader Thom Robb, who had started a KKK sect that was supposedly less hateful, or more careful in its public displays of hate and use of racist language. But, wrote Victor Lewis-Smith for the London *Evening Standard* (3 Aug.

1999), "once Ronson began doing what he does best, ingratiating himself with his subjects, winning their trust," they spoke openly, revealing their hateful, racist views.

His next documentary, also amusing and disturbing, was a five-part series titled *Secret Rulers of the World* (2001). It came out in England the same year as his book *Them: Adventures with Extremists* and covered similar territory. In the documentary, he interviews a variety of people—some of whom are virulent anti-Semites—who believe that the world is ruled by a secret elite that controls the world's finances, launches wars, and takes part in various shadowy machinations. Some of the people he interviews, such as British author David Icke and American talk radio host Alex Jones, also appear in *Them*. Three years later, on a similar theme, Ronson's three-part series *Crazy Rulers of the World* (2004) aired on Channel 4. The first part of that series was titled "The Men Who Stare at Goats," which accompanied a book of the same name that was published that year. It examined the US military's attempt, starting in 1979, to try to train some of its soldiers to use supernatural powers.

BOOKS

In *Them: Adventures with Extremists*, Ronson enters the world of Muslim radicals, conspiracy theorists, Christian separatists, and white supremacists. He explores their lives and their beliefs, and he mines both for absurdity and humor. When the book came out in England, in the spring of 2001, it received many good reviews. "This book is chilling and hilarious by turns," wrote David V. Barrett for the London *Independent* (25 May 2001). "Ronson's trademark laid-back attitude is a delight and probably the only reason he gets away with saying the things he does to hate-filled extremists." However, A. C. Grayling, in a review for the London *Independent on Sunday* (15 Apr. 2001), offered a less positive assessment: "When Muslim fanatics dispense leaflets on London streets denouncing Israel and homosexuality, or white supremacists waste ammunition on rows of tins in their Idaho fastness, they seem merely comical. But they, and all extremists, cease to be comical when they bomb, assassinate, foment hatreds, issue fatwahs, get into gunfights with the police—and even start wars. . . . Ronson's account of them is amusing but superficial, and nowhere near angry enough."

Them: Adventures with Extremists came out in the United States on December 31, 2001, not quite four months after the devastating terrorist attacks of September 11, 2001. Aside from Muslim extremist Omar Bakri and KKK leader Thom Robb, American readers were also introduced to Austin, Texas, radio talk-show host and conspiracy theorist Alex Jones as well as another conspiracy theorist, David Icke, who believes that the world is secretly controlled by twelve-foot "Annunaki lizards . . . from the lower fourth dimension." But the obsessions and fears of some extremists, wrote Ronson, form the foundation for acts of terrorism. That "unamusing conclusion," wrote Jonathan Yardley for the *Washington Post* (3 Jan. 2002), can be drawn from "this most amusing book."

Some American reviewers, even while praising the book, took issue with Ronson for his cool detachment. Writing for the *New York Times* (18 Jan. 2002), Patricia Cohen noted, "The irreverence is refreshing and strangely comforting. Mr. Ronson's hate-spewing extremists are buffoons, so pathetically foolish at times that they're almost endearing." But she went on to caution, "The problem is that after September 11, it's hard to be quite so detached about extremists. They are linked to terror, as Mr. Ronson himself acknowledges when he lifts the bemused neutrality for a moment toward the end of the book. . . . Such observations are curiously absent for most of the book, however."

In his next book, *The Men Who Stare at Goats* (2004), Ronson described the history and modern uses of the First Earth Battalion, a secret US Army unit established in 1979 to train a select group of soldiers in supernatural and paranormal abilities. Among the skills the soldiers attempted to master were becoming invisible, walking through walls, reading minds, and killing someone simply by staring (using goats as test subjects). In 1995 the Central Intelligence Agency (CIA) declassified the black-op program. "For much of the book, readers can be forgiven if they think they are reading fiction," wrote Jai Singh for the *Boston Globe* (17 Apr. 2005). "Soldiers attempt to kill goats by staring at them and telepathically stopping the goat's heart. The only man said to have been successful in felling a goat spends a day with Ronson, but offers only a home video that demonstrates his telepathic power on a hamster." Singh added, "The seemingly fictional, however, bumps into reality. In 2004, the Special Forces call in the original goat killer—a martial arts instructor named Guy Savelli—for consultations in the wake of the Abu Ghraib scandal."

One of the "nonviolent" ideas of the old program was the use of jarring and dissonant sounds as a weapon of war, an idea that was transformed and implemented in the United States' War on Terror by continuously blasting Barney the Purple Dinosaur songs into the cells of some Iraqi prisoners. Singh later added, "Ronson comes off as an unusual cross between Comedy Central's Jon Stewart and the *New Yorker*'s Seymour Hersh. He is too serious and inquisitive to be pure comedian and too personality driven and anecdotal to be an investigative reporter." In yet another positive review, Janet Maslin for the *New York Times* (7 Apr. 2005) observed, "Mr. Ronson

sets his book up beautifully. It moves with wry, precise agility from crackpot to crackpot in its search for the essence of this early New Age creativity." In conclusion, Maslin pointed out that Ronson "remains terrifically adept at capturing the horror of these developments without losing track of their lunacy."

In his next best seller, *The Psychopath Test: A Journey through the Madness Industry* (2011), Ronson examined contemporary concepts of madness and the role madness plays in our lives. The name of the book is a reference to the standard diagnostic checklist, called the Hare PCL-R Checklist, developed by noted psychopathy expert and psychologist Robert Hare. Ronson took a three-day seminar from Hare and intently studied the checklist, which enumerates twenty traits, such as "glibness/superficial charm," "lack of remorse or guilt," and "callous/lack of empathy." To be labeled a psychopath, one must receive a certain score, which is compiled based on both the amount and intensity of traits present.

In search of real-life psychopaths, Ronson interviewed the imprisoned Haitian death-squad leader Toto Constant, who had committed grave atrocities, and "Chainsaw Al" Dunlap, a businessman known for his ruthlessness. The book takes yet another turn when describing Ronson's meeting with a twenty-nine-year-old inmate at Broadmoor, a psychiatric hospital in England. The man told Ronson that he had pretended to be insane to get out of a long jail sentence but for the past twelve years has been unable to convince the system that he is in fact sane. Ronson also interviewed the editor of the fourth edition of the *Diagnostic and Statistical Manual of Mental Disorders* (*DSM-IV*), the American Psychiatric Association's catalog of conditions and disorders. Ronson's account also considers the relationship between common conceptions of madness and how madness is portrayed in the media.

The Psychopath Test was generally well received. Ronson's "winning style pervades most" of the book, wrote Janet Maslin for the *New York Times* (16 May 2011). Carolyn Kellogg for the *Los Angeles Times* (19 May 2011) called it "cheerily kooky as it is well researched." Some critics, however, wanted more depth. Rachel Cooke, in a mixed review for the London *Observer* (11 June 2011), pointed out, "Ronson's new book is provocative and interesting, and you will, I guarantee, zip merrily through it. But it also reveals, sometimes painfully, the limitations of his journalistic technique. He skates when you want him to dig; he does that amazed, disingenuous thing, when a little old-fashioned anger and indignation would serve him far better."

Ronson is also the author of *Clubbed Class* (1994), *Out of the Ordinary: True Tales of Everyday Craziness* (2006), and *What I Do: More True Tales of Everyday Craziness* (2007). The last two are collections of his humor columns for the London *Guardian*.

Jon Ronson and his wife, culture journalist Elaine Ronson, live in London. They have a son named Joel.

SUGGESTED READING

Cohen, Patricia. "Hopping Rides with a Range of Extremists." *New York Times* 18 Jan. 2002: E55. Print.

Cooke, Rachel. "A Touch Too Much of the Funny-ha-ha." *Observer* 12 June 2011: BR40. Print.

Jonronson.com. Jon Ronson, 2011. Web. 7 Feb. 2012.

Kellogg, Carolyn. "The Disputed Borders of Sane." *Los Angeles Times* 19 May 2011: D9. Print.

Maslin, Janet. "True Tales Odd Enough to Stop a Farm Animal's Heart." *New York Times* 7 Apr. 2005: E12. Print.

Rosenbaum, Ron. "Beyond the Fringe." *New York Times* 13 Jan. 2002: 7.10. Print.

Singh, Jai. "When 'The X-Files' Met the Army." *Boston Globe* 17 Apr. 2005: C7. Print.

—*Dmitry Kiper*

AFP/Getty Images

Philip Rosedale

Born: September 29, 1968
Occupation: Entrepreneur and founder of Linden Lab

To the uninitiated, Second Life, a virtual world launched by Philip Rosedale in 2003, may seem little more than a computer game. But, as Joe Stafford wrote for the *Austin American-Statesman* (23 Jan. 2005), "Second Life is not about armed conquest, explosions, or amassing point totals. It simply is about living in a different place, a place where virtually nothing is impossible." That place, he explained, "is a tiny Xanadu existing only on the servers of a California company and in the minds and hard drives of its subscribers."

Second Life never became the online juggernaut that Rosedale had originally hoped. After a flurry of positive media attention, which included cover stories in such major publications as *BusinessWeek* and *Newsweek*, the excitement surrounding the enterprise died down within a few years. Reporters began noting disparagingly that much of the activity in Second Life was either mind-numbingly prosaic or sexual in nature. "The problem with creating an immersive 3-D experience is that it is just too involved, and so it's hard to get people to engage," Rosedale admitted to Quentin Hardy for the *New York Times* (8 Nov. 2011). "Smart people in rural areas, the

handicapped, people looking for companionship—they love it. But you have to be highly motivated to get on and learn to use it."

While Rosedale, who has since gone on to other ventures, may not have changed the world in the way he had envisioned, Second Life still boasts a million active users. Although the website seemingly consists, for the most part, of virtual night clubs and beach resorts, several universities and nonprofit organizations maintain a presence there as well, extending their educational and philanthropic missions beyond the usual boundaries.

EARLY LIFE AND EDUCATION

Rosedale, the oldest of four siblings, was born in San Diego, California, on September 29, 1968. His mother was an English teacher who stopped working outside the home in order to raise her children; his father was a US Navy jet-fighter pilot who became an architect after retiring from the military.

Rosedale was a curious and technologically adept child. "I . . . always wanted to kind of make the world's biggest Lego kit," he told David Pogue for the CBS News program *Sunday Morning* (18 Feb. 2007). He was intensely interested in exploring other worlds. "I would build cardboard rockets in my parents' basement," he recalled to John Preston for the London *Sunday Telegraph* (11 Nov. 2007). "I'd sit inside my rocket, look up at the sky and think about going into space. For me, computers have the same liberating potential. I always thought, from the very beginning, that you should be able to use computers to imagine and simulate a place that frees us from all the problems that we have with reality."

When Rosedale was in fourth grade, he built a rudimentary analog computer using a kit he had ordered from the back of *Popular Mechanics*. When he was in middle school, however, his parents purchased him an Apple IIe, a desktop computer that was considered to be on the cutting edge when it was introduced in 1983.

In addition to teaching himself computer programming, Rosedale built his own music synthesizer and rigged his bedroom door with a garage-door opener so that it swung up and out of sight when a button was pressed. He imagined, as he has told interviewers, that the door on a spaceship would work in a similar way. At the age of seventeen, he started his own company, Automated Management Systems. The company sold, installed, and serviced software that Rosedale created for architectural firms, car dealerships, and other businesses.

Rosedale used the proceeds from Automated Management Systems to fund his tuition at the University of California, San Diego, where he majored in physics. Because he was used to coasting by on his wits, creativity, and natural talent, college provided a rude awakening. "I remember taking an honors physics sequence, and it was one of the most depressing experiences I had ever had," he told Kelli Anderson for @UCSD, an online alumni publication (May 2009). "I thought I was so smart, yet those classes absolutely punished me." During his senior year, Rosedale, who eventually learned to relish the hard work necessitated by college-level courses, served as a teaching assistant for a class in experimental physics, in which students were given ten weeks to develop and construct their own inventions. He earned his bachelor of science degree in 1992.

EARLY CAREER

After graduating from the University of California, Rosedale drove his 1972 Cadillac convertible to San Francisco. There, he and Gary Greenbaum, a fellow physics student whom he had met in San Diego, founded FreeVue, a company that developed software for use in the still-new practice of videoconferencing. In 1996, FreeVue was purchased by RealNetwork, a Seattle-based firm involved in streaming media— content that can be viewed or heard while it is in the process of being delivered. Welcoming the chance to gain experience in engineering management, Rosedale signed on as the chief technology officer (CTO) for the company.

Rosedale remained with RealNetwork until 1999, when a combination of factors made it appear as though his youthful dream of building a virtual world might actually be feasible. "When networks [had first] started emerging, I was struck by the idea that the most fantastic thing you could possibly do was get a whole bunch of computers together and then in some manner simulate the laws of physics," he told Andrew Cave for the London *Daily Telegraph* (20 Dec. 2008). "You could potentially, through the looking glass of a computer screen, create a world that has similar physical properties to ours. You could build the dream gadgets, cars, houses, and stuff that you could only imagine but that are difficult to actually create in the real world."

Among the factors making Rosedale's vision seem within reach was the advent of broadband Internet access for the home market. Prior to that time, most users logged onto the Internet using dial-up modems that tied up their phone lines and required several hours to download even a short video. With broadband access through a cable modem, the savvy computer users of 1999 enjoyed much speedier connection times and no longer had to consider adding a second phone line to their homes. However, even if the average computer user had enjoyed broadband access before the end of the decade, there were few websites or services offering truly appealing 3-D computer graphics. That changed when a company called Nvidia introduced its revolutionary GeForce2, a graphic processing unit (GPU) that allowed for an unprecedented level of realism and capability.

INSPIRATION FOR VIRTUAL LIFE

In addition to the technological factors that made Rosedale's vision seem possible, he was also inspired by two cultural phenomena. The year 1999 marked his first attendance at Burning Man, an annual gathering held in the Black Rock Desert of Nevada, which attracts thousands of artists, spiritual seekers, and free-thinkers. Greeted by a large sign that declared "No Spectators," Rosedale was transfixed. "As I wandered around Burning Man, I was struck by a couple of things," he related in a video interview for *Examiner.com* (22 June 2012). "One was that . . . you can build a lot of crazy stuff if you just remove the inhibitions and a lot of the physical constraints around building. . . . The other thing I was struck by is the mind-boggling sense of community. . . . It really motivated me." Rosedale conducted the video interview in the guise of his Second Life avatar—the computer-generated figure that represents him online. The avatar, which shares few physical traits with him aside from being a Caucasian male, is known on the Internet as Philip Linden.

Rosedale had also been influenced by a book given to him by his wife, Yvette. *Snow Crash*, by Neal Stephenson, was published in 1992 and was billed by its publisher as the "gigathriller of the information age." The cyberpunk novel follows the adventures of the aptly named Hiro Protagonist, who is a pizza deliveryman in the real world but a warrior prince with a vital mission in the Internet, or "Metaverse." Second Life bears marked similarities to Stephenson's virtual world, as many observers have pointed out, and Rosedale has stated that although he had long harbored the idea for Second Life, he was still inspired and encouraged by reading Stephenson's work.

LINDEN LAB AND SECOND LIFE
Leaving RealNetwork, Rosedale joined Accel Partners, a venture-capital firm, as an entrepreneur-in-residence. Although his ideas did not ultimately attract funds from Accel, one of the firm's principals, Mitch Kapor—best known as the designer of the Lotus computer application—was impressed. Later in 1999, using money he had saved from the sale of FreeVue, plus an infusion of cash from Kapor personally, Rosedale founded Linden Lab, naming his new company after the San Francisco street on which it was originally located. Focusing on hardware development, he began trying to develop a haptic device that would allow users to interact realistically in a virtual world. The term haptic refers to sense of touch; robotic arms, for example, employ haptic technology.

Soon, however, Rosedale turned his energies to creating the virtual world itself, and in March 2002, a testing version of Second Life—originally called Linden World—was launched. Its first inhabitant was an avatar named Stellar Sunshine, who was controlled, in reality, by a mother of four from southern California. During her first evening in the virtual world, the woman, who had been chosen because she was a longtime participant in the world of virtual reality and computer gaming, created a cabin with smoke rising from its chimney and a giant beanstalk, which her avatar was able to climb by moving from leaf to leaf.

Second Life was opened to subscribers from the general public in June 2003, and within two years it had attracted its first 100,000 users. After that, the pace accelerated, and by 2006 the subscriber base was growing at an estimated rate of 20 percent a month, even without a concerted effort by Linden Labs. "The main reason is that there are [now] enough people and content for it to be interesting," Rosedale told Andrew McCormick for *New Media Age* (19 Oct. 2006). "Doing a marketing campaign at launch would have been futile as there was [almost] nothing there. . . . It has grown virally and organically— almost all recruitment is by word of mouth and general awareness. As more people come to the service, it becomes more compelling."

THE ATTRACTIONS OF SECOND LIFE
Those who sign up for a no-cost, basic subscription to Second Life are given an avatar with a nondescript outfit and hairstyle and are free to roam the various environments that have been built by other users. Few have remained satisfied with that option for long. For a small fee, avatars can be personalized, and for a monthly "property tax" of about $10, a person can obtain a plot of virtual land on which to design a personalized structure or environment. While some people have created futuristic landscapes, gothic castles, or sylvan fairylands, others have been slightly more rooted in reality. "They want oceanfront property . . . and they want palm trees, and they want a cantilevered Frank Lloyd Wright house, up a little bit from a beach at a pier with a little power boat," Rosedale told Toby Sterling for the Associated Press Financial Wire (9 Oct. 2006). "And then they watch the sun set on the deck."

Depeche Mode and Duran Duran, among other music groups, have held concerts in Second Life, using avatars that closely resemble their members, and some big companies have also made their presence felt. Toyota, for example, arranged test-drives of its new models for avatars who dropped by a virtual showroom. Several colleges saw advantages to establishing a presence in the virtual world and built campuses in Second Life, where their students can gather to obtain information or listen to streaming lectures. In one instance, a Ball State University English class, scheduled to be conducted on Second Life with eighteen students, attracted more than three hundred applicants.

High-profile politicians, including John Edwards and Nicolas Sarkozy, set up virtual campaign offices, and in 2008 the US House Energy and Commerce Committee's subcommittee on telecommunications held a hearing in Second Life. Those who gathered to watch subcommittee chair Edward Markey's avatar conduct the session included several female Second Life inhabitants in bikinis, a naked man, a pink catlike creature, and a gothic character sporting feathered wings.

MONEY-MAKING OPPORTUNITIES
Individual entrepreneurial ventures quickly sprang up in Second Life. For example, for a fee, an experienced Second Life user might sell you a deluxe "skin" for your avatar; unsurprisingly the best-selling female models tend to be slim and large-breasted, while the most popular male versions boast sculpted muscles and trendy hairstyles. An enterprising businessperson can also offer to decorate a fellow user's virtual home, provide a new virtual wardrobe, or plan a virtual wedding for two avatars. It has not been uncommon for two people who are totally unknown to each other in real life to marry in Second Life, and the phenomenon has been known to cause friction between legal spouses. Users can also buy virtual pets from virtual pet shops, virtual meals from virtual gourmet shops, or virtual tattoos from a virtual tattoo artist. All of Second

Life's vendors legally own the intellectual rights to their creations. This means, for example, that if online pet-shop owner has written computer code that enables a virtual dog to do a particular trick, a rival cannot simply copy the code for his own use.

While business on Second Life is conducted in an imaginary currency known as Lindens, users can cash in their virtual earnings at online currency exchanges. As in the real-life financial world, exchange rates vary, and some companies, such as the gaming site *IGN*, buy Lindens when prices are low and later resell them at a profit. Lindens are not the only such currency traded in that manner; the "gold" coins used in various online adventure games are also actively bought and sold. In a single month, Gaming Open Market, a major player in the industry, has been known to handle trades worth an estimated $200,000—in real US dollars.

A Chinese German businesswoman named Ailin Graef, who controls an avatar she calls Anshe Chung, reportedly earned $100,000 in 2005, at the height of Second Life's popularity, by leasing land in virtual locations considered particularly desirable. Some journalists have faulted Rosedale for publicizing that figure, asserting that it is exceptionally rare for Second Life entrepreneurs to gross even $1,000 a month and that to do so requires countless hours of time in front of the computer.

THE HYPE SLOWS

In 2007, the editors of *Time* magazine named Rosedale one of the most influential people in the world; that same year he was deemed by *PC World* as one of the fifty most important people on the Web. Eventually, however, journalists—who were once delighted to sign up for an avatar and interview Rosedale while strolling through Second Life's more fantastic landscapes—moved on to other topics. The number of dedicated users who log on to the site on a regular basis has leveled out at about a million, according to most estimates.

In 2008, Rosedale stepped down as CEO of Linden Lab, believing that his time would be better spent working on the company's technology issues rather than management problems. He was briefly reinstated as interim CEO in 2010.

OTHER PROJECTS

While working on Second Life, Rosedale in 2009 created a system called the LoveMachine, which allows one employee to leave a public message of recognition or approval for another, effectively turning performance reviews into a bonding experience. The system was implemented at Linden Lab; when a worker receives a message, he or she is also entitled to a small monetary bonus from the company. Other firms, including the consumer-deals company LivingSocial use the technology as well.

In 2011, Rosedale, who remained Linden Lab's chairman of the board even after stepping down as CEO for the second time, launched a new company, Coffee & Power. The company allows users to bid on jobs, such as software development or costume design, posted by others on its website. "There are so many amazing and useful things that we could all do for each other if we just had a way to quickly find, explain, and pay for them," Rosedale said in a press release quoted by Dean Takahashi for *Venture Beat* (1 Nov. 2011). "The remarkable range of jobs and services in Second Life was the inspiration to create Coffee & Power—we wanted to bring the same thing to the real world."

Rosedale and his wife, the former Yvette Forte, have four children and live in San Francisco. Rosedale boxes as a form of exercise and is also a devotee of daily meditation.

SUGGESTED READING

Anderson, Kelli. "Age of Avatars." *@UCSD*. University of California, May 2009. Web. 16 Aug. 2012.

Hardy, Quentin. "Bit by Bit, Work Exchange Site Aims to Get Jobs Done." *New York Times*. New York Times Co., 6 Nov. 2011. Web. 16 Aug. 2012.

Maney, Kevin. "The King of Alter Egos Is a Surprisingly Humble Guy." *USA Today*. Gannett Co. Inc., 4 Feb. 2007. Web. 16 Aug. 2012.

McCormick, Andrew. "Building a Better World." *New Media Age*. 19 Oct. 2006. *Ebscohost*. Web. 16 Aug. 2012.

Preston, John. "Second Life: Unreality Check." *Telegraph* [London]. Telegraph Media Group, 11 Nov. 2007. Web. 16 Aug. 2012.

Stafford, Joe. "Welcome to Your Second Life." *Austin360.com*. Austin American-Statesman, 23 Jan. 2005. Web. 16. Aug. 2012.

Takahashi, Dean. "Philip Rosedale's New Start-up Creates Marketplace for Small, Fun Jobs." *Venture Beat*. VentureBeat, 1 Nov. 2011. Web. 18 July 2012.

—*Mari Rich*

Rick Ross

Born: January 28, 1976
Occupation: Rapper

Rick Ross first burst onto the hip-hop scene in 2005, with the rap single "Hustlin'," an anthem that glorified Miami, Florida, as a haven for drug trafficking. He achieved commercial success following the release of his first two studio albums, which contain songs in which he rhapsodizes about dealing drugs. However, the self-proclaimed hustler-turned-rapper found his credibility in question after it was revealed that he was once a Florida corrections officer. Despite the revelation, Ross's third album reached the top of album charts while his next one achieved platinum status.

EARLY LIFE AND EDUCATION
The rapper Rick Ross was born William Leonard Roberts II on January 28, 1976, in Coahoma County, Mississippi. He and his sister were raised by their single mother, Tommie Roberts, in Carol City, a poverty-stricken suburb located north of Miami with a predominantly African American population. His father left the family when Ross was young and has since passed away. During his early teens, Ross began to take an interest in rap music, writing and recording rap lyrics with his childhood friend Elric "E-Class" Prince and then selling the mixtapes to his junior high school classmates. (A mixtape is a collection of original and exclusive tracks recorded by aspiring hip-hop artists and DJs to showcase their talents and generate interest in their music.) He continued to hone his writing skills when he was a student at Carol City Senior High School. "At fifteen, I was writing rhymes, songs with structure, choruses, bridges, and intros," Ross told the Associated Press in an interview for the *Victoria* (Texas) *Advocate* (Aug. 11, 2006). In addition to music, Ross turned his attention to sports, becoming a member of his high school football team. Following his 1994 graduation from Carol City Senior High, Ross was awarded an athletic scholarship to Albany State University (ASU), a historically black institution in Albany, Georgia. He briefly attended ASU, where he majored in criminal justice before dropping out after only one semester.

EARLY MUSIC CAREER
Upon returning to Florida in 1995, Ross decided to pursue a career in rap music. He renewed acquaintances with his childhood friend "E-Class" Prince and signed with Poe Boy Entertainment (now known as Poe Boy Music Group), a management company founded by Prince and Alex "Gucci Pucci" Bethune, another childhood friend. Over the next few years, Ross performed at events in the local hip-hop scene with the Carol City Cartel, a group Ross founded, and also spent a significant amount of time writing lyrics and recording demos. In 2000 Ross, performing under the moniker Teflon Da Don (a reference to the nickname of the late mafia boss John Gotti, known as the "Teflon Don"), was featured on the single "Ain't SHHH to Discuss," a track on fellow hip-hop artist Erick Sermon's third studio album, *Erick Onasis*. That same year Ross accepted an offer

Getty Images

from Tony Draper to join the Houston, Texas–based Suave House Records, an independent Southern hip-hop label. Ross spent the next two years continuing to work on his solo material before moving to another record label, following a failed distribution deal. "Unfortunately, I was in a bad situation with Jcor Entertainment," Draper told the Ballerstatus.com website (6 Sep. 2007). "I had a joint venture deal with Jcor, who had their distribution deal with Interscope Records. Jcor was supposed to supply marketing dollars, but they didn't. They only paid $500,000 on a $5 million tab. So to not tie up my artist, I allowed Ross to go to Slip-N-Slide Records in 2002."

Under the new label Ross continued to independently produce a series of mixtapes while also serving as a ghostwriter for fellow Miami rappers and new labelmates Trick Daddy and Trina. Ross, who also toured with Trick Daddy, earned co-writing credit for the single "Told Ya'll," a track from Trina's 2002 platinum-selling album *Diamond Princess*, which peaked at number 64 on the *Billboard* Hot R&B/Hip-Hop Songs chart. In return, Trina championed Ross's music. "I was on tour and I was taking his mixtapes on tour, promoting, pushing him before people knew who he was," she told HiphopDX.com (26 July 2011). Three years later the duo renewed their collaboration on the track "I Gotta," featured on Trina's 2005 disc *Glamorest Life*, which reached the top five of *Billboard*'s Top R&B/Hip-Hop Albums and Top Rap Albums.

SOLO CAREER

Ross jump-started his solo career in November 2005, with the recording of the song "Hustlin'," a Miami anthem about drug trafficking. "When I finished 'Hustlin','' I knew it was gonna be a hit," Ross told *Billboard* magazine (3 June 2006). He handed his single to several local urban radio announcers, including DJ Khaled, a producer and host at WEDR. The single became a regional hit after receiving frequent airplay from several local stations. At about this time Ted Lucas, the chief executive officer of Slip-N-Slide Records, was seeking to renegotiate his distribution deal with Atlantic Records and was being heavily courted by representatives from other record companies. One of these executives was Shakir Stewart, the senior vice president of A&R at Def Jam Records (headed by rapper and label president Jay-Z). "What made Rick Ross stand out was that he's a real lyrical guy," Stewart told *Billboard* (3 June 2006), adding, "It's not just about the beat and a one-liner." In January 2006 Def Jam Records reached a distribution agreement with Slip-N-Slide Records and offered Ross a four-album deal reportedly worth $10 million.

Port of Miami, Ross's major-label debut, was released in August 2006. The record sold 187,000 units in its first week, reaching the pinnacle of the *Billboard* 200 chart, as well as the number-one spot on *Billboard*'s Top R&B/Hip-Hop Album chart. *Port of Miami* eventually attained gold status, with sales of at least 500,000 units. A review of the album for *Entertainment Weekly* (7 Aug. 2006) noted, "On *Port of Miami*, Ross turns the minute details of drug distribution and dealing into ominous, slow-rolling songs, like the hypnotic, organ-driven hit single 'Hustlin'' and the Scarface-goes-South Beach stomp of 'Cross That Line.' In general, the whole 'crack-rap' trend . . . is a disheartening one, but Ross's pulpy debut manages to enthrall despite the drug-centric lyrics." Brendan Frederick, who reviewed the album for *XXL* magazine (18 Aug. 2006), was equally complimentary, adding that "while the runaway success of 'Hustlin'' could have positioned Ross for one-hit-wonder status, he confidently sidesteps this fate by delivering the goods on *Port of Miami*. With a cohesive sound the city can call its own, the bearded rapper gets the release he needs by exposing the dark side of the Sunshine State."

The album's success was spurred by the lead single, "Hustlin'," which was certified platinum by the Recording Industry Association of American (RIAA), with sales of at least a million units. "Hustlin'" had an accompanying music video that received heavy rotation on MTV, MTV2, and its hip-hop sister channel, MTV Jams, and peaked at number 11 on the *Billboard* Hot R&B/Hip-Hop Songs chart and reached the top 10 of *Billboard*'s Hot Rap Tracks. Ross was featured on the remix of singer Nelly Furtado's 2006 hit single "Promiscuous" and appeared on three tracks from DJ Khaled's 2006 release, *Listennn... the Album*: "Born-N-Raised," "Holla at Me," and "Watch Out." Ross also made several appearances on *We the Best Forever* (2007), DJ Khaled's follow-up. In September 2007, after reaching a compromise with Def Jam Records, the rapper's former label Suave House Records released *Rise to Power*, a collection of songs that were written and recorded by Ross when he was a member of the label's roster.

In March 2008 Ross released his second studio album, *Trilla*, whose title drew inspiration from Michael Jackson's best-selling record. "I just remember bein' a kid when Michael Jackson's album *Thriller* came out. It was one of the first vinyl albums I bought, along with Run DMC's *Walk This Way*," Ross said in an interview on DJBooth.net. "I just played it over and over for a year long. I just wanted to make my sophomore album that intense; just wanted to electrify everyone." Like its predecessor, the disc debuted at the top spot of *Billboard*'s 200 and Top R&B/Hip-Hop Album charts and went on to achieve gold certification; *Trilla* also reached number one on the *Billboard* Top Rap Albums chart. Notable tracks included the singles "Speedin'," a collaboration with R. Kelly that was a top-30 hit on *Billboard*'s Bubbling Under Hot 100 Singles chart; and "The Boss," the platinum-selling second single that featured T-Pain and reached the top five of two *Billboard* categories: Hot R&B/Hip-Hop Songs and Hot Rap Tracks.

CONTROVERSIES

In July 2008, Ross found himself embroiled in controversy when a photograph of someone identified as Ross wearing a corrections uniform surfaced on the Internet after reportedly being leaked by fellow rapper Trick Daddy. Ross, who claimed to have been a drug trafficker and a member of the Carol City Cartel, a violent street gang, vehemently denied the allegations and claimed that the image in question had been doctored. However, the Smoking Gun website subsequently posted documentation (including employment application containing Ross's Social Security number and a certificate for perfect attendance) obtained from the Department of Corrections that revealed that he was employed as a corrections officer (at Dade County's South Florida Reception Center) from December 1995 to June 1997.

In January 2009, "Mafia Music," the lead track from Ross's third studio album, *Deeper than Rap*, was released. It featured lyrics that disparaged fellow rapper 50 Cent, whose real name is Curtis Jackson: "I love to pay her bills / Can't wait to pay her rent / Curtis Jackson baby mama / I ain't asking for a cent." The song sparked a feud with 50 Cent, who answered with the song "Officer Ricky (Go Head, Try Me)" and posted a series of Officer Ricky cartoons on the You-Tube video-sharing website. In February 2009, 50 Cent also taped an interview with the mother of one of Ross's children and made it available on YouTube. That same month Ross's reported criminal past and gang member affiliations were again under dispute after the Smoking Gun posted the copy of a deposition by Rey Hernandez, a Miami Beach police officer who had arrested Ross in January 2008 on gun and drug charges. In the transcript Hernandez revealed that Ross had no arrests in the Miami-Dade County area prior to 2008; he also indicated that he could not find evidence that Ross had been affiliated with any local gangs. In March 2009, after months of denial, Ross made a complete reversal regarding the photo, confessing that the image was indeed authentic and admitting that he had previously worked as a corrections officer.

This revelation did not, however, affect the sales of Ross's recordings. In April 2009 *Deeper than Rap* became Ross's third consecutive album to debut at number one on the *Billboard* 200, with sales of 158,000 copies during its first week of release. It featured the single "Magnificent," a collaboration with the R&B singer John Legend that reached the top 10 of *Billboard*'s Hot R&B/Hip-Hop Songs and Hot Rap Tracks. The disc, which also topped the charts in two other *Billboard* categories (Top R&B/Hip-Hop Albums and Top Rap Albums), was well received by the critics. "*Deeper than Rap* is just as certain as his first two studio albums, *Port of Miami* and *Trilla*, but reflects the view from the top, not the bottom. Now, instead of climbing up to success, he's achieved it," Jon Caramanica wrote for the *New York Times* (22 Apr. 2009). Adding that the album is "a throwback to a time of sonic and attitudinal ambition in hip-hop—the Bad Boy era of the mid- to late '90s, with its warm soul samples connoting the new hip-hop luxury comes to mind. Few rap albums have sounded this assured, this sumptuous, in years." In a review for *Billboard* (9 May 2009), Monica Herrera added: "The Miami-bred MC Rick Ross has faced a number of career obstacles in recent months—from damaged street credibility to a multi-episodic beef—so it's all the more impressive that on his third album, *Deeper than Rap*, he presents his most cohesive work yet."

In June 2010 "Freeway" Rick Ross, a convicted Los Angeles drug lord, filed a $10 million copyright infringement suit against the rapper and his record labels, Def Jam and Universal Music Group, accusing them of unlawfully capitalizing on his name and image. The federal lawsuit was dismissed in November 2010 and he filed an appeal in state court the following April. Another measure by "Freeway" Rick Ross to block the release of the rapper's upcoming album also proved unsuccessful. *Teflon Don*, the rapper's fourth studio album, was released in July 2010 and narrowly missed the top spot of the *Billboard* 200. It debuted in second place, selling more than 176,000 copies during its first week; the disc went on to achieve platinum status.

In February 2011 Ross secured a distribution deal for his label, Maybach Music Group (MMG), with Warner Bros., who beat out several record companies, including Bad Boy Records and Cash Money Records. As a solo artist Ross remained signed to Def Jam. In May 2011 MMG released its first compilation album, *Self Made Vol. 1*, featuring artists on the label's roster such as Wale, Meek Mill, and Pill. Ross made headlines again on October 14, 2011, when he was hospitalized twice in the same day following seizures during two separate flights to Memphis, Tennessee, where he was scheduled to perform. After a two-day hospital stay, Ross, who cited lack of sleep as the cause of his seizures, postponed several concert dates in order to rest and recover from his health scare. In November the rapper also announced plans to push back the release date for his next solo effort—*God Forgives, I Don't*—set for release in 2012. Ross was back in the news in February 2012, after a man was found murdered in front of a Miami home owned by the rapper, who has been ruled out as a suspect by local police.

PERSONAL LIFE

In addition to his record label, MMG, Ross has also launched Rick Ross Charities, whose mission is to "strengthen the lives of today's at-risk youth from all backgrounds and create diversity by providing solid resources through education advocacy, mentoring programs, and financial resources to deserving students," according to the organization's website. The rapper also owns a Wingstop restaurant franchise in Memphis, Tennessee.

SUGGESTED READING

Caramanica, Jon. "Beyond Authenticity: A Rapper Restages." *New York Times*. New York Times, 22 Apr. 2009. Web. 18 Mar. 2012.

Herrera, Monica. "Deeper than Rap." *Billboard.com*. Billboard, 9 May 2009. Web. 18 Mar. 2012.

Hoard, Christian. "Rick Ross: Miami Hustler." *Rolling Stone* 15 June 2006: 30–32. Print.

Reid, Shaheem. "Rick Ross Finally Admits Prison-Guard Past." *MTV.com*. MTV, 12 Mar. 2009. Web. 18 Mar. 2012.

"Rick Ross's Hood Dreams." *The Smoking Gun*. The Smoking Gun, 9 Feb. 2009. Web. 18 Mar. 2012.

—*Bertha Muteba*

Dilma Rousseff

Born: December 14, 1947
Occupation: President of Brazil

When Dilma Rousseff assumed the presidency of Brazil on January 1, 2011, she became the first female head of state in the country's history. "It's not easy being the first woman to govern your country," Michelle Bachelet, who led Chile from 2006 to 2010, wrote for *Time* magazine (21 Apr. 2011, online). "Beyond the honor it signifies, there are still prejudices and stereotypes to confront. Nor is it easy to govern an emerging nation: when societies begin to see the light of development at the end of the tunnel, there is a surge of optimism and enthusiasm, but the challenges become more complex and the citizenry more demanding. It's harder still to govern a country as large and globally relevant as Brazil." Bachelet continued, "Brazil is living a unique moment in its history, one of great opportunity, which requires a leader with solid experience and firm ideals. Dilma offers precisely that virtuous combination of wisdom and conviction that her country needs." In addition to her readily apparent wisdom and conviction, Rousseff is an ex-guerrilla who fought against Brazil's once-powerful military dictatorship and was imprisoned and tortured in the 1970s. As a presidential candidate, she offered another exceptionally important quality to Brazilian voters: she received an enthusiastic endorsement from her predecessor, President Luiz Inácio Lula da Silva. Known as "Lula," he is the most popular leader in Brazil's modern history. "In an age when 'change' is a common political battle cry," Bradley Brooks wrote for the Associated Press (20 Sep. 2010), "in Brazil the majority just want more of the same."

EARLY LIFE AND EDUCATION

Rousseff was born on December 14, 1947 in Belo Horizonte, the capital of the Brazilian state of Minas Gerais. Her mother, Dilma Jane da Silva, hailed from a family of ranchers, and worked as a teacher. Rousseff's father, Pedro Rousseff, was born in Bulgaria as Petar Russav. He was a lawyer, contractor, and real estate developer. Russav left Bulgaria in the late 1920s, leaving behind a pregnant first wife, Evdokiya Yankova. (Dilma Rousseff had a half-brother, Lyuben-Kamen, from that union.) Some sources speculate that he was forced to leave because his involvement with the Bulgarian Communist Party made him susceptible to political persecution; others state that he left because his business interests were doing poorly.

Whatever the reason for emigrating from his native land, Russav settled in France for several years before moving on to Argentina and then Brazil, where he changed his surname to

AFP/Getty Images

Rousseff. There he met Dilma Jane da Silva, and they married in 1946. The couple had three children—Igor (born in January 1947), Dilma, and Zana (born in 1951). Their son Pedro died in 1962, and their daughter Zana died at the age of twenty-six. Lyuben-Kamen, reportedly always longed to go to Brazil to visit his half-siblings, but he died in 2007, never having done so.

Rousseff's father provided a comfortable life for the family in Belo Horizonte, with a large home, membership in a tennis club, and a staff of household help. Rousseff has said that she had no political aspirations in her youth. She attended Nossa Senhora de Sion, an all-girls school, before transferring as a teenager to the Colégio Estadual Central do Brasil, a co-ed public school that, at the time, was a hotbed of student activism.

TUMULTUOUS YEARS

In March 1964, Brazil's president, João Goulart, was deposed in a bloodless coup. The event ushered in two decades of authoritarian military rule. Coup leaders enjoyed the backing of the US government, which feared the spread of communism in South America. Still a student, Rousseff joined the *Organização Revolucionária Marxista-Política Operíria* (Revolutionary Marxist Political Worker's Organization, or POLOP), one of many leftist groups that opposed Brazil's military rulers.

In 1967, Rousseff married her first husband, Cláudio Galeno Linhares, a journalist and fellow leftist. Soon after, amid dissension in POLOP's ranks about engaging in armed struggle, Rousseff joined the militant Comando de Libertação Nacional (National Liberation Command, or COLINA).

Rousseff's exact role in COLINA has been debated in the media. While some assert that her duties were largely clerical and organizational, others have claimed that she developed a deep familiarity with weapons and was an influential leader with the group. Rousseff has admitted only to transporting weapons on occasion, and she claims never to have engaged in actual shooting, in part because of her poor vision. Nonetheless, COLINA's activities in Minas Gerais were limited. The group undertook some small bank robberies, car thefts, and organized two bombings that resulted in no casualties.

Following one of the organization's robberies, several members of the COLINA guerillas were arrested. As COLINA members gathered to discuss the arrests, police raided their meeting place. In the melee that ensued, two officers were killed by machine-gun fire. Following the incident, COLINA found itself the target of an intense police investigation. Linhares and Rousseff, who had just finished her fourth semester as an economics student at the Universidade Federal de Minas Gerais (Federal University of Minas Gerais), began sleeping in separate, hidden locations. *Soon, they travelled to Rio de Janeiro, and took shelter with one of Rousseff's aunts, who believed that the fugitive couple was on vacation.*

When Linhares was ordered by COLINA's leadership to travel to Porto Alegre, the capital of Rio Grande do Sul, Rousseff remained in *Rio de Janeiro, where she continued working for the organization and where she met a leftist lawyer named Carlos Franklin Paixão de Araujo, with whom she fell in love. Rousseff and* Linhares split amicably, and she and Araujo, ten years her senior, embarked on a relationship that, although rocky, lasted some thirty years.

Araujo, the son of a prominent Brazilian defense attorney, was head of a dissident offshoot of the Partido Comunista Brasileiro (Brazilian Communist Party), and was chosen as one of the leaders of the Vanguarda Armada Revolucionária Palmares (Palmares Armed Revolutionary Vanguard). The VAR Palmares, as the group was commonly known, was formed when COLINA merged with another leftist group, the Vanguarda Popular Revolucionária. Rousseff also played a role in VAR Palmares. A military prosecutor once referred to her as the group's "Joan of Arc," referring to the fifteenth-century French peasant girl who led the French army to several victories during the Hundred Years' War.

VAR Palmares funded their activities partly by robberies. Among their most notorious exploits was the theft of more than $2 million in cash from a safe in the home of Anna Gimel Benchimol Capriglione, the secretary and mistress of Adhemar de Barros, a former governor of São Paulo known for his corruption. Rousseff has always steadfastly denied involvement in the storied caper, and her exact role remains a matter of debate.

In January 1970, Brazilian authorities captured and imprisoned Rousseff. She remained jailed in a facility on the outskirts of São Paulo for almost three years, during which time she was subjected to repeated beatings and torture by electrical shocks. Some forty years later, charges were filed against Mauricio Lopes Lima, a former army captain whom Rousseff was able to name as one of her tormentors. She was released from custody in 1972, and went to live in Porto Alegre, where Araujo, who had also been arrested, was finishing his jail sentence. She resided during that time with his parents, and was able to visit him often, bringing along books and newspapers.

LIFE AFTER PRISON

Unable to re-enter the Federal University of Minas Gerais because she had been branded a subversive, Rousseff entered a university in Rio Grande do Sul. In 1975, she earned an undergraduate degree in economics, completing an internship at the Foundation of Economics and Statistics, which was affiliated with the Rio Grande do Sul state government. The following year, she gave birth to her only child, a daughter she named Paula. Rousseff entered a graduate economics program at the state university in Campinas in 1978, but she never completed her thesis. Despite her academic work and obligations to her children, Rousseff remained politically active, participating in a movement to win amnesty for expelled or persecuted dissidents.

POLITICAL CAREER

In the early 1980s, Rousseff worked with politician Leonel Brizola to establish the Partido Democratico Trabalhista (Democratic Labour Party, or PDT). Brizola, the former governor of the state of Rio Grande do Sul, was the brother-in-law of former President Goulart. Rousseff and Araujo threw themselves into party politics; she served as an economic adviser to PDT members of the Rio Grande do Sul Legislative Assembly, and he won a post as a state deputy for the party.

In 1985, following mass protests related to Brazil's economic recession, the country's military rulers peacefully ceded power. A new era of democracy in Brazil began. Rousseff and Araujo worked for the successful campaign of Alceu Collares for mayor of Porto Alegre. After Collares took office in 1986, he appointed Rousseff as the municipal secretary of the treasury. She remained in that post until 1988, when she stepped down to aid Araujo's mayoral bid. Araujo's mayoral campaign was unsuccessful.

In 1989, Brazil held its first direct presidential election in decades. President Tancredo Neves had won the presidency indirectly in 1985 via electoral college. When Neves died one day before being inaugurated, his vice president, José Sarney, had assumed power. Rousseff intially supported her political colleague Brizola in the 1989 election. When Brizola lost the first round of voting, she transferred her allegiance to Luiz Inácio Lula da Silva, who represented the Partido dos Trabalhadores (Workers' Party or PT). The election was ultimately won by Fernando Collor de Mello, a former governor of Alagoasa.

In 1990, Collares was elected governor of Rio Grande do Sul. He appointed Rousseff as president of the Foundation of Economics and Statistics, where she had served as an intern more than a decade earlier. In 1993, she was named State Secretary of Mines, Energy and Communications under Collares.

Rousseff left public service in 1994 after she learned that Araujo had fathered a child with another woman. She served briefly as the editor of the magazine *Indicadores Econômicos* (*Economic Indicators*) in 1995, and also enrolled in a doctoral program. However, she did not complete her PhD. Rousseff was reappointed as State Secretary of Mines, Energy and Communications for Rio Grande do Sul following Olívio Dutra's election as governor in 1998. As secretary, she handled one of the largest blackouts in the region's history.

Rousseff and Araujo divorced in 2000. In 2002, Lula da Silva was elected president of Brazil. He appointed Rousseff Minister of Energy and Mines. Shortly before taking office, at a time when Brazil was facing a severe energy crisis, Lula had called a meeting of economic experts, which included Rousseff. "She arrived with a laptop and would press the little buttons all the time while telling me, 'No, Mr. President, it's not like that, it's like this,'" he later recalled in a speech, as quoted by Alexei Barrionuevo for the *New York Times* (31 Oct. 2010).

As energy minister, Rousseff launched a program dubbed Luz para Todos (Light for All), which made electricity available to more than ten million Brazilians living in rural areas. She also oversaw an increase in research into the development of alternative fuel sources in Brazil. During Rousseff's tenure as energy minister, Brazil's energy company, Petrobas, added thousands of new jobs.

In 2005, Rousseff was appointed Lula's chief of Staff and minister of the Civil House. She became the first Brazilian woman named as minister of the Civil House, which includes management of all domestic functions of the national government, and oversight of all other cabinet ministers. Rousseff was instrumental in launching the Programa de Aceleração do Crescimento (Growth Acceleration Program, or PAC), an ambitious effort to improve Brazil's infrastructure through an unprecedented increase in economic investment and the undertaking of numerous social initiatives. She also helped establish the public housing program known as Minha Casa, Minha Vida (My House, My Life), which provides homes to tens of thousands of disadvantaged Brazilians. Minha Casa, Minha Vida precipitated a boom in construction jobs throughout Brazil.

PRESIDENTIAL CAMPAIGN

Rousseff underwent treatment for lymphatic cancer in 2009. Despite speculation in the media regarding her health, her name was widely circulated as a potential replacement for President Lula as he approached the end of his term-limited tenure in office. In June 2010, Rousseff officially announced her candidacy in Brazil's 2011 presidential election. Her opponents in the race included Marina Silva, an environmental activist with whom Rousseff had clashed in the past as a director of Petrobras, and José Serra, a social democrat and former governor of São Paulo. Rousseff's campaign had the advantage of President Lula's unequivocal support.

Critics protested that Rousseff was merely riding Lula's coattails, that she had never before held elected office, and that she lacked her mentor's charisma. Some suggested that Lula was using her until the constitution could be changed, allowing him to run again. In the first round of voting, in early October 2010, Rousseff received almost 40 percent of the vote to Serra's 32.5 percent. Political observers speculated that her refusal to denounce abortion caused her to fall short of the decisive 50 percent mark in the first round of voting. Silva's presence on the ballot also contributed; representing Brazil's Green party, she garnered a respectable 19.3 percent of the total vote. In the run-off election held later in the month, Rousseff emerged the victor, earning 56 percent of the vote.

PRESIDENT ROUSSEFF

Rousseff was sworn in on January 1, 2011, becoming Brazil's first woman president. In her inauguration speech, she stated, "I didn't come here to extol my [own] biography, but to glorify the life of each Brazilian woman. My supreme commitment is to honor women, protect the [weak] and govern for all." Political analysts wondered whether as president she would manage to step out of Lula's shadow.

Soon after she took office, Rousseff's cabinet underwent a significant period of political controversy. Antonio Palocci, her chief of staff, resigned in the wake of accusations that he had used his political connections to earn lucrative consulting contacts. Alfredo Nascimento, Rousseff's Minister of Transportation, resigned over allegations of corruption in his department, as did the Minister of Agriculture, Minister of Tourism, and Minister of Sports. Nelson Jobim, the Minister of Defense, was forced to step down after publicly insulting two fellow cabinet members. While some political observers complained that Rousseff was tainted by her association with these cabinet members, others saw the fact that she had called for their resignations as proof that she would be tougher on corruption than Lula had been.

Despite the doubts of her detractors, Rousseff has differentiated herself in other ways as well. "Less than three months into the job, Ms. Rousseff, once thought to be a potential puppet of Mr. da Silva, has swiftly moved out of [his] shadow," Alexei Barrionuevo wrote for the *International Herald Tribune* (19 Mar. 2011), praising the fact that she "is more likely to pursue foreign policy driven by economic goals than by a desire for the kind of global grandeur that Mr. da Silva often sought." Similarly, Mac Margolis asserted for *Newsweek* (26 Sep. 2011), "Barely nine months in office, Rousseff has stamped her understated style on a country Lula had owned."

Brazil's economic growth, which began under Lula, has continued during Rousseff's tenure. Brazil is readying for two important moments on the world stage as it prepares to play host to the 2014 FIFA World Cup and the 2016 Olympics. "[A]mong the world's major economic powers, [Brazil] has achieved a rare trifecta: high growth (unlike the United States and Europe), political freedom (unlike China), and falling inequality (unlike practically everywhere)," Nicholas Lemann wrote for the *New Yorker* (5 Dec. 2011). "Brazilians usually rank at the very top in international measures of how optimistic the citizens of a nation are about its future."

PERSONAL LIFE

Rousseff lives with her mother and aunt in the Palácio da Alvorado, Brazil's official presidential residence. Rousseff enjoys the opera and has a pet Labrador retriever.

SUGGESTED READING

Bachelet, Michele. "The 2011 *Time* 100." *Time*. Time, 21 Apr. 2011. Web. 10 Apr. 2012.

Barrionuevo, Alexei. "Poised to Lead Brazil, an Ally of the Current President Faces Unfinished Tasks." *New York Times* 31 Oct. 2010: A06.

Lemann, Nicholas. "The Anointed." *New Yorker* 05 Dec. 2011: 50.

Margolis, Mac. "Don't Mess with Dilma." *Newsweek* 26 Sep. 2011: 36.

—*Mari Rich*

Kay Ryan

Born: September 21, 1945
Occupation: Poet, educator

Kay Ryan has been publishing her unique brand of short, smart, witty poetry since the early 1980s, but her work did not receive much notice until the late 1990s, and it would take yet another decade for her to receive substantial national recognition. Some of Ryan's most notable poetry collections include *Flamingo Watching* (1994), *Elephant Rocks* (1996), *Say Uncle* (2000), *The Niagara River* (2005), and *The Best of It: New and Selected Poems* (2010). For *The Best of It*, Ryan received the 2011 Pulitzer Prize for Poetry. Also in 2011, she received the MacArthur Foundation Fellowship, commonly referred to as the MacArthur "genius" grant. From 2008 until 2010, Ryan served as the US poet laureate, a great honor for American poets. Her poetry has also been published in various literary magazines, including the *New Yorker*, the *Atlantic Monthly*, and the *Paris Review*.

EARLY LIFE

Kay Ryan was born on September 21, 1945, in San Jose, California, a city south of San Francisco. Her mother was an elementary school teacher, while her father held many different jobs, which caused the family to move frequently around California. Ryan grew up in the San Joaquin Valley, where her father was a ranch hand; then in Fruitvale, not far from Bakersfield, where he worked as an oil driller. When Ryan was in the sixth grade, her family moved again, this time to Rosemond, a small town in the Mojave Desert. "My father worked away from home a lot," Ryan told Katy Butler for the Mill Valley, California, *Pacific Sun* (5 Sep. 2008). "He was better at working than he was at being a businessman, and he went through a series of enterprises that didn't work out. . . . We didn't feel poor. We were clean, we had food. But we worked for it in a sense, in that my mother had to experience a lot of anxiety about where the rent was going to come from." To a degree, Ryan internalized some of that anxiety.

EDUCATION

After high school, Ryan attended Antelope Valley College, a community college in Southern California. It was around this time, at the age of nineteen, that she began to write. Her father died that same year of a heart attack, leading Ryan to write what she considered her first poem, titled "After Zeno" (1965), which begins with the following lines: "When he was / I was. / But I still am / and he is still." The entire poem is only fourteen lines long, with three or four words per line, and the content and style are a kind of

Wirelmage

foreshadowing of what Ryan's poetry would look and sound like many years later.

Ryan transferred from Antelope Valley College to the University of California, Los Angeles (UCLA), where she submitted some of her poems to the poetry club—and was denied membership. She majored in English, receiving her bachelor's degree in 1967 and her master's degree in 1968. She then enrolled in a literary-criticism doctorate program at the University of California, Irvine, but soon decided that she did not want to pursue literary criticism and dropped out of the program.

BECOMING A POET

In 1971, Ryan moved to Marin County, in the San Francisco Bay Area. There, she found part-time work teaching remedial English at the College of Marin, a local community college, where she would continue to teach the same class for decades. She was still writing poetry on her own, something she had continued to do since her father's death, but she was not yet sure if she should become a poet. In 1976, five years after arriving in Marin County, Ryan went on a cross-country bicycle trip, and while riding through the Rocky Mountains in Colorado, she had an epiphany. In a moment when her senses were heightened, she decided to become a poet.

The following year, she met Carol Adair, who worked for the San Quentin State Prison education department, where Ryan taught English. The two fell in love and, in 1979, moved in together. They were unofficially married in 2004

and officially married in 2008. Not only Ryan's spouse but also her biggest supporter, Adair was determined to see her poetry published in respectable magazines, and they both worked hard to send out Ryan's work to editors and publishers.

For the first few years, their efforts were fruitless. Adair raised some funds so that Ryan could self-publish her first book of poetry, *Dragon Acts to Dragon Ends* (1983). The following year, Ryan finally got her first break when *Poetry* magazine published two of her poems. In 1985, a small press published her second book of poems, *Strangely Marked Metal*, which also went unnoticed. It would take Ryan nearly a decade to produce another book of poetry. When *Flamingo Watching* finally came out, it also received very little notice. *Flamingo Watching* includes such poems as "Flamingo Watching," "This Life," "The Mock Ruin," "Spring," "Turtle," and "Every Painting by Chagall."

GAINING RECOGNITION

Two years after the publication of *Flamingo Watching*, prestigious New York City–based publishing house Grove Press released Ryan's next collection of poetry, *Elephant Rocks*; the company would go on to publish many of her subsequent collections. By this point, Ryan had placed a few poems in such literary magazines as the *New Yorker*, the *Atlantic Monthly*, and the *Paris Review*.

Elephant Rocks finally earned Ryan some attention in the mainstream press, but not very much. Patricia Holt, in a review for the *San Francisco Chronicle* (7 May 1996), acknowledged that Ryan has been compared to the poets Emily Dickinson and Ralph Waldo Emerson. However, wrote Holt, "the first thing you notice about her poems is an elbow-to-the-ribs playfulness equally reminiscent of Ogden Nash." Holt went on to add that, like Ryan's previous collection of poems, *Elephant Rocks* has a "kind of internal rhyming that doubles up on itself." Ryan's poems delve into such broad topics as life, animals, and nature; yet each poem manages to convey something original, the writer's unique observations and perspectives, in a very tight and condensed style.

Prominent poet and critic Dana Gioia, in an essay for the poetry magazine *Dark Horse* (Winter 1998–99), was one of the first critics to strongly and passionately advocate for Ryan's efforts. He began his *Dark Horse* essay by writing, "Over the past five years no new poet has so deeply impressed me with her imaginative flair or originality as Kay Ryan." Ryan's fifth collection of poems, *Say Uncle*, came out in 2000. Like *Elephant Rocks*, it received some notice in the mainstream press, but not a lot. In her online review for *Slate* magazine (8 Nov. 2000), Katha Pollitt called *Say Uncle* "wonderful" and wrote,

"Kay Ryan comes out of the Dickinsonian tradition of compression, verbal playfulness, humor, and—that word again!—wit, the sort of wit that brevity is the soul of, for her poems are rarely even one hundred words long." Pollitt also commended Ryan on her ability to blend "cleverness with openness." The collection features many poems, such as "Mockingbird," "Patience," "Why We Must Struggle," and "Coming and Going."

After winning both a Guggenheim Fellowship and the Ruth Lilly Poetry Prize, the latter a $100,000 prize awarded to living US poets for lifetime achievement, in 2004, Ryan released her seventh collection of poems, *The Niagara River*, the following year. For the first time in her career, Ryan's work was widely reviewed by a great variety of publications. And according to most of them, Ryan's new poems were not only generally excellent but also a significant and original addition to the world of poetry and the English language.

Writing for the *New York Times* (18 Dec. 2005), David Kirby observed, "A Kay Ryan poem is maybe an inch wide, rarely wanders onto a second page, and works in one or two muted colors at most. Rather than raise a righteous old hullabaloo, a Ryan poem sticks the reader with a little jab of smarts and then pulls back as fast as a doctor's hypodermic." In a similar vein, in a review for the *Los Angeles Times* (9 Dec. 2005), Laurel Maury wrote, "Ryan may be a miniaturist, but she doesn't try to contain the world in a grain of sand, or eternity in an hour. Hers is a small, sensible voice of wisdom, one that knows that our huge Western ideas of self are so much blustery untruth. She believes that propriety and small motions are the only thing that can really save anyone, although even these might not work."

As other critics have done before him, David Yezzi, writing for the *Weekly Standard* (21 Nov. 2005), discussed how Ryan manages to balance wit and emotion: "Her willfully low-key ingredients are then leavened by one of the finest (and funniest) caustic wits in contemporary poetry, and by a humane melancholia that lends the poems urgency, and grounds them in deep feeling." In this collection, as in her previous work, Ryan played with clichés, reimagining and reconstructing them until they took on new meaning. One such twist on a familiar phrase can be seen in her poem "Home to Roost," in which "chickens / are circling and / blotting out the / day" until they "come home / to roost—all / the same kind / at the same speed."

In the summer of 2008, Ryan learned that she would be the sixteenth US poet laureate, a high national honor. She succeeded the poet Charles Simic, who had held the post for a single one-year term. This news was widely covered, and many journalists made much of the fact that Ryan, at sixty-two years old, had been virtually unknown for much of her career, and had not tried to cultivate success by attending writers' workshops or seminars, pursuing an MFA, or networking in any major way.

During her time as poet laureate, Ryan started a project called "Poetry for the Mind's Joy," which celebrated the work of community college students across the country. As a result of her new status, sales of her books increased, and she was suddenly being interviewed by journalists all over the country on a regular basis. When James H. Billington, the librarian of Congress, appeared with Ryan on the PBS interview program *Charlie Rose* (6 Nov. 2008), Rose asked Billington why he had selected Ryan to be poet laureate; Billington replied, "Kay Ryan is really and truly an original. And that's what strikes you when you have to read a great deal of poetry and consult with a great many people, as I do." Ryan served two terms as poet laureate, from 2008 to 2010.

After Ryan's wife, Carol Adair, was diagnosed with terminal cancer, the two worked together on a collection of Ryan's published poems. Adair died in 2009, and the following year, Grove Press published *The Best of It: New and Selected Poems*, which features poems from *Flamingo Watching*, *Elephant Rocks*, *Say Uncle*, and *The Niagara River*, as well as twenty-three new poems, including "The Edges of Time," "Repetition," "Bitter Pill," and "Spiderweb." The book's dedication reads, "For Carol / who knew it."

The Best of It received very good reviews. "Ryan has become a classic American poet," declared John Freeman in the *Los Angeles Times* (25 Apr. 2010). Freeman also observed, "Everything her eye falls upon takes on a brisk, beautifully complete clarity. Her tidy lines disguise an enormous intelligence and tonal warmth: a ferocious capacity for finding the essence of things." In a review for the *New Yorker* (12 Apr. 2010), Adam Kirsch pointed out that Ryan's "most startling discovery is that melancholy, with its tendency to brood and spread, is best contained in a form that is tight, witty, almost sprightly sounding. Her poems are often built on the logic of the pun, taking an ordinary word or dead cliché as a title and then jolting it to unexpected life." *The Best of It* was named one of the best books of 2010 by many publications, including the *New York Times*, the *Los Angeles Times*, the *San Francisco Chronicle*, and the *New Yorker*, and received the Pulitzer Prize for Poetry in 2011.

Kay Ryan lives in Fairfax, California.

SUGGESTED READING

Freeman, John. "Lean and Precise, the Message Is Clear." *Los Angeles Times* 25 Apr. 2010: E10. Print.

Kirsch, Adam. "Think Small: America's Quiet Poet Laureate." *New Yorker* 12 Apr. 2010: 76. Print.

O'Rourke, Meghan. "The Outsider Artist." *Slate. com.* Slate Group, 29 July 2008. Web. 14 Feb. 2012.

Thomas, Louisa. "The Reluctant Poet Laureate." *Newsweek* 13 July 2009: 63. Print.

Thompson, Bob. "Verse of the Turtle." *Washington Post* 17 July 2008: C1. Print.

—Dmitry Kiper

Janette Sadik-Khan

Born: 1960
Occupation: Commissioner of the New York City Department of Transportation

Janette Sadik-Khan is the polarizing, if prolific, commissioner of the New York City Department of Transportation (DOT). Taking her cues from cities abroad, Sadik-Khan's extensive reimagining of New York City's roadways have inspired other American cities to revamp their automobile-focused designs. What some call her almost self-righteous enthusiasm for bicycles and public space has won her fervent supporters and equally fervent detractors. "She's preparing us for a future that will have fewer cars," Sam Schwartz, a traffic consultant, columnist, and former traffic commissioner told Lisa Taddeo for *Esquire* magazine (Dec. 2010). For a city of commuters, Sadik-Khan's vision of the future is difficult to fathom. Since 2007, when Sadik-Khan assumed her post, she has implemented more significant changes to the city's roadways than any of her predecessors since Robert Moses—the transportation czar who made New York City the paved paradise that it is today. Sadik-Khan disparages New York's labyrinth of bureaucratic red tape and her methods of reclaiming space for cyclists and pedestrians are often unusual. Ron Shiffman, a former commissioner of New York's Department of City Planning, told Dana Goldstein for the *American Prospect* (21 Nov. 2008) of Sadik-Khan: "She's a guerilla bureaucrat."

EARLY LIFE AND CAREER

Sadik-Khan was born in 1960 to parents Orhan Sadik-Khan and Jane McCarthy, who divorced when their daughter was seven. Her father was the late managing director of PaineWebber, an investment banking firm. McCarthy is an author and former journalist for the *New York Post* where she worked the city hall beat. She was also an environmental activist who worked with the Citizens Housing and Planning Council. Sadik-Khan grew up in the city, but traveled to California to attend Occidental College in Los Angeles. She graduated with a bachelor of arts in political science in 1982. She earned a law degree from Columbia University and became a

Bloomberg via Getty Images

member of the New York State bar. Sadik-Khan worked as a corporate lawyer before entering public service.

In 1990, Sadik-Khan joined the administration of New York City Mayor David Dinkins, a Democrat. She served as a senior advisor on mass transit. As a policy maker for DOT, she introduced several transportation initiatives that never came to fruition. In 1991, she suggested a toll at the East River bridges. The measure was inspired by a concept known as congestion pricing, in which motorists are charged for the use of heavily trafficked areas in an effort to tame gridlock. The project was shelved, as was Sadik-Khan's plan to install a light rail service, or above ground train, across Forty-Second street, amid objections from the Mass Transit Authority (MTA) and community groups. (She would reintroduce iterations of both projects under Mayor Michael Bloomberg.) During her tenure, Sadik-Khan was most famous for going after diplomats with unpaid parking tickets. When Dinkins lost his reelection bid to Republican Rudy Giuliani in 1993, Sadik-Khan moved to Washington, DC, where she worked for the Department of Transportation under President Bill Clinton. She worked on reforms to the bus manufacturing industry and developed an art-in-transit program before becoming deputy administrator at the Federal Transit Administration (FTA) where she managed the capital construction budget as well as federal assistance programs and policies.

In 1997, Sadik-Khan returned to the private sector as the senior vice president of the international engineering firm, Parsons Brinck-erhoff. She travelled extensively with the firm, meeting with international transportation officials and generating ideas that would be fodder for her work in New York City. She was briefly considered for the position of commissioner of DOT in 2000 under Giuliani. She caught the attention of Bloomberg while consulting on the rebuilding of the World Trade Center in Manhattan.

TRANSPORTATION COMMISSIONER

In 2007, Bloomberg was considering two candidates for commissioner: Sadik-Khan and a man named Michael Horodniceanu, a former traffic commissioner in the Dinkins administration. Bloomberg was in his second term and looking to replace Iris Weinshall who was taking a teaching position at the City University of New York. Horodniceanu had ties to Weinshall, and was seen as the more "car-friendly" candidate, Annie Karni wrote for the (now defunct) *New York Sun* (14 Mar. 2007). Sadik-Khan on the other hand, made her interest in mass transit clear. Gene Russianoff, the chief attorney of the transport advocacy Straphangers Campaign, told Karni: "If the mayor is creative enough to pick someone like Janette, it sends a message that he wants to have a legacy in taming city traffic." Sadik-Khan was officially named transportation commissioner in April 2007.

Sadik-Khan oversees New York City's six thousand miles of street and twelve thousand miles of sidewalk, nontoll bridges, tunnels, and the Staten Island Ferry, which transports over sixty-five thousand commuters each day. While she does not control the city's sprawling system of subways, trains and buses, she often works in partnership with the MTA. As New York City's population continues to grow, the DOT has become concerned with issues of public and environmental health as well as traffic flow.

Although her changes have been implemented in a piecemeal fashion, Sadik-Khan is pleased with her progress. "There have been lots of things that have changed in New York City in the last 20 to 30 years. Our streets are not one of them," Sadik-Khan told Goldstein. "Our streets have really been designed as more utilitarian corridors to get cars as quickly as possible from point A to point B. Now there's a recognition that we can't keep doing that."

PLANYC AND CONGESTION PRICING

Sadik-Khan's appointment came the same month that Bloomberg unveiled a major sustainability agenda called PlaNYC. The 127 reforms on the agenda are based on reports that New York City will add one million people to its population by 2030. The goals of PlaNYC are to reduce New York City's carbon footprint by 30 percent, provide more public space and improve public health in a city where car exhaust permeates all breathable air. The blueprint—Sadik-Khan, in an interview with the European Cyclists Federation (14 June 2012) called the plan "a roadmap for managing the growth of the city"—was an abrupt departure from Bloomberg's earlier rhetoric concerning the future of the city; but his continuing support for Sadik-Khan has proven to critics that the administration is serious about sustainability. In 2008, Sadik-Khan introduced DOT's own "roadmap," a strategic plan called Sustainable Streets. Several of the policies outlined in the plan have been implemented, perhaps due to a lesson learned in Sadik-Khan's first year with DOT.

The original centerpiece of Bloomberg's PlaNYC was an effort to implement congestion pricing, charging cars eight dollars (twenty-one dollars for trucks) to travel below Sixtieth Street in Manhattan on weekdays. Sadik-Khan hoped to reduce the number of cars on the road—encouraging those who choose to drive within the city to use public transportation or a bicycle—and use the revenues to improve public transit. A majority of city dwellers supported the plan, as did the city hall, which approved the plan with a 30–20 vote in March 2008. The federal government promised the city $354 million to improve the mass transit system if the bill was approved by the state. Sadik-Khan and Bloomberg traveled to Albany to negotiate the plan, and adjusted it to appeal to suburb and outer borough citizens. Daily toll charges became tax deductible and the fee for taxis was dropped to one dollar. Still, state legislators in Albany crushed the initiative. They voiced their objections to Bloomberg's PlaNYC and Sadik-Khan, arguing that many of the initiatives benefitted people in the city at the expense of those in the suburbs. Assemblyman Jeffrey Dinowitz, as quoted by Michael Crowley for *New York Magazine* (17 May 2009), called Sadik-Khan an "anti-car extremist." Sadik-Khan's often brusque and some perceived, self-righteous, tone didn't win her any fans either. Queens City Council member John Liu told Crowley, "There is a sense of the elite telling the everyday people what's good for them, and that's simply not appreciated."

To her critics, Sadik-Khan argues that congestion pricing, an expansion of public space, and—perhaps her most divisive project—bicycle lanes aren't matters of elitism but of practicality. More than half of the city's residents do not own a car. As far as everyday people, she has told sources, the neediest New Yorkers rely almost entirely on public transportation while their health is seriously affected by car exhaust. And in response to anticar allegations, Sadik-Khan told Goldstein: "I'm radically pro-choice. I'm pro-all modes of transportation, not one mode elevated above all others, which I think has been the case in the past. We're really just trying to rebalance our system."

CYCLING ADVOCATE

Sadik-Khan seeks to improve the city from the perspective of cyclists and pedestrians as well as motorists and has looked to cities around the world for inspiration. She took a five-hour bike tour with the former mayor of Bogotá, Colombia. She visited Curitiba, Brazil, where they are making way for light rail through designated bus lanes. She has also traveled to Paris and London, where they successfully implemented congestion pricing in 2003. But one city in particular stood out to her for its innovative design. The city center of Copenhagen, Denmark—with its protected bike lanes, pedestrian promenades, and eighteen designated car-free areas—is a haven for cyclists and pedestrians. Sadik-Khan was so impressed that she hired Copenhagen's urban planner, seventy-two-year-old Jan Gehl, as a consultant in New York. (His fee was paid for with funds raised from private foundations.)

With the help of Gehl, Sadik-Khan implemented several designs similar to those in Copenhagen. In the Chelsea neighborhood of Manhattan, Gehl and Sadik-Khan erected what Sadik-Khan calls a "complete street," in which bike lanes are protected by a single lane of parked cars. Controversially, Sadik-Khan has turned over 250 miles of roadway to cyclists in the form of designated bike lanes. Though the number of cyclists in New York has increased, a majority of citizens do not own a bicycle.

Sadik-Khan has also painted hundreds of miles of bike lanes. Bike lanes have rapidly usurped auto lanes in the city, and some argue, without the input of the surrounding community. Businesses have complained that bike lanes and their surrounding buffers discourage motorists from pulling over to make quick purchases. Others, like Iris Weinshall who filed a lawsuit challenging a particular bike lane on Prospect Park West in Brooklyn, point to a larger issue. On his blog for the *New Yorker* website, John Cassidy wrote of the movement to create city bike lanes (8 Mar. 2011): "I support it. But the way it has been implemented . . . irks me to no end. I view the Bloomberg bike-lane policy as a classic case of regulatory capture by a small faddist minority intent on foisting its bipedalist views on a disinterested or actively reluctant populace."

Sadik-Khan insists that while she is committed to a sustainable future for the city, her greatest concern is safety. She argues that vehicle injuries are down 63 percent because of bike lanes and pedestrians plazas. Traffic fatalities in the city are at an all-time low. Sadik-Khan admits that her fervor to implement changes has made her unpopular in some circles, but Paul Steely White, the executive director of the advocacy group Transportation Alternatives, has defended her efficiency. "She takes her agency's mission of improving safety very, very seriously," he told Michael M. Grynbaum for the *New York Times* (4 Mar. 2011). "It's why she does things quickly, and it's why she does things sometimes too aggressively for people, but ultimately it's to save lives and to achieve a better balance on our streets."

Sadik-Khan is currently putting the finishing touches on a privately funded bike share program—another Copenhagen-inspired plan—in which people would pay a minimal fee to ride public bikes across the city. Stations for the bikes are planned throughout Manhattan and Brooklyn. It will be the largest bike sharing program in North America.

GUERRILLA BUREAUCRAT

As Manhattan real-estate prices indicate, space in New York City does not come cheap, and Sadik-Khan has bemoaned the lack of public space in the city for citizens to escape cramped apartments and for tourists to take refuge from the bustle. Working with Gehl, Sadik-Khan hopes to make the city friendlier to pedestrians. She launched a CityBench program, in which DOT installed a number of comfortable benches across the city to encourage walkers, and she's hoping to make the city easier to navigate with signage pointing the way to various neighborhoods and tourist destinations.

So far her most successful project, also designed with Gehl, has been a series of pedestrian plazas known as Broadway Boulevard. The creation of Broadway Boulevard involved the appropriation of two car lanes to create a public plaza in the middle of Times Square. The plaza features tables and chairs where people can gather and sit amid the billboards and traffic. White lines and barrier blocks made of recycled concrete separate the space. Similar plazas can be found along Broadway, which cuts through Manhattan's grid diagonally. Businesses surrounding the plazas—which are almost always full—report higher revenues, and help the city by storing the plaza furniture after hours in return. The success of Broadway Boulevard, has led to similar transformations in other places throughout the city including Madison Square and Herald Square. The plazas, like the bike lanes, appeared with surprising speed. One plaza in the Down Under the Manhattan Bridge Overpass (DUMBO) neighborhood of Brooklyn was created in one weekend. She told Taddeo that she made the space to send a message. "It was a quick way of showing you can transform a space in a matter of hours instead of a matter of years," she said.

Sadik-Khan has also instituted a program called Summer Streets. In its inaugural year, 2008, Sadik-Khan shut down Park Avenue for three Saturdays during the month of August. She opened the street to events like yoga classes and salsa dancing lessons.

As for mass transit, Sadik-Khan created a Select Bus Service, which operates like a bus rapid transit. The bus routes features designated bus lanes, new curbside fare collection and express stops. The service would greatly improve the city's reputation as one of the largest bus fleets in North America with some of the slowest routes. "I can't wish people onto a bus that's moving at two miles per hour," Sadik-Khan told Goldstein. "I have to give them service that encourages them to do it." Sadik-Khan hopes that bus lanes might encourage the city to move toward a light rail service. She points to Bogotá and Curitiba, two cities that are pursuing this tactic. She also hopes to create new ferry routes on the East River.

OTHER WORK
Sadik-Khan is president of the National Association of City Transportation Officials (NACTO), a coalition of transportation commissioners from thirteen major American cities; the group drafts national transportation policy and hopes to find direct federal funding for transportation projects for cities like New York, which must seek funding from the state's capitol in Albany. State representatives, most representing constituencies outside of the city, have been some of Sadik-Khan's most vocal critics. Sadik-Khan is also chair of the Transportation Research Board's Committee on Transportation Issues in Major US Cities and chair of the Reconnecting America board of directors, a national nonprofit organization. She is the founding president of a communications consulting company called Company 39. In 2011, Sadik-Khan won the Jane Jacobs Medal, named after the late urban activist who famously clashed with Robert Moses in the 1950s. In 2012, Sadik-Khan was selected as a David Rockefeller Fellow by the Rockefeller Foundation; the distinction encourages engagement between the public and private sector.

PERSONAL LIFE
Sadik-Khan met her husband Mark Geistfeld, now a law professor at New York University, while attending law school at Columbia University. The two married in 1990 and have one teenage son named Max. The family lives in New York City's West Village. Sadik-Khan often rides her bike—a Specialized Globe—to her office in the financial district.

SUGGESTED READING
Crowley, Michael. "Honk, Honk, Aaah." *New York Magazine*. New York Media, 17 May 2009. Web. 17 Aug. 2012.

Goldstein, Dana. "Street Fighter." *American Prospect*. American Prospect, 21 Nov. 2008. Web. 17 Aug. 2012.

Grynbaum, Michael M. "For City's Transportation Chief, Kudos and Criticism." *New York Times*. New York Times, 4 Mar. 2011. Web. 19 Aug. 2012.

"Janette Sadik-Khan: North America's Bicycle Super Star: Velo-city Talk." *European Cyclists Federation*. European Cyclists Federation, 14 Jun. 2012. Web. 17 Aug. 2012.

Karni, Annie. "Traffic Tsar Candidates Have Vastly Differing Visions." *New York Sun*. TWO SL, 14 Mar. 2007. Web. 17 Aug. 2012.

Taddeo, Lisa. "Janette Sadik-Khan: Urban Re-engineer." *Esquire*. Hearst Communications, Dec. 2010. Web. 16 Aug. 2012.

—Molly Hagan

Brian Sandoval

Born: August 5, 1963
Occupation: Governor of Nevada (Republican)

When Brian Sandoval, a Republican was sworn in as the governor of Nevada, on January 3, 2011, he became the first Hispanic politician ever to hold that post. It has not been the only such milestone in his career. In 2003, after winning the race for attorney general, Sandoval became the first Hispanic candidate ever elected to statewide office in Nevada, and two years later he became the first Hispanic Nevadan ever to take the bench as a US district-court judge. "The label 'rising Republican star' has been used so often to describe Brian Sandoval over the years that it seemed his name could scarcely appear in print without it," David McGrath Schwartz wrote for the *Las Vegas (Nevada) Sun* (9 May 2010).

EARLY LIFE AND EDUCATION
Brian Edward Sandoval was born on August 5, 1963, in Redding, California. When he was five years old, his family settled in northern Nevada, living first in Fallon and then in rural Sparks, just east of Reno. Sandoval's father, Ron, a Federal Aviation Administration maintenance supervisor, served for a time as a deputy sergeant-at-arms in the Nevada legislature. His mother, Gloria, was a legal secretary. "[She] worked for US Attorney Larry Semenza and a magistrate judge. That was my first exposure to the law," Sandoval told Mae Flennoy for *This Month @ Moritz* (Apr. 2006), published by the Ohio State University's Moritz School of Law. "I would sit at the courthouse and wait for her to get off work. At 13, I worked at the cafeteria at the old federal courthouse in Reno. As I grew older, I became very interested in government and law." Although the family was of Mexican descent, Ron and Gloria spoke only English at

home, so Sandoval and his two siblings did not grow up speaking Spanish.

Sandoval attended Bishop Manogue Catholic High School, in Reno, the only Catholic secondary school in northern Nevada. There, he played football and basketball and was elected president of the student body. He purchased his first car, a 1971 orange Volkswagen Beetle, using money he earned raising lambs with his brother. After he completed high school, in 1981, Sandoval entered the University of Nevada at Reno, where he studied English and economics. He earned a BA degree in 1986. Although he had reportedly thought about attending veterinary school—having enjoyed his experience in raising lambs—he decided instead to pursue his interest in law and enrolled at Moritz. While there he worked in the office of US senator Paul Laxalt, a Republican from Nevada, and as an extern for the Supreme Court of Ohio.

EMBARKS ON LEGAL CAREER

After earning a law degree, in 1989, Sandoval passed the Nevada and California bar exams on his first try and entered private practice. He was hired by a firm now known as McDonald, Carano, and Wilson, which had been cofounded by Alan Bible, a former Nevada attorney general and Democratic US senator. He greatly impressed those with whom he worked. "Here we had a young lawyer who is just starting his legal practice and he was frankly just as interested in being involved in public service as he was in his practice of law," Larry Hicks, then a partner at the firm, told Benjamin Spillman for the *Las Vegas Review-Journal* (2 May 2010). Sandoval remained there for two years, working mainly on matters of business litigation. In 1991 he joined another firm, Robison, Belaustegui, Robb and Sharp, where he focused on environmental law. One of his most high-profile cases, undertaken for Sparks, his hometown, resulted in an $18 million settlement from a group of oil and pipeline companies. Again, he was greatly admired by his colleagues; Kent Robinson, a partner, described him to Jane Ann Morrison for the *Las Vegas Review-Journal* (15 July 2002) as a "plow horse," who consistently worked the longest hours and was among the most productive attorneys in the office.

In 1994, at the suggestion of Nevada state assemblyman Jim Gibbons, who was planning to run in Nevada's gubernatorial race, Sandoval announced that he would vie for the Assembly seat Gibbons would be vacating. Sandoval's office colleagues were seemingly unhappy that he needed to cut back on his work hours to make a political run, so he left Robinson's firm and cofounded his own: Gamboa, Sandoval, and Stovall. Most of the fledgling firm's individual clients were Hispanic; one major group client was the Utility Shareholders Association of

Nevada, a corporation consisting of power-company stockholders. Some journalists have asserted that the group acted as a proxy for utilities managers who wanted to keep rates high, rather than as an advocate for stockholding consumers. "I don't want to sound defensive one bit," Sandoval told Morrison when asked about those assertions. "I'm proud of representing thousands of senior citizens who have invested their life savings in a power company and rely on it to buy their groceries and medicine and pay their rent."

POLITICAL CAREER BEGINS

While Gibbons lost his bid, Sandoval—who had the financial backing of the Republican Party as well as the mining and gaming industries—won election to the Assembly; he won reelection two years later. During his two terms he was a member of several committees, including those devoted to the judiciary, taxation, and natural resources, and he sponsored more than a dozen bills that became law. They included one that prohibited felons from suing victims if they were injured while committing crimes, one that increased the penalties for operating a boat while drunk, and one that allowed poor defendants to perform community service to help defray the costs of their legal battles.

In 1998 Sandoval, who had continued to practice law privately while serving in the Assembly, was appointed to the state's gaming commission by Governor Bob Miller, the Democrat who had defeated Gibbons in 1994. Because his law partners were engaged in arguing cases before the commission, Sandoval left Gamboa, Sandoval, and Stovall to avoid any conflicts of interest and established himself as a solo practitioner.

After the Republican Kenny Guinn took over as governor, in 1999, he appointed Sandoval chairman of the Nevada Gaming Commission; at age thirty-five he was the youngest person ever to serve as the state's chief gaming regulator. Gambling was legal in Nevada between 1869 and 1910; in the following two decades, illegal gambling flourished there. In 1931 state legislators, realizing that stopping the practice was virtually impossible—and hoping to expand on the tourist boom that was expected when the Hoover Dam was completed—legalized most forms of gaming. The industry took off in earnest after the end of World War II, when newly prosperous Americans began flocking to Nevada to try their luck at the gaming tables. The Nevada Gaming Commission was set up in 1959; its primary responsibilities, according to its website, "include acting on the recommendations of the State Gaming Control Board in licensing matters and ruling in work permit appeal cases. . . . Additionally, the Commission is charged with the responsibility of promulgating regulations to implement and enforce the State laws governing gaming." As the chairman of the commission, Sandoval—who was called on at times to testify before Congress—adopted regulations that limited gambling in certain neighborhoods, fought national efforts to block gambling on college sports, and prohibited slot machines with themes appealing to children.

NEVADA'S ATTORNEY GENERAL

Sandoval resigned from the gaming commission in August 2001, in order to run for state attorney general against the Democrat John Hunt. (No gaming commissioner can hold elected office.) On November 5, 2002, he trounced Hunt, garnering almost 60 percent of the vote. Some observers attributed the victory to his campaign war chest: he had collected $1.6 million, $470,000 of which had been contributed by gaming interests. The race marked "another impressive bullet point on Sandoval's resume, as well as another instance in which he moved easily between the interconnected worlds of public service and private interest . . . ," J. Patrick Coolican and David McGrath Schwartz wrote for the *Las Vegas Sun* (9 May 2010). "Sandoval's career . . . offers a window on the inner workings of the elite echelons of Nevada politics and business. It's a tight network with just a handful of figures in gaming and a few other industries. Lobbyists for those industries deliver campaign money to candidates. Lobbyists have the elected officials' ear. Lobbyists win legislative and regulatory battles, helping businesses earn more profit, which means more money for campaigns. And the cycle continues."

Sandoval, the first Hispanic candidate ever elected to statewide office in Nevada, was sworn in as attorney general on January 6, 2003. He promised to help fight nuclear-waste storage at Yucca Mountain, stop school violence, punish consumer fraud, and prevent child abuse. In his new post Sandoval oversaw a staff of 350 and administered a budget of more than $40 million. Concurrently, he served on several state bodies, including the Nevada Board of Pardons and the Nevada Cyber-Crime Task Force.

NEVADA'S FIRST HISPANIC FEDERAL JUDGE

In early 2005 Harry Reid and John Ensign, Nevada's US senators, put forth Sandoval's name for a lifetime appointment as a federal judge. (Reid had originally approached Sandoval years earlier to gauge his interest in a judgeship, but Sandoval had wanted to gain more experience before exploring that option.) Many observers theorized that Reid had ulterior motives: if Sandoval were on the federal bench, he would pose no political competition as a rising GOP star. On March 1, 2005, President George W. Bush formally nominated Sandoval to the seat on the US District Court for Nevada, which was being vacated by Howard D. McKibben. Sandoval underwent a grueling mock hearing in preparation for his actual confirmation hearing. "I'm still trying to get the singe marks off my suit," he quipped to Benjamin Grove for the *Las Vegas Sun* (30 Sep. 2005). He was confirmed by the US Senate on October 24, 2005, by a vote of 89–0 (with 11 senators not voting). He thus became Nevada's first Hispanic federal judge. At 42 he was also among the youngest US district-court judges in the country and one of the youngest in Nevada history. (McKibben was 44, and Phillip Pro was 41, when they were appointed, in 1984 and 1987, respectively, to Nevada's federal district court.)

"I'm very confident in my litigation skills and confident in the courtroom . . . ," Sandoval told Flennoy a half-year after his arrival at the court. "As attorney general you are confronted with litigation from every part of the legal spectrum, criminal, habeas corpus, and civil. You're exposed to complex litigation that some lawyers won't see in their entire legal careers. I believe it prepared me well." He continued, "I want the legal community to be confident that I will be well prepared when they come in my courtroom. I want to be the best possible judge I can be. I want to be seen as somebody who is fair. I want individuals to know they are going to be treated with dignity and respect."

Sandoval surprised many when he announced, on August 15, 2009, that in one month he would give up his lifetime appointment to the federal bench. Immediately speculations about his intentions began to circulate. "When Brian Sandoval announced this month that he was resigning from the federal bench, the complexion of next year's race for governor changed instantly," David McGrath Schwartz wrote for the *Las Vegas Sun* (30 Aug. 2009). "Republican leaders buzzed excitedly, some declaring the 45-year-old former assemblyman, gaming commissioner and attorney general to be the future of Nevada's GOP. A few Democrats privately acknowledged he would be a likeable, articulate and formidable opponent. All that reaction came without his granting an interview or formally announcing that he is running." Schwartz pointed out that until Sandoval's resignation took effect, on September 15, he was prohibited from speaking publicly about running for elected office and continued, "When he does start talking about his decision to resign after nearly four years on the U.S. District Court bench in Reno, the first question he'll likely encounter is this: Why give up a prestigious, lifetime appointment paying $174,000 a year to beg voters for a job that pays $33,000 less and will involve leading a state with a looming $2 billion . . . deficit and a host of other troubles? The speculation ranges on how Sandoval would answer that question. Some say he was bored by the federal bench. Others hint that it's his prominent competitive streak, which dates to his days playing high school basketball in Reno. Still others say he sees his state struggling and wants to take an active role in turning it around."

RUNNING FOR GOVERNOR

As predicted, the day Sandoval's resignation took effect, he announced his gubernatorial bid. His decision to resign from the federal bench to run for office was a rare one. Since 1795 fewer than twenty federal judges had done so, the most recent in 1970. Sandoval's detractors quickly began painting him as a quitter. "Brian Sandoval quit mid-term in the Nevada Assembly," the Republican gubernatorial candidate and former Las Vegas mayor Mike Montandon charged in a fund-raising letter, as quoted by Anjeanette Damon in the *Reno Gazette-Journal* (15 Sep. 2009). "Brian Sandoval quit in the middle of his term as attorney general, virtually handing the office to a liberal Democrat in the next election. And now, Brian Sandoval says he will quit his job as a federal judge and give [President] Barack Obama the opportunity to appoint another liberal judge to the federal bench. Since when is quitting a qualification for governor?" Sandoval countered by pointing out to Damon, "My entire adult life has been committed to public service. My job titles may have changed, but the thing that has remained the same is my commitment to the people of Nevada."

In the Republican primary Sandoval faced Montandon and Jim Gibbons, who had served in Congress for five terms, beginning in 1997, and then won Nevada's gubernatorial race on his second try, in 2006. As governor Gibbons had been plagued by numerous scandals: a young woman charged that an intoxicated Gibbons had assaulted her in a parking garage, and his wife alleged that he was involved in a long extramarital affair, misusing state funds to cover it up. In early 2010 he was named the worst governor in the country by the watchdog group Citizens for Responsibility and Ethics in Washington. As expected, Sandoval easily triumphed in the primary, with 55.5 percent of the vote. (Gibbons garnered slightly more than 27 percent, and Montandon captured about 12.5 percent.)

In the general election Sandoval faced the Democrat Rory Reid, the eldest son of Harry Reid, who had become the majority leader of the US Senate in 2007. The younger Reid, who was serving as the Clark County commissioner, was not considered a strong candidate. In an article for the *Las Vegas Sun* (2 Nov. 2010), David McGrath Schwartz asserted that Sandoval was "a near-perfect candidate for governor. He had the resume, the message, the jaw line and hair that gave his candidacy an air of inevitability. He looked like a Hispanic Ronald Reagan, one Democrat griped." Still, Sandoval faced a few stumbling blocks on his road to the governor's mansion. His Hispanic base was dismayed, for example, when he asserted during an interview for the Spanish-language channel Univision that he avidly supported neighboring Arizona's tough anti-immigration law and that he opposed offering amnesty to anyone who was in the United States illegally. He further alienated voters during that same interview when he stated that he was not worried about his own children being stopped on the street and forced to produce identification, because his offspring "don't look Hispanic." Then, a few weeks before the election, a woman went to the media claiming that she had worked in the 1990s without documentation as a housekeeper for Sandoval; the candidate and his wife denied knowing her and asserted that she had been recruited by the Reid camp to make that false accusation.

During the campaign Democrats tried to tar Sandoval by highlighting his role as attorney general in the imposition of a state tax increase in 2003. That year a longstanding stalemate regarding insufficient revenue to fund education had prevented the legislature from completing the budget, and at the behest of Kenny Guinn, then the governor, Sandoval filed suit, asking the state's high court to force legislators to meet their constitutional duties by approving a balanced budget. The justices ruled that the legislature could ignore the state's constitutional stipulation that a two-thirds legislative majority is required to raise taxes, calling instead for a simple majority. By then one assemblyman had changed his mind and given the legislature the vote needed to approve the tax increase, so "the issue became moot," as Benjamin Stillman wrote for the *Las Vegas Review-Journal* (13 Apr. 2010). (The court's ruling was later overturned.) The tax increase was the largest in Nevada history up to that date, and Democrats—working with the Committee to Protect Nevada Jobs—pounced on the issue, arguing in an ad that Sandoval had "worked to overthrow the will of the people" by "using the courts to force an $800 million tax increase," according to Stillman. Despite such charges, on Election Day Sandoval garnered more than 53 percent of the vote. He was sworn in on January 3, 2011, inheriting a record state deficit of $3 billion.

A CONSERVATIVE GOVERNOR

While Sandoval was considered for many years to be a moderate Republican, he expressed increasingly conservative views while campaigning and has stuck by them since he became governor. He has pledged not to raise taxes, and on his website, he states the importance of maintaining Nevada's "business-friendly, low tax environment." In an effort to increase revenue by bringing jobs to the state, he launched a new Economic Development Board, staffed in part with appointees from McDonald, Carano, and Wilson and the gaming industry. Sandoval is a vocal supporter of Second Amendment rights and has also advocated strongly for states' rights, asserting on his website, "I have a profound respect for the United States Constitution and believe it should be strictly interpreted. The Tenth Amendment, which is the foundation for the expression of state's rights, is extremely important in the face of continued federal intrusion upon state's rights."

Sandoval has endorsed Texas governor Rick Perry for the 2012 Republican presidential nomination.

Sandoval has been married to the former Kathleen Teipner since 1990. A speech pathologist by training, his wife now directs the Family and Youth Intervention program at the Children's Cabinet, a civic organization in Reno. The couple have three children: James, Madeline, and Marisa.

SUGGESTED READING

Nevada Governor Brian Sandoval. State of Nevada, 2011. Web. Jan. 2012.

Schwartz, David McGrath. "Brian Sandoval Defeats Rory Reid in Governor's Race, Now Must Govern." *Las Vegas Sun.* Las Vegas Sun, 2 Nov. 2010. Web. Jan. 2012.

Spillman, Benjamin. "Sandoval Takes Hits Left, Right." *Las Vegas Review-Journal.* Las Vegas Review Journal, 2 May 2010. Web. Jan. 2012.

—*Mari Rich*

Kenny Scharf

Born: November 23, 1958
Occupation: Artist

"I want to have fun when I'm painting. And I want people to have fun looking at the paintings," the artist Kenny Scharf told Gerald Marzorati for ARTnews (September 1985). "When I think, what should I do next? I think: more, newer, better, nower, funner." Scharf, who coined the term "pop surrealism" to describe his creations, gained prominence in New York City's East Village art scene in the early 1980s, when he was in his early 20s, along with his friends and fellow artists Keith Haring and Jean-Michel Basquiat. His paintings, sculptures, collages, installations, and decorated appliances, cars, and other objects are distinguished by their lightheartedness, phosphorescent colors, cartoony characters and other comic-like fauna and flora, settings in outer space, and realistic images of items common in popular culture. His work reflects the ongoing influence of the animated cartoons he watched on television for thousands of hours as a child, as well as the so-called Googie architecture favored in and around Los Angeles while he was growing up and the artwork produced by the Surrealists, which he studied as an undergraduate. "What the Surrealist painters in Europe, in particular Dali, Tanguy and Ernst, introduced to modern culture, Kenny has taken to a new level by infusing it with the genius and animated comedy of Hanna-Barbera (The Jetsons and The Flintstones) and Walt Disney (Fantasia)," the gallery owner Tony Shafrazi wrote about Scharf for Artnet.com. "Kenny Scharf has brought back to art the wonder of perpetual imagination with zing and boundless humor. His art is electrically charged with the 'grooviest' and 'zaniest' innovations at the frontier of creative and playful discovery."

Nearly every year from 1979 to the present, work by the extraordinarily prolific Scharf has been exhibited in art galleries and museums in the United States and abroad. He has had more than 70 solo shows, and his work has been included in upwards of 130 group shows. After visiting one of his recent installations—Cosmic Cavern, a room densely decorated with painted found objects and plastic toys—Penelope Green described Scharf for the *New York Times* (June 4, 2009) as an "ever-youthful psychedelic painter, performance artist and 'customizer,' as he puts it, of home appliances like ovens and blenders." "Nearly 30 years ago," she wrote, "Mr. Scharf's cartoony do-it-yourself environments were a retort to a grimly professional art world—and a whole lot of fun. They still are." The Guggenheim Museum and the Whitney Museum of American Art, in New York City, are among the institutions that have works by Scharf in their permanent collections.

EARLY LIFE AND EDUCATION

Kenny Paul Scharf was born into a Jewish family in Hollywood, California, on November 23, 1958. His father, Roy Scharf, worked in the knitwear business, and his mother, Rose, was a homemaker. Scharf and his two older brothers grew up in Sherman Oaks, a suburb of Los Angeles. As a boy Scharf enjoyed looking in his parents' set of Time/Life art books at reproductions of works by such masters as Michelangelo and Leonardo da Vinci. A neighbor's book about the Surrealist artist Salvador Dali impressed him greatly. From early childhood he loved to watch animated cartoons on television and was "obsessed with utopia, the future," he recalled to Jane McCarthy for the Web site *Flavorwire* (June 5, 2009). Growing up in the 1960s, he said, "That whole promise of the future was very much ingrained in my aesthetic. Back then everything had a futuristic tinge—the cars and the fast food and the supermarkets." Also influencing this futuristic aesthetic was Googie architecture, a genre that developed in southern California in the 1950s in response to the postwar technology boom, and which, Scharf said, "not only shapes things visually, it shapes your mind too because it's pounding in, 'the future's going to be great!' As a little kid, I believed it. I thought I was going to buy a ticket and go to space." In the early 1960s Scharf created what he called "The Book of Everything," in which he drew pictures of inventions that evoked the Stone Age aesthetics of *The Flintstones* and the futuristic environment of *The Jetsons*, his favorite TV cartoons. When the Scharfs bought their first color television, in 1965, young Kenny would gaze at the screen from a distance of a few inches, captivated by the vivid hues. He has traced his fondness for bright colors to the countless vivid images he saw as a young TV viewer.

In 1969 Scharf began taking lessons in painting still lifes in oils at an art shop a short bike ride from where he lived. At home he preferred to copy photographs from *National Geographic* magazine and the paintings in Time/Life books and on art postcards. In 1974 his family moved to Beverly Hills, California. As a student at Beverly Hills High School, he took full advantage of the school's abundant art supplies. (In 1995 a dozen paintings he completed in high school were exhibited at the Yoshii Gallery, in New York City, along with other samples of his early work.) In his free time, too, Scharf devoted himself to drawing and painting.

After his high-school graduation, in 1976, Scharf entered the University of California–Santa Barbara, where he concentrated on art history, printmaking, and painting. In a course taught by the art patron and historian Eileen Guggenheim,

Courtesy of Emmanuel Dunand/AFP/Getty Images

he learned about Andy Warhol and the New York studio known as the Factory where Warhol worked in the 1960s. ("The Factory" was the name of each of Warhol's subsequent studios, too.) "Something clicked in me," Scharf told McCarthy. "For a whole bunch of other kids like Keith Haring and Basquiat and for me, Andy was kind of our impetus, our inspiration."

In 1978 Scharf moved to New York City and enrolled at the School of Visual Arts (SVA), where he studied photorealist and airbrush painting, collage, photography, and videography. In a sculpture class he met Keith Haring, and the two soon became roommates. He and Haring socialized with a group that came to include Jean-Michel Basquiat, the artists Julian Schnabel, Jenny Holzer, and Francesco Clemente, the actresses and performance artists Grace Jones and Ann Magnuson, and many others. Scharf and his new friends and acquaintances frequented establishments such as Club 57 and the Mudd Club, where they sometimes performed and displayed their work. As did others, Scharf took his art to the streets, spray-painting images of cartoon characters on buildings. "The reason why we did art in the street is that art had nothing to do with what was happening in people's lives," he told Sarah Douglas for Artinfo.com (May 11, 2007). "And most people . . . don't go to museums, to galleries, but seeing things in the street gets people to think differently, it inspires them. That's what we enjoyed. Reaching people, getting out into the real world. It's not as though we were saying we wanted nothing to do with the art world, but it was a way of recognizing that the art world can be a very elitist place that doesn't include Joe Schmoe from the street. I've always been against an elitist sensibility."

CAREER

In 1979 Scharf mounted an exhibition called *Celebrating the Space Age* at Club 57. In the same year he had his first official solo show, an exhibit of *The Estelle Series*, paintings depicting "the adventures of . . . a jet set woman of the future," according to Artnet.com. It was held at Fiorucci, in New York, a fashionable department store and artists' mecca, and on its opening day its organizer, the performer Joey Arias, along with the innovative singer known as Klaus Nomi, entertained attendees. During the next decade Scharf often joined Arias, Nomi, and the performance artist John Sex to entertain in clubs and galleries. As a participant in the Times Square Show in 1980 (not 1979, as many sources report), Scharf submitted an air-conditioning unit that he had decorated; a photo of it later appeared in *Arts Magazine*.

After Scharf earned a B.F.A. degree from SVA, in 1980, he formed a company, Van Chrome's Customized Appliances. As Van Chrome, he would visit people's homes and "customize" gas meters, appliances, and other things by painting on them and attaching toys and other objects to them. "I'd arrive with my kit and spend the day customizing," he told Francesco Spampinato for the magazine *apartamento* (Spring, 2011). "I'd do the phone and the blender, then I'd survey the house and recommend other items, like, 'I'll do your TV and toaster for just $200 extra!'" Customization, he told Green at the *Times*, "is a way to make your mundane tasks and objects magical. If your appliance breaks down or wears out, it's still useful because it remains . . . art." Scharf would advertise his service by "walking" his own decorated vacuum cleaner on New York streets. He also began selling items adorned with small objects and painted designs. "It was a way of making art accessible to everyone," he told Spampinato. For some years in the 1980s, Scharf sold decorated T-shirts and other work in his own shop, in the SoHo district of New York, and in the 1990s and early 2000s, in a shop in Miami.

Scharf began exhibiting his *Jetsons*- and *Flintstones*-inspired work at the Fun Gallery on New York's Lower East Side, soon after the gallery opened in 1981. He held parties in what he dubbed the Cosmic Closet, a room in the Times Square apartment he shared with Haring for two years. He decorated its walls with discarded cans and other trash that he had painted with Day-Glo colors, and he illuminated everything with black light (ultraviolet light rays). He recreated the Cosmic Closet for the New York/New Wave show mounted in 1981 by the art

curator, agent, and teacher Diego Cortez at P.S. 1, a public school turned art gallery in the Long Island City section of the New York borough of Queens. Since then he has fabricated more than two dozen similar installations.

In 1982 Scharf exhibited two of his cartoon-inspired paintings, Judy on the Beach and The Flintstones, in a joint show with the graffiti artist Futura 2000 at the Tony Shafrazi Gallery in New York City. In his first solo exhibition at that gallery, in 1983, his oil-and-spray-painted pictures included Felix on a Pedestal, in which the cartoon character Felix the Cat appears; Plasmospace, in which a mob of overlapping, bloblike cartoon figures cavort in outer space; and The Fun's Inside. The background of the last-named work, which measures about 7.5 feet by 9 feet, is a complex tangle of squiggles; the foreground shows the spherical, dark- and light-blue head of a cartoon creature with yellow eyes and a green balloonlike nose, its neck emerging from the stem of a plant; within its gigantic, smiling, lipless, gaping mouth are two stylized mountain peaks set against an otherworldly magenta-and-pink sky in which float strangely shaped clouds consisting of opaque bubbles. Scharf's other solo 1983 show was mounted at the American Graffiti Gallery, in Amsterdam, the Netherlands.

Later in that decade Scharf had a total of 10 solo shows, among them two at the Akira Ikeda Gallery, in Tokyo, Japan, and one at the Galerie L. J. Beaubourg, in Paris, France. His "customized" 1961 Cadillac, titled Ultima Suprema Deluxa, debuted at the Gagosian Gallery in Los Angeles in 1984 and was exhibited later that year at a solo exhibition at the Shafrazi Gallery. In a review for the *New York Times* (December 7, 1984) of the Shafrazi show, Grace Glueck characterized the artist as "the Hieronymus Bosch of our Kool-Aid, sci-fi, space-age." She continued, "Taking cues from . . . comic strips, television cartoons, Walt Disney, earlier art and the anthropomorphic signs that line our highways, Scharf works in two and three dimensions. His chef d'oeuvre here on canvas is When Worlds Collide"—which measures slightly more than 10 feet by 17 feet—"an exuberant apocalypse presided over by a jolly man-mountain in shiny red toy color behind whose goofy smile is a bright, barren desert. Disporting in the picture's cosmic space (Scharf is good at cosmic space) are bubble gum clouds, octopoid creatures and blasts, bursts and puffs of candy-colored stuffs, a Bugs Bunny take on intergalactic calamity. . . . Stealing the show is Suprema Ultima Deluxa. On its hood, toy dinosaurs and plastic fighter planes consort together, and the rest of the car is so bedizened with paint, toys, and plastic baubles as to make an uptown disco seem austere. Our culture is in good hands." Along with a large black-light installation called Closet #7, When Worlds Collide was exhibited at the 1985

Whitney Biennial; since then it has been part of the Whitney's permanent collection.

In 1983 Scharf also participated in nine group shows in the United States and five overseas, the latter at the Bienalle de São Paulo in Brazil; the Kunstmuseum in Lucerne, Switzerland; the Palais des Beaux-Arts in Charleroi, Belgium; the Salvatore Ala Gallery in Milan, Italy; and the Palacio de Cristal in Madrid, Spain. According to Artnet.com, at the Madrid show, called *Tendencias en Nueva York* ("Trends in New York"), waiting lines stretched a quarter mile, not only on opening day but afterward as well; the show later traveled to Barcelona, Spain, and Paris, France. Later in the 1980s Scharf's work appeared in 32 group shows, in places including the Museum of Modern Art in San Francisco, California; the Montreal Museum of Contemporary Art in Canada; the Museum of Contemporary Art in London, England; the Venice Bienalle in Italy; the Wacoal Art Center and the Sogetsu Museum in Tokyo, Japan; sites in two cities in Poland; and the Thomas Cohn Gallery in Rio de Janeiro, Brazil. In 1985 Scharf, Basquiat, Haring, and Clemente each decorated a portion of the new Palladium Nightclub in Manhattan, at the invitation of its owners. After inebriated customers began defacing his paintings, Scharf removed them. The Palladium was later demolished.

FAMILY AND RECENT WORK

Earlier, in 1983, Scharf had flown to Brazil with his friend Bruno Schmidt, a Brazilian-born artist. During the flight he met another Brazilian native, Tereza Goncalves. He and Goncalves married later that year, and what Scharf had originally envisioned as a vacation led to his living and working in a coastal town near a rain-forested area of Bahia for more than three years. "I felt I had to get out of New York," he told Scarlet Cheng for the *Los Angeles Times* (December 2, 2001). "There was too much hype. I felt I was losing my sense of self and getting carried away by the media." He also recalled to Cheng, "I just painted, and it was really good for me, anchored me in what I'm really about—it's not to be a star, but to make art." Scharf's first daughter was born in Brazil in 1984.

For about two years starting in 1987, Scharf and his family (a second daughter was born in 1988) lived in a house overlooking the Hudson River, about 90 miles north of New York City. In 1989 they moved to the Greenwich Village section of the city and then, in mid-1992, to Miami Beach, Florida, where they remained until 1999, when they settled in Los Angeles. All the while they maintained their home in Brazil, too. The lush greenery of the Brazilian rain forest and luxuriant Florida gardens inspired the artist's many paintings of cartoony, imaginary plants and wildlife, subjects to which he still returns. Alarmed by the extensive logging and clearcutting of the Brazilian rain forest by timber companies and cattle ranchers, Scharf organized lavish events in New York City, called "Don't Bungle the Jungle," in 1989 and 1992 to raise money for the foundation Companions of Arts and Nature to use for research, education, and the purchase of rainforested land. Both events attracted many celebrities and together raised close to $1 million.

Earlier, in 1983, Klaus Nomi had died of AIDS. Along with Robert Mapplethorpe, Keith Haring, Tseng Kwong Chi, and David Wojnarowicz, Nomi was one of hundreds of East Village residents active in the arts who succumbed to AIDS in the 1980s and 1990s. Additionally among Scharf's friends, Andy Warhol died after routine surgery in 1987, and Basquiat died of a drug overdose in 1988. "It's strange to feel like you're the only one left," Scharf told Nicole Winfield for the Associated Press (June 23, 1995). "It had a big impact on me. And for a while, I think I was more serious." According to his daughter Malia in a blurb about *The Fun's Inside* (2011), a documentary about Scharf that she made with Nathan Meier, during the 1990s the artist "felt as though he was being 'punished for being alive,' while the price of works by fallen comrades Haring, Basquiat and Warhol reached astronomic heights," and he "struggled to remain relevant" in the art market. "I've been out of fashion so many times," Scharf told Carolina A. Miranda for *ARTnews* (June 1, 2011, online). "The first time it happened, I was like, 'Oh my god, this is terrible—they've dropped me!' But then I was popular again. And then suddenly no one was calling anymore. . . . These days, I don't take it too seriously."

In the 1990s Scharf took part in 32 solo and 51 group shows, and since 2000, his work has been seen in a total of more than three dozen solo and group shows. His one-man shows included *Scharf-O-Rama Vision: 1978–1995*, at the Museum of Art in Fort Lauderdale, Florida (1995); *El Mundo de Kenny Scharf*, at the Museo de Arte Contemporaneo in Monterrey, Mexico (1996); *Kenny Scharf: Paintings 1990–1997*, at the Cotthem Gallery, in Brussels, Belgium (2003); *Kenny Scharf: Superdeluxa*, at the Waddington Galleries, in London (2008); and *Naturalfutura and Three Dozen!*, at the Paul Kasmin Gallery, in New York (2011). The last exhibit included *Oil Painting*, which, by his own account, Scharf made to express his anger about the BP oil spill in the Gulf of Mexico in 2010, and 36 paintings of huge doughnuts adrift in the sky or in space. A sugary pastry, Scharf told Katy Donoghue for *Whitewall* magazine (January 27, 2011, online), is "a great pop symbol of what consumerist America is selling us, packaging it in such a beautiful way, making it enticing, when it's really pretty bad for you."

Dennis Hopper, Paul Reubens, Ann Magnuson, and RuPaul were among the performers who lent their voices to *The Groovenians*, a half-hour animated film that Scharf made with the director and animator Jordan Reichek and several others. A pilot for a television series that never materialized, *The Groovenians* aired once, on the Cartoon Network, in 2002. A mural about 15 feet high and 50 feet long that Scharf filled with cartoonish figures remained on a wall on the Bowery, in Lower Manhattan, for about six months in 2010 and 2011. The artist is currently spray-painting 100 metal storefront security gates in Manhattan for a public-art project sponsored by the Mediacy Group.

Writing for dot429.com (June 8, 2011), Corey A. Rosenberg described Scharf as "playful, carefree, captivating, silly, colorful and brilliant." Scharf's marriage ended in divorce. His daughters, Zena and Malia, turned 27 and 23, respectively, in 2011. Scharf works in his home studios in Brooklyn, New York, and Culver City, California.

SUGGESTED READING

Green, Penelope. "That's Not a Basement, It's Art." *New York Times*. New York Times, 3 June 2009. Web. 19 Dec. 2011.

"Kenny Scharf Catalogue." *Artnet.com*. Artnet Worldwide, n.d. Web. 19 Dec. 2011.

McCarthy, Jane. "Artist Kenny Scharf on Warhol, Donuts, and the Art of Throwing Parties." *Flavorwire*. Flavorpill, 5 June 2009. Web. 19 Dec. 2011.

Rosenberg, Corey A. "Kenny Scharf Makes Art That Pops." *dot429.com*. dot429, 8 June 2011. Web. 19 Dec. 2011.

Scharf, Kenny. Interview by Sarah Douglas. *Artinfo.com*. Louise Blouin Media, 11 May 2007. Web. 8 Dec. 2011.

Spampinato, Francesco. "Kenny Scharf: Bringing the Fantasy into Reality." *apartamento* May 2011: 193–204. Print.

—*Molly Hagan*

Getty Images

Stuart Scott

Born: July 19, 1965
Occupation: Television sportscaster, actor

Stuart Scott has distinguished himself among sportscasters with his laid-back style and use of hip-hop patois to deliver sports news and highlights. As an anchor and analyst for the cable-television channel ESPN, the country's leading sports network, Scott has become famous for his trademark catchphrases, dubbed "Stu-isms"—"Booyah!," "Cool as the other side of the pillow," "Must be buttah 'cause he's on a roll," and "Can I get a witness to the congregation?" He is also known for his journalistic integrity and the wealth of statistics and other information that he offers on air. A graduate of the University of North Carolina at Chapel Hill, Scott worked for a series of television stations in South Carolina, North Carolina, and Florida before joining ESPN, in 1993, when ESPN2 debuted. In 1995 he moved to ESPN, and soon afterward he became an anchor of *SportsCenter*, one of the network's flagship programs. He gained many fans as the cohost, with Rich Eisen, of *SportsCenter*'s live 2:00 a.m. edition. During that time he began working on other ESPN programs, particularly on National Football League (NFL) and National Basketball Association (NBA) broadcasts. Currently, he serves as ESPN's NBA studio host, NBA Draft anchor, *Monday Night Football* anchor, and occasional *SportsCenter* host. "What I've done on television is try to work hard, try to be factually correct, try and write creatively and compellingly . . . ," he said, as quoted by James Andrew Miller and Tom Shales in their book *Those Guys Have All the Fun: Inside the World of ESPN* (2011). "I think that, more than most people, as an African American you have to make sure that you can carry yourself wherever you go and keep it real. What I do on television is part of who I am. I'm not trying to be anyone else. I've always been of the mindset 'Be who you are; just do the job and work hard.'"

EARLY LIFE AND EDUCATION

The youngest of the four children of Ray Scott, a postal inspector, and Jaqueline Scott, Stuart Scott was born on July 19, 1965, in Chicago, Illinois. He has two sisters and a brother. When Scott was seven years old, he moved with his family to Winston-Salem, North Carolina; he returned to Chicago each summer to visit his cousins. As a youngster he developed a love of sports and dreamed of becoming a professional football player. He often played catch with his father and took up football, basketball, swimming, and gymnastics. He became an avid University of North Carolina (UNC) Tar Heels fan after both of his sisters enrolled at the school. In an interview for the *Chapel Hill (North Carolina) Herald* (20 May 2001), Scott told Eric Ferreri, "My idols weren't sportscasters. . . . All my idols were athletes, from Phil Ford to Dr. J. to Walter Payton, Dick Butkus. . . . Muhammad Ali was the biggest one. Sportscasting wasn't what I set out to do."

Scott attended R. J. Reynolds High School, in Winston-Salem, where he played on the football, basketball, baseball, and tennis teams. He also acted in school productions and served as vice president of the student body. Determined to make it as a football player despite his poor eyesight, he became a star wide receiver and defensive back for the R. J. Reynolds Demons. He was voted a team captain and, as a senior, was recruited by four small colleges, including Lenoir-Rhyne, Catawba, and Western Carolina (which his brother attended). Scott chose instead to enroll at UNC at Chapel Hill and begin as a walk-on, after his brother encouraged him to fulfill his dream of attending that school.

At UNC Scott could not play football for over two years because of a series of eye operations, including two to replace his corneas. He channeled his passion for sports into broadcasting, working at UNC's student radio station, WXYC-FM, as a sports and news reporter. During the summer after his junior year, he interned at the television station WTVD, an ABC affiliate in Durham. When his eyes healed, during his junior year, he played wide receiver and defensive back for a semiprofessional football team, and he continued to do so as a senior. He has said that his firsthand experience in sports competitions proved to be invaluable in his career as a reporter. "I've always believed playing sports, at any level, will make you a more accurate and efficient journalist," he told an interviewer for *Jet* (15 Apr. 2002). "Not so much for knowing what it feels like to catch the game-winning touchdown, but more importantly, what it feels like to drop the game-winning pass or strike out when it counts most. Relating to that feeling will help you relate to the athlete on a deeper level. It keeps you grounded in your reporting and it makes it less likely that you'll clown an athlete in

a mean way." Scott earned a BA degree in communications (specifically radio, television, and motion pictures) in 1987.

STARTS CAREER AS A TELEVISION JOURNALIST

After graduating from college Scott landed a job with the television station WPDE-TV, an ABC affiliate in Florence, South Carolina. As a general-assignment reporter during the week and a sports anchor on weekends, he was responsible for everything from writing his own scripts to setting up camera shots to editing. Scott later described his hands-on training to a writer for the *Myrtle Beach (South Carolina) Sun-News* (11 Apr. 2006) as "one of the best experiences of my life. Your first job is always special, and for me it was learning how to write and how to get certain shots, things that helped me down the road." In 1988 he was hired as a news reporter at WRAL-TV, in Raleigh, North Carolina. Scott left WRAL in August 1990, when he was hired as a sports reporter and sports anchor for the NBC affiliate WESH-TV, in Orlando, Florida. While he was with WESH, his feature story on rodeo earned him first-place honors in a competition held by the Central Florida Press Club.

A demo tape that he sent to ESPN at the urging of his wife led ESPN to interview him and then, in 1993, hire him as one of the first anchors at the newly launched ESPN2. Scott started out by anchoring *SportSmash*, a five-minute sports update for ESPN2's *SportsNight*. In 1994 he replaced Keith Olbermann as Suzy Kolber's cohost on *SportsNight*, after Olbermann returned to his anchor chair on *SportsCenter*. Scott hosted several other shows on ESPN2, including the thirty-minute NFL preview show *Edge NFL Matchup*, the NBA news-and-highlights program *NBA 2Night*, and *SportsNight: College Football Edition*.

ESPN ANCHOR AND COMMENTATOR

In 1995 Scott joined ESPN as a *SportsCenter* anchor and commentator on the network's NFL and NBA broadcasts. He has appeared on shows including *NFL Prime Time, Sunday NFL Countdown,* and *Monday Night Countdown* and covered such events as the NBA Draft, the NBA All-Star Game, and the NBA Finals. Scott has also covered Major League Baseball play-offs and National Collegiate Athletic Association Final Four contests and served as an anchor for ESPN's *Dream Job* reality series and game show *Stump the Schwab*. He hosted the network's 2005 *New Year's Eve Special* and David Blaine's "Drowned Alive" stunt, in 2006. Also in 2006, after *Monday Night Football* (MNF) moved to ESPN, Scott began serving as an on-site host for the ninety-minute edition of *Monday Night Countdown*, which airs live from 7:00 to 8:30 p.m. and previews that night's football match. He also provides post-game coverage of *MNF* games on *SportsCenter*. In 2008 Scott became the lead host for NBA on ESPN and ABC (which are both owned by the Walt Disney Co.), and he currently leads a studio team consisting of Jon Barry, Michael Wilbon, and Magic Johnson. In 2009 he helped ESPN launch its West Coast production of *SportsCenter* and hosted a select number of 1:00 a.m. Eastern Time (ET) editions from the newly constructed L.A. Live complex, a state-of-the-art entertainment facility located across the street from the Staples Center. Scott can now most often be seen anchoring *SportsCenter*'s 11:00 p.m. ET edition.

Many have cited as especially memorable Scott's pairing with Rich Eisen as coanchors for the live 2:00 a.m. ET edition of *SportsCenter* in the late 1990s. Repeats of the one-hour show aired several times a day and reached millions of sports fans nationwide. Scott and Eisen became known for their shtick and catchphrases. Maile Carpenter, writing for the Raleigh, North Carolina, *News and Observer* (5 Oct. 1997), described the duo as "an odd but workable match, Scott the high-energy pep guy, Eisen the witty, sardonic sidekick."

While Eisen spiced his comments with wry, Jewish humor and pop-culture references, Scott mixed urban street slang with his own catchphrases: he would exclaim "Boo-yah!" after extraordinary dunks and home runs, "Cool as the other side of the pillow" to describe athletes who remain calm under pressure, and "Can I get a witness to the congregation?" following a spectacular play. Scott "gives the sports news as if he's talking to his boys on the street corner, a style that separates him from most anchors," Sam Adams wrote for the Denver, Colorado, *Rocky Mountain News* (8 Dec. 2001). "Call it factual rap—sports news delivered with mad, hip-hop flavor."

Scott told Ernest Hooper for the *St. Petersburg (Florida) Times* (16 May 1997) that as one of the few African American sports anchors on television then, he "wanted to represent a segment of the audience that wasn't really being represented." He said to Adams, "I do my sportscasts how I talk. My nouns and verbs don't necessarily match up. But that's how I talk, so that's what I'm going to bring. I'm not going to say anything on TV that I don't say in my normal conversation. If I talk to you a lot and you don't use big words, I don't want to hear you use big words on TV. If that's not who you are, who are you trying to impress? If you do your work, you can be who you are."

Scott has received criticism and even hate mail for his use of hip-hop colloquialisms, but he is widely credited with helping to attract younger, more diverse viewers to ESPN. In *Those Guys Have All the Fun*, Keith Clinkscales, ESPN's senior vice president of content development, told James Andrew Miller and Tom Shales, "I don't want to commit hyperbole here, but Stuart's delivery on *SportsCenter*—his willingness to stick with it despite getting complaints, and the producers letting him stick with it—is one of the great cultural moments that African American culture has ever had. It made us relevant in sports." "I'm proud of what I do, but I'm proud of all us who work there," Scott told the *Myrtle Beach Sun-News* writer. "Everybody brings their own style to the table. I'm proud of ESPN for allowing us to have our own personalities on air. I really appreciate that a lot."

Scott has conducted exclusive one-on-one interviews with such high-profile figures as Michael Jordan, Tiger Woods, President Bill Clinton, and, during the 2008 presidential campaign, Barack Obama. He has appeared in the films *He Got Game* (1998), *Enchanted* (1998), *Drumline* (2002), *Mr. 3000* (2004), *The Longest Yard* (2005), *The Game Plan* (2007), and *Just Wright* (2010) and on the television shows *Arli$$*, *Soul Food*, and *One on One*. He has also been cast in commercials and music videos and has been spoofed on *Saturday Night Live*.

PERSONAL LIFE

On April 3, 2002, while participating in a New York Jets mini-camp for a three-part ESPN special, Scott was struck in the left eye with a football launched from a football-throwing machine. He underwent emergency surgery to repair the cornea and lens and missed two months of work. The accident also damaged his eyelid.

In November 2007 Scott had an emergency appendectomy after becoming ill during a *Monday Night Football* broadcast. During the surgery a malignant tumor was discovered, and he later had another operation to remove possibly cancerous tissue in his abdomen. Scott underwent chemotherapy, and the cancer went into remission. It reappeared in 2011, and Scott completed another round of chemotherapy. Scott, who works out regularly, talked about his disease to Shannon J. Owens for the Fort Lauderdale, Florida, *Sun-Sentinel* (10 Aug. 2011): "To me, it's like a football game. I'm facing this, this wants to win. You can try, but I'm just gonna come harder than you . . . all day long." In 2011 Scott received the Spirit of Jimmy V Award from the V Foundation for Cancer Research.

Scott lives in Avon, Connecticut. From his marriage to Kimberley, in 1993, he has two daughters, Taelor and Sydni, who were sixteen and eleven in mid-2011.

SUGGESTED READING

Miller, James Andrew, and Tom Shales. *Those Guys Have All the Fun: Inside the World of ESPN* Boston: Little, 2011.

"On the Set with ESPN's Stuart Scott." *Courant. com*. Hartford Courant, 23 May 1999. Web. Jan. 2012.

—*Christopher Cullen*

Kazuyo Sejima

Born: 1956
Occupation: Architect

"Analytic and poetic, assertive and recessive, Kazuyo Sejima is the moonwalker of architecture, gliding in opposite directions with mind-bending grace," Arthur Lubow wrote for *W* magazine (Sep. 2010). Sejima and her partner, Ryue Nishizawa, are the principals of the Japanese architecture firm SANAA, which has been responsible for such high-profile projects as the New Museum in New York City; the Glass Pavilion at the Toledo Museum of Art in Ohio; the Rolex Learning Center in Lausanne, Switzerland; and the 21st Century Museum of Contemporary Art in Kanazawa, Japan. Sejima is only the second female architect to win the prestigious Pritzker Prize, widely acknowledged to be the field of architecture's equivalent of the Nobel Prize. "The world of architecture is still very masculine, as is Japanese public culture, so the glass ceiling Sejima has broken is double-thickness Plexiglas," Rowan Moore wrote for *Vogue* (Nov. 2006).

EARLY LIFE AND EDUCATION
Sejima was born in 1956 in Ibaraki Prefecture, Japan, a coastal region located northeast of Tokyo. Her mother hailed from an aristocratic and educated family that once owned one of Japan's noteworthy castles. Her father was an engineer. Because girl's names generally end in "ko," his decision to name her Kazuyo was an unusual one. "'Yo' is a little bit different," Sejima explained to Lubow. "My mother said my father gave me that name because he wanted me to make my own way."

Sejima has joked to journalists that when she was small her main ambition was to become a grandmother, because the elderly women she encountered always looked so comfortable and happy. Still, as she told Moore, she had a mild interest in architecture even as a youngster. "When I was a child I saw a photograph of the Sky House by Kiyonori Kikutake [an iconic structure consisting of a single room mounted on four pylons]," she recalled. "It was very striking for me. Is this a house? I thought. But then I forgot about it until I started at university. I had to decide a direction, and then I remembered that as a child I had been interested in that house. When I got to university, I saw it in the library in a publication and realized it was very famous."

Getty Images

Sejima attended the Japan Women's University, the country's oldest private institute of higher learning for female students. She graduated with a degree in architecture in 1981.

CAREER
Upon graduating, Sejima was hired to work in the firm of Toyo Ito, who is known for such buildings as the Sendai Mediatheque, a library and exhibition space, and the Kaohsiung National Stadium, built for the World Games in Taiwan. In a fitting coincidence, Ito once worked for the firm of Kikutake, whose Sky House had inspired Sejima as a child. Sejima was greatly influenced by Ito's dramatic yet practical aesthetic. She remained at the firm until 1987, when she established her own company, Kazuyo Sejima and Associates. Nishizawa soon joined her as a staffer while studying architecture at Yokohama National University, from which he graduated in 1990.

Among Sejima's first projects as the head of her own firm was a series of small "platform" homes with such features as corrugated iron roofs and glass facades, used as vacation homes or primary dwellings in Chiba and Yamanichi. She was also commissioned to design numerous pachinko parlors, arcades at which patrons play a colorful and noisy game that is somewhat similar to pinball. As the decade came to a close, Sejima began to win both higher-profile commissions and formal recognition from her peers. In 1990 she began work on the Saishunkan Seiyaku Women's Dormitory, which provided housing for several dozen female workers in the city of Kumamoto. Although conventional wisdom in Japan held that such facilities should provide the greatest privacy possible for their residents, Sejima, now working closely with Nishizawa, created a series of four-person bedrooms flanking a large, soaring public area. "She would like to make a community of eighty people like one family," her fellow architect Riken Yamamoto told Arthur Lubow for *T* (9 Oct. 2005). "Architects can sometimes change the system with their design. She believed that."

Sejima was named the Japan Institute of Architects' Young Architect of the Year in 1992. That same year, she was commissioned to design what became known as the Villa in the Forest for a wealthy client who wanted to be able to host artists visiting his area of Nagano. She conceived a two-part structure composed of living quarters and a studio space, with walls made of thick concrete to provide insulation from the cold in the mountainous region. Because of its curving outer walls and white concrete, the project, completed in 1994, is often likened to a modernist igloo. Among her other unusual projects of the early 1990s was a *kōban*, one of the small community police kiosks that dot Japan.

In 1995 Nishizawa announced that he wanted to leave the firm to work on projects of his own. Sejima had come to consider him an equal and rely heavily on his judgments, and she offered, instead, to make him a partner. The two formed the firm Sejima and Nishizawa and Associates, commonly known as SANAA. Observers have noted that the decision to capitalize and give equal weight to proper names and conjunctions alike can be seen as symbolic of the collaborative and egalitarian spirit of their enterprise. In addition to their collaborative work, Sejima and Nishizawa have continued to take on independent, individual projects.

Sejima completed a number of major projects in the mid-1990s, receiving a great deal of acclaim for her work. "She won the commission to restore a historic quarter of Salerno, in Italy's southern rust-bucket district," Ian Perlman wrote for the *Sydney Morning Herald* (15 Aug. 2000). "She won competitions to add new art museums to the dowager samurai city of Kanazawa and Iida, a hinterland way station, for a site hard against medieval ramparts. Deep in Japanese suburbia she has designed an apartment block in which walls pivot, expressing interior life like a musical score."

Among the projects to which Perlman referred, the Kitagata apartment block in central Japan's Gifu Prefecture is considered particularly worthy of note by both architectural experts and social scientists. Sejima was a member of an international team of female architects, including Akiko Takahashi of Japan, Christine Hawley of England, and Elizabeth Diller of the United States, which was chosen to reimagine the possibilities of public housing. "[Their] task was straightforward but far from simple: to design a set of apartments that could serve as an alternative to the reductivist postwar system blocks common to most towns and cities," Phoebe Chow wrote for the *Architectural Review* (Apr. 2001, online). Each of the 107 units in Sejima's portion of the project includes a terrace open to the outside. The interior passageway linking rooms within each individual unit is framed with glass, allowing exposure to the outside world, and each unit has at least two direct entrances from a public corridor. The units themselves vary widely in layout; Sejima designed numerous different configurations in acknowledgment of the fact that various nontraditional family groups would inhabit them. Her work was considered so visionary that it inspired a lavishly illustrated monograph, *Kazuyo Sejima in Gifu*, published in 2001. Sejima has been the subject of other books as well, including *Kazuyo Sejima + Ryue Nishizawa/SANAA: Works 1995–2003* (2003); *Houses: Kazuyo Sejima + Ryue Nishizawa, SANAA* (2007); *Shift: SANAA and the New Museum* (2008); and, *The SANAA Studios 2006–2008: Learning from Japan; Single Story Urbanism* (2009).

Sejima received equal attention for Small House, a project on an entirely different scale than the multiunit apartment block in Gifu. As space in Tokyo is at a premium, many houses there are extremely small, and Sejima was hired to design a home that could fit on "the 388-square-foot buildable area of a 646-square-foot lot. The challenge was practically like performing a magic trick," Naomi Pollock, a Tokyo-based correspondent, wrote for the *Architectural Record* (April 2001). The resulting house has four levels: a bedroom and a tiny bathroom with a shower occupy the lowest level; the main entrance and family room are on the next; a space for cooking, eating, and socializing takes up another; and the top level contains a deep soaking tub and a covered terrace with sweeping views of the city. Her work was praised by numerous other industry insiders, and the home was considered a marvel of simplicity and efficiency.

In 2004 SANAA completed its largest, most prestigious project to that date: the 21st Century Museum of Contemporary Art in Kanazawa, a coastal city with a rich feudal history. For the project Sejima and Nishizawa designed a labyrinth of separate galleries connected by a system of corridors, all contained within a main outer wall of curving glass. In addition to exhibition spaces, the museum incorporates several free community facilities and four glass-enclosed courtyards. The project won a Golden Lion award at the 2004 Venice Biennale of Architecture. It was not Sejima's first proud moment at the biennale; in 2000 she had curated the Japanese Pavilion at the exhibition.

INTERNATIONAL ACCLAIM

In 2006 Sejima completed her first major US project, an addition to the Toledo Museum of Art in Ohio, which was in need of a space in which to exhibit its extensive collection of glass works. Sejima designed a pavilion that was built in a small park across from the main building. "Just as theater-in-the-round radically changes the relationship between actors and audience, so the new Glass Pavilion at the Toledo Museum of Art subverts many of the old rules of displaying art," Clifford A. Pearson wrote for the *Architectural Record* (Jan. 2007). "By using mostly clear-glass walls for both the building's envelope and its interior partitions, the architects . . . have performed the museum equivalent of stripping away the proscenium stage and creating a more fluid dynamic between art and viewer." Many critics and industry professionals found the decision to house glass artwork in a glass building to be a bold one, although it brought up such issues as where to mount thermostats (the solution was to place them on freestanding rods) and how to protect the art from ultraviolet rays (the designers called for translucent curtains that can be drawn when needed).

Now with an increased profile in the United States, Sejima and Nishizawa were hired to design a museum in New York City. "They were the firm that every other firm we interviewed admired," Lisa Phillips, the director of the New Museum, as the venue is called, explained to Lubow for *T*. "Wherever we went, there were SANAA books on the shelves." Located on the Bowery, in downtown Manhattan, the structure was completed in 2007 and contains a carefully curated selection of contemporary art from around the world. Resembling, as many observers have noted, a series of boxes haphazardly stacked by a child, the striking building comprises seven stories built around a steel core, cantilevered to accommodate skylights and terraces.

Sejima received even greater attention in 2009 for her work on the Serpentine Gallery Pavilion in London, England. Every year since 2000 the gallery, one of the most prestigious in the world, has tapped a top architectural firm that has not yet completed a building in England to design a temporary structure, which is then used as a venue for a program of public talks and other events. Other Serpentine Pavilion laureates have included Frank Gehry, Rem Koolhaas, and Daniel Libeskind. Viewed from above, SANAA's design, which was widely considered a major triumph for the firm, resembled a meandering stream of water mounted atop a series of slim, almost ethereal columns.

The year 2010 was a stellar one for SANAA and its principals. The Rolex Learning Center, a library and student center in Switzerland, was completed, earning the firm much praise. Sejima also served as director of that year's Venice Biennale of Architecture, becoming the first woman and the first native of Japan to hold the position. When invited, she requested that Nishizawa be allowed to codirect, but biennale officials decreed that only one director was permitted. She agreed to take the position but subsequently enlisted both Nishizawa and Yuko Hasegawa, a former chief curator of the 21st Century Museum, as advisers. In explaining Sejima's appointment, Paolo Baratta, who heads the group that oversees the biennale, told Lubow for *W*, "[She] is really the architect who refuses to conceive architecture as a way of representing the power of somebody, or the money of somebody else, or the ambitions of the client. She instead comes back to an idea of architecture where functions, relations, and the division of space are what matters." That year's event was widely considered one of the best in recent memory, and much of the credit was given to Sejima.

The most newsworthy event of the year came with the announcement that Sejima and Nishizawa were being jointly awarded the Pritzker Prize, the highest honor in the field of architecture. The prize is given annually to architects whose work has made "consistent and significant contributions to humanity." Sejima is the second female recipient in the history of the prize, after Zaha Hadid in 2004. The jury cited specific works such as New York's New Museum, Toledo's Glass Pavilion, and Kanazawa's 21st Century Museum of Contemporary Art and asserted that Sejima and Nishizawa deserved the prize for their "architecture that is simultaneously delicate and powerful, precise and fluid, ingenious but not overly or overtly clever; for the creation of buildings that successfully interact with their contexts and the activities they contain, creating a sense of fullness and experiential richness; for a singular architectural language that springs from a collaborative process that is both unique and inspirational; [and] for their notable completed buildings and the promise of new projects together."

Sejima has taught architecture at the Polytechnique de Lausanne, Princeton University, and Keio University, among other institutions. In 2005, SANAA was selected from a pool of more than 120 international architectural firms to design a new branch of the famed Louvre to be located in Lens, a former coal-mining town in the Nord-Pas de Calais region of France. Created in collaboration with the firm Imrey Culbert and various other teams, the Louvre-Lens was scheduled to open to the public in 2012. Sejima has also become deeply involved in efforts to rebuild Miyatojima, an island that is part of the city of Higashimatsushima in Miyagi Prefecture, which was heavily damaged in the 2011 earthquake and subsequent tsunami.

Sejima maintains an office in a warehouse space located in the Shinagawa waterfront district of Tokyo, where she works with Nishizawa and a team of architects.

SUGGESTED READING

Lubow, Arthur. "Disappearing Act." *T* 9 Oct. 2005: 148. Print.

---. "Kazuyo Sejima: The Closet Starchitect." *W* Sep. 2010: 206. Print.

Moore, Rowan. "A Light Touch." *Vogue* Nov. 2006: 326. Print.

Nomura, Hiroko. "Architect Sejima Keeps Creative Juices Flowing." *Nikkei Weekly* 19 Sep. 2011: 32. Print.

Pearson, Clifford A. "SANAA's Sejima and Nishizawa Create Layers of Reflections and Perspectives." *Architectural Record* Jan. 2007: 78. Print.

Perlman, Ian. "Vision-Impaired Syndrome City." *Sydney Morning Herald* 15 Aug. 2000: 14. Print.

Pollock, Naomi. "On a Tiny Lot in Downtown Tokyo, Kazuyo Sejima Shapes a Sculptural Jewel, Aptly Named Small House." *Architectural Record* Apr. 2001: 120. Print.

—*Mari Rich*

Getty Images

Daniel Shechtman

Born: January 24, 1941
Occupation: Scientist, educator

Israeli scientist Dan Shechtman won the 2011 Nobel Prize in Chemistry for his 1982 discovery of a previously undescribed form of crystal. Quasiperiodic crystals, or quasicrystals, are informally known as shechtmanite. Before Shechtman's discovery, scientists believed that such crystalline solids not only did not, but could not, exist; their existence would defy the laws of nature. The very definition of crystals ruled them out. For that reason, the immediate, virtually universal reaction to Shechtman's discovery among his colleagues in the fields of chemistry, physics, metallurgy, and crystallography was widespread rejection and ridicule.

Foremost among Shechtman's detractors was Linus Pauling, who won the Nobel Prize in Chemistry in 1954 for his work in elucidating the nature of chemical bonds, as well as the Nobel Peace Prize in 1962. Pauling did not question Shechtman's experimental results, but until his death in 1994, he refused to accept Shechtman's interpretation of those results, which indicated the reality of quasicrystals. Since Pauling was highly revered among members of the American Chemical Society, some chemists never voiced doubts about his views during his lifetime. Nevertheless, by the late 1980s, increasing numbers of scientists had replicated Shechtman's work and confirmed his conclusions. In 1991, the International Union of Crystallography changed the definition of a crystal to encompass quasicrystals. Tel Aviv University physicist Ron Lifshitz described Shechtman's discovery to Asaf Shtull-Trauring for *Haaretz.com* (1 Apr. 2011) as "a scientific revolution that is still going on."

Thousands of scientists now study quasicrystals in laboratories around the world. They have created hundreds of new types of alloys that are quasicrystals, and in 2010, scientists found a naturally occurring form in a rock sample from Russia. Most quasicrystals are stable and easy to create. Characteristics such as extraordinary hardness and a low coefficient of friction make them useful as components of surgical equipment and other products. Additional uses are expected to emerge as more is learned about them and as technology advances.

Several scientists came across quasicrystals before Shechtman, but none considered them worthy of study. Shechtman has attributed his discovery to the availability of the transmission electron microscope, which enabled him to examine much smaller crystals than had previously been possible; his professionalism and expertise; his tenacity; and his courage in the face of enormous opposition. "Usually, great discoveries come by serendipity, when you stumble upon something new," Shechtman said at a Jerusalem press conference on October 9, 2011, "and you have to be able to realize it is something that wasn't there before, and then try to explain what you see. Then, when you start to talk about it, you will face opposition. And here is the real test: If you believe in yourself, then listen to others but don't let them discourage you as long as you are not convinced that they are right and you are wrong. In my case, I knew I was right."

In 1975, Shechtman joined the faculty of his alma mater, the Technion–Israel Institute of Technology in Haifa, Israel. He was named a distinguished professor in 1998 and now holds the Philip Tobias chair in materials science. He is a member of the Technion's Department of Materials Engineering and heads the school's Louis Edelstein Centre for Quasicrystals. Since 2004, he has also served four months a year as a professor of materials science and researcher at the Ames Laboratory, a US Department of Energy national laboratory on the Iowa State University campus at Ames.

EARLY LIFE

Shechtman was born on January 24, 1941, in Tel Aviv, in what was then Palestine, a territory administered by Great Britain; he was seven years old when Israel became an independent nation. Shechtman's grandparents emigrated from Russia early in the twentieth century. Shechtman was raised in Ramat Gan and Petah Tikva, suburbs of Tel Aviv.

As a boy, Shechtman read Jules Verne's fantasy *The Mysterious Island* (1874) many times. He greatly admired the character Cyrus Smith, whose knowledge included mechanics, chemistry, and other sciences. Smith, Shechtman told a *Technion Live* interviewer (6 Oct. 2011), "could do everything. He was an engineer, and I wanted to be like him." Shechtman also recalled being powerfully impressed by his first look through a microscope at school; afterward, he dreamed of working with microscopes. In another vivid memory, his high-school physics teacher praised him when he solved a problem concerning the resistance of a complicated electrical circuit. "Danny knows his physics," the teacher said.

Shechtman did well in school but was not the top student in his class. For years he participated in the left-leaning Zionist youth movement Hashomer Hatzair (Young Guard). "In my youth group . . . we were educated to become physically and mentally independent. You threw us on a desert island and we would survive," he said at the Jerusalem press conference. As a high school student, he underwent rigorous paramilitary training; Shechtman has said that this training and his experiences in the Hashomer Hatzair helped prepare him to withstand the later belittlement directed at him by his colleagues. In 1959, he began his mandatory service in the

Israeli army. During that period of two and a half years, he met his future wife.

UNDERGRADUATE AND GRADUATE EDUCATION

After completing military service, Shechtman enrolled at the Technion, Israel's oldest university. He studied mechanical engineering and earned a bachelor of science degree in 1966. Unable to find a job in his field, he returned to the Technion and pursued a master's degree in materials science and engineering. He chose that field by chance: as a college senior, he had accepted the invitation of a classmate to collaborate on a project in metallurgy. "If that guy hadn't approached me, I would be in a different place," he told Shtull-Trauring. Materials science and engineering draws from chemistry, physics, mathematics, and other disciplines to determine the structure, properties, and ways of forming materials. Shechtman earned a master's degree in 1968 and a PhD in 1972, both at the Technion.

EARLY CAREER

For the next three years, Shechtman worked in the United States for the American air force as a postdoctoral researcher. In 1975, the air force offered him "a marvelous position," he told Shtull-Trauring. When he and his wife, Zipora, discussed whether to remain in the United States or return to Israel, they came up with far more reasons for the former than the latter. Shechtman was about to sign a contract with the air force when the Technion offered him a faculty position, which he accepted. "I am a Zionist and I try to do many things for Israel's good," he told Shtull-Trauring.

Shechtman taught and conducted research at the Technion for the next six years. He then became eligible for a sabbatical leave, and he accepted an offer from the US National Bureau of Standards (now called the National Institute of Standards and Technology) in Gaithersburg, Maryland, to conduct research in its materials department for two years. Supported by the US Defense Advanced Research Projects Agency (DARPA), Shechtman joined a group that was developing and examining the characteristics of metallic alloys for potential use in the aerospace industry. As part of that research, he used a transmission electron microscope to examine the diffraction patterns produced by crystals of new alloys of his own invention. At that time, he was among the few people in materials science who had become expert in the use of that tool.

CRYSTALLOGRAPHY IN BRIEF

The field of crystallography dates from 1912, when the German scientist Max von Laue (1879–1960) used single-wavelength x-rays to produce the diffraction pattern of a crystal. Von Laue won the Nobel Prize in Physics in 1914 for his discovery of x-ray diffraction. The diffraction pattern of a crystal reveals characteristics of its atomic structure. During the next seventy years, x-ray diffraction investigations of hundreds of thousands of crystals showed that all crystals—whether in metallic materials, rocks or ceramic materials, or any other crystalline solid—have three characteristics: order, periodicity, and rotational symmetry. Thus, a crystal was defined as a material whose atoms or molecules are always arranged in a specific order that repeats itself periodically, with the arrangement remaining symmetrical if it is rotated a certain number of times. All crystallographers agreed that that number can be one, two, three, four, or six—never five, and never seven or more. In other words, rotational symmetry can only be single-fold, twofold, threefold, fourfold, or sixfold. Three-dimensional repeating units form what is called a crystal lattice.

To illustrate the three characteristics of crystals, one can imagine using triangular, square, or hexagonal tiles to cover a surface. Such shapes will cover the surface completely, with no gaps. They will display order and periodicity, as in a checkerboard or a honeycomb. If one rotates an arrangement of squares by 90 degrees, it will look exactly the same. Rotating it by 90 degrees three more times brings it back to its original position.

THE DISCOVERY OF QUASICRYSTALS
On the morning of April 8, 1982, while working alone in his laboratory at the Bureau of Standards, Shechtman was examining an alloy of 75 percent aluminum and 25 percent manganese that he had created as a molten mass. He cooled it rapidly, and it became solid. When he first looked at a sliver of the mass through his electron microscope, he saw only blackness. He made a thinner sample and then, magnifying the crystals 36,000 times, he saw the aluminum-manganese alloy's diffraction pattern. Shechtman could scarcely believe his eyes: as he noted in his log book, he saw ten bright spots arranged equidistantly in each of a series of concentric circles.

According to definitions and descriptions of crystals in all physics, chemistry, and crystallography textbooks published in the previous seventy years, no crystal could produce such a diffraction pattern, because it would arise from fivefold rotational symmetry. Such a pattern was simply not possible. Shechtman has recalled in interviews that when he counted the ten spots, he said to himself, "There is no such creature." Eager to have someone else see what the microscope had revealed, Shechtman left the lab and looked for another researcher in the corridor outside, but nobody was there. He then conducted repeated experiments, thinking that perhaps the explanation for the anomaly was that the

aluminum-manganese crystals were twinned. But there was no evidence of twinning.

Although Shechtman's notation in his logbook for image 1725 reads "10-fold???," the question marks reflect astonishment rather than doubt, because he soon became convinced that he had discovered something completely new: a diffraction pattern that had order and symmetry but not periodicity. Referring to the multifaceted solids known as icosahedrons, which have twenty faces, Shechtman noted during his Nobel lecture at Stockholm University in Sweden (8 Dec. 2011) that "many of the quasiperiodic crystals have icosahedral symmetry" with "six fivefold axes, ten threefold axes, and fifteen twofold axes." An accompanying slide displayed an image labeled "the first view of the icosahedral phase" of a quasicrystal, in which the pentagonal crystals, which measure about 0.5 micrometers, or 500 nanometers across (about five thousand times the diameter of a helium atom), are clearly visible. "A few days later all my work was complete, and everything was ready for the announcement," Shechtman told Istvan Hargittai for the *Israel Journal of Chemistry* (Dec. 2011).

REACTIONS TO SHECHTMAN'S DISCOVERY
Although Shechtman believed that "everything was ready" to be made public, he discovered that none of his colleagues accepted his conclusions or were willing to challenge crystallographic dogma. "I told everyone who was ready to listen that I had material with pentagonal symmetry," he told Shtull-Trauring. "People just laughed at me." Those people included the leader of his group at the Bureau of Standards. One day, he came into Shechtman's lab "with a sheepish smile" and placed on his desk a well-known textbook of crystallography. He advised Shechtman to read the book so that he would realize that what he thought he had discovered was not possible. Shechtman responded that he had used that very textbook in courses that he had taught, and that despite its assertions about the impossibility of fivefold rotational symmetry, he knew that he was right. "The main lesson that I have learned over time is that a good scientist is a humble and listening scientist and not one that is sure 100 percent in what he reads in the textbooks," Shechtman said at a news conference in Haifa (5 Oct. 2011). Soon afterward, the same man told Shechtman that he was a disgrace to their group and could no longer be associated with it.

Shechtman joined a different group at the bureau, remaining in the same lab to continue his work. A great number of scientists heard Shechtman denigrated at conferences by Linus Pauling, often in his capacity as the keynote speaker. Shechtman was talking nonsense, Pauling would declare from the podium, adding, "There is no such thing as quasicrystals, only quasi-scientists." Until the end of his life, Pauling insisted that Shechtman's diffraction patterns showed only evidence of twinning. "After a while, I enjoyed every moment of this scientific battle, knowing that he was wrong," Shechtman recalled during an interview at Iowa State University (5 Oct. 2011).

Back at the Technion, Shechtman convinced one of his colleagues, the materials scientist Ilan Blech, that he had indeed discovered a never-before-identified crystal. He and Blech coauthored an article entitled "The Microstructure of Rapidly Solidified Al_6Mn" and submitted it to the *Journal of Applied Physics* in September 1984. The journal's editors immediately rejected it as of no interest to physicists. The following month, Shechtman and Blech submitted their paper to the journal *Metallurgical Transactions*, which published it in June 1985.

Meanwhile, during a trip to the United States in September 1984, Shechtman showed the paper to John W. Cahn, a highly respected senior scientist at the Bureau of Standards. Cahn, who had originally dismissed Shechtman's findings as impossible, reversed his position. He offered to add his name to Shechtman and Blech's paper and recruited Denis Gratias, a French crystallographer, to confirm the accuracy of Shechtman's work. The men rewrote the article, entitling it "Metallic Phase with Long-Range Orientational Order and No Translational Symmetry." They submitted the article in October 1984 to the journal *Physical Review Letters*, an American Physical Society publication. It was accepted and appeared in the November 12, 1984, issue.

Within days, Shechtman was bombarded by phone calls from scientists who had replicated his experiments and drawn the same conclusions. Still, his work was not accepted by the majority of crystallographers until 1987, when An-Pang Tsai, a scientist at Tohoku University in Japan, created an alloy of zinc, magnesium, and holmium whose aperiodic crystals were large enough to produce x-ray diffraction patterns; a French team produced similarly large crystals. (Crystallography was long known as x-ray crystallography, and for years electron microscopy had been disdained among crystallographers.) In 1991, the executive committee of the International Union of Crystallography announced a new definition: "By crystal we mean any solid having an essentially discrete diffraction diagram, and by aperiodic crystal we mean any crystal in which three-dimensional lattice periodicity can be considered to be absent."

Since then, Shechtman has continued to study alloys and quasicrystals at the Technion and the Ames Laboratory. In the mid-1980s, he introduced a Technion course in technological entrepreneurship, which he has called "my baby" and to which he invites expert lecturers in fields such as patent law. He has been recognized many times at the Technion as an outstanding teacher.

NOBEL PRIZE AND OTHER HONORS

Shechtman's honors include the American Physical Society's International Award for New Materials (1988), the Weizmann Science Award (1993), the Israel Prize for Physics (1998), the Wolf Prize in Physics (1999), the Gregori Aminoff Prize of the Royal Swedish Academy of Sciences (2000), and the European Materials Research Society 25th Anniversary Award (2008).

On December 10, 2011, in introductory remarks preceding the Swedish king's presentation of the Nobel Prize in Chemistry to Shechtman, Nobel Committee for Chemistry member Sven Lidin said, "Your discovery of quasicrystals has created a new cross-disciplinary branch of science, drawing from and enriching chemistry, physics, and mathematics. This is in itself of the greatest importance. It has also given us a reminder of how little we really know and perhaps even taught us some humility. That is a truly great achievement."

Shechtman's wife, Zipora Shechtman, is a professor in the Department of Counseling and Human Development at Haifa University. The couple have four children and nine grandchildren. Shechtman is saving his Nobel Prize money for his grandchildren's education.

SUGGESTED READING

"Ames Laboratory, Iowa State University, Technion Scientist Wins Nobel Prize in Chemistry." *Iowa State University News Service*. ISU University Relations, 5 Oct. 2011. Web. 5 Feb. 2012.

Blizovsky, Avi. "Crystal Clear—All the Way to the Nobel." *Hayadan: Israeli Science and Technology News*. Hayadan, 6 Oct. 2011. Web. 5 Feb. 2012.

Chang, Kenneth. "Israeli Scientist Wins Nobel Prize for Chemistry." *New York Times*. New York Times, 5 Oct. 2011. Web. 5 Feb. 2012.

Hargittai, Istvan. "Dan Shechtman's Quasicrystal Discovery in Perspective." *Israel Journal of Chemistry* 51.11–12 (2011): 1144–52. Print.

Leichman, Abigail Klein. "The Scorned Scientist Who Became a Nobel Laureate." *Israel21c*. Israel21c, 10 Oct. 2011. Web. 5 Feb. 2012.

Shtull-Trauring, Asaf. "Clear as Crystal." *Haaretz.com*. Haaretz, 1 Apr. 2011. Web. 5 Feb. 2012.

"Who is Dan Shechtman?" *Technion Live*. Technion–Israel Institute of Technology, 6 Oct. 2011. Web. 5 Feb. 2012.

—Miriam Helbok

Rachel Sklar

Born: December 8, 1973
Occupation: Media blogger, author, attorney

Journalist, media critic, and former lawyer Rachel Sklar is editor-at-large for the blog *Mediaite*. She is also the former media editor and a founding contributor at the Huffington Post, as well as the cofounder of both Change the Ratio, a project that promotes women in business, and Charitini, a website devoted to collecting monetary donations that are then passed on to nonprofit organizations. Sklar was spotlighted in the British media and marketing blog *The Wall* in a post called "Social Media Movers and Shakers: The Ones to Watch in 2011." She proved herself worthy of the distinction with her abundance of self-attributed titles, and as she told the website We Are NY Tech (Feb. 28, 2011, online), the one she chooses to use "depends [on] who I'm meeting with."

Sklar has managed to maintain her position as online media critic as she joined the ranks of New York's media elite. "I'm always aware that I live in a glass house surrounded by giant stones," she told Rachel Kramer Bussel for the website Gothamist (Aug. 19, 2005, online), "and I try to be even-handed." Once considered a protégé for media maven Arianna Huffington of the Huffington Post, Sklar has become somewhat of a tech fairy godmother in her own right for startups such as the social and professional networking site Hashable. She is also an advisor to the online sports network SBNation as well as the content-marketing platform Kapost. She is a TechStars mentor and the cohost of the television program *The Salon* on The Jewish Channel. As a freelance journalist Sklar has written for print publications such as *Glamour*, the *Financial Times*, the *Chicago Tribune*, *Wallpaper*, and the *New York Post*. She has been described as "witty" and "offbeat" and is popular both for her irreverent blog and Twitter postings as well as for her media expertise, which she is routinely invited to share on news networks such as CNN, MSNBC, and Fox News.

EARLY LIFE AND EDUCATION

Rachel Sklar was born on December 8, 1973, in Toronto, Ontario, Canada. Her father, Donald Sklar, is a psychiatrist, and her mother, Corinne Sklar, is a lawyer. Sklar has an older sister named Michelle. Her older brother, Robert, died in 1991. Sklar and her siblings spent many childhood summers at Camp Winnebagoe on Fox Lake in Ontario. As a counselor at the camp, Sklar directed plays, and, as she joked to Matt Haber for the *New York Observer* (Aug. 1, 2008, online), she "may have been the first person to mount a version of [the movie] *Grease Two*."

AP Photo

Sklar also referenced her time at the *Winnebugler*, the camp's weekly magazine.

She attended high school at York Mills Collegiate Institute followed by the University of Western Ontario, where she was the vice president for communications in the University Students' Council. Sklar was also a contributor to the school newspaper, the *Gazette*, and a member of the Debating Society. After graduation Sklar nearly pursued a musical-theater education at New York University's Tisch School of the Arts but instead chose to attend the University of Toronto Faculty of Law, her mother's alma mater. While a student there she wrote for the school humor magazine, the *Hearsay*, and wrote and performed in the musical-comedy sketch "Law Follies." Sklar graduated with honors in 1998 and was the class valedictorian.

FROM LAW TO JOURNALISM

From law school Sklar was recruited to the New York City–based international law firm White & Case. In her second year, she was invited to spend six months at the firm's Stockholm office. "I should clarify that I didn't practice Swedish law—I was there as a liaison for the office on matters of U.S. law," she told the website We Are NY Tech. She added, "That was how I learned that it's not always what you know, but knowing who to ask. I would send thank-you presents of Swedish chocolate back through the inter-office diplomatic pouch, and word spread quickly that people should answer my emails." In Sweden Sklar dabbled in numerous creative projects. She recorded four pop-dance tracks for a producer friend, one of which was recorded by a Swedish pop singer and achieved moderate success. She also began freelance writing small articles. "I always knew I wanted to write—it's just what I've always done," she told Bussel, and she credited her law degree with making her a better writer. "I had never really wanted to practice law—something which was borne out by the practice of law—but I loved law school and I was really engaged by the material. I always knew I'd leave, it was just a matter of when."

Sklar's first big break into journalism landed her on the front page of the sports section for the Don Mills, Ontario, *National Post* on May 15, 2000. The story, about the World Hockey Championships in St. Petersburg, Russia, was titled "Prib Becomes Paradise for Sports Fans: Hotel Guests Share Space with Movers and Shakers from World Hockey Scene." "Prib" was a reference to the luxury Pribaltiyskaya Hotel, which Sklar described as "a 1,200-room monolith on the shores of the Baltic Sea." The piece came about by coincidence. Sklar was living in Stockholm and was visiting St. Petersburg for pleasure. While staying at the Prib she befriended a number of hockey players and wrote what became a sketch of life in the hotel. After the publication of her article, Sklar developed a relationship with the *National Post*. "I got unique stories because I traveled for them—the World Cup of Lawyers in Malta, the Nobel Museum in Stockholm," she told Bussel. "So, ironically, what made me broke is also what helped get me a career."

In 2002 Sklar enrolled in a writing course through the website MediaBistro. For her first assignment, she wrote a poem called "A Canadian Moves South," about her own move to New York City. She scribbled the words to the poem on a legal pad in a partner's office. On a whim Sklar sent the poem to the *New York Times*, and it ran in the paper's Metropolitan Diary section two weeks later. Speaking with Bussel, she recalled, "I remember I closed my office door and jumped up and down." Using a MediaBistro connection and the aid of the website's "How to Pitch" guide, Sklar saw several of her stories published in the *New York Times* stand-alone City Section. She profiled Karyn Bosnak of Save-Karyn.com, who, after running up over $20,000 in credit-card debt, began a tongue-in-cheek website asking strangers to help her pay it off—which they did. Sklar also wrote profiles of Lynn Harris, the creator of the Breakup Girl character and subsequent dating blog, and Blaire Allison, who created MarryBlaire.com with the tagline "I'm ready to get married—Do you know my husband?" as she searched for the perfect mate. "For a while," Sklar told Bussel, "'quirky net innovators' was my beat." Though she was still working as a lawyer, Sklar was as successful as she

was relentless. "I would just watch my inbox," she explained to Bussel. "When I'd get an email that someone just had to pass on I would see if it had legs."

Despite her early success with the *New York Times*, Sklar characterized her path from lawyer to journalist as difficult—especially the brutal pay cut. "I went from being a lawyer at a top New York firm to being a freelance writer with no contacts," she told Geoff Wolinetz for the website Bundle (Mar. 4, 2010, online). Describing being invited to a wedding in Toronto, she said, "Everyone was bringing something to contribute and they knew I was struggling, so they just asked me to bring paper plates and cups for a get-together one night prior to the wedding." She continued, "I spent like $40 on all this stuff—it was like 40 percent of my total net worth—and when I got to the party, a bridesmaid said, 'Oh, thanks. But we already have this stuff.' Not mean or anything, but she tossed it in the trash. . . . The $40 I'd spent on it was so much money to me."

Sklar lived off her savings after quitting her job at the law firm. After eighteen months of freelancing, she moved out of her old apartment and sold her old work clothes on Craig's List. Sklar later taught a class for MediaBistro called Mastering the Lateral Move: How to Get out of Your Current Position and into Full-Time Journalism, warning, "Do not quit your day job until you have established yourself as a freelancer!" Referring to her class, she added, "That seminar was basically a 'do as I say not as I did' cautionary tale."

MEDIA BLOGGER

In 2004, Sklar contributed several pieces to the now-defunct web magazine *The Black Table*, including an article where she covered the 2004 Republican National Convention and recalled crashing the invitation-only Creative Coalition Gala Benefit and witnessing a "Republican Conga Line." In 2005 Elizabeth Spiers, then the editor in chief at MediaBistro, was looking to launch several blogs, one of which was the media gossip blog *FishbowlNY*. Sklar was recommended to Spiers by A. J. Daulerio, a former editor of *The Black Table* and was initially hired as a blogger for the site, later becoming its coeditor and main writer. She was hired, as she told Bussel, "out of the blue," and added, "I don't even know if I had initial expectations—there honestly wasn't time." She continued, "The learning curve was incredibly steep, and I was paranoid about making mistakes so I was following every link on every story. . . . But [blogging] was so much fun and such a total rush—and it felt really familiar too, like the goofy emails I used to send my friends during all-nighters at the law firm." Spiers allowed Sklar creative control over her posts—she once posted a rewrite of the epic Billy Joel song "We Didn't Start the Fire" to reflect the big news stories of the day and included a link to each story. Referring back to her law training, she told Lisa Bryn Rundle for the *University of Toronto Magazine* (Winter 2012), "There's nothing I love more than to find five hours to really wonk out on a nice juicy post."

The same year Sklar became a founding contributor to the fledgling Huffington Post. At the time, the news and opinion site boasted only six employees. "When [Arianna Huffington] launched her group blog in 2005, skeptics dismissed it as a vanity outlet for her and her Hollywood friends," Howard Kurtz wrote for the *Washington Post* (July 9, 2007). "But the Huffington Post has become an undeniable success, its evolution offering a road map of what works on the Web."

Sklar became the editor of the site's media blog, *Eat the Press*, and was one of the first to truly tap into the marketing possibilities of blogging. "The blogosphere isn't covered with crazy ranters," she told a reporter for *Inside Health Media* (Sep. 13, 2007). "It's becoming more and more professional, more and more rigorous in terms of scanning the reporting and fact-checking. It's just really evolving."

Sklar left the Huffington Post after the 2008 election and became a consultant with Abrams Research, which is owned by MSNBC journalist and web entrepreneur, Dan Abrams. Abrams funded *Mediaite*, the media blog of which Sklar became editor-at-large. The site posts news and opinion stories as well as objective rankings of media figures on a power grid according to their weekly popularity.

ONLINE INITIATIVES AND PHILANTHROPY

Along with digital strategist Emily Gannett, Sklar is a cofounder of the Change the Ratio project, which promotes visibility for and provides opportunities to women in media and technology. The project was inspired by a 2010 *New York Magazine* article, "Tweet Tweet Boom Boom," about tech startup companies. The article featured only six women in the fifty-three-person "all-star" line up. Sklar wrote a response to the article on *Mediaite* titled "If We Can Make a City Smarter, Why Can't We Do the Same with Its VC Firms?" and began a tireless campaign to promote women in technology fields. Sklar says recognition is the basis of Change the Ratio. "There has always been a ratio problem at conferences, [on] panels and on [power] lists," she told Lisa Bryn Rundle. "They typically tend to be disproportionate to the number of women in the fields." When asked about whether sexism continues in new media, Sklar replied, "I wouldn't characterize [the gender discrepancy] as sexism. I think of sexism as something deliberate. . . . It's more institutional bias. The ease of men referring to men."

Through Change the Ratio, Sklar became acquainted with and began brainstorming with the marketing head of Hashable, Emily Hickey. Hashable is a mobile and desktop application that manages a user's personal and business contacts. Sklar has been spreading the good news of the networking site as a "Hashvangelist" ever since their meeting.

Sklar is also the cofounder of the microgiving website Charitini, which encourages a small donation to charity in lieu of buying a friend a birthday drink. She launched the site on her thirty-sixth birthday in 2009. On that day sixty-two of her friends donated more than $1,000. "It's not about shaming people for not giving 'enough,'" Sklar told Elizabeth Glover for the *Washington Times* (May 20, 2009). "There is no 'enough' in times like this. Everything needs to be more affordable, and that includes karma. The idea is to introduce the idea of giving back, and to make the point that disposable income— what we use to buy drinks at a bar for a birthday party—can be used to do a little good."

Sklar is also involved with a number of non-profit organizations including the Elie Wiesel Foundation, the Robin Hood Foundation, and TeachAIDS.org.

BOOKS, TELEVISION, AND THEATER

Sklar coauthored the book *Stroke of Luck: Life, Crisis and Rebirth of a Stroke Survivor* with Howard Rocket, the father of a childhood friend. It was published by the Toronto Rehabilitation Institute Foundation in 1999, and all of the proceeds from the sale of the book go to agencies involved in stroke research and rehabilitation. Sklar's next project is a humorous book titled *Jew-ish: Who We Are, How We Got Here, and All the Ish in Between*.

Sklar is a frequent cohost of the show *The Salon* on The Jewish Channel, hosted by *Forward* editor Jane Eisner. The program is billed as the first-ever television show devoted to Jewish women's issues. Sklar is also a contributing writer to Jewcy, a Jewish news and culture website.

Sklar studied improvisational acting with the Upright Citizens Brigade and has performed in numerous comedy shows. In the summer of 2005, she was a part of Gotham City Improv's *Weekly Review: A Media Musical*, which billed itself, according to Bussel, as "the first ever musical comedy based entirely on ever-changing events in politics and the media," and featured a new musical each week. Sklar told Bussel her "big moment was performing 'Look at Me, I'm Sandra D. (O'Connor)' as Ruth Bader Ginsberg." At the 2004 New York City Midnight Moviemaking Madness Film Competition, Sklar also won an award for best leading actress for her role in the short Western *Behind the Badge*.

SUGGESTED READING

Bussel, Rachel Kramer. "Rachel Sklar, Co-Editor and Writer of *FishbowlNY*." *Gothamist*. Gothamist, 19 Aug. 2005. Web. 17 Jan. 2012.

"Depends Who I'm Meeting with." *We Are NY Tech*. Onepager, 28 Feb. 2011. Web. 17 Jan. 2012.

Glover, Elizabeth. "'Toast' to Web Charity Network." *Washington Times* 20 May 2009: B3. Print.

Haber, Matt. "Sklar Comes Alive!" *New York Observer*. New York Observer. 1 Aug. 2008. Web. 17 Jan. 2012.

Kurtz, Howard. "A Blog That Made It Big: The Huffington Post, Trending up and Left." *Washington Post* 9 July 2007: C1. Print.

"Rachel Sklar, the Huffington Post, Media and Special Projects Editor." *Inside Health Media* 1.677 (13 Sep. 2007): n. pag. Print.

Rundle, Lisa Bryn. "60 Seconds with Rachel Sklar: Online Media Maven." *University of Toronto Magazine* 39.2 (Winter 2012): 62. Print.

Sklar, Rachel. "If We Can Make a City Smarter, Why Can't We Do the Same with Its VC Firms?" *Mediaite*. Mediaite, 19 Apr. 2010. Web. 18 Jan. 2012.

---. "Prib Becomes Paradise for Sports Fans: Hotel Guests Share Space with Movers and Shakers from World Hockey Scene." *National Post* [Don Mills, Ontario] 15 May 2000: B6. Print.

Wolinetz, Geoff. "Other People's Money: Media Blogger Rachel Sklar on Selling Her Clothes, Giving to Charity and the 'Toonie.'" *Bundle*. Bundle Corporation, 4 Mar. 2010. Web. 17 Jan. 2012.

—*Molly Hagan*

Courtesy of Kevin C. Cox/Getty Images

Josh Smith

Born: December 5, 1985
Occupation: Basketball player

The six-foot-nine Atlanta Hawks' power forward Josh Smith is widely regarded as one of the most athletically gifted players in the National Basketball Association (NBA). His exceptional scoring, rebounding, and blocking abilities and a quickness rare for a player his size have earned him comparisons to the Miami Heat's LeBron James, arguably the league's best player. Smith entered the NBA right out of high school, in 2004, and has spent his seven seasons in the league with the Hawks. He has led the team in total blocks and average number of blocks per game in each season and has finished in the league's top five in both categories in four of them. He has also achieved several other distinctions, including becoming the youngest player in NBA history

to block 10 or more shots in a game and the youngest to record 500 career blocks (in 2007) and 1,000 career blocks (in 2010). In 2005 he became the second-youngest player to win the NBA Sprite Slam Dunk contest.

Along with the Hawks' All-Star shooting guard Joe Johnson and the All-Star center Al Horford, Smith has transformed the squad from being one of the league's worst to being a consistent playoff contender: the team earned playoff berths in each of the last four seasons (2007–10). Smith is known as the Hawks' spark plug and a vocal leader on the court, and many consider him the key to the team's success. "If Joe Johnson is cool and quiet as the team captain," Michael Cunningham wrote for the *Atlanta Journal-Constitution* (March 13, 2010), referring to the Hawks' All-Star guard, "then Smith is the drill sergeant barking to give their best." Smith told Cunningham, "I feel that Joe Johnson, first and foremost, is our leader. But he sort of leads by how he plays the game, until he gets real, real mad. I guess I am the other one that uses his voice, is vocal, is policing it. Not even always policing but telling people where they need to be at certain spots at different times." Horford told Jeff Schultz for the *Atlanta Journal-Constitution* (April 21, 2010), "Joe is one of those players who lives for the big moment—he's our go-to guy. But I think Josh is the biggest key for us. He gets everybody going. He makes things happen. When he's rebounding the ball, scoring the ball, he's the guy who makes us go."

EARLY LIFE AND EDUCATION

Joshua Smith was born on December 5, 1985, in Atlanta, Georgia, to Walter "Pete" Smith and Paulette (Reaves) Smith. He has a brother, Walter, an older sister, Kasola, and a younger sister, Phebe. Kasola Smith was a champion long jumper for the University of Tennessee at Chattanooga; Phebe Smith was an All-American basketball star at Columbus State University, in Georgia. (According to some sources Smith has a third sister, Shanti.) He and his siblings grew up in the Atlanta suburb of College Park. Smith's father was a truck driver; his mother was a homemaker who also ran a hair salon. Earlier, in the 1970s, as Paulette Reeves, she was an R&B singer, recording hits including "Jazz Freak" and "Your Real Good Thing's About to Come to an End"; she resumed her career as a gospel artist a decade ago.

Smith "was brought up in a spiritual environment, taught to do right and to always respect other people and respect himself," his mother told Steve Hummer for the *Atlanta Journal-Constitution* (January 3, 2005). He began playing basketball at a young age. He told Mark Wiedmer for the *Chattanooga (Tennessee) Times Free Press* (October 27, 2005) that playing basketball was "all I've ever wanted to do." Smith's father, who had tried out with several American Basketball Association teams in the 1970s, repeatedly reminded young Josh that becoming a professional required an enormous amount of hard work. "I always tell him [basketball] is a privilege, not a pleasure," his father told Hummer. "Don't turn it into a pleasure." Heeding his father's advice, Smith worked daily on his basketball game, usually putting his skills on display in pickup games with his siblings in which he often beat all of them.

By the time Smith entered McEachern High School, in Powder Springs, another Atlanta suburb, he was already taller and more athletic than most of his peers: at six feet five inches, he was able to dunk a basketball. During his three years at McEachern High, he was selected twice for the All-State team. He also played on the Atlanta Celtics, a highly touted Amateur Athletic Union (AAU) team that competed in tournaments all over the country. His Celtics teammates included the future NBA players Randolph Morris and Dwight Howard. Karl McCray, then the AAU Celtics' coach and now the team's president, told Ken Sugiura for the *Atlanta Journal-Constitution* (May 10, 2010), "We all knew that those three kids could be NBA players. We've been doing this a long time. You can kind of tell the kids coming through who really have a legitimate chance."

As a high-school senior, Smith transferred to Oak Hill Academy, a private, Baptist-affiliated boarding school in Mouth of Wilson, Virginia, that is nationally famous for its basketball program; the school has produced a slew of current and former NBA players, including Carmelo Anthony, Michael Beasley, Brandon Jennings, and Kevin Durant. The future Boston Celtics' All-Star point guard Rajon Rondo was Smith's teammate and roommate at Oak Hill. During his one year at the school (2003–04), Smith averaged 25.8 points, 7.4 rebounds, six blocks, and three steals per game and set a single-season school record for most points scored—980. He helped lead the Oak Hill Warriors to a 38–0 record and a number-one national ranking by *USA Today*, while he himself was named a finalist for the Naismith Award. He also earned McDonald's All-American honors and played in the McDonald's All-American Game.

Viewed as one of the nation's top high-school basketball players, Smith indicated that he was considering making the jump to the NBA, by playing in several other postseason All-Star games, including the EA Sports Roundball Classic and the Nike Hoop Summit. He was named the latter game's Most Valuable Player (MVP) after leading the US team with 27 points in a 99–79 victory over the World Select team. That performance and others helped convince NBA scouts that Smith was ready for the professional ranks, and although he had signed a letter of intent to attend Indiana University, he abandoned his college plans and entered the NBA draft. (Two years later the NBA instituted a rule requiring players to be at least 19 years old and one year past high school before entering the draft.)

CAREER

In the 2004 NBA draft, Smith was selected by the Atlanta Hawks in the first round, with the 17th overall pick. Later that summer he signed a three-year, $3.4 million contract with the team. Billy Knight, then the Hawks' general manager, told Paul Newberry for the Associated Press (June 24, 2004), "He has things you can't teach. He's long, rangy and plays above the rim. We have to work on his skills set. He hasn't had to work on those because he's been so good athletically. Players like that have a tendency to do what they need to do. Now, he's going to be facing players who are just as athletic as he is."

Questions concerning Smith as he entered the league centered on his shooting and ball-handling skills, maturity, work ethic, and ability to adapt to NBA coaching. Such doubts led the ESPN analyst Jay Bilas to predict that Smith would be the likeliest draftee to become a bust. Smith entered his rookie season determined to prove his detractors wrong, and under the guidance of the first-year head coach, Mike Woodson, he dedicated himself to working on his weaknesses. "He was 18 years old, and he'd never really been coached," Woodson said to Mark Bradley for the *Atlanta Journal-Constitution*

(January 18, 2010). "That was a major jump. He had to learn everything."

During his rookie season (2004–05), Smith made 59 starts in 74 games and averaged 27.7 minutes per game. He played in 15 games off the bench for the Hawks before breaking into the team's starting lineup in the second month of the season. He made his NBA debut on November 3, 2004, in a game against the Phoenix Suns, scoring seven points, with seven rebounds, three assists, and one block in 24 minutes. The Hawks lost the game, 112–82. Smith made his debut as a starter in a December game against the Detroit Pistons, scoring 12 points and grabbing five rebounds, with four blocks and two assists in 27 minutes. Later that month Smith put his natural athleticism and raw talent on full display during a game against the Dallas Mavericks, in which he blocked 10 shots—an NBA season high. He became, at 19, the youngest player in league history to block 10 or more shots in a game and became only the third NBA player to accomplish that feat without committing a personal foul. While the Hawks finished that season with the league's worst record—13 wins and 69 losses—Smith stood out as one of the team's few bright spots. He finished that season with a total of 144 blocks, more than any of his teammates and good for 12th in the league and first among all rookies. He also led the Hawks and all rookies in average number of blocks per game (1.9) and finished among rookie leaders in several other statistical categories, ranking third in rebounds (an average of 6.2), eighth in points (an average of 9.7), 10th in steals (an average of 0.8) and tied for 12th in assists (1.7) per game. He was subsequently named to the NBA's All-Rookie Second Team.

A highlight of Smith's impressive rookie campaign came during the NBA's 2005 All-Star Weekend, when he competed in the Rookie Challenge and the NBA Sprite Slam Dunk Contest. He won the latter event with a dazzling array of dunks, including one from the foul line and another in which he honored the former Hawks legend and two-time Slam Dunk champion Dominique Wilkins by wearing Wilkins's jersey. Smith became the second-youngest player (after Kobe Bryant, who won the event at 18 in 1997) and only the third Hawk to win the event (after Wilkins and Spud Webb). Despite his successes Smith experienced difficulties as an NBA rookie. "I came in not knowing anything," he recalled to Ian Thomsen for *Sports Illustrated* (November 30, 2007, online). "I'd get in the game and I needed help all the time."

Smith solidified his role as a starter in 2005–06, making 73 starts in 80 games and averaging 32.0 minutes per game. He led the Hawks in total blocks (206) and average number of blocks per game (2.6), placing second and fourth, respectively, in those categories in the league. He

became only the fourth Hawk and the first non-center to post at least 200 blocks in one year. He also finished third on the team in average number of rebounds per game (6.6) and fourth in average number of points (11.3) and assists (2.4) per game. The Hawks, meanwhile, won twice as many games as they had the previous season, finishing with a record of 26–56. At the end of the regular season, the Hawks presented Smith with the inaugural Lou Hudson Award, which recognizes the team's most improved player.

Smith continued to show significant improvement during the 2006–07 season. He started each of the 72 games in which he participated and averaged 16.4 points, 8.6 rebounds, 2.9 blocks, 3.3 assists, 1.4 steals, and 36.8 minutes per game. He finished second in the NBA in total blocks (207) and blocks per game and led the Hawks in blocks and rebounds per game, while finishing second on the team in points and steals and third in assists and minutes played; he was one of only three players in the league to finish in the top 20 in three categories—rebounds, steals, and blocks. He also led the Hawks with 32 double-doubles and was the team's leading scorer in 19 games; he recorded 20 or more points 27 times. Smith additionally reached several career milestones, scoring his 2,000th point, grabbing his 1,000th rebound, and reaching 500 blocks. (He was the youngest player in NBA history to achieve that number of blocks.) The Hawks, who improved their record to 30–52, again honored him with the team's Lou Hudson Award.

During the summer of 2007, Smith worked with the All-Star guard Calvin Murphy and the Hall of Fame center Hakeem Olajuwon to further improve his game. At that point he was known primarily as a shot-blocker and finisher with a talent for making notable dunks. While many in basketball circles acknowledged his superior athletic abilities, others criticized him for relying too heavily on his strengths at the cost of defense, ball security, and shot selection. His lack of self-discipline led to many clashes between Smith and Woodson, who suspended him for two games late in the 2006–07 season following a confrontation during a game. Nevertheless, Woodson acknowledged to Sekou Smith for the *Atlanta Journal-Constitution* (April 20, 2008) that "a lot of [the team's] success has been because of Josh Smith's endurance and his unique ability to do some things that, quite frankly, very few guys in this league can do."

In 2007–08 Smith made a career-high 81 starts and achieved career-high averages in points (17.4), assists (3.4), and steals (1.5) per game, while averaging 8.2 rebounds and 2.8 blocks per game. He became only the third player (and the first non-center) in NBA history to average at least 17 points, eight rebounds, three assists, 2.8 blocks, and 1.5 steals per game in one season. He also recorded a career-high 227 blocks and 25 three-pointers, making him the first player to ever record at least 225 blocks and 25 three-pointers in the same season. Thanks largely to Smith's versatile all-around play, the Hawks improved their record to 37–45 and clinched their first playoff spot since the 1998–99 season. In the opening round of the playoffs, the team lost to the Boston Celtics, the eventual NBA champions, in seven games; Smith averaged 15.7 points, 6.4 rebounds, and 2.9 assists per game.

After signing a five-year, $58 million contract extension with the Hawks during the summer of 2008, Smith returned to help the team reach the playoffs again in 2008–09. Despite appearing in a career-low 69 games—he missed 11 games due to a left-ankle injury—he led the team in average number of blocks (1.6) and steals (1.4) per game, while finishing second in average number of points (15.6), second in average number of rebounds (7.2), and tied for third in average number of assists (2.4) per game. The Hawks achieved their first winning season since 1999, with a record of 47–35, and advanced to the Eastern Conference semifinals, where they were swept by the Cleveland Cavaliers in four games.

In 2009–10 Smith received All-Star consideration, with averages of 15.7 points and 2.1 blocks per game and career highs in average number of rebounds (8.7), assists (4.2), and steals (1.6) per game. In February 2010 he became the youngest player ever to reach 1,000 shots, doing so in a game against the Oklahoma City Thunder. That year he finished second to the Orlando Magic's Dwight Howard in the voting for the NBA's Defensive Player of the Year Award. "Josh is a beast," Howard told Sekou Smith. "He's always been able to do stuff on the floor that most people can only do on video games. He's on another level than most guys in the league already." The Hawks finished the 2009–10 season with a record of 53–29, reaching at least 50 wins for the first time since 1997. After defeating the Milwaukee Bucks in the opening round of the playoffs—a highly competitive seven-game series—they were swept in the Eastern Conference semifinals for the second consecutive year, losing to the Orlando Magic in four games.

Following the 2009–10 season, the Hawks replaced Mike Woodson with the team's longtime assistant coach Larry Drew, a former NBA player. Smith, who had worked hard on his jump shot during the off-season, showed significant improvements in his perimeter shooting in 2010–11, shooting 48 percent from the field and a career-best 33 percent from beyond the three-point arc. He averaged 16.5 points, 8.5 rebounds, 3.3 assists, 1.6 blocks, and 1.3 steals per game. The Hawks reached the playoffs for the fourth consecutive season. The team again failed to advance past the Eastern Conference semifinals, losing to the Chicago Bulls in six games.

As of late November 2011, the 2011–12 NBA season had not started because of a standoff between team owners and players in collective bargaining.

PERSONAL LIFE

Smith, whose nickname is "J-Smoove," married his longtime girlfriend, the former Alexandria Lopez, in July 2010. The couple have a daughter, Genesis, and a son, Josh. Smith has been active in the Hawks' Player Assist Program, in which players purchase tickets to Hawks home games for underprivileged youths. He has also devoted time to other local charitable endeavors. In 2009 he hosted a Thanksgiving dinner for 200 women and children from My Sister's House, an Atlanta shelter.

SUGGESTED READING

Cunningham, Michael. "Hawks' Smith Likes Role as Leader; Forward Not Shy in Giving Teammates Verbal Encouragement on Floor." *Atlanta Journal-Constitution* 13 Mar. 2010, first replate ed., Sports: C1. Print.

Schultz, Jeff. "Smith Remains Atlanta's X-Factor." *Atlanta Journal-Constitution* 21 Apr. 2010, first replate ed., Sports: C1. Print.

Sugiura, Ken. "Smith, Howard Have Deep Roots as Friends." *Atlanta Journal-Constitution* 10 May 2010, first replate ed., Sports: C4. Print.

Thomsen, Ian. "Dunking His Reputation: Josh Smith Trying to Show He's a Man of Many Talents." *SI Vault*. Time, 30 Nov. 2007. Web. 19 Dec. 2011.

Wiedmer, Mark. "Hawks' Smith has Visited McKenzie." *Chattanooga Times Free Press* 27 Oct. 2005, Local Sports: D1. Print.

—*Christopher Cullen*

Hope Solo

Born: July 30, 1981
Occupation: Soccer player

Few goalkeepers have enjoyed the same level of mainstream popularity as Hope Solo, a starter for the US women's national soccer team. Solo has developed a loyal fan base, including more than 400,000 followers on Twitter. She also appeared on the thirteenth season of the ABC show *Dancing with the Stars*, finishing in fourth place. "I don't think we've had such [a] superstar like that—maybe since Mia Hamm," national women's soccer teammate Megan Rapinoe told Geoffrey C. Arnold for the *Oregonian* (22 Sep. 2011). Following a highly decorated college career, Solo joined the US national team in 2000 and became the starting goalkeeper in 2005. In 2007 she found herself in the midst of controversy as a result of postgame comments she made during the FIFA Women's World Cup and was benched for the rest of the season. She rejoined the team for the 2008 Beijing Olympics, where she helped them win the gold medal. Solo was named as part of the national team that will defend its title at the 2012 Summer Olympic Games in London, England.

EARLY LIFE AND CAREER

Hope Amelia Solo was born on July 30, 1981 to Judy and Jeffrey Solo in the city of Richland, Washington, outside of Seattle. A self-described tomboy, Solo liked sports and wild animals and even owned a pet rat. She was five years old when she first began playing soccer in her backyard with her father, a Vietnam War veteran. Her parents divorced when she was six and Solo lived with her mother and her older brother Marcus. (She also has another older half brother, David, from her father's previous marriage.) Solo remained close to her father, who had adopted a nomadic existence, living on the streets of Seattle or in a tent in the woods. However, at age eight, she lost touch with him following an incident in which he took her and Marcus to Seattle for three weeks without telling their mother.

Growing up, Solo immersed herself in soccer, playing locally for the Three Rivers Soccer Club and the Tri-City Admirals. She also successfully tried out for the US Youth Soccer Olympic Development Program (ODP), which identifies elite players across the United States. From 1995 to 1999 Solo gained experience as a member of US junior national teams. In 1996 she was named the starting goalkeeper for the under-sixteen girls' team, despite never having previously played the position. "I didn't take it that seriously," she told Lieber Steeg for *USA Today* (24 July 2007). "Once I was on the field, I was going to be the best athlete. My competitive nature is deeply inbred. It always takes over." Solo had an impressive performance in 1999, at the inaugural women's soccer tournament at the Pan American Games in Winnipeg, Manitoba. She served as the starting goalkeeper in three of the games, including the gold-medal match against Mexico's team, in which she had eleven saves en route to a shutout victory.

Solo was also a standout at Richland High School, where she served as the forward for the girls' soccer team. "My goal, when I got serious about soccer, was to have my college education paid for," she told Steve Kelley for the *Seattle Times* (21 May 2000). "I was having fun, plenty of fun playing; but I wanted more than that." During her high-school career, Solo compiled one hundred and nine goals and earned All-America accolades from *Parade* magazine in 1997 and 1998.

FIFA via Getty Images

STANDOUT ON COLLEGE AND NATIONAL TEAMS

After turning down offers to attend Santa Clara University and the University of Virginia (UVA), Solo remained in her home state and attended the University of Washington (UW) in Seattle, where she was a reluctant goalie for the Huskies women's soccer team. "I never wanted to become a goalkeeper," Solo confided to John F. Molinaro for *CBC Sports* (15 June 2011). "I was just a little kid having all sorts of fun . . . but as soon as I hit college, I realized I could not go far [as a forward]." Although she only appeared in twelve games, Solo, who shared goalkeeping duties with Leslie Weeks, recorded seventy-seven saves—the fourth-best total in team history—and had three shutouts. As a result of her performance in 1999, Solo was named the Huskies' rookie of the year and voted to the Pacific-10 (Pac-10) All-Conference second team.

In March 2000 Solo received an invitation from April Heinrichs, the head coach of the US Women's national soccer team and a former recruiter at UVA, to join its thirty-player pre-Olympic residency camp. The offer surprised Solo, who had turned down Heinrichs's recruitment effort to attend UW. "When she was hired as the national team coach, I was really scared. I thought, 'There went my career. There went my dreams, my hopes, everything,'" she recalled to Kelley. Solo made her senior debut on April 5, at a tournament in Davidson, North Carolina; she held Iceland scoreless and helped her team win by eight points. Solo had identical results in her only other national appearance, against Mexico, in the semifinals of the Nike US Women's Cup, held on May 5. However, Solo was not among the eighteen players selected to the 2000 US Women's Olympic team.

Solo continued to dominate her opponents at the college level. During her sophomore year she allowed just fifteen goals in twenty-one games and recorded six shutouts for the Huskies, who had an overall record of eighteen victories (a school record) and three losses. Her ninety-five saves were the third-best single-season total in school history. Solo's performance in 2000 catapulted her team to its first-ever appearance in the Pac-10 Conference championships. She surrendered five goals in nine conference games, culminating in the Huskies' inaugural title. Solo's team received the number-two seed in the National Soccer Coaches Association of America (NSCAA) tournament and reached the fourth round, also known as "the Sweet Sixteen," for the first time. Solo was voted an NSCAA All-American; she was also named to the Pac-10 All-Conference first team and garnered a nomination as the *Seattle Post-Intelligencer* female athlete of the year.

In early September 2001, while attending training camp for the women's national team, Solo suffered a torn adductor muscle in her right leg; she was preparing for the upcoming Nike US Women's Cup at the time. Despite the injury, Solo still managed seventy-seven saves, along with seven shutouts, while only allowing twelve goals. With an overall record of thirteen wins, five losses, and two tie games, the Huskies went on to compete again in the Pac-10 championship, where they won six conference games while losing two and tying one to finish in second place. The team also reached the second round of the NSCAA tournament. Solo was a candidate for the 2001 Hermann Trophy, which is regarded as the collegiate version of the Heisman Trophy, and the prestigious Missouri Athletic Club Collegiate Soccer Player of the Year award. For the second time she earned NSCAA All-American and Pac-10 All-Conference first team honors; she was also a finalist for the *Seattle Post-Intelligencer*'s Female Athlete of the Year.

In 2002, her final year at UW, Solo played in eighteen games, amassing seventy-six saves and two shutouts for the Huskies, who compiled a record of nine wins, eight losses, and three tie games. The team came in fifth at the Pac-10 championship, with four conference wins, four losses, and one tie. Solo, an NSCAA All-American and first-team All–Pac-10 selection for the third time, ended her college career as the team's all-time leader in three categories: shutouts (18), saves (325), and goals against average (1.02). While attending UW she also reconnected with her father, who was a fixture at all of her home games. "I'd make him macaroni and cheese,

and we'd sit in the woods in a tent and talk for hours," she told Sal Ruibal and Jill Lieber Steeg for *USA Today* (30 Sep. 2007).

LAUNCHES PROFESSIONAL AND INTERNATIONAL CAREER

After graduating from the University of Washington with a bachelor's degree in speech communications, Solo was selected fourth overall by the Philadelphia Charge in the 2003 Women's United Soccer Association (WUSA) Draft. Solo saw limited action, however, due to a back injury. She played in eight games during her first year with the team, who had five regular-season wins and eleven losses. However, Solo's tenure with the WUSA was short-lived. In mid-September 2003, a month after the season had ended, the league, which had consisted of eight teams including the Charge, disbanded. The following year Solo moved to Europe, where she played for the Kopparbergs/Göteborg FC, a team in Sweden's top-tier league for women's soccer. In August she represented the United States at the 2004 Summer Olympics, in Athens, Greece, where she served as an alternate for the US women's national soccer team, which included Mia Hamm, Brandi Chastain, and Brianna Scurry, the designated goalkeeper. However, Solo never took the field of play during the US squad's surprising run, which culminated in an overtime win against Brazil in the gold-medal match. As a result she was not awarded a medal.

In 2005, following her nine-month stint with the Kopparbergs/Göteborg FC, Solo spent five months with the Olympique Lyonnais women's team, which competes in Féminine D1, one of Europe's top professional women's leagues. She was also part of the US women's national squad that competed at the 2005 Algarve Cup, the women's soccer exhibition tournament held annually in Portugal from late February to early March. Under new head coach Greg Ryan, who had replaced Heinrichs, Solo made three starts and recorded shutouts in each game, including the championship match against Germany. She cited her experience playing abroad as valuable. "Playing in those leagues really helped my decision making," Solo recalled in an interview posted on the US Soccer website (7 July 2005). "I couldn't communicate very well with my Swedish or French teammates, so I had to rely on my own ability to read the game and make my own decisions. It made me become comfortable with myself in uncomfortable situations." Three months after winning the Algarve Cup, she was designated as the starting goalkeeper for the US women's national squad. In 2006 Solo made eighteen appearances for the national team, allowing just one goal while compiling a record of fourteen wins, no losses, and four ties.

CONTROVERSY AND FALLOUT AT 2007 FIFA WOMEN'S WORLD CUP

In June of the following year, the national squad was scheduled to play six warm-up matches prior to the 2007 FIFA Women's World Cup. Solo's father, who had never seen her play in a national tournament, planned to attend her upcoming match on June 23 at Giants Stadium in New Jersey. "He was so excited to go back to his hometown, to see me in my USA jersey, to show me where he grew up [in the Bronx]," she told Ruibal and Steeg. However, Solo's father would never get the chance; he suffered a fatal heart attack on June 15, just one day before the six-game series. After missing the first two games, Solo resumed her goalkeeping duties for the remaining four games.

Solo was in the starting lineup for the US women's team at the 2007 FIFA Women's World Cup, held in Shanghai, China. (FIFA is an acronym for the Fédération Internationale de Football Association, soccer's international governing body.) After surrendering two goals to North Korea in the first game, which ended in a tie, Solo held her opponents (Sweden, Nigeria, and England) scoreless in the next three games. Despite the impressive performance, Ryan decided to start Scurry, in place of Solo, for the semifinal match, relying on the veteran, who was undefeated against Brazil. The decision proved fateful, as the US squad was soundly defeated in a four-run shutout. In a postgame interview, Solo was openly critical of Ryan's decision to replace her with Scurry. Elizabeth Merrill for the ESPN website (18 Aug. 2008) quoted Solo as saying: "It was the wrong decision, and I think anybody that knows anything about the game knows that. There's no doubt in my mind I would have made those saves. And the fact of the matter is, it's not 2004 anymore."

Solo was ostracized as a result of her remarks. Ryan banned her from team practice and benched her for the next day's bronze-medal match, in which the United States defeated Norway. She was forbidden from attending the medal ceremony and was forced to fly home alone. Within a few days she apologized to her teammates on her MySpace page, although she claimed that her words were misconstrued. In October 2007, prior to a three-game exhibition against Mexico, Solo issued a formal apology to both her teammates and her coach. She also announced that she would not play in the series—the team's final three games of the season—and would focus instead on regaining their trust.

REDEMPTION AT THE 2008 OLYMPICS

On October 22, 2007, it was announced that Ryan's contract, which was due to expire at the end of the year, would not be renewed. A month later Pia Sundhage, a former Swedish national team player who had also coached in her native country and in the United States, was named as his replacement, becoming the team's first foreign-born coach. In December Solo was among twenty-four players invited by Sundhage to attend the US women's national team training camp; the roster also included sixteen players from the World Cup squad. Among her first actions was to address the 2007 World Cup incident. "I knew I had to do something, so I pretty much listened," Sundhage told Jeré Longman for the *New York Times* (15 July 2011). "I asked the players, 'What do you want to happen?' The other question was, 'Do you want to win?' Yes, of course, they said. Then I said, 'We need good goalkeepers.'"

In the months preceding the Summer Olympics, Solo made sixteen starts and registered nine shutouts while leading the national team to victories in the Four Nations Tournament, the Algarve Cup, and the Peace Queen Cup. She also held Costa Rica scoreless in the semifinals of the Olympic Women's qualifying tournament; with this victory the United States earned an Olympic berth. In late June, Sundhage selected Solo as the team's starting goalkeeper for the Olympics, in Beijing, China; Scurry was named an alternate. Solo started all six games and played every minute. Despite conceding two goals in the opening loss to Norway, she quickly rebounded, recording shutouts in her next two games. Following quarterfinal and semifinal victories—against Canada and Japan, respectively—the United States reached the finals, setting up a rematch with Brazil, whom Solo held scoreless to help her team capture the gold medal in overtime.

CAREER IN THE WPS

In mid-September of 2008, twenty-one national team members, including Solo, were made available to the teams comprising the newly created Women's Professional Soccer (WPS) league. Solo was drafted by the St. Louis Athletica and played well during the inaugural season, which began in April 2009. She ranked second-best in the league in saves and shutouts, leading her club to a second-place finish and capturing the WPS Goalkeeper of the Year award. On the national team front, Solo recorded one shutout in six games; her lone goal was yielded in the Algarve Cup final, in which she was named MVP.

After the Athletica disbanded in May 2010, Solo joined the Atlanta Beat, a stint that was not without controversy. In August she took to Twitter, condemning fans of the Boston Breakers for allegedly making crude and racist remarks toward her. Solo vented again on Twitter in early September following the Washington Freedom's playoff-clinching victory over Atlanta. She accused the league and one of the referees of siding with the opposing team; as a result of her actions, Solo received a $2,500 fine, a one-day suspension, and eight days of community service. After the season ended, she had shoulder surgery and recuperated for the rest of the year.

While playing for the magicJack franchise during the 2011 season, Solo also served as the starting goalie at the FIFA Women's World Cup, in Germany, where she won the Golden Glove and Bronze Ball awards. Solo's tenure with magicJack ended in January 2012 after the WPS suspended operations; the league was eventually dissolved four months later. In February Solo signed with the Seattle Sounders Women, a United Soccer Leagues W-League team. Three months later she was named to the roster for the 2012 Summer Olympics in London.

Solo has capitalized on her increasing popularity in an effort to bring attention to women's soccer. In 2011 she was among the athletes featured in *ESPN The Magazine*'s third annual *Body Issue*.

SUGGESTED READING

Arnold, Geoffrey C. "Hope Solo, U.S. National Team Taking Women's Soccer to New Heights." *Oregonian*. Advance Publications, 21 Sep. 2011. Web. 10 June 2012.

Kelley, Steve. "UW's Solo Gets Her Shot with National Soccer Team." *Seattle Times*. Seattle Times Co., 21 May 2000. Web. 26 May 2012.

Lieber Steeg, Jill. "Solo's Success as USA's Goalie Is No Accident." *USA Today*. Gannett Co., 24 July 2007. Web. 25 May 2012.

Lieber Steeg, Jill, and Sal Ruibal. "Hope Solo's World Cup Quest Was for Her Father." *USA Today*. Gannett Co., 30 Sep. 2007. Web. 25 May 2012.

Longman, Jeré. "A Whole New Pitch for the U.S." *New York Times*. New York Times Co., 15 July 2011. Web. 30 May 2012.

Merrill, Elizabeth. "Solo No More: Goalkeeper Regains Starting Spot and Teammates' Trust." *ESPN*. ESPN Internet Ventures, 18 Aug. 2008. Web. 30 May 2012.

Molinaro, John F. "Hope Solo Puts '07 Controversy behind Her." *CBC Sports*. CBC Inc., 15 July 2011. Web. 30 May 2012.

U.S. Soccer. "U.S. WNT Goalkeeper Hope Solo Reflects on Her Winding Road to the U.S. Goal." U.S. Soccer, 2005. Web. 10 June 2012.

—*Bertha Muteba*

Omar Souleyman

Born: 1966
Occupation: Musician

Singer Omar Souleyman started performing his own unique style of traditional Middle Eastern dance-folk-pop music in his native Syria in the mid-1990s. After a decade of performing

Redferns

at weddings and other celebrations and releasing hundreds of cassette tapes of these shows, Souleyman made his worldwide debut with the album *Highway to Hassake*, in 2007. It was well received by critics and the public. In 2009, Souleyman and his band began touring the United States, the United Kingdom, and Australia, where he performed at concert halls and big music festivals. Like his first worldwide release, Souleyman's subsequent albums *Dabke 2020* (2009) and *Jazeera Nights* (2010) are compiled from live recordings at weddings and parties in his native country. However, the next album, *Haflat Gharbia: The Western Concerts* (2011), is a collection of his live performances while on tour. Souleyman also collaborated with the eclectic Icelandic singer Björk on several remixes in 2011.

EARLY LIFE AND STARTING OUT AS A SINGER

Omar Souleyman was born in 1966 and grew up in Ras Al Ain, a small town in Syria's northeastern region, close to the Turkey's southern border. Souleyman was not raised in a musical family. However, as a boy he heard instruments such as the *rebab*, a Middle Eastern instrument with similarities to a violin and a banjo, though it usually has just one string; and the *bouzouki*, a type of lute often used in Balkan music. Souleyman dropped out of school—because of an eye injury, he has explained—and went on to work a variety of jobs, including as a stonemason.

Souleyman got the idea to pursue singing full-time because of encouragement from friends who had heard him sing at a few weddings. In the mid-1990s, he started performing at weddings and family parties, where he would sing folk poetry over traditional dance beats. In 1996, he met Rizan Sa'id, a young multi-instrumentalist who was playing keyboards. Souleyman asked Sa'id to join him, and the two slowly built up a reputation as a great party band. They continued to perform at weddings and family parties, with Souleyman singing folk poetry and Sa'id playing keyboards and synthesizers and driving the rhythm. Sa'id played not only Syrian styles of dance music but also blended in other Middle Eastern styles, such as Kurdish, Iraqi, and Arabic. The kind of music they performed is known as *dabke*, a style of dance and party music particular to the Levant region of the Middle East, which mainly includes Syria, Lebanon, Israel, Jordan, and the Palestinian territories. The duo would sometimes perform with other musicians, such as violin players and percussionists. They also performed with musicians who played the *saz*, a kind of lute with a pear-shaped body; the *ney*, a kind of flute; and the bouzouki. By then, Souleyman's trademark look was set: large, dark sunglasses and a keffiyeh scarf on his head.

A RISING STAR IN SYRIA

Souleyman's journey to wider mass appeal began when Zuhir Maksi, a local producer who had his own label, recorded him live at those parties and weddings and released a good deal of the recordings as cassette tapes for the general public. The Syrian people of the region soon developed a high opinion of Souleyman as a musician, and demand increased for his band to perform at parties and weddings. The tapes themselves were of inferior sound and production quality, but people who bought those tapes could hear the spirit and energy of the singer, and so the dynamic singer continued to be in demand.

Aside from helping to spread the word about Souleyman, Maksi would occasionally perform with him, whispering lines of poetry into his ear during the live show. Mark Gergis wrote about this phenomenon, which is unfamiliar to most Westerners, for the official Omar Souleyman website (May 2011): "This age old poet and singer relationship is a tradition in the region and often employs the poetry form called the *ataba*—a form of folk poetry still employed today. During a concert, the poet often stands very near to Souleyman, following him into the circle of dabke line-dancers, and whispering verses relevant to the event and the families that host it into Omar's ears. Acting as a conduit, Souleyman strides into the audience, vocalizing the prose in song before returning for the next verse." Souleyman later continued that tradition with Hassan Hamadi and Mahmoud Harbi, both well-respected local poets. The latter, Harbi, would

eventually go on to tour internationally with Souleyman.

In 1996, *Jani*, a live recording of Souleyman's performance at a wedding, was released. The recording was so successful that within a few years, Souleyman released hundreds of such recordings of different wedding performances. As his popularity continued to rise, he began performing at weddings and parties all over Syria. He was soon performing in other Middle Eastern countries, such as the United Arab Emirates, Lebanon, and Saudi Arabia. A recording that helped Souleyman gain further acclaim across the Middle East was his studio album *Khataba* (2005), which had a solidly produced sound and did not have any of the technical glitches of live cassette recordings. Although Souleyman's popularity was growing in the Arab world, he was still unknown to Western audiences at this time.

WORLDWIDE RECOGNITION: TOURS AND ALBUMS

Highway to Hassake: Folk and Pop Sounds of Syria (2007) was the first collection of Souleyman's music released outside the Middle East. In 1998, almost a decade before the album's release, American musician Mark Gergis heard Souleyman's music during a visit to Syria. He did not see Souleyman live but did hear his wedding recordings, which were by this point fairly ubiquitous in Syrian cassette kiosks. Over the years and several trips to Syria, Gergis collected many such tapes. In 2006, he finally met Souleyman, which ultimately led to the release of *Highway to Hassake* on the Sublime Frequencies label, where Gergis had connections.

Highway to Hassake is a compilation of Souleyman's cassette recordings spanning more than a decade, starting from around 1996. On the compact disc, Souleyman sings his unique version of the dabke style, but he also incorporates Turkish pop music, the distinctive beat of Iraqi *choubi*, and ataba. Many music critics in the West, particularly the United States and England, wrote enthusiastically of the album's raw energy, which they viewed as a combination of Middle Eastern music—particularly Syrian folk styles—and electronic dance music. The CD features thirteen songs, including "Leh Jani" ("When I Found Out"), "Jani" ("She Came to Me"), and "Jalsat Atabat" ("Atabat Session"). In a review for the *Washington Post* (8 Jan. 2008), Chris Richards wrote, "The sonic anarchy on *Highway to Hassake* always stays tethered to Souleyman's voice. His vocal cords strain with startling urgency as he pleads his way through narratives worthy of Shakespeare (even though he's not singing in English). According to the liner notes, these songs recount tales of unrequited passion, meddling parents, star-crossed lovers and double-crossed fools."

Souleyman was not the only one to receive praise for *Highway to Hassake*. Music critics took note of Sa'id's talent as well. Commenting on Sa'id, Richards stated, "Equally compelling: the keyboard fireworks of Rizan Sa'id—a synthesizer virtuoso so nimble he could probably ace your favorite Van Halen guitar solo on the keypad of a touch-tone phone. Sa'id's riotous blips and drum machine thwacks jostle for position in Souleyman's breakneck beatscape, giving these tracks a kinetic energy that shines through the cassette tape hiss and across the cultural divide." *Highway to Hassake* also received enthusiastic reviews in the *Village Voice*, *Seattle Weekly*, and the London *Observer*, as well as many other publications across the globe. In addition to the album, a video widely available on YouTube featured Souleyman singing the song "Leh Jani" and helped the singer draw in even more fans.

Souleyman's next two albums were released internationally in 2009 and 2010. Like *Highway to Hassake*, they are compilations of his performances from a career that by that point spanned nearly a decade and a half. *Dabke 2020: Folk and Pop Sounds of Syria* (2009) features eight songs. Some have elaborate titles, such as "La Sidounak Sayyada" ("I'll Prevent the Hunters from Hurting You"), "Laqtuf Ward Min Khaddak" ("I Will Pick a Flower from Your Cheek"), and "Kaset Hanzal" ("Drinking from the Glass of Bitterness"). Souleyman's third album, *Jazeera Nights* (2010), also features dramatic titles, including "Labji Wa Bajji Il Hajar" ("My Tears Will Make the Stones Cry"), "Hafer Gabrak Bidi" ("I Will Dig Your Grave with My Hands"), and "Hot Il Khanjar Bi Gleibi" ("Stab My Heart"). The album, like the two that came before it, received a great deal of glowing, if short, reviews.

Even though Souleyman sings in Arabic, reviewers have called attention not only to his song titles but also the lyrics, which are provided by a variety of poets. In a review of *Jazeera Nights* for the *New York Times* (30 May 2010), Ben Ratliff wrote, "The songs are grave, direct, and Mr. Souleyman cheerleads around the lyrics." Ratliff added that the lyrics are "worth pondering" and provided a sample translation for readers: "'I will cry, and make the stones cry on everybody who said I made them cry,' Mr. Souleyman sings. 'I spent my life being afraid to die before we embraced / I will embrace you.'" In addition to the lyrics of *Jazeera Nights*, Ratliff praised the album's music, particularly the "high-speed beats and microtonal synth wails." In a profile of Souleyman for the Abu Dhabi–based publication the *National* (28 May 2010), Dan Hancox wrote that there is a "tendency to see any folk music as an established set of standards, preserved in amber. Blessedly, its reality is one of complexity and constant evolution. Indeed, Souleyman has witnessed the Syrian musical scene change a great deal, even in the last few years." Souleyman told Hancox that his brand of Syrian/Arabic folk music has "sped up." When asked whether this was due to foreign influences, Souleyman replied, "No, we developed the speed. We started out with slower rhythms, but each year it's got faster by about ten beats per minute. The change came from the electronic keyboards—you can just turn the speed up and make it faster with your hand."

Souleyman and his band went on their first tour of Europe and the United States in 2009, during which they received positive reviews and much enthusiasm from concert attendees. The following year, the band went on tour again, playing such venues as New York City's SummerStage concert series in Central Park and at the hip London venue Scala. Writing about Souleyman's performance in the United Kingdom, Hancox stated: "It is amusing to behold an English crowd attempting to dance to something it doesn't quite know how to relate to. Fortunately, with Souleyman's help, inhibitions are quickly cast aside. He paces the edge of the stage clapping his hands, beckoning to the crowd. His most successful maneuver is to sweep his arm along and then up, an injunction to raise one hand into the air as the leader in a dabke dance would. It may be a long way from a Syrian wedding, but the crowd soon realizes that a lack of knowledge of the right steps is not a problem, and begin to make up their own: a mixture of naive attempts at dabke, flamenco, Bollywood hand-flourishes, fist-pumping, foot-stomping, rock moshing, even the festive footwork of an Irish ceilidh. It's a mess, but a glorious one."

Souleyman returned to New York City in the fall of 2010 to yet another hip music venue, the Music Hall of Williamsburg, in Brooklyn. Unlike some of his other live performances in the West, Souleyman was accompanied only by Sa'id, his keyboardist and composer, which created a mellower atmosphere than the typically frenzied state aroused by the up-tempo dance numbers with percussion. In a review of the concert for the *New York Times* (3 Nov. 2010), Ratliff wrote, "Mr. Souleyman wore his typical clothes: brown leather jacket over a floor-length tunic, aviator sunglasses, a red-and-white-checked keffiyeh. He started singing a poem in slow rubato over a single synthesizer chord. Mr. Sa'id filled in the pauses with fast, fluttering, modal figures; there were no percussion sounds. It wasn't as guttural and rending as this kind of song has been on his records; it was orderly and calming, quite beautiful."

In 2011, Souleyman went on tour once again to perform at festivals worldwide, including the Perth International Arts Festival in Perth, Australia; the Chaos in Tejas Festival in Austin, Texas; the Bonnaroo Festival in Manchester, Tennessee; the Field Day Festival in London, England; and the Isle of Wight

Bestival on the British Isle of Wight. Souley-man also played shows in Germany, France, Belgium, and the Netherlands. Despite playing concerts and music festivals all over the United States, Australia, and Europe, Souleyman did not play general-admission concerts in his home country of Syria. As before, he continued to perform regularly at parties and weddings there.

Souleyman's fourth album, also released by Sublime Frequencies, is titled *Haflat Gharbia: The Western Concerts* (2011). The album is another collection of live material, this time compiled from Souleyman's concerts in the United States, Europe, and Australia, between 2009 and 2011. *Haflat Gharbia* was favorably received, peaking at number ten on the Billboard Top World Albums chart after its release. In a review for Allmusic (2011), Thom Jurek commented on how lively and exciting the sound is, a general consensus among music critics: "Sa'id is able to make his wildly modified keyboards and samplers capture the sounds of the ney, violin, and numerous percussion instruments, while [Ali] Shaker's electric saz is as expertly played as any guitar virtuoso's axe. Its amplified sound resembles a dead cross between a Fender Stratocaster and a sitar. In addition to these two, poet Zuhir Maksi literally stands close to Souleyman on-stage and whispers poetry or prose (both traditional and modern) into his ear. The singer transforms this in real time into a wailing live vocalization that is pure lightning-bolt energy, wailing with abandon atop the numerous rhythms, harmonies, and melodies being played with nonstop kinetic musical fire behind him." Jurek concluded that *Haflat Gharbia* is "among the finest live albums of the twenty-first century thus far."

Music critics and music fans have not been the only ones singing the praises of Souleyman's band. On the National Public Radio (NPR) program *All Things Considered* (29 June 2009), on the series called *You Must Hear This*, on which musicians discuss other musicians they greatly admire, the eclectic singer-songwriter Björk, of Iceland, recalled that the first time she heard Souleyman was on You-Tube. "Some people," said Björk, "call what he plays Syrian techno [sound bite of laughter]. . . . But I think what's refreshing about Omar Souleyman is just the party and fun, and it's really alive and very urgent, and he's not shy of using synths and electronics and drum machines and YouTube. So he's, like, really eager to make something that's vibrant today." In 2011, Björk and Souleyman collaborated on several remixes of Björk's songs, including "Tesla" and "Crystalline," for her musical and interactive project titled *Biophilia* (2011).

Omar Souleyman lives in Syria.

SUGGESTED READING

Carroll, Jim. "If You See One Syrian Wedding Singer This Year . . ." *Irish Times*. Irish Times, 9 Sep. 2010. Web. 11 June 2012.

Gehr, Richard. "Omar Souleyman, Arabian Idol." *Village Voice*. Village Voice LLC, 22 June 2010. Web. 11 June 2012.

Gergis, Mark. "Bio." *Omar Souleyman*. Sublime Frequencies and Omar Souleyman, May 2011. Web. 11 June 2012.

Hancox, Dan. "Highway to Hipsterville." *Abu Dhabi National*. Abu Dhabi Media Company, 28 May 2010. Web. 11 June 2012.

Ratliff, Ben. "Cool Alchemy: Merging East and West for a Universal Beat." *New York Times*. New York Times, 3 Nov. 2010. Web. 11 June 2012.

SELECTED WORKS

Highway to Hassake: Folk and Pop Sounds of Syria, 2007; *Dabke 2020: Folk and Pop Sounds of Syria*, 2009; *Jazeera Nights*, 2010; *Haflat Gharbia: The Western Concerts*, 2011

—*Dmitry Kiper*

Katie Jacobs Stanton

Born: 1969
Occupation: Internet executive

Since July 2010, Katie Jacobs Stanton has served as the vice president of international strategy for the social networking and microblogging giant Twitter, Inc., leading the Internet firm's rapid overseas expansion. Describing her achievements in that regard, a writer for *Forbes* magazine (Aug. 2011) observed, "Katie Jacobs Stanton now has 70 percent of all Tweets [the term for a Twitter message] coming from outside the United States, and a fifth of world leaders are now on the service, including Russian president [Dmitry] Medvedev . . . and President [Barack] Obama. . . . The platform became a lifeline in the aftermath of Japan's earthquake and tsunami (one quarter of all Tweets now hail from Japan) and a bullhorn during [the] Arab spring."

With prior stints at both Yahoo! and Google, Stanton has enjoyed remarkable success in the technology sector, playing an integral role in the development of Yahoo! Finance, Google Finance, and the OpenSocial and Google Moderator applications, among other projects. But her achievements are not limited to the leading Silicon Valley–based Internet companies. In March of 2009, she joined the Obama administration as the first director of citizen participation, working through new media platforms to make the government more accessible to the public.

Getty Images

From the White House, she moved on to the US State Department in January 2010 as a special adviser to the Office of Innovation, where she sought new-media solutions to the problems of international diplomacy. Because of her impressive track record in both the public and private sectors, as well as her influential position at Twitter, Stanton was ranked fifty-sixth on *Forbes* magazine's August 2011 list of the "World's Most Powerful Women."

EARLY LIFE AND EDUCATION

Katie Jacobs Stanton was born in 1969. Her father was a banker, her mother a nurse. Raised in the Hudson River hamlet of Cortlandt Manor near Peekskill, New York, in northern Westchester County, Stanton graduated from Hendrick Hudson High School, in Montrose, New York, in 1987 and went on to attend Rhodes College, a small liberal arts institution in Memphis, Tennessee. Although she was initially unsure if Rhodes would be a good fit, Stanton quickly made herself at home, declaring to Christina Huntington for *Rhodes Magazine* (Winter 2010), "When I got there, everyone was very friendly; it was very warm. I loved it so much that I wanted to stay."

Majoring in political science, Stanton displayed an abiding interest in both public and global affairs. She studied under Mike Kirby, who encouraged her to take her research outside of the confines of Rhodes College. "Getting real-world experience and injecting it into the classroom, making it relevant, was really important," she told Huntington. For one assignment,

Stanton worked with the Shelby County Department of Corrections. A committed volunteer throughout her undergraduate career, she donated her time to both Habitat for Humanity and Tex-Mex Border Ministry.

While at Rhodes, Stanton spent two semesters overseas, studying at the American University in Paris and in Jerusalem, where she explored the Israeli-Palestinian conflict. "One of the best things I did was go abroad," she explained to Huntington. She also worked for a summer in Washington, DC, serving as an intern for the late Senator Ted Kennedy of Massachusetts.

Though she would make her name at such technology-driven companies as Yahoo!, Google, and Twitter, Stanton showed little interest in such endeavors during her days at Rhodes. As an undergraduate, she recalled to Huntington, "Never in a million years" did she expect to end up in the technology sector. "I took an intro to computer science class and let's just say, it didn't come naturally to me."

Stanton graduated from Rhodes in 1991. Two years later, she entered Columbia University's School of International and Public Affairs, in New York City, as a Jacob K. Javits Fellow, working for a master's degree in international affairs. She completed her degree in 1995 and, continuing her fellowship, spent the next year in Washington, DC, as a staff member for the Senate Committee on Foreign Relations.

FROM BANKING TO THE TECH SECTOR

With the conclusion of her fellowship in Washington, Stanton returned to New York City, where she accepted an associate position at Chase Securities, a division of JP Morgan Chase Bank. For the next two and a half years or so, she researched emerging markets as a member of Chase's corporate emerging markets group. Dissatisfied with banking, Stanton started looking for a new direction in her career, "Whatever I did next," she explained to Huntington, "I wanted to be able to sit next to a stranger on a plane and be really proud of what I did."

She soon zeroed in on the Internet company Yahoo! The company was in the midst of creating its financial news division, Yahoo! Finance, and Stanton, with her background at Chase, proved an ideal fit to help with its launch. She moved out to the San Francisco Bay Area and started work in April 1999 as group production manager, a post she would hold for about three and a half years.

In October 2002, Stanton decided to take a break from her career. As she explained to Huntington, "Yahoo! was my first professional love, but I left it to spend more time with my greater loves, my newborn twins and toddler." About six months later, Stanton started looking to return to the job market.

"When I was ready to go back to work," she remarked to Huntington, "I wanted to go somewhere that could possibly be as good as Yahoo! or even better. Google was the only company I could even think of, and I wasn't disappointed. I was really proud to be a 'Googler.'" Stanton's Google tenure commenced in April 2003 and extended over the next six years. At first, she served on the company's search team, but soon moved to Google's new business development team. There, she worked on a host of new product launches, including the 2006 launch of Google's financial news resource, Google Finance. She also had a hand in the debuts and management of, among other initiatives, OpenSocial, an application that helps social networking programs function on different websites, and Google Moderator, a crowdsourcing application wherein users pose and rank potential questions.

WHITE HOUSE AND STATE DEPARTMENT

Stanton's efforts at Google did not go unnoticed. Google Moderator, in particular, had proven useful to the presidential campaign of Barack Obama, allowing visitors to his website to submit questions to the candidate. Over one hundred thousand users sent in queries and nearly two million votes were registered. The most popular questions were in turn answered by the campaign. Following his victory in the 2008 election, president-elect Obama asked Stanton, who had volunteered for his campaign, to join his White House new media team as the first director of citizen participation. "When the president calls, you have to come," Stanton remarked according to a writer for the *Washington Post*'s WhoRunsGov webpage. "I wasn't really looking to leave Google but I thought if the White House calls I would definitely do it, so here I am."

After moving to Washington, DC, with her family, she went to work at the White House in March 2009. For the next year, she sought to facilitate dialogue between the administration and the public. She saw her mission as helping to build "Government 2.0." As she commented to Juanita Cousins for the Memphis, Tennessee, *Commercial Appeal* (23 Sep. 2009), "We have so many enormous challenges in our country from the economy to health care. . . . The Internet is a platform to address these challenges."

Stanton had the president's speeches posted on YouTube and other popular websites, rather than just official platforms, and set up a White House Twitter account. In conjunction with the Department of Health and Human Services, she sponsored a contest to raise awareness about the H1N1 flu virus. The public was invited to submit videos sounding the alarm about H1N1 and detailing how to avoid infection. The best videos were then posted across the web. "It was a low-cost, effective way to get people talking about the flu," Stanton observed to Huntington. "It's not just the government talking, but it's people talking to one another: 'Hey, did you see this funny video on Flu.gov?' Or 'Hey, I heard you're sick, check this out, it might help you.'"

As director of citizen participation, she encouraged officials to join socialnet working sites and dialogue with their constituents. To facilitate this, she negotiated the terms-of-use protocols with social networking companies like Twitter. "We made it easier for the government to communicate with and back-and-forth to our citizens," she said to the *Washington Post*'s WhoRunsGov. "Technology is enabling unprecedented levels and types of collaboration," Stanton told Huntington. "It's not necessarily the government talking to people, it's talking with people. And the web enables so many more people to participate."

In January 2010, Stanton moved from the White House to the US State Department's Office of Innovation to take a position as special adviser to Alec Ross, senior innovation adviser to Secretary of State Hillary Rodham Clinton. While at the White House, Stanton had sought to use the Internet and social media to connect government officials with their constituents. At the State Department, in a process she described to Huntington as "twenty-first-century statecraft," she would apply those same techniques to the world of international diplomacy.

On January 12, 2010, a devastating earthquake struck the Caribbean nation of Haiti, shattering the capital of Port au Prince, affecting nearly three million people, and incurring a death toll of between 92,000 and 316,000. Though only a few days into her new job at the State Department, Stanton acted quickly. "With every crisis," she commented to WhoRunsGov, "there is opportunity." In a matter of hours and in coordination with the mobile phone network Mobile Accords, she organized the creation of a mechanism through which Americans could donate funds to help relief efforts. By texting "HAITI" to 90999 on their cell phones, texters donated ten dollars to the American Red Cross. As to what the mobile platform would actually accomplish, Stanton set the bar low. "We had no idea what to expect," she explained to WhoRunsGov. "We thought we would make $100,000 at max." By the end of its first week, however, donations totaled $32 million, making it the largest campaign of its kind in history.

But Stanton's Haitian efforts didn't stop there. "We saw on television these stories of people trapped under the buildings using a mobile phone to tell people where they were, and they were saved," she remembered. "So we thought, we should have this for everybody." Stanton reached out to Haiti's cell phone operators and convinced them to set up an emergency code that would allow Haitians to communicate their emergency needs to medical and security personnel via text message. Her team's new-media approach to the Haitian crisis demonstrated, in Stanton's words to WhoRunsGov, "a great example of what government can do."

Stanton brought similar strategies to two other diplomatic hot spots. To ensure the integrity of the April 2010 elections in the African nation of Sudan, she coordinated with cell phone companies and with public interest groups to establish SudanVoteMonitor.com, through which voters and poll watchers could report any potential malfeasance or irregularities. "Election monitors or citizens can text in any election-related problems: missing ballots, polls closing too early, acts of voter intimidation," Stanton reported to WhoRunsGov. "We want this to be a free and fair election." Based on the success of the Sudan operation, officials at the US embassy in the West African nation of Guinea requested that similar measures be implemented there.

To help fight drug violence in Mexico, Stanton worked with Mexican citizen organizations and cell phone companies to create an anonymous tip line that would allow people to report suspected crimes to law enforcement and emergency personnel via text message. "We've seen this unprecedented rise of violence in that area," Stanton remarked as quoted by WhoRunsGov. "This is an effort to make the whole process more transparent."

A major moment in Stanton's State Department tour came in May 2010, when she accompanied Secretary of State Clinton on a diplomatic visit to China.

Stepping down from her post at the State Department in August 2010, Stanton returned to the San Francisco Bay Area with her family to serve as vice president of international strategy at Twitter. Looking back on her work in Washington, DC, she couldn't help but compare her time in government with her work experience in the technology sector. "Being used to a fast-paced environment that isn't afraid to fail, where risk-takers are rewarded," she commented to blogger Nancy Scola for the Tech-President website (9 July 2010), "government is just a very different environment." While praising her colleagues for their efforts to create what she called a "passionate bureaucracy," she felt that government could use an infusion of tech-sector vigor. "In Silicon Valley," she said, "you need more adult supervision. Here, you could use a lot more youthful energy. . . . We're almost missing a generation. I'm 40 years old, and I don't feel like there are many others like me." Nevertheless, Stanton is optimistic that social media and other Internet tools can be employed to address challenges both at home and overseas. As she said to WhoRunsGov, "It's possible to solve these problems using technology, but also using the power of our communities. When we see people just working together,

using simple but powerful technology, we can save the world."

AT TWITTER

Twitter is a social media and microblogging service that allows users to post, read, and forward "tweets" of up to 140 characters across multiple digital platforms. Since its launch in July 2006, the service has exploded in popularity and become a vital agent in global affairs. As of April 2012, Twitter reported 140 million active users and an average of 340 million tweets per day.

Twitter performed a valuable role in the aftermath of the March 11, 2011, earthquake in Japan. The earthquake sent a tsunami crashing into the country's western shore, killing over 15,000 people and creating a nuclear disaster at the Fukushima Daiichi nuclear power plant. With the phone systems overburdened by the volume of calls, Twitter became a forum for transmitting news within Japan and for checking in with friends and relatives. The US State Department used it to transmit emergency information to American nationals and to inform Japanese Americans how to get in touch with their families and loved ones back in Japan.

Twitter also served a central function in the Arab Spring uprisings of 2011, with demonstrators in Tunisia, Bahrain, Syria, and Egypt, among other nations, using it as a means of organizing protests and bypassing the state-controlled media, transmitting the news to readers both at home and abroad. During the upheaval in Egypt, for example, the Egyptian American journalist Mona Eltahawy was arrested by security forces in November 2011. Beaten and sexually assaulted, she nevertheless managed to send out a tweet, alerting those who followed her Twitter account that she had been detained. The news spread throughout the globe and an almost instant campaign for her release developed. After being held for twelve hours, Eltahawy once again took to Twitter, this time to announce "I AM FREE." Commenting to Jacob Weisberg for *Vogue* (12 Feb. 2012), Stanton remarked, "It's stuff like that that moves us . . . that makes us excited that we can provide some kind of service to allow that important story to find its way out there, to have happy outcomes like this."

Stanton's task at Twitter is to "[get] the world tweeting," a writer for *Forbes* observed (Aug. 2011). Judging by the overseas statistics and the growing international consequence of the medium, she is performing that task admirably. Following expansion efforts in Ireland and Japan, Stanton led a major push into Germany in February 2012.

Like her colleagues at Twitter, Stanton sees the company's mission as more than just a commercial one. Twitter's core values emphasize free speech and open communication. "We want to build our business in a way that makes us proud," she explained to Weisberg. "If it means that we have to start censoring people's tweets, that violates a core ethos of our company. While it might help us get more users in China, it would ruin what we're about."

PERSONAL LIFE

Stanton makes her home in Los Altos, outside of San Francisco, where she lives with her husband Patrick, who works on green technology for the Danish Foreign Ministry, and their three children—Ellie and the twins, Declan and Caleigh. Balancing career and family hasn't always been an easy task. "It's hard as a working mom," Stanton commented to Huntington. "When you're working, you feel like you should be with the kids, and when you're with the kids, you feel like you should be working." Her position at Twitter allows her some flexibility, however, and she is able to avoid the late nights required of her during her earlier tours in the tech sector.

SUGGESTED READING

Cousins, Juanita. "Obama Staffer Speaks on Relevance of New Media." *Commercial Appeal* [Memphis, TN]. Scripps Interactive Newspapers, 23 Sep. 2009. Web. 10 Apr. 2012.

Huntington, Christina. "Building Government 2.0." *Rhodes Magazine*. Rhodes College, Winter 2010. Web. 10 Apr. 2012.

Scola Nancy. "Headed West to Twitter, Katie Stanton Reflects on Washington." *TechPresident*. Personal Democracy Media, 9 July 2010. Web. 10 Apr. 2012.

Weisberg, Jacob. "Fast Company: The Women of Twitter." *Vogue*. Condé Nast. 12 Feb. 2012. Web. 10 Apr. 2012.

WhoRunsGov. "Katie Jacobs Stanton: Twitter, International Business Strategy." *Washington Post*. Washington Post, 2012. Web. 10 Apr. 2012.

—*Paul McCaffrey*

Jeremy Stoppelman

Born: November 10, 1977
Occupation: CEO and cofounder of Yelp

"It would be easy to mock Yelp, the crowdsourced cityguide with a slightly goofy style, or the fact that it doesn't build anything, or employ legions of staff writers. . . . That, however, would be stupid," Brian Caulfield wrote for *Forbes* (18 Dec. 2009). "Beneath this web site's friendly, casual demeanor is a truly clever business model." Yelp, which was cofounded by PayPal veteran Jeremy Stoppelman, is a website that combines user-generated reviews of products and services with elements of social media. The mix has

Bloomberg via Getty Images

proven exceptionally popular, particularly among young urbanites, and Yelp—despite some degree of criticism from naysayers and a spate of lawsuits from disgruntled participants—is being widely credited with changing the way in which small businesses engage with their customers.

EARLY LIFE AND EDUCATION

Jeremy Stoppelman was born on November 10, 1977, in Great Falls, Virginia. He and his family eventually moved to McLean, Virginia, where Stoppelman attended school. His family has endured its share of tragedy. In 1993 Stoppelman's brother Andrew, who suffered from a heart condition called arrhythmogenic right ventricular dysplasia (ARVD), died of the disease when he was a teenager. Stoppelman's father John S. Stoppelman was a securities lawyer who had cofounded On-Site Sourcing, a company that sold document-management software for accountants and lawyers, in the early 1990s. In 1998, unable to cope with personal problems, John Stoppelman shot himself, leaving behind Jeremy, his brother Michael (who is now a software engineer at Yelp), and their mother Lynn Ballard Stoppelman.

Lynn Stoppelman, responded to her son Andrew's death by setting up a memorial fund to research a cure for ARVD, which is responsible for a statistically significant percentage of the deaths of young athletes. (Her efforts were also said to be instrumental in attracting a large research grant from the National Institutes of Health.) She became fascinated by the question of how families learned to cope with such traumatic events, and she eventually left her thriving career in marketing to earn an advanced degree in marriage counseling and family therapy.

Jeremy Stoppelman became interested in business and finance early on. By the age of fourteen, he had opened his first brokerage account and began subscribing to business magazines. After graduating from Langley High School in McLean, in 1995, he entered the Electrical and Computer Engineering (ECE) program at the University of Illinois College of Engineering. The university has a rich history of accomplishment in the fields of engineering and computing. Among its instructors were Joseph Tykociner, who first invented a method for putting sound on film in the 1920s, and Nobel Prize winner John Bardeen, the only physics laureate to have won twice: in 1956 as coinventor of the transistor and in 1972 for his theory of superconductivity. A computer engineering curriculum was created for the university in 1973, and in 1986 the Center for Supercomputing Research and Development was founded there. Mosaic, the first user-friendly web browser, was developed at Illinois by Marc L. Andreessen and Eric J. Bina shortly before Stoppelman's admission. Among Stoppelman's fellow students were Max Levchin and Russ Simmons, who would later figure prominently in his life.

EARLY CAREER

Stoppelman earned a bachelor's degree in computer engineering in 1999 and soon found work as a software engineer at Excite@Home, a company that had been formed that year by the merger of Excite, then one of the most recognized online portals and search engines on the web, and the @Home Network, a high-speed cable Internet service provider (ISP). While the merger of the two web giants caused great excitement in the business world, Stoppelman was unhappy with the corporate culture there. "I quickly realized [it] was not for me," he explained to Cris Valerio, a San Francisco–based technology reporter and host of the Bloomberg Television program *Venture* (28 May 2010). "About four months into the job I decided maybe there's a start-up . . . that [might be] a better fit." He continued, "And, you know, I was fortunate. It was a very exciting time in [Silicon] Valley. . . . So many start-ups were calling engineers every day, saying, 'Come join us, come join us.'"

Almost immediately after he made the decision to leave Excite@Home, which went bankrupt in 2001, Stoppelman was hired by X.com. The company was founded in early 1999 by a South African–born Stanford dropout named Elon Musk, using $10 million from the sale of an earlier venture, Zip2, which developed, hosted, and maintained websites for newspaper publishers and other media companies. (He had

reportedly earned more than $20 million in total from the deal.) Musk's new idea was to provide online banking services and an innovative way to transfer funds via the Internet. He had competition, however, from a company called Confinity, which had been cofounded in late 1998 by Peter Thiel and Stoppelman's fellow University of Illinois grad Max Levchin. Confinity's flagship service, called PayPal, allowed users to store encrypted financial information on their personal digital assistants (PDAs); because the information could not be stolen as readily as a wallet filled with cash, Levchin and Thiel touted the security benefits of their brainchild, as well as its ease of use.

PayPal was setting the tech world abuzz even before its official release. "The bill for lunch arrives, but you've left your wallet in the car," Karlin Lillington wrote for *Wired* (27 July 1999). "Your lunch mate doesn't want to pick up the tab. So she pulls out her Palm III [PDA], beams you a little program called PayPal, and suggests you beam back your share of the bill. Later that day, the cash comes out of your account and drops into hers. That scenario should be a reality by September, when Confinity, a Palo Alto, California, software start-up, launches PayPal, an application that will allow individuals to 'beam' sums of money between handheld devices such as mobile phones, Palm Pilots, and pagers." Thiel told Lillington, "All these devices will become one day just like your wallet. Every one of your friends will become like a virtual, miniature ATM." Soon, Levchin and Thiel had unveiled a method of making payments via e-mail in addition to PDAs, and in January 2000 the online auction giant eBay began displaying the PayPal logo and encouraging its participants to pay for their purchases using the service.

In March 2000 Confinity and X.com merged. While they briefly considered retaining the name X.com for the new company, consumer surveys showed that many people considered it either too vague or objected to its mildly pornographic overtones. It was decided instead to call the venture PayPal, which tested well with its alliterative and cheerfully friendly sound. The month of the merger, PayPal attracted its millionth user.

Stoppelman served as the vice president of engineering at the newly merged company, which did not enjoy immediate financial success. A New York–based company called CertCo filed a patent-infringement lawsuit, and there were also rumblings from legislators in a handful of states that PayPal was acting as an unlicensed banking institution. Despite those admitted difficulties, when the company conducted its initial public offering (IPO), in February 2002, investors were excited by its prospects, and when trading opened, shares shot from their $13 offering price up to $18.50. By the end of the day, the stock had reached $20, and the IPO ultimately raised more than $70 million.

In October 2002 PayPal was acquired by eBay for an astounding $1.5 billion. Many of the company's key executives, who profited richly from the deal, left to pursue other avenues. Stoppelman decided to enter Harvard Business School to earn an advanced degree. "I thought, hey, this might be a good time to just take a little break from [Silicon] Valley and experience something different [from engineering] and learn some other part of what it means to build a business," he told Valerio.

Stoppelman remained at Harvard for just a year before dropping out to join Levchin in his next project: MRL Ventures, a small group of engineers and entrepreneurs, many of them from either PayPal or the University of Illinois, who worked together to incubate new ideas. Stoppelman explained to Valerio, "Every day we came in we were brainstorming about what could be next in the world of consumer internet, what would be another useful service."

The previous summer Stoppelman had caught the flu and needed to find a doctor. He had turned, naturally, to the web. "And the only sites that existed were really rudimentary—you could only look up the doctor's name, maybe where he went to school, nothing beyond that," he said in an article for *Newsweek* (21 Oct. 2009). "So [fellow University of Illinois and PayPal alum Russ Simmons] and I started obsessing over social networking and reviews—maybe those two things fit together?" During a birthday lunch for Levchin, who had turned twenty-nine shortly after forming MRL Ventures, the pair brought the subject up to the group. "We thought the best way to find local recommendations is to ask friends," he wrote for *Newsweek*. "How can we capture that, bring it online, and make it a useful tool where you can actually search by word of mouth?"

YELP IS LAUNCHED

By the time they had returned to the office, the idea for Yelp had been born. Levchin agreed to provide an early round of capital. Stoppelman and Simmons initially considered naming the company Yocal, a combination of *yokel* and *local* before deciding that it lacked appeal. A colleague searching for available domain names discovered that Yelp.com was available and made that suggestion. The founders immediately vetoed it, asserting that it sounded like the noise a dog would make upon being kicked. Still, after no better options presented themselves, Yelp began to grow on everyone, and the domain name was secured for $5,000.

The initial version of the site was launched in October 2004. While users seemed to like the general idea, the actual experience of navigating Yelp left something to be desired. "The actual mechanism of the site proved to be painful, noisy, spammy," Stoppelman wrote for *Newsweek*. "The person looking for a business wasn't always promised a response from their friends—and those friends were often annoyed by questions to which they didn't have answers." Still, one minor feature of the site generated a lot of interest: the ability for a user to write an unsolicited—and presumably unbiased—review of a business or service.

By February 2005 the site had been redesigned to highlight the review-writing feature. With limited capital, Stoppelman and Simmons initially focused only on the San Francisco Bay area, where Yelp quickly proved to be a hit. Modeling the business on Craigslist, a classified-ad provider that had gradually expanded across the country, Stoppelman and Levchin rolled out sites for other urban areas, including New York, Austin, and Seattle, where it was equally popular.

THE PAYPAL MAFIA

Stoppelman and Simmons were far from the only PayPal veterans launching other successful ventures. Among the most successful is the video-sharing service YouTube, the work of Chad Hurley, Steven Chen, and Jawed Karim. The site now records more than two billion page views per day. Peter Thiel started a hedge fund, Clarium Capital, and Roelof Botha, PayPal's chief financial officer, became a partner at Sequoia Capital, a venture firm involved with Apple and Google, among other Internet behemoths. Reid Hoffman, a PayPal executive vice president, founded the successful business-networking site LinkedIn, and David Sacks, a chief operating officer, started a production company called Room 9 Entertainment whose first film, the darkly satirical *Thank You for Smoking* (2005), grossed almost $25 million at the box office. Elon Musk, one of the more iconoclastic PayPal alumni, now heads Space Explorations Technology (SpaceX), which develops relatively low-cost rockets, some of which have been purchased by NASA.

Collectively, these young engineers and entrepreneurs became known as the "PayPal Mafia," thanks in large part to a *CNN Money* article (26 Nov. 2007) by Jeffrey M. O'Brien. Headlined "Meet the PayPal Mafia," the piece included a novelty photo of Stoppelman, Levchin, Thiel, and several others dressed in an array of leather jackets, pin-striped suits, velour track outfits, and thick gold chains, evoking the style of mobsters in recent films and television series. "This group of serial entrepreneurs and investors represents a new generation of wealth and power," O'Brien wrote. "In some ways they're classic characters of Silicon Valley, where success and easy access to capital breed ambition and further success. It's the reason people come to the area from all over the world. But even by that standard, PayPal was a Petri dish for entrepreneurs."

"The story of engineers and executives leaving a company to start new ones is as old as Silicon Valley itself. . . . But the network of PayPal alumni is unusual," Miguel Helft wrote for the *New York Times* (17 Oct. 2006). "The effectiveness of the PayPal network stems, in part, from the fact that it includes all the elements needed to put together a start-up: Talented engineers and entrepreneurs with innovative ideas and a love of the start-up life; experienced managers who can turn ideas into businesses; and financiers. . . ." Helft continued, "The fact that most key PayPal employees were in their 20s and 30s, and not ready for retirement, helped too." He pointed out that several of the men had known each other from either Stanford or the University of Illinois and that those "long-standing bonds created an atmosphere of openness and trust, which not only helped PayPal succeed, but also made it easier for members of the network to embrace each other's post-PayPal projects."

The mafia appellation became ironic when allegations surfaced that members of Yelp's sales force were guilty of extorting advertising dollars in exchange for the deletion of negative reviews, and in 2010 the site was hit by a spate of class-action suits. While the lawsuits were ultimately dismissed, they caused a public-relations nightmare for the company that has not entirely abated. Stoppelman told Kermit Pattison for the *New York Times* (24 Mar. 2010): "The way Yelp works is very counterintuitive to a lot of folks, which is the source of the problem. In 2005, we created a review filter. It's automated and algorithmic and screens out certain reviews that it just doesn't know enough about. When a consumer encounters a business's page, the reviews they're seeing aren't necessarily every review that's been written about the business. It's a selection of those reviews. It ensures that the consumer sees generally useful, trustworthy information that gives them a good idea of what to expect when they patronize that business." He asserted that his salespeople had absolutely no control over which reviews appeared, saying, "The review filter is automated. It doesn't take into account advertiser status. It works the same for everybody." Stoppelman explained that many of the issues arose when business owners tried to circumvent the system by soliciting fake positive reviews from customers or friends; conversely, he also acknowledged the need to protect businesses against false and malicious reviews from competitors.

Another recurring issue is Yelp's on-going adversarial relationship with Google, which tried unsuccessfully to purchase the smaller company in 2009. In 2011 Yelp cooperated with a Federal Trade Commission investigation into the search engine's practices. "We have . . . told officials that we believe Google has acted anti-competitively in at least two key ways: by misusing Yelp review content in their competing Places product and by favoring their own competing Places product in search results," Stoppelman wrote in a 2011 blog post.

YELP TODAY

Despite those troublesome factors, Yelp has expanded at a rapid rate. The site boasts some twenty-five million reviews of restaurants, salons, doctors, repairmen, hotels, and other businesses and is visited more than sixty-five million times per month—almost six million times via Yelp's mobile apps. (Yelp apps were named among the best of 2011 by *PC Magazine*, *Time*, and *Travel & Leisure* magazines.) Reviews now cover more than 150 American cities as well as locations throughout Canada and Europe.

PERSONAL LIFE

Stoppelman was named one of the food world's most powerful people in 2012 by TheDailyMeal.com, a popular site; he also appears frequently on lists of the country's most eligible or "hottest" bachelors. He lives in the Bay Area with his dog, Darwin, and frequently posts Yelp reviews, which reveal that he is particularly fond of burritos.

FURTHER READING

Caulfield, Brian. "The Not-So-Evil Genius of Jeremy Stoppelman." *Forbes*. Forbes. 18 Dec. 2009. Web. 6 Apr. 2012.

Helft, Miguel. "It Pays to Have Pals in Silicon Valley." *New York Times*. New York Times. 17 Oct. 2006. Web. 6 Apr. 2012.

Lillington, Karlin. "PayPal Puts Dough in Your Palm." *Wired*. Wired. 27 July 1999. Web. 6 Apr. 2012.

O'Brien, Jeffrey M. "Meet the PayPal Mafia." *Fortune*. CNNMoney. 26 Nov. 2007. Web. 6 Apr. 2012.

Pattison, Kermit. "Talking to the Chief of Yelp, the Site That Businesses Love to Hate." *New York Times*. New York Times. 24 Mar. 2010. Web. 6 Apr. 2012.

Stoppelman, Jeremy. "For Yelp, Locals Aren't Yokels." *Newsweek*. Newsweek. 21 Oct. 2009. Web. 6 Apr. 2012.

Shaun Tan

Born: 1974
Occupation: Illustrator, author

"I think there is great similarity between science and art. The fact that they are fairly separate disciplines in our time says something about our culture. What they have in common is a curiosity about reality, and casting of the imagination over initial perception."

In the Hampton Roads, Virginia, *Virginian-Pilot* (Apr. 17, 2011), Caroline Luzzatto described the work of writer Shaun Tan, saying, "In the alternate universe of Shaun Tan's books, despair hangs overhead like a milky-eyed dead fish. Homesick strangers puzzle over vending machines with impenetrable instructions. An unexpected friend has tentacles. An unfriendly city has tubes, dials and warnings not to look too closely at anything that doesn't make sense." According to Luzzatto, that "alternate universe" originates in Tan's "startling take on the world—one that has won him legions of fans and a raft of awards, including, just in the past few months, an Oscar for a short film he co-directed, based on his own book, and the Astrid Lindgren Memorial Award, an international prize regarded as a Nobel for children's books." She added, "Look at his work, and it's clear he is calling on inner child and inner alien."

Tan is known for such evocative picture books as *The Lost Thing*, published in 2000 by the Australian imprint Lothian Books, and *The Red Tree*, published in 2001 by Lothian. Although the term "picture book" implies to some readers a volume meant solely for children, Tan's work appeals to those of all ages. "[Books like mine] really are a problematic art form in terms of audience perception, though I don't see why this needs to be the case," Tan explained to Chuan-Yao Ling for *World Literature Today* (Sep. 2008). "Picture books are very similar to short animation, or a typical painting exhibition (with about the same number of images), or an adult short story. It just so happens that the vast majority of picture books are for young children, but I think this is just a cultural convention—it varies from country to country. Artists' books demonstrate that the form itself is open to all levels of sophistication, constrained only by two ingredients, words and pictures." So devoted are many of Tan's adult fans that they have his artwork tattooed on their bodies. Tan told Neil Gaiman for the London *Guardian* (Dec. 2, 2011), "The first time [I saw one] it freaked me out. I felt: 'Are you sure you want to do this?' People ask me for permission because they think there's some copyright issue. My response is, 'Unless you're going to sell your arm and make a profit I don't think there is one, so go ahead.'"

Getty Images

draw," he told Carlo Rotella for the *New York Times Magazine* (Apr. 22, 2011, online), "than as the short kid." Tan's father gave him his first paying job, providing him with some pocket change to sketch a palm tree on an architectural drawing. Tan was heavily influenced by his architect father, as well as by American science-fiction films such as *Star Wars* and by television series such as *The Twilight Zone*, which featured tales of the supernatural.

An introspective child, Tan collected seashells and tried to fit into his predominantly white school by sharing his drawings. The Tans owned a variety of pets, a fact reflected in the many creatures that populate his books. "My family's first pet was a stray cat with a broken leg that my brother brought home one day, and we kept it in the shed," Tan told Karl Quinn for the Melbourne *Age* (Feb. 21, 2011), adding, "After that we always had these strange, broken animals as pets. We had a budgie with an underbite at one stage."

EARLY LIFE

Shaun Tan was born in 1974 in Western Australia. He grew up in Hillarys, a suburb of Perth. (Some sources alternatively mention the city of Fremantle.) His Chinese Malaysian father was an architect, who had come to Australia in his twenties to study, and his mother was a third-generation Australian of English and Irish descent. His older brother, Paul, is a geologist.

Tan exhibited artistic talent at an early age. "It was better to be known as the kid who could

EDUCATION

While attending Balcatta High School, Tan, who had been admitted into a special program for gifted art students, began earning money by illustrating stories for science-fiction and horror magazines. He briefly considered studying science. Tan told Chris Thomson for *Western Australia Today* (Mar. 16, 2010, online), "I think there is great similarity between science and art." He continued, "The fact that they are fairly separate disciplines in our time says something about our culture. What they have in common is a curiosity about reality, and casting of the imagination over initial perception. Scientific ideas are profound acts of the imagination, prior to all testing and calculation, and similarly, all works of art are a series of hypotheses that have been put to experimental test on paper or canvas."

Tan attended the University of Western Australia, where he decided to major in fine arts and English literature. He had no set career plans and never seriously planned on becoming a professional illustrator, considering his artistic pursuits hobbies rather than vocations. Tan, who in 1992 became the first Australian ever to be honored as an L. Ron Hubbard Illustrator of the Future, graduated with a bachelor of arts degree in 1995. Despite his initial disinclination to consider his drawing a reliable source of income, he subsequently embarked upon a freelance career, "taking on every kind of work he could get, from diagrams of microscopes to sword-wielding warriors on the covers of fantasy novels," as Carlo Rotella described it.

BREAKTHROUGH WORK

Tan first gained widespread attention with his illustrations for *The Rabbits*, a 1998 book whose sparse but powerful text was written by fellow Australian John Marsden. The initial setting of the book calls to mind the vast, unspoiled tracts of land that characterized Australia or the American Midwest before colonization, in this case populated only by a variety of birds, reptiles, and small mammals. Once the titular rabbits arrive, the landscape begins to change; the suited and bespectacled colonizers build strange-looking houses rather than living in trees like the native wildlife, introduce foods that sicken the original inhabitants of the land, and start fights that, because of their greater numbers, they always win. *The Rabbits* was almost universally considered an insightful and sensitive examination of colonialism and postindustrial environmental damage by its reviewers. It was named the Picture Book of the Year by the Children's Book Council of Australia; won the Aurealis Conveners Award for Excellence, an Australia science-fiction honor; and received the Spectrum Gold Award for Book Illustration, which is presented annually to an artist working in the fantasy, horror, or science-fiction genre. To prepare for the task of illustrating *The Rabbits,* Tan conducted research ranging from observing animals at the Perth Zoo to studying centuries-old photographs, architecture, and drawings. His art was influenced by landscapes as well as elements from his neighborhood and everyday life. Tan has also said that he was influenced, in part, by George Orwell's novel *Animal Farm* (1945), which his mother read to him when he was young, mistakenly believing that it was a children's book.

Tan collaborated with Gary Crew, known for his work in the horror field, on *The Viewer* (1997)—the tale of Tristan, a young boy who haunts junkyards in search of discarded items with which he can tinker. Upon the book's 2004 publication in Canada, a critic for *Publishers Weekly* (May 3, 2004, online) wrote, "Ominous words and violent imagery fuel this dystopia, which is equal parts science fiction and life-as-we-know-it. . . . Crew's language is foreboding, while Tan loads his marvelous, shadowy images with post-apocalyptic clutter. The audience can almost feel the power that [one item Tristan finds] exudes in this unsettling walk through history and its cautionary perspective."

The Children's Book Council of Australia honored Tan again in 2000 for *Memorial* (1999), which also won an Australian Publishers Association (APA) Design Award and was short-listed for the Queensland Premier's Book Awards. Written by Crew and illustrated by Tan, the book revolves around a tree planted by returning servicemen next to a war memorial in a small town. As the years pass, the tree begins to grow so large that it damages the statue next to it and creates a traffic hazard. When town officials consider cutting it down, questions arise as to the significance of such war memorials and whether they really serve to keep valuable memories alive.

THE LOST THING

Among the best known of Tan's books is *The Lost Thing*, whose introverted protagonist finds a strange creature while wandering on the beach one day to collect bottle caps, much as the introspective young Tan collected shells as a child. The large red creature, while indisputably machine-like, also possesses tentacles and a tail. After asking several bystanders for information, to no avail, the boy concludes that the creature has no owner nearby and is lost. He takes it home, where his parents are too engrossed in watching television to notice. When they finally do, they demand that the boy return it to the beach. Instead, he hides it in the family's shed and feeds it for a time (calling to mind Tan's first pet, the cat with the broken leg, for those familiar with his life story). As the reviewer Emma Jane wrote for the *Weekend Australian* (Feb. 26, 2011), "The narrator learns of a new place, a utopia for lovely anomalies. Here, the lost thing can exist in splendid singularity with other organic-machine hybrids such as the X873 water grinder, the symbiotic passenger pear and the four-stroke nectar-diesel coelacanth with adopted daughter. And they all live oddly ever after."

In 2010, after a lengthy period of development, Tan and producer Andrew Ruhemann codirected a fifteen-minute film version of the *Lost Thing*, which won an Academy Award in the category of best-animated short. The award greatly increased Tan's profile, prompting Emma

Jane to write, "While it's tempting to tell California to keep its grabby hands to itself, Tan really should be shared." Although Tan had been a design consultant and concept artist on the computer-animated films *Wall-E* (2008) and *Horton Hears a Who* (2008), he expressed little interest in making a feature film of his own, not wanting to endure the financial and artistic pressure that venture might entail.

LATER WORKS AND AWARDS

Tan made a similar splash as author and illustrator of the picture book *The Red Tree*, which follows a depressed young girl through her day. Drawn morose and mouthless, she wakes in a dismal bedroom into which a few dead leaves have drifted. By the time she dresses and opens the door, the leaves have engulfed the bed and reached her waist. As she walks down the street, a large open-mouthed fish with expressionless eyes looms over her head. Her day continues in that vein, with the girl becoming increasingly more isolated and confused by her surroundings. When she finally returns to her room, however, she is greeted by the sight of a colorfully drawn, flame-leaved tree growing from her floor. "Suddenly there it is, right in front of you, bright and vivid. Just as you imagined it would be," Tan writes just on one of the last pages of the book. Critic Emma Jane admitted, "As someone who has experienced sensations akin to being eclipsed by an enormous fish, I wept the first time I reached this page. Tan's metaphorical depiction of the fragility yet stubborn resilience of happiness is extraordinarily moving." Many agree with Jane's assessment; the small red leaf that Tan drew on each page, even the gloomiest, is often seen tattooed on his fans, and the volume has become a favorite with therapists and those in recovery from depression, substance abuse, and other such challenges. *The Red Tree* was adapted for the stage by the Barking Gecko Theatre Company in 2010.

The Arrival, Tan's 2006 book about one man's journey to a strange land, is also among his most beloved and critically acclaimed. In the volume Tan follows his protagonist, drawn in a painstakingly photorealistic manner, as he leaves his family and native land behind. In his new home he is confronted with unfamiliar looking buildings and indecipherable street signs; so alien is everything around him that when he finds a job hanging posters, he is unsure as to which way they should face. He is soon befriended, however, by more experienced immigrants, who feed him and help him to settle in. Ultimately, he is joined by his wife and child, and their touching reunion provides the climax of the book. A reviewer for *Publishers Weekly* (July 16, 2007, online) wrote, "With this haunting, wordless sequence about a lonely emigrant in a bewildering city, Tan finds in the graphic novel format an ideal outlet for his sublime imagination." The reviewer added, "Nearly all readers will be able to relate—either through personal or ancestral experience—to the difficulties of starting over, be it in another country, city, or community. And few will remain unaffected by this timeless stunner." Among other laurels, *The Arrival* was chosen by the Children's Book Council of Australia as Picture Book of the Year in 2007.

Tan's later books include *Tales from Outer Suburbia* (2008), an illustrated collection of short stories, and *Lost and Found* (2011), an omnibus containing *The Rabbits*, *The Lost Thing*, and *The Red Tree*.

Tan won the coveted Hugo Award for best professional artist in both 2010 and 2011. In 2011 he also garnered what is arguably the most prestigious honor of his career: the Astrid Lindgren Memorial Award, which comes with 5 million krona prize, making it among the most lucrative literary honors in the world. Named for the beloved author of the Pippi Longstocking series, the prize is given by the government of Sweden to those who further the cause of children's literature. Prior recipients have included authors Maurice Sendak and Philip Pullman. Tan's own name graces an annual award given by the Western Australian city of Subiaco to a budding school-age artist; Tan acts as patron of the contest and has also painted two large murals on the walls of the city's public library that are the source of much civic pride.

PERSONAL LIFE

Despite the number of accolades he has received in the last several years, Tan is said to be a quiet person, with an unassuming demeanor. He told Will Brodie for the *Sydney Morning Herald* (Feb. 28, 2011, online), "I'm a pretty average person in terms of my behaviour and how I approach things. People often expect me to be weird, or kookie or eccentric or dressed in a funny way, but then I've had other interviews where journalists have written afterwards that I look like an accountant, and I do."

Tan lives in Melbourne with his wife, Finnish graphic designer and jewelry maker Inari Kiuru. They own three birds, which, as journalists often remark upon, they allow to fly around the house.

SUGGESTED READING

Brodie, Will. "Underdog Aussie's Oscar Triumph." *Sydney Morning Herald*. Fairfax Media, 28 Feb. 2011. Web. 30 Dec. 2011.

Gaiman, Neil. "In Conversation: Neil Gaiman Talks to Shaun Tan." *Guardian* [London] 2 Dec. 2011: 12. Print.

Henderson, Scott. "Shaun Tan: Interview." *Vine*. Fairfax Media, 9 Feb. 2011. Web. 30 Dec. 2011.

Jane, Emma. "Go, You Lost Thing, Bring Back an Oscar." *Weekend Australian* 26 Feb. 2011: 11. Print.

Ling, Chuan-Yao. "A Conversation with Illustrator Shaun Tan." *World Literature Today* Sep. 2008: 44–47. Print.

Luzzatto, Caroline. "Inner Child Meets Inner Alien." *Virginian-Pilot* [Hampton Roads] 17 Apr. 2011: E5. Print.

Quinn, Karl. "Short Road to the Oscars." *Age* [Melbourne] 21 Feb. 2011, Life sec.: 24. Print.

Rotella, Carlo. "Shaun Tan's Wild Imagination." *New York Times Magazine*. New York Times, 22 Apr. 2011. Web. 30 Dec. 2011.

Thomson, Chris. "Shaun Tan Headlines World Sci-Fi Convention." *Western Australia Today*. Fairfax Media, 16 Mar. 2010. Web. 30 Dec. 2011.

SELECTED WORKS

The Viewer (with Gary Crew), 1997; *The Rabbits* (with John Marsden), 1998; *Memorial* (with Gary Crew), 1999; *The Lost Thing*, 2000; *The Red Tree*, 2001; *The Arrival*, 2006; *Tales from Outer Suburbia*, 2008; *Lost and Found*, 2011

—*Mari Rich*

Wirelmage

Catherine Tate

Born: May 12, 1968
Occupation: Actor and comedian

Catherine Tate is a British comedian and actor best known in the United States for her role as special projects manager Nellie Bertram on the NBC television series *The Office*. In the United Kingdom, Tate is known as the beloved star and creator of the sketch-comedy program, *The Catherine Tate Show*, which aired from 2004 to 2009. Tate played a bevy of characters known for their underlying pathos and memorable catchphrases.

Tate created one such character, the sarcastic fifteen-year-old character Lauren Cooper, as a caricature of both modern British youth and a send-up of the injustices of adolescence; Lauren desperately yearns to be cool but always ends up the butt of the joke. When faced with a humiliating situation, she breezily asks her offenders or a mortified onlooker, "Look at my face: am I bovvered?" The character became so popular, Sara Phillips noted for the London *Guardian* (12 Oct. 2006), that the phrase was "inadvertently reclaimed" by the very teenagers Tate had sought to satirize. To Britain's delight, Tate has even parroted the phrase "Am I bovvered?" when meeting former Prime Minister Tony Blair and the Queen. In 2006, the word *bovvered*, meaning "bothered," officially entered the national lexicon when it was added to the *Oxford English Dictionary* in 2006.

The popularity of *The Catherine Tate Show* landed Tate a starring role on the long-running television program and British institution, *Doctor Who,* from 2006 to 2010, and a number of film and theater roles. Her role on *The Office* in 2011 may even suggest the beginning of a larger international career. Such a level of fame was never the expectation of the classically trained actor turned stand-up comedian, though Tate has taken the success of the show that might well become her legacy in stride. However, she told Brian Viner for the London *Independent* (23 Dec. 2006), "If in five years' time the only thing that I've done that is remembered is a teenager saying, 'Am I bovvered?' then I'd worry."

EARLY LIFE AND EDUCATION

Tate was born Catherine Ford on May 12, 1968, in London, England. She changed her name to Catherine Tate when she became an actor and received her card from the British Equity (actors' association). She grew up in Bloomsbury in central London and was raised by her mother, a florist named Josephine, who left Tate's father before Tate was born. As a child, Tate was surrounded by women, including her grandmother, aunts, and godmother. It was a matriarchy, she told Liz Hoggard for the *London Evening Standard* (14 July 2008); since then, she added, "It's never been a point of reference [for me] to look to a man."

As an only child, Tate was adored by her family, though she has described herself as a very shy and nervous child. She suffered from an obsessive disorder that derived from word association. In an oft-cited example, Tate explains that she could not bear to leave her jumper (sweater) crumpled on the floor because the word "jumper" begins with the same letter as her mother's first name. She would imagine her mother lying crumpled on the floor and pick up the sweater. To cope with her compulsion and the awkwardness of childhood, Tate turned to comedy. "I used humor to deflect attention," she told Simon Hattenstone for the *Guardian* (4 Apr. 2008). "It was a controlling mechanism. Because I could use it to control my image." She would rather be the "funny one," she reasoned, than the "ginger one" or the "red-faced one."

At Notre Dame High School, Tate was by no means the class clown, but she took an interest in the stand-up comedians at the Comedy Store in Leicester Square. She was already showing promise as an actor, so much so that she began attending a boy's Catholic school at the age of sixteen because her own school did not have an acting program to suit her. Tate decided to seriously pursue theater and left school before beginning her A-levels (Advanced Level General Certificate of Education). She applied to the prestigious Central School of Speech and Drama—the alma mater of actors such as Lawrence Olivier and Judi Dench—four times before she was accepted. She then moved to Spain for nearly a year before beginning her studies at Central in 1990.

STAND-UP COMIC AND EARLY ACTING ROLES

After graduating from Central in 1993, Tate played small roles with the Royal Shakespeare Company and the National Theatre in London. On television, she landed several bit parts on the police procedural *The Bill*, uncredited roles on the medical drama *Casualty*, and an appearance on the comedy *Men Behaving Badly*. Despite these roles, Tate was frustrated with her acting career and what she saw as a lack of control over her future. In 1996, when Tate was in her late twenties, she decided to take a break from acting and auditions and try her hand at stand-up comedy. For three years, she worked as a receptionist during the day and performed at comedy clubs at night. Tate recalled the "delicious danger" of stand-up comedy to Hattenstone: "I really did like the gladiatorial aspect of it—if it was a particularly rough club and you would get a bit of trouble. I liked the fact that people want to have a go. There's an arrogance involved in doing stand-up comedy because what you're saying is, 'Yeah, have a go, but know this, I believe I'm funnier than you,' and when the audience gets behind you and acknowledges that, it's brilliant." Tate performed on the British comedy circuit for five years.

Tate's stand-up earned her appearances on the Channel 4 sketch-comedy show *Barking*, the television comedy *That Peter Kay Thing*, and another sketch show called *Harry Hill*. In 2000, she was invited to the Edinburgh Fringe Festival as a part of stand-up comedian Lee Mack's show, *New Bits*. Mack was impressed by Tate's stand-up and had asked her to be a part of the show. Tate played the character of an old woman who would later evolve into the familiar character Nan on *The Catherine Tate Show*. *New Bits* was nominated for the competitive Perrier Award (now known as the Edinburgh Comedy Award), given to the best comedy show at the festival.

EDINBURGH FRINGE FESTIVAL

The following year, Tate returned to the festival with a one-woman show. After putting off writing its script—and cancelling all of her London previews—Tate arrived in Edinburgh with only a rough idea of the fifty-minute show in her head. "That night—the opening night—the show somehow went well," Tate wrote for the *Guardian* (21 Sep. 2008). "It was part-improvised and entirely raw, being the first time I'd performed any of it in front of any one, let alone a paying crowd." After the show, Tate wrote down what she remembered from the performance and continued to improvise and revise throughout the run. Tate wrote for the *Guardian* that the Edinburgh performance, which was also nominated for a Perrier Award, taught her the importance of vetting bits in front of an audience. "When it came to recording the first series [season] of my show," she wrote, "almost every sketch had been tried out in front of a live crowd and was all the better for it."

Tate's performance at the Edinburgh Fringe led to several major breaks in her career. The late Geoffrey Perkins, a major comedy producer for the BBC, saw the show and offered Tate a chance to star in her own comedy sketch show. He also gave her a role on the small town sitcom *Wild West* (2002–04). Tate played Angela Davis, a lesbian shopkeeper, alongside fellow comedian Dawn French. At first, Tate turned down the television offers to tour with the Royal Shakespeare Company. She returned a year later and began negotiations for her own show.

THE CATHERINE TATE SHOW

The Catherine Tate Show premiered, with Perkins as producer, on BBC Two in 2004. It won Tate the best newcomer award at the British Comedy Awards in its first season and was nominated for a BAFTA award. Tate won another Comedy Award for the show's 2006 Christmas special. On the show, Tate played a number of characters, including Lauren Cooper. Some, like the elderly, foul-mouthed Nan, required hours in the makeup chair. Another such character was the effeminate, middle-aged Derek Faye, who utters the catchphrase, "How very dare you!" in response to insinuations that he might be gay. With or without stage makeup, Tate was able to transform herself into an impressive array of people. Miranda Sawyer for the London *Observer* (14 Oct. 2006) noted similarities between *The Catherine Tate Show* and another character-based sketch show, *Little Britain* (2003–06), with comedians David Walliams and Matt Lucas. Sawyer wrote that Tate's characters, by comparison, were "quirkier" and "less cartoony; rooted more in everyday life somehow."

Other fan favorites included Geordie Georgie, a woman who guilts her coworker Martin into giving money to her various charity campaigns. In one sketch, Georgie pledges to run forty-two miles dressed as a bottle of Cinzano to aid the plight of battered husbands. Another character, the upper-middle class Aga Saga Woman, goes into shock when confronted with problems like being unable to find "good brie" and nearly running out of extra virgin olive oil. In addition to acting, Tate served as the show's head writer, working with a team that included Aschlin Ditta, Derren Litten, Mathew Horne—all of whom appeared on many episodes alongside Tate—Arthur Matthews, and director Gordon Anderson.

The popularity of the show, which ran for three seasons, was evident when sitting Prime Minister Tony Blair chose to appear in a sketch with Tate as Lauren Cooper to earn populist points with voters. In 2005, Tate made headlines when she appeared in the 77th Royal Variety Performance. She addressed the Queen from the stage during her sketch asking, "Is one bovvered?" At the end of the show's third season, Tate killed off Lauren in a kayaking incident, but alludes to her eventual return. Lauren's tombstone reads: "I still ain't bovvered."

DOCTOR WHO AND OTHER ROLES

After *The Catherine Tate Show*, Tate was offered the role of the Doctor's companion on the popular science fiction television series *Doctor Who*. The show, which has been on the air since 1963, follows the exploits of an alien time traveler known as the Doctor, who regenerates into a new form—played by a new actor—if his current body dies. The Doctor has been played by eleven different actors, including William Hartnell, Tom Baker, and Matt Smith. Tate joined the cast first as "the bride" in the July 2006 episode "Doomsday," and then as Donna Noble on the episode "The Runaway Bride," which aired on Christmas Day in 2006. At that time, the Doctor was being played by the Scottish Shakespearean actor David Tennant. The episode was so popular that Tate returned as Noble for fifteen more

episodes as the Doctor's companion, until the end of Tennant's run as the Doctor in 2010. In 2011, Tate appeared as Beatrice opposite Tennant's Benedick in Shakespeare's *Much Ado About Nothing* on London's West End. The well-reviewed production was set in England during the raucous 1980s.

In 2005, Tate starred in the Neil LaBute play *Some Girl(s)* with American actor David Schwimmer. She joked with a reporter about not being able to talk to Schwimmer for fear of asking him about his role on the popular television show *Friends* (1994–2004). Her comments were misconstrued—or perhaps deliberately spun—to make it sound as if the two were feuding. In 2006, Tate appeared in a play about death row called *The Exonerated*, with Stockard Channing, Richard Dreyfuss, Kristin Davis, Danny Glover, Kate Mulgrew, Aidan Quinn, and four actual death row exonerees.

In addition to her stage roles, Tate has appeared in a handful of films. She was in the romantic comedy *Love and Other Disasters* (2006) with the late Brittany Murphy, who played an American intern working for British *Vogue*. The same year, Tate starred as the aunt of a young boy in *Sixty Six*, a drama set in 1966 during the World Cup; the movie also starred Helena Bonham Carter and Stephan Rea. In *Scenes of a Sexual Nature* (2006), a comedic drama that examines the love lives of several Londoners, Tate played Sara, who considers divorcing her husband, played by Adrian Lester. In 2007, she appeared as the middle-aged mother of a boy about to enter college in the comedy *Starter for 10*. Tate also starred in a comedy called *Mrs. Ratcliffe's Revolution* (2007). The film is based on a true story about a Yorkshire family who moves to East Germany, only to question their allegiance to the Communist Party. In 2010, Tate played Queen Isabelle in the film *Gulliver's Travels*, starring comedian Jack Black.

THE OFFICE

Tate joined the cast of the American version of *The Office* in 2011 as British special projects manager Nellie Bertram. Based on a popular British television show of the same name created by comedian Ricky Gervais, the show, which is shot in a mock-umentary style, first aired in 2005. Bertram was hired by chairman of the board, Jo Bennett, played by Kathy Bates. Tate's character first appeared as a contender for the regional manager position at the paper company Dunder Mifflin (the office of the show's title)—a job vacated by Michael Scott, the show's former starring role played by Steve Carrell. Though her character did not get Scott's job, Tate was kept on for a larger storyline involving a romance with Dunder Mifflin CEO Robert California, played by James Spader.

Initially, Bertram had flirted with Rainn Wilson's character, Dwight Schrute.

Reviews of Tate's performance were mixed. Some critics saw Tate as a hilarious addition to the show, while others saw her character as so outrageous as to be out of step with reality and another example of *The Office*'s steady decline. The creators of the show announced in August 2012 that the 2013 season would be its last.

Tate, who counts Gervais among her own admirers, was a fan of the *The Office* long before becoming a cast member. "It's a double-edged sword," she told Will Harris for *New York Magazine* (16 Feb. 2012). "Once you're in it, you almost can no longer be an audience member. Which is kind of bittersweet."

PERSONAL LIFE

Tate has one child, a daughter named Erin, with her ex-partner Twig Clark, a stage manager whom she met while working with the Royal Shakespeare Company. Erin was born in January 2003, before Tate was scheduled to begin filming *The Catherine Tate Show*. Tate later spoke about suffering from postpartum depression, but regrets having done so publicly. She believes that the press has glamorized her struggle with the disease. "That's so much the image of the crying clown," she told Hattenstone. "And I'm not one."

Tate, who is single, lives with her daughter in London. She counters her pessimistic and nervous personality by studying astrology. She also has a knack for languages and speaks French, Spanish, and Italian.

SUGGESTED READING

Harris, Will. "Catherine Tate on Her Return to *The Office* and Getting a Word Into the Oxford English Dictionary." *New York Magazine*. New York Media, 16 Feb. 2012. Web. 22 Aug. 2012.

Hattenstone, Simon. "What I'm Not Is a Cheery Person." *Guardian* [London]. Guardian News and Media, 4 Apr. 2008. Web. 22 Aug. 2012.

Hoggard, Liz. "Catherine Tate's Modern Outlook." *London Evening Standard*. ES London, 14 Jul. 2008. Web. 22 Aug. 2012.

Phillips, Sarah. "'Bovvered' Wins Word of the Year Award." *Guardian* [London]. Guardian News and Media, 12 Oct. 2006. Web. 22 Aug. 2012.

Sawyer, Miranda. "Catherine the Great." *Observer* [London]. Guardian News and Media, 14 Oct. 2006. Web. 22 Aug. 2012.

Tate, Catherine. "Joke's on You." *Guardian* [London]. Guardian News and Media, 21 Sep. 2008. Web. 22 Aug. 2012.

Viner, Brian. "Catherine Tate: The Shy Star." *Independent* [London]. Independent Print, 23 Dec. 2006. Web. 22 Aug. 2012.

SELECTED TELEVISION SHOWS

The Bill, 1993–97; "Casualties," *Men Behaving Badly*, 1994; *Big Train*, 1998–2002; *The Harry Hill Show*, 2000; "Leonard," *That Peter Kay Thing*, 2000; *Attention Scum*, 2001; *Wild West*, 2002–4; *The Catherine Tate Show*, 2004–9; *Doctor Who*, 2006–10; *The Office*, 2011–12

SELECTED FILMS

Love and Other Disasters, 2006; *Scenes of a Sexual Nature*, 2006; *Mrs. Ratcliffe's Revolution*, 2007; *Starter for 10*, 2007; *Gulliver's Travels*, 2010

—*Molly Hagan*

Susan Tedeschi

Born: November 9, 1970
Occupation: Blues and soul guitarist

The influential editor and musicologist Timothy White wrote for *Billboard* (30 Jan. 1999) that Susan Tedeschi's voice can "seethe, whoop, and soar with enough sensual blunder to break the seal on whiskey bottles and tear the leaves from the trees." Music journalists writing today are fond of quoting the line, and most almost inevitably go on to compare Tedeschi to Bonnie Raitt or Janis Joplin. Tedeschi takes the comparisons in stride. "[R]eally, there aren't a lot of women you can be compared to when you do the blues, especially if you're white," she told Steve Morse for the *Boston Globe* (16 May 1993). "I'm not going to be compared to Koko Taylor, Etta James, or Big Mama Thornton, even though they're big influences on me."

Like many recording artists, Tedeschi's personal life seemingly receives as much press attention as her music. She is married to guitarist Derek Trucks of the Allman Brothers Band, and the two frequently collaborate on projects.

FAMILY BACKGROUND

Tedeschi (pronounced teh-DESK-ee) was born on November 9, 1970, in Boston, Massachusetts. The third and last of three children, she grew up in nearby Norwell. Her father, Richard, became interested in genealogy after he retired from his video business, and taught Tedeschi a great deal about her ancestry. Reportedly, the land on which she was raised had been given to the family centuries before by a British monarch, and Tedeschi is said to be a distant cousin of the late Diana, Princess of Wales. Several of her ancestors sailed to America on the *Mayflower*, and Abraham Lincoln appears on a distant branch of the family tree. Tedeschi's mother, Patricia, is of Irish ancestry.

Getty Images

The Tedeschi name may be familiar even to those who are not blues fans, because it is prominently displayed on some two hundred convenience stores throughout the Northeast. Tedeschi's paternal great-grandfather, Angelo, had opened his first location in 1923, selling imported Italian meats and cheeses from his home in Rockland, Massachusetts, and the chain is still run by members of the family.

EARLY LOVE OF MUSIC

Growing up, Tedeschi's home was always filled with music. Richard, who played the acoustic guitar and harmonica, had a large and eclectic record collection, and Tedeschi loved hearing him play music by the Beatles, Buddy Holly, and the Everly Brothers, as well as works by such blues artists as Lightnin' Hopkins and Mississippi John Hurt. Her family recalls that she was singing while still in her crib—even before she could talk—and by the time she was six years old, Pat, who was active in community theater, began arranging performances for her. Tedeschi made her theatrical debut in a production of *Oliver!*, playing a workhouse urchin.

At the age of ten, Tedeschi traveled to New York to audition for a role in the musical *Annie*. Although she did not win the part, during the trip she met country legend Johnny Cash, who was staying in the same hotel. "I ran into [him]. Literally," she recalled to Kathaleen Roberts for the *Albuquerque Journal* (9 Feb. 2009). "He said, 'Slow down, little girl.' I didn't realize who he was

at the time. I told him I was a singer and he said, 'I'm a singer too. Maybe we can sing together sometime.'"

Tedeschi, who played the clarinet as a teenager, wrote her first song at age fourteen. She performed as a member of the Norwell High School concert band. By age sixteen, she was playing with a cover band called Third Rail, which performed songs by Heart, the Beatles, and the Eagles at private parties. She later joined a band called the Smoking Section, which had regular gigs at clubs around Massachusetts. "I really liked the biker bars," she recalled to Morse. "A lot of those Harley guys can be the best audience." Tedeschi admits that, early in her career, she sometimes used an ID card with a fake birth date in order to participate in open-mic nights or blues jams at certain venues. Despite those forays into rock, Tedeschi continued work in musical theater. When she was seventeen, she played the lead role in a production of *Evita* at the Hingham Civic Music Theater.

EDUCATION

While deeply devoted to music, Tedeschi was unsure about pursuing it as a career and toyed instead with the idea of becoming a marine biologist. As a gift for her high school graduation, she was given tuition to attend a five-week summer program at the Berklee College of Music, in Boston. Already accepted at a college in Ithaca, New York, Tedeschi changed her mind midway through the summer and decided to stay at Berklee. Her parents were supportive of the decision, and in the fall of 1988, she became a full-time music student.

Tedeschi remained interested in musical theater, and she initially based her singing style on that of popular female performers like Linda Rondstadt. She preferred, as she has told interviewers, to sing in a "pretty" manner. Her attitude changed when she joined Berklee's Reverence Gospel Ensemble, under the direction of Dennis Montgomery III, whom she still counts as a major influence. "I wanted to find something with a little more guts, a little more soul," she explained to Mark Small for *Berklee Today* (Fall 2000). "I loved the gospel choir. I had never been shy about singing in front of people, but singing in front of a whole bunch of people who could really sing was a little frightening."

As much as she loved singing gospel and performing in churches around Boston, Tedeschi saw little future in focusing solely on that genre. "I knew that as a young white girl, I couldn't make a living singing gospel," she told Small. Remembering her father's old Lightnin' Hopkins and Mississippi John Hurt albums—and influenced by a boyfriend who loved Magic Sam, Otis Rush, and Freddie King—she turned her attention to the blues. "The blues bring people together," she explained to Morse. "It doesn't matter what color or background you're from. Everyone can get inspired by the blues."

AFTER GRADUATION

Tedeschi, who earned extra cash as a student by singing show tunes on the *Spirit of Boston*, a dinner-cruise ship, graduated from Berklee in 1991 with a degree in musical composition and performance. She began appearing regularly at area clubs, including Johnny D's in Somerville, the House of Blues in Cambridge, and the Yard Rock in Quincy. Wielding a new Fender guitar, she often worked with Adrienne Hayes, a fellow Boston-based guitarist and vocalist. In 1993, the pair joined forces with Annie Raines, a harmonica player, to form the first incarnation of the Susan Tedeschi Band. While the backup performers changed occasionally, the band ultimately featured a semiregular lineup that included the bassist Jim Lamond and the drummer Tom Hambridge. In 1994, the group won a Boston Battle of the Bands competition, and the following year they placed second in the National Blues Talent Competition held in Memphis, Tennessee.

THE START OF A RECORDING CAREER

In 1995, Tedeschi borrowed $10,000 and released her debut album, *Better Days*, which included several original tracks, as well as covers of such blues standards as Leiber and Stoller's "Hound Dog" and Elmore James's "It Hurts Me Too." The album—coupled with multiple Boston Music Award nods, increased Tedeschi's visibility greatly. Soon she was being invited to open for such performers as Buddy Guy and B. B. King.

Tedeschi also found herself in great demand on the club and festival circuit, and for many days out of the year, she was on the road. She was backed on tour by her boyfriend at the time, guitarist Sean Costello, and his band, the Jive Bombers. Costello, who was widely considered among the most promising blues guitarists of his generation, suffered from bipolar disorder; he died in 2008, right before his thirtieth birthday, of an accidental drug overdose.

In 1998, Tedeschi released her next album, *Just Won't Burn*, on the Massachusetts indie label Tone-Cool Records. Richard Rosenblatt, Tone-Cool's president, was a musician himself—he had played the harmonica in a group called the Eleventh Hour Blues Band—and Tedeschi knew that he loved and appreciated roots music. She also trusted his business integrity. "I don't want to be in debt, and [major] record labels are banks," she told Jim Beal Jr. for the *San Antonio Express-News* (12 May 2000). "Everything they give you, you owe them, and they're banks with very high interest rates. They'll try to sell you in a certain way. I don't want any part of that. I want to be known as a regular girl making good music." Most critics agreed that she was making good music. Jim McGuinness, for example, wrote for

the Bergen County, New Jersey, *Record* (27 Feb. 1998), "*Just Won't Burn* brims with powerful vocals, blistering guitar licks, and a white-hot energy that suggest Tedeschi will be a major blues figure for years to come." Many music journalists were especially impressed at her brave inclusion of John Prine's "Angel from Montgomery," a song most people associated with Bonnie Raitt, whose cover version was widely considered definitive. Later that year, in the wake of *Just Won't Burn*'s success, *Better Days* was reissued.

DEREK TRUCKS

In 1999, while opening for the Southern blues/ rock legends the Allman Brothers Band, Tedeschi met Derek Trucks. His uncle, Butch Trucks, had been a founding member of the Allman Brothers, and Derek, a child prodigy who had learned the guitar at age nine, began touring with the group as a guest artist when he was thirteen. Considered a master slide guitarist, he had formed his own eponymous band in 1996, and in 1999, the year he met Tedeschi, he also became a formal member of the Allman Brothers. "The first time I heard Derek play, I got butterflies in my stomach and I actually cried," Tedeschi told Wayne Bledsoe for the *Knoxville News-Sentinel* (26 Sep. 2003). Despite the difficulties of conflicting tour schedules, the two began dating, traveling to see each other whenever their performance schedules allowed.

THE GRAMMYS

Tedeschi's schedule became even more grueling in 2000, after she was nominated for a Grammy Award in the category of best new artist. She seemed an anomaly in a field that included Britney Spears, Christina Aguilera, Kid Rock, and Macy Gray. Many industry observers expressed shock. "Tedeschi has no music video. She doesn't do Tommy Hilfiger ads or bare her bellybutton on stage," Letta Tayler wrote for New York *Newsday* (20 Feb. 2000). "And she's up against some of the biggest names in pop, stars whose faces are plastered across billboards and whose songs are ubiquitous on radio and MTV."

Some cynically suggested that the National Academy of Recording Arts and Sciences, the organization that oversees the awards, was desperate to prove its credibility by nominating an artist with undeniable musical ability. (For one thing, none of the other nominees was an especially skilled instrumentalist.) Others maintained that the Academy's relatively new voting system was ensuring that skill and artistry, rather than merely sales figures, were being rewarded. Under the overhauled system, the nominees in the four top categories—album of the year, record of the year, song of the year, and best new artist—would be chosen by a blue-ribbon panel of twenty-five industry experts, rather than by the Academy's ten thousand rank-and-file members.

Nevertheless, Christina Aguilera took home the 2000 Grammy for Best New Artist.

OTHER RECORDING WORK

Tedeschi, who married Trucks on December 5, 2001, now faced the difficulties of juggling an increasingly high-profile career with a family life. Their son, Charles Khalil (named for saxophonist Charlie Parker, guitarist Charlie Christian, and writer Khalil Gibran), was born in 2002, and their daughter, Sophia Naima (whose middle name is derived from a John Coltrane ballad), followed in 2004. "The biggest problem that I have, career wise, is finding time to play music and write music when I'm not onstage," she told Jesse Fox Mayshark for the *New York Times* (5 Mar. 2006). "Because I'm Mom from six or seven in the morning up until a few minutes before I go onstage sometimes. So there's really no break."

With her mother-in-law providing childcare, Tedeschi continued touring, and although there were long gaps between albums, she continued to record. In 2002, she released *Wait for Me.* "With classy yet scorching performances and songs infused with roots rock, blues, funk, and even pop, it's a crossover album that oozes with integrity, terrific playing, and a loose yet distinctive direction," Hal Horowitz wrote in an undated review for the All Music Guide website.

Tedeschi next recorded the gospel-inspired cover album *Hope and Desire*, which was released on the Verve label in 2005, and she followed that in 2008 with *Back to the River*, which debuted at number one on the *Billboard* blues chart. The river referred to in the title is the St John's, in Jacksonville, Florida, where she and Trucks live when not on the road. "I've always been near a river it seems, whether this one in Jacksonville, or the North River in Norwell, and both reflect very peaceful, calming places in my heart," she told Jay N. Miller for the *Patriot Ledger* (10 Nov. 2008). Referring to the title track, which she cowrote with guitarist Tony Joe White, she said, "It is a song by someone who's been on the road a bit too long and reflects your desire to get back to your roots, your home, your family, all the more important things in life."

Although *Wait for Me*, *Hope and Desire*, and *Back to the River* were each nominated for a Grammy Award in the category of best contemporary blues album, it was not until Tedeschi and Trucks teamed up that she received one of the coveted statuettes.

COLLABORATION

During the early years of their marriage, Tedeschi and Trucks always toured and recorded separately. "He's got his thing and I've got my thing and they're both important," she told a reporter for the *Lancaster Intelligencer Journal* (31 Oct. 2003). "Both need to be [heard]." They backed an occasional track on each other's albums, and from time to time they performed gigs together as part of a casual band they called the Soul Stew Revival, which also included Trucks's younger brother, Duane, on drums.

That changed in 2010, when they decided to join forces as the Tedeschi Trucks Band. The eleven member group also featured Allman Brothers bassist Oteil Burbridge and his brother, Kofi Burbridge, a flutist/keyboard player from the Derek Trucks Band; drummers J. J. Johnson and Tyler Greenwell; vocalists Mike Mattison of the Derek Trucks Band and Mark Rivers; trombonist Saunders Sermons; saxophonist Kebbi Williams; and trumpet player Maurice Brown. The group's powerful sound and versatility have won over fans of both the Susan Tedeschi Band and the Derek Trucks Band.

The new group's first album, *Revelator*, recorded in their home studio, was released in 2011 and won the Grammy Award for best contemporary blues album of the year. The following year, they released their sophomore effort, a live double album titled *Everybody's Talkin'*. In addition to their work in the studio, they tour widely, often accompanied by Charlie and Sophia. "I see Derek and I at seventy or eighty in rocking chairs, playing guitar together," Tedeschi told Mike Devlin for the Victoria, British Columbia, *Times Colonist* (22 June 2008). "We are doing this for life. It is our life."

SINGING STYLE

Journalists frequently comment about the disparity between Tedeschi's blistering, bluesy voice and her outward "girl-next-door" appearance. She favors a fresh-scrubbed look, often wears flowery sundresses while performing, and plays a guitar decorated with stickers—some of them depicting storybook characters like Winnie the Pooh. Her background also strikes many as an unconventional one for a blues musician. Martin L. Johnson wrote for the *Mountain Xpress* (7 Oct. 2003), a North Carolina–based alternative paper, "While she'll never be able to boast the tortured biography of the musicians she most admires—[bluesman] Dr. John, for instance, took up piano after his 'strummin finger' was shot off in a barroom fight—Tedeschi's talent and voice foretell a lengthy career."

Tedeschi believes that those disparities allow her to make music that transcends expectations. "If your intentions are good, and if the music's good, it doesn't matter if you're playing Indian classical music and you're from San Francisco, or if you're a girl from suburbia playing the blues," she told Joan Anderman for the *Boston Globe* (27 July 2001).

SUGGESTED READING

Anderman, Joan. "Blues to Her Roots." *Boston Globe* 27 July 2001: D14.

Beal, Jim Jr. "Tedeschi Keeps Focus on Music, Not Image." *San Antonio Express-News* 12 May 2000: H14.

Bledsoe, Wayne. "Bliss amid the Blues." *Knoxville News-Sentinel* 26 Sep. 2003: 5.

Devlin, Mike. "Living a Blues Dream." (Victoria, British Columbia) *Times Colonist.* 22 June 2008: B1.

Johnson, Martin L. "Berklee Blues." *Mountain Xpress* 7 Oct. 2003: 41.

Mayshark, Jesse Fox. "Ramblin' Man and Woman, Married With Kids." *New York Times.* New York Times, 5 Mar. 2006. Web. 10 June 2012.

Mcguinness, Jim. "Pure as Her Driven Blues." (Bergen County, New Jersey) *Record* 27 Feb. 1998: 3.

—*Mari Rich*

AFP/Getty Images

Sophie Theallet

Born: 1964
Occupation: Fashion designer

French-born designer Sophie Theallet became an overnight sensation in April 2009 when First Lady Michelle Obama wore one of her dresses to a public function. Theallet first honed her skills while serving as an assistant to Jean Paul Gaultier for five years before spending another decade as Azzedine Alaïa's right-hand woman. Since being catapulted into the international spotlight, she has launched her eponymous clothing line. Theallet credits her success to a simple formula: "I just try to make beautiful clothes done in a beautiful way," she said in an interview posted on the *New York Observer* website (11 Nov. 2008).

EARLY LIFE AND EDUCATION

The youngest of six children, Sophie Theallet was born in 1964 in Bagnères-de-Bigorre, a town in the southwest of France where she grew up with her parents and five older brothers. Theallet, whose father worked as a doctor, credits her family with instilling in her a love of fashion. "I have always wanted to be a fashion designer; I was almost predestined to be one by my history. My father's mother was a fashion illustrator and a very eccentric bourgeoisie woman in the thirties," she said in an interview posted on the *CIRCA Jewels* blog (14 Sep. 2011). "On my mother's side, they were industrials from the South of France and owned a factory that produced high-end wool blankets and dressing gowns."

Theallet was eight years old when she sketched her first collection. Her turning point came six years later, while visiting cousins in London. "[The trip] was a revelation. It was the peak of the punk movement, and I loved music.

At the same time, Vivienne Westwood and Malcolm McLaren really inspired me with their strong fashions," she told Renée Schettler Ross for *France Magazine* (Summer 2010). Upon completing secondary school, Theallet decided to pursue fashion as a career. In 1982 the eighteen-year-old moved to Paris and attended Studio Berçot, a prestigious fashion design school.

APPRENTICESHIPS WITH GAULTIER AND ALAÏA

In 1984, after graduating a year early and winning the National Young Designer Award, Theallet was enlisted to create her own line of clothing for the Paris-based Printemps department store. Although her collection was a success, she decided against launching a fashion label and dedicated herself to learning her craft. She spent the next five years working for the renowned French couturier Jean-Paul Gaultier, whose avant-garde designs have since been worn by some of the world's biggest celebrities, including Madonna, Rihanna, and Beyoncé. During this period, she also worked with the fashion-forward Belgian designer Martin Margiela.

Theallet regarded her apprenticeship with Gaultier as a valuable learning experience. "I learnt from Gaultier to be fearless, to not be scared of your ideas and to have a unique voice," she recalled to Robert Cordero for the *National* (12 July 2009). "With him, I learnt my individual color palette and to create stories."

In 1989, Theallet served as the apprentice for another well-known designer: the Tunisian-born Azzedine Alaïa, dubbed the "King of Cling" for his body-hugging silhouettes. As Alaïa's right-hand woman, she regularly traveled with him and assisted him with his main collection, as well as his accessories and knitwear lines. He also helped enhance her cutting and draping talents. "Fit is very important, the way that clothes are done and cut, the woman has to feel the clothes," she explained to Hillary Latos in an interview for *Resident* magazine (Feb. 2012). "With Alaïa he made my eyes very sharp, and taught me how to do a fitting and defined what fashion is. It was the best experience you can have as a designer, if you want to learn, you learn from the best."

NEW YORK AND COLLABORATION WITH FRANÇOIS NARS

In 1999, a decade after she had started working for Alaïa, Theallet fell in love and moved from France to New York City. Over the next four years, she lived with her boyfriend at the Chelsea Hotel, a historic landmark in downtown Manhattan. Theallet served as a consultant, continuing to collaborate part time with Alaïa while also performing freelance work for other fashion designers, including Diane von Furstenburg and Rachel Roy. Theallet also created cosmetics bags, uniforms, and T-shirts for Nars Cosmetics, a skincare and makeup line established by the celebrity makeup artist François Nars, who eventually sold his cosmetics empire in 2000.

In 2005 Theallet teamed up with Nars to establish Motu Tané, an exclusive, limited quantity line of upscale resort wear named after a French Polynesian island owned by Nars. The idea for the clothing line came from Nars, who was working on a book about Tahiti at the time. "I was really frustrated with the fact that I couldn't find any great fabrics to photograph," he told Marc Karimzadeh for *Women's Wear Daily* (28 June 2005). "I called Sophie and asked her if she could remake some vintage prints . . . and that's when we started talking about creating a collection and a lifestyle."

At the invitation of Nars, Theallet, who also held the title of chief creative officer for the collection, briefly took up residence on the main island of Bora Bora, which Motu Tané is next to, and which is renowned for the luxury resorts that overlook its famous turquoise lagoon. While there, Theallet conducted research on the original Polynesian textile designs for the line, which embodied a chic and jet-setting lifestyle. She also tried out different color combinations, dyed the original fabrics by hand in her kitchen, and incorporated a Polynesian patchwork method that is usually reserved for bed linens. "I try to mix the artisanal feeling of the island with what I learned in couture," she told Karimzadeh for *Women's Wear Daily*.

Launched in mid-October, the eighty-piece collection targeted upscale department stores and specialty boutiques, including Barneys New York and Jeffrey. The Motu Tané featured items made of lightweight and floaty fabrics, such as dresses made of Polynesian silk chiffon that contained details such as raffia halters and shell necklines; dresses with empire waists and gathered sleeves; crinkle chiffon blouses that were Victorian-inspired; and high-end printed T-shirts made of jersey. Other items in the collection included caftans, skirts, and bathing suits, as well as footwear and headgear. Following the launch, Theallet and Nars announced plans to make the line available year-round and to expand into fashion and home accessories.

SPRING 2009 COLLECTION

In 2007, after two years of collaborating with Nars, Theallet made the decision to launch her own collection with the help of her American-born husband, Steven Francoeur, who supervises production and sales. (The two met at a dinner party thrown at Alaïa's home.)

At that time, the couple's apartment, located in the New York neighborhood of Brooklyn Heights, served as Theallet's makeshift studio, while the kitchen table became the hub where Theallet performed her sketching and sewing, with the assistance of only one seamstress. Theallet would subsequently send the patterns that she had drawn for her clothing line to South Korea, Vietnam, and India, where they were printed on textiles and shipped back to her. From there, she would create a prototype of the garment, which she produced at a local factory. Theallet would then conduct a final appraisal of the item for quality control, wrapping, and labeling.

Theallet's clothing line made its runway debut in September 2008, at New York's Spring/Summer Fashion Week, which is considered the unofficial kickoff of the runway season. (It is among the four major fashion shows held in the fashion capitals of the world, including Paris, London, and Milan.) Theallet's ready-to-wear collection drew raves for her attention to feminine detail, which included pin tucks and draping. Cathy Horyn wrote for the *New York Times* (9 Sep. 2008), "The lines of her dresses—shirtwaists in boldly striped cotton, skimmy shifts in tropical prints or vivid orange silk with delicately pleated hems—were as modest as they were feminine."

Equally complementary was Laird Borrelli-Persson for *Style* (9 Sep. 2008), who wrote: "It's well-known that Theallet worked with Azzedine Alaïa for a decade before establishing Motu Tané, a resort line, with François Nars. But it was the influence of the makeup king . . . that was most notable in this extremely summery collection, which featured djellaba shapes, head scarves, crisp cottons circled with bright ribbon stripes, and tropical flowers appliquéd with satin."

Theallet also garnered headlines for her choice to cast only African American models. "I was thinking about colors, and they look amazing on dark skin, so it came naturally," she told Borrelli-Persson. She also said her decision paid homage to the legendary designer Yves Saint Laurent, who had recently passed away; the pioneering couturier was the first to have a show that exclusively featured black models.

RISING PROFILE IN FASHION CIRCLES

Theallet's fall/winter 2009 collection, which debuted in February 2009, drew inspiration from Native American styles. Similar to her spring collection, Theallet showcased a bold color palette and adorned her dresses with feminine details, including pleats, tiers, and pin tucks. Many of her outfits were accessorized with moccasin boots that were jointly designed with footwear manufacturer Sorel.

In April 2009 Theallet further raised her visibility in the fashion industry, when First Lady Michelle Obama donned one of her cotton shirtwaist dresses for a statue presentation ceremony at the US Capitol Visitor Center, in Washington, DC. In August of that year, Theallet was among ten emerging designers vying for the prestigious Council of Fashion Designers of America (CFDA) and Vogue Fashion Fund initiative, which provides the winners with a cash award and a yearlong mentorship from established fashion designers and executives.

A month later, Theallet unveiled her spring/summer 2010 line, which was a clear departure from her earlier collections. "Sophie Theallet is all fired up this season—showcasing, as she did, a collection that drew on a firey palette of oranges, burnt umber, ochre, peach and satiny saffron before moving onto striking color clashes; magenta and egg yolk yellow, egg yolk yellow and teal," according to Jessica Bumpus for *Vogue UK* (14 Sep. 2009). "Low-key and sparing use of print and pattern kept the collection to a safe wardrobe bet—as did wearable silky cami vests tucked into safari skirts, shirt dresses and the occasional frou frou number."

Theallet found herself back in the headlines in November 2009, when she was named recipient of the CFDA/*Vogue* Fashion Fund award. As the winner, Theallet received a cash award totaling two hundred thousand dollars; Oscar de la Renta also agreed to serve as her mentor. In February 2010, Theallet was one of twelve designers who were awarded affordable studio space in the Garment District from the CFDA Fashion Incubator program.

REMAINING A FORCE ON THE RUNWAY

With her winnings, Theallet expanded her fall/winter 2010 line to include knitwear. The ready-to-wear collection, which was also unveiled in February, embraced a bohemian style that revolved around fairy tale themes. "I was thinking about folklore and old children's stories that little girls grow up with around the world," she told *Interview* magazine (2010). "I want to bring back to women the lost memories and the magic we felt when we fell in love with our first princess dress."

Theallet's show, which was attended by renowned fashion editors such as Carine Roitfield and Suzy Menkes, also drew critical praise. "The show started with cozy knitwear but quickly morphed [into] hippy gypsy French floral dresses paired with tassled boots," Raakhee Mirchandani wrote for the *New York Post* (19 Feb. 2010). "The beauty is in the delicate nature of her fabrics, a smooth charmeuse, a sheer georgette and luxe velvets sell her message of bohemian beauty. And the standout piece was the soft pink pleated skirt paired with a red velvet off-the-shoulder top that solidified her place among the designers to watch."

Theallet's spring/summer 2011 line—a nod to Mexican culture—featured models in Frida Kahlo–inspired hairstyles sporting peasant blouses, tiered skirts, traditional lace, and bohemian printed sundresses. Strong women have influenced her subsequent collections. Female outlaw Bonnie Parker, of Bonnie and Clyde fame, served as the inspiration for Theallet's fall/winter 2011 collection, in which her models donned black berets, pencil skirts, printed and chiffon silk dresses, as well as wool coats and tailored suits. "Theallet's vision for winter was an ode to Parisian charm. The opening look, a black knee-length silk pencil skirt paired with a supple cerise deep V-neck blouse complete with beatnik black beret and choker, was a taste of the tough-chic masculine-feminine wares to follow," Indigo Clarke wrote for *Vogue UK* (15 Feb. 2011). "Menswear was also a reference point— a Forties-inspired oversized tailored trouser and suit jacket made an entrance along with a double-breasted silk overcoat, and boxy men's-style overcoat cropped and paired with a gossamer slip of a skirt."

In February 2011, Theallet teamed up with Nine West to launch a line of accessories, including shoes, handbags, and jewelry. Four months later she launched a resort collection that was inspired by the writer F. Scott Fitzgerald's wife, Zelda. Theallet's spring/summer 2012 line made its debut in September 2011 and was influenced by the classic 1969 French film *La Piscine*, a sexy psychological thriller. In her next collection (fall/winter 2012), Theallet presented vintage-inspired clothing, including floor-length gowns, wrap dresses, and slit skirts in a color palette that included red, burgundy, and fuchsia. The dragonfly served as the inspiration for her most recent ready-to-wear collection (spring/summer 2013).

In addition to her own collection, Theallet has also designed uniforms for the employees at New York's Gramercy Park Hotel. Theallet, a recipient of the International Woolmark Award in July 2012, also has plans to expand her company in the future. "I want to make a lifestyle brand, just everything a woman needs," she told Tracey Lomrantz for *Glamour* (1 Feb. 2010). "At Gaultier and Alaïa I learned the accessories, so you will definitely see those at some point, but I can't say when or how for now—it's too soon."

Theallet lives in New York City with Francoeur, with whom she has a son.

SUGGESTED READING

Borrelli-Persson, Laird. "Sophie Theallet: Review Spring 2009." *Style*. Fairchild Fashion Group, 9 Sep. 2008. Web. 14 Sep. 2012.

Bumpus, Jessica. "Sophie Theallet Spring/Summer 2010." *Vogue UK*. Condé Nast Digital, 14 Sep. 2009. Web. 14 Sep. 2012.

Clarke, Indigo. "Sophie Theallet Autumn/Winter 2011–12." *Vogue UK*. Condé Nast Digital, 15 Feb. 2011. Web. 14 Sep. 2012.

Cordero, Robert. "Every Stitch and Detail Has a Purpose." *The National*. Mubadala Development, 12 July 2009. Web. 14 Sep. 2012.

Horyn, Cathy. "Pledging Allegiance." *New York Times*. New York Times, 9 Sep. 2008. Web. 14 Sep. 2012.

Karimzadeh, Marc. "Motu Tané Offering Resort All Year Long." *Women's Wear Daily*. Fairchild Fashion Media, 28 June 2005. Web. 14 Sep. 2012.

Mirchandani, Raakhee. "Sophie Theallet Fashion Week Review." *New York Post*. NYP Holdings, 19 Feb. 2010. Web. 14 Sep. 2012.

"Sophie Theallet's Making All The Right Choices." *Interview*. Brant Publications, 2010. Web. 14 Sep. 2012.

"Très Tree-Lined Chic." *New York Observer*. New York Observer, 11 Nov. 2008. Web. 15 Sep. 2012.

—*Bertha Muteba*

Justin Theroux

Born: August 10, 1971
Occupation: Actor, screenwriter, film director

Although Justin Theroux is best known as a film actor, he is also a stage actor, a screenwriter, and a film director. Theroux got his professional start as an actor in the New York theater world, where he took the stage with the likes of Paul Giamatti and Philip Seymour Hoffman. After a minor role in the psychological thriller *American Psycho*

WireImage

(2000), Theroux appeared—in a bigger role playing a film director—in David Lynch's subversive thriller *Mulholland Drive* (2001); he would later costar in Lynch's dreamlike thriller *Inland Empire* (2006). Theroux has also appeared in big-budget Hollywood movies: he played an Irish gangster in *Charlie's Angels: Full Throttle* (2003) and a detective in *Miami Vice* (2006). He has directed one film, the quirky romantic comedy *Dedication* (2007), and he has written several screenplays, including those for the war-film spoof *Tropic Thunder* (2008) and the superhero action film *Iron Man 2* (2010). The 2006 Broadway jukebox musical *Rock of Ages* is set to be released as a movie in 2012. Theroux is credited as a cowriter of the screenplay. The movie musical stars well-known actors Tom Cruise, Bryan Cranston, Alec Baldwin, Catherine Zeta-Jones, Paul Giamatti, Russell Brand, and many others.

EARLY LIFE AND EDUCATION

The youngest of three children, Justin Paul Theroux was born on August 10, 1971, in Washington, DC. His father, Eugene, was a lawyer, and his mother, Phyllis, was an essayist, columnist, and book author. The marriage ultimately ended in divorce.

Theroux had trouble staying for a long time at any one school until his early teens, when he began his studies at Buxton, a boarding school in Willamstown, Massachusetts. At Buxton, Theroux tried acting for the first time. He liked it enough to want to study it as an undergraduate. At Bennington College in Vermont, he double-majored in drama and the visual arts, and after graduating he entered the prestigious British American Drama Academy, in London, England, where he took part in Shakespearean plays, including *A Midsummer Night's Dream* and *Twelfth Night*.

NEW YORK AND THE THEATER WORLD

Theroux moved to New York City in the early 1990s. Before diving into the theater world, he first made a living as a visual artist, painting murals, billboards, ads, T-shirts, restaurant walls, and whatever else was available. This went on for a few years until the mid-1990s, when he began taking part in plays staged by such respectable New York City companies as the Theatre Workshop and Actors' Playhouse. His first New York acting role, in the spring of 1994, was in the Actors' Playhouse production of *Hide Your Love Away: The Ballad of Brian Epstein*, a play about The Beatles' manager. Theroux's first film role was a minor part in Mary Harron's *I Shot Andy Warhol* (1996), and his first Broadway role, a year later, was in Anton Chekhov's play *The Three Sisters*, which also featured Paul Giamatti, Calista Flockhart, Billy Crudup, Robert Bogue, Jerry Stiller, and Jeanne Tripplehorn. At the time Tripplehorn was dating the actor Ben Stiller—who is also the son of actor Jerry Stiller—and through her, Theroux met Ben Stiller. That contact would prove valuable a few years later.

Meantime, Theroux kept busy, acting in such Off-Broadway plays as *Shopping and F***ing* (1998), with actor Philip Seymour Hoffman, and appearing in episodes of such television shows as *New York Undercover* (1998), *Spin City* (1998), *Ally McBeal* (1998), and *Sex and the City* (1998–99). Theroux reunited with director Mary Harron for *American Psycho* (2000), a film adaptation of the eponymous 1991 book by Bret Easton Ellis. Like the book, the film is a dark, satirical, disturbing psychological thriller about a Manhattan businessman who becomes a serial killer. Christian Bale played the lead role and Theroux, in a minor role, played his business associate. From 2000 to 2001, Theroux played public relations chief Nick Pierce on the television series *The District*, a CBS police drama.

A NEW DIRECTION

Theroux's career took a new direction when he played a self-important, hotshot director in *Mulholland Drive* (2001), a film written and directed by the highly lauded, imaginative filmmaker David Lynch. Lynch—whose work is often strange, layered, cerebral, and occasionally dreamlike and surreal—had previously directed such films as *The Elephant Man* (1980), *Blue Velvet* (1986) and *Twin Peaks: Fire Walk with Me* (1992). *Mulholland Drive* earned Lynch the Palme d'Or, the highest prize at the Cannes Film Festival, as well as an Oscar nomination

for best director. The film can be described as a postmodern thriller or as a nonlinear story of a woman's relationship to Hollywood and celebrity. Theroux, speaking to Gary Arnold for the *Washington Times* (Oct. 12, 2001), summarized the film as follows: "There's a person who lives on the fringe of Hollywood, and you sort of enter the movie midfantasy as she gets to L.A. She gushes over being able to use this beautiful apartment owned by her aunt and encounters only sunny days. . . . Then, when the film turns dark, gets turned on its head, we see things as they really are: The sunshine girl is a desperate, weak-minded hanger-on who lives on the fringes of power and celebrity and everything." That year, in a very different role, Theroux made a brief albeit memorable appearance as Evil DJ in the comedy *Zoolander* (2001), which was cowritten and directed by Ben Stiller, who also starred in the film. *Zoolander*, an offbeat spoof of the world of male modeling, gave Theroux a chance to show off his real-life break-dancing moves.

Despite a burgeoning film career, Theroux continued to occasionally appear in theater productions. In 2002, at the Wilbur Theatre in Boston, he starred in Frank McGuinness's antiwar drama *Observe the Sons of Ulster Marching Towards the Somme*. Directed by Nicholas Martin, the production opened on Broadway in New York in February 2003, a few weeks before the US invasion of Iraq. *Observe the Sons* is about a platoon of Protestant Irish soldiers in the British Army during World War I. The action moves from the barracks to the battle, namely the Battle of the Somme, on July 1, 1916. In a review for the *New York Times* (Feb. 25, 2003), Bruce Weber observed that although "all eight performances are vibrant," Theroux's portrayal of the young soldier Kenneth Pyper was "especially good." That same year, in yet another very different role, Theroux costarred in the big-budget action-comedy film *Charlie's Angels: Full Throttle* (2003). He played Seamus, an Irish gangster seeking revenge because one of the Angels had once turned him over to the authorities. Also that year Theroux joined the cast of *Six Feet Under*, a dark, critically acclaimed HBO drama-comedy show about a family that runs a funeral home. He appeared in eight episodes as Brenda Chenowith's neighbor Joe. He last appeared on the series in 2004, after which he got involved in more obscure projects, with small roles in the comedies *Strangers with Candy* (2005) and *The Baxter* (2005). The summer of 2006 saw the release of the big-budget action movie *Miami Vice* (2006). Directed by Michael Mann and starring Jamie Foxx and Colin Farrell, the movie was a remake of the 1980s series of the same name, which Mann had produced. Theroux, playing Detective Larry Zito, had a fairly small role in the movie.

Later that year Theroux reunited with director David Lynch for the film *Inland Empire* (2006), which, like *Mulholland Drive*, also focused on the world of Hollywood filmmaking, but unlike that film, was even more fragmentary, nonlinear, surreal, and symbolic. In *Inland Empire*, Nikki Grace (Laura Dern) is offered a lead role in a film that is being directed by Kingsley Stewart (Jeremy Irons). The film, titled "On High in Blue Tomorrows," had previously stopped production because the two main actors were murdered. For Nikki, the line between "On High in Blue Tomorrows" and reality soon becomes blurred and liquid, particularly when she begins an affair with Devon (Theroux), her costar in the Kingsley production. The dreamlike and hallucinatory moods of each scene set the aesthetic for Lynch's film, which received many positive reviews, although there were plenty of mixed and negative ones, too. In a mostly negative review for the *New Yorker* (Dec. 11, 2006, online), Richard Brody wrote, "When Lynch sticks with his straightforward view of how things are done in Hollywood, the film briefly comes alive as a trenchant, nuanced report from the front. But he also shoehorns in lugubrious scenes from Poland, a sitcom apartment inhabited by people wearing rabbit heads, and mysterious appearances and disappearances, and jumbles the strands together as a pretentious puzzle. The resulting grab bag of Lynchian motifs and methods . . . quickly devolves into self-parody." But there were plenty of positive, glowing reviews, such as one offered by Manohla Dargis for the *New York Times* (Dec. 6, 2006). Dargis observed that *Inland Empire* is "one of the few films I've seen this year that deserve to be called art," but she qualified her praise by pointing out that the three-hour film "has the power of nightmares and at times the more prosaic letdown of self-indulgence." She then concluded, "*Inland Empire* isn't a film to love. It is a work to admire, to puzzle through, to wrestle with. Its pleasures are fugitive, even frustrating. The first time I saw it, I was repulsed by the shivers of Lynchian sadism, a feeling doubtless informed by my adoration of the far more approachable, humanistic *Mulholland Drive*. On second viewing, though, *Inland Empire* seemed funnier, more playful and somehow heartfelt." Theroux's role in the film, although not as prominent as that of costar Laura Dern, was still substantial, and it increased his reputation as an actor with immense power to transform himself.

BEHIND THE CAMERA

Theroux's next role would be behind the camera. The film *Dedication*, which premiered in January 2007 at the Sundance Film Festival, marked Theroux's directorial debut. He took the directorial job after it was offered to him by Plum Pictures. In the summer of 2007 the film came out

in the United States in a very limited release. *Dedication* is the story of Henry (Billy Crudup), a pessimistic children's book author who cares little for children. When his illustrator and only friend Rudy, played by Tom Wilkinson, finds himself in a losing battle for his health, Henry is forced to use another illustrator. The new illustrator is a pretty, young woman named Lucy, played by Mandy Moore. Henry and Lucy initially appear to be a complete mismatch, and the film progresses like a quirky romantic comedy. *Dedication* received few reviews, and most were mixed. In a generally good review for *Screen International* (Jan. 26, 2007, online), Patrick Z. McGavin wrote, "It's an extreme work in many respects, confrontational, occasionally mean-spirited. . . . The movie's too feverish and knotty to achieve widespread appeal, though it is bound to resonate with contemporary hipsters and urban men and women that identify with its portrait of artistic seriousness. The excellent cast, headed by Billy Crudup and Mandy Moore, supported by excellent work from Tom Wilkinson, Bob Balaban and Dianne Wiest, lifts this above the fray." McGavin then concluded his review by making the following case: "As its title suggests *Dedication* is meant to inflame, to make you feel uncomfortable and unsettled. The script and direction are sometimes prickly and difficult to take. The lack of polish, the raggedness of the material, underscores its faults though it also makes it distinctive and difficult to forget." The soundtrack of the film was provided by the experimental rock band Deerhoof, whom Theroux had asked to contribute.

A NEW CHALLENGE: SCREENWRITING

Having acted and directed, Theroux then took on a new challenge, being a screenwriter. With Ben Stiller, he cowrote the big-budget comedy *Tropic Thunder* (2008). Starring and directed by Stiller, the movie is a satirical look at big-budget Hollywood movies, which often involve big egos, convoluted negotiations, and extended periods of shooting. In *Tropic Thunder* Stiller plays Tugg Speedman, an action hero trying to do a more "serious" film; Robert Downey Jr. plays Kurk Lazarus, an Australian actor so committed to the role of playing a black man that he undergoes a skin-coloring procedure; and Jack Black plays Jeff Portnoy, a comedian who is also trying to change his image—that of a bloated, drug-addicted goofball—by taking on a new kind of film. Steve Coogan plays Damien Cockburn, the film's director, who decides that the best way to shoot the movie would be to drop off his actors in the Vietnam jungle and film them with hidden cameras. Then all goes wrong when the actors discover a heroin-making site and are taken captive—without realizing that the situation is all too real. Tugg Speedman thinks it is all some kind of improvisational-acting challenge and is convinced that it is all being captured by hidden cameras. *Tropic Thunder* received very mixed reviews, striking some critics as tasteless and some as quite funny. Manohla Dargis for the *New York Times* (Aug. 12, 2008) observed that Stiller, as a director, has "little sense of modulation." In other words, he never knows how to tone it down, so everything is exaggerated. By contrast, Peter Bradshaw for the London *Guardian* (Sep. 18, 2008) gave it four stars out of five and concluded, "*Tropic Thunder* isn't a masterpiece, but it is supremely effective entertainment."

Theroux next penned the screenplay for *Iron Man 2* (2010), the sequel to the 2008 superhero movie *Iron Man*, which also starred Robert Downey Jr. *Iron Man 2*, despite a mixed reception from critics, became one of the highest-grossing films of 2010. In the film there is plenty of trouble for Tony Stark, who, in front of the international press, admits to being Iron Man. Justin Hammer, a major rival, is planning an army of specialized suits; Congress expects Stark to consent to being a part of the US military system; and in Russia, Ivan Vanko (Mickey Rourke) seeks revenge on Stark, believing that Stark's father did his own father terribly wrong. For the *Chicago Sun-Times* (May 5, 2010, online), Robert Ebert wrote, "*Iron Man 2* is a polished, high-octane sequel, not as good as the original but building once again on a quirky performance by Robert Downey Jr." He added, "The superhero genre doesn't necessarily require good acting, but when it's there (as in *Iron Man* and *The Dark Knight*), that takes it up a level. Downey here gives us a Tony Stark who is cockier and more egotistical than ever. Or, and here's the key, he seems to be." On that note, Anthony Lane for the *New Yorker* (May 10, 2010, online) observed, "One of the pleasures of Jon Favreau's movie, with its reams of alert dialogue by Justin Theroux, is that it manages to celebrate a full-time narcissist without sucking up to him or letting him shrink into a pest."

Despite his additional role as a screenwriter, Theroux continued to act. In 2008 he appeared as John Hancock in two episodes of the seven-part HBO mini-series *John Adams*, which starred Paul Giamatti. Based on a book by historian David McCullough, *John Adams* went on to win multiple Emmy Awards. Two years later Theroux appeared in five episodes of the NBC television series *Parks and Recreation*, which stars Amy Poehler of *Saturday Night Live* fame. That year he also played a creepy wizard, a minor role, in the fantasy-comedy film *Your Highness* (2010), which starred Danny McBride, James Franco, Natalie Portman, and Zooey Deschanel. The movie was both a commercial and critical failure—panned by nearly all the critics.

According to the *New York* magazine (Dec. 12, 2011), Theroux is working on a half-hour cartoon-comedy program for the Fox television network. The show takes place in New York City and features a curmudgeon as the lead character.

PERSONAL LIFE

Theroux lives in Manhattan. Although he has received critical recognition for his work, particularly his acting, he started receiving a lot more press in June 2011 after beginning a romantic relationship with the actress Jennifer Aniston.

SUGGESTED READING

Adalian, Josef. "Justin Theroux to Create Cartoon for Fox." *New York*. New York Media, 12 Dec. 2011. Web. 10 Jan. 2012.

Arnold, Gary. "Smoke and Mirrors." *Washington Times* 12 Oct. 2001: B5. Print.

Bradshaw, Peter. "Tropic Thunder." *Guardian* [London] 18 Sep. 2008, Film & Music: 9. Print.

Brody, Richard. "Inland Empire." *New Yorker*. New Yorker, 11 Dec. 2006. Web. 10 Jan. 2012.

Dargis, Manohla. "The Trippy Dream Factory of David Lynch." *New York Times* 6 Dec. 2006: E1. Print.

---. "War May Be Hell, but Hollywood Is Even Worse." *New York Times* 12 Aug. 2008: E1. Print.

Ebert, Roger. "Iron Man 2: Slick Sequel Sports a Sick Superhero." *Chicago Sun-Times*. Sun-Times Media, 5 May 2010. Web. 10 Jan. 2012.

Lane, Anthony. "Fighting Form." *New Yorker*. New Yorker, 10 May 2010. Web. 10 Jan. 2012.

McGavin, Patrick Z. "Dedication." *Screen Daily*. Screen International, 26 Jan. 2007. Web. 10 Jan. 2012.

Weber, Bruce. "Eight Men Facing the Horrors of the Battlefield." *New York Times* 25 Feb. 2003: E3. Print.

SELECTED WORKS

American Psycho, 2000; *Mulholland Drive*, 2001; *Charlie's Angels: Full Throttle*, 2003; *Strangers with Candy*, 2005; *Inland Empire*, 2006; *Miami Vice*, 2006; *Dedication*, 2007; *Tropic Thunder*, 2008; *Iron Man 2*, 2010; *Your Highness*, 2010

—*Dmitry Kiper*

Tim Thomas

Born: April 15, 1974
Occupation: Hockey player with the Boston Bruins

"I do play differently than just about anybody in the world," the Boston Bruins goaltender Tim Thomas told Fluto Shinzawa for the *Boston Herald* (30 Jan. 2011). Thomas was referring to his highly unorthodox goaltending style, which has come to be known as the "battle-fly"—an acrobatic, aggressive variation on the traditional butterfly style of goaltending in which goalies drop to their knees and spread out their legs to block shot attempts. "When a forward tiptoes into his crease, Thomas doesn't hesitate to chop him with his stick or step around him to get a better view of the play," writes Shinzawa. "If a shooter slashes into his shot, Thomas often employs a backstroke-like swim move to foil any second shot—he's assuming he'll stop the first—that might be coming. When a stray puck bobbles into his view and teammates are nowhere in sight, Thomas will go into a full swan dive to nudge it out of dangerous situations."

Similar to his unconventional style, Thomas followed an unorthodox career path. He was drafted in the ninth round of the 1994 National Hockey League (NHL) Entry Draft after his freshman season at the University of Vermont (UVM). Thomas opted to finish his education, and after graduating from UVM in 1997, he spent a combined eight seasons playing in the minor leagues and Europe before emerging in 2005 at the age of thirty-one as a regular NHL starter with the Boston Bruins. Since that debut, Thomas has established himself as one of the best goaltenders in the league, and he has helped the Bruins establish themselves as a perennial playoff contender.

Thomas has been named to four All-Star teams (2008, 2009, 2011, and 2012) and won the Vezina Trophy as the league's best goaltender in 2009 and 2011. During the 2010–11 season, he broke the NHL regular-season record for save percentage (.938), and he led the Bruins to their first Stanley Cup title in thirty-nine years. In addition to the Vezina Trophy, Thomas won the NHL's Conn Smythe Trophy as the Most Valuable Player (MVP) of the 2011 Stanley Cup playoffs. Commenting on his long journey to NHL stardom, Thomas said, as quoted by Jeff Z. Klein for the *New York Times* (25 Aug. 2011), "You can do whatever you want if you're willing to work long enough and hard enough at it. It's kind of the American dream, so to speak, but a lot of people have kind of given up on that."

EARLY LIFE AND EDUCATION

The eldest of the two sons born to Tim Thomas Sr. and Kathy Thomas, Timothy James Thomas was born on April 15, 1974, in Flint, Michigan, about sixty miles northwest of Detroit. He and his younger brother Jake grew up in the Flint suburb of Davison and were raised in a close-knit, working-class family. Thomas's father worked as a car salesman in and around the Flint area, but he often struggled to make ends meet due to the declining automobile industry. "We were never poor poor, but we were never rich either," his father told Klein. "We always paid the bills."

NHLI via Getty Images

Thomas started playing hockey at an early age, beginning with a foam stick and ball. As a young boy, Thomas idolized the Detroit Red Wings' longtime captain Steve Yzerman and the American goaltender Jim Craig. Craig is best known for being the backstop of the US Olympic hockey team, which defeated the Soviet Union in 1980 to win the gold medal. Thomas told David Shoalts for the Toronto, Canada, *Globe and Mail* (26 Jan. 2009), "When I was a kid . . . my goal was to play in the Olympics. The 1980 Olympics made a huge impact on me, being from the US, I didn't even think about the NHL until maybe high school."

Thomas began playing on youth hockey teams at the age of five, and he further honed his skills in pickup "garage" games with his father and his uncles who quickly recognized his athletic talent and his competitiveness. His father would leave him for hours at a time at an ice rink in Flint, where Thomas developed his skating skills. Tim's Uncle Bill noted to Klein that Tim was already skating pirouettes and doing leg saves at an age when other children were still learning how to skate. Both of Thomas's parents played a major role in his development as a hockey player. They sold their wedding rings to ensure that he would be able to attend a goalie camp as a youth.

In 1989, Thomas enrolled as a sophomore at Davison High School, where he played football, hockey, and baseball. As a goalie on Davison's varsity hockey team, he began honing the unorthodox, sprawling style that he would later become famous for. Thomas first garnered attention as a goaltender during his junior year when he made sixty-two saves in a regional play-off game that lasted six overtimes. During his senior year, he became the first player in Davison history to earn First-Team All-State honors. However, college and professional scouts ignored Thomas after he graduated due to his unimposing size— he stands just five feet eleven—and the fact that he did not play on any elite junior or travel teams. As a result, he spent one season playing junior hockey with the now defunct Lakeland Jets of the North American Hockey League (NAHL). After proving his worth with the Jets during the 1992–93 season, Thomas accepted a hockey scholarship to the University of Vermont (UVM) in Burlington.

Thomas spent four seasons as the starting goaltender for the UVM Catamounts, during which he established himself as one of the best collegiate goaltenders in the nation. After a superb freshman campaign in 1993–94, he was selected by the Quebec Nordiques in the ninth round as the 217th overall pick of the 1994 NHL Entry Draft. Instead of signing with the Nordiques, he chose to resume his hockey career at UVM in the Eastern College Athletic Conference (ECAC), where he earned a number of accolades. Thomas earned NCAA All-American and All-ECAC First-Team honors during his sophomore and junior seasons. He was named ECAC Goaltender of the Year in 1995–96 after posting a record of 26 wins and 7 losses with a 2.34 GAA (goals against average), a .924 save percentage, and three shutouts. Thomas helped lead the Catamounts to their first-ever NCAA Frozen Four in 1996. His teammates, Martin St. Louis and Eric Perrin, went on to careers in the NHL. Thomas graduated from UVM in 1997 after compiling a career record of 81–43–15, with a 2.70 GAA, and nine shutouts in 140 games.

LONG ROAD TO THE NHL

After concluding his career with the Catamounts, Thomas participated in a professional training camp for the NHL's Colorado Avalanche, but he was released from the team before the start of the 1997–98 season. The Avalanche had obtained Thomas's rights in 1995 when the Quebec Nordiques franchise relocated to Denver, Colorado. At the time, many coaches and scouts were unconvinced that Thomas's unorthodox goaltending style would carry over to the NHL. Undaunted, Thomas joined the minor leagues, playing a combined seven games with the Birmingham Bulls and Houston Aeros of the East Coast Hockey League (ECHL) and the International Hockey League. He then travelled to Finland to play for HIFK, a Finnish team based in Helsinki and part of SM-liiga, one of the top professional hockey leagues in Europe. Thomas proved his detractors wrong by posting a record

of 13–4–1, with a 1.61 GAA, and a .947 save percentage in eighteen games. He enjoyed even greater success in the playoffs, going 9–0 with a 1.52 GAA and leading HIFK to the 1998 Finnish championship.

During the summer of 1998, Thomas returned to North America. He signed a free-agent deal with the NHL's Edmonton Oilers, who assigned him to the Hamilton Bulldogs, their American Hockey League (AHL) affiliate in Hamilton, Ontario, Canada. Thomas only appeared in fifteen games with the Bulldogs before returning to Europe to close out the 1998–99 season with HIFK, where he went 8–3–3 with a 2.23 GAA in fourteen games. For the 1999–2000 season, Thomas joined the Detroit Vipers of the IHL, where he posted a mediocre 10–21–3 record with 3.53 GAA in thirty-six games. He returned to Europe for the following two seasons, playing with AIK of Sweden's Elite League in 2000–01 and with the Finish club Oulun Kärpät in the SM-liiga in 2001–02.

In the summer of 2002, Thomas signed as a free agent with the Boston Bruins of the NHL. The team assigned him to their AHL Rhode Island affiliate, the Providence Bruins, which is also known as the "Baby B's." Thomas spent most of the 2002–03 season with the Baby B's, where he earned a record of 18–12–5 with a 2.87 GAA and a .906 save percentage in thirty-five games. That season he earned three separate call-ups to the Boston club, making his NHL debut with the Bruins on October 19, 2002, against the Edmonton Oilers and earning his first career win after recording thirty-one saves on thirty-four shots in a 4–3 Bruins' victory. Thomas appeared in three other games with the Bruins in 2002–03, finishing with a 3–1–0 record. Thomas played the entire 2003–04 season with the Baby B's, dominating with nine shutouts and a 1.84 GAA in forty-three games.

Despite experiencing one of his best professional seasons, Thomas lost his opportunity for a regular NHL goaltending job in 2004–05 due to the NHL lockout, which led to the cancellation of the entire season and lasted a total of 310 days before ending in July 2005. During this time, Thomas returned to Europe for the fifth time in his career and spent the 2004–05 season with the Finnish club Jokerit in the SM-liiga. He would go on to post some of the best numbers of his career as he led the league in wins (34), GAA (1.58), games played (54), and shutouts (15), the latter of which set a league record. He also posted an 8–4 record with a 1.83 GAA in twelve play-off games to help lead Jokerit to runner-up status in the 2005 Finnish championship.

At the end of the season, Thomas received the Lasse Oksanen Trophy, which is awarded annually by SM-liiga to the league's best player. Commenting on his MVP season in Finland, Thomas said, as noted by Steve Conroy for the

Boston Herald (1 Mar. 2006), "I really thought that the [NHL] lockout was going to hurt my career. But I was able to turn a negative into a huge positive."

Thomas was then lured back to the United States after the Bruins promised him an opportunity to compete for the team's backup goaltending job. Determined to give the NHL one last shot, Thomas signed a one-year deal with the Bruins for the league minimum, then worth $450,000. "I thought I was finally getting my chance," he told David Shoalts. "I told them I was only coming back with a one-way contract and a chance to play in the NHL." Those hopes were dashed after training camp when the Bruins sent Thomas back down to the AHL for a third stint with the Providence Baby B's.

Disappointed but undeterred, Thomas opened the 2005–06 season playing with the Baby B's, where he had a .923 save percentage in twenty-six games. In January 2006, he was called back up to the Bruins after both Raycroft and Toivonen suffered injuries. Thomas stepped in as the Bruins' starting goaltender and took advantage of the opportunity, finishing with a 12–13–7 record, a 2.77 GAA, a .917 save percentage, and his first NHL shutout. He told Luke DeCock, writing for the Raleigh, North Carolina, *News & Observer* (10 Feb. 2008), "I always believed I had the talent to play in the NHL and play at a high level in the NHL. But at that point in my career . . . I actually pretty much made peace with the fact it was never going to happen."

For his gutsy regular-season performance, Thomas was honored with the Bruins' Seventh Player Award, which is presented each year by Bruins fans to the player who far exceeds expectations. During that off-season, the Bruins signed Thomas to a three-year contract extension.

CAREER WITH THE BOSTON BRUINS

Thomas began the 2006–07 season backing up Hannu Toivonen, who had been named the starter after the Bruins traded Raycroft to the Toronto Maple Leafs for the Finnish goaltending prospect Tuukka Rask. Thomas was given the starting job after Toivonen struggled early in the season. In 2006–07, Thomas had a .905 save percentage in a career-high sixty-six games and compiled a record of 30–29–4, becoming the first Bruins goaltender to reach thirty wins since the 2001–02 season. Thomas received the Bruins' Seventh Player Award for the second consecutive season, and he became the first goalie in franchise history to win the award more than once. Despite his solid play, the Bruins were mostly inconsistent throughout the season and missed out on the playoffs for the second straight year after finishing last in the Northeast Division with a 35–41–6 record. Dave Lewis, the team's first-year head coach, was fired and replaced by Claude Julien, who had most recently coached the New Jersey Devils.

During the 2007–08 off-season, the Bruins traded Toivonen to the St. Louis Blues and acquired goaltender Manny Fernandez from the Minnesota Wild. As a result, Thomas was again relegated to a backup role, this time behind Fernandez. However, it was while filling in for an injured Fernandez that Thomas would emerge as the Bruins' clear-cut starter and finished fourth in the league in save percentage (.921) and posted a record of 28–19–6 in fifty-seven games. He earned his first career All-Star selection, backing up Devils goaltender Martin Brodeur in the 2008 NHL All-Star Game in Atlanta, Georgia. Thomas was credited as the winning goalie for the Eastern Conference, and he helped propel the Bruins into the playoffs for the first time since the 2003–04 season. In the 2008 Stanley Cup playoffs, the Bruins advanced to the Eastern Conference quarterfinals where they lost to the Montreal Canadians in seven games.

In 2008–09, Thomas not only settled in as the Bruins' starting goaltender, he also established himself as one of the best in the NHL. During the 2008–09 season, he led the league in GAA (2.10) and save percentage (.933) and earned a career-high thirty-six wins and five shutouts. He was named to his second consecutive All-Star team and earned the most wins in the Eastern Conference for the second straight year. In April 2009, the Bruins signed Thomas to a four-year contract extension worth $20 million.

After sweeping the Canadians in the first round of the playoffs that year, the Bruins lost to the Carolina Hurricanes in the Eastern Conference semifinals. In eleven playoff games, Thomas posted a league-best 1.85 GAA, a .935 save percentage, and one shutout. In June 2009 Thomas received the Vezina Trophy, awarded annually to the NHL's best goaltender. He also shared the William M. Jennings Trophy with teammate Manny Fernandez for allowing the fewest team goals (196) during the regular season.

During the 2009–10 season, Thomas's performance was hampered by a left hip injury. The season also saw the emergence of Bruins' rookie goaltender Tuukka Rask, who replaced Fernandez as the team's backup. In forty-three games, Thomas compiled a record of 17–18–8 with a 2.56 GAA, a .915 save percentage, and five shutouts.

Thomas's otherwise down season was highlighted by his selection to the US men's hockey team for the 2010 Winter Olympics, held in Vancouver, Canada. He served as the backup goaltender for Ryan Miller on the silver-medal-winning US squad that lost to Canada 3–2 in a dramatic overtime final. (Thomas has also represented the United States in six world championships: 1995, 1996, 1998, 1999, 2005, and 2008.)

Upon returning from the Olympic break in early March, Thomas served mostly as a backup to Rask who led the NHL in GAA (1.97) and save percentage (.931) and guided the Bruins back to the Eastern Conference semifinals, where they lost to the Philadelphia Flyers in seven games.

RECORD-BREAKING SEASON

One week after the Bruins lost to the Flyers in May 2010, Thomas underwent surgery to repair a torn labrum in his left hip. After dedicating the entire 2010–11 off-season to rehabilitation and training, he returned to the ice hoping to reclaim his job as the Bruins' starting goaltender. "I was prepared that Tuukka was going to get a good opportunity," he explained to Stephen Harris for the *Boston Herald* (20 Jan. 2011). "But I also knew that I was going to get some opportunity. I was trying to be ready to take advantage of it when I did get to play." Thomas went on to have one of the best goaltending seasons in NHL history. He set an NHL regular-season record with a league-best .938 save percentage, breaking Dominik Hašek's mark of .937 in 1998–99. He led the league with a 2.00 GAA while earning nine shutouts and thirty-five wins, and he also set a franchise record by opening the season with eight consecutive victories. He received his third consecutive All-Star selection and became the only goaltender in NHL history to win three straight All-Star games.

The Bruins finished the 2010–11 season with a division-best record of 46–25–11, advancing to the play-offs for the fourth consecutive year. After defeating the Montreal Canadians, Philadelphia Flyers, and Tampa Bay Lightning in the first three rounds of the play-offs, the team advanced to their first Stanley Cup Finals since 1990. Facing the Vancouver Canucks, the Bruins took the series in seven games to capture their first Stanley Cup in thirty-nine years. Thomas was awarded the Conn Smythe Trophy as the play-off MVP after leading all goaltenders with sixteen wins, a GAA of 1.98, and a save percentage of .940. He finished with a record 738 saves during the 2011 postseason. At thirty-seven, Thomas became the oldest player and second American-born player to win the Conn Smythe Trophy. In June 2011, he was awarded his second Vezina Trophy in three seasons, making him the second goalie in history (after the Philadelphia Flyers' Bernie Parent in 1974–75) to win the Conn Smythe Trophy, a Stanley Cup, and a Vezina Trophy in the same season.

CONTROVERSY

Thomas returned as the Bruins' starting goaltender during the 2011–12 season, and in January 2012, he found himself at the center of controversy when he chose not to attend the team's White House visit with President Barack Obama, which was held in honor of the team's 2011 Stanley Cup championship. Thomas later issued a public statement, attributing his decision to political and ideological reasons.

On January 29, 2012, Thomas broke his own record by winning his fourth consecutive All-Star game, going 3–4 with a 2.14 GAA and a .923 save percentage. He finished the season strong with a 35–19–1 record, a 2.36 GAA, and a .923 save percentage. The team qualified for their fifth consecutive playoffs but lost to the Washington Capitals in the first round of a seven-game series.

In late May of 2012, the Bruins announced that Thomas was taking time off and would not play during the final year of his four-year contract. According to Bruins general manager Peter Chiarelli, Thomas cited "fatigue and the desire to spend time with his family" as the reasons for his decision, but Chiarelli also told Fluto Shinzawa for the *Boston Globe* (2 June 2012) that "it would be hard for a 38-year-old not to play and come back [to professional hockey]." Thomas then waived the no-trade clause in his contract, which opened the door for Bruins management to trade Thomas and release their obligation to pay out the remainder of his contract. In July, however, Thomas was once again at the center of controversy when he publically supported fast-food restaurant owner Dan Cathy and his statements denouncing same-sex marriage. This left many sports critics questioning whether trading the two-time Vezina Trophy winner would be smooth and easy for the Bruins.

PERSONAL LIFE

Thomas lives in the Boston area with his wife Melissa, their daughters Kiley and Kelsey, and son Keegan. He conducts youth and adult hockey camps across the United States during the offseason and recently established the Tim Thomas Foundation, a charitable organization that aims to help people struggling with illness as well as victims of natural disasters.

SUGGESTED READING

"Bruins' Tim Thomas Has Had Season to Remember." *PostStar*. Associated Press, 15 June 2011. Web. 17 Aug. 2012.

Klein, Jeff Z. "A Jubilant Return Home." *New York Times* 25 Aug. 2011: B10. Print.

Olshansky, Elliot. "NHL Trade Rumors: How Does Tim Thomas Chick-Fil-A Facebook Post Affect Trade Possibilities?" *SWR*. Sports World Report, 27 July 2012. Web. 17 August 2012.

Shinzawa, Fluto. "Thomas Has Taken His Unorthodox Style on a Long Journey to NHL Stardom." *Boston Globe* 30 Jan. 2011: 1. Print.

—*Chris Cullen*

Alexis Thompson

Born: February 10, 1995
Occupation: Professional golfer

Alexis Thompson made headlines on the international golf scene in 2007, when at age twelve she became the youngest player to qualify for the US Women's Open. Three years later, she decided to turn professional. "I just thought my game was ready, and I wanted to take my game to the next level and play against the best in the world," Thompson told Bob Cohn for the *Pittsburgh Tribune-Review* (7 July 2010, online). In 2011, she had a record-setting victory at the Navistar Classic, becoming the youngest Ladies Professional Golf Association (LPGA) tournament winner. Also that year, the sixteen-year-old Thompson became the second-youngest winner of the Ladies European Tour (LET) and gained official membership to the LPGA Tour.

EARLY LIFE

The youngest of three children, Alexis "Lexi" Thompson was born on February 10, 1995, to Scott and Judy Thompson in Coral Springs, Florida. Her father is an engineer and her mother is an insurance claims processor. Thompson has two older brothers, Nicholas and Curtis.

Thompson hails from an athletic family. Her mother was a competitive golfer in high school and junior college, and her father is a former baseball player. Both Nicholas and Curtis briefly played in Little League baseball before they were introduced to golf by their father, a self-taught recreational player. "Golf was never a chore. It was never, 'You have to go hit two pyramids of balls today at the range.' Scott always made it fun, with games, closest-to-the-pin contests," Judy Thompson told Randall Mell for the Golf Channel (15 Nov. 2011, online). "Scott never read a golf book or a golf magazine. It's all come from the heart." Nicholas was the first of the three competitive siblings to embrace golf and pursue a professional career in the sport.

A year after Thompson was born, her family moved to a home in Coral Springs that was located by the private golf course of the Tournament Players Club at Eagle Trace. Thompson picked up a golf club at an early age. "I started off when I was five," she told Michelle King for *Seventeen* (6 Sep. 2011, online). "I have two older brothers and they're really good, so that's what got me into it. I feel a competitive element with them." The siblings would often challenge each other to chipping and putting contests to get out of doing household chores.

THE JUNIOR CIRCUIT

Thompson first began competing in tournaments at the age of six, when she entered the girls seven-and-under division at the 2001 Doral-Publix

Getty Images

Junior Golf Classic, a prestigious national tournament held each December. Thompson shot a two-round total of 90, finishing in third place—eleven shots back of the winner, Marissa Kay. "I remember it distinctly," Judy Thompson told Mick Elliott for *espnW* (15 Nov. 2011, online). "My husband put her in Doral and someone beat her by ten shots. She was terrible. [Scott] saw the ability of the other players and said, 'I have one year to get her better.' . . . She was so determined. They went out to practice every day. She took it on."

A seven-year-old Thompson made her debut at the US Kids Golf World Championship in 2002. She came in third place, in the girls eight-and-under category, finishing the tournament with a score of 63—nine shots back of the winner. Thompson fared significantly better in December of that year, when she made her second consecutive appearance at the Doral-Publix Junior Golf Classic. She captured her first title, with a total score of 61. In August of the following year, Thompson claimed the second junior title of her career, at the 2003 US Kids Golf World Championship, again in the girls eight-and-under division. With a final score of 91, she finished four strokes ahead of the second-place finisher. Her older brother Curtis came in third at the same event, in the boys age ten group. Thompson ended 2003 on a high note, successfully defending her title at the Doral-Publix Junior Golf Classic. She continued to excel on the junior circuit in 2004. Following her first-place finish in the girls eight-and-under division at the Jekyll Island Cup, a regional, invitation-only tournament, Thompson earned an invitation to participate in the US Kids Golf World Championship. She advanced to the girls age nine group and won the event in that category.

BREAKING RECORDS

In 2005, Thompson made her second consecutive appearance at the Jekyll Island Cup, where she was the runner-up in the girls age nine group. Thompson garnered attention in May of that year, when she entered a local qualifying event for the 2005 US Women's Open Championship. At age ten, she was the youngest player ever to file for entry to that event. Amateur female golfers are eligible to compete for a spot in the US Women's Open either by receiving an exemption or by competing successfully in both local and sectional qualifying tournaments. Thompson's bid for entry fell short. She had scored a 77 and came within one shot of advancing to a playoff to claim one of the four remaining sectional spots. The decision by Thompson's parents to enter her in the qualifier drew criticism from fellow competitor Dede Cusimano, who questioned her ability to handle the pressure. "I think players need to be a little older to try this because of the level of maturity. The first six holes, she was crying and stomping off greens and that's a distraction," Cusimano told Randall Mell for the South Florida *Sun Sentinel* (20 May 2005, online).

Undaunted by negative comments on her bid for the US Women's Open, Thompson started competing on the Florida Junior Tour (FJT), often playing against high-school-aged junior golfers between thirteen and eighteen years old. In September 2005, she earned a special exemption to play in her first FJT event. The ten-year-old shot a total of 146 to finish second in the girls thirteen to fifteen age group, only two strokes behind first place. Thompson earned her first FJT title at an event that took place in October at the PGA (Professional Golfers' Association) Golf Club. Playing under another special exemption, she won the girls age thirteen to fifteen division. A month later, Thompson claimed her second FJT title. She ended the year with a fifth-place finish in the FJT girls sixteen to eighteen division.

Thompson enjoyed ongoing success on the Florida Junior Tour in 2006, particularly in the girls thirteen to fifteen age group. Her first win of the year came in January. Thompson erased a two-stroke deficit and scored a 153 to finish one stroke ahead of the runner-up. That same month, she tied for third at the 2006 Dixie Amateur Championship. In February, the eleven-year-old Thompson won a two-stroke victory at an FJT event. She added a fifth FJT title to her collection at a tournament two months later, finishing first by a two-stroke margin.

In 2006, Thompson also competed in six FJT events in the girls sixteen to eighteen age group. She came in third place at two of these events. Her lone victory in the sixteen to eighteen division—and sixth overall FJT title—came in November. A month later, Thompson made headlines at the Doral-Publix Junior Golf Classic. The eleven-year-old won in the girls sixteen to eighteen division, claiming her third Doral title. She was the first player in the tournament's twenty-five year history to receive permission to compete three age groups ahead of her peers. A week after the Doral victory, Thompson placed eighth at the Junior Orange Bowl International Golf Championship, which is considered among the world's most prestigious junior golf tournaments.

At the Dixie Amateur Championship in January 2007, Thompson won an impressive eight-stroke victory. She began working with renowned golf instructor Jim McLean that year and also started homeschooling. In April, Thompson made her first appearances at American Junior Golf Association (AJGA) events: the Mizuno Junior, where she placed fourth, and the Aldila Junior Classic. At the Aldila Junior Classic, she scored a four-over-par 148 en route to a one-stroke win. With the victory, Thompson became the second-youngest winner in the history of the AJGA. This earned her invitations to three other AJGA tournaments: the Rolex Girls Junior Championship, the Betsy Rawls Girls Championship, and the Polo Golf Junior Classic.

Prior to her top-ten finish at the Rolex Girls Junior Championship in June 2007, Thompson bid a second time for the US Women's Open. This time, she succeeded. At the age of twelve years, four months, and one day old, she broke the record for the youngest person to qualify for the championship. The record had previously been held by Morgan Pressel, who was twelve years, eleven months, and twenty-one days old when she broke the record in 2001. Although Thompson succeeded in her bid for the 2007 US Women's Open, she finished in a tie for 141st place and did not qualify to continue the event.

Nevertheless, Thompson reached another milestone in July 2007, when she took first place at the Westfield Junior PGA Championship and became the youngest winner in its thirty-two-year history. Following an eleventh-place finish at the McDonald's Betsy Rawls Girls Championship, also held in July, Thompson made headlines again in August, when she became the youngest quarterfinalist in the 107-year history of the US Women's Amateur Golf Championship. After earning first-team Rolex Junior All-America honors in October, she finished twenty-eighth overall at the Polo Golf Junior Classic in November.

The following January, Thompson was nearly successful in defending her Dixie Amateur title but came up short, finishing in second place. She won the stroke-play championship and reached the quarterfinals in match play at the 2008 Ione D. Jones/Doherty Women's Amateur Championship, also held in January. In April, she earned the girls junior title at the AJDA Laredo Energy Junior at Traditions. After that victory, Thompson qualified for her second US Women's Open in June. She missed the cut by two strokes and finished in a tie for eighty-fifth place, unable to go on to the next round. (To "make the cut" in a golfing event, the golfer must achieve a final score at or above the event's target in order to advance.) Despite her performance at the US Women's Open, Thompson stood atop the podium at the 2008 US Girls Junior Golf Championship a month later, where the thirteen-year-old became the second-youngest winner in the history of the tournament.

Thompson made her second consecutive appearance at the US Women's Amateur Golf Championship in the summer of 2008, but she was eliminated in the first round. She fared better in September, at the 2008 Junior Ryder Cup, during which the US team triumphed over the European team. For the second straight year, Thompson was named a first-team Rolex Junior All-American. In January 2009, she once again claimed runner-up status at the Dixie Amateur Championship. She also made a thirteen-stroke victory at the South Atlantic Ladies Amateur (the SALLY) and won the match-play title at the Ione D. Jones/Doherty Championship. In February 2009, Thompson captured the girls junior title at the Verizon Heritage Junior Classic. She and her brother Curtis, the winner of the boys junior title, became the first brother and sister to win the tournament. The duo accomplished that same feat in April, at the Laredo Energy Junior at Traditions.

SUCCESS AT THE US WOMEN'S OPEN

Later in February 2009, Thompson began playing against men on Florida's Fuzion Minor League Golf Tour; she finished tied for eighth at the Jacaranda Shootout. She also appeared at the Kraft Nabisco Championship, where she finished tied for twenty-first place. In June, the fourteen-year-old defeated Virginia Derby Grimes, an opponent more than three times her age, to win the Women's Southern Amateur.

The next month, Thompson qualified for her third US Women's Open. This time, she made the cut. Thompson finished in a tie for thirty-fourth place—eleven shots behind the winner, Eun-Hee Ji of South Korea. In August, Thompson captured her second Junior PGA Championship, reached the semifinals of the US Women's Amateur, and represented the United States at the Junior Solheim Cup, a winning effort against the European squad. She was also a member of the triumphant US team at the Spirit International Amateur, a biennial event. Next came two more titles: the Polo Golf Junior Classic in November and the Junior Orange Bowl in December. *Golfweek* praised Thompson's success, naming her the 2009 Women's Amateur Player of the Year and the 2009 Junior Girls Player of the Year.

Thompson continued to compete as an amateur during the first half of 2010. In March, she entered the Handa Women's Australian Open and tied for sixteenth place—twelve strokes behind the winner, Taiwan's Yani Tseng. A month later, she tied for twenty-fourth place at the Kraft Nabisco Championship, another tournament that was won by Tseng; Thompson was the event leader in the driving distance category. In early June, Thompson represented the United States in the 2010 Curtis Cup and helped lead her team to victory against Great Britain and Ireland.

TURNING PROFESSIONAL

On June 16, 2010, Thompson made headlines when she announced that she was turning professional and would compete on the Ladies Professional Golf Association (LPGA) Tour. She also signed a sponsorship deal with Cobra-PUMA Golf and Red Bull. Since the LPGA does not accept members who are under eighteen, Thompson was forced to depend on sponsors' exemptions. Nonmembers of the LPGA are only allowed six sponsor exemptions per season. Shortly after turning professional, Thompson was granted a sponsor's exemption to compete in the ShopRite LPGA Classic—her first professional appearance—but failed to make the cut. In July, Thompson entered her fourth consecutive US Women's Open, where she made the cut for the second time. Playing her best game at the event thus far, she finished in a tie for tenth place.

Following her success at the 2010 US Women's Open, Thompson competed at the Evian Masters in France. She placed second, narrowly missing a chance to become the youngest winner on the LPGA Tour. From August to early October 2010, she appeared in three more LPGA events: the CN Canadian Women's Open, where she missed the cut; the P&G NW Arkansas Championship (now called the Walmart NW Arkansas Championship), where she was tied for fifty-seventh place; and the Navistar LPGA Classic, where she finished in a tie for sixteenth place, eight strokes behind the winner. Thompson spent October and November playing on Florida's Fuzion Minor League Golf Tour and had top-five finishes in every tournament she entered. In December 2010, she unsuccessfully applied to the LPGA to increase her sponsors' exemptions from six to twelve. Instead, the commissioner, Mike Whan, announced a change in the LPGA rules, allowing nonmembers to compete in qualifiers. This change worried some veteran players, who thought that nonmembers might gain greater access and playing privileges than players who earned tour membership.

Thompson remained a fixture on the Fuzion Golf Tour in 2011. She achieved top-ten placement at three tournaments in January. Her first victory on the circuit came at the TPC February Shootout, when she became the second woman to win an event on the tour; Carrie Dykstra was the first to accomplish this in 2004. Thompson also competed on the LPGA Tour and the Ladies European Tour (LET), with February appearances at the Women's Australian Open and the ANZ Ladies Masters. The following month, Thompson placed in the top ten in three more tournaments on the Fuzion Tour.

In July 2011, the sixteen-year-old Thompson successfully appealed to the LPGA to enter Qualifying School, or Q-School, for membership. Q-School consists of three stages, or qualifying competitions. Those who finish at the top of the final stage—the number of whom is determined on a yearly basis—receive an LPGA Tour card. Following her second consecutive appearance at the Evian Masters, Thompson recorded a ten-stroke victory at the first stage of the 2011 Q-School. Her first win on the LPGA Tour came in September, at the Navistar LPGA Classic, where she became the tour's youngest winner. Shortly after her five-stroke victory at Navistar, Thompson withdrew from the second stage of Q-School and was granted an age waiver, giving her full membership and playing privileges on the 2012 LPGA Tour schedule. She made golfing headlines again in December 2011, when her four-stroke win at the Dubai Ladies Masters made her the second-youngest winner on the Ladies European Tour.

Since the start of the 2012 LPGA Tour season, Thompson has played four events: the Women's Australian Open, where she placed in the top thirty; the Honda LPGA Thailand, where she was a top-twenty finisher; the Kia Classic; and the RR Donnelley LPGA Founders Cup. The latter was Thompson's first tournament with her new caddie, Greg Johnston. Thompson's previous caddie, her father, had decided to caddie for her older brother Nicholas, who has been looking to regain his PGA Tour card. Her other brother, Curtis, plays for Louisiana State University's golf team.

Thompson continues to be homeschooled so that she can travel and regularly compete.

SUGGESTED READING

Cohn, Bob. "Teenager Takes Tentative Steps onto LPGA Tour." *Pittsburgh Tribune-Review*. Trib Total Media, 7 July 2010. Web. 17 Apr. 2012.

Elliott, Mick. "There's Nothing Typical About Lexi Thompson." *espnW*. ESPN Internet Ventures, 15 Nov. 2011. Web. 17 Apr. 2012.

King, Michelle. "Meet 16 Y/O Golf Pro Alexis Thompson." *Seventeen*. Hearst Communications, 6 Sep. 2011. Web. 17 Apr. 2012.

Mell, Randall. "Daddy's Girl." *Golf Channel*. Golf Channel, 15 Nov. 2011. Web. 17 Apr. 2012.

Randall Mell. "Girl, 10, Comes Up Shot Short." *Sun Sentinel* [South Florida]. Sun Sentinel, 20 May 2005. Web. 17 Apr. 2012.

—*Bertha Muteba*

Helle Thorning-Schmidt

Born: December 14, 1966
Occupation: Prime minister of Denmark

On October 3, 2011, in a ceremony led by Danish head of state Queen Margrethe II in Copenhagen, Helle Thorning-Schmidt became her country's first female prime minister. Her inauguration came on the heels of the nationwide elections held on September 15, 2011, in which her center-left coalition—composed of the Social Democratic Party, the Social Liberal Party, and the Socialist People's Party—gained control of Denmark's legislature, the 179-seat Folketing, by a 5-seat margin.

The election results continued a long legacy of coalition government in Denmark. Because any Danish political party garnering 2 percent or more of the total vote can send representatives to the Folketing, no party has succeeded in winning an absolute majority since the early twentieth century. Other representatives who won election or reelection that day include center-right or rightist politicians whose coalition had ruled Denmark for the previous ten years, most recently under Liberal Party leader Lars Løkke Rasmussen, who became prime minister in April 2009.

Rasmussen acknowledged Thorning-Schmidt's victory on election night and led a caretaker government while his successor formed her cabinet during the eighteen days before her swearing in. His defeat was attributed to the lingering effects of the global recession that began in late 2007. The recession has hurt Denmark significantly less than it has hurt Greece, Spain, and many other countries within the European Union (EU), in part because Denmark has not adopted the euro, and Rasmussen was said to have handled Denmark's economic problems fairly well. Nevertheless, many Danes complained that the country's recovery was too slow, and they responded favorably to Thorning-Schmidt's campaign platform, which called for take any radical steps. As Ian Traynor and Lars Eriksen wrote for the London *Guardian* (15 Sep. 2011, online), "In a society that prizes consensus, major changes in key policy areas were unlikely." They added, "Given the austerity policies favored across Europe by the dominant center-right as the response to the lack of growth, Denmark will be watched to see whether the new government will take a different approach and succeed."

DENMARK: A BRIEF LOOK

The small Scandinavian country of Denmark has a relatively homogeneous population of about 5.51 million. Most Danes are descendants of people from the Nordic group, and more than 80 percent are members of the Danish Lutheran National Church. In 2009, the government reported that 9.1 percent of the population were recent immigrants or their descendants, and more than half of those were Muslims.

Fears among some Danes regarding the influence of immigrants on Danish society led in 2002 to the formation of the Danish People's Party. On its website, the party declares, "Denmark is not an immigrant-country and never has been. Thus we will not accept transformation to a multiethnic society. Denmark belongs to the Danes and its citizens must be able to live in a secure community founded on the rule of law, which develops along the lines of Danish culture." The party does allow that citizenship should be available to nonnative Danes "to a limited extent and according to special rules and in conformity with the stipulations of the Constitution."

Denmark is among the world's wealthiest nations, ranking fifty-fourth in terms of overall gross domestic product and purchasing power and twenty-second in per capita gross domestic product, according to the US Central Intelligence Agency. The Danish government asserts that income inequality in Denmark is lower than in any of the other thirty-four nations in the Organisation for Economic Co-operation and Development, and poverty is rare.

The tax rate for individuals approaches 50 percent, but because of Denmark's extensive system of social welfare, the effective rate is much less. Education at all levels is virtually free. Workers are entitled to about six weeks of vacation every year; women are allowed four weeks' leave during pregnancy and twenty weeks of maternity leave, and many male workers receive three weeks of paternity leave at full pay. The government provides free day care for the children of all working people, health care, generous unemployment income, and automatic academic or vocational retraining for those who have lost jobs. "I am a welfare society Dane," Thorning-Schmidt said, as quoted by Jennifer Buley in the *Copenhagen Post* (20 Sep. 2011).

Getty Images

raising the taxes of the wealthiest Danes and banks; increasing spending on infrastructure, education, hospitals, and welfare programs; lengthening the workday by twelve unpaid minutes (one extra unpaid hour per week); and ending some of the barriers to immigration erected in recent years. According to Lisa Mullins, speaking for the *World* (16 Sep. 2011, online), "In the past decade, the Danish right and far-right pushed through tough anti-immigrant measures, but this time around, it looks like Denmark's stagnant economy trumped all other concerns."

Thorning-Schmidt earned master's degrees in political science and European studies before launching her career, which began in a supervisory back-office job with a Danish delegation to the European Parliament (1994–97). After working as a consultant to the Danish Confederation of Trade Unions, she won election to the European Parliament in 1999, where she served one five-year term before her entrance into domestic Danish politics. She was elected to the Folketing as a representative of a district in Copenhagen in February 2005 and became leader of the Social Democratic Party in April of that year.

As prime minister, Thorning-Schmidt's challenges include boosting the economy, reducing government deficits, and grappling with disagreements among Danes concerning issues such as immigration, social-welfare policies, and Denmark's role within the EU. But most observers have predicted that her government will not

"Someone before me made the welfare system I was born into and grew up in. I went to a public kindergarten and primary school and was in the municipal after-school program. I am shaped by the welfare society."

EARLY YEARS AND EDUCATION

The youngest of three siblings, Helle Thorning-Schmidt was born on December 14, 1966, in Rødovre, a Copenhagen suburb. She has a sister, Hanne, and a brother, Henrik. Her father, Holger Thorning-Schmidt, was an associate professor of mathematics and economics at the University of Copenhagen. Her mother, Grete, worked in business. After their parents divorced in 1976, Hanne lived with their father and Helle and Henrik with their mother, but the parents maintained amicable relations and made sure that the children spent time with their noncustodial parent every week.

Thorning-Schmidt grew up in Ishøj, near Copenhagen. During her childhood, Ishøj grew from a small, mainly agricultural community into a multicultural town that became the home of many immigrants to Denmark, mainly from Turkey. According to its website, Ishøj outpaced other Danish communities in terms of "immigrant integration initiatives." The town is an example of "how the welfare society grew and created new opportunities for people who hadn't experienced that kind of prosperity," Thorning-Schmidt once said, as quoted by Lars Eriksen and Luke Harding in the London *Guardian* (16 Sep. 2011, online).

Thorning-Schmidt graduated from the local high school, Ishøj Gymnasium, in 1985. As a high school student, she supported peace movements and groups that called for the end of apartheid in South Africa. In 1992, having completed undergraduate work in political science at the University of Copenhagen, she was admitted to the College of Europe in Bruges, Belgium. While there, she met her future husband, Stephen Kinnock, whose father, Neil Kinnock, was a major figure in British politics. Thorning-Schmidt earned a master's degree in European studies from the College of Europe in 1993. She then returned to Denmark, where she joined the Social Democratic Party, and earned a master's degree in political science from the University of Copenhagen in 1994.

PROFESSIONAL LIFE

Also in 1994, Thorning-Schmidt was hired to head the secretariat of the Danish Social Democrats' delegation to the European Parliament. The European Parliament and the Council of the European Union monitor the operations of all EU institutions, approve the EU's annual budget, and draft policy and legislate on a wide array of social and political issues. The secretariat of each delegation provides administrative and technical support and expertise to the parliamentarians, who are elected to five-year terms by the citizens of the EU member states. As of January 2012, 736 parliamentarians represented some five hundred million inhabitants of the EU's twenty-seven member states.

Thorning-Schmidt married Stephen Kinnock in 1996. In 1997, she left the secretariat to become an international consultant for the Danish Confederation of Trade Unions, commonly known as the LO, the largest of Denmark's three umbrella organizations for unions. About three-quarters of Danish workers belong to unions, making Denmark one of the most highly unionized nations in the world, and around half of them belong to one of the twenty-five organizations in the confederation. Denmark is famous for maintaining conditions that benefit its working people by means of what is called "flexicurity." The European Commission's web page on "employment, social affairs, and inclusion" defines flexicurity as "an integrated strategy for enhancing, at the same time, flexibility, and security in the labor market [that] attempts to reconcile employers' need for a flexible workforce with workers' need for security—confidence that they will not face long periods of unemployment."

POLITICAL CAREER

In 1999, Thorning-Schmidt ran successfully for a seat in the European Parliament as a representative of Denmark's Social Democrats. Her five-year term began on June 10, 1999. In 2003, while still with the European Parliament, she ran unsuccessfully to represent Østerbro, one of Copenhagen's ten official districts, in the Folketing. She left the European Parliament in early July 2004.

In February 2005, Thorning-Schmidt won election to a seat in the Folketing as the Østerbro representative; two months later, she was elected to head the Social Democratic Party. Her party fared poorly in the next national elections, held on November 13, 2007. The election had been moved up from its normally scheduled date at the request of the ruling coalition, led by Liberal Party head Anders Fogh Rasmussen (no relation to Lars Løkke Rasmussen), ostensibly to avoid distractions that might arise if necessary discussions regarding the EU were held during an election campaign. According to Carter Dougherty for the *New York Times* (14 Nov. 2007, online), however, the prime minister sought to take advantage of the healthy economy then prevailing in Denmark. Dougherty reported that unemployment had dropped to 3.1 percent, "the lowest in over three decades," while the economy had grown by 3.5 percent.

Rasmussen's optimism proved to be correct. His party and its coalition partner, the Conservative People's Party, remained in power, with the

Danish People's Party supporting the coalition in the Folketing but not included in the cabinet. Meanwhile, the Social Democrats attracted fewer votes they had in more than a hundred years. Speaking right after the election, Thorning-Schmidt said, as quoted by Lee Moran in the London *Daily Mail* (16 Sep. 2011, online), "Danes need more time before they hand over responsibility to us."

As it turned out, a worldwide recession struck almost immediately after the election. During the next four years, Denmark's budget surplus vanished, and the recession led to the failure of nine Danish banks. According to Eurostat, the statistics-generating arm of the European Union, the jobless rate in Denmark had reached about 7.7 percent by October 2011. (In comparison, the rates in Ireland, Greece, and Spain were far worse—14.4, 19.2, and 22.7 percent, respectively.) Lars Løkke Rasmussen, who became prime minister in 2009 when Anders Fogh Rasmussen was named the secretary-general of NATO, "took credit for steering Denmark through the financial crisis in better shape than many other European countries," according to Associated Press reporter Karl Ritter (15 Sep. 2011). He continued, "However, the rebound has been slower than in neighboring Nordic nations and the government projects budget deficits of 3.8 percent of gross domestic product in 2011 and 4.6 percent in 2012."

During the 2011 national election campaign, the slowness of the rebound led many voters to respond favorably to Thorning-Schmidt's promises to boost the economy by raising taxes on Danes in the highest income brackets and on banks, and by increasing spending on social programs and infrastructure. Fewer voters supported the platform espoused by Rasmussen, who rejected both tax increases and the allocation of more money for domestic programs, advocating instead the continuation of various austerity measures.

Some criticism of Thorning-Schmidt surfaced during the campaign regarding her predilection for designer clothing. More potentially serious were revelations that her husband, Stephen Kinnock, had failed to pay his share of taxes in Denmark for several years. Kinnock had become the director of the Europe and Central Asia division of the World Economic Forum, headquartered in Geneva, Switzerland, in 2009, and had paid taxes in Switzerland on the grounds that it was his main residence, while he only spent weekends in Copenhagen. Thorning-Schmidt publicly apologized for what she termed an "honest mistake," and, according to Buley, "after an investigation, the tax authorities found [the couple] not guilty of intentional tax evasion." Thorning-Schmidt also vigorously denied some reports, published right before the 2011 election, that her husband is homosexual.

Nearly 88 percent of Denmark's more than four million eligible voters turned out on September 15, 2011, to cast their ballots in the national elections. The Social Democrats captured forty-four seats in the Folketing, and the members of their coalition, dubbed the Red Alliance, secured another forty-eight seats, for a total of ninety-two. The so-called Blue Alliance—the Liberals, along with the Conservatives, the Danish People's Party, the Liberal Alliance, and a member of the Union Party from the Faroe Islands—won a total of eighty-seven seats. In terms of individual votes, the Red Alliance won just over half the total.

Rasmussen conceded defeat that night. He led a caretaker government until October 3, 2011, when Thorning-Schmidt became prime minister. On the same day, she announced the names of the ministers in her twenty-two-member cabinet, all of whom were either Social Democrats or members of the Social Liberal Party or the Socialist People's Party. One of the first actions of the Thorning-Schmidt administration was the rejection of border restrictions that the previous government had threatened to impose. As of early January 2012, her government had not yet acted on other parts of her platform.

Richard Howitt, who represents the British Labour Party in the European Parliament, characterized Thorning-Schmidt to Eriksen and Harding as "personable, funny and warm," while Denis McShane, a Labour Party member of the British Parliament, described her to them as "steady" and "serious." Thorning-Schmidt and her husband have two daughters, Camilla and Johanna.

SUGGESTED READING

Boyd, Clark. "Helle Thorning-Schmidt Becomes Denmark's First Female Prime Minister." Interview by Lisa Mullins. *World*. Public Radio International, 16 Sep. 2011. Web. 10 Jan. 2012.

Dougherty, Carter. "Danish Prime Minister Narrowly Wins 3rd Term." *New York Times*. New York Times, 14 Nov. 2007. Web. 10 Jan. 2012.

Moran, Lee. "Kinnock Success at Last: Former Labour Leader's Daughter-in-Law Becomes Denmark's First Female Prime Minister (Despite 'Gay Husband' Slurs)." *Mail Online*. Associated Newspapers, 16 Sep. 2011. Web. 10 Jan. 2012.

Traynor, Ian, and Lars Eriksen. "Danes Vote for Their First Female Prime Minister." *Guardian*. Guardian News and Media, 15 Sep. 2011. Web. 10 Jan. 2012.

—*Miriam Helbok*

Tomas Tranströmer

Born: April 15, 1931
Occupation: Writer and poet

The Nobel Prize–winning Swedish poet Tomas Gösta Tranströmer published his first collection of poetry in 1954, when he was in his early twenties and still in college. He went on to publish more than twelve collections of poetry, which have been translated into more than fifty languages. Tranströmer's books of poetry and his impressionistic memoir have been collected and translated into English, most notably by the poets Robert Bly and Robin Fulton, who have been great advocates of his work since the 1970s and 1980s.

In 1990, at the age of fifty-nine, Tranströmer suffered a stroke that left him partially immobile on the right side of his body and practically unable to speak. Yet he continued to publish poetry and gain acclaim. Some of his most recent collections in English translation include *New Collected Poems* (1997; translated by Fulton) and *The Deleted World* (2006; translated by Robin Robertson). In 2011, at the age of eighty, Tranströmer was awarded the Nobel Prize for Literature.

AFP/Getty Images

EARLY LIFE AND EDUCATION

Tomas Tranströmer was born on April 15, 1931 in Stockholm, Sweden. His father, Gösta, was a journalist, and his mother, Helmy, was a schoolteacher. Tranströmer was an only child. His parents divorced when he was three years old. From then on, he was raised in Stockholm by his mother. In 1956, he received his BA from Stockholm University in the history of literature, poetics, the history of religion, and psychology.

POET AND PSYCHOLOGIST

In 1957, Tranströmer found work as an assistant at Stockholm University's Institution for Psychometrics. Working as a psychologist from 1960 to 1966, he provided rehabilitation and therapy services at the Roxtuna Prison for Boys near Linköping, Sweden. Later on, Tranströmer moved with his wife and two young daughters to Västerås, a town west of Stockholm, where he continued to work with convicts, drug addicts, and juvenile delinquents.

Tranströmer became a published poet while an undergraduate at Stockholm University. Having already published some of his poems in various journals, Tranströmer made his solo publishing debut in 1954 with the book *17 dikter* (*17 Poems*). In that first poetry collection, written in his teens and early twenties, Tranströmer's passion for music, nature, and the mysteries of life was already palpable. He was still in his twenties when he published his second collection in 1958, *Hemligheter på vägen* (*Secrets along the Way*), which would later be translated into English and other languages and anthologized, much like the rest of his poetry. Most critics agree that his third collection, *Den halvfärdiga himlen* (*The Half-Finished Heaven*; 1962), marked a new point of arrival for the young poet, whose verse by this point had become more resonating, substantial, and layered. In "Lament," one of the poems from the collection, Tranströmer alludes to a writer struggling with his work: "He laid aside his pen. / It rests still on the table. / It rests still in the empty room. / He laid aside his pen. // Too much that can neither be written nor kept secret! / He is paralyzed by something happening far away" (1–6).

The Half-Finished Heaven was followed by *Klanger och spar* (*Bells and Tracks*; 1966), *Mörkerseende* (*Seeing in the Dark*; 1970), and *Stilgar* (*Paths*; 1973). As the 1960s spilled into the 1970s, accompanied by much social and political change and turmoil, Tranströmer felt—but did not yield to—real pressure in his native Sweden to write on social and political topics. Instead, his poems were philosophical, introspective, and musical, embracing the mysteries of life. One reason for this was the nature of his job, working with troubled teens. "I felt more free than most of my colleagues because I was working with these issues as a psychologist, so I didn't feel very guilty about writing poetry," Tranströmer told Elizabeth Kastor for the *Washington Post* (2 Apr. 1986). Robert Bly, a longtime friend and translator of Tranströmer's work, elaborated on Tranströmer's unique role as both poet and psychologist, explaining to Kastor that Tranströmer considered his poetry and his psychologist's work as equally important and mutually influential.

Baltics, his longest poem to date, was published as a book in Sweden in 1974. Continuing on with the musical qualities that had already begun to emerge in *The Half-Finished Heaven*, *Baltics* is divided into six parts, each addressing some aspect of Tranströmer's past and family history, or reflecting on more recent events, ideas, or nature. *Baltics*, a sort of family chronicle in verse, was released in English translation in 1975.

INCREASED RECOGNITION ABROAD

In the 1970s Tranströmer was still largely unknown in the United States and England, but by the following decade he had gained more of a following (albeit a small one) and serious recognition there. Although his entire oeuvre was impressive in its own right, his burgeoning acclaim in the English-speaking world, particularly in England and America, was due in large part to the efforts of Fulton and Bly, who not only translated his work but also advocated for his recognition as one of the great poets of our time. Tranströmer's main work of the late 1970s was *Sanningsbarriären* (*Truth Barriers*; 1978). Several years after it was published in Swedish, Bly translated and published it in English.

The first comprehensive collection of Tranströmer's poetry in English was released in 1981 as *Selected Poems*, translated by Fulton. It included poems from all eight poetry books Tranströmer had published in Swedish; and three of those eight books were included in the collection unabridged. In an enthusiastic review for the *New York Times* (2 Apr. 1981), Rolf Fjelde called Tranströmer's poems "spare and incisive" and acknowledged "his claim on a growing audience of American readers." Fjelde observed: "Mr. Tranströmer has traveled extensively, and much of the pleasure of his art is in the wit and accuracy of his imagination as it expands our awareness and renews the familiar. In a smoky hut in Madeira, two fish are frying with 'tiny garlic explosions.' New York City seen at night from a distant prospect is like 'a spiral galaxy seen from the side,' the dozing bodies in its subway cars becoming 'catacombs in motion.'" Fjelde goes on to comment on Tranströmer's reliance on metaphor and both native Swedish and international imagery in his exploration of life: "Sometimes these deft formulations go beyond pungent perception to express an esthetic credo, a moral stance, as in a prose-poem titled 'Upright,' which captures the condition of living 'free but wary' in the memory of a visit to the Sara tribe in Africa. . . . The exotic provenance of these images is balanced in Mr. Tranströmer's work by the stones, forests, villages and cities of his native Sweden, the chief metaphors of his meditations on existence."

Toward the end of the review, Fjelde quotes a line from Tranströmer: "The language marches in step with the executioners. / Therefore we must get a new language." Using that line as a jumping-off point, Fjelde concludes that the poet works on his craft from a variety of overlapping ways: "In Mr. Tranströmer's work one senses . . . the novelist who refuses to sell experience short . . . the dramatist unable to cheapen life for a lucrative effect, the poet who lives like his squat pine tree in the swamp, of whom 'what you see is nothing / compared to the roots, the widespread, secretly / creeping, immortal or halfmortal / root system'—are all partisans in a common resistance movement that will not collaborate with literal, or figurative, death-dealers." Tranströmer, in other words, is not "marching with the executioners" of language but is instead on the forefront of creating a new language, a new way of expressing the reality of human feelings and perceptions.

CAREER MILESTONES

By the mid-1980s there was serious talk among some poets that Tranströmer would someday win the Nobel Prize for Literature. The year 1987 saw the release of two separate collections of his poetry in English translation: *Collected Poems*, translated by Fulton; and *Tomas Tranströmer: Selected Poems, 1954–86*, edited by the poet Robert Hass. The latter featured more than one hundred poems adapted into English by twelve different translators, including Hass. In the latter part of the decade, Tranströmer published two books of poetry in Swedish, *Det blå huset* (*The Blue House*; 1987) and *För levande och döda* (*For the Living and the Dead*; 1989). The following year, his life changed dramatically.

In November of 1990, at the age of fifty-nine, Tranströmer suffered a massive stroke that left him partially immobile on the right side of his body and nearly unable to speak. Yet despite losing his ability to converse, Tranströmer could still write poetry of the highest order. In 1993 he published *Minnena ser mig* (*Memories Look at Me*), a short memoir of his life in the 1930s and 1940s. A few years later, a new wave of English translations appeared, as did new discussions about Tranströmer deserving the Nobel Prize. In 1996, Ecco Press published *For the Living and the Dead: New Poems and a Memoir*, containing seventeen poems from *For the Living and the Dead*, most of the poems from *Sorgegondolen* (*The Grief Gondola*; 1996), and all but the last section of *Memories Look at Me*. Aside from Fulton and Bly, translators contributing to the English publication of this collection included Joanna Bankier, Samuel Charters, and Malena Morling.

The following decade saw the publication of even more translations and collections. *The Half-Finished Heaven: The Best Poems of Tomas Transtromer* (2001), chosen and translated by Bly, received a glowing review from Noah Isenberg for the *New Yorker* (18 Nov. 2001). Isenberg wrote: "This extraordinary collection of work by one of Sweden's greatest contemporary poets presents a rich sampling of Tomas Transtromer's verse published during the past five decades. Selected and deftly translated by Robert Bly, *The Half-Finished Heaven* draws on 10 separate volumes and is replete with evocative riffs on historical narratives—a dramatic moment from the French Revolution or an imagined African tour by Goethe 'disguised as Gide'—and affecting first-person meditations on matters like escaping death and the stark landscape of Scandinavia in winter." Isenberg also noted a degree of resonance with classical music history that he saw emerging in Transtromer's writing: "references to Schubert, Wagner, and Liszt abound." Isenberg concluded his review by pointing out that Transtromer's "elegant style" could be described in a line from his poem "Preludes": "Truth doesn't need any furniture." Five years later, in 2006, two more translated collections came out: *The Deleted World*, translated by Robin Robertson, and *The Great Enigma: New Collected Poems*, translated by Fulton.

That same year, in an essay for the London *Guardian* (28 Oct. 2006), Robertson reflected on how complicated it is to translate Transtromer: "His exquisite compression and vividly cinematic imagery are instantly attractive, but the elemental sparseness of his language can often be rendered as colourless and bland." Speaking to the unique quality of Transtromer's writing in his native language, Robertson explained that "the supple rhythms of the original poems are hard to replicate and, equally, the plosive musicality of Swedish words like 'domkyrkoklocklang' lose all their aural resonance when they become a 'peal of cathedral bells.'" Later in the essay, Robertson mentions that he had at one point visited Transtromer and his wife at their Stockholm home in May and that they had approved of his translations.

In February of the following year, however, Transtromer's longtime translator Fulton wrote a strongly worded letter to the editor of the *Times Literary Supplement*, alleging that Robertson had "excessively" borrowed from Fulton's own translations and was lacking in his understanding of the Swedish language. Five years later, Fulton published yet another updated collection, titled *New Collected Poems* (2011). In a positive review for the London *Guardian* (18 June 2011), Paul Batchelor concluded, "Fulton is to be applauded for bringing into English a unique sensibility, a haunting voice, and images of such incisive clarity that they can permanently alter your perceptions."

A few months after the publication of that new collection, Transtromer won the Nobel Prize for Literature, in October of 2011, marking the first time a Swede won the literature prize since 1974. Aside from the honor and prestige that goes with the Nobel Prize, Transtromer received a cash award of about $1.4 million. Soon after his victory, the New York publisher Farrar, Straus & Giroux bought the rights to the short Transtromer collection *The Deleted World*, translated by Robertson, and released the book later that year, in December. *Air Mail: The Correspondence of Robert Bly and Tomas Transtromer*, a collection of about two hundred letters written between the two poets from 1964 to 1990, is set to be published in English in 2013.

According to the Poetry Foundation, Transtromer's other honors include the Lifetime Recognition Award from the Griffin Trust for Excellence in Poetry, the Petrarch Prize in Germany, and the Aftonbladets Literary Prize, along with many other awards and recognitions.

Tomas Transtromer married Monica Bladh in 1958. They have two grown daughters together, Paula and Emma. The couple lives in the Sodermalm district of Stockholm, not far from where Transtromer grew up.

SUGGESTED READING

Batchelor, Paul. "Poetry: Root and Branch." *Guardian* [London] 17 June 2011: R14.

Fjelde, Rolf. "Poems as Meeting Places." *New York Times* 26 Apr. 1981: 7.24.

Kastor, Elizabeth. "The Poet and His Double Life." *Washington Post* 2 Apr. 1986: D1.

Lesser, Rika. "The Nobel Prize for Pain." *Los Angeles Times* 12 May 1996: BR6.

"Biography." *Tomas Transtromer: The Official Website*. WordPress.com, n.d. Web. 6 Apr. 2012.

—*Dmitry Kiper*

Ming Tsai

Born: March 29, 1964
Occupation: Chef and restaurateur

Most people recognize the face of award-winning chef Ming Tsai from his successful shows on the Food Network and PBS, but few know that he got his start behind the scenes at his family's Chinese restaurant in Dayton, Ohio. He began working the wok at Mandarin Kitchen as a young adult. The Chinese American chef later studied cuisine in Paris and Japan, but also boasts a mechanical engineering degree from Yale University. He debuted his first television show, the Emmy Award–winning *East Meets West*, on the Food Network in 1998, the same year he opened his Blue Ginger restaurant in Wellesley, Massachusetts. Upon opening, Blue Ginger was nominated for Best New Restaurant by the prestigious James Beard Foundation. In 2002, Tsai won the coveted James Beard Award for Best Chef Northeast.

Becoming famous for his East-meets-West style of cooking, Tsai's rise coincided with the popular fusion movement that joins techniques and ingredients from different countries and cultures. "My fusion, because I'm Chinese by birth and trained in Paris and Japan and had a Southeast Asian restaurant—primarily Thai and Indonesian and Vietnamese—becomes 'East-meets-West,'" Tsai explained to Jim Frost for the *Chicago-Sun Times* (19 Jan. 2000). "Unfortunately, fusion cuisine has gotten a bad rap— what I call con-fusion cuisine, because there are a lot of young [chefs] who are finding all these wonderful ingredients and products and putting them into food without understanding the traditional use of the product." But Tsai insists that his food is about more than fusion; he aims to make Asian cooking more accessible to Americans by using Asian ingredients to put a spin on classic Western dishes. Eating healthy on a budget and teaching others to do the same is another of Tsai's motivations. He believes that chefs can use their skills to make a difference outside the realm of fine dining. He has collaborated with the mass-retailer Target on a line of moderately priced kitchen supplies and packaged food. He also teamed up with Iron Chef Cat Cora as a founding member of Chefs for Humanity, a charity that got its start feeding rescue workers and people affected by Hurricane Katrina.

EARLY LIFE

Tsai was born on March 29, 1964, in Newport Beach, California, to Iris and Stephen Tsai. The elder Tsai is a mechanical engineer. Tsai's mother taught cooking classes and later co-owned a restaurant with her husband in Dayton, Ohio, where Tsai grew up. The restaurant, which opened in 1980, was called Mandarin Kitchen, and Tsai soon began working there himself. He recalls the first dishes he made, fried rice and Mongolian beef. Tsai told Bob Batz for the *Dayton Daily News* (9 Dec. 1998) that from that moment, he was "hooked on cooking."

Tsai attended Southdale Elementary School and the Miami Valley School. He later transferred to and graduated from Phillips Academy in Andover, Massachusetts. Tsai's parents are originally from Beijing, China, and his grandparents lived in Taipei. As a child in California, Tsai's father, a Yale graduate, worked as a professor of aeronautical engineering at Stanford University. When it came time to decide an academic path, Tsai decided to follow in his father's

Getty Images

footsteps and pursue a mechanical engineering degree from Yale. While he graduated in 1986, Tsai says that he experienced a moment of epiphany during a physics exam during his junior year. "I realized then—as everyone was punching furiously on their calculators—that I really didn't give a flying hoot what the separation point of a rotating disc was," he told Kathryn Matthews for the California *Knight Ridder-Tribune* (24 May 1999). He realized that his true passion was much more creative. He explained to Marion Kane for the *Toronto Star* (13 Dec. 2003), "All the culture, all the experiences, everything I'd done, I found I could put it on a plate."

At Yale, Tsai was an all-American squash player. He began playing the game at Andover, he recalls, when it became clear that he would never make the competitive basketball team. He was a good player, and has suggested that his skill was a major factor in his acceptance to Yale, where he played for coach Daniel Talbott's first class. Talbott became one of Tsai's best friends and introduced him to his sister, Polly, who later became Tsai's wife.

As a college student, Tsai had spent several summers in Paris as an unpaid apprentice, working at city bakeries and restaurants. The summer before his junior year, he studied at the famous Le Cordon Bleu cooking school, where he later was a pastry chef. After graduation, Tsai moved to Paris, where he worked at the acclaimed restaurant Natacha as a sous chef, and the Parisian gourmet food company Fauchon under famed pastry chef Pierre Hermé. During that time, Tsai had no official papers to work in France and thus was forced to work unpaid. To support himself, he played in professional squash tournaments on weekends. He also spent time in Osaka, Japan, where he studied classical Japanese cooking with sushi master Hiroko Kobayashi. After two years, Tsai returned to the United States. He attended Cornell University and graduated with a master's degree in restaurant and hotel management in 1989.

For the next two and half years, Tsai worked at the Chicago InterContinental Hotel as a food and beverage director. He realized, however, that he missed working in the kitchen. In 1992 he took a job in San Francisco at the Silks restaurant inside the Mandarin Oriental Hotel, where he worked with the Chinese cookbook author Ken Hom, who became Tsai's mentor (Hom later wrote the foreword to Tsai's first cookbook). He also worked at San Francisco's Ginger Club before moving to Santa Fe, New Mexico, in 1991. He became the executive chef of Santa-café restaurant, where he honed his East/West-style cuisine. It was exhilarating for Tsai to be cooking again, and Santacafé won rave reviews from local critics; however, Tsai dreamed of owning his own restaurant. "If you're going to express yourself as a chef," he told Matthews, "you need to be at least part owner." Tsai and his wife scoured the country for the best possible location for his prospective restaurant. In the interim, Tsai worked as a consulting chef, though he has joked that the title is a euphemism for "unemployed chef."

BLUE GINGER

Tsai and his family finally decided on the Boston suburb of Wellesley for their prospective restaurant. The decision was a strategic one. Boston was a city large enough to support a Chinatown (where Tsai gathers fresh ingredients) but was also not saturated with upscale restaurants. Additionally, Wellesley was (and is) a community affluent enough to frequent the fine dining establishment that Tsai was interested in founding. Tsai and his wife, Polly, the restaurant's co-owner, envisioned a casual bistro that emphasized Tsai's East/West style. They chose the name Blue Ginger for several reasons. They thought the name sounded whimsical, and it was a marriage of Tsai's favorite color—blue, connoting flowing water—and a favorite Asian ingredient. When they settled on the name, they didn't realize that there actually is such a thing as blue ginger, an Indonesian root with medicinal properties. For Blue Ginger's design, Tsai consulted a feng shui master. According to the master's suggestions, the restaurant features a water fountain just inside the entrance.

Blue Ginger officially opened its doors in February 1998, going on to earn a slew of accolades, including three stars from the *Boston Globe*. *Boston* magazine named Blue Ginger Best New Restaurant, and Tsai was heralded as the Chef of the Year by *Esquire* magazine. But the most prestigious recognition came from the James Beard Foundation, as Blue Ginger was nominated as one of the best new restaurants in the country. Following the success of Tsai's television shows and cookbooks, Blue Ginger has drawn diners from all over the world. In 2002, Tsai cobranded the Blue Ginger name with the mass-retailer Target and agreed to sell a line of cooking products and frozen food. Tsai even participated in the design of a few products, including the Blue Ginger knife, which in true East/West fashion combines a Chinese cleaver and a French knife. Tsai's previous cobranding effort was an *East Meets West* brand based on his popular television show. The brand was sold at higher-end retailers, including Marshall Field's. He also boasts a Ming Tsai signature knife series manufactured by Kyocera.

Before its tenth anniversary, Blue Ginger underwent a renovation that nearly doubled its size. The new Blue Ginger now boasts a lounge with its own separate menu. Reviewing the restaurant in 2008, Devra First for the *Boston Globe* (6 Aug. 2008) lamented the lackluster yet now-classic dishes in the main dining room and praised the more intriguing menu in Blue Ginger's lounge. She also wrote of Blue Ginger's evolution and Tsai's unusual conundrum: "Celebrity chefs, like rock stars, can find themselves in a strange position: Having become known for something, they are doomed to keep repeating it. It's hard to believe the Stones relish playing 'Satisfaction' after all this time, but they still have to trot it out live for the fans. Blue Ginger's lounge menu is like Tsai's new album. The dining room dishes may be his bread and butterfish [referring to restaurant favorite], but it was time for some fresh material. There's something to be said for classic. There's also something to be said for change."

TELEVISION CAREER

Tsai received his first encouragement to pursue a career in television while working at Santacafé. He appeared on the Food Network series *Dining Around*, in which hosts Alan Richman and Nina Griscom reviewed three restaurants from across the country on each episode. The show's producer, Marilyn O'Reilly, commented on his natural presence in front of the camera and invited Tsai to appear on *Ready, Set, Cook!*, another Food Network show, on which famous chefs competed against each other over the course of five episodes (all shot in one day) to create the best meal. The show had launched the careers of Mario Batali and Food Network host Bobby Flay. Tsai's competition was the legendary Asian fusion chef Susur Lee. Tsai was invited back to the Food Network as a guest on the program *Chef du Jour*, and then spent a week filling in for chef

Sara Moulton on the show *Cooking Live*. His episodes were tremendously popular with audiences. Tsai decided to invest in an expensive two-day session with a media trainer, who instructed Tsai on all aspects of television cooking. Tsai learned to move quickly while providing a detailed explanation for each ingredient that he used. He also learned how to engage the cameras while pulling a dish out of the oven. The training paid off; after appearing on an assortment of shows, Food Network executives invited Tsai to film his own show.

Tsai's first program, *East Meets West with Ming Tsai*, premiered on the Food Network in September 1998. The show became wildly popular and often featured celebrity guest chefs such as Mario Batali, Ken Oringer, and Douglas Rodriguez. His parents even appeared in a few episodes. For Tsai, the shooting schedule was hectic—he travelled to New York to film thirty episodes in a two-week period—but he hit just the right note with audiences. Tsai worked hard, as he has told numerous sources, to "demystify" Asian cuisine; though some of the recipes he shared on *East Meets West* were more complicated, he taught viewers how to build a pantry of Asian ingredients and incorporate them into their daily cooking. During this time, Tsai was also a frequent guest on the CBS morning program *The Early Show* with Bryant Gumbel. In 1998, *East Meets West with Ming Tsai* was awarded a daytime Emmy.

After *East Meets West* ended in 2003, Tsai moved to PBS, where he premiered a new show called *Simply Ming*. Hoping to appeal to families cooking on a budget, he prides himself on showcasing cost-effective, healthy recipes that use as few ingredients as possible. Tsai serves as the show's executive producer as well as its host; he even designed parts of the set. In 2009, *Simply Ming* was nominated for two Emmy Awards for outstanding culinary program and outstanding culinary/lifestyle host. Tsai also broadcasts a series of podcast tutorials through the show.

Beginning in 2000, Tsai hosted a show on the Food Network and the Fine Living Network called *Ming's Quest*, in which Tsai traveled the world in search of unusual cooking ingredients. In 2008, he travelled to the Olympics in Beijing with the show. Tsai also served as a guest judge, alongside Todd English and Michael Ruhlman, on the PBS cooking competition show *Cooking Under Fire* in 2005. A predecessor to Bravo's popular *Top Chef* competition, *Cooking Under Fire* allowed aspiring chefs to compete for a spot at one of English's New York City restaurants.

COOKBOOKS

Tsai signed a book deal in 1998, the same year he opened Blue Ginger and premiered *East Meets West with Ming Tsai*. His first book capitalized on both endeavors. Coauthored with Arthur Boehm, it was called *Blue Ginger: East Meets West Cooking with Ming Tsai* and was published by Clarkson-Potter in 1999. The book shares more advanced recipes from Blue Ginger and includes beer and wine pairings—often a tricky realm with fusion recipes. His second book, also coauthored with Boehm, was *Simply Ming: Easy Techniques for East-Meets-West Meals* (2003). The book's format was intentionally designed to be conducive to improvisation, appealing to both advanced and less experienced home cooks. Each chapter features a sauce, oil, marinade, or broth that could be used in several different ways and in several different recipes. Usually, this base contains more ingredients, but many can be made and stored for future use. Tsai's third book, *Simply Ming: Ming's Master Recipes* (2005), features twenty recipes from the second season of Tsai's PBS show of the same name.

Most of Tsai's books contain a glossary listing the essentials of an East/West pantry, but his fourth book, *Simply Ming: One-Pot Meals* (2010; cowritten with Boehm), provides an in-depth exploration of seven different cooking techniques that require only one pot. Each chapter focuses respectively on wokking, braising, sautéing, high-temperature cooking, roasting, tossing, and soups. The book provides a thorough how-to course for beginners, but also focuses heavily on healthy and affordable eating. Tsai also coauthored the books *The Food of Asia* (2002; with Kong Foong Ling and Cheong Liew) and *The Asian Kitchen* (2007; with Kong Foong Ling, Cheong Liew, and Luca Invernizzi Tettoni).

PERSONAL LIFE

Tsai married his wife Polly Talbott Tsai, who is also from Dayton, in 1996. The couple has two sons named David and Henry. David is seriously allergic to soy, dairy products, and nuts. Due to his son's potentially life-threatening allergies, Tsai has become a national spokesperson for the Food Allergy and Anaphylaxis Network (FAAN). He also developed a Food Allergy Reference Book that lists potential allergens in all Blue Ginger recipes. The book, which Tsai and his staff refer to as the "bible," served as the catalyst for a new Massachusetts food allergy law requiring restaurants to provide adequate safeguards and training. Tsai worked with state senator Cynthia Stone Creem to pass the bill, which was signed into law on January 15, 2009, and went into effect the following year. It was the first law of its kind in the country, and Tsai hopes to get similar legislation passed in other states.

Tsai, a wine lover, dreams of one day having his own vineyard. He is fluent in Mandarin Chinese and French. He lives with his family outside Boston, a few minutes away from Blue Ginger.

SUGGESTED READING

Batz, Bob. "TV Chef's Dayton Background Adds Seasoning to Show." *Dayton Daily News* 9 Dec. 1998: 1C. Print.

Frost, Jim. "Ming Style; Blue Ginger's Energetic Founder Blends East and West with Grace and Humor." *Chicago Sun-Times* 19 Jan. 2000, late ed.: 1. Print.

Kane, Marion. "Old Friends Cook Up East-West Feast." *Toronto Star* 13 Dec. 2003: M02. Print.

Matthews, Kathryn. "Ming Tsai Adds Emmy to Growing List of Awards." *Knight Ridder-Tribune* 24 May 1999: Print.

SELECTED BOOKS

Blue Ginger: East Meets West Cooking with Ming Tsai, 1999; *The Food of Asia*, 2002; *Simply Ming: Easy Techniques for East-Meets-West Meals*, 2003; *Simply Ming: Ming's Master Recipes*, 2005; *The Asian Kitchen*, 2007; *Simply Ming: One-Pot Meals*, 2010

SELECTED TELEVISION SHOWS

East Meets West with Ming Tsai, 1998–2003; *Ming's Quest*, 2000–04; *Simply Ming*, 2003–present; *Cooking Under Fire*, 2005

—*Molly Hagan*

Getty Images

Julie Verhoeven

Born: 1969
Occupation: Fashion designer, illustrator

British designer and artist Julie Verhoeven never intended to have a successful career in fashion, but after working as designer John Galliano's assistant in the early 1990s, she received her big break when designer Marc Jacobs asked her to put her spin on the classic Louis Vuitton handbag design in 2002. Her whimsical appliqués—frogs, mushrooms, and rainbows reminiscent of the psychedelic 1960s—dotted a limited number of bags obscuring the familiar Louis Vuitton monogram and sent the fashion world into a frenzy. The bags were so popular that when asked if she would be toting her own work on her shoulder that season, Verhoeven replied that she was still on the waiting list to receive one. The exclusivity of the Vuitton bags made Verhoeven a fashion celebrity and her illustrations of spooky female forms "the next big thing." Her "Verhoeven girls," rendered wide-eyed in ink with painterly flourishes, became her calling card. After spending much of the 1990s as a design consultant, Verhoeven's dreamy aesthetic had finally converged with popular taste.

"I never wanted to be a designer," Verhoeven admitted to Lee Carter for the Don Mills, Ontario *National Post* (6 Apr. 2002). "I just like drawing and researching old designs. Who wants to be constantly reminded that the bag or dress you bought is identical to thousands more?" Though Verhoeven keeps one foot firmly planted in the fashion world—for instance, designing prints for Versace and linens for the retailer H&M, for instance—she is most interested in pursuing her art. Her work, including illustrations and installations, has been shown in major cities all over the world, including New York, Cologne, Amsterdam, and her home city of London. Her solo exhibitions include *Unforgiving* (2003), *Saint James in Bloom* (2006), *Still Life and Woman* (2007), *Dull as Dishwater* (2007), *Verheaven* (2006), *Rubber Necking* (2009), *Man Enough to be a Woman* (2009), *Gluteus Maximus Part 1: Domestic Hiss* (2011) and *Gluteus Maximus Part 2: Her Indoors* (2011). The two-part exhibit *Gluteus Maximus* explores the contemporary female experience.

EARLY LIFE

Verhoeven was born in 1969 in Sevenoaks, a town west of Kent, England. Her Dutch father worked as a corporate graphic designer, and her mother was an illustrator. Influenced by her creative parents, Verhoeven was captivated by art from a young age. Her father took her to the National Gallery in London, where she has said that two paintings in particular—George Seurat's *Bathers at Asnières* and Pierre-August

Renoir's *The Umbrellas*—had an impact on her early aesthetic. Popular art and surrealism also made an impression on the young Verhoeven. Still, she says her parents tried to discourage her when she said that she wanted to be an artist, warning her and her brother, Leo, that they would not make any money in the arts. (Verhoeven's brother became a painter.)

Verhoeven attended a girl's school but left at the age of sixteen to study fashion because, as she told Penny Martin for the SHOWstudio website (3 Apr. 2002, online), it "was considered to be a bit more sensible" than art. She enrolled at Medway College (now the Kent Institute of Art and Design) in 1985. After graduating with a fashion diploma in 1987, she twice applied to London's prestigious Central Saint Martins College of Art and Design at the University of the Arts London, but she was not accepted. Verhoeven maintains that her quiet demeanor and her homemade leopard-fur Bermuda shorts cost her a slot. Despite that, she caught the attention of a tutor who recommended her to up-and-coming designer and Central Saint Martins graduate John Galliano, who was seeking help at the time. At the age of eighteen, Verhoeven began working for Galliano as his first design assistant.

GALLIANO'S ASSISTANT

Galliano's offices were in London's Covent Garden in the late 1980s. Verhoeven described the space as "romantic" to Rachel K. Ward for *Gravure* magazine (2008, online). In two cramped rooms above a theater, they were "literally surrounded by clothes, hanging from every corner," she recalled. Galliano, by Verhoeven's account, was obsessed with research. He would spend several weeks in the library—the London College of Fashion or the Victoria and Albert Museum—at the beginning of every collection. "Because that was my first ever experience in fashion I assumed that the research and fashion team work was normal but I realize now it was quite exceptional the way he created these stories, scenarios, and everyone followed the stories and the characters in the collection," she told Ward. "It is unique to go to that extent." The experience left a huge impression on Verhoeven. After assisting Galliano, she approached her own work in much the same manner. For over a year, Verhoeven did odd jobs for Galliano, including making his morning cappuccino. She began taking evening classes in fashion drawing at Central Saint Martins, and after a while, she began posting her drawings at work. Soon she found herself doing some artwork for T-shirts, invitations, and prints, and accompanying Galliano to the library to do research.

Verhoeven continued to take evening drawing classes for the next five years, studying fashion drawing with her mentor, Howard Tangye, at Central Saint Martins and life drawing at Morley Adult College. While working for Galliano, Verhoeven lived in Regent's Park Terrace in a basement flat owned by designer Jasper Conran, whom Galliano was dating at the time. At twenty-two Verhoeven left her job with Galliano to try her hand as a freelance illustrator. She taught at her alma mater, Medway College, three days a week while traveling the outskirts of London. She also did a lot of design work for Conran in theater, including costume sketches for Simon Callow's 1992 production of the musical *My Fair Lady*.

In 1993 Verhoeven moved to Paris to work for the designer Martine Sitbon. She lived in the historic Marais district in a small studio apartment for two years. "I didn't like Paris," she later told Tessa Williams-Akoto for *Independent Property* (10 Oct. 2007). "It lacks grittiness, and I like grittiness. It seemed too clean. You don't see that many colorful or dodgy characters there as you do here [in London]." Though she returned to London, Verhoeven continued to consult for Sitbon over the next seven years. During that time she continued to do work for Conran and, from 1996 to 1998, Australian-born fashion designer Richard Tyler. She also consulted with the London design house Ghost, renowned Irish milliner Philip Treacy, and women's perfumer Cacharel. In 2000 Verhoeven left her position with Sitbon to pursue a career in illustration. However, the fashion world kept calling, and Verhoeven soon found herself in the running to design a handbag with superbrand Louis Vuitton.

THE COVETED PATCHWORK BAGS

American designer Marc Jacobs took over as creative director at the French design house Louis Vuitton in 1997. He has since collaborated with a number of artists to reinvigorate the brand, including graffiti artist Stephen Sprouse in 2001. Jacobs was immediately attracted to Verhoeven's work. "Fashion is semi, if not totally, escapist," he told Carter. "Julie and I both use imagination and childhood memories in our work. I can remember what my sixth-grade teacher wore and I'm sure Julie can, too. We refuse to grow up." Despite their artistic similarities, Verhoeven was surprised when she was chosen to collaborate with the popular designer. "Marc just rang out of the blue. I nearly fell off my chair. And I had to pretend to be cool," Verhoeven told Laura Craik for the London *Evening Standard* (10 Dec. 2001). "He just rang and said what he wanted—he had this clear idea of a fairytale appliquéd patchwork bag. So I finished the roughs at home and then went to Paris and worked in the studio there." The bag debuted in the Vuitton 2002 Spring/Summer collection and became the season's hottest commodity. The patchwork bags were so prized that Verhoeven herself could not get one.

GIBO AND BEYOND

Verhoeven's success with Louis Vuitton brought her to the attention of Franco Pene, the president of the Italian fashion label Gibo. The label had already produced the work of such respected yet subversive designers as Helmut Lang, Alexander McQueen, Viktor & Rolf, and Hussein Chalayan, and had risen to fame in the 1970s for manufacturing the early works of haute-couture designers Georgio Armani and Jean Paul Gaultier. In early 2002 Pene approached Verhoeven about designing her own line, a first for her.

Verhoeven debuted her highly anticipated Spring/Summer 2003 collection at London Fashion Week in the fall of 2002. She had begun work on the collection the previous March. Her ideas were born, unsurprisingly, from the libraries at the London College of Printing and Camberwell Art School. With the assistance of Calvin Klein's casting agent and well-known stylist Suzanne Koller of the Parisian fashion magazine *Self Service*, Verhoeven choreographed the show down to the last detail, including the music that would play as the models made their way down the catwalk. A handful of fashion's toughest customers were in attendance: designers Alexander McQueen, Stella McCartney, and Katherine Hamnett, as well as *Vogue* editor in chief Anna Wintour. The standing-room-only crowd gave the show a "visibly good response," wrote Johnny Davis Main for the London *Independent on Sunday* (29 Sep. 2002). Verhoeven's bold prints and artist's palette motif became the hit of the week. Wintour even bestowed upon Verhoeven a rare and reserved congratulations after the show. As Pene and Gibo had hoped, Verhoeven's aesthetic as an artist also proved to be commercially appealing. Her collection—with most pieces retailing for about five hundred dollars—was sold in a London boutique that opened in February 2003. The shop, which once sold designs by McQueen, was partially gutted by Verhoeven before the opening. She exposed plaster walls in the space and covered them in her signature inking. Verhoeven went on to design several more collections with Gibo.

In 2007 Verhoeven joined old friend and former student Stuart Vevers of English luxury brand Mulberry to design a collection. For inspiration Vevers gave her only the image of a rose. "Stuart really wanted me to treat this as an art-based project, so we started with the square scarf, using it like a canvas," Verhoeven told Rhiannon Harries for the *Belfast Telegraph* (10 Sep. 2007, online). "He wanted it to be bold, and I was keen for my drawings to be less willowy. I wanted it to read like a floral on first sight—an expressive and energetic pattern. But I couldn't not draw a face. I'm just inspired and fascinated by them." Among Verhoeven's designs for Mulberry was a print in which it appears that a woman's face is turning into the bud of a rose. The effect was dark yet beautiful, adjectives that might also describe the Verhoeven-inspired Mulberry pop-up store in London that was decorated with the surrealist flair of the Mad Hatter's tea party in the Lewis Carroll novel *Alice in Wonderland*.

In 2009 Verhoeven teamed up with another old friend, Danish designer Peter Jensen. The collection was inspired by the films of American actress Jodie Foster. (Jensen's previous collection was inspired by actresses Sissy Spacek and Alison Steadman.) "It felt very appropriate," Jensen told Harriet Walker for the *Independent Magazine* (18 Apr. 2009), "because the elements of [Verhoeven's] illustration fit so well into the Jodie Foster universe. They are feisty and colorful, a bit girly and so youthful." Verhoeven paid homage to such Foster classics as *Freaky Friday* and *The Hotel New Hampshire* in her designs. That same year, Verhoeven also paired up with the fashion powerhouse, Versace, to design prints for their 2009 Spring/Summer collection that Suzy Menkes for the *New York Times* (26 Sep. 2008, online) called "pop . . . with a feminine touch."

BEING JULIE

Verhoeven finds inspiration for her work from a range of sources. From the sounds of punk music's New Wave to the "characters" she says she sees on the street outside of her house. By all accounts, it seems that Verhoeven defies common description in her tastes, personal style, and demeanor. She has been called the least charismatic person in the fashion industry for her lack of ego and self-effacing charm, but while her voice is notoriously quiet, her wardrobe is jarringly loud. She rarely wears her own pieces, favoring paint-spattered smocks, candy-colored hair, and painted cheeks akin to what one might expect to see on a doll. She has inhabited the same London home for over eighteen years and has decorated it according to her tastes—sketches and strips of colored vinyl line the walls. Though Verhoeven is eccentric, Dominic Lutyens wrote for the *Saturday Magazine* (31 Mar. 2007), she is not "off her rocker." He remarked, "It's just that she's keenly aware of the absurdities and ironies of life and of the ridiculous constraints imposed on us by convention." He reported of his own experience, "The incongruity of my conducting a rational interview with her in the idiosyncratic environment of her home, for example, isn't lost on her and she finds it (entertainingly) weird."

ART PROJECTS

As an illustrator Verhoeven's designs have been published in art and fashion magazines such as the *Face, Dazed & Confused, Self Service, ACNE paper, Grey, Dansk, Tokion, Flaunt,* and *Numéro.* Other projects have included cover design for the 2005 Penguin edition of F. Scott Fitzgerald's *A Diamond as Big as the Ritz* and Christmas cards designed for British clothes retailer Topshop, the Royal College of Art, and Vogue.com.

Verhoeven has also designed a number of products for various retailers. In 2006, she created a deck chair for the Royal Parks Foundation, V&A teacup and saucer, carrier bags for Selfridges, and chairs for Sketch restaurant in London. Among her other creative endeavors were a makeup bag for Lancôme and jewelry for Dover Street Market in 2007, totes and linens for H&M Home in 2010, and a cotton scarf for ASOS and a limited-edition Sky HD box in 2011.

In 2002, Verhoeven put up an exhibit entitled *Fat Bottomed Girls* after the Queen song of the same name. That year she published *Fat Bottomed Girls* as a collection of illustrations inspired by her forty favorite pop songs of all time. *A Bit of Rough*, a collection of illustrations and photographs of Verhoeven's installations, was published in conjunction with an exhibition at the MU gallery in Eindhoven, the Netherlands, in 2009. Verhoeven also provided illustrations for a children's book called *Cicely Scissors*, written by her friend Adrian Self. The book follows the story of a pair of scissors that wonders why she is a pair while everything else is one; it has yet to be published.

Verhoeven's murals can be seen throughout the United Kingdom, including at the Bellini Bar and Hospital Club in London and the Bristol Harbourside and the Mulberry boutique in Leeds. Solo art exhibitions have taken place at ZINGERpresents in Amsterdam and Riflemaker in London.

In addition to her design and illustration work, Verhoeven has made a number of films. Her short art films include *Knee Deep in Your Eyes* (2008); *Commercial Break* (2009); and *Gilding the Lily* (2009), commissioned by Versace for its 2009 Spring/Summer show; *I Want You* (2010), in collaboration with the Scottish alternative rock band Primal Scream; and *If You are Happy and You Know It* (2011) for AnOthermag.com. Among her animated films are *New Year* (2000) with the English pop-music group Sugababes; *Some Velvet Morning* (2003), in collaboration with Primal Scream and Kate Moss; and *Fischerspooner* (2005), commissioned by Deitch Projects in New York for the electro-pop artist of the same name. She has also collaborated with graphic designer Peter Saville on two web-based projects for SHOWstudio.com: *Forget Me Knot* (2002) and *Dress Me Up, Dress Me Down* (2005).

PERSONAL LIFE

Verhoeven lives in Camberwell in South London. She was married to Brazilian artist Fabio Almeida for a time, but the couple divorced in the early 2000s. As of early 2012 she is in a relationship with Dutch art dealer Steven van Grinsven.

SUGGESTED READING

Carter, Lee. "It's on the Bag: There's a Story behind Julie Verhoeven's Fairy-Tale Drawings." *National Post* [Don Mills, Ontario] 6 Apr. 2002, natl. ed.: SP9. Print.

Harries, Rhiannon. "Malice in Wonderland." *Belfast Telegraph* 10 Sep. 2007. Web. 8 Feb. 2012.

Lutyens, Dominic. "Colour Me Happy." *Independent* 31 Mar. 2007, first ed.: 48. Print.

Verhoeven, Julie. *Fat Bottomed Girls*. London: TDM, 2002. Print.

---. *A Bit of Rough*. Eindhoven: MU, 2009. Print.

Walker, Harriet. "Dream Team." *Independent Magazine* 18 Apr. 2009, first ed.: 32. Print.

Ward, Rachel K. "Interview with Julie Verhoeven." *Gravure* 3 (2008): n. pag. Web. 31 Jan. 2012.

Williams-Akoto, Tessa. "Swirl Power." *Independent Property* 10 Oct. 2007, first ed.: 2. Print.

—*Molly Hagan*

Justin Verlander

Born: February 20, 1983
Occupation: Baseball player

Among the elite pitchers in Major League Baseball (MLB), the Detroit Tigers' right-hander Justin Verlander has frequently been compared to his boyhood idol, the Hall of Fame pitcher Nolan Ryan, for possessing the kind of dominant pitches that give him the chance to throw a no-hitter anytime he steps on the mound. Those pitches include a blistering fastball, which regularly reaches speeds between ninety-five and one hundred miles per hour, and a complementary arsenal of devastating off-speed and breaking pitches, which includes a changeup, curveball and slider. Like Ryan, who remains baseball's all-time leader in strikeouts and no-hitters, the six-foot-five, 225-pound Verlander is known as a reliable pitcher who can throw a high number of innings and pitches and for having the extraordinary ability to sustain triple-digit speed on his pitches deep into games. Morgan Campbell, writing for the *Toronto Star* (19 July 2011, online), called him "a once-in-a-generation power pitcher who not only hits triple digits with his fastball . . . but combines that raw power with skill and endurance." Paul White for *USA Today* (8 July 2011) has declared that he "is as close as this era of baseball—with its careful handling of pitchers—has to a time when pitchers threw more and science knew less about the stressful nature of throwing a baseball."

Verlander was drafted second overall by the Tigers in the 2004 MLB Draft and then spent one season in the minor leagues before earning a spot in the Tigers' starting rotation in 2006. That season he was named the American League (AL) Rookie of the Year after seventeen wins and nine

AP Photo

his mother, who works in customer relations at a telephone company, was a competitive swimmer in her youth and continues to compete as a tennis player. Hyperactive as a child, Verlander naturally gravitated toward sports and started playing baseball at an early age. One of his biggest influences growing up was his father, the local president of the Communication Workers of America (CWA) union and a baseball enthusiast. He taught Verlander how to pitch and helped coach many of his youth-baseball teams. Verlander also idolized the legendary pitcher Nolan Ryan as a child and fostered dreams of breaking Ryan's hallowed strikeout record.

Verlander's baseball talent was evident by the time he started playing T-ball, but his parents kept him grounded by instilling in him the importance of humility. His father first recognized his astonishing throwing ability when Verlander was about nine or ten years old, while the two were skipping rocks across a pond near their home. Despite his age, Verlander was able to throw his rocks twice as far as his father could. His father recalled to Campbell, "It was somewhat humbling. It was one of those moments I refer to as 'pinch me' moments. There have been quite a few with Justin." Verlander's arm proved no match for his peers, and when he pitched in Little League, other children "would weep in the batter's box and on-deck circle," Steve DiMeglio wrote for *USA Today* (26 June 2006). His uncanny pitching velocity, however, came with extreme wildness, and he frequently walked and hit batters due to a lack of control.

HIGH SCHOOL AND COLLEGE BASEBALL

When Verlander was thirteen years old, his father sent him to the Richmond Baseball Academy, an instructional facility in Richmond, Virginia, run by former major-league scout Bob Smith. There, he began working with Smith on developing his pitching mechanics and control. Smith oversaw his pitching development as he attended Goochland High School. Verlander pitched for Goochland's varsity baseball team as a freshman, when his fastball hit eighty-one miles per hour. (He was nicknamed Skippy after skipping junior-varsity baseball.) The velocity on his fastball rose steadily throughout high school, hitting ninety-three miles per hour during his senior year, when he posted 144 strikeouts and an astonishing 0.29 ERA in seventy-two innings.

Despite a dominant high school career, Verlander garnered little interest from major-league scouts. Many of those scouts had watched him pitch at the beginning of his senior year while he was battling a debilitating case of strep throat. At the time, the illness diminished his fastball velocity to eighty-six miles per hour, leaving many scouts unimpressed. Verlander noted to John Powers for the *Boston Globe* (30 Sep. 2011), "By the end of the year, I was back up to where I

losses with a 3.63 earned-run average (ERA). Verlander has since won at least seventeen games four times and pitched two hundred or more innings in each of the last five seasons and recorded two hundred or more strikeouts in each of the last three. He has also earned four All-Star selections (2007, 2009, 2010, and 2011) and thrown two no-hitters, once in 2007 and again in 2011.

Verlander was the talk of the baseball world in 2011, when he became only the tenth pitcher in MLB history to win the Cy Young and Most Valuable Player (MVP) awards in the same year, after leading the AL in wins (24), ERA (2.40), and strikeouts (250)—the coveted "triple crown" of pitching. With those awards, he became the second player ever to have won the Rookie of the Year, Cy Young, and MVP Awards in his career. "He's got the best stuff of anybody I've ever had, no question," Tigers' manager Jim Leyland told Campbell. "He's still in the process of becoming the best pitcher. He's starting to figure things out. If he lets himself, he should be real special for a really long time."

EARLY LIFE

The older of the two sons, Justin Brooks Verlander was born to Richard and Kathy Verlander on February 20, 1983, in Manakin-Sabot, Virginia. Verlander comes from an athletic family. His maternal grandmother, Olympia Ryder, played softball and competed on women's semiprofessional basketball teams in the 1940s, and normally was, but there was nobody around to see it."

After graduating high school undrafted, Verlander accepted a baseball scholarship to Old Dominion University (ODU), in nearby Norfolk, Virginia. He chose the school after head coach Tony Guzzo promised him that they would protect his arm by limiting his appearances and keeping him on closely monitored pitch counts. (Power pitchers like Verlander are more prone to serious long-term arm injuries due to the extreme stress put on their elbows and shoulders.)

Verlander pitched for three seasons at ODU, during which he went 21–18 with a 2.57 ERA in 335.7 innings and broke several records. In 2002, his freshman year, he posted a 7–6 record and led the Colonial Athletic Association (CAA) conference with a 1.90 ERA, while striking out 137 in 113.2 innings. That year Verlander broke a school record for most strikeouts in a game with seventeen, during a start against James Madison University. He was named CAA Rookie of the Year and earned first-team All-America honors. Verlander again won All-Conference and All-America honors as a sophomore in 2003, when he went 7–6 with a team-best 2.40 ERA and led the CAA with 139 strikeouts. Later that summer, he pitched for Team USA at the Pan American Games in Santo Domingo, Dominican Republic, where he went 5–1 with a 1.29 ERA and helped lead the United States to the silver medal.

By the time Verlander entered his junior year, he had added a curveball and changeup to his pitching repertoire. The effectiveness of those pitches helped complement his fastball, which was now reaching triple-digit speeds, thanks to strenuous off-season conditioning programs that added fifteen pounds to his once-lanky frame. As a junior in 2004, Verlander went 7–6 with a 3.49 ERA in sixteen starts and set ODU's single-season strikeout record with 151, which led the conference and was good for fifth among all National Collegiate Athletic Association (NCAA) Division I pitchers. He earned first-team All-Conference and All-America honors for the third consecutive year and was named ODU's Alumni Association Male Athlete of the Year. After three seasons of college baseball, Verlander, who was rated by *Baseball America* as the fifth-best pitching prospect, impressed the Detroit Tigers—who were then coming off a franchise-worst 119-loss season—enough to select him with the second overall pick in the 2004 MLB Draft. "Our people thought he had a tremendous makeup," the Tigers' president and general manager, Dave Dombrowski, told John Powers. "We didn't think he'd ever be content in what he was achieving. We always thought he would strive to get better." Verlander finished his college career at ODU as the school's and the conference's all-time leader in strikeouts, with 427. In October 2004 the Tigers signed him to a five-year, $4.5 million contract that included a $3.12 million signing bonus.

DETROIT TIGER

Verlander spent just one season in the Tigers' farm system. During the winter of 2005, he was sent to Florida to work with the team's minor-league pitching instructor, Jon Matlack, on his mechanics and delivery. He then began his professional career and opened the 2005 season with the Lakeland Tigers, the organization's advanced single-A affiliate in Florida. In thirteen starts with the Lakeland Tigers, Verlander compiled a 9–2 record and 1.67 ERA with 104 strikeouts in eighty-six innings. He was then promoted to the Tigers' double-A affiliate in Erie, Pennsylvania. After a series of stellar starts with the Erie SeaWolves, Verlander earned his first call-up to the majors on July 4, 2005, starting the night game of a day-night doubleheader against the Cleveland Indians. He took a loss in his major-league debut after allowing four runs on seven hits in 5.1 innings. Afterward, Verlander was relegated to Erie, where he remained for just two weeks before earning a second call-up to the majors on July 23, in a start against the Minnesota Twins. He earned his second career loss after giving up five runs on eight hits in six innings. Verlander subsequently returned to Erie, where he made only several more starts before being sidelined for the remainder of the year due to a shoulder strain. In seven total starts with the Erie SeaWolves, he went 2–0 with a 0.28 ERA and thirty-two strikeouts.

Verlander entered the 2006 season rated by *Baseball America* as the Tigers' top prospect. After putting up solid numbers in the Tigers' spring training camp that year, he convinced the organization's management that he was major-league ready and was awarded a permanent spot on the Tigers' five-man rotation. Verlander wasted little time proving his worth, and despite opening his rookie campaign as the number-five man in the rotation, he quickly emerged as the Tigers' most valuable starting pitcher. He picked up his first career win on April 8, 2006, in a game with the Texas Rangers, allowing just two hits and two walks over seven scoreless innings. He then pitched his first complete-game shutout in May against the Kansas City Royals. Verlander was named the American League (AL) Rookie of the Month for May, after compiling a record of 4–1 with a 1.73 ERA in five starts. He then headed into the 2006 All-Star break with a record of 10–4, becoming the first Tigers rookie pitcher ever to reach ten wins prior to the season's midpoint. Despite fighting through lingering arm fatigue during the second half of the season, Verlander finished his first full year in the majors with impressive numbers, going 17–9 with a 3.63 ERA in thirty starts and recording 124 strikeouts in 186 innings. He led all Tigers starters in ERA and tied for the team lead in wins—his seventeen wins were the most by a Tigers rookie pitcher since 1976—and his strikeout total set a franchise record for most by a right-handed rookie pitcher. He also led all AL rookies in wins, games started, and innings pitched.

Along with fellow starters Kenny Rogers, Jeremy Bonderman, and Nate Robertson, Verlander served as a key contributor on a Tigers' pitching staff that led the major league in ERA and shutouts and helped the Tigers earn their first postseason since 1987, as they finished second in the AL Central Division with a record of 95–67. The Tigers went on to defeat the New York Yankees and the Oakland Athletics in the American League Division Series (ALDS) and American League Championship Series (ALCS), respectively. In doing so, they earned their first AL pennant and went to the World Series for the first time since 1984. Verlander started game one and game five of the series against the National League (NL) champion St. Louis Cardinals. He lost both games after allowing a combined seven earned runs on twelve hits in eleven innings. The Tigers ultimately lost the series to the Cardinals in five games. Two weeks after the World Series, Verlander was named the AL Rookie of the Year, receiving twenty-six of twenty-eight first-place votes from the Baseball Writers' Association of America (BBWAA). He became only the fourth Tigers player to win the honor and the first since second baseman Lou Whitaker in 1978.

Verlander spent the 2007 off-season rethinking his strength and conditioning program, in an effort to prevent the same arm fatigue that had plagued him toward the end of his rookie year and during the postseason. He began focusing more on strengthening his legs and core and used resistance training to hone his mechanics. Verlander explained to Morgan Campbell, "If your legs and core are strong and you have proper mechanics, your arm is kind of along for the ride. It all starts from the ground up. You kind of think of it like a whip." Aided by improved strength, agility, and mechanics, he enjoyed even greater success in 2007. That season he earned his first career All-Star selection after achieving a record of 18–6 with a 3.66 ERA and striking out 183 in 201.2 innings. He led the Tigers in wins, innings pitched, and strikeouts, and led the AL with a .750 winning average.

Verlander won attention around the league on June 12, when he threw his first career no-hitter against the Milwaukee Brewers and struck out a career-high twelve batters. He became only the fifth Tigers pitcher to throw a no-hitter and the first since Jack Morris in 1984. He also became the first pitcher ever to throw a no-hitter, start a World Series game, and earn both All-Star and Rookie of the Year honors in his first two seasons in the major league. Verlander's achievements notwithstanding, the Tigers failed to return to the playoffs and defend their AL crown after finishing second in the Central Division with an 88–74 record.

Verlander's pitching success foundered during the 2008 season. He finished with the first and only losing record in his career, going 11–17 with a career-worst 4.84 ERA. He led the AL in losses and finished among the league leaders in several other dubious categories. He ranked third in hit batsmen (14), tied for third in walks (87), and tied for fifth in earned runs allowed (108). The Tigers, meanwhile, struggled as a whole and finished last in their division, with a 74–88 record.

RECORD-SETTING COMEBACK

After making adjustments to his pitching mechanics, such as lowering the arm angle on his delivery and adding an effective slider to his pitching repertoire, Verlander reestablished himself as one of the game's best young pitchers in 2009. He went 19–9 with a 3.45 ERA and led the majors in games started (35), innings pitched (240), and strikeouts (269), while tying for the major-league lead in wins. He was named to his second All-Star team and finished third in the voting for that year's Cy Young Award.

In February 2010 Verlander signed a five-year, $80 million contract extension with the Tigers. He rewarded their faith in him by having another successful season in 2010, posting a record of 18–9 with a 3.37 ERA and earning his third All-Star selection. That year he tied for fourth in the AL in wins, tied for third in the league in innings (224.1), and finished fourth in the league in both strikeouts (219) and games started (33). With his win total, Verlander became the first pitcher since Dwight Gooden to record at least seventeen wins in four of his first five seasons. The Tigers finished the 2009 and 2010 seasons with records of 86–77 and 81–81, second and third in their division, respectively.

In 2011 Verlander made a valid case for being the best pitcher in the game after posting one of the most dominant pitching campaigns in recent memory. He recorded his one-thousandth career strikeout in his fifth start of the season in an April game against the Chicago White Sox, becoming the fifteenth Tigers pitcher to accomplish the feat.

Three starts later, on May 7, he threw his second career no-hitter and barely missed a perfect game against the Toronto Blue Jays in which he struck out four and walked just one. Reaching triple-digit speeds with his fastball in the ninth inning of that game, Verlander became the thirtieth pitcher in baseball history to throw more than one hitter and joined Virgil Trucks as the only other Tigers pitcher to accomplish the feat. He went on to gain nine consecutive victories, from May 24 to June 30 and to be named the AL Pitcher of the Month for June after going

6–0 with a 0.92 ERA and fifty-four strikeouts in forty-nine innings. He was then named to his fourth career All-Star team, after entering the 2011 midseason break with a record of 12–4 and superb 2.15 ERA.

Instead of cooling off, Verlander was even more dominant during the second half of the season and ended the year winning his last twelve games to finish with a record of 24–5, becoming the first Tigers pitcher to reach twenty wins since Bill Gullickson in 1991. He led the AL in wins, ERA (2.40), and strikeouts (250) to win that league's pitching triple crown, becoming the first AL pitcher to do so since the Minnesota Twins' Johan Santana in 2006. He also led the majors in wins and strikeouts, as well as in games started (34) and innings (251), while allowing a career-low fifty-seven walks. His twenty-four wins are the most by a major-league pitcher since Randy Johnson reached the same total in 2002 and the most by an AL pitcher since Bob Welch won twenty-seven games in 1990.

Verlander's dominating regular-season performance helped lead the Tigers back to the playoffs, as they finished with a 95–67 record to win their first-ever AL Central Division title (since being moved to the division in 1998). The Tigers advanced to the ALCS, where they lost to the Texas Rangers in six games. In November 2011 Verlander was unanimously selected as the winner of the AL Cy Young Award and was named the AL MVP, becoming only the tenth pitcher in history to win both awards in the same year; he is the third Tigers pitcher to achieve this (after starter Denny McClain in 1968 and closer Guillermo "Willie" Hernandez in 1984). He is only the AL's ninth unanimous selection for the Cy Young Award and the first since Johan Santana in 2006. In addition, he is the first pitcher to win the MVP Award since reliever Dennis Eckersley in 1992 and the first starting pitcher since Roger Clemens in 1986. With his 2011 accolades, Verlander joined the Brooklyn Dodgers' Don Newcombe as one of two players in MLB history to win the Rookie of the Year, Cy Young, and MVP awards in his career. Despite those achievements, he entered the 2012 season with even greater goals in mind. "I was blessed with a great arm," he told Steve Kornacki for the *Grand Rapids (Michigan) Press* (27 Mar. 2011). "I can do things with my arm that others can't. But I want to be the best. I want to go to the Hall of Fame."

PERSONAL LIFE

Verlander lives in Goochland County, Virginia, with his longtime girlfriend, Emily Yuen, whom he has dated since high school. He spends his off-seasons in Lakeland, Florida, where the Tigers hold their annual spring-training camp. An avid car collector, Verlander boasts a collection that includes an Aston Martin DBS, Ferrari Italia 458, and Mercedes-Benz SLS Roadster.

SUGGESTED READING

Barnas, Jo-Ann. "Verlander's Journey: From Roots in Virginia to All-Star Phenom." *Detroit Free Press* 10 July 2011: A1. Print.

Campbell, Morgan. "Training, and Science, Help Verlander Defy Power Pitcher's Odds." *TheStar.com*. Toronto Star, 19 July 2011. Web. 6 Feb. 2012.

DiMeglio, Steve. "Banking on the Rookie." *Baseball Digest* 1 Sep. 2006: 60. Print.

Kornaci, Steve. "Verlander Eyes Bigger Target; Tigers' Ace Wants to Deliver Hall of Fame Stats." *Grand Rapids Press* 27 Mar. 2011: C10. Print.

Powers, John. "Motor City Gas; Formidable Verlander Provides the Fuel that Tigers Run On." *Boston Globe* 30 Sep. 2011: 10. Print.

Waldrop, Melinda. "The Right Stuff." *Daily Press* [Newport News] 8 July 2007: C1. Print.

White, Paul. "Justin Verlander: The Koufax of His Era." *USA Today* 9 July 2011: 1C. Print.

—*Chris Cullen*

Justin Vernon

Born: April 30, 1981
Occupation: Singer and songwriter

Singer-songwriter Justin Vernon is the founder, singer, and front man of the band Bon Iver. Vernon's first album as Bon Iver, *For Emma, Forever Ago* (2008), was recorded in his father's cabin in his home state of Wisconsin. Music critics praised the album for its spare, subtle instrumentation, lyrical language, and—most notably—the deep emotion of Vernon's multitracked falsetto voice. Many publications nationwide dubbed the album one of the year's best. Vernon's second full-length album, *Bon Iver, Bon Iver* (2011), showed him expanding his musical style while maintaining the emotional depth and sensitive multitracked vocals of his debut. Bon Iver has been nominated for four 2012 Grammy Awards: record of the year (for the song "Holocene"), song of the year (also for "Holocene"), best new artist, and best alternative album.

At the request of hip-hop megastar Kanye West, Vernon contributed his vocals to nearly half of West's album *My Beautiful Dark Twisted Fantasy* (2010). Vernon and three multi-instrumentalists have been touring extensively as Bon Iver in Europe and North America. Bon Iver has also performed on various TV shows, such as the *Colbert Report* and the *Late Show with David Letterman*.

EARLY YEARS

The middle of three children, Justin DeYarmond Edison Vernon was born on April 30, 1981 in Eau Claire, Wisconsin. Along with his brother, Nate, and sister, Kim, Vernon was raised in Eau Claire in a musical household. Vernon's parents, Justine and Gil, were supportive of Vernon's varied musical interests. His mother played organ and French horn and would sometimes sing in the car while driving her children. Vernon also listened to his parents' record collection, which included albums by Bob Dylan, Tom Waits, and John Prine. Vernon was also a fan of Jackson Browne, Primus, and the Indigo Girls.

During his teens, while attending Eau Claire Memorial High School, Vernon—by then a tall young man—played on the football team and served as the team's captain. He was also involved in several music projects: playing guitar in his high school's jazz band and playing saxophone in the school's marching band. He also served as the front man for Mount Vernon, a ska-influenced jazz/pop/rock group that at times had as many as ten members. Apparently, even then, Vernon had the ability to touch an audience. His friend Drew Christopherson, speaking to Andrea Swensson for the Minneapolis *City Pages* (31 Aug. 2011), recalled, "It's very easy for him to get people to feel connected. He played our graduation party in high school, and our whole gymnasium filled with the graduating class was practically up in arms watching him play these songs. Everyone was kind of tearing up."

COLLEGE AND A NEW BAND

After high school Vernon went on to attend college in his hometown, the University of Wisconsin, Eau Claire, where he majored in world religious studies and minored in women's studies. Speaking to Jon Caramanica for the *New York Times* (5 June 2011), Vernon explained why he did not want to major in music: "I didn't want to be proficient . . . It seemed like other people were valuing things that were more about technical ability and not, like, feel." Vernon continued to make music, this time with a new band named DeYarmond Edison after his two middle names. A four-member band, DeYarmond Edison had elements of Wilco, old blues, indie rock, The Band, acoustic Americana, and folk; Vernon sang in a low voice similar to his actual speaking voice. In 2005, the year after Vernon graduated from the University of Wisconsin, all the band members (and their girlfriends) left Wisconsin and moved to Raleigh, North Carolina, to explore new terrain and make a name for themselves in a new music scene that was somewhat bigger than that of their hometown.

NORTH CAROLINA BREAKDOWN

They all lived together in a big house in Raleigh and worked on their music. When they got an

Getty Images

opportunity to play multiple shows at the multimedia space known as the Bickett Gallery, they decided to push their music even further by letting each band member focus on exploring his or her own musical and artistic strengths prior to one of the shows: the drummer, for example, focused on free jazz improvisation, and the keyboard player explored early American music. Vernon asked that everyone in the band sing during one Bickett Gallery concert—they did—and he even sang a song in a falsetto voice, which was new for him at that point.

The four-concert residency at the Bickett Gallery led to the band's breakup, however, as it became evident that Vernon and the rest of the band members had conflicting ideas about the direction DeYarmond Edison should pursue. Speaking to Grayson Currin of the Durham, North Carolina, *Independent Weekly* (27 July 2011), Vernon recalled, "The Bickett residency, ironically, was the most I've ever learned about music and simultaneously the reason we started to break apart. We realized there were so many things we'd never explored as musicians." He went on to say, "I had this intense friendship with all these guys, and it was like we had gotten divorced. We made all these life commitments to each other. I couldn't imagine going through something deeper." Although breaking up with his band was painful, Vernon had more trouble ahead: he was diagnosed with mononucleosis of the liver and mostly stayed in bed for three months. Because he had quit his job at a local restaurant, he had no money; Vernon's situation worsened when he lost a few hundred dollars playing poker online. He also broke up with his girlfriend.

DeYarmond Edison went on to perform without Vernon as a trio called Megafaun. Vernon, meanwhile, recorded a solo EP—as Justin Vernon—titled *Hazelton* (2006), of which he made one hundred copies to sell. He also served as a producer and collaborator for an album by the band The Rosebuds. In the fall of 2006, Vernon left Raleigh, overwhelmed, tired, and broke.

THE CABIN TALE

After spending some time at his parents' home in Wisconsin, Vernon drove to his father's hunting cabin in Dunn County, northwest of Eau Claire, where he would spend the winter months mostly in solitude. He had no plans to record an album or write songs but just wanted to get away and retrieve some sense of self. He did practical chores like chopping wood, and he even hunted deer. In a revealing interview with Guy Raz for the National Public Radio program *All Things Considered* (3 Jan. 2009), Vernon talked about his time at the cabin, describing it as "an attempt to still my life, I think. I think you can lose track of your inner voice because there are so many people around, there are so many distractions, there are so many voices and influences. And for me, it was really beautiful to sort of reconnect with this person that I felt like I haven't really had that much quiet time with since I was a little boy." And with regard to making music in the cabin, Vernon said: "I brought my musical gear with me because I thought, you know, it would be a smart idea to have it with me. But I think I was so confused; it was at a point in my life that I think everybody goes through where something needs to budge and then something needs to change, and you just—you can't really be aware of that because you're so within it, you're so in the present moment. And that present moment seems to be constantly fleeting at the same time."

After a few weeks of near solitude in the woods, Vernon felt that he had to start making music—so he played his guitar and sang. In his singing he emphasized emotions and feelings, and he began to work on his falsetto; he also experimented with voice-manipulation effects. Some of the songs he played and recorded in the cabin he had already written prior to leaving North Carolina, but his singing and overall approach to how the music should feel and sound was new. Vernon had no idea how popular his cabin recordings would become.

MAKING IT BIG

As a kind of tribute to his time in the cabin, Vernon decided to adopt the stage name Bon Iver, which is an intentional misspelling of the French greeting *bon hiver*, "good winter." Vernon, as Bon Iver, released *For Emma, Forever Ago* in 2007.

He only made a few hundred CDs to sell at concerts and online. But word of his music spread, especially after the album got positive mentions on music review websites such as Pitchfork and BrooklynVegan. As a result of this attention, Bon Iver was asked to perform at the CMJ music marathon festival in New York City, a potentially big opportunity for up-and-coming musicians. Vernon was approached by many record labels eager to sign him. He ultimately went with the record label Jagjaguwar, which officially released *For Emma, Forever Ago* in February 2008. The record received nearly unanimous positive reviews in all sorts of mainstream publications. In an elaborate review for the *Village Voice* (19 Feb. 2008), Melissa Giannini wrote: "Equal parts awe and nostalgia, hearing Vernon's muted strums and granular falsetto fade like spun sugar into breath vapor is like seeing the Grand Canyon for the first time. With idiosyncratic vocals and the simple acoustics of a man alone in this world (plus guitar), the tunes could've easily melted into monotony. But each track folds seamlessly yet distinctively into the next, like imperfect logs split and added to the pile; audible is the intensifying beat of a heart burdened by physical/emotional labor, and the layered echoes of a ghost chorus cascading across a chasm or against the walls of a creaky cabin-turned-cloister."

For Emma, Forever Ago has only nine songs, most of which feature guitar and multiple tracks of Vernon's voice. The latter allowed Vernon to harmonize with himself, creating interesting textures and layers of sound. Also featured on the album are spare drums and horns, all working subtly beneath his voice. The song "Skinny Love" contains a few of his voices (some in falsetto), acoustic guitars, a slide guitar, electric guitars, and quiet drums. The album's opening track, "Flume," opens with a simple, strumming acoustic guitar, which continues to provide the rhythm, but what stands out are the many falsetto voices that soon enter the song, sounding almost choral. Most of the album's lyrics focus less on meaning than on sound and on the emotion conveyed by Vernon's singing. In a profile for the *New Yorker* (12 Jan. 2009), Sasha Frere-Jones wrote, "Sometimes I am surprised by the fragmentary lyrics on *For Emma*; more often, I am moved by the beauty of Vernon's massed voice, and held in place by the force of each careful, dogged song." In yet another positive review, Kitty Empire for the London *Observer* (17 May 2008) called *For Emma* a "very full and emotionally rich record."

The media attention surrounding Vernon's debut album as Bon Iver led to a successful series of tours in 2008, both in the United States and Europe. In the former, his concerts included New York's Bowery Ballroom, as well as the South by Southwest Music Festival in Austin, Texas. Performing live as Bon Iver, Vernon usually had two or three musicians (all multi-instrumentalists) with him onstage. The songs—alongside Vernon's now famous voice—usually featured some of the following instruments: drums, guitars, keyboard, bass, and violin; his bandmates also sang backup. In December 2008, the band appeared on the *Late Show with David Letterman*, performing the song "Skinny Love." Bon Iver also contributed a new song to *The Twilight Saga: New Moon Soundtrack* (2009).

Bon Iver's popularity continued to grow with the release of *Blood Bank* (2009), an EP of four new songs. The title track, "Blood Bank," was written and recorded when Vernon was making *For Emma*. The last track on the EP, "Woods," is a quiet, meditative song sung a cappella that builds with multiple voices that have been manipulated in various ways by the pitch-correcting audio processor Auto-Tune. Because *Blood Bank* was only a four-song EP, it did not receive nearly the amount of attention in the mainstream press that *For Emma* did. But the popular rapper Kanye West heard it and was so enthralled with the song "Woods" that he asked Vernon if he could sample it on his album, *My Beautiful Dark Twisted Fantasy* (2010). Vernon agreed and "Woods" ended up as the basis for West's song "Lost in the World." West had something bigger in mind, however: he flew Vernon out to Hawaii, where the album was being recorded, and Vernon ended up singing on almost half of the album's songs. In the spring of 2011, Vernon, as Bon Iver, performed with West, who headlined the Coachella music festival in California. Soon after that, Vernon made the cover of the May 2011 edition of *Billboard* magazine and, according to that article, sales of *For Emma* reached 323,000 copies.

June 2011 saw the release of Bon Iver's second full-length album, *Bon Iver, Bon Iver*, which received mostly positive reviews. It was recorded at April Base, a studio Vernon had built in Fall Creek, Wisconsin. Although the new album features more instruments than *For Emma* and delved into different musical styles (1970s country rock, 1980s synthesizer-driven rock, 1990s art rock, and others), it still has Vernon's voice—falsetto and multiple tracks—as its central musical foundation and emotional force. Once again the lyrics are more focused on sound and feel rather than on concrete meaning. All the song titles are geographic names, some real and some made up. The song "Calgary" transitions from a mellow, acoustic mood to a more rock-centered one. "Perth" features heavy drums and "Lisbon, OH" has synthesizers.

Perhaps the most controversial song on the album is "Beth/Rest," the last track: it has a 1980s soft-rock feel that is very different from Vernon's previous Bon Iver works. The critics who did not like the album singled out this song as a primary example of the record's faults.

In a review for the *Chicago Sun-Times* (20 July 2011), Thomas Conner argued that "there's a crucial missing ingredient: soul." Conner called most of the album's songs "claustrophobic and flat compositions." Most critics, however, did not share that view. As Chris Richards wrote for the *Washington Post* (21 June 2011): "The best album of our halfway-over year proves that rock-and-roll isn't dead—it's only sleeping. And dreaming. Vividly." Similarly, Dorian Lynskey put *Bon Iver* on the "best albums of 2011" list for the London *Guardian* (12 Dec. 2011), calling the album "rich and expansive without being the least bit grandiose." Writing for the *San Francisco Chronicle* (19 June 2011), Aidin Vaziri observed, "The music feels as if it's suspended in air, as if getting a taste of mainstream pop only confirmed Vernon's desire to make music that sets a mood but doesn't require motion. The naive charm of the first album has dissipated a bit, but *Bon Iver, Bon Iver* still feels like a shot of integrity in a world of fake."

In February 2012, Bon Iver competed with The Band Perry, Nicki Minaj, J. Cole, and Skrillex to win the Grammy Award for Best New Artist. The band's album, *Bon Iver* also won the Grammy for Best Alternative Album, beating out albums from Death Cab for Cutie, Foster the People, and Radio Head.

SUGGESTED READING

Braiker, Brian. "Into the Wild with Bon Iver." *Rolling Stone* 19 Feb. 2009: 19. Print.

Caramanica, Jon. "Kanye's Boy in Eau Claire." *New York Times* 5 June 2011: MM28. Print.

Eells, Josh. "The Sound of Silence." *Rolling Stone* 23 June 2011: 70–73. Print.

Frere-Jones, Sasha. "Into the Woods: The Bon Iver Sound." *New Yorker* 12 Jan. 2009: 70–71. Print.

Greenwald, Andy. "Bon Iver." *Entertainment Weekly* 24 June 2011: 73. Print.

—*Dmitry Kiper*

Bradley Voytek

Born: June 18, 1981
Occupation: Neuroscientist

Neuroscientist Bradley Voytek is primarily interested in such topics as working memory and attention. His research has been published in a variety of journals, including *Neuron* and the *Journal of Cognitive Neuroscience*. Voytek is also interested in questions of meta-neuroscience—that is, questions about the field itself—related to issues such as data collection and peer reviews. He has written about these topics in his blog, *Oscillatory Thoughts*, and the blog of the

Courtesy of Bradley Voytek

magazine *Scientific American*. Voytek has also been interviewed by such major media outlets as the *New York Times*, the *Washington Post*, *Wired*, and *Forbes*. In 2008, he received a two-year grant from the National Institute of Neurological Disorders and Stroke, part of the National Institutes of Health (NIH); in 2011, he received a four-year grant from the NIH's National Institute of General Medical Sciences. Voytek holds a PhD in neuroscience from the University of California, Berkeley.

EARLY LIFE

Bradley Thomas Voytek was born in Phoenix, Arizona, on June 18, 1981. He grew up primarily in San Diego, California. An only child, he was raised by his father, Tom Voytek, during the first part of his childhood, but at the age of ten he moved in with the parents of his stepmother, Kim Isler.

From an early age, Voytek was fascinated by science fiction, a passion he still holds dear. Voytek wanted to become a physicist—most likely an astrophysicist—and by the time he was in high school, he had become an avid reader of popular physics and cosmology books by authors such as Stephen Hawking, Richard Feynman, and Carl Sagan. Voytek's step-grandfather was an electrical engineer who loved his work, and he was instrumental in getting Voytek interested in science, especially physics.

UNDERGRADUATE EDUCATION

Voytek graduated from high school a year early and went on to attend the University of Southern California (USC) in Los Angeles, where for the first two years he was a physics major. "I really learned how to socialize in college and I made a lot of friends," Voytek wrote in an e-mail to *Current Biography* (the source of all quotes unless otherwise noted). He continued, "During my first week of college in August 1997 it was really hot in Los Angeles, so I organized a series of evening 'fountain hopping' trips where a group of a dozen or more of us freshmen would jump around in the fountains around USC's campus. My dorm room became the de facto hangout place, and later my house became a party spot."

But Voytek's life journey took a big turn when his step-grandfather's mental faculties started to decline. In 1996, Voytek's grandfather had been was diagnosed with Parkinson's disease, a disorder of the brain mostly known for its motor symptoms, such as shaking and problems with balance and walking. In a talk at the TEDx-Berkeley conference on April 3, 2010, Voytek discussed this experience in relation to his interest in neuroscience. Aside from the physical signs of decline, Voytek noticed that his step-grandfather had "a lot of changes in personality: he became very anxious and paranoid; he would often wake up after nightmares where people were chasing him."

This started happening during the end of Voytek's high school days, and it would continue—and only get worse—when he entered college. At the time he began his studies at USC, Voytek said in his speech, "I believed in reductionism. I believed that psychology reduced to biology, which reduced to chemistry, which reduced to physics. But there is this thought that kept gnawing in the back of my mind: how is it this small group of cells that have died off in my grandfather's brain caused such *drastic* personality changes?" What Voytek wanted to know most was, "in terms of our minds, who are we?" So after about two years as a physics major, Voytek switched to psychology, because USC did not have a neuroscience major at the time. He also took classes outside his new major that focused on such topics as the philosophy of mind, computer programming, and artificial intelligence.

At USC, Voytek made a discovery. "As an undergrad," he told Alex Knapp for *Forbes* (17 Oct. 2011), "I joined a lab, and the professor wanted me to take a bunch of data stored as .txt files and open them and copy and paste them into Excel. He gave me three weeks to finish. Instead, I wrote a program to crank out the data in an afternoon, came to him the next day. He was blown away. I was blown away that he was blown away. That started my path to how I can combine technical skills with neurosciences to utilize computers to make data connections. . . . What can we learn from that data? How can we combine data to discover new things?"

Voytek received his BA in psychology from USC in 2002. From 2002 to 2004, he served as a staff research associate to Edythe D. London at the University of California, Los Angeles (UCLA).

GRADUATE EDUCATION AND RESEARCH

Voytek then went on to attend the University of California, Berkeley, where he pursued a doctorate in neuroscience. Of his graduate studies at UC Berkeley, Voytek told Knapp, "I was interested in how different brain areas communicate to give rise to cognition. Particularly, how does the brain balance learning—which is dependent on malleability, flexibility—with a stable sense of self and cognition? So I ended up doing research with Dr. Robert Knight, who basically made his career by working with patients with brain lesions. What we were interested in is how circumscribed lesions to one brain area affect behavior? And can we see that effect using an EEG?"—that is, an electroencephalogram, a test that measures and records the electrical activity of the brain using electrodes attached to the head and hooked by wires to a computer.

During his time in graduate school, Voytek held several positions at other universities. In 2007, he was the technology chair at the UC Berkeley Graduate Assembly Executive Board; from 2008 to 2010, he was a trainee at the Department of Neurology at the Johns Hopkins University School of Medicine in Baltimore; and in 2009, he was an electrophysiology consultant at the University Hospital in Oslo, Norway.

Back at UC Berkeley, Voytek worked on his PhD thesis, for which Robert Knight was his adviser. His dissertation, titled "Frontal and Basal Ganglia Contributions to Memory and Attention," explored the role of the basal ganglia and prefrontal cortex in visual working memory and attention by examining patients with focal, unilateral lesions to these brain regions. As part of his research, Voytek combined his EEG studies with his studies of patient-based behavioral research. He received his PhD in neuroscience in May 2010.

POSTDOCTORAL RESEARCH AND WORK

After earning his doctorate, Voytek worked as a postdoctoral researcher under UC Berkeley's Mark D'Esposito until 2011. In the fall of 2010, Voytek and Knight published two papers in the journals *Neuron* and *Proceedings of the National Academy of Sciences* that supported the hypothesis that memory is not simply stored in one area of the brain but is, rather, distributed throughout its various regions; therefore, they concluded, memory is a brain-wide network. Then, starting in 2011, Voytek began work as a postdoctoral fellow under Adam Gazzaley at the University of California, San Francisco (UCSF). Together, they examined the limits and plasticity (ability to

adapt) of human attention and how it is distributed in the brain.

In addition to questions of neuroscience, Voytek is also fascinated by meta-neuroscience questions, ones about the methods and approach of the field itself. For example, he has written about the peer-review process. In an article for the *Scientific American* blog (2 Nov. 2011), he asked non-rhetorically, "What is scientific peer review for?" His answer: "The scientific peer-review process increases the probability that the scientific literature converges—*at long time scales*—upon scientific truth via distributed fact-checking, replication, and validation by other scientists." In the article, Voytek made it clear that he is not attacking peer review, which he believes to be very important; rather, he wrote, "I'm attacking peer-review [that is] based on journal editors hand-picking one to three scientists who then read a biased presentation of the data without being given the actual data used to generate the conclusions." Voytek concluded that although peer review is necessary, it does not mean that all new research should be published in journals or even on paper (as opposed to only online); furthermore, he argued, the scientific papers could be shorter, publishing only the new findings without rehashing old studies. All this would also make the publication process faster, which Voytek sees as crucial to advancing science.

In a meta-neuroscience undertaking of his own, Voytek is working on a project that should help scientists better analyze data. With the help of his wife, Jessica, a web designer and developer, Voytek is working on a website to distill the millions of neuroscience research studies into something more manageable. The website, called brainSCANr, is a database in which scientists can look up key words and concepts to see papers that examine two or more concepts or faculties. Voytek explained the project to *Current Biography* thusly: "[There are] so many little pieces of facts about how this kind of neuron responds to this kind of behavior, and how this neurotransmitter modulates neuronal firing in this brain region, and how people with this disease process faces differently from 'normal' people, and so on. It's too much, and no one person will ever be capable of integrating all of this stuff. So we're seeing if we can't do it algorithmically, at least a little, to help ease the burden and speed up discovery."

Besides his serious scientific endeavors, Voytek is interested in zombies and is involved in something he calls "zombie sciences." This goes back to his love for the fantasy and science-fiction genres. Starting from the time when he was a doctoral student at UC Berkeley, he and neuroscientist Timothy Verstynen created a "map of the zombie brain," based on observable information they gathered from such movies as

28 *Days Later* (2002) and *Shaun of the Dead* (2004). They then created a Zombie Apocalypse Survival Guide. "This entire endeavor is partly an academic 'what if' exercise for us and partly a tongue-in-cheek critique of the methods of our profession of cognitive neuroscience," Verstynen told *Wired* (30 June 2011). Voytek added, "If someone accidentally learns something about the brain along the way, then I've achieved my goal."

Voytek started working as a consultant for the National Academy of Sciences' Science and Entertainment Exchange in 2011, in addition to his academic employment. In 2012, he also began to serve as a data evangelist for Uber, Inc., an on-demand car service. Although Voytek lists himself on his resume as the winner (split prize) of *Time* magazine's Person of the Year award, in both 2006 and 2011, this is not quite accurate: in 2006 the winner was "You," and in 2011 it was "The Protestor." (Voytek told *Current Biography* that this is very much tongue-in-cheek and a "good conversation piece.")

Voytek has published work in such journals as *Biological Psychiatry* and the *Journal of Cognitive Neuroscience*, and he has two coauthored papers in the books *Mind and the Frontal Lobes: Cognition, Behavior, and Brain Imagining* (2010) and *Multiscale Analysis and Nonlinear Dynamics: From Molecules to the Brain* (2012).

PERSONAL LIFE

Voytek describes himself as a "big gamer," referring to his passion for video games and tabletop role-playing games such as Dungeons and Dragons. He is also a dedicated weight lifter and likes to partake in outdoor activities, including snowboarding and rock climbing. But his biggest passions, he told *Current Biography*, are "writing and talking to people, meeting new people, and listening to who they are," as a result of which his wife calls him a "social butterfly."

SUGGESTED READING

Knapp, Alex. "Neuroscientist Bradley Voytek Is Bringing the Silicon Valley Ethos into Academia." *Forbes*. Forbes.com, 17 Oct. 2011. Web. 23 Mar. 2012.

Sanders, Robert. "Phantom Images Stored in Flexible Network throughout Brain." *UC Berkeley News Center*. U of California, Berkeley, 3 Nov. 2010. Web. 23 Mar. 2012.

Voytek, Bradley. *Oscillatory Thoughts*. Bradley Voytek, n.d. Web. 23 Mar. 2012.

---. "What Is Peer Review For?" *Scientific American*. Scientific American, 2 Nov. 2011. Web. 23 Mar. 2012.

Watercutter, Angela. "How to Survive the Zombie Apocalypse Using Science." *Wired*. Condé Nast, 30 June 2011. Web. 23 Mar. 2012.

—*Dmitry Kiper*

Elizabeth Warren

Born: June 22, 1949
Occupation: Lawyer, politician

In the wake of the financial crisis that hit the United States in 2008, Elizabeth Warren, a Harvard law professor and bankruptcy expert, was appointed by Senate Majority Leader Harry Reid to chair the Congressional Oversight Panel for the Troubled Asset Relief Program (TARP). Warren's deep knowledge of financial matters and blunt style of questioning won her many supporters in her effort to track the bailout funds that had been awarded to major banks and other institutions, but she also made enemies, especially in Republican circles and in the financial industry. According to Suzanna Andrews for *Vanity Fair* (November 2011, online), her detractors called her "incompetent, power hungry, [and] ignorant," and in one well-publicized instance, she was branded a "liar." Republicans saw her as a threat to their long-held beliefs about government and business and vowed to block her confirmation as head of the newly created Consumer Financial Protection Bureau (CFPB), a mandate of the Dodd-Frank Wall Street Reform and Consumer Protection Act of 2010. Although Warren had conceived the plans for the CFPB in the first place and had spent several months building the agency and hiring personnel, President Barack Obama worried that her contentious relationship with Republicans—as well as with some members of his own party—might undermine its mission. He chose instead to nominate former Ohio attorney general Richard Cordray for the post, "kneecapping" Warren, as Andrews phrased it, and giving her "a Judas kiss" after the announcement.

Warren had first been tapped by Reid because of her 2007 paper "Unsafe at Any Rate," in which she argued that the difference between buying a tangible consumer product (like a toaster) and a financial product (like a mortgage) lies in how the two markets are regulated. "It is impossible to buy a toaster that has a one-in-five chance of bursting into flames and burning down your house," she wrote. "But it is possible to refinance an existing home with a mortgage that has the same one-in-five chance of putting the family out on the street—and the mortgage won't even carry a disclosure of that fact to the homeowner. Similarly, it's impossible to change the price on a toaster once it has been purchased. But long after the papers have been signed, it is possible to triple the price of the credit used to finance the purchase of that appliance, even if the customer meets all the credit terms, in full and on time."

Referring to the 2008 financial crisis, economist Paul Krugman wrote in an op-ed piece for the *New York Times* (March 20, 2011, online) that Warren was one of the "foresighted few" in

Courtesy of Brendan Hoffman/Getty Images

her prediction that high debt levels and predatory lending would spell financial disaster for America's middle class. "[Warren] took the lead in pushing for consumer protection as an integral part of financial reform," Krugman asserted, "arguing that many debt problems were created when lenders pushed borrowers into taking on obligations they didn't understand."

In creating the CFPB Warren had envisioned a government agency that would regulate such egregious practices and promote transparency between businesses and consumers—much like the Federal Trade Commission's Bureau of Consumer Protection—but her plan was met with harsh opposition from Republicans, who accused her of interfering with the free market. "I've never been an ideologue," Warren, a former Republican, told Joe Nocera for the *New York Times* (July 22, 2011, online). "And I thought the best way to deal with [the] perception [that I am anti-business] was to put our vision out there. The vision is clear. Consumers should be able to tell the price and risk of any credit product before they buy it. We want to mow down the fine print." But as Nocera noted, the accusations "never did go away."

Although Warren was passed over for the nomination to head the bureau that she had created, and despite the browbeating she took from legislators, she received strong support and praise from the ordinary citizens she had championed during her months of preparing the CFPB for operation. In 2012 she ran for the US Senate seat once held by the late Edward Kennedy of Massachusetts, winning the Democratic primary and facing Republican incumbent Senator Scott Brown in November of that year. Her message struck an undeniable chord with many economically struggling voters. "We cannot run a democracy without a strong middle class," she said in a campaign speech quoted by Andrews. "If we hollow out the middle class then the country we know is gone."

EARLY LIFE AND EDUCATION

The future law professor and Senate candidate was born on June 22, 1949, in Norman, Oklahoma to Donald J. and Pauline Reed Herring. The youngest of four siblings, she was the only girl. Before she was born, her father's business partner had absconded with money earmarked for starting a car dealership. It was a financial blow from which it would take the Herrings years to recover. During Warren's childhood, Donald worked as a traveling salesman, but he suffered a debilitating heart attack when she was 12. He later found work as a maintenance man in an apartment building. Pauline took a job answering phones at Sears so the family could pay its mortgage. Warren, who had begun babysitting for her neighbors at the age of nine, started waiting tables at her Aunt Alice's Mexican restaurant at age 13. She attended Northwest Classen High School and was named Oklahoma's top high-school debater at age 16. Because she had skipped a grade, she graduated that year and was awarded a full scholarship to George Washington University, in Washington, DC. She left the school after two years, however, to marry her childhood sweetheart, Jim Warren, a National Aeronautics and Space Administration (NASA) engineer. At 19, she moved with him to Houston, Texas, where he worked on the Apollo program. Warren subsequently enrolled at the University of Houston, and in 1970 she earned a BS degree in speech pathology.

Jim Warren was later assigned to work in New Jersey on an antiballistic-missile program, and there his wife began teaching children with disabilities at a local public school. She soon became frustrated with the school's bureaucracy, however, and quit. Recalling how she had loved to debate in high school, Warren decided to pursue a law career and enrolled at Rutgers University shortly after having her first child, Amelia, in 1972. When Warren graduated in 1976, she was nine months pregnant with her second child, Alexander. She set up a private law practice in her home and also began teaching in a newly created evening program at the Rutgers School of Law. At 26 years old, she was younger than many of her students.

ACADEMIC CAREER

In 1978 Warren and her husband divorced. She found work teaching law at the University of

Houston and the University of Michigan, among other schools, and conducting extensive research on bankruptcy. "As a teacher at that level, you do research—that's just part of the job," she told Don Mecoy for the *Oklahoman* (August 1, 2010, online). "The areas where I was teaching were all the money courses—commercial law, contract law, bankruptcy law." Warren had just started teaching when the United States Bankruptcy Reform Act was passed in 1978. The law, which went into effect in 1979, made it easier for businesses and individuals to file for bankruptcy. Warren decided to investigate the new code and enlisted the help of fellow law professor Jay Lawrence Westbrook and sociologist Teresa A. Sullivan to conduct a study. "I get this clever idea," she recalled to Charles P. Pierce for the *Boston Globe Sunday Magazine* (December 20, 2009, online). "I'm going to expose these sleazy debtors who are exploiting the bankruptcy system and their poor, hapless creditors and enriching themselves as far as the law allows by going through bankruptcy court. I go out with these other two folks [Sullivan and Westbrook] and we start collecting data about the families who are filing for bankruptcy. We end up doing this big study . . . and it completely turns me around. I knew what I was going to find before I went out there, and I discovered that it doesn't work that way."

Warren and her colleagues discovered that most bankruptcy cases occurred in middle-class families and commonly arose from job loss, divorce, and medical debt, thus countering the popular notion that people declared bankruptcy as an easy way to avoid paying their bills. The initial study was, as Fred Waddell wrote for the *Journal of Financial Counseling and Planning* (1991), perhaps "the most extensive empirical study of consumer bankruptcy ever undertaken" and took almost six years to complete. Written with Sullivan and Westbrook, the resulting book, *As We Forgive Our Debtors: Bankruptcy and Consumer Credit in America* was first published in 1989 by Oxford University Press. "The authors describe the law and statistics in clear, nontechnical language," Waddell wrote, "combining a thorough statistical description of the social and economic position of consumer bankrupts with human portraits of the debtors and creditors whose journey has ended in bankruptcy court." The study found that less than five percent of all bankruptcy debtors were found to be "abusing the system," as Waddell explained. He quoted *As We Forgive Our Debtors*: "We found virtually no debtors who seemed to take bankruptcy on a lark (or) to deal with relatively minor debts in relation to their incomes. Instead, the debtors . . . were in so much financial trouble we had to wonder how they had stayed out of bankruptcy so long and what it must have been like in the months or years before filing as they dealt with debts that grew mountainous beside unsteady income. The fact that the debtors in our sample did not choose bankruptcy earlier, given the disastrous state of their affairs, suggests to us that many of them tried longer than was reasonable to avoid discharging their debts. If the economic theorists are correct that moral conviction and stigma are the principal deterrents to bankruptcy, the data suggest that these deterrents work. One out of five bankrupt individuals reaffirm some of their debts, often for no discernable reason other than their sense of obligation."

The three authors teamed up again in 2000 to publish *The Fragile Middle Class: Americans in Debt*, the fruits of a survey of more than 2,000 people who had filed for bankruptcy in the United States during the 1990s. The study reaffirmed many of their earlier findings. They found, as paraphrased by David Cay Johnston for the *New York Times* (September 3, 2000, online), that "people in every occupation go bankrupt in rough proportion to their numbers." "Many people in bankruptcy were solid bill payers until something knocked their legs out from under them," Warren told Johnston. "Bankruptcy is a solution invoked one at a time by families who have fallen through the social safety net." A reviewer for *Publisher's Weekly* (March 13, 2000, online) concluded: "While the authors offer no comprehensive solutions to this societal malaise, their chilling diagnosis of middle class affliction demonstrates that we all may be only a job loss, medical problem or credit card indulgence away from a downward spiral leading to bankruptcy."

In 2003 Warren wrote *The Two Income Trap: Why Middle-Class Mothers and Fathers Are Going Broke* with her daughter, Amelia Warren Tyagi, a former financial consultant. "When a family builds a budget around two paychecks, they are in big trouble if either paycheck goes away," Warren told Melissa Block for the National Public Radio (NPR) program *All Things Considered* (September 8, 2003). "A two-income family has two chances for someone to get laid off, two chances for someone to get too sick to work and, most importantly, no safety net if anything goes wrong." *The Two Income Trap* became immensely popular and marked, in some respects, Warren's transformation from academic to advocate.

In 2005, the same year she and Tyagi published the best-selling book *All Your Worth: The Ultimate Lifetime Money Plan*, Warren was invited to speak on the television show *Dr. Phil*. On the program, one family told her that they had taken out a second mortgage in order to consolidate their debts. Warren patiently explained that such a decision put them in danger of foreclosure. After speaking, she recalled thinking: "I've been doing scholarly work for more than 20 years, and I may have just done more good in the last 90 seconds than I ever accomplished with anything else I wrote," as she told Daniel

McGinn for the *Daily Beast* (April 10, 2009, online). "I began to think that instead of writing one more thing to impress other academics or to reassure myself that I'm a serious scholar, I should [focus] on the question of change, of real impact, of how to be helpful." (Over the course of her career, Warren has co-authored several textbooks, including *The Law of Debtors and Creditors: Text, Cases, and Problems*; *Secured Credit: A Systems Approach*; and *Commercial Transactions: A Systems Approach*. Each has been reprinted several times.)

PUBLIC POLICY WORK

In 1995, the year she joined the faculty of Harvard Law School, Warren was asked to advise the National Bankruptcy Review Commission (NBRC), which had been created under the authority of the Bankruptcy Reform Act of 1994. The independent commission solicited various views on the bankruptcy system to be included in a report that Warren later helped draft; the legislation suggested in the report became the source of a brutal debate in Congress. The legislative director of the Consumer Federation of America described the opposing factions to Andrews: "On the one side you had a huge business alliance, starting with the credit card companies. And on the other side you had a sort of ragtag public-interest coalition." Ultimately, the legislation that passed was characterized as a win for the business alliance and a resounding loss for consumers and Warren's commission.

Warren played a lead role in a similar public-policy debate in 2008, when Senator Harry Reid asked her to head the congressional panel formed to oversee the $700 billion government bailout known as TARP. The money was dispersed among such large institutions as the insurance corporation AIG, which received $150 billion for its lost assets. When Warren took the position, her role was relatively undefined, but she soon created an investigative committee, interviewing government officials and demanding open communication with banks who had received TARP funds. (Her job was particularly difficult because the TARP money had been doled out without requiring companies to report how the money would be spent.) Warren televised the public hearings, and her blunt style of questioning greatly embarrassed the financiers and government officials brought before the panel. (One video clip, labeled "Elizabeth Warren Makes [Secretary of the Treasury] Timothy Geitner Squirm" enjoyed great popularity on You-Tube and quickly went viral.) Warren repeatedly asked how the TARP money had been spent at Chrysler, Citibank, and the other recipient companies, but her questions were met with vague responses and incredulity. "These people aren't used to simple questions," a frustrated Warren told Mecoy. "They don't expect to hear them and

they somehow, when you do (ask them), act like you're not half-bright or you're somehow asking something nasty." Warren was also frustrated by the lack of accountability her subjects seemed to feel. "What's begun to hit me is that people have enormous power and yet nobody's ever responsible," Warren told Mecoy. "How does that happen? Nobody's ever accountable. Nothing is ever anybody's fault."

While Warren succeeded in turning public attention to the mismanagement behind the crisis, she also made her next appointed task—the creation of the CFPB—more difficult. Wall Street executives tried to ruin her credibility by suggesting that she had only a tenuous grasp on financial reality. "But her sin was actually the opposite: she knew what she was talking about," Andrews asserted. "Wall Street's power in Washington, says a former congressional staffer who worked on the Dodd-Frank bill, has been built partly on the fact that few people outside Wall Street understand the esoterica of finance—the intricacies of C.D.O.'s [collateralized debt obligations] and the labyrinthian structures of credit-default swaps. And that knowledge is used to control and confuse." Warren made the exposure of the "tricks and traps" hidden by that esoterica and jargon the driving mission of the CFPB, but she faced enormous resistance at every step of the process. Opponents of the CFPB, backed by powerful business lobbies, attempted to defang or eliminate the bureau in Congress, but Warren fought back by speaking out in public. "My first choice is a strong consumer agency," she told Shahien Nasiripour for the *Huffington Post* (March 3, 2010, online). "My second choice is no agency at all and plenty of blood and teeth left on the floor."

Worried that a bitter battle over Warren's nomination to run the bureau would undermine the CFPB's purpose, President Obama nominated former Ohio attorney general Richard Cordray to the post instead. Warren's struggles with the CFPB have made her a populist icon; she officially announced her candidacy for the US Senate on September 14, 2011. After triumphing in the Massachusetts Democratic primary on September 18, 2012, Warren faced incumbent Scott Brown, a Republican with deep ties to the financial industry.

Buoyed by the nascent Occupy Wall Street protests across the country, Warren's message has been given significant exposure. "There is nobody in this country who got rich on his own," she said in one campaign speech that has since gone viral. "You built a factory out there? Good for you. But I want to be clear: you moved your goods to market on the roads the rest of us paid for; you hired workers the rest of us paid to educate; you were safe in your factory because of police forces and fire forces that the rest of us paid for. . . . Now look, you built a factory and it turned into something terrific, or a great idea? God bless. Keep a big hunk of it. But part of the underlying social contract is you take a hunk of that and pay forward for the next kid who comes along." She told Andrews that the stakes were high in her race for the US Senate. "[Middle-class families] are getting *hammered* and you know Washington doesn't get it," she stated. "G.E. doesn't pay any taxes and we are asking college kids to take on even more debt to get an education, and asking seniors to get by on less. These aren't just economic questions. These are *moral* questions." On November 6, Warren's message concerning Wall Street excess resonated with voters as she defeated Brown to become the first woman elected to the Senate from Massachusetts.

Warren is now married to Bruce Mann, a fellow law professor at Harvard. They live in Cambridge, Massachusetts.

SUGGESTED READING

Andrews, Suzanna. "The Woman Who Knew Too Much." *Vanity Fair.* Condé Nast Digital, Nov. 2011. Web. 19 Dec. 2011.

"Elizabeth Warren Discusses Her Book *The Two-Income Trap: Why Middle-Class Mothers and Fathers Are Going Broke.*" *All Things Considered.* NPR. 8 Sep. 2003. Radio.

Krugman, Paul. "The War on Warren." *New York Times.* New York Times, 20 Mar. 2011. Web. 19 Dec. 2011.

Nocera, Joe. "The Travails of Ms. Warren." *New York Times.* New York Times, 22 July 2011. Web. 19 Dec. 2011.

Warren, Elizabeth. "Unsafe at Any Rate." *Democracy.* Democracy: A Journal of Ideas, Summer 2007. Web. 19 Dec. 2011.

— *Molly Hagan*

Niobe Way

Born: 1964
Occupation: Professor of applied psychology

Niobe Way is a professor of applied psychology and a co-director of the Center for Research on Culture, Development, and Education in the Department of Applied Psychology at New York University (NYU). She is also the author of *Everyday Courage: The Lives and Stories of Urban Teenagers* (1998), and most recently, *Deep Secrets: Boys' Friendships and the Crisis of Connection* (2011). Way has been researching the behaviors of adolescent boys for nearly 20 years, and in *Deep Secrets,* she "debunks the age-old assumption that the capacity and need for close intimate relationships is inherently female," Debra Weinstein wrote for NYU's Web site (July 1, 2010). Way criticizes masculine stereotypes that encourage boys and men to closet their emotions. "Data from a wide

Courtesy of Harvard University Press

range of experts, from neuroscientists [and] developmental psychologists to primatologists and evolutionary anthropologists, indicate that empathy, close relationships, and love are not only human capacities and needs, they are at the root of why we have thrived as a species," Way wrote in an opinion piece for the *Huffington Post* Website (June 7, 2011). "Yet we continue to make valuing close relationships and being empathic into something girly or gay rather than simply human or critical for well-being."

In addition to researching gender, Way studies how schools and families influence teenage development and ethnic identity, and the effects of racial stereotyping in education, specifically during the crucial early teen years. In a comprehensive study over several years, Way conducted hundreds of interviews with urban students attending schools in New York City. "According to our research, a primary reason for the ineffectiveness of middle school reform lies with the fact that most efforts do not address a critical problem faced by many middle school students, namely racial stereotypes, discrimination and harassment in middle schools," she wrote with Diane Hughes for the *New York Times* (March 25, 2007, online). With Bonnie J. Leadbeater, Way is also the author of *Growing Up Fast: Transitions to Adulthood among Adolescent Mothers* (2001), which won the Best Book Award for Social Policy from the Society for Research on Adolescence in 2002. She has co-edited several other books, including *Urban Girls: Resisting Stereotypes,*

Creating Identities (1996); Adolescent Boys: Exploring Diverse Cultures of Boyhood (2004); and Urban Girls Revisited: Building Strengths (2007). Way was named president of the Society for Research on Adolescence (SRA) in 2010.

EARLY LIFE AND EDUCATION

Way was born in 1964 in Paris, France, to parents Brenda (Bolte) Way and Peter Way. She has three siblings—Justin, Thaisa, and Lucan—including the stepbrother from her mother's second marriage. Peter Way is an independent classics scholar and, according to Jan Hoffman for the New York Times (September 21, 2011, online), named her for Niobe, the ancient Queen of Thebes who boasted to the gods about her fourteen children. As punishment for her pride, Niobe's children were slaughtered, and in her mourning she turned to stone. Way's mother Brenda is an accomplished dancer who studied ballet with famed choreographer George Balanchine as a teenager in New York City. Brenda founded the Oberlin Dance Collective (ODC) at the college of the same name in Oberlin, Ohio in 1971, by which time she and Peter Way were divorced. Way moved to the Bay Area of California with the ODC, her mother, and her siblings in 1976. Brenda married Way's stepfather, Henry Erlich, director of human genetics at Roche, in 1981.

In an interview with Hoffman, Way recalled watching the friendship between her younger brother Lucan and his best friend when she was a teenager. The boys were inseparable, until one day when Way's mother caught them destroying a cherished rag doll. The seemingly insignificant incident ruptured the boys' friendship completely, and Way maintains that her brother was so wounded by the separation that he has trouble talking about it today. She cites the event as an early inspiration for what would become much of her life's work. "That's when I first saw the significance of friendships for boys, in both my brother's love and his sense of loss," she said. Way attended the University of California, Berkeley. Her first ambition was acting, but as she told Deborah Cameron for Times Higher Education (April 7, 2011, online), she "chickened out." Way changed her focus to psychology, and graduated with dual degrees in social welfare and psychology in 1985.

In the late 1980s, Way worked as a counselor at an urban public high school. The boys she met while working at the school often came to her to talk about their struggles with "friendship, betrayal, and heartbreak," Vanna Le summarized for the New Yorker (March 16, 2011, online). Way added to Le, "I became fascinated by the discrepancy between the stereotypes of boys and what boys actually sounded like. I wanted to learn about their social and emotional developments, particularly during adolescence—the

age during which boys are most heavily stereotyped as stoic and only interested in one thing (i.e., sex). I discovered that while boys do sound and act like stereotypes at times, they also often implicitly challenge such stereotypes especially in the context of their closest male friendships."

Way completed her doctorate in human development and psychology at Harvard University in 1994, where she studied with Carol Gilligan, whose research on adolescent girls in the early 1980s put her at the forefront of gender studies. Gilligan's research focused on the "missing voices of girls and women in developmental theory," a reporter wrote on NYU's Steinhardt Web site, and as Way continued in her own studies, she realized that the voices of urban youths seemed to be missing as well. "Theories about how young people navigate adolescence have been largely based on studies of predominantly white suburban schools," Way is quoted as saying on the site; in her postdoctoral work, Way sought to bring the experiences of inner-city teenagers into a larger understanding of what she called "normative developmental processes."

CAREER

Way was a National Institute of Mental Health postdoctoral fellow through Yale University's Department of Psychology from 1994 to 1996. During that time, she spent six months in New York City at the helm of a research project in which she interviewed over 120 adolescent mothers in the New York's Harlem neighborhood. The information culled from these interviews was included in Growing Up Fast: Transitions to Adulthood among Adolescent Mothers (2001), the book she co-wrote with psychologist Bonnie J. Leadbeater. Growing Up Fast received the Best Book Award for Social Policy from the SRA in 2002. According to the summary provided by the book's publisher, Psychology Press (2001), Way and Leadbeater's portrayal of young, inner-city mothers defies stereotype. "[The mothers'] often-creative solutions to living in poverty, the intensity of their desires to make their children's lives better, the height of their youthful ambition when they succeed, and the depth of their pain when they fail, all show a surprising range. The authors argue that adolescent mothers who enter young adulthood with the skills and desires to care for themselves and their children are not the resilient few and present a lengthy analysis of the multidimensional processes that lead to and characterize this resilience."

After co-editing Urban Girls: Resisting Stereotypes, Creating Identities (1996) with Leadbeater (the two also co-edited Urban Girls Revisited: Building Strengths in 2007); Way published Everyday Courage: The Lives and Stories of Urban Teenagers in 1998. In the book, Way explores the lives of 24 teenagers living in a northwestern city; her aim, she wrote on the NYU Steinhardt

Web site, was to address the "huge misconceptions [that] exist about urban teenagers. Many people's impression of these kids is that their lives are about gangs, drugs, violence, and teen pregnancy." Instead, *Everyday Courage* presented nuanced portraits of teens dealing with "betrayal, trust, racism, sexism, single motherhood, and death," Antoinette Brinkman summarized for the *Library Journal* (1998, online). Way's mentor, Gilligan, praised the book as a "brilliant example of voice-centered research," adding that it was "essential reading for anyone hoping to work effectively with adolescents." Way's subjects, according to the NYU Press, included Malcolm, an honor-roll student who became a teen father and suffered from depression as his younger sister was dying of cancer; and Eva, a talented basketball player and poet who struggles to maintain a relationship with her mother as she pursues a college scholarship. "Contradictory and surprisingly conservative viewpoints are expressed by these young people, who seem to value relationships and community above all," Brinkman wrote. "Though based on a small sample, the book is meticulous, provocative, and innovative."

In 2004, Way and Judy Y. Chu co-edited *Adolescent Boys: Exploring Diverse Cultures of Boyhood*. The book was divided into five parts, focusing respectively on identity development, family relationships, friends and peers, sexuality and romantic relationships, and schooling. "*Adolescent Boys* expands the discourse on what it means to be a boy and masculine in both a Western and non-Western context through its amplification of boys' voices across various cultural contexts," Lionel C. Howard concluded in his review for the *Harvard Education Review* (Winter 2005, online). He added that the book "brings together a coherent and consistent body of literature on a topic that is often relegated to a single chapter or afterthought in similar books and edited volumes." However, Howard noted some flaws in the execution of Way and Chu's research: "The authors utilize an assortment of methodological and analytical strategies and techniques to provide empirically grounded evidence that ultimately contributes to a deeper understanding of boys' lives," he wrote. "While a few studies have some methodological shortcomings (e.g. using a single item to measure suicide ideation, self-reports, and secondary data) and limited conclusions (e.g. failing to discuss issues of trust for gay or bisexual boys, and the complexity of having multiple marginal identities, like being Latino and gay), they still contribute to an expanded view of masculinity (beyond hegemonic and stereotypical definitions) by attending the nuances that not only celebrate the unique factors of adolescent boys from diverse backgrounds, but also highlight the aspects that make them similar."

The same year *Adolescent Boys* was published, Way and fellow NYU professor Diane Hughes began conducting a study called "Raising Academic Performance: A Study of School, Peer, and Parental Influences on Academic Engagement and Performance Among Diverse Urban Youth." In the first phase of the federally financed study, Way and Hughes asked sixth-grade students to fill out, according to Anindita Dasgupta for the New York *Villager* (August 30, 2006, online), a substantive, 40-page survey about their experiences, interactions, and opinions. "We feel that there could be a lot of improvement in the way schools serve kids in school, as well as outside of school," Way told Julia Levy for the *New York Sun* (November 12, 2004). "We want to try to really locate the factors that seem most important from the kids' perspective. We want to find what's most important in making a difference and have that feed back into the schools."

The same group of students—from public middle schools in the East Harlem, Manhattan Valley, Gramercy, and Chinatown neighborhoods of New York City, numbering about 800—answered similar questions in the seventh grade and again in eighth grade. In the second phase of the research, Way and Hughes interviewed a subset of that group—both children and their parents—and asked follow-up questions that did not appear in the larger survey. Two hundred voluntary participants were interviewed. Though the psychologists went through a rigorous screening process to communicate with the New York City schools in which the study took place, some parents were troubled by the survey questions which, Dasgupta reported, included: "On average, how often do you see your father?"; "How much does this person (mother, father, guardian) like or love you?"; "Some people don't expect me to do well in life because of my ethnicity—(strongly disagree, disagree, in between, agree, strongly agree)"; and, "A lot of people don't expect my ethnic group to do well in life." However, despite criticism, most parents allowed their children to participate in the survey. Way pointed out that none of the questions asked students about topics she considered to be truly invasive, such as drug use or sex, though she acknowledged that some of the questions might make students uncomfortable. "You'll never get real answers and learn real perspectives without asking sensitive questions," she told Dasgupta.

The results of their study were surprising. "We found that 40 percent to 45 percent of black, Hispanic, and white middle school students and 60 percent to 65 percent of Asian-American middle school students report being discriminated against or harassed by their peers because of their race or ethnicity," Way wrote with Hughes for the *Times*. "Such harassment ranges from slurs to violence. One student said she was told she couldn't play a game with other students because she was Dominican. Other students spoke of being teased, spit on, pushed, tripped in the stairwell and even punched in the face by their peers because of their ethnicity. This information is important because racial and ethnic stereotypes, discrimination and harassment create a hostile learning environment for everyone." Way and Hughes offered solutions in their report. They called for the topic of race and ethnicity and "the way it influences the experiences and expectations of students, teachers, and parents" to become a part of the middle school curriculum and a significant part of teacher-training programs.

Way addressed two negative effects of racial stereotyping in the school environment in an article for the *Huffington Post* Web site (September 5, 2011). First, she cited the Pygmalion effect, an oft-replicated experiment conducted by Robert Rosenthal and Lenore Jacobson in the 1960s in which children in classrooms were randomly labeled exceptionally smart before the school year began. Way noted, "The teachers were told about the labels, but the children were not." As a result of the experiment, the children with the randomly assigned labels showed a significant improvement in their intelligence scores. "The impact of teacher (or employer, parent, etc.) expectations and support—and the consequences of a lack thereof—should not be underestimated for black and Latino men," Way wrote. Similarly, she cited the "stereotype threat," a result of an experiment conducted by psychologists Claude Steele and Joshua Aronson. Steele and Aronson found that black students and white students score equally well on achievement tests "when they do not think that their race will be considered in the assessment." Conversely, the experiment also found that black students "score significantly lower than white students" when they are led to believe that their race will be considered in the assessment. Way wrote that this "stereotype threat . . . is at the root of the achievement gap." Adding, "When schools and families do not support the emotional and social needs of children . . . they struggle to achieve their goals."

RECENT WORK

Way's most recent book is *Deep Secrets: Boys' Friendships and the Crisis of Connection* (2011). As quoted by Weinstein, Way wrote in the book: "The boys in our studies felt the pressure to accommodate to 'conventional male standards' and occasionally said it directly: 'Now I'm a man, I need to take care of myself and not depend on others,' or 'I don't need to speak about my feelings anymore, I'm growing up,' or simply 'I don't have close friendships with other boys. . . . I'm not gay.' Having intimate male friends and being a heterosexual male were perceived contradictions. 'I sound so gay,' says an 18-year-old

boy after he claims that it 'wouldn't be so bad' if he still had a close male friend." *Deep Secrets* addresses what Way has deemed a social crisis: she writes that boys and men are sacrificing necessary and healthy relationships under pressure to adhere to what is considered gender-appropriate behavior. Way reports that, as children, both boys and girls enjoy close same-sex friendships, but as boys reach adolescence this behavior—or generally emotionally expressive behavior—is discouraged. "As they reached late adolescence, boys described how their close relationships with parents and friends were fading," Way wrote for the *Huffington Post* Web site (June 17, 2011), "'like a DJ uses his cross fader to start fading it slowly and slowly and now I'm like halfway through the cross fade,' as one 17-year-old described it to me. At the ages of 16 and 17 years old, when the suicide rate among boys in the United States increases to five times the rate of girls, boys spoke of losing their close relationships and feeling increasingly isolated." Way says that neurological differences between males and females have been largely exaggerated. Culturally, we tend to associate emotional behavior with women, but Way and numerous researchers agree that exhibiting emotion and sharing close friendships have nothing to do with gender roles—that they are, in fact, fundamentally human.

Further, Way believes that such gender bias has influenced the way we think about school and parenting. Way suggests that social skills and encouraged empathy are crucial to a child's development. "[I]n this culture, [maturity] is equated with independence, autonomy, and separating from others. I think maturity should be defined as the ability to have mutually supportive, intimate, and deeply empathetic relationships," she told Le. "If that was the epitome of maturity, the way we think about parenting and schooling our children would radically change."

Way has been a professor of applied psychology at NYU since 1995. In 2005, Way visited China for research. She returned in 2007 and taught in NYU's Shanghai program. Way is separated from her husband of 18 years. She has two young children and lives in the Greenwich Village neighborhood of New York City.

SUGGESTED READING

Cameron, Deborah. "Deep Secrets: Boys' Friendships and the Crisis of Connection." *Times Higher Education*. TSL Education, 7 Apr. 2011. Web. 23 Dec. 2011.

Hoffman, Jan. "Allowing Teenage Boys to Love Their Friends." *New York Times*. New York Times, 21 Sep. 2011. Web. 23 Dec. 2011.

Le, Vanna. "Ask an Academic: The Secrets of Boys." *New Yorker*. Condé Nast Digital, 16 Mar. 2011. Web. 23 Dec. 2011.

Levy, Julia. "NYU Researchers Hope to Decipher Turmoil of Preteens." *New York Sun*. 12 Nov. 2004, New York: 4. Print.

Way, Niobe. "Properly Addressing the Crisis Facing Black and Latino Men." *Huffington Post*. TheHuffingtonPost.com, 5 Sep. 2011. Web. 23 Dec. 2011.

Weinstein, Debra. "In Studies Across Disciplines, Steinhardt's Social Scientists Challenge Deeply Held Beliefs About Gender." *NYU Steinhardt*. New York University, 1 July 2010. Web. 23 Dec. 2011.

SELECTED WORKS

Urban Girls: Resisting Stereotypes, Creating Identities (with Bonnie J. Leadbeater), 1996; *Everyday Courage: The Lives and Stories of Urban Teenagers*, 1998; *Growing Up Fast: Transitions to Adulthood Among Adolescent Mothers* (with Bonnie J. Leadbeater), 2001; *Adolescent Boys: Exploring Diverse Cultures of Boyhood* (with Judy Y. Chu), 2004; *Urban Girls Revisited: Building Strengths* (with Bonnie J. Leadbeater), 2007; *Deep Secrets: Boys' Friendships and the Crisis of Connection*, 2011

—*Molly Hagan*

Getty Images

Matthew Weiner

Born: 1965
Occupation: Television writer, director, producer

Matthew Weiner is the creator, writer, producer, and occasional director of the smart, critically acclaimed AMC television series *Mad Men*, which is set at an advertising agency in the early 1960s. For four years in a row, starting with its first season in 2007, the show won the Emmy Award for best drama, along with many other honors. *Mad Men* stars Jon Hamm, Elizabeth Moss, John Slattery, Vincent Kartheiser, January Jones, and Christina Hendricks, among others. Weiner is in charge of every aspect of the show, and he is famous for his obsession with detail and his interest in making his show a story about people's lives rather than simply a period drama.

During its fourth season, which aired in 2010, approximately three million people tuned in each week to watch the show, which has had a palpable impact on American popular culture. Various popular television shows, such as *Saturday Night Live* and *The Simpsons*, have made multiple *Mad Men* references, the clothing store Banana Republic put out their *Mad Men* collection, and the show has also inspired several books, including *Mad Men and Philosophy: Nothing Is as It Seems* (2010). Before *Mad Men*, Weiner's most notable position, from 2004 to 2007, was that of writer and executive producer on *The Sopranos*, yet another critically acclaimed drama. In 2011 *Time* magazine put Weiner on its list of the hundred people deemed the most influential that year.

EARLY LIFE AND EDUCATION

The third of four children, Matthew Weiner (pronounced WHY-ner) was born in Baltimore, Maryland, in 1965. His father, Leslie, was a respected neuroscientist, and his mother, Judith, had a law degree, although she never practiced. Both Leslie and Judith grew up in New York City. In 1975, when Weiner was nine years old, the family moved to Los Angeles, California.

Weiner grew up in an intellectual household, where knowledge was prized and debate encouraged. At a young age Weiner read J. D. Salinger's novel *Catcher in the Rye* (1951) and Joseph Heller's novel *Catch-22* (1961). He also loved watching reruns of *The Twilight Zone*, a 1960s television show that depicted everyday people experiencing strange and paranormal events. He also read about beat-generation writers such as Jack Kerouac and about blacklisted Hollywood filmmakers, who were put out of work for alleged ties to the Communist Party.

By the time Weiner was a teenager, he had become deeply fascinated by American history and popular culture in the period between the late 1950s and the early 1960s. Around the age of twelve he saw *Star Wars* (1977), the popular George Lucas motion picture, and, unlike nearly every young boy in America, was neither taken aback nor delighted by what he saw. Weiner told Bruce Handy for *Vanity Fair* (Sep. 2009), "Oh my God, my friends were nuts. We saw it twice the first day, and I was like, 'Why are we seeing this *again*?' And they were like, 'Who's your favorite character?' And I was like, 'There's *no* characters in this movie.'" Weiner continued to develop his critical eye for film, largely because of the influence of his parents, as he described to Alex Witchel in an interview for the *New York Times* (June 22, 2008): "My parents made us see good movies—you had to be able to identify movie stars. They also made us go to the opera. You were expected to know all their references. . . . Half of the reason I was interested in the '50s was just to communicate with them." Although Weiner was a fairly precocious young man outside of school, he was not a particularly good student in high school, but he still managed to gain acceptance to a good university.

For his undergraduate studies, Weiner attended Wesleyan University in Middletown, Connecticut, a small, private liberal arts school. His major was a combination of history, philosophy, and literature. He graduated in 1987. Because the undergraduate program at Wesleyan offered no grades, Weiner faced a considerable challenge when applying to the film school at the University of Southern California (USC) in Los Angeles. However, his father, a prominent neuroscientist at the university, petitioned the dean to admit his son to the program. (The neuromuscular program at the University of Southern California is now called the Leslie P. Weiner Neurological Care and Research Center.) Weiner did well at USC, and soon after receiving his MFA, in December 1990, he married architect Linda Brettler.

After spending several years writing screenplays that did not sell, Weiner was encouraged by his wife to write, direct, and produce his own movie. His film *What Do You Do All Day?* (1996), a largely autobiographical comedy about a struggling writer, received very little notice. Weiner then decided to try comedy writing. He did stand-up comedy, wrote for a few short-lived sitcoms, and finally, in 1999, joined the writing staff of the fairly successful sitcom *Becker*, in which actor Ted Danson played a misanthropic New York City doctor. After about two years as a writer on *Becker*—he was on the show for a total of three years—Weiner became dissatisfied with his job. He wanted to do something else, something bigger, so on his own time he started writing the pilot episode of *Mad Men*. After completing the script in 2001, Weiner sent it around to various producers and received nothing but rejections.

GANGSTERS AND AD MEN

Weiner then sent the *Mad Men* pilot to David Chase, the creator, producer, and occasional writer of the highly acclaimed HBO series *The Sopranos*. By this point *The Sopranos*, which premiered in 1999 to nearly unanimous critical praise, had been on HBO for a few years. The show starred James Gandolfini as Tony Soprano, a middle-aged Mafia boss who is having problems with both his family and "the family business." Critics and audiences were calling it one of the best shows in the history of television. Chase read Weiner's *Mad Men* pilot, loved it, and hired Weiner as an executive producer and writer for *The Sopranos*. Chase told Bruce Handy for his piece in *Vanity Fair*, "To me, Matt's number-one strength is his originality. . . . When he was writing a character [on *The Sopranos*] you would always be delighted because it was not the stock version of the character. That's what I mean by 'originality.' Maybe it's another word for 'intelligence' or 'insight.'" It did not take long for Weiner's efforts to be recognized by the entertainment industry. The producers of *The Sopranos*, including Weiner, won the Emmy Award for outstanding drama series in 2004 and 2006. Along with Terence Winter, he also received an Emmy nomination for outstanding writing in the 2004 episode "Unidentified Black Males." Weiner earned another Emmy nomination in 2007 for cowriting the episode "Kennedy and Heidi" with Chase, and he won a 2007 Writers Guild Award for the series.

As *The Sopranos* series finale was approaching in June 2007, there was even more buzz than usual. Media watchers were ruminating over the meaning of the show and speculating about how it would end. Writing for the *New Yorker* (June 4, 2007, online), David Remnick noted, "*The Sopranos*, like its predecessor, Martin Scorsese's *Goodfellas*, is about the ruthlessness of petty lying crooks, but the beat-downs, strangulations, and shootings are the least of the violence. [Chase] has immersed us for years in an examination of addiction, twelve-step recoveries, teenage depression, modern pharmacology, suicides, sexual indulgence, family betrayals, financial manipulation, accidents, heart attacks, strokes, death and dying—and always, afterward, the inability to summon a language to equal the emotion." Remnick concluded with this reflection: "The end is a mystery, but we know one thing: *The Sopranos* defied Aristotelian conventions. It is a comedy that ends with a litany of the dead and missing."

Keeping in mind how incredibly successful *The Sopranos* had been and how Weiner helped contribute to that success during the series' last few seasons, it came as a surprise to Weiner when HBO rejected his *Mad Men* pilot. According to Handy, Chase "championed the script" and gave it to HBO executives, but they passed. Handy added: "Even as the pilot script languished, piling up rejections, not just at HBO but elsewhere on your cable box, Weiner refused to move on, evincing the kind of stubborn, even touching faith in his work that is usually knocked out of people in Hollywood by that point in their careers." His persistence eventually paid off in 2006, when AMC, best known for airing classic movies, ordered *Mad Men*, its first original drama series.

Weiner, who is well known for his obsession with the smallest details, is not only the show's creator, head writer, and producer, but also the show-runner, which means he has final say over all aspects of the show including casting, costume, hairstyles, wardrobe, and set design. In an interview with Alex Witchel for the *New York Times* (June 22, 2008), Weiner said, "I do not feel any guilt about saying that the show comes from my mind and that I'm a control freak." Among the most important people to lend a critical eye to the show is not even on the staff. Weiner explained to Witchel, "Every single script goes through my wife. She inevitably says, 'What is it about?' We talk about it and I'm always angry when she's talking." He added, "She went to Harvard, she's really smart and I just stand there literally with my hands out like—'What?' I argue with her, and I always swear I'm not going to show it to her again because I'm so defensive. I mean, my writers come up with lots of good ideas, but she is really something."

THE MEN AND WOMEN OF STERLING COOPER

Mad Men premiered on AMC in July 2007, a month after *The Sopranos* series finale. It was an immediate hit with the critics, but averaged fewer than a million viewers per episode—a modest but committed audience that would grow with every season. (The "Mad" in *Mad Men* stands for Madison Avenue, in Manhattan, where many advertising firms had their offices in the 1960s.)

In a review for the *Chicago Tribune* (July 19, 2007), television critic Maureen Ryan wrote, "It'd be very easy to be seduced by the surfaces of this vibrant show, which is set among the Manhattan ad men (and women) of 1960, when the highballs started flowing at 4:30 p.m. and smoking wasn't just accepted but almost required. . . . But don't expect a snappy, superficial, retro homage to the Rat Pack—*Mad Men* is first and foremost an intelligently made character drama. One of the interesting things about this show is how quickly the expertly done period re-creation falls away, once we get to know the yearning, confused, confident people who inhabit the Sterling Cooper Advertising Agency. They're not period pieces—they're just like us." Lynn Smith, writing for the *Los Angeles Times* (July 15, 2007), made a similar point about the show's relevance: "Like science fiction, period dramas often reflect current concerns and *Mad Men* aims to explore the complications of our office-based lives, which Weiner believes have similarities to those at the end of the '50s."

The first episode takes place in the spring of 1960, the year of the Kennedy-Nixon presidential debates and subsequent election of John F. Kennedy. The pilot episode is about an ad agency's efforts to keep an account with its biggest client, Lucky Strike cigarettes. In her review for the *Chicago Tribune*, Ryan wrote, "*Mad Men* has what we expect from truly addictive cable fare—moral gray areas, flawed characters and knotty, intriguing plots that contain digressions we don't mind because the worlds we're watching are so compelling and complete."

Although all of the main characters are important, the show's hero, or antihero—Weiner makes it a point to write nuanced, morally ambiguous characters—is Don Draper, creative director of the Sterling Cooper ad agency. Writing for *Vanity Fair* (Sep. 2009), Bruce Handy described him thus: "He's a man in flight from his own past, a Gatsby-esque figure without the romance of a Daisy; or rather, he seems to be looking for a Daisy everywhere but his home in the suburbs, where his beautiful, bored, emotionally stunted wife, Betty, is stranded in what feels at times like an improbably compelling adaptation of *The Feminine Mystique*. But in the show's central irony he is able to plumb human needs and desires with an artist's intuition." Handy concluded, "In short, Don Draper is an advertising Mozart, or at least he's the best Sterling Cooper has to offer, for another of the show's ironies is that Don and his colleagues are dinosaurs not just in terms of the impending social revolutions of the 1960s but also in terms of the creative revolution that would roil advertising that decade."

MAD MEN WINS SCRUTINY AND PRAISE

The show's second season, set in 1962, continued to receive a great deal of critical praise and nearly doubled its viewership, with an approximate 1.8 million people watching each week. During the third season, set in 1963, aside from all the personal and professional troubles, all the characters experienced one of the most traumatic events of the unfolding decade: the assassination of President John F. Kennedy. The fourth season, which aired in 2010 and takes place between November 1964 and October 1965, continued to demonstrate the series' quality and relevance—and its growing place in popular culture. Nearly three million people tuned in each week to watch the increasingly layered drama unfold.

The show has also invited a great deal of scrutiny, due in part to Weiner's obsessive attention to detail. Although wardrobe and set design have generated plenty of discussion—mostly involving critics and everyday viewers marveling at the accuracy and seamlessness of it all—the show's language is the area that is dissected most fanatically, especially by academics, linguists, and loyal fans. Some took issue when one of the characters, Joan, bid farewell to the old year by saying, "1960, I am so over you," or when another character, Peggy, said, "I'm in a very good place right now," or when Don Draper said, "The window for this apology is closing." Some linguists contended that these idioms or manners of speaking did not yet exist in 1960. Weiner has been known to counter some of these objections—he has defended Joan's use of "I am so over you"—but speaking to Ben Zimmer for the *New York Times* (July 25, 2010) about this issue, he said that he welcomes the "fault-finding from fans," in large part because he sees himself as "one of the most nitpicky people in the world." He then added, "I'm glad that we're held to a high standard, and I'm glad that people get pleasure from picking it apart."

After the end of the fourth season, convoluted contract negotiations ensued. Most significantly, AMC wanted to cut Weiner's budget and reduce the size of the cast. Weiner refused the offer and ultimately prevailed. In the spring of 2011, Lionsgate, the studio behind *Mad Men*, signed a two-season deal (with an option for a third season) with Weiner. The first episode of the fifth season is scheduled to air on AMC in March 2012.

The number of awards Weiner has earned for the show is extensive. The series has earned four Emmy Awards for outstanding drama series; three Golden Globe Awards for best television drama series; a Peabody Award; three Producers Guild Awards; four Writers Guild Awards; the 2008 and 2009 British Academy of Film and Television Arts (BAFTA) Award, the 2008 Royal Television Society Award for International Program; and five Television Critics Association Awards, including Program of the Year. The show was also named among the top ten outstanding television programs of 2007, 2008, 2009, and 2010 by the American Film Institute (AFI). Weiner himself has won a number of awards and nominations for individual episodes he wrote or cowrote, including Emmy Awards for outstanding writing for a drama series. Additionally, he has been nominated twice by the Directors Guild for his work behind the camera.

Weiner lives in Los Angeles with his wife and four sons.

SUGGESTED READING

Handy, Bruce. "Don and Betty's Paradise Lost." *Vanity Fair* Sep. 2009: 268. Print.

Remnick, David. "Family Guy." *New Yorker*. New Yorker, 4 June 2007. Web. 9 Jan. 2012.

Ryan, Maureen. "'Mad Men' More Than a Sleek Period Piece." *Chicago Tribune* 19 July 2007: C1. Print.

Witchel, Alex. "Smoking, Drinking, Writing, Womanizing, Smoking, Drinking . . ." *New York Times Magazine* 22 June 2008: MM32. Print.

Zimmer, Ben. "'Mad Men'-ese." *New York Times Magazine* 25 July 2010: MM18. Print.

—*Dmitry Kiper*

Florence Welch

Born: August 28, 1986
Occupation: Singer

Florence Welch is the lead singer of the British pop/rock band Florence and the Machine. Her debut album *Lungs* (2009) yielded five hit singles and has sold over four million copies worldwide. Her follow-up album *Ceremonials* (2011) has been climbing the charts as Welch tours with her band, which includes key player and *Lungs* co-creator, Isabella Summers, as well as a four-piece band and string section. Welch, who has no formal musical training, is known for her otherworldly compositions and her booming, soulful voice. She described her unique sound to Tom Lamont for the London *Observer* (30 Oct. 2011), as "big, tribal goth pop." After several musical false starts—a stint as a folk singer and earlier, at the age of thirteen, as the lead in a band called Toxic Cockroaches—Welch found her sound after an emotional breakup with longtime boyfriend Stuart Hammond. Welch and Summers, who was also going through a rough breakup, sequestered themselves in Summers's small London recording studio and created *Lungs*, a record which Lamont deemed "one of the best breakup albums in years."

Welch has successfully managed several crossovers that remain a challenge for other musical acts. After performing at the 2010 MTV Video Music Awards in Los Angeles, at which she recreated live the music video for her hit single "Dog Days Are Over," her hype extended well beyond her native England; the song was even used in the film *Eat, Pray, Love* in 2010. She leapt from her status as an "indie" icon to a mainstream music staple—performing a tribute to the "Queen of Soul" Aretha Franklin alongside Christina Aguilera, Martina McBride, Jennifer Hudson, and Yolanda Adams at the 2011 Grammy Awards. She was also asked to write the song "Heavy in Your Arms" for the soundtrack of the *Twilight* film *Eclipse* (2010).

With her bright red hair and gothic vintage flair, Welch has captured the attention of designers, including British retailer Topshop and Chanel director Karl Lagerfeld. While the art and fashion world celebrate Welch's softer, more wraithlike qualities, Welch celebrates dark impulses that drive her personal aesthetic. "I want my music to sound like throwing yourself out of a tree, or off a tall building, or as if you're being sucked down into the ocean and you can't

FilmMagic

breathe," she says in the "About" section on her website, florenceandthemachine.net. "It's something overwhelming and all-encompassing that fills you up, and you're either going to explode with it, or you're just going to disappear."

EARLY LIFE

Florence Leontine Mary Welch was born on August 28, 1986 in Camberwell in South London, England. Her mother, Evelyn Welch, is a professor of Renaissance studies and the dean of arts at the University of London, Queen Mary. Her father, Nick Welch, was formerly in the advertising business. Welch names her mother as an early artistic influence for introducing her to gothic architecture and Renaissance and Egyptian mythology. The gruesomeness of the latter captivated the young Welch's imagination. Her father, on the other hand, introduced her to the punk rock band the Ramones. A self-described "dreamy" child, Welch attended Alleyn's School, located in Dulwich in Southeast London, where she sang in the choir and frequently got in trouble for bursting into song during lessons. Early on, Welch was diagnosed with both dyslexia and dyspraxia. She has suffered from insomnia since she was a child and used to draw crosses on her bed to protect her from lurking werewolves and vampires.

When Welch was ten years old, her parents divorced. Three years later, her mother fell in love with their next-door neighbor, Peter Openshaw, a professor of medicine at Imperial College, London. Evelyn Welch moved in with Openshaw, bringing Florence and her two younger siblings, Grace and John James, with her. Openshaw was a widower with three teenage children of his own. Welch has described early years with her new brothers and sisters as chaotic. To escape the household bickering, she turned to punk rock and a growing fascination with witchcraft.

Around the same time, Welch's grandfather fell ill and died in a coma, and her manic-depressive grandmother died by suicide. She sang at both of their funerals. Welch then took to writing songs. The songs were mostly about breakups, even though she had never had a boyfriend. By the time Welch was sixteen, she was seriously pursuing a musical career and spent a lot of time in London clubs. Her family was supportive; her mother and stepfather read books on the music business while her stepbrother, Nick, drove her and her early bands to gigs. Her father was an early tour manager.

The first of Welch's bands was called Toxic Cockroaches. It began in 1999 when Welch was only thirteen. Another, more recent predecessor to Florence and the Machine was a band called Ashok, which she fronted in her late teens. She signed a music deal with Ashok but decided to walk away from it. In 2006, Welch started playing the drums with her longtime friend and musical collaborator, Isa Summers, a keyboardist. They called themselves Florence Robot and Isa Machine, then later shortened the name to Florence and the Machine. The band played small London venues, and Welch became known for her on-stage antics and crowd surfing. Welch briefly attended Camberwell College of the Arts, though she left after eighteen months to continue her music career. She was officially discovered in December 2006 during a black-tie event. In the restroom, a tipsy Welch cornered Mairead Nash of the indie/pop DJ duo Queens of Noize and sang the Etta James song "Something's Got a Hold on Me." Nash was impressed and asked Welch to sing at her Christmas party. Weeks later, Nash became Welch's manager.

FLORENCE AND THE MACHINE

In 2007, Welch signed with the independent label Moshi Moshi Records, and then with Island Universal Records in 2008. Prior to either deal, Welch and Summers spent time at various London pubs, partying and performing. Welch, who had just ended a tumultuous relationship with literary editor Stuart Hammond, told Gareth Grundy for the *Observer* (20 Dec. 2009) that her life during that period was "spinning out of control." She recalled waking up one morning after a particularly raucous night and finding herself on the roof of a pub wearing a Captain America costume. Nash intervened and told Welch that she needed to make a change. "Things were very much in the balance," she told Grundy. "There was a moment when it could have tipped either way and I could have completely gone under. But I resurfaced and life got itself back on track, I think."

For an entire summer, Welch and Summers kept to Summers's London recording studio and wrote most of what would become Florence and the Machine's debut album, *Lungs*. Inspired by the music of Madonna, among others, the two composed songs on Summers's keyboard and a drum set borrowed from a neighboring band. Welch claims that it was due to these sessions that she found the gothic, thundering pop sound for which she has become famous. For Welch, writing the song "Between Two Lungs," which she recorded pounding the studio walls with her hands in lieu of drums, was a revelation. Armed with their new material, Florence and the Machine attracted the attention of Island Universal Records in 2008. By early 2009, Welch had won a Critic's Choice Brit Award—a new prize within the recording industry given to the year's most promising acts. Though the band's first single, "A Kiss with a Fist," was released in 2008, *Lungs* was officially released in July of 2009.

Lungs, produced by Paul Epworth, debuted at the number two slot on the charts due to the death of pop icon Michael Jackson that year. The album peaked at number one the following year. Critics praised Welch and compared her to musicians like P. J. Harvey, Björk, David Bowie, and Kate Bush for her mystical, gothic imagery and persona. *Lungs* successfully lived in two worlds; it was considered both macabre ("My Boy Builds Coffins") and euphoric ("Cosmic Love"). The album garnered five singles, including "You've Got the Love," a cover of the 1986 Candi Staton song that became wildly popular in the United Kingdom.

The song "Dog Days Are Over," a heart-pounding crescendo with tribal drums, made Welch a star across the pond. She described the song to Korina Lopez for *USA Today* (9 Aug. 2010) as a symbol of "apocalyptic euphoria, chaotic freedom, and running really, really fast with your eyes closed." Welch was asked to perform "Dog Days Are Over" live for the MTV Video Music Awards in Los Angeles in 2010. She was encouraged to recreate the song's strange and ritualistic music video, which was nominated for Best Video at the awards. The song was also used that year in the film *Eat, Pray, Love*, starring Julia Roberts. Welch attributes the successful performance at the VMA's with her newfound popularity in America. By her own account, the search term "Florence and the Machine" ignited Internet search engines that night following her performance. In a matter of minutes, Welch had gone global.

TOURING AND CEREMONIALS

In 2010, Florence and the Machine returned to the Brit Awards, where they won Best Album.

Welch also wrote and recorded a song called "Heavy in Your Arms" for the soundtrack of the film *Twilight: Eclipse* (2010). The song is available on a repackaged edition of *Lungs*. In early 2011, she sang at the Nobel Peace Prize ceremony in Oslo. She was also invited to the Grammys and asked to participate in a tribute to soul singer Aretha Franklin. Standing beside Christina Aguilera, Martina McBride, Jennifer Hudson, and Yolanda Adams, Welch sang part of Franklin's famous song "Think." Two weeks later, she filled in for pop singer Dido at the 2011 Academy Awards. She performed one of the Best Original Song nominees, "If I Rise," written by Indian composer A. R. Rahman for the movie *127 Hours* (2010). Dido, who originally performed the song with Rahman, could not make the event. Rahman called Welch, whom he had seen at the Nobel Prize ceremony in Norway, and asked her to perform the song. At the after-party, Welch sang a duet with Elton John.

After the release of *Lungs*, Welch's fan base expanded to include celebrities such as Beyoncé, who told Welch that the album was an inspiration for her own latest release, to the popular television show *Glee*, whose cast sang "Dog Days Are Over" in a November 2010 episode. For much of the time between 2009 and the release of *Ceremonials* in 2011, Welch was on tour. It was an exhausting schedule, but Welch learned to keep up. Reversing the drunken, crowd-surfing persona associated with her London days, Welch made the decision to no longer drink on the road. Meanwhile, her live performances became famous. "During 'Dog Days Are Over' she invites the crowd to howl like wolves and leap into the air, which they do, spectacularly," a London *Sunday Times* (20 Sep. 2009) reporter wrote of Welch's performance at the Lowlands Festival in Holland in 2009. "By the end of 'Cosmic Love,' a girl at the front is in tears." Before the release of *Ceremonials*, Florence and the Machine toured with the Irish rock band U2.

After the whirlwind of touring, Welch returned to both her childhood home in Camberwell and a small Soho recording studio—the legendary Studio 3 of Abbey Road Studios—where she recorded her follow-up album, *Ceremonials*. She again worked with producer Paul Epworth but also collaborated with writer Francis "Eg" White, who has created songs with popular singers such as Natalie Imbruglia and Adele Adkins. White and Welch cowrote "What the Water Gave Me," the album's five-minute-long first single. The song and the album as a whole employ imagery associated with death and drowning. "To me, this album is almost like a battle cry," she told Cameron Adams for Australia's *Courier Mail* (27 Oct. 2011). "People thought I might be coming back with something more ethereal and twinkly; I wanted to come back with something tough and heavier." Her original plan was to record the album in Los Angeles in a larger studio, but ultimately she felt more comfortable returning to London. If there were any doubts about Welch's decisions on *Ceremonials*, they were quickly dispelled when the album shot up the UK charts to the number-one spot upon its October 2011 release. After a little more than three months, the album had sold over 1.8 million copies worldwide.

Reviewers have described *Ceremonials* using various synonyms for the word "epic." Welch has said that she wanted the album, in all respects, to be bigger than her first. From the soaring vocals and orchestra backing to lyrics about conquering life and death, *Ceremonials* operates on different scale than *Lungs* in almost every respect—certainly it is a good fit for the larger venues Florence and the Machine continue to sell out. Music critic Jon Pareles for the *New York Times* called *Ceremonials* an "album of anthems" (8 Nov. 2011). He added, however, that "soon after the songs make their initial splash, grandeur turns to grandiosity. In making the songs so monumental, Florence and the Machine have also made them impersonal."

Ceremonials experiments with various styles, including soul, as evidenced on the track "Lover to Lover." Welch also included songs that dealt with her second breakup with Hammond, "Breaking Down" and "No Light, No Light." Although *Ceremonials* has its darker tones, her single "Shake It Out" is an anthem of positivity that draws on American gospel. The song "Spectrum," which prominently features a harp, showcases Welch's voice at its most restrained. The album reached number six on the music charts in the United States.

PERSONAL LIFE

A lifelong lover of vintage fashion, Welch is known for elaborate, Victorian-inspired stage costumes. Her free-flowing style and striking bone structure has attracted designers such as Topshop and Chanel director Karl Lagerfeld, whom many consider to be the king of couture. For the latter's "Under the Sea"–themed 2012 Spring/Summer runway show on October 4, 2011, Welch emerged singing from a giant shell. Lagerfeld also photographed Welch for the cover of her single "Shake it Out." Welch has additionally worked with Aldene Johnson, a London-based stylist and fashion editor of the British magazine *Vice* since 2009.

Though its members are in constant flux due to the expanding nature of Welch's sound, the core of "the Machine" has been composed of keyboardist Summers, guitarist Rob Ackroyd, drummer Chris Hayden, and harpist Tom Monger. Welch is in a relationship with events organizer James Nesbitt and lives with her family in Camberwell. Her younger sister, Grace, is her personal handler and travels with her on tour.

SUGGESTED READING

Adams, Cameron. "Rise of the Machine." *Courier Mail* [Brisbane] 27 Oct. 2011, first ed.: 44. Print.

Grundy, Gareth. "The Faces of 2009: Florence Welch." *Observer* [London] 20 Dec. 2009: 4. Print.

Lamont, Tom. "'Do I Want to Be Stuck in Teenage Land, Where Everything Is Free and Easy?'" *Observer* [London] 30 Oct. 2011: 27. Print.

Lopez, Korina. "Fortuitous Bathroom Visit Propels Her Career; A Chance Meeting Led to a Big Musical Break." *USA Today* 9 Aug. 2010, final ed.: D5. Print.

Pareles, Jon. "New Music." *New York Times* 8 Nov. 2011, late ed.: C3. Print.

— *Molly Hagan*

Wes Welker

Born: May 1, 1981
Occupation: Football player with the New England Patriots

Many football coaches and players have called the New England Patriots' wide receiver Wes Welker, who stands a mere five feet nine inches and weighs 185 pounds, the toughest pound-for-pound player in the National Football League (NFL). Known for his elusive quickness, sure-handedness, and precise route-running skills, Welker has used his unique skill set to emerge as one of the best slot receivers in the league. Despite posting record-breaking numbers in high school and college, Welker was repeatedly overlooked by scouts because of his unimposing size and subsequently went undrafted in the 2004 NFL draft. He began his NFL career when he signed with the San Diego Chargers as an undrafted rookie free agent but was released from the team after only one game, leading him to sign with the Miami Dolphins.

After spending three modestly successful seasons with the Dolphins, Welker was traded to the New England Patriots. He has since established himself as a key member of a high-powered Patriots offense that consistently ranks among the best in the league, and he played a major role in securing the team American Football Conference (AFC) East Division titles in 2007, 2009, 2010, and 2011 and berths in Super Bowl XLII and Super Bowl XLVI. One of the NFL's most prolific receivers, Welker recorded at least one hundred receptions and one thousand yards receiving in four of his first five seasons with the Patriots. He has made four straight Pro Bowl teams (2008–11) and earned four Associated Press (AP) All-Pro selections (2007,

2008, 2009, and 2011) and has also set several franchise and league records.

EARLY LIFE AND EDUCATION

The younger of the two sons of Leland and Shelley Welker, Wesley Carter Welker was born on May 1, 1981, in Oklahoma City, Oklahoma. His father worked as an engineer for Southwestern Bell for nearly three decades; his mother worked as a nurse. Welker was drawn to sports through the influence of his brother, Lee, who is four years older. The two boys loved to play soccer and football and spent countless hours playing in the family backyard. Their parents signed them up for youth-league soccer teams in an attempt to delay their entry into organized football and other dangerous sports.

Welker's athletic talents were evident from an early age. Intuitive, strong willed, and extremely competitive, he developed a knack for scoring goals in soccer, and on one occasion, according to his father, he scored an astonishing seventeen goals in a single game. Like his brother, Welker attended Heritage Hall School in Oklahoma City, a small, independent, private school that educates children from kindergarten through high school. He started playing football in sixth grade after the school's coaches invited him to join the team based on his speed, which he had showcased while running sprints alongside some of his football friends during a practice. Welker came to the attention of Heritage Hall's varsity football coaches the following year, when his coach, Craig Brown, declared that Welker would become the best athlete in the school's history.

HIGH SCHOOL CAREER

Brown's bold declaration proved true as Welker emerged as an all-around star on Heritage Hall's varsity football squad. Under head coach Rod Warner, he became a standout on offense, defense, and special teams, as a running back, defensive back, placekicker, and punt returner, respectively. Despite his relatively small size, Welker became known for his hard-nosed and unrelenting style of play. Warner recalled to Jim McCabe for the *Boston Globe* (3 Dec. 2007), "He was a machine. . . . He would go at it so hard, all the time. He would not only kick off, he would be the first downfield to make the tackle. He would make a sixty- or seventy-yard play, handle the extra-point try, tilt his facemask back to throw up, then go out and kick off. He just never quit. I mean, never."

Welker's dogged versatility was put on full display during his junior season, when he rushed for 1,228 yards, made sixty-two receptions, and scored thirty-seven touchdowns while adding ten interceptions and eight field goals. That year he teamed up with his best friend, quarterback and future country music star Graham Colton,

Getty Images

to lead Heritage Hall to a perfect 15–0 record and a Class 2A state title with a thrilling 35–34 victory over the Tishomingo Indians. In the state title game, Welker accumulated over two hundred all-purpose yards (rushing, receiving, and returning), scored three touchdowns, and recorded one interception. In another remarkable game, he scored ten points in the final thirteen seconds—scoring a touchdown, converting the extra point, booting an onside kick, and kicking a field goal—to lead Heritage Hall to a come-from-behind victory.

During his senior season, Welker led Heritage Hall to a 12–1 record and was named Oklahoma Player of the Year by the *Daily Oklahoman* and *USA Today*. He finished his high school career at Heritage Hall having accumulated 8,231 all-purpose yards. He scored a combined ninety touchdowns along with nearly two hundred tackles, twenty-two interceptions, and nine fumble recoveries.

COLLEGE CAREER

Despite his extraordinary accomplishments in high school, Welker was considered by college scouts to be too small and too slow to play National Collegiate Athletic Association (NCAA) Division I-A football (later renamed Division I Football Bowl Subdivision), the highest level of college football. Also working against him was the fact that he had competed in Oklahoma's Class 2A division, the second lowest of the six high-school athletic levels in the state, which prompted doubts about how he would fare against stiffer competition. Consequently, Welker received no scholarship offers from Division I-A schools.

In an effort to secure Welker a scholarship, Warner sent out more than one hundred DVDs of Welker's high school highlights to football coaches throughout the United States. One of those coaches was Texas Tech University's Mike Leach, who was intrigued by Welker's unique combination of skills. "When you saw him, he was slow and not really big," Leach explained to Jarrett Bell for *USA Today* (29 Jan. 2008), "but he just had a great sense of the field and how to play football." After another recruit opted to attend Boston College instead of Texas Tech, Leach offered Welker the university's last remaining football scholarship, which he immediately accepted.

As a freshman Welker joined the Texas Tech Red Raiders' starting lineup as a slot receiver and punt returner, roles he retained over the next four years. He thrived in Leach's pass-oriented offensive system and emerged as one of the most accomplished athletes in Texas Tech history, with coaches and teammates nicknaming him "the Natural." During his college career, he appeared in a total of fifty games and finished as Texas Tech's all-time leader in receptions (259) and receiving yards (3,069) while also setting NCAA career records for punt return yards (1,761) and punt return touchdowns (eight). Welker received the Mosi Tatupu Award for being the best special teams player in college football in 2003 and was selected to the All-Big 12 Conference First-Team in 2000, 2002, and 2003. Welker graduated from Texas Tech with a degree in management.

PROFESSIONAL CAREER

Welker's record-breaking college numbers notwithstanding, professional scouts once again labeled him too small and too slow to play in the NFL, and he was passed over by every team in the 2004 NFL Draft. He eventually secured a spot on an NFL roster after signing with the San Diego Chargers as an undrafted rookie free agent. "I knew I had a chance to at least see what I could do," he explained to Monique Walker for the *Boston Globe* (2 Oct. 2011). "I didn't know if I'd make the team or what would happen or anything like that leading up to the day before cuts. I had a good preseason. I didn't know what was going on." Welker made his professional debut on September 12, 2004, in the Chargers' season opener against the Houston Texans. In the game, which the Chargers won, 27–20, he returned four kickoffs for 102 yards. However, Welker was released from the team days later to clear roster space for safety Clinton Hart.

Soon after his release from the Chargers, Welker was signed by the Miami Dolphins. In fourteen games during his rookie season with the Dolphins, he returned fifty-seven kicks for 1,313 yards (an average of 23 yards per return) and scored his first career kickoff return touchdown on a 95-yard return in a game against the Baltimore Ravens. He also fielded forty-three punts for 464 yards, with an average of 10.8 yards per return. That season, Welker made NFL history in a matchup against the New England Patriots, during which he served as an emergency replacement for injured kicker Olindo Mare and became the first player ever to kickoff, make a tackle, kick a field goal, kick an extra point, and return a kickoff and a punt in the same game. He was subsequently named the AFC Special Teams Player of the Week for accomplishing the feat.

During the 2005 season, Welker served as a kickoff and punt return specialist for the Dolphins and also emerged as a wide receiver. That year he recorded twenty-nine receptions, sixty-one kickoff returns, and forty-three punt returns. Despite rumors that he would be cut from the Dolphins, Welker played in all sixteen games during the 2006 season, scoring his first career touchdown reception in a game against the Chicago Bears. Welker finished the season as the Dolphins' all-time leader in kickoff returns (166), kickoff return yards (3,756), and combined kickoff and punt return yards (4,988). The Dolphins, however, missed out on the playoffs for a fifth straight year after finishing last in the AFC East Division, with a record of 6–10.

NEW ENGLAND PATRIOTS

During the 2007 off-season, the Dolphins traded Welker, who had become a restricted free agent, to the New England Patriots for second- and seventh-round draft picks. The Patriots signed him to a five-year, $18.1 million contract. Impressed with Welker's elusiveness as a returner and receiver, Patriots head coach Bill Belichick recalled to Paul Tenorio for the *Washington Post* (29 Jan. 2008), "He killed us just about every time we played him. The only way we could really handle him was to double-team him." In his first season with the Patriots, Welker enjoyed a breakthrough year, starting thirteen of sixteen games and shattering career highs in every statistical category. Serving as the team's slot receiver, he set the Patriots' single-season record for receptions with 112, tying the Cincinnati Bengals' T. J. Houshmandzadeh for most in the NFL and breaking the record for most receptions by a player in his first season with a new team.

Along with fellow wide receivers Randy Moss and Donté Stallworth, both of whom also signed with the Patriots in 2007, and perennial All-Pro quarterback Tom Brady, Welker was part of an explosive Patriots offense that broke numerous NFL records, including most touchdowns in a season (seventy-five). The Patriots won a franchise-record fifth consecutive AFC

East Division title and became the first team in league history to finish with a record of 16–0 during the regular season. The team won its first two playoff games, against the Jacksonville Jaguars and San Diego Chargers, respectively, and advanced to Super Bowl XLII. During the game, Welker tied the Super Bowl record for most receptions with eleven catches. The Patriots lost to the New York Giants, 17–14; nevertheless, the season was a significant one for the team, which became the first ever to win eighteen consecutive games in one season and the third team in league history to finish the year with a record of 18–1.

At the end of the season, Welker was named to his first AP All-Pro Second Team and received the Patriots' 12th Player Award for his invaluable contributions to the team. Describing Welker as a "tough, hard-nosed football player," Brady explained to Walker, "Different guys create different separation different ways. Wes uses his quickness a lot of the time and you see he gets a lot of separation because he is so good in and out of his breaks." Nick Caserio, the Patriots' director of player personnel, told Ian R. Rapoport for the *Boston Herald* (23 Dec. 2009) about Welker, "As a receiver, you have basically two jobs: to get open and catch the football. The one thing that separates him from other folks is his quickness and change of direction. He knows one speed and that's one hundred miles per hour."

Welker duplicated his success in 2008, when he led the Patriots in receptions (111) and receiving yards (1,165). He caught six or more passes per game during the Patriots' first eleven games, making him the first player in league history to accomplish that feat. Welker subsequently was named the Patriots' MVP for the 2008 season by *USA Today* and earned his first career Pro Bowl selection as a reserve for the AFC squad. He was also named to the AP All-Pro Second Team for the second consecutive year. The Patriots finished second in the AFC East with an 11–5 record after losing the division crown to the Dolphins in a tiebreaker.

INJURIES

During the 2009 season, Welker firmly established himself as a slot receiver, leading the league and setting a Patriots franchise record with a career-high 123 receptions and becoming only the fourth receiver in NFL history to record one hundred or more receptions in three consecutive seasons. He tied Herman Moore, who had caught the same number of passes for the Detroit Lions in 1995, for the second-highest reception total in league history. Welker also caught ten or more passes per game in seven games, matching the record Andre Johnson set with the Houston Texans in 2008, and ranked first in the AFC and second in the NFL with a 12.5 yards-per-return average (twenty-seven punt returns for 338 yards). Welker put up impressive numbers despite missing the second and third weeks of the season due to a knee injury and most of the regular-season finale against the Houston Texans after tearing two ligaments in his left knee early in the game. He earned his second Pro Bowl selection and was named to the AP All-Pro First Team for the first time in his career. The Patriots won the AFC East Division with a record of 10–6 and returned to the playoffs but were defeated by the Baltimore Ravens in the wild card round, 33–14. Welker did not play in the game due to his injury, which required off-season surgery.

Because of the severity of his knee injury, many analysts predicted Welker would miss most, if not all, of the 2010 NFL season. Nonetheless, after months of intense rehabilitation, Welker returned to the field to play in the Patriots' season opener. He appeared in fifteen of sixteen regular-season games and led the Patriots in receptions (eighty-six) while finishing second on the team in touchdown receptions (seven). He earned his third selection to the Pro Bowl, serving as a replacement for Johnson, who had been injured. The Patriots ended the season with a 14–2 record but lost to the New York Jets in the AFC Divisional playoff round, 28–21.

2011 SEASON

Welker had arguably the best season of his career to date in 2011, leading the NFL in receptions (122) for the third time and leading the AFC in receiving yards (1,569) and receiving yards per game (98.1), both of which were career highs. He also tied the NFL record for longest touchdown reception, catching a ninety-nine-yard touchdown pass in the season opener against the Miami Dolphins. He was named to his fourth consecutive Pro Bowl, earned his second Associated Press First-Team All-Pro selection, and helped the Patriots return to the Super Bowl for the second time in five seasons. Welker recorded seven receptions for sixty yards during Super Bowl XLVI; however, the Patriots again lost to the Giants, 21–17. During the 2012 off-season, Welker signed a one-year franchise tender with the Patriots worth $9.5 million.

PERSONAL LIFE

On June 24, 2012, Welker married his longtime girlfriend, Anna Burns, in a ceremony in Aspen, Colorado. The couple resides in the Boston area. Welker has established the Wes Welker Foundation (originally the 83 Foundation) to help assist at-risk youths in Oklahoma City. In 2010, he was recognized with the Ed Block Courage Award, an award named for the respected humanitarian and longtime trainer of the Baltimore Colts and awarded to one player from each NFL team each year for demonstrating exceptional sportsmanship on and off the field.

SUGGESTED READING

Bell, Jarrett. "Welker's View Improves: Patriots Receiver Moves from Sideline Festivity to Center of Super Bowl." *USA Today* 29 Jan. 2008: 1C. Print.

Bishop, Greg. "A Small Patriots Receiver Ends Up Being the Biggest Target of All." *New York Times* 4 Feb. 2008: D3. Print.

Carlson, Jenni. "Working Together: Wes Welker's Family Recalls Hard Work, Heartache and What It Took for Him to Reach the Top." *Oklahoman* [Oklahoma City] 27 Jan. 2008: 1A. Print.

Evans, Murray. "Back in Oklahoma, Story of Welker's Rise to Glory is Often Told." *Associated Press*. Associated Press, 2 Feb. 2008. Web. 16 July 2012. Print.

Grossfeld, Stan. "Passion is in Fashion: Boston Has Four of the League Leaders in Intensity, and They Wear it Well." *Boston Globe* 24 June 2011, Sports sec.: 1. Print.

McCabe, Jim. "Yes Welker: Patriot's Refusal to Take No for Answer Got Him Where He is Today." *Boston Globe* 3 Dec. 2007: D1. Print.

Rapoport, Ian R. "Little Engine That Does: Pats' Welker Defies Odds as One of NFL's Best." *Boston Herald* 23 Dec. 2009: 64. Print.

Tenorio, Paul. "Young Receivers Are Rooting for the Little Guy: Pats' Welker Is a Big Influence." *Washington Post* 29 Jan. 2008: E4. Print.

—*Chris Cullen*

Tim Westergren

Born: December 21, 1965
Occupation: Cofounder of Pandora Radio

After stints as a musician and composer, Tim Westergren founded Pandora Radio, a popular streaming music website that enables listeners to select songs based on their personal preferences. Its precursor, Savage Beast Technologies, was launched in 2000 in the wake of the dot-com crash and initially licensed its software to retailers while struggling to survive financially. By 2005 Westergren had reinvented the company to establish Pandora as a consumer-oriented radio Internet service largely supported by advertising revenue.

By 2007, however, Pandora faced near extinction due to a protracted legal battle between Internet radio broadcasters and the Recording Industry Association of America (RIAA) regarding royalty rates. Westergren took the conflict to the Internet and rallied support from Pandora users. He also became a prominent figure on Capitol Hill, lobbying Congress to lower royalty rates for streaming music.

Bloomberg via Getty Images

After an agreement was reached in 2009, Pandora went public two years later. Westergren credits his company's longevity to one thing—the music. "We have a saying at Pandora: 'It's the play-list, stupid,'" he revealed to Laura Green for *Smart Business* (1 Feb. 2012). "It's as simple as that—making it a super easy, intuitive experience and nailing the music choices. That's really the basis for Pandora's success so far."

EARLY LIFE AND EDUCATION

Tim Westergren was born on December 21, 1965, in Minneapolis, Minnesota, and at the age of six, his father's career forced a family move to France. Westergren's passion for music began soon after. "I started playing [the] piano when I was about seven years old, and I just really fell in love with [it]," he told Andy Mannix in an interview for *City Pages*, a weekly alternative newspaper in the Minneapolis–St. Paul region (10 July 2012). Westergren, who had initially taught himself to play, briefly received some lessons from a blues pianist but lacked discipline. While attending high school in England, he joined the choir and also learned to play several other instruments, including the clarinet, the bassoon, the drums, and the recorder.

In 1982 Westergren returned to the United States and his parents enrolled him at Cranbrook Schools, a private, college preparatory school in Bloomfield Hills, Michigan. After graduating in 1984, Westergren attended Stanford University in Palo Alto, California, where he majored in political science. Music remained an active interest for Westergren who took elective courses in jazz and classical theory. "The last couple of years, though, I really got [deeper] into music and recording technology," he revealed to Sam Devine for the *San Francisco Bay Guardian* (9 Jan. 2008). "There's a place [at Stanford] called the Center for Computer Research in Music and Acoustics. It's a place where science and music come together. There's a lot of study of sound and sound creation and sound recording, and I [practically] lived there my senior year."

FIRST YEARS AS A MUSICIAN
In 1988 Westergren earned his BA degree from Stanford. He remained in California and worked part-time as an afternoon nanny and in his off-time, formally trained with a jazz pianist in Berkeley. Westergren also pursued a career in music, playing keyboards with three local acoustic rock groups: Barefoot, Late Coffee and Oranges, and Yellowwood Junction.

Westergren cofounded Yellowwood Junction with singer/guitarist Brian Wachhorst in 1993. The group, which local radio station KFOG-FM had voted one of the Bay Area's most promising unsigned bands in 1994, toured mostly on the West Coast and developed a loyal following in California, Oregon, Washington, and Colorado. "We signed with a record label, had 300 or 400 people at our shows," Westergren told Rick Newman for *U.S. News & World Report* (15 June 2011). Despite releasing their debut album *After Today* (1994), Yellowwood Junction failed to reach a wider audience. Westergren noted the similarities that his group and other struggling local musicians faced in their efforts to gain greater visibility and exposure. "There were some great bands, but they were only known to the people who saw them play live," he recalled to Michael V. Copeland in an interview for *CNNMoney.com* (29 June 2010). "I remember thinking, 'If only these bands could get some kind of exposure.'"

MUSIC COMPOSER AND A MUSIC DATABASE
Unable to earn a living, Westergren gave up touring and performing with the band in the mid-1990s. He then spent the next four years working as a music composer for various student films and low-budget productions, including the independent drama *The Last Best Sunday* (1999). He also owned and operated Nightfly Studios, a digital recording company.

The process of writing and producing music enabled Westergren to recognize the need for a tool that could help analyze and then profile music choices according to listeners' preferences. "When you're a film composer your job is to figure out someone else's taste. So you'll sit down with a film director with a stack of CDs and play stuff for them and try and learn what they like

about music," he explained to Devine. "Then, as a composer, you've got to go back to your recording studio and write a piece of music they'll like. So what you're doing is, you're [encoding] that feedback into musicological information."

Westergren came up with the idea of creating a customized music database after he read a story about Aimee Mann who first gained prominence as the lead singer of the popular 1980s new-wave group 'Til Tuesday. Following the release of two critically acclaimed and modestly successful solo albums—*Whatever* (1993) and *I'm with Stupid* (1995), Mann parted ways with her record label (Geffen Records), who shelved her third album (*Bachelor No. 2*, 2000) for not being commercial or mainstream enough.

Westergren was convinced there had to be a way that fans could be notified of Mann's new album, which she eventually released under her own label. "I thought, if I could do a kind of Myers-Briggs [personality map] for music and tell people what songs they'd probably like based on musical similarities, the Internet could solve the problem of access," he recalled to Linda Tischler for *Fast Company* (1 Dec. 2005).

SAVAGE BEAST TECHNOLOGIES
Westergren shared his vision with Jon Kraft, a fellow Stanford classmate and successful Silicon Valley entrepreneur who had sold his own software firm four years earlier. In late 1999 and at the height of the dot-com era, the duo collaborated on a business plan for Westergren's Internet-based music search-and-recommendation company. They also recruited Will Glaser, a computer scientist and mathematician, to help create the software technology.

In January 2000 Westergren, along with Kraft and Glaser, officially launched Savage Beast Technologies, which was initially based out of a one-bedroom apartment in the San Francisco neighborhood of Potrero Hill. Westergren and Kraft pitched their idea to numerous potential investors and managed to raise $1.5 million in first-round funding in March 2000, shortly before the NASDAQ stock market crash and the burst of the dot-com bubble.

Westergren expanded his staff, hiring several part-time music analysts and a musicologist, Nolan Glasser, to develop the Music Genome Project—software that contained a mathematical algorithm used to generate a comprehensive library (database) of individual songs catalogued according to a series of distinct characteristics. "We spent many months brainstorming, whiteboarding, testing and retesting with a collection of musicians/technologists. . . . It was a very interesting combination of musical and mathematical/computer science skills coming together," Westergren explained to Jim Smalley for the *DCist* (7 June 2006). "The first few thousand songs were analyzed around my living room table. It took close to a year to complete the first production version."

FINANCIAL STRUGGLES

In the wake of the economic downturn in 2001, the initial funding for Savage Beast Technologies was exhausted. Despite having to take out personal loans and borrow against nearly a dozen credit cards, Westergren remained undaunted. "We had a choice: Cut our losses and throw in the towel or find a way to keep going. We decided to keep the company alive and start deferring salaries. Ultimately, over 50 people deferred almost $1.5 million over the course of two years," he told Katy Finneran for *Forbes* (21 Jan. 2010). The company relocated from San Francisco to Oakland to save on rent.

In May 2001 Barnes and Noble introduced its Jazz Discovery service, which was created by Savage Beast Technologies. Following Kraft's departure in March 2002, Westergren became solely responsible for pitching the company to potential investors and obtaining additional financing. By the end of that year, he had managed to license the Music Genome Project, the startup's patented and proprietary technology, as a music recommendation engine to other businesses including America Online (AOL) and to online retailers with in-store, self-service kiosks such as Tower Records, Best Buy, and Borders. However, these licensing deals barely generated sufficient revenue to keep the company going.

PANDORA MEDIA

The turning point for Westergren came in 2004 when he garnered the interest of Larry Marcus, a fellow musician and the managing director of Walden Venture Capital. "The pitch that he gave wasn't that interesting," Marcus told Claire Cain Miller for the *New York Times* (7 Mar. 2010). "But what was incredibly interesting was Tim himself. We could tell he was an entrepreneur who wasn't going to fail."

After Westergren secured $7.8 million in funding, Savage Beast Technologies restructured its management team, which included newly appointed CEO and president, Joseph J. Kennedy, formerly the president and chief operating officer of the financial services firm E-Loan. Westergren became chief strategy officer of the company, which changed its name to Pandora Media in July 2005.

Under the new management, Pandora was relaunched as a customized radio station that targeted the consumer rather than the retailers. "In scanning the landscape, we found that 80 percent of the time people spend listening to music they're not playing their own music; they're listening to the radio," Kennedy explained to Jennifer Pellet for *Chief Executive.net* (27 Jan. 2012). "And, hey, we had this intellectual property that

would enable us, we believed, to be the best in the world at bringing personalization to radio."

In August 2005 Pandora released a public beta version of the radio service, offering its customers access to ten hours of free music before charging them with a monthly three dollar subscription fee. The site received heavy traffic in the first six weeks and attracted 50,000 trial users and 500 subscribers. Following the success of the subscription-based service, Westergren and his partners launched in November 2005 a second version of Pandora—one that was entirely supported by advertising.

Westergren credited James Feuille of Crosslink Capital General with this strategy. "Jim advocated for a free service, which at the time was far from obvious," Westergren told Kambiz Foroohar for *Bloomberg Markets* (4 Oct. 2011). This new business model option was financed with $12 million in venture capital from Crosslink Capital, along with several other investment firms. The free service amassed 450,000 registered users and 700 new subscribers in the first six weeks.

By 2007, Pandora had branched out into the mobile phone arena by making its personalized music service available on several Sprint cell phone devices. In the summer of 2008, Pandora introduced a streaming radio application for Apple iPhone users—a strategy that paid off. "We went from 20,000 listeners to 40,000 a day," Westergren told Eric Benderoff for the *Chicago Tribune* (14 Aug. 2008). By May 2009 Pandora announced that it had amassed fifty million registered users and introduced Pandora One, a premium service with several new features including ad-free listening and higher-quality audio.

ROYALTY RATES THREATEN PANDORA

In March 2007 Pandora's revenue stream, and its survival, was threatened by the Copyright Royalty Board's (CRB) decision to triple the licensing fees paid by online radio sites each time they play a copyrighted song. (The Copyright Royalty Board is a regulatory body that determines the rates paid by webcasters for copyright licenses.) Under the old system, royalty rates involved paying a yearly fee plus a percentage of the revenue to SoundExchange, the nonprofit organization that collects the fees on behalf of sound recording copyright owners for digital transmissions. Broadcast radio stations do not have to pay royalty rates to artists or labels.

Westergren responded by helping to launch SaveNetRadio, a nationwide grassroots campaign to rescue radio and audio streaming sites, and by appealing to Pandora customers to sign an online petition to delay the royalty hikes. On June 26, 2007, Pandora, along with other Internet radio sites, went off the air as part of a nationwide "Day of Silence" protest against the increases, which were scheduled to take effect in mid-July. Westergren also lobbied Congress for passage of the Internet Radio Equality Act (2007) that was aimed at overturning CRB's ruling.

Westergren's efforts paid off: Prior to the July 15 deadline, SoundExchange announced that it would indefinitely postpone the royalty rate increases while it worked out a new deal with webcasters. In September 2008, Congress passed the Webcaster Settlement Act of 2008 that gave Internet radio stations until February 2009 to negotiate a lower royalty fee that would override CRB's rates.

SoundExchange and the Internet radio broadcasters failed to reach a deal by the February 2009 deadline, and in June Congress passed the Webcaster Settlement Act of 2009, which extended negotiations an additional thirty days. By July 2009, after two years of negotiating, SoundExchange and the webcasters reached a decision regarding the royalty rates. According to Greg Sandoval for *CNET.com* (7 July 2009), under the terms of the new agreement, "large ad-supported radio services, such as Pandora . . . either share 25 percent of revenue with the music industry or pay a per-stream rate of 0.08 cent retroactive to 2006, whichever is greater. That rate will increase until reaching 0.14 cent in 2015." To help offset the increased royalty rates, Pandora required listeners whose usage exceeded the forty-hours-a-month free limit to pay ninety-nine cents to keep listening. (This listening cap was lifted in September 2011.) Shortly after the royalty deal, Pandora received a reported $35 million in venture capital funding.

PANDORA GROWS AND GOES PUBLIC

By the end of 2009, Pandora had forty-three million registered users and revenues of $50 million that came primarily from advertising and songs purchased on iTunes and Amazon's music store (via Pandora's affiliate program). This marked the company's first profitable quarter. Pandora's royalty payments to SoundExchange, however, totaled $28 million—more than half of its revenue.

In 2010 Pandora sought to diversify, and early in the year it partnered separately with Pioneer Electronics and Alpine Electronics to create car stereos that could access the Pandora iPhone application. By April, Pandora introduced a new application for Apple's iPad tablet and the company reported fifty million registered listeners. By July 2010 the figure had grown to sixty million, and by 2011, Pandora reported over eighty million registered users.

In October 2010 Pandora set its sights on making its service available in as many vehicles as possible. "Simply put, half of radio listening happens in the car. People spend 20 hours a week listening to music; 17 hours of that is from radio," Westergren told Alex Pham for the *Los Angeles Times* (21 Oct. 2010). "About half of that radio listening, or 8.5 hours, occurs while they're in a car. So that's the Holy Grail." In 2011, Pandora Radio was factory installed in Mini Coopers and cars made by BMW, Mercedes-Benz, Toyota, and Hyundai. That same year several Ford vehicles (Fiesta, Fusion, Mustang, and Lincoln MKZ) and all new General Motors cars came with factory installed Pandora Radio. To help celebrate Chevrolet's centennial anniversary, General Motors also created the Chevrolet Centennial channel on Pandora, which offers the top one hundred songs that mention Chevrolet cars.

In June 2011 Pandora Media went public on the New York Stock Exchange. According to the registration statement filed four months earlier with the Securities and Exchange Commission, Westergren owns less than three percent of Pandora and will receive 3.6 million shares of the company. However, as of June 2012, those shares have seen a 38 percent decline in value. Furthermore, Pandora radio, which was listed as one of *Time* magazine's 50 Best iPhone Apps in February 2012, faces increased competition from rival digital music services, namely, Rhapsody, iHeartRadio, and Spotify—Europe's top streaming service now available in the United States. To meet these challenges, Pandora Media plans to expand into overseas markets.

As chief strategy officer at Pandora, Westergren spends most of the year traveling the country and getting feedback from listeners at numerous town hall meetings. He also continues to lobby Congress for lower royalty rates for music streaming services. Westergren lives in San Francisco, California, with his wife, an academic political scientist, and his daughter.

SUGGESTED READING

Gray, Tyler. "Pandora Pulls Back the Curtain on Its Magic Music Machine." *Fast Company*. Mansueto Ventures, 21 Jan. 2011. Web. 23 July 2012.

Green, Laura. "How Tim Westergren Dials In Approval from Pandora's Customers and Employees to Drive Growth." *Smart Business*. Smart Business Network, 1 Feb. 2012. Web. 14 Aug. 2012.

Mannix, Andy. "Pandora Radio's Tim Westergren on Congress, Spotify, and Emily White." *City Pages*. Village Voice Media, 10 July 2012. Web. 17 July 2012.

Newman, Rick. "How Pandora Became an Unlikely Hit." *U.S. News & World Report*. U.S. News & World Report, L.P., 15 June 2011. Web. 19 July 2012.

Sisario, Ben. "Pandora Faces Rivals for Ears and Ads." *New York Times*. New York Times, Inc., 20 June 2012. Web. 30 July 2012.

Smalley, Jim. "Interview with Pandora Founder Tim Westergren." *DCist.* Gothamist, LLC, 7 June 2006. Web. 23 July 2012.

—*Bertha Muteba*

Joss Whedon

Born: June 23, 1964
Occupation: Writer, filmmaker

Joss Whedon made a name for himself in television writing strong female characters, first as a staff writer for the ABC comedy *Roseanne* and then as the creator of the popular WB/UPN series *Buffy the Vampire Slayer*, a small-screen adaptation of his 1992 movie. When questioned about his knack for writing female characters, he told Luke Benedictus for the Melbourne *Sunday Age* (25 Sep. 2005, online): "To me, the question isn't how you do it. It's how can you possibly avoid doing it?" In the late 1990s and early 2000s, Whedon achieved an enthusiastic following with *Angel* and *Firefly*, two other television shows he developed. Most recently he has garnered headlines for his big-screen work on *The Avengers* (2012), which upon its release became the highest-grossing movie of the year.

EARLY LIFE AND EDUCATION

Born on June 23, 1964, in New York City, Joseph Hill Whedon hails from a family of writers. In addition to being the head of the history department at Riverdale Country School, an exclusive private school in the Bronx, his mother, Lee Stearns, was an aspiring novelist; his father, Tom Whedon, was an Emmy Award–winning television writer and producer whose credits include the popular 1970s children's programs *The Electric Company* and *Captain Kangaroo*, as well as the hit 1980s comedies *Alice*, *Benson*, and *The Golden Girls*; and his grandfather, John Whedon, wrote screenplays for several iconic television sitcoms, including *The Donna Reed Show*, *The Andy Griffith Show*, *The Dick Van Dyke Show*, and *Leave It to Beaver*.

Whedon has two older brothers, Samuel and Matthew. After his parents divorced when he was nine, he and his brothers remained in New York with their mother. It was around this time that Whedon became fascinated with comic books. Both of his parents eventually moved on to new relationships, and he has two half brothers, Zach and Jed, from his father's second marriage.

During his junior year of high school, Whedon left Riverdale Country School, which he had attended since the first grade, and transferred abroad to a highly renowned all-male boarding school in Winchester, England. "My mother suggested it, because she was on

Getty Images

sabbatical, and enjoyed England, and didn't trust the schools in California where my father was. So I was to go for half a year, because she was taking a half a year sabbatical," he recalled to Kenneth Plume for IGN.com (23 June 2003, online). "I was lazy, I was terrible, but through osmosis, I was learning more than I ever had before. It was so extraordinary. My family went back to America, and the school asked me to stay along, and I did."

After completing his studies at boarding school, Whedon returned to the United States. He enrolled in Wesleyan University in Middletown, Connecticut, where he pursued a major in film studies. While there he continued to explore an ongoing interest in gender and feminism that had first been nurtured by his mother, a women's-rights activist. "She was an extraordinary inspiration—a radical feminist, a history teacher and just one hell of a woman. What she did was provide a role model of someone who is completely in control of her life," he told Ryan Gilbey for the *Observer* (21 Apr. 2012, online). "It was only when I got to college that I realized that the rest of the world didn't run the way my world was run and that there was a need for feminism." This was reflected in his student films, most notably his senior project, a postapocalyptic Western whose heroine was based on the Clint Eastwood film character Man with No Name.

HOLLYWOOD BOUND

After obtaining his BA in film and gender studies in 1987, Whedon, who had adopted Joss

(Chinese for "luck") as his first name, moved to Los Angeles, California, to become a screenwriter. He lived with his father and stepmother, writing unsolicited screenplays (also known as spec scripts) while working in a video store. Whedon wrote spec scripts for four network comedies—*It's a Living*, on which his father was a writer; the short-lived *Just in Time*; *The Wonder Years*; and *It's Garry Shandling's Show*—before landing his first staff writing position on the second season (1989–90) of *Roseanne*. He penned four of the show's episodes before leaving the series. "Having been rewritten almost to death, I got shut out of the process—and I thought the producers were talented and good friends, but I couldn't work for them anymore, because I don't like getting paid to do nothing," he told Plume.

In 1990 Whedon served as a writer and coproducer for the television adaptation of Ron Howard's comedy television series *Parenthood*, which was canceled after twelve episodes. Following his mother's untimely death in 1992 from a brain aneurysm, he sold his first movie screenplay: *Buffy the Vampire Slayer*, a dark comedy with a strong female heroine. "The first thing I thought of when I thought of *Buffy*—the movie—was the little blonde girl who goes into a dark alley and gets killed in every horror movie. The idea of *Buffy* was to subvert that idea and create someone who was a hero where she had always been a victim," he said to Gilbey.

To Whedon's disappointment, his script for *Buffy the Vampire Slayer* was reworked into a campy, tongue-in-cheek movie whose heroine is a shallow, ditzy cheerleader at a posh Los Angeles high school. "I really thought I'd never work again," he recalled to Emily Nussbaum for the *New York Times* (22 Sep. 2002, online). "It was that devastating." Although the film grossed less than $17 million domestically, it gained a cult following on video. Whedon subsequently landed uncredited behind-the-scenes work as a script doctor, refining the screenplays of several films, including the 1994 remake of Sam Peckinpah's crime caper *The Getaway*; the Keanu Reeves action film *Speed* (1994); Kevin Costner's postapocalyptic thriller *Waterworld* (1995); the computer-animated Disney film *Toy Story* (1995), for which he received an Academy Award nod for Best Original Screenplay; and *Alien Resurrection* (1997), the third sequel to Ridley Scott's 1979 science-fiction thriller, *Alien*.

DARLING OF THE WB

In 1997 Whedon was contacted by Fran Rubel Kuzui, the director and executive producer of *Buffy*, and Gail Berman, an executive at Sandollar Productions (the company that also owned the film's rights), about adapting the movie for the small screen. Whedon and Berman successfully pitched the concept to the fledgling WB Television Network, whose programming chief,

Garth Ancier, picked up the series as a midseason replacement. Whedon's newly formed company, Mutant Enemy Productions, would coproduce the twelve episodes of the *Buffy* television series, along with Sandollar Television and Kuzui Enterprises. Whedon also had complete creative control. "As far as I'm concerned, the first episode of *Buffy* was the beginning of my career. It was the first time I told a story from start to finish the way I wanted," he told A. J. Jacobs for *Entertainment Weekly* (25 Apr. 1997, online). Whereas the original film portrays the protagonist as vapid and popular, the small-screen adaptation, which is darker in tone and set in a suburban high school that sits atop a portal to hell, presents the Buffy character as someone with whom younger viewers can identify.

Buffy debuted on March 10, 1997, with Sarah Michelle Gellar in the title role. Most of the first season's episodes center on Buffy's attempt to live a normal teenage life while leading a secret life as a slayer of evil beings. Whedon also focused on Buffy's inner circle of evil-fighting sidekicks: fellow outcast Willow, a shy, mousy computer geek, and her equally nerdy best friend, Xander; Cordelia, a popular, snobby cheerleader who is Buffy's high-school rival; Giles, the school librarian, who is also her guide and trainer; and Angel, a handsome, brooding stranger whom she discovers to be a vampire with a soul.

In anticipation that the show would not be renewed, Whedon conceived the episodes as standalone stories, in which he explored common teenage issues such as peer pressure ("The Pack"), alienation ("Invisible Girl"), and virginity ("Teacher's Pet"). He received writing credit for six episodes, including the season finale, "Prophecy Girl," which culminates in the long-awaited showdown between Buffy and that season's villain, an ancient vampire known as the Master. The first season averaged 3.7 million viewers per episode and became a hit with critics and viewers alike. It performed well in the 18-to-49 demographic and was renewed for twenty-two episodes.

When the series returned for a second season on September 15, 1997, Whedon introduced two new vampire villains: Spike and Drusilla, Angel's former partners in crime. The show remained in its Monday night time slot, behind the family drama *Seventh Heaven*, until January 20, 1998, when it was paired with the network's new teen drama *Dawson's Creek* on Tuesday nights. Whedon wrote and directed "Innocence," the first episode in the new time slot, which went on to become the highest-rated episode in the show's history. He also received writing and directing credits for the two-part season finale, "Becoming." The show outperformed its first season, averaging about 5.2 million viewers and finishing the sophomore season as one of the network's top-rated programs.

The third season, which debuted in September 1998, took on a darker tone with the introduction of Faith, a fellow slayer with a rebellious, reckless, and violent nature. Other story arcs involved Willow's exploration of witchcraft and Angel's resurrection from a hell dimension. Whedon wrote and directed five episodes, including the controversial two-part finale that culminates in an attack on the graduating seniors, the airing of which was delayed in the wake of the 1999 Columbine High School shootings.

CULT HERO STATUS

Following a successful third season of *Buffy*, Whedon launched a spinoff series that revolves around the character of Angel as he seeks redemption in Los Angeles by opening a detective agency that specializes in fighting supernatural evil. Although the series has a darker and heavier tone than *Buffy*, Whedon, who also served as the executive producer of *Angel*, sought to inject humor into the scripts. "We're very strict about making a dark, scary, challenging show that isn't relentless and blue," he told Josh Wolk for *Entertainment Weekly* (19 Aug. 1999, online). In early October 1999, *Angel* made its Tuesday night premiere on the WB network. With *Buffy* serving as the lead-in, the series averaged 4.8 million viewers. *Buffy*, already in its fourth season, continued in popularity with an average of 4.7 million viewers.

Whedon's work on Buffy included the first prime-time TV depiction of a lesbian couple involving a main character, Willow, who develops a romantic relationship with fellow witch Tara. Whedon also garnered attention for an episode he wrote and directed called "Hush," in which a group of demons terrorize the townspeople by stealing their voices. The episode, which contains minimal dialogue, earned him a 2000 Emmy Award nomination in the category of Outstanding Writing for a Drama Series.

During the fifth season Whedon drew critical praise for another *Buffy* episode. "The Body" deals with the aftermath of Buffy's mother's unexpected death from a brain aneurysm—the same condition that claimed the life of Whedon's mother. "Joss Whedon delivers an intense yet quiet one-hour masterpiece," David Bianculli wrote in a review of the episode for the New York *Daily News* (27 Feb. 2001, online). "The hour, written and directed with brave intensity by Whedon, does nothing more—and nothing less—than detail how Buffy and her friends react to the situation. It's an hour almost without artifice. There are no music cues whatsoever on the soundtrack; scenes play out at a deliberately slow pace, with all the silences and tensions intact." Whedon also focused on death in the season finale, which ends with Buffy sacrificing her life to save the world by diving into a portal, or gateway, to a dimension of hell.

The series received nods for Program of the Year, Outstanding Achievement in Drama, and Individual Achievement in Drama at the 2001 Television Critics Association (TCA) Awards. It also averaged nearly four and a half million viewers, while its spinoff, *Angel*, was not far behind, with a little over four million in its sophomore season.

Although *Buffy* was the network's second-highest-rated program (behind *Seventh Heaven*), the WB lost its broadcasting rights to the rival United Paramount Network (UPN), which picked up the series for two seasons. Whedon continued to serve as executive producer but handed the show's reins to coproducer Marti Noxon. *Buffy*'s sixth season premiered on October 2, 2001, and the show continued to air on Tuesday nights. The overarching story dealt with Buffy's resurrection and her subsequent depression after being pulled from her peaceful resting place.

Whedon received his sole writing and directing credit of the sixth season for the musical episode "Once More, with Feeling." "My father wrote Off-Off-Broadway musical lyrics, so did his father, before they both worked in TV. I was raised on a steady diet of Sondheim," Whedon shared with Tasha Robinson in an interview posted on the AV Club website (8 Aug. 2007, online). "I made a musical because I was six years into a show, and I knew that nobody was going to stop me. . . . 'Once More, with Feeling' took me four months to write." The critically acclaimed episode sparked some controversy in June 2002 when the Academy of Television Arts and Sciences failed to include it on the Emmy Award nomination ballot in the category for Outstanding Writing in a Drama Series. Despite the Academy informing Emmy voters about the error and giving them the opportunity to change their selection, the episode failed to earn a nod for writing and was nominated instead for Outstanding Music Direction. Whedon's other credits during that year included writing and directing an episode of *Angel*'s third season.

After seven seasons on network television, Whedon decided to bring *Buffy* to a close, citing the grueling schedule as the major reason. "Ultimately, I wasn't going on set as much, wasn't directing as many episodes. I was still very much involved, but the physicality of being there was less," he told Laura Miller for *Salon* (20 May 2003, online). "I feel like we did the best we could for a long . . . time and it's time to tell the next story." Whedon penned the seventh-season premiere as well as the final episode of the series, which concludes with the destruction of the Hellmouth and the entire town of Sunnydale. "Chosen," the series finale, was nominated in the category of Outstanding Special Visual Effects for a Series.

During *Buffy*'s last season, Whedon also served as the writer, director, and executive producer of *Firefly*, a futuristic Western series that first premiered on the Fox network in December 2002. Despite attaining a cult following, the ratings-starved *Firefly* was soon canceled. "I stopped having ideas, which for me is an extremely rare experience," Whedon explained to Bernard Zuel for the *Sydney Morning Herald* (25 Aug. 2010, online). "It was something much more subtle [than losing hope], it took away my ability to think in terms of episodic television. For years." Whedon's sole remaining television series, *Angel*, remained on the air for a fourth and fifth season before being canceled by the WB network in 2004.

LIFE AFTER BUFFY
After a failed 2004 animated pilot based on the Buffy character, Whedon signed on to write and direct a feature film about the DC Comics female superhero Wonder Woman in March 2005. His previous experience with fantasy and comic book movies included his screenwriting contributions to the comic-book film *X-Men* (2000) and the animated science-fiction films *Titan A.E.* (2000) and *Atlantis: The Lost Empire* (2001). Later in 2005, *Serenity*, a film continuation of *Firefly*, was released, receiving mostly favorable reviews. "To the uninitiated, *Serenity* may seem like just another *Star Trek* knockoff, but to so easily dismiss writer Joss Whedon's feature directing debut . . . would be to miss out on a highly entertaining piece of genre-blending fun," Kevin Crust wrote in a review for the *Los Angeles Times* (30 Sep. 2005, online). "A strongly acted, well-written story fortified by riveting action sequences—a rarity these days among studio releases—*Serenity* should delight Whedon novices as much as the already converted." Equally complimentary was Robert K. Elder for the *Chicago Tribune* (30 Sep. 2005, online), who called the movie "a brash, funny, action-packed bit of sci-fi ecstasy." The film failed to attract an audience, however, grossing less than $40 million worldwide.

In 2007 Whedon dropped out of the Wonder Woman movie project when his script failed to meet approval. He also directed two episodes of the NBC comedy *The Office* that year. Whedon then returned to weekly television with the short-lived Fox series *Dollhouse*, which aired for two seasons (2009–10) on the Fox network. His other television directorial credits include a 2010 episode of the Fox musical comedy show *Glee*. Also in 2010, Whedon turned down an offer to participate in a big-screen remake of *Buffy*; Warner Bros. has announced plans for a 2012 release.

BOX-OFFICE SUCCESS
Whedon directed the post-credits scene of the 2011 film *Thor*, the big-screen adaptation featuring the Marvel Comics superhero. He was also the uncredited co-writer of another comic-book adaptation, *Captain America: The First Avenger* (2011), which grossed nearly $177 million worldwide. Whedon then went on to write and direct *The Cabin in the Woods* (2012), a psychological thriller about five vacationing college friends who become unwitting pawns in a sadistic scientific experiment. "*The Cabin in the Woods* . . . showcases one of Whedon's greatest strengths: his ability to take previously disrespected genres—in this case the slasher film—and turn them inside-out and upside-down and every which way but loose," Connie Ogle wrote for the *Miami Herald* (11 Apr. 2012, online). She added, "The film is also surprisingly funny, too, thanks to the clever screenplay by Whedon and [Drew] Goddard." Whedon also produced the film, which grossed nearly $60 million worldwide.

His most successful film to date is *The Avengers* (2012), another entry in the franchise that includes *Thor* and *Captain America*, featuring the title characters of those films as well as fellow Marvel superheroes Iron Man and the Incredible Hulk. Released domestically on May 4, 2012, the movie quickly reached $1 billion in worldwide ticket sales. Upcoming projects include two independent films, one the science-fiction romance *In Your Eyes* and the other a modern-day version of the William Shakespeare play *Much Ado about Nothing*.

In addition to his film and television work, Whedon has penned comics for Marvel and created several series for Dark Horse Comics. Whedon and his wife, architect Kai Cole, live in Los Angeles with their two children.

SUGGESTED READING
Benedictus, Luke. "The Ladies' Man." *Sunday Age* [Melbourne]. Fairfax Media, 25 Sep. 2005. Web. 23 May 2012.

Crust, Kevin. "Finding Joy on Starship *Serenity*." *Los Angeles Times*. Los Angeles Times, 30 Sep. 2005. Web. 23 May 2012.

Gilbey, Ryan. "Joss Whedon: Hollywood's Golden Boy." *Observer*. Guardian News and Media, 21 Apr. 2012. Web. 23 May 2012.

Miller, Laura. "The Man behind the Slayer." *Salon*. Salon Media Group, 20 May 2003. Web. 23 May 2012.

Nussbaum, Emily. "Must See Metaphysics." *New York Times*. New York Times, 22 Sep. 2002. Web. 19 May 2012.

Ogle, Connie. "The Cabin in the Woods." *Miami.com*. Miami.com, 11 Apr. 2012. Web. 23 May 2012.

Plume, Kenneth. "An Interview with Joss Whedon." *IGN.com.* IGN Entertainment, 23 June 2003. Web. 23 May 2012.

—*Bertha Muteba*

Beau Willimon

Born: 1978
Occupation: Playwright, screenwriter

Beau Willimon became nationally known when his screenplay for the film *The Ides of March* (2011), cowritten with George Clooney and Grant Heslov, was nominated for an Academy Award. *The Ides of March* was adapted from his play *Farragut North*, which Willimon wrote in 2004 and was first staged in 2008. The New York–based organization Outer Critics Circle included *Farragut North* among its nominations for Outstanding New Off-Broadway Play in 2008 and nominated Willimon for that year's John Gassner American Playwriting Award.

Farragut North follows campaign organizers behind the scenes as they work for a presidential hopeful during a primary season. The play conjures "the high-stakes, adrenalin-filled atmosphere" that Willimon experienced while working on the campaigns of several high-profile Democratic candidates between 1998 and 2004, he told Richard Patterson for *musicOMH* (Nov. 2008, online). But "the subject of the play is not politics," he continued. "The subjects are power, ambition, and hubris—and those are relevant not just in the political world, but also on Wall Street, in Hollywood, in any world where power dynamics are at play, even within the microcosm of a family." Willimon told Kristin Sterling for *Columbia News* (8 Aug. 2002, online), "I strongly believe in the power of art to shape our understanding of the political, economic, and social dilemmas which face our world."

Willimon, who studied playwriting at Columbia University, has said that all of his one-act and full-length plays, screenplays, and television scripts deal with the same subjects. "The topics seem disparate, but Willimon insists that the theme that runs throughout his works is the ways power plays out in everyday relationships," Amanda Erickson wrote for *Columbia College Today* (May/June 2009, online).

"I love writing movies, and they certainly help pay the bills, but if someone were to tell me I could never write another play, I'd quickly end up in the loony bin," Willimon told Sara Cardace for the *New York Post's Page Six Magazine* (23 Nov. 2008, online). For Willimon, a major appeal of writing plays is that he is always able to find aspiring directors eager to mount them and aspiring actors eager to appear in them, "even

Getty Images

if it's for half a dozen people in a living room," he told Winter Miller for *Variety* (22 Apr. 2008, online). He told Christopher Wallenberg for the *Boston Globe* (25 Apr. 2010, online), "There were many years when I was hand-to-mouth and didn't know how I was gonna make rent. I've done every job under the sun. . . . So to be able to make a living where all I do is write is absolutely liberating."

EARLY YEARS

Beau Willimon was born in 1978 in Washington, DC, the first of two sons of Henry Pack Willimon Jr. and his wife, Nancy. According to some sources, his original given name was Pack. His younger brother, Charles "Chas" Willimon, is a teacher, singer/songwriter, and instrumentalist; in their first collaboration, Chas wrote the music for Beau's play *Spirit Control*. Henry Willimon was a captain in the US Navy, and the family moved "every two or three years," Beau Willimon told Adam Szymkowicz in an interview for Szymkowicz's blog (18 Apr. 2010). From Washington, the Willimons moved to Hawaii, San Francisco, and Philadelphia. After Henry Willimon retired from the military, when Beau Willimon was ten, the family put down roots in St. Louis, Missouri. Willimon's father, an attorney, went on to practice family law.

Willimon told Szymkowicz that his family's frequent moves during his childhood forced him to adapt to new neighborhoods and schools and to make new friends repeatedly; consequently, he met "a wide spectrum of people" and became "deeply curious about the world." He added, "I think a strong sense of curiosity is important to any writer. It's what compels us to tell other people's stories, not just our own. And it helps us ask questions of ourselves and others that are both difficult and unexpected. It's what helps us tap into the mysteries which breathe life and magic into the stories we hope to tell."

HIGH SCHOOL AND COLLEGE

Willimon attended the John Burroughs School, a coeducational college-preparatory day school in St. Louis. He was introduced to theater through road-show productions of the musicals *The Unsinkable Molly Brown* and *Brigadoon* that came to St. Louis. In high school, he appeared in student theatrical productions and took courses in theater. After his graduation from the Burroughs School in 1995, he entered Columbia University in New York City, where he studied fine arts, primarily painting, with the goal of becoming a professional artist; he made history his second major. As a junior, Willimon told Erickson, he found that "there was something [about painting] that felt constricting and claustrophobic." To Wallenberg, he said, "I could make facile, pretty-looking paintings that would impress people. But they just felt like lies to me."

Willimon decided to write a play "to cleanse my brain," he told Erickson. His play won that year's Seymour Brick Memorial Prize, an award from Columbia College's Department of English and Comparative Literature that recognizes the best play submitted by an undergraduate. "That was when I began seriously considering this as a career," Willimon said to Erickson. He told Wallenberg, "Writing plays supplied for me everything that painting didn't, which is the ability to tell stories in real time, in a real space, in three dimensions, in flesh and blood. I realized I had been trying to cram all this narrative into my paintings, but ultimately painting was a static medium. So it just opened up this whole new door."

As an undergraduate, Willimon spent a summer engaged in public service in Tallinn, the capital of Estonia, supported by an Eesti Fellowship. During his senior year at Columbia, he told Erickson, he and a friend worked "twenty hours a day, seven days a week" as volunteers in the successful campaign of Charles Schumer, then a Democratic New York State assemblyman, for the US Senate seat held by the Republican Alfonse D'Amato, who had been seeking a fourth term. Willimon and his friend devoted much of their time to polling and posting fliers.

GRADUATE EDUCATION

After earning his BA degree, in 1999 Willimon audited a course taught by Eduardo Machado, then head of Columbia's MFA program in playwriting. Encouraged by Machado, whom he has named as one of his mentors, Willimon enrolled in the program and spent the next three years at Columbia. There, he told Wallenberg, he wrote "lots of bad stuff" and "learn[ed] what my voice was." In 2000, he aided Hillary Clinton's successful campaign for a US Senate seat and worked in former senator Bill Bradley's failed attempt to win the Democratic presidential election.

During the summer of 2001, Willimon traveled in South Africa. The September 11, 2001, terrorist attacks on the United States occurred right after his return to New York. In pondering the attacks, he concluded that "if we are to gain any insight from our own national tragedy . . . we must also attempt to understand the tragedies which confront the rest of the world," he told Sterling. "We must not reflect on our losses alone, but rather place them in the context of global culture which is routinely afflicted with loss."

He decided to return to South Africa to record some of the lasting effects of apartheid that he had observed, prominent among them pervasive fear, mistrust, and paranoia. "Perhaps by reflecting on South Africa, a nation whose political realities have sustained decades-long forms of paranoia, Americans can gain insight into their own relationship with terror," he said to Sterling. Supported by a Mortimer Hays-Brandeis Traveling Fellowship, he made two trips to South Africa in the 2002–2003 academic year. He later made several dozen lithographs based on his photographs and drawings of South African places and people.

As a graduate student, Willimon teamed up with Tomas Vu-Daniel, director of the LeRoy Neiman Center for Print Studies at Columbia, to found an organization called Pangea Arts, which aimed to support and present theatrical works, films, and visual art representing "a global spectrum of cultures," Sterling wrote. Springboard 2002, a festival of exhibitions, lectures, films, and performances organized by Pangea Arts, took place at Columbia in April 2002. In the same year, Willimon winnowed his full-length play *Baby Blue* into a one-act drama that became a finalist for the Hangar Theatre New Play Festival in Ithaca, New York. *Baby Blue* "focuses on a middle-aged mother attempting to help her twenty-two-year-old son recover from a nervous breakdown resulting from his alcoholism," Willimon told Sterling. "The play is about how unconditional love can prove to be fatal." In early 2002, Willimon served as an intern with the Wooster Group, which mounted a production of *To You, the Birdie*, based on Paul Schmidt's translation of Jean Racine's seventeenth-century play *Phèdre* and directed by Elizabeth LeCompte at St. Ann's Warehouse in Brooklyn, New York.

CAREER AFTER GRADUATE SCHOOL

Willimon earned a master's degree in dramatic writing from Columbia in 2003. He then went to Iowa, where, in his last involvement to date with a political campaign, he assisted in the ultimately unsuccessful presidential bid by Howard Dean, former governor of Vermont, for the 2004 Democratic nomination. The experience was "extraordinary," he told Erickson. "When I came back from that campaign, politics was what I wanted to write about."

That desire led Willimon to write what became *Farragut North*. The play was named best new work at the 2005 Dayton Playhouse FutureFest, a weekend festival in Ohio in which six new and unproduced plays are presented. But of the several dozen theater companies nationwide that Willimon mailed the script to, none responded positively, and for the next four years it lay untouched.

One of his next scripts was inspired by what he had learned about the American South during the Civil War in a course taught by renowned historian Eric Foner. Called *Hickory Hill*, the drama is set in the South and told "from the perspective of the slaves on a plantation," Willimon told Scott Myers for a videotaped interview posted on Myers's website Go into the Story (19 Feb. 2012). AMC Networks bought the script with the aim of making an original television series from it, but nothing has yet come of that project.

Willimon earned two successive Lila Acheson Wallace Juilliard Playwriting Fellowships, which supported his writing at the Juilliard School from 2006 to 2008. *Lower Ninth*, one of the full-length plays that he wrote during that period, was inspired by the horrific conditions endured by thousands of New Orleanians and other Americans living along the Gulf Coast in the wake of Hurricane Katrina in 2005. The floods caused by breached levees in New Orleans destroyed the homes of many of the African Americans who lived in the Lower Ninth Ward. In Willimon's drama, Malcolm, a middle-aged African American, and E. Z., the teenage son of one of his former girlfriends, are stranded on the roof of a house nearly submerged by floodwaters, along with the tarpaulin-covered body of a third man, Lowboy. Weakened by heat, hunger, and fear, Malcolm and E. Z. talk about their lives, the racism they have experienced, and the absence of rescuers. In one scene, Malcolm dreams about Lowboy, who briefly comes to life on the stage. *Lower Ninth* premiered at the Flea, an off-Broadway theater, in early 2008. It was performed in 2010 at the Donmar Warehouse in London, England, where Willimon had served as writer in residence in 2008.

When Szymkowicz asked Willimon what advice he would give to playwrights just starting out, he responded, "I think the single most important thing is to find the friends and peers you really believe in, and who really believe in you, and stick together. It's a tough business and a hard life, and you'll get strength from those people. Nobody can do it alone. When things are going good for you, help your friends out, and when things are going good for your friends, hopefully they'll return the favor." He added, "If you need to do a day job, I recommend work that's easy on the brain and leaves you enough energy for your *real* job, which is writing plays." Until *The Ides of March* began to open doors for him, Willimon supported himself with a variety of jobs; according to Szymkowicz, he has also been a "pool shark" and an airplane pilot.

In 2008, Willimon's newly acquired agent mailed the *Farragut North* script to acting companies, as well as several Hollywood offices. The campaigns for the 2008 presidential nominations were in full swing, and as Willimon and others have speculated, it may be the excitement and news coverage surrounding the campaigns that led several theater companies to greet *Farragut North* with great enthusiasm. Moreover, even before its first staging, Warner Bros. expressed interest in optioning the rights to the script and making a film adaptation with George Clooney and Leonardo DiCaprio in starring roles. Warner Bros. ultimately abandoned that plan, and the film was made by Sony Pictures. Clooney remained on board, recruiting Willimon to collaborate on a filmscript with him and his longtime writing partner Grant Heslov. During the next few years, the trio rewrote the script. Among other changes, they made the presidential candidate a leading character, broadened the story, and added many new scenes and locations.

Meanwhile, *Farragut North* had made its stage debut in November 2008, in an off-Broadway production mounted by the Atlantic Theater Company and directed by Doug Hughes. It starred John Gallagher Jr. as Stephen, who at age twenty-five has accumulated enough experience and admiration to land him the position of press secretary to a politician (unseen in the play) seeking the Democratic presidential nomination; Chris Noth as Stephen's mentor Paul, a veteran campaign manager; Kate Blumberg as Ida, a *New York Times* reporter; Olivia Thirlby as Molly, a savvy young campaign intern; and Isiah Whitlock Jr. as Tom, who works for a rival camp. *Farragut North* premiered on the West Coast in June 2009 at the Geffen Playhouse in Los Angeles, and it has since been staged at many other venues, though not on Broadway, as had been rumored.

Named for a Washington, DC, subway station near K Street, where many lobbyists have offices, *Farragut North* is "a universal story that can always seem fresh," Willimon said to Erickson. He told Cardace that the play, while fictional, reflects his observations of people and events during the electoral campaigns he participated in.

"In terms of the affairs and some of the particulars of the backroom meetings, that's all made up," he said. "But the atmosphere of it, the paranoia, the bald ambition, the gluttony for power, and the ways in which all those things can warp your soul—it was all there."

In 2009, the year that marked the fortieth anniversary of the premiere of *Butch Cassidy and the Sundance Kid*, Willimon organized a free outdoor showing of that film for the Tribeca Film Festival in honor of its screenwriter, William Goldman, whom he has cited as another of his mentors. In 2010, Willimon's play *Spirit Control* premiered at the Manhattan Theatre Club (MTC) in New York City. Written as an MTC commission and directed by Henry Wishcamper, *Spirit Control* starred Jeremy Sisto as an air-traffic controller whose seemingly enviable life is upended after a harrowing incident involving a pilot who suffers a heart attack during a flight. According to the MTC website, the play "is a chilling and mesmerizing look at how we navigate a crisis, and the demons that haunt us long after."

The Ides of March, which George Clooney directed, premiered in October 2011. The film received a mostly positive critical response. In a representative review, Russell Florence Jr. described it for Ohio-based website Cityfolk (11 Oct. 2011, online) as "a powerful, intimate, fast-paced look at the schemes and pitfalls of a heated Democratic presidential primary in must-win Ohio." In words echoed by many other critics, he also wrote in the Dayton, Ohio, online magazine *Most Metro*, "The story doesn't break new ground, but still addresses its core themes of hubris and loyalty with thought-provoking insight." *The Ides of March* earned Academy Award, Golden Globe Award, and BAFTA Award nominations in the categories of best screenplay and best adapted screenplay, while Willimon, Clooney, and Heslov shared the Australian Academy of Cinema and Television Arts (AACTA) International Award for Best Screenplay.

Willimon has since written the pilot for and helped to develop the series *House of Cards*, based on the 1990 BBC miniseries of the same title. The miniseries was adapted from the 1989 political novel by Michael Dobbs, a one-time chief of staff for the British Conservative Party. The new series will be streamed on Netflix (it will not air on television) and is scheduled to begin in late 2012. Set in the United States rather than Great Britain, it will star Kevin Spacey in "a satirical tale of power, corruption and lies," according to a Netflix press release (18 Mar. 2011). David Fincher will direct the pilot; Willimon is writing thirteen hours' worth of scripts and serving as the series' co–executive producer. Willimon is also writing the script for an American version of Kasper Barfoed's Danish film *Kandidaten* (*The Candidate*, 2008).

PERSONAL LIFE

Willimon has lived in Brooklyn since about 2002. "Most days I'm alone in my apartment with my cat trying to punch out pages, although I'm usually more successful procrastinating with online Scrabble or Risk," he admitted to Szymkowicz. He told Szymkowicz that he owns "dozens of maps and map-books" and enjoys traveling; he has made many long-distance solo walks since the late 1990s, when he "trekked the Dingle Peninsula and Northeast Coast of Ireland on foot." The London-based agent Fay Davies has represented Willimon since 2009.

SUGGESTED READING

Erickson, Amanda. "Beau Willimon '99 Brings Politics Alive on Stage." *Columbia College Today*. Columbia U, May/June 2009. Web. 17 Feb. 2012.

Wallenberg, Christopher. "A Political Drama with Powerful Ambitions." *Boston.com*. New York Times, 25 Apr. 2010. Web. 17 Feb. 2012.

Willimon, Beau. "I Interview Playwrights Part 148: Beau Willimon." Interview by Adam Szymkowicz. *ASzym.blogspot.com*. Adam Szymkowicz, 18 Apr. 2010. Web. 17 Feb. 2012.

---. "Q&A: Beau Willimon." Interview by Richard Patterson. *MusicOMH*. OMH, Nov. 2008. Web. 23 Mar. 2012.

Woodward, Adam. "Beau Willimon." *Little White Lies*. Church of London, 26 Oct. 2011. Web. 17 Feb. 2012.

—Miriam Helbok

Yukiko Yamashita

Born: 1972
Occupation: Developmental biologist

The research of developmental biologist Yukiko Yamashita has focused on the behavior of adult stem cells in order to gain a better understanding of the processes that control asymmetric stem cell division. This type of cell division, which is crucial to the growth of multicellular organisms, results in two distinct daughter cells—one that is identical to the original stem cell and another type of specialized cell that can be found in specific tissues or organs throughout the body. Preserving a balance between the number of stem cells and differentiated cells is essential for maintaining normal tissue development and organ stability. Too few cells can lead to cell death, and a proliferation of such cells can lead to a tumor.

Yamashita's investigations, which involve the use of the germ line stem cells of a male fruit fly, have yielded many groundbreaking findings. During a postdoctoral fellowship at Stanford

University, Yamashita discovered that after the centrosome is duplicated, one of the centrosomes remains close to the niche, or the habitat where the stem cell resides and reproduces, while the other centrosome moves to the opposite end of the cell prior to cell division. Since making this discovery Yamashita has been successful in identifying that the positioning for the two centrosomes is not random: The centrosome located close to the stem cell microenvironment is the parent centrosome, and the one that travels away from the niche is the daughter centrosome.

The research of Yamashita and her collaborators has paved the way for many studies that have speculated that the chromosomes of germ line stem cells are not randomly segregated, much in the same way as the centrosomes, a theory that has been challenged by Yamashita. In an account of her work published in the *Journal of Cell Science* (Mar. 15, 2011), the author stated, "In recent years, the finding that some stem cell populations preferentially retain mother centrosomes during division . . . raised the possibility that this could provide a mechanism for the retention of template DNA strands. . . . However, our present study clearly demonstrates that this is not necessarily the case. That is, in male GSCs that consistently asymmetrically segregate the mother centrosome, the chromosome strands are randomly segregated. It remains possible that centrosomes are asymmetrically segregated to segregate fate determinants such as protein and RNA . . . or other factors such as damaged proteins." The article continued, "It is also important to note that *Drosophila* female GSCs have been reported to non-randomly segregate DNA strands . . . even though centrosomes are not stereotypically segregated in these cells. . . . Thus, it remains possible that chromosome strands are asymmetrically segregated in some cells, but stem cells that asymmetrically segregate centrosomes do not necessarily asymmetrically segregate chromosome strands."

Yamashita's efforts in the field of cell biology have been celebrated in the scientific community. In 2011 she was among twenty-two individuals to be honored with the prestigious five-year, $500,000 fellowship from the John D. and Catherine T. MacArthur Foundation. According to the foundation's website, the MacArthur Genius Grant, as it is more commonly known, is awarded annually to "talented individuals who have shown extraordinary originality and dedication in their creative pursuits and a marked capacity for self-direction." Upon learning that she had won the coveted award, Yamashita was initially skeptical. "I called my husband right after I hung up my phone call with the foundation," she said in an article in *The Node* (Oct. 13, 2011), a website launched by *Development*, a research journal dedicated to developmental

Courtesy the John D. & Catherine T. MacArthur Foundation

biology. "[He] seriously warned me that 'if you get a second phone call asking your bank account and pin number, so that they can transfer the award money, don't give it to them.'"

Since January 2007 Yamashita has taught and conducted research at the University of Michigan Medical School, as well as the Life Sciences Institute (LSI); that same year, she established her own lab at the university. In addition to the MacArthur Fellowship, Yamashita has received many other honors, including the Searle Scholar prize (2008), the March of Dimes Basil O'Connor Starter Scholar Research Award (2008), and the American Society for Cell Biology Women in Cell Biology Junior Career Recognition Award (2009). She is a member of the American Society for Cell Biology (ASCB) and serves on the editorial board of the Faculty of 1000.

EARLY LIFE

The oldest of four siblings, Yukiko Yamashita was born in 1972 in Akashi, an industrial city located to the west of Kobe, Japan. Her mother worked as a pharmacologist, and her father was a longtime employee at a patent office and an amateur inventor. His patented devices included a capless and retractable highlighter pen.

Yamashita, whose interest in living things dates back to a childhood spent collecting butterflies and dragonflies, credits her parents for instilling in her a love of science. In her ASCB award-winning essay, "A Tale of Mother and Daughter," which appeared in the journal

Molecular Biology of the Cell (Jan. 1, 2010), Yamashita wrote, "My parents hardly treated me as a girl (or a boy), with their only expectation being that I explain things. . . . This certainly influenced me in that I did not think my gender would matter in my future pursuits—which turned out to be biology." She went on to credit her pursuit of a career in biology to "a combination of [her] fascination with all living creatures and [her] inclination toward the logical."

Yamashita has commented that the works of French writer Albert Camus (1913–60), which she read in high school, also had a significant impact on her career choice. In her essay, she said of him, "I decided that he was the most logical person of those who have addressed the meaning of life. His ultimate question was whether there is a meaning to life or not. . . . Although biology cannot directly answer this philosophical question, it gives us good ideas as to why human beings have evolved to have a brain capable of asking such a question."

EDUCATION

Upon completing high school, Yamashita studied biology at Kyoto University, Japan's second-oldest university, where she earned her bachelor of science degree in 1994. She continued her studies at the Kyoto University Graduate School of Science under the direction of Professor Mitsuhiro Yanagida, whose lab was world renowned for its study of mitotic control. Yamashita's research focused on the processes responsible for the cell-division cycle, which results in the creation of two exact copies of the original cell, also known as daughter cells. But Yamashita felt stifled by the countless hours spent in the research lab, which impeded her natural curiosity, and likewise by the traditional gender roles of Japanese society. "Certainly, the way I was nurtured by my parents prepared me to become a biologist," she recounted in her ASCB essay. "However, during my undergraduate and graduate school years, I was shocked by people's expectation that I, as a female, must fill a woman's role. These years were the toughest of my life, as I was unwilling to adopt such a role. It was around this time that I almost decided not to pursue a career as a scientist."

After receiving her PhD in biophysics in 1999, Yamashita remained undaunted, pursuing her postdoctoral training at Kyoto University under the guidance of Professor Shunichi Takeda, whose lab was at the forefront of DNA-repair research. In 2001 Yamashita, who was now married, applied to postdoctoral programs in the United States at the suggestion of her husband, Kentaro Nabeshima, who had also conducted his graduate studies in Yanagida's lab. That year both received fellowship offers from the Department of Developmental Biology at Stanford University in Palo Alto, California; Nabeshima accepted a postdoctoral position in the lab of Dr. Anne Villeneuve, while Yamashita served as a postdoctoral fellow in the lab of Dr. Margaret T. "Minx" Fuller.

At Stanford, Yamashita became intrigued with the processes that control asymmetric stem cell division. This kind of mitosis produces two daughter cells—an identical stem cell that retains the self-renewing capability of the original stem cell and a differentiated cell that divides a limited number of times and eventually develops into another type of cell, such as a skin, muscle, or nerve cell. As is common in genetic research, Yamashita used *Drosophila melanogaster*, a species of fruit fly, as a model organism. What makes the *Drosophila* genus so popular is that it is easy to breed in a lab and produces a large number of offspring in a relatively short amount of time, giving scientists an unlimited supply of subjects to study. It also has a short life span, which means that scientists can study many generations in a short period. Additionally, its genetic system is not only similar in structure and function to that of a human being but also easy to manipulate.

Yamashita's investigations focused on germ line stem cells from the *Drosophila melanogaster* testis (male gonad), which undergo asymmetric divisions. In studying these adult stem cells, she adopted a unique approach, deciding to monitor the behavior of a single stem cell rather than an entire group as they divide. As she explained to Danielle LaVaque-Manty for *exploreLSI* newsletter (Fall 2007, online), "I see stem cells as being cells first, before they are stem cells."

BREAKTHROUGHS

While working in Fuller's lab from 2001 to 2006, Yamashita made an important breakthrough when the cell-imaging technique that she was using to track the asymmetrical mitosis in the dividing stem cells through green fluorescent proteins (GFPs) finally proved successful. "Often we do not know what we really love until we have found it," Yamashita wrote in her ASCB essay. She described her discovery in glowing detail, "The GSCs were nicely aligned in a rosette around the hub cells, illustrating the beautiful nature of cellular arrangements in the context of tissue architecture. Hub cells function as a major component of the stem cell 'niche,' which specifies stem cell identity by sending a signaling ligand [a molecule that binds to another molecule] to GSCs." Yamashita then added, "I really fell in love with this system upon seeing the GSC mitotic spindle for the first time. Seeing the GSC mitotic spindle nicely oriented toward the hub cells was almost like being in outer space and realizing that the Earth was not everything after all. The shape of the mitotic spindle in male GSCs was almost boringly exactly what I was accustomed to seeing. However, this spindle was nicely oriented perpendicularly toward the hub. . . . I remember having the distinct feeling that this is where cell biology must meet developmental biology."

This was not the only discovery Yamashita made while under Fuller's guidance. In a profile of Yamashita in the *ASCB Newsletter* (Oct. 2009, online), John Fleischman wrote, "According to Fuller, Yamashita first demonstrated that the stem cell sticks close to the niche, maintaining a stereotypical position with its centrosome at right angles to the hub. In the G1 phase of the cell cycle (also known as interphase), the centrosome duplicates itself, creating two daughter centrosomes. One centrosome copy stays in the niche and remains within a stem cell. The other copy migrates to the opposite pole of the soon-to-divide cell." Yamashita was also able to distinguish these two daughter centrosomes.

Yamashita explained in her ASCB essay that after this discovery, she and Fuller were often asked whether her findings might be caused by mother-daughter centrosome differences. She noted, "By then, it had long been known that the mother centrosome differs from the daughter because of the age difference in centrioles. . . . I began looking for a way to distinguish mother and daughter centrosomes. However, because *Drosophila* did not have any known mother centriole-specific components . . . simple antibody staining would not work." She continued, "One day, I saw a newly published article describing a new *Drosophila* centriolar component that is incorporated into the centriole only during duplication and stays there forever (or at least for a very long time. . . . Almost at that moment, I ordered oligos to construct a transgene for transient expression of a tagged form of this centriolar marker (PACT). I tried multiple tags and expression systems . . . hoping I might be able to label the mother centrosome green and the daughter centrosome red. I also tried the gal4/gal80 temperature-sensitive system for temporal control of expression. In the end, the unexciting method of heat-shock-induced GFP-PACT worked. This approach allowed me to clearly see that the GFP-marked daughter centrosome is always away from the hub." Yamashita has commented that the mother-daughter centrosome poses a profound fascination for her and that making these observations was "one of the best moments of my life."

A LAB OF HER OWN

Only a year after joining the faculty of the University of Michigan in 2006, Yamashita founded her own lab, where she has continued to study the mechanisms that govern cell behavior. Recent findings by the lab are listed on the MacArthur Foundation website. "She and her colleagues have identified specific proteins expressed by support cells that surround each stem cell, providing a spatial frame of reference for the stem cell. Within the dividing cell, chromosome-separating assemblies need to be oriented precisely relative to the support cells for the division to complete—stem cell division stalls if the chromosomes are improperly aligned," the MacArthur website reads. "Yamashita has extended this result, observing that misalignment occurs more frequently with age, with errors beginning considerably earlier than other, more conventional markers of organism aging would suggest."

In early 2011 an account of Yamashita's work challenging the time-honored strand theory was published in the *Journal of Cell Science*. Later that year she was awarded the prestigious MacArthur Fellowship, with which she hopes to be able to fund research that seeks to understand the manner in which different stem cell populations collaborate with each other in tissues and interact to control their self-renewal capabilities and life cycles.

Yamashita lives in Ann Arbor, Michigan, with her husband and daughter.

SUGGESTED READING

Fleischman, John. "ASCB Profile: Yukiko Yamashita." *ASCB Newsletter: October 2009.* The American Society for Cell Biology, 1 Oct. 2009. Web. 18 Jan. 2012.

LaVaque-Manty, Danielle. "Under the Scope: Curiouser and Curiouser." *exploreLSI* 3.2 (2007): 5. Web. 18 Jan. 2012.

Terashima, Sasha. "Yukiko Yamashita, a Developmental Biologist at U-M, Named One of This Year's MacArthur Fellows." *The Node.* The Company of Biologists, 13 Oct. 2011. Web. 18 Jan. 2012.

Yadlapalli, Swathi, Jun Cheng, and Yukiko M. Yamashita. "Drosophila Male Germline Stem Cells Do Not Asymmetrically Segregate Chromosome Strands." *Journal of Cell Science* 124.6 (2011): 933–39. Print.

Yamashita, Yukiko. "A Tale of Mother and Daughter." *Molecular Biology of the Cell* 21.1 (2010): 7–8. Print.

—Bertha Muteba

Carl Zimmer

Born: July 13, 1966
Occupation: Science writer

Carl Zimmer is considered by many to be one of the best popular science writers living in the United States. Zimmer is the author of many well-received books, including *At the Water's Edge: Fish with Fingers, Whales with Legs, and How Life Came Ashore but Then Went Back to*

Sea (1998), *Parasite Rex: Inside the Bizarre World of Nature's Most Dangerous Creatures* (2000), *Soul Made Flesh: The Discovery of the Brain—and How It Changed the World* (2004), and *A Planet of Viruses* (2011).

From 1994 to 1999 Zimmer served as the senior editor of *Discover* magazine. He still serves as a contributing editor and writes for the *Loom*, his *Discovery* blog. *Brain Cuttings*, a collection of his columns for the magazine, was published in 2010. Zimmer also contributes articles to the *New York Times*, as well as the *Wall Street Journal* and the London *Guardian*. Zimmer teaches a seminar and a workshop on science writing at Yale University, in New Haven, Connecticut. Zimmer has also published two textbooks: *The Tangled Bank: An Introduction to Evolution* (2009), for non-science majors; and *Evolution: Making Sense of Life* (2012), for science majors.

Zimmer has received many honors and awards for his writing. According to his website, he has won fellowships from the John Simon Guggenheim Memorial Foundation and the Alfred P. Sloan Foundation; he has also won the Pan-American Health Organization Award for Excellence in International Health Reporting, the American Institute Biological Sciences Media Award, and the Everett Clark Award for science writing. In 2007 he received the National Academies of Science Communication Award. Several years later, he was admitted to the board of directors of the Council for the Advancement of Science Writing.

EARLY LIFE

Carl Zimmer was born on July 13, 1966, in New Haven, Connecticut, where he spent the first two years of his life. The family then moved to the New York City borough of Brooklyn, and after three years they all moved to New Jersey. Zimmer's father, Richard, worked as a lawyer and a local congressman, and his mother, Mary, was a homemaker; he has a brother, Ben. During his teen years, Zimmer made comic strips and wrote short stories; he also wrote for his high school newspaper. He was a voracious reader, particularly of the Sherlock Holmes mysteries, Isaac Asimov's science fiction, and American fiction authors like Mark Twain. He graduated from high school in 1983.

EDUCATION

Zimmer attended Yale University, where he majored in English. He took a few science classes, and perhaps he would have taken more if it were not for the fact that the classes "always seemed to be at eight in the morning and pretty far away in the science part of the campus," he told *Current Biography*, the source of quotes for this biography unless otherwise stated. Zimmer received his BA in English in 1987.

Ben Stechschulte

Upon graduation, Zimmer moved to Philadelphia, where he worked as a carpenter. After his then-girlfriend left for the Peace Corps, he decided to find a new direction in life. Zimmer had some friends in New York City who invited him to share an apartment with them. In New York he started looking for entry-level jobs at various magazines. He sent out applications to publications all over the city and got only one response: a letter from *Discover* magazine informing him that there was an opening for an assistant copy editor. As Zimmer recalled to *Current Biography*, it was around the year 1990.

DISCOVER

Discover is a monthly magazine with a strong focus on science, medicine, and technology. Zimmer started out as an assistant copy editor but, as he recalled to *Current Biography*, he "turned out to be pretty bad at copy editing." After a year with the magazine, the editors put him on other entry-level duties, such as fact checking. He was also given a chance to write short articles for the magazine on everything from physics and mathematics to earth sciences. A few years later he was promoted to associate editor. In 1994 he became the magazine's senior editor, a position that he would hold for about five years. In 1999 Zimmer stepped down as senior editor, but he would continue to serve as a contributing editor.

During his time at the magazine, Zimmer became increasingly more interested in biology. "Originally, I was just hoping to get a job in the magazine industry, period," Zimmer told Andrew Goldstein for *Yale Scientific* (18 Mar. 2012), the United States' oldest college science publication. "But it didn't take me long to realize that I was really fascinated by science and by the challenge of writing about these things, explaining these things, telling these stories to other people." Although Zimmer started out by writing about a great variety of sciences, he was increasingly fascinated by biology.

AT THE WATER'S EDGE (1998)

Zimmer's first book, *At the Water's Edge: Fish with Fingers, Whales with Legs, and How Life Came Ashore but Then Went Back to Sea*, was published during his last year as the senior editor at *Discover*. Zimmer found evolution to be one of the most interesting aspects of biology. He was fascinated by how "things had gotten to be the way they are," he told *Current Biography*. During his last few years at *Discover*, he wrote about findings that advanced our understanding of evolution in significant ways: for example, he wrote about a paleontologist in Pakistan who discovered the fossils of a whale with legs—after which other scientists began to find similar evidence. Zimmer was also writing about fossils that showed how vertebrates came out of the water to live on land. As much as he loved writing about these findings, he could only dedicate a few thousand words to each article. Zimmer wanted to delve into the topic deeper and write a book.

In *At the Water's Edge*, Zimmer explores in detail how vertebrates that lived in water became four-footed land animals, an evolutionary process that took place around 365 million years ago, over a time period of about 10 million years: feet evolved from fins, the ribcage evolved in a manner more suitable for land living, and other changes took place as well. Zimmer also delves deeply into an even less-understood process: the evolution of some land mammals back into creatures that live in water, which also took about ten million years. That process started about 50 million years ago, Zimmer wrote. A reviewer for *New Scientist* (7 Nov. 1998) observed that Zimmer "tracks the story expertly." In his review for the *Times Higher Education Supplement* (24 July 1998), Harry Miller called *At the Water's Edge* "a lovely book, beautifully and freshly written, that few could resist reading."

PARASITE REX (2000)

Parasite Rex: Inside the Bizarre World of Nature's Most Dangerous Creatures tells the story of what Zimmer considers to some of the most fascinating and sophisticated organisms our planet has to offer—parasites. They are capable of controlling the brain and immune system of any creature they are using as a host. The stories almost seem as if they are out of science fiction, but they are all true. The *Sacculina*, for example, is a genus of parasites

that use a crab as host and eventually go on to feed on what the crab eats, ultimately making the crab a "walking corpse," Zimmer writes in the book. Also fascinating is how some parasites, such as *Euhaplorchis californiensis*, go from one species to another: the parasite lives in a horn snail, but after it is eaten by a fish it then goes on to live in that fish, and after that fish is eaten by a bird, it then goes on to live in that bird. Some parasites go so far as to change the brain of its host by, for example, making a rat completely unafraid of the smell of a cat; once the rat is eaten, the parasite continues living inside the cat. In the book Zimmer narrates these seemingly unbelievable tales, putting them in a biological context and examining their role in evolution. As part of his research, Zimmer traveled across the globe to such places as California, Costa Rica, and Sudan. In a review for the *Los Angeles Times* (26 Sep. 2000), Michael Harris made the case that Zimmer's writing is a "model of liveliness and clarity." And *Parasite Rex*, Harris added, "is a book capable of changing how we see the world." Kevin Padian wrote for the *New York Times* (22 Oct. 2000), "The detective work behind all this is fascinating and frequently ingenious. Zimmer follows medics treating sleeping sickness in Sudan, fieldworkers assessing internal parasites in Costa Rica, curators tending the National Parasite Collection in a disused guinea pig barn in Maryland. And everywhere he finds that the scientists themselves are as amazed as he is at the complexity and cleverness of parasites." *Parasite Rex* was reissued in 2011 with a new epilogue.

EVOLUTION: THE TRIUMPH OF AN IDEA (2001)

In 2001 Zimmer put out his third book, *Evolution: The Triumph of an Idea*. The idea for the book was born when Zimmer was contacted by the Boston-based public television station WGBH, which was working on a series about the life and work of English naturalist Charles Darwin. Zimmer was asked to write a companion book for the series. He agreed. His goal was to write an introduction to evolution for the general public, both for people who had seen the program and those who had not. In the book Zimmer shows not only how and why Darwin's theories have now been confirmed as correct. After Darwin died, in 1882, scientists would go on to discover the various means by which natural selection works, such as genes. In the book Zimmer covers a great variety of topics: extinction, evolution of disease, DNA, Darwin's discoveries in South America, new scientific discoveries, and many other related topics. Writing for *New Scientist* (2 Feb. 2002), Douglas Palmer opened his review by asking if we need yet more books about Darwin. "Yes, we do," he wrote, "but only if they are as good as Carl Zimmer's *Evolution*, which brings the great man's ideas bang up to date." The book was reissued in 2006 with a new introduction.

Ever since Zimmer started writing about evolution, aside from getting positive responses, he has received many angry letters, emails, and comments on his blog from those who consider the story of creation told in the Bible to be the absolute, literal truth. To them, what Zimmer is writing and saying is heretical. When *Current Biography* asked if this bothers him, Zimmer explained "[p]eople are going to believe what they're going to be believe," adding that one should not get too upset with individuals about such things. But when it comes to public policy, he said, it is a different matter. As an example, he mentioned the state of Louisiana, which provides funding to some Christian private schools that teach that the Loch Ness monster is real, that this can be seen as proof that dinosaurs never became extinct, and that, therefore, evolution is wrong. "Ultimately, the state is supporting that kind of nonsense," Zimmer said, "and as a citizen I find that outrageous."

SOUL MADE FLESH (2004)

Zimmer's next book, *Soul Made Flesh: The Discovery of the Brain—and How It Changed the World*, is a history of a major development in science that changed how scientists, philosophers, and laypeople think of the mind and consciousness. Before the mid-1600s there was a predominant belief that each human being had an immaterial soul; but many, including the French philosopher René Descartes, had a hard time accounting for how an immaterial soul—which was thought to be responsible for a person's reasoning, memory, and character—could control and influence the actions of a material body. The book is mainly set in seventeenth-century England and focuses on a daring group of scientists and philosophers known as the Oxford circle. It emphasizes one member of the circle in particular, Thomas Willis, who is considered to be the founder of modern neurology. Among other things, Zimmer describes in great and sometimes gory detail the experiments conducted, such as the dissection of human brains. The book was very well received. A reviewer for *Newsday* (15 Feb. 2004) called it an "instructive and engaging account." And Ross King, writing for the *Los Angeles Times* (21 Mar. 2004), dubbed Zimmer "one of our most gifted science writers." King then concluded that Zimmer "has produced a top-notch work of popular science, chock-full of fascinating lore and inspired quotations."

MICROCOSM: E. COLI AND THE NEW SCIENCE OF LIFE (2008)

Zimmer's next book, *Microcosm: E. coli and the New Science of Life*, is both a biological history of the evolution of the bacterium *Escherichia coli* (*E. coli*) and a vivid biological portrait of its current state and significance to our science and culture. Scientists have been able to engineer and reengineer various strains of *E. coli* to study how genes function as well as to make pharmaceutical drugs. In his book, Zimmer shows how diverse *E. coli* is, and how some strains—including several common to the human digestive system—are harmless or beneficial, while others can make people sick or even kill them. In a positive review for the *New York Times* (29 June 2008), Peter Dizikes called the book "engrossing." Druin Burch wrote for *New Scientist* (10 May 2008), "It is a powerful account of the dynamic, complicated and social world we share with this ordinary yet remarkable bug. Evolution and genetics glitter among the pages, as do the lives and experiments of the scientists who have studied them. *Microcosm* is exciting, original and wholly persuasive of the beauty and utility of looking at the largest of issues from the smallest perspectives."

A PLANET OF VIRUSES (2011)

For his next book, *A Planet of Viruses*, Zimmer stayed on the small side, both in terms of the book's size, which is about one hundred pages, and its content: as the title indicates, it is about viruses, which are the smallest living things in the world known to current science. He discusses viruses living in human beings, as well as oceans, caves, and other places. He also gets into the history and biology of such viruses as HIV, West Nile, the flu, the common cold, and others. While promoting the book, Zimmer was asked by Karen Weintraub for the *Boston Globe* (12 Dec. 2011) to explain the difference between viruses and bacteria. Zimmer replied: "Bacteria are a lot more like us—they've got lots of DNA in them, lots of proteins inside of them. They can feed, they can grow, they can divide. Most viruses are just protein cells with just a few genes inside. All they can do is insert their genes and proteins into a cell and force that cell to make new viruses. They're not quite alive in the sense that bacteria or we are alive." The reviews for the book were generally positive. In a review for *New Scientist* (10 May 2011), Debora MacKenzie called the book "a mostly well-told tale with lots of 'wow' moments," but she took issue with what she considered to be not enough context with regard to what all those viruses mean for us in our daily lives. However, James Norton for the *Washington Post* (13 Sep. 2011) could not disagree more. "Zimmer," Norton wrote, "accomplishes in a mere 100 pages what other authors struggle to do in 500: He reshapes our understanding of the hidden realities at the core of everyday existence."

SCIENCE INK: TATTOOS OF THE SCIENCE OBSESSED (2011)

The idea for Zimmer's next book has its roots in the summer of 2007, when he noticed that his friend, neurobiologist Sandeep Robert Datta, had a tattoo of a DNA code. It was not the first time he saw a scientist with a science-related tattoo. So that year Zimmer posted a question on the *Loom* blog asking whether this is common. Before long, he started receiving a great many responses—stories as well as photos of tattoos. And the stories and photos kept coming. (Zimmer himself does not have any tattoos.) Eventually, in 2011, Zimmer selected the best stories and photos—some that had been published on his blog and some that had not—and put them together in a book, *Science Ink: Tattoos of the Science Obsessed*. "Many [of the tattoos] are literal representations of a scientist's obsession with their profession: a tree of life covering a zoology graduate's back, or a cross section through a mountain chain for a geology student," Catherine de Lange wrote for *New Scientist* (2 Nov. 2011). De Lange went on to comment: "[o]thers tell more personal stories, such as the neuroscientist with a tattoo of the type of nerve cell that is damaged in Lou Gehrig's disease, which killed her father. This book gathers up the marvels of science that have touched people so deeply they wanted to embody them. Zimmer's explanations of these concepts turn what could have been a gimmicky coffee-table picture book into an informative guide to some of the most captivating ideas in science."

Zimmer lives in Connecticut with his wife, Grace, and their two children, Charlotte and Veronica. Grace works as a garden designer.

SUGGESTED READING

Dizikes, Peter. "E. Coli and You." *New York Times* 29 June 2008, sec. BR: 11. Print.

King, Ross. "When the Brain Was Named King." *Los Angeles Times*. Los Angeles Times, 21 Mar. 2004. Web. 10 Aug. 2012.

Miller, Harry. "A Search for Whales in the Sahara." *Times Higher Education Supplement*. TSL Education Ltd., 24 July 1998. Web. 10 Aug. 2012.

Padian, Kevin. "Here's Your Host." *New York Times* 22 Oct. 2000, sec. 7: 18. Print.

Palmer, Douglas. "Prime Time for Darwin." *New Scientist* 2 Feb. 2002: 48. Print.

—Dmitry Kiper

OBITUARIES

Svetlana Alliluyeva

Born: Moscow, Russia; February 28, 1926
Died: Richland Center, Wisconsin;
November 22, 2011
Occupation: Author, political figure

Svetlana Alliluyeva was born Svetlana Stalina in Moscow on February 28, 1926, to Soviet dictator Joseph Stalin and his wife, Nadezhda Alliluyeva. By her own account, Alliluyeva's early childhood was idyllic until the suicide of her mother in 1932, when Alliluyeva was only six years old. While alive, Stalin exerted a disturbing amount of control over his daughter's life; when Alliluyeva first fell in love, with Jewish filmmaker Aleksei Kapler, Stalin had Kapler sent to a prison camp in Siberia for over five years. Even after her father's death in 1953, Alliluyeva lived under his political shadow and with the memories of his cruelty. "He broke my life," she said in a rare late interview with the *Wisconsin State Journal* in 2010, as quoted in her *New York Times* obituary. "I want to explain to you. He broke my life."

After her highly publicized immigration to the United States in the spring of 1967, Alliluyeva published her first memoir, *Twenty Letters to a Friend*, in the fall of that year. Despite the Soviet backlash, or perhaps because of it, the book was an American success. In it, Alliluyeva detailed her early life and marriages. Her first marriage was in 1944 to a Jewish student named Grigory Morozov, with whom she had a son, Joseph; then, in 1949, she married the son of Stalin's "right-hand man," Yuri Zhdanov, with whom she had a daughter named Yekaterina, or Katya for short. Both marriages ended in divorce.

In 1963, Alliluyeva met an Indian communist named Brijesh Singh. The Soviet government would not let the couple marry because Singh was a foreigner, and when he fell seriously ill in 1966, officials forbade Alliluyeva to visit him in India. The government begrudgingly allowed her to travel there after Singh's death to retrieve his ashes. While in India, she sought political asylum at the American embassy in New Delhi. She publicly denounced her birth country and her father's legacy and moved to the United States. This journey is recounted in her second memoir, *Only One Year* (1969).

In 1970, Alliluyeva married William Wesley Peters, an apprentice to the architect Frank Lloyd Wright. The couple had a daughter, Olga, before divorcing in 1973. Alliluyeva continued to use the name Lana Peters until her death.

Alliluyeva wavered in her opinion of her father and the Soviet Union in the 1980s, when she traveled to Moscow asking for forgiveness, ostensibly to see the children she had left twenty years before. She returned to the United States in 1986 and settled in Wisconsin.

Alliluyeva died of colon cancer on November 22, 2011, in a nursing home in Richland Center, Wisconsin. She is survived by her daughters Katya, who still lives in Russia, and Olga, who has since changed her name to Chrese Evans.

See Current Biography 1968.

Ray C. Anderson

Born: West Point, Georgia; July 28, 1934
Died: Atlanta, Georgia; August 9, 2011
Occupation: Founder and CEO of Interface, Inc.

Businessman and industrial engineer Ray C. Anderson founded a carpet manufacturing business called Carpets International of Georgia, later renamed Interface, Inc., in 1973. For nearly two decades, Interface and Anderson raked in profits thanks to their innovative tile designs. But in 1994, Anderson, then age sixty, read a book by environmentalist Paul Hawken called *The Ecology of Commerce: A Declaration of Sustainability* (1993), and his view of his profitable enterprise changed completely. Anderson, who claims to have wept when he realized the pollution for which companies like his were responsible, began an extensive campaign to make Interface and its products sustainable. The endeavor won him accolades from environmentalists as well as businesspeople, and Interface's profits surged. In his later years, Anderson devoted a significant portion of his time to promoting sustainable business practices all over the world; as Anderson told Gwen Kinkead for *Fortune* (24 May 1999), "Business and industry—the largest, wealthiest, most powerful, most pervasive institutions on earth, and the ones doing the most damage—must take the lead."

Anderson was born in rural West Point, Georgia, on July 28, 1934, to postal worker William Henry Anderson and teacher Ruth McGinty. He was the youngest of three siblings. Anderson graduated from the Georgia Institute of Technology, which he attended on a football scholarship, in 1956 with a bachelor of science degree in industrial engineering. He worked for Procter & Gamble and the Callaway Mills Company before founding Interface.

Anderson is the author of several books on business and the environment, including *Mid-Course Correction: Toward a Sustainable Enterprise; The Interface Model* (1998) and *Confessions of a Radical Industrialist: Profits, People, Purpose; Doing Business by Respecting the Earth* (2009). He is a coauthor, along with Charlie Eitel and J. Zink, of *Face It: A Spiritual Journey of Leadership* (1996).

Anderson died of cancer at his home in Atlanta on August 9, 2011. He is survived by his wife, Patricia Adams Anderson, and two daughters from a previous marriage, Mary Anne Lanier and Harriet Langford.

See Current Biography 2005.

Theodoros Angelopoulos

Born: Athens, Greece; April 27, 1936
Died: Piraeus, Greece; January 24, 2012
Occupation: Film director, screenwriter

The dreamlike films of Greek filmmaker Theodoros "Theo" Angelopoulos are not widely known in the United States, but they have amassed an international critical following. Angelopoulos, who briefly attended law school, began making films while working as a cinema critic in Athens in the 1960s. His first feature was called *Reconstruction (Anaparastasi)* and was released in 1970.

Though he was not without his detractors, Angelopoulos's greatest fans compared his vision to the works of filmmakers Michelangelo Antonioni and Jean-Luc Godard. His film *Eternity and a Day (Mia aioniothta kai mia mera,* 1998), about the contemplations of a terminally ill writer, won the prestigious Palme d'Or—the top prize at the Cannes Film Festival—in 1998. Angelopoulos, who claimed a handful of other prizes during his fruitful career, was not known for modesty; the fiery director famously made a scene in Cannes in 1995 when his film *Ulysses' Gaze,* released that year, took second-place honors at the festival. "I planned my speech for the Palme d'Or," he said "contemptuously," according to the *Sydney Morning Herald,* as quoted in his *New York Times* obituary by Margalit Fox (25 Jan. 2012), "but now I've forgotten it."

Angelopoulos was born in Athens, Greece, on April 27, 1936. He died on January 24, 2012, due to injuries he sustained after being hit by a motorcycle while on location for a film in Piraeus, Greece. Angelopoulos is survived by his wife, film producer Phoebe Economopoulou, and his three daughters.

See Current Biography Illustrated 1997.

John Arden

Born: Barnsley, England; October 26, 1930
Died: Galway, Ireland; March 28, 2012
Occupation: Playwright

Experimental playwright John Arden, along with a group of writers that included Harold Pinter and John Osborne, came of age during the British cultural unrest of the 1950s and 1960s. Rebelling against what he saw as the stuffiness of midcentury British drama and social norms, Arden sought to create theater that would satisfy his own sense of artistry, his political convictions, and the experiences of his generation. Though he never reached a level of commercial success comparable to that of his peers, Arden remains a leading figure in the British dramatic canon for his intellectual curiosity and his bold (and arguably radical) use of masks, mime, and clowning. He has often been compared to German revolutionary political playwright Bertolt Brecht. One of Arden's best-known works, *Serjeant Musgrave's Dance: An Unhistorical Parable,* premiered at the Royal Court in 1959. Arden was inspired by an incident in which British soldiers killed five innocent people in Cyprus in 1958; in the play, set in late nineteenth-century England, five British soldiers return the body of a fallen comrade to his hometown in hopes of convincing the townspeople to renounce the war.

Arden was born in Barnsley in Yorkshire, England, on October 26, 1930. His father, Charles Alwyn Arden, was the manager of a glass factory, and his mother, Elizabeth Layland Arden, was a former teacher. After serving in the Intelligence Corps from 1949 to 1950, Arden attended King's College, Cambridge University, where he earned his bachelor's degree in 1953, then went on to study architecture at the Edinburgh College of Art. It was in Edinburgh that Arden wrote his first play, a Victorian romantic comedy called *All Fall Down,* which was performed at the school in 1955, the same year he graduated. For the next two years, he worked as an assistant architect in London, but he gave up his architecture career to pursue playwriting in 1957. His major works include *Live like Pigs* (1958) and *Armstrong's Last Goodnight* (1964).

Arden wrote for radio as well as for the stage, and he often collaborated with his wife, playwright and actress Margaretta D'Arcy, whom he married in 1957. Arden also wrote several novels, including *Silence among the Weapons* (1982), which is set in the Roman Empire; a short-story collection; and several collections of essays.

Arden died at his home in Galway, Ireland, on March 28, 2012. He is survived by his wife and four sons.

See Current Biography 1988.

Neil Armstrong

Born: Wapakoneta, Ohio; August 5, 1930
Died: Cincinnati, Ohio; August 25, 2012
Occupation: American astronaut

Neil Armstrong made history on July 20, 1969, as the first person to set foot on the moon. As he stepped off the lunar module's ladder onto the moon's surface, Armstrong made the now-famous statement, "That's one small step for man, one giant leap for mankind." He became an immediate international celebrity, although Armstrong was said to be uncomfortable with taking credit for an achievement that had taken the efforts of thousands of people at the National Aeronautics and Space Administration (NASA).

Armstrong was born in Wapakoneta, Ohio, on August 5, 1930. At age fourteen, he started learning how to fly a plane at the Wapakoneta Airport; he earned his pilot's license at the age of sixteen. In 1947, he entered Purdue University on a naval scholarship. He was placed on active duty and flew seventy-eight combat missions during the Korean War. After his service, Armstrong returned to Purdue, graduating in 1955 with a bachelor's degree. He performed flight tests on more than two hundred different models of aircraft for the National Advisory Committee for Aeronautics (which would become NASA in 1958).

In 1962, Armstrong volunteered for and was accepted to NASA's astronaut program. In 1966, he commanded Gemini 8, a mission in which Armstrong and his copilot accomplished the first manual docking of two spacecraft in orbit. Soon after the two craft were docked, however, a jet-thruster malfunction occurred, sending the spacecraft into a rapid—and potentially fatal—spin. Armstrong took the controls and successfully navigated back to earth.

In January 1969, NASA announced the flight crew of Apollo 11. Armstrong was selected for the moon mission, along with Edwin "Buzz" Aldrin and Michael Collins. The crew took off on July 16, 1969, and reached the moon four days later. Collins maintained the command module in lunar orbit while Armstrong and Aldrin spent several hours working on the moon's surface.

Upon their return to Earth, the Apollo 11 astronauts were celebrated in a world tour that took them to twenty-five countries in thirty-five days. Armstrong returned to NASA as a deputy associate administrator for aeronautics in the Office of Research and Technology, where he worked until 1971. In 1970 he graduated from the University of Southern California with a master's degree in aerospace engineering, and became a professor of engineering at the University of Cincinnati, where he taught for eight years. In 1986, he served as vice chair on the committee investigating the space shuttle *Challenger* disaster. He also served on the boards of several technology and aeronautics companies.

Armstrong married Janet Shearon in 1956; the couple had three children and divorced in 1994. In 1999, Armstrong married Carol Knight. She survives him, as do two sons from his first marriage, Mark and Eric. (A daughter, Karen, died of cancer in 1962.) Armstrong is also survived by his siblings, Dean Armstrong and June Armstrong Hoffman; two stepchildren; and ten grandchildren. Armstrong underwent heart by-pass surgery in the month before his death; he died on August 25, 2012, of complications from the procedure.

See Current Biography 1969.

Eve Arnold

Born: Philadelphia, Pennsylvania; April 21, 1912
Died: London, England; January 4, 2012
Occupation: Photojournalist

Renowned photojournalist Eve Arnold took more than 750,000 photographs during her lifetime, though she did not even pick up a camera until she was twenty-eight years old. During her prolific career, Arnold formed close relationships with various iconic figures, including Marilyn Monroe, Joan Crawford, and Malcolm X, resulting in startlingly intimate celebrity portraits. But it would be a mischaracterization of Arnold to classify her solely as a celebrity photographer; she traveled to some of the darkest and most obscure regions of the earth, taking pictures of such diverse subjects as horse trainers in Mongolia and the women of a Havana brothel. It is a credit to her skill that all of her subjects are represented with equal care. "If a photographer cares about the people before the lens and is compassionate, much is given," Arnold once said. "It is the photographer, not the camera, that is the instrument."

Arnold was born Eve Cohen to Ukrainian immigrant parents in Philadelphia, Pennsylvania, on April 21, 1912. Her father was a rabbi, and Arnold was one of nine children. After high school, she worked at a real-estate firm while taking classes in medicine at night. At age twenty-eight, she moved to New York City, where a boyfriend introduced her to photography. She married industrial designer Arnold Arnold in 1948; the couple later divorced.

Though she was largely self-taught, Arnold briefly studied with *Harper's Bazaar* photographer Alexey Brodovitch at the New School, during which time she documented impromptu fashion shows in Harlem. These photographs were printed in the British magazine *Picture Post*, marking the first time her work was published.

The photographs caught the attention of the co-operative agency Magnum Photos, and in 1951, Arnold became one of the first women ever hired by the agency.

Arnold's early work has become synonymous with images of postwar America, with her earliest assignments including the 1952 Republican National Convention and a day in the life of aging film star Joan Crawford. Arnold's numerous accolades include a Lifetime Achievement Award from the American Society of Media Photographers. She was also named a master photographer by the International Center of Photography in New York, an accolade many consider to be the highest in the field.

Arnold has published several books of photography, including *The Unretouched Woman* (1976), *In China* (1980), *In America* (1983), and *Marilyn Monroe: An Appreciation* (1987). She continued to accept assignments until the late 1990s.

Arnold died in London on January 4, 2012. She is survived by her son, Frank, and three grandchildren.

See Current Biography 2005.

Roy Ash

Born: Los Angeles, California; October 20, 1918
Died: Los Angeles, California; December 14, 2011
Occupation: Founder and president of Litton Industries

Roy Lawrence Ash was a successful business-man and a powerful force in the Nixon administration. As the founder and president of Litton Industries, Ash grew a small electronics company into a conglomerate, with annual sales exceeding $1.5 billion as early as 1968. The same year, President Richard Nixon asked Ash to head an advisory council to restructure and consolidate functions within the executive branch. During his tenure in the Nixon administration, Ash oversaw the creation of the Environmental Protection Agency, the Nuclear Regulatory Commission, the National Oceanic and Atmospheric Administration, and the Office of Management and Budget (OMB). He was named director of the OMB in 1972.

Ash was born in Los Angeles, California, on October 20, 1918. He graduated from high school in 1935 but was unable to afford college. He took a job with the Bank of America National Trust and Savings Association in Los Angeles, where he remained until he enlisted in the army in 1942, during World War II. Ash, who would later be referred to by journalists and contemporaries as the "human computer," was selected to join the US Army Air Forces Office of Statistical Control. He was discharged after the war in

1945 with the rank of captain. Despite his lack of an undergraduate degree, Ash was accepted to the Harvard Graduate School of Business, where he graduated first in his class after eighteen months.

Ash joined Charles Thornton, the head of the statistical control service during the war, at the Hughes Aircraft Company in 1949. In 1953, Ash and Thornton organized their own company, the Electro-Dynamics Corporation, which would later become a part of Litton Industries. Conglomerates were a relatively new business enterprise at the time, and Nixon, impressed by Ash's ability to successfully manage the numerous companies under the Litton umbrella, hoped that he could apply the same management skills to government. Beginning in 1968, Ash was the head of a panel that advised the creation of a number of government agencies. In 1972, Nixon appointed him the director of the OMB, which oversaw the budget of the executive branch and managed the presidential cabinet. Ash would hold this position until February 1975.

Ash died of Parkinson's disease at his home in Los Angeles on December 14, 2011. He is survived by his wife, Lila; his children, Charles, James, Robert, Loretta Danko, and Marilyn Hanna; nine grandchildren; and two great-grandchildren.

See Current Biography 1968.

Ahmed Ben Bella

Born: Marnia, Algeria; December 25, 1918
Died: Algiers, Algeria; April 11, 2012
Occupation: Revolutionary, former Algerian president

Ahmed Ben Bella, the son of an Algerian farmer, was a fighter from the age of sixteen until his death. During World War II, he was a decorated soldier in the French Army. Less than a decade later, he was one of the founding members of the Algerian Front of National Liberation (FLN), leading the 1954 revolution for freedom from France. In 1963, he was elected without opposition as the president of Algeria, only to be ousted in a coup led by a former ally in 1965. After years in confinement, Ben Bella emerged as a voice for freedom in developing countries across the world. He even took to the streets during the 2010–11 Arab Spring at the age of ninety-three.

Ben Bella was born in the small mountain town of Marnia (now Maghnia), Algeria, on December 25, 1918. His father was a farmer and merchant. Ben Bella attended a French government school, but his education was cut short when he was pulled out of school by his father to work. Conscripted as a soldier in the

French Army at the age of sixteen, Ben Bella became a decorated soldier—he was awarded the Free French Forces' highest honor, the Médaille Militaire, by Charles de Gaulle himself—as well as a celebrated soccer player. But Ben Bella was already becoming involved in the underground movement for revolution, and he turned down an opportunity to play professional soccer in France in order to return to Algeria after the war.

In 1950, Ben Bella was arrested for staging an armed robbery the year before to garner funds for the nationalist movement. He was sentenced to eight years in prison but escaped in 1952 using a blade smuggled to him in his food. He became a fugitive, earning himself the nickname "the invisible one," until he emerged as one of the original nine members of the Revolutionary Committee for Unity and Action (CRUA), later the FLN, in 1954. On November 1, 1954, the FLN and the Army for National Liberation (ANL) launched a long and bloody campaign, during which Ben Bella was imprisoned and nearly assassinated on several occasions. On March 18, 1962, French and Algerian leaders signed a cease-fire agreement, and the struggle for power in Algeria began in earnest.

In 1962, Algeria held elections in which Ben Bella ran a slate of candidates, including himself, without opposition. He was elected to a five-year presidential term in 1963. As president, Ben Bella aligned himself politically with other communist regimes but notably did not sever ties with France or the United States. Ben Bella was deposed in 1965 in a coup led by Colonel Houari Boumedienne. He was kept isolated in a remote village for the next fourteen years, during which time his mother arranged a marriage for him with Algerian journalist Zohra Sellami. The couple adopted two children.

After Boumedienne's death in 1978, Ben Bella served his exile in Lausanne, Switzerland. In the 1990s, he returned to Algeria to participate in protests there. He died at his home in Algiers on April 11, 2012.

See Current Biography 1963.

role of the state in economic, political, and social issues. Bendjedid was also responsible for initiating civil rights in Algeria via the Constitution of 1989.

After the decline of Algeria's economy in the late 1980s—largely due to falling oil prices—civil unrest took control and sparked the 1988 October Riots, which spread across cities in Algiers leaving several hundred rioters dead. As president, Bendjedid installed a multi-party political system in Algeria and democratic reform that gave power to voters in elections. These principles clashed with Islamic ideals, and tensions rose as the old system resisted the political changes implemented by Bendjedid. This pressure between the fundamentalist Islamic population and the president's regime escalated, and in January 1992, the Algerian military staged a bloodless coup, cancelled the upcoming multi-party legislative elections, and forced Bendjedid to resign from office. He was placed under house arrest in the city of Oran, hundreds of miles from the capital, until 1999 when he was freed.

The coup, combined with the current state of instability and conflict in the country, ultimately led to the long and bloody Algerian Civil War, which was waged between the government and Islamist rebel groups. The death toll from this conflict, which lasted from 1991 to 2002, was between 150,000 and 200,000.

Bendjedid's military career began in 1954 during the Algerian War of Independence against France, which claimed over 300,000 lives before Algeria won its independence in 1962. Following the war, Bendjedid, who was a protégé of future Algerian president Houari Boumediene, was rewarded with the military command of Constantine and Oran, in western Algeria. In 1969, he was promoted to the prestigious rank of colonel in the Algerian military. He also served as the minister of defense from November 1978 until February 1979 when he became president of Algiers following the death of Boumediene in December of 1978.

Bendjedid was married and had four sons. He died from cancer on October 6, 2012, while being treated in a military hospital in Ain Naadja, Algiers. Algeria called for eight days of national mourning after his death.

See Current Biography Illustrated 1991.

Chadli Bendjedid

Born: Bouteldja, Algeria; April 14, 1929
Died: Ain Naadja, Algiers; October 6, 2012
Occupation: Algerian president, political leader

Chadli Bendjedid, who served as Algeria's third president from 1979 to 1992, was known for implementing democratic principles in a country dominated by Arab radicals and supreme governmental control. Bendjedid strongly opposed communism and introduced reforms to reduce the

Maeve Binchy

Born: Dalkey, Ireland; May 28, 1940
Died: Dublin, Ireland; July 30, 2012
Occupation: Irish novelist and playwright

Maeve Binchy was an Irish novelist celebrated for her keen-eyed depictions of her home country and her sensitive characterizations of ordinary individuals. Though the majority of her novels are set in Ireland, Binchy's stories about Irish provincial life nevertheless held universal appeal, and her work has been translated into thirty-seven languages. In a December 8, 1991, review of Binchy's short story collection *The Lilac Bus*, John Kenny Crane wrote for the *New York Times*, "Plot has never been Ms. Binchy's strong suit or first love. It is, instead, her well-drawn characters and their dynamic interaction with one another in the most ordinary circumstances that characterize her fiction."

Binchy was born the eldest of four children on May 28, 1940, in Dalkey, a suburb of Dublin. Her father was a lawyer and her mother a nurse. Binchy graduated from University College, Dublin with a degree in history and French in 1961, and she began work as a teacher in Dublin soon after. She travelled briefly to Israel and wrote letters home to her father describing her experience, which he forwarded to an Irish newspaper, where the letters were published. In 1968 Binchy took a job with the *Irish Times*, working as an editor and a columnist.

Throughout the 1970s, Binchy published two collections of her newspaper writings, as well as a play, a collection of short stories, and a television screenplay. Her agent encouraged her to produce a longer work of fiction, and in 1982, Binchy published her first novel, *Light a Penny Candle*, which became a best seller. Though she was forty-two at the time, Binchy went on to publish fifteen more novels in her lifetime, including *Circle of Friends* (1990), which was made into a film in 1995 starring Chris O'Donnell and Minnie Driver, and *Tara Road* (1998), an Oprah's Book Club selection.

Binchy married journalist Gordon Snell in 1977. He survives her, as do her brother, William, and sister, Joan Ryan. Binchy died on July 30, 2012, in a Dublin hospital, following a brief illness.

See Current Biography 1995.

Osama bin Laden

Born: Riyadh, Saudi Arabia; ca. March 1957
Died: Abbottabad, Pakistan; May 2, 2011
Occupation: Terrorist; leader of al-Qaeda

Osama bin Laden was a Saudi Arabian terrorist and al-Qaeda leader who orchestrated the attacks on the World Trade Center and the Pentagon on September 11, 2001. Four planes were hijacked and crashed, killing more than three thousand people in New York and Washington, DC, and causing countless more injuries. Bin Laden, a fundamentalist Muslim, declared a jihad, or holy war, against the United States in 1996 for their presence in Saudi Arabia. He revised his decree in 1998, ordering the killing of any American wherever possible. In addition to planning the devastating

attacks on September 11, he was also behind the bombings of US embassies in East Africa and the USS *Cole* before it.

Bin Laden was born to a wealthy family in Riyadh, Saudi Arabia, most likely in March 1957. His father, Mohammed bin Laden, owned the largest construction company in the country and was hired by the government to oversee the refurbishment of Mecca and Medina, the holiest shrines in Islam. While studying engineering at King Abdulaziz University, bin Laden met a professor who was a member of the fundamentalist group, the Muslim Brotherhood. He became an extremist and when the Soviet Union invaded Afghanistan in 1979, bin Laden considered it his holy duty to travel there and fight with the Afghan mujahideen, which was backed by the CIA. He returned to Saudi Arabia in the late 1980s, after the withdrawal of Soviet forces from Afghanistan. He had his Saudi citizenship revoked in 1994 for criticizing the royal family's ties to the United States and moved to Afghanistan, which had come under the strict rule of the Taliban militia. Bin Laden and the Taliban formed a powerful collaborative, as did he and the members of al-Qaeda, a loosely connected network of fundamentalist terrorists. After the September 11 attacks, bin Laden evaded US officials for nearly ten years, though he occasionally appeared on videotaped messages and Arab television.

After a decade-long manhunt through the Middle East, American forces killed bin Laden at his compound in Abbottabad, Pakistan, on May 2, 2011. The attack was ordered by President Barack Obama. Not much is known of his late personal life, but bin Laden was said to have at least four wives and several children.

See Current Biography 2001.

Ernest Borgnine

Born: Hamden, Connecticut; January 24, 1917
Died: Los Angeles, California; July 8, 2012
Occupation: American film and television actor

Ernest Borgnine was an Academy Award–winning film and television actor best known for his onscreen reputation as a tough but endearing everyman. Borgnine's Hollywood career took off in 1953 when he played Sgt. "Fatso" Johnson alongside Burt Lancaster, Donna Reed, and Frank Sinatra in *From Here to Eternity*. After several roles playing thugs and heavies, Borgnine broke type, starring as an insecure, lonely Bronx butcher in 1955's *Marty*. The performance won him a best actor Oscar and solidified his status as a rising star.

Borgnine would go on to act in acclaimed action and adventure films like *The Dirty Dozen*, *Ice Station Zebra*, and *The Wild Bunch*. His presence in Hollywood was rivaled only by his prolific television career. Borgnine began working in television with two appearances on *Captain Video and His Video Rangers* in 1951. From there, he would go on to play the titular role in the World War II comedy series *McHale's Navy* in addition to landing parts on some of the classic television programs of the twentieth century including *Love Boat*; *Magnum P.I.*; *Murder, She Wrote*; and *ER*; garnering several Emmy nominations in the process. Borgnine lent his characteristically gruff voice to numerous animated projects throughout his career including a stint as the geriatric, undersea superhero Mermaid Man on Nickelodeon's *SpongeBob SquarePants* in the early 2000s.

Borgnine served in the Navy in the years leading up to and during World War II. He received the honorary title of chief petty officer in 2004 for his work with veterans support organizations. In 2011, the Screen Actors Guild presented Borgnine with a lifetime achievement award. His personal life was tumultuous and included four failed marriages—most notoriously his one-month marriage to Broadway singer Ethel Merman. Borgnine died of renal failure at Cedars-Sinai Medical Center. He was ninety-five. Borgnine is survived by his wife of thirty-nine years, Tova, and his four children.

See Current Biography 1956.

Ray Bradbury

Born: Waukegan, Illinois; August 22, 1920
Died: Los Angeles, California; June 5, 2012
Occupation: American science-fiction writer

Ray Bradbury was a science-fiction writer, novelist, and essayist whose stories captured the imaginations of generations of readers. Bradbury never attended college; instead, he sought his education in libraries, especially from the books of his hero, Aldous Huxley. Some of Bradbury's best-known works are the short-story collection *The Martian Chronicles* (1950) and the novel *Something Wicked This Way Comes* (1962). His stories of technology, magic, and horror gave voice to the hopes and fears of postwar America. In his most famous novel, the dystopian *Fahrenheit 451* (1953), Bradbury imagines the desolation of a world without books. Though Bradbury never won a Pulitzer Prize for any of his individual works, he was awarded a Pulitzer special citation for his life's work in 2007.

Bradbury was born in Waukegan, Illinois, on August 22, 1920. He had an excellent memory of his childhood and even claimed to remember his own birth. His father was a lineman with the local power company, and his mother, a homemaker originally from Sweden, read him stories by the Grimm brothers and L. Frank Baum before bed. Bradbury had an older brother named Leonard; another brother and a sister died as infants. He took tremendous inspiration from the events of his childhood, especially his relationship with his aunt, Neva Bradbury, a costume designer and artist who introduced him to the theater and the work of Edgar Allan Poe.

As a teenager, Bradbury moved with his family to Los Angeles, California, where he took an interest in science-fiction writing and film. In high school, he began a lasting habit of writing one thousand words each day. He sold his first short story, cowritten with Henry Hasse, to a science-fiction magazine in 1941.

Bradbury began the most successful stretch of his career in 1947, when he submitted one of his most celebrated stories, "Homecoming," to a young Truman Capote, then an editor at *Mademoiselle* magazine. The story went on to be selected as one of the O. Henry Prize Stories of 1947, an annual collection of the best American short stories. That same year, he married Marguerite McClure, a former English instructor at UCLA; she died in 2003 after fifty-seven years of marriage.

Bradbury has written several screenplays, and his stories have been adapted for television and film. The successful film version of *Fahrenheit 451*, directed by François Truffaut, was released in 1966. Bradbury was awarded the National Medal of Arts by President George W. Bush in 2004.

Bradbury died in Los Angeles, the city where he had lived for over fifty years, on June 5, 2012. He continued to write until his death. He is survived by his daughters, Susan Nixon, Ramona Ostergen, Bettina Karapetian, and Alexandra Bradbury, as well as eight grandchildren.

See Current Biography 1982.

Andrew F. Brimmer

Born: Newellton, Louisiana; September 13, 1926
Died: Washington, DC; October 7, 2012
Occupation: American economist, financial consultant, and member of the Federal Reserve Board

Andrew Brimmer achieved national notoriety when he became the first African American member of the Federal Reserve Board, which sets the country's monetary policy and interest rates. He was appointed to the position by

President Lyndon B. Johnson in 1966 and had previously been the assistant secretary of commerce for economic affairs under President John F. Kennedy.

During his term as a member of the Reserve Board, Brimmer called for lowering tax rates and the rate of inflation and reversing the balance-of-payments deficit. He also advocated for improving the economic conditions of African Americans and called for programs that would address and amend the financial dissimilarities between them and white Americans. Brimmer fought to spread the message that racial discrimination undermined the US economy by serving to further degrade African American workers who were vital to the country's economy.

Brimmer was the son of a Louisiana sharecropper and attended segregated schools growing up. He joined the US Army in 1945 at the end of WWII and achieved the rank of staff sergeant. After his service ended in 1946, he used the G.I. Bill of Rights to attend the University of Washington in Seattle and earned his bachelor's degree in economics in 1950. He received his master's degree the following year. He was a recipient of the Fulbright scholarship—a prestigious scholarly award that offers grants to students to study internationally—which allowed him to study in India. He then attended the Massachusetts Institute of Technology (MIT) and went on to earn his PhD from the Harvard Business School in 1957. He taught economics at Michigan State University and the Wharton School of Finance and Commerce at the University of Pennsylvania.

In 1965, Brimmer became a member of the Board of Trustees for Alabama's Tuskegee University and then became its chair in 1982, stepping down from that position and the board in 2010. The university named its school of business and information science after him.

Brimmer left the Federal Reserve Board in 1974 and taught at the Harvard Business School for two years. He also established a financial consulting firm, Brimmer & Company, which is based in Washington, DC.

Brimmer died on October, 7, 2012, at the age of eighty-six. He is survived by his daughter, Esther Brimmer, and his wife, Doris Scott Brimmer.

See Current Biography 1968.

Chuck Brown

Born: Gaston, North Carolina; August 22, 1936
Died: Baltimore, Maryland; May 16, 2012
Occupation: Musician

A musical hero local to Washington, DC, Chuck Brown was known as the "Godfather of Go-Go," after the style of music he helped to create. In go-go music—so named, Brown once

said, because it "just goes and goes"—Brown combined funk, soul, big band, jazz, Latin rhythms, and African call-and-response to create a unique sound. Go-go music sustained its popularity throughout the mid-Atlantic states, though Brown enjoyed only brief periods of success nationally. His 1978 hit single "Bustin' Loose" held the number-one R&B spot on the Billboard Top 40 for four consecutive weeks. In 2011, he was nominated for a Grammy Award for his song "Love," featuring singer Jill Scott and bassist Marcus Miller.

Brown was born in Gaston, North Carolina, on August 22, 1936. In 1942, his family moved to Washington, DC. After working a slew of jobs during his childhood to help support his mother, Brown began robbing local jewelry stores and pawnshops as a teenager. During one robbery, Brown shot a man who later died from his injuries, and Brown was sentenced to serve four years in prison at Lorton Penitentiary in Virginia. While in prison, Brown earned his high school diploma and learned to play the guitar. After his release in 1962, he formed a group called the Soul Searchers, with whom he began to develop his go-go sound. The Soul Searchers' first hit was the 1971 song "We the People," from the album of the same name. Brown also found success with his 1984 album, *We Need Some Money.*

In 2005, Brown was awarded the National Endowment for the Arts National Heritage Fellowship. In 2009, a block of Seventh Street in Washington, DC, was renamed Chuck Brown Way in his honor.

Brown died of multiple organ failure as a result of sepsis on May 16, 2012, in Baltimore. He is survived by his wife and four children. One child, a son, died in the 1990s.

See Current Biography Illustrated 2001.

Helen Gurley Brown

Born: Green Forest, Arkansas; February 18, 1922
Died: New York, New York; August 13, 2012
Occupation: Former editor in chief of *Cosmopolitan*

The editor in chief of *Cosmopolitan* magazine for more than three decades, Helen Gurley Brown gave the magazine its edge when she took over the failing magazine in 1965. She transformed the unprofitable magazine targeted at housewives into a slick and trendy publication that celebrated the sex lives of young single women. The frank sex advice she offered in every edition of the magazine shocked some readers in the 1960s, but under Gurley Brown's leadership, the magazine's circulation more than quadrupled. Brown's successor at *Cosmo,*

Bonnie Fuller, said in an interview with CNN, "Helen was a modern career woman in a time when there weren't many. She saw that the next generation of women would be her."

Helen Gurley Brown was born in Green Forest, Arkansas, on February 18, 1922. At the age of ten, her father was killed in an elevator accident, and she moved to Los Angeles with her mother and sister. In 1939 she graduated from high school as class valedictorian. She graduated from Woodbury Business College (now Woodbury University) in 1941. She worked as a secretary for several different companies, and in 1948 she took a job with the advertising agency Foote, Cone & Belding. Her boss was impressed by her witty and animated writing style, and encouraged her to pursue copywriting. She took extension courses in writing and entered an essay to *Glamour* magazine's "Ten Girls with Taste" contest, which she won. She joined the ad agency Kenyon & Eckhardt in 1958, where she became one of the highest-paid woman copywriters in the country.

In 1962, Gurley Brown published the book *Sex and the Single Girl*, offering advice to single women on how to attain a great sex life and fulfilling career. The book became a runaway best-seller and was among the top ten nonfiction sellers of the year. She followed that success with a second book, *Sex and the Office*, in 1964. In 1965, she was asked to become editor of *Cosmopolitan*, a poorly selling women's magazine. Under Gurley Brown's leadership, *Cosmo* became one of the highest-selling women's magazines in the world. After heading the magazine for thirty-two years, Gurley Brown stepped down in 1997, but stayed on as the editor of Hearst Magazine International, where she managed *Cosmo*'s sixty-four international editions.

Gurley Brown married movie producer David Brown in 1959. He died in 2010. The couple never had children and no immediate family survives her. Gurley Brown died in a Manhattan hospital on August 13, 2012, following a brief illness.

See Current Biography 1999.

Priscilla L. Buckley

Born: New York City, New York; October 17, 1921
Died: Sharon, Connecticut; March 25, 2012
Occupation: Magazine editor, journalist

Priscilla Langford Buckley served as the managing editor of the conservative magazine *National Review* from 1959 to 1985, then as the magazine's senior editor until her retirement in 1999. Born to a wealthy family of ten in New York City on October 17, 1921, Buckley attended Smith College and worked as a reporter for the Central Intelligence Agency and the United Press during World War II. She recounted her exploits as one of the nation's few female journalists during the 1940s and 1950s in the first volume of her memoirs, *String of Pearls: On the News Beat in New York and Paris* (2001). The second volume, published in 2005, is called *Living It Up with National Review*.

Buckley's younger brother, William F. Buckley Jr., persuaded her to leave the United Press and join the staff of *National Review* as an assistant editor in 1956. Upon becoming managing editor, Buckley oversaw the daily workings of the magazine and its writers. It was during her tenure that *National Review* gained prominence in conservative circles. Jeffrey Hart wrote of her managerial style in *National Review* (16 Apr. 2001): "Priscilla, with her buoyant soul, optimism that never fractured, and strong common sense, kept the ship plowing through the waves."

Buckley died of kidney failure at her home in Sharon, Connecticut, on March 25, 2012. She never married. Buckley is survived by her siblings F. Reid Buckley, Carol Buckley, and James L. Buckley, the latter a retired judge and former state senator.

See Current Biography Illustrated 2002.

Willard C. Butcher

Born: Bronxville, New York; October 25, 1926
Died: Hobe Sound, Florida; August 25, 2012
Occupation: Former chairman and CEO of Chase Manhattan Bank

Willard C. Butcher, who was the chief executive officer of Chase Manhattan Corporation, oversaw the bank's rapid growth and expansion into the international market during the 1980s. Under Butcher's leadership, Chase Manhattan began operations in more than fifty countries and opened the first US banks in countries such as the Soviet Union and China.

Butcher was born on October 25, 1926, in Bronxville, New York, and was raised in Scarsdale. His mother worked as a teacher and his father was an executive for the utilities company Consolidated Edison. Butcher served in the US Navy before enrolling at Brown University, where he was elected to the academic honor society Phi Beta Kappa. Butcher graduated magna cum laude in 1947 with a bachelor's of arts degree. That same year, he entered the management training program at Chase National Bank and was hired as a junior executive soon after. In

1955, Chase National merged with the Bank of Manhattan Company, becoming Chase Manhattan Bank. Butcher was made area executive for the bank's European and sub-Saharan African divisions in 1968 and was promoted to executive vice president of international operations the following year.

The 1960s and early 1970s marked a period of weak earnings growth for Chase, and the bank's primary competitor, Citibank, was beginning to edge ahead of Chase by earning significantly higher profits and rapidly expanding its operations overseas. In 1972, Chase's president, Herbert P. Patterson, was asked to step down due to the bank's poor performance, and Butcher was named president and chief operating officer. Butcher streamlined the bank's operations in an effort to maximize profitability, and he aggressively expanded into the global market. By 1979, Chase had experienced nine straight quarters of rising earnings, and in December of that year, Chase's board of directors elected Butcher as the bank's chief executive officer. The following year, Butcher succeeded David Rockefeller Sr. as Chase's CEO. In 1981, Butcher became chair of the board. Butcher retired in 1991, but he continued to serve as vice chair of the Chase International Advisory Committee.

Butcher was widowed twice. He married his third wife, Carole McMahon Butcher, in 1979. She survives him, as do his children (John, Willard Jr., Sarah Garonzik, Helen Bennet, and Barbara Uboe), and his eleven grandchildren. Butcher died of kidney cancer at his home in Hobe Sound, Florida, on August 25, 2012.

See Current Biography 1980.

Adolfo Calero

Born: Managua, Nicaragua; December 22, 1931
Died: Managua, Nicaragua; June 2, 2012
Occupation: Nicaraguan rebel leader

The Nicaraguan rebel leader Adolfo Calero was a major figure in the anti-Sandinista resistance movement in Nicaragua during the 1980s. He was involved in the Iran-Contra scandal during the administration of President Ronald Reagan in 1986. The United States supported Calero and the Contra rebel army in their struggle to overthrow the country's Marxist Sandinista regime, funneling money to them despite a congressional ban. Calero, who was educated in the United States, had lobbied US politicians for funds and later testified before Congress during an investigation of the affair. The Contras and the Sandinistas reached a cease-fire agreement in 1988.

Under the agreement, the Contras disbanded and the Sandinistas agreed to free elections, in which they lost power.

Calero was born Adolfo Calero Portocarrero in Managua, Nicaragua, on December 22, 1931. His father was the writer Adolfo Calero Orozco. He graduated from the University of Notre Dame in Indiana in 1953 and studied industrial management at Syracuse University in New York. He returned to Nicaragua and became the manager at a Coca-Cola bottling plant. As a prominent member of the Conservative Party, Calero opposed Nicaragua's Communist government. He participated in and organized antigovernment strikes and was briefly jailed in 1978. The Central Intelligence Agency (CIA) installed him as the leader of the Nicaraguan Democratic Force, a Contra army, in 1983.

Calero published his memoirs, *Chronicles of a Contra*, in 2011. He died of pneumonia in Managua on June 2, 2012. He is survived by his wife, María Ernestina Lacayo; his daughter, Myriam; and three grandchildren.

See Current Biography 1987.

Santiago Carrillo

Born: Gijón, Spain; January 18, 1915
Died: Madrid, Spain; September 18, 2012
Occupation: Spanish politician

Santiago Carrillo was a key figure in twentieth-century Spanish politics who was respected for his efforts to transform the far-left Spanish Communist party into a more moderate force, thus helping the country move beyond its violent and divisive past during Spain's transition to democracy.

Carrillo was born in the northern Spanish town Gijón on January 18, 1915. His father was a metalworker and an active member in the Socialist Workers Party. As a teenager, Carrillo joined the Socialist Youth Federation. Following the collapse of the Spanish monarchy in 1931, he organized an antifascist militia in response to right-wing political obstruction during Spain's Second Republic. In 1934, he was elected secretary general of the Socialist Youth Federation. When civil war broke out in 1936, Carrillo was made councilor for public order in the Defense Junta organized to defend Madrid from General Francisco Franco's advancing forces. There were concerns that Franco's sympathizers in the city would assist the approaching army, and Carrillo moved to relocate thousands of imprisoned right-wing supporters to outside the city. During the transfer, thousands of prisoners were massacred in the town of Paracuellos. Though he was responsible for maintaining public order at the time of the massacre, Carrillo has denied any responsibility for the murders.

When Franco came to power in 1939, Carrillo fled to France, where he acted as the de facto leader of the Spanish Communist Party in France. His political stance became increasingly moderate while in exile, as he worked to form an alliance against Franco among Communists and non-Communists alike. In 1960 he was elected secretary general of the Spanish Communist Party. Following Franco's death in 1975, Carrillo returned to Spain, where he lobbied for the Communist Party to be allowed to compete in elections. In 1977, he published the book *Eurocommunism and the State*, advancing a more moderate form of democratic socialism. That same year, the Spanish Communist Party was legalized, and Carrillo was elected to the Congress of Deputies. In 1986 and again in 1989 he ran unsuccessfully in the parliamentary elections. He officially retired from politics in 1991.

Carrillo separated from his first wife in 1944. He married Carmen Menéndez in 1949. She survives him, as do his sons, Santiago Jr., José, and Jorge. Carrillo died in his home in Madrid on September 18, 2012.

See Current Biography 1977.

Don Carter

Born: St. Louis, Missouri; July 29, 1926
Died: Miami, Florida; January 5, 2012
Occupation: Professional bowler

Don Carter, once known as Mr. Bowling, was professional bowling's first superstar. During the heyday of the sport in the 1950s and 1960s, Carter dominated the lanes and signed an unprecedented $1 million endorsement contract in 1964. During his career, Carter won five World Invitational bowling titles and four all-star titles awarded by the Bowling Proprietors Association of America. He was inducted into the Professional Bowlers Association Hall of Fame in 1975.

Carter was born in St. Louis, Missouri, on June 29, 1926. Though his family could scarcely afford it, his mother gave him thirteen cents on his thirteenth birthday to bowl his first game. During high school, Carter was a member of the bowling team and excelled at baseball and football. After graduating in 1944, he served in the Pacific during World War II. He was discharged in 1946 and was offered a position as an infielder on the former Philadelphia Athletics minor-league baseball team. Carter, however, asked to be released from his contract at the end of the season to pursue bowling. For the next several years, Carter worked odd jobs and ran a bowling alley to support himself and practice his technique.

(Carter was known for a unique and seemingly clumsy stance.) In 1951, he was selected to join the *Bowlers Journal* all-American team. In 1952, he won his first all-star bowling championship; the next year, he was named Bowler of the Year for the first time. Also in 1953, Carter married fellow bowler LaVerne Haverly, née Thompson. The two divorced in 1964.

Carter died of complications from pneumonia at his home in Miami, Florida, on January 5, 2012. His second wife, Paula Sperber, also a professional bowler, survives him. Carter is also survived by his three children, Jim, Cayce Carter, and John; three grandchildren; and five great-grandchildren.

See Current Biography 1963.

Gilbert Cates

Born: New York City, New York; June 6, 1934
Died: Los Angeles, California; October 31, 2011
Occupation: Film director, television producer

Gilbert Cates was a film director and an Emmy Award–winning television producer who oversaw fourteen televised Academy Awards ceremonies. Credited with recruiting emcees like Billy Crystal, Chris Rock, Steve Martin, and Whoopi Goldberg, Cates is considered the most successful producer in the show's history. He also held powerful positions in the Directors Guild of America, including serving as its president from 1983 to 1987, and was known in the guild as a diplomat in Hollywood business matters.

Cates was born Gilbert Katz in the Bronx neighborhood of New York City on June 6, 1934. After he graduated from Syracuse University in 1955, Cates and his brother, Joe, began producing television programs, including the game shows *Haggis Baggis* (1959) and *Camouflage* (1961). He began a fruitful collaboration with playwright Robert Anderson in 1967 when he directed Anderson's comedy *You Know I Can't Hear You When the Water's Running* on Broadway. Cates adapted Anderson's 1968 play *I Never Sang for My Father* for film in 1970. The movie, starring Gene Hackman, was nominated for several Academy Awards. Cates's next film, *Summer Wishes, Winter Dreams* (1973), starring Joanne Woodward, also garnered several Oscar nominations.

Cates became the producer of the Oscar telecast in 1989. Though critics were often divided on his work, Cates drew the best ratings in the show's history. He won an Emmy Award for best producer in 1991.

In 1990, Cates became the founding dean of the School of Theater, Film, and Television at the University of California, Los Angeles

(UCLA). He was also the founder and production director of the Geffen Playhouse there.

Cates reportedly died in the UCLA parking lot on October 31, 2011. The cause of death was unknown, although he was recovering from heart surgery. His wife, Judith Reichman Cates, survives him. He is also survived by his four children, David, Jonathan, Gil Jr., and Melissa; two stepchildren, Anat and Ronit Reichman; and five grandchildren.

See Current Biography 1997.

Elizabeth Catlett

Born: Washington, DC; April 15, 1915
Died: Cuernavaca, Mexico; April 2, 2012
Occupation: Sculptor, printmaker

African American artist and sculptor Elizabeth Catlett created works that were rooted in her experience as a black woman living in an age of segregation. Her depictions of African American women and children hold an especially wide appeal; Catlett's strong and maternal figures in wood and bronze served as social symbols for the working class, African Americans, and women. In her introduction to the 1998 book *Elizabeth Catlett Sculpture: A Fifty-Year Retrospective*, poet Maya Angelou wrote that Catlett "boldly uses all media to make public the best of our most private selves."

Catlett was born in Washington, DC, on April 15, 1915. She won a scholarship to the Carnegie Institute of Technology (Carnegie Mellon University) but was rejected when the school found out that she was black. Instead, she attended Howard University, graduating with a bachelor's degree in art in 1935. She taught briefly in Durham, North Carolina, before pursuing her master's degree in sculpture at the University of Iowa, where she studied with the painter Grant Wood. Wood encouraged Catlett to sculpt what she knew. The result was her thesis and one of her best-known works, a black woman and child chiseled in limestone called *Mother and Child* (1940).

After receiving her MFA, Catlett worked, studied, and taught at various places around the country, including Dillard University in New Orleans; New York City, where she studied with French sculptor Ossip Zadkine; the Art Institute of Chicago; and the Hampton Institute, now Hampton University, in Virginia. While teaching at the George Washington Carver School in Harlem, Catlett decided she wanted to create art for a larger, more working-class audience, and her work became more political.

Catlett moved to Mexico in the late 1940s. Her efforts toward social justice put her in the crosshairs of Senator Joseph McCarthy, and

Catlett became a suspected Communist and was labeled an undesirable alien. She later gave up her American citizenship. Catlett became the first female professor and head of the sculpture department at the National Autonomous University of Mexico's School of Fine Arts in 1958.

Catlett was briefly married to the artist Charles White. They divorced in 1946. She met and married artist Francisco Mora while working at the Taller de Gráfica Popular workshop in Mexico City. Mora died in 2002.

Catlett died in her sleep at her home in Cuernavaca, Mexico, on April 2, 2012. She is survived by her three sons, Francisco, Juan, and David Mora Catlett; ten grandchildren; and six great-grandchildren.

See Current Biography 1998.

Dick Clark

Born: Bronxville, New York; November 30, 1929
Died: Santa Monica, California; April 18, 2012
Occupation: Television personality and producer

Dick Clark was the producer and host of the television program *American Bandstand* from 1956 until 1989. He also hosted the television quiz show *The $10,000 Pyramid* (later *The $100,000 Pyramid*, then simply *Pyramid*) and *Dick Clark's New Year's Rockin' Eve*. His career spanned over half a century, and as the host of *American Bandstand*, Clark oversaw the debuts of numerous musicians, from Buddy Holly and the Jackson 5 to Madonna and the Talking Heads. In addition to being at the forefront when it came to rock music, *American Bandstand* is also noted for its early dance-floor integration and for showcasing teenagers as the driving force of popular culture.

Clark was born Richard Wagstaff Clark on November 30, 1929, in Bronxville, New York, and grew up in the nearby town of Mount Vernon. His older brother, Bradley, was killed in World War II, and the death had a profound effect on the teenage Clark, who listened to the radio to assuage his grief. He idolized the radio announcer Arthur Godfrey and decided to pursue radio as a career.

Clark attended Syracuse University, where he was a disc jockey at the student-run radio station. He graduated in 1951. After a brief stint working for his father, who was then a station manager, Clark moved to Philadelphia, where he hosted a weekday radio show called *Dick Clark's Caravan of Music* at WFIL in 1952. The same year, the station's television affiliate launched an afternoon program called *Bandstand*, hosted by Bob Horn and Lee Stewart. In 1955, Clark was serving as a substitute host for Horn; in 1956, when Horn was arrested and fired for drunk driving, Clark took over.

Bandstand grew from a Philadelphia program featuring such local acts as Chubby Checker and

Frankie Avalon to a national broadcast, earning the new name *American Bandstand* in 1957. The show popularized rock-and-roll music and dance steps like the twist, and Clark became the clean-cut ambassador of youth culture in America. In 1959, however, Clark's reputation was marred by the so-called payola scandal, in which Clark was accused of taking money to play certain records on the show. He testified before Congress but was never found guilty of any crime.

Over the course of his career, Clark hosted a slew of television programs, including the various incarnations of *Pyramid* (1973–88) and *Dick Clark's New Year's Rockin' Eve* (1972–2012). A shrewd businessman, he served as the producer and creator of many of his entertainment ventures under the umbrella corporation Dick Clark Productions. He won four Emmy Awards as a producer and host and has written or cowritten several books, including his autobiography, *Rock, Roll & Remember* (1976), cowritten with Richard Robinson.

Clark, who suffered a stroke in 2004, died of a heart attack at Saint John's Health Center in Santa Monica, California, on April 18, 2012. He is survived by his third wife, Kari Wigton; three children, Richard, Duane, and Cindy; and three grandchildren.

See Current Biography 1959, Current Biography Illustrated 1987.

Charles W. Colson

Born: Boston, Massachusetts; October 16, 1931
Died: Falls Church, Virginia; April 21, 2012
Occupation: Lawyer, politician, evangelical preacher

Charles Wendell Colson, who went by the name Chuck, was a young lawyer who became a major player in the illegal activities surrounding the 1972 reelection campaign of President Richard Nixon. He was sentenced to five years in prison but served only seven months. Upon his release in 1976, Colson founded Prison Fellowship Ministries, an evangelical criminal justice reform group.

Colson was born in Boston, Massachusetts, on October 16, 1931. Although he came from a struggling, working-class family, he attended the prestigious Browne & Nichols (now Buckingham Browne & Nichols) preparatory school in Cambridge. After graduating in 1949, he reportedly turned down a full scholarship to Harvard University; Colson claimed that the admissions officer had treated him in a condescending manner. He graduated with distinction from Brown University in 1953, then served in the Marines before earning his law degree from George Washington University in 1959.

Colson became involved in Republican politics and earned a reputation for his aggressive and often dirty campaign tactics. He worked on Richard Nixon's successful 1968 presidential campaign and was appointed special counsel to the president in 1969. Colson wrote in his 1975 memoir *Born Again* that he and Nixon "understood each other." They were "prideful men seeking that most elusive goal of all—acceptance and the respect of those who had spurned us." This was evident in 1972 when the administration went out of its way to discredit Daniel Ellsberg, the man who had leaked the Pentagon Papers, and when Colson was linked to the break-in at the Democratic National Committee headquarters at the Watergate complex in Washington, DC.

For his work with Prison Fellowship Ministries, Colson was awarded the $1 million Templeton Prize for Progress in Religion in 1993. He became involved in the political evangelical movement and encouraged President George W. Bush to pursue faith-based policies. In 2006, a federal judge ruled that Prison Fellowship Ministries violated the separation of church and state in Iowa because the program allotted special privileges, using tax money, to inmates who were "born again." Colson stepped down as the group's chairman shortly thereafter.

Colson, who was convicted of a felony, had his rights to practice law, vote, and serve on a jury restored by Florida governor Jeb Bush in 2000.

Colson died of complications from a brain hemorrhage on April 21, 2012, in Falls Church, Virginia. He had homes in both Leesburg, Virginia, and Naples, Florida. Colson, whose first marriage ended in divorce, is survived by his second wife, Patricia Ann Hughes; three children, Wendell Ball II, Christian, and Emily Ann; and five grandchildren.

See Current Biography 2000.

Barry Commoner

Born: Brooklyn, New York; May 28, 1917
Died: Manhattan, New York; September 30, 2012
Occupation: American biologist and environmentalist

Dr. Barry Commoner was an American biologist and a pioneer of modern ecology and the environmental movement. His scientific work not only includes the study of viruses, cell metabolism, and free radicals, but also the study of the detrimental effects of nuclear fallout. His experiments concerning the impact of nuclear fallout focused on the study of the baby teeth of children who had been exposed to radiation from nuclear tests. These studies uncovered the detrimental effects of nuclear radiation, and became part of a petition drafted by the St. Louis Committee of Nuclear Information, which Commoner helped found in 1958. This petition received international support from the scientific community, and provided the foundation for President John F. Kennedy's Nuclear Ban Treaty of 1963.

Commoner attended Columbia University as an undergraduate student and earned his master's and doctoral degrees in biology from Harvard University. He was a professor at Washington University, where he taught plant physiology for thirty-four years.

Commoner was influential in educating the public on the potential dangers of nuclear weapons and nuclear waste. Likewise, he was also a pioneer of the environmental movement. Named the "Paul Revere of Ecology" by *Time* magazine in 1970, Commoner was influential in educating the public on the importance of recycling and the potential benefits of solar power and other sustainable forms of energy. He was the author of numerous books, such as *The Closing Circle* (1971), and *The Poverty of Power* (1976). In *The Closing Circle*, Dr. Commoner explained his four laws of ecology, including the philosophy that "there is one ecosphere for all living organisms and what affects one, affects all." These four laws continue to have a significant impact on ecology and the scientific community.

In 1980, Dr. Commoner ran for president of the United States as the Citizens Party candidate and used his ecological message as the keystone for his campaign. Ronald Reagan, however, won the election. Commoner never ran for office again; instead, he focused his attention on his scientific endeavors.

On September 30, 2012, Dr. Commoner died in Manhattan from natural causes. He was 95 years old. Commoner is survived by his second wife, Lisa Feiner; Lucy and Frederic, his two children from his first marriage to Gloria Gordon; and a granddaughter.

See Current Biography 1970.

Don Cornelius

Born: Chicago, Illinois; September 27, 1936
Died: Los Angeles, California; February 1, 2012
Occupation: Television host and producer

Don Cornelius was the host and creator of the Chicago television program *Soul Train*, which showcased African American music, fashion, and dance. Cornelius began the show in 1970 and funded the pilot himself. He served as the host in national syndication for over thirty-five years, introducing soul, funk, and eventually rap acts to homes across America.

Cornelius was born on the South Side of Chicago on September 27, 1936. After he had left the Marines and a series of odd sales jobs, he decided to take an introductory course in broadcasting. In 1967, he became a fill-in disc jockey at WVON-AM in Chicago. He also worked for a television news program on Chicago's WCIU-TV station that was aimed at an African American audience. It was there that he pitched to studio executives a show that he called a soul-music version of the popular television show *American Bandstand*.

Soul Train, which was written, produced, and hosted by Cornelius, premiered on WCIU-TV on August 17, 1970. It was such a success that less than a year later, the show moved to Los Angeles and went into national syndication. Scores of black artists performed and got their start on *Soul Train*, including Aretha Franklin, the Jackson 5, Barry White, and James Brown. During its heyday, the program was at the forefront of black youth culture. In 1985, Cornelius began the Soul Train Music Awards.

When ratings began to decline in the late 1980s and early 1990s, Cornelius stepped down as *Soul Train*'s host to allow for a rotating roster of young emcees and comedians. He stopped producing new shows in 2006.

In 2008, Cornelius was arrested after a domestic dispute with his second wife. He was sentenced to three years probation.

Cornelius died of a self-inflicted gunshot wound at his home in Los Angeles on February 1, 2012. His survivors include two sons from his first marriage, Anthony and Raymond.

See Current Biography Illustrated 2000.

Stephen R. Covey

Born: Salt Lake City, Utah; October 24, 1932
Died: Idaho Falls, Idaho; July 16, 2012
Occupation: American business consultant, author

Stephen Covey was already a highly successful manager of the multimillion-dollar management consulting business Covey Leadership Center when he published *The 7 Habits of Highly Effective People* in 1989. The book sold more than twenty million copies in forty different languages and spent more than two hundred weeks on the *New York Times* Best Sellers list. Covey's book combined a self-help approach with business management principles, with an emphasis on developing personal integrity and responsibility as a way to achieve success.

In 1952 Covey completed a bachelor's degree in business administration at the University of Utah, with the intention of joining the family's hospitality business, which was founded by his grandfather. However, after graduation he travelled to the United Kingdom to serve as a Mormon missionary for two years. There he was responsible for training the new heads of Mormon congregations, gaining his first experience in leadership training. He returned to the United States and earned his MBA from Harvard University in 1957.

Covey began working as an assistant to the president of Brigham Young University, eventually teaching organizational behavior and business management at the school. He completed his doctorate degree in business and education in 1976. In 1983 he quit teaching and founded the Covey Leadership Center, which offered leadership programs and training seminars. The center merged with Franklin Quest to become FranklinCovey in 1997. Within twelve years of its founding, the center's annual revenues had reached about $75 million and, in 1995, the center attracted nearly 250,000 people to Covey's seminars. Covey published *The 7 Habits of Highly Effective People* in 1989, and followed that success with several other best sellers, including *The 7 Habits of Highly Effective Families* (1997) and *The 8th Habit: From Effectiveness to Greatness* (2004).

In April 2012, Covey sustained serious injuries in a bicycle accident, including several broken ribs and a partially collapsed lung, from which he never fully recovered. He died in a hospital in Idaho Falls on July 16, 2012. He is survived by his wife, Sandra Merrill Covey, whom he wed in 1956; their nine children; three siblings; fifty-two grandchildren; and six great-grandchildren.

See Current Biography 1998.

she clinched first place in thirty-four National Amateur Union championships, more than any other woman in history. Her success earned her the prestigious James E. Sullivan Award in 1944, an annual award given to outstanding amateur athletes in the United States. Curtis was the first woman and the first swimmer to receive the honor. She was featured on the cover of magazines such as *Collier's* and *Newsweek*, and was even offered a movie deal by MGM, but turned it down for personal reasons.

Cuneo opened the Ann Curtis School of Swimming in San Rafael in 1959, where she coached accomplished athletes such as Olympic swimmer Rick DeMont, who won gold in the 400-meter freestyle at the 1972 Olympics in Munich, Germany. Curtis was inducted into the International Swimming Hall of Fame in 1966.

Curtis began swimming and training at a boarding school in Santa Rosa California and started competing at the age of eleven. During her training at the well known Crystal Plunge pool in San Francisco, she swam three miles a day, six days a week, under the direction of esteemed Olympic coach Charlie Sava. In addition to her intensive training regimen, Curtis's five-foot-ten, 160-pound frame was the ideal swimmer's body.

On June 26, 2012, Curtis died at her home in San Rafael from Alzheimer's disease. She was predeceased by her husband, Gordon Cuneo, whom she married in 1949; she was also predeceased by her son Brian Cuneo. Curtis is survived by the couple's other four children, Carrie, Susan, David, and Brian; nine grandchildren; and four great-grandchildren. Her daughter Carrie continues Curtis's legacy and now runs the Ann Curtis School of swimming.

See Current Biography 1945.

Ann Curtis

Born: San Francisco, California; March 6, 1926
Died: San Rafael, California; June 26, 2012
Occupation: American Olympic swimming champion

Ann Curtis was one of the most accomplished female swimmers of her time. In the 1948 London Olympics games, she won gold in the women's 400-meter freestyle—setting a new Olympic record with a time of 5:17:8—and the women's 4×100-meter freestyle relay. She also took home a silver medal in the women's 100-meter freestyle event, narrowly missing the gold by two-tenths of a second behind Greta Anderson of Denmark.

Before her international success at the Olympic Games, Curtis was already a rising athletic star in the United States. From 1943 to 1948,

Hal David

Born: Brooklyn, New York; May 25, 1921
Died: Los Angeles, California; September 1, 2012
Occupation: American lyricist

Hal David was a Grammy and Academy Award–winning lyricist whose collaboration with composer Burt Bacharach produced some of the greatest hits of the 1960s and 1970s. He was known for his down-to-earth and emotionally direct lyrics, which captured the spirit of the sixties in songs such as "What the World Needs Now Is Love" and "Do You Know the Way to San Jose."

Hal David was born to Austrian immigrants on May 25, 1921, in Brooklyn, New York. One of three brothers, David spent much of his childhood writing stories and poems and later decided to study journalism at New York University and worked as a copywriter for the *New York Post* after graduation.

Throughout this time, David maintained his interest in writing lyrics, and, in 1949, he achieved his first top-ten hit with "The Four Winds and the Seven Seas." In 1957, he met Bacharach and the duo collaborated on the song "The Story of My Life," which was recorded by Marty Robbins and reached the number-one spot on the Billboard country charts. In 1962, they began producing music for up-and-coming vocalist Dionne Warwick. The song "Don't Make Me Over" was the first of many hits for David, Bacharach, and Warwick, followed by "Walk on By," and "I'll Never Fall in Love Again."

David and Bacharach also wrote music for film, and four of the duo's songs were nominated for Academy Awards, including "Raindrops Keep Fallin' on My Head," which earned them an Oscar in 1970. Bacharach and David wrote the score for the Broadway musical comedy *Promises, Promises*, which was nominated for a Tony Award and won a Grammy for best score from an original cast show album in 1969. Following their collaboration on the 1973 movie musical *Lost Horizon*, which flopped at the box office, the songwriting team parted ways. Soon after, they were sued by Warwick for their failure to produce new music for her. The three would not work together for nearly twenty years, when they reunited in 1992 to record "Sunny Weather Lover."

David produced dozens of top-ten songs and was elected to the Songwriters Hall of Fame in 1972 and the Nashville Songwriters Hall of Fame in 1984. He served for many years as president of the American Society of Composers, Authors and Publishers. In 2011, David and Bacharach received the Gershwin Prize from the Library of Congress.

David died at Cedars-Sinai Medical Center in Los Angeles, following a stroke. He is survived by his wife, Eunice; two sons, Jim and Craig; and three grandchildren. His first wife, Anne, died in 1987.

See Current Biography 1980.

Miguel de la Madrid Hurtado

Born: Colima, Mexico; December 12, 1934
Died: Mexico City, Mexico; April 1, 2012
Occupation: Former Mexican President

Miguel de la Madrid Hurtado was elected president of Mexico as a member of the ruling Institutional Revolutionary Party in 1982. He took power during an economic crisis and imposed unpopular austerity measures to direct Mexico toward a free-market economy. In 1985, a magnitude 8.1 earthquake struck Mexico City, leveling buildings and killing nearly ten thousand people. De la Madrid initially refused to address the disaster and turned down offers of foreign aid. Mexican citizens banded together to look for survivors in the rubble until the government took action. The misstep permanently colored de la Madrid's presidency and the capabilities of his party.

De la Madrid was born in Colima, Mexico, on December 12, 1934. He received a master's degree from Harvard's Kennedy School of Government and began his career working for Mexico's central bank. He was the chosen successor for President José López Portillo. When de la Madrid's term ended in 1988, his chosen successor won in a national election, but the Institutional Revolutionary Party appeared to be losing significant ground with the electorate. After his presidency, de la Madrid became the director of a state-owned publishing company.

De la Madrid died in Mexico City on April 1, 2012. He had been hospitalized for emphysema. He is survived by his wife, Paloma Cordero, and children, Miguel, Enrique, Federico, Gerardo, and Margarita de la Madrid Cordero, as well as several grandchildren.

See Current Biography 1983.

Shelagh Delaney

Born: Salford, England; November 25, 1938
Died: Suffolk, England; November 20, 2011
Occupation: Playwright, screenwriter

English playwright and screenwriter Shelagh Delaney reached the height of her career at the age of nineteen with the debut of her first play, *A Taste of Honey*, in 1958. Born in the industrial town of Salford, Lancashire, on November 25, 1938, the teenage Delaney left school at age seventeen to work a series of odd jobs. She was writing a novel when she saw the Terence Rattigan play *Variations on a Theme*, which also premiered in 1958 and sought to address difficult subjects such as homosexuality. Disliking the play for its timidity, Delaney decided to rewrite her novel, which dealt with the stark realities of the British working class, as a play.

A Taste of Honey became a huge hit in London's West End. It premiered on Broadway in 1960 and ran for over three hundred performances. The original Broadway production was directed by Tony Richardson and starred Angela Lansbury and Joan Plowright, the latter of whom won a Tony Award for her role as the play's heroine. Richardson and Delaney collaborated on the well-received 1962 film version of the play as well. *A Taste of Honey* enjoyed a Broadway revival with Amanda Plummer in 1981.

Delaney is often included in the group of British playwrights who came of age during the 1950s and rejected the stuffiness of British high culture for the grittiness of the working class, known as the "angry young men." In keeping with this moniker, Delaney was often called an "angry young woman," a label she detested. Her other works include several screenplays, collections of short stories, and nonfiction.

Delaney died of heart failure and breast cancer at her daughter's home in Suffolk, England, on November 20, 2011. Delaney, who never married, is survived by her daughter, Charlotte Jo Delaney, and three grandchildren.

See Current Biography 1962.

Edward J. Derwinski

Born: Chicago, Illinois; September 15, 1926
Died: Oak Brook, Illinois; January 15, 2012
Occupation: American secretary of veterans affairs

In 1989, Edward J. Derwinski, a Chicago politician who had served in the Pacific theater during World War II, was sworn in under President George H. W. Bush as the first secretary of veterans affairs. Derwinski was born to Polish parents living in Chicago, Illinois, on September 15, 1926. He enlisted in the military after graduating high school in 1944. After his discharge in 1946, Derwinski pursued a bachelor's degree in history at Chicago's Loyola University and took over the family savings-and-loan business following his father's death. He was elected to the Illinois General Assembly in 1957, and in 1958, he was elected to the US House of Representatives, representing Illinois's Fourth District as a conservative Republican.

In 1971, Derwinski, the ranking Republican on the House Post Office and Civil Service Committee, was the principal architect of legislation that transformed the post office from a cabinet department into an independent government agency that functioned like a private business. In 1977, he was involved in a scandal when he was accused of leaking information to South Korean government officials; he denied any wrongdoing, though during confirmation hearings in 1989 he admitted that he let the information "slip" in conversation. Derwinski lost his seat to redistricting in 1982 but continued to work in Washington, DC, until he was appointed secretary of veterans affairs in 1989.

As secretary, Derwinski expanded health-care coverage for Vietnam veterans who were exposed to the herbicide Agent Orange, which has been linked to non-Hodgkin lymphomas. He moved to improve the quality of care in veterans' hospitals but was criticized for letting veterans' cemeteries fall into disrepair. Though he initially won high ratings from veterans, Derwinski was booed at the 1992 American Legion convention. Upon his resignation, Derwinski was named George H. W. Bush's campaign manager for ethnic coalitions.

Derwinski died of cancer at a nursing home in Oak Brook, Illinois, on January 15, 2012. He is survived by his second wife, Bonita Derwinski; two children, Maureen Quattrocki and Michael; two stepchildren, Kevin and Maggie Hickey; and seven grandchildren.

See Current Biography 1991.

Phyllis Diller

Born: Lima, Ohio; July 17, 1917
Died: Los Angeles, California; August 20, 2012
Occupation: American actress and comedian

Legendary comedian Phyllis Diller was known for her spot-on comedic timing and outsize stage persona. She appeared on stage as a wildly flamboyant housewife, telling stories about her fictional husband "Fang" and joking about her age, her appearance, and her home life. Diller has been called a pioneer for subsequent generations of women comedians; on the talk show *Watch What Happens Live*, Joan Rivers stated that Diller "broke the way for every woman comedian."

Diller was born in Lima, Ohio, on July 17, 1917. She briefly attended the Sherwood Conservatory of Music in Chicago, where she trained as a classical pianist. She eventually transferred to Bluffton College in Ohio, where she met Sherwood Anderson Diller. The two married in 1939 and relocated to California. Diller worked various jobs in San Francisco and Oakland, and eventually began writing comedy routines and taking unpaid performing jobs at local hospitals, schools, and other events. In 1955, she performed on stage at a San Francisco nightclub called the Purple Onion, making her professional debut. Beginning in 1958, Diller appeared on several dozen episodes of Jack Paar's *Tonight Show*, and she began performing stand-up comedy at nightclubs across the country. In 1959 she met comedian Bob Hope, and the two performed together in several USO tours, three movies, and various television specials. In 1968, Diller hosted a short-lived variety show called *The Beautiful Phyllis Diller Show*. Her career, however, was not limited to comedy; she starred in the 1969 Broadway production of *Hello, Dolly!* and performed as a piano soloist with hundreds of different symphony orchestras in the 1970s and 1980s. Throughout her career, Diller appeared in more than two dozen movies. She suffered from a near-fatal heart attack in 1999 and retired from standup comedy three years later. In 2005, she released an autobiography called *Like a Lampshade in a Whorehouse: My Life in Comedy*, written with Richard Buskin. In her later years, she did voice-over work for several television shows, including *Hey Arnold* and *Family Guy*.

Diller died at her home in Los Angeles on August 20, 2012. She is survived by her children, Perry, Sally Diller, and Suzanne Mills; four grandchildren; and a great-granddaughter.

See Current Biography 1967.

Michael Clarke Duncan

Born: Chicago, Illinois; December 10, 1957
Died: Los Angeles, California; September 3, 2012
Occupation: American actor

Michael Clarke Duncan was an American actor best known for his 1999 portrayal of John Coffey, a wrongfully convicted prisoner on death row, in the film adaptation of Stephen King's novel *The Green Mile*. Duncan was nominated for an Academy Award for best supporting actor in 2000 for his performance in this film.

Duncan was born on the South Side of Chicago on December 10, 1957. His father left the family when Duncan was young, and Duncan was raised by his mother and older sister. He briefly attended Alcorn State University in Mississippi, but he returned to Illinois after his mother fell ill; he later transferred to Kankakee Community College, about an hour south of Chicago, where he majored in communications and played basketball. He then took a job as a ditch digger for the Peoples Gas Company in Chicago and often spoke of becoming a Hollywood actor. After six years, he quit his job and moved to Los Angeles.

With his massive height and muscular frame, Duncan landed a series of jobs as a bodyguard for celebrities such as Will Smith, Jamie Foxx, and rapper The Notorious B.I.G. This led to a string of bit parts on television and in film. In 1998, Duncan landed his first major role, as Bear in *Armageddon*, and acted alongside Bruce Willis, Steve Buscemi, and Ben Affleck. He befriended Willis on the set, who recommended Duncan to director Frank Darabont while he was casting *The Green Mile*. Reading the script, Duncan said he immediately felt a connection with the character of John Coffey and, after accepting the part, he stunned audiences with his sensitive portrayal of the massive yet childlike prisoner. This success led to a series of other film roles, including *The Scorpion King* (2002), *Daredevil* (2003), and *Sin City* (2005).

Duncan was engaged to be married sometime in 2013. His fiancée, Omarosa Manigault, performed life-saving CPR when she found him unresponsive in his Los Angeles home following a heart attack in July. He died at Cedars-Sinai Medical Center in Los Angeles on September 3, 2012. He is survived by his fiancée; his mother, Jean Duncan; and his sister, Judy Duncan. At the time of his death, Duncan was slated to appear in two films in 2012, *In the Hive* and *The Challenger*.

See Current Biography 2000.

Nora Ephron

Born: New York, New York; May 19, 1941
Died: New York, New York; June 26, 2012
Occupation: Screenwriter, playwright, essayist, filmmaker

Nora Ephron was an essayist and journalist who, after writing the Academy Award–nominated screenplay for the film *Silkwood* (1983), went on to achieve a highly successful career as a writer and director of films. Her most celebrated films include *When Harry Met Sally . . .* (1989), *Sleepless in Seattle* (1993) (both of which were nominated for an Academy Award for best screenplay), *You've Got Mail* (1998), and *Julie & Julia* (2009).

Known for her candid personal essays and incredible wit, Ephron has been compared to the satirist and poet Dorothy Parker. Several of Ephron's essay collections—including *Wallflower at the Orgy* (1970), *Crazy Salad: Some Things About Women* (1975), and *Scribble Scribble* (1978)—compiled her writings from *New York Magazine*, *Esquire* (where Ephron was a contributing editor and columnist), and other magazines to which she was a contributor. Two later collections of personal essays, *I Feel Bad About My Neck: And Other Thoughts on Being a Woman* (2006) and *I Remember Nothing: And Other Reflections* (2010), became best-sellers. A pragmatic optimist, Ephron was a master of the romantic-comedy genre. Charles McGrath wrote in an obituary for the *New York Times* on June 26, 2012, that Ephron had a "gift . . . for delayed but happy endings."

Ephron's most memorable work was biting but never venomous; it was often poignant but always funny. Even when Ephron wrote about her painful divorce from journalist Carl Bernstein (first in the 1983 novel *Heartburn* and then in the 1986 film of the same name), she dealt her blows with humor and grace.

Ephron was born in New York City on May 19, 1941. Her parents, Henry and Phoebe Ephron, were screenwriters and playwrights. Ephron was the eldest of four daughters, all of whom became writers. (In 2008, Ephron and her sister Delia wrote the play *Love, Loss and What I Wore*, based on the novel of the same name by Ilene Beckerman.) Ephron's family moved to Beverly Hills, California, when she was four years old. She attended Beverly Hills High School and then Wellesley College in Massachusetts. In the summer of 1961, she was an intern at the White House during the Kennedy administration.

After graduating from college in 1962, Ephron moved to New York City. She worked as a mail girl for *Newsweek* and landed her first reporting job for the *New York Post* in 1963. Ephron made a name for herself at the *Post* writing short celebrity profiles. She began freelance writing in 1968, and her first collection of writing (*Wallflower at the Orgy*) was published in 1970. Ephron's first two marriages—the first to writer Dan Greenburg, the second to Bernstein—ended in divorce. In 1987 she married screenwriter Nicholas Pileggi, who survives her.

Ephron's directing credits include *This is My Life* (1992), *Sleepless in Seattle* (1993), *Mixed Nuts* (1994), *Michael* (1996), *You've Got Mail* (1998), *Lucky Numbers* (2000), *Bewitched* (2005), and *Julie & Julia* (2009).

Ephron died on June 26, 2012, in New York City. She had been diagnosed with acute myeloid leukemia, and her death was a result of contracting pneumonia brought on by the leukemia. In addition to Pileggi, Ephron is survived by sons Max and Jacob from her marriage to Bernstein, and by her sisters Delia, Amy, and Hallie.

See Current Biography 1990.

Fang Lizhi

Born: Beijing, China; February 12, 1936
Died: Tucson, Arizona; April 6, 2012
Occupation: Chinese astrophysicist

Fang Lizhi was a theoretical astrophysicist who studied the structure of the universe. He was also one of China's best-known dissidents and the man who inspired the pro-democracy protests that culminated in Tiananmen Square in 1989. Born to a railroad clerk in Beijing on February 12, 1936, Fang established himself as a brilliant student at Beijing University in the 1950s. At the founding meeting of the university's Communist Youth League, he took the podium and encouraged students to think independently. After graduation, Fang studied nuclear reactor theory at the Chinese Academy of Sciences' Institute of Physics. He was among the one hundred intellectuals invited to speak their minds by Mao Zedong in 1956; Fang wrote a

paper calling for education reform and was subsequently expelled from the party.

Fang continued to study and teach at Beijing's University of Science and Technology of China (USTC) until the Cultural Revolution began in 1966, at which time he was imprisoned for a year, then sent to work among peasants in the rural Anhui Province. He brought a copy of Lev Landau's *Classical Theory of Fields* (1951) with him, which inspired him to shift his focus from solid-state physics to cosmology while in exile. During this time, the USTC was moved to Anhui, and after Fang was allowed to resume teaching there, he caused controversy by introducing the big bang theory to Chinese physics.

After Mao's death in 1976, Fang traveled extensively and, for the first time in several years, began to publish research under his own name instead of a pseudonym. During the brief period of openness and intellectual exchange that followed, Fang became a well-known advocate for education reform and an outspoken critic of the Communist Party, helping to organize student demonstrations. In 1987, he was again expelled from the party and stripped of his job as the vice president of the USTC. Fang's ousting and other forced resignations sparked a slew of student demonstrations that ended in the bloody assault on protesters in Tiananmen Square in 1989.

Following the protests, Fang and his family sought refuge at the American embassy, which soured relations between the United States and China for over a year. In 1990, after Fang experienced heart trouble, Chinese leaders allowed him to travel to the United Kingdom for medical treatment. He and his family subsequently left for the United States. Fang taught physics at the University of Arizona in Tucson and continued to travel and lecture on human rights until his death.

Fang died of unknown causes in Tucson on April 6, 2012. His survivors include his son, Fang Ke.

See Current Biography 1989.

Dietrich Fischer-Dieskau

Born: Berlin, Germany; May 28, 1925
Died: Starnberg, Germany; May 18, 2012
Occupation: Opera singer

Dietrich Fischer-Dieskau was a celebrated German opera singer, teacher, and orchestra conductor. He was born Alfred Dietrich Fischer to Albert Fischer, a scholar and amateur pianist, and teacher Theodora Klingelhoffer in Berlin on May 28, 1925; his father later added Dieskau, from his mother's family, to the family name. A shy child who loved music and performance,

Fischer-Dieskau often entertained his mentally disabled brother with puppet shows.

After losing his father at a young age, Fischer-Dieskau was inducted into the Hitler Youth as a child and drafted into the Wehrmacht at age eighteen, whereupon he was sent to Russia to care for army horses. While he was gone, his brother was sent to an institution, where he died. In 1945, Fischer-Dieskau was captured by American forces and sent to a prisoner-of-war camp in Italy, where he entertained troops with his beautiful voice. He was so popular that he was one of the last prisoners to be released in 1947. When he returned home, he found that his mother's apartment had been bombed. Few of his family's possessions survived the war.

Though only twenty-two, Fischer-Dieskau found immediate fame as a singer of German lieder, or poems set to music. He made his debut as an opera singer in 1948 as Posa in Giuseppe Verdi's *Don Carlos*. In 1955, he debuted in New York by singing Franz Schubert's *Winterreise* cycle without intermission. Fischer-Dieskau performed hundreds of recitals throughout his career, often accompanied by pianist Gerald Moore. He retired from the opera in 1978 and performed his last recital in 1992. After his retirement, he continued to teach and conduct. He also wrote several books about music and a memoir called *Reverberations* (1989).

Fischer-Dieskau married cellist Irmgard Poppen in 1949; she died after giving birth to their third child in 1963. He was married again in 1965, 1968, and finally 1977, the last time to Hungarian soprano Júlia Várady.

Fischer-Dieskau died at his home in Starnberg, Bavaria, on May 18, 2012. He is survived by Várady and by his three sons from his first marriage, Matthias, Martin, and Manuel.

See Current Biography 1967.

Manuel Fraga Iribarne

Born: Vilalba, Spain; November 23, 1922
Died: Madrid, Spain; January 15, 2012
Occupation: Spanish political leader

The conservative Spanish politician Manuel Fraga Iribarne was the last surviving minister of the government of Spanish dictator Francisco Franco. Unlike his compatriots, Fraga remained active in the Spanish government for nearly sixty years, most notably serving as president of the Galicia region (1990–2005) and then in the Senate of Spain.

Fraga was born in Vilalba, Spain, on November 23, 1922. He studied law before entering politics, and he held several important posts before being named minister of information and tourism in 1962. While in this post, he coined the slogan "Spain is different." Fraga served as the interior minister after Franco's death in 1975. In 1976, he began to form the country's modern conservative party, the Alianza Popular (People's Alliance), now the Partido Popular (People's Party). Two years later, he helped write Spain's democratic constitution.

Fraga died in Madrid on January 15, 2012. His wife, Carmen Estevez, died in 1996. The couple had five children.

See Current Biography 1965.

Helen Frankenthaler

Born: New York, New York; December 12, 1928
Died: Darien, Connecticut; December 27, 2011
Occupation: Painter

Helen Frankenthaler was part of an art movement known as second-generation abstract expressionism and refined a painting technique, first developed by Jackson Pollock, in which she poured washed-out paint directly onto raw canvas. She first used the technique on a painting called "Mountains and Sea" (1952), which has become one of her best-known works. Art critics have called her bleeding color stains lyrical, and her free-flowing forms have earned her the label of "poet's painter."

Frankenthaler was born to a wealthy New York family on December 12, 1928. She studied art with Paul Feeley at Bennington College in Vermont and returned to New York City's thriving art community after her graduation in 1949. She began a relationship with the critic Clement Greenberg who introduced her to the abstract expressionists of the day, including Pollock and Willem and Elaine de Kooning. Frankenthaler had her first solo show in 1951 at the Tibor de Nagy gallery. Her first major show was in 1960 at the Jewish Museum. The Whitney Museum of American Art organized a retrospective of her work in 1969. Some of her work can also be seen at the Museum of Modern Art.

In 1958, Frankenthaler married the painter Robert Motherwell, a prominent member of the first generation of abstract expressionists. They divorced in 1971. Frankenthaler married investment banker Stephen M. DuBrul Jr. in 1994.

Frankenthaler died after a long illness at her home in Darien, Connecticut, on December 27, 2011. She is survived by her husband; two stepdaughters, Jeannie Motherwell and Lise Motherwell; and six nieces and nephews.

See Current Biography 1966.

Joe Frazier

Born: Beaufort, South Carolina; January 12, 1944
Died: Philadelphia, Pennsylvania; November 7, 2011
Occupation: Boxer

Joe Frazier, known in the ring as Smokin' Joe, was a former heavyweight champion and the famous rival of Muhammad Ali. Frazier became a professional boxer in 1965, after winning the heavyweight gold medal at the 1964 Tokyo Olympic Games.

Frazier was born in Beaufort, South Carolina, on January 12, 1944. His family owned a small farm, and Frazier (known in his childhood as Billy) proved to be a hard worker at an early age. He showed an interest in boxing as a teenager but after beating up a white man for calling him a racial slur, Frazier's mother sent him to live with one of his brothers in Philadelphia. Frazier dropped out of school and found a job at a slaughterhouse. To lose weight, Frazier began working out at Philadelphia Police Athletic League gym. It was there that he was discovered by his manager, Yank Durham.

"I've had plenty of other boxers with more raw talent," Durham told the *New York Times Magazine* in 1970, as quoted in Frazier's obituary (7 Nov. 2011), "but none with more dedication and strength." With an unbeaten record, Frazier first fought Ali on March 8, 1971. The match was touted as the fight of the century; Ali (formerly Cassius Clay) was making his return to boxing after being stripped of his title for evading the Vietnam draft. He too was unbeaten. The match lasted twelve rounds, with Frazier emerging the undisputed victor.

Ali had his comeuppance on Frazier in 1975 in what became known as the Thrilla in Manila. Many consider the fight one of the greatest in boxing history. Both men were battered, but Frazier, whose left eye was swollen shut, did not emerge to fight a fifteenth round.

In the ring, Frazier was constantly on the attack and knocked out many opponents with his deadly left hook. But his rivalry with Ali extended beyond the physical; the two prizefighters taunted each other relentlessly. Ali, who was politically outspoken and given to poetic turns of phrase, called blue-collar Frazier ignorant and referred to him as a gorilla. Bad blood reportedly existed between them long after the two men retired. (Ali publicly apologized to Frazier on the thirtieth anniversary of their 1971 fight. Frazier accepted.)

Frazier announced his retirement in 1976 at the age of thirty-two after losing a match to George Foreman. (He lost only four matches in his career: two to Ali and two to Foreman.)

Frazier died of liver cancer at his home in Philadelphia on November 7, 2011. His survivors include his sons, Marvis, Hector, Joseph Rubin, Joseph Jordan, Brandon Marcus, and Derek Dennis; and his daughters, Jacqui, Weatta, Jo-Netta, Renae, and Natasha. Frazier's marriage to his wife Florence ended in divorce.

Frazier's daughter Jacqui Frazier-Lyde also became a boxer. She fought Ali's daughter Laila Ali in 2001 when they were both unbeaten; Ali won.

See Current Biography 1971.

Benedict Freedman

Born: New York, New York; December 19, 1919
Died: Corte Madera, California; February 24, 2012
Occupation: Novelist, aeronautical engineer, mathematician

Benedict Freedman wore many hats during his long life, but is most well known as the coauthor, with his wife, the late Nancy Freedman, of the 1947 novel *Mrs. Mike*. A fictionalized account of a friend's life as a turn-of-the-century pioneer living with her husband in the Canadian wilderness, the novel became an immediate hit upon its publication—and later, a cult favorite of teenage girls. *Mrs. Mike* was adapted for film in 1949; the movie stars Dick Powell and Evelyn Keyes. The Freedmans published two sequels to *Mrs. Mike*: *The Search for Joyful* (2002) and *Kathy Little Bird* (2004).

Freedman was born in New York City on December 19, 1919. His father was David Freedman, a popular writer who created the character of Baby Snooks for the actress Fanny Brice. Freedman proved himself to be a child prodigy in mathematics and graduated high school at the age of thirteen.

Barely a teenager, Freedman began a premedical degree at Columbia University, but dropped out when his father died. Freedman was seventeen. He took up writing and contributed to programs that starred Al Jolson and Robert Benchley. In 1939, he moved to California to pursue a degree in aeronautical engineering. The same year he met his wife, Nancy. Nancy was believed to be terminally ill at the time with rheumatic fever, and when Freedman asked for her hand her father said he didn't believe that she would live to see the wedding. She and Freedman were married until she passed away in 2010.

During World War II, Freedman worked for the famously eccentric aviator and engineer Howard Hughes. Before his interview with Hughes, Freedman was asked to bathe twice and wipe himself down with alcohol.

Freedman returned to college as a middle-aged man. He earned a bachelor's degree and doctorate in mathematics from the University of

California, Los Angeles. He taught mathematics at Occidental College in Los Angeles.

Freedman died at his home in Corte Madera, California, on February 24, 2012. He is survived by his children, Johanna Shapiro, Deborah Jackson, and Michael Freedman; eight grandchildren; and four great-grandchildren.

See Current Biography 1947.

Carlos Fuentes

Born: Panama City, Panama; November 11, 1928
Died: Mexico City, Mexico; May 15, 2012
Occupation: Mexican novelist, short story writer, former diplomat

Carlos Fuentes was a novelist and writer in the manner of his colleagues Gabriel García Márquez and Mario Vargas Llosa. Many consider the novel *The Death of Artemio Cruz* (1962) to be his masterpiece. The novel, about a newspaper tycoon on his deathbed, traces Mexico's history and what Fuentes suggests is the country's failure to live up to the revolutionary ideals on which it was founded.

Fuentes was born in Panama City on November 11, 1928. His father was a Mexican diplomat and Fuentes spent his childhood living in several Latin American countries. In 1936, the family moved to Washington, DC, where Fuentes enrolled in public school. He began writing as a teenager living in Santiago, Chile, making the conscious decision to write in Spanish and not English, though he was fluent in both. He returned to Mexico at the age of sixteen; he cited his grandmothers, who were well versed in Mexican folklore, as the inspirations for his fiction.

Fuentes continued to write while he earned a law degree, studying in both Mexico and Geneva, Switzerland. He was working for the government when his first novel, *When the Air is Clear*, was published in 1958.

Fuentes's 1985 novel, *The Old Gringo*, became a bestseller in the United States. The book was adapted into a film starring Gregory Peck and Jane Fonda in 1989. His last novel, *Destiny and Desire*, was published in 2011; *New York Times Book Review* critic Michael Wood likened it to a "playful revision" of *War and Peace*. Fuentes's body of work includes novels, short stories, essays, newspaper articles (the last published in a French journal on the day of his death), plays, and an opera.

Throughout his career, Fuentes was an outspoken critic of oppressive regimes across the globe. He served briefly as the ambassador to France but resigned in 1977 to protest the appointment of former Mexican president Gustavo Díaz Ordaz as the ambassador to Spain.

Fuentes died of an internal hemorrhage at Angeles del Pedregal hospital in Mexico City. He is survived by his wife, Silvia Lemus, and a daughter, Cecilia, from his first marriage to Rita Macedo. Macedo died in 1993. His two children with Lemus, Carlos and Natasha, are also deceased.

See Current Biography 1972.

Ben Gazzara

Born: New York, New York; August 28, 1930
Died: New York, New York; February 3, 2012
Occupation: Film and stage actor

Ben Gazzara was an Emmy Award–winning actor who played Brick in the original Broadway production of Tennessee Williams's *Cat on a Hot Tin Roof* in 1955. Gazzara, who studied acting with Lee Strasburg at the famed Actors Studio in New York City, was also a favorite collaborator of the filmmaker John Cassavetes.

Gazzara was born in New York City to Sicilian immigrants on August 28, 1930. He began acting at the Madison Square Boys Club at the age of eleven. As a high school graduate, Gazzara quit night school, where he was studying engineering, to join the Dramatic Workshop at the New School with Erwin Piscator. In 1951, he won a spot at the Actors Studio where he studied method acting with Strasburg, one of the studio's founders. Gazzara once described method acting to Ben Gross for the *New York Daily News* (8 Dec. 1963) as "the ability of an actor to think real thoughts on stage."

Gazzara appeared in a number of Broadway and Off-Broadway productions, including *Cat on a Hot Tin Roof* (starring opposite Burl Ives, 1955), *A Hatful of Rain* (1955), *Duet* (1975), *Hughie* (1975), and the revival of *Awake and Sing!* (2006). He was nominated for several Tony Awards.

In the 1960s, Gazzara starred in the television program *Run for Your Life* in which he played Paul Bryan, a man with a terminal disease who lived his last days to their fullest potential. He was nominated for two Emmy Awards in this role. He won an Emmy for the HBO movie *Hysterical Blindness* (2002) in which he starred opposite Gena Rowlands.

With Cassavetes, Gazzara appeared in the films *Husbands* (1970), *The Killing of a Chinese Bookie* (1976), and *Opening Night* (1977). Gazzara worked with several other noted film directors, including Otto Preminger (*Anatomy of a Murder*, 1959), Peter Bogdanovich (*They All Laughed*, 1981), the Coen Brothers (*The*

Big Lebowski, 1998), and Spike Lee (*The Son of Sam*, 1999).

Gazzara died of pancreatic cancer on February 3, 2012. He lived in Manhattan. He is survived by his third wife, Elke; his daughters Elizabeth and Danja; and his brother, Anthony.

See Current Biography 1967.

Julian Goodman

Born: Glasgow, Kentucky; May 1, 1922
Died: Juno Beach, Florida; July 2, 2012
Occupation: American television executive

Julian Goodman was a broadcast executive and longtime president of NBC, who started out at the network on the nightly news desk in Washington, DC, and rapidly rose through the ranks. He negotiated an unprecedented $1 million contract deal to keep Johnny Carson on *The Tonight Show*, helped to establish Chet Huntley and David Brinkley's long-running partnership anchoring the nightly news, and clashed with the Nixon administration over the network's coverage of the Vietnam War.

Goodman was born in Glasgow, Kentucky, on May 1, 1922. While in high school, he worked as a part-time reporter for the *Glasgow Daily News*. He enrolled in what is now Western Kentucky University, majoring in English, but left the university at the start of World War II to enlist in the US Army. In 1945, he began work as a radio newswriter for the NBC-owned radio station WRC, in Washington, DC. He enrolled at George Washington University, where he completed his bachelor's degree in economics in 1948.

In 1950 Goodman became manager of news and special events for NBC's radio network, and in 1952 and 1956 he was placed in charge of covering the Democratic and Republican conventions. In 1955 Goodman secured permission to broadcast congressional committee hearings. Goodman relocated to New York in 1959 after being promoted to director of news and public affairs for the NBC News division. In 1960 he was responsible for producing the second presidential debate between John F. Kennedy and Richard Nixon. Goodman was appointed vice president of NBC News in 1961, working to significantly expand the network's coverage by improving broadcasting on current events and implement new technology. He worked on the development of "instant news specials," which were short broadcasts that were developed within hours to cover current, fast-breaking news topics. Goodman also helped to create NBC's electronic news service, which the news network used to share film coverage of breaking news with affiliated stations.

In December 1965, Goodman was named executive vice president of NBC, and by January 1966 he was elected to the NBC board of directors. In March, he was promoted to the president of the company.

Goodman, who retired from the network in 1974, died of kidney failure in Juno Beach, Florida, on July 2, 2012. Goodman's wife of sixty-six years, Betty Davis, survives him, as do their four children, John, Jeffrey, Gregory, and Julie Koerner, and six grandchildren.

See Current Biography 1967.

Wilson Greatbatch

Born: Buffalo, New York; September 6, 1919
Died: Williamsville, New York; September 27, 2011
Occupation: Biomedical engineer, inventor of the pacemaker

Wilson Greatbatch was a biomedical engineer who first developed a pacemaker small enough to be implanted into a human chest in 1958. His discovery was the result of a happy accident. He was working at the Chronic Disease Research Institute with a doctor who was recording the sound of a heartbeat. Greatbatch was using silicon transistors to make an oscillator to record the sound. He grabbed the wrong resistor and plugged it into the circuit he was making. The circuit began pulsing the rhythm of a human heart. The discovery took years to perfect, but in 1960 Greatbatch and his collaborator, a surgeon named William C. Chardack, had successfully implanted the device inside a human. He perfected the battery life of the pacemaker in 1970. His company, Wilson Greatbatch Inc., is a leading supplier of pacemakers and other medical devices.

Greatbatch was born in Buffalo, New York, on September 6, 1919; he was named in honor of President Woodrow Wilson. His father was a construction contractor from the United Kingdom. His mother was a secretary. Greatbatch was a radioman and then a tail gunner during World War II. The violence of the war led him to embrace religion. He worked briefly as a telephone repairman before attending Cornell University on the GI bill. He received his master's degree in engineering in 1957. While working on the pacemaker, Greatbatch quit his job and supported his family with $2,000 in savings and a large home vegetable garden. Greatbatch holds more than 150 patents, including those for a solar-powered canoe and tools used in AIDS research.

Greatbatch married his childhood sweetheart, Eleanor Wright, after he returned from the war. She died in January 2011.

Greatbatch died at his home in Williamsville, New York, on September 27, 2011. He is survived by his children Anne, Warren, Kenneth, and John; twelve grandchildren; and eight great-grandchildren. Another son, Peter, died in 1998.

See Current Biography Illustrated 2001.

Andy Griffith

Born: Mount Airy, North Carolina; June 1, 1926
Died: Manteo, North Carolina; July 3, 2012
Occupation: American actor

Andy Griffith's entertainment career spanned more than fifty years, with appearances on stage, in film, and on television. But after all his years in show business, Griffith is best known for his role as the affable Sheriff Andy Taylor on *The Andy Griffith Show*.

Andrew Samuel Griffith was born in the small town of Mount Airy, North Carolina, on June 1, 1926. As a child, he learned trombone and sang in his church. His pastor recommended him for a scholarship to the University of North Carolina at Chapel Hill, where Griffith earned a music degree. He graduated in 1949 and married Barbara Edwards. The couple took jobs as schoolteachers and in their spare time enjoyed performing at local theaters and clubs.

In 1953, Griffith was performing at a local civic club; the comedic monologue he gave that night was recorded and aired on a local radio station. It became a hit and Griffith was increasingly offered gigs at nightclubs and small roles on television.

In 1955 he was cast in the television production of *No Time for Sergeants*; he reprised the role later that year on Broadway. The play ran for almost two years and Griffith was nominated for a Tony Award for his performance. He earned his first film credit in 1957 with the lead role in *A Face in the Crowd*. His portrayal of the character's rapid fall from fame and emotional unraveling garnered Griffith critical acclaim, and he returned to Broadway appearing in the 1959 musical comedy *Destry Rides Again*, which earned Griffith his second Tony nomination.

In early 1960, Griffith created the down-home character of Sheriff Andy Taylor for a skit he performed on *The Danny Thomas Show*. The show's producer, Sheldon Leonard, offered Griffith his own sitcom based on the performance, and Griffith accepted after negotiating for 50 percent ownership of the show. *The Andy Griffith Show* first aired in 1960 and ran for eight years, never dropping out of the top-ten shows on television. Griffith was often confused with his character on the show, the even-tempered and wise sheriff of Mayberry, which he took as a great credit to his acting skill.

Throughout the 1970s, Griffith performed in three other short-lived television series and several made-for-TV movies, never matching the popularity of *The Andy Griffith Show*. In 1986, he landed the title role in the series *Matlock*, playing a tough-minded defense attorney. The show became immensely popular and ran until 1995.

In 1996, Griffith recorded the gospel album *I Love To Tell the Story: 25 Timeless Hymns*, which won a Grammy Award. A statue was erected in Raleigh, North Carolina, in 2002 to commemorate *The Andy Griffith Show* and was inscribed, "A simpler time, a sweeter place, a lesson, a laugh, a father and a son."

Griffith died at his home on Roanoke Island on July 3, 2012, following a heart attack. He is survived by his third wife, Cindi Knight Griffith, and a daughter from his first marriage, Dixie Nan Griffith. His son, Andrew Samuel Griffith Jr., died in 1996.

See Current Biography 1960.

Floyd D. Hall

Born: Lamar, Colorado; April 4, 1916
Died: Woodstock, Vermont; April 26, 2012
Occupation: Chief executive of Eastern Airlines, former airline pilot

Floyd D. Hall was a former airline pilot and executive who changed the fate of Trans World Airlines (TWA) but was unable to do the same with Eastern Airlines. He was born on April 4, 1916, in Lamar, Colorado, where his father owned a hotel. Hall, who had two brothers who also became pilots, learned to fly as a teenager in the late 1920s. He earned his bachelor of science degree from the University of Colorado in 1938. After a two-year training period, he accepted a job as a professional pilot at TWA, but soon after, he was called upon to serve during World War II, where he attained the rank of lieutenant colonel. After the war he studied business at the University of California, Los Angeles and the University of Michigan.

Hall returned to TWA as a pilot in 1946. He accepted his first management job at the airline in 1956. For the next several years, Hall rose through the ranks of the company. He introduced several successful ad campaigns and, as an executive in 1963, he was able to turn an $18 million profit after a $10.8 million deficit in 1962.

Hall was offered the chief executive position at Eastern Airlines in late 1963. The company was struggling but Hall was eager to accept the challenge; he introduced a new jet fleet and improved management. The airline showed signs of a turnaround during the late 1960s, but was never quite able to catch up to its competitors. Hall stepped down in 1975, reporting a net loss of $20.7 million. Eastern Airlines folded in 1991.

Hall's first marriage to the late Mary Feild ended in divorce. His wife Kimathea (née Griffis) died in 2000.

Hall died at a nursing home in Woodstock, Vermont, on April 26, 2012. He is survived by his daughter, Nancy Morton; his stepson, Nixon Griffis; five grandchildren; and eleven great-grandchildren.

See Current Biography 1970.

Marvin Hamlisch

Born: New York, New York; June 2, 1944
Died: Los Angeles, California; August 6, 2012
Occupation: American composer

Marvin Hamlisch was a prolific composer who scored the music for over forty feature films and several Broadway musicals He was awarded three Academy Awards, four Emmys, four Grammys, one Tony, two Golden Globes, and the 1976 Pulitzer Prize for drama. He is one of only eleven people to have won all the major creative prizes in the United States.

Hamlisch was born on June 2, 1944, in New York City. His father was an accordionist and, by the age of five, Hamlisch was able to play songs on the piano that he had heard on the radio. At the age of seven he became the youngest person to be accepted to the Juilliard School. He later attended Queens College in New York, earning his bachelor's degree in music and graduating cum laude. While in school, Hamlisch worked as a music counselor at a summer camp where he wrote music for shows put on by the campers. He later reworked one of these early songs, called "Travelin' Man," for Liza Minnelli, which she recorded on her first album.

At the age of twenty-one, Hamlisch had his first hit song with "Sunshine, Lollipops, and Rainbows," sung by Lesley Gore. In 1964, Hamlisch began work as an assistant on the Broadway musical productions of *Funny Girl* and *Fade Out—Fade In*. He met movie producer Sam Spiegel at a party in 1968 where he learned Spiegel was looking for music for a movie adaptation of John Cheever's short story "The Swimmer." Three days later, Hamlisch presented Spiegel with theme music he had written for the movie and was immediately hired. After scoring *The Swimmer*, he went on to write the music for a number of films, earning an Oscar nomination for his song "Life Is What You Make It" from the 1971 film *Kotch*.

One of Hamlisch's greatest successes came with his score for the film *The Way We Were* in 1973. The title song, written in collaboration with lyricists Marilyn and Alan Bergman and recorded by Barbra Streisand, became a number-one pop single. At the 1974 Academy Awards, Hamlisch set a record when he won all three of the music awards that year: best song and best original dramatic score for *The Way We Were* as well as best scoring for his adaptation of Scott Joplin's "The Entertainer" for *The Sting*. He went on to produce the music for *A Chorus Line* and earned a Tony Award and shared the Pulitzer Prize for drama for his work on the play. In 1994, Hamlisch garnered two Emmy Awards as the music director for Streisand's televised special *Barbra Streisand: The Concert*. In 2002 he was again nominated for a Tony Award, for best original musical score for *Sweet Smell of Success* with lyricist Craig Carnelia.

Hamlisch died in Los Angeles on August 6, 2012, following a brief illness. He is survived by his wife, Terre Blair whom he married in 1989.

See Current Biography 1976.

Václav Havel

Born: Prague, Czechoslovakia; October 5, 1936
Died: Hrádeček, Czech Republic; December 18, 2011
Occupation: Czech president, playwright, dissident

The Czech dissident and playwright Václav Havel inspired a generation of Czechs to dispose of Communist rule in the 1989 Velvet Revolution after the fall of the Berlin Wall. Havel provoked the oppressive regime in Prague with his essays and plays throughout the 1960s and 1970s. On several occasions, he was sent to prison for subversion. Once, for founding the human rights organization Charter 77, he was imprisoned for nearly four years. Havel's reputation as a political philosopher and artist grew in intellectual circles and abroad before it took hold in larger Czechoslovakia. He was at the forefront of the Prague demonstrations that led to the Velvet Revolution. When the peaceful revolution ended, Havel was installed as the country's first post-Communist president.

Havel, a fervent idealist and counterculture icon, took slowly to his new and more dignified position. He was known to sign his name with a small heart and ride a child's scooter through the corridors of the Prague Castle from where he governed. But Havel surprised his detractors, serving the office successfully for fourteen years. He resigned in 1992 as the country began to split, but was later elected as the first president of the Czech Republic. Havel reached out to the West and arranged for the withdrawal of Soviet troops from the country. For better or worse, he led by his own moral compass; campaigning for the rights of Gypsies (an unpopular stance) and condemning the financial gains of corrupt capitalists despite the Czech Republic's ostensibly smooth transition to a market democracy. He was succeeded by the more conservative Václav Klaus in 2003.

Havel was born to a wealthy family in Prague on October 5, 1936. His father was a successful commercial real-estate developer. When the Communists came to power in 1948, the government seized his family's property. Havel began his military service in 1957. He wrote his first play while in the army. Throughout the 1960s, Havel worked with the Theater on the Balustrade, first as a stagehand and then as a playwright. His play *The Garden Party* was performed in 1963. In 1968, New York's Public Theater invited him to a production of his play *In Memorandum*. The experience had a profound effect on him. Havel's plays were considered avant-garde comedies that mirrored the absurdities of life under a Communist regime. Havel, who also wrote a number of influential essays including "Power of the Powerless" in 1978, was incredibly prolific throughout this period. His writing was so influential that when he was imprisoned, he was allowed to write only letters about family matters to his wife, Olga. These letters were also later published—and revered—as *Letters to Olga* (1988).

After Havel retired from politics, he returned to writing. His play *Leaving* was produced in 2008. His memoirs include *Disturbing the Peace* (1991) and *To the Castle and Back* (2007).

Havel married the actress Olga Šplíchalová in 1964. She died of cancer in 1996. He married his second wife, actress Dagmar Veškrnová, the following year. He did not have any children.

A lifelong smoker, Havel died of complications from lung cancer at his cottage in northern Bohemia on December 18, 2011. He is survived by his second wife and his brother, Ivan.

See Current Biography 1985, 1995.

Ben W. Heineman

Born: Wausau, Wisconsin; February 10, 1914
Died: Waukesha, Wisconsin; August 5, 2012
Occupation: American businessman, corporate lawyer

Ben W. Heineman Sr. was a successful businessman and corporate lawyer who revitalized the Chicago and Northwestern Railway Company when he became chair of the troubled business in 1956. In addition to being an adept business leader, Heineman served at the local, state, and national levels of government as chair of a number of conferences and as advisor to President Lyndon B. Johnson, Illinois governor Adlai Stevenson, and Chicago mayor Richard Daley. Heineman also organized the sale of sixty-six acres of lakefront property in Milwaukee from his rail company to Milwaukee County, saving the land from private development; the land will remain open to public use in perpetuity.

Heineman was born on February 10, 1914, in Wausau, Wisconsin, where his grandfather had established a successful lumber business nearly forty-five years earlier. Heineman's father ran the family business until 1930, when the company went bankrupt following the Great Depression and his father committed suicide. Also in 1930, Heineman matriculated at the University of Michigan, where he remained until his junior year when he was accepted to Northwestern University Law School. He left Michigan without completing his bachelor's degree, graduating from Northwestern at the top of his class several years later.

From 1936 until 1941, Heineman worked for the Chicago law firm Levinson, Becker, Peebles and Swiren, specializing in corporate law. During this time, he contributed a number of highly regarded papers to the *Illinois Law Review*. Blind in one eye, Heineman was permanently deferred for military service during World War II, and he worked as the assistant general counsel with the Office of Price Administration, and later worked with the State Department on several assignments.

In 1951 Heineman was asked by Governor Stevenson to serve as special assistant district attorney in the investigation of a cigarette-tax fraud. Heineman prosecuted a number of high-profile cases against the racketeers. He was active in fundraising and organizational efforts for Stevenson's first presidential campaign, even acting as a speechwriter. In 1956, Heineman became chair of the board of the Chicago and Northwestern Railway; he introduced a number of new accounting techniques and returned the company to profitability. Heineman led the railway for nearly thirty years. He also served as chair of the White House Conference on Civil Rights in 1966 and on the Illinois Board of Higher Education from 1962 to 1969.

Heineman died in Waukesha, Wisconsin, on August 5, 2012, following a stroke. His wife of nearly seventy-five years, Natalie Goldstein Heineman, died in 2010. He is survived by his children, Ben Jr. and Martha Pieper; six grandchildren; and two great-grandchildren.

See Current Biography 1962.

Christopher Hitchens

Born: Portsmouth, United Kingdom; April 13, 1949
Died: Houston, Texas; December 15, 2011
Occupation: British-born American journalist, polemicist

Christopher Hitchens was a journalist and author, known for his sharp wit, incredible extemporaneous abilities, and fiery indictments of public figures ranging from former US secretary of state Henry Kissinger to Mother Teresa. He frequently attended parties and was rarely seen without a glass of liquor in his hand or a cigarette dangling from his lips. Still, his appearance—often disheveled after a night of debauchery—was at odds with his voracious intelligence. He began following the news at the age of seven and, as a young man at Oxford, embraced socialism and fell in with a literary circle that included Martin Amis, James Fenton, and Ian McEwan. He wrote columns for both the *New Statesman* and the *Nation*; later in life, he wrote a column for *Vanity Fair*. His first book, *Cyprus* (1984), a history of the country where he spent time as a correspondent, marked the beginning of a prolific career.

Hitchens was born in Portsmouth, United Kingdom, on April 13, 1949. His father was a career officer in the British navy. Hitchens was the first in his family to attend private school. Despite his conservative upbringing, he turned toward leftist politics at the age of fifteen with his objection to the war in Vietnam. He attended Balliol College, Oxford and joined the International Socialists, a Trotskyite party. He graduated with a degree in philosophy, politics, and economics in 1970. Hitchens began his career reviewing books for the *New Statesman* while still a student.

During his career, Hitchens became a US citizen and surprised his friends and readers when he also embraced the US war in Iraq. As a personality, he was often invited on television programs where he relished debates with his detractors like the conservative host Sean Hannity. As a writer, he wrote about his love of the writer George Orwell, his hatred for Henry Kissinger (whom he called a war criminal), and his fervent atheism. His last book, published months before his death, was a collection of essays called *Arguably*.

Hitchens married Eleni Meleagrou in 1981. The marriage ended in divorce, but their children, Alexander and Sophia, survive him. Hitchens is also survived by his second wife, Carol Blue; their daughter, Antonia; and his brother, Peter.

Hitchens died while undergoing treatment for esophageal cancer on December 15, 2011, at a medical center in Houston, Texas. He was diagnosed with the disease only a year earlier, while on a tour promoting his memoir *Hitch-22* (2010).

See Current Biography 1999.

E. J. Hobsbawm

Born: Alexandria, Egypt; June 9, 1917
Died: London, England; October 1, 2012
Occupation: British historian

E. J. Hobsbawm is considered one of the greatest historians of modern times and the most distinguished Marxist historian in Great Britain. His influential three-volume economic history of industrial capitalism, *The Age of Revolution: Europe 1789–1848*; *The Age of Capital: 1848–1875*; and *The Age of Empire: 1875–1914*, encapsulated what Hobsbawm referred to as the "long nineteenth century," a period that ranged from the French Revolution in 1789 to World War I in 1914. In 1994, he published the concluding portion, *The Age of Extremes: A History of the World, 1914–1991*. Hobsbawm is also well-known for his analysis of the French Revolution, the British Industrial Revolution, and the labor movements of the nineteenth century.

Hobsbawm was born in Egypt in 1917 to European Jewish parents. The family moved to Vienna in 1919 after the end of World War I. When Hobsbawm was twelve, his father died suddenly, and his mother died of lung disease two years later in 1931. Hobsbawm was sent to live with relatives in Berlin, Germany, but with the increase in Hitler's power throughout Germany in the 1930s, Hobsbawm was sent to live with another group of relatives in London. He was enrolled in the St. Marylebone Grammar School and then studied at King's College in Cambridge. He received his PhD in history from Cambridge University.

Hobsbawm joined the Communist Party in 1936. After World War II, he continued to be a devoted member and advocate for the party and remained so for the duration of his life and career as an eminent historian.

In 1947, after serving in the Royal Engineers and the Royal Army Educational Corps, Hobsbawm was a history professor at Birkbeck, University of London and became president of the college in 2002. Hobsbawm was named a Fellow of the British Academy in 1976, and in 1998, British Prime Minister Tony Blair appointed him to the Order of the Companion of Honour, one of Britain's highest civilian awards, which recognizes contributions to national service, especially in the advancement of culture.

On October 1, 2012, Hobsbawm died in London from pneumonia. He was ninety-five years old. He is survived by his wife, Marlene; three children; seven grandchildren; and one great-grandchild.

See *Current Biography* 2003.

Celeste Holm

Born: New York, New York; April 29, 1917
Died: New York, New York; July 15, 2012
Occupation: American stage, film, and television actress

Celeste Holm was an Academy Award–winning actress best known for her performance in *Gentleman's Agreement* (1947), for which she won the Oscar for best-supporting actress in addition to a Golden Globe. She was also a two-time Academy Award–nominee for her roles in *Come to the Stable* (1949) and *All About Eve* (1950). But Holmes was not only a decorated film actress—she was also a notable presence on the stage and appeared in Broadway productions such as *The Time of Your Life* (1939) and, most notably, her role as Ado Annie in the musical *Oklahoma* (1943), which made her a Broadway star.

Celeste Holm studied theater at the University of Chicago before she began her professional acting career in a production of *Hamlet* as an understudy to Leslie Howards's role of Ophelia. She did not make her Broadway debut, however, until the 1938 production of *Gloriana*, which opened the door to a successful career on Broadway. She made the transition to film in 1946, when 20th Century Fox offered her a movie deal in *Three Little Girls in Blue*.

In 1954, after a successful career in film, Celeste Holm moved to television with the series, *Honestly, Celeste*, and, in 1958, *The Celeste Holm Show*. Overall, her acting career spread across film, the stage, and television, and her impressive filmography includes appearances—both minor and major roles—in well over one hundred productions. She received numerous awards, including the Sarah Siddons Award for theater, the Lifetime Achievement Award by Brandeis University's SunDeis Film Festival in 2006, and was inducted into the American Theater Hall of Fame in 1992. She also served on the National Council of Arts after being appointed by President Reagan in 1982.

In addition to a distinguished acting career, Celeste Holm was acclaimed for her philanthropic work. She performed for mentally ill patients in psychiatric awards and was on the board for the National Mental Health Association. She also raised money for the United Nations Children's Fund (UNICEF) and helped spread awareness of their mission to protect the rights of children.

On July 15, 2012, Celeste Holm died of a heart attack in her Upper Park West apartment in New York City. She was ninety-five years old. Holm is survived by her husband Frank Basile; two sons, Daniel and Ted, and seven grandchildren.

See *Current Biography* 1944.

Whitney Houston

Born: Newark, New Jersey; August 9, 1963
Died: Beverly Hills, California; February 11, 2012
Occupation: Pop singer, actress

The Grammy Award–winning singer and actress Whitney Houston left an enduring legacy as one of the twentieth century's greatest voices. Houston, who boasts familial ties to Aretha Franklin (her godmother) and Dionne Warwick (her cousin), set Billboard records throughout the late 1980s with singles like "Saving All My Love for You," "How Will I Know," "The Greatest Love of All," and "I Wanna Dance with Somebody (Who Loves Me)." She made her acting debut in the 1992 film *The Bodyguard* opposite Kevin Costner. The film's soundtrack includes the song that became her signature, a cover of Dolly Parton's "I Will Always Love You." Houston began a turbulent and abusive marriage to the singer Bobby Brown in 1992; around the same time, she began using marijuana and cocaine. By the early 2000s, Houston's career and her incredible voice were on the decline. She attempted several comebacks, more personal than professional. Her albums sold well but in her live performances she appeared unstable. Houston briefly starred in a reality television show about her family life called "Being Bobby Brown." The couple's marriage ended in 2007.

Houston was born on August 9, 1963, in Newark, New Jersey. Her mother, who survives her, is Cissy Houston, a former back-up singer for Aretha Franklin. Houston began singing in church when she was nine. As a teenager she began a modeling career and sang back-up for Lou Rawls and Chaka Khan, among others. Still, Houston's parents insisted she finish high school and she graduated in 1981. She was discovered by Clive Davis, the president and founder of Arista Records who become her mentor, at a New York City club called Sweetwaters in 1983. Davis and Houston spent the next two years crafting her debut album *Whitney Houston* (1985), which yielded three number one singles. As her fame grew, Houston extended her musical reach to R&B and gospel. Regardless of genre, all of Houston's albums were bestsellers. As an actress, her other films include *Waiting to Exhale* (1995) and *The Preacher's Wife* (1996).

Houston died on February 11, 2012, in Beverly Hills, California. She was staying at the Beverly Hilton hotel with friends and family and was scheduled to attend a pre-Grammy party thrown by Davis that night. Paramedics were unable to revive Houston after she was found unconscious in her hotel bathtub. The cause of death was later ruled to be drowning and the effects of heart disease and cocaine use. In addition to her mother, Houston is survived by her teenage daughter, Bobbi Kristina.

See Current Biography 1986.

Robert Hughes

Born: Sydney, Australia; July 28, 1938
Died: New York, New York; August 6, 2012
Occupation: Art critic, documentarian, historian

As a college student at the University of Sydney, Robert Hughes became involved with the Sydney Push, a collective of left-wing political commentators, writers, artists, and academics. He left school in the early 1960s and began work as an art critic for the Sydney-based publication the *Observer*. Hughes relocated to London in 1965, where he continued working as an art critic. His work appeared in the *Times*, the *Spectator*, and the *Daily Telegraph*. In 1966, Hughes published a history of Australian painting entitled *The Art of Australia*.

Hughes moved to New York City in 1970 after taking a position as art critic for *Time* magazine. Through associates in New York, he began working on various film and television projects. Hughes narrated the 1975 film *Protected*, which is an exposé of the native population of Australia's Palm Island.

In 1980, Hughes created the BBC documentary television series *The Shock of the New*, focusing on controversial and notable works of contemporary art. Critics praised the project for its sense of humor and its ability to explain the confounding nature of modern works of art. *The Shock of the New* was released with a companion series of books.

Hughes was involved in numerous film and television projects throughout his career, including *American Visions* (1997) and *Goya: Crazy Like a Genius* (2002). He received an International Emmy Award in 2009 for his work on *The Mona Lisa Curse* (2008).

In 1987, Hughes published *The Fatal Shore*, a history of Australia that traces the country's origins as a prison colony for the British Empire. The book was awarded the 1987 Duff Cooper Prize and the 1988 WH Smith Literary Award. In 2011, *Time* magazine chose the book for its All-TIME 100 Nonfiction Books list, which is an annual selection of the magazine's choices for the top one hundred nonfiction books written in English since 1923.

Throughout his career, Hughes remained an active commentator on Australian politics. He was a vociferous supporter of Australia's Republican movement, which seeks to end the country's status as a constitutional monarchy under the Queen of England. Hughes died at the age of seventy-four in New York City on August 6, 2012. He is survived by his third wife, Doris Downes.

See Current Biography 1987.

Hal Jackson

Born: Charleston, South Carolina; ca. November 3, 1915
Died: New York, New York; May 23, 2012
Occupation: Disc jockey, radio executive

Hal Jackson was a prominent disc jockey and radio executive for over fifty years. He was also a civil rights fundraiser and sports broadcaster. He began his career in Washington, DC, where he was the first African American disc jockey to be nationally broadcasted on network radio. In 1971, he became one of the first African American radio station owners in New York City. He was also the first African American inducted to the National Association of Broadcasters Hall of Fame in 1990. Jackson continued to host his popular New York program, begun in the 1980s, called *Sunday Morning Classics* until his death.

Jackson was born the youngest of five children on approximately November 3, 1915, in Charleston, South Carolina. (Like many Southern black children during that time, his birth was never officially recorded.) His parents died when he was a child and he lived with relatives in New York, Charleston, and Washington, DC. He attended Howard University, where he broadcasted sports events, though he did not graduate. In 1939, Jackson began a radio program called *The Bronze Review* out of WINX, a station owned by the *Washington Post*. It was fifteen minutes long. He landed the gig by appealing to an advertiser after being told by an executive that the station would never hire an African American host. In 1949, he hosted a short-lived television variety show. He appeared on a program broadcast out of Howard University. By the 1950s, he was hosting three radio programs in New York. His career was briefly rocked by the payola scandal—in which disc jockeys were accused of accepting gifts from record companies in exchange for airtime—but the charges were later dropped.

In 1949, Jackson established his familiar smooth-talking persona in a program called *The House that Jack Built*; the name is also the title of his autobiography, cowritten with Jim Haskins and published in 2001.

Jackson died on May 23, 2012, in New York City. He is survived by his fourth wife, Debi, the cohost of *Sunday Morning Classics*. His previous marriages ended in divorce. He is also survived by his children, Jane, Jewell, and Hal Jackson Jr., as well as his grandchildren and great-grandchildren.

See Current Biography 2002.

Nicholas deB. Katzenbach

Born: Philadelphia, Pennsylvania; January 17, 1922
Died: Skillman, New Jersey; May 8, 2012
Occupation: Former US attorney general

Nicholas deB. Katzenbach was an influential lawyer during the 1960s. As attorney general in the Johnson administration, he defended the 1964 Civil Rights Act before the Supreme Court. Before that, in 1963, Katzenbach faced down Alabama governor George C. Wallace on the steps of the University of Alabama in Tuscaloosa to admit two African American students—Vivian Malone and James Hood. In 1965, he sought a federal court order that barred Alabama officials from interfering with Dr. Martin Luther King's march to Selma.

Katzenbach was born Nicholas deBelleville Katzenbach on January 17, 1922, in Philadelphia, Pennsylvania. His father was a former New Jersey attorney general and his mother served on the state's board of education. Katzenbach attended Phillips Exeter Academy in New Hampshire and then Princeton University in 1939. After the attack on Pearl Harbor, he enlisted in the Air Force where he became a second lieutenant and navigator. After he was shot down during a bombing mission in 1943, he was captured by the Italians. He escaped imprisonment twice and was turned over to the Germans. According to his *New York Times* obituary, Katzenbach read over four hundred books during his captivity. When he was discharged, with the rank of first lieutenant, he convinced Princeton administrators to graduate him based on his reading as a prisoner of war. He graduated from Yale Law School in 1947 and was a Rhodes scholar in England.

Katzenbach was studying international law and teaching at Yale and the University of Chicago when he was approached to join the Kennedy administration as Attorney General Robert Kennedy's assistant attorney general in 1962. Katzenbach worked to protect the voices of the civil rights movement and wrote a legal briefing about the Cuban missile crisis. After President Kennedy's assassination, Katzenbach wrote a memo in which he determined that Lee Harvey Oswald was the lone killer. He succeeded Robert Kennedy as the US attorney general in the administration of President Lyndon B. Johnson in 1965. He resigned in 1966 after altercations with J. Edgar Hoover, the head of the FBI. He resigned from any involvement in the State Department in 1968, after the election of President Richard Nixon.

Katzenbach joined the International Business Machines (IBM) Corporation as a senior vice president. He represented the company in a thirteen-year antitrust suit filed by President Johnson that was later dropped by President Ronald Reagan.

Katzenbach died on May 8, 2012, at his home in Skillman, New Jersey. He is survived by his wife, Lydia, and his children, Christopher, John (the novelist), Mimi, and Anne. He is also survived by six grandchildren.

See Current Biography 1965.

John Keegan

Born: London, England; May 15, 1934
Died: Kilmington, England; August 2, 2012
Occupation: Writer, lecturer, historian

Sir John Desmond Patrick Keegan is best known for his work as a military historian. Over a career that spanned sixty years, he published dozens of books on the history and analysis of warfare. In addition, he served as a war correspondent for the London-based *Daily Telegraph*.

Born in 1934, Keegan suffered from tuberculosis as a child. The health effects of the disease prevented him from joining the military. Keegan's father was a World War I veteran, and he developed an interest in warfare at a young age. After graduating from Balliol College in Oxford in 1953, he took a position at the American Embassy in London. Keegan served as a lecturer of military history at the Royal Military Academy Sandhurst for over twenty-five years.

Keegan's influential work, *The Face of Battle*, surveying the history and methods of the English military at the battles of Agincourt, Waterloo, and the Somme, was published in 1976. He was a prolific writer, producing works that detailed military strategy and the psychology of warfare ranging from World War I to the Iraq War. He published two books on World War II, *The Second World War* (1989), and *Atlas of the Second World War* (1989). Keegan's work covered naval, ground, and air warfare. In 2002, he published *Winston Churchill*, an acclaimed biography of the British wartime leader.

Keegan served as a lecturer at Sandhurst until 1986, when he became defense editor at the *Daily Telegraph*. During his career at the newspaper, he also served as a visiting professor at Princeton University and Vassar College. As a journalist, Keegan became widely known for his staunch support of the US–led military action aimed at toppling Iraqi dictator Saddam Hussein. In 2000, he was knighted by the Queen of England in recognition for his contributions to the field of military history. Keegan died on August 2, 2012, at the age of seventy-eight.

See Current Biography 1989.

David Kelly

Born: Dublin, Ireland; July 11, 1929
Died: Dublin, Ireland; February 12, 2012
Occupation: Irish actor

David Kelly was an Irish character actor who was best known for roles he played later in life, including Grandpa Joe in Tim Burton's *Charlie and the Chocolate Factory* (2005) and the lead in the 1998 comedy *Waking Ned Devine*. In 2005, he was presented a lifetime achievement award by the Irish Film and Television Academy.

Kelly was born on July 11, 1929, in Dublin, Ireland. He began acting at the age of twelve at the Gaiety Theatre in Dublin. He was a stage actor working in Dublin and New York before making his film debut with a bit part in the 1958 British film *Dublin Nightmare*. He later transitioned to television. One of his most memorable roles was on the BBC show *Fawlty Towers* in the 1970s.

Kelly died on February 12, 2012, in Dublin. He is survived by his wife, the actor Laurie Morton, and their two children.

See Current Biography 2005.

Har Gobind Khorana

Born: Raipur, India (now Pakistan); ca. January 9, 1922
Died: Concord, Massachusetts; November 9, 2011
Occupation: Indian biochemist

The Nobel Prize–winning biochemist Har Gobind Khorana made landmark discoveries in genetics and, in 1972, constructed the first artificial gene. He was born in a village called Raipur in the Punjab region of India, now a part of eastern Pakistan. His family was poor but valued education; his first four years of school took place with the village teacher under a tree. He studied chemistry at Punjab University in Lahore. For his doctorate and postdoctoral studies in organic chemistry, Khorana moved to Liverpool, United Kingdom, and Zurich, Switzerland,

where he was interested in proteins and nucleic acids.

Khorana received the Nobel Prize in Physiology or Medicine in 1968, along with Robert W. Holley and Marshall W. Nirenberg, for demonstrating how genetically encoded proteins carry out the functions of a living cell. In the 1970s, Khorana created the first artificial cell and made strides in technical biochemistry that laid the foundation for genetic engineering and biotechnology.

Khorana served as a professor at the Massachusetts Institute of Technology from 1970 to 2007. He received the National Medal of Science in 1987.

Khorana died on November 9, 2011, in Concord, Massachusetts. His wife, Esther, died in 2001; a daughter, Emily Anne, died in 1979. He is survived by his children Julia Elizabeth and Dave Roy.

See Current Biography 1970.

Kim Jong Il

Born: Siberia, Russia; February 16, 1941 or 1942
Died: Seoul, North Korea; December 17, 2011
Occupation: North Korean head of state

Kim Jong Il, the elusive Communist leader of North Korea who was known to his people as "Dear Leader," pursued a nuclear arsenal even in the face of widespread starvation and the near-collapse of his country. Kim's origins have been heavily mythologized. He is believed to have been born on February 16, 1941, in a camp in Siberia where his father was being trained by the Soviet military (although all official records in North Korea indicate that he was born in 1942). His father, Kim Il Sung, who is known to North Koreans as the "Great Leader," established a Communist government in North Korea in 1948. The younger Kim graduated from Kim Il Sung University in 1964. During his youth, Kim rose through the party hierarchy and developed a reputation for his love of women and lavish parties.

Kim became a member of North Korea's Central Committee in 1980. He was suspected of ordering a bombing attack on Rangoon, Burma, which killed several South Korean cabinet members in 1983. He was also linked to the deaths of two American soldiers in 1976. In 1991, he became the commander of the country's armed forces.

Kim Il Sung died unexpectedly in 1994. Few believed that Kim Jong Il would be the son—he has two brothers—to replace his father. In the 1990s, the country began a program to develop nuclear missiles. After taking power, Kim tested one of the missiles over

Japan. Other countries panicked. "On the brink of collapse and with its people racked by starvation, North Korea's most successful business is one that involves pulling cash and aid out of South Korea, the US, and Japan in exchange for abandoning an arms buildup," Tim Larimer wrote for *Time* magazine (23 Aug. 1999).

During the 1990s, President Bill Clinton engaged in talks with Kim, but when President George W. Bush took office in 2001, he refused to continue a precedent of what he considered to be appeasement. In the years before Kim's death, the country was building a uranium enrichment plant and testing missiles.

Kim was in poor health as early as 2008. He died of a heart attack on December 17, 2011, while traveling on his train. His successor is his youngest son, Kim Jong Un.

See Current Biography 2002.

Thomas Kinkade

Born: Placerville, California; January 19, 1958
Died: Los Gatos, California; April 6, 2012
Occupation: American painter

Thomas Kinkade was a painter who successfully mass-marketed his work. As the cofounder of Media Arts Group Inc. (now called the Thomas Kinkade Company), Kinkade licensed his paintings—often idealized rural or suburban landscapes with religious connotations—to appear on mugs, tote bags, greeting cards, and furniture. A self-described "painter of light" because his paintings appeared to glow, Kinkade favored sentimental scenes. Though his work was unpopular with critics, Kinkade once estimated that his work could be found in some form in one household for every twenty in the United States, according to his *New York Times* obituary.

Kinkade was born in Placerville, California, on January 19, 1958, and was attracted to art at a young age. He studied art at the University of California, Berkeley and then the Art Center College of Design in Pasadena where he met fellow artist James Gurney. The two young artists traveled cross-country after graduation, sketching local landscapes. In 1982, they cowrote a book called *The Artist's Guide to Sketching*. The two also worked on the 1983 animated film *Fire and Ice*.

In the 1980s, Kinkade experimented with luminism, the technique that makes his paintings appear to light up from within, and began to paint the scenes for which he became famous. He also became a born-again Christian. Tired of the gallery system, Kinkade founded the

Media Arts Group in 1990 and soon became a multimillionaire.

Kinkade died from an accidental overdose of alcohol and Valium on April 6, 2012. He is survived by his wife, Nanette, and their four children.

See Current Biography 2000.

Jack Layton

Born: Montreal, Canada; July 18, 1950
Died: Toronto, Canada; August 22, 2011
Occupation: Canadian politician

Jack Layton was the head of the New Democrat Party (NDP) in Canada. Born in Montreal on July 18, 1950, Layton was raised in the English-speaking Hudson neighborhood. He came from a prosperous family and a long line of politicians. He studied political science and economics at McGill University and pursued his master's and doctorate degrees at York University in Toronto.

Layton was elected to the Toronto city council in 1982 where he was known as an outspoken liberal politician. In 1985, he switched his focus from protesting problems to solving them through the legislature. In 2001, Layton ran for mayor in Toronto and lost. In 2003, Layton became the leader of the NDP. He is credited with transforming the party from one of internal strife to an effective organizational body. He is the author of the 2006 book *Speaking Out Louder: Ideas That Work for Canadians*. Before his death, he was also an active member of Parliament.

Layton died at his home in Toronto on August 22, 2011, of cancer. Layton's first marriage ended in divorce but produced two children, Sarah and Michael, who survive him. He is also survived by his wife, Olivia Chow, also a politician, whom he married in 1988.

See Current Biography 2009.

Evelyn Lear

Born: Brooklyn, New York; January 8, 1926
Died: Sandy Spring, Maryland; July 1, 2012
Occupation: American opera singer

Evelyn Lear was a celebrated American operatic soprano. She appeared in over forty productions, including *Rueben, Rueben, Alkmene,* and *Die Verlobung.* One of her more notable roles, however, was in the 1960 production of Berg's *Lulu* in Austria. Despite having only three weeks to prepare for the title role, her performance brought her international recognition, and she was asked to play the role again at the 1962 Vienna Festival under the direction of Karl Böhm. Her career ascended dramatically after that production, and in 1966, she won a Grammy award for Best Opera Recording for Berg's *Wozzeck*.

In addition to Hunter College and New York University, Lear attended the world-renowned Juilliard School of Music in New York City. She received a Fulbright scholarship—a scholarly award that offers grants to students to study internationally—along with her husband and fellow Juilliard classmate, Thomas Stewart, to study at the Hochschule für Musik und Theater München (University of Music and Performing Arts Munich) in Germany.

Lear began her professional operatic career in Berlin in Richard Strauss's production *Ariadne auf Naxos*. She is also well-known for her long-term affiliation with another Strauss opera, *Der Rosenkavalier*, where she showed her versatility by singing all three lead female roles in the production.

Lear performed at many of the world's famous opera houses—including La Scala in Milan, Italy; the Metropolitan Opera in New York City; and London's Royal Opera House. In addition to a Grammy, the Senate of West Berlin bestowed upon Lear the title of *Kammersängerin*, which is the German honorific title for notable singers. The Salzburg Festival in Austria also presented her with the Max Reinhardt Award.

Lear made her final professional performance at the Metropolitan Opera in 1985. In 1999, Lear and her husband formed the Evelyn Lear and Thomas Stewart Emerging Singers Program (ESP) in partnership with the Wagner Society of Washington, DC. ESP continues to help rising singers by offering vocal education and performance opportunities.

On July 1, 2012, Evelyn Lear died in a nursing home in Sandy Spring, Maryland. She was eighty-six years old. Lear is survived by her son, Jan; a daughter, Bonni Stewart; and two grandchildren.

See Current Biography 1973.

Bernard Lovell

Born: Oldland Common, England; August 31, 1913
Died: Swettenham Village, England; August 6, 2012
Occupation: English physicist and radio astronomer

Sir Bernard Lovell was an innovator in physics and radio astronomy who lent his skills to the British effort in World War II and occupied a uniquely independent position in the United States and Soviet space race.

Lovell was born near Bristol, England, in 1913. He earned his bachelor and doctorate degrees from the University of Bristol, and upon receiving his doctorate, he was named assistant lecturer in physics at Manchester University. Following a stint developing guidance radar for British bombers during World War II, Lovell began work on an ambitious, 250-foot radio dish on land owned by the university. It would later be named the Jodrell Bank radio telescope.

Lovell is best known for creating the Jodrell Bank radio telescope and for founding the Jodrell Bank Centre for Astrophysics. At the time, the Jodrell telescope was the only antenna in the world capable of tracking rockets as they travelled through space.

One of Lovell's intended uses for the radio telescope was to track space satellites. The chance to test his creation came two months after its completion, when the Soviet's launched the satellite Sputnik 1 in October 1957. Western officials called upon Lovell and his telescope to track the rudimentary satellite through its launch. Then, twenty-two days into the satellite's orbit, the battery powering its radio signal ran out, and the Soviets then turned to Lovell for help tracking it during the next three months of orbit.

Lovell was the author of more than two dozen published books and lectures, and he frequently made appearances on BBC science programming. He became a fellow of the Royal Society in 1955 and was knighted in 1961. In 2011, the Jodrell observatory was nominated by the United Kingdom for UNESCO (United Nations Educational, Scientific and Cultural Organization) World Heritage Site status.

Lovell died at his home in Swettenham Village, England. He was ninety-eight. He is survived by four children, fourteen grandchildren, and fourteen great-grandchildren.

See Current Biography 1959.

Lynn Margulis

Born: Chicago, Illinois; March 5, 1938
Died: Amherst, Massachusetts; November 22, 2011
Occupation: American microbiologist

Microbiologist Lynn Margulis spearheaded a controversial theory known as serial endosymbiotic theory in 1967. After enduring years of ridicule, Margulis's theory was accepted in the 1980s; her work fundamentally changed the way scientists view evolution. Lynn Margulis was born Lynn Alexander on March 5, 1938, in Chicago, Illinois. She graduated from the University of Chicago, where she met her first husband, the cosmologist Carl Sagan, at the age of eighteen. They married in 1957. Margulis received her master's degree in genetics and zoology from the University of Wisconsin, and her doctorate degree from the University of California, Berkeley.

In Wisconsin, Margulis became interested in instances in which a cell's makeup could not be directly traced to the genes within a cell's nucleus. She hypothesized that these cells evolved as a result of symbiotic relationships with bacteria. Her findings were published in 1967 in the *Journal of Theoretical Biology*. The theory was widely unpopular for many years because it was in direct conflict with evolutionary theories of the day, including chance mutation. She wrote a book called *Origin of Eukaryotic Cells*, which was revised in 1981 as *Symbiosis in Cell Evolution*.

Margulis taught at Boston University for twenty-two years and then joined the faculty at the University of Massachusetts, Amherst. Her marriage to Sagan ended in divorce, as did her second marriage to chemist Thomas N. Margulis. She is survived by her children, Jennifer Margulis, Jeremy Sagan, Zachary Margulis-Ohnuma, and Dorion Sagan—a science writer who often collaborated with his mother. Other survivors include three sisters, three half-brothers, and nine grandchildren.

Margulis died on November 22, 2011, in Amherst, Massachusetts, after suffering a hemorrhagic stroke.

See Current Biography 1992.

Ante Markovic

Born: Konjic, Kingdom of Serbs, Croats and Slovenes; November 25, 1924
Died: Zagreb, Croatia; November 28, 2011
Occupation: Former Yugoslav prime minister

Ante Markovic was the last prime minister of Yugoslavia before the country split into seven independent states. Markovic was born on November 25, 1924, in a town called Konjic, which is now in Bosnia and Herzegovina. He joined the League of Communist Youth and fought with Josip Broz Tito's resistance army against the Germans and Italians during World War II. He received an electrical engineering degree from Zagreb University. Markovic rose through the ranks of the Communist Party, and in 1989, Yugoslavia's collective presidency, representing six republics and two provinces, named him prime minister. Economic and ethnic tensions were coming to a head among the states; the presidency hoped that Markovic could hold the country together. After Croatia, Slovenia, and Macedonia declared independence and ignited a decade-long war, Markovic resigned his post in 1991.

Markovic died in Zagreb, Croatia, on November 28, 2011.

See Current Biography 1991.

Paul Winston McCracken

Born: Richland, Iowa; December 29, 1915
Died: Ann Arbor, Michigan; August 3, 2012
Occupation: American economist, teacher

Paul Winston McCracken served as chair of President Nixon's Council of Economic Advisors (CEA) from 1969 to 1971. Previously, he had served as an economic advisor for presidents John F. Kennedy and Lyndon B. Johnson.

Born in Iowa in 1915, McCracken earned a bachelor's degree at William Penn University in 1937. While teaching at Berea College in Kentucky, he earned his master's degree in economics from Harvard University in 1942. In 1943, he took a position as a researcher with the Federal Reserve Bank of Minneapolis and remained in that position until 1948. After earning his PhD in economics, McCracken became a faculty member at the Ross School of Business at the University of Michigan.

During his time at the University of Michigan, McCracken served as an economic adviser to the Kennedy and Johnson administrations. President Nixon then named him to his Council of Economic Advisers with the aim of curbing rising inflation in the US economy. McCracken advocated for centrist policies to combat inflation, serving as an arbiter between conservative, market-based approaches and other advisors who were pushing for new tax policies. Although McCracken theorized that a managed reduction in economic growth would alleviate inflation, prices continued to increase. In order to prevent a serious recession and stabilize the economy, Nixon chose to detach the value of US currency from the gold standard and put temporary price controls in place. McCracken suggested that Nixon take a more gradual approach to control inflation, and although Nixon's abrupt economic measures may have helped earn him reelection in 1972, they did not help to curb the nation's inflation. Slow growth and high inflation continued to plague the American economy until the 1980s.

In 1971, McCracken returned to teach at the University of Michigan and retired in 1986. Over the course of his career, McCracken published dozens of economic papers and articles, and in 1996 he wrote an essay recounting Nixon's economic policies and his experiences as a presidential advisor.

McCracken died on August 3, 2012, at the age of ninety-six. He is survived by two daughters, Linda Langer and Paula McCracken.

See Current Biography 1969.

George McGovern

Born: Avon, South Dakota; July 19, 1922
Died: Sioux Falls, South Dakota; October 21, 2012
Occupation: American senator and candidate for president

A champion of liberal progressivism in the Senate and an infamously unsuccessful presidential candidate, George McGovern was a figurehead of the anti–Vietnam War movement who helped define the values of the Democratic Party for years to come. In the presidential election of 1972, McGovern, the Democratic nominee, lost forty-nine of fifty states to incumbent President Richard Nixon. His campaign—though staffed with political stars-to-be, including a young Bill and Hillary Rodham Clinton—was marred by a haphazard national convention, and the disparaging of his running mate, Senator Thomas F. Eagleton, over electroshock therapy he received in the 1960s.

McGovern was elected to his first of three terms as a senator from South Dakota in 1962. While his legislative impact was minimal, he voted a consistently liberal line in favor of civil rights and antipoverty bills. He played a key role in the development and expansion of food stamp and nutrition programs, and was an unabashedly vocal opponent of the war in Vietnam. It was this ardent antiwar platform that McGovern rode to the Democratic nomination in 1972. In later years, McGovern would speculate that it was a disregard for image, and an insistence on an issues-driven campaign that led to his as-yet unrivaled defeat at the polls. He was painted by his Republican opponents as spineless and antimilitary, a leftist radical outside the mainstream of America. But his reputation as a voice on agricultural issues, and the unintended advantage afforded to Democrats nationwide following the Watergate scandal, led him to a third term as senator in 1974.

The son of a Methodist pastor, McGovern was born in Avon, South Dakota, a town of about six hundred, on July 19, 1922. He was enrolled at Daktota Wesleyan University when Japanese forces attacked Pearl Harbor. The young McGovern enlisted in the Army Air Corps in 1942, and was tasked with flying B-24 bombers in thirty-five missions over Austria, Germany, and Italy. He earned a Distinguished Flying Cross for his successful crash landing of his plane after sustaining damage from enemy fire. He married Eleanor Stegeberg in 1943, and resumed his studies at Dakota Wesleyan following his discharge from the military in 1945, graduating the following year with a BA, magna cum laude.

After earning his master's degree in history from Northwestern University, McGovern continued working on his doctoral dissertation for Northwestern while teaching political science and history at Dakota Wesleyan. He earned his PhD in history in 1953, but left teaching that year when he accepted the position of executive secretary of the South Dakota Democratic Party. In this role, he built a strong base in a typically Republican state, travelling relentlessly to set up county organizations and build support among farmers and other New Deal Democrats. He was elected to the House of Representatives in 1956, becoming the first Democratic congressman from South Dakota in more than two decades. McGovern followed his two-term stint in the House with an unsuccessful bid for Senate against sitting Republican Karl E. Mundy. He became special assistant to President John F. Kennedy in 1961, and was appointed as director of Kennedy's Food for Peace program.

McGovern died at a hospice in Sioux Falls, South Dakota on October 21, 2012. He was ninety. No cause of death was announced. He is survived by three daughters, ten grandchildren, and one great-grandchild. His daughter Teresa died in 1994 and his son Steven died in July 2012. McGovern's wife, Eleanor, died in 2007.

See Current Biography Illustrated 1967.

Dom Mintoff

Born: Cospicua, Malta; August 6, 1916
Died: Tarxien, Malta; August 20, 2012
Occupation: Maltese prime minister

An ideological hero to some and a ruthless tyrant to others, twice former Maltese prime minister Dom Mintoff transformed the perpetually colonized island nation into a self-sufficient republic, complete with socialized medicine, diverse industrial pursuits, and a booming tourism industry.

Mintoff rose to political prominence as an architect and civil engineer with the goal of rebuilding Malta after the bombing by Axis powers in World War II. He became an ardent socialist and Labor Party member and served his first term as prime minister from 1955 to 1958, when Malta was still a British colony. Mintoff resigned following a failed effort to integrate with Britain, and although Malta gained its independence in 1964, constitutional terms allowed for continued British influence in trade, banking, communications, military, and law enforcement. While out of office, Mintoff was a fervent advocate for the expulsion of all British interests from Malta. In 1971, he was once more elected prime minister. Tense negotiations with Britain during his first few years in office led to Malta becoming a fully independent republic in 1974, with the last of the British military presence withdrawing from the island in 1979. Mintoff closed all British–run NATO bases and took great care to clear Maltese institutions of any lingering British influence.

Mintoff shunned Western powers, turning to countries like Libya, China, and the Soviet Union for funding and aid during the republic's infancy. His domestic policies often caused controversy, and accusations of cronyism, gerrymandering, and general corruption came frequently from critics. Mintoff resigned in 1984, leaving behind a legacy of swift, resolute change in the eyes of supporters and a trail of political coercion in the eyes of his opponents.

Mintoff died at his home in the village of Tarxien on August 20, 2012. He was ninety-six. He is survived by his daughters, Yana and Anne.

See Current Biography 1984.

Sun Myung Moon

Born: Korea; February 25, 1920
Died: Gapyeong, South Korea; September 3, 2012
Occupation: Korean religious leader and businessman

Sun Myung Moon, evangelist, business mogul, and self-proclaimed messiah, was the founder of the Unification Church, an international organization that rose to prominence during the new religious movement of the 1960s and 1970s. An ardent capitalist and political conservative, Moon's influence reached far beyond the religious realm. Through the church and its countless affiliates, Moon held business interests in media, real estate, publishing, automobile manufacturing, fishing, and seafood processing. Moon and his church were frequently subjects of heavy scrutiny, drawing the ire of anticult organizations and the Internal Revenue Service, alike.

Moon was born in a small, rural village in what is now North Korea, on February 25, 1920. When he was ten, his family joined the Presbyterian Church, where Moon was first acquainted with Christianity. According to Unification Church teachings, Moon was visited by Jesus Christ around Easter 1935. Moon claimed that Jesus came bearing a message from God, saying that Moon would be the one to establish the kingdom of heaven on earth. He also claimed that Jesus confided in him that the crucifixion was not meant to occur, rather it was intended that he marry and beget the "True Family," a task now entrusted to Moon. Unification's heavy focus on marriage—the church is famous for its mass weddings—stems from this alleged visitation.

Moon began developing his theology in the early 1950s, leaving his then wife (a fact reluctantly acknowledged in church literature), and moving to Seoul, where he founded the Unification Church in 1954. He published the church's main theological text, called the *Divine Principle*, in 1956. In keeping with his professed holy mandate, Moon married seventeen-year-old Hak Ja Han in 1960, and began to build the "True Family," which would end up consisting of thirteen children, many of whom hold prominent church leadership roles today.

As the Unification Church's popularity grew in Korea, Moon toured the world proselytizing. He found a particularly fertile demographic in young Americans, leading Moon to settle in the United States in 1972. Many American "Moonies" (a term the church now considers derogatory) were recruited from college campuses, being urged to drop out and surrender their worldly possessions to the church. The church drew scrutiny for its recruitment efforts and internal policies. Defectors wrote damning exposés, and hundreds of church members were abducted by their families to be "deprogrammed" from alleged brainwashing. Despite the negative attention, church membership remained steady and Moon maintained public visibility, becoming heavily involved in conservative politics—even leading a call to forgive President Nixon for his role in the Watergate scandal. It was during the church's rapid expansion in the United States that Moon established many of his ultimately fruitful business ventures, including America's largest distributor of raw fish used by sushi restaurants.

But the 1980s marked the beginning of a decline in prosperity for the Unification Church. Moon was indicted on charges that he failed to report $150,000 in income in 1981. In 1982, he was convicted of conspiracy to obstruct justice and tax fraud, and started serving a thirteen-month federal prison term. During the 1990s, the church, seeing a decline in membership expansion, refocused its recruiting efforts on Africa and Latin America.

Moon died on September 3, 2012, in Gapyeong, South Korea, of complications from pneumonia, including kidney failure. He was ninety-two. He is survived by his wife and ten of his children.

See Current Biography 1983.

Rudolf L. Mössbauer

Born: Munich, Germany; January 31, 1929
Died: Grünwald, Germany; September 14, 2011
Occupation: Physicist

Rudolf L. Mössbauer was a Nobel Prize–winning German physicist whose work on recoilless nuclear resonance absorption led to the discovery of nuclear resonance fluorescence, also known as the Mössbauer effect. He was born in Munich on January 31, 1929. After receiving his graduate degree, he began researching gamma rays at the Institute for Physics of the Max Planck Institute of Medical Research in Heidelberg. The Mössbauer effect, which he discovered in 1958, describes the recoil-free emission of gamma rays from an atom's nucleus. Mössbauer, along with Robert Hofstadter, was awarded the Nobel Prize for Physics in 1961. Mössbauer retired from research and academia in 1997. He died on September 14, 2011, in Grünwald, Germany.

See Current Biography 1962.

Patrick V. Murphy

Born: Brooklyn, New York; May 15, 1920
Died: Wilmington, North Carolina; December 16, 2011
Occupation: Former New York City police commissioner

Patrick V. Murphy was the New York City police commissioner during the 1970s. He spearheaded reforms aimed at eradicating widespread corruption within the New York Police Department (NYPD). He encouraged officers to get to know the communities on their beats and cracked down on an established system of police payoffs. By the time he stepped down in 1973, he had become a national figure for his leadership not only in New York, but also in Detroit and Washington, DC. He wrote about his policing philosophy in the 1977 book *Commissioner: A View from the Top of American Law Enforcement*. In 1978, he helped found the Police Executive Research Forum that investigates issues including race, poverty, and immigration and their effects on the work of a police force.

Murphy was born in Brooklyn, New York, on May 15, 1920. His father and two of his brothers were officers in the NYPD. After serving in World War II, he, too, joined the NYPD, where he was assigned to patrol the Red Hook neighborhood in Brooklyn, in 1945. He later became a training officer and taught classes in police science at the City College of New York. After moving to Washington, DC, he served as director of the Law Enforcement Assistance Administration in the 1960s. He became the police commissioner of Detroit in 1970. The same year, he accepted Mayor John V. Lindsay's invitation to return to New York and head the NYPD.

Murphy died of complications after a heart attack at a hospital in Wilmington, North Carolina, on December 16, 2011. He is survived by his wife, Martha, and their children, Patrick Jr., Kevin, Paul, Mark, Sallie Kelley, Eileen Karam, and Anne Zabriskie. Another son, Gerard, works for the Police Executive Research Forum. Murphy is also survived by twenty-one grandchildren and seventeen great-grandchildren.

See Current Biography 1972.

LeRoy Neiman

Born: St. Paul, Minnesota; June 8, 1921
Died: New York, New York; June 20, 2012
Occupation: American painter

LeRoy Neiman was a popular and prolific American painter whose work, which included bright sketches of sporting events and lively parties, often appeared in *Playboy* magazine. As a person, Neiman was nearly as flamboyant as his art. He smoked cigars and wore a long handlebar mustache. He created the *Playboy* feature "Man at His Leisure," which depicted illustrated versions of the glamorous locales around the globe to which he travelled. Though he was largely ignored or disparaged by critics, Neiman became the official artist of five Olympic Games, where millions of people tuned in to watch him paint events in real-time on television. In 1972, Neiman was on hand to paint Bobby Fischer and Boris Spassky at the world chess championship in Iceland.

Neiman was born LeRoy Runquist in St. Paul, Minnesota, on June 8, 1921. His biological father left the family when Neiman was young, and Neiman took the surname of one of his stepfathers. (His mother, Lydia Runquist, remarried twice.) Neiman took an early interest in painting. As a teenager, he found a job painting sale items and shopkeeper portraits on grocery store windows. In 1942, Neiman enlisted in the army. Stationed in Europe as a cook, he gained celebrity among the troops for painting suggestive murals on the walls of the kitchens and dining halls.

After his discharge in 1946, Neiman attended the St. Paul Gallery and School of Art (now the Minnesota Museum of American Art) and the School of the Art Institute of Chicago (SAIC) where, after his graduation, he taught classes in fashion illustration and figure drawing for several years. In 1953, he was inspired by his discovery of several discarded cans of enamel house paint. He used the paint to develop his frenetic style, recognizable for its short, quick brushstrokes. Neiman met Hugh Hefner in 1953, shortly before Hefner published the first issue of *Playboy*. Hefner was impressed with Neiman's style and asked him to contribute illustrations to the magazine.

Neiman published numerous collections of his work. His memoir, titled *All Told: My Art and Life Among Athletes, Playboys, Bunnies and Provocateurs*, was published in 2012.

Neiman died on June 20, 2012, in New York City. He is survived by his wife, Janet Byrne, whom he married in 1957.

See Current Biography 1996.

John Neville

Born: Willesden, United Kingdom; May 2, 1925
Died: Toronto, Canada; November 19, 2011
Occupation: Stage and screen actor

John Neville was a Shakespearean actor who appeared onstage opposite Claire Bloom, Judi Dench, and Richard Burton. He was praised by critics in both the United Kingdom and the United States. Later in his career, he appeared on the American television show *The X-Files* and in the film *The Adventures of Baron Munchausen* (1988). Neville was born in Willesden, in Greater London, on May 2, 1925. He served in the Royal Navy during World War II; after his service he enrolled in the Royal Academy of Dramatic Art in London where he changed his working-class accent to become a Shakespearean actor. Over a six-year period in the 1950s, Neville appeared in all of Shakespeare's plays. He recalls these years as his greatest achievement. Neville was the artistic director of the Stratford Shakespeare Festival in Canada from 1986 to 1989. He died of Alzheimer's disease in Toronto on November 19, 2011. He is survived by his wife, Caroline, six children, and six grandchildren.

See Current Biography 1959.

Chukwuemeka Odumegwu Ojukwu

Born: Zungeru, Nigeria; November 4, 1933
Died: London, United Kingdom; November 26, 2011
Occupation: Former Nigerian political leader and colonel

Chukwuemeka Odumegwu Ojukwu was a Nigerian colonel who led eastern Nigeria to declare independence from Nigeria as the Republic of Biafra in 1967. The civil war that followed cost millions of lives; the conflict shocked the world with reporters' images of starving children and famine. Ojukwu was born in Zungeru, Nigeria, on November 4, 1933. His father, Sir Louis Phillipe Odumegwu Ojukwu, became one of Nigeria's wealthiest businessmen during Ojukwu's childhood, and Ojukwu attended the most prestigious private schools in the country. In 1947, he moved to the United Kingdom where he attended Epsom College prep school and Lincoln College, Oxford.

As a young man, Ojukwu earned a reputation as both an intellectual who loved Shakespeare and a playboy of conspicuous wealth. He returned to Nigeria, but refused a junior partnership in his father's business. He served in the Nigerian military in 1957, and sought advanced officer training in the United Kingdom. Upon his return to Nigeria in 1963, Ojukwu became a lieutenant colonel. After a violent uprising led by general Yakubu Gowon in northern Nigeria in 1966, Ojukwu led the eastern region of Nigeria, of which he was military governor, to secede in 1967 as the independent Republic of Biafra. The same year, the civil war began. Biafrans were cut off from food supplies and citizens died at an incredible rate due to both starvation and warfare. The secession was defeated in 1970. Ojukwu fled abroad, but returned after receiving a presidential pardon in 1982.

Ojukwu, who was living in Enugu, Nigeria, died in a London hospital on November 26, 2011, after suffering a stroke in 2010. He was married three times. He is survived by his third wife, Bianca Odinaka Onoh, whom he married in 1994.

See Current Biography 1969.

John R. Opel

Born: Kansas City, Missouri; January 5, 1925
Died: Fort Myers, Florida; November 3, 2011
Occupation: Computer executive

John R. Opel was the chief executive of IBM Corporation from 1981 to 1985. During his tenure, the company began manufacturing personal computers and nearly doubled its profits. Opel was born in Kansas City, Missouri, on January 5, 1925. He graduated from high school and served with the army in the South Pacific during World War II. He earned a bachelor's degree from Westminster College and a master's of business administration from the University of Chicago in 1949. That same year, he joined IBM as a sales representative. He became president of the company in 1974 and CEO in 1981. During Opel's second year as chief executive, the US Justice Department dropped a thirteen-year antitrust lawsuit against the company. IBM began manufacturing new products and became a fierce competitor in the market. For his shrewd leadership, Opel was featured on the cover of *Time* magazine in 1983. Opel stepped down as chief executive in 1985, but remained a chairman until 1986 and a board member until 1993.

Opel died in Fort Myers, Florida, on November 3, 2011. He is survived by his wife, Carole; five children, Robert, Julie Conlee, John E., Nancy Wickham, and Mary Porteus; and fifteen grandchildren.

See Current Biography 1986.

Joe Paterno

Born: Brooklyn, New York; December 21, 1926
Died: State College, Pennsylvania; January 22, 2012
Occupation: College football coach

Joe Paterno, the head football coach at Pennsylvania State University for forty-six years, once had the most wins of any coach in major college football. In 2011, Paterno, a Pennsylvania fixture who was revered as a symbol of integrity in college sports, was fired amid allegations that he had concealed the sexual abuse of children by his former defense coordinator Jerry Sandusky. These allegations were later confirmed and made public after Paterno's death.

Paterno was born in the Brooklyn borough of New York City on December 21, 1926. He attended Brooklyn Preparatory where he played football and basketball. Paterno earned a scholarship to Brown University in 1945 but was inducted into the army during his freshman year. He returned to Brown after a year of military service, studying English and playing quarterback on the football team. He graduated in 1950. He was planning to pursue a law degree in Boston when his coach at Brown, Charles "Rip" Engle accepted a coaching job at Penn State and asked Paterno to come along as an offensive backfield coach. Paterno intended to stay only a little while, but succeeded Engle as head coach in 1966 and remained with the college until 2011.

During his career, Paterno coached 409 winning games. He drew national attention to the school in the late 1960s with a couple of breakout seasons, and in 1982 and 1986, Penn State was the top-ranked team in the country. In 1973, Paterno turned down a lucrative contract to coach the New England Patriots. His dedication to Penn State made him a state icon and earned him the affectionate nickname "JoePa." His coaching philosophy emphasized education and he encouraged players to participate in activities and studies off the field, setting the expectation that his players would be top students as well as winners.

The same day that Paterno announced his retirement, it was reported that Sandusky, who retired in 1999 but retained access to school grounds, had sexually abused a number of young boys involved in a charity program he created, called the Second Mile. Paterno, who was informed about a particular incident in which Sandusky was witnessed raping a young boy in the Penn State showers as early as 1998, was fired. Subsequent reports, including a comprehensive report undertaken by Louis Freeh, revealed that Paterno convinced college officials not to report Sandusky to the police, fearing bad publicity for the program. The crime tainted Paterno's career and memory after his death; in 2012, the NCAA revoked 111 past Penn State wins (making Paterno's record 298) reaching back to 1998. The college also removed a statue of Paterno from the stadium.

Paterno died of lung cancer on January 22, 2012, in State College, Pennsylvania. He is survived by his wife, Sue; his children, Joseph Jr. (known as Jay), David, Scott, Diana Giegerich, and Mary Kathryn Hort; and many grandchildren.

See Current Biography 1984.

Oswaldo Payá

Born: Havana, Cuba; February 29, 1952
Died: Bayamo, Cuba; July 22, 2012
Occupation: Cuban political activist

Cuban political activist Oswaldo Payá Sardiñas was born in Havana, Cuba, in 1952. He was seven years old when the Communist government of Fidel Castro took power. Payá was raised in a Roman Catholic family, and during its early years in power, the Castro regime placed restrictions on the practice of religion. Nonetheless, Payá made an effort to remain close to the church, joining the youth group and becoming a catechist, or teacher of the Roman Catholic faith. As a teenager, Payá was sentenced to three years in prison after refusing to transport political prisoners during his mandatory military service.

Payá studied physics and telecommunications and worked for a time at a state-run surgical equipment company. He repeatedly refused opportunities to leave Cuba for the United States, and in 1987, he founded the Christian Liberation Movement (*Movimiento Cristiano de Liberación*, or MCL). The purpose of the group was to use acts of nonviolent civil disobedience to protest the rule of the Cuban Communist Party. MCL also advocated internationally for the improvement of Cuban human rights and for the rights of political prisoners on the island. In addition to serving as the group's executive director, Payá connected the organization with citizens and governments worldwide. In 2002, Payá's organization presented the Cuban government with 11,000 signatures of people advocating their support of free speech and political discourse in the country. The Cuban government responded to the effort by stating that it was a US-supported effort to overthrow them.

Payá was a critic of the US embargo on Cuba, believing that it had more of a negative impact on the Cuban people than it did on the Cuban government. In addition, Payá's social and economic policies for Cuba were based in Catholicism, and he often disagreed with the neoliberal economic proposals espoused by Miami-based Cuban dissident groups.

On July 22, 2012, Payá and MCL youth league chair Harold Cepero died in a car crash near the city of Bayamo. After Payá's death, US President Barack Obama praised his record of political activism, and the European Union released a statement recognizing Payá's work.

Payá was sixty years old when he died. He is survived by his wife and three children.

See Current Biography 2003.

John Payton

Born: Los Angeles, California; December 27, 1946
Died: Baltimore, Maryland; March 22, 2012
Occupation: American lawyer and civil rights activist

John Payton was a lawyer and civil rights activist who served as the president of the NAACP Legal Defense and Educational Fund. In this position he argued several important cases in front of the Supreme Court, including the successful *Lewis v. City of Chicago* (2010) in which a group of African American firefighters charged the city with discriminatory hiring practices. In 2010, the *National Law Journal* named him one of the most influential lawyers of the decade.

Payton was born in Los Angeles, California, on December 27, 1946. He attended Ponoma College in Claremont, California, where he lobbied the school to recruit more black students and to offer a black studies program. Working his way through school, he graduated in 1973. He graduated from Harvard Law in 1977 and became a corporate lawyer with Wilmer Cutler Pickering Hale and Dorr. Payton served as corporate counsel for the District of Columbia in 1991, and was nominated by President Bill Clinton to be the assistant attorney general for civil rights in 1993. However, Payton clashed with the Congressional Black Caucus and chose to withdraw his name from consideration for the position. He was named president of the NAACP Legal Defense and Educational Fund in 2008.

Payton died in Baltimore, Maryland, on March 22, 2012. He is survived by his wife, Gay McDougall, two brothers, and one sister.

See Current Biography 2010

Dory Previn

Born: Rahway, New Jersey; October 22, 1925
Died: Southfield, Massachusetts; February 14, 2012
Occupation: Singer-songwriter

Dory Previn was a singer and songwriter who earned three Academy Award nominations for her work as a composer and lyricist. She released several successful solo albums in the 1970s, and was praised for the beauty of her prose, which chronicled her turbulent past. Previn was born Dorothy Veronica Langan in Rahway, New Jersey, on October 22, 1925. Her father was a World War I veteran and failed musician who pushed Previn to pursue an entertainment career. (At one point, he left the family to live in the attic; Previn believed he was deranged from the gassing he endured during the war.) Working as a club singer in the 1950s, she was hired by MGM as a songwriter in 1959. It was the same year she married the composer André Previn.

With her husband, Previn wrote the lyrics to several famous film songs including "Come Saturday Morning" from *The Sterile Cuckoo* (1969), which was later recorded by the Sandpipers, and the theme for *The Valley of the Dolls* (1967), which was later recorded by Dionne Warwick. In 1970, Previn suffered a public emotional breakdown after her husband left her for the actress Mia Farrow. She spent several months in a psychiatric hospital where she began writing the confessional poems that would become the lyrics for her solo albums. She also wrote short stories, screenplays, and a musical.

Previn died on February 14, 2012, at her home in Southfield, Massachusetts. She is survived by her husband, Joby Baker, a painter whom she married in 1984. A first marriage, prior to André Previn, ended in divorce. She is also survived by three stepchildren, Michelle Wayland, Fredricka Baker, and Scott Zimmerman, as well as six step-grandchildren.

See Current Biography 1975.

George C. Price

Born: Belize City, Belize; January 15, 1919
Died: Belize City, Belize; September 19, 2011
Occupation: First prime minister of Belize

George Cadle Price was a politician who negotiated for Belizean independence from Great Britain and, in 1981, became Belize's first prime minister. Price, born in Belize City on January 15, 1919, was the eldest son in a wealthy family of ten. As a young man, he attended seminary school in Mississippi, but soon chose politics over the priesthood and was elected to the Belize City council in 1947. Price was central to the struggle for Belize independence through the 1950s and 1960s as a politician and the founder of the People's United Party (PUP). (Independence was delayed due to a looming threat from neighboring Guatemala, which laid claim to the colony.) He became prime minister in 1981 and again from 1989 to 1993. During this time he was known for his simple lifestyle and lack of affectation. He served as minister under the leadership of Said Musa in 1998. In 2010, he became the first person to receive Belize's highest honor, the Order of National Hero. Price died on September 19, 2011.

See Current Biography Illustrated 1984.

David Rakoff

Born: Montreal, Canada; November 27, 1964
Died: New York, New York; August 9, 2012
Occupation: Writer, journalist, actor

David Rakoff is best known for his work on Public Radio International's *This American Life*. His success on the show helped him to become a well-respected writer known for his autobiographical nonfiction works. Rakoff also appeared on television and in several films.

Rakoff was born in Montreal, Quebec, on November 27, 1964. His mother was a psychotherapist and his father was a psychiatrist. After graduating from high school in Toronto, Rakoff enrolled at Columbia University in New York City, where he graduated with a degree in East Asian Studies in 1986. At the age of twenty-two, Rakoff was diagnosed with Hodgkin's disease. After receiving an eighteen-month course of chemotherapy and undergoing surgery, he was given a clean bill of health.

Rakoff first worked in the publishing industry as an assistant and a publicist. In 1992, he and humorist David Sedaris became friends, and he began working with Sedaris and his sister on theater projects. Rakoff was also introduced to Sedaris's colleague Ira Glass, who was putting together his radio show, *This American Life*. Rakoff first appeared on the show in 1996, presenting "Christmas Freud," an autobiographical account of his experience playing Sigmund Freud in a department store window scene during the holiday season.

Audiences resonated with Rakoff's candor and humor. His nonfiction essays portrayed a wry and self-deprecating personality. Rakoff was unabashed about his homosexuality and his Jewish identity, and he routinely touched on his experiences with the stereotypes he encountered.

Throughout the 2000s, Rakoff appeared regularly on *This American Life*. Additionally, his writing appeared in *GQ, New York Times Magazine, Salon, Vogue,* and *Harper's Bazaar.* In 2001, he published a collection of essays entitled *Fraud,* and the collection *Don't Get Too Comfortable* was published in 2005. Rakoff's 2010 book, *Half Empty,* earned him the 2011 Thurber Prize for American Humor. Rakoff also acted on stage, television, and in film, appearing in, among other things, the Sedaris's theatrical production, *One Woman Shoe,* in 1995; the soap opera *As the World Turns* in 1998; and the 2009 short film *The New Tenants.*

Rakoff was again diagnosed with cancer in 2010. He died on August 9, 2012. Following his death, Glass and the other producers at *This American Life* compiled a tribute essay entitled "Our Friend David."

See Current Biography 2007.

Norman Foster Ramsey

Born: Washington, DC; August 27, 1915
Died: Wayland, Massachusetts; November 4, 2011
Occupation: American physicist

Norman Foster Ramsey was a Nobel Prize–winning physicist who studied the nuclei of atoms. He created a technique called the separated oscillatory fields method, now called the Ramsey Method, that improved upon the way atomic energy levels were measured and that also made way for the invention of the atomic clock. His research laid the foundation for several other technologies including magnetic resonance imaging (MRI) and the atomic hydrogen maser, an extremely precise form of atomic clock used to track global positioning satellites.

Ramsey was born in Washington, DC, on August 27, 1915. His mother was a mathematics teacher and his father was an officer in the US Army. Ramsey attended Columbia University in New York City and received his bachelor's degree in 1935. He was awarded a fellowship to Cambridge University in England where he received a second bachelor's degree and a master's degree, both in physics. He then returned to Columbia to pursue his PhD, which he received in 1940. While at Columbia, Ramsey studied under physicist and future Nobel laureate Isidor Isaac Rabi. Ramsey improved upon Rabi's technique of measuring atomic energy and developed what would become known as the Ramsey Method.

During World War II, Ramsey worked at the Massachusetts Institute of technology (MIT) Radiation Laboratory where he played a major role in creating the three-centimeter-wavelength radar system, which was the first of its kind and was used extensively during the war. He was appointed expert radar consultant to the secretary of war in 1942, and in 1943, Ramsey went to Los Alamos, New Mexico, where he was assigned a leadership role on the Manhattan Project, the multinational research program that produced the first atomic bomb.

Ramsey began teaching at Harvard University in 1947 and officially retired in 1986. He managed the construction and operation of two important particle accelerator laboratories: Fermilab, near Chicago, and the Brookhaven National Laboratory in Long Island, New York. He served on the general advisory committee for the Atomic Energy Commission and later as the first science adviser to the North Atlantic Treaty Organization (NATO). Ramsey was awarded the Nobel Prize in Physics in 1989 for the separated oscillatory fields method and the development of hydrogen masers.

Ramsey died in Wayland, Massachusetts, on November 4, 2011, at the age of ninety-six. He married his first wife, Elinor Jameson, in 1940; she died in 1983. He is survived by his second wife, Ellie Welch Ramsey, four daughters, two stepchildren, eight grandchildren, and nine great-grandchildren.

See Current Biography 1963.

William Raspberry

Born: Okolona, Mississippi; October 12, 1935
Died: Washington, DC; July 17, 2012
Occupation: American public affairs columnist and academic

William Raspberry was a well-known public affairs columnist for the *Washington Post*, where he wrote an opinion column for over forty years. His writing focused on social issues such as urban poverty, race relations and racial discrimination, crime, education, and politics.

Raspberry was among the first African American writers to gain nationwide recognition in the press. He was the second African American to win the Pulitzer Prize, which he received in 1994 for his commentaries on social and political topics. That same year, he also received the National Association of Black Journalists Lifetime Achievement Award. Ten years later in 2004, the National Press Club presented Raspberry with its highest award, the Fourth Estate Award.

Raspberry was born on October 12, 1935. He was raised in Mississippi and attended racially segregated schools. Despite his upbringing in what he referred to as "apartheid," Raspberry excelled in his education. He graduated in 1958 from Indiana Central College (now the University of Indianapolis). In 1962 he joined the *Washington Post* first as a teletypist and

then as a reporter. After reporting on the 1965 Watts riots in Los Angeles, he won the Capital Press Club's Journalist of the Year award and was subsequently promoted to a columnist for the paper.

Raspberry wrote over five thousand opinion columns for the *Washington Post* and was syndicated in an additional two hundred newspapers nationwide. In 1991 he published *Looking Backward at Us*, a collection of his columns from the previous decade. In addition to writing, Raspberry taught journalism at Duke University in Durham, North Carolina, from 1995 through 2008, commuting weekly from his home in Washington, DC.

After retiring from the *Post* in 2005, Raspberry established Baby Steps in his hometown of Okolona, Mississippi. Baby Steps is devoted to educating and empowering low-income and at-risk parents of preschoolers in order to help these parents prepare their children for school and the future.

On July 17, 2012, William Raspberry died at his home in Washington, DC, from prostate cancer. He is survived by his wife of forty-six years, Sondra Raspberry; two daughters, Patricia Raspberry and Angela Raspberry Jackson; a son, Mark; a foster son, Reginald Harrison; a brother and a sister; and his mother, Willie Mae Tucker Raspberry, who is 106 years old.

See Current Biography 2001.

Stanley R. Resor

Born: New York, New York; December 5, 1917
Died: Washington, DC; April 17, 2012
Occupation: US Secretary of the Army

Stanley R. Resor served as the US secretary of the army from 1965 to 1971 during the Vietnam War and oversaw an increase in troops from 117,000 to 360,000 between 1966 and 1968. Resor, a decorated World War II veteran, also investigated the massacre by US soldiers of three hundred unarmed Vietnamese civilians at My Lai in 1968. Under President Richard Nixon, Resor began implementing Vietnamization, a policy in which South Vietnamese fighting forces were trained with the goal to steadily replace US troops stationed in South Vietnam.

Resor was born Stanley Burnet Resor, named after his father, in New York City on December 5, 1917. Resor's father was a well-known advertising executive, and Resor, according to his April 19, 2012, *New York Times* obituary, changed his middle name to Rogers to differentiate himself from his famous father.

Resor graduated from Yale University in 1939 and then entered the Yale School of Law but left during World War II to enlist in the US Army. While stationed in Bastogne, Belgium, in 1944, Resor and his unit were surrounded by German forces during the siege, and Resor was wounded while defending the city during the Battle of the Bulge. For his service, Resor was awarded the Bronze Star, the Silver Star, and the Purple Heart. After the war, Resor finished his law degree and began practicing at the New York City law firm now known as Debevoise & Plimpton, but he left in 1965 to serve under President Lyndon Johnson as undersecretary of the army. Resor was promoted to secretary of the army three months later after the resignation of Stephen Ailes. He remained in the post under President Richard Nixon and resigned in 1971 to return to his law practice.

During his tenure as secretary of the army, Resor established the framework for an all-volunteer army, which went into effect in 1973. Additionally, in 1970, Resor appointed, for the first time in US history, two women to the rank of general and in 1971 worked to end discrimination against African American soldiers in off-base housing.

In 1978, President Jimmy Carter appointed Resor as undersecretary of defense, but he resigned less than a year later. He became an outspoken advocate of nuclear arms reduction and served as chair of the Arms Control Association (ACA) from 1992 to 2000. In 1997, Resor, along with ACA and fifty military and diplomatic experts, wrote a letter to President Bill Clinton opposing the expansion of the North Atlantic Treaty Organization (NATO).

Resor died at his home in Washington, DC, of kidney failure on April 17, 2012, at the age of ninety-four. His first wife, Jane Lawler Pillsbury, died in 1994. He is survived by his second wife, Louise Mead Walker, as well as his seven sons, twenty grandchildren, and two great-grandchildren.

See Current Biography 1969.

Adrienne Rich

Born: Baltimore, Maryland; May 16, 1929
Died: Santa Cruz, California; March 27, 2012
Occupation: American poet

Adrienne Rich was a prolific and celebrated American poet whose work challenged conventional poetic forms as well as social constructs. She was a young prodigy and budding feminist when W. H. Auden hand-selected her first collection, *A Change of World*, for publication in the Yale Series of Younger Poets in 1951. She came out as a lesbian in the 1970s and soon after became a fierce voice against the oppression of all women.

Rich was born in Baltimore, Maryland, on May 16, 1929. Her father was a physician and professor who pushed Rich as a child to write and read poetry. Although she was raised in the Episcopal Church, Rich embraced her Jewish roots later in life, and much of her later poetry examined that part of her history. She attended Radcliffe College where, in her senior year, her first collection of poetry was chosen for publication. Several acclaimed collections followed, including *Snapshots of a Daughter-In-Law: Poems 1954–1962* (1963) and, what many consider her finest work, *Diving into the Wreck: Poems 1971–1972* (1973). Rich's prose included collections of essays such as *On Lies, Secrets, and Silence* (1979), and the powerful and influential essay, "Compulsory Heterosexuality and Lesbian Existence" (1980).

While Rich's poetry was often controversial, receiving literary awards became controversial as well. When told she had won the National Book Award in 1974 for *Diving into the Wreck*, Rich refused to accept the award for herself alone and instead accepted it with two other finalists, African American poets Alice Walker and Audre Lorde. The three women accepted the award together "on behalf of all women." Then in 1997, Rich turned down the prestigious National Medal of Arts, which is the highest award granted by the US government to artists and arts patrons. In a letter addressed to actor Jane Alexander, chair of the National Endowment for the Arts at the time, Rich explained that "the very meaning of art . . . is incompatible with the cynical politics of [the Clinton] administration" and that art "means nothing if it simply decorates the dinner table of power which holds it hostage." Rich was also the recipient of the Academy of American Poets Fellowship in 1992; a MacArthur Foundation Fellowship, or "genius grant," in 1994; and the Lannan Lifetime Achievement Award in 1999.

Rich married Harvard economist Alfred Haskell Conrad in 1953. He committed suicide in 1970. Rich died on March 27, 2012, and is survived by her partner of thirty years, writer Michelle Cliff; her three sons; her sister; and two grandchildren.

See Current Biography 1976.

Sally K. Ride

Born: Los Angeles, California; May 26, 1951
Died: San Diego, California; July 23, 2012
Occupation: American astronaut, physicist, and college professor

Sally Ride is best known for being the first American woman in space. But she was also the youngest astronaut in history when she joined the National Aeronautics and Space Administration (NASA) in 1978 at the age of thirty-two. She beat over one thousand applicants for the position. Ride entered Earth's orbit on June 18, 1983, aboard NASA's *Challenger*. Her position as part of the *Challenger*'s five-person crew was the ground-based capsule communicator, and she was partly responsible for developing the robotic arm used on the space shuttle. She was the first woman to operate the robotic arm in space, using it to retrieve a satellite.

Ride was bombarded by media attention for overcoming gender boundaries and entering the previously male-dominated realm of NASA. Ride, however, insisted on fair treatment and was considered an equal among her male colleagues. She is credited for paving the way for gender equality in America's space program and for women in all professions. In 1984, a year after her first space flight, Ride joined the crew of the *Challenger* again and spent approximately fourteen days in space. She was scheduled for a third mission, but this was cancelled after the space shuttle *Challenger* (mission STS-51-L) exploded seventy-three seconds after takeoff on January 28, 1986. Seven astronauts lost their lives in the incident.

Sally Ride double-majored in physics and English as an undergraduate student, and she earned her master's degree and PhD in physics with a research concentration in astrophysics from Stanford University. After her time working with NASA, Sally Ride became a physics professor at the University of California, San Diego. In 2001, Ride founded the Sally Ride Science Company, which provides elementary and middle school students with the opportunity to take science programs. With her long-time partner, Tam O'Shaughnessy, she cowrote six children's books that were intended to introduce children to space and science.

On July 23, 2012, Sally Ride died of pancreatic cancer in her home in San Diego. She was sixty-one years old. Ride is survived by O'Shaughnessy, her mother, sister, niece, and nephew.

See Current Biography 1983.

Andrew A. Rooney

Born: Albany, New York; January 14, 1919
Died: New York, New York; November 4, 2011
Occupation: American broadcast journalist and humorist

Andrew A. Rooney was the commentator and "resident curmudgeon" who appeared every week on the television program *60 Minutes* on CBS. From 1978 to 2011, he filled his segment, "A Few Minutes with Andy Rooney," with musings on everything from modern public art ("I don't like most of the stuff passing for art and it's everywhere") to Ernest Hemingway, whom he had met personally and called a "jerk." According to his humorous monologues, he had similar complaints about blue jeans, baseball, large cereal boxes, and music he could not hum. But not everyone found Rooney's grumbling funny; on a few occasions he got into trouble for his dismissive or offensive comments about black and gay people. He denied making several of these comments (which were never made on the show) and apologized for another comment he had made on the air about "homosexual unions," for which he was briefly suspended from *60 Minutes* in 1990.

Rooney was born in Albany, New York, on January 14, 1919. His father worked in the newspaper business, and Rooney began his career in journalism as a copy boy at the *Albany Knickerbocker News*. He worked briefly for the campus newspaper at Colgate University before being drafted into the army three months before the attack on Pearl Harbor in 1941. In the army, he wrote for the US military newspaper *Stars and Stripes* in London. He covered the invasion of France and won a Bronze Star for reporting under fire while in Saint-Lô, France. He was one of the first Americans to enter the concentration camps at Buchenwald and Thekla in Germany. Rooney and his *Stars and Stripes* colleague, Bud Hutton, wrote *Air Gunner* (1944) and *The Story of the Stars and Stripes* (1946), recounting their experiences and the experiences of soldiers they had known.

After the war, Rooney worked as a freelance journalist and a writer for the entertainment broadcaster Arthur Godfrey. In the late 1950s and early 1960s, he wrote several World War II documentaries for CBS News where he met journalist Harry Reasoner. Rooney's association with Reasoner would lead to his job as a writer and then broadcaster on *60 Minutes* in 1978.

Rooney published several books and wrote a newspaper column for Tribune Media Services from 1979 until 2011. In 2003, he was awarded lifetime achievement awards from the Academy of Television Arts and Sciences and the National Society of Newspaper Columnists.

On October 2, 2011, Rooney announced during his regular segment on *60 Minutes* that he was stepping down. He died on November 4, 2011 in New York City, several weeks after undergoing minor surgery. Rooney's wife, Marguerite Howard, predeceased him in 2004. Rooney is survived by four children, Ellen Rooney, Martha Fishel, Emily Rooney, and Brian Rooney; five grandchildren; and two great-grandchildren.

See Current Biography 1982.

Murray Rose

Born: Birmingham, England; January 6, 1939
Died: Sydney, Australia; April 15, 2012
Occupation: Australian swimmer

Olympic gold-medalist Murray Rose was a celebrated Australian swimmer who enjoyed a brief Hollywood acting career. At seventeen, Rose became the youngest triple-gold medalist in the history of the Olympics at the 1956 Summer Games in Melbourne, Australia. He won gold in the 400-meter freestyle, the 1,500-meter freestyle, and the 4×200-meter freestyle relay. At the 1960 Games in Rome, he won gold in the 400-meter freestyle, silver in the 1,500-meter freestyle, and bronze in the 4×200-meter freestyle relay. Rose would have competed at the 1964 games in Tokyo, but he was barred from competition after missing the Australian trials because he was filming a movie in Hawaii. Rose studied drama and television at the University of Southern California and graduated in 1962. He had small parts in the films *Ride the Wild Surf* (1964) and *Ice Station Zebra* (1968), starring Rock Hudson.

Rose was born Iain Murray Rose in Birmingham, England, on January 6, 1939. With the outbreak of World War II, Rose's family moved to Sydney, Australia, when he was one year old. He learned to swim at the age of three and began taking lessons at five.

As a young man, Rose's talent and clean-cut looks made him an Australian superstar. His celebrity there was on par with that of the baseball player Mickey Mantle in the United States, according to journalist Gay Talese in 1957, as quoted in Rose's *New York Times* obituary. Rose attributed his athletic success to his vegetarian (other sources have reported vegan) diet; in reference to his eating habits, he acquired the nickname "The Seaweed Streak."

During his career, Rose set fifteen world records. Within the sport of competitive swimming, he is still considered among the greatest of all time. Rose was active in the Australian charity The Rainbow Club, which teaches swimming to mentally and physically disabled children.

Rose died of leukemia on April 15, 2012, in Sydney. His first marriage ended in divorce; a daughter from that marriage, Somerset, survives him. He is also survived by his wife, Jodi; his son, Trevor; and his granddaughter, Tess.

See Current Biography 1962.

Albert D. Rosellini

Born: Tacoma, Washington; January 21, 1910
Died: Seattle, Washington; October 10, 2011
Occupation: Former US governor

Albert D. Rosellini was the progressive governor of Washington State from 1957 until 1965. Rosellini was a Democrat who sought reform in the state's prisons and mental institutions. He also oversaw the creation of the Evergreen Point floating bridge, which was later renamed in his honor.

Rosellini was born to Italian immigrants in Tacoma, Washington, on January 21, 1910. He attended the University of Washington as an undergraduate and decided to get his law degree after his father was sentenced to one year in jail for attempting to smuggle drugs out of Mexico.

Rosellini served in Washington's state senate for eighteen years; during his tenure he introduced a bill to establish medical and dental schools at the University of Washington, and he appointed a commission on sex discrimination and equal rights for women. He then served two terms as the state's governor, losing his second reelection to Republican Dan Evans. Rosellini lost again to Evans in 1972. In his later years, he became a mentor to Democratic politicians in Washington State.

Rosellini died in Seattle on October 10, 2011, from complications related to pneumonia. His wife, Ethel, whom he met while working on a case in which she served as a witness, died in 2002. Rosellini is survived by his children, John, Albert Jr., Jane Campbell, Sue Stiller, and Lynn Rosellini; fifteen grandchildren; and several great-grandchildren.

See Current Biography 1958.

Barney Rosset

Born: Chicago, Illinois; May 28, 1922
Died: New York, New York; February 21, 2012
Occupation: American publisher and editor

Barney Rosset was the former owner of the controversial publishing company Grove Press, which, during the 1950s, 1960s, and 1970s, published works by Beat writers such as Allen Ginsberg, William S. Burroughs, and Jack Kerouac; European absurdists Samuel Beckett, Eugène Ionesco, and Jean Genet; and leftist revolutionaries Che Guevara, Ho Chi Minh, and Malcolm X. Rosset, who was the son of a wealthy Chicago family, bought the Greenwich Village press in 1951. He hoped to publish *Tropic of Cancer*, Henry Miller's sexually explicit autobiographical novel published in Paris in 1934 but banned in the United States, and the 1928 D. H. Lawrence novel, *Lady Chatterley's Lover*. The publication of these novels as well as *Naked Lunch* by William S. Burroughs ignited censorship battles that took Rosset and Grove Press to the Supreme Court. The Court ruled in favor of Grove Press in 1964, creating a landmark ruling on the topics of free speech, censorship, and the First Amendment. Rosset expanded his influence with varying degrees of success to theater and film; he clashed again with censors in 1968 when he purchased the American distribution rights to the Swedish film *I Am Curious (Yellow)*.

Rosset was born in Chicago on May 28, 1922. He attended the progressive Francis W. Parker School where he dated Joan Mitchell, who later become a famous abstract expressionist painter and Rosset's wife. Rosset considered his high school experience the favorite time of his life, and after graduation, he spent several wandering years at Swarthmore College, the University of Chicago, and the University of California, Los Angeles. He joined the army during World War II and served as a photographer in China. After the war, he earned a degree in philosophy from the University of Chicago and produced a poorly received documentary about the discrimination that returning African American soldiers faced, called *Strange Victory*. After spending a brief time in Paris, Rosset and Mitchell returned to New York City in 1949 where Rosset attended the New School for Social Research, receiving a bachelor's degree in 1952. He bought Grove Press in 1951 for $3,000.

Rosset made many enemies throughout his career. The Grove Press office was bombed by Cuban exiles in 1968, though no one was hurt, and in 1970, some of Rosset's employees accused him of sexism. Rosset, who also published the influential *Evergreen Review* from 1957 to 1973, sold Grove in 1985. It was later bought by the Atlantic Monthly Press in 1993 and renamed Grove/Atlantic. A documentary about Rosset, titled *Obscene*, was released in 2008.

Rosset died after a double-heart-valve replacement in New York City on February 21, 2012. His first four marriages, including his marriage to Mitchell, ended in divorce. He is survived by his wife, Astrid Myers; his children, Peter, Tansey Rosset, Beckett, and Chantal R. Hyde; four grandchildren; and four step-grandchildren.

See Current Biography 1972.

Ken Russell

Born: Southampton, England; July 3, 1927
Died: Lymington, England; November 27, 2011
Occupation: English film director

Ken Russell was a controversial English film director whose movies included *The Devils* (1971) and *Women in Love* (1969), an adaptation of the D. H. Lawrence novel of the same name, for which Russell was nominated for an Academy Award for best director in 1971. Russell sought to shock his audience with scenes of over-the-top violence and sex, and critics alternatively praised his films as brilliant or condemned them as tasteless and crass. His adaptation of The Who's rock album *Tommy* (1975) perfectly showcased his flamboyant style; *Newsweek* called the movie "exhilarating." His science-fiction film *Altered States* (1980), starring William Hurt, has become a cult classic. Throughout the remainder of his career, Russell primarily directed short films, documentaries, and films for television.

Russell was born in Southampton, England, on July 3, 1927. By his own account, he led a lonely childhood, spending his time with his mother or alone at the movies. He served briefly in the British Merchant Navy and the Royal Air Force. After his discharge in 1949, Russell moved to London where he studied dance and photography. Beginning in 1959, he made a number of biographical films about artists for the British Broadcasting Corporation (BBC), including dancer Isadora Duncan, painter Henri Rousseau, and composer Claude Debussy. These films marked the beginning of Russell's filmmaking career.

Later in life, Russell returned to directing documentaries for television. He wrote several novels—including erotica about famous composers—and a column for the *Times of London*. In 2007, the same year he published his novel *Beethoven Confidential: Brahms Gets Laid*, Russell joined the cast of the reality television program *Celebrity Big Brother*.

Russell died at his home in Lymington, England, on November 27, 2011. His first three marriages ended in divorce. He married actress Lisi Tribble in 2001. She survives him, as do his children from his previous marriages, Alex, James, Xavier, Toby, Victoria, Molly, Rupert, and Rex.

See Current Biography 1975.

Andrew Sarris

Born: New York City, New York; October 31, 1928
Died: New York City, New York; June 20, 2012
Occupation: American film critic

Andrew Sarris was an influential American film critic who introduced European auteur theory to American film criticism from his posts at the *Village Voice* and the *New York Observer*. Sarris was a part of a generation of critics that included Pauline Kael, the stinging resident film critic at the *New Yorker*, with whom he sparred frequently, most famously over the use of the term "auteur." (Fans of Sarris and Kael lifted the feud off the page, dividing themselves as "Sarristes" and

"Paulettes.") Sarris learned of the word (French for "author") and its application to film criticism during a fruitful year spent in Paris, where he met the celebrated French New Wave directors Jean-Luc Godard and François Truffaut. Auteur theory holds that a director's role is paramount to that of any great artist. Sarris counted among those artists Godard, Truffaut, Ingmar Bergman, Orson Welles, and Alfred Hitchcock. "[Sarris] brought to American film criticism its crucial idea, its crucial word ("auteur"), and the crucial taste that it signifies," Richard Brody, a film critic for the *New Yorker*, wrote of Sarris after his death.

Sarris was born to Greek immigrants in the Brooklyn borough of New York City on October 31, 1928. He recalls watching films from age three or four. He graduated from Columbia College in 1951 and joined the Army Signal Corps where, in his off-duty hours, he reviewed movies for the local paper. In 1960, Sarris began writing film reviews for the avant-garde newspaper the *Village Voice*. He caused a stir with his inaugural article, a ringing endorsement for the director Alfred Hitchcock and his film *Psycho* (1960). He refined many of his theories—Sarris was known, and sometimes mocked, for his highly analytical writing voice—and published his essay "Notes on the Auteur Theory" in 1962. He published his masterwork, *The American Cinema: Directors and Directions, 1929–1968*, several years later in 1968.

Sarris taught film at Columbia University, Yale University, Julliard, and New York University. He married Molly Haskell, also a film critic, in 1969. She is his only immediate survivor. Sarris's younger brother, George, died in a skydiving accident in 1961.

Sarris died on June 20, 2012, of complications of an infection developed after a fall.

See Current Biography 2007.

Vidal Sassoon

Born: London, United Kingdom; January 17, 1928
Died: Los Angeles, California; May 9, 2012
Occupation: British hairstylist and products executive

Vidal Sassoon was a hairstylist whose easy-to-care-for designs for women's hair changed perceptions of beauty and popular notions about the level of maintenance women needed to make themselves beautiful in the late 1950s and early 1960s. Bucking an arduous tradition of upkeep that included curlers, up-dos, and sprays, his cuts were often short and geometrical to complement an individual's bone structure. He created cuts for celebrities like actress Mia Farrow (her signature pixie) and fashion designer

Mary Quant. Sassoon became an institution. He opened salons across Europe and the United States, and began producing his own line of hair care products in the late 1960s. According to his *New York Times* obituary, sales of Vidal Sassoon products like shampoos and conditioners reached annual sales figures of $100 million before Sassoon sold the company in 1983.

Sassoon was born in London on January 17, 1928. He grew up in a poor family and, after his father left, spent several years with his brother in an orphanage before his mother remarried. His mother sensed that the teenage Sassoon would be a hairdresser and took him to a local shop where he began an apprenticeship at age fourteen. In 1948, Sassoon, who was Jewish, travelled to Israel to fight in the country's War of Independence. As quoted by Sean O'Hagan for the *New Statesman*, Sassoon recalled that he returned from the war with "a sense of purpose." He opened his first salon on Bond Street in London in 1954, where he developed the architecturally inspired designs that would become his signature. A film about his life, *Vidal Sassoon: The Movie*, was released in 2010.

Sassoon was diagnosed with leukemia in 2009, but it was reported that he died of natural causes on May 9, 2012, at his home in Los Angeles, California. His first three marriages ended in divorce. He is survived by his wife, Rhonda; and children, Eden, Elan, and David. A daughter named Catya died in 2002.

See Current Biography 1999.

Alexander Saxton

Born: Great Barrington, Massachusetts; July 16, 1919
Died: Lone Pine, California; August 20, 2012
Occupation: American historian, novelist, and labor activist

Best known for his tenacious chronicling of race in America, Alexander Saxton was a post–World War II renaissance man. Before settling into academia, Saxton ditched his privileged Manhattan upbringing for labor fields and factory floors. After dropping out of Harvard during his junior year, Saxton moved to Chicago, taking the first of many low-paying, manual labor jobs. He remained active in the labor and Socialist movements before being blacklisted during the McCarthy era. His first nonfiction book, *The Indispensable Enemy: Labor and the Anti-Chinese Movement in California*, was published in 1972 to critical acclaim and is considered a landmark piece of labor history.

Born on July 16, 1919, in Massachusetts, Saxton spent his childhood living on the Upper East Side of Manhattan with his parents and older brother. His father was editor in chief for

Harper & Brothers, putting the young Saxton in the proximity of legendary literary figures like Aldous Huxley and Thornton Wilder, who often joined the family for dinner. In his early twenties, Saxton worked full-time as an organizer for maritime workers in San Francisco while penning three novels and writing for left-wing publications. He published his first novel, *Grand Crossing*, when he was twenty-four. Saxton was active in the American Communist Party, and was called to testify before the House Un-American Activities Committee in the mid-1950s.

When anti-Communist fervor made it impossible for Saxton to find publishers for his fiction, he reentered the academic sphere, earning a bachelor's degree from the University of Chicago and a PhD in history from the University of California, Berkeley. He took a professorial position teaching American history at the University of California Los Angeles in 1968. Saxton made his mark as a historian during his time at UCLA. He cofounded the university's Asian American Studies Center—a program among the first of its kind—in the early 1970s.

Saxton died on August 20, 2012, at his home in Lone Pine, California, of a self-inflicted gunshot wound following several years of declining health. He was ninety-three. His daughter, Catherine Steele, told the *New York Times* that Saxton "felt the terms of his life were his to decide." He was predeceased by his wife, Trudy, and daughter Christine, and is survived by Steele, a grandson, and a great-grandson.

See Current Biography 1943.

Barbara Ann Scott

Born: Sandy Hill, Ottawa, Canada; May 9, 1928
Died: Amelia Island, Florida; September 30, 2012
Occupation: Canadian figure skater

A Canadian figure skater and national heroine, Barbara Ann Scott was the first North American to win the world and European figure skating championships. A nineteen-year-old Scott captured international attention in 1948 when she won an Olympic gold medal in women's figure skating—the only Canadian ever to do so to date—at the St. Moritz Winter Games in Switzerland. With her win, she became the only person to hold the European, North American, world, and Olympic women's figure skating titles simultaneously.

Scott was born on May 9, 1928, in Ottawa, Canada, and began skating at the age of six. At the age of eleven, she won her first Canadian junior championship, and went on to win four senior titles by her Olympic debut. She was the first woman to land a double Lutz in competition. Her gentle demeanor and effortless charm made Scott a media darling and respected figure among her peers. At home in Canada, Scott garnered unanimous esteem, becoming a symbol of postwar national pride. She was recognized as the nation's top athlete three times as the winner of the Lou Marsh Trophy in 1945, 1947, and 1948. A generation of Canadian girls cherished their Barbara Ann Scott dolls.

Following her Olympic win in 1948, Scott embarked on a professional career, touring the world with several productions to rave reviews. She performed professionally until 1955, when she married Tom King, the press agent for the Hollywood Ice Revue in which Scott was a featured skater. She was inducted into the Canadian Figure Skating Hall of Fame that same year.

Scott bore the Olympic torch in 2010, presenting it to Canada's House of Commons prior to the Vancouver Games. In August 2012, Ottawa's City Hall unveiled an exhibit featuring artifacts from Scott's illustrious athletic career. Scott had previously donated the items to the city archives.

Scott and King lived in Fernandina Beach on Florida's Amelia Island, where she died on September 30, 2012, at the age of eighty-four. The cause of death was not made public. Scott is survived by her husband.

See Current Biography 1948.

Tony Scott

Born: North Shields, England; June 21, 1944
Died: San Pedro, California; August 19, 2012
Occupation: British film director and producer

Tony Scott was a British director best known for his blockbuster films *Top Gun* (1986), *Beverly Hills Cop II* (1987), and *Crimson Tide* (1995). He was referred to as one of the most influential film directors of the past quarter century.

Scott's career took off after the success of *Top Gun*, which brought in an impressive $176 million at the US box office and nearly $345 million internationally, making it the highest grossing film in 1986. The film was associated with numerous awards, including an Oscar and a Golden Globe for the song "Take My Breath Away," a Grammy for "Top Gun Anthem," and a People's Choice Award for favorite motion picture. Consequently, Scott became a household name and one of the most in-demand action film directors in Hollywood.

Scott followed in the footsteps of his older brother, Hollywood director Ridley Scott, who is well-known for films such as *Alien* (1979), *Blade Runner* (1982), and *Black Hawk Down* (2001). Scott received fine arts degrees from the West

Hartlepool College of Art and the Sunderland Art School. His film career began as an actor in his brother's production *Boy and Bicycle* (1962). In 1967, Scott and his brother created the RSA, a commercial production company in London, and, in 1995, they founded Scott Free Productions.

Scott made his debut as a director in the 1983 film *The Hunger*. But it was his commercial for automaker Saab Corporation in the early 1980s, in which a car races a jet, that prompted Hollywood producer Jerry Bruckheimer to sign Scott on as director for *Top Gun*.

Scott's directorial style included a mixture of fast-cutting shots, slow motion, and interesting angles. Over the years, it had evolved into a signature vivacious style with impressive special effects, high energy, momentum, and gimmicks that revolutionized action films. His most recent films include *The Taking of Pelham 1 2 3* (2009) and *Unstoppable* (2010). A film adaptation of the book, *Killing Lincoln*, which Scott was producing with his brother, is scheduled for release in 2013.

On August 19, 2012, Scott fell to his death from the Vincent Thomas Bridge in Los Angeles, in what was later deemed a suicide. He was sixty-eight. He is survived by his twin sons, Max and Frank; his wife, Donna Scott; and his brother, Ridley Scott.

See Current Biography 2004.

Junior Seau

Born: California; January 19, 1969
Died: Oceanside, California; May 2, 2012
Occupation: American football player

Junior Seau was a professional football player who spent twenty seasons as an NFL linebacker playing for the San Diego Chargers, the Miami Dolphins, and the New England Patriots. He was voted to twelve consecutive Pro Bowls and played in two Super Bowls. Seau was even named to the 1990s All-Decade Team by the Pro Football Hall of Fame. "If the football gods made a perfect linebacker," Sam Farmer and Rick Rojas wrote for the *Los Angeles Times* after his death, "it would be Seau." He officially retired after the 2009 season (he had announced his retirement in 2006 but then joined the New England Patriots for four more seasons).

Seau was born Tiaina Baul "Junior" Seau on January 19, 1969, to Samoan immigrants. He played football for the University of Southern California Trojans before being selected fifth overall by the Chargers in the 1990 NFL draft. After his first year in the NFL, Seau established the Junior Seau Foundation, which, as of 2010,

had distributed more than $4 million to child-abuse prevention and educational scholarships. In 2010, Seau was arrested on suspicion of domestic violence; later that day, he drove his car off a cliff and landed on the beach in Carlsbad, California. Rumors circulated that the accident was a suicide attempt, but Seau insisted that he had fallen asleep at the wheel.

On May 2, 2012, Seau's girlfriend, Megan Noderer, found him dead at their Oceanside home. His death was ruled a suicide, inflicted from a gunshot wound to the chest. Less than two weeks before his death, another retired NFL player, Ray Easterling, committed suicide in the same manner. Easterling was the leading plaintiff in a lawsuit against the NFL for its inadequate treatment of concussions, head injuries, and chronic traumatic encephalopathy (CTE), a disease caused by repeated brain trauma. Seau's autopsy did not show brain damage, but could not rule out CTE. Seau's family asked that the National Institutes of Health study his brain to determine if CTE was present and if it may have been a factor in his death.

Seau is survived by his mother, Luisa; his father, Tiaina Seau Sr.; his ex-wife, Gina Deboer; Noderer; and three children, Sydney, Jake, and Hunter.

See Current Biography 2001.

Maurice Sendak

Born: New York, New York; June 10, 1928
Died: Danbury, Connecticut; May 8, 2012
Occupation: American children's book author and illustrator

Maurice Sendak was a renowned children's book author and illustrator who was considered by many critics to be the best of his time. Sendak redefined a genre long devoted to well-behaved children and modest mores with his 1963 book, *Where the Wild Things Are*, which won the prestigious Caldecott Medal. Other successful books followed, including *In the Night Kitchen* (1970), *Outside Over There* (1981), and *Higglety Pigglety Pop!* (1967), which was written for his beloved dog Jennie. His books are beloved among children and abhorred by some adults who have called for them to be removed from library shelves (in particular, *In the Night Kitchen* caused controversy because the book's protagonist runs naked through his dreams). But Sendak, whose inspiration was often rooted in his own childhood memories, told Stephen Colbert for the *Colbert Report* in 2012, "I don't write for children. I write."

Sendak was born to Jewish immigrants from Poland in the Brooklyn borough of New York

City on June 10, 1928. He was often sick as a child, and recalled spending a lot of time looking out of his window and drawing. His adolescence was marked by the onslaught of World War II and the horrors of the Holocaust, in which many of his European relatives died. Sendak, who hated school, began drawing part-time for All-American Comics while he was still in high school. He then began work as a window dresser for the toy store FAO Schwarz in Manhattan, where his storefront illustrations caught the attention of the publisher Harper & Row. Sendak illustrated children's books for other authors; the first book he both wrote and illustrated himself, *Kenny's Window*, was released in 1956.

Later in life, Sendak designed sets for the theater. In 1996, Sendak was honored for his achievements with the prestigious National Medal of Arts. Working together with playwright Tony Kushner, Sendak illustrated *Brundibar* (2003), a children's book based on an opera that had been performed in the Nazi concentration camp Theresienstadt during the Holocaust.

Sendak was predeceased by psychiatrist Eugene Glynn, his partner of fifty years, who died in 2007. (Sendak never told his family that he was gay.) Sendak died from complications of a stroke on May 8, 2012 at Danbury Hospital in Connecticut.

See Current Biography Illustrated 1968, 1989.

Yitzhak Shamir

Born: Ruzhinoy, Russia; October 22, 1915
Died: Tel Aviv, Israel; June 30, 2012
Occupation: Israeli prime minister

Yitzhak Shamir served two terms as prime minister of Israel: 1983–1984 and 1988–1992. He was also a member of the Stern gang, an organization of Zionist activists that sought to establish a Jewish state by gaining control of Palestine from Britain following World War II.

Shamir was born in Russia on October 22, 1915. He was raised in a Jewish family in the village of Ruzhinoy, now Ruzhany. During this time, strong (and often violent) anti-Semitism existed throughout Russia and Europe. Shamir dreamed of returning to Palestine, the spiritual and ancestral home of Judaism, and in 1935, Shamir migrated to Palestine, after studying for a time at Warsaw University in Poland. While in Palestine, Shamir's parents and two sisters we killed during the Holocaust.

Shamir became a member of the Zionist group Irgun Zvai Leumi when he was living in British-occupied Palestine. When the group was reorganized in 1940, he joined its new militant faction, Lehi. Shamir allegedly took part in assassinations and bombings aimed at ending British control of Palestine, and as a result of these allegations and his association with Lehi (also known as the Stern Gang), British officials labeled him a terrorist. The Stern Gang later disbanded and was absorbed into the Israeli army following the founding of the state of Israel in 1948.

After a short career in business, Shamir joined Israel's national intelligence agency, the Mossad, in 1955. He remained in the intelligence field for over ten years before his election to the Knesset (Israel's parliament) as a member of the Likud Party in 1973. In 1980, Prime Minister Menachem Begin named Shamir to the post of foreign minister where he worked to normalize Israel's relations with Egypt after the two countries signed a peace agreement in 1979. Shamir succeeded Begin as prime minister in 1983, but in response to economic problems related to inflation, he and the Likud Party lost their majority in the Israeli parliament in 1984, and Shimon Peres took over as prime minister. Shamir remained active in Israeli politics, however, and was again elected prime minister in October 1986.

During his second term as prime minister, Shamir worked to cultivate diplomatic and economic ties between Israel and countries in Africa and Asia. Furthermore, during the US–led Gulf War in 1990, Israel endured missile strikes from Iraq. Although Shamir deployed Israeli aircraft to protect its airspace, he did not order retaliatory strikes against Iraq.

The Likud Party was defeated in the 1992 election by Yitzhak Rabin's Labor Party. Shamir retained a seat in the parliament until 1996.

Shamir died on June 30, 2012. He was ninety-six years old. Upon his death, Shimon Peres commemorated Shamir's accomplishment as a Jewish leader and Israeli politician. He is survived by his daughter, Gilada Diamant; his son, Yair Shamir; five grandchildren; and seven great-grandchildren.

See Current Biography, 1996.

Carroll Shelby

Born: Leesburg, Texas; January 11, 1923
Died: Dallas, Texas; May 10, 2012
Occupation: American racecar driver and manufacturer

Carroll Shelby was an American racecar driver and manufacturer of sports cars with Shelby American Inc. His sleek designs—most famously the Shelby Cobra for Ford in the early 1960s—were inspired by, and soon became competitive with, top-performing European models. As a racer, Shelby served as codriver on the British Aston Martin team that won the prestigious endurance race, the 24 Hours of Le Mans, in France in 1959—he was the second American-born driver ever to win the race.

After being diagnosed with angina pectoris, Shelby quit racing and founded Shelby American in 1962. Shelby developed the Shelby Cobra after purchasing a discontinued chassis from the British automaker AC Bristol and combining the lightweight frame with a powerful Ford V8 engine. Ford then asked Shelby to develop the GT40, which went on to win Le Mans four straight years in a row for Ford, beginning in 1966. He worked with Lee Iacocca of Ford to design a high-performance Mustang, the GT350, which made its debut in 1965. In the 1980s, Shelby produced a handful of other high-performance models for Iacocca, this time at Chrysler, including the Dodge Shelby Charger.

Shelby was born in Leesburg outside of Dallas, Texas, on January 11, 1923. He enlisted in the Air Force during World War II where he served as a flight instructor. After the war, Shelby worked on a Texas oil rig and then borrowed money to start an ill-fated chicken ranch. He began drag racing in 1952. As the story goes, Shelby was late to the track one day and did not have time to change his clothes. He raced in his overalls and they became his customary uniform. He began racing professionally in Europe in 1954.

Shelby, who had a heart transplant in 1990, founded the Carroll Shelby Foundation in 1991 to provide financial assistance and medical care for children undergoing treatment for serious heart and kidney conditions.

Shelby died in Dallas on May 10, 2012. He is survived by his wife, Cleo; his children, Patrick, Michael, and Sharon; and his sister, Anne Shelby Ellison.

See Current Biography 1993.

Norodom Sihanouk

Born: Phnom Penh, French Indochina; October 31, 1922
Died: Beijing, China; October 15, 2012
Occupation: King of Cambodia

Norodom Sihanouk served two reigns as king of Cambodia: from 1941 to 1955 and again from 1993 to 2004. During his later career, his role as monarch was more ceremonial than political. Although his title changed several times, Sihanouk wielded political influence in Cambodia for over six decades.

Sihanouk was born in 1922 as a prince in Cambodia's Norodom royal family. When he was nineteen, King Sisowath Monivong, Sihanouk's grandfather, passed away. Cambodia was still a French colony, and French officials arranged for Sihanouk to be selected by the Crown Council.

France preferred Sihanouk be named king because he spoke French, and it was thought he would remain loyal to French interests.

After Japan occupied Cambodia in 1945, King Sihanouk declared Cambodia's independence from France. Other countries, including Vietnam and Laos, were also calling for the end to French colonial authority from Indochina. In response to threats from France, Sihanouk lived in exile in Thailand before Cambodia's independence became official in November 1953.

In March 1955, Sihanouk abdicated the throne to his father, which allowed him to run Cambodia's first election following independence. Sihanouk's party, the People's Socialist Community (Sangkum Reastr Niyum), won the election handily, although he was accused of vote rigging and active repression of other candidates.

Sihanouk served as Cambodia's head of state until 1970. He became notorious for his lavish lifestyle and maintaining the country's close cultural and economic relations with France. While many Cambodians remained impoverished, Sihanouk spent much of his time producing films. He developed nineteen movies during his lifetime, serving at various times as director, composer, and lead actor. Although Sihanouk tried to keep Cambodia out of the Vietnam War, he eventually allowed Vietnamese Communist troops to make use of Cambodian land, thus subjecting the country to bombing raids by the US military.

Cambodia's prime minister, General Lon Nol, led a vote to depose King Sihanouk in March 1970, while Sihanouk was on a diplomatic mission abroad. Nol's colleague in the overthrow, Prince Sirik Matak, was made king. Nol and Matak allowed the US military to invade Cambodia in order to assist its efforts against Vietnamese Communists. Sihanouk fled to Beijing, and he began to work toward bringing the Khmer Rouge to power in Cambodia and overthrowing the Lon Noi government. Sihanouk recruited legions of Cambodian peasants to fight in support of their cause, and between 1975 and 1979, the Khmer Rouge killed approximately two million Cambodian nationals during a reign of oppression that isolated the country from the rest of Asia and the world.

The Khmer Rouge lost its control in Cambodia in 1975, and Sihanouk returned. The Khmer Rouge leader, Pol Pot, remained the head of state until December 1978, when Vietnam invaded. Throughout the 1980s, Sihanouk served as a Cambodian figurehead in an effort to oust Vietnam from the country. He was made king again in 1993, serving a ceremonial and advisory role in the Cambodian government.

Sihanouk died on October 15, 2012. After his death, United Nations Secretary General Ban Ki-moon commemorated Sihanouk's dedication to Cambodia.

See Current Biography, 1993.

John R. Silber

Born: San Antonio, Texas; August 15, 1926
Died: Brookline, Massachusetts; September 27, 2012
Occupation: Former president of Boston University

John R. Silber served as president of Boston University (BU) for twenty-five years, working to expand what was a second-tier commuter school into a top-ranked research university. Silber was often a controversial figure—BU's faculty twice voted for his dismissal—but he raised the university's admission and hiring standards, recruited top-notch faculty members, and significantly expanded and improved BU's facilities and campus.

Silber was born in San Antonio, Texas, on August 15, 1926. He graduated summa cum laude from Trinity University in 1947 with degrees in fine arts and philosophy. He earned his master's degree from Yale University in 1952 and completed his doctorate there in 1956. In 1957, Silber returned to Texas as an assistant professor of philosophy at the University of Texas at Austin. He became department chair in 1962 and dean of the College of Arts and Sciences in 1967. As dean, Silber clashed with a member of the university's board of regents and was dismissed in 1970. Despite this setback, he was selected to serve as BU's seventh president in January 1971.

As president of BU, Silber grew the university's endowment from $18 million to $422 million and greatly expanded the school's campus and research funding. He began an aggressive recruitment campaign, attracting future Nobel Prize–winners Elie Wiesel and Derek Walcott to the faculty in 1976 and 1982, respectively. As president, he also recruited US poet laureate Robert Pinsky, Nobel– and Pulitzer–prize winner Saul Bellow, and Nobel-winning physicist Sheldon Glashow to the university's faculty.

In 1988, Silber established the university's long-running partnership with Chelsea Public Schools, known as the Boston University/Chelsea Partnership, which provided tutoring, scholarships, and enrichment programs to the troubled public school system until 2008. Silber also doubled the size the school's campus and added a number of programs including the Prison Education Program in 1972; the Boston Scholars Program in 1973; and Boston University Academy, a college-preparatory school for gifted high school students, in 1993.

In 1990, Silber secured the Democratic nomination in the Massachusetts gubernatorial campaign against Republican William Weld. Silber lost by a narrow margin to Weld. From 1995 until 1999, he chaired the Massachusetts Board of Education.

Silber's wife, Kathryn Underwood, whom he married in 1947, died in 2005. Their son, David, died in 1994. Silber died at his home in Brookline, Massachusetts, on September 27, 2012, of kidney failure. He is survived by seven children, Rachel Devlin, Martha Hathaway, Judith Ballan, Alexandra Silber Mock, Ruth Belmonte, Caroline Lavender; Charles Hiett; a brother, Paul; twenty-six grandchildren; and three great-grandchildren.

See Current Biography 1984.

Louis Aston Marantz Simpson

Born: Kingston, Jamaica; March 27, 1923
Died: Stony Brook, New York; September 14, 2012
Occupation: American poet

Louis Aston Marantz Simpson was a Jamaican-born American poet whose conversational yet multi-layered poetry earned him the 1964 Pulitzer Prize. He is known for his sophisticated and multifaceted poetry about everyday American life.

Simpson was born in Kingston, Jamaica, on March 27, 1923. His mother had emigrated from Russia and his father was of Scottish and African descent. At age fourteen, Simpson began producing poetry and by age sixteen, his poems were being published in the Jamaican periodical *Public Opinion*. Simpson's parents divorced, and when his father died, his stepmother disinherited him, which prompted Simpson to move to New York City where he enrolled at Columbia University. In 1943 he left Columbia to enlist in the US Army, serving with the 101st Airborne Division and earning his US citizenship. He then returned to Columbia and earned his bachelor's degree in English in 1948. Simpson's first book of poetry, *The Arrivistes*, was published that same year.

Simpson earned a master's degree from Columbia in 1950 and began work as an editor for the Bobbs-Merrill publishing company. From 1955 to 1959, he worked as an instructor at Columbia, earning his PhD and then joining the faculty at the University of California, Berkeley. In 1963 Simpson published his fourth book of poetry, *The End of the Open Road*, which won him the 1964 Pulitzer Prize in poetry. In 1967 he began teaching at the State University of New York at Stony Brook, remaining on the faculty there until the 1990s.

In addition to his many volumes of poetry, Simpson was also known for his acclaimed literary criticism, particularly his 1975 study, *Three on the Tower*, which examined the works of Ezra Pound, T. S. Eliot, and William Carlos Williams. In 1976 Simpson received the American Academy of Arts and Letters award in literature.

Simpson, who had been diagnosed with Alzheimer's disease in 2005, died in Stony Brook, New York, on September 14, 2012. He is survived by his three children, Matthew, Anthony, and Anne Simpson, as well as two grandchildren.

See Current Biography 1964.

Arlen Specter

Born: Wichita, Kansas; February 12, 1930
Died: Philadelphia, Pennsylvania; October 14, 2012
Occupation: United States senator

As one of the most divisive, yet respected, senators in United States history, Arlen Specter was an enduring figurehead of American politics known for his centrism, as well as his wavering party affiliation. He began his political career as a Democrat, switching to the Republican ticket during an ultimately successful bid for Philadelphia district attorney in 1965. After serving twenty-nine years as a Republican senator from Pennsylvania, Specter announced he would run for reelection as a Democrat in 2010. He ended up losing during the primaries, bringing an end to his storied career.

During his nearly half-century as a public figure, Specter's antics and aura became the stuff of political legend. As a young lawyer investigating the JFK assassination as part of the Warren Commission, Specter originated the lone gunman theory, proposing that President John F. Kennedy and Texas Governor John B. Connally were struck by the same bullet. Specter's courtroom know-how earned him a reputation as one the Senate's brightest legal thinkers. On the Senate Judiciary Committee, Specter played the role of contrarian and relentless inquisitor during a number of Supreme Court confirmation hearings. He left fellow Republicans dumbfounded in 1987 when he helped vote down conservative nominee Robert Bork, but earned reluctant praise from Republicans and scorn from feminists with the confirmation of Clarence Thomas following lengthy hearings on charges of sexual harassment levied against Thomas by law professor Anita Hill. Specter was heavily criticized for his aggressive questioning of Hill, but maintained his conduct was justified and professional. Specter went on to serve as Judiciary Committee chairman for two years beginning in 2005.

Specter took a considered, yet resolute position during the impeachment of President Bill Clinton on charges of perjury and obstruction of justice, calling the proceedings "a sham trial" and voting to acquit. But it was his abrupt party shift in 2009 for which he will be best remembered. Ever the moderate, Specter took issue with the growing profile of the Tea Party movement and right-wing extremism within Republican ranks, and decided running as a Democrat would be more politically advantageous. "I am not prepared to have my 29-year record in the United States Senate decided by the Pennsylvania Republican primary electorate," he told the *New York Times.* Despite an endorsement from President Barack Obama, Specter lost the primary race, drawing only 46 percent of the vote.

Specter was born on February 12, 1930, in Wichita, Kansas, to Jewish immigrant parents hailing from present-day Ukraine. He worked in his father's junkyard as a boy before the family left Kansas for Philadelphia, where he attended the University of Pennsylvania. Specter served in the Air Force, and earned a law degree from Yale in 1956. His later years were marked by numerous health issues, including a brain tumor and heart bypass surgery. He died at his home in Philadelphia from complications of non-Hodgkin's lymphoma. He was eighty-two. Specter is survived by his wife Joan, whom he married in 1953; their two sons; and four grandchildren.

See Current Biography 2009.

Bert Randolph Sugar

Born: Washington, DC; June 7, 1937
Died: Mount Kisco, New York; March 25, 2012
Occupation: American sportswriter

With his signature fedora and a cigar dangling from his teeth, sportswriter Bert Randolph Sugar was one of the most recognizable figures in American boxing. Though he studied to become a lawyer and passed the Washington bar, Sugar was a prolific writer, television and radio commentator, and sports fanatic, though boxing was his passion. He was a former magazine and author of more than eighty books, including *Sting like a Bee: The Muhammad Ali Story* (1971) with José Torres and *Boxing's Greatest Fighters* (2006), in which he ranked the one hundred best boxers of all time. Sugar was inducted into the International Boxing Hall of Fame in 2005.

Sugar was born Herbert Randolph Sugar in Washington, DC, on June 7, 1937. He attended the University of Maryland and obtained his business and law degrees from the University of Michigan. Rather than practice law, Sugar moved to New York City where he worked in advertising for ten years. In 1969, he bought the magazine *Boxing Illustrated* and was its editor until 1973. From 1979 until 1983, he served as editor of *The Ring* magazine. Sugar also briefly edited the men's magazine *Argosy.*

Sugar was diagnosed with lung cancer and after a lengthy battle he died of cardiac arrest at the Northern Westchester Hospital in Mount

Kisco, New York, on March 25, 2012. His home was in Chappaqua, New York. He is survived by his wife, Suzanne; children, JB Sugar and Jennifer Frawley; brother, Steven; and four grandchildren.

See Current Biography 2002.

Arthur Ochs Sulzberger

Born: New York, New York; February 5, 1926
Died: Southampton, New York; September 29, 2012
Occupation: American publisher and business-person

Arthur Ochs Sulzberger Sr. is best known for his work as publisher of the *New York Times* and as chair of the newspaper's parent company, The New York Times Company. As publisher, Sulzberger oversaw the expansion of the company into a multibillion-dollar media giant and led the newspaper through a transition from traditional printing-press production to new digital formats. Sulzberger was also responsible for a host of staffing changes and for the expansion of the paper's coverage into business, sports, and the arts.

Sulzberger was named publisher of the *New York Times* and chair of the New York Times Company in June 1963. He immediately began improving the organization's finances and expanding its business platforms. Sulzberger took the company public in 1969, raising considerable revenue in the process, which was used to purchase Cowles Communication in 1971. This expanded the company's holdings from newspaper, radio, and shares of power and paper companies into interests in magazines and television.

In 1971, and under Sulzberger's supervision, the *New York Times* published a series of articles revealing the classified government history of America's involvement in the Vietnam War. The Pentagon Papers, which provided evidence that the administrations of President Richard M. Nixon and President Lyndon B. Johnson had lied to Congress and the public about the expansion of US military operations in Southeast Asia, caused a national uproar. The Nixon administration mounted a legal effort to prevent the further publishing of the government archive, but in June 1971, the US Supreme Court ruled that the government had failed to provide significant justification for censorship of the Pentagon Papers. In choosing to publish these articles, Sulzberger had risked his professional reputation as well as the reputation of the *New York Times*. The Court's decision helped to vindicate Sulzberger: The *New York Times* received a Pulitzer Prize in 1972 for its series of articles, and the case provided legal clarity to the right to free speech as described in the First Amendment to the US Constitution.

Sulzberger remained chair of the New York Times Company until 1997. At the time of his retirement, he had successfully secured the company's finances and ensured that future generations of the Sulzberger family would continue to run the company. Sulzberger had expanded the New York Times Company into a media empire while also protecting and nurturing the journalistic integrity of its flagship newspaper.

Sulzberger died on September 29, 2012, in Southampton, New York. He is survived by his children, Arthur Jr., Karen, Cynthia, and Cathy; two sisters; and nine grandchildren. Arthur Sulzberger Jr. succeeded his father as publisher of the *New York Times* in 1992 and as chair of The New York Times Company in 1997.

See Current Biography 1966.

Donna Summer

Born: Boston, Massachusetts; December 31, 1948
Died: Englewood, Florida; May 17, 2012
Occupation: American singer and songwriter

Grammy Award–winning songstress Donna Summer rose to fame in the 1970s as the queen of disco after her seventeen-minute club hit "Love to Love You Baby" was released in the United States. She later transitioned to funk, pop, R&B, rock, and gospel in the 1980s and 1990s. Her other hits include "Hot Stuff," "Bad Girls," "Last Dance," and "She Works Hard for the Money." Summer's first American hit album, *Love to Love You Baby* (1975) and the two albums that followed, *A Love Trilogy* (1976) and *Four Seasons of Love* (1976), explored the synthesized and sexualized tones of the disco era. But Summer, a religious woman who counted among her idols the gospel singer Mahalia Jackson, was uncomfortable with her reputation as a sex symbol. She became depressed and attempted suicide in 1976 and became a born-again Christian in 1979.

The 1980s heralded the dawn of a new era for both disco music and Summer's career. She successfully distanced herself from the fading genre with the anthem of female empowerment "She Works Hard for the Money," among other hits. She also recorded several gospel songs including "Forgive Me" from the album *Cat Without Claws* (1984). The song earned Summer a Grammy for best inspirational performance. All told, Summer won five Grammys during her career, though she was nominated seventeen times. Summer wrote songs for herself and other artists, including country star Dolly Parton. In 2009, she performed a concert in Oslo, Norway, honoring Nobel Peace Prize recipient, President Barack Obama.

Summer was born LaDonna Adrian Gaines in Boston on December 31, 1948. She was one of seven children. As a teenager, Summer joined a touring production of the rock musical *Hair*. She moved to Germany where she lived for several years and married an Austrian actor named Hellmuth Sommer in 1972. (The marriage ended in divorce.) She worked as a backup singer and released her debut album, *Lady of the Night* in Europe in 1974. "Love to Love You Baby," her first American single the next year, coincided with the rise of disco and became an international sensation.

Summer married songwriter Bruce Sudano in 1980. He survives her, as do Summer's three daughters, Brooklyn Sudano, Amanda Sudano, and Mimi Dohler; her four grandchildren; and her siblings, Ricky Gaines, Dara Bernard, Mary Ellen Bernard, Linda Gaines, and Jeanette Yancey. Summers died of cancer at her home in Englewood, Florida, on May 17, 2012.

See Current Biography 1979.

Thomas Stephen Szasz

Born: Budapest, Hungary; April 15, 1920
Died: Manlius, New York; September 8, 2012
Occupation: Hungarian American psychiatrist

Thomas Stephen Szasz, a Hungarian-born American psychiatrist, was a leading critic of contemporary psychiatric practices and claimed they were unethical and unscientific, particularly in regard to compulsory mental health treatment and the use of mental illness as a defense in court. He also staunchly defended the right of a patient to be fully informed before giving consent to participation in studies or treatment.

Szasz was born in Budapest, Hungary, on April 15, 1920. His family immigrated to the United States in 1938 after Hungary aligned with Nazi Germany. The family settled in Cincinnati, Ohio, where Szasz earned his bachelor's degree from the University of Cincinnati in 1941 and his medical degree in 1944. He studied psychoanalysis at the Chicago Institute, working there until 1951 when he joined the faculty at what is now the State University of New York (SUNY) Upstate Medical University.

In 1961 Szasz rose to prominence with the publication of *The Myth of Mental Illness: Foundations of a Theory of Personal Conduct*, in which he argued that most psychological diagnoses were not scientifically legitimate and many psychiatric treatments were unnecessary and exploitative. In 1969, Szasz joined with the Church of Scientology to establish the anti-psychiatry Citizens Commission on Human Rights; Szasz later distanced himself from the church.

The author of more than thirty books and hundreds of papers, Szasz's later publications include *The Myth of Psychotherapy: Mental Healing as Religion, Rhetoric, and Repression* (1978), *The Medicalization of Everyday Life* (2007), and *Psychiatry: The Science of Lies* (2010). Szasz retired from SUNY Upstate in 1990. Two years after his retirement, he was sued for malpractice by the widow of a former patient who had committed suicide after Szasz suggested he discontinue his medication for bipolar disorder. The case was settled out of court in 1994, but Szasz gave up his private practice soon afterward.

Szasz died at his home in Manlius, New York, on September 8, 2012, following a fall. Szasz's wife, Rosine, died in 1971. He is survived by two children, Margot Szasz Peters and Suzy Szasz Palmer; a brother; and one grandchild.

See Current Biography 1975.

Dorothea Tanning

Born: Galesburg, Illinois; August 25, 1910
Died: New York, New York; January 31, 2012
Occupation: American artist and writer

Dorothea Tanning was an American surrealist painter and celebrated writer and poet who saw her poems published in the *New Yorker*, the *Yale Review*, and the *Paris Review*. For thirty years, Tanning was married to Max Ernst, the acclaimed German surrealist and Dadaist painter. During her long and prolific career, Tanning produced paintings such as *Maternity* (1946) and *Birthday* (1942) and created costume and set designs for choreographer George Balanchine. She took her exploration of surrealist art to new heights with the more prismatic style of her paintings in the 1950s and 1960s and the soft forms of her installations and sculptures in the 1970s. Tanning's autobiography, *Between Lives: An Artist and Her World*, was published in 2001.

Tanning was born in Galesburg, Illinois, on August 25, 1910. She attended Knox College in Galesburg but left after two years to attend the Chicago Academy of the Arts. After several weeks there, she decided she would rather teach herself.

In 1935, Tanning moved to New York City where she found a job as a commercial illustrator. The Modern Museum of Art exhibition "Fantastic Art, Dada and Surrealism" in 1936 was a watershed moment in her career: "I saw in the exhibition that here were people doing things like me," she told Michael Kimmelman for the *New York Times* (24 Aug. 1995). In 1939, Tanning moved to Paris to be among other surrealists but returned to the United States after the outbreak of World War II. In 1942, Tanning met Max Ernst, who was married to wealthy art collector Peggy Guggenheim. Ernst had asked Tanning to show her work at Guggenheim's gallery in an exhibition featuring female surrealists. Tanning and Ernst were later married—in a double ceremony with the artist Man Ray and dancer Juliet Browner—in 1946.

Tanning and Ernst initially lived in Sedona, Arizona, in a home that Tanning designed. They then moved to France after Ernst, who was German, was denied American citizenship during the McCarthy era. Tanning returned to New York after Ernst's death in 1976. She died on January 31, 2012, at her home in New York City. She is survived by three nieces and a nephew.

See Current Biography Illustrated 2001.

Antoni Tàpies

Born: Barcelona, Spain; December 13, 1923
Died: Barcelona, Spain; February 6, 2012
Occupation: Spanish painter and sculptor

Antoni Tàpies was a Spanish abstract artist—though he hated the characterization "abstract"—whose work often made use of unusual materials, such as sand and gravel, and who experimented with graffiti-like techniques, such as etching. Tàpies came to national attention as a founding member, with poet Joan Brossa, of the Catalonian Dau al Set artistic movement in 1948. His early work was largely collage, but after receiving a scholarship to study in Paris, where he met Picasso, he began to produce paintings. He began exhibiting his work in the United States in 1953. In the 1960s and 1970s, he began to work in sculpture and mixed media as his work shifted away from surrealism and abstract expressionism toward pop art and conceptualism. He founded the Tàpies Foundation, an institution devoted to the study of modern art, in Barcelona in 1984.

Tàpies was born in Barcelona to an elite Catalonian family on December 13, 1923. His father was a prominent lawyer who worked in government. Tàpies was a teenager during the Spanish Civil War and the Catalan nationalist movement—events that would later influence his symbolic, yet ambiguous paintings. At age seventeen, he nearly died of a heart attack brought on by tuberculosis. He spent the next two years recovering and painting, though he enrolled in the University of Barcelona to study law in 1943 at the behest of his father. Several years later he abandoned his studies to devote his life to art.

Tàpies married Teresa Barba Fàbregas in 1954. The couple had three children together, Antonio, Clara, and Miguel. Tàpies died in Barcelona on February 6, 2012.

See Current Biography 1966.

Ron Taylor

Born: Sydney, Australia; March 8, 1934
Died: Sydney, Australia; September 9, 2012
Occupation: Australian shark expert and filmmaker

A dedicated conservationist and renowned documentarian, Ron Taylor was an Australian shark expert who lent his undersea cinematography skills to iconic scenes in Steven Spielberg's *Jaws.* Together with his wife, Valerie, Taylor built a robust catalog of footage chronicling the behavior of the ocean's deadliest predators.

Taylor was an avid spear fisher in his youth and turned pro as a young adult, hunting fish for food and sport. He also became enthralled with capturing his prey on film. Taylor began experimenting with underwater cinematography, and in 1962 won the Encyclopedia Britannica news photography award for a film titled *Playing With Sharks.* His international profile got a boost in 1963 when he sold a documentary called *Shark Hunters* to NBC. That same year he married Valerie Heighes, a champion swimmer and avid spear fisher whom he had met at the St. George Spear Fishing Club in Sydney. The Taylors competed as a successful professional spearfishing team, winning the New South Wales Open Water Championship several times. Ron Taylor also competed individually, winning the 1965 World Spearfishing Championship.

When the Taylors realized that spearfishing was causing fish populations to disappear for good, they stopped fishing to become full-time underwater photographers and filmmakers instead. It was a career-spanning partnership that would yield some of the most thrilling and important undersea film work of all time, including the documentary *Blue Water, White Death* (1971).

Taylor is perhaps best remembered for his contributions to the 1975 summer blockbuster *Jaws.* The scene in which a scientist played by Richard Dreyfuss is attacked by a great white shark while floating in an iron cage was filmed by the Taylors. A small cage and short stuntman were used to make the attacking shark appear larger. The *Jaws* sequence put the Taylors on the map, and cemented their status as in-demand producers of shark footage.

With time, however, Taylor began to question the implications of his involvement with *Jaws,* fearing that the film enforced negative stereotypes about sharks. His later years were devoted to marine conservation efforts; in 2003 he was named a member of the Order of Australia on the merits of his work. Taylor died on September 9, 2012, of leukemia in his hometown of Sydney. He was seventy-eight. Taylor is survived by his wife and filmmaking partner, Valerie.

See Current Biography 2007.

Russell E. Train

Born: Jamestown, Rhode Island; June 4, 1920
Died: Bozman, Maryland; September 17, 2012
Occupation: Administrator of the Environmental Protection Agency (EPA)

Russell Errol Train served as the administrator of the Environmental Protection Agency (EPA) from 1973 to 1977 under US President Richard Nixon. As a public servant, he helped to establish a serious consideration of environmental issues at the federal level. Later in his career, he worked with numerous environment organizations on such issues as pollution and animal welfare.

Train earned a degree in political science from Princeton University in 1941. After college, he served in the US Army during World War II, and then earned a law degree from Columbia University Law School in 1948. Beginning in 1949, Train served as a legal advisor to various congressional committees. From 1957 to 1965, he served as a US Tax Court judge. During the late 1950s, Train took several safaris in East Africa. These trips inspired in him a desire to become more involved in environmental protection and preservation.

Train founded the African Wildlife Leadership Foundation in 1961. The organization, which was later renamed the African Wildlife Foundation, works on issues related to preserving African wildlife, protecting ecologically sensitive lands, and instituting sustainable arrangements between wildlife and human populations.

In 1969, Train was named under secretary of the Department of the Interior in the Nixon administration. He served as chair of the Council on Environmental Quality (CEQ) from 1970 to 1973. President Nixon named him administrator of the EPA in 1973. Train, who served in the position until 1977, was the second administrator in the organization's history. During his tenure as administrator, Train oversaw the passage of the Clean Air Act, the Toxic Substances Control Act (TSCA), and the National Pollutant Discharge Elimination Systems (NPDES). After leaving the White House, Train was named president of the US arm of the World Wildlife Fund. He served as the organization's president until 1985, its chair from 1985 to 1994, and he became chairman emeritus in 2000.

Train was awarded the 1983 J. Paul Getty Wildlife Conservation Prize for his work on environmental issues. In 1991, President George Bush gave Train the Presidential Medal of Freedom, and in 2001, he was awarded the Seventh Annual Heinz Award Chairman's Medal for his career-long dedication to wildlife conservation.

Train died on September 17, 2012, in Bozman, Maryland. He was ninety-two years old.

He is survived by his wife of fifty-eight years, Aileen; his daughters, Nancy Smith, Emily Rowan, and Errol Giordano; his son, Charles Train; and twelve grandchildren.

See Current Biography, 1970.

Gore Vidal

Born: West Point, New York; October 3, 1925
Died: Hollywood Hills, California; July 31, 2012
Occupation: Writer

A World War II veteran, Gore Vidal became a renowned writer and political commentator. A political liberal, he criticized the US government, and wrote frankly about topics such as homosexuality during a time when American culture was pointedly conservative. In addition to his works of nonfiction, Vidal wrote plays, novels, and screenplays. Vidal earned a reputation for his sense of humor, which was often as scathing as it was shrewd.

Eugene Luther Gore Vidal was born in West Point, New York, on October 3, 1925. His family was politically connected. After serving in the military, Vidal's father worked in the administration of US President Franklin Delano Roosevelt. His grandfather was US Senator Thomas Gore of Oklahoma. Senator Gore, a proponent of American isolationism, influenced his grandson's philosophy on US foreign policy.

After graduating from Phillips Exeter Academy in New Hampshire, Vidal enlisted in the Army. His first novel, *Williwaw* (1946), was based on his experience as a US service member stationed in Alaska. *Williwaw* earned favorable reviews. Vidal caused controversy in 1948, with the publication of his second novel, *The City and the Pillar.* The novel caused an uproar for its unabashed portrayal of a homosexual relationship.

While continuing to publish works of fiction under the pen name Edgar Box, Vidal helped to rewrite the screenplay for the 1959 film *Ben Hur,* which was a critical and commercial success. During the 1960s, he resumed publishing novels under his real name, including *Julian* (1964), *Washington, D.C.* (1967), and *Myra Breckinridge* (1968). Over the next thirty years, he continued publishing novels, including *Kalki* (1978), *Creation* (1981), *Hollywood* (1989), and *The Golden Age* (2000).

As his career progressed, Vidal became known for his nonfiction work, including political essays and works of literary criticism. His work appeared regularly in *The New York Review of Books, Esquire,* and the *New Statesman.* A social commentator, his work focused on sex, religion, partisan politics, and American foreign policy. Vidal cherished his role as a public figure, and proved more than willing to enter into public arguments (either in his writing or during television appearances) with other literati of his day, including Norman Mailer and William F. Buckley. Throughout his life, Vidal made numerous appearances in films, and on television, as both an actor and a political commentator. Several documentary works have been made about Vidal's career, including *Gore Vidal: The Man Who Said No* (1982) and *The Education of Gore Vidal* (2003).

During his later years, Vidal became a vociferous critic of the Republican Party and the administration of US President George W. Bush. Vidal never married, but remained in a relationship with his partner Howard Austin throughout his life. Vidal died on July 31, 2012, in Hollywood Hills, California.

See Current Biography Illustrated 1965 and 1983.

Mike Wallace

Born: Brookline, Massachusetts; May 9, 1918
Died: New Canaan, Connecticut; April 7, 2012
Occupation: American broadcast journalist and news anchor

Mike Wallace was a broadcast journalist who made his name as a tough interrogator on the CBS news magazine *60 Minutes*. Wallace took on celebrities and politicians ranging from singer and actress Barbra Streisand, to Nixon administrator John D. Ehrlichman during the Watergate scandal, to Iranian leader Ayatollah Khomeini in 1979, whom he asked how he felt about being called a lunatic by Egyptian President Anwar el-Sadat. Wallace's outsize personality and propensity to speak the unspeakable earned him devoted viewers and many disgruntled subjects. He was known to preface his most biting remarks with the disingenuous phrase "Forgive me. . . ." In a 2006 interview with the *New York Times*, Wallace conceded that his interview style walked "a fine line between sadism and intellectual curiosity." Still, from his start as an interviewer on the 1950s program *Night Beat* to his thirty-eight years on *60 Minutes*, Wallace was an icon of the journalistic pursuit for truth with an actor's carriage. (Though there were times when he drew criticism for using deceitful gimmicks to obtain information or for paying large sums to score exclusive interviews.) For his work, he earned twenty-one Emmy Awards.

Wallace was born Myron Leon Wallace in Brookline, Massachusetts, on May 9, 1918. He attended Brookline High School and worked his way through the University of Michigan where he worked for the university radio station. He became an announcer for popular programs like "The Lone Ranger" and "The Green Hornet" at radio stations in Illinois and Michigan

before he enlisted in the US Navy in 1943. He appeared on the radio and television talk show "Mike and Buff" with his second wife, Buff Cobb; the show ended when the couple divorced in 1954. Wallace honed his interviewing skills on the television *Night Beat*, beginning in 1956. He became so popular that ABC picked up the show and renamed it *The Mike Wallace Interview* in 1957; the show was cancelled in 1958. He briefly took up acting but decided to seriously pursue journalism in 1962 after the death of his nineteen-year-old son, Peter, in a mountain-climbing accident in Greece. Wallace became the successful anchor of the *CBS Morning News with Mike Wallace* and, after turning down a job as President Nixon's press secretary, became the first cohost of *60 Minutes* when it premiered in 1968. He retired from the program in 2006.

Wallace had two sons, including Peter, with his first wife, Norma Kaphan, whom he divorced in 1948. His son Chris, who survives him, is a journalist for Fox News. Wallace and his third wife, Lorraine Perigord, divorced in 1983. His wife, Mary Yates, survives him, as do his stepchildren, Pauline Dora, Eames Yates, and Angus Yates; seven grandchildren; and four great-grandchildren. Wallace, who had a history of heart problems, died at a care facility in New Canaan, Connecticut, on April 7, 2012.

See Current Biography Illustrated 1957, 1977.

James D. Watkins

Born: Alhambra, California; March 7, 1927
Died: Alexandria, Virginia; July 26, 2012
Occupation: US Navy admiral, US Secretary of Energy

After a career in the US navy that spanned three decades, James D. Watkins served as US Secretary of Energy under President George H. W. Bush. He was chief of naval operations, the highest rank in the Department of the Navy, during the administration of President Ronald Reagan. During his tenure in the federal government, he served as chair of commissions on HIV/AIDS and ocean policy.

Born in Alhambra, California, on March 7, 1927, Watkins graduated from the US Naval Academy at Annapolis in 1949. While serving in the navy, he earned a master's degree in engineering from the US Naval Postgraduate School. Watkins served on destroyers, cruisers, and submarines during the Korean War and the Vietnam War. Having worked his way up the ranks of the navy, he was named commander of the Pacific Fleet. In 1982, he was appointed chief of naval operations, where he helped manage the presence of the

American navy in the Persian Gulf, Grenada, and Lebanon.

Admiral Watkins retired from the navy in 1986. In 1987, President Reagan appointed Watkins as chair of the ten-member President's Commission on the HIV Epidemic, which became known as the Watkins Commission. Although Watkins was not experienced in the issue, he rose to the challenge, and worked with the committee to help formulate policy recommendations to the Reagan administration. The commission's report recommended, among other things, increased research, education, medical treatment, and a policy of nondiscrimination against those with AIDS. Although some criticized the White House for not implementing the suggestions proposed by the commission, its work helped introduce the complicated and serious nature of the AIDS/HIV problem to the American public.

In 2001, President George W. Bush named Watkins chair of the Commission on Ocean Policy, which helped introduce new measures related to overfishing and coastal pollution. During his later career, Watkins served on the board of numerous organizations, including Southern California Edison Company, the Carnegie Corporation, and the Joint Ocean Commission Initiative.

Watkins died at his home in Alexandria, Virginia, on July 26, 2012. He was predeceased by his first wife, Sheila Jo (McKinney). He is survived by his second wife, Janet McDonough Watkins; his brother, John; six children; four stepchildren; fourteen grandchildren; and three great-grandchildren.

See Current Biography 1989.

which influenced the generations of folk and country musicians that followed him. He played with folk music greats like Clarence "Tom" Ashley, Jean Ritchie, Mother Maybelle Carter, and Earl Scruggs. For a large part of his career, Watson recorded and toured with his son, Merle Watson, who died in 1985. Before his own death, Watson played concerts with Merle's son, Richard.

Arthel Lane Watson was born in Stony Fork, North Carolina, on March 3, 1923. His father, who led the church choir in which Watson's mother sang, made a banjo out of a cat's hide for Watson when he was eleven. He received his first guitar at thirteen. Watson briefly attended school at the Governor Morehead School for the Blind in Raleigh, but dropped out in the seventh grade to go to work with his father. He played local shows as a youth and received the name "Doc" from an audience member when it was decided that "Arthel" was too difficult to pronounce. To support his family, Watson worked as a piano tuner and played in a band called Jack Williams and the Country Gentleman, where he perfected his banjo-like guitar style. Watson was "discovered" by folklorist Ralph Rinzler when he played a show with Clarence "Tom" Ashley in 1960.

During his long career, Watson won seven Grammy Awards. He founded a music festival called Merlefest in honor of his son in 1988.

Watson died in a hospital in Winston-Salem on May 29, 2012, after undergoing abdominal surgery earlier that week. He is survived by his wife, Rosa Lee Carlton; his daughter, Nancy Ellen Watson; his brother, David; two grandchildren; and several great-grandchildren.

See Current Biography 2003.

Doc Watson

Born: Stony Fork, North Carolina; March 3, 1923
Died: Winston-Salem, North Carolina; May 29, 2012
Occupation: American singer and guitarist

"There may not be a serious, committed baby boomer alive who didn't at some point in his or her youth try to spend a few minutes at least trying to learn to pick a guitar like Doc Watson," President Bill Clinton said when he presented Watson with the prestigious National Medal of the Arts in 1997, as quoted in Watson's *New York Times* obituary. A Grammy Award–winning bluegrass musician and guitar virtuoso, Doc Watson was a North Carolina native who rose to national prominence during the resurgence of American folk music during the 1960s. Watson, who lost his vision due to an illness when he was a baby, was famous for his flat-picking and fingerpicking techniques,

Alexis Weissenberg

Born: Sofia, Bulgaria; July 26, 1929
Died: Lugano, Switzerland; January 8, 2012
Occupation: Bulgarian-born French pianist

Alexis Weissenberg was a Bulgarian-born virtuoso pianist who alternately compelled and repelled critics during his long performance career. Weissenberg, who escaped a concentration camp in 1941 after he earned the sympathies of a guard with his accordion playing, studied at Julliard, and became a French citizen in the 1950s. He made his New York debut at Carnegie Hall in 1948 while he was still a teenager. His specialties included Schumann, Chopin, and Rachmaninoff.

Weissenberg's popularity waned in the late 1950s and early 1960s; critics argued that his performances (and his performance demeanor)

were cold, detached, and often aggressive. In turn, the outspoken Weissenberg told Canada's *Globe and Mail* in 1983: "You cannot lose your control physically and be precise as to what your hands do. Can you imagine a surgeon operating on somebody, and swooning and looking up at the ceiling and being very excited about it? The patient would die. That is what happens in music too. The patient dies, because there's too much going on besides the actual performance." After a decade-long sabbatical, Weissenberg re-emerged in 1966.

Alexis Sigismond Weissenberg was born in Sofia, Bulgaria, to a Jewish family on July 26, 1929. His only marriage ended in divorce. Sources report that he had children, but no information about survivors was available. Weissenberg, who had Parkinson's disease, died in Lugano, Switzerland, on January 8, 2012.

See Current Biography Illustrated 1978.

Jacqueline Grennan Wexler

Born: Sterling, Illinois; August 2, 1926
Died: Orlando, Florida; January 19, 2012
Occupation: College president, former nun

Jacqueline Grennan Wexler, once known as Sister Jacqueline of the Sisters of Loretto, was an education reformer who served as the president of Webster College in St. Louis, Missouri, and then as the president of Hunter College in New York City. Wexler oversaw the transition of Webster, a Roman Catholic college, into a secular institution in 1967—the same year that she petitioned the church to be released from her vows. "The very nature of higher education is opposed to juridical control by the church," she announced to Webster students in January 1967. "The academic freedom which must characterize a college or university would provide continuing embarrassment for the church if her hierarchy were forced into endorsing or negating the action of the college or university."

Jean Marie Grennan was born on August 2, 1926, in Sterling, Illinois, where her parents owned a large farm. (She chose the name Jacqueline for her brother Jack, who died at the age of twenty-one, when she took her vows.) Wexler received a bachelor's degree from Webster in 1948 and took her vows the following year. She spent several years teaching high school, during which time she received a master's degree in English from Notre Dame University in 1957. She began work as an administrator at Webster in 1959. Wexler displayed a knack for leadership and rose through the educational ranks, becoming Webster's president in 1965. Raising millions of dollars in private funds, Wexler equipped the

college, then women-only, with state-of-the-art facilities for both the arts and science departments. Even before she was released from her vows, Wexler was often an outspoken critic of church policies on several issues, including birth control.

Wexler became the president of Hunter College in New York in 1970, where she fielded student demonstrations and expanded health care education before stepping down in 1979. From 1982 to 1990, Wexler was the president of the National Conference of Christians and Jews. She married a widower named Paul Wexler in 1969 and adopted his two children, Wendy Wexler Branton and Wayne Wexler. They survive her, as do two sisters, four grandchildren, and two great-grandchildren. Wexler died at her home in Orlando, Florida, on January 19, 2012.

See Current Biography 1970.

Kevin H. White

Born: Boston, Massachusetts; September 25, 1929
Died: Boston, Massachusetts; January 27, 2012
Occupation: Former mayor of Boston

Kevin H. White served four terms (1968–1984) as the Democratic mayor of Boston, Massachusetts. He began his career as secretary of state of Massachusetts and was elected mayor in 1967. As mayor, White oversaw the enforced desegregation of Boston schools amid a violent backlash, and revitalized the city, particularly the downtown area near Faneuil Hall. During his fourth term, Boston's economy plummeted and the finances of White's administration were subjected to a federal investigation that officially closed in 1989. White was never charged with a crime though an estimated twenty city officials and a number of businessmen were convicted of extortion, bribery, and other corruption charges.

Kevin Hagan White was born to a family of Boston politicians on September 25, 1929. He received his bachelor's degree from Williams College in 1952 and his law degree from Boston College in 1955. White was elected as Massachusetts's secretary of state in 1960 at the age of thirty-one, and won his mayoral bid against Louise Day Hicks in 1968. The year of his election saw the assassination of Rev. Dr. Martin Luther King Jr. With the existing racial tensions in the city, White feared riots in the days following King's death. To quell any public unrest, White decided to air an already scheduled James Brown concert in Boston that night on public television. The legendary concert became known as "the night James Brown saved Boston." The significance of the event was captured in a 2008 television documentary of the same name.

In 1983, White announced that he would not pursue a fifth mayoral term. From 1984 to 2002 he served as the director of the Institute for Political Communication at Boston University. He was diagnosed with Alzheimer's disease in 2003 and died at his home in Boston on January 27, 2012. He is survived by his wife, Kathryn; his brother, Terrence; his children, Christopher, Mark, Caitlin, Elizabeth, and Patricia; and seven grandchildren.

See Current Biography 1974.

Tom Wicker

Born: Hamlet, North Carolina; June 18, 1926
Died: near Rochester, Vermont; November 25, 2011
Occupation: American journalist

Tom Wicker was a political reporter, Washington news bureau chief, and columnist for the *New York Times*. Wicker, who was also a novelist, was a little-known White House correspondent traveling with President John F. Kennedy on November 22, 1963, when the president was assassinated in Dallas. Wicker covered the story and, less than a year later, earned a job as the chief of the paper's news bureau in Washington, DC. In 1966, he took over the thrice-weekly op-ed column, "In the Nation," from retiring *New York Times* columnist Arthur Krock. He served as associate editor of the *Times* from 1968 until 1991. Wicker, whose political views fell to the left of the conservative Krock, retired in 1991.

Thomas Grey Wicker was born to a poor family in Hamlet, North Carolina, on June 18, 1926. After serving in the Navy during World War II, he worked his way through the University of North Carolina at Chapel Hill and graduated with a degree in journalism in 1948. He worked for several small newspapers before getting a job with the Washington news bureau of the *New York Times* in 1960. Gay Talese, author of *The Kingdom and the Power* (1969), a history of the *New York Times*, wrote of Wicker's career-changing coverage of JFK's assassination, "It was a remarkable achievement in reporting and writing, in collecting facts out of confusion, in reconstructing the most deranged day in his life, the despair and bitterness and disbelief, and then getting on a telephone to New York and dictating the story in a voice that only rarely cracked with emotion."

Wicker was an outspoken observer who occasionally became an active participant in the stories he covered. In 1971, he became involved in the uprising of 1,300 prisoners at Attica in upstate New York, serving as a mediator between the inmates and prison officials. The standoff ended violently, with ten hostages and twenty-nine inmates dead after state troopers stormed the prison. Wicker wrote about the ordeal in a book called *A Time to Die* (1975). He authored a number of other nonfiction books and ten novels, some of which are published under the pen name Paul Connolly.

Wicker died at his Vermont home on November 25, 2011. His first marriage ended in divorce. He is survived by his wife, Pamela Hill Wicker; two children, Cameron Wicker and Thomas Grey Wicker Jr.; and three step-children, Kayce Freed Jennings, Lisa Freed, and Christopher Hill.

See Current Biography 1973.

Andy Williams

Born: Well Lake, Iowa; December 3, 1927
Died: Branson, Missouri; September 25, 2012
Occupation: American singer and television host

The voice behind "Moon River" and a crooner of countless Christmas classics, Andy Williams brought family-friendly pop music to living rooms across the United States in the 1960s and for decades thereafter. His Emmy Award–winning television variety program "The Andy Williams Show" and seasonal television specials cemented his reputation as an entertainer of the masses at a time when America's musical landscape was in flux.

Williams began his music career at the age of eight, appearing with his three brothers on local—and eventually national—radio stations as the Williams Brothers Quartet in the mid 1930s. He went solo in the 1950s, landing regular spots performing on *The Tonight Show* with Steve Allen. Williams had a Billboard Top 10 hit with a version of "Canadian Sunset" in 1956, and continued that streak with other charting singles including "Can't Get Used to Losing You," "The Shadow of Your Smile," and "The Hawaiian Wedding Song," for which he garnered his first of five Grammy nominations. While Williams would never nab a Grammy for himself, he did host the first seven live telecasts of the awards program, and continued to score hits throughout his singing career.

In 1991, Williams visited Branson, Missouri, a small Ozark town undergoing an unlikely transformation into one of the nation's premier country music destinations. He opened the Andy Williams Moon River Theater the following year, bringing the town its first non-country-music performance venue.

Williams lived a life relatively free of scandal, aside from a 1976 incident in which his ex-wife—French songstress Claudine Longet—was charged with fatally shooting her boyfriend, ski racing champion Spider Sabich. Longet held that the shooting was accidental, and Williams supported her, frequently accompanying Longet to court dates.

Williams, who continued to perform until 2011, died on September 25, 2012, at his home in Branson, Missouri, of complications due to bladder cancer. He was eighty-four. He is survived by his wife, Debbie, whom he married in 1991; three children; and six grandchildren.

See Current Biography 1960.

Camilla Williams

Born: Danville, Virginia; October 18, 1919
Died: Bloomington, Indiana; January 29, 2012
Occupation: American opera singer

Soprano Camilla Williams became the first black woman to perform with a major opera company in the United States when she appeared as Cio-Cio-San in Puccini's "Madama Butterfly" with the New York City Opera on May 15, 1946. (The distinction is often misattributed to her late colleague and friend Marian Anderson, who performed at the Metropolitan Opera in 1955.) Williams was a concert singer who appeared in a number of operas throughout her career and sang "The Star-Spangled Banner" on the steps of Lincoln Memorial before Rev. Dr. Martin Luther King Jr. delivered his "I Have a Dream" speech in 1963.

Williams was born in Danville, Virginia, on October 18, 1919. After studying music education at Virginia State University (then Virginia State College for Negroes), she taught music at an elementary school in Danville. With the financial help of several Virginia State alumni, Williams moved to Philadelphia to study with Marion Szekely-Freschl and eventually began her concert career. Performing in Stamford, Connecticut, in 1944, Williams was discovered by the legendary Met soprano Geraldine Farrar, who became her mentor.

Williams retired from singing in 1971. She began teaching voice at Indiana University in Bloomington in 1977; she retired from the university in 1997. Her husband, civil rights lawyer Charles T. Beavers, died in 1969. Williams, who died at her Bloomington home on January 29, 2012, never had children.

See Current Biography 1952.

Nicol Williamson

Born: Hamilton, Scotland; September 14, 1936
Died: Amsterdam, the Netherlands; December 16, 2011
Occupation: British actor

Nicol Williamson was a celebrated stage and screen actor with a career playing some of the most coveted leading roles in classical theater, including William Shakespeare's Hamlet and Macbeth, and Anton Chekov's Vanya. Williamson, who also played a drug-addicted Sherlock Holmes in the film *The Seven-Per-Cent Solution* (1976) and Merlin in the 1981 film *Excalibur*, was known for his uneven temperament, a trait that often yielded brilliant, if unorthodox portrayals.

Williamson was born in Hamilton, Scotland, on September 14, 1936, though he was raised in Birmingham, England. He served in the British Army and went on to pursue acting in 1960. In 1964, he appeared as Bill Maitland in the John Osborne play *Inadmissible Evidence* at the Royal Court in London. The play was transferred to Broadway in New York where Williamson was nominated for a Tony Award and received a New York Drama Critics Circle Award. Williamson divided critics throughout his career, but the praise he received was vehement. Of his rough-hewn Hamlet, a reviewer for *Time* magazine wrote, as quoted in Williamson's *New York Times* obituary, that Williamson "burns with incandescence and carries with him the smell of smoldering cordite." They added, "If he were not lit by inner fire, he would be singularly unprepossessing."

Williamson died after a two-year struggle with esophageal cancer at his home in Amsterdam on December 16, 2011. His 1971 marriage to the actress Jill Townsend ended in divorce in 1977. He is survived by his son, Luke.

See Current Biography 1970.

James Q. Wilson

Born: Denver, Colorado; May 27, 1931
Died: Boston, Massachusetts; March 2, 2012
Occupation: American social scientist

James Q. Wilson was a social scientist who proposed the influential "broken windows" theory of law enforcement that was implemented in the 1990s by New York City mayor Rudy Giuliani and police commissioner William "Bill" Bratton. The theory was later taken to Los Angeles to transform the city's corrupt and distrusted police department and to aid in crime reduction. The theory focuses on community maintenance and quality of life; as the psychologically based theory goes, if a broken window is fixed it signifies that the community is cared for and that disturbances in that community are not tolerated. Wilson and criminologist George L. Kelling wrote in an article for the *Atlantic*, "one unrepaired broken window is a signal that no one cares, and so breaking more windows costs nothing" (Mar. 1982). In New York, these "broken windows" included panhandling, prostitution, public drunkenness, and graffiti. Under Giuliani, the city's crime rate fell significantly, though he was not immune to criticism in his implementation of Wilson's theory.

Wilson was born in Denver, Colorado, on May 27, 1931, though he grew up in Long Beach, California. He graduated from the University of Redlands and served in a noncombat role in the US Navy during the Korean War. He received his doctorate in political science, specializing in urban politics and policing, from the University of Chicago in 1959. Wilson, who taught at Harvard University from 1961 to 1987, published a number of books about social issues related to crime, urban politics, and the relationships between individuals and institutions, including *Bureaucracy: What Government Agencies Do and Why They Do It* (1989).

Wilson died in Boston from complications of leukemia on March 2, 2012. He is survived by his wife, Roberta; his children, Matthew Wilson and Annie Gilbert; his sister, Diane Gray; and five grandchildren.

See Current Biography 2002.

Adam Yauch

Born: Brooklyn, New York; August 5, 1964
Died: New York, New York; May 4, 2012
Occupation: American rapper

Rapper Adam Yauch was born in Brooklyn, New York, on August 5, 1964. More popularly known as MCA, he was a founding member of the revolutionary hip-hop group the Beastie Boys.

The group signed with Def Jam and audiences first regarded the white, Jewish Beastie Boys as a novelty act. But their continuing reinvention of the rap-rock genre—from songs like the early parody-anthem "(You Gotta) Fight For Your Right (To Party)" to the breakthrough album *Paul's Boutique* (1989)—made fans out of many of their critics, and the group is largely credited for bringing hip-hop beats into the mainstream.

The Beastie Boys, comprised of Yauch (MCA), Michael Diamond (Mike D), and Adam Horovitz (Ad-Rock), began as a punk rock band in 1981 and initially incorporated rap and hip-hop into their music as a joke. (Their first single "Cooky Puss" was a track of prank phone calls played over scratching and guitar riffs.) They began as pranksters, but drew fans by the millions; the Beastie Boys maintained their popularity from their debut album, *Licensed to Ill* in 1986, to their most recent, *Hot Sauce Committee Part Two* in 2011, which would be Yauch's final recording. But as they aged, they matured and turned their clever lyrics to political issues (Yauch was especially active in the Free Tibet movement) and apologized for their earlier sexist and homophobic themes. The band was inducted into the Rock and Roll Hall of Fame in 2012.

Yauch founded the Milarepa Fund to raise awareness and funds for Tibetan independence in 1994; the fund hosted the Tibetan Freedom Concert series from 1996 until 2001. Yauch also directed several Beastie Boys music videos and *Gunnin' for That #1 Spot* (2008), a documentary about basketball. He began the film distribution and production company Oscilloscope Laboratories, which distributed the Academy Award–nominated film *The Messenger* (2009), as well as a number of acclaimed documentaries.

Yauch married Dechen Wangdu in 1998. She survives him, as do his parents, Noel and Frances Yauch, and his daughter, Tenzin Losel. Yauch was diagnosed with salivary gland cancer in 2009. He died in New York City on May 4, 2012.

See Current Biography Illustrated 1998.

CLASSIFICATION BY PROFESSION

ACTIVISM
Devi, Mahasweta
Friedman, Kinky
Gbowee, Leymah
Harris, Sam
Honkala, Cheri
Lasn, Kalle
Namegabe, Chouchou
Okolloh, Ory
Prendergast, John
Rodgers, Nile

ARCHITECTURE
Gang, Jeanne
Sejima, Kazuyo

ART
Höller, Carsten
Lee, Jim
Scharf, Kenny
Tan, Shaun

ASTRONAUTICS
Burbank, Daniel C.

BUSINESS
Adelson, Jay
Ahrendts, Angela
Arrington, Michael
Cloninger, Kathy
Cohen, Lyor
Cook, Tim
Dubuc, Nancy
Ek, Daniel
Ells, Steve
English, Todd
Fong, Dennis
Gass, Michelle
Giffords, Gabrielle
Houston, Drew
Huntsman, Jon, Jr.
Koch, Jim
Kraft, Robert K.
Lyne, Susan
Mooney, Beth
Morrison, Denise
Moskovitz, Dustin
Mulleavy, Kate and Laura
Murphy, Mark
Mutawa, Naif Al-
Ortega Gaona, Amancio
Rometty, Virginia
Rosedale, Philip
Stanton, Katie Jacobs
Stoppelman, Jeremy

Theallet, Sophie
Westergren, Tim

COMEDY
Bamford, Maria
Buress, Hannibal
Hardwick, Chris
Tate, Catherine

DANCE
Askegard, Charles

ECONOMICS
Amin, Samir
Diamond, Peter
Fryer, Roland
Moyo, Dambisa
Reinhart, Carmen

EDUCATION
Agacinski, Sylviane
Augenbraum, Harold
Ayala, Francisco
Bloom, Paul
Chaon, Dan
Clement, Paul D.
Desmond-Hellmann, Susan
Deutscher, Guy
Devi, Mahasweta
Diamond, Peter
Eagleman, David
Fryer, Roland
Greiner, Markus
Hayhoe, Katharine
Herr, Hugh
Miles, Tiya
Reinhart, Carmen
Riess, Adam
Ryan, Kay
Shechtman, Daniel
Warren, Elizabeth
Way, Niobe
Yamashita, Yukiko

FASHION
Ahrendts, Angela
Monroque, Shala
Mulleavy, Kate and Laura
Ortega Gaona, Amancio
Theallet, Sophie
Verhoeven, Julie

FILM
Bamford, Maria
Carr, Kris

FILM (continued)
Common
Cousteau, Fabien
Deschanel, Zooey
Hardwick, Chris
Harris, Naomie
Lasn, Kalle
Mara, Rooney
McCarthy, Thomas
Papamichael, Phedon
Pike, Rosamund
Ronson, Jon
Scott, Stuart
Theroux, Justin
Whedon, Joss
Willimon, Beau

GASTRONOMY
DiSpirito, Rocco
English, Todd
Florence, Tyler
Lahlou, Mourad
McCalman, Max
Pépin, Jacques
Redzepi, René
Tsai, Ming

GOVERNMENT AND POLITICS, FOREIGN
Lucas, Caroline
Nasheed, Mohamed
Rousseff, Dilma
Thorning-Schmidt, Helle

GOVERNMENT AND POLITICS, U.S.
Clement, Paul D.
Friedman, Kinky
Giffords, Gabrielle
Huntsman, Jon, Jr.
Landry, Jeffrey M.
Olsen, Matthew
Prendergast, John
Priebus, Reince
Sadik-Khan, Janette
Sandoval, Brian
Stanton, Katie Jacobs
Warren, Elizabeth

HISTORY
Ferguson, Niall
Miles, Tiya

JOURNALISM
Arrington, Michael
Belluck, Pam
Burnett, Erin
Devi, Mahasweta
Fager, Jeff
Ferguson, Niall
Friedman, Kinky
Goldberg, Michelle
Granderson, LZ
Hafezi, Parisa

Hedges, Chris
Lewis, Michael
Monroque, Shala
Morgan, Piers
Namegabe, Chouchou
Ronson, Jon
Scott, Stuart
Sklar, Rachel
Zimmer, Carl

LAW
Clement, Paul D.
Okolloh, Ory
Priebus, Reince
Sandoval, Brian
Sklar, Rachel
Warren, Elizabeth

LITERATURE
Abouet, Marguerite
Billingsley, Franny
Chabon, Michael
Chaon, Dan
Collins, Suzanne
Devi, Mahasweta
Friedman, Kinky
Grahame-Smith, Seth
Johnson, Brian David
Levine, Philip
Longfellow, Ki
Lunge-Larsen, Lise
Ryan, Kay
Tan, Shaun
Tranströmer, Tomas

MILITARY
Meyer, Dakota

MUSIC
Balsom, Alison
Cohen, Lyor
Common
Deschanel, Zooey
Edwards, Kathleen
Friedman, Kinky
Hardwick, Chris
Herbert, Matthew
Kweli, Talib
Kwiecien´, Mariusz
Lambert, Miranda
Luisi, Fabio
Perry, Katy
Popper, John
Prieto, Dafnis
Rodgers, Nile
Ross, Rick
Souleyman, Omar
Tedeschi, Susan
Vernon, Justin
Welch, Florence
Westergren, Tim

NONFICTION
Agacinski, Sylviane
Belluck, Pam
Bradley, Raymond S.
Carr, Kris
DiSpirito, Rocco
Eagleman, David
English, Todd
Ferguson, Niall
Friedman, Kinky
Gimlette, John
Goldberg, Michelle
Hardwick, Chris
Harris, Sam
Johnson, Brian David
Lahlou, Mourad
Lasn, Kalle
Lewis, Michael
McCalman, Max
Pendergast, John
Pépin, Jacques
Redzepi, René
Rodgers, Nile
Tsai, Ming
Zimmer, Carl

ORGANIZATIONS
Augenbraum, Harold
Cloninger, Kathy
Heuer, Rolf-Dieter
Lasn, Kalle

PHILANTHROPY
Kraft, Robert K.
Moskovitz, Dustin

PHILOSOPHY
Agacinski, Sylviane

PSYCHOLOGY
Bloom, Paul
Way, Niobe

PUBLISHING
Lee, Jim

RADIO
Abumrad, Jad

SCIENCE
Ayala, Francisco
Bradley, Raymond S.
Cousteau, Fabien
Desmond-Hellmann, Susan
Eagleman, David
Greiner, Markus
Harris, Sam
Hayhoe, Katharine
Herr, Hugh
Heuer, Rolf-Dieter
Lisi, Antony Garrett
Riess, Adam

Shechtman, Daniel
Voytek, Bradley
Yamashita, Yukiko

SOCIAL SCIENCES
Agacinski, Sylviane
Deutscher, Guy
Moyo, Dambisa
Way, Niobe

SPORTS
Carpenter, Chris
Coughlin, Natalie
Datsyuk, Pavel
Djokovic, Novak
Griffin, Blake
Hernández, Félix
Herr, Hugh
Kraft, Robert K.
Kvitova, Petra
Lomu, Jonah
Maddon, Joe
Murphy, Mark
Peterson, Adrian
Reid, Andy
Rhéaume, Manon
Rivera, Mariano
Rodgers, Aaron
Scott, Stuart
Smith, Josh
Solo, Hope
Thomas, Tim
Thompson, Alexis
Verlander, Justin
Welker, Wes

TECHNOLOGY
Adelson, Jay
Cook, Tim
Ek, Daniel
Herr, Hugh
Houston, Drew
Hunicke, Robin
Johnson, Brian David
Moskovitz, Dustin
Rosedale, Philip
Stanton, Katie Jacobs
Stoppelman, Jeremy
Westergren, Tim

TELEVISION
Bamford, Maria
Buress, Hannibal
Burnett, Erin
Collins, Suzannea
Deschanel, Zooey
Dubuc, Nancy
English, Todd
Fager, Jeff
Florence, Tyler
Grahame-Smith, Seth
Hardwick, Chris

TELEVISION *(continued)*
Kaling, Mindy
McCarthy, Thomas
Morgan, Piers
Scott, Stuart
Tate, Catherine
Weiner, Matthew
Whedon, Joss

THEATER
Askegard, Charles
Longfellow, Ki
McCarthy, Thomas
Theroux, Justin
Willimon, Beau